Lecture Notes in Computer Science   10427

Commenced Publication in 1973
Founding and Former Series Editors:
Gerhard Goos, Juris Hartmanis, and Jan van Leeuwen

More information about this series at http://www.springer.com/series/7407

Rupak Majumdar · Viktor Kunčak (Eds.)

Computer Aided Verification

29th International Conference, CAV 2017
Heidelberg, Germany, July 24–28, 2017
Proceedings, Part II

 Springer

Editors
Rupak Majumdar
Max Planck Institute for Software Systems
Kaiserslautern, Rheinland-Pfalz
Germany

Viktor Kunčak
School of Computer and Communication
  Sciences
EPFL - IC - LARA
Lausanne
Switzerland

ISSN 0302-9743   ISSN 1611-3349   (electronic)
Lecture Notes in Computer Science
ISBN 978-3-319-63389-3   ISBN 978-3-319-63390-9   (eBook)
DOI 10.1007/978-3-319-63390-9

Library of Congress Control Number: 2017946069

LNCS Sublibrary: SL1 – Theoretical Computer Science and General Issues

Printed on acid-free paper

This Springer imprint is published by Springer Nature
The registered company is Springer International Publishing AG
The registered company address is: Gewerbestrasse 11, 6330 Cham, Switzerland

Preface

It has been our privilege to serve as the program chairs for CAV 2017, the 29th International Conference on Computer-Aided Verification. CAV 2017 was held in beautiful Heidelberg, Germany, during July 22–28, 2017. The pre-conference workshops took place at the Crowne Plaza Hotel in Heidelberg City Centre. The main conference took place at the Stadthalle by the river Neckar.

The CAV conference series is dedicated to the advancement of the theory and practice of computer-aided formal analysis of hardware and software systems. The conference covers the spectrum from theoretical results to concrete applications, with an emphasis on practical verification tools and the algorithms and techniques that are needed for their implementation. CAV considers it vital to continue spurring advances in hardware and software verification while expanding to new domains such as biological systems and computer security.

Out of 191 submissions to the conference, we chose 50 regular papers and seven tool papers. These papers cover a wide range of topics and techniques, from algorithmic and logical foundations of verification to practical applications in distributed, networked, and cyber-physical systems. One direction of topical interest is the increasingly sophisticated combination of "traditional" techniques for reasoning and search with data-driven techniques. The program featured invited talks by Chris Hawblitzel (Microsoft), Marta Kwiatkowska (Oxford), and Viktor Vafeiadis (MPI-SWS), as well as invited tutorials, by Loris D'Antoni and Mayur Naik. As traditional, one of the winners of the CAV award also gave a presentation. We also had a special workshop to celebrate David Dill's many contributions to CAV on the occasion of his 60th birthday.

In addition to the main conference, CAV hosted the Verification Mentoring Workshop for junior scientists entering the field and six pre-conference technical workshops: the Workshop on Synthesis (SYNT), Satisfiability Modulo Theories (SMT), Verified Software: Theories, Tools, and Experiments (VSTTE), Design and Analysis of Robust Systems (DARS), Formal Approaches to Explainable Verification (FEVER), and Numerical Software Verification (NSV).

Organizing a conference is a community effort. The Program Committee for CAV consisted of 56 members; we kept the number large to ensure each PC member would have a reasonable number of papers to review and be able to provide thorough reviews. In addition, we used 104 external reviewers. All together, the reviewers drafted over 730 reviews and put in enormous effort in ensuring a good-quality program.

This year, we made artifact evaluation mandatory for tool submissions and optional but encouraged for regular submissions. We used an artifact evaluation committee of 26 members. Our goal for artifact evaluation was to provide friendly "beta-testing" to tool developers; we recognize that developing a stable tool on a cutting-edge research topic is certainly not easy and we hope the constructive comments provided by the AEC were of help to the developers. Needless to say we were impressed by the quality of the artifacts and in fact all accepted tools passed artifact evaluation. We are grateful to the reviewers for their outstanding efforts in making sure each paper got a fair chance.

We would like to thank Eva Darulova for chairing the workshop organization process, Barbara Jobstmann and Thomas Wahl for managing sponsorship and student fellowships, respectively, Mikaël Mayer for maintaining the CAV website, and the always helpful Steering Committee members Orna Grumberg, Aarti Gupta, Daniel Kroening, and Kenneth McMillan. We worked closely with Pavithra Prabhakar, Andrey Rybalchenko, and Damien Zufferey, who organized the Verification Mentoring Workshop. Finally, we would like to thank Roslyn Stricker, who helped us tremendously in the administration and organization of CAV.

We hope that you find the proceedings of CAV 2017 thought provoking!

July 2017   Rupak Majumdar
                                                                Viktor Kunčak

Organization

Program Chairs

Rupak Majumdar   Max Planck Institute for Software Systems, Germany
Viktor Kunčak   EPFL, Switzerland

Workshop Chair

Eva Darulova   Max Planck Institute for Software Systems, Germany

Sponsorship Chair

Barbara Jobstmann   EPFL, Switzerland and Cadence Design Systems

Fellowship Chair

Thomas Wahl   Northeastern University, USA

Program Committee

Aws Albarghouthi   University of Wisconsin, USA
Christel Baier   TU Dresden, Germany
Per Bjesse   Synopsys, USA
Jasmin Blanchette   Inria Nancy – Grand Est, France
Sergiy Bogomolov   Australian National University, Australia
Ahmed Bouajjani   IRIF, Paris Diderot University, France
Rohit Chadha   University of Missouri, USA
Bor-Yuh Evan Chang   University of Colorado at Boulder, USA
Swarat Chaudhuri   Rice University, USA
Wei-Ngan Chin   National University of Singapore, Singapore
Hana Chockler   King's College London, UK
Alessandro Cimatti   Fondazione Bruno Kessler, Italy
Isil Dilig   University of Texas at Austin, USA
Dino Distefano   Facebook and Queen Mary University of London, UK
Michael Emmi   Nokia Bell Labs, USA
Javier Esparza   TU Munich, Germany
Georgios Fainekos   Arizona State University, USA
Azadeh Farzan   University of Toronto, Canada
Aarti Gupta   Princeton University, USA
Gerard Holzmann   Nimble Research, USA
Marieke Huisman   University of Twente, The Netherlands
Radu Iosif   Verimag, France

Artifact Evaluation Committee

Swen Jacobs	Saarland University, Germany
Moa Johansson	Chalmers, Sweden
Dejan Jovanovic	SRI International, USA
Ralf Jung	Max Planck Institute for Software Systems, Germany
Ivan Kuraj	MIT, USA
Andreas Lochbihler	ETH Zurich, Switzerland
Jose Morales	IMDEA Software, Spain
Van Chan Ngo	Carnegie Mellon University, USA
Zvonimir Pavlinovic	New York University, USA
Markus Rabe	University of California, Berkeley, USA
Mukund Raghothaman	University of Pennsylvania, USA
Andrew Reynolds	University of Iowa, USA
Nima Roohi	University of Illinois, Urbana-Champaign, USA
Christian Schilling	University of Freiburg, Germany
Muralidaran Vijayaraghavan	MIT, USA
Nicolas Voirol	EPFL, Switzerland

Additional Reviewers

Alireza Abyaneh	Constantin Enea	K. Narayan Kumar
Mahmudul Faisal Al Ameen	Chuchu Fan	Sebastian Küpper
	Samira Farahani	Axel Legay
Sebastian Arming	Grigory Fedyukovich	Sorin Lerner
Konstantinos Athanasiou	Pierre Flener	Peizin Liu
Mohamed Faouzi Atig	Matthias Fleury	Le Quang Loc
Domagoj Babic	Wan Fokkink	Andreas Lochbihler
Michael Backenköhler	Zhoulai Fu	Alexander Lück
Gogul Balakrishnan	Nils Gesbert	Ravichandran Madhavan
Clark Barrett	Shilpi Goel	Victor Magron
Matthew Bauer	Yijia Gu	Assaf Marron
Ryan Beckett	Arie Gurfinkel	Umang Mathur
Harsh Beohar	Vahid Hashemi	Todd Millstein
Olaf Beyersdorff	Bardh Hoxha	Sergio Mover
Pavol Bielik	Johannes Hölzl	Suvam Mukherjee
Armin Biere	Catalin Hritcu	Daniel Neider
Jesse Bingham	Mens Irini-Eleftheria	Dennis Nolte
Stefan Blom	Himanshu Jain	Peter O'Hearn
Stefan Bucur	Chuan Jiang	Wytse Oortwijn
Dario Cattaruzza	George Karpenkov	Gustavo Petri
Ed Cerny	Dileep Kini	Lauren Pick
Le Ton Chanh	Hui Kong	Markus Rabe
Dmitry Chistikov	Aamod Kore	Jaideep Ramachandran
Andreea Costea	Jan Křetínský	Rajarshi Ray
Eva Darulova	Thilo Krüger	Andrew Reynolds

Nima Roohi
Philipp Ruemmer
Sarah Sallinger
Anne-Kathrin Schmuck
Peter Schrammel
Daniel
  Schwartz-Narbonne
Cristina Serban
Alexey Solovyev
Sadegh Soudjani
Benno Stein

Ofer Strichman
Kausik Subramanian
Rob Sumners
Sol Swords
Michael Tautschnig
Nguyen Toan Thanh
Dmitriy Traytel
Nikos Tzevelekos
Viktor Vafeiadis
Freark van der Berg
Jules Villard

Mike Whalen
Christoph Wintersteiger
Xiao Xu
Shakiba Yaghoubi
Eugen Zalinescu
Qirun Zhang
Yiji Zhang
Cai Zhouhong
Florian Zuleger

Steering Committee

Orna Grumberg	Technion, Israel
Aarti Gupta	Princeton University, USA
Daniel Kroening	Oxford University, UK
Kenneth McMillan	Microsoft Research, USA

CAV Award Committee

Tom Ball (Chair)	Microsoft Research, USA
Kim G. Larsen	Aalborg University, Denmark
Natarajan Shankar	SRI International, USA
Pierre Wolper	Liege University, Belgium

Verification Mentoring Workshop

Pavithra Prabhakar	Kansas State University, USA
Andrey Rybalchenko	Microsoft Research, UK
Damien Zufferey	Max Planck Institute for Software Systems, Germany

Publicity Chair

Mikaël Mayer	EPFL, Switzerland

Contents – Part II

Software Analysis

Contents – Part I

Data Driven Techniques

Runtime Verification

Cyber-Physical Systems

Concurrency

Analysis of Software and Hardware

Verified Compilation of Space-Efficient Reversible Circuits

Matthew Amy[1,2]([✉]), Martin Roetteler[3], and Krysta M. Svore[3]

[1] Institute for Quantum Computing, Waterloo, Canada
[2] David R. Cheriton School of Computer Science,
University of Waterloo, Waterloo, Canada
meamy@uwaterloo.ca
[3] Microsoft Research, Redmond, USA

Abstract. The generation of reversible circuits from high-level code is an important problem in several application domains, including low-power electronics and quantum computing. Existing tools compile and optimize reversible circuits for various metrics, such as the overall circuit size or the total amount of space required to implement a given function reversibly. However, little effort has been spent on verifying the correctness of the results, an issue of particular importance in quantum computing. There, compilation allows not only mapping to hardware, but also the estimation of resources required to implement a given quantum algorithm, a process that is crucial for identifying which algorithms will outperform their classical counterparts. We present a reversible circuit compiler called REVERC, which has been formally verified in F* and compiles circuits that operate correctly with respect to the input program. Our compiler compiles the REVS language [21] to combinational reversible circuits with as few ancillary bits as possible, and provably cleans temporary values.

1 Introduction

The ability to evaluate classical functions coherently and in superposition as part of a larger quantum computation is essential for many quantum algorithms. For example, Shor's quantum algorithm [26] uses classical modular arithmetic and Grover's quantum algorithm [11] uses classical predicates to implicitly define the underlying search problem. There is a resulting need for tools to help a programmer translate classical, irreversible programs into a form which a quantum computer can understand and carry out, namely into reversible circuits, which are a special case of quantum transformations [19]. Other applications of reversible computing include low-power design of classical circuits. See [15] for background and a critical discussion.

Several tools have been developed for synthesizing reversible circuits, ranging from low-level methods for small circuits such as [14,16,17,25,29] (see also [23] for a survey) to high-level programming languages and compilers [10,21,28,31,33]. In this paper we are interested in the latter class—i.e., methods

© Springer International Publishing AG 2017
R. Majumdar and V. Kunčak (Eds.): CAV 2017, Part II, LNCS 10427, pp. 3–21, 2017.
DOI: 10.1007/978-3-319-63390-9_1

for compiling high-level code to reversible circuits. Such compilers commonly perform optimization, as the number of bits quickly grows with the standard techniques for achieving reversibility (see, e.g. [24]). The question, as with general purpose compilers, is whether or not we can trust these optimizations.

In most cases, extensive testing of compiled programs is sufficient to establish the correctness of both the source program and its translation to a target architecture by the compiler. Formal methods are typically reserved for safety- (or mission-) critical applications. For instance, formal verification is an essential step in modern computer-aided circuit design due largely to the high cost of a recall. Reversible – specifically, quantum – circuits occupy a different design space in that (1) they are typically "software circuits," i.e., they are not intended to be implemented directly in hardware, and (2) there exist few examples of hardware to actually run such circuits. Given that there are no large-scale universal quantum computers currently in existence, one of the goals of writing a quantum circuit compiler at all is to accurately gauge the amount of physical resources needed to perform a given algorithm, a process called *resource estimation*. Such resource estimates can be used to identify the "crossover point" when a problem becomes more efficient to solve on a quantum computer, and are invaluable both in guiding the development of quantum computers and in assessing their potential impact. However, different compilers give wildly different resource estimates for the same algorithms, making it difficult to trust that the reported numbers are correct. For this reason compiled circuits need to have some level of formal guarantees as to their correctness for resource estimation to be effective.

In this paper we present REVERC, a lightly optimizing compiler for the REVS language [21] which has been written and proven correct in the dependently typed language F* [27]. Circuits compiled with REVERC are certified to preserve the semantics of the source REVS program, which we have for the first time formalized, and to reset or *clean* all ancillary (temporary) bits used so that they may be used later in other computations. In addition to formal verification of the compiler, REVERC provides an assertion checker which can be used to formally verify the source program itself, allowing effective end-to-end verification of reversible circuits.

Contributions. The following is a summary of the contributions of our paper:

- We give a formal semantics of REVS.
- We present a compiler for REVS called REVERC, written in F*. The compiler currently has three modes: direct to circuit, eager-cleaning, and Boolean expression compilation.
- We develop a new method of eagerly cleaning bits to be reused again later, based on *cleanup expressions*.
- Finally, we verify correctness of REVERC with machine-checked proofs that the compiled reversible circuits faithfully implement the input program's semantics, and that all ancillas used are returned to their initial state.

Related Work. Due to the reversibility requirement of quantum computing, quantum programming languages and compilers typically have methods for generating reversible circuits. Quantum programming languages typically allow compilation of classical, irreversible code in order to minimize the effort of porting existing code into the quantum domain. In QCL [20], "pseudo-classical" operators – classical functions meant to be run on a quantum computer – are written in an imperative style and compiled with automatic ancilla management. As in REVS, such code manipulates registers of bits, splitting off subregisters and concatenating them together. The more recent Quipper [10] automatically generates reversible circuits from classical code by a process called *lifting*: using Haskell metaprogramming, Quipper lifts the classical code to the reversible domain with automated ancilla management. However, little space optimization is performed [24].

Verification of reversible circuits has been previously considered from the viewpoint of checking equivalence against a benchmark circuit or specification [30,32]. This can double as both *program verification* and *translation validation*, but every compiled circuit needs to be verified separately. Moreover, a program that is easy to formally verify may be translated into a circuit with hundreds of bits, and is thus very difficult to verify. Recent work has shown progress towards verification of more general properties of reversible and quantum circuits via model checking [4], but to the authors' knowledge, no verification of a reversible circuit compiler has yet been carried out. By contrast, many compilers for general purpose programming languages have been formally verified in recent years – most famously, the CompCert optimizing C compiler [13], written and verified in Coq. Since then, many other compilers have been developed and verified in a range of languages and logics including Coq, HOL, F*, etc., with features such as shared memory [6], functional programming [7,9] and modularity [18,22].

2   Reversible Computing

Reversible functions are Boolean functions $f : \{0,1\}^n \rightarrow \{0,1\}^n$ which can be inverted on all outputs, i.e., precisely those functions which correspond to permutations of a set of cardinality 2^n, for some $n \in \mathbb{N}$. As with classical circuits, reversible functions can be constructed from universal gate sets – for instance, it is known that the Toffoli gate which maps $(x,y,z) \mapsto (x,y,z \oplus (x \wedge y))$, together with the controlled-NOT gate (CNOT) which maps $(x,y) \mapsto (x,x \oplus y)$ and the NOT gate which maps $x \mapsto x \oplus 1$, is universal for reversible computation [19].

An important metric that is associated with a reversible circuit is the amount of scratch space required to implement a given target function, i.e., temporary bits which store intermediate results of a computation. In quantum computing such bits are commonly denoted as *ancilla* bits. A very important difference to classical computing is that scratch bits cannot just be overwritten when they are no longer needed: any ancilla that is used as scratch space during a reversible computation must be returned to its initial value—commonly assumed to be 0—computationally. Moreover, if an ancilla bit is not "cleaned" in this way, in a quantum computation it may remain entangled with the computational registers which in turn can destroy the desired interferences that are crucial for many quantum algorithms.

Figure 1 shows a reversible circuit over NOT, CNOT, and Toffoli gates computing the NOR function. Time flows left to right, with input values listed on the left and outputs listed on the right. NOT gates are depicted by an $\oplus$, while CNOT and Toffoli gates are written with an $\oplus$ on the *target* bit (the bit whose value changes) connected by a vertical line to, respectively, either one or two *control* bits identified by solid dots. Two ancilla qubits are used which both initially are 0; one of these ultimately holds the (otherwise irreversible) function value, the other is returned to zero. For larger circuits, it becomes a non-trivial problem to assert (a) that indeed the correct target function f is implemented and (b) that indeed all ancillas that are not outputs are returned to 0.

REVS From Bennett's work on reversible Turing machines it follows that any function can be implemented by a suitable reversible circuit [5]: if an n-bit function $x \mapsto f(x)$ can be implemented with K gates over $\{\text{NOT}, \text{AND}\}$, then the reversible function $(x, y) \mapsto (x, y \oplus f(x))$ can be implemented with at most $2K + n$ gates over the Toffoli gate set. The basic idea behind Bennett's

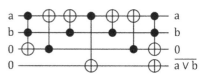

Fig. 1. A Toffoli network computing the NOR function $f(a, b) = \overline{a \vee b}$.

method is to replace all AND gates with Toffoli gates, then perform the computation, copy out the result, and undo the computation. This strategy is illustrated in Fig. 2, where the box labelled U_f corresponds to f with all AND gates substituted with Toffoli gates and the inverse box is simply obtained by reversing the order of all gates in U_f. Bennett's method has been used to perform classical-to-reversible circuit compilation in the quantum programming language Quipper [10]. One potential disadvantage of Bennett's method is the large number of ancillas it requires as the required memory scales proportional to the circuit *size* of the initial, irreversible function f.

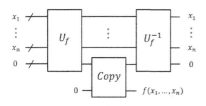

Fig. 2. A reversible circuit computing $f(x_1, \ldots, x_m)$ using the Bennett trick. Input lines with slashes denote an arbitrary number of bits.

In recent work, an attempt was made with the REVS compiler (and programming language of the same name) [21] to improve on the space-complexity of Bennett's strategy by generating circuits that are *space-efficient* – that is, REVS is an optimizing compiler with respect to the number of bits used. Their method makes use of a dependency graph to determine which bits may be eligible to be cleaned *eagerly*, before the end of the computation and hence be reused again. We build on their work in this paper, formalizing REVS and developing a *verified* compiler without too much loss in efficiency. In particular, we take the idea of eager cleanup and develop a new method analogous to garbage collection.

Var x,   **Bool** $b \in \{0,1\} = \mathbb{B}$,   **Nat** $i, j \in \mathbb{N}$,   **Loc** $l \in \mathbb{N}$

Val $v ::= \mathsf{unit} \mid l \mid \mathsf{reg}\ l_1 \ldots l_n \mid \lambda x.t$

Term $t ::= \mathsf{let}\ x = t_1\ \mathsf{in}\ t_2 \mid \lambda x.t \mid (t_1\ t_2) \mid t_1; t_2 \mid x \mid t_1 \leftarrow t_2 \mid b \mid t_1 \oplus t_2 \mid t_1 \wedge t_2$
$\qquad\quad \mid \mathsf{clean}\ t \mid \mathsf{assert}\ t \mid \mathsf{reg}\ t_1 \ldots t_n \mid t.[i] \mid t.[i..j] \mid \mathsf{append}\ t_1\ t_2 \mid \mathsf{rotate}\ i\ t$

Fig. 3. Syntax of REVS.

3   Languages

In this section we give a formal definition of REVS, as well as the intermediate and target languages of the compiler.

3.1   The Source

The abstract syntax of REVS is presented in Fig. 3. The core of the language is a simple imperative language over Boolean and array (register) types. The language is further extended with ML-style functional features, namely first-class functions and *let* definitions, and a reversible domain-specific construct *clean* which asserts that its argument evaluates to 0 and frees a bit.

In addition to the basic syntax of Fig. 3 we add the following derived operations:

$$\neg t \stackrel{\Delta}{=} 1 \oplus t, \qquad t_1 \vee t_2 \stackrel{\Delta}{=} (t_1 \wedge t_2) \oplus (t_1 \oplus t_2),$$

$$\mathsf{if}\ t_1\ \mathsf{then}\ t_2\ \mathsf{else}\ t_3 \stackrel{\Delta}{=} (t_1 \wedge t_2) \oplus (\neg t_1 \wedge t_3),$$

$$\mathsf{for}\ x\ \mathsf{in}\ i..j\ \mathsf{do}\ t \stackrel{\Delta}{=} t[x \mapsto i]; \cdots ; t[x \mapsto j].$$

Note that REVS has no *dynamic* control – i.e. control dependent on run-time values. In particular, every REVS program can be transformed into a straight-line program. This is due to the restrictions of our target architecture (see below).

The REVERC compiler uses F# as a meta-language to generate REVS code with particular register sizes and indices, possibly computed by some more complex program. Writing an F# program that generates REVS code is similar in effect to writing in a hardware description language [8]. We use F#'s *quotations* mechanism to achieve this by writing REVS programs in quotations <@...@>. Note that unlike languages such as Quipper, our strictly combinational target architecture doesn't allow computations in the meta-language to depend on computations within REVS.

Example 1. Figure 4 gives an example of a carry-ripple adder written in REVS. Naïvely compiling this implementation would result in a new bit being allocated for every carry bit, as the assignment on line 8 is irreversible (note that carry_ex 1 1 0 = 1 = carry_ex 1 1 1, hence the value of c can not be uniquely computed given a, b and the output). REVERC reduces this space usage by automatically cleaning the old carry bit, allowing it to be reused.

```
1  fun a b ->
2    let carry_ex a b c = (a ∧ (b ⊕ c)) ⊕ (b ∧ c)
3    let result = Array.zeroCreate(n)
4    let mutable carry = false

6    result.[0] ← a.[0] ⊕ b.[0]
7    for i in 1 .. n-1 do
8      carry ← carry_ex a.[i-1] b.[i-1] carry
9      result.[i] ← a.[i] ⊕ b.[i] ⊕ carry
10   result
```

Fig. 4. Implementation of an n-bit adder.

Semantics. We designed the semantics of REVS with two goals in mind:

1. keep the semantics as close to the original implementation as possible, and
2. simplify the task of formal verification.

The result is a somewhat non-standard semantics that is nonetheless intuitive for the programmer. Moreover, the particular semantics naturally enforces a style of programming that results in efficient circuits and allows common design patterns to be optimized.

The big-step semantics of REVS is presented in Fig. 5 as a relation $\Rightarrow \subseteq$ Config × Config on configuration-pairs – pairs of terms and Boolean-valued stores. A key feature of our semantics is that Boolean, or bit values, are always allocated on the store. Specifically, Boolean constants and expressions are modelled by allocating a new location on the store to hold its value – as a result all Boolean values, including constants, are mutable.

The allocation of Boolean values on the store serves two main purposes: to give the programmer fine-grain control over how many bits are allocated, and to provide a simple and efficient model of *registers* – i.e. arrays of bits. Specifically, registers are modelled as static length lists of bits. This allows the programmer to perform array-like operations such as bit modifications ($t_1.[i] \leftarrow t_2$) as well as list-like operations such as slicing ($t.[i..j]$) and concatenation (append $t_1\ t_2$) without copying out entire registers. We found that these were the most common access patterns for arrays of bits in low-level bitwise code (e.g. arithmetic and cryptographic implementations).

The semantics of $\oplus$ (Boolean XOR) and $\wedge$ (Boolean AND) are also notable in that they first reduce both arguments to locations, *then* retrieve their value. This results in statements whose value may not be immediately apparent – e.g., $x \oplus (x \leftarrow y; y)$, which under these semantics will always evaluate to 0. The benefit of this definition is that it allows the compiler to perform important optimizations without a significant burden on the programmer.

3.2 Boolean Expressions

Our compiler uses XOR-AND Boolean expressions – single output classical circuits over XOR and AND gates – as an intermediate language. Compilation from Boolean expressions into reversible circuits forms the main "code generation" step of our compiler.

$$\text{Store } \sigma : \mathbb{N} \rightharpoonup \mathbb{B}$$

$$\text{Config } c ::= \langle t, \sigma \rangle$$

$$[\text{LET}] \frac{\langle t_1, \sigma \rangle \Rightarrow \langle v_1, \sigma' \rangle \quad \langle t_2[x \mapsto v_1], \sigma' \rangle \Rightarrow \langle v_2, \sigma'' \rangle}{\langle \text{let } x = t_1 \text{ in } t_2, \sigma \rangle \Rightarrow \langle v_2, \sigma'' \rangle}$$

$$[\text{REFL}] \frac{}{\langle v, \sigma \rangle \Rightarrow \langle v, \sigma \rangle} \qquad [\text{BEXP}] \frac{\langle t_1, \sigma \rangle \Rightarrow \langle l_1, \sigma' \rangle \quad \langle t_2, \sigma' \rangle \Rightarrow \langle l_2, \sigma'' \rangle \quad l_3 \notin \text{dom}(\sigma'')}{\langle t_1 \star t_2, \sigma \rangle \Rightarrow \langle l_3, \sigma''[l_3 \mapsto \sigma''(l_1) \star \sigma''(l_2)]\rangle}$$

$$[\text{BOOL}] \frac{b \in \mathbb{B} \quad l \notin \text{dom}(\sigma)}{\langle b, \sigma \rangle \Rightarrow \langle l, \sigma''[l \mapsto b]\rangle} \qquad [\text{APP}] \frac{\langle t_1, \sigma \rangle \Rightarrow \langle \lambda x.t_1', \sigma' \rangle \langle t_2, \sigma' \rangle \Rightarrow \langle v_2, \sigma'' \rangle}{\langle t_1'[x \mapsto v_2], \sigma'' \rangle \Rightarrow \langle v, \sigma''' \rangle}{\langle (t_1 \ t_2), \sigma \rangle \Rightarrow \langle v, \sigma''' \rangle}$$

$$[\text{SEQ}] \frac{\langle t_1, \sigma \rangle \Rightarrow \langle \text{unit}, \sigma' \rangle \quad \langle t_2, \sigma' \rangle \Rightarrow \langle v, \sigma'' \rangle}{\langle t_1; t_2, \sigma \rangle \Rightarrow \langle v, \sigma'' \rangle} \qquad [\text{ASSN}] \frac{\langle t_1, \sigma \rangle \Rightarrow \langle l_1, \sigma' \rangle \quad \langle t_2, \sigma' \rangle \Rightarrow \langle l_2, \sigma'' \rangle}{\langle t_1 \leftarrow t_2, \sigma \rangle \Rightarrow \langle \text{unit}, \sigma''[l_1 \mapsto \sigma''(l_2)]\rangle}$$

$$[\text{APPEND}] \frac{\langle t_1, \sigma \rangle \Rightarrow \langle \text{reg } l_1 \ldots l_m, \sigma' \rangle \quad \langle t_2, \sigma' \rangle \Rightarrow \langle \text{reg } l_{m+1} \ldots l_n, \sigma'' \rangle}{\langle \text{append } t_1 \ t_2, \sigma \rangle \Rightarrow \langle \text{reg } l_1 \ldots l_n, \sigma'' \rangle}$$

$$[\text{INDEX}] \frac{\langle t, \sigma \rangle \Rightarrow \langle \text{reg } l_1 \ldots l_n, \sigma' \rangle \quad 1 \le i \le n}{\langle t.[i], \sigma \rangle \Rightarrow \langle l_i, \sigma' \rangle}$$

$$[\text{SLICE}] \frac{\langle t, \sigma \rangle \Rightarrow \langle \text{reg } l_1 \ldots l_n, \sigma' \rangle \quad 1 \le i \le j \le n}{\langle t.[i..j], \sigma \rangle \Rightarrow \langle \text{reg } l_i \ldots l_j, \sigma' \rangle}$$

$$[\text{REG}] \frac{\langle t_1, \sigma \rangle \Rightarrow \langle l_1, \sigma_1 \rangle}{\langle t_2, \sigma \rangle \Rightarrow \langle l_2, \sigma_2 \rangle} \\ \vdots \\ \frac{\langle t_n, \sigma \rangle \Rightarrow \langle l_n, \sigma_n \rangle}{\langle \text{reg } t_1 \ldots t_n, \sigma \rangle \Rightarrow \langle \text{reg } l_1 \ldots l_n, \sigma_n \rangle}$$

$$[\text{ROTATE}] \frac{\langle t, \sigma \rangle \Rightarrow \langle \text{reg } l_1 \ldots l_n, \sigma' \rangle \quad 1 < i < n}{\langle \text{rotate } t \ i, \sigma \rangle \Rightarrow \langle \text{reg } l_i \ldots l_{i-1}, \sigma' \rangle}$$

$$[\text{CLEAN}] \frac{\langle t, \sigma \rangle \Rightarrow \langle l, \sigma' \rangle \quad \sigma'(l) = 0}{\langle \text{clean } t, \sigma \rangle \Rightarrow \langle \text{unit}, \sigma'|_{\text{dom}(\sigma') \setminus \{l\}} \rangle} \qquad [\text{ASSERT}] \frac{\langle t, \sigma \rangle \Rightarrow \langle l, \sigma' \rangle \quad \sigma'(l) = 1}{\langle \text{assert } t, \sigma \rangle \Rightarrow \langle \text{unit}, \sigma' \rangle}$$

Fig. 5. Operational semantics of REVS.

A Boolean expression is defined as an expression over Boolean constants, variable indices, and logical $\oplus$ and $\wedge$ operators. Explicitly, we define

$$\textbf{BExp } B ::= 0 \mid 1 \mid i \in \mathbb{N} \mid B_1 \oplus B_2 \mid B_1 \wedge B_2.$$

Note that we use the symbols $0, 1, \oplus$ and $\wedge$ interchangeably with their interpretation in $\mathbb{B}$. We use $\text{vars}(B)$ to refer to the set of free variables in B.

We interpret a Boolean expression as a function from (total) Boolean-valued states to Booleans. In particular, we define $\textbf{State} = \mathbb{N} \to \mathbb{B}$ and denote the semantics of a Boolean expression by $[\![B]\!] : \textbf{State} \to \mathbb{B}$. The formal definition of $[\![B]\!]$ is obvious so we omit it.

3.3 Target Architecture

REVERC compiles to *combinational, reversible circuits* over NOT, controlled-NOT and Toffoli gates. By combinational circuits we mean a sequence of logic gates applied to bits with no external means of control or memory – effectively pure logical functions. We chose this model as it is suitable for implementing classical functions and oracles within quantum computations [19].

Formally, we define

$$\textbf{Circ } C ::= - \mid \text{NOT } i \mid \text{CNOT } i\ j \mid \text{Toffoli } i\ j\ k \mid C_1 :: C_2,$$

i.e., **Circ** is the free monoid over NOT, CNOT, and Toffoli gates with unit – and the append operator ::. All but the last bit in each gate is called a *control*, whereas the final bit is denoted as the *target* and is the only bit *modified* or changed by the gate. We use $\text{use}(C)$, $\text{mod}(C)$ and $\text{control}(C)$ to denote the set of bit indices that are used in, modified by, or used as a control in the circuit C, respectively. A circuit is *well-formed* if no gate contains more than one reference to a bit – i.e., the bits used in each controlled-NOT or Toffoli gate are distinct.

Similar to Boolean expressions, a circuit is interpreted as a function from states (maps from indices to Boolean values) to states, given by applying each gate which updates the previous state in order. The formal definition of the semantics of a reversible circuit C, given by $[\![C]\!] : \textbf{State} \rightarrow \textbf{State}$, is straightforward:

$$[\![\text{NOT } i]\!]s = s[i \mapsto \neg s(i)]$$
$$[\![\text{CNOT } i\ j]\!]s = s[j \mapsto s(i) \oplus s(j)]$$
$$[\![\text{Toffoli } i\ j\ k]\!]s = s[k \mapsto (s(i) \wedge s(j)) \oplus s(k)]$$
$$[\![-]\!]s = s \qquad [\![C_1 :: C_2]\!]s = ([\![C_2]\!] \circ [\![C_1]\!])s$$

We use $s[x \mapsto y]$ to denote the function that maps x to y, and all other inputs z to $s(z)$; by an abuse of notation we use $[x \mapsto y]$ to denote other substitutions as well.

4 Compilation

In this section we discuss the implementation of REVERC. The compiler consists of around 4000 lines of code in a common subset of F* and F#, with a front-end to evaluate and translate F# quotations into REVS expressions.

4.1 Boolean Expression Compilation

The core of REVERC's code generation is a compiler from Boolean expressions into reversible circuits. We use a modification of the method employed in REVS.

As a Boolean expression is already in the form of an irreversible classical circuit, the main job of the compiler is to allocate ancillas to store sub-expressions whenever necessary. REVERC does this by maintaining a (mutable) heap of ancillas $\xi \in \textbf{AncHeap}$ called an *ancilla heap*, which keeps track of the currently available (zero-valued) ancillary bits. Cleaned ancillas (ancillas returned to the zero state) may be pushed back onto the heap, and allocations return previously used ancillas if any are available, hence not using any extra space.

The function COMPILE-BEXP, shown in pseudo-code below, takes a Boolean expression B and a target bit i and then generates a reversible circuit computing $i \oplus B$. Note that ancillas are only allocated to store sub-expressions of $\wedge$ expressions, since $i \oplus (B_1 \oplus B_2) = (i \oplus B_1) \oplus B_2$ and so we compile $i \oplus (B_1 \oplus B_2)$ by first computing $i' = i \oplus B_1$, followed by $i' \oplus B_2$.

function COMPILE-BEXP(B, i, ξ)
    if $B = 0$ **then** –
    else if $B = 1$ **then** NOT i
    else if $B = j$ **then** CNOT j i
    else if $B = B_1 \oplus B_2$ **then** COMPILE-BEXP(B_1, i, ξ)::COMPILE-BEXP(B_2, i, ξ)
    else // $B = B_1 \wedge B_2$
        $a_1 \leftarrow$ pop-min(ξ); $C \leftarrow$ COMPILE-BEXP(B_1, a_1, ξ);
        $a_2 \leftarrow$ pop-min(ξ); $C' \leftarrow$ COMPILE-BEXP(B_2, a_2, ξ);
        $C :: C' ::$ Toffoli a_1 a_2 i
    end if
end function

Cleanup. The definition of COMPILE-BEXP above leaves many garbage bits that take up space and need to be cleaned before they can be re-used. To reclaim those bits, we clean temporary expressions after every call to COMPILE-BEXP.

To facilitate the cleanup – or *uncomputing* – of a circuit, we define the *restricted inverse* uncompute(C, A) of C with respect to a set of bits $A \subset \mathbb{N}$ by reversing the gates of C, and removing any gates with a target in A. For instance:

$$\text{uncompute(CNOT } i\ j, A) = \begin{cases} - & \text{if } j \in A \\ \text{CNOT } i\ j & \text{otherwise} \end{cases}$$

The other cases are defined similarly. Note that since uncompute produces a subsequence of the original circuit C, no ancillary bits are used.

The restricted inverse allows the temporary values of a reversible computation to be uncomputed without affecting any of the target bits. In particular, if $C = $ COMPILE-BEXP(B, i), then the circuit $C :: $ uncompute($C, \{i\}$) maps a state s to $s[i \mapsto [\![B]\!]s \oplus s(i)]$, allowing any newly allocated ancillas to be pushed back onto the heap. Intuitively, since no bits contained in the set A are modified, the restricted inverse preserves their values; that the restricted inverse uncomputes the values of the remaining bits is less obvious, but it can be observed that if the computation doesn't *depend* on the value of a bit in A, the computation will be inverted. We formalize and prove this statement in Sect. 5.

4.2 REVS Compilation

In studying the REVS compiler, we observed that most of what the compiler was doing was evaluating the non-Boolean parts of the program – effectively bookkeeping for registers – only generating circuits for a small kernel of cases. As a result, transformations to different Boolean representations (e.g., circuits, dependence graphs [21]) and the interpreter itself reused significant portions of this bookkeeping code. To make use of this redundancy to simplify both writing and verifying the compiler, we designed REVERC as a *partial evaluator* parameterized by an abstract machine for evaluating Boolean expressions. As a side effect, we arrive at a unique model for circuit compilation similar to staged computation (see, e.g. [12]).

REVERC works by evaluating the program with an abstract machine providing mechanisms for initializing and assigning locations on the store to Boolean expressions. We call an instantiation of this abstract machine an *interpretation* $\mathscr{I}$, which consists of a domain D equipped with two operators:

$$\mathsf{assign} : D \times \mathbb{N} \times \mathbf{BExp} \to D$$
$$\mathsf{eval} : D \times \mathbb{N} \times \mathbf{State} \rightharpoonup \mathbb{B}.$$

We typically denote an element of an interpretation domain D by σ. A sequence of assignments in an interpretation builds a Boolean computation or circuit within a specific model (i.e., classical, reversible, different gate sets) which may be simulated on an initial state with the eval function – effectively an operational semantics of the model. Practically speaking, an element of D abstracts the store in Fig. 5 and allows delayed computation or additional processing of the Boolean expression stored in a cell, which may be mapped into reversible circuits immediately or after the entire program has been evaluated. We give some examples of interpretations below.

Example 2. The standard interpretation $\mathscr{I}_{standard}$ has domain $\mathbf{Store} = \mathbb{N} \rightharpoonup \mathbb{B}$, together with the operations

$$\mathsf{assign}_{standard}(\sigma, l, B) = \sigma[l \mapsto [\![B]\!]\sigma]$$
$$\mathsf{eval}_{standard}(\sigma, l, s) = \sigma(l).$$

Partial evaluation over the standard interpretation coincides exactly with the operational semantics of REVS.

Example 3. The *reversible circuit* interpretation $\mathscr{I}_{circuit}$ has domain $D_{circuit} = (\mathbb{N} \rightharpoonup \mathbb{N}) \times \mathbf{Circ} \times \mathbf{AncHeap}$. In particular, given $(\rho, C, \xi) \in D_{circuit}$, ρ maps heap locations to bits in C, and ξ is an ancilla heap. Assignment and evaluation are further defined as follows:

$$\mathsf{assign}_{circuit}((\rho, C, \xi), l, B) = (\rho[l \mapsto i], C :: C', \xi)$$
$$\text{where } i = \text{ pop-min}(\xi),$$
$$(C', \xi') = \text{ COMPILE-BEXP}\,(B[l' \in \mathsf{vars}(B) \mapsto \rho(l')], i, \xi)$$
$$\mathsf{eval}_{circuit}((\rho, C, \xi), l, s)) = ([\![C]\!]s)\,(\rho(l))$$

Interpreting a program with $\mathscr{I}_{circuit}$ builds a reversible circuit executing the program, together with a mapping from heap locations to bits. Since the circuit is required to be reversible, when a location is overwritten, a new ancilla i is allocated and the expression $B \oplus i$ is compiled into a circuit. Evaluation amounts to running the circuit on an initial state, then retrieving the value at the bit associated with a heap location.

Given an interpretation $\mathscr{I}$ with domain D, we define the set of $\mathscr{I}$-configurations as $\mathbf{Config}_{\mathscr{I}} = \mathbf{Term} \times D$ – that is, $\mathscr{I}$-configurations are pairs of programs and elements of D which function as an abstraction of the heap. The relation

$$\Rightarrow_{\mathscr{I}} \subseteq \mathbf{Config}_{\mathscr{I}} \times \mathbf{Config}_{\mathscr{I}}$$

gives the operational semantics of REVS over the interpretation $\mathscr{I}$. We do not give a formal definition of $\Rightarrow_{\mathscr{I}}$, as it can be obtained trivially from the definition of $\Rightarrow$ (Fig. 5) by replacing all heap updates with assign and taking $\mathsf{dom}(\sigma)$ to mean the set of locations on which eval is defined. To compile a program term t, REVERC evaluates t over a particular interpretation $\mathscr{I}$ (for instance, the reversible circuit interpretation) and an initial heap $\sigma \in D$ according to the semantic relation $\Rightarrow_{\mathscr{I}}$. In this way, evaluating a program and compiling a program to a circuit look almost identical. This greatly simplifies the problem of verification (see Sect. 5).

REVERC currently supports three modes of compilation, defined by giving interpretations: a default mode, an eagerly cleaned mode, and a "crush" mode. The default mode evaluates the program using the circuit interpretation, and simply returns the circuit and output bit(s), while the eager cleanup mode operates analogously, using instead the garbage-collected interpretation defined below in Sect. 4.3. The crush mode interprets a program as a list of Boolean expressions over free variables, which while unscalable allows highly optimized versions of small circuits to be compiled, a common practice in circuit synthesis. We omit the details of the Boolean expression interpretation.

Function Compilation. While the definition of REVERC as a partial evaluator streamlines both development and verification, there is an inherent disconnect between the treatment of a (top-level) function expression by the interpreter and by the compiler, in that we want the compiler to evaluate the function body. Instead of defining a two-stage semantics for REVS we took the approach of applying a program transformation, whereby the function being compiled is evaluated on special heap locations representing the parameters. This creates a further problem in that the compiler needs to first determine the size of each parameter; to solve this problem, REVERC performs a static analysis we call *parameter interference.* We omit the details of this analysis due to space constraints and instead point the interested reader to an extended version of this paper [3].

4.3   Eager Cleanup

It was previously noted that the circuit interpretation allocates a new ancilla on every assignment to a location, due to the requirement of reversibility. Apart from REVERC's additional optimization passes, this is effectively the Bennett method, and hence uses a large amount of extra space. One way to keep the space usage from continually expanding as assignments are made is to clean the old bit as soon as possible and then reuse it, rather than wait until the end of the computation. Here we develop an interpretation that performs this automatic, eager cleanup by augmenting the circuit interpretation with a *cleanup expression* for each bit. Our method is based on the eager cleanup of [21], and was intended as a more easily verifiable alternative to mutable dependency diagrams.

The *eager cleanup* interpretation $\mathscr{I}_{GC}$ has domain

$$D = (\mathbb{N} \rightharpoonup \mathbb{N}) \times \mathbf{Circ} \times \mathbf{AncHeap} \times (\mathbb{N} \rightharpoonup \mathbf{BExp}),$$

where given $(\rho, C, \xi, \kappa) \in D$, ρ, C and ξ are as in the circuit interpretation. The partial function κ maps individual bits to a Boolean expression over the bits of C which can be used to return the bit to its initial state, called the cleanup expression. Specifically, we have the following property:

$$\forall i \in \mathsf{cod}(\rho), s'(i) \oplus [\![\kappa(i)]\!]s' = s(i) \qquad \text{where } s' = [\![C]\!]s.$$

Intuitively, any bit i can then be cleaned by simply computing $i \mapsto i \oplus \kappa(i)$, which in turn can be done by calling COMPILE-BEXP($\kappa(i)$, i).

Two problems remain, however. In general it may be the case that a bit *can not* be cleaned without affecting the value of other bits, as it might result in a loss of information – in the context of cleanup expressions, this occurs exactly when a bit's cleanup expression contains an irreducible self-reference. In particular, if $i \in \mathsf{vars}(B)$, then COMPILE-BEXP(B, i) does not compile a circuit computing $i \oplus B$ and hence won't clean the target bit correctly. In the case when a garbage bit contains a self-reference in its cleanup expression that can not be eliminated by Boolean simplification, REVERC simply ignores the bit and performs a final round of cleanup at the end.

The second problem arises when a bit's cleanup expression references another bit that has itself since been cleaned or otherwise modified. In this case, the modification of the latter bit has invalidated the correctness property for the former bit. To ensure that the above relation always holds, whenever a bit is modified – corresponding to an XOR of the bit, i, with a Boolean expression B – all instances of bit i in every cleanup expression is replaced with $i \oplus B$. Specifically we observe that, if $s'(i) = s(i) \oplus [\![B]\!]s$, then

$$s'(i) \oplus [\![B]\!]s = s(i) \oplus [\![B]\!]s \oplus [\![B]\!]s = s(i).$$

The function CLEAN, defined below, performs the cleanup of a bit i if possible, and validates all cleanup expressions in a given element of D:

```
function CLEAN((ρ, C, ξ, κ), i)
    if i ∈ vars(κ(i)) then return (ρ, C, ξ, κ)
    else
        C' ← COMPILE-BEXP(κ(i), i, ξ)
        if i is an ancilla then insert(i, ξ)
        κ' ← κ[i' ∈ dom(κ) ↦ κ(i')[i ↦ i ⊕ κ(i)]]
        return (ρ, C :: C', ξ, κ')
    end if
end function
```

Assignment and evaluation are defined in the eager cleanup interpretation as follows. Both are effectively the same as in the circuit interpretation, except the assignment operator calls CLEAN on the previous bit mapped to l.

$$\mathsf{assign}_{GC}((\rho, C, \xi, \kappa), l, B) = \text{CLEAN}((\rho[l \mapsto i], C :: C', \xi, \kappa[i \mapsto B']), i)$$
$$\text{where } i = \text{pop-min}(\xi),$$
$$B' = B[l' \in \mathsf{vars}(B) \mapsto \rho(l')]$$
$$C' = \text{COMPILE-BEXP}(B', i, \xi)$$
$$\mathsf{eval}_{GC}((\rho, C, \xi, \kappa), l, s)) = (\llbracket C \rrbracket s)(\rho(l))$$

The eager cleanup interpretation coincides with a reversible analogue of *garbage collection* for a very specific case when the number of references to a heap location (or in our case, a bit) is trivially zero. In fact, the CLEAN function can be used to eagerly clean bits that have no reference in other contexts. We intend to expand REVERC to include a generic garbage collector that uses cleanup expressions to more aggressively reclaim space – for instance, when a bit's unique pre-image on the heap leaves the current scope.

4.4   Optimizations

During the course of compilation it is frequently the case that more ancillas are allocated than are actually needed, due to the program structure. For instance, when compiling the expression $i \leftarrow B$, if B can be factored as $i \oplus B'$ the assignment may be performed reversibly rather than allocating a new bit to store the value of B. Likewise if i is provably in the 0 or 1 state, the assignment may be performed reversibly without allocating a new bit. Our implementation identifies some of these common patterns, as well as general Boolean expression simplifications, to further minimize the space usage of compile circuits. All such optimizations in REVERC have been formally verified.

5   Verification

In this section we describe the formal verification of REVERC and give the major theorems proven. All theorems given in this section have been formally specified and proven using the F* compiler [27]. We first give theorems about our Boolean expression compiler, then use these to prove properties about whole program compilation. The total verification of the REVERC core's approximately 2000 lines of code comprises around 2200 lines of F* code, and took just over 1 person-month. We feel that this relatively low-cost verification is a testament to the increasing ease with which formal verification can be carried out using modern proof assistants. Additionally, the verification relies on only 11 unproven axioms regarding simple properties of lookup tables and sets, such as the fact that a successful lookup is in the codomain of a lookup table.

Rather than give F* specifications, we translate our proofs to mathematical language as we believe this is more enlightening. The full source code of REVERC including proofs can be obtained at https://github.com/msr-quarc/ReVerC.

5.1   Boolean Expression Compilation

Correctness. Below is our main theorem establishing the correctness of the function COMPILE-BEXP with respect to the semantics of reversible circuits and Boolean expressions. It states that if the variables of B, the bits on the ancilla heap and the target are non-overlapping, and if the ancilla bits are 0-valued, then the circuit computes the expression $i \oplus B$.

Theorem 1. *Let B be a Boolean expression, ξ be an ancilla heap, $i \in \mathbb{N}$, $C \in$* **Circ** *and s be a map from bits to Boolean values. Suppose* $\mathsf{vars}(B)$, ξ *and $\{i\}$ are all disjoint and $s(j) = 0$ for all $j \in \xi$. Then*

$$(\llbracket \text{COMPILE-BEXP}(B, i, \xi) \rrbracket s)\,(i) = s(i) \oplus \llbracket B \rrbracket s.$$

Cleanup. As remarked earlier, a crucial part of reversible computing is cleaning ancillas both to reduce space usage, and in quantum computing to prevent entangled qubits from influencing the computation. Moreover, the correctness of our cleanup is actually necessary to prove correctness of the compiler, as the compiler re-uses cleaned ancillas on the heap, potentially interfering with the precondition of Theorem 1. We use the following lemma to establish the correctness of our cleanup method, stating that the uncompute transformation reverses all changes on bits not in the target set under the condition that no bits in the target set are used as controls.

Lemma 1. *Let C be a well-formed reversible circuit and $A \subset \mathbb{N}$ be some set of bits. If $A \cap \mathsf{control}(C) = \emptyset$ then for all states s, $s' = \llbracket C :: \mathsf{uncompute}(C, A) \rrbracket s$ and any $i \notin A$,*

$$s(i) = s'(i)$$

Lemma 1 largely relies on the following important lemma stating in effect that the action of a circuit is determined by the values of the bits used as controls:

Lemma 2. *Let $A \subset \mathbb{N}$ and s, s' be states such that for all $i \in A$, $s(i) = s'(i)$. If C is a reversible circuit where* $\mathsf{control}(C) \subseteq A$, *then*

$$(\llbracket C \rrbracket s)(i) = (\llbracket C \rrbracket s')(i)$$

for all $i \in A$.

Lemma 1, together with the fact that COMPILE-BEXP produces a well-formed circuit under disjointness constraints, gives us our cleanup theorem below that Boolean expression compilation with cleanup correctly reverses the changes to every bit except the target.

Theorem 2. *Let B be a Boolean expression, ξ be an ancilla heap and $i \in \mathbb{N}$ such that* $\mathsf{vars}(B)$, ξ *and $\{i\}$ are all disjoint. Suppose* COMPILE-BEXP$(B, i, \xi) = C$. *Then for all $j \neq i$ and states s we have*

$$(\llbracket C \circ \mathsf{uncompute}(C, \{i\}) \rrbracket s)\,(j) = s(j).$$

5.2 REVS Compilation

It was noted in Sect. 4 that the design of REVERC as a partial evaluator simplifies proving correctness. We expand on that point now, and in particular show that if a relation between elements of two interpretations is preserved by assignment, then the evaluator also preserves the relation. We state this formally in the theorem below.

Theorem 3. *Let $\mathscr{I}_1, \mathscr{I}_2$ be interpretations and suppose whenever $(\sigma_1, \sigma_2) \in R$ for some relation $R \subseteq \mathscr{I}_1 \times \mathscr{I}_2$,*

$$(\mathsf{assign}_1(\sigma_1, l, B), \mathsf{assign}_2(\sigma_2, l, B)) \in R$$

for any l, B. Then for any term t, if $\langle t, \sigma_1 \rangle \Rightarrow_{\mathscr{I}_1} \langle v_1, \sigma_1' \rangle$ and $\langle t, \sigma_2 \rangle \Rightarrow_{\mathscr{I}_2} \langle v_2, \sigma_2' \rangle$, then $v_1 = v_2$ and $(\sigma_1', \sigma_2') \in R$.

Theorem 3 lifts properties about interpretations to properties of evaluation over those abstract machines – in particular, we only need to establish that *assignment* is correct for an interpretation to establish correctness of the corresponding evaluator/compiler. In practice we found this significantly reduces boilerplate proof code that is otherwise currently necessary in F* due to a lack of automated induction.

Given two interpretations $\mathscr{I}, \mathscr{I}'$, we say elements σ and σ' of $\mathscr{I}$ and $\mathscr{I}'$ are *observationally equivalent* with respect to a supplied set of initial values $s \in \mathbf{State}$ if for all $i \in \mathbb{N}$, $\mathsf{eval}_{\mathscr{I}}(\sigma, i, s) = \mathsf{eval}_{\mathscr{I}'}(\sigma', i, s)$. We say $\sigma \sim_s \sigma'$ if σ and σ' are observationally equivalent with respect to s. As observational equivalence of two domain elements σ, σ' implies that any location in scope has the same valuation in either interpretation, it suffices to show that any compiled circuit is observationally equivalent to the standard interpretation. The following lemmas are used along with Theorem 3 to establish this fact for the default and eager-cleanup interpretations – a similar lemma is proven in the implementation of REVERC for the crush mode.

Lemma 3. *Let σ, σ' be elements of $\mathscr{I}_{standard}$ and $\mathscr{I}_{circuit}$, respectively. For all $l \in \mathbb{N}, B \in \mathbf{BExp}, s \in \mathbf{State}$, if $\sigma \sim_s \sigma'$ and $s(i) = 0$ whenever $i \in \xi$, then*

$$\mathsf{assign}_{standard}(\sigma, l, B) \sim_s \mathsf{assign}_{circuit}(\sigma', l, B).$$

Moreover, the ancilla heap remains 0-filled.

We say that $(\rho, C, \xi) \in D_{circuit}$ is *valid* with respect to $s \in \mathbf{State}$ if and only if $s(i) = 0$ for all $i \in \xi$. For elements of D_{GC} the validity conditions are more involved, so we introduce a relation, $\mathcal{V} \subseteq D_{GC} \times \mathbf{State}$, defining the set of valid domain elements:

$$((\rho, C, \xi, \kappa), s) \in \mathcal{V} \iff \forall i \in \xi, s(i) = 0 \wedge \forall l, l' \in \mathsf{dom}(\rho), \rho(l) \neq \rho(l')$$
$$\wedge \forall i \in \mathsf{cod}(\rho), [\![i \oplus \kappa(i)]\!]([\![C]\!]s) = s(i)$$

Informally, $\mathcal{V}$ specifies that all bits on the heap have initial value 0, that ρ is a one-to-one mapping, and that for every active bit i, XORing i with $\kappa(i)$ returns the initial value of i – that is, $i \oplus \kappa(i)$ *cleans* i.

Lemma 4. *Let σ, σ' be elements of $\mathscr{I}_{standard}$ and $\mathscr{I}_{GC}$, respectively. For all $l \in \mathbb{N}, B \in \mathbf{BExp}, s \in \mathbf{State}$, if $\sigma \sim_s \sigma'$ and $(\sigma', s) \in \mathcal{V}$, then*

$$\mathsf{assign}_{standard}(\sigma, l, B) \sim_s \mathsf{assign}_{GC}(\sigma', l, B).$$

Moreover, $(\mathsf{assign}_{GC}(\sigma', l, B), s) \in \mathcal{V}$.

By setting the relation R_{GC} as

$$(\sigma_1, \sigma_2) \in R_{GC} \iff \sigma_2 \in \mathcal{V} \wedge \sigma_1 \sim_{s_0} \sigma_2$$

for $\sigma_1 \in D_{standard}$, by Theorem 3 and Lemma 4 it follows that partial evaluation/compilation preserves observational equivalence between $\mathscr{I}_{standard}$ and $\mathscr{I}_{GC}$. A similar result follows for $\mathscr{I}_{circuit}$.

To formally prove correctness of the compiler we need initial values in each interpretation (and an initial state) which are observationally equivalent. We don't describe the initial values here as they are dependent on the program transformation applied to expand top-level functions.

6 Experiments

We ran experiments to compare the bit, gate and Toffoli counts of circuits compiled by REVERC to the original REVS compiler. The number of Toffoli gates in particular is distinguished as such gates are generally much more costly than NOT and controlled-NOT gates – at least 7 times as typical implementations use 7 CNOT gates *per Toffoli* [19], or up to hundreds of times in most fault-tolerant architectures [2]. We compiled circuits for various arithmetic and cryptographic functions written in REVS using both compilers and reported the results in Table 1. Experiments were run in Linux using 8 GB of RAM.

Table 1. Bit and gate counts for both compilers in default and eager cleanup modes. In cases when not all results are the same, entries with the fewest bits used or Toffolis are bolded.

Benchmark	REVS			REVS (eager)			REVERC			REVERC (eager)		
	Bits	Gates	Toffolis	Bits	Gates	Toffolis	Bits	Gates	Toffolis	Bits	Gates	Toffolis
carryRippleAdd 32	129	281	**62**	129	467	124	128	281	**62**	**113**	361	90
carryRippleAdd 64	257	569	**126**	257	947	252	256	569	**126**	**225**	745	186
mult 32	128	6016	4032	128	6016	4032	128	6016	4032	128	6016	4032
mult 64	256	24320	16256	256	24320	16256	256	24320	16256	256	24320	16256
carryLookahead 32	160	345	**103**	**109**	1036	344	165	499	120	146	576	146
carryLookahead 64	424	1026	**307**	**271**	3274	1130	432	1375	336	376	1649	428
modAdd 32	65	188	62	65	188	62	65	188	62	65	188	62
modAdd 64	129	380	126	129	380	126	129	380	126	129	380	126
cucarroAdder 32	65	98	32	65	98	32	65	98	32	65	98	32
cucarroAdder 64	129	194	64	129	194	64	129	194	64	129	194	64
ma4	17	24	8	17	24	8	17	24	8	17	24	8
SHA-2 round	449	1796	**594**	353	2276	754	452	1796	**594**	449	1796	**594**
MD5	7841	81664	**27520**	7905	82624	27968	4833	70912	**27520**	**4769**	70912	**27520**

The results show that both compilers are more-of-less evenly matched in terms of bit counts across both modes, despite REVERC being certifiably correct. REVERC's eager cleanup mode never used more bits than the default mode, as expected, and in half of the benchmarks reduced the number of bits. Moreover, in the cases of the carryRippleAdder and MD5 benchmarks, REVERC's eager cleanup mode produced circuits with significantly fewer bits than either of REVS' modes. On the other hand, REVS saw dramatic decreases in bit numbers for carryLookahead and SHA-2 with its eager cleanup mode compared to REVERC.

While the results show there is clearly room for optimization of gate counts, they appear consistent with other verified compilers (e.g. [13]) which take some performance hit when compared to unverified compilers. In particular, unverified compilers may use more aggressive optimizations due to the increased ease of implementation and the lack of a requirement to prove their correctness compared to certified compilers. In some cases, the optimizations are even known to not be correct in all possible cases, as in the case of fast arithmetic and some loop optimization passes in the GNU C Compiler [1].

7 Conclusion

We have described our verified compiler for the REVS language, REVERC. Our method of compilation differs from the original REVS compiler by using partial evaluation over an interpretation of the heap to compile programs, forgoing the need to re-implement and verify bookkeeping code for every internal translation. We described two interpretations implemented in REVERC, the circuit interpretation and a garbage collected interpretation, the latter of which refines the former by applying eager cleanup.

While REVERC is verified in the sense that compiled circuits produce the same result as the program interpreter, as with any verified compiler project this is not the end of certification. The implementation of the interpreter may have subtle bugs, which ideally would be verified against a more straightforward adaptation of the semantics using a relational definition. We intend to address these issues in the future, and to further improve upon REVERC's space usage.

References

1. Using the GNU Compiler Collection. Free Software Foundation, Inc. (2016). https://gcc.gnu.org/onlinedocs/gcc/
2. Amy, M., Maslov, D., Mosca, M., Roetteler, M.: A meet-in-the-middle algorithm for fast synthesis of depth-optimal quantum circuits. IEEE Trans. Comput. Aided Des. Integr. Circuits Syst. **32**(6), 818–830 (2013)
3. Amy, M., Roetteler, M., Svore, K.M.: Verified compilation of space-efficient reversible circuits. arXiv e-prints (2016). https://arxiv.org/abs/1603.01635
4. Anticoli, L., Piazza, C., Taglialegne, L., Zuliani, P.: Towards quantum programs verification: from quipper circuits to QPMC. In: Devitt, S., Lanese, I. (eds.) RC 2016. LNCS, vol. 9720, pp. 213–219. Springer, Cham (2016). doi:10.1007/978-3-319-40578-0_16

5. Bennett, C.H.: Logical reversibility of computation. IBM J. Res. Dev. **17**, 525–532 (1973)
6. Beringer, L., Stewart, G., Dockins, R., Appel, A.W.: Verified compilation for shared-memory C. In: Shao, Z. (ed.) ESOP 2014. LNCS, vol. 8410, pp. 107–127. Springer, Heidelberg (2014). doi:10.1007/978-3-642-54833-8_7
7. Chlipala, A.: A verified compiler for an impure functional language. In: Proceedings of the 37th Annual ACM SIGPLAN-SIGACT Symposium on Principles of Programming Languages (POPL 2010), pp. 93–106. ACM (2010)
8. Claessen, K.: Embedded languages for describing and verifying hardware. Ph.D. thesis, Chalmers University of Technology and Göteborg University (2001)
9. Fournet, C., Swamy, N., Chen, J., Dagand, P.E., Strub, P.Y., Livshits, B.: Fully abstract compilation to JavaScript. In: Proceedings of the 40th Annual ACM SIGPLAN-SIGACT Symposium on Principles of Programming Languages (POPL 2013), pp. 371–384. ACM (2013)
10. Green, A.S., LeFanu Lumsdaine, P., Ross, N.J., Selinger, P., Valiron, B.: Quipper: a scalable quantum programming language. In: Proceedings of the 34th Annual ACM SIGPLAN Conference on Programming Language Design and Implementation (PLDI 2013). ACM (2013)
11. Grover, L.K.: A fast quantum mechanical algorithm for database search. In: Proceedings of the 28th Annual ACM Symposium on the Theory of Computing (STOC 1996), pp. 212–219. ACM (1996)
12. Jones, N.D., Gomard, C.K., Sestoft, P.: Partial Evaluation and Automatic Program Generation. Prentice-Hall Inc., Upper Saddle River (1993)
13. Leroy, X.: Formal certification of a compiler back-end or: programming a compiler with a proof assistant. In: Proceedings of the 34th Annual ACM SIGPLAN-SIGACT Symposium on Principles of Programming Languages (POPL 2006), pp. 42–54. ACM (2006)
14. Lin, C.C., Jha, N.K.: RMDDS: Reed-Muller decision diagram synthesis of reversible logic circuits. J. Emerg. Technol. Comput. Syst. **10**(2), 14 (2014)
15. Markov, I.L.: Limits on fundamental limits to computation. Nature **512**, 147–154 (2014)
16. Maslov, D., Miller, D.M., Dueck, G.W.: Techniques for the synthesis of reversible Toffoli networks. ACM Trans. Des. Autom. Electron. Syst. **12**(4), 42 (2007)
17. Miller, D.M., Maslov, D., Dueck, G.W.: A transformation based algorithm for reversible logic synthesis. In: Proceedings of the 40th Annual Design Automation Conference (DAC 2003), pp. 318–323 (2003)
18. Neis, G., Hur, C.K., Kaiser, J.O., McLaughlin, C., Dreyer, D., Vafeiadis, V.: Pilsner: a compositionally verified compiler for a higher-order imperative language. In: Proceedings of the 20th ACM SIGPLAN International Conference on Functional Programming (ICFP 2015), pp. 166–178. ACM (2015)
19. Nielsen, M.A., Chuang, I.L.: Quantum Computation and Quantum Information. Cambridge University Press, Cambridge (2000)
20. Ömer, B.: Quantum programming in QCL. Master's thesis, Technical University of Vienna (2000)
21. Parent, A., Roetteler, M., Svore, K.M.: Reversible circuit compilation with space constraints. arXiv e-prints (2015). https://arxiv.org/abs/1510.00377
22. Perconti, J.T., Ahmed, A.: Verifying an open compiler using multi-language semantics. In: Shao, Z. (ed.) ESOP 2014. LNCS, vol. 8410, pp. 128–148. Springer, Heidelberg (2014). doi:10.1007/978-3-642-54833-8_8
23. Saeedi, M., Markov, I.L.: Synthesis and optimization of reversible circuits. ACM Comput. Surv. **45**(2), 21 (2013)

24. Scherer, A., Valiron, B., Mau, S.C., Alexander, S., van den Berg, E., Chapuran, T.E.: Resource analysis of the quantum linear system algorithm. arXiv e-prints (2015). https://arxiv.org/abs/1505.06552

25. Shafaei, A., Saeedi, M., Pedram, M.: Reversible logic synthesis of k-input, m-output lookup tables. In: Proceedings of the Conference on Design, Automation and Test in Europe (DATE 2013), pp. 1235–1240 (2013)

26. Shor, P.W.: Polynomial-time algorithms for prime factorization and discrete logarithms on a quantum computer. SIAM J. Comput. **26**(5), 1484–1509 (1997)

27. Swamy, N., Hriţcu, C., Keller, C., Rastogi, A., Delignat-Lavaud, A., Forest, S., Bhargavan, K., Fournet, C., Strub, P.Y., Kohlweiss, M., Zinzindohoue, J.K., Zanella-Béguelin, S.: Dependent types and multi-monadic effects in F*. In: Proceedings of the 43rd Annual ACM SIGPLAN-SIGACT Symposium on Principles of Programming Languages (POPL 2016), pp. 256–270. ACM (2016)

28. Thomsen, M.K.: A functional language for describing reversible logic. In: Proceedings of the 2012 Forum on Specification and Design Languages (FDL 2012), pp. 135–142. IEEE (2012)

29. Wille, R., Drechsler, R.: Towards a Design Flow for Reversible Logic. Springer, Heidelberg (2010)

30. Wille, R., Grosse, D., Miller, D., Drechsler, R.: Equivalence checking of reversible circuits. In: Proceedings of the 39th IEEE International Symposium on Multiple-Valued Logic (ISMVL 2009), pp. 324–330 (2009)

31. Wille, R., Offermann, S., Drechsler, R.: Syrec: a programming language for synthesis of reversible circuits. In: Proceedings of the 2010 Forum on Specification and Design Languages (FDL 2010), pp. 1–6 (2010)

32. Yamashita, S., Markov, I.: Fast equivalence-checking for quantum circuits. In: Proceedings of the 2010 IEEE/ACM Symposium on Nanoscale Architectures (NANOARCH 2010), pp. 23–28 (2010)

33. Yokoyama, T., Glück, R.: A reversible programming language and its invertible self-interpreter. In: Proceedings of the 2007 Symposium on Partial Evaluation and Semantics-Based Program Manipulation (PEPM 2007), pp. 144–153. ACM (2007)

Ascertaining Uncertainty for Efficient Exact Cache Analysis

Valentin Touzeau[1,2(✉)], Claire Maïza[1,2], David Monniaux[1,2], and Jan Reineke[3]

[1] Univ. Grenoble Alpes, VERIMAG, 38000 Grenoble, France
{valentin.touzeau,claire.maiza,david.monniaux}@univ-grenoble-alpes.fr
[2] CNRS, VERIMAG, 38000 Grenoble, France
[3] Saarland University, Saarland Informatics Campus, Saarbrücken, Germany
reineke@cs.uni-saarland.de

Abstract. Static cache analysis characterizes a program's cache behavior by determining in a sound but approximate manner which memory accesses result in cache hits and which result in cache misses. Such information is valuable in optimizing compilers, worst-case execution time analysis, and side-channel attack quantification and mitigation.

Cache analysis is usually performed as a combination of "must" and "may" abstract interpretations, classifying instructions as either "always hit", "always miss", or "unknown". Instructions classified as "unknown" might result in a hit or a miss depending on program inputs or the initial cache state. It is equally possible that they do in fact always hit or always miss, but the cache analysis is too coarse to see it.

Our approach to eliminate this uncertainty consists in (i) a novel abstract interpretation able to ascertain that a particular instruction may definitely cause a hit and a miss on different paths, and (ii) an exact analysis, removing all remaining uncertainty, based on model checking, using abstract-interpretation results to prune down the model for scalability. We evaluated our approach on a variety of examples; it notably improves precision upon classical abstract interpretation at reasonable cost.

1 Introduction

There is a large gap between processor and memory speeds termed the "memory wall" [21]. To bridge this gap, processors are commonly equipped with caches, i.e., small but fast on-chip memories that hold recently-accessed data, in the hope that most memory accesses can be served at a low latency by the cache instead of being served by the slow main memory. Due to temporal and spatial locality in memory access patterns caches are often highly effective.

In hard real-time applications, it is important to bound a program's *worst-case execution time* (WCET). For instance, if a control loop runs at 100 Hz, one must show that its WCET is less than 0.01 s. In some cases, measuring the program's execution time on representative inputs and adding a safety margin

© Springer International Publishing AG 2017
R. Majumdar and V. Kunčak (Eds.): CAV 2017, Part II, LNCS 10427, pp. 22–40, 2017.
DOI: 10.1007/978-3-319-63390-9_2

may be enough, but in safety-critical systems one may wish for a higher degree of assurance and use static analysis to cover all cases. On processors with caches, such a static analysis involves classifying memory accesses into cache hits, cache misses, and unclassified [20]. Unclassified memory accesses that in reality result in cache hits may lead to gross overestimation of the WCET.

Tools such as OTAWA[1] and AIT[2] compute an upper bound on the WCET of programs after first running a static analysis based on abstract interpretation [11] to classify memory accesses. Our aim, in this article, is to improve upon that approach with a refined abstract interpretation and a novel encoding into finite-state model checking.

Caches may also leak secret information [2] to other programs running on the same machine—through the shared cache state—or even to external devices—due to cache-induced timing variations. For instance, cache timing attacks on software implementations of the Advanced Encryption Standard [1] were one motivation for adding specific hardware support for that cipher to the x86 instruction set [15]. Cache analysis may help identify possibilities for such *side-channel attacks* and quantify the amount of information leakage [7]; improved precision in cache analysis then translates into fewer false alarms and tighter bounds on leakage.

An ideal cache analysis would statically classify every memory access at every machine-code instruction in a program into one of three cases: (i) the access is a cache hit in all possible executions of the program (ii) the access is a cache miss in all possible executions of the program (iii) in some executions the access is a hit and in others it is a miss. However, no cache analysis can perfectly classify all accesses into these three categories.

One first reason is that perfect cache analysis would involve testing the reachability of individual program statements, which is undecidable.[3] A simplifying assumption often used, including in this article, is that all program paths are feasible—this is safe, since it overapproximates possible program behaviors. Even with this assumption, analysis is usually performed using sound but incomplete abstractions that can safely determine that some accesses always hit ("∀Hit" in Fig. 1) or always miss ("∀Miss" in Fig. 1). The corresponding analyses are called *may* and *must* analysis and referred to as "classical AI" in Fig. 1. Due to incompleteness the status of other accesses however remains "unknown" (Fig. 1).

Contributions. In this article, we propose an approach to eliminate this uncertainty, with two main contributions (colored red and green in Fig. 1):

1. A novel abstract interpretation that safely concludes that certain accesses are hits in some executions ("∃Hit"), misses in some executions ("∃Miss"), or hits

---

[1] http://www.otawa.fr/: an academic tool developed at IRIT, Toulouse.

[2] https://www.absint.com/ait/: a commercial tool developed by Absint GmbH.

[3] One may object that given that we consider machine-level aspects, memory is bounded and thus properties are decidable. The time and space complexity is however prohibitive.

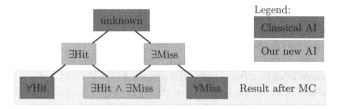

Fig. 1. Possible classifications of classical abstract-interpretation-based cache analysis, our new abstract interpretation, and after refinement by model checking. (Color figure online)

in some and misses in other executions ("∃Hit ∧ ∃Miss" in Fig. 1). Using this analysis and prior must- and may- cache analyses, most accesses are precisely classified.

2. The classification of accesses with remaining uncertainty ("unknown", "∃Hit", and "∃Miss") is refined by model checking using an exact abstraction of the behavior of the cache replacement policy. The results from the abstract interpretation in the first analysis phase are used to dramatically reduce the complexity of the model.

Because the model-checking phase is based on an exact abstraction of the cache replacement policy, our method, overall, is *optimally precise*: it answers precisely whether a given access is always a hit, always a miss, or a hit in some executions and a miss in others (see "Result after MC" in Fig. 1).[4] This precision improvement in access classifications can be beneficial for tools built on top of the cache analysis: in the case of WCET analysis for example, a precise cache analysis not only improves the computed WCET bound; it can also lead to a faster analysis. Indeed, in case of an unclassified access, both possibilities (cache hit and cache miss) have to be considered [10,17].

The model-checking phase would be sufficient to resolve all accesses, but our experiments show this does not scale; it is necessary to combine it with the abstract-interpretation phase for tractability, thereby reducing (a) the number of model-checker calls, and (b) the size of each model-checking problem.

2   Background: Caches and Static Cache Analysis

Caches. Caches are fast but small memories that store a subset of the main memory's contents to bridge the latency gap between the CPU and main memory. To profit from spatial locality and to reduce management overhead, main memory is logically partitioned into a set of *memory blocks* M. Each block is cached as a whole in a cache line of the same size.

---

[4] This completeness is relative to an execution model where all control paths are feasible, disregarding the functional semantics of the edges.

When accessing a memory block, the cache logic has to determine whether the block is stored in the cache ("cache hit") or not ("cache miss"). For efficient look up, each block can only be stored in a small number of cache lines known as a *cache set*. Which cache set a memory block maps to is determined by a subset of the bits of its address. The cache is partitioned into equally-sized cache sets. The size k of a cache set in blocks is called the *associativity* of the cache.

Since the cache is much smaller than main memory, a *replacement policy* must decide which memory block to replace upon a cache miss. Importantly, replacement policies treat sets independently[5], so that accesses to one set do not influence replacement decisions in other sets. Well-known replacement policies are least-recently-used (LRU), used, e.g., in various Freescale processors such as the MPC603E and the TriCore17xx; pseudo-LRU (PLRU), a cost-efficient variant of LRU; and first-in first-out (FIFO). In this article we focus exclusively on LRU. The application of our ideas to other policies is left as future work.

LRU naturally gives rise to a notion of *ages* for memory blocks: The age of a block b is the number of pairwise different blocks that map to the same cache set as b that have been accessed since the last access to b. If a block has never been accessed, its age is ∞. Then, a block is cached if and only if its age is less than the cache's associativity k.

Given this notion of ages, the state of an LRU cache can be modeled by a mapping that assigns to each memory block its age, where ages are truncated at k, i.e., we do not distinguish ages of uncached blocks. We denote the set of cache states by $C = M \rightarrow \{0, \ldots, k\}$. Then, the effect of an access to memory block b under LRU replacement can be formalized as follows[6]:

$$update : C \times M \rightarrow C$$

$$(q, b) \mapsto \lambda b'. \begin{cases} 0 & \text{if } b' = b \\ q(b') & \text{if } q(b') \geq q(b) \\ q(b') + 1 & \text{if } q(b') < q(b) \wedge q(b') < k \\ k & \text{if } q(b') < q(b) \wedge q(b') = k \end{cases} \quad (1)$$

Programs as Control-Flow Graphs. As is common in program analysis and in particular in work on cache analysis, we abstract the program under analysis by its control-flow graph: vertices represent control locations and edges represent the possible flow of control through the program. In order to analyze the cache behavior, edges are adorned with the addresses of the memory blocks that are accessed by the instruction, including the instruction being fetched.

For instruction fetches in a program without function pointers or computed jumps, this just entails knowing the address of every instruction—thus the program must be linked with absolute addresses, as common in embedded code. For data accesses, a pointer analysis is required to compute a set of possible addresses for every access. If several memory blocks may be alternatively

---

[5] To our best knowledge, the only exception to this rule is the *pseudo round-robin* policy, found, e.g., in the ARM Cortex A-9.

[6] Assuming for simplicity that all cache blocks map to the same cache set.

accessed by an instruction, multiple edges may be inserted; so there may be multiple edges between two nodes. We therefore represent a control-flow graph by a tuple $G = (V, E)$, where V is the set of vertices and $E \subseteq V \times (M \cup \{\bot\}) \times V$ is the set of edges, where $\bot$ is used to label edges that do not cause a memory access.

The resulting control-flow graph G does not include information on the functional semantics of the instructions, e.g. whether they compute an addition. All paths in that graph are considered feasible, even if, taking into account the instruction semantics, they are not—e.g. a path including the tests $x \leq 4$ and $x \geq 5$ in immediate succession is considered feasible even though the two tests are mutually exclusive. All our claims of completeness are relative to this model.

As discussed above, replacement decisions for a given cache set are usually independent of memory accesses to other cache sets. Thus, analyzing the behavior of G on all cache sets is equivalent to separately analyzing its projections onto individual cache sets: a projection of G on a cache set S is G where only blocks mapping to S are kept. Projected control-flow graphs may be simplified, e.g. a self-looping edge labeled with no cache block may be removed. Thus, we assume in the following that the analyzed cache is fully associative, i.e. of a single cache set.

Collecting Semantics. In order to classify memory accesses as "always hit" or "always miss", cache analysis needs to characterize for each control location in a program *all* cache states that may reach that location in any execution of the program. This is commonly called the *collecting semantics*.

Given a control-flow graph $G = (V, E)$, the *collecting semantics* is defined as the least solution to the following set of equations, where $R^C : V \to \mathcal{P}(C)$ denotes the set of reachable concrete cache configurations at each program location, and $R_0^C(v)$ denotes the set of possible initial cache configurations:

$$\forall v' \in V : R^C(v') = R_0^C(v') \cup \bigcup_{(v,b,v') \in E} update^C(R^C(v), b), \tag{2}$$

where $update^C$ denotes the cache update function lifted to sets of states, i.e., $update^C(Q, b) = \{update(q, b) \mid q \in Q\}$.

Explicitly computing the collecting semantics is practically infeasible. For a tractable analysis, it is necessary to operate in an abstract domain whose elements compactly represent large sets of concrete cache states.

Classical Abstract Interpretation of LRU Caches. To this end, the classical abstract interpretation of LRU caches [9] assigns to every memory block at every program location an interval of ages enclosing the possible ages of the block during any program execution. The analysis for upper bounds, or *must analysis*, can prove that a block must be in the cache; conversely, the one for lower bounds, or *may analysis*, can prove that a block may not be in the cache.

The domains for abstract cache states under may and must analysis are $\mathcal{A}_{May} = \mathcal{A}_{Must} = C = M \to \{0, ..., k\}$, where ages greater than or equal to the cache's associativity k are truncated at k as in the concrete domain. For reasons of brevity, we here limit our exposition to the must analysis. The set of concrete cache states represented by abstract cache states is given by the concretization function: $\gamma_{Must}(\hat{q}_{Must}) = \{q \in C \mid \forall m \in M : q(m) \leq \hat{q}_{Must}\}$. Abstract cache states can be joined by taking their pointwise maxima: $\hat{q}_{M1} \sqcup_{Must} \hat{q}_{M2} = \lambda m \in M : \max\{\hat{q}_{M1}(m), \hat{q}_{M2}(m)\}$. For reasons of brevity, we also omit the definition of the abstract transformer $update_{Must}$, which closely resembles its concrete counterpart given in (1), and which can be found e.g. in [16].

Suitably defined abstract semantics R_{Must} and R_{May} can be shown to over-approximate their concrete counterpart:

Theorem 1 (Analysis Soundness [9]**).** *The may and the must abstract semantics are safe approximations of the collecting semantics:*

$$\forall v \in V : R^C(v) \subseteq \gamma_{Must}(R_{Must}(v)), R^C(v) \subseteq \gamma_{May}(R_{May}(v)). \tag{3}$$

3   Abstract Interpretation for Definitely Unknown

All proofs can be found in Appendix A of the technical report [19]. Together, may and must analysis can classify accesses as "always hit", "always miss" or "unknown". An access classified as "unknown" may still be "always hit" or "always miss" but not detected as such due to the imprecision of the abstract analysis; otherwise it is "definitely unknown". Properly classifying "unknown" blocks into "definitely unknown", "always hit", or "always miss" using a model checker is costly. We thus propose an abstract analysis that safely establishes that some blocks are "definitely unknown" under LRU replacement.

Our analysis steps are summarized in Fig. 2. Based on the control-flow graph and on an initial cache configuration, the abstract-interpretation phase classifies some of the accesses as "always hit", "always miss" and "definitely unknown". Those accesses are already precisely classified and thus do not require a model-checking phase. The AI phase thus reduces the number of accesses to be classified by the model checker. In addition, the results of the AI phase are used to simplify the model-checking phase, which will be discussed in detail in Sect. 4.

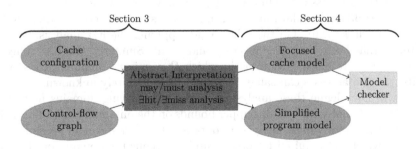

Fig. 2. Overall analysis flow.

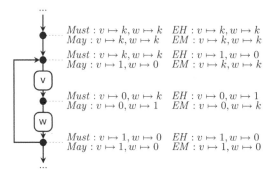

Fig. 3. Example of two accesses in a loop that are definitely unknown. May/Must and EH/EM analysis results are given next to the respective control locations.

An access is "definitely unknown" if there is a concrete execution in which the access misses and another in which it hits. The aim of our analysis is to prove the existence of such executions to classify an access as "definitely unknown". Note the difference with classical may/must analysis and most other abstract interpretations, which compute properties that hold *for all executions*, while here we seek to prove that *there exist* two executions with suitable properties.

An access to a block a results in a hit if a has been accessed recently, i.e., a's age is low. Thus we would like to determine the minimal age that a may have in a reachable cache state immediately prior to the access in question. The access can be a hit if and only if this minimal age is lower than the cache's associativity. Because we cannot efficiently compute exact minimal ages, we devise an *Exists Hit* (EH) analysis to compute safe upper bounds on minimal ages. Similarly, to be sure there is an execution in which accessing a results in a miss, we compute a safe lower bound on the maximal age of a using the *Exists Miss* (EM) analysis.

Example. Let us now consider a small example. In Fig. 3, we see a small control-flow graph corresponding to a loop that repeatedly accesses memory blocks v and w. Assume the cache is empty before entering the loop. Then, the accesses to v and w are definitely unknown in fully-associative caches of associativity 2 or greater: they both miss in the first loop iteration, while they hit in all subsequent iterations. Applying standard may and must analysis, both accesses are soundly classified as "unknown". On the other hand, applying the EH analysis, we can determine that there are cases where v and w hit. Similarly, the EM analysis derives that there exist executions in which they miss. Combining those two results, the two accesses can safely be classified as definitely unknown.

We will now define these analyses and their underlying domains more formally. The EH analysis maintains upper bounds on the minimal ages of blocks. In addition, it includes a must analysis to obtain upper bounds on all possible ages of blocks, which are required for precise updates. Thus the domain for abstract cache states under the EH analysis is $\mathcal{A}_{EH} = (M \to \{0, \ldots, k-1, k\}) \times \mathcal{A}_{Must}$. Similarly, the EM analysis maintains lower bounds on the minimal ages of blocks and includes a regular may analysis: $\mathcal{A}_{EM} = (M \to \{0, \ldots, k-1, k\}) \times \mathcal{A}_{May}$. In the following, for reasons of brevity, we limit our exposition to the EH analysis. The EM formalization is analogous and can be found in the technical report [19].

The properties we wish to establish, i.e. bounds on minimal and maximal ages, are actually *hyperproperties* [6]: they are not properties of individual reachable states but rather of the entire *set* of reachable states. Thus, the conventional approach in which abstract states concretize to sets of concrete states that are a superset of the actual set of reachable states is not applicable. Instead, we express the meaning, γ_{EH}, of abstract states by *sets of sets* of concrete states. A set of states Q is represented by an abstract EH state $(\hat{q}, \hat{q}_{Must})$, if for each block b, $\hat{q}(b)$ is an upper bound on b's minimal age in Q, $\min_{q \in Q} q(b)$:

$$\gamma_{EH} : \mathcal{A}_{EH} \to \mathcal{P}(\mathcal{P}(C))$$

$$(\hat{q}, \hat{q}_{Must}) \mapsto \left\{ Q \subseteq \gamma_{Must}(\hat{q}_{Must}) \mid \forall b \in M : \min_{q \in Q} q(b) \leq \hat{q}(b) \right\} \qquad (4)$$

The actual set of reachable states is an element rather than a subset of this concretization. The concretization for the must analysis, γ_{Must}, is simply lifted to this setting. Also note that—possibly contrary to initial intuition—our abstraction cannot be expressed as an underapproximation, as different blocks' minimal ages may be attained in different concrete states.

The abstract transformer $update_{EH}((\hat{q}_{EH}, \hat{q}_{Must}), b)$ corresponding to an access to block b is the pair $(\hat{q}'_{EH}, update_{Must}(\hat{q}_{Must}, b))$, where

$$\hat{q}'_{EH} = \lambda b'. \begin{cases} 0 & \text{if } b' = b \\ \hat{q}(b') & \text{if } \hat{q}_{Must}(b) \leq \hat{q}(b') \\ \hat{q}(b') + 1 & \text{if } \hat{q}_{Must}(b) > \hat{q}(b') \wedge \hat{q}(b') < k \\ k & \text{if } \hat{q}_{Must}(b) > \hat{q}(b') \wedge \hat{q}(b') = k \end{cases} \qquad (5)$$

Let us explain the four cases in the transformer above. After an access to b, b's age is 0 in all possible executions. Thus, 0 is also a safe upper bound on its minimal age (case 1). The access to b may only increase the ages of younger blocks (because of the LRU replacement policy). In the cache state in which b' attains its minimal age, it is either younger or older than b. If it is younger, then the access to b may increase b''s actual minimal age, but not beyond $\hat{q}_{Must}(b)$, which is a bound on b's age in every cache state, and in particular in the one where b' attains its minimal age. Otherwise, if b' is older, its minimal age remains the same and so may its bound. This explains why the bound on b''s minimal age does not increase in case 2. Otherwise, for safe upper bounds, in cases 3 and 4, the bound needs to be increased by one, unless it has already reached k.

Lemma 1 (Local Consistency). *The abstract transformer* $update_{EH}$ *soundly approximates its concrete counterpart* $update^C$:

$$\forall (\hat{q}, \hat{q}_{Must}) \in \mathcal{A}_{EH}, \forall b \in M, \forall Q \in \gamma_{EH}(\hat{q}, \hat{q}_{Must}) :$$

$$update^C(Q, b) \in \gamma_{EH}(update_{EH}((\hat{q}, \hat{q}_{Must}), b)). \quad (6)$$

How are EH states combined at control-flow joins? The standard must join can be applied for the must analysis component. In the concrete, the union of the states reachable along all incoming control paths is reachable after the join. It is thus safe to take the *minimum* of the upper bounds on minimal ages:

$$(\hat{q}_1, \hat{q}_{Must1}) \sqcup_{EH} (\hat{q}_2, \hat{q}_{Must2}) = (\lambda b. \min(\hat{q}_1(b), \hat{q}_2(b)), \hat{q}_{Must1} \sqcup_{Must} \hat{q}_{Must2}) \quad (7)$$

Lemma 2 (Join Consistency). *The join operator $\sqcup_{EH}$ is correct:*

$$\forall((\hat{q}_1, \hat{q}_{M1}), (\hat{q}_2, \hat{q}_{M2})) \in \mathcal{A}^2_{EH}, Q_1 \in \gamma_{EH}(\hat{q}_1, \hat{q}_{M1}), Q_2 \in \gamma_{EH}(\hat{q}_2, \hat{q}_{M2}) :$$
$$Q_1 \cup Q_2 \in \gamma_{EH}((\hat{q}_1, \hat{q}_{M1}) \sqcup_{EH} (\hat{q}_2, \hat{q}_{M2})). \quad (8)$$

Given a control-flow graph $G = (V, E)$, the *abstract EH semantics* is defined as the least solution to the following set of equations, where $R_{EH} : V \to \mathcal{A}_{EH}$ denotes the abstract cache configuration associated with each program location, and $R_0^C(v) \in \gamma_{EH}(R_{EH,0}(v))$ denotes the initial abstract cache configuration:

$$\forall v' \in V : R_{EH}(v') = R_{EH,0}(v') \sqcup_{EH} \bigsqcup_{(v,b,v') \in E} update_{EH}(R_{EH}(v), b). \quad (9)$$

It follows from Lemmas 1 and 2 that the abstract EH semantics includes the actual set of reachable concrete states:

Theorem 2 (Analysis Soundness). *The abstract EH semantics includes the collecting semantics: $\forall v \in V : R^C(v) \in \gamma_{EH}(R_{EH}(v))$.*

We can use the results of the EH analysis to determine that an access results in a hit in at least some of all possible executions. This is the case if the minimum age of the block prior to the access is guaranteed to be less than the cache's associativity. Similarly, the EM analysis can be used to determine that an access results in a miss in at least some of the possible executions.

Combining the results of the two analyses, some accesses can be classified as "definitely unknown". Then, further refinement by model checking is provably impossible. Classifications as "exists hit" or "exists miss", which occur if either the EH or the EM analysis is successful but not both, are also useful to reduce further model-checking efforts: e.g. in case of "exists hit" it suffices to determine by model checking whether a miss is possible to fully classify the access.

4 Cache Analysis by Model Checking

All proofs can be found in Appendix B of the technical report [19]. We have seen a new abstract analysis capable of classifying certain cache accesses as "definitely unknown". The classical "may" and "must" analyses and this new analysis classify a (hopefully large) portion of all accesses as "always hit", "always miss", or "definitely unknown". But, due to the incomplete nature of the analysis the exact status of some blocks remains unknown. Our approach is summarized at a high level in Listing 1.1. Functions May, Must, ExistsHit and ExistsMiss return the result of the corresponding analysis, whereas CheckModel invokes the model checker (see Listing 1.2). Note that a block that is not fully classified as "definitely unknown" can still benefit from the *Exists Hit* and *Exists Miss* analysis during the model-checking phase. If the AI phase shows that there exists a path on which the block is a hit (respectively a miss), then the model checker does not have to check the "always miss" (respectively "always hit") property.

Listing 1.1. Abstract-interpretation phase

```
function ClassifyBlock(block) {
  if (Must(block))        //Must analysis classifies the block
    return AlwaysHit;
  else if (!May(block))    //May analysis classifies the block
    return AlwaysMiss;
  else if (ExistHit(block) && ExistMiss(block))
    return DefinitelyUnknown; //DU analysis classifies the block
  else // Otherwise, we call the model checker
    return CheckModel(block, ExistsHit(block), ExistsMiss(block));
}
```

Listing 1.2. Model-checking phase

```
function CheckModel(block, exist_hit, exist_miss) {
  if (exist_hit) { //block can not always miss
    if (CheckAH(block)) return AlwaysHit;
  }
  else if (exist_miss) { //block can not always hit
    if (CheckAM(block)) return AlwaysMiss;
  } else { //AI phase did not provide any information
    if (CheckAH(block)) return AlwaysHit;
    else if (CheckAM(block)) return AlwaysMiss;
  }
  return DefinitelyUnknown;
}
```

We shall now see how to classify these remaining blocks using model checking. Not only is the model-checking phase *sound*, i.e. its classifications are correct, it is also *complete* relative to our control-flow-graph model, i.e. there remain no unclassified accesses: each access is classified as "always hit", "always miss" or "definitely unknown". Remember that our analysis is based on the assumption that each path is semantically feasible.

In order to classify the remaining unclassified accesses, we feed the model checker a finite-state machine modeling the cache behavior of the program, composed of (i) a model of the program, yielding the possible sequences of memory accesses (ii) a model of the cache. In this section, we introduce a new cache model, focusing on the state of a particular memory block to be classified, which we further simplify using the results of abstract interpretation.

As explained in the introduction, it would be possible to directly encode the control-flow graph of the program, adorned with memory accesses, as one big finite-state system. A first step is obviously to slice that system per cache set to make it smaller. Here we take this approach further by defining a model sound and complete with respect to a given memory block a: parts of the model that have no impact on the caching status of a are discarded, which greatly reduces the model's size. For each unclassified access, the analysis constructs a model focused on the memory block accessed, and queries the model checker. Both the simplified program model and the focused cache model are derived automatically, and do not require any manual interaction.

The *focused cache model* is based on the following simple property of LRU: a memory block is cached if and only if its age is less than the associativity k, or in other words, if there are less than k younger blocks. In the following, w.l.o.g., let $a \in M$ be the memory block we want to focus the cache model on. If we are only interested in whether a is cached or not, it suffices to track the set of blocks younger than a. Without any loss in precision concerning a, we can abstract from the relative ages of the blocks younger than a and of those older than a.

Thus, the domain of the focused cache model is $C_{\odot} = \mathcal{P}(M) \cup \{\varepsilon\}$. Here, ε is used to represent those cache states in which a is not cached. If a is cached, the analysis tracks the set of blocks younger than a. We can relate the focused cache model to the concrete cache model defined in Sect. 2 using an abstraction function mapping concrete cache states to focused ones:

$$\alpha_{\odot} : C \to C_{\odot}$$

$$q \mapsto \begin{cases} \varepsilon & \text{if } q(a) \geq k \\ \{b \in M \mid q(b) < q(a)\} & \text{if } q(a) < k \end{cases} \tag{10}$$

The focused cache update $update_{\odot}$ models a memory access as follows:

$$update_{\odot} : C_{\odot} \times M \to C_{\odot}$$

$$(\widehat{Q}, b) \mapsto \begin{cases} \emptyset & \text{if } b = a \\ \varepsilon & \text{if } b \neq a \wedge \widehat{Q} = \varepsilon \\ \widehat{Q} \cup \{b\} & \text{if } b \neq a \wedge \widehat{Q} \neq \varepsilon \wedge |\widehat{Q} \cup \{b\}| < k \\ \varepsilon & \text{if } b \neq a \wedge \widehat{Q} \neq \varepsilon \wedge |\widehat{Q} \cup \{b\}| = k \end{cases} \tag{11}$$

Let us briefly explain the four cases above. If $b = a$ (case 1), a becomes the most-recently-used block and thus no other blocks are younger. If a is not in the cache and it is not accessed (case 2), then a remains outside of the cache. If another block is accessed, it is added to a's younger set (case 3) unless the access causes a's eviction, because it is the kth distinct younger block (case 4).

Example. Figure 4 depicts a sequence of memory accesses and the resulting concrete and focused cache states (with a focus on block a) starting from an empty cache of associativity 2. We represent concrete cache states by showing the two blocks of age 0 and 1. The example illustrates that many concrete cache states may collapse to the same focused one. At the same time, the focused cache model does not lose any information about the caching status of the focused block, which is captured by the following lemma and theorem.

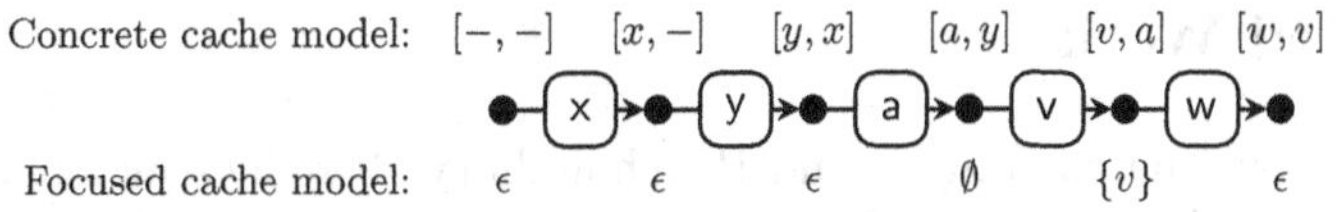

Concrete cache model: $[-,-]$ $[x,-]$ $[y,x]$ $[a,y]$ $[v,a]$ $[w,v]$

Focused cache model: ϵ ϵ ϵ $\emptyset$ $\{v\}$ ϵ

Fig. 4. Example: concrete vs. focused cache model.

Lemma 3 (Local Soundness and Completeness). *The focused cache update abstracts the concrete cache update exactly:*

$$\forall q \in C, \forall b \in M : \alpha_{\odot}(update(q,b)) = update_{\odot}(\alpha_{\odot}(q),b). \tag{12}$$

The *focused collecting semantics* is defined analogously to the *collecting semantics* as the least solution to the following set of equations, where $R_{\odot}^{C}(v)$ denotes the set of reachable focused cache configurations at each program location, and $R_{\odot,0}^{C}(v) = \alpha_{\odot}^{C}(R_0^C(v))$ for all $v \in V$:

$$\forall v' \in V : R_{\odot}^{C}(v') = R_{\odot,0}^{C}(v') \cup \bigcup_{(v,b,v') \in E} update_{\odot}^{C}(R_{\odot}^{C}(v),b), \tag{13}$$

where $update_{\odot}^{C}$ denotes the focused cache update function lifted to sets of focused cache states, i.e., $update_{\odot}^{C}(Q,b) = \{update_{\odot}(q,b) \mid q \in Q\}$, and $\alpha_{\odot}^{C}$ denotes the abstraction function lifted to sets of states, i.e., $\alpha_{\odot}^{C}(Q) = \{\alpha_{\odot}(q) \mid q \in Q\}$.

Theorem 3 (Analysis Soundness and Completeness). *The focused collecting semantics is exactly the abstraction of the collecting semantics:*

$$\forall v \in V : \alpha_{\odot}^{C}(R^C(v)) = R_{\odot}^{C}(v). \tag{14}$$

Proof. From Lemma 3 it immediately follows that the lifted focused update $update_{\odot}^{C}$ exactly corresponds to the lifted concrete cache update $update^C$.

Since the concrete domain is finite, the least fixed point of the system of Eq. 2 is reached after a bounded number of Kleene iterations. One then just applies the consistency lemmas in an induction proof.   □

Thus we can employ the focused cache model in place of the concrete cache model without any loss in precision to classify accesses to the focused block as "always hit", "always miss", or "definitely unknown".

For the program model, we simplify the CFG without affecting the correctness nor the precision of the analysis: (i) If we know, from may analysis, that in a given program instruction a is never in the cache, then this instruction cannot affect a's eviction: thus we simplify the program model by not including this instruction. (ii) When we encode the set of blocks younger than a as a bit vector, we do not include blocks that the may analysis proved not to be in the cache at that location: these bits would anyway always be 0.

5   Related Work

Earlier work by Chattopadhyay and Roychoudhury [4] refines memory accesses classified as "unknown" by AI using a software model-checking step: when abstract interpretation cannot classify an access, the source program is enriched with annotations for counting conflicting accesses and run through a software model checker (actually, a bounded model checker). Their approach, in contrast to ours, takes into account program semantics during the refinement step; it is thus likely to be more precise on programs where many paths are infeasible for semantic reasons. Our approach however scales considerably better, as shown in Sect. 6: not only do we not keep the program semantics in the problem instance passed to the model checker, which thus has finite state as opposed to being an arbitrarily complex program verification instance, we also strive to minimize that instance by the methods discussed in Sect. 4.

Chu et al. [5] also refine cache analysis results based on program semantics, but by symbolic execution, where an SMT solver is used to prune infeasible paths. We also compare the scalability of their approach to ours.

Our work complements [12], which uses the classification obtained by classical abstract interpretation of the cache as a basis for WCET analysis on timed automata: our refined classification would increase precision in that analysis. Metta et al. [13] also employ model checking to increase the precision of WCET analysis. However, they do not take into account low-level features such as caches.

6   Experimental Evaluation

In industrial use for worst-case execution time, cache analysis targets a specific processor, specific cache settings, specific binary code loaded at a specific address. The processor may have a hierarchy of caches and other peculiarities. Loading object code and reconstructing a control-flow graph involves dedicated tools. For data caches, a pointer value analysis must be run. Implementing an industrial-strength analyzer including a pointer value analysis, or even interfacing in an existing complex analyzer, would greatly exceed the scope of this article. For these reasons, our analysis applies to a single-level LRU instruction cache, and operates at LLVM bitcode level, each LLVM opcode considered as an elementary instruction. This should be representative of analysis of machine code over LRU caches at a fraction of the engineering cost.

We implemented the classical may and must analyses, as well as our new definitely-unknown analysis and our conversion to model checking. The model-checking problems are produced in the NuSMV format, then fed to nuXmv [3].[7] We used an Intel Core i3-2120 processor (3.30 GHz) with 8 GiB RAM.

Our experimental evaluation is intended to show (i) precision gains by model checking (number of unknowns at the may/must stage vs. after the

---

[7] https://nuxmv.fbk.eu/: nuXmv checks for reachability using Kleene iterations over sets of states implicitly represented by binary decision diagrams (BDDs). We also tried nuXmv's implementation of the IC3 algorithm with no speed improvement.

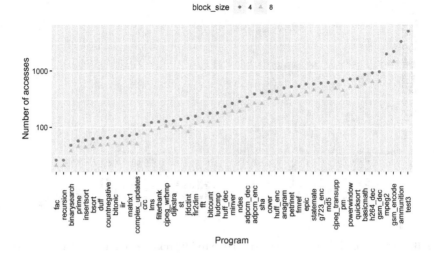

Fig. 5. Size of benchmarks in CFG blocks of 4 and 8 LLVM instructions.

full analysis) (ii) the usefulness of the definitely-unknown analysis (number of definitely-unknown accesses, which corresponds to the reduced number of MC calls, reduced MC cumulative execution time) (iii) the global analysis efficiency (impact on analysis execution time, reduced number of MC calls).

As analysis target we use the TACLeBench benchmark suite [8][8], the successor of the Mälardalen benchmark suite, which is commonly used in experimental evaluations of WCET analysis techniques. Figure 5 (log. scale) gives the number of blocks in the control flow graph where a block is a sequence of instructions that are mapped to the same memory block. In all experiments, we assume the cache to be initially empty and we chose the following cache configuration: 8 instructions per block, 4 ways, 8 cache sets. More details on the sizes of the benchmarks and further experimental results (varying cache configuration, detailed numbers for each benchmark,...) may be found in the technical report [19].

6.1 Effect of Model Checking on Cache Analysis Precision

Here we evaluate the improvement in the number of accesses classified as "always hit" or "always miss". In Fig. 6 we show by what percentage the number of such classifications increased from the pure AI phase due to model checking.

As can be observed in the figure, more than 60% of the benchmarks show an improvement and this improvement is greater than 5% for 45% of them.

We performed the same experiment under varying cache configurations (number of ways, number of sets, memory-block size) with similar outcomes.

---

[8] http://www.tacle.eu/index.php/activities/taclebench.

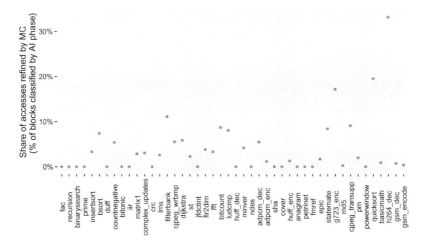

Fig. 6. Increase in hit/miss classifications due to MC relative to pure AI-based analysis.

6.2   Effect of the Definitely-Unknown Analysis on Analysis Efficiency

We introduced the definitely-unknown analysis to reduce the number of MC calls: instead of calling the MC for each access not classified as either always hit or always miss by the classical static analysis, we also do not call it on definitely-unknown blocks. Figure 7(a) shows the number of MC calls with and without the definitely-unknown analysis. The two lines parallel to the diagonal correspond to reductions in the number of calls by a factor of 10 and 100. The definitely-unknown analysis significantly reduces the number of MC calls: for some of the larger benchmarks by around a factor of 100. For the three smallest

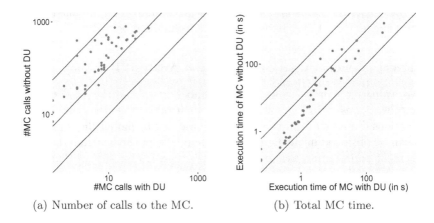

(a) Number of calls to the MC.   (b) Total MC time.

Fig. 7. Analysis efficiency improvements due to the definitely-unknown analysis.

benchmarks, the number of calls is even reduced to zero: the definitely-unknown analysis perfectly completes the may/must analysis and no more blocks need to be classified by model checking. For 28 of the 46 benchmarks, fewer than 10 calls to the model checker are necessary after the definitely-unknown analysis.

This reduction of the number of calls to the model checker also results in significant improvements of the whole execution time of the analysis, which is dominated by the time spent in the model checker: see Fig. 7(b). On average (geometric mean) the total MC execution time is reduced by a factor of 3.7 compared with an approach where only the may and must analysis results are used to reduce the number of MC calls.

Note that the definitely-unknown analysis itself is very fast: it takes less than one second on all benchmarks.

6.3   Effect of Cache and Program Model Simplifications on Model-Checking Efficiency

In all experiments we used the focused cache model: without this focused model, the model is so large that a timeout of one hour is reached for all but the 6 smallest benchmarks. This shows a huge scalability improvement due to the focused cache model. It also demonstrates that building a single model to classify all the accesses at once is practically infeasible.

Figure 8 shows the execution time of individual MC calls (on a log. scale) with and without program-model simplifications based on abstract-interpretation results. For each benchmark, the figure shows the maximum, minimum, and mean execution time of all MC calls for that benchmark. We observe that the maximum execution time is always smaller with the use of the AI phase due to the simplification of program models. Using AI results, there are fewer MC calls and many of the suppressed MC calls are "cheap" calls: this explains why the

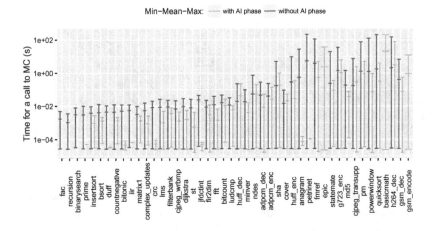

Fig. 8. MC execution time for individual call: min, mean, and max.

average may be larger with AI phase. Some benchmarks are missing the "without AI phase" result: this is the case for benchmarks for which the analysis did not terminate within one hour.

6.4 Efficiency of the Full Analysis

First, we compare our approach to that of the related work [4,5]. Both tools from the related work operate at C level, while our analysis operates at LLVM IR level. Thus it is hard to reasonably compare analysis precision. To compare scalability we focus on total tool execution time, as this is available. In the experimental evaluation of [4] we see that it takes 395 s to analyze statemate (they stop the analysis at 100 MC calls). With a similar configuration, 64 sets, 4 ways, 4 instructions per block (resp. 8 instructions per blocks) our analysis makes 3 calls (resp. 0) to the model checker (compared with 832 (resp. 259) MC calls without the AI phase) and spends less than 3 s (resp. 1.5 s) on the entire analysis. Unfortunately, among all TACLeBench benchmarks [4] gives scalability results only for statemate, and thus no further comparison is possible. The analysis from [5] also spends more than 350 s to analyze statemate; for ndes it takes 38 s whereas our approach makes only 3 calls to the model checker and requires less than one second for the entire analysis. This shows that our analysis scales better than the two related approaches. However, a careful comparison of analysis precision remains to be done.

To see more generally how well our approach scales, we compare the total analysis time with and without the AI phase. The AI phase is composed of the may, must and definitely-unknown analyses: without the AI phase, the model checker is called for each memory access and the program model is not simplified. On all benchmarks the number of MC calls is reduced by a factor of at least 10, sometimes exceeding a factor of 100 (see Fig. 9(a)). This is unsurprising given the strong effect of the definitely-unknown analysis, which we observed in the previous section. Additional reductions compared with those seen in Fig. 7(a) result

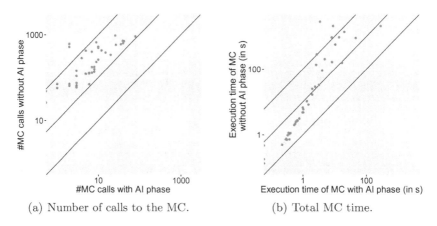

(a) Number of calls to the MC.   (b) Total MC time.

Fig. 9. Analysis efficiency improvements due to the entire AI phase.

from the classical may and must analysis. Interestingly, the reduction in total MC time appears to increase with increasing benchmark sizes: see Fig. 9(b). While the improvement is moderate for small benchmarks that can be handled in a few seconds with and without the AI phase, it increases to much larger factors for the larger benchmarks.

It is difficult to ascertain the influence our approach would have on a full WCET analysis, with respect to both execution time and precision. In particular, WCET analyses that precisely simulate the microarchitecture need to explore fewer pipeline states if fewer cache accesses are classified as "unknown". Thus a costlier cache analysis does not necessarily translate into a costlier analysis overall. We consider a tight integration with a state-of-the-art WCET analyzer as interesting future work, which is beyond the scope of this paper.

7   Conclusion and Perspectives

We have demonstrated that it is possible to precisely classify all accesses to an LRU cache at reasonable cost by a combination of abstract interpretation, which classifies most accesses, and model checking, which classifies the remaining ones.

Like all other abstraction-interpretation-based cache analyses, at least those known to us, ours considers all paths within a control-flow graph to be feasible regardless of functional semantics. Possible improvements over this include: (i) encoding some of the functional semantics of the program into the model-checking problem [4,13] (ii) using "trace partitioning" [18] or "path focusing" [14] in the abstract-interpretation phase.

References

1. Bernstein, D.J.: Cache-timing attacks on AES (2005). https://cr.yp.to/antiforgery/cachetiming-20050414.pdf
2. Canteaut, A., Lauradoux, C., Seznec, A.: Understanding cache attacks. Technical report 5881, INRIA, April 2006. https://hal.inria.fr/inria-00071387/en/
3. Cavada, R., et al.: The NUXMV symbolic model checker. In: Biere, A., Bloem, R. (eds.) CAV 2014. LNCS, vol. 8559, pp. 334–342. Springer, Cham (2014). doi:10.1007/978-3-319-08867-9_22
4. Chattopadhyay, S., Roychoudhury, A.: Scalable and precise refinement of cache timing analysis via path-sensitive verification. Real-Time Syst. **49**(4), 517–562 (2013). http://dx.doi.org/10.1007/s11241-013-9178-0
5. Chu, D., Jaffar, J., Maghareh, R.: Precise cache timing analysis via symbolic execution. In: 2016 IEEE Real-Time and Embedded Technology and Applications Symposium (RTAS), Vienna, Austria, 11–14 April 2016, pp. 293–304. IEEE Computer Society (2016). http://dx.doi.org/10.1109/RTAS.2016.7461358
6. Clarkson, M.R., Schneider, F.B.: Hyperproperties. In: Proceedings of the 21st IEEE Computer Security Foundations Symposium, CSF 2008, Pittsburgh, Pennsylvania, 23–25 June 2008, pp. 51–65 (2008). http://dx.doi.org/10.1109/CSF.2008.7
7. Doychev, G., Köpf, B., Mauborgne, L., Reineke, J.: CacheAudit: a tool for the static analysis of cache side channels. ACM Trans. Inf. Syst. Secur. **18**(1), 4:1–4:32 (2015). http://doi.acm.org/10.1145/2756550

8. Falk, H., Altmeyer, S., Hellinckx, P., Lisper, B., Puffitsch, W., Rochange, C., Schoeberl, M., Sorensen, R.B., Wägemann, P., Wegener, S.: TACLeBench: a benchmark collection to support worst-case execution time research. In: 16th International Workshop on Worst-Case Execution Time Analysis, WCET 2016, Toulouse, France, 5 July 2016, pp. 2:1–2:10 (2016). http://dx.doi.org/10.4230/OASIcs.WCET.2016.2

9. Ferdinand, C., Wilhelm, R.: Efficient and precise cache behavior prediction for real-time systems. Real-Time Syst. **17**(2–3), 131–181 (1999)

10. Lundqvist, T., Stenström, P.: Timing anomalies in dynamically scheduled microprocessors. In: 20th IEEE Real-Time Systems Symposium (RTSS) (1999)

11. Lv, M., Guan, N., Reineke, J., Wilhelm, R., Yi, W.: A survey on static cache analysis for real-time systems. Leibniz Trans. Embedded Syst. **3**(1), 05:1–05:48 (2016). http://ojs.dagstuhl.de/index.php/lites/article/view/LITES-v003-i001-a005

12. Lv, M., Yi, W., Guan, N., Yu, G.: Combining abstract interpretation with model checking for timing analysis of multicore software. In: Proceedings of the 31st IEEE Real-Time Systems Symposium, RTSS 2010, San Diego, California, USA, 30 November–3 December 2010, pp. 339–349. IEEE Computer Society (2010). http://dx.doi.org/10.1109/RTSS.2010.30

13. Metta, R., Becker, M., Bokil, P., Chakraborty, S., Venkatesh, R.: TIC: a scalable model checking based approach to WCET estimation. In: Kuo, T., Whalley, D.B. (eds.) Proceedings of the 17th ACM SIGPLAN/SIGBED Conference on Languages, Compilers, Tools, and Theory for Embedded Systems, LCTES 2016, Santa Barbara, CA, USA, 13–14 June 2016, pp. 72–81. ACM (2016). http://doi.acm.org/10.1145/2907950.2907961

14. Monniaux, D., Gonnord, L.: Using bounded model checking to focus fixpoint iterations. In: Yahav, E. (ed.) SAS 2011. LNCS, vol. 6887, pp. 369–385. Springer, Heidelberg (2011). doi:10.1007/978-3-642-23702-7_27

15. Mowery, K., Keelveedhi, S., Shacham, H.: Are AES x86 cache timing attacks still feasible? In: Cloud Computing Security Workshop, pp. 19–24. ACM, New York (2012)

16. Reineke, J.: Caches in WCET analysis: predictability, competitiveness, sensitivity. Ph.D. thesis, Universität des Saarlandes (2008)

17. Reineke, J., et al.: A definition and classification of timing anomalies. In: 6th International Workshop on Worst-Case Execution Time Analysis (WCET), July 2006

18. Rival, X., Mauborgne, L.: The trace partitioning abstract domain. ACM Trans. Program. Lang. Syst. (TOPLAS) **29**(5), 26 (2007)

19. Touzeau, V., Maiza, C., Monniaux, D., Reineke, J.: Ascertaining uncertainty for efficient exact cache analysis. Technical report TR-2017-2, VERIMAG (2017)

20. Wilhelm, R., Engblom, J., Ermedahl, A., Holsti, N., Thesing, S., Whalley, D.B., Bernat, G., Ferdinand, C., Heckmann, R., Mitra, T., Mueller, F., Puaut, I., Puschner, P.P., Staschulat, J., Stenström, P.: The worst-case execution-time problem - overview of methods and survey of tools. ACM Trans. Embedded Comput. Syst. **7**(3) (2008). Article 36

21. Wulf, W.A., McKee, S.A.: Hitting the memory wall: implications of the obvious. SIGARCH Comput. Archit. News **23**(1), 20–24 (1995). http://doi.acm.org/10.1145/216585.216588

Non-polynomial Worst-Case Analysis of Recursive Programs

Krishnendu Chatterjee[1], Hongfei Fu[2(✉)],
and Amir Kafshdar Goharshady[1]

[1] IST Austria, Klosterneuburg, Austria
[2] State Key Laboratory of Computer Science,
Institute of Software, Chinese Academy of Sciences,
Beijing, People's Republic of China
fuhf@ios.ac.cn

Abstract. We study the problem of developing efficient approaches for proving worst-case bounds of non-deterministic recursive programs. Ranking functions are sound and complete for proving termination and worst-case bounds of non-recursive programs. First, we apply ranking functions to recursion, resulting in measure functions, and show that they provide a sound and complete approach to prove worst-case bounds of non-deterministic recursive programs. Our second contribution is the synthesis of measure functions in non-polynomial forms. We show that non-polynomial measure functions with logarithm and exponentiation can be synthesized through abstraction of logarithmic or exponentiation terms, Farkas' Lemma, and Handelman's Theorem using linear programming. While previous methods obtain worst-case polynomial bounds, our approach can synthesize bounds of the form $\mathcal{O}(n \log n)$ as well as $\mathcal{O}(n^r)$ where r is not an integer. We present experimental results to demonstrate that our approach can efficiently obtain worst-case bounds of classical recursive algorithms such as Merge-Sort, Closest-Pair, Karatsuba's algorithm and Strassen's algorithm.

1 Introduction

Automated analysis to obtain quantitative performance characteristics of programs is a key feature of static analysis. Obtaining precise worst-case complexity bounds is a topic of both wide theoretical and practical interest. The manual proof of such bounds can be cumbersome as well as require mathematical ingenuity, e.g., the book *The Art of Computer Programming* by Knuth presents several mathematically involved methods to obtain such precise bounds [52]. The derivation of such worst-case bounds requires a lot of mathematical skills and is not an automated method. However, the problem of deriving precise worst-case bounds is of huge interest in program analysis: (a) first, in applications such as hard real-time systems, guarantees of worst-case behavior are required; and (b) the bounds are useful in early detection of egregious performance problems in large

© Springer International Publishing AG 2017
R. Majumdar and V. Kunčak (Eds.): CAV 2017, Part II, LNCS 10427, pp. 41–63, 2017.
DOI: 10.1007/978-3-319-63390-9_3

code bases. Works such as [36,37,40,41] provide an excellent motivation for the study of automatic methods to obtain worst-case bounds for programs.

Given the importance of the problem of deriving worst-case bounds, the problem has been studied in various different ways.

1. *WCET Analysis.* The problem of worst-case execution time (WCET) analysis is a large field of its own, that focuses on (but is not limited to) sequential loop-free code with low-level hardware aspects [67].
2. *Resource Analysis.* The use of abstract interpretation and type systems to deal with loop, recursion, data-structures has also been considered [1,37,50], e.g., using linear invariant generation to obtain disjunctive and non-linear bounds [19], potential-based methods for handling recursion and inductive data structures [40,41].
3. *Ranking Functions.* The notion of ranking functions is a powerful technique for termination analysis of (recursive) programs [8,9,20,25,58,61,64,68]. They serve as a sound and complete approach for proving termination of non-recursive programs [31], and they have also been extended as ranking supermatingales for analysis of probabilistic programs [12,14,16,29].

Given the many results above, two aspects of the problem have not been addressed.

1. *WCET Analysis of Recursive Programs Through Ranking Functions.* The use of ranking functions has been limited mostly to non-recursive programs, and their use to obtain worst-case bounds for recursive programs has not been explored in depth.
2. *Efficient Methods for Precise Bounds.* While previous works present methods for disjunctive polynomial bounds [37] (such as $\max(0, n) \cdot (1 + max(n, m)))$, or multivariate polynomial analysis [40], these works do not provide efficient methods to synthesize bounds such as $\mathcal{O}(n \log n)$ or $\mathcal{O}(n^r)$, where r is not an integer.

We address these two aspects, i.e., efficient methods for obtaining non-polynomial bounds such as $\mathcal{O}(n \log n)$, $\mathcal{O}(n^r)$ for recursive programs, where r is not an integer.

Our Contributions. Our main contributions are as follows:

1. First, we apply ranking functions to recursion, resulting in *measure* functions, and show that they provide a sound and complete method to prove termination and worst-case bounds of non-deterministic recursive programs.
2. Second, we present a sound approach for handling measure functions of specific forms. More precisely, we show that *non-polynomial* measure functions involving logarithm and exponentiation can be synthesized using *linear programming* through abstraction of logarithmic or exponentiation terms, Farkas' Lemma, and Handelman's Theorem.
3. A key application of our method is the worst-case analysis of recursive programs. Our procedure can synthesize non-polynomial bounds of the form

$\mathcal{O}(n \log n)$, as well as $\mathcal{O}(n^r)$, where r is not an integer. We show the applicability of our technique to obtain worst-case complexity bounds for several classical recursive programs:

- For *Merge-Sort* [24, Chap. 2] and the divide-and-conquer algorithm for the *Closest-Pair problem* [24, Chap. 33], we obtain $\mathcal{O}(n \log n)$ worst-case bound, and the bounds we obtain are asymptotically optimal. Note that previous methods are either not applicable, or grossly over-estimate the bounds as $\mathcal{O}(n^2)$.
- For *Karatsuba's algorithm* for polynomial multiplication (cf. [52]) we obtain a bound of $\mathcal{O}(n^{1.6})$, whereas the optimal bound is $n^{\log_2 3} \approx \mathcal{O}(n^{1.585})$, and for the classical *Strassen's algorithm* for fast matrix multiplication (cf. [24, Chap. 4]) we obtain a bound of $\mathcal{O}(n^{2.9})$ whereas the optimal bound is $n^{\log_2 7} \approx \mathcal{O}(n^{2.8074})$. Note that previous methods are either not applicable, or grossly over-estimate the bounds as $\mathcal{O}(n^2)$ and $\mathcal{O}(n^3)$, respectively.

4. We present experimental results to demonstrate the effectiveness of our approach.

In general, our approach can be applied to (recursive) programs where the worst-case behaviour can be obtained by an analysis that involves only the structure of the program. For example, our approach cannot handle the Euclidean algorithm for computing the greatest common divisor of two given natural numbers, since the worst-case behaviour of this algorithm relies on Lamé's Theorem [52]. The key novelty of our approach is that we show how non-trivial non-polynomial worst-case upper bounds such as $\mathcal{O}(n \log n)$ and $\mathcal{O}(n^r)$, where r is non-integral, can be soundly obtained, even for recursive programs, using linear programming. Moreover, as our computational tool is linear programming, the approach we provide is also a relatively scalable one (see Remark 2). Due to page limit, we omit the details for syntax, semantics, proofs, experiments and other technical parts. They can be found in the full version [15].

2   Non-deterministic Recursive Programs

In this work, our main contributions involve a new approach for non-polynomial worst-case analysis of recursive programs. To focus on the new contributions, we consider a simple programming language for non-deterministic recursive programs. In our language, (a) all scalar variables hold integers, (b) all assignments to scalar variables are restricted to linear expressions with floored operation, and (c) we do not consider return statements. The reason to consider such a simple language is that (i) non-polynomial worst-case running time often involves non-polynomial terms over integer-valued variables (such as array length) only, (ii) assignments to variables are often linear with possible floored expressions (in e.g. divide-and-conquer programs) and (iii) return value is often not related to worst-case behaviour of programs.

For a set A, we denote by $|A|$ the cardinality of A and $\mathbf{1}_A$ the indicator function on A. We denote by $\mathbb{N}$, $\mathbb{N}_0$, $\mathbb{Z}$, and $\mathbb{R}$ the sets of all positive integers, non-negative integers, integers, and real numbers, respectively. Below we fix a set $\mathcal{X}$ of *scalar* variables.

Arithmetic Expressions, Valuations, and Predicates. The set of *(linear) arithmetic expressions* $\mathfrak{e}$ over $\mathcal{X}$ is generated by the following grammar: $\mathfrak{e} ::= c \mid x \mid \lfloor \frac{\mathfrak{e}}{c} \rfloor \mid \mathfrak{e} + \mathfrak{e} \mid \mathfrak{e} - \mathfrak{e} \mid c * \mathfrak{e}$ where $c \in \mathbb{Z}$ and $x \in \mathcal{X}$. Informally, (i) $\frac{\cdot}{c}$ refers to division operation, (ii) $\lfloor . \rfloor$ refers to the floored operation, and (iii) $+, -, *$ refer to addition, subtraction and multiplication operation over integers, respectively. In order to make sure that division is well-defined, we stipulate that every appearance of c in $\frac{\mathfrak{e}}{c}$ is non-zero. A *valuation* over $\mathcal{X}$ is a function ν from $\mathcal{X}$ into $\mathbb{Z}$. Informally, a valuation assigns to each scalar variable an integer. Under a valuation ν over $\mathcal{X}$, an arithmetic expression $\mathfrak{e}$ can be *evaluated* to an integer in the straightforward way. We denote by $\mathfrak{e}(\nu)$ the evaluation of $\mathfrak{e}$ under ν. The set of *propositional arithmetic predicates* ϕ over $\mathcal{X}$ is generated by the following grammar: $\phi ::= \mathfrak{e} \le \mathfrak{e} \mid \mathfrak{e} \ge \mathfrak{e} \mid \neg \phi \mid \phi \wedge \phi \mid \phi \vee \phi$ where $\mathfrak{e}$ represents an arithmetic expression. The satisfaction relation $\models$ between valuations and propositional arithmetic predicates is defined in the straightforward way through evaluation of arithmetic expressions. For each propositional arithmetic predicate ϕ, $\mathbf{1}_\phi$ is interpreted as the indicator function $\nu \mapsto \mathbf{1}_{\nu \models \phi}$ on valuations, where $\mathbf{1}_{\nu \models \phi}$ is 1 if $\nu \models \phi$ and 0 otherwise.

Syntax of the Programming Language. Due to page limit, we present a brief description of our syntax. The syntax is a subset of C programming language: in our setting, we have *scalar variables* which hold integers and *function names* which corresponds to functions (in programming-language sense); assignment statements are indicated by ':=', whose left-hand-side is a scalar variable and whose right-hand-side is a linear arithmetic expression; '**skip**' is the statement which does nothing; while-loops and conditional if-branches are indicated by '**while**' and '**if**' respectively, together with a propositional arithmetic predicate indicating the relevant condition (or guard); demonic non-deterministic branches are indicated by '**if**' and '$\star$'; function declarations are indicated by a function name followed by a bracketed list of non-duplicate scalar variables, while function calls are indicated by a function name followed by a bracketed list of linear arithmetic expressions; each function declaration is followed by a curly-braced compound statement as function body; finally, a program is a sequence of function declarations with their function bodies. Given a recursive program in our syntax, we assign a distinct natural number (called *label* in our context) to every assignment/skip statement, function call, if/while-statement and terminal line in the program. Each label serves as a program counter which indicates the next statement to be executed.

Semantics Through CFGs. We use control-flow graphs (CFGs) to specify the semantics of recursive programs. Informally, a CFG specifies how values for scalar variables and the program counter change in a program.

Definition 1 (Control-Flow Graphs). *A* control-flow graph *(CFG) is a triple which takes the form* (†) $\left(F, \left\{\left(L^f, L_b^f, L_a^f, L_c^f, L_d^f, V^f, \ell_{in}^f, \ell_{out}^f\right)\right\}_{f \in F}, \{\rightarrow_f\}_{f \in F}\right)$ *where:*

- *F is a finite set of* function names*;*
- *each L^f is a finite set of* labels *attached to the function name* f*, which is partitioned into (i) the set L_b^f of* branching *labels, (ii) the set L_a^f of* assignment *labels, (iii) the set L_c^f of* call *labels and (iv) the set L_d^f of* demonic non-deterministic *labels;*
- *each V^f is the set of* scalar variables *attached to* f*;*
- *each ℓ_{in}^f (resp. ℓ_{out}^f) is the* initial label *(resp. terminal label) in L^f;*
- *each $\rightarrow_f$ is a relation whose every member is a triple of the form (ℓ, α, ℓ') for which ℓ (resp. ℓ') is the source label (resp. target label) of the triple such that $\ell \in L^f$ (resp. $\ell' \in L^f$), and α is (i) either a propositional arithmetic predicate ϕ over V^f (as the set of scalar variables) if $\ell \in L_b^f$, (ii) or an* update function *from the set of valuations over V^f into the set of valuations over V^f if $\ell \in L_a^f$, (iii) or a pair (g, h) with $g \in F$ and h being a* value-passing function *which maps every valuation over V^f to a valuation over V^g if $\ell \in L_c^f$, (iv) or $\star$ if $\ell \in L_d^f$.*

W.l.o.g, we consider that all labels are natural numbers. We denote by Val_f the set of valuations over V^f, for each $f \in F$. Informally, a function name f, a label $\ell \in L^f$ and a valuation $\nu \in Val_f$ reflects that the current status of a recursive program is under function name f, right before the execution of the statement labeled ℓ in the function body named f and with values specified by ν, respectively.

Example 1. We consider the running example in Fig. 1 which abstracts the running time of BINARY-SEARCH. The CFG for this example is depicted in Fig. 2.   □

It is intuitive that every recursive program in our setting can be transformed into a CFG. Based on CFGs, the semantics models executions of a recursive program as runs, and is defined through the standard notion of call stack. Below we fix a recursive program P and its CFG taking the form (†). We first define the notion of *stack element* and *configurations* which captures all information within a function call.

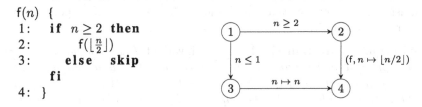

Fig. 1. A program for BINARY-SEARCH   **Fig. 2.** The CFG for Fig. 1

Stack Elements and Configurations. A *stack element* c (of P) is a triple (f, ℓ, ν) (treated as a letter) where $f \in F$, $\ell \in L^f$ and $\nu \in Val_f$; c is non-terminal if $\ell \in L^f \setminus \{\ell_{out}^f\}$. A *configuration* (of P) is a finite word of non-terminal stack elements (including the empty word ε). Thus, a stack element (f, ℓ, ν) specifies that the current function name is f, the next statement to be executed is the one labelled with ℓ and the current valuation w.r.t f is ν; a configuration captures the whole trace of the call stack.

Schedulers and Runs. To resolve non-determinism indicated by $\star$, we consider the standard notion of *schedulers*, which have the full ability to look into the whole history for decision. Formally, a scheduler π is a function that maps every sequence of configurations ending in a non-deterministic location to the next configuration. A stack element c (as the initial stack element) and a scheduler π defines a unique infinite sequence $\{w_j\}_{j \in \mathbb{N}_0}$ of configurations as the execution starting from c and under π, which is denoted as the *run* $\rho(c, \pi)$. This defines the semantics of recursive programs.

We now define the notion of termination time which corresponds directly to the running time of a recursive program. In our setting, execution of every step takes one time unit.

Definition 2 (Termination Time). *For each stack element c and each scheduler π, the* termination time *of the run $\rho(c, \pi) = \{w_j\}_{j \in \mathbb{N}_0}$, denoted by $T(c, \pi)$, is defined as $T(c, \pi) := \min\{j \mid w_j = \varepsilon\}$ (i.e., the earliest time when the stack is empty) where $\min \emptyset := \infty$. For each stack element c, the* worst-case termination-time function $\overline{T}$ *is a function on the set of stack elements defined by: $\overline{T}(c) := \sup\{T(c, \pi) \mid \pi$ is a scheduler for $P\}$.*

Thus $\overline{T}$ captures the worst-case behaviour of the recursive program P.

3 Measure Functions

In this section, we introduce the notion of measure functions for recursive programs. We show that measure functions are sound and complete for nondeterministic recursive programs and serve as upper bounds for the worst-case termination-time function. In the whole section, we fix a recursive program P together with its CFG taking the form (†). We now present the standard notion of *invariants* which represent reachable stack elements. Due to page limit, we omit the intuitive notion of *reachable stack elements*. Informally, a stack element is *reachable* w.r.t an initial function name and initial valuations satisfying a prerequisite (as a propositional arithmetic predicate) if it can appear in the run under some scheduler.

Definition 3 (Invariants). *A (linear)* invariant I *w.r.t a function name f^* and a propositional arithmetic predicate ϕ^* over V^{f^*} is a function that upon any pair (f, ℓ) satisfying $f \in F$ and $\ell \in L^f \setminus \{\ell_{out}^f\}$, $I(f, \ell)$ is a propositional arithmetic predicate over V^f such that (i) $I(f, \ell)$ is without the appearance of floored expressions (i.e. $\lfloor \cdot \rfloor$) and (ii) for all stack elements (f, ℓ, ν) reachable w.r.t $f^*, \phi^*, \nu \models I(f, \ell)$. The invariant I is in* disjunctive normal form *if every $I(f, \ell)$ is in disjunctive normal form.*

Obtaining invariants automatically is a standard problem in programming languages, and several techniques exist (such as abstract interpretation [26] or Farkas' Lemma [19]). In the rest of the section we fix a(n initial) function name $f^* \in F$ and a(n initial) propositional arithmetic predicate ϕ^* over V^{f^*}. For each $f \in F$ and $\ell \in L^f \backslash \{\ell^f_{out}\}$, we define $D_{f,\ell}$ to be the set of all valuations ν w.r.t f such that (f, ℓ, ν) is reachable w.r.t f^*, ϕ^*. Below we introduce the notion of measure functions.

Definition 4 (Measure Functions). *A measure function w.r.t f^*, ϕ^* is a function g from the set of stack elements into $[0, \infty]$ such that for all stack elements (f, ℓ, ν), the following conditions hold:*

- **C1:** *if $\ell = \ell^f_{out}$, then $g(f, \ell, \nu) = 0$;*
- **C2:** *if $\ell \in L^f_a \backslash \{\ell^f_{out}\}$, $\nu \in D_{f,\ell}$ and (ℓ, h, ℓ') is the only triple in $\to_f$ with source label ℓ and update function h, then $g(f, \ell', h(\nu)) + 1 \leq g(f, \ell, \nu)$;*
- **C3:** *if $\ell \in L^f_c \backslash \{\ell^f_{out}\}$, $\nu \in D_{f,\ell}$ and $(\ell, (g, h), \ell')$ is the only triple in $\to_f$ with source label ℓ and value-passing function h, then $1 + g(g, \ell^g_{in}, h(\nu)) + g(f, \ell', \nu) \leq g(f, \ell, \nu)$;*
- **C4:** *if $\ell \in L^f_b \backslash \{\ell^f_{out}\}$, $\nu \in D_{f,\ell}$ and $(\ell, \phi, \ell_1), (\ell, \neg\phi, \ell_2)$ are namely two triples in $\to_f$ with source label ℓ, then $\mathbf{1}_{\nu \models \phi} \cdot g(f, \ell_1, \nu) + \mathbf{1}_{\nu \models \neg\phi} \cdot g(f, \ell_2, \nu) + 1 \leq g(f, \ell, \nu)$;*
- **C5:** *if $\ell \in L^f_d \backslash \{\ell^f_{out}\}$, $\nu \in D_{f,\ell}$ and $(\ell, \star, \ell_1), (\ell, \star, \ell_2)$ are namely two triples in $\to_f$ with source label ℓ, then $\max\{g(f, \ell_1, \nu), g(f, \ell_2, \nu)\} + 1 \leq g(f, \ell, \nu)$.*

Intuitively, a measure function is a non-negative function whose values strictly decrease along the executions regardless of the choice of the demonic scheduler. By applying ranking functions to configurations, one can prove the following theorem stating that measure functions are sound and complete for the worst-case termination-time function.

Theorem 1 (Soundness and Completeness). *(1) (Soundness). For all measure functions g w.r.t f^*, ϕ^*, it holds that for all valuations $\nu \in Val_{f^*}$ such that $\nu \models \phi^*$, we have $\overline{T}(f^*, \ell^{f^*}_{in}, \nu) \leq g(f^*, \ell^{f^*}_{in}, \nu)$. (2) (Completeness). $\overline{T}$ is a measure function w.r.t f^*, ϕ^*.*

By Theorem 1, to obtain an upper bound on the worst-case termination-time function, it suffices to synthesize a measure function. Below we show that it suffices to synthesize measure functions at cut-points (which we refer as *significant labels*).

Definition 5 (Significant Labels). *Let $f \in F$. A label $\ell \in L^f$ is significant if either $\ell = \ell^f_{in}$ or ℓ is the initial label to some while-loop appearing in the function body of f.*

We denote by L^f_s the set of significant locations in L^f. Informally, a significant label is a label where valuations cannot be easily deduced from other labels, namely valuations at the start of the function-call and at the initial label of a while loop.

The Expansion Construction (from g to $\widehat{g}$). Let g be a function from $\{(f, \ell, \nu) \mid f \in F, \ell \in L_s^f, \nu \in Val_f\}$ into $[0, \infty]$. One can obtain from g a function $\widehat{g}$ from the set of all stack elements into $[0, \infty]$ in a straightforward way through iterated application of the equality forms of C1–C5.

4   The Synthesis Algorithm

By Theorem 1, measure functions are a sound approach for upper bounds of the worst-case termination-time function, and hence synthesis of measure functions of specific forms provide upper bounds for worst-case behaviour of recursive programs. We first define the synthesis problem of measure functions and then present the synthesis algorithm, where the initial stack element is integrated into the input invariant. Informally, the input is a recursive program, an invariant for the program and technical parameters for the specific form of a measure function, and the output is a measure function if the algorithm finds one, and fail otherwise.

The RecTermBou Problem. The RecTermBou problem is defined as follows:

- *Input:* a recursive program P, an invariant I in disjunctive normal form and a quadruple (d, op, r, k) of technical parameters;
- *Output:* a measure function h w.r.t the quadruple (d, op, r, k).

The quadruple (d, op, r, k) specifies the form of a measure function in the way that $d \in \mathbb{N}$ is the degree of the measure function to be synthesized, $\text{op} \in \{\log, \exp\}$ signals either logarithmic (when $\text{op} = \log$) (e.g., $n \ln n$) or exponential (when $\text{op} = \exp$) (e.g., $n^{1.6}$) measure functions, r is a rational number greater than 1 which specifies the exponent in the measure function (i.e., n^r) when $\text{op} = \exp$ and $k \in \mathbb{N}$ is a technical parameter required by Theorem 3. In the input for RecTermBou we fix the exponent r when $\text{op} = \exp$. However, iterating with binary search over an input bounded range we can obtain a measure function in the given range as precise as possible. Moreover, the invariants can be obtained automatically through e.g. [19]. Below we present our algorithm SynAlgo for synthesizing measure functions for the RecTermBou problem. The algorithm is designed to synthesize one function over valuations at each function name and appropriate significant labels so that C1–C5 are fulfilled. Due to page limit, we only illustrate the main conceptual details of our algorithm. In the following, we fix an input from the RecTermBou problem to our algorithm.

Overview. We present the overview of our solution which has the following five steps.

1. *Step 1.* Since one key aspect of our result is to obtain bounds of the form $\mathcal{O}(n \log n)$ as well as $\mathcal{O}(n^r)$, where r is not an integer, we first consider general form of upper bounds that involve logarithm and exponentiation (Step 1(a)), and then consider templates with the general form of upper bounds for significant labels (Step 1(b)).

2. *Step 2.* The second step considers the template generated in Step 1 for significant labels and generate templates for all labels. This step is relatively straightforward.
3. *Step 3.* The third step establishes constraint triples according to the invariant given by the input and the template obtained in Step 2. This step is also straightforward.
4. *Step 4.* The fourth step is the significant step which involves transforming the constraint triples generated in Step 3 into ones without logarithmic and exponentiation terms. The first substep (Step 4(a)) is to consider abstractions of logarithmic, exponentiation, and floored expressions as fresh variables. The next step (Step 4(b)) requires to obtain linear constraints over the abstracted variables. We use Farkas' lemma and Lagrange's Mean-Value Theorem (LMVT) to obtain sound linear inequalities for those variables.
5. *Step 5.* The final step is to solve the unknown coefficients of the template from the constraint triples (without logarithm or exponentiation) obtained from Step 4. This requires the solution of positive polynomials over polyhedrons through the sound form of Handelman's Theorem (Theorem 3) to transform into a linear program.

We first present an informal illustration of the key ideas through a simple example.

Example 2. Consider the task to synthesize a measure function for Karatsuba's algorithm [52] for polynomial multiplication which runs in $c \cdot n^{1.6}$ steps, where c is a coefficient to be synthesized and n represents the maximal degree of the input polynomials and is a power of 2. We describe informally how our algorithm tackles Karatsuba's algorithm. Let n be the length of the two input polynomials and $c \cdot n^{1.6}$ be the template. Since Karatsuba's algorithm involves three sub-multiplications and seven additions/subtractions, the condition C3 becomes (*) $c \cdot n^{1.6} - 3 \cdot c \cdot \left(\frac{n}{2}\right)^{1.6} - 7 \cdot n \geq 0$ for all $n \geq 2$. The algorithm first abstracts $n^{1.6}$ as a stand-alone variable u. Then the algorithm generates the following inequalities through properties of exponentiation: (**) $u \geq 2^{1.6}, u \geq 2^{0.6} \cdot n$. Finally, the algorithm transforms (*) into (***) $c \cdot u - 3 \cdot \left(\frac{1}{2}\right)^{1.6} \cdot c \cdot u - 7 \cdot n \geq 0$ and synthesizes a value for c through Handelman's Theorem to ensure that (***) holds under $n \geq 2$ and (**). One can verify that $c = 1000$ is a feasible solution since

$$\left(1000 - 3000 \cdot (1/2)^{1.6}\right) \cdot u - 7 \cdot n =$$

$$\frac{7}{2^{0.6}} \cdot \left(u - 2^{0.6} \cdot n\right) + \frac{1000 \cdot 2^{1.6} - 3014}{2^{1.6}} \cdot \left(u - 2^{1.6}\right) + \left(1000 \cdot 2^{1.6} - 3014\right) \cdot 1.$$

Hence, Karatsuba's algorithm runs in $\mathcal{O}(n^{1.6})$ time. □

4.1   Step 1 of SynAlgo

Step 1(a): General Form of a Measure Function

Extended Terms. In order to capture non-polynomial worst-case complexity of recursive programs, our algorithm incorporates two types of extensions of terms.

1. *Logarithmic Terms.* The first extension, which we call log-extension, is the extension with terms from $\ln x, \ln (x - y + 1)$ where x, y are scalar variables appearing in the parameter list of some function name and $\ln (\cdot)$ refers to the natural logarithm function with base e. Our algorithm will take this extension when op is log.

2. *Exponentiation Terms.* The second extension, which we call exp-extension, is with terms from $x^r, (x - y + 1)^r$ where x, y are scalar variables appearing in the parameter list of some function name. The algorithm takes this when op = exp.

The intuition is that x (resp. $x - y + 1$) may represent a positive quantity to be halved iteratively (resp. the length between array indexes y and x).

General Form. The general form for any coordinate function $\eta(\mathsf{f}, \ell, \cdot)$ of a measure function η (at function name f and $\ell \in L_\mathsf{s}^\mathsf{f}$) is a finite sum

$$\mathfrak{e} = \sum_i c_i \cdot g_i \tag{1}$$

where (i) each c_i is a constant scalar and each g_i is a finite product of no more than d terms (i.e., with degree at most d) from scalar variables in V^f and logarithmic/exponentiation extensions (depending on op), and (ii) all g_i's correspond to all finite products of no more than d terms. Analogous to arithmetic expressions, for any such finite sum $\mathfrak{e}$ and any valuation $\nu \in \mathit{Val}_\mathsf{f}$, we denote by $\mathfrak{e}(\nu)$ the real number evaluated through replacing any scalar variable x appearing in $\mathfrak{e}$ with $\nu(x)$, provided that $\mathfrak{e}(\nu)$ is well-defined.

Semantics of General Form. A finite sum $\mathfrak{e}$ at f and $\ell \in L_\mathsf{s}^\mathsf{f}$ in the form (1) defines a function $\llbracket \mathfrak{e} \rrbracket$ on Val_f in the way that for each $\nu \in \mathit{Val}_\mathsf{f}$: $\llbracket \mathfrak{e} \rrbracket(\nu) := \mathfrak{e}(\nu)$ if $\nu \models I(\mathsf{f}, \ell)$, and $\llbracket \mathfrak{e} \rrbracket(\nu) := 0$ otherwise. Note that in the definition of $\llbracket \mathfrak{e} \rrbracket$, we do not consider the case when log or exponentiation is undefined. However, we will see in Step 1(b) below that log or exponentiation will always be well-defined.

Step 1(b): Templates. As in all previous works (cf. [12,16,20,25,40,58,61,68]), we consider a template for measure function determined by the triple (d, op, r) from the input parameters. Formally, the template determined by (d, op, r) assigns to every function name f and $\ell \in L_\mathsf{s}^\mathsf{f}$ an expression in the form (1) (with degree d and extension option op). Note that a template here only restricts (i) the degree and (ii) log or exp extension for a measure function, rather than its specific form. In detail, the algorithm sets up a template η for a measure function by assigning to each function name f and significant label $\ell \in L_\mathsf{s}^\mathsf{f}$ an expression $\eta(\mathsf{f}, \ell)$ in a form similar to (1), except for that c_i's in (1) are interpreted as distinct *template variables* whose actual values are to be synthesized. In order to ensure that logarithm and exponentiation are well-defined over each $I(\mathsf{f}, \ell)$, we impose the following restriction (§) on our template: $\ln x, x^r$ (resp. $\ln (x - y + 1), (x-y+1)^r$) appear in $\eta(\mathsf{f}, \ell)$ only when $x-1 \geq 0$ (resp. $x-y \geq 0$) can be inferred from the invariant $I(\mathsf{f}, \ell)$. To infer $x - 1 \geq 0$ or $x - y \geq 0$ from $I(\mathsf{f}, \ell)$, we utilize Farkas' Lemma.

Theorem 2 (Farkas' Lemma [28,60]). *Let* $\mathbf{A} \in \mathbb{R}^{m \times n}$, $\mathbf{b} \in \mathbb{R}^m$, $\mathbf{c} \in \mathbb{R}^n$ *and* $d \in \mathbb{R}$. *Assume that* $\{\mathbf{x} \mid \mathbf{Ax} \leq \mathbf{b}\} \neq \emptyset$. *Then* $\{\mathbf{x} \mid \mathbf{Ax} \leq \mathbf{b}\} \subseteq \{\mathbf{x} \mid \mathbf{c}^\mathsf{T}\mathbf{x} \leq d\}$ *iff there exists* $\mathbf{y} \in \mathbb{R}^m$ *such that* $\mathbf{y} \geq \mathbf{0}$, $\mathbf{A}^\mathsf{T}\mathbf{y} = \mathbf{c}$ *and* $\mathbf{b}^\mathsf{T}\mathbf{y} \leq d$.

By Farkas' Lemma, there exists an algorithm that infers whether $x - 1 \geq 0$ (or $x - y \geq 0$) holds under $I(\mathsf{f}, \ell)$ in polynomial time through emptiness checking of polyhedra (cf. [59]) since $I(\mathsf{f}, \ell)$ involves only linear (degree-1) polynomials in our setting.

Then η naturally induces a function $[\![\eta]\!]$ from $\big\{(\mathsf{f}, \ell, \nu) \mid \mathsf{f} \in F, \ell \in L_\mathsf{s}^\mathsf{f}, \nu \in \mathrm{Val}_\mathsf{f}\big\}$ into $[0, \infty]$ parametric over template variables such that $[\![\eta]\!](\mathsf{f}, \ell, \nu) = [\![\eta(\mathsf{f}, \ell)]\!](\nu)$ for all appropriate stack elements (f, ℓ, ν). Note that $[\![\eta]\!]$ is well-defined since logarithm and exponentiation is well-defined over satisfaction sets given by I.

4.2 Step 2 of SYNALGO

Step 2: Computation of $\widehat{[\![\eta]\!]}$. Let η be the template constructed from Step 1. This step computes $\widehat{[\![\eta]\!]}$ from η by the expansion construction of significant labels (Sect. 3) which transforms a function g into $\widehat{g}$. Recall the function $[\![\mathsf{e}]\!]$ for e is defined in Step 1(a). Formally, based on the template η from Step 1, the algorithm computes $\widehat{[\![\eta]\!]}$, with the exception that template variables appearing in η are treated as undetermined constants. Then $\widehat{[\![\eta]\!]}$ is a function parametric over the template variables in η.

By an easy induction, each $\widehat{[\![\eta]\!]}(\mathsf{f}, \ell, \centerdot)$ can be represented by an expression in the form

$$\max\big\{\textstyle\sum_j \mathbf{1}_{\phi_{1j}} \cdot h_{1j}, \; \ldots, \; \sum_j \mathbf{1}_{\phi_{mj}} \cdot h_{mj}\big\} \tag{2}$$

where each ϕ_{ij} is a propositional arithmetic predicate over V^f such that for each i, $\bigvee_j \phi_{ij}$ is tautology and $\phi_{ij_1} \wedge \phi_{ij_2}$ is unsatisfiable whenever $j_1 \neq j_2$, and each h_{ij} takes the form similar to (1) with the difference that (i) each c_i is either a scalar or a template variable appearing in η and (ii) each g_i is a finite product whose every multiplicand is either some $x \in V^\mathsf{f}$, or some $\lfloor \mathsf{e} \rfloor$ with e being an instance of $\langle expr \rangle$, or some $\ln \mathsf{e}$ (or e^r, depending on op) with e being an instance of $\langle expr \rangle$. For this step we use the fact that all propositional arithmetic predicates can be put in disjunctive normal form.

4.3 Step 3 of SYNALGO

This step generates constraint triples from $\widehat{[\![\eta]\!]}$ computed in Step 2. By applying non-negativity and C2–C5 to $\widehat{[\![\eta]\!]}$ (computed in Step 2), the algorithm establishes constraint triples which will be interpreted as universally-quantified logical formulas later.

Constraint Triples. A *constraint triple* is a triple $(\mathsf{f}, \phi, \mathsf{e})$ where (i) $\mathsf{f} \in F$, (ii) ϕ is a propositional arithmetic predicate over V^f which is a conjunction of atomic formulae of the form $\mathsf{e}' \geq 0$ with e' being an arithmetic expression, and (iii) e is an expression taking the form similar to (1) with the difference that

(i) each c_i is either a scalar, or a template variable c appearing in η, or its reverse $-c$, and (ii) each g_i is a finite product whose every multiplicand is either some $x \in V^f$, or some $\lfloor e \rfloor$ with e being an instance of $\langle expr \rangle$, or some $\ln e$ (or e^r, depending on op) with e being an instance of $\langle expr \rangle$. For each constraint triple (f, ϕ, e), the function $\llbracket e \rrbracket$ on Val_f is defined in the way such that each $\llbracket e \rrbracket(\nu)$ is the evaluation result of e when assigning $\nu(x)$ to each $x \in V^f$; under ($\S$) (of Step 1(b)), logarithm and exponentiation will always be well-defined.

Semantics of Constraint Triples. A constraint triple (f, ϕ, e) encodes the following logical formula: $\forall \nu \in Val_f. (\nu \models \phi \to \llbracket e \rrbracket(\nu) \geq 0)$. Multiple constraint triples are grouped into a single logical formula through conjunction.

Step 3: Establishment of Constraint Triples. Based on $\widehat{\llbracket \eta \rrbracket}$ (computed in the previous step), the algorithm generates constraint triples at each significant label, then group all generated constraint triples together in a conjunctive way. To be more precise, at every significant label ℓ of some function name f, the algorithm generates constraint triples through non-negativity of measure functions and conditions C2–C5; after generating the constraint triples for each significant label, the algorithm groups them together in the conjunctive fashion to form a single collection of constraint triples.

Example 3. Consider our running example (cf. Example 1). Let the input quadruple be $(1, \log, -, 1)$ and invariant (at label 1) be $n \geq 1$ (length of array should be positive). In Step 1, the algorithm assigns the template $\eta(f, 1, n) = c_1 \cdot n + c_2 \cdot \ln n + c_3$ at label 1 and $\eta(f, 4, n) = 0$ at label 4. In Step 2, the algorithm computes template at other labels and obtains that $\eta(f, 2, n) = 1 + c_1 \cdot \lfloor n/2 \rfloor + c_2 \cdot \ln \lfloor n/2 \rfloor + c_3$ and $\eta(f, 3, n) = 1$. In Step 3, the algorithm establishes the following three constraint triples q_1, q_2, q_3:

- $q_1 := (f, n - 1 \geq 0, c_1 \cdot n + c_2 \cdot \ln n + c_3)$ from the logical formula $\forall n.(n \geq 1) \to c_1 \cdot n + c_2 \cdot \ln n + c_3 \geq 0$ for non-negativity of measure functions;
- $q_2 := (f, n - 1 \geq 0 \wedge 1 - n \geq 0, c_1 \cdot n + c_2 \cdot \ln n + c_3 - 2)$ and $q_3 := (f, n - 2 \geq 0, c_1 \cdot (n - \lfloor n/2 \rfloor) + c_2 \cdot (\ln n - \ln \lfloor n/2 \rfloor) - 2$ from resp. logical formulae
  - $\forall n.(n \geq 1 \wedge n \leq 1) \to c_1 \cdot n + c_2 \cdot \ln n + c_3 \geq 2$ and
  - $\forall n.(n \geq 2) \to c_1 \cdot n + c_2 \cdot \ln n + c_3 \geq c_1 \cdot \lfloor n/2 \rfloor + c_2 \cdot \ln \lfloor n/2 \rfloor + c_3 + 2$
  for C4 (at label 1). □

4.4   Step 4 of SYNALGO

Step 4: Solving Constraint Triples. To check whether the logical formula encoded by the generated constraint triples is valid, the algorithm follows a sound method which abstracts each multiplicand other than scalar variables in the form (2) as a stand-alone variable, and transforms the validity of the formula into a system of linear inequalities over template variables appearing in η through Handelman's Theorem and linear programming. The main idea is that the algorithm establishes tight linear inequalities for those abstraction variables by investigating properties for the abstracted arithmetic expressions, and use linear programming to solve the formula based on the linear inequalities for abstraction variables. We note that validity of such logical formulae are generally undecidable since they involve non-polynomial terms such as logarithm [33].

Below we describe how the algorithm transforms a constraint triple into one without logarithmic or exponentiation term. Given any finite set Γ of polynomials over n variables, we define $\mathsf{Sat}(\Gamma) := \{x \in \mathbb{R}^n \mid h(x) \geq 0 \text{ for all } h \in \Gamma\}$. In the whole step, we let $(\mathsf{f}, \phi, \mathsf{e}^*)$ be any constraint triple such that $\phi = \bigwedge_j \mathsf{e}_j \geq 0$; moreover, we maintain a finite set Γ of linear (degree-1) polynomials over scalar and freshly-added variables. Intuitively, Γ is related to both the set of all e_j's (so that $\mathsf{Sat}(\Gamma)$ is somehow the satisfaction set of ϕ) and the finite subset of polynomials in Theorem 3. Due to lack of space, we only illustrate the part of the algorithm for logarithmic terms (i.e., the case when op $=$ log); exponentiation terms can be treated in a similar fashion.

Step 4(a): Abstraction of Logarithmic, Exponentiation, and Floored Expressions. The first sub-step involves the following computational steps, where Items 2–4 handle variables for abstraction, and Item 6 is approximation of floored expressions, and other steps are straightforward.

1. *Initialization.* First, the algorithm maintains a finite set of linear (degree-1) polynomials Γ and sets it initially to the empty set.
2. *Logarithmic and Floored Expressions.* Next, the algorithm computes the following subsets of $\langle expr \rangle$:
   - $\mathcal{E}_L := \{\mathsf{e} \mid \ln \mathsf{e} \text{ appears in } \mathsf{e}^* \text{ (as sub-expression)}\}$ upon op $=$ log.
   - $\mathcal{E}_F := \{\mathsf{e} \mid \mathsf{e} \text{ appears in } \mathsf{e}^* \text{ and takes the form } \lfloor \frac{\cdot}{c} \rfloor\}$.
   Let $\mathcal{E} := \mathcal{E}_L \cup \mathcal{E}_F$.
3. *Variables for Logarithmic and Floored Expressions.* Next, for each $\mathsf{e} \in \mathcal{E}$, the algorithm establishes fresh variables as follows:
   - a fresh variable u_e which represents $\ln \mathsf{e}$ for $\mathsf{e} \in \mathcal{E}_L$;
   - a fresh variable w_e indicating e for $\mathsf{e} \in \mathcal{E}_F$.
   After this step, the algorithm sets N to be the number of all variables (i.e., all scalar variables and all fresh variables added up to this point). In the rest of this section, we consider an implicit linear order over all scalar and freshly-added variables so that a valuation of these variables can be treated as a vector in $\mathbb{R}^N$.
4. *Variable Substitution (from e to $\widetilde{\mathsf{e}}$).* Next, for each e which is either t or some e_j or some expression in $\mathcal{E}$, the algorithm computes $\widetilde{\mathsf{e}}$ as the expression obtained from e by substituting (i) every possible $u_{\mathsf{e}'}$ for $\ln \mathsf{e}'$, and (ii) every possible $w_{\mathsf{e}'}$ for e' such that e' is a sub-expression of e which does not appear as sub-expression in some other sub-expression $\mathsf{e}'' \in \mathcal{E}_F$ of e. From now on, any e or $\widetilde{\mathsf{e}}$ or is treated as a polynomial over scalar and freshly-added variables. Then any $\mathsf{e}(x)$ or $\widetilde{\mathsf{e}}(x)$ is the result of polynomial evaluation under the correspondence between variables and coordinates of x specified by the linear order.
5. *Importing ϕ into Γ.* The algorithm adds all $\widetilde{\mathsf{e}}_j$ into Γ.
6. *Approximation of Floored Expressions.* For each $\mathsf{e} \in \mathcal{E}_F$ such that $\mathsf{e} = \lfloor \frac{\mathsf{e}'}{c} \rfloor$, the algorithm adds linear constraints for w_e recursively on the nesting depth of floor operation as follows.

- *Base Step.* If $\mathfrak{e} = \lfloor \frac{\mathfrak{e}'}{c} \rfloor$ and $\mathfrak{e}'$ involves no nested floored expression, then the algorithm adds into Γ either (i) $\widetilde{\mathfrak{e}'} - c \cdot w_{\mathfrak{e}}$ and $c \cdot w_{\mathfrak{e}} - \widetilde{\mathfrak{e}'} + c - 1$ when $c \geq 1$, which is derived from $\frac{\mathfrak{e}'}{c} - \frac{c-1}{c} \leq \mathfrak{e} \leq \frac{\mathfrak{e}'}{c}$, or (ii) $c \cdot w_{\mathfrak{e}} - \widetilde{\mathfrak{e}'}$ and $\widetilde{\mathfrak{e}'} - c \cdot w_{\mathfrak{e}} - c - 1$ when $c \leq -1$, which follows from $\frac{\mathfrak{e}'}{c} - \frac{c+1}{c} \leq \mathfrak{e} \leq \frac{\mathfrak{e}'}{c}$. Second, given the current Γ, the algorithm finds the largest constant $t_{\mathfrak{e}'}$ through Farkas' Lemma such that $\forall \boldsymbol{x} \in \mathbb{R}^N . \left(\boldsymbol{x} \in \mathsf{Sat}(\Gamma) \to \widetilde{\mathfrak{e}'}(\boldsymbol{x}) \geq t_{\mathfrak{e}'} \right)$ holds; if such $t_{\mathfrak{e}'}$ exists, the algorithm adds the constraint $w_{\mathfrak{e}} \geq \left\lfloor \frac{t_{\mathfrak{e}'}}{c} \right\rfloor$ into Γ.
- *Recursive Step.* If $\mathfrak{e} = \lfloor \frac{\mathfrak{e}'}{c} \rfloor$ and $\mathfrak{e}'$ involves some nested floored expression, then the algorithm proceeds almost in the same way as for the Base Step, except that $\widetilde{\mathfrak{e}'}$ takes the role of $\mathfrak{e}'$. (Note that $\widetilde{\mathfrak{e}'}$ does not involve nested floored expresions.)

7. *Emptiness Checking.* The algorithm checks whether $\mathsf{Sat}(\Gamma)$ is empty or not in polynomial time in the size of Γ (cf. [59]). If $\mathsf{Sat}(\Gamma) = \emptyset$, then the algorithm discards this constraint triple with no linear inequalities generated, and proceeds to other constraint triples; otherwise, the algorithm proceeds to the remaining steps.

Example 4. We continue with Example 3. In Step 4(a), the algorithm first establishes fresh variables $u := \ln n$, $v := \ln \lfloor n/2 \rfloor$ and $w := \lfloor n/2 \rfloor$, then finds that (i) $n - 2 \cdot w \geq 0$, (ii) $2 \cdot w - n + 1 \geq 0$ and (iii) $n - 2 \geq 0$ (as Γ) implies that $w - 1 \geq 0$. After Step 4(a), the constraint triples after variable substitution and their Γ's are as follows:

- $\widetilde{\mathfrak{q}_1} = (\mathsf{f}, n - 1 \geq 0, c_1 \cdot n + c_2 \cdot u + c_3)$ and $\Gamma_1 = \{n - 1\}$;
- $\widetilde{\mathfrak{q}_2} = (\mathsf{f}, n - 1 \geq 0 \wedge 1 - n \geq 0, c_1 \cdot n + c_2 \cdot u + c_3 - 2)$ and $\Gamma_2 = \{n - 1, 1 - n\}$;
- $\widetilde{\mathfrak{q}_3} := (\mathsf{f}, n - 2 \geq 0, c_1 \cdot (n - w) + c_2 \cdot (u - v) - 2)$ and $\Gamma_3 = \{n - 2, n - 2 \cdot w, 2 \cdot w - n + 1, w - 1\}$. □

For the next sub-step we will use Lagrange's Mean-Value Theorem (LMVT) [6, Chap. 6] to approximate logarithmic and exponentiation terms.

Step 4(b): Linear Constraints for Abstracted Variables. The second sub-step consists of the following computational steps which establish into Γ linear constraints for logarithmic or exponentiation terms. Below we denote by $\mathcal{E}'$ either the set $\mathcal{E}_L$ when $\mathsf{op} = \log$ or $\mathcal{E}_E$ when $\mathsf{op} = \exp$. Recall the $\widetilde{\mathfrak{e}}$ notation is defined in the Variable Substitution (Item 4) of Step 4(a).

1. *Lower-Bound for Expressions in $\mathcal{E}_L$.* For each $\mathfrak{e} \in \mathcal{E}_L$, we find the largest constant $t_{\mathfrak{e}} \in \mathbb{R}$ such that the logical formula $\forall \boldsymbol{x} \in \mathbb{R}^N . (\boldsymbol{x} \in \mathsf{Sat}(\Gamma) \to \widetilde{\mathfrak{e}}(\boldsymbol{x}) \geq t_{\mathfrak{e}})$ holds, This can be solved by Farkas' Lemma and linear programming, since $\widetilde{\mathfrak{e}}$ is linear. Note that as long as $\mathsf{Sat}(\Gamma) \neq \emptyset$, it follows from (§) (in Step 1(b)) that $t_{\mathfrak{e}}$ is well-defined (since $t_{\mathfrak{e}}$ cannot be arbitrarily large) and $t_{\mathfrak{e}} \geq 1$.
2. *Mutual No-Smaller-Than Inequalities over $\mathcal{E}_L$.* For each pair $(\mathfrak{e}, \mathfrak{e}') \in \mathcal{E}_L \times \mathcal{E}_L$ such that $\mathfrak{e} \neq \mathfrak{e}'$, the algorithm finds real numbers $r_{(\mathfrak{e}, \mathfrak{e}')}, b_{(\mathfrak{e}, \mathfrak{e}')}$ through Farkas'

Lemma and linear programming such that (i) $r_{(\mathfrak{e},\mathfrak{e}')} \geq 0$ and (ii) both the logical formulae

$$\forall \boldsymbol{x} \in \mathbb{R}^N. \left[\boldsymbol{x} \in \mathsf{Sat}(\Gamma) \to \widetilde{\mathfrak{e}}(\boldsymbol{x}) - \left(r_{\mathfrak{e},\mathfrak{e}'} \cdot \widetilde{\mathfrak{e}'}(\boldsymbol{x}) + b_{\mathfrak{e},\mathfrak{e}'} \right) \geq 0 \right] \quad \text{and}$$

$$\forall \boldsymbol{x} \in \mathbb{R}^N. \left[\boldsymbol{x} \in \mathsf{Sat}(\Gamma) \to r_{\mathfrak{e},\mathfrak{e}'} \cdot \widetilde{\mathfrak{e}'}(\boldsymbol{x}) + b_{\mathfrak{e},\mathfrak{e}'} \geq 1 \right]$$

hold. The algorithm first finds the maximal value $r_{\mathfrak{e},\mathfrak{e}'}^*$ over all feasible $(r_{\mathfrak{e},\mathfrak{e}'}, b_{\mathfrak{e},\mathfrak{e}'})$'s, then finds the maximal $b_{\mathfrak{e},\mathfrak{e}'}^*$ over all feasible $(r_{\mathfrak{e},\mathfrak{e}'}^*, b_{\mathfrak{e},\mathfrak{e}'})$'s. If such $r_{\mathfrak{e},\mathfrak{e}'}^*$ does not exist, the algorithm simply leaves $r_{\mathfrak{e},\mathfrak{e}'}^*$ undefined. Note that once $r_{\mathfrak{e},\mathfrak{e}'}^*$ exists and $\mathsf{Sat}(\Gamma) \neq \emptyset$, then $b_{\mathfrak{e},\mathfrak{e}'}^*$ exists since $b_{\mathfrak{e},\mathfrak{e}'}$ cannot be arbitrarily large once $r_{\mathfrak{e},\mathfrak{e}'}^*$ is fixed.

3. *Mutual No-Greater-Than Inequalities over $\mathcal{E}_L$.* For each pair $(\mathfrak{e}, \mathfrak{e}') \in \mathcal{E}_L \times \mathcal{E}_L$ such that $\mathfrak{e} \neq \mathfrak{e}'$, the algorithm finds real numbers $r_{(\mathfrak{e},\mathfrak{e}')}, b_{(\mathfrak{e},\mathfrak{e}')}$ through Farkas' Lemma and linear programming such that (i) $r_{(\mathfrak{e},\mathfrak{e}')} \geq 0$ and (ii) the logical formula

$$\forall \boldsymbol{x} \in \mathbb{R}^N. \left[\boldsymbol{x} \in \mathsf{Sat}(\Gamma) \to \left(r_{\mathfrak{e},\mathfrak{e}'} \cdot \widetilde{\mathfrak{e}'}(\boldsymbol{x}) + b_{\mathfrak{e},\mathfrak{e}'} \right) - \widetilde{\mathfrak{e}}(\boldsymbol{x}) \geq 0 \right]$$

holds. The algorithm then finds the minimal value $(r_{\mathfrak{e},\mathfrak{e}'}^*, b_{\mathfrak{e},\mathfrak{e}'}^*)$ similarly as above.

4. *Constraints from Logarithm.* For each variable $u_{\mathfrak{e}}$, the algorithm adds into Γ first the polynomial expression $\widetilde{\mathfrak{e}} - \left(\mathbf{1}_{t_{\mathfrak{e}} \leq e} \cdot e + \mathbf{1}_{t_{\mathfrak{e}} > e} \cdot \frac{t_{\mathfrak{e}}}{\ln t_{\mathfrak{e}}} \right) \cdot u_{\mathfrak{e}}$ from the fact that the function $z \mapsto \frac{z}{\ln z}$ $(z \geq 1)$ has global minima at e (so that the inclusion of this polynomial expression is sound), and then the polynomial expression $u_{\mathfrak{e}} - \ln t_{\mathfrak{e}}$ due to the definition of $t_{\mathfrak{e}}$.

5. *Mutual No-Smaller-Than Inequalities over $u_{\mathfrak{e}}'s$.* For each pair $(\mathfrak{e}, \mathfrak{e}') \in \mathcal{E}_L \times \mathcal{E}_L$ such that $\mathfrak{e} \neq \mathfrak{e}'$ and $r_{\mathfrak{e},\mathfrak{e}'}^*, b_{\mathfrak{e},\mathfrak{e}'}^*$ are successfully found and $r_{\mathfrak{e},\mathfrak{e}'}^* > 0$, the algorithm adds $u_{\mathfrak{e}} - \ln r_{\mathfrak{e},\mathfrak{e}'}^* - u_{\mathfrak{e}'} + \mathbf{1}_{b_{\mathfrak{e},\mathfrak{e}'}^* < 0} \cdot \left(t_{\mathfrak{e}'} + \frac{b_{\mathfrak{e},\mathfrak{e}'}^*}{r_{\mathfrak{e},\mathfrak{e}'}^*} \right)^{-1} \cdot \left(-\frac{b_{\mathfrak{e},\mathfrak{e}'}^*}{r_{\mathfrak{e},\mathfrak{e}'}^*} \right)$ into Γ.

This is due to the fact that $[\![\mathfrak{e}]\!] - \left(r_{\mathfrak{e},\mathfrak{e}'}^* \cdot [\![\mathfrak{e}']\!] + b_{\mathfrak{e},\mathfrak{e}'}^* \right) \geq 0$ implies the following:

$$\ln [\![\mathfrak{e}]\!] \geq \ln r_{\mathfrak{e},\mathfrak{e}'}^* + \ln \left([\![\mathfrak{e}']\!] + (b_{\mathfrak{e},\mathfrak{e}'}^* / r_{\mathfrak{e},\mathfrak{e}'}^*) \right)$$

$$= \ln r_{\mathfrak{e},\mathfrak{e}'}^* + \ln [\![\mathfrak{e}']\!] + \left(\ln \left([\![\mathfrak{e}']\!] + (b_{\mathfrak{e},\mathfrak{e}'}^* / r_{\mathfrak{e},\mathfrak{e}'}^*) \right) - \ln [\![\mathfrak{e}']\!] \right)$$

$$\geq \ln r_{\mathfrak{e},\mathfrak{e}'}^* + \ln [\![\mathfrak{e}']\!] - \mathbf{1}_{b_{\mathfrak{e},\mathfrak{e}'}^* < 0} \cdot \left(t_{\mathfrak{e}'} + (b_{\mathfrak{e},\mathfrak{e}'}^* / r_{\mathfrak{e},\mathfrak{e}'}^*) \right)^{-1} \cdot \left(-b_{\mathfrak{e},\mathfrak{e}'}^* / r_{\mathfrak{e},\mathfrak{e}'}^* \right),$$

where the last step is obtained from LMVT and by distinguishing whether $b_{\mathfrak{e},\mathfrak{e}'}^* \geq 0$ or not, using the fact that the derivative of the natural-logarithm is the reciprocal function. Note that one has $t_{\mathfrak{e}'} + \frac{b_{\mathfrak{e},\mathfrak{e}'}^*}{r_{\mathfrak{e},\mathfrak{e}'}^*} \geq 1$ due to the maximal choice of $t_{\mathfrak{e}'}$.

6. *Mutual No-Greater-Than Inequalities over $u_{\mathfrak{e}}'s$.* Similar to the previous item, the algorithm establishes mutual no-greater-than inequalities over $u_{\mathfrak{e}}$'s.

Although in Item 4 and Item 6 above, we have logarithmic terms such as $\ln t_{\mathfrak{e}}$ and $\ln r_{\mathfrak{e},\mathfrak{e}'}^*$, both $t_{\mathfrak{e}}$ and $r_{\mathfrak{e},\mathfrak{e}'}^*$ are already determined constants, hence their approximations can be used. After Step 4, the constraint triple $(\mathsf{f}, \phi, \mathfrak{e}^*)$ is transformed into $(\mathsf{f}, \bigwedge_{h \in \Gamma} h \geq 0, \widetilde{\mathfrak{e}^*})$.

Example 5. We continue with Example 4. In Step 4(b), the algorithm establishes the following non-trivial inequalities:

- *(From Item 2,3 in Step 4(b) for $\widetilde{\mathfrak{q}}_3$)* $w \geq 0.5 \cdot n - 0.5, w \leq 0.5 \cdot n$ and $n \geq 2 \cdot w, n \leq 2 \cdot w + 1$;
- *(From Item 4 in Step 4(b) for $\widetilde{\mathfrak{q}}_1, \widetilde{\mathfrak{q}}_2$)* $n - e \cdot u \geq 0$ and $u \geq 0$;
- *(From Item 4 in Step 4(b) for $\widetilde{\mathfrak{q}}_3$)* $n - e \cdot u \geq 0, u - \ln 2 \geq 0$ and $w - e \cdot v \geq 0, v \geq 0$;
- *(From Item 6,7 in Step 4(b) for $\widetilde{\mathfrak{q}}_3$)* $u - v - \ln 2 \geq 0$ and $v - u + \ln 2 + \frac{1}{2} \geq 0$.

After Step 4(b), Γ_i's $(1 \leq i \leq 3)$ are updated as follows:

- $\Gamma_1 = \{n - 1, n - e \cdot u, u\}$ and $\Gamma_2 = \{n - 1, 1 - n, n - e \cdot u, u\}$;
- $\Gamma_3 = \{n - 2, n - 2 \cdot w, 2 \cdot w - n + 1, w - 1, n - e \cdot u, u - \ln 2, w - e \cdot v, v, u - v - \ln 2, v - u + \ln 2 + \frac{1}{2}\}$.   □

Remark 1. The key difficulty is to handle logarithmic and exponentiation terms. In Step 4(a) we abstract such terms with fresh variables and perform sound approximation of floored expressions. In Step 4(b) we use Farkas' Lemma and LMVT to soundly transform logarithmic or exponentiation terms to polynomials.

    □

4.5   Step 5 of SynAlgo

This step is to solve the template variables in the template established in Step 1, based on the sets Γ computed in Step 4. While Step 4 transforms logarithmic and exponentiation terms to polynomials, we need a sound method to solve polynomials with linear programming. We achieve this with Handelman's Theorem.

Definition 6 (Monoid). *Let Γ be a finite subset of some polynomial ring $\Re[x_1, \ldots, x_m]$ such that all elements of Γ are polynomials of degree 1. The* monoid *of Γ is defined by:* $\mathsf{Monoid}(\Gamma) := \left\{ \prod_{i=1}^{k} h_i \mid k \in \mathbb{N}_0 \text{ and } h_1, \ldots, h_k \in \Gamma \right\}.$

Theorem 3 (Handelman's Theorem [38]). *Let $\Re[x_1, \ldots, x_m]$ be the polynomial ring with variables $x_1, \ldots, x_m$ (for $m \geq 1$). Let $g \in \Re[x_1, \ldots, x_m]$ and Γ be a finite subset of $\Re[x_1, \ldots, x_m]$ such that all elements of Γ are polynomials of degree 1. If (i) the set $\mathsf{Sat}(\Gamma)$ is compact and non-empty and (ii) $g(\boldsymbol{x}) > 0$ for all $\boldsymbol{x} \in \mathsf{Sat}(\Gamma)$, then*

$$g = \sum_{i=1}^{n} c_i \cdot u_i \tag{3}$$

for some $n \in \mathbb{N}$, non-negative real numbers $c_1, \ldots, c_n \geq 0$ and $u_1, \ldots, u_n \in \mathsf{Monoid}(\Gamma)$.

Basically, Handelman's Theorem gives a characterization of positive polynomials over polytopes. In this paper, we concentrate on Eq. (3) which provides a sound form for a non-negative polynomial over a general (i.e. possibly unbounded) polyhedron.

Step 5: Solving Unknown Coefficients in the Template. Now we use the input parameter k as the maximal number of multiplicands in each summand at the right-hand-side of Eq. (3). For any constraint triple (f, ϕ, e^*) which is generated in Step 3 and passes the emptiness checking in Item 7 of Step 4(a), the algorithm performs the following steps.

1. *Preparation for Eq. (3).* The algorithm reads the set Γ for (f, ϕ, e^*) computed in Step 4, and computes $\widetilde{e}^*$ from Item 4 of Step 4(a).
2. *Application of Handelman's Theorem.* First, the algorithm establishes a fresh coefficient variable λ_h for each polynomial h in Monoid(Γ) with no more than k multiplicands from Γ. Then, the algorithm establishes linear equalities over coefficient variables λ_h's and template variables in the template η established in Step 1 by equating coefficients of the same monomials at the left- and right-hand-side of the following polynomial equality $\widetilde{e}^* = \sum_h \lambda_h \cdot h$. Second, the algorithm incorporates all constraints of the form $\lambda_h \geq 0$.

Then the algorithm collects all linear equalities and inequalities established in Item 2 above conjunctively as a single system of linear inequalities and solves it through linear-programming algorithms; if no feasible solution exists, the algorithm fails without output, otherwise the algorithm outputs the function $[\![\eta]\!]$ where all template variables in the template η are resolved by their values in the solution. We now state the soundness of our approach for synthesis of measure functions.

Theorem 4. *Our algorithm, SYNALGO, is a sound approach for the RECTERMBOU problem, i.e., if SYNALGO succeeds to synthesize a function g on $\{(f, \ell, \nu) \mid f \in F, \ell \in L_s^f, \nu \in \text{Val}_f\}$, then $\widehat{g}$ is a measure function and hence an upper bound on the termination-time function.*

Example 6. Continue with Example 5. In the final step (Step 5), the unknown coefficients c_i's ($1 \leq i \leq 3$) are to be resolved through (3) so that logical formulae encoded by $\widetilde{q}_i$'s are valid (w.r.t updated Γ_i's). Since to present the whole technical detail would be too cumbersome, we present directly a feasible solution for c_i's and how they fulfill (3). Below we choose the solution that $c_1 = 0$, $c_2 = \frac{2}{\ln 2}$ and $c_3 = 2$. Then we have that

- (From $\widetilde{q}_1$) $c_2 \cdot u + c_3 = \lambda_1 \cdot u + \lambda_2$ where $\lambda_1 := \frac{2}{\ln 2}$ and $\lambda_2 := 2$;
- (From $\widetilde{q}_2$) $c_2 \cdot u + c_3 - 2 = \lambda_1 \cdot u$;
- (From $\widetilde{q}_3$) $c_2 \cdot (u - v) - 2 = \lambda_1 \cdot (u - v - \ln 2)$.

Hence by Theorem 1, $\overline{T}(f, 1, n) \leq \eta(f, 1, n) = \frac{2}{\ln 2} \cdot \ln n + 2$. It follows that BINARY-SEARCH runs in $\mathcal{O}(\log n)$ in worst-case.   □

Remark 2. We remark two aspects of our algorithm. (i) *Scalability.* Our algorithm only requires solving linear inequalities. Since linear-programming solvers have been widely studied and experimented, the scalability of our approach directly depends on the linear-programming solvers. Hence the approach we present is a relatively scalable one. (ii) *Novelty.* A key novelty of our approach is to obtain non-polynomial bounds (such as $\mathcal{O}(n \log n)$, $\mathcal{O}(n^r)$, where r is not integral) through linear programming. The novel technical steps are: (a) use of abstraction variables; (b) use of LMVT and Farkas' lemma to obtain sound linear constraints over abstracted variables; and (c) use of Handelman's Theorem to solve the unknown coefficients in polynomial time.   □

5   Experimental Results

We apply our approach to four classical recursive algorithms, namely Merge-Sort [24, Chap. 2], the divide-and-conquer algorithm for the Closest-Pair problem [24, Chap. 33], Strassen's Algorithm for matrix multiplication [24, Chap. 4] and Karatsuba's Algorithm for polynomial multiplication [52]. We implement our algorithm that basically generates a set of linear constraints, where we use lp_solve [56] for solving linear programs. Our experimental results are presented in Table 1, where all numbers are rounded to 10^{-2} and n represents the input length of those algorithms. All results were obtained on an Intel i3-4130 CPU 3.4 GHz 8 GB of RAM. For Merge-Sort and Closest-Pair, our algorithm obtains the worst-case bound $\mathcal{O}(n \log n)$. For Strassen's Algorithm, we use a template with $n^{2.9}$ so that our algorithm synthesizes a measure function, hence proving that its worst-case behaviour is no greater than $\mathcal{O}(n^{2.9})$, near the worst-case complexity $\mathcal{O}(n^{2.8074})$. For Karatsuba's Algorithm, we use a template with $n^{1.6}$ so that our algorithm synthesizes a measure function (basically, using constraints as illustrated in Example 2), hence proving that $\mathcal{O}(n^{1.6})$ is an upper bound on its worst-case behaviour, which is near the worst-case complexity $\mathcal{O}(n^{1.5850})$. In the experiments we derive simple invariants from the programs directly from the prerequisites of procedures and guards of while-loops. Alternatively, they can be derived automatically using [19].

Table 1. Experimental results where $\eta(\ell_0)$ is the part of measure function at the initial label.

Example	Time (in seconds)	$\eta(\ell_0)$
Merge-Sort	6	$25.02 \cdot n \cdot \ln n + 21.68 \cdot n - 20.68$
Closest-Pair	11	$128.85 \cdot n \cdot \ln n + 108.95 \cdot n - 53.31$
Karatsuba	3	$2261.55 \cdot n^{1.6} + 1$
Strassen	7	$954.20 \cdot n^{2.9} + 1$

6   Related Work

The termination of recursive programs or other temporal properties has already been extensively studied [5, 21–23, 27, 53–55, 66]. Our work is most closely related to automatic amortized analysis [4, 32, 40, 42–46, 50, 51, 63], as well as the SPEED project [35–37]. There are two key differences of our methods as compared to previous works. First, our methods are based on extension of ranking functions to non-deterministic recursive programs, whereas previous works either use potential functions, abstract interpretation, or size-change. Second, while none of the previous methods can derive non-polynomial bounds such as $\mathcal{O}(n^r)$, where r is not an integer, our approach can derive such non-polynomial bounds through linear programming.

Ranking functions for intra-procedural analysis have been widely studied [8,9,20,25,58,61,64,68], and have been extended to ranking supermartingales [12–14,16,17,29] for probabilistic programs. Most works focus on linear or polynomial ranking functions/supermartingales [12,14,16,20,25,58,61,64,68]. Polynomial ranking functions alone can only derive polynomial bounds, and needs additional structures (e.g., evaluation trees) to derive non-polynomial bounds such as $\mathcal{O}(2^n)$ (cf. [10]). In contrast, we directly synthesize non-polynomial ranking functions without additional structures. The approach of recurrence relations for worst-case analysis is explored in [1–3,30,34]. A related result is by Albert et al. [2] who considered using evaluation trees for solving recurrence relations, which can derive the worst-case bound for Merge-Sort. Their method relies on specific features such as branching factor and height of an evaluation tree, and cannot derive bounds like $\mathcal{O}(n^r)$ where r is not an integer. Another approach through theorem proving is explored in [65]. This approach is to iteratively generate control-flow paths and then to obtain worst-case bounds over generated paths through theorem proving (with arithmetic theorems). Several other works present proof rules for deterministic programs [39] as well as for probabilistic programs [49,57]. None of these works can be automated. Other related approaches are sized types [18,47,48], and polynomial resource bounds [62]. Again none of these approaches can yield bounds like $\mathcal{O}(n \log n)$ or $\mathcal{O}(n^r)$, for r non-integral.

7 Conclusion

In this paper, we developed a ranking-function based approach to obtain non-polynomial worst-case bounds for recursive programs through (i) abstraction of logarithmic and exponentiation terms and (ii) Farkas' Lemma, LMVT, and Handelman's Theorem. Moreover our approach obtains such bounds using linear programming, thus is an efficient approach. Our approach obtains non-trivial worst-case complexity bounds for classical recursive programs: $\mathcal{O}(n \log n)$-complexity for both Merge-Sort and the divide-and-conquer Closest-Pair algorithm, $\mathcal{O}(n^{1.6})$ for Karatsuba's algorithm for polynomial multiplication, and $\mathcal{O}(n^{2.9})$ for Strassen's algorithm for matrix multiplication. The bounds we obtain for Karatsuba's and Strassen's algorithm are close to the optimal bounds. An interesting future direction is to extend our technique to data-structures. Other future directions include investigating the application of our approach to invariant generation and using integer linear programming instead in our approach.

Acknowledgements. We thank all reviewers for valuable comments. The research is partially supported by Vienna Science and Technology Fund (WWTF) ICT15-003, Austrian Science Fund (FWF) NFN Grant No. S11407-N23 (RiSE/SHiNE), ERC Start grant (279307: Graph Games), the Natural Science Foundation of China (NSFC) under Grant No. 61532019 and the CDZ project CAP (GZ 1023).

References

1. Albert, E., Arenas, P., Genaim, S., Gómez-Zamalloa, M., Puebla, G., Ramírez-Deantes, D.V., Román-Díez, G., Zanardini, D.: Termination and cost analysis with COSTA and its user interfaces. Electr. Notes Theor. Comput. Sci. **258**(1), 109–121 (2009)

2. Albert, E., Arenas, P., Genaim, S., Puebla, G.: Automatic inference of upper bounds for recurrence relations in cost analysis. In: Alpuente, M., Vidal, G. (eds.) SAS 2008. LNCS, vol. 5079, pp. 221–237. Springer, Heidelberg (2008). doi:10.1007/978-3-540-69166-2_15

3. Albert, E., Arenas, P., Genaim, S., Puebla, G., Zanardini, D.: Cost analysis of Java bytecode. In: Nicola, R. (ed.) ESOP 2007. LNCS, vol. 4421, pp. 157–172. Springer, Heidelberg (2007). doi:10.1007/978-3-540-71316-6_12

4. Alias, C., Darte, A., Feautrier, P., Gonnord, L.: Multi-dimensional rankings, program termination, and complexity bounds of flowchart programs. In: Cousot, R., Martel, M. (eds.) SAS 2010. LNCS, vol. 6337, pp. 117–133. Springer, Heidelberg (2010). doi:10.1007/978-3-642-15769-1_8

5. Alur, R., Chaudhuri, S.: Temporal reasoning for procedural programs. In: Barthe, G., Hermenegildo, M. (eds.) VMCAI 2010. LNCS, vol. 5944, pp. 45–60. Springer, Heidelberg (2010). doi:10.1007/978-3-642-11319-2_7

6. Bartle, R.G., Sherbert, D.R.: Introduction to Real Analysis, 4th edn. Wiley, Hoboken (2011)

7. Bodík, R., Majumdar, R. (eds.): POPL. ACM, New York (2016)

8. Bournez, O., Garnier, F.: Proving positive almost-sure termination. In: Giesl, J. (ed.) RTA 2005. LNCS, vol. 3467, pp. 323–337. Springer, Heidelberg (2005). doi:10.1007/978-3-540-32033-3_24

9. Bradley, A.R., Manna, Z., Sipma, H.B.: Linear ranking with reachability. In: Etessami, K., Rajamani, S.K. (eds.) CAV 2005. LNCS, vol. 3576, pp. 491–504. Springer, Heidelberg (2005). doi:10.1007/11513988_48

10. Brockschmidt, M., Emmes, F., Falke, S., Fuhs, C., Giesl, J.: Analyzing runtime and size complexity of integer programs. ACM Trans. Program. Lang. Syst. **38**(4), 13:1–13:50 (2016)

11. Castagna, G., Gordon, A.D. (eds.): POPL. ACM, New York (2017)

12. Chakarov, A., Sankaranarayanan, S.: Probabilistic program analysis with martingales. In: Sharygina, N., Veith, H. (eds.) CAV 2013. LNCS, vol. 8044, pp. 511–526. Springer, Heidelberg (2013). doi:10.1007/978-3-642-39799-8_34

13. Chatterjee, K., Fu, H.: Termination of nondeterministic recursive probabilistic programs. CoRR abs/1701.02944 (2017). http://arxiv.org/abs/1701.02944

14. Chatterjee, K., Fu, H., Goharshady, A.K.: Termination analysis of probabilistic programs through Positivstellensatzs. In: Chaudhuri, S., Farzan, A. (eds.) CAV 2016. LNCS, vol. 9779, pp. 3–22. Springer, Cham (2016). doi:10.1007/978-3-319-41528-4_1

15. Chatterjee, K., Fu, H., Goharshady, A.K.: Non-polynomial worst-case analysis of recursive programs. CoRR abs/1705.00317 (2017). https://arxiv.org/abs/1705.00317

16. Chatterjee, K., Fu, H., Novotný, P., Hasheminezhad, R.: Algorithmic analysis of qualitative and quantitative termination problems for affine probabilistic programs. In: Bodík and Majumdar [7], pp. 327–342

17. Chatterjee, K., Novotný, P., Žikelić, Đ.: Stochastic invariants for probabilistic termination. In: Castagna and Gordon [11], pp. 145–160

18. Chin, W., Khoo, S.: Calculating sized types. Higher-Order Symbolic Comput. **14**(2–3), 261–300 (2001)

19. Colón, M.A., Sankaranarayanan, S., Sipma, H.B.: Linear invariant generation using non-linear constraint solving. In: Hunt, W.A., Somenzi, F. (eds.) CAV 2003. LNCS, vol. 2725, pp. 420–432. Springer, Heidelberg (2003). doi:10.1007/978-3-540-45069-6_39

20. Colón, M.A., Sipma, H.B.: Synthesis of linear ranking functions. In: Margaria, T., Yi, W. (eds.) TACAS 2001. LNCS, vol. 2031, pp. 67–81. Springer, Heidelberg (2001). doi:10.1007/3-540-45319-9_6

21. Cook, B., Podelski, A., Rybalchenko, A.: Termination proofs for systems code. In: Schwartzbach, M.I., Ball, T. (eds.) PLDI, pp. 415–426. ACM (2006)

22. Cook, B., Podelski, A., Rybalchenko, A.: Summarization for termination: no return!. Form. Methods Syst. Des. **35**(3), 369–387 (2009)

23. Cook, B., See, A., Zuleger, F.: Ramsey vs. lexicographic termination proving. In: Piterman, N., Smolka, S.A. (eds.) TACAS 2013. LNCS, vol. 7795, pp. 47–61. Springer, Heidelberg (2013). doi:10.1007/978-3-642-36742-7_4

24. Cormen, T.H., Leiserson, C.E., Rivest, R.L., Stein, C.: Introduction to Algorithms, 3rd edn. MIT Press, Cambridge (2009)

25. Cousot, P.: Proving program invariance and termination by parametric abstraction, lagrangian relaxation and semidefinite programming. In: Cousot, R. (ed.) VMCAI 2005. LNCS, vol. 3385, pp. 1–24. Springer, Heidelberg (2005). doi:10.1007/978-3-540-30579-8_1

26. Cousot, P., Cousot, R.: Abstract interpretation: a unified lattice model for static analysis of programs by construction or approximation of fixpoints. In: Graham, R.M., Harrison, M.A., Sethi, R. (eds.) POPL, pp. 238–252. ACM (1977)

27. Cousot, P., Cousot, R.: An abstract interpretation framework for termination. In: Field, J., Hicks, M. (eds.) POPL, pp. 245–258. ACM (2012)

28. Farkas, J.: A fourier-féle mechanikai elv alkalmazásai (Hungarian). Mathematikaiés Természettudományi Értesitö **12**, 457–472 (1894)

29. Fioriti, L.M.F., Hermanns, H.: Probabilistic termination: soundness, completeness, and compositionality. In: Rajamani, S.K., Walker, D. (eds.) POPL, pp. 489–501. ACM (2015)

30. Flajolet, P., Salvy, B., Zimmermann, P.: Automatic average-case analysis of algorithm. Theor. Comput. Sci. **79**(1), 37–109 (1991)

31. Floyd, R.W.: Assigning meanings to programs. Math. Aspects Comput. Sci. **19**, 19–33 (1967)

32. Gimenez, S., Moser, G.: The complexity of interaction. In: Bodík and Majumdar [7], pp. 243–255

33. Gödel, K., Kleene, S.C., Rosser, J.B.: On undecidable propositions of formal mathematical systems. Institute for Advanced Study Princeton, NJ (1934)

34. Grobauer, B.: Cost recurrences for DML programs. In: Pierce, B.C. (ed.) ICFP, pp. 253–264. ACM (2001)

35. Gulavani, B.S., Gulwani, S.: A numerical abstract domain based on *expression abstraction* and *max operator* with application in timing analysis. In: Gupta, A., Malik, S. (eds.) CAV 2008. LNCS, vol. 5123, pp. 370–384. Springer, Heidelberg (2008). doi:10.1007/978-3-540-70545-1_35

36. Gulwani, S.: SPEED: symbolic complexity bound analysis. In: Bouajjani, A., Maler, O. (eds.) CAV 2009. LNCS, vol. 5643, pp. 51–62. Springer, Heidelberg (2009). doi:10.1007/978-3-642-02658-4_7

37. Gulwani, S., Mehra, K.K., Chilimbi, T.M.: SPEED: precise and efficient static estimation of program computational complexity. In: Shao, Z., Pierce, B.C. (eds.) POPL, pp. 127–139. ACM (2009)

38. Handelman, D.: Representing polynomials by positive linear functions on compact convex polyhedra. Pacific J. Math. **132**, 35–62 (1988)

39. Hesselink, W.H.: Proof rules for recursive procedures. Formal Asp. Comput. **5**(6), 554–570 (1993)

40. Hoffmann, J., Aehlig, K., Hofmann, M.: Multivariate amortized resource analysis. ACM Trans. Program. Lang. Syst. **34**(3), 14 (2012)

41. Hoffmann, J., Aehlig, K., Hofmann, M.: Resource aware ML. In: Madhusudan, P., Seshia, S.A. (eds.) CAV 2012. LNCS, vol. 7358, pp. 781–786. Springer, Heidelberg (2012). doi:10.1007/978-3-642-31424-7_64

42. Hoffmann, J., Hofmann, M.: Amortized resource analysis with polymorphic recursion and partial big-step operational semantics. In: Ueda, K. (ed.) APLAS 2010. LNCS, vol. 6461, pp. 172–187. Springer, Heidelberg (2010). doi:10.1007/978-3-642-17164-2_13

43. Hoffmann, J., Hofmann, M.: Amortized resource analysis with polynomial potential. In: Gordon, A.D. (ed.) ESOP 2010. LNCS, vol. 6012, pp. 287–306. Springer, Heidelberg (2010). doi:10.1007/978-3-642-11957-6_16

44. Hofmann, M., Jost, S.: Static prediction of heap space usage for first-order functional programs. In: Aiken, A., Morrisett, G. (eds.) POPL, pp. 185–197. ACM (2003)

45. Hofmann, M., Jost, S.: Type-based amortised heap-space analysis. In: Sestoft, P. (ed.) ESOP 2006. LNCS, vol. 3924, pp. 22–37. Springer, Heidelberg (2006). doi:10.1007/11693024_3

46. Hofmann, M., Rodriguez, D.: Efficient type-checking for amortised heap-space analysis. In: Grädel, E., Kahle, R. (eds.) CSL 2009. LNCS, vol. 5771, pp. 317–331. Springer, Heidelberg (2009). doi:10.1007/978-3-642-04027-6_24

47. Hughes, J., Pareto, L.: Recursion and dynamic data-structures in bounded space: Towards embedded ML programming. In: Rémi, D., Lee, P. (eds.) ICFP. pp. 70–81. ACM (1999)

48. Hughes, J., Pareto, L., Sabry, A.: Proving the correctness of reactive systems using sized types. In: Boehm, H., Jr., G.L.S. (eds.) POPL. pp. 410–423. ACM Press (1996)

49. Jones, C.: Probabilistic non-determinism. Ph.D. thesis, The University of Edinburgh (1989)

50. Jost, S., Hammond, K., Loidl, H., Hofmann, M.: Static determination of quantitative resource usage for higher-order programs. In: Hermenegildo, M.V., Palsberg, J. (eds.) POPL, pp. 223–236. ACM (2010)

51. Jost, S., Loidl, H.-W., Hammond, K., Scaife, N., Hofmann, M.: "Carbon Credits" for resource-bounded computations using amortised analysis. In: Cavalcanti, A., Dams, D.R. (eds.) FM 2009. LNCS, vol. 5850, pp. 354–369. Springer, Heidelberg (2009). doi:10.1007/978-3-642-05089-3_23

52. Knuth, D.E.: The Art of Computer Programming, vols. I–III. Addison-Wesley, Reading (1973)
53. Kuwahara, T., Terauchi, T., Unno, H., Kobayashi, N.: Automatic termination verification for higher-order functional programs. In: Shao, Z. (ed.) ESOP 2014. LNCS, vol. 8410, pp. 392–411. Springer, Heidelberg (2014). doi:10.1007/978-3-642-54833-8_21
54. Lee, C.S.: Ranking functions for size-change termination. ACM Trans. Program. Lang. Syst. **31**(3), 10:1–10:42 (2009)
55. Lee, C.S., Jones, N.D., Ben-Amram, A.M.: The size-change principle for program termination. In: Hankin, C., Schmidt, D. (eds.) POPL, pp. 81–92. ACM (2001)
56. lp_solve 5.5.2.3 (2016). http://lpsolve.sourceforge.net/5.5/
57. Olmedo, F., Kaminski, B.L., Katoen, J., Matheja, C.: Reasoning about recursive probabilistic programs. In: Grohe, M., Koskinen, E., Shankar, N. (eds.) LICS, pp. 672–681. ACM (2016)
58. Podelski, A., Rybalchenko, A.: A complete method for the synthesis of linear ranking functions. In: Steffen, B., Levi, G. (eds.) VMCAI 2004. LNCS, vol. 2937, pp. 239–251. Springer, Heidelberg (2004). doi:10.1007/978-3-540-24622-0_20
59. Schrijver, A.: Theory of Linear and Integer Programming. Wiley-Interscience Series in Discrete Mathematics and Optimization. Wiley, Hoboken (1999)
60. Schrijver, A.: Combinatorial Optimization - Polyhedra and Efficiency. Springer, Heidelberg (2003)
61. Shen, L., Wu, M., Yang, Z., Zeng, Z.: Generating exact nonlinear ranking functions by symbolic-numeric hybrid method. J. Syst. Sci. Complex. **26**(2), 291–301 (2013)
62. Shkaravska, O., Kesteren, R., Eekelen, M.: Polynomial size analysis of first-order functions. In: Rocca, S.R. (ed.) TLCA 2007. LNCS, vol. 4583, pp. 351–365. Springer, Heidelberg (2007). doi:10.1007/978-3-540-73228-0_25
63. Sinn, M., Zuleger, F., Veith, H.: A simple and scalable static analysis for bound analysis and amortized complexity analysis. In: Biere, A., Bloem, R. (eds.) CAV 2014. LNCS, vol. 8559, pp. 745–761. Springer, Cham (2014). doi:10.1007/978-3-319-08867-9_50
64. Sohn, K., Gelder, A.V.: Termination detection in logic programs using argument sizes. In: Rosenkrantz, D.J. (ed.) PODS, pp. 216–226. ACM Press (1991)
65. Srikanth, A., Sahin, B., Harris, W.R.: Complexity verification using guided theorem enumeration. In: Castagna and Gordon [11], pp. 639–652
66. Urban, C.: The abstract domain of segmented ranking functions. In: Logozzo, F., Fähndrich, M. (eds.) SAS 2013. LNCS, vol. 7935, pp. 43–62. Springer, Heidelberg (2013). doi:10.1007/978-3-642-38856-9_5
67. Wilhelm, R., et al.: The worst-case execution-time problem - overview of methods and survey of tools. ACM Trans. Embed. Comput. Syst. **7**(3), 1–53 (2008)
68. Yang, L., Zhou, C., Zhan, N., Xia, B.: Recent advances in program verification through computer algebra. Front. Comput. Sci. China **4**(1), 1–16 (2010)

Automated Resource Analysis with Coq Proof Objects

Quentin Carbonneaux[1][(✉)], Jan Hoffmann[2],
Thomas Reps[3,4], and Zhong Shao[1]

[1] Yale University, New Haven, USA
quentin.carbonneaux@yale.edu
[2] Carnegie Mellon University, Pittsburgh, USA
[3] University of Wisconsin, Madison, USA
[4] GrammaTech, Inc., Ithaca, USA

Abstract. This paper addresses the problem of automatically performing resource-bound analysis, which can help programmers understand the
performance characteristics of their programs. We introduce a method for
resource-bound inference that (i) is compositional, (ii) produces machine-
checkable certificates of the resource bounds obtained, and (iii) features a
sound mechanism for user interaction if the inference fails. The technique
handles recursive procedures and has the ability to exploit any known
program invariants. An experimental evaluation with an implementation
in the tool Pastis shows that the new analysis is competitive with state-
of-the-art resource-bound tools while also creating Coq certificates.

1 Introduction

To help developers better understand the performance of programs at compile
time, the programming-language research community has been developing techniques and tools that can automatically and statically analyze the resource consumption of programs [1,2,4,7,13,20,23,28,31]. Most of these techniques derive
symbolic worst-case bounds that depend on the sizes of program variables or
the arguments of a function. Deriving such bounds for arbitrary programs is an
undecidable problem. However, existing tools deliver impressive results for certain classes of programs. Tools deriving bounds on imperative programs include

Supported, in part, by a gift from Rajiv and Ritu Batra; by NSF under grants
1521523 and 1319671; by AFRL under DARPA MUSE award FA8750-14-2-0270,
DARPA STAC award FA8750-15-C-0082, and DARPA award FA8750-16-2-0274;
and by the UW-Madison Office of the Vice Chancellor for Research and Graduate
Education with funding from the Wisconsin Alumni Research Foundation. The U.S.
Government is authorized to reproduce and distribute reprints for Governmental
purposes notwithstanding any copyright notation thereon. Any opinions, findings,
and conclusions or recommendations expressed in this publication are those of the
authors, and do not necessarily reflect the views of the sponsoring agencies.

R. Majumdar and V. Kunčak (Eds.): CAV 2017, Part II, LNCS 10427, pp. 64–85, 2017.
DOI: 10.1007/978-3-319-63390-9_4

KoAT [10], Rank [5], CoFloCo [16], Loopus [30], and C4B [11]. RAML [17] is able to derive complex bounds on functional programs.

State-of-the-art bound analysis tools suffer from two major shortcomings. First, when the inference of a resource bounds fails, the user has no other choice than to either rewrite the input program or modify the tool itself (the second option being only available to experts). Second, many automated tools are based on sophisticated algorithms relying on subtle invariants for their correctness. Even tools based on time-tested programming-language devices like type systems and program logics have complex implementations that are prone to bugs.

The goal of this paper is to address these shortcomings. We base our work on automatic amortized resource analysis (AARA), a technique that statically derives concrete (non-asymptotic) resource bounds. AARA is implemented in the tools C4B for imperative programs and RAML for functional programs. The benefits of AARA include compositionality—by generating compositional and local constraint systems—and reduction of resource-bound inference to efficient off-the-shelf linear programming (LP).

Contributions. First, we present a new unifying framework for proving the soundness of AARA-based systems for low-level code. The framework applies directly to low-level programs parameterized with abstract base constructs. This parameterized presentation allows, similarly to the theory of abstract interpretation, multiple instantiations depending on the programs to be analyzed. We also introduce *rewrite functions*, a new technical device to encode weakening that is amenable to sound user interaction.

Second, to demonstrate the effectiveness of these new ideas, we have implemented them in a new tool called Pastis.

- Thanks to our new parametric framework, Pastis is the first AARA-based tool to generate polynomial bounds on low-level integer programs with recursive procedures.
- Thanks to rewrite functions, Pastis is the first resource analysis tool to provide a sound mechanism for user interaction when the inference of a bound fails.
- Thanks to the logical foundations of our framework, and to the certificates provided by the LP solver, Pastis is the first resource analysis tool able to automatically generate proof certificates of the validity of its bounds.

Third, to show that Pastis is practical, we have implemented an LLVM frontend to our new analysis and evaluated it on more than 200,000 lines of C code against state-of-the-art tools. Surprisingly for a tool generating proof objects, we are able to report that Pastis is competitive and can successfully generate many polynomial bounds.

2   Setting

Programs will be represented as standard interprocedural control-flow graphs. This assumption does not tie the presentation of our analysis to a specific set of statements; moreover, it allows the technique to be applied to unstructured input programs, including ones written in bytecode and other low-level languages.

Syntax. A program is represented as a directed graph where nodes are *program points* and edges bear program *actions*. Intuitively the program counter jumps from node to node following edges and updates the program state according to the actions it encounters. We use the three sets $\mathcal{L}$, $\mathcal{V}$, and $\mathcal{P}$, respectively, for the program points, the variable names, and the procedure names.

A procedure is represented by a tuple (L, ℓ_e, ℓ_x) where $L \subseteq \mathcal{V}$ is the set of local variables for the procedure and $\ell_e, \ell_x \in \mathcal{L}$ are respectively the entry and exit points of the procedure.

$$Act := v \leftarrow e \mid \mathsf{call}\ P \mid \mathsf{guard}\ e \mid \mathsf{weaken}$$

An action can be the assignment of a variable $v \leftarrow e$ where $v \in \mathcal{V}$ and e is an expression. We leave the syntax of expressions abstract because it is irrelevant for most of the presentation that follows. An action can also be a call $\mathsf{call}\ P$ to a procedure $P \in \mathcal{P}$. The arguments and return values are passed using global variables. We also include guards as actions. They are used to represent conditional statements and block the execution if their condition is not validated at runtime. Finally, an action can be an explicit weakening hint weaken. Such a hint can be inserted by the user or by a pre-processing heuristic; it does not have any semantic effect but is used by our analysis to perform potential rewrites.

We now define a program as a triple (E, Δ, G) where:

- $E \subseteq (\mathcal{L} \times Act \times \mathcal{L})$ is the set of all edges in the program;
- Δ is a map from procedure names $\mathcal{P}$ to procedures;
- and $G \subseteq \mathcal{V}$ is the set of global variables.

In addition, we require that no two procedures in the program share any local variables, and that the sets of global variables and local variables are disjoint. These properties can be ensured by pre-processing.

Semantics. An execution state is a pair (ℓ, σ) where $\sigma \in \Sigma$ is a program state that maps variables $\mathcal{V}$ to a value domain $\mathcal{D}$, and $\ell \in \mathcal{L}$ is the program counter.

We define single-step execution of the program as a transition relation on execution states. When evaluating an edge of the program, the change made to the program state is determined by the action labelling the edge. For each program state σ we assume that we have an evaluation function $[\![\cdot]\!]_\sigma$ that maps expressions to the value domain $\mathcal{D}$. We also require the presence of a predicate $\mathsf{OK} \subseteq \mathcal{D}$ on the value domain to check the validity of conditions in guards (e.g., a singleton $\{\mathsf{true}\}$). We use $\sigma[u/v]$ to denote a new program state that extends σ by updating the binding of v to the value u. The complete operational semantics of programs is given in Fig. 1. We write $\rightarrow^*$ to denote the reflexive transitive closure of the step relation $\rightarrow$.

$$\frac{(\ell, v \leftarrow e, \ell') \in E}{(\ell, \sigma) \rightarrow (\ell', \sigma[\![e]\!]_\sigma/v])} \qquad \frac{(\ell, \mathsf{weaken}, \ell') \in E}{(\ell, \sigma) \rightarrow (\ell', \sigma)} \qquad \frac{(\ell, \mathsf{guard}\ e, \ell') \in E \qquad [\![e]\!]_\sigma \in \mathsf{OK}}{(\ell, \sigma) \rightarrow (\ell', \sigma)}$$

$$\frac{(\ell, \mathsf{call}\ P, \ell') \in E \qquad \begin{matrix} \Delta(P) = (\_, \ell_e, \ell_x) \\ (\ell_e, \sigma) \rightarrow^* (\ell_x, \sigma') \end{matrix} \qquad \sigma''(v) = \begin{cases} \sigma'(v) & \text{if } v \in G \\ \sigma(v) & \text{otherwise} \end{cases}}{(\ell, \sigma) \rightarrow (\ell', \sigma'')}$$

Fig. 1. Mixed-step semantics of a program (E, Δ, G). Non-call steps use a classic small-step transition while calls are atomically executed using $\rightarrow^*$.

3   Introductory Example

We now illustrate the potential-based technique on the program shown in Fig. 2. For presentation purposes, we use a Python-like syntax; the control-flow graph is derived in a standard way from this syntax.

The essence of the potential method is to *annotate* each program point ℓ with a *potential function* $\Gamma_\ell \in (\Sigma \rightarrow \mathbb{Q})$, which maps a program state to a rational number. In the example, the potential functions are displayed between curly braces. The potential functions are subject to local constraints that enforce the condition that, during each program execution, the values of the successive potential functions encountered are *non-increasing*. Thus, if the constraints are met, for any execution $(\ell_0, \sigma_0) \rightarrow^* (\ell_n, \sigma_n)$, the value $\Gamma_{\ell_0}(\sigma_0)$ of the annotation of the initial program point

```
1  {3.25}
2  k, z = 0, 0
3  {1/4 · (13 − k) + z}
4  while k < 10 and random:
5      {1/4 · (13 − k) + z} =
6      {1/4 · (13 − (k+4)) + 1 + z}
7      k = k + 4
8      {1/4 · (13 − k) + 1 + z}
9      z = z + 1
10     {1/4 · (13 − k) + z}
11 ≥ {z}
```

Fig. 2. Example.

is an upper bound on the value $\Gamma_{\ell_n}(\sigma_n)$ of the annotation of the final point. The full set of constraints is given in Sect. 4; annotations matching them are said *admissible*.

As we will see, the annotation of the example is admissible, which lets us deduce that 3.25 is an upper bound on the final value of loop counter z. We often refer to the final annotation as a potential *goal*, because that potential function defines the quantity we are looking to bound. In the example, the goal is $\{z\}$.

We now argue that the annotation of the example is admissible: (i) for each assignment "$v \leftarrow e$" in the program, the annotations Γ and Γ', before and after the assignment, respectively, are such that for any state σ, $\Gamma(\sigma) = \Gamma'(\sigma[\![e]\!]_\sigma/v])$ (that is, they are non-increasing around the assignments); and (ii) for any state σ reachable at line 11, the potential annotations $\Gamma_{10} := \{1/4 \cdot (13 - k) + z\}$ and $\Gamma_{11} := \{z\}$ satisfy $\Gamma_{10}(\sigma) \geqslant \Gamma_{11}(\sigma)$ (indeed, $\sigma(k) \leqslant 13$ at that point). Thus, all steps taken by the program keep the potential non-increasing, and the annotation is admissible.

It is sometimes useful to understand a potential-function annotation "$\{e(v)\}$" over $v \subseteq V$ as an assertion "$\{e(v) \geq goal_{final}\}$." From this point of view, a potential-function annotation is a two-vocabulary assertion, where $e(\boldsymbol{v})$ is an expression in the current-state vocabulary (and evaluated in the current state), and $goal_{final}$ is an expression (over $\mathcal{V}$) in the final-state vocabulary (and evaluated in the final state). Thus, line 5 can be read as the assertion "$\{1/4 \cdot (13 - k) + z \geq z_{final}\}$," and line 1 can be read as the assertion "$\{3.25 \geq z_{final}\}$."

In the remainder of the paper, we explain how to generalize the reasoning we did in this section to programs with multiple procedures, and how to automate it using linear programming. To this end, we formally define admissibility conditions of potential annotations and then encode these conditions into linear programs. As in the example, our framework separates assignment constraints from weakening constraints. To handle the latter we introduce *rewrite functions*.

4   Interprocedural Potential Annotations

In this section, we consider a fixed program (E, Δ, G). A procedure P in the program has entry and exit points $P_e, P_x \in \mathcal{L}$, respectively. A state σ at $\ell \in \mathcal{L}$ is *reachable from* (P_e, σ_0) when there is an *execution trace*

$$(P_e, \sigma_0) \to (\ell_1, \sigma_1) \ldots \to (\ell_n, \sigma_n),$$

such that $\sigma_n = \sigma \wedge \ell_n = \ell$, or $(\ell_n, \mathsf{call}\ Q, \_) \in E$ and σ at ℓ is reachable from (Q_e, σ_n). The latter disjunct is necessary because we use mixed-step semantics: calls are represented by a single step $\to$, and $\to^*$ always relates two points in the same procedure. Finally, we say that σ at ℓ is *reachable (from P_e)*, when there is an initial state σ_0 such that σ at ℓ is reachable from (P_e, σ_0).

A *potential function* is a function that maps program states to rational numbers. A *procedure annotation* Γ associates a potential function Γ_ℓ with each program point ℓ in a procedure. An *interprocedural potential annotation* (IPA) Ψ maps each procedure name P to a set of procedure annotations $\Psi(P)$. Sets of annotations are used because, depending on the context in which a procedure is called, different annotations might be used. A *goal* is a potential function of special interest: it is the quantity at the end of the program that we are seeking to bound in terms of the initial state.

Definition 1 (Admissible IPA). *We say that an IPA Ψ for the program (E, Δ, G) is admissible for a goal g and an entry and exit point S_e and S_x in a procedure S when:*

(A1) $\exists \Gamma \in \Psi(S). \Gamma_{S_x} = g$;

and for every procedure P, edge $(\ell, a, \ell') \in E$, annotation $\Gamma \in \Psi(P)$, and state σ reachable (from S_e) at ℓ:

(A2) if a is weaken, then $\Gamma_\ell(\sigma) \geqslant \Gamma_{\ell'}(\sigma)$;
(A3) if a is guard e, then $\Gamma_\ell(\sigma) = \Gamma_{\ell'}(\sigma)$;
(A4) if a is $v \leftarrow e$, then $\Gamma_\ell(\sigma) = \Gamma_{\ell'}(\sigma[e/v])$;
(A5) if a is call Q, then $\exists \Gamma' \in \Psi(Q). \Gamma_\ell = \Gamma'_{Q_e} \wedge \Gamma_{\ell'} = \Gamma'_{Q_x}$.

The reachability condition in Definition 1 ensures that the inequalities are required to hold only for states that can actually appear in an actual execution trace. These admissibility conditions provide us with a principled way to obtain upper bounds on the potential goal, as demonstrated by Proposition 1. Moreover, the local nature of these conditions makes the generation of constraints described in Sect. 6 a local and compositional process.

Proposition 1. *For every program state σ reachable at ℓ, if Ψ is an admissible IPA and (ℓ', σ') is such that $(\ell, \sigma) \to^* (\ell', \sigma')$, then for all $\Gamma \in \Psi(P)$, $\Gamma_\ell(\sigma) \geqslant \Gamma_{\ell'}(\sigma')$.*

Proposition 1 and (A1) imply the existence of a procedure annotation $\Gamma \in \Psi(S)$ such that any execution state (ℓ, σ) on a trace $(S_e, \sigma_e) \to^* (S_x, \sigma_x)$ gives an upper bound $\Gamma_\ell(\sigma)$ on the goal evaluated on the final state $g(\sigma_x)$; in particular, $\Gamma_{S_e}(\sigma_e) \geqslant g(\sigma_x)$. This property is intuitively clear as all the admissibility conditions of Definition 1 constrain the values of the potential functions to decrease as the program progresses. Suppose now that g measures, in the final state, the size of the value stored in a variable v (e.g., the length of a list or the absolute value of an integer). Then each of the potential functions in the procedure annotation Γ expresses an upper bound on the size of v in the final state in terms of the *local state* at other program points. That is, our analysis tracks the size of v backwards through the program points.

Note that the negation of any admissible IPA for a goal $-g$ will provide *lower bounds* on the goal g. This observation shows that the orientation we chose for the inequality of (A2) is irrelevant and allows computation of both upper and lower bounds.

Resource Analysis. When the potential goal g is set, finding an admissible IPA for a program gives upper bounds on g at all program points. These bounds can be readily used to account for the resource consumption of a program. For instance, if a bound on the number of iterations of a loop is desired, the loop can be instrumented with a counter z initially set to 0 and incremented at every iteration.

```
z = 0          # instrumentation counter
while ...:
    ...
    z = z + 1  # counting iterations
```

The final value of z is the number of times the loop body was executed. So if we write ℓ_1 and ℓ_2 for the program points before and after the loop, respectively, an admissible IPA Ψ for $g(\sigma) := \sigma(z)$ will provide a bound Γ_{ℓ_1} for the number of loop iterations. The actual number of iterations when the loop starts in state σ_1 is bounded by $\Gamma_{\ell_1}(\sigma_1)$. Note that the bound on the value of z in the *final* state is expressed in terms of the values of variables in the *initial* state: Annotations provide cross-program invariants.

High-Water Mark Resource Consumption. For resources that can be freed (e.g. memory, connections, etc.), we often want to know the highest amount of resource required: the "net" consumption at the end of the program is not enough. On this aspect, our admissibility departs slightly from previous works on automated amortized analysis [11,17]. In these papers, a sound annotation bounds not only the final value of a resource counter, but also the high-water mark of this counter. So if a program allocates 3 integers, then frees them, an admissible annotation in this paper is 0, since no memory is in use at the end of the execution. However, the high-water mark consumption of this program is 3.

We will now explain how to modify our setting to accommodate this difference. In contrast to previous work that has the resource counter as a semantic instrumentation, we can use a standard program variable z to track the available resources. Allocation grows this counter variable and freeing lessens it. We now show that from an admissible IPA Ψ, by adding an additional requirement, we can obtain a *water-mark-tracking* IPA.

Proposition 2. *A water-mark-tracking IPA Ψ, is an admissible IPA such that:*
$(\star)$ *for any point ℓ, $\Gamma \in \Psi(P)$, and state σ reachable at ℓ, $\Gamma_\ell(\sigma) \geqslant \sigma(z)$.*
Given such an IPA Ψ, a trace $(\ell_0, \sigma_0) \rightarrow (\ell_1, \sigma_1) \rightarrow \ldots \rightarrow (\ell_n, \sigma_n)$, and $\Gamma \in \Psi(P)$, we have $\Gamma_{\ell_i}(\sigma_i) \geqslant \max_{j \geqslant i} \sigma_j(z)$.

Proof. We give the intuition on a trace with no procedure calls. By induction on $n - i$. If $n = i$, the result holds by $(\star)$. Otherwise, we have $\Gamma_{\ell_i}(\sigma_i) \geqslant \Gamma_{\ell_{i+1}}(\sigma_{i+1})$ and, by induction, $\Gamma_{\ell_i}(\sigma) \geqslant \max_{j \geqslant i+1} \sigma_j(z)$. We conclude using $(\star)$ on σ_i.

Note that, like admissibility conditions, the condition $(\star)$ is *local* but implies a *global* water-mark property. In a practical implementation, the condition $(\star)$ can be enforced naturally using the framework we describe in Sect. 5. The non-negativity requirement of the potential in previous works is exactly the condition $(\star)$, since their potential functions are essentially $\Gamma - z$ in this work.

5   Rewrite Functions

Because of admissibility condition (A2), any automated analysis using the potential method needs to enforce *weakening* conditions of the form $\Gamma \geqslant \Gamma'$ on potential functions. In this section, we present a new principled approach to weakening in AARA-based systems: *rewrite functions*. To our knowledge, they subsume all the existing potential-weakening and potential-rewriting mechanisms. Moreover, they provide a language for a user to interact with an AARA-based system, which is a feature unique to this work.

Definition 2 (Rewrite Function). *We say that F_ℓ is a rewrite function at a program point ℓ when for any state σ reachable at ℓ, $F_\ell(\sigma) \geqslant 0$.*

In other words, F_ℓ is the left-hand side of a program invariant $F_\ell(\sigma) \geqslant 0$.

Example. Assume that the potential function at program point ℓ is $\Gamma := 2y + z$, and we are looking for a weakening $\Gamma' := k' + k'_x \cdot x + k'_y \cdot y + k'_z \cdot z$ such that $\Gamma \geqslant \Gamma'$ holds. We will assume that nothing is known about the sign of variables x, y, and z, and thus pointwise constraints $2 \geqslant k'_y$, $1 \geqslant k'_z$, $0 \geqslant k'_x$, and $0 \geqslant k'$ would not ensure that $\Gamma \geqslant \Gamma'$ holds.

Now assume that $y \geqslant z + x$ and $z \geqslant x$ are invariants that hold at ℓ, which means that we have two rewrite functions $F_1 := -x + y - z$ and $F_2 := -x + z$. Write Γ as follows:

$$\Gamma = 2y + z - (0 \cdot F_1 + 0 \cdot F_2). \tag{1}$$

Because F_1 and F_2 mean that $-x + y - z \geq 0$ and $-x + z \geq 0$, respectively, we obtain a value that is less than or equal to Γ by choosing any positive coefficients to replace either/both of the 0s in Eq. (1). For instance, by choosing both coefficients to be 2, we have

$$\Gamma = 2y + z - (0 \cdot F_1 + 0 \cdot F_2) \geq 2y + z - (2 \cdot F_1 + 2 \cdot F_2) = 4x + z,$$

and thus we can choose Γ' to be $4x + z$. (Rather than making specific choices for the coefficients $\{u_i\}$, however, we will leave it to the LP solver to choose values that allow it to solve the overall constraint system generated for the program.)

In short, we can systematize potential weakening as a two-step process.

1. If the original potential at ℓ is V, write the weakened potential as $V - \sum u_i \cdot F_i$, where $\{F_i\}$ is the set of rewrite functions available at ℓ. (In the example, $V = 2y + z$.)
2. Choose values for the coefficients $\{u_i\}$ such that $u_i \geqslant 0$, for all i. (In the example, $u_1 = 2 \geq 0$, and $u_2 = 2 \geq 0$.)

We can express this process using standard linear-algebra notation. Let the coefficients of Γ (i.e., k), Γ' (k'), and u be column vectors, and let the matrix F represent the set $\{F_i\}$ of rewrite functions, with each F_i a column of F. The constraints generated to express the allowable rewrites of Γ into Γ' as per items 1 and 2 are

$$(k' = k - Fu) \wedge (u \geq 0). \tag{2}$$

In the example above, we have

$$\begin{pmatrix} k' \\ k'_x \\ k'_y \\ k'_z \end{pmatrix} = \begin{pmatrix} 0 \\ 0 \\ 2 \\ 1 \end{pmatrix} - \begin{pmatrix} 0 & 0 \\ -1 & -1 \\ 1 & 0 \\ -1 & 1 \end{pmatrix} \begin{pmatrix} u_1 \\ u_2 \end{pmatrix} \wedge \begin{pmatrix} u_1 \\ u_2 \end{pmatrix} \geq \begin{pmatrix} 0 \\ 0 \end{pmatrix}.$$

There are many solutions to this system. The LP solver is free to pick any one that allows the overall system of constraints to be satisfied.

Rewrite Idempotence. An interesting consequence of the algebraic formulation of weakenings introduced above is that, for a fixed set of rewrite functions, multiple compositions of the linear weakening system are never necessary. In practice, this property means that our automated system never needs to apply a weakening operation twice consecutively: once is always sufficient.

We call the set of coefficients for the initial and final potential in a satisfying assignment of a linear weakening system a *solution*. Then the following property holds:

Proposition 3 (Rewrite Idempotence). *The set of solutions for one weakening application and the set of solutions for two or more composed weakening applications are identical.*

Rewrite Hints. In practice, a system needs a source of rewrite functions to use at the different points in the program. Because rewrite functions are obtained from program invariants, abstract interpretation [15]—using various abstract domains—can be used to obtain rewrite functions for the different points in the program: given such a source of invariants, a system would employ heuristics to choose which invariants should be used as rewrite functions in the constraint system passed to the LP solver.

Occasionally, however, a program requires a complex transfer of potential. With previous implementations of amortized analysis, one was faced with two choices: either rewrite the program, or modify the analysis. Both alternatives have drawbacks.

- Rewriting the program provides only an indirect means for obtaining the desired effect, and it can be hard to understand whether a given program rewriting will allow the analyzer to establish the desired bound.
- Modifying the analysis to enable more complex transfers of potential requires the whole soundness proof to be redone as well as a good knowledge of the implementation of the analyzer.

Rewrite functions offer a third option. A programmer can manually specify rewrite functions as hints to be used to analyze the complex parts of a program. These hints, in contrast with typical assertions, both have no runtime effect and do not compromise soundness. In particular, before using a rewrite function, the analyzer would ask an oracle (e.g., an SMT solver or an abstract interpreter) if the value of the user-supplied rewrite function is provably non-negative at that program point. This approach provides a good fallback mechanism in case the heuristics of the analyzer are not sophisticated enough to identify an appropriate set of rewrite functions.

6   Automatic Potential Inference

In this section, we describe a general framework to automate the inference of potential. To emphasize the modularity of the method presented, we leave expressions and base potential functions $(b_i)_{1 \leqslant i \leqslant N}$ unspecified. However, we make two formal requirements necessary to automate the inference process.

Requirement 1: Basis Stability. Ideally, we would like the basis to be linearly stable under all expression substitutions. However, this requirement is too strong in practice. As an escape hatch, for each assignment "$x \leftarrow e$", we assume an *exclusion set* $X_{v \leftarrow e}$ of all the base functions that are not expressible as linear combinations of the basis after the substitution $[e/v]$. An important consequence of this definition is that if $b \notin X_{v \leftarrow e}$, there is a family of coefficients (k_i) such that $b[e/v] = \sum_i k_i \cdot b_i$.

As an example, we show that the requirement is met if the expressions are increments by a constant $u + c$ where $c \in \mathbb{Z}$, the base functions $(b_i)_i$ are all the monomials over program variables of total degree d or less, and $X_{v \leftarrow e} = \varnothing$ for all assignments. If the maximum power of v in b is v^n (with $n \leqslant d$), then

$$b[u + c/v] = \sum_{0 \leqslant j \leqslant n} \binom{n}{j} c^{n-j} \frac{u^j b}{v^n}.$$

In this sum, the products $\binom{n}{j} c^{n-j}$ are the constant coefficients (k_i) above and the multiplicands $u^j b / v^n$ are base functions. Indeed, they are monomials over program variables of degree $n \leqslant d$. Note that when v does not appear in b, n is 0 and the above sum correctly degenerates to b.

The exclusion set enables the implementation of practical tools. For example, during pre-processing it is often desirable to abstract a statement into one or more non-deterministic assignments "$v \leftarrow \star$". These assignments cause any base function that depends on the assigned variable to not be linearly stable. This situation leads us to define $X_{v \leftarrow \star} = \{b_i \mid v \in b_i\}$, where we write $v \in b_i$ to express that b_i depends on v.

Requirement 2: Rewrite Functions. We also assume that we are provided with a set of rewrite functions for every program point. Recall that, by Definition 2, for any program point ℓ and any program state σ reachable at that point, such a rewrite function F_ℓ satisfies $F_\ell(\sigma) \geqslant 0$.

Generating a Linear System. In the following, we explain how to generate a procedure annotation for a procedure S, given a potential goal g. We assume that procedure annotations of all the procedures called by S are available. In an actual implementation, the method described here would be implemented by a function calling itself recursively to generate all the procedure annotations needed transitively by the input program. The annotation generated is parameterized by LP variables that are constrained by a linear system. We also sketch the proof that a satisfying assignment of the linear system describes an admissible potential annotation, as specified in Definition 1.

The potential function associated with each program point of S is a "template" potential function $\Gamma_\ell(\sigma) = \sum_i k_i \cdot b_i(\sigma)$, where each k_i belongs to LP, a set of LP variables, and $(b_i)_i$ is the family of base functions. For every program edge (ℓ, a, ℓ'), we constrain the coefficients $(k_i)_i$ and $(k'_i)_i$ of Γ_ℓ and $\Gamma_{\ell'}$ by case analysis on the kind of the action a. To be able to use matrix notation, we define the column vectors $\boldsymbol{k} := (k_1, \ldots, k_N)^\mathsf{T}$ and $\boldsymbol{k}' := (k'_1, \ldots, k'_N)^\mathsf{T}$.

- **Case $v \leftarrow e$.** Because of Requirement 1, substituting an expression e for v in a base function $b_i \notin X_{v \leftarrow e}$ is a linear operation. Without loss of generality, assume that the exclusion set $X_{v \leftarrow e}$ is $\{b_i \mid N_X < i \leqslant N\}$. The constraints generated are

$$(\boldsymbol{k} = Q\boldsymbol{k}') \wedge \bigwedge_{N_X < i \leqslant N} k'_i = 0.$$

The $N \times N$ matrix Q contains zeroes everywhere but in the first N_X columns. The jth column ($j \leqslant N_X$) is the result of the substitution $b_j[e/v]$; that is: $b_j[e/v] = \sum_i q_{i,j} \cdot b_i$. The expansion exists because $b_j \notin X_{v \leftarrow e}$ when $j \leqslant N_X$. These coefficients are constants known before the generation of the linear program, and only depend on the choice of the basis.

The transformation $\Gamma_{\ell'}[e/v]$ on $\Gamma_{\ell'}$ is constrained to be linear by setting the coefficients of base functions in the exclusion set to zero. This linear transformation is then encoded as a matrix multiplication. Thus, for all states σ, $\Gamma_\ell(\sigma) = \Gamma_{\ell'}[e/v](\sigma) = \Gamma_{\ell'}(\sigma[e/v])$ and the admissibility condition (A4) is satisfied.

- **Case weaken.** To encode a weakening via a set of linear constraints, we make use of the rewrite functions provided in Requirement 2. As explained in Sect. 5, we relate the potential functions Γ_ℓ and $\Gamma_{\ell'}$ using an ℓ-specific set of unknowns, $\boldsymbol{u}_\ell$, as coefficients in a linear combination of the rewrite functions available at ℓ. Following Eq. (2), let F_ℓ denote the matrix of rewrite functions available at ℓ (in which the ith column of F is the ith rewrite function F_i). In matrix notation, the constraints generated are

$$(\boldsymbol{k}' = \boldsymbol{k} - F_\ell \boldsymbol{u}_\ell) \wedge (\boldsymbol{u} \geq 0).$$

- **Case call P.** When calling a procedure, we need to know what base functions depend only on global variables and what depend only on local variables of the caller. We call these sets GF and LF, respectively. Note that these two sets do not form a partition: some potential functions in the complement of $GF \cup LF$ depend on both local and global variables. We write $(k_i^e)_i$ and $(k_i^x)_i$ for the entry and exit annotations of P. With this notation, the analysis generates the following system of constraints.

  - The potential associated with global variables only is passed from the caller to the callee, and fetched back after the return: $\bigwedge_{i \in GF} k_i = k_i^e \wedge k_i^x = k_i'$.
  - Local variables of the callee start and end without making any contribution to the potential: $\bigwedge_{i \notin GF} k_i^e = 0 \wedge k_i^x = 0$.
  - The potential associated with local variables before the call can be recovered after: $\bigwedge_{i \in LF} k_i' = k_i$.
  - Finally, we consider the coefficients of base functions that depend on both local and global variables. Such coefficients are constrained to be zero at the call and return sites in the caller because we do not know how their base function will evolve through the call: $\bigwedge_{i \notin GF \cup LF} k_i = 0 \wedge k_i' = 0$.

  The admissibility argument in this case is more subtle than the ones given before. It follows from inductive reasoning and leverages a *framing* lemma to pass the potential of local variables through the call. Our implementation also makes use of *resource polymorphism*, as explained in greater detail below.

- **Case guard e.** We require that $\boldsymbol{k}' = \boldsymbol{k}$, and the admissibility condition (A3) is trivially satisfied.
- **Potential Goal.** Finally, we constrain the annotation of the exit point Γ_{S_x} to be the potential goal g pointwise, as in the guard case above. This fulfills (A1).

Constraint Solving. The generated constraints can be solved by an off-the-shelf LP solver. To derive the best possible bound, we minimize the potential $\sum_i k_i^e \cdot b_i(\sigma)$ that is associated with the entry point of the procedure. When all the base functions $b_i(\sigma)$ are non-negative, we use a weighted sum $\sum_i w_i k_i^e$ as objective function in the linear program. The weights w_i can be set to assign a higher priority to the coefficients of higher-degree base functions b_i.

A more robust method for non-negative base functions that allows us to prioritize the minimization of the coefficients of high-degree base functions is to use the support for efficient iterative solving that is provided by modern LP solvers: We first use the objective function $\sum_i k_{j_i}^e$ to minimize the coefficients $k_{j_i}^e$ of the base functions b_{j_i} with the highest degree. If the LP solver finds a solution, then we add the constraint $\sum_i k_{j_i}^e = o_0$ where o_0 is the objective value, and re-run the solver to optimize the coefficients for the lower-degree base functions.

It is not always the case that all base functions are non-negative in the initial state. In the implementation, we use a linear system to rewrite the initial potential as $X + \sum k_i F_i$ where $(F_i)_i$ is a family of rewrite functions in the initial state. We then constrain X to be 0 and minimize the coefficients k_i as described before.

Resource Polymorphism. In practice, constraining procedures to always use the same initial and final potential is too restrictive because procedures can be executed in different contexts. In the absence of recursion, procedure bodies can be inlined, and different bounds will be derived for the various call sites. However, inlining strategies are not applicable to recursive procedures.

An example of such a situation is displayed in Fig. 3(a). In this example, we look for an upper bound on n at the program exit. It is easy to show by induction that n is invariant across a call of P. However, if the analysis naively uses the equality constraints $\Gamma_e = \Gamma_c$ and $\Gamma_r = \Gamma_x$, no bound can be found. Indeed, Γ_x has to be set to the goal n, and then $\Gamma_r = \Gamma_x[n + 1/n] = \{n+1\}$ by the admissibility condition (A4); but $n + 1 \neq n$, preventing $\Gamma_r = \Gamma_x$. One solution to this problem is to allow a framing to be performed at call sites. In the example in Fig. 3(a), the frame used is 1.

With non-linear procedures, frames can be of higher degree. However, we cannot merely add a term like $5n$ to a potential function before and after a procedure call because the variable n can be modified by the procedure. A sound and practical approach to infer frames that we use in our implementation has been pioneered in [18]; it uses as a frame an annotation obtained by another run of the analysis on the callee with a smaller set of base functions.

```
def P():
    Γe := {n}
    if n > 0:
        n = n - 1
        Γc := {n+1}
        P()
        Γr := {n+1}
        n = n + 1
    Γx := {n}
    (a)
```

```
def Q():
    Γe := {z+(n 2)}
    if n > 0:
        n = n - 1
        Γc := {z+(n 2)+n}
        Q()
        Γr := {z+n}
        z = z + n
            {z}
        n = n + 1
    Γx := {z}
    (b)
```

Fig. 3. Procedures where resource-polymorphic recursion is used to infer a bound.

Consider, for example, the procedure Q in Fig. 3(b). It is a variant of P in which we added the assignment "z = z + n" after the recursive call. Assume that our potential goal is $\Gamma_x = \{z\}$. If z_0 and n_0 are the values of z and n before the call of Q then we have $z = z_0 + \binom{n_0}{2}$ after the call. Consequently, Γ_e is a sound potential annotation for the entry point of Q. To justify this potential annotation, we attempt to use the same annotation Γ_e for the potential before the recursive call. Note, however, that we have some additional potential n available in Γ_c. To transfer this potential to the return point Γ_r we have to analyze how n changes during a call to Q. As with the example on Fig. 3(a), n is invariant across the call, and we can perform a similar analysis on Q to derive $\Gamma'_e = \{n\}$ and $\Gamma'_x = \{n\}$ for the entry and exit points of Q. The annotations before and after the recursive call can now use the combined annotations $\Gamma_e + \Gamma'_e$ and $\Gamma_x + \Gamma'_x$, respectively.

7   Pastis: A Practical Implementation for Integer Programs

We implemented the framework of Sect. 6 in a tool that computes polynomial resource bounds for imperative integer programs. Programs are internally represented as described in Sect. 2, but the tool accepts as input both a minimal imperative language and LLVM bitcode. The expressions accepted are additions, subtractions, and multiplications of constants and program variables; a special random expression is used to represent all other operations (e.g., shifts and divisions). The base functions are picked among the monomials M defined below.

$$\text{(Monomials)} \qquad M := 1 \mid v \mid M_1 \cdot M_2 \mid \max(0, P) \qquad v \in \mathcal{V}$$

$$\text{(Polynomials)} \qquad P := k \cdot M \mid P_1 + P_2 \qquad\qquad k \in \mathbb{Q}$$

Heuristics to Select Base and Rewrite Functions. In Pastis, we make use of invariants generated by abstract interpretation to generate basis and rewrite functions. For example, if some variable v can be proved non-negative at one program point, we add the base function $\max(0, v)$ and a set of rewrite functions that will be needed to transfer potential to and from this base function. For instance, we register the rewrite function $\max(0, v) - \max(0, v - 1) - 1$.

```
if v > 0:
  {max(0, v)} ≥
  {max(0, v−1)+1}
v = v - 1
  {max(0, v)+1}
```

Fig. 4.

As shown in Fig. 4, this rewrite function can be used before a decrement when $v \geqslant 1$. Higher-degree base functions are introduced by considering successive powers and products of linear base functions.

By using as base functions the lengths of intervals that can be formed by pairs of program variables (e.g., $\max(0, b-a)$), Pastis strictly generalizes C4B [11]: any derivation in that system can be encoded in the framework of Sect. 6. Moreover, our work is more general because it allows higher-degree base functions, as well as base functions that do not match exactly the interval pattern.

Simple Polynomial Example. The program shown in Fig. 5 has a polynomial bound on the loop counter z. In the annotations, we use a saturating subtraction operation $a \mathrel{\dot-} b := \max(0, a - b)$. (In our implementation, $\max(0, \cdot)$ is used, as explained above.) As we will see, the annotations of the example already form a valid certificate. We found them by solving the system of linear constraints derived using the method of Sect. 6 on this program text. In this example, because there are no procedure calls, there are only two kinds of checks to do: (i) assignment checks, and (ii) potential-rewrite checks. The potential rewrites are all marked with a "$\geqslant$" sign (lines 4, 10, 15, and 16).

```
1  def nested():
2     {(ⁿ⁻⁰ 2) + z}
3     while n > 0:
4        ≥ {(ⁿ⁻¹ 2) + (n ∸ 1) + z}
5        n = n - 1
6        {(ⁿ⁻⁰ 2) + (n ∸ 0) + z}
7        m = n
8        {(ⁿ⁻⁰ 2) + (m ∸ 0) + z}
9        while m > 0:
10          ≥ {(ⁿ⁻⁰ 2) + (m ∸ 1) + (z+1)}
11          m = m - 1
12          {(ⁿ⁻⁰ 2) + (m ∸ 0) + (z+1)}
13          z = z + 1
14          {(ⁿ⁻⁰ 2) + (m ∸ 0) + z}
15       ≥ {(ⁿ⁻⁰ 2) + z}
16    ≥ {z}
```

Fig. 5. Polynomial example.

The most interesting parts of the reasoning are the "potential transfers" in this program. The core idea is that the quadratic potential associated with the counter of the outer loop will, at each decrement (line 5), generate a linear potential used to pay for the increments of the counter z in the inner loop. The potential behavior of the inner loop is then very similar to the one given in the introductory example of Sect. 3. The only difference is that all annotations carry an extra quadratic part $\binom{n \dot- 0}{2}$ that remains unchanged through the loop.

The validity of the potential rewrites can be justified with rewrite functions as explained in Sect. 5. For example, on line 4, we use the rewrite function $F := \binom{n \dot- 0}{2} - \binom{n \dot- 1}{2} - (n \mathrel{\dot-} 1)$ to show that $\binom{n \dot- 0}{2} + z \geqslant \binom{n \dot- 1}{2} + (n \mathrel{\dot-} 1) + z$. Indeed, the right-hand side of the inequality can be rewritten as $\binom{n \dot- 0}{2} + z - (1 \cdot F)$. Note that the rewrite function F can be used on line 4 because it is under the check "while n > 0". It could not be used on line 2, where no information about n is known yet.

Polynomial Example with Recursion. Figure 6 contains an implementation of the core of the Quicksort algorithm. All array operations are abstracted away and we look for a bound on the variable z at the end of the procedure. Note that we pass two arguments to the procedure qsort. In our implementation, as in the programs of Sect. 2, the arguments are passed via global variables. This approach is similar to machine calling conventions that use registers to pass arguments.

The bound Γ_e on z is quadratic. We can express it precisely using the binomial basis. Indeed, we will see below that Γ_e is a tight worst-case bound on z. We left all the annotations on the inner loop unspecified because they follow exactly the same pattern as the ones in the inner loop above. The interesting parts of the derivation are the two weakening hints on lines 4 and 12, and the two recursive calls. The first weakening uses the binomial identity $\binom{X+1}{2} = \binom{X}{2} + X$. This identity is applied with $X := h \doteq (l+1)$ because in this branch $h \doteq (l+1) = h \doteq l - 1$. The current implementation of our system is not able to infer this rewrite function from the body of the recursive function alone; we thus use an explicit rewrite hint. Similarly on line 12, we use a hint to prove that

```
1  def qsort(l, h):
2      Γₑ := {(ʰ⁻ˡ₂) + z}
3      if l < h:
4          hint
5              ≥ {(ʰ⁻⁽ˡ⁺¹⁾₂) + (h ÷ (l+1)) + z}
6          m = 1
7          {(ʰ⁻⁽ˡ⁺¹⁾₂) + (h ÷ (m+1)) + z}
8          while m < h-1 and random:
9              m = m + 1
10             z = z + 1
11         {(ʰ⁻⁽ˡ⁺¹⁾₂) + z}
12         hint
13             ≥ {(ʰ⁻⁽ᵐ⁺¹⁾₂) + (ᵐ⁻ˡ₂) + z}
14         qsort(l, m)
15         {(ʰ⁻⁽ᵐ⁺¹⁾₂) + z}
16         qsort(m+1, h)
17     {z}
```

Fig. 6. Quicksort core.

$$\binom{X+Y}{2} \geq \binom{X}{2} + \binom{Y}{2} + X \cdot Y \geq \binom{X}{2} + \binom{Y}{2}, \quad (3)$$

where $X := h \doteq (m+1)$ and $Y := m \doteq l$.

Note that $X + Y = h \doteq (l+1)$ because $l \leqslant m < h$.

Let us now discuss the recursive calls on lines 14 and 16. As in Sect. 6, we can describe the potential before and after the calls piecewise. On line 14, after the arguments are assigned, $\binom{m \doteq l}{2} + z$ will become $\binom{h \doteq l}{2} + z = \Gamma_e$. This quantity is the potential passed to the recursive call. The term $\binom{h \doteq (m+1)}{2}$ only depends on local variables and remains unchanged by the call; it is thus framed and retrieved on line 15. Finally, z, the final potential of qsort, is returned on line 15 and added to the frame. The call of line 16 follows a similar logic, but without any frame.

The procedure qsort exhibits its worst-case behavior when the internal loop goes all the way from l to $h-1$. Note that all the weakenings of the derivation are actually pure potential rewrites ($\geqslant$ is in fact $=$), except for the one on line 13. On that line, the term $X \cdot Y$ of Eq. 3 is lost potential. However, in the worst-case scenario, $m = h - 1$ on line 13 and thus $X \cdot Y = 0$, making the weakening a pure potential rewrite, too. Thus, in the worst case of Quicksort, no potential is ever lost and the bound $\binom{h \doteq l}{2} + z$ is exact: $\Gamma_e(\sigma_e) = \sigma_x(z)$, where σ_e and σ_x are, respectively, the entry and exit states of qsort.

8   Generation of Coq Proof Objects

In the framework of Sect. 6, IPAs are natural candidates for proof certificates. In this section, we explain how to leverage this observation and generate Coq proofs from the coefficients returned by a successful run of the LP solver. The Coq files generated depend on a small library described below, and can be checked completely automatically without modifications. The certified theorems state that the derived bounds are sound with respect to a Coq formalization of our interprocedural control-flow graphs and do not rely on any unproved assumptions. In particular, the certificates also include a soundness proof of the invariants that we derived with a simple abstract interpretation.

Benefits of Formal Verification. The benefits of checking bounds with a proof assistant are three-fold. First, it greatly increases the confidence in generated bounds, which is especially critical considering that we observed LP solvers silently overflow and return an unsound solution. All resource-analysis tools using LP solvers are currently vulnerable to this issue. Second, proof certificates are a license to implement aggressive heuristics and optimizations in our tool without risking unnoticed soundness issues. Third, it allows the integration of resource bounds into larger formal developments. We think that automating the inference of resource-bound theorems will enable a new class of software verification where not only the correctness is proved, but also quantitative properties are proved, such as real-time guarantees and memory usage, which are often neglected.

Coq Support Library. We implemented a support library that is used by all the Coq certificates generated. This library contains a formal definition of the control-flow graphs presented in Sect. 2, and a generalized version of the IPAs presented in Sect. 4. These generalized IPAs (Coq terms of type IPA) express in a single annotation the results of both the abstract interpretation and the potential annotations. A set of admissibility conditions on IPAs is defined as a predicate "IPA_VC: IPA $\rightarrow$ Prop", which is designed to be easily checked automatically. A theorem similar to Proposition 1 gives a semantic meaning to this verification condition.

   Finally, to automate fully the checking of the certificates produced, a set of relatively small tactics is defined (130 lines of Coq); they are tightly coupled with the proof-generation module of Pastis. The checking of IPAs is split into two tasks for each edge: (i) checking the validity of the abstract-state transformation, and (ii) checking the corresponding admissibility condition in Definition 1. For (i), we use the Coq decision procedure lia for linear-integer arithmetic. This logic is sufficient because the abstract interpretation merely derives linear constraints between program variables. Similarly for (ii), the inequalities to check on potential annotations are linear in program variables with coefficients in $\mathbb{Q}$. Because the coefficients are constants, the checking of inequalities is reduced to $\mathbb{Z}$, and also automated using lia. Equalities are checked with the generic ring tactic. Finally, one ad hoc tactic handles the normalization of potential annotations using the $\max(0, \cdot)$ function, which is not handled natively by lia.

Importantly, according to the Coq reference manual [32], the `lia` tactic is complete. This property means that a failure when checking a proof certificate can only be explained by an invalid certificate. Invalid certificates can be the result of a bug in our tool—we found one in the abstract interpreter during the development—or of invalid coefficients in the potential annotations (e.g., because of overflows or rounding errors in the LP solver).

Generated Coq Files. A generated file starts by defining the program analyzed as a control-flow graph with procedure calls. Then, for each procedure and program point, the results of the abstract-interpretation procedure and the potential annotations are listed. From these two pieces of information, multiple procedure annotations are defined and aggregated in a single global IPA for the complete program (referred to as "ipa" in the Coq file). This IPA is proved to satisfy the verification condition in a theorem

```
Theorem admissible_ipa: IPA_VC ipa.
Proof. prove_ipa_vc. Qed.
```

The proof of admissibility is always a single call to the tactic `prove_ipa_vc` imported from the library described above. This tactic call is where the bulk of the checking happens. Finally, a user-readable theorem expresses the soundness of the bound that was generated. For example

```
Theorem bound_valid: forall s1 s2,
  steps P_start (proc_start P_start) s1 (proc_end P_start) s2 →
  ( s2 G_z <= (3#2) * s1 G_g + (1#2) * s1 G_g^2 )%Q.
Proof. prove_bound ipa admissible_ipa P_start. Qed.
```

In this theorem, `s1` and `s2` are the initial and final program states, respectively, of the execution of the `start` procedure (which appears in the hypothesis as "`steps P_start ...`"). In this example, the goal was set to $\{z\}$, i.e., the value of the global variable z at the end of the execution (shown as "`s2 G_z`"). It is bounded in terms of the initial value of another global variable g. A rational number a/b is represented in Coq using the notation `a#b`. The proof of this theorem leverages both the main theorem about admissible IPAs—proved once and for all in our library—and one annotation of the `start` procedure that has the goal as final potential.

Rewrite Functions. Rewrite functions are also checked for validity in the Coq implementation. One challenge in this step is that rewrite functions often contain non-linear expressions (e.g., the binomial functions used in Sect. 7). This issue prevents us from using the built-in automation of Coq directly. To solve this issue, we used a small domain-specific language (DSL). Elements of this DSL are interpreted (in Coq) as a pair of an actual rewrite function (a map from states to rationals) and a conjunction of linear conditions. The conjunction is, by design of the DSL, a sufficient condition proving the non-negativity of the rewrite function. This trick lets us once more reuse Coq's linear-integer automation to lighten the proof burden. When checking weakening steps in the tactic `prove_ipa_vc`, all the rewrite functions that were used by the LP solver are put in the proof context as hints for `lia` to use.

9   Experimental Evaluation

Benchmark Set. To evaluate the performance of Pastis, we used the benchmark suite of the paper that presented Loopus'15 [30]. That paper compares Loopus'15 to Loopus'14 [29], KoAT [10], and CoFloCo [16]. The comprehensive program set used is based on the compiler optimization Collective Benchmark (cBench) which contains 211,892 lines of C code. These C files are pre-processed to extract all functions into independent files; those files are then translated to the various input formats of the tools compared. Pastis accepts directly LLVM bitcode and processes it to extract a control-flow graph as described in Sect. 2. The benchmark was run in intraprocedural mode because only KoAT and Pastis support procedure calls.

Machine. The experimental evaluation was run on a machine equipped with an Intel Xeon CPU clocked at 3.10 GHz and 32 GB of memory.

Results. Table 1 contains a digest of the experiments. The results for Loopus'14, KoAT, and CoFloCo were taken from the evaluation done by Sinn et al. [30]. By the number of examples only, Pastis is in the same ballpark as the majority of other tools. We also found that Pastis infers bounds quickly in most cases: 98% are found in less than 3 s.

Loopus'15 deserves special mention as it performs remarkably well; we were impressed by its versatility on this benchmark set. In addition to its sophisticated intraprocedural loop-analysis algorithm, Loopus'15 implements many practical ad hoc features. Among others, the C types are retrieved from the debugging information in the LLVM bitcode; some heuristics to identify loops on null-terminated C strings and files are built in; and finally, at the expense of compositionality, large sections of code can be represented symbolically with a Scheme-like syntax in the case where top-level loops are preceded with complex straight-line code. Similar features are not yet implemented in Pastis.

From the "Proof ✓" column, we can see that most but not all the bounds that Pastis generated were successfully checked by Coq. Coq usually processes the generated files quickly: 311 files take less than 10 s to check, and another 83 files take less than 20 s. The checking failures are caused by imprecision in the

Table 1. Experimental evaluation of Pastis on 1659 functions from the cBench benchmark. Only Pastis can generate proof certificates, whence the four occurrences of "N/A" in the last column. The tools were run with a timeout of 60 s.

Tool	Bounded	$O(1)$	$O(n)$	$O(n^2)$	$>O(n^2)$	Timeout	Proof ✓
Loopus'15	806	205	489	97	15	6	N/A
Pastis	459	187	229	43	0	127	424
Loopus'14	431	200	188	43	0	20	N/A
KoAT	430	253	138	35	4	161	N/A
CoFloCo	386	200	148	38	0	217	N/A

LP certificates and by our conversion function from floating-point numbers to rational numbers. Especially on higher-degree problems, it is common to see a base function in a loop invariant assigned a small, non-zero, bogus coefficient. Past a certain threshold, our extraction mechanism will output a small rational number when zero is actually needed. On examples with large constants, we also observed LP-solver overflows leading to obviously unsound bounds. As a practical counter-measure, our LLVM-bitcode reader replaces all "large" constants with non-deterministic expressions.

10   Related Work

Resource-Bound Analysis. The analysis method presented is based on automatic amortized resource analysis (AARA). This analysis technique has been introduced for functional programs [17,19,20,33] and has also been applied to derive bounds for object-oriented programs [21] and heap-manipulating imperative programs [6]. In contrast to our work, none of the previous work focuses on proof certificates or deriving bounds for imperative code that depend on integers. Most related to our work is the recent application of AARA to derive linear bounds for imperative integer programs [11]. The main benefits of our work are the derivation of polynomial bounds, the flexibility introduced by rewrite functions, and the automatic verification of resource certificates in Coq.

Amortized analysis has been formalized in the proof assistants Isabelle/HOL and Coq to verify manually the complexity of algorithms and data-structures [14, 26]. Our focus is on integer programs rather than sophisticated data-structures and algorithms, and our technique verifies programs automatically.

Resource-bound analyses that focus on integer programs include CAMPY [31], KoAT [10], Rank [5], CoFloCo [16], COSTA [4] and Loopus [30]. The advantages of our method include LP-based bound inference, natural compositionality, bound inference for recursive procedures, and automatically-checked Coq certificates. Recent work on an interprocedural analysis that finds procedure summaries in non-linear arithmetic [22] has shown how such information can be used to find resource bounds.

We are only aware of three other papers that describe tools that can generate bounds with machine-verified certificates. Carbonneaux et al. [12] use Coq and the verified CompCert C compiler to derive stack bounds for assembly code that are verified by Coq. In contrast to the present paper, their technique does not use linear constraint solving and automatic verification is limited to constant stack bounds. Blazy et al. [9] describe a loop-bound estimation for WCET analysis that is formally verified in Coq. An advantage of our method is that we generate complex symbolic bounds and can naturally handle recursive functions. Albert et al. [3] have used the KeY program verifier to automatically verify bounds generated by the COSTA bound analyzer. While the overall methodology is similar, we show that we can handle a large set of benchmarks, perform bounds inference via linear programming, and focus on integer bounds rather than bounds that depend on the sizes of data structures.

Template-Based Methods. Several program-analysis methods use the idea of (i) choosing a template that characterizes the kind of invariants of a program that are sought, (ii) extracting an appropriate set of (linear) constraints from the program, and (iii) solving the constraints. For example, Template Constraint Matrices (TCMs) are a parameterized family of linear-inequality domains for expressing invariants in linear real arithmetic. Sankaranarayanan et al. [27] gave meet, join, and a set of abstract transformers for all TCM domains. Monniaux [24] gave an algorithm that finds the best transformer in a TCM domain across a straight-line block and good transformers across more complicated control flow.

Müller-Olm and Seidl [25] showed how to obtain invariants that are polynomial equalities of bounded degree. Their method uses a finite-height domain that is a vector space whose basis elements are (transformers on) the set of monomials in which polynomial invariants can be expressed.

Bagnara et al. [8] presented a technique to generate invariants that are polynomial inequalities of bounded degree. Their technique introduces additional variables (dimensions) to represent nonlinear terms, and uses convex polyhedra to represent polynomial cones in the extended set of variables.

Acknowledgments. We thank Vilhelm Sjöberg and Lionel Rieg for their helpful suggestions during the implementation of proof certificates in Coq.

References

1. Albert, E., Arenas, P., Genaim, S., Gómez-Zamalloa, M., Puebla, G.: Automatic inference of resource consumption bounds. In: Bjørner, N., Voronkov, A. (eds.) LPAR 2012. LNCS, vol. 7180, pp. 1–11. Springer, Heidelberg (2012). doi:10.1007/978-3-642-28717-6_1

2. Albert, E., Arenas, P., Genaim, S., Puebla, G., Zanardini, D.: Cost analysis of Java bytecode. In: Nicola, R. (ed.) ESOP 2007. LNCS, vol. 4421, pp. 157–172. Springer, Heidelberg (2007). doi:10.1007/978-3-540-71316-6_12

3. Albert, E., Bubel, R., Genaim, S., Hähnle, R., Román-Díez, G.: Verified resource guarantees for heap manipulating programs. In: Lara, J., Zisman, A. (eds.) FASE 2012. LNCS, vol. 7212, pp. 130–145. Springer, Heidelberg (2012). doi:10.1007/978-3-642-28872-2_10

4. Albert, E., Fernández, J.C., Román-Díez, G.: Non-cumulative resource analysis. In: Baier, C., Tinelli, C. (eds.) TACAS 2015. LNCS, vol. 9035, pp. 85–100. Springer, Heidelberg (2015). doi:10.1007/978-3-662-46681-0_6

5. Alias, C., Darte, A., Feautrier, P., Gonnord, L.: Multi-dimensional rankings, program termination, and complexity bounds of flowchart programs. In: Cousot, R., Martel, M. (eds.) SAS 2010. LNCS, vol. 6337, pp. 117–133. Springer, Heidelberg (2010). doi:10.1007/978-3-642-15769-1_8

6. Atkey, R.: Amortised resource analysis with separation logic. In: Gordon, A.D. (ed.) ESOP 2010. LNCS, vol. 6012, pp. 85–103. Springer, Heidelberg (2010). doi:10.1007/978-3-642-11957-6_6

7. Avanzini, M., Lago, U.D., Moser, G.: Analysing the complexity of functional programs: higher-order meets first-order. In: ICFP (2012)

8. Bagnara, R., Rodríguez-Carbonell, E., Zaffanella, E.: Generation of basic semi-algebraic invariants using convex polyhedra. In: Hankin, C., Siveroni, I. (eds.) SAS 2005. LNCS, vol. 3672, pp. 19–34. Springer, Heidelberg (2005). doi:10.1007/11547662_4

9. Blazy, S., Maroneze, A., Pichardie, D.: Formal verification of loop bound estimation for WCET analysis. In: Cohen, E., Rybalchenko, A. (eds.) VSTTE 2013. LNCS, vol. 8164, pp. 281–303. Springer, Heidelberg (2014). doi:10.1007/978-3-642-54108-7_15

10. Brockschmidt, M., Emmes, F., Falke, S., Fuhs, C., Giesl, J.: Alternating runtime and size complexity analysis of integer programs. In: Ábrahám, E., Havelund, K. (eds.) TACAS 2014. LNCS, vol. 8413, pp. 140–155. Springer, Heidelberg (2014). doi:10.1007/978-3-642-54862-8_10

11. Carbonneaux, Q., Hoffmann, J., Shao, Z.: Compositional certified resource bounds. In: PLDI (2015)

12. Carbonneaux, Q., Hoffmann, J., Ramananandro, T., Shao, Z.: End-to-end verification of stack-space bounds for C programs. In: PLDI (2014)

13. Černý, P., Henzinger, T.A., Kovács, L., Radhakrishna, A., Zwirchmayr, J.: Segment abstraction for worst-case execution time analysis. In: Vitek, J. (ed.) ESOP 2015. LNCS, vol. 9032, pp. 105–131. Springer, Heidelberg (2015). doi:10.1007/978-3-662-46669-8_5

14. Charguéraud, A., Pottier, F.: Machine-checked verification of the correctness and amortized complexity of an efficient union-find implementation. In: Urban, C., Zhang, X. (eds.) ITP 2015. LNCS, vol. 9236, pp. 137–153. Springer, Cham (2015). doi:10.1007/978-3-319-22102-1_9

15. Cousot, P., Cousot, R.: Abstract interpretation: A unified lattice model for static analysis of programs by construction or approximation of fixpoints. In: POPL (1977)

16. Flores-Montoya, A., Hähnle, R.: Resource analysis of complex programs with cost equations. In: Garrigue, J. (ed.) APLAS 2014. LNCS, vol. 8858, pp. 275–295. Springer, Cham (2014). doi:10.1007/978-3-319-12736-1_15

17. Hoffmann, J., Das, A., Weng, S.C.: Towards automatic resource bound analysis for OCaml. In: POPL (2017)

18. Hoffmann, J., Hofmann, M.: Amortized resource analysis with polymorphic recursion and partial big-step operational semantics. In: Ueda, K. (ed.) APLAS 2010. LNCS, vol. 6461, pp. 172–187. Springer, Heidelberg (2010). doi:10.1007/978-3-642-17164-2_13

19. Hoffmann, J., Aehlig, K., Hofmann, M.: Multivariate amortized resource analysis. In: POPL (2011)

20. Hofmann, M., Jost, S.: Static prediction of heap space usage for first-order functional programs. In: POPL (2003)

21. Hofmann, M., Jost, S.: Type-based amortised heap-space analysis. In: Sestoft, P. (ed.) ESOP 2006. LNCS, vol. 3924, pp. 22–37. Springer, Heidelberg (2006). doi:10.1007/11693024_3

22. Kincaid, Z., Breck, J., Forouhi Boroujeni, A., Reps, T.: Compositional recurrence analysis revisited. In: PLDI (2017)

23. Madhavan, R., Kulal, S., Kuncak, V.: Contract-based resource verification for higher-order functions with memoization. In: POPL (2017)

24. Monniaux, D.: Automatic modular abstractions for template numerical constraints. LMCS 6(3:4) (2010)

25. Müller-Olm, M., Seidl, H.: Precise interprocedural analysis through linear algebra. In: POPL (2004)

26. Nipkow, T.: Amortized complexity verified. In: Urban, C., Zhang, X. (eds.) ITP 2015. LNCS, vol. 9236, pp. 310–324. Springer, Cham (2015). doi:10.1007/978-3-319-22102-1_21

27. Sankaranarayanan, S., Sipma, H.B., Manna, Z.: Scalable analysis of linear systems using mathematical programming. In: Cousot, R. (ed.) VMCAI 2005. LNCS, vol. 3385, pp. 25–41. Springer, Heidelberg (2005). doi:10.1007/978-3-540-30579-8_2

28. Serrano, A., López-García, P., Hermenegildo, M.V.: Resource usage analysis of logic programs via abstract interpretation using sized types. TPLP **14**(4–5), 739–754 (2014)

29. Sinn, M., Zuleger, F., Veith, H.: A simple and scalable static analysis for bound analysis and amortized complexity analysis. In: Biere, A., Bloem, R. (eds.) CAV 2014. LNCS, vol. 8559, pp. 745–761. Springer, Cham (2014). doi:10.1007/978-3-319-08867-9_50

30. Sinn, M., Zuleger, F., Veith, H.: Difference constraints: an adequate abstraction for complexity analysis of imperative programs. In: FMCAD (2015)

31. Srikanth, A., Sahin, B., Harris, W.R.: Complexity verification using guided theorem enumeration. In: POPL (2017)

32. The Coq development team: Reference manual (v8.6). https://coq.inria.fr/distrib/current/refman/index.html. Accessed May 2017

33. Vasconcelos, P., Jost, S., Florido, M., Hammond, K.: Type-based allocation analysis for co-recursion in lazy functional languages. In: Vitek, J. (ed.) ESOP 2015. LNCS, vol. 9032, pp. 787–811. Springer, Heidelberg (2015). doi:10.1007/978-3-662-46669-8_32

Look for the Proof to Find the Program: Decorated-Component-Based Program Synthesis

Adrià Gascón[1(✉)], Ashish Tiwari[2],
Brent Carmer[3], and Umang Mathur[4]

[1] University of Warwick and The Alan
Turing Institute, London, UK
agascon@turing.ac.uk
[2] SRI International, Menlo Park, USA
tiwari@csl.sri.com
[3] Oregon State University, Corvallis, USA
carmerb@eecs.oregonstate.edu
[4] University of Illinois at Urbana-Champaign, Champaign, USA
umathur3@illinois.edu

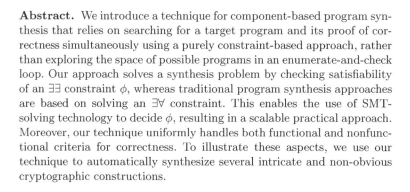

Abstract. We introduce a technique for component-based program synthesis that relies on searching for a target program and its proof of correctness simultaneously using a purely constraint-based approach, rather than exploring the space of possible programs in an enumerate-and-check loop. Our approach solves a synthesis problem by checking satisfiability of an $\exists\exists$ constraint ϕ, whereas traditional program synthesis approaches are based on solving an $\exists\forall$ constraint. This enables the use of SMT-solving technology to decide ϕ, resulting in a scalable practical approach. Moreover, our technique uniformly handles both functional and nonfunctional criteria for correctness. To illustrate these aspects, we use our technique to automatically synthesize several intricate and non-obvious cryptographic constructions.

1 Introduction

Automated program synthesis has a rich history in computer science. This problem has been studied from several perspectives, and currently lies at the intersection between logic, artificial intelligence, and software engineering. The seminal work by Manna and Waldinger [23], commonly referred to as *deductive synthesis*, is based in the observation that a program with input x and output y, specified by a formula $\phi(x, y)$, can be extracted from a constructive proof of $\forall x \exists y : \phi(x, y)$, as this formula is equivalent to a second-order formula of the form $\exists f \ \forall x : \phi(x, f(x))$.

A. Gascón—Part of this work was done while the author was at the University of Edinburgh, supported by the SOCIAM Project under EPSRC grant EP/J017728/2.
A. Tiwari—Supported in part by the National Science Foundation under grant CCF 1423296.

R. Majumdar and V. Kunčak (Eds.): CAV 2017, Part II, LNCS 10427, pp. 86–103, 2017.
DOI: 10.1007/978-3-319-63390-9_5

More recently, program synthesis has taken the form of *inductive synthesis*, where programs are not deduced, but synthesized iteratively by finding candidate programs that work correctly on an ever-increasing input space. In practice, this search is implemented using powerful constraint solvers, typically Boolean Satisfiability (SAT) solvers and Satisfiability Modulo Theory (SMT) solvers. The various choices in the synthesis approach, correctness specification, and restrictions on the program search space, have been explored extensively [2,16, 19,28,29].

Manna and Waldinger [23] foresee the possibility that the user could suggest program segments, i.e. snippets, to the synthesizer, which it could use to construct a full solution. This idea was pursued in the work on *component-based program synthesis* [16,32], where the target program is constructed from a set of predefined components (library calls). The component-based synthesis problem is also naturally encoded as an ∃∀ problem: there *exists some* placement of components on the different program lines such that *for all* inputs, the function computed by the resulting program satisfies the given property.

Although it comes in many flavors, a synthesis problem is essentially parameterized by a *target language*, i.e. the language of the target program to be synthesized, and a *specification language*, i.e. the formalism in which the functionality of the target program is expressed. Moreover, synthesis may be subject to nonfunctional constraints, such as optimizing for certain metrics like program size or power consumption, or enforcing security properties. Examples of target languages include MapReduce-style programs [27], bit-vector manipulations [16], recursive programs [20], high-level circuit descriptions [13], and domain-specific languages for cryptographic constructions [18,22]. On the other hand, examples of specification languages include formulas in several modal temporal logics, input-output examples [19,27], flattened verilog circuits given as SMT/Boolen formulas [13], and assertions in imperative program sketches [29].

Generally speaking, the synthesis problem seeks to find a program P in the target language, such that P satisfies the specification ϕ given in the specification language. As ϕ is often a relation between input-output pairs, this naturally corresponds to an exists-forall check. In fact, inductive synthesis algorithms often consist of two procedures: a procedure to generate candidate programs from the target language, and a procedure for checking ϕ on a given candidate. In that setting, synthesis consists of an enumerate-and-check feedback loop, similar to a Counterexample-Guided Abstraction Refinement (CEGAR) loop, that continues until a valid candidate, i.e. a candidate satisfying ϕ, is found, or no more candidates can be generated. Note that, to achieve scalability, the verification check is often conservative, i.e. ϕ is replaced by a sufficient, but not necessary condition. This is often the case with security properties, as they are costly to check in a sound and complete way.

The paradigm of "enumerate-and-check" for solving synthesis problems is fairly widespread in literature [13,16,22,27]. In this context, the general idea of looking for a program and its proof simultaneously has been also considered in previous work on type-directed synthesis [12,26], where program candidates that are not type correct are pruned early in the enumerate-and-check. Also, the deductive phase of the Leon synthesizer [20] is also based on proof search.

In this paper, we pursue a framework that enables synthesis using a single search, and avoids quantifier alternation. Inspired by the challenge posed by Manna and Waldinger [23] pertaining to incorporation of user-defined proof systems in synthesis, and building on the framework of component-based synthesis [16], we present an approach for synthesis that allows users to define simple proof systems, in the form of *constraint-generation rules* for the components of the synthesized program. This framework, which we call *decorated-component-based synthesis*, provides a way for the user to not only easily encode nonfunctional properties, as in [32], but also replace the validity check in the synthesis process by a search for a proof in the provided proof system. This effectively removes a quantifier alternation and hence turns the enumerate-and-check approach into a search problem in which, intuitively, the space of target programs and their corresponding correctness proofs are explored simultaneously, resulting in a much more scalable approach.

Contributions. We make three key contributions in this work. First, we formulate the *decorated-component-based program synthesis* problem, which allows users to encode a bounded search for proof (in a user-picked proof system) in the synthesis problem. Second, we show that decorated-component-based synthesis problem reduces to an exists-forall constraint in general, just as the component-based synthesis problem [16]. However, the additional "decorations" enable users to either augment a synthesis constraint with additional existential parts (similar to the work in [32]), or entirely replace the forall by a existential in the synthesis constraint. This second application of decorations is appealing because solving a purely existential constraint is significantly faster than solving an exists-forall constraint. Third, we demonstrate that security is an ideal domain for application of automated program synthesis technology, thus solidifying preliminary evidence in this regard [3,7,18,22,32]. Decorated-component-based synthesis eases the task of specifying security requirements. Our synthesizer and all the examples mentioned in this paper, as well as instructions for running them, are available at the SYNUDIC project's public repository [14].

Outline. We start by illustrating our approach (with complete details) on an example synthesis problem (Sect. 2). We then formally define decorated-component-based synthesis (Sect. 3), and show that it reduces to an $\exists\forall$ constraint (Sect. 4). We then present our main result that enables conservative replacement of the $\forall$ by an $\exists$ in the synthesis constraint (Sect. 5). Finally, we show its application to synthesis of cryptographic schemes (Sect. 6).

2   An Illustrative Example

Secure Multi-party Computation (MPC) is a subfield of cryptography with the goal of creating protocols for multiple parties to jointly compute a function over their inputs without disclosing the inputs to each other. Here we consider the problem of designing an information secure two-party multiplication protocol, which is a basic component in many privacy-preserving algorithms [5,10].

Our problem is as follows: find a protocol for Alice and Bob to compute an additive share of the product of Alice's and Bob's private input values. Let Alice's (private input) value be $\texttt{input}(A) \in \mathbb{Z}_q$, and Bob's value be $\texttt{input}(B) \in \mathbb{Z}_q$, for some natural q, say 2^{32}. For *correctness*, our functional requirement is that

$$\texttt{output}(A) + \texttt{output}(B) = \texttt{input}(A) * \texttt{input}(B)$$

In other words, each party computes a *share* of the result. We assume that Alice and Bob can rely on a third *untrusted* party Carol that aids in the computation.

Now that we have the functional correctness requirement, let us consider the nonfunctional security requirement. Informally, the main security requirement is that Alice and Carol should not learn the value $\texttt{input}(B)$, and Bob and Carol should not learn the value $\texttt{input}(A)$. In the static honest-but-curious adversary model, one assumes that the parties – Alice, Bob, and Carol – have an incentive to deduce as much information as possible from the transcripts of the protocol, but they do not deviate from it nor collude. (Formally, the security requirement is formulated in the so-called "simulation paradigm", see [21] for details.)

How do we use our new decorated-component-based synthesis technique to discover a secure multiplication protocol? We first identify the components that we could use in the protocol. These are the three arithmetic operations $\texttt{plus}$, $\texttt{minus}$, and $\texttt{times}$, along with a few calls to a pseudo-random generator, say $\texttt{genx}$, $\texttt{geny}$, $\texttt{genr}$, and $\texttt{genu}$ (that generate random numbers x, y, r, u), and the identity function $\texttt{identity}$.

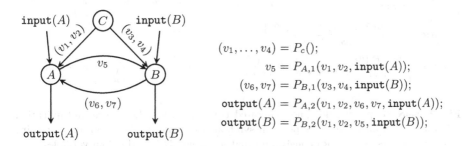

$$(v_1, \ldots, v_4) = P_c();$$
$$v_5 = P_{A,1}(v_1, v_2, \texttt{input}(A));$$
$$(v_6, v_7) = P_{B,1}(v_3, v_4, \texttt{input}(B));$$
$$\texttt{output}(A) = P_{A,2}(v_1, v_2, v_6, v_7, \texttt{input}(A));$$
$$\texttt{output}(B) = P_{B,2}(v_1, v_2, v_5, \texttt{input}(B));$$

Fig. 1. High-level synthesis sketch for secure multiplication. The diagram (left) shows the structure of the protocol to be synthesized. Solving the corresponding template (right) involves finding programs $P_C, P_{A,1}, P_{B,1} P_{A,2}, P_{B,2}$, built out of components $\texttt{genx}, \texttt{geny}, \texttt{genr}, \texttt{genu}, \texttt{identity}, \texttt{plus}, \texttt{minus}, \texttt{times}$ in the library, satisfying (i) the functional requirement, i.e. $\texttt{output}(A) + \texttt{output}(B) = \texttt{input}(A) * \texttt{input}(B)$), and (ii) the security requirement. Moreover, $P_C, P_{A,1}, P_{B,1} P_{A,2}, P_{B,2}$ must have no more than 5, 1, 3, and 2 operations, respectively.

Next, let us fix a communication schedule between the parties. The structure of the protocol, depicted in Fig. 1(left) is as follows: (1) C computes some values $(v_1, \ldots, v_4)$ first (5 lines), (2) C sends (v_1, v_2) to A and (v_3, v_4) to B,

(3) A computes v_5 (1 line) and sends it to B, (4) B computes some values (3 lines), sends a pair (v_6, v_7) to A and picks one value as its output, (5) A computes its output (2 lines). Note that instances of this template are constant-round protocols, as opposed to approaches to secure multiplication based on Oblivious Transfer [15]. Our tool [14] takes a description of the library and a template of a straight-line program similar to the one in Fig. 1(right) as input.

If we give each of the components its natural interpretation (that is, all variables are integer valued, plus is arithmetic addition, and so on), then the correctness requirement is simply the arithmetic equality $\mathtt{output}(A) + \mathtt{output}(B) = \mathtt{input}(A) * \mathtt{input}(B)$. Now, synthesis can be performed as in [16] or [32] – the synthesis problem is reduced to an $\exists\forall$ formula over a suitable theory, where the $\exists$ quantifier searches over the space of possible programs, and the $\forall$ quantifier checks correctness over the space of all possible inputs.

Our new decorated-component-based synthesis framework allows us to (a) conservatively turn the validity check above into a satisfiability check over an alternate theory, and (b) provide a natural way of also specifying a nonfunctional security requirement. The key idea behind our approach is associating a constraint with each use of a component in the (yet to be discovered) program, by defining a *decoration*, or a *constraint generation rule*, for every component.

genx $\quad \dfrac{}{\{\theta\}\; v := \mathtt{genx}\; \{\theta \circ \{v \mapsto pol2vec(``x")\}\}} \quad v_x = 1 \wedge \bigwedge_{i \neq x} v_i = 0$

plus $\quad \dfrac{}{\{\theta\}\; x := \mathtt{plus}(y, z)\; \{\theta \circ \{x \mapsto \theta(y) + \theta(z)\}\}} \quad \bigwedge_{i \in I} x_i = y_i + z_i$

times $\quad \dfrac{[\theta(y) * \theta(z) \text{ is quadratic}]}{\{\theta\}\; x := \mathtt{times}(y, z)\; \{\theta \circ \{x \mapsto \theta(y) * \theta(z)\}\}} \quad \bigwedge_{i,j \in L} x_{ij} = y_i z_j + y_j z_i \wedge \bigwedge_{i \in NL} y_i = z_i = 0$

compose $\quad \dfrac{\{\theta_0\}\; P_1\; \{\theta_1\} \qquad \{\theta_1\}\; P_2\; \{\theta_2\}}{\{\theta_0\}\; P_1; P_2\; \{\theta_2\}}$

check $\quad \dfrac{\{\theta_0\}\; P\; \{\theta\} \qquad \theta(v) + \theta(w) = \theta(a)\theta(b)}{\{\theta_0\}\; P\; \{\mathtt{assert}(\mathtt{v} + \mathtt{w} = \mathtt{a} * \mathtt{b})\}} \quad v_{ab} + w_{ab} = 1 \wedge \bigwedge_{i \neq ab} v_i + w_i = 0$

Fig. 2. Selected proof rules and generated constraints for the secure multiplication example. Essentially, the rules perform symbolic execution of the program. The third column shows (some of the) constraints that are generated on the dual variables.

As a first step in defining the decorations, consider an abstract domain $\mathcal{A}$ that consists of symbolic polynomial expressions of degree at most 2 over the six variables: the two inputs a, b and the four random numbers x, y, r, u.

$$\mathcal{A} = \{p(a, b, x, y, r, u) \mid p \text{ is quadratic with no constant term}\}$$

where polynomials in $\mathcal{A}$ are represented in *canonical form* as a sum of ordered monomials.

Let us say we wish our program (that is yet to be discovered) to have a functional correctness proof in this abstract domain. We can design proof rules that essentially perform symbolic execution to check the correctness assertion.

Let $\theta : V \mapsto \mathcal{A}$ map a *program variable* $v \in V$ to the symbolic polynomial value of v. We can compute θ by starting with any substitution, and updating it using the rules in Fig. 2. For example, the rule `genx` says that after execution of $v := \texttt{genx}$, we get a new substitution that maps v to the symbolic polynomial x. Similarly, the rule `plus` handles program lines of the form $v := \texttt{plus}(x, y)$ by setting $\theta(v)$ to the polynomial $(\theta(x) + \theta(y)) \in \mathcal{A}$. In Fig. 2 we omitted rules for `minus`, `geny`, `genr`, `genu`, and `identity`. Once we have computed the substitution θ at the end of the program, we use the rule `check` to prove an assertion $v + w = a * b$ by checking if $\theta(v) + \theta(w)$ and $\theta(a) * \theta(b)$ are syntactically equal (recall elements of $\mathcal{A}$ are represented in canonical form). The proof rule for `times` in Fig. 2 has a condition that allows multiplication to be used only on linear polynomials (so that the result is atmost quadratic).

Note that this proof system for checking correctness turns the validity question over integers into an evaluation over $\mathcal{A}$. Our goal now is to have our synthesizer use this proof system to, instead of searching for a program satisfying the postdondition $\texttt{output}(A) + \texttt{output}(B) = \texttt{input}(A) * \texttt{input}(B)$, search for a program while *simultaneously* searching for its correctness proof. To see how this is done, first note that the elements in the chosen abstract domain can be uniquely identified by 27 parameters – namely, the coefficients of all degree 1 and degree 2 monomials over the six variables ($C(6, 1) + C(6, 2) + C(6, 1) = 6 + 15 + 6 = 27$). Let $L = \{x, y, r, u, a, b\}$ and $NL = \{ij \mid i \neq j, i \in L, j \in L\} \cup \{ii \mid i \in L\}$. Hence, every program variable v is associated with 27 *new variables*, namely, v_i, where index i ranges over the set $I = L \cup NL$ of all indices. If variable v gets a symbolic value $p \in \mathcal{A}$ and p is quadratic, then the new variables v_i's get the value of the coefficient of the monomial i in p. Now, let us say we could prove our functional requirement using quadratic symbolic values. Then, there exists a value of the new variables that witnesses this proof. The converse is even more important for our goal: if we find a consistent valuation for the new variables, then we would establish our functional requirement. Restricting $\mathcal{A}$ to contain *quadratic* polynomials makes the set of new variables, and the proof search, finite.

A sound proof rule application (on the abstract values) induces certain constraints on the new variables. Hence, as mentioned above, we associate to every component a constraint generation rule, also called a *decoration*, that produces the suitable constraint to encode the corresponding proof rule. The generated constraint essentially says what combinations of the 27 parameters for its inputs and outputs are consistent with the proof rule. For example, the Column 3 in Fig. 2 shows such constraints for selected components.

Note that the correctness requirement was an equivalence of polynomial expressions, and in our abstract domain $\mathcal{A}$, this maps to equality of coefficients (see right column on last row in Fig. 2). Thus, ignoring the security requirement, the synthesis problem is reduced to finding $27 * l$ values, where l is the length of the program, that satisfy some big constraint generated using decorations. This is an $\exists\exists$ problem: we are finding a program (first $\exists$) and a proof of its correctness over the chosen abstract domain (second $\exists$). Decorations have enabled us to replace the $\forall$ check by an $\exists$ check. Note that, although the task of finding a proof system requires human intuition, the process of designing constraint generation rules, i.e. parameterizing the abstract domain and building the constraint for every component of the library, is systematic (Sect. 5.1).

We have not yet solved our original problem because we still need to include the security requirement. The formal security requirement, which is based on showing a simulation of the ideal functionality in the actual functionality (see [21] for details on this proof technique), is difficult to capture precisely. We take a very practical approach here: we replace the security requirement by another easily checkable requirement that is sufficient (but not necessary) for security. The new check can itself be described by proof rules, and we can again search for a bounded-size proof to establish security. The sufficiency of the proof rules may itself be proved as a meta-theorem by hand. In our example, we use ideas from [32], which were in turn inspired by [22], to synthesize block cipher modes of operation. Essentially, the decorations rely on a simple type system that propagates a qualifier stating whether a variable always has a "random" value on any program line, in a sound, and possibly incomplete, way.

Using this encoding of the security requirement, our sketch is complete, we run our synthesis tool, and it returns the following protocol:

1. C generates random numbers x, y, r, and computes xy and $r - xy$.
2. C sends (x, r) to A and $(r - xy, y)$ to B.
3. A computes $\texttt{input}(A) - x$ and sends it to B.
4. B computes $\texttt{output}(B) = (\texttt{input}(A) - x)b + (r - xy)$ and sends $y + \texttt{input}(B)$ to A.
5. A computes $\texttt{output}(A) = (y + \texttt{input}(B))x - r$.

We were not aware of this protocol before it was synthesized by our tool. Note that the protocol did not use the fourth random number (u), whereas we were expecting the synthesized protocol to need it.

3   Decorated-Component-Based Program Synthesis

We define the component-based synthesis problem in this section, as introduced in [16]. We then extend it to decorated-component-based synthesis, where components are additionally allowed to be associated with certain constraint-generation rules.

A component library Σ is a set of symbols. Each symbol is associated with an arity, but without loss of generality and for simplicity, we will often implicitly assume that the arity of each symbol in Σ is two. The symbols in Σ should be regarded as functions that can be invoked by a program.

The functions in Σ compute over some values. For simplicity again, let us say these values come from a domain $\texttt{Domp}$ of all values. The semantics of the functions in Σ is given over the domain $\texttt{Domp}$ by $\texttt{Semp}$.

$$\texttt{Semp} : \ \Sigma \ \mapsto \ 2^{\texttt{Domp}^3} \tag{1}$$

That is, if $f \in \Sigma$, then $\texttt{Semp}(f)$ is a ternary relation on $\texttt{Domp}$. Intuitively, $c = f(a, b)$ iff $(a, b, c) \in \texttt{Semp}(f)$.

$$l0 : x_0 := \textbf{input}$$
$$l1 : x_1 := f_1(a_{11}, a_{12});$$
$$l2 : x_2 := f_2(a_{21}, a_{22});$$
$$\vdots$$
$$l9 : x_9 := f_9(a_{91}, a_{92});$$

Variables: Domain
$f_1, \ldots, f_9 : \Sigma$
$a_{11}, \ldots, a_{92} : 0..8$
$vx_0, \ldots, vx_9 : \text{Domp}$
$tx_0, \ldots, tx_9 : \text{Domd}$

Fig. 3. A template for an arbitrary straight-line program with 9 lines.

We want to synthesize straight-line programs (SLPs) using calls to functions in Σ. A generic template of such a 9-line program is shown in Fig. 3. The semantics Semp of one component can be extended to semantics of a straight-line program P (such as the one shown in Fig. 3) that takes one input x_0 and produces one output x_9 so that $\text{Semp}(P) \subseteq \text{Domp}^2$ contains all pairs (a, b) where $x_9 = b$ is reachable starting with $x_0 = a$.

A specification, ϕ_{fspec}, of a program P that takes one input and produces one output is given as binary relation on Domp.

Definition 1. (Component-Based Synthesis, or CoS [16]). *A CoS problem is a tuple $(\Sigma, \text{Domp}, \text{Semp}, \phi_{\text{fspec}}, n)$ consisting of a library Σ of functions, a domain Domp of values, a semantics function $\text{Semp} : \Sigma \mapsto 2^{\text{Domp}^3}$, a specification relation $\phi_{\text{fspec}} \subseteq \text{Domp}^2$, and an integer n. The goal is to find a straight-line program P of length n that only calls functions in Σ to compute a function that refines ϕ_{fspec}; that is, $\forall x, y : \text{Semp}(P)(x, y) \Rightarrow \phi_{\text{fspec}}(x, y)$.*

3.1 Decorated-Component-Based Synthesis

We now allow the library components $f \in \Sigma$ to be associated with additional constraint-generation rules, and introduce the problem of synthesizing straight-line programs (SLPs) that use such decorated components.

Let V denote all program variables. The semantics Semp interpreted V as elements in Domp. Now, let Domd be an alternate domain of values, and consider valuations $\sigma : V \mapsto \text{Domd}$ that interpret V in this new domain Domd. Each function $f \in \Sigma$ is given an alternate meaning:

$$\text{Semd} : \Sigma \mapsto 2^{\text{Domd}^3} \qquad (2)$$

That is, if $f \in \Sigma$, then $\text{Semd}(f)$ is a ternary relation on Domd. Intuitively, if we use the statement $z = f(x, y)$ in a Program P, then we would require the existence of three values in Domd – one value tx associated with x, a value ty associated with y, and a value tz associated with z – such that $(tx, ty, tz) \in \text{Semd}(f)$. The alternate meaning of a SLP P is simply the conjunction of the alternate meaning of each statement.

$$\text{Semd}(P) = \{\sigma \in \text{Domd}^V \mid (\sigma(x), \sigma(y), \sigma(z)) \in \text{Semd}(f) \; \forall (z := f(x, y) \in P)\} \; (3)$$

Definition 2. (Decorated-CoS, or DCoS) *A DCoS problem is an 8-tuple* $(\Sigma, \mathsf{Domp}, \mathsf{Semp}, \phi_{\mathsf{fspec}}, n, \mathsf{Domd}, \mathsf{Semd}, \phi_{\mathsf{dspec}})$, *where* $(\Sigma, \mathsf{Domp}, \mathsf{Semp}, \phi_{\mathsf{fspec}}, n)$ *is a CoS problem,* Domd *is an alternate domain of values,* Semd *is a mapping* $\Sigma \mapsto 2^{\mathsf{Domd}^3}$, *and* $\phi_{\mathsf{dspec}} \subseteq \mathsf{Domd}^2$ *is an additional constraint on input* x *and output* y. *The goal is to synthesize both a straight-line program* P *and a valuation* $\sigma : V \mapsto \mathsf{Domd}$ *such that* P *solves the component-based synthesis problem and* σ *is a model of* $\mathsf{Semd}(P)$ *and* $(\sigma(x), \sigma(y)) \in \phi_{\mathsf{dspec}}$.

In a DCoS problem, the Semp part could be redundant (if $\phi_{\mathsf{fspec}} = \mathsf{Domp}^2$), or the Semd part could be redundant (if $\mathsf{Semd}(f) = \mathsf{Domd}^3$ and $\phi_{\mathsf{dspec}} = \mathsf{Domd}^2$). Hence, DCoS generalizes CoS, and supports Semd-only problem formulations too.

Note that decorations are useful to enforce nonfunctional constraints on the target program, such as a bound on the number of a component function to use.

4   Solving the Synthesis Problems

We solve the synthesis problems by converting them to an $\exists\forall$ constraint and using an off-the-shelf $\exists\forall$ SMT solver to solve the constraint. This approach was used in earlier work on component-based synthesis [16]. We note here that the decorated components introduce additional existential constraints, and hence, the overall synthesis constraint continues to be an $\exists\forall$ formula.

4.1   Component-Based Program Synthesis as $\exists\forall$

Consider an instance of the CoS problem, depicted in Fig. 3, where, for notational convenience, we fixed $n = 9$. Synthesizing the program amounts to finding values for the 9 variables $f_1, \ldots, f_9$ from the set Σ, and values for the 18 variables $a_{11}, a_{12}, \ldots, a_{91}, a_{92}$ from the set $\{0, 1, \ldots, 8\}$. If the value of a_{ij} is k, then it means the j-th argument of the function call on Line i is equal to x_k.

We have the following well-formedness constraint on the a_{ij} variables, which guarantees that the synthesized programs will indeed be a SLP.

$$\phi_1 = \bigwedge_{i \in 1..9} (a_{i1} < i \wedge a_{i2} < i). \quad \text{More generally, } \phi_1 = \bigwedge_{i \in 1..9} \bigwedge_{j \in 1..\mathsf{arity}(f_i)} a_{ij} < i$$

With each left-hand side variable $x_1, \ldots, x_9$ in the program sketch in Fig. 3, we associate one first-order variable vx_i, which denotes the value in Domp of x_i. The following constraint imposes consistency of vx_i values with respect to the semantics Semp.

$$\phi_2 = \bigwedge_{\substack{i,j,k \in 1..9 \\ f \in \Sigma}} (a_{i1} = j \wedge a_{i2} = k \wedge f_i = f) \Rightarrow (vx_j, vx_k, vx_i) \in \mathsf{Semp}(f)$$

The constraint above says that if the first argument of the functional call on Line i comes from Line j, the second argument comes from Line k, and the function on Line i is $f \in \Sigma$, then the value vx_i should be such that $(vx_j, vx_k, vx_i) \in \mathsf{Semp}(f)$.

We are now ready to write our $\exists\forall$ *synthesis constraint* $\Phi_{\exists\forall}$:

$$\exists f_1, \ldots, f_9 \in \Sigma \; \exists a_{11}, \ldots, a_{92} \in [0..8] \;\; (\phi_1 \;\wedge$$
$$\forall vx_0, \ldots, vx_9 \in \text{Domp} \;\; (\phi_2 \Rightarrow \phi_{\text{fspec}}(vx_0, vx_9)))$$

The satisfiability of $\Phi_{\exists\forall}$ is equivalent to the existence of an instance of the sketch in Fig. 3 that satisfies the functional requirement f_{spec}. Thus, we can solve the CoS problem by generating the above formula and solving it using an $\exists\forall$ solver, as described in [16].

4.2   Decorated-Component-Based Program Synthesis as $\exists\forall$

Let $tx_0, tx_1, \ldots, tx_9$ denote new variables (interperted over Domd) corresponding to the 10 lines in the program sketch shown in Fig. 3. (We assume program P does not assign twice to the same variable, so there is a 1–1 correspondence between program variables and program lines.) The following constraint imposes consistency of the Domd values (assigned to the new variables) with respect to the semantics Semd.

$$\phi_3 = \bigwedge_{\substack{i,j,k \in 1..9 \\ f \in \Sigma}} (a_{i1} = j \wedge a_{i2} = k \wedge f_i = f) \;\Rightarrow\; (tx_j, tx_k, tx_i) \in \text{Semd}(f)$$

Now, the decorated-component-based synthesis problem reduces to satisfiability of the following exists-forall formula $\Psi_{\exists\forall}$:

$$\exists f_1, \ldots, f_9 \in \Sigma \; \exists a_{11}, \ldots, a_{92} \in [0..8]$$
$$\exists tx_0, \ldots, tx_9 \in \text{Domd} \;\; (\phi_1 \wedge \phi_3 \wedge \phi_{\text{dspec}}(tx_0, tx_9) \wedge$$
$$\forall vx_0, \ldots, vx_9 \in \text{Domp} \;\; (\phi_2 \Rightarrow \phi_{\text{fspec}}(vx_0, vx_9)))$$

where $\phi_{\text{fspec}}(vx_0, vx_9)$ captures the functional requirement and $\phi_{\text{dspec}}(tx_0, tx_9)$ captures the alternate requirement.

The following claim follows from definition of the two synthesis problems and noting that ϕ_2 captures $\text{Semp}(P)$ and ϕ_3 captures $\text{Semd}(P)$.

Proposition 1. *The CoS problem, respectively DCoS problem, has a solution (a desired program) iff the constraint $\Phi_{\exists\forall}$, respectively $\Psi_{\exists\forall}$, is satisfiable.*

5   Component-Based Synthesis Using $\exists$ Solving

Our main result is that, in some cases, given a CoS problem, one can design a decoration for the components that is an "abstraction" of its primary semantics. Such a decoration allows us to completely ignore the main functional specification while performing synthesis. Since the function specification was the only source of $\forall$ in the synthesis constraint, the synthesis constraint simplifies to an $\exists$ constraint, which can be solved using standard SMT solvers [24,30].

Consider any program P. Let V be the set of program variables in P, and let V be partitioned into $I \uplus O$, where I are the input variables, and O are the variables defined in P. Let PSp denote the set of all program states Domp^V, and let PSd denote the set of all alternate states Domd^V. A *concretization function* γ is a mapping from the set PSd to the powerset 2^{PSp}.

Definition 3. *A set $Sd \subseteq \mathsf{PSd}$ is an* abstraction *of a set $Sp \subseteq \mathsf{PSp}$ with respect to a concretization function γ and a subset $W \subseteq V$ of variables, if*

$$Sp|_W \ \subseteq \ \bigcap_{\theta \in Sd} \gamma(\theta)|_W$$

where $X|_Y$ denotes the projection of the set X onto the Y components (that is, we consider assignments to the variables in Y and ignore the other variables).

Remark 1. In sharp contrast to Definition 3, recall that in the usual notion of abstraction, we say Sp_2 is an abstraction of Sp_1 if $Sp_1 \subseteq \bigcup_{s \in Sp_2} \gamma(s)$.

Definition 4. *The alternate semantics* Semd *is an <u>abstraction</u> of the primary semantics* Semp *in a program P if there exists a* concretization *function $\gamma : \mathsf{PSd} \rightarrow 2^{\mathsf{PSp}}$ such that for every $Sp \subseteq \mathsf{PSp}$, for every $Sd \subseteq \mathsf{PSd}$, if Sd is an abstraction of Sp w.r.t γ and I, then* $\mathsf{Semd}(P)(Sd)$ *is an abstraction of* $\mathsf{Semp}(P)(Sp)$ *w.r.t γ and $I \uplus O$.*

Remark 2. The definition of abstraction of programs given in Definition 4 is similar to the usual notion of abstraction: if we start with an abstraction of initial states, and apply the abstract transformer, we should get back an abstraction of the concretely transformed initial states. Definition 4 says the same thing, but with the difference that we restrict to the set I when checking abstraction on the initial states, and use the new notion of when a set of alternate program states is said to abstract a set of primary program states (Definition 3).

We note that Definition 4 allows us to compose programs while preserving abstractions if the composed programs modify a disjoint set of variables. More precisely, if the decoration of P_1 is an abstraction, and the decoration of P_2 is an abstraction, then the decoration of $P_1; P_2$ is an abstraction too, under the assumption that P_2 does not change the value of any variable in P_1 (and only treats those values as its inputs).

The main point of having a decoration that is an abstraction is that now, if we can find an interpretation for the program in the alternate semantics, then we know the program is functionally correct in its primary semantics.

Theorem 1. *Let ϕ_{fspec} and ϕ_{dspec} be primary and alternate specifications such that $\gamma(\{\sigma \mid (\sigma(x_0), \sigma(x_9)) \in \phi_{\mathsf{dspec}}\}) \subseteq \{\sigma \mid (\sigma(x_0), \sigma(x_9)) \in \phi_{\mathsf{fspec}}\}$. If Semd is an abstraction of* Semp *(as in Definition 4) with respect to the concretization function γ, then, whenever ϕ_{dspec} holds in P, then ϕ_{fspec} holds in P.*

The main consequence of Theorem 1 is that now we can solve a CoS problem, which is an $\exists\forall$ problem, by checking satisfiability of an existentially quantified constraint (no quantifier alternation). We can do this only if we have a decoration Semd that is an abstraction of Semp. Given such an Semd, we can solve the CoS problem by checking satisfiability of the following existential formula $\Phi_{\exists\exists}$:

$$\exists f_1, \ldots, f_9 \in \Sigma \ \exists a_{11}, \ldots, a_{92} \in [0..8]$$
$$\exists tx_0, \ldots, tx_9 \in \text{Domd} \ (\phi_1 \wedge \phi_3 \wedge \phi_{\text{dspec}}(tx_0, tx_9))$$

This formula is the same as $\Psi_{\exists\forall}$, but with all references to $vx_0, \ldots, vx_9$ removed. Since these were the only universally quantified variables, we get rid of the $\forall$ and get the above *quantifier-alternation-free synthesis constraint*, which can be solved using existing Satisfiability Modulo Theory (SMT) solvers [24,30].

Theorem 1 can be viewed a "weak" form of duality because it constructs an $\exists$ formula that implies a $\forall$, but not vice-versa. Also, it must be understood as a template for meta-theorems that argue that a given decoration enables $\exists\exists$ synthesis, such as the one that we used in our example of Sect. 2.

If we use enumeration over all possible values to check a $\forall$ verification condition, we may find a violation of the $\forall$ formula after some finite search and thus, we may find a bug. If we use enumeration over all possible values to check the sufficient $\exists$ formula, we may find a suitable valuation of the exists-variables after some finite search, and thus we may find a proof (for the $\forall$ formula). Hence, our notion of abstraction here, and the resulting weak duality in Theorem 1 has an interesting use in program verification: it replaces a "search for bugs" approach (violation of $\forall$) by a "search for proofs" approach (satisfiability of the dual $\exists$). One may wonder if program analysis community has ever implicitly used Theorem 1 to perform verification. The answer is yes: template-based methods for verification, also called constraint-based verification [17,31], are an instance of the weak duality principle. We next outline a template-based technique to construct abstract decorations, which can be used to solve CoS problems.

5.1   Constructing Abstract Decorations

We describe a generic approach for constructing abstract decorations. Note that we followed this recipe when constructing the decoration for our secure multiplication example in Sect. 2. Let us assume we have an abstract domain PSa; for example, one over which we could have created an abstract interpreter, or performed predicate abstraction. Let us see how we would generate decorations from PSa. Let us say we have proof rules that generate valid Hoare triples $\{\phi_1\}P\{\phi_2\}$ over the abstract states, where P is a program, ϕ_1, ϕ_2 are elements of PSa. Now, to define the decoration Semd, we first parameterize the elements of PSa. Say, we have a template $\Phi(u)$ that contains parameters u such that

$$\text{PSa} = \{\Phi(c) \mid c \in \text{Domd}\}, \text{ for some set Domd}$$

In other words, we can generate all abstract program states by instantiating the parameters u from the set Domd. The set Domd forms our alternate domain.

If $l1, l2, \ldots$ are all the program locations (nodes in the program graph), then $\boldsymbol{u}_{l1}, \boldsymbol{u}_{l2}, \ldots$ are our new program variables that are interpreted over Domd. Finally, we need to define the alternate meaning Semd for each program statement. This is achieved by considering proof rules comprising of valid Hoare triples $\{\phi_1\}z := f(x, y)\{\phi_2\}$, and trying to generate a constraint $\psi_f(\boldsymbol{u}, \boldsymbol{v})$ such that

$$\forall \boldsymbol{u}, \boldsymbol{v} : \psi_f(\boldsymbol{u}, \boldsymbol{v}) \Rightarrow \{\varPhi(\boldsymbol{u})\}z := f(x, y)\{\varPhi(\boldsymbol{v})\}$$

If we can find such a ψ_f (not equivalent to *false*) forall $f \in \Sigma$, then $(\psi_f)_{f \in \Sigma}$ defines Semd. By construction, Semd is an abstraction of Semp. An example of this process of constructing an abstract Semd can be found in Fig. 2.

We would like to emphasize two points here. First, the task of constructing an abstract decoration Semd will not succeed always, because we may not find such ψ_f. Second, while abstract decorations are a powerful concept, decorations that are *not* abstractions of Semp also prove to be immensely useful, especially in the application to synthesis, where they can be used to capture nonfunctional properties. This latter use of decorations was explored in [32], and reused here.

6　Cryptographic Schemes

In this section, we present some examples of cryptographic schemes that we synthesized using the DCoS framework. These are summarized in Table 1. Our synthesis tool takes as input a program sketch, such as the one in Sect. 2, multiple primal semantics (Semp), and multiple decorations (Semd) on components, along with requirements specified on these semantics. It solves the synthesis problem by generating and solving either the $\varPhi_{\exists\forall}$ formula (in case there are some primal semantics) or the $\varPhi_{\exists\exists}$ formula (in case there are only decorations on components). Our tool, along with all the examples and corresponding SMT instances, is available at [14].

Table 1. Summary of examples of synthesized cryptographics schemes. Details on the BC modes, secure multiplication, and oblivious transfer examples are given in Sects. 6.1, 6.2, and 6.3, respectively. The sketches of all examples are available at [14]. The decorations SPOLY and RAND are the ones introduced informally in Sect. 2, DEC and SEC are described in Sect. 6.1 and were inspired by the work of [22], SARITH corresponds to symbolic arithmetic expressions (used to approximate operations in a group), and SBOOL corresponds to symbolic Boolean expressions.

Synthesis problem	Search space size	Solution size	Decorations	Synthesis time
BC modes	$\sim 1 \times 10^9$	11 lines	DEC + SEC	~ 1 s
Secure multiplication	$\sim 2 \times 10^{13}$	21 lines	SPOLY + RAND	~ 50 s
Oblivious transfer	$\sim 2 \times 10^7$	9 lines	SARITH	~ 1 s
Du-Atallah multiplication	$\sim 3 \times 10^{19}$	11 lines	SPOLY + RAND	~ 1 s
Dining Cryptographers	$\sim 2 \times 10^{25}$	12 lines	RAND + SBOOL	~ 1 s

$$\frac{u = f(v, w), \quad \texttt{know}(v), \quad \texttt{know}(w)}{\texttt{know}(u)} \text{ if } f \text{ is known} \quad \Bigg| \quad \frac{u = v \oplus w, \quad \texttt{know}(u), \quad \texttt{know}(w)}{\texttt{know}(v)}$$

Fig. 4. Decryptability check: Assuming that initially only the encrypted message is "known", we can apply the above rules to check if message m can be "known". A k-step (bounded size) proof search can be encoded using decorated components by having k-*length arrays* of alternate values for each program variable.

6.1 Block Cipher Modes

Block ciphers are keyed, invertible functions that map a fixed length bit string (say 128 bits) to a random bit string of the same length. A *block cipher mode Enc* uses a block cipher to encrypt messages longer than this fixed length. We have *two* requirements: *correctness* of *Enc*, which is captured by the existence of a decryption algorithm *Dec* such that $\forall k, m : Dec_k(Enc_k(m)) = m$, and *security*, which is expressed by the fact that no adversary with oracle access to *Enc* is able to learn anything about random ciphertexts.

Malozemoff et al. [22] proposed an algorithm for synthesis of block cipher modes that follows the enumerate-and-check paradigm. The algorithm proceeds by carefully enumerating candidate straight-line programs and checking correctness and security for each of them. The security property is approximated using a labeling system that guarantees that if a candidate straight-line program can be labeled satisfying certain constraints, then it implements a secure block cipher. The search for the *existence* of a correct labeling is then implemented using an SMT solver. Regarding correctness, the authors propose a fix-point algorithm analogous to our encoding of decryptability check as a decoration; see Fig. 4.

We used both the $\exists\forall$ and the $\exists\exists$ approach to synthesize block cipher modes, which highlights the flexibility of the DCoS framework. Our formulation of the problem is analogous to the one in [22]; that is, our sketches do not provide additional "hints" to the synthesis tool. In the $\exists\forall$ approach, we specify correctness directly using a primal semantics; that is, we synthesize ($\exists$) both an encryption scheme *Enc and* a decryption scheme *Dec* such that for all ($\forall$) input messages m, $Dec(Enc(m)) = m$. By having a primal semantics for specifying correctness, and a decoration for specifying security, we solved the synthesis problem by generating and solving the $\Psi_{\exists\forall}$ formula shown in Sect. 4. The $\exists\forall$ approach has two main drawbacks: first, solving $\Psi_{\exists\forall}$ turned out to be expensive because it required us to synthesize two programs at once, *Dec* and *Enc*. Moreover, it requires us to specify primal semantics for the block cipher function itself. This is not ideal, since a bad choice might be a source of unsoundness in the decryptability check.

The new $\exists\exists$ approach, enabled by Theorem 1, addresses both these issues. The crucial observation is that the correctness check used in [22] is in fact an instance of the weak duality of Theorem 1, and hence it can be encoded as a second decoration. Hence, to ensure correctness, it is not necessary to synthesize a decryption scheme, but instead check for "decryptability" (Fig. 4). The new $\exists\exists$ approach resulted in a reduction in running time from $\sim 100\,\text{s}$ (using the $\Psi_{\exists\forall}$ approach) to $\sim 1\,\text{s}$, to synthesize well-known encryption schemes such as CBC,

OFB, CFB, OFB, and PCBC. Moreover, another benefit is that we can leverage the incremental solving capabilities of SMT solvers, such as Yices and Z3, to efficiently find hundreds of variants of block cipher modes. Our $\exists\exists$ approach found hundreds of correct modes of operation in less than 5 min on a regular laptop, including all the common ones mentioned above.

6.2   Secure Multiplication

In Sect. 2, we presented an application of our synthesis methodology to synthesize a secure 2-party computation multiplication protocol. The synthesis time for the sketch described in Sect. 2 is $\sim 50\,$s. As explained above, our synthesis tool takes as input a sketch of the solution, i.e. a description of a finite family of protocols $\mathcal{F}$ in this case, and searches for a protocol $P \in \mathcal{F}$ that satisfies the requirements.

Figure 5 reports running times and approximated search space size, i.e. $|\mathcal{F}|$, for 30 variants of our sketch presented in Sect. 2.

The first 15 variants of our sketch are satisfiable (blue trace in the plot), and were obtained in the following way: we started from a sketch whose only completion is the solution reported in Sect. 2; that is, $|\mathcal{F}| = 1$, and then increasingly relaxed it until we obtained a most general one.

Hence, the leftmost data point of the satisfiable instances corresponds to simply a verification check. The second one corresponds to a sketch where everything is fixed but the first line of A's program. In subsequent data points (3)–(15), the part of the protocol to be determined is (3) messages from C, (4) messages from C and B, (5) arithmetic operations in A and B, (6) arithmetic operations in C, and messages from C and B, (7) arithmetic operations, (8) arithmetic operations and messages from B, (9) arithmetic operations and messages from C and A, (10) arithmetic operations and messages from C and B, (11) arithmetic operations in A and B, and program for C, (12) arithmetic operations in A, and programs for C and B, (13) everything but first line of A's program, and programs for C and B, (14) programs for A, B, and C, (15) programs for A, B, and C, letting A have a total of 4 lines.

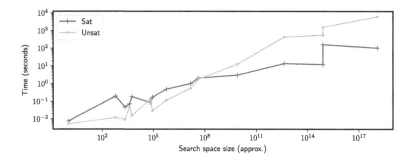

Fig. 5. Running times for satisfiable and unsatisfiable variants of the secure multiplication sketch. The experiments were run using Yices as backend solver on a 2.30 GHz machine with 8 Gb of memory.

The unsatisfiable instances are obtained from (1)–(15) by adding the additional restriction that C cannot use multiplication. This prevents C from generating appropriately correlated random data, which results in unsatisfiable sketches.

Although it is difficult to make definitive statements about the behaviour of SMT solvers, the plot in Fig. 5 confirms a tendency that we have often observed: our approach scales well for satisfiable instances, and hence using general sketches spanning a large $\mathcal{F}$ is fine as long as $\mathcal{F}$ contains a solution. On the other hand, if the synthesis problem is not realizable, proving so for large families of programs may not scale well.

6.3 Oblivious Transfer

In the two-party version of oblivious transfer (OT), one party, the Sender, has two messages m_0 and m_1, and the other party, the Chooser, can pick which message she wants to receive. The goal of oblivious transfer is to achieve this transfer of message from Sender to the Chooser, but with the requirements that (a) the Sender does not learn the choice made by the Chooser, and (b) the Chooser does not learn the content of the other message (that was not chosen).

We wish to base the protocol on the decisional Diffie-Hellman (DDH) assumption [6]: given a cyclic group with generator g, the DDH assumption states that (g^a, g^b, g^{ab}) is computationally indistinguishable from (g^a, g^b, g^c) for randomly and independently chosen elements a, b, c from $\mathbb{Z}$. We provide a sketch to the synthesis tool that consists of four blocks of straight-line code (executed by Sender, Chooser, Sender, Chooser in turns), where the Sender and the Chooser are allowed use of upto 3 random numbers each.

While approches based on $\exists\forall$ paradigm timed out due to the complexity of the protocol, we were able to perform $\exists\exists$ synthesis by using only suitably designed decorations. We synthesized two different OT protocols: the first one was also recently reported in [8], and the second one is the well-known Naor-Pinkas protocol [25]. The solutions were obtained in about 1 and 100 seconds, respectively, on a regular laptop using Yices as backend solver.

Due to technical difficulties in formalizing the security requirements, we used approximate requirements that eliminated a large number insecure protocols, but not necessarily all of them. Consequently, there is a need here for *a posteriori* verification of security of the synthesized scheme (using other verification tools; such as, Easycrypt [4]). Program synthesis, however, remains a fast and effective tool to quickly generate plausible schemes.

7 Conclusion

We formulated the decorated-component-based synthesis framework and showed how component decorations can be used to enable a weak duality principle, which allows us to replace a desired $\forall$ check by a stronger $\exists$ check. Besides its applications to speed up program synthesis, it is important to recognize the use of this duality principle in different verification techniques, such as constraint-based verification [17,31]. Decorations can abstract the concrete meaning, and thus provide sufficient checks for functional properties. They can also be unrelated to the concrete meaning, and encode nonfunctional properties of programs.

It is worth emphasizing that decorations are not abstract interpreters [9]: in abstract interpretation, assertion checking is still a "forall" check (just over abstract values). In contrast, decorations on components behave as constraints, and hence our extension of primal semantics with decorations has flavors of constraint programming [11] and combining inductive and co-inductive constructs [1].

Exploring extension of DCoS to programs with loops, designing decorations to encode more sophisticated proof systems, and studying algebraic properties of decorations remain future challenges.

References

1. Abel, A., Pientka, B., Thibodeau, D., Setzer, A.: Copatterns: programming infinite structures by observations. In: 40th ACM Symposium Principles of Programming Languages POPL (2013)
2. Alur, R., Bodík, R., Juniwal, G., Martin, M.M.K., Raghothaman, M., Seshia, S.A., Singh, R., Solar-Lezama, A., Torlak, E., Udupa, A.: Syntax-guided synthesis. In: Formal Methods in Computer-Aided Design, FMCAD, pp. 1–17 (2013)
3. Barthe, G., Crespo, J.M., Kunz, C., Schmidt, B., Gregoire, B., Lakhnech, Y., Zanella-Beguelin, S.: Fully automated analysis of padding-based encryption in the computational model (2013). http://www.easycrypt.info/zoocrypt/
4. Barthe, G., Dupressoir, F., Grégoire, B., Kunz, C., Schmidt, B., Strub, P.-Y.: EasyCrypt: A Tutorial. In: Aldini, A., Lopez, J., Martinelli, F. (eds.) FOSAD 2012-2013. LNCS, vol. 8604, pp. 146–166. Springer, Cham (2014). doi:10.1007/978-3-319-10082-1_6
5. Bogdanov, D., Laur, S., Willemson, J.: Sharemind: a framework for fast privacy-preserving computations. In: Jajodia, S., Lopez, J. (eds.) ESORICS 2008. LNCS, vol. 5283, pp. 192–206. Springer, Heidelberg (2008). doi:10.1007/978-3-540-88313-5_13
6. Boneh, D.: The decision Diffie-Hellman problem. In: Buhler, J.P. (ed.) ANTS 1998. LNCS, vol. 1423, pp. 48–63. Springer, Heidelberg (1998). doi:10.1007/BFb0054851
7. Carmer, B., Rosulek, M.: Linicrypt: a model for practical cryptography. In: Robshaw, M., Katz, J. (eds.) CRYPTO 2016. LNCS, vol. 9816, pp. 416–445. Springer, Heidelberg (2016). doi:10.1007/978-3-662-53015-3_15
8. Chou, T., Orlandi, C.: The simplest protocol for oblivious transfer. Cryptology ePrint Archive, Report 2015/267 (2015). http://eprint.iacr.org/
9. Cousot, P., Cousot, R.: Abstract interpretation: a unified lattice model for static analysis of programs by construction or approximation of fixpoints. In: 4th ACM Symposium on Principles of Programming Languages, POPL, pp. 238–252 (1977)
10. Du, W., Atallah, M.J.: Protocols for secure remote database access with approximate matching. In: Ghosh, A.K. (ed.) E-Commerce Security and Privacy, pp. 87–111. Springer, Heidelberg (2001)
11. Felgentreff, T., Millstein, T., Borning, A., Hirschfeld, R.: Checks and balances: constraint solving without surprises in object-constraint programming languages. In: Proceedings Conference on Object-oriented Programming, Systems, Languages, and Applications, OOPSLA (2015)

12. Frankle, J., Osera, P., Walker, D., Zdancewic, S.: Example-directed synthesis: a type-theoretic interpretation. In: POPL, pp. 802–815. ACM (2016)
13. Gascón, A., Subramanyan, P., Dutertre, B., Tiwari, A., Jovanovic, D., Malik, S.: Template-based circuit understanding. In: Formal Methods in Computer-Aided Design, FMCAD, pp. 83–90. IEEE (2014)
14. Gascón, A., Tiwari, A.: Synudic: synthesis using dual interpretation on components (2016). https://github.com/adriagascon/synudic
15. Gilboa, N.: Two party RSA key generation. In: Wiener, M. (ed.) CRYPTO 1999. LNCS, vol. 1666, pp. 116–129. Springer, Heidelberg (1999). doi:10.1007/3-540-48405-1_8
16. Gulwani, S., Jha, S., Tiwari, A., Venkatesan, R.: Synthesis of loop-free programs. In: Proceedings of ACM Conference on Programing Language Design and Implementation PLDI, pp. 62–73 (2011)
17. Gulwani, S., Srivastava, S., Venkatesan, R.: Program analysis as constraint solving. In: Proceedings of ACM Conference on Programming Language Design and Implementation, PLDI, pp. 281–292 (2008)
18. Hoang, V., Katz, J., Malozemoff, A.: Automated analysis and synthesis of authenticated encryption schemes. In: ACM CCS (2015)
19. Jha, S., Gulwani, S., Seshia, S.A., Tiwari, A.: Oracle-guided component-based program synthesis. In: Proceedings of ICSE, vol. 1, pp. 215–224. ACM (2010)
20. Kneuss, E., Kuraj, I., Kuncak, V., Suter, P.: Synthesis modulo recursive functions. In: OOPSLA, pp. 407–426. ACM (2013)
21. Lindell, Y.: How to simulate it - a tutorial on the simulation proof technique. Cryptology ePrint Archive, Report 2016/046 (2016). http://eprint.iacr.org/2016/046
22. Malozemoff, A.J., Katz, J., Green, M.D.: Automated analysis and synthesis of block-cipher modes of operation. In: IEEE 27th Computer Security Foundations Symposium, CSF, pp. 140–152. IEEE (2014)
23. Manna, Z., Waldinger, R.J.: Toward automatic program synthesis. Commun. ACM **14**(3), 151–165 (1971)
24. Microsoft Research: Z3: an efficient SMT solver. http://research.microsoft.com/projects/z3/
25. Naor, M., Pinkas, B.: Efficient oblivious transfer protocols. In: Proceedings of 12th ACM-SIAM Symposium on Discrete Algorithms, SODA, pp. 448–457 (2001)
26. Polikarpova, N., Kuraj, I., Solar-Lezama, A.: Program synthesis from polymorphic refinement types. In: PLDI, pp. 522–538. ACM (2016)
27. Smith, C., Albarghouthi, A.: Mapreduce program synthesis. In: PLDI, pp. 326–340. ACM (2016)
28. Solar-Lezama, A., Rabbah, R.M., Bodík, R., Ebcioglu, K.: Programming by sketching for bit-streaming programs. In: PLDI (2005)
29. Solar-Lezama, A., Tancau, L., Bodík, R., Saraswat, V., Seshia, S.: Combinatorial sketching for finite programs. In: ASPLOS (2006)
30. SRI International: Yices: an SMT solver. http://yices.csl.sri.com/
31. Srivastava, S., Gulwani, S., Foster, J.S.: Template-based program verification and program synthesis. STTT **15**(5–6), 497–518 (2013)
32. Tiwari, A., Gascón, A., Dutertre, B.: Program synthesis using dual interpretation. In: Felty, A.P., Middeldorp, A. (eds.) CADE 2015. LNCS (LNAI), vol. 9195, pp. 482–497. Springer, Cham (2015). doi:10.1007/978-3-319-21401-6_33

E-QED: Electrical Bug Localization During Post-silicon Validation Enabled by Quick Error Detection and Formal Methods

Eshan Singh[(✉)], Clark Barrett, and Subhasish Mitra

Stanford University, Stanford, USA
{esingh, clarkbarrett, subh}@stanford.edu

Abstract. During post-silicon validation, manufactured integrated circuits are extensively tested in actual system environments to detect design bugs. Bug localization involves identification of a bug trace (a sequence of inputs that activates and detects the bug) and a hardware design block where the bug is located. Existing bug localization practices during post-silicon validation are mostly manual and *ad hoc*, and, hence, extremely expensive and time consuming. This is particularly true for subtle electrical bugs caused by unexpected interactions between a design and its electrical state. We present E-QED, a new approach that automatically localizes electrical bugs during post-silicon validation. Our results on the OpenSPARC T2, an open-source 500-million-transistor multicore chip design, demonstrate the effectiveness and practicality of E-QED: starting with a failed post-silicon test, in a few hours (9 h on average) we can automatically narrow the location of the bug to (the fan-in logic cone of) a handful of candidate flip-flops (18 flip-flops on average for a design with ~ 1 Million flip-flops) and also obtain the corresponding bug trace. The area impact of E-QED is $\sim 2.5\%$. In contrast, determining this same information might take weeks (or even months) of mostly manual work using traditional approaches.

1 Introduction

For complex integrated circuits (*ICs*), difficult design flaws (bugs) increasingly escape pre-silicon design verification and are only detected during post-silicon validation when manufactured ICs are extensively tested in actual system environments (Foster 2015). Design bugs can be broadly classified into *logic bugs* that are caused by (logic) design errors and *electrical bugs* that are caused by unexpected interactions between a design and its electrical state. Examples include errors introduced by crosstalk, power-supply noise, thermal effects or process variations. Traditional pre-silicon verification is slow; but, more importantly, it is generally incapable of detecting electrical bugs that appear only after ICs are manufactured. **This paper focuses on electrical bugs.**

Typical post-silicon validation involves: 1. bug detection by applying a variety of test stimuli (e.g., random instruction tests, end-user applications) at various voltage,

This work is supported in part by DARPA and the Semiconductor Research Corporation (SRC).

R. Majumdar and V. Kunčak (Eds.): CAV 2017, Part II, LNCS 10427, pp. 104–125, 2017.
DOI: 10.1007/978-3-319-63390-9_6

temperature, and clock frequency corners; 2. *bug localization* which identifies a *bug trace* (a sequence of inputs that activates and detects the bug) and a hardware design block where the bug is located; and, 3. bug fixing using techniques such as software patches, clock frequency/operating voltage selection, or silicon respin. Existing post-silicon validation and debug practices are mostly manual and *ad hoc*, and, hence, very expensive (Mishra et al. 2017). The effort to localize bugs from observed system failures (e.g., crashes, output errors) dominates the overall cost (Dusanapudi et al. 2015; Friedler et al. 2014; Nahir 2014). For example, it might take weeks (or even months) of (manual) work to localize a single bug (Dusanapudi et al. 2015; Reick 2012; Vermeulen and Goossens 2014).

Post-silicon bug localization is difficult because of long error detection latencies. *Error detection latency* is the time elapsed between when a test activates a bug and creates an error and when that error manifests as an observable failure (e.g., system crash). Error detection latencies of difficult bugs can exceed several millions or even billions of clock cycles (Hong et al. 2010; Lin et al. 2014). It is extremely difficult to trace that far back into the history of system operation for complex ICs. In addition, IC design size and complexity pose major challenges. Full-chip simulation to obtain expected responses (for various internal states, not just software-visible states) is several orders of magnitude slower than actual silicon and may be impractical. Formal analysis and Boolean Satisfiability techniques can be severely limited by design size. System-level failure reproduction, which involves returning the system to an error-free state and re-running the system (perhaps with some modifications) to reproduce the "exact" failure, is difficult (due to non-deterministic behaviors such as asynchronous I/Os and multiple-clock domains). In order to limit the number of cycles that must be traced and analyzed during bug localization, techniques such as Quick Error Detection (*QED* (Lin et al. 2014)) that ensure short error detection latencies are crucial. An overview of existing bug localization approaches is presented in Sect. 4.

New techniques are essential to overcome post-silicon bug localization challenges. There have been some recent publications that address detection and localization of logic bugs (e.g. (Lin et al. 2015)) during pre-silicon and post-silicon validation. Here, we present E-QED, a new technique to automatically localize electrical bugs during post-silicon validation and debug. Key features of E-QED are: 1. It is broadly applicable to most digital designs. 2. It can localize electrical bugs inside processor cores as well as in uncore components (interconnection networks, cache controllers, memory controllers) that occupy large portions of System-on-Chip (*SoC*) designs. 3. It does not require manual intervention during design or during post-silicon validation and debug. 4. It does not rely on full system-level simulation. 5. It scales to large designs.

We demonstrate the effectiveness and practicality of E-QED using OpenSPARC T2, a 500-million-transistor open-source SoC. Our results (details in Sect. 3) show that: 1. E-QED correctly and automatically localizes electrical bugs in a few hours (between 7–13 h). Such bugs would generally take weeks (or even months) of manual work to localize using traditional approaches. 2. E-QED achieves very fine-grained electrical bug localization. For each localized electrical bug, using formal analysis, E-QED automatically generates a small list of candidate flip-flops (*FFs*) that might have captured error(s) caused by the bug. For the OpenSPARC T2 SoC with ~ 1 Million FFs, E-QED automatically localizes electrical bugs to only 18 candidate FFs on average. Thus, E-QED achieves a *localization factor* (total number of FFs in a design divided by the total number of candidate FFs that an electrical bug is localized to) of over 50,000. 3. For each localized electrical bug, E-QED automatically generates a short bug trace using formal analysis. 4. E-QED incurs only a small area overhead (∼2.5% for OpenSPARC T2) and has practically no clock-speed impact. 5. E-QED enables flexible trade-offs between area overhead, electrical bug localization granularity, and bug localization runtime. For example, with 1.5% area overhead (vs. 2.5%) the average FF candidate count increases only by a factor of 3 (i.e., E-QED still achieves a localization factor of four orders of magnitude).

E-QED uses the following three steps that work together in a coordinated fashion to overcome electrical bug localization challenges: 1. Low-cost hardware structures called E-QED signature blocks are automatically inserted during the design phase (Sect. 2.1). 2. QED tests that achieve short error detection latencies are run during post-silicon validation.[1] 3. Formal techniques are used to reason about the signatures collected by the E-QED signature blocks, automatically localizing bugs to a handful of candidate FFs (Sects. 2.2–2.4).

Motivating Example

Consider the following electrical bug example for the OpenSPARC T2 SoC (OpenSPARC), shown in Fig. 1. Suppose that a bug occurs during the following sequence of events: (1) Processor core 0 writes the value 0 to the crossbar (in order to store the value 0 in address [C]); (2) the entry corresponding to address [C] in L2 cache bank 0 is updated with value 0 (from the crossbar); (3) in response to a request to load

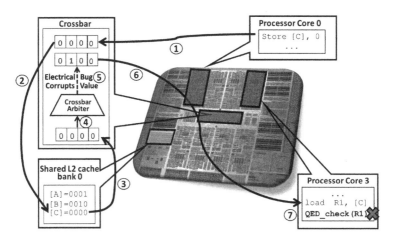

Fig. 1. An example of an electrical bug corrupting the value (corresponding to address [C]) stored by processor core 0 to L2 cache bank 0 (steps 1–2) as it passes through the arbitration logic of the crossbar (steps 3–5) while being loaded by processor core 3 (step 6). The bug is detected by a QED test (step 7).

---

[1] We use Quick Error Detection (*QED*) tests that typically achieve error detection latencies of 1,000 clock cycles or fewer (Lin et al. 2014); however, our approach can work with other tests that achieve similar error detection latencies.

from address [C] by processor core 3, the cached value corresponding to address [C] is written into the crossbar; (4) when this value passes through the crossbar arbitration logic, (5) an electrical bug causes a single-bit error to be captured in the output register of the crossbar arbiter; (6) the corrupted value is loaded into core 3; and then, (7) the corrupted value is detected by a QED test.

Note that without QED, the error may not be detected by the post-silicon validation test or the error detection latency can be millions of clock cycles; e.g., the error may be detected during an end-result check (which checks for expected output values upon test completion). Using a QED test, the error detection latency improves (i.e., reduces) to only a few hundred cycles. This drastically reduces the amount of data that needs to be analyzed to localize the bug. However, upon error detection by the QED test in processor core 3, it is impossible to <u>directly</u> determine where the error actually occurred and consequently how to localize the bug to a specific design block. An error in the datapath during any of steps 1–6 (in processor core 0, the crossbar, L2 cache bank 0, or processor core 3) would have been detected in the same way by the QED test running on processor core 3 (using the QED check in Fig. 1, step 7).

E-QED automatically localizes this bug not only to the crossbar (containing 40,000 of the nearly 1 million FFs in the design), but to a subset of 8 candidate FFs within the crossbar that could have captured this single-bit error. The 8 candidates include the FF in the output register that did capture the actual error. E-QED also provides a 544-Kbit bug trace, the sequence of inputs to the crossbar that triggered the bug during post-silicon validation. The total runtime required to obtain this result by running E-QED is 488 min, and the hardware area overhead is 2.5%.

In contrast, traditional post-silicon bug localization approaches would require significant manual effort, additional hardware (e.g., trace buffers, details in Sect. 4) with significantly higher area overhead, or both. For example, even if the bug was detected quickly using a QED test, saving a full trace of all inputs and outputs of the crossbar alone (instead of using E-QED signature blocks, details in Sect. 2.1) for just 1,000 cycles would require over 34 Mbits of data.

The rest of the paper is organized as follows. Section 2 presents our new E-QED technique. Results are then presented in Sect. 3, followed by related work in Sect. 4. We conclude in Sect. 5. An extended version of this paper appears in (Singh et al. 2017).

2 Electrical Bug Localization Using E-QED

E-QED relies on several steps that are summarized in Fig. 2. During the chip design phase, E-QED signature blocks are automatically inserted (details in Sect. 2.1). These E-QED signature blocks are used during post-silicon validation to capture and compress the logic values of selected signals (*signatures*). During post-silicon validation, a suite of tests is run—it is crucial to run tests with short error-detection latencies (e.g., QED tests (Lin et al. 2014)). When an error is detected by such a test, the test is immediately halted, and all the captured signatures are scanned out (using on-chip scan chains (Abramovici et al. 1990)). In the last phase, formal analysis, the collected signatures are analyzed by a Bounded Model Checking (*BMC*) tool to first identify which design block produced the error(s), and then to find the FFs in that block that could have captured the error(s), and finally to narrow this list even further by checking for consistency with signatures captured by neighboring design blocks. We explain each of these steps in more detail below.

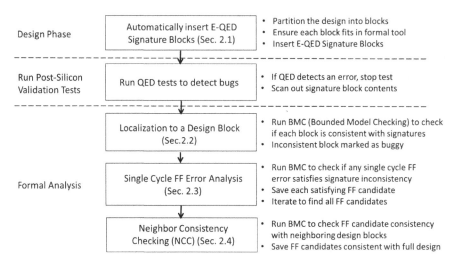

Fig. 2. An overview of E-QED.

2.1   Automatic Insertion of E-QED Signature Blocks

E-QED relies on being able to use a formal tool to perform bug localization after error detection by a post-silicon validation test. If the entire design can be loaded into the formal tool and analyzed, then this requirement can be satisfied by externally tracing the design's inputs and outputs during post-silicon testing (i.e., by saving all the signals at the external design interface). In this case, no additional internal hardware is required. However, most designs (particularly large SoCs) cannot be analyzed by existing formal tools without being partitioned into smaller blocks. In order to be able to analyze these smaller design blocks, we insert additional hardware (*E-QED Signature Blocks)* to capture logic values of signals at the boundaries of these smaller design blocks.

Design Partitioning. As mentioned above, unless it is possible to fit the full design into a formal tool, the design must be divided into smaller blocks. We use a simple algorithm that builds a list of design blocks by recursively descending through the design hierarchy. At each step, the current design block is tested to see if it can be loaded into the formal tool. If so, the recursion terminates and the block is added to the list. The result is a partition of the design into design blocks, each of which can be analyzed by the formal tool. Next, input and output signals for each block are grouped into *interfaces* as follows. For each design block A, the set of output signals driven by A and captured by the same design block B (or the same set of design blocks in the case that the signals fan out to more than one design block) are grouped into a single interface. In addition, if a design block C receives inputs from a design block in a different clock domain, then all such input signals for design block C are also grouped into a separate interface. Each interface gets a single E-QED Signature Block (explained next) as illustrated in Fig. 3. As explained above, the primary inputs and outputs are traced externally.

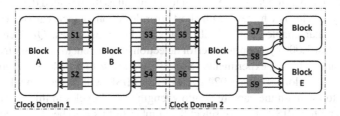

Fig. 3. Insertion of E-QED Signature Blocks. A and B use the same clock, so they can share signature blocks S1 and S2 at their interfaces. Since C is in a separate clock domain, the interfaces between B and C require separate signature blocks within each clock domain. Each signal from C captured in signature block S8 fans out to both D and E.

In our evaluation in Sect. 3, we explored one further enhancement beyond this algorithm. We observed that uninitialized memory arrays contributed too many degrees of freedom during formal analysis. To overcome this issue, we inserted additional signature blocks. Specifically, we added signature blocks to the signals between each cache bank and the cache controller logic and to the signals between the instruction cache and the instruction fetch unit for each thread on each processor core. This provided additional information on the data values being stored and loaded in the caches and the instructions being executed by the processors. As shown in Fig. 12 (in Sect. 3.2), this significantly improves the precision of E-QED.

E-QED Signature Block Design. E-QED Signature Blocks store logic values called signatures that represent a (lossy) compression of the sequence of logic values for a set of signals over time. We use multiple-input signature registers or *MISRs* (which have been extensively used for circuit test response compaction (Saxena and McCluskey 1997)) for this purpose. A MISR is a shift-register in which certain bits are XORed and fed back into the first bit, and, at the same time, a set of input signals are XORed with the values being shifted. An example of a 6-bit MISR is shown in Fig. 4.

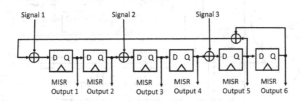

Fig. 4. An example of a 6-bit Multiple Input Signature Register (MISR) with 3 input signals and feedback generated from bits 5 and 6.

If a MISR has been operating for N cycles since reset, we refer to the number N of captured cycles as the *capture window* of the MISR. For post-silicon bug localization, it is crucial that the capture window is long enough to include the point when a bug gets activated and an error is created. However, the capture window must also not be too long, since the design behavior over the entire window is analyzed using the formal tool (see Sects. 2.2–2.4). If N is too large, the formal tool will fail as the unrolled design grows too large to analyze. This is why tests with short error detection latencies are necessary, and QED in particular enables our E-QED approach. For most cases, QED ensures that capturing the last 1,000 cycles prior to error detection is sufficient to also capture the point of bug activation. In our experiments (Sect. 3), we set N to 1,024. Since post-silicon validation tests run longer than 1,024 cycles, each MISR will be reset to a known state periodically to maintain the capture window length (1,024 cycles in this case).

In choosing the MISR size, we select the number of bits K to be at least equal to the number of signal bits being captured (M). K should also be large enough such that the MISR has more states than the capture window length (i.e., K must be greater than $\log_2(N)$). For M signal bits over N cycles, a complete trace would require $M*N$ bits. Thus, if K is $M*b$ (can be viewed as b MISR bits per input signal), the parameter b decides the compression ratio N/b.

Based on empirical analysis (discussed in Sect. 3.2), we used $b = 8$ for all the blocks in the OpenSPARC T2 design except for inside the processor core, where we used $b = 4$. After selecting the MISR size, the choice of which bits to use as feedback can be made based on extensive existing work which optimizes for various good properties of MISRs (e.g. (Bardell et al. 1987)).

As mentioned above, we periodically reset each MISR to a known state (to mark the start of a capture window). However, this raises the possibility that the error might be captured right after the MISR is reset, in which case the number of cycles captured will be much less than our target N (and the point when the bug got activated may not be included in the capture window as a result). To avoid this situation, in our *E-QED Signature Block* (shown in Fig. 5), we use two MISRs (operating in parallel) for each signature block. The two MISRs are paired with a counter, and they are reset (the MISRs to a defined starting

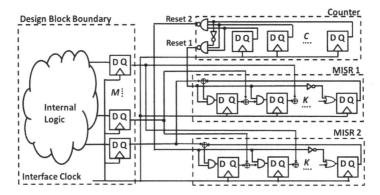

Fig. 5. The complete E-QED Signature Block design, with M interface signals generating a K-bit signature and the reset logic shown with the FFs of a C-bit counter (detailed counter implementation and MISR feedback not shown).

state and the counter to 0) when the design is powered on with a global reset. After that, the counter repeatedly counts to $2N$, alternately resetting one of the MISRs (to its starting state) every N cycles (waveforms in Fig. 6). This ensures that at the instant an error is detected, at least one of the MISRs has captured a signature covering at least N (and no more than $2N$) cycles. By setting N to a value greater than the expected error detection latency (e.g., 1,000 cycles for typical QED tests), we can ensure that with high likelihood, at least one signature covers the entire period between bug activation and error detection. The counter is sized to C, the ceiling of $\log_2(2N)$. The logic values in the MISRs and the counter can be scanned out when an error is detected by the QED test.

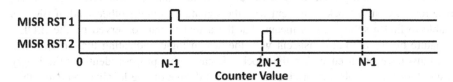

Fig. 6. Reset of MISR 1 and MISR 2, each resetting every $2N$ cycles. Note that at any instant, one MISR has captured data covering at least N cycles.

2.2   Bug Localization to a Design Block

We now explain how our design partitioning approach in Sect. 2.1 supports the first step in the electrical bug localization process: isolating an error detected by a post-silicon validation test to a specific design block. Following the detection of an error by QED tests, the logic values captured in the counters and MISRs are scanned out from each E-QED signature block. Formal analysis of the signature values is then performed using BMC (Clarke et al. 2001). BMC works by taking a model of the system (e.g., Verilog RTL), unrolling it some fixed number of time steps, and employing iterative time frame expansion to model sequential operation over this window of time. Then, automated tools such as Boolean Satisfiability solvers are used to check whether a set of constraints on the unrolled design is consistent. Constraints can be placed on any part of the unrolled design, commonly including the initial state, the inputs, and the final state.

Recall that when an error is detected, at least one of the two MISRs in each E-QED signature block has captured at least N cycles. Let T be the larger of the two capture windows (obtained from the counter in the E-QED signature block). For each design block B to be analyzed, we set up a BMC problem over T unrolled cycles (time frames), where T is the larger of the two windows captured by the E-QED Signature Blocks for the interfaces associated with B (i.e., signals that are either inputs or outputs for B).[2] In the BMC problem, we constrain the appropriate MISR (the one capturing T cycles) in each signature block to be equal to its scanned-out value in the final state following error detection, and also to be equal to its reset value at the beginning of the capture

---

[2] We assume that all interfaces for a design block are in the same clock domain and thus all have the same value of T. This assumption can easily be satisfied by modifying the design partitioning algorithm to continue its recursive descent if the current design block uses more than one clock domain.

window (*T* cycles before the final state). This corresponds to whether the design can satisfy the following property:

```
MISR reset = 1
##<T>
Input MISRs = <Input Signatures> && Output MISRs = <Output Signatures>
```

If the BMC tool is able to solve these constraints (note that, the initial state of the design block is not specified and so can be chosen arbitrarily by the BMC tool), we conclude that no bug occurred in this particular design block during the captured cycles. The solution produced by BMC also provides one possible error free *T*-cycle trace for the design block consistent with the signatures. On the other hand, if BMC is unable to find a solution, this means that the actual signals observed by the E-QED signature blocks are not consistent with the design logic, indicating that an electrical bug must have occurred within the block.[3] Because this process identifies the buggy design block, it can already produce a significant degree of bug localization. Note that, it is theoretically possible for all design blocks to pass the BMC test, either because (i) the bug triggered (and produced error) outside the capture window; or (ii) some valid trace shares the same set of signatures as the actual captured buggy trace (because of lossy compression by E-QED signature blocks); or (iii) the symbolic initial states (corresponding to internal flip-flops in the design block where E-QED signature blocks are not inserted) introduce too many degrees of freedom. However, in our simulations based on injected errors (see Sect. 3), using QED tests and $N = 1024$, we did not encounter any such scenario: we always found exactly one block that failed the BMC test. These points are discussed in more detail in (Singh et al. 2017).

We illustrate the analysis above through a simple example, shown in Fig. 7. The inputs and outputs are both compressed using the 6-bit MISR shown in Fig. 4. For the Input MISR, its inputs, signals 1, 2, and 3 (corresponding to Fig. 4), are B, A, and 0 respectively. For the Output MISR, signals 1, 2, and 3 are Z, Y, and X respectively. During cycle 1, the MISRs are at their initial state (000001) and the circuit inputs A and B are 1 and 0. The initial outputs at cycle 1 are the contents of F6, F7 and F8 (011), and they are compressed into the output MISR on the next clock edge. A transient electrical bug occurring somewhere in the circuit results in the output X having the incorrect value 1 at cycle 5. At cycle 6, the error is captured in the output MISR signature, making it 110010 (instead of the correct output MISR signature 110000). A BMC run for this design over the 6 cycles (based on the captured output MISR signature 110010 and the captured input MISR signature 111010) reports unsatisfiable, indicating that an error has occurred in the circuit[4].

---

[3] As an optimization, in this case, we also run the BMC analysis with the smaller value of *T* for the block. If this analysis is also inconsistent, it provides a much shorter window in which the bug occurred.

[4] E-QED uses symbolic initial values for FFs. To keep this example simple, we set the initial values of the FFs as shown in Fig. 7.

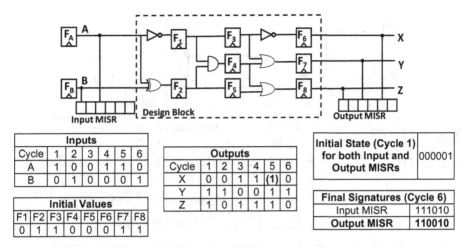

Inputs						
Cycle	1	2	3	4	5	6
A	1	0	0	1	1	0
B	0	1	0	0	0	1

Initial Values							
F1	F2	F3	F4	F5	F6	F7	F8
0	1	1	0	0	0	1	1

Outputs						
Cycle	1	2	3	4	5	6
X	0	0	1	1	(1)	0
Y	1	1	0	0	1	1
Z	1	0	1	1	1	0

Initial State (Cycle 1) for both Input and Output MISRs	000001

Final Signatures (Cycle 6)	
Input MISR	111010
Output MISR	110010

Fig. 7. A simple design block, a sequence of inputs and outputs, the initial values in the FFs and MISRs, the final signature captured by the Input MISR and the expected and captured (corrupted) signature in the Output MISR.

2.3 Single-Cycle FF Error Analysis with Bounded Model Checking

After the electrical bug has been localized to a single block (recall that in Sect. 2.1, we choose block sizes based on what fits within the BMC tool), E-QED performs further localization within the block by using an error model. In this paper, we use a *single-cycle FF error model*, which assumes that the electrical bug causes a transient error that affects one (arbitrary) flip–flop in the design during a single (arbitrary) cycle. Such an error model has been commonly used in the literature (e.g. (McLaughlin et al. 2009)) for electrical bugs. Our E-QED approach can be extended to include other models as discussed in (Singh et al. 2017). To demonstrate how error analysis can find a list of candidates, one of which corresponds to the FF and cycle that captured the single-cycle error due to an electrical bug, consider the earlier example of Fig. 7 presented again in Fig. 8.

For simplicity, let us first assume that we can directly observe all of the inputs and outputs on every cycle (we will consider the case where we have only the MISR signatures next). Recall that the expected output at cycle 5 is XYZ = 011, but we observe: XYZ = 111; i.e., the value of X is incorrect. In this simple example, there are only three FFs along the path to the X output; F_1, F_3 and F_6. According to our error model, an electrical bug could have caused an error in any one of them, and all three could have potentially caused the observed error at X; so there are three possible error scenarios. In the first, the error causes F_6 to capture a 0 instead of a 1 in cycle 4 (due to an electrical bug along the path from F_3 to F_6). In the second, the error causes F_3 to capture a 0 instead of a 1 in cycle 3 (due to an electrical bug along the path from F_1 to F_3). This error then propagates to F_6 and then to X. In the third, the error causes F_1 to capture a 0 instead of a 1 in cycle 2 (due to an electrical bug along the path from F_A to F_1). But notice that in this case, the input to F_4 in cycle 3 would then change to 0, and crucially, the input to F_7 in cycle 4 would also change to 0, and therefore output Y would be 0 in cycle 5. Since the error did not affect Y, this third scenario is not

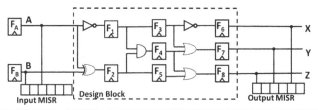

Inputs						
Cycle	1	2	3	4	5	6
A	1	0	0	1	1	0
B	0	1	0	0	0	1

Input Sequence (A B)	(Erroneous) Output Sequence (X Y Z)	
10, 01, 00, 10, 10, 01	011, 010, 101, 101, **(111)**, 010	Trace 1
10, 01, 00, 10, 10, 01	011, 010, **(111)**, 101, 011, 010	Trace 2

Trace	Single-Cycle FF Error Candidates
1	Cycle 3 FF3, Cycle 4 FF6
2	Cycle 1 FF4, Cycle 2 FF7

Outputs						
Cycle	1	2	3	4	5	6
X	0	0	1	1	(1)	0
Y	1	1	0	0	1	1
Z	1	0	1	1	1	0

Trace	Input MISR Signature Sequence (Cycle 1 to Cycle 6)
1	000001, 101000, 110100, 011010, 100101, 111010
2	000001, 101000, 110100, 011010, 100101, 111010

Trace	Output MISR Signature Sequence (Cycle 1 to Cycle 6)
1	000001, 001000, 001100, **100100, 110000, 110010**
2	000001, 001000, 001100, **101100, 110100, 110010**

Fig. 8. The results of single-cycle FF error analysis for the example from Fig. 7. Each candidate (cycle and FF pair) has the property that if an error occurs at the input of the candidate FF at the candidate cycle (captured in the following cycle), it would result in the captured Output MISR signature at cycle 6. Note that, the candidates that generate Trace 1 match the actual sequence but the candidates that generate Trace 2 are aliased candidates in that they correspond to a different output sequence but result in the same final output MISR signature.

consistent with the observed outputs, leaving only errors in FFs F_3 and F_6 as viable candidates. Importantly, observe that, given our error model, this is an exhaustive list of the potential sources of the error observed at X in cycle 5.

Now, consider the case where we do not have direct access to the input or output signals, but only to the compressed 6-bit MISR signatures. Figure 8 once again lists the captured Output MISR signatures in sequence ending at cycle 6. The two candidate FFs that were identified as possible sources of the error above both generate the captured erroneous output signature by recreating the exact output sequence (corresponding to Trace 1) that was captured due to the error. However, there are also other traces that can be created with different candidates that end with the same final signatures in the MISRs. We call these *aliased* FF candidates and traces. An example is shown as Trace 2 in Fig. 8. Aliasing occurs due to lossy compression in the MISRs: errors introduced into the output MISR at different times can result in the same final signature. Observe from the output sequences in Fig. 8 that for Trace 2, the erroneous candidate FFs cause an output error at Y in cycle 3. This error shifts through the output MISR (as shown in the MISR sequence for Trace 2) to still match the final captured output MISR signature. Since in practice we do not have the actual output signals, but only work with the MISR signatures, aliasing can increase the number of candidate FFs and traces returned by the formal analysis, reducing the resolution of the bug diagnosis. We discuss a technique for significantly improving (i.e., reducing and potentially eliminating) these aliased candidates in the next section.

We use BMC to systematically compute all candidate FFs consistent with the signature values for the interfaces of the buggy design block. To do this, we first modify the design (this modification is only to support the formal analysis at this step; the actual manufactured design is **not** affected). In the modified design, a two-input multiplexer is added before the data input of every FF in the design (Fig. 9(a)). The inputs to the multiplexer are the original data input to the FF and an inverted data input value to help inject an error as needed. By setting the select line of the multiplexer, an error is captured in the FF, matching the model for electrical bugs described earlier.

The select lines are all controlled by a decoder, allowing an error to be injected into a single FF on exactly one cycle as shown in Fig. 9(b). The decoder inputs are left unconstrained and provided to the BMC tool to control. The least significant output bit is not used, so an input combination of all 0s to the decoder generates an output of all 0s (on decoder output bits $1...R$), meaning no error is injected into the design on that cycle. An additional FF (Fig. 9(b)) is added to ensure that only one single FF in the design block is chosen to have an error for only one cycle during a single BMC run. This additional FF (in Fig. 9(b)) is initially reset to 0 (reset is asserted at the start of BMC) and is then set to 1 (and remains 1) once the decoder produces a non-zero value on output bits $1...R$. Once the value of this FF is 1, it forces the "Error Select" signals to all be 0 for all remaining cycles.

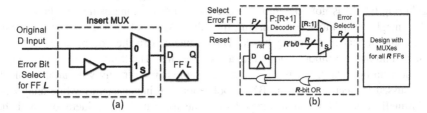

(a)   (b)

Fig. 9. (a) The inserted multiplexer allows an error to be injected into FF L. (b) control logic to inject an error during one cycle into the design when the BMC provides a FF index as input "Select Error FF" to the decoder. No error is injected when P is all 0s. The first time a non-zero input is provided, exactly one of the bits of the R "Error Select Lines" is set, causing the corresponding FF to capture an error during the next cycle.

Thus, the BMC, in its attempt to satisfy the error trace, can only inject an error into a single FF in the design, and only in one cycle.

As before, a BMC problem is set up with an unroll limit of T cycles, and constraints are added corresponding to the reset and final signature values. This time, however, the BMC tool can additionally control the decoder so that it can attempt to satisfy the input and output constraints by injecting a single error into a FF in the design block sometime during the T cycles. If BMC finds a solution, it provides a candidate FF which could (potentially) be the source of the erroneous bit flip (bug) that caused the error, together with a trace of length T of the input and output signals that is consistent with the

MISR signatures. Of course, it is possible that there is more than one way to achieve this. Therefore, the BMC tool is run repeatedly (each time with an added constraint to rule out all previously found FF candidates) until no more candidate FFs can be found.

2.4   Neighbor Consistency Checking

As explained in the example in Sect. 2.3 above, a consequence of using compressed signatures to constrain BMC is that aliasing can occur: different candidates for a single FF error can lead to the same output signature. Aliasing can be reduced by increasing the number of bits in the MISRs. However, in this section we introduce an alternative technique for reducing aliasing that does not require longer MISRs. This technique, which we call *Neighbor Consistency Checking (NCC)*, checks whether the trace generated by BMC corresponding to a particular candidate FF is consistent with the signatures captured in the MISRs at the interfaces of **other** blocks in the rest of the design. Any inconsistency can rule out the candidate FF as the one which captured the error, thereby improving diagnosis resolution.

The NCC strategy is as follows. Recall that for each FF candidate in the buggy block, the BMC tool also returns a full sequence of input and output values for T cycles (where T is the number of time frames analyzed). These values are applied as input or output constraints, as appropriate, to each of the neighboring blocks. The BMC tool is then used to check each neighboring block to see whether these newly-added constraints are consistent with the block's logic and the signatures on its interfaces. Note that, because the initial state of a neighboring block (initial states of FFs in the neighboring block) is not known, these checks cannot be done using simulation.

If a neighboring block is consistent, then the BMC tool returns a trace for inputs and outputs of that neighboring block. This sequence can then be recursively tested against additional neighbors, continuing across the chip. The limit would be reaching a clock domain boundary, where the interface is not shared directly with another block (as discussed in Sect. 2.1). If the BMC tool reports an inconsistency while analyzing the **immediate** neighbors of a buggy block, the trace under consideration (and the corresponding candidate FFs) can be eliminated. If the analysis has progressed further, then we backtrack to the previously analyzed neighbor and check to see if a different trace can be found that is consistent with its signatures. We continue the analysis in this way until either a fully consistent (across the whole design) set of traces is found or no such set of traces can be found in which case the candidate trace is eliminated.

Let us return to our running example. This time, we add a small neighboring block whose three inputs are driven by the three outputs (X, Y, Z) as shown in Fig. 10. The outputs of this block are captured using another 6-bit MISR (identical to Output MISR 1, capturing U, V, W instead of X, Y, Z respectively). Recall from Sect. 2.3 (Fig. 8) that there are 4 FF candidates and 2 traces consistent with the signature from Output MISR 1 at cycle 6. If we now use those two traces as the input constraints on the neighboring block, we can test if they are consistent with Output MISR 2. As seen in Fig. 10, the output sequence for aliased Trace 2 (in Fig. 8) results in a different final signature (at cycle 6) in Output MISR 2. This means it can be ruled out as a candidate, narrowing the candidate FFs to those from Trace 1 (in Fig. 8).

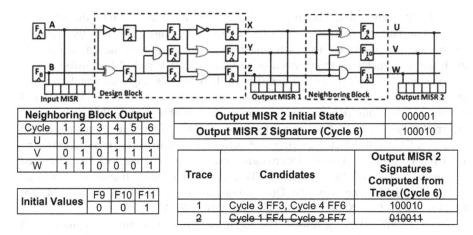

Neighboring Block Output					
Cycle	1	2	3	4	5	6
U	0	1	1	1	1	0
V	0	1	0	1	1	1
W	1	1	0	0	0	1

Initial Values	F9	F10	F11
	0	0	1

Output MISR 2 Initial State	000001
Output MISR 2 Signature (Cycle 6)	100010

Trace	Candidates	Output MISR 2 Signatures Computed from Trace (Cycle 6)
1	Cycle 3 FF3, Cycle 4 FF6	100010
2	~~Cycle 1 FF4, Cycle 2 FF7~~	~~010011~~

Fig. 10. Example circuit (continuing from Fig. 8) demonstrating NCC.

3   Results

In this section, we present simulation results demonstrating the effectiveness and practicality of E-QED. For our simulations, we use the OpenSPARC T2 SoC (Open-SPARC), an open-source version of the UltraSPARC T2 SoC (a 500-million-transistor SoC with 8 processor cores with private L1 caches supporting 64 hardware threads, 8 banks of shared L2 cache memory using a directory-based cache coherence protocol, 4 on-chip memory controllers, and a crossbar-based interconnect). We used the following design parameters for the E-QED Signature Blocks (Sect. 2.1): target capture window $N = 1,024$ cycles, counter size $C = 11$ bits; MISR size $K = M * b$, where $b = 8$ for all MISRs except those inside the processor core, where $b = 4$. A total of 118 E-QED Signature Blocks were used, adding 185,057 FFs, with an area impact of 2.5%.

In addition to an overview of results (in Sect. 3.1) with the parameters listed above, we also present an analysis of various trade-offs (in Sect. 3.2) that influence total area impact (by varying the parameter b in various signature blocks and also the signature block locations) and the granularity of electrical bug localization (in terms of candidate FFs as well as the number of candidate traces). The results in this section are for the single-cycle FF error model of electrical bugs (Sect. 2.3). We present an expanded set of results in (Singh et al. 2017).

3.1   Overview of Results

We randomly injected single-cycle FF errors in the OpenSPARC T2 design (with E-QED signature blocks inserted using our algorithm in Sect. 2.1) through RTL simulations (using Synopsys VCS). We ran 1,000,000 simulation runs, half with the SPLASH-2 Fast Fourier Transform (FFT) benchmark (Woo et al. 1995) and the other half with an in-house version of the Matrix Multiply (MMULT) benchmark. We ran 64-threaded versions of both benchmarks to ensure all threads on all processor cores of

OpenSPARC were active. The single-cycle FF errors were injected into: the processor core (all instances), crossbar, L2 cache controller (all instances) and the memory control unit (all instances). For each simulation run, we ran both the original benchmark and the benchmark transformed using QED (EDDI-V and PLC transforms with *Inst_min* and *Inst_max* set to 100, see (Lin et al. 2014)). During each simulation run, the injected error was allowed to propagate until it either vanished (i.e., was masked before impacting any program outputs) or resulted in observable failure (e.g., crash, incorrect outputs, exception or error detection by QED versions of the benchmarks). As soon as a QED test detected an error, we performed electrical bug localization using E-QED (Fig. 2). E-QED results for errors that cause hangs and deadlocks are discussed in (Singh et al. 2017) (they require QED tests with CFTSS-V transform (Lin et al. 2014)). For BMC, we used the Questa Formal tool (version 10.5) from Mentor Graphics on an Intel Xeon E5-2640 with 128 GB of RAM.

Table 1 summarizes the results. The bug trace size is the number of signals for all input and output interfaces captured in the signature blocks for that design block, multiplied by the length of the trace generated by the BMC tool. Recall that this length is determined by the counter value (T in Sect. 2.2) used to set up BMC analysis.

In Table 1, the "Number of Detected Errors" is the number of injected errors detected by the corresponding validation test (deadlocks and hangs caused by either test were not included). Note that, the vast majority of injected errors vanished (which is consistent with published literature (Cho et al. 2015; Sanda et al. 2008)). QED tests detected many more errors than the original tests (~ 4x more than original tests due to fine-grained QED checks, which is also consistent with published literature (Hong et al. 2010; Lin et al. 2014)).

Table 1. Electrical bug localization results for 1,000,000 single-cycle FF error simulations in the OpenSPARC T2 SoC.

	Original tests (no QED)	E-QED (after running QED versions of the original tests)
Number of detected errors	2,832	12,555
Error detection latency (cycles) [min, avg, max]	[2K, 976K, 8.8M]	[19, 168, 763]
Number of FF candidates [min, avg, max]	$9.3 * 10^5$ ($\sim$all flip-flops in the design)	[5, 18, 36]
Number of candidate bug traces [min, avg, max]	N/A	[1, 1, 1]
Number of bits in a bug trace [min, avg, max]	N/A	[109k, 483k, 1.74M]
BMC runtime (minutes)	N/A	[420, 526, 772]
Total E-QED signature block area impact	N/A	2.5%
Clock speed impact	N/A	~ 0%
Localization factor [min, avg, max]	1x	[25,837x, 51,674x, 186,025x]

Observation 1: E-QED automatically localized every error detected by the EDDI-V and PLC checks in the QED tests, and produced a list of 18 candidate FFs on average (out of a total of close to a million FF candidates) – a localization factor of over four orders of magnitude. These results were achieved with BMC runtime of 7–13 h. Very importantly, in every case, E-QED was able to report a unique trace with an average trace size of 483 kbits.

Table 2 shows the breakdown of results with respect to various design blocks of the OpenSPARC T2 SoC and various techniques presented in Sects. 2.2, 2.3 and 2.4.

Table 2. Electrical bug localization results (similar to Table 1) with a detailed breakdown.

		Design Block localization (Sect. 2.2)	Single-cycle FF error localization (Sect. 2.3)	NCC localization (Sect. 2.4)
Processor core (Core)	Number of traces [min, avg, max]	N/A	[1, 3, 8]	[1, 1, 1]
	Number of FF candidates [min, avg, max]	44,084	[11, 54, 91]	[8, 16, 29]
	Avg. localization factor	22x	17,224x	58,133x
	BMC runtime (minutes) [min, avg, max]	[62, 74, 77]	[303, 416, 478]	[49, 85, 114]
L2 cache (L2C)	Number of traces [min, avg, max]	N/A	[2, 14, 19]	[1, 1, 1]
	Number of FF candidates [min, avg, max]	31,675	[28, 77, 154]	[7, 19, 33]
	Avg. localization factor	29x	12,080x	48,954x
	BMC runtime (minutes) [min, avg, max]	[51, 58, 64]	[468,504,535]	[42,187,242]
Crossbar (CCX)	Number of traces [min, avg, max]	N/A	[2, 12, 17]	[1, 1, 1]
	Number of FF candidates [min, avg, max]	41,521	[31, 74, 130]	[5, 23, 36]
	Avg. localization factor	22x	12,569x	40,440x
	BMC runtime (minutes) [min, avg, max]	[53, 61, 72]	[379,421,450]	[54,142,205]
Memory control unit (MCU)	Number of traces [min, avg, max]	N/A	[3, 19, 24]	[1, 1, 1]
	Number of FF candidates [min, avg, max]	18,068	[21, 67, 143]	[5, 11, 18]
	Avg. localization factor	51x	13,882x	84,557x
	BMC runtime (minutes) [min, avg, max]	[35, 37, 41]	[315,387,428]	[78,163,251]
Total E-QED signature block area impact		2.5%		
Clock speed impact		~0%		

Observation 2: Signature-based electrical bug localization at the design block level (Sect. 2.2) achieves a localization factor of 22–51x. Single-Cycle FF Error Localization improves the localization factor by another 200–1,000x. Neighbor Consistency Checking (NCC) further improves localization factor by another 5–10x (for an average overall localization factor of 50,000x) and produces just a single candidate trace.

3.2   Design Trade-Offs

For the results in Tables 1 and 2, the total area impact of E-QED signature blocks is 2.5% (obtained through synthesis of the OpenSPARC T2 SoC using the Synopsys Design Compiler with the Synopsys EDK 32 nm library for standard cells and memories). In Fig. 11, we analyze the area impact vs. the granularity of electrical bug localization. We vary the MISR parameter b (recall from Sect. 2.1 that the MISR size is $b*M$, where M is number of signals captured by the signature) from 2 to 14.[5] For the entire design, this varies the total number of FFs in the signature blocks from 48,436 to 338,930. We use the number of candidate traces here for comparison since the primary aim of NCC is to reduce the number of candidate traces found (ideally to 1). Reducing the number of candidate traces also reduces the number of FF candidates.

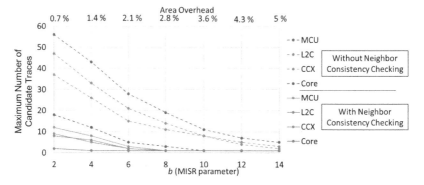

Fig. 11. The maximum number of unique candidate traces observed, before and after Neighbor Consistency Checking (NCC), for different area overheads, varied by changing the size of the MISRs in the signature blocks (MISR size is $b*M$, where M is number of signals captured by the signature).

Observation 3: Neighbor Consistency Checking is able to reduce the number of candidate traces to just 1 when the area impact is 2.8% (this corresponds to a design where MISRs are constructed with $b = 8$ for the entire design). The area impact can be further reduced to 2.5% (while still ensuring only a single candidate trace is found) by using a hybrid set of parameters (the parameters used in Sect. 3.1), namely $b = 4$ within the processor cores and $b = 8$ everywhere else.

---

[5] Note that in our simulation experiments, above (in Sect. 3.1), we used different fixed values of b for different parts of the design. In this section, we allow b to vary but all MISRs use the same value of b.

As discussed in Sect. 2.1, we made two enhancements to our approach to signature block insertion: signature blocks were added for signals around the L1 and L2 cache memory array banks (adding 16,640 FFs for all L2 banks and 3,840 FFs for all L1 banks), and signature blocks were also added at the instruction fetch units of the processors (adding 8,192 FFs across all 8 cores). As shown in Fig. 10, NCC analysis with these additional E-QED signature blocks significantly reduces the number of candidate traces for each value of b.

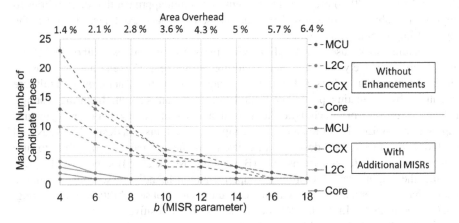

Fig. 12. The maximum number of unique candidate traces observed after performing NCC, with and without the addition of extra signature blocks around the L2 and L1 caches and processor instruction fetch unit, for different MISR parameters b (From Sect. 2.1, MISR size is $b*M$, where M is number of signals captured).

4 Related Work

Most existing publications on post-silicon bug localization (especially for electrical bugs) focus on ways to improve observability as well as techniques for localizing bugs inside the design (and combinations thereof). For example, many existing techniques capture system behavior (logic values of various signals during post-silicon validation runs) using trace buffers: small on-chip memories that record logic values of a selected set of internal signals (Abramovici 2006; Anis and Nicolici 2007; Ma et al. 2015, and many others). However, with typical long error detection latencies (millions or billions of clock cycles) trace buffers can quickly become ineffective. E-QED leverages the QED technique (Lin et al. 2014) to create post-silicon validation tests with sufficiently short error detection latencies. (Other techniques that create tests with short error detection latencies can also be used with E-QED). Even when tests with short error detection latencies are available, inserting trace buffers for fine-grained electrical bug localization still imposes unacceptably high area overheads. For example, as discussed in Sect. 1, saving a full trace of all inputs and outputs of the crossbar block alone of the OpenSPARC T2 SoC for just 1,000 cycles would require over 34 Mbits of data.

Recorders that store microarchitectural information in processor cores (e.g. (Park et al. 2009, 2010)) require much less area. But they are applicable for processor cores only (while uncore components and accelerators occupy large portions of complex SoCs). Moreover, approaches in (Park et al. 2009, 2010) require manual analysis. Techniques for compressing trace buffer contents generally provide limited benefits. Trace compression techniques such as state restoration (Ko and Nicolici 2009)) (or related approaches that use RTL simulation to restore signals from partial traces) cannot be used for electrical bugs (because electrical bugs are not present in the RTL description). (Vali and Nicolici 2016) presents a trace signal selection approach that directly tries to improve the ability to diagnose FF errors caused by electrical bugs. However, the reported improvements are modest.

Signature blocks used by E-QED overcome these limitations. Although MISRs have been extensively used for manufacturing testing (e.g. (Saxena and McCluskey 1997 and numerous others)), E-QED does not require the generation of fault-free signatures by simulating post-silicon validation tests (unlike manufacturing testing). Instead, it uses formal techniques to reason about consistency between signatures captured by E-QED signature blocks at the inputs and outputs of a design block, as well as the logic inside the design block itself. While it may be possible to use hardware-implemented assertions (e.g. (Bayazit and Malik 2005)) to enhance E-QED, finding the "right" set of (hardware implementation-friendly) assertions remains a major challenge for automatic assertion generation. Other observability techniques (e.g. (DeOrio et al. 2011; Li et al. 2010)) can result in false positives.

The problem of electrical bug localization is similar to the classical fault diagnosis problem in manufacturing testing (Abramovici et al. 1990). The use of Scan Design for Testability makes the problem somewhat simpler for manufacturing testing vs. post-silicon validation. Many publications have used formal techniques for these purposes (e.g. (Larrabee 1992; Mangassarian et al. 2007, and others)). Similarly (Zhu et al. 2011, 2014) use formal techniques, aided by backbones and a sliding window approach, for electrical bug localization. Techniques such as BackSpace and its derivatives (De Paula et al. 2008, 2011, 2012; Le et al. 2013; Sengupta et al. 2012) also use formal methods for bug localization purposes. However, as explained in Sect. 2, the biggest challenge is to create an automatic approach that scales for large SoCs without incurring large area impact. Some of the above techniques attempt to overcome the scalability challenge by "consistently" reproducing the buggy behavior over multiple runs; this can be very difficult for complex designs, as explained in (De Paula et al. 2011). Our E-QED approach overcomes these challenges: E-QED signature blocks enable scalability for large SoC designs with small area impact; short error detection latencies of QED tests enable us to apply BMC in conjunction with the E-QED signature blocks; and, E-QED analysis techniques in Sect. 2 enable us to perform bug localization despite lossy compression by E-QED signature blocks (with minimal reliance on consistent reproduction of buggy behaviors). Note that, the E-QED Neighbor Consistency Checking technique in Sect. 2.4 is different from consistency checking techniques presented in (Jones et al. 1996; Park et al. 2009, 2010, and others).

5 Conclusion

E-QED overcomes electrical bug localization challenges during post-silicon validation and debug. It automatically localizes electrical bugs and provides a comprehensive list of components that may contain the bugs (together with corresponding bug traces). It is an automatic approach which is highly effective and practical for large designs, as demonstrated on the OpenSPARC T2 SoC: automatic electrical bug localization in a few hours (9 h on average) that can narrow an electrical bug to a handful of candidate flip-flops (18 flip-flops on average for a design with ~ 1 Million flip-flops) and identify a single candidate bug trace. The area impact of E-QED is $\sim 2.5\%$. In contrast, it might take weeks (or even months) of mostly manual work (per bug) using traditional approaches. E-QED is made possible through a unique combination of Quick Error Detection techniques for bug detection, E-QED signature blocks that are automatically inserted during design, and new consistency checking techniques enabled by formal methods.

There are several future directions. E-QED can be extended to: 1. leverage already-existing Scan Design for Testability techniques to further enhance bug localization; 2. localize bugs in in analog and mixed-signal components of SoCs; 3. understand the interplay between scalability of BMC tools for bug localization vs. error detection latencies of QED tests vs. design of more sophisticated E-QED signature blocks; 4. diagnose defects that are detected using system-level testing during manufacture; 5. enable full system-level (consisting of many ICs chips) bug localization; and, 6. correct/fix bugs after manufacture.

References

Abramovici, M., Breuer, M.A., Friedman, A.D.: Digital Systems Testing and Testable Design. Computer Science Press, New York (1990)

Abramovici, M.: A reconfigurable design-for-debug infrastructure for SoCs. In: Proceedings of IEEE/ACM Design Automation Conference, pp. 7–12 (2006)

Anis, E., Nicolici, N.: On using lossless compression of debug data in embedded logic analysis. In: Proceedings of 2007 IEEE International Test Conference (ITC) (2007)

Bardell, P.H., McAnney, W.H., Savir, J.: Built-in test for VLSI: Pseudorandom Techniques. Wiley, New York (1987)

Bayazit, A.A., Malik, S.: Complementary use of runtime validation and model checking. In: Proceedings of ICCAD-2005, IEEE/ACM International Conference on Computer-Aided Design, pp. 1052–1059 (2005)

Cho, H., et al.: Understanding soft errors in uncore components. In: Proceedings of 2015 52nd ACM/EDAC/IEEE Design Automation Conference (DAC), pp. 1–6 (2015)

Clarke, E., Biere, A., Raimi, R., Zhu, Y.: Bounded model checking using satisfiability solving. Formal Methods Syst. Des. **19**(1), 7–34 (2001)

DeOrio, A., Khudia, D.S., Bertacco, V.: Post-silicon bug diagnosis with inconsistent executions. In: Proceedings of 2011 IEEE/ACM International Conference on Computer-Aided Design (ICCAD), San Jose, CA, pp. 755–761 (2011)

De Paula, F.M., et al.: BackSpace: formal analysis for post-silicon debug. In: Proceedings of International Conference on Formal Methods in Computer-Aided Design, pp. 1–10 (2008)

De Paula, F.M., et al.: TAB-BackSpace: unlimited-length trace buffers with zero additional on-chip overhead. In: Proceedings of IEEE/ACM Design Automation Conference (2011)

De Paula, F.M., Hu, A.J., Nahir, A.: nuTAB-BackSpace: rewriting to normalize non-determinism in post-silicon debug traces. In: Madhusudan, P., Seshia, S.A. (eds.) CAV 2012. LNCS, vol. 7358, pp. 513–531. Springer, Heidelberg (2012). doi:10.1007/978-3-642-31424-7_37

Dusanapudi, M., et al.: Debugging post-silicon fails in the IBM POWER8 bring-up lab. IBM J. Res. Dev. **59**(1), 1–10 (2015)

Foster, H.D.: Trends in functional verification: a 2014 industry study. In: Proceedings of IEEE/ACM Design Automation Conference, pp. 48–52 (2015)

Friedler, O., et al.: Effective post-silicon failure localization using dynamic program slicing. In: Proceedings of IEEE/ACM Design Automation Test in Europe, pp. 1–6 (2014)

Hong, T., et al.: QED: quick error detection tests for effective post-silicon validation. In: Proceedings of IEEE International, Test Conference, pp. 1–10 (2010)

Jones, R.B., Seger, C.-J.H., Dill, D.L.: Self-consistency checking. In: Srivas, M., Camilleri, A. (eds.) FMCAD 1996. LNCS, vol. 1166, pp. 159–171. Springer, Heidelberg (1996). doi:10.1007/BFb0031806

Ko, H.F., Nicolici, N.: Algorithms for state restoration and trace-signal selection for data acquisition in silicon debug. IEEE Trans. Comput.-Aided Des. Integr. Circ. Syst. **28**(2), 285–297 (2009)

Larrabee, T.: Test pattern generation using Boolean satisfiability. IEEE Trans. Comput.-Aided Des. Integr. Circ. Syst. **11**(1), 4–15 (1992)

Le, B., Sengupta, D., Veneris, A., Poulos, Z.: Accelerating post silicon debug of deep electrical faults. In: Proceedings of 2013 IEEE 19th International On-Line Testing Symposium (IOLTS), Chania, pp. 61–66 (2013)

Li, W., Forin, A., Seshia, S.A.: Scalable specification mining for verification and diagnosis. In: Proceedings of Design Automation Conference (DAC), pp. 755–760 (2010)

Lin, D., et al.: Effective post-silicon validation of system-on-chips using quick error detection. IEEE Trans. Comput. Aided Des. Integr. Circ. Syst. **33**(10), 1573–1590 (2014)

Lin, D., et al.: A structured approach to post-silicon validation and debug using symbolic quick error detection. In: Proceedings of 2015 IEEE International Test Conference (ITC), October 2015

Ma, S., et al.: Can't see the forest for the trees: state restoration's limitations in post-silicon trace signal selection. In: Proceedings of 2015 IEEE/ACM International Conference on Computer-Aided Design (ICCAD), pp. 1–8 (2015)

Mangassarian, H., et al.: A performance-driven QBF-based iterative logic array representation with applications to verification, debug and test. In: Proceedings of International Conference on Computer-Aided Design (ICCAD) (2007)

McLaughlin, R., Venkataraman, S., Lim, C.: Automated debug of speed path failures using functional tests. In: Proceedings of 2009 IEEE VLSI Test Symposium, pp. 91–96 (2009)

Mishra, P., Morad, R., Ziv, A., Ray, S.: Post-silicon validation in the SoC era: a tutorial introduction. In: IEEE Design & Test, April 2017

Nahir, A., et al.: Post-silicon validation of the IBM POWER8 processor. In: Proceedings of IEEE/ACM Design Automation Conference, pp. 1–6 (2014)

OpenSPARC: World's First Free 64-bit Microprocessor. http://www.opensparc.net

Park, S.-B., Hong, T., Mitra, S.: Post-silicon bug localization in processors using instruction footprint recording and analysis (IFRA). IEEE Trans. Comput. Aided Des. Integr. Circ. Syst. **28**(10), 1545–1558 (2009)

Park, S.-B., et al.: BLoG: post-silicon bug localization in processors using bug localization graph. In: Proceedings of IEEE/ACM Design Automation Conference, pp. 368–373 (2010)

Reick, K.: Post-silicon debug – DAC workshop on post-silicon debug: technologies, methodologies, and best-practices. In: Proceedings of IEEE/ACM Design Automation Conference (2012)

Sanda, P.N., et al.: Soft-error resilience of the IBM POWER6 processor. IBM J. Res. Dev. **52**(3), 275–284 (2008)

Saxena, N.R., McCluskey, E.J.: Parallel signature analysis design with bounds on aliasing. IEEE Trans. Comput. **46**(4), 425–438 (1997)

Sengupta, D., et al.: Lazy suspect-set computation: fault diagnosis for deep electrical bugs. In: Proceedings of the Great Lakes Symposium on VLSI. ACM (2012)

Singh, E., Barrett, C., Mitra, S.: E-QED: electrical bug localization during post-silicon validation enabled by quick error detection and formal methods, arXiv:1705.0125 [cs.OH] (2017)

Vali, A., Nicolici, N.: Bit-flip detection-driven selection of trace signals. In: Proceedings of 2016 21th IEEE European Test Symposium (ETS), Amsterdam, pp. 1–6 (2016)

Vermeulen, B., Goossens, K.: Debugging Systems-on-Chip: Communication-Centric and Abstraction Based Techniques. Springer, Heidelberg (2014)

Woo, S.C., et al.: The SPLASH-2 programs: characterization and methodological considerations. In: Proceedings of International Symposium on Computer Architecture (1995)

Zhu, C.S., Weissenbacher, G., Malik, S.: Post-silicon fault localisation using maximum satisfiability and backbones. In: Proceedings of IEEE/ACM Formal Methods Computer-Aided Design, pp. 63–66 (2011)

Zhu, C.S., Weissenbacher, G., Malik, S.: Silicon fault diagnosis using sequence interpolation with backbones. In: Proceedings of 2014 IEEE/ACM International Conference on Computer-Aided Design (ICCAD), San Jose, CA (2014)

SMTCoq: A Plug-In for Integrating SMT Solvers into Coq

Burak Ekici[1], Alain Mebsout[1], Cesare Tinelli[1(✉)],
Chantal Keller[2], Guy Katz[3], Andrew Reynolds[1],
and Clark Barrett[3]

[1] The University of Iowa, Iowa City, USA
`cesare-tinelli@uiowa.edu`
[2] LRI, Univ. Paris-Sud, CNRS,
Université Paris-Saclay, Orsay, France
[3] Stanford University, Stanford, USA

Abstract. This paper describes SMTCoq, a plug-in for the integration of external solvers into the Coq proof assistant. Based on a checker for generic first-order proof certificates fully implemented and proved correct in Coq, SMTCoq offers facilities to check answers from external SAT and SMT solvers and to increase Coq's automation using such solvers, all in a safe way. The current version supports proof certificates produced by the SAT solver ZChaff, for propositional logic, and the SMT solvers veriT and CVC4, for the quantifier-free fragment of the combined theory of fixed-size bit vectors, functional arrays with extensionality, linear integer arithmetic, and uninterpreted function symbols.

1 Introduction and Overview

SMTCoq is an open-source plugin for the Coq proof assistant that allows users to dispatch proof goals to external solvers for Boolean satisfiability (SAT) and Satisfiability Modulo Theories (SMT). It is aimed mostly at users doing verification in Coq, and is a sophisticated tool that lets them harness the power of these solvers in a trustworthy way. SMTCoq sends selected Coq (sub)goals to external solvers. When the solvers succeed in proving a goal they are required to return a proof witness, or *certificate*, which is then used by SMTCoq to effectively reconstruct a proof of the goal within Coq in a fully automated way.

SMTCoq's two main objectives are (1) to increase the level of automation in Coq by providing safe tactics for solving a class of Coq goals automatically by means of external solvers, and (2) to increase the confidence in SAT and SMT solvers in general by providing an independent and certified checker for

This work was partially sponsored by the Air Force Research Laboratory (AFRL) and the Defense Advanced Research Projects Agency (DARPA) under contracts FA8750-13-2-0241 and FA8750-15-C-0113. Any opinions, findings, and conclusions or recommendations expressed here are those of the authors and do not necessarily reflect the views of AFRL or DARPA.

R. Majumdar and V. Kunčak (Eds.): CAV 2017, Part II, LNCS 10427, pp. 126–133, 2017.
DOI: 10.1007/978-3-319-63390-9_7

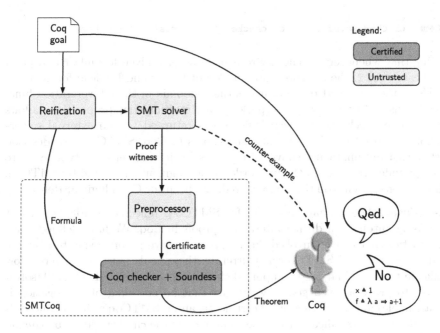

Fig. 1. SMTCoq's architecture

SAT/SMT proof witnesses. SMTCoq has been designed to be modular along two dimensions: supporting new theories, and incorporating new solvers. Correspondingly, its main checker is an extensible combination of several independent small checkers, and its kernel relies on a fairly general certificate format, close to the one proposed by Besson *et al.* [3].

An initial implementation of SMTCoq [11] incorporated only the ZChaff SAT solver [12] and the veriT SMT solver [5], supporting for the latter the combined theory of equality over uninterpreted symbols (EUF) and linear integer arithmetic (LIA). *We describe a recent major extension of the tool that incorporates the CVC4 SMT solver [1] and supports, additionally, the theory of arrays and the theory of fixed-sized bit vectors.*[1]

General Architecture. The heart of SMTCoq is a checker for SMT proof certificates, in SMTCoq's own format, that is implemented and proved correct inside Coq (see Fig. 1). The checker is written to be executable inside Coq. Its Coq signature is `checker : formula → certificate → bool` where `certificate` is the type of proof certificates and `formula` is a type representing SMT formulas. SMTCoq implements a *deep embedding* in Coq of SMT formulas via a function $\llbracket \_ \rrbracket$: `formula → bool` that interprets each SMT formula as a corresponding Boolean term in Coq. The correctness of the checker is guaranteed by a Coq lemma of the form:

---

[1] A version incorporating this extension is available at https://smtcoq.github.io/.

Lemma checker_sound : ∀ f c, checker f c = true → ⟦f⟧ = true

stating that whenever the checker returns `true` for a given formula `f` and proof certificate `c` for `f`, the interpretation in Coq of `f` is a valid Boolean formula.

Using the type `bool` of Booleans as the codomain of the interpretation function ⟦_⟧ instead of Coq's own type `Prop` of (intuitionistic) propositions allows SMTCoq to check the classical logic proofs returned by the external solvers without the need to add classical logic axioms to Coq. SMTCoq provides Coq tactics that automatically convert Coq goals (which are terms of type `Prop`) to `bool`, provided they fall in the first-order logic fragment supported by SMTCoq. This conversion relies on the `reflect` predicate from the Coq plugin SSReflect [6].

Use Cases. The primary use case for SMTCoq, reflected in Fig. 1, aims at increasing automation during interactive proofs in Coq. We have defined a few Coq tactics that can be invoked during an interactive proof session to dispatch goals to an external SMT solver. Currently, these goals must be universal formulas in the combination of supported theories listed earlier. If the SMT solver is able to prove a given goal (by proving that an encoding of its negation is unsatisfiable) and produce a proof certificate, and if SMTCoq's checker succeeds in validating the certificate, then the soundness of the checker yields, by *computational reflection*, a Coq proof of the original goal. In this use case, the trusted base consists only of Coq itself: if something else goes wrong (e.g., the SMT solver fails to prove the goal or SMTCoq's checker fails to validate the certificate), the tactic will fail. However, no unsoundness will be introduced into the system.

A secondary use of SMTCoq, not reflected in Fig. 1 for space constraints, is simply as a correct-by-construction independent checker for proof certificates generated by certifying SMT solvers like CVC4 and veriT. In this case, the trusted base is both Coq and SMTCoq's parser for input problems written in the SMT-LIB standard format [2]. The parser must be trusted to guarantee that SMTCoq is effectively verifying a proof of the actual problem that was sent to the external solver—as opposed to a proof of some other formula. However, this parser is fairly straightforward, and so its correctness is easy to verify by other means (e.g., [9]), although that is left for future work.

A crucial aspect of both use cases is the need to *preprocess* proof certificates before sending them to SMTCoq's checker because, for instance, they may not be in the format accepted by the checker—which is the case with CVC4-generated certificates. However, there is no need to trust this preprocessing stage or prove anything about it. If the preprocessor is buggy, SMTCoq will fail to validate the proof certificate and so no unsoundness will be introduced into Coq in this case either. This preprocessing stage allows us to easily extend SMTCoq with new solvers as long as their certificates can be faithfully converted to the SMT-Coq format. SMTCoq's current support for ZChaff, veriT and CVC4 is indeed provided through a preprocessor for each solver. Using a preprocessor is also beneficial for efficiency: proof certificates may be further compacted or simplified before or after their translation, thus potentially improving performance and scalability. We do all that in the extension described next.

2   The CVC4 Extension

For this work, we leveraged the proof-producing capabilities of the CVC4 SMT solver [7,10]. CVC4 uses the LFSC proof format [14] also used by its predecessor CVC3 [13]. LFSC is appealing because of its flexibility, generality, and ability to represent fine-grained proofs. To increase compactness and scalability, LFSC extends the Edinburgh Logical Framework (LF) [8] by allowing types with computational *side conditions*, explicit checks defined as programs in a simple functional programming language. Proof rules in LFSC are defined as operators whose type may include a side condition on the rule's premises. Proof certificates are then encoded as LFSC terms and proof checking reduces to type checking, with the twist that, when checking the application of a proof rule with a side condition, an LFSC checker must compute the actual parameters and then execute the side condition, rejecting the rule application as ill-typed if the side condition fails.

The validity of an LFSC proof certificate thus relies on the correctness of the proof rules it uses, including the correctness of their side conditions, if any. CVC4 defines its own proof rules, in LFSC modules called *signatures*, for the various theories it supports. These signatures contain definitions for variables, clauses, and rules for propositional reasoning; they also contain definitions for terms, formulas, and rules for theory reasoning. More specifically, the signatures include: resolution rules; CNF-conversion rules; rules for equality and congruence over uninterpreted functions; types, constructors and rules for the theory of arrays with extensionality; and types and constructors for the theory of fixed-size bit vectors together with *bit-blasting* rules for that theory. They currently do not include definitions and rules for integer arithmetic since CVC4 does not yet produce proof certificates for that theory.

To extend SMTCoq to CVC4 we have developed (in OCaml) a translator/pre-processor from the fragment of LFSC used by CVC4 to the certificate format used by SMTCoq. A proof certificate in SMTCoq is a sequence of proof steps, where each proof step is either an input clause or the application of a *rule* to a (potentially empty) list of *derived* clauses together with a resulting clause. Each clause in the certificate is identified by a unique number. Before our extension, SMTCoq already had a set of predefined rules whose checkers had been proven correct in Coq.

A major difference between the two proof formats lies in the presentation of the deduction rules. In SMTCoq, the small checkers deduce new formulas from already known formulas (possibly with the help of a certificate produced by an external solver), making the proof format inherently linear. In contrast, the LFSC proof format is more general, not only because of the side conditions but also because it allows natural deduction-style rules which enable the construction of nested proofs. As a consequence, in some cases, our LFSC-to-SMTCoq translator needs to replay parts of the side conditions in LFSC rule applications in order to produce the premises, conclusions, and certificates needed by the small checkers in SMTCoq. The translator also linearizes nested proofs, adding intermediate resolution steps to the generated SMTCoq certificate. The whole transformation is feasible because LFSC proofs are more *fine-grained* than SMTCoq proofs; hence, they contain all the information needed by the SMTCoq checker. In particular, and contrary to other proof formats such as the one used by the Z3 SMT solver [4], there is no need to perform proof reconstruction on LFSC proof certificates.

2.1   Bit Vectors and Functional Arrays

We instrumented CVC4 to produce LFSC proofs for the quantifier-free fragment of the SMT theories of *fixed-width bit vectors* and *functional arrays with extensionality* [7, 10]. We extended SMTCoq correspondingly to accept and check proof certificates in these new theories. This involved two major steps:

1. We extended the Coq `formula` type with the function symbols of the bit vector and array theories, and provided a suitable encoding of bit vectors and arrays in Coq.
2. We extended the SMTCoq proof format with proof rules for the new theories, extended SMTCoq's checker correspondingly to check certificates containing applications of those rules, and proved the extended checker correct in Coq.

Step 2 was achieved by adding new certified small checkers to the SMTCoq checker for the new theories. Thanks to SMTCoq's original design, neither the existing small checkers nor their proofs of correctness had to be changed as a result of this addition.

Since Coq itself has limited support for bit vectors and arrays as defined in the SMT-LIB standard supported by CVC4, for Step 1 we had to design and implement complete Coq libraries for them.[2] Our bit vector library represents bit vectors with a dependent type `bitvector` parameterized by a positive integer n, for the bit vector size. It provides a complete formalization in Coq of the SMT-LIB theory of bit vectors with the exception of the division operator which is currently unsupported. The type `bitvector` is implemented as a list of Booleans together with a proof that the list has length n.

Our array library is inspired by Coq's own `FMapList` library. We encode arrays, which in SMT-LIB are just maps from some index type to some value type, as finite maps from keys to values together with a default value for all key that are not explicitly listed in the finite map.[3] This library provides a type `farray` parameterized by the key type and the value type, and makes extensive use of Coq's type classes to express necessary properties of the parameter types. For instance, key types are required to be endowed with a *total ordering*. This ordering ensures that arrays have a unique finite map encoding, allowing array equality to be reduced to structural equality over finite maps.

---

[2] These libraries are publicly available as part of the SMTCoq distribution.

[3] While not faithful to the SMT-LIB semantics, this encoding is adequate for universal goals.

2.2   Coq Tactics and Proof Holes

SMTCoq brings the power of SAT and SMT solvers to Coq users by providing sound Coq tactics for solving subgoals with the aid of such solvers. Those tactics add an unprecedented level of automation to Coq, one that is still lacking in most interactive theorem provers. The original SMTCoq had two tactics, respectively for ZChaff and for veriT. We have developed two additional ones: cvc4, which relies only on CVC4, and smt, which takes advantage of CVC4 and veriT by falling back on the cvc4 and the verit tactics as needed. Coq users may resort to these tactics whenever they can express some of their goals in terms of the SMTCoq libraries for EUF, LIA, bit vectors and functional arrays. We believe the latter is possible in many instances where Coq is used for verification purposes, given the usefulness of those theories in modeling verification problems, and considering the generality and extensibility of our Coq libraries.

Currently, CVC4 is not fully proof-producing for the theories above. As a result, its proof certificates may contain *holes*; that is, they may refer to lemmas that, while proven valid by CVC4 internally, are assumed without proof in the proof certificate. These include linear arithmetic lemmas as well as lemmas corresponding to equivalence-preserving simplification steps performed by CVC4 on the input formula encoding the goal. To account for these *partial proofs*, we have extended SMTCoq's proof system with a new rule that permits holes in SMTCoq's proof certificates by introducing *cuts* in the proof. The result of this addition is that SMTCoq recognizes unproven lemmas and lifts them to Coq subgoals that are either further processed by the tactic that invoked SMTCoq or are returned to the user.

To illustrate this with a concrete example, Fig. 2a shows a Coq goal involving all the theories now supported by SMTCoq. The first call to the cvc4 tactic in the proof would be able to prove the goal fully automatically if it wasn't for the presence of a hole in the proof certificate produced by CVC4 due to

```
Goal
  ∀ (a b: farray Z Z) (v w x y: Z)
    (r s: bitvector 4)
    (f: Z → Z)
    (g: farray Z Z → Z)
    (h: bitvector 4 → Z),
    a[x ← v] = b ∧ a[y ← w] = b →
    r = s ∧ h r = v ∧ h s = y →
    v < x + 1 ∧ v > x - 1 →
    f (h r) = f (h s) ∨ g a = g b.
Proof.
  cvc4.
  verit.
Qed.
```

(a)

```
1 subgoal, subgoal 1 (ID 10899)
  a, b : farray Z Z
  v, w, x, y : Z
  r, s : bitvector 4
  f : Z → Z
  g : farray Z Z → Z
  h : bitvector 4 → Z
  ========================================
  (a[x ← v] = b ∧ a[y ← w] = b →
   r = s ∧ h r = v ∧ h s = y →
   v < x + 1 ∧ x - 1 < v →
   f (h r) = f (h s) ∨ g a = g b)
  ↔ (a[x ← v] = b ∧ a[y ← w] = b →
     r = s ∧ h r = v ∧ h s = y →
     1 ≤ v + -1 * x ∧ 0 ≤ v + -1 * x →
     f (h r) = f (h s) ∨ g a = g b)
```

(b)

Fig. 2. SMTCoq tactics. $a[i ← v]$ denotes array updates; Z is Coq's own integer type.

an unproven rewriting step. The corresponding *subgoal* returned by the tactic, shown in Fig. 2b, requires the user to prove the equivalence of a formula and its rewritten version (with the rewritten parts highlighted). This is a goal that the `verit` tactic, invoked by the user later in the proof, is able to solve in full by considering the symbols from the theory of arrays and bit vectors, which are not supported by veriT, as uninterpreted. The composite tactic `smt` can actually solve the original goal of Fig. 2a with no user assistance by combining the other tactics automatically.

3   Conclusion and Future Work

SMTCoq has been designed to be easily extensible to new theories and/or solvers. We presented one such extension with CVC4 as a background solver and the theories of bit vectors and arrays as new supported theories. We argued that the various tactics provided by SMTCoq greatly increase the automation capabilities of Coq. We have verified that by developing and testing several examples not discussed here but available in the SMTCoq distribution. In our extension, SMT solvers are not required to justify all their steps in a proof thanks to a cut mechanism that allows part of the proof to be discharged manually or by other means. We see this as a crucial feature in practice since it allows SMTCoq to take advantage of the automated reasoning power of SMT solvers, even when they do not provide full proof-generation support for all theories of interest to a particular problem.

We are working on extending the SMTCoq proof system to allow nested proofs, which will simplify the conversion from CVC4 proofs. In future work, we plan to continue expanding the scope of CVC4's proof generator to additional theories and proof steps, and extend SMTCoq correspondingly. Finally, we plan to add proof support in both tools for goals with quantifier alternations. This is a major extension that might require us to represent SMT formulas in Coq natively as propositions, instead of Boolean terms, and handle classical reasoning either by adding classical logic axioms to Coq or by restricting attention to decidable predicates.

References

1. Barrett, C., Conway, C.L., Deters, M., Hadarean, L., Jovanović, D., King, T., Reynolds, A., Tinelli, C.: CVC4. In: Gopalakrishnan, G., Qadeer, S. (eds.) CAV 2011. LNCS, vol. 6806, pp. 171–177. Springer, Heidelberg (2011). doi:10.1007/978-3-642-22110-1_14
2. Barrett, C., Stump, A., Tinelli, C.: The SMT-LIB standard: version 2.0. In: Proceedings of 8th International Workshop on Satisfiability Modulo Theories (SMT), p. 14 (2010)
3. Besson, F., Fontaine, P., Théry, L.: A flexible proof format for SMT: a proposal. In: Proceedings of 1st International Workshop on Proof eXchange for Theorem Proving (PxTP), pp. 15–26 (2011)

4. Böhme, S., Weber, T.: Fast LCF-style proof reconstruction for Z3. In: Kaufmann, M., Paulson, L.C. (eds.) ITP 2010. LNCS, vol. 6172, pp. 179–194. Springer, Heidelberg (2010). doi:10.1007/978-3-642-14052-5_14

5. Bouton, T., de Oliveira, D.C.B., Déharbe, D., Fontaine, P.: veriT: an open, trustable and efficient SMT-solver. In: Schmidt, R.A. (ed.) CADE 2009. LNCS (LNAI), vol. 5663, pp. 151–156. Springer, Heidelberg (2009). doi:10.1007/978-3-642-02959-2_12

6. Gonthier, G., Mahboubi, A.: An Introduction to small scale reflection in coq. J. Formaliz. Reason. **3**(2), 95–152 (2010)

7. Hadarean, L., Barrett, C., Reynolds, A., Tinelli, C., Deters, M.: Fine grained SMT proofs for the theory of fixed-width bit-vectors. In: Davis, M., Fehnker, A., McIver, A., Voronkov, A. (eds.) LPAR 2015. LNCS, vol. 9450, pp. 340–355. Springer, Heidelberg (2015). doi:10.1007/978-3-662-48899-7_24

8. Harper, R., Honsell, F., Plotkin, G.: A framework for defining logics. J. ACM **40**(1), 143–184 (1993)

9. Jourdan, J.-H., Pottier, F., Leroy, X.: Validating $LR(1)$ parsers. In: Seidl, H. (ed.) ESOP 2012. LNCS, vol. 7211, pp. 397–416. Springer, Heidelberg (2012). doi:10. 1007/978-3-642-28869-2_20

10. Katz, G., Barrett, C., Tinelli, C., Reynolds, A., Hadarean, L.: Lazy proofs for DPLL(T)-based SMT solvers. In: Proceedings of 16th International Conference on Formal Methods in Computer-Aided Design (FMCAD), pp. 93–100 (2016)

11. Keller, C.: A matter of trust: skeptical communication between coq and external provers. Ph.D. thesis, École Polytechnique, June 2013

12. Mahajan, Y., Fu, Z., Malik, S.: Zchaff 2004: an efficient SAT solver. In: Proceedings of 7th International Conference on Theory and Applications of Satisfiability Testing (SAT), pp. 360–375 (2004)

13. Reynolds, A., Hadarean, L., Tinelli, C., Ge, Y., Stump, A., Barrett, C.: Comparing proof systems for linear real arithmetic with LFSC. In: Proceedings of 8th International Workshop on Satisfiability Modulo Theories (SMT) (2010)

14. Stump, A., Oe, D., Reynolds, A., Hadarean, L., Tinelli, C.: SMT proof checking using a logical framework. Formal Methods Syst. Des. **41**(1), 91–118 (2013)

Foundations of Verification

Efficient Parallel Strategy Improvement
for Parity Games

John Fearnley[(⊠)]

Department of Computer Science, University of Liverpool, Liverpool, UK
john.fearnley@liv.ac.uk

Abstract. We study strategy improvement algorithms for solving parity games. While these algorithms are known to solve parity games using a very small number of iterations, experimental studies have found that a high step complexity causes them to perform poorly in practice. In this paper we seek to address this situation. Every iteration of the algorithm must compute a best response, and while the standard way of doing this uses the Bellman-Ford algorithm, we give experimental results that show that one-player strategy improvement significantly outperforms this technique in practice. We then study the best way to implement one-player strategy improvement, and we develop an efficient parallel algorithm for carrying out this task, by reducing the problem to computing prefix sums on a linked list. We report experimental results for these algorithms, and we find that a GPU implementation of this algorithm shows a significant speedup over single-core and multi-core CPU implementations.

1 Introduction

Parity Games. A parity game is a zero-sum game played on a finite graph between two players called Even and Odd. Each vertex of the graph is labelled with an integer *priority*. The players move a token around the graph to form an infinite path, and the winner is determined by the *parity* of the largest priority that is visited infinitely often: Even wins if and only if it is even.

Parity games have attracted much attention in the verification community, because they capture the expressive power of nested least and greatest fixpoint operators, as formalized in the modal μ-calculus and other fixpoint logics [11]. In particular, deciding the winner in parity games is polynomial-time equivalent to checking non-emptiness of non-deterministic parity tree automata, and to the modal μ-calculus model checking, two fundamental algorithmic problems in automata theory, logic, and verification [7,11,27].

Strategy Improvement. We study *strategy improvement* for solving parity games, which is a local search technique that iteratively improves the strategy of one of the two players until an optimal strategy is found. Much like

This work was supported by EPSRC grant EP/P020909/1 "Solving Parity Games in Theory and Practice."

© Springer International Publishing AG 2017
R. Majumdar and V. Kunčak (Eds.): CAV 2017, Part II, LNCS 10427, pp. 137–154, 2017.
DOI: 10.1007/978-3-319-63390-9_8

the simplex method for linear programming, and policy iteration algorithms for MDPs, strategy improvement algorithms can solve large parity games in a very small number of iterations in practice. The first strategy improvement algorithm devised specifically for parity games was given by Vöge and Jurdziński [30], and since then several further algorithms have been proposed [2,20,26].

Every strategy improvement algorithm uses a *switching rule* to decide how to proceed in each step. Theoretically, the best known switching rule is the *random-facet* rule, which provides a $2^{O(\sqrt{n \log n})}$ upper bound on the number of strategy improvement iterations [21]. However, this is a *single switch* rule, which only switches one edge in each iteration. In practice, we would expect an arbitrarily chosen initial strategy to differ from an optimal strategy by $O(n)$ edges, and so a single switch rule will necessarily cause the strategy improvement algorithm to take at least $O(n)$ iterations.

In this paper, we focus on the *greedy all-switches* switching rule, which switches every vertex that can be switched in each iteration. This rule has been found to perform very well in practice, and as our experimental results confirm, greedy all-switches strategy improvement can solve games with more than ten million vertices in under one-hundred iterations.

Practical Aspects of Strategy Improvement. Although strategy improvement can solve large games using only a handful of iterations, experimental work has found that it performs very poorly in practice. For example, Friedmann and Lange performed an experimental study [10] in which the all-switches variant of the Vöge-Jurdziński algorithm was compared with Jurdziński's *small-progress measures* algorithm [16] and Zielonka's *recursive* algorithm [32]. They found that, in some cases, the Vöge-Jurdziński algorithm takes longer than an hour to solve games with under one-hundred thousand vertices, whereas the recursive algorithm can scale to problems that are an order of magnitude larger.

The reason for this is that, although the algorithm uses a very small number of iterations, the cost of performing each step is very high. In particular, the Vöge-Jurdziński algorithm, which has served as the standard benchmark for strategy improvement algorithms, has a step complexity of $O(n^2)$, even in games with a small number of priorities[1].

In fact, there are existing algorithms that avoid this high step complexity. Björklund, Sandberg and Vorobyov present an algorithm whose step complexity is $O(n \cdot d)$, where d is the number of distinct priorities used in the game. While d can be as large as n in the case where every vertex has a distinct priority, in practice d is often a very small constant such as 2 or 4. Luttenberger observed [20] that a particularly simple algorithm is obtained if one combines the Björklund-Vorobyov strategy improvement algorithm for mean-payoff games [2], with the discrete valuation used by the Vöge-Jurdziński algorithm. This algorithm also has $O(n \cdot d)$ step complexity, and is the one that we will focus on in this paper.

---

[1] This is because the algorithm requires that every vertex has a distinct priority, and so comparing two valuations requires $O(n)$ time.

Our Contribution. Our goal in this paper is to show that all-switches strategy improvement can be used in practice to solve large parity games efficiently. As we have mentioned above, the number of iterations needed by the algorithm is usually tiny, and so our effort is dedicated towards improving the cost of computing each step. The main contributions of this paper are:

Best Response Computation. In each iteration of strategy improvement, the algorithm has a strategy for one of the two players, and must compute a best response strategy for the opponent. This can be a very expensive operation in practice. For the algorithm studied in this paper, this boils down to solving a solving a shortest paths problem that can contain negative weights. The natural approach is to apply the Bellman-Ford algorithm. However, the first contribution of this paper is to show that there is a better approach: best responses can be computed using a one-player version of strategy improvement.

The performance of strategy improvement algorithms on shortest paths problems was studied by Cochet-Terrasson and Gaubert [3]. While they showed that the number of improvement iterations is at most $O(|V||E|)$, their experimental results on random graphs found that strategy improvement was outperformed by the Bellman-Ford algorithm. They found that, while they typically both take the same number of iterations, one iteration of strategy improvement is more expensive than one iteration of Bellman-Ford.

Nevertheless, for the case of parity games, we give experimental evidence to show that one-player strategy improvement outperforms the Bellman-Ford algorithm when computing best responses. The experimental data shows that part, but not all, of this improvement is due to the fact that we can initialize the algorithm with the best response from the previous iteration.

A Parallel Algorithm for Strategy Improvement. Once we fix the decision to use one-player strategy improvement to compute best responses, we turn our attention towards the best way to implement this. In recent years, hardware manufacturers have made little progress in speeding up single-core CPU workloads, but progress continues to be made by adding more cores to CPUs. Moreover, GPUs continue to be made more powerful, and the rise of general purpose computing on GPUs has found many prominent applications, for example, in the training of deep neural networks. For this reason, we argue that good parallel implementations are required if we are to use an algorithm in practice.

The second contribution of this paper is to develop an efficient parallel algorithm for computing a strategy improvement iteration. The decision to use one-player strategy improvement to compute best responses means that the only non-trivial task is to compute the *valuation* of a pair of strategies. We show that this task can be reduced to an instance of *list ranking*, a well-studied problem that requires us to compute the prefix-sum of a linked list. The first work optimal parallel algorithm for list ranking was given by Cole and Vishkin [4]. However, their algorithm is complex and difficult to implement in practice. Helman and Jájá give a simpler randomized algorithm that is work efficient with high probability [12], and in particular it has been shown to work well on modern GPU hardware [31]. We give a modification of the Helman-Jájá algorithm that can be used to compute a valuation in a parity game.

Experimental Results. We have produced CPU and GPU implementations of the aforementioned parallel algorithm. The third contribution of this paper is to provide experimental results. We use the recently developed benchmark suite of Keiren [18], which unlike previous benchmarks from PGSolver [10], contains large parity games derived from real verification tasks.

We find that our implementation scales to parity games with tens of millions of vertices, and that the limiting factor is memory rather than run time. We also compare a single-threaded sequential CPU implementation with a multi-threaded parallel CPU implementation and a GPU implementation, which both use list ranking algorithm described above. While the parallel CPU implementation fails to deliver a meaningful speedup, the GPU implementation delivers an average speedup of 10.37.

Related Work. Strategy improvement originated from the *policy iteration* algorithms that are used to solve Markov decision processes [25], and can be seen as a generalisation of this method to the two-player setting. The method was first proposed by Hoffman and Karp in order to solve two-player concurrent stochastic games [1]. It was then adapted by Condon [5] to solve simple-stochastic games, and by Puri to solve discounted games [24]. Parity games can be reduced in polynomial time to discounted and simple-stochastic games [15,33], so both of these algorithms could, in principle, be used to solve parity games, but both reductions require the use of large rational numbers, which makes doing so impractical.

The greedy all-switches switching rule has received much attention in the past. Its good experimental performance inspired research into whether it always terminates after polynomially many iterations. However, Friedmann showed that this was not the case [9], by giving an example upon which the algorithm takes exponential time. Recently, it has even been shown that deciding whether a given strategy is visited by the algorithm is actually a PSPACE-complete problem [8].

There has been much previous work on solving parity games in parallel. Most of the work so far has focused on the small progress measures algorithm [16], because it can be, implemented in parallel in an straightforward way. In the first paper on this topic, van de Pol and Weber presented a multi-core implementation of the algorithm [28], and Huth et al. presented further optimizations to that algorithm [14]. Two papers have reported on implementations on the parallel Cell processor used by the Playstation 3 [17,29].

For parallel implementations of strategy improvement, there are two relevant papers. Hoffman and Luttenberger have given GPU implementations of various algorithms for solving parity games [13]. In particular, they implemented the strategy improvement algorithm that is studied in this paper, but they used the Bellman-Ford algorithm to compute best responses. Meyer and Luttenberger have reported on a GPU implementation of the Björklund-Vorobyov strategy improvement algorithm for mean-payoff games [22].

2   Preliminaries

Parity Games. A parity game is played between two players called Even and Odd. Formally, it is a tuple $\mathcal{G} = (V, V_{\text{Even}}, V_{\text{Odd}}, E, \text{pri})$, where (V, E) is a directed graph. The sets V_{Even} and V_{Odd} partition V into the vertices belonging to player Even, and the vertices belonging to player Odd, respectively. The *priority* function pri $: V \rightarrow \mathbb{N}$ assigns a positive natural number to each vertex. We define $D_{\mathcal{G}} = \{p \in \mathbb{N} : \text{pri}(v) = p \text{ for some } v \in V\}$ to be the set of priorities that are used in $\mathcal{G}$. We make the standard assumption that there are no terminal vertices, which means that every vertex is required to have at least one outgoing edge.

A *positional strategy* for player Even is a function that picks one outgoing edge for each Even vertex. More formally, a positional strategy for Even is a function $\sigma : V_{\text{Even}} \rightarrow V$ such that, for each $v \in V_{\text{Even}}$ we have that $(v, \sigma(v)) \in E$. Positional strategies for player Odd are defined analogously. We use Σ_{Even} and Σ_{Odd} to denote the set of positional strategies for players Even and Odd, respectively. Every strategy that we consider in this paper will be positional, so from now on, we shall refer to positional strategies as strategies.

A *play* of the game is an infinite path through the game. More precisely, a play is a sequence $v_0, v_1, \ldots$ such that for all $i \in \mathbb{N}$ we have $v_i \in V$ and $(v_i, v_{i+1}) \in E$. Given a pair of strategies $\sigma \in \Sigma_{\text{Even}}$ and $\tau \in \Sigma_{\text{Odd}}$, and a starting vertex v_0, there is a unique play that occurs when the game starts at v_0 and both players follow their respective strategies. So, we define $\text{Play}(v_0, \sigma, \tau) = v_0, v_1, \ldots$, where for each $i \in \mathbb{N}$ we have $v_{i+1} = \sigma(v_i)$ if $v_i \in V_{\text{Even}}$, and $v_{i+1} = \tau(v_i)$ if $v_i \in V_{\text{Odd}}$.

Given a play $\pi = v_0, v_1, \ldots$ we define:

$$\text{MaxIo}(\pi) = \max\{p : \exists \text{ infinitely many } i \in \mathbb{N} \text{ s.t. } \text{pri}(v_i) = p\},$$

to be the largest priority that occurs *infinitely often* along π. The winner is determined by the parity of this priority: a play π is *winning* for player Even if $\text{MaxIo}(\pi)$ is even, and we say that π is winning for Odd if $\text{MaxIo}(\pi)$ is odd.

A strategy $\sigma \in \Sigma_{\text{Even}}$ is a *winning strategy* for a vertex $v \in V$ if, for every (not necessarily positional) strategy $\tau \in \Sigma_{\text{Odd}}$, we have that $\text{Play}(v, \sigma, \tau)$ is winning for player Even. Likewise, a strategy $\tau \in \Sigma_{\text{Odd}}$ is a winning strategy for v if, for every (not necessarily positional) strategy $\sigma \in \Sigma_{\text{Even}}$, we have that $\text{Play}(v, \sigma, \tau)$ is winning for player Odd. The following fundamental theorem states that parity games are *positionally determined*.

Theorem 1 [6,23]. *The set of vertices V can be partitioned into winning sets $(W_{\text{Even}}, W_{\text{Odd}})$, where Even has a positional winning strategy for all $v \in W_{\text{Even}}$, and Odd has a positional winning strategy for all $v \in W_{\text{Odd}}$.*

The computational problem that we are interested in is, given a parity game, to determine the partition $(W_{\text{Even}}, W_{\text{Odd}})$.

3   Strategy Improvement

In this section, we describe the strategy improvement algorithm that we will consider in this paper. The algorithm, originally studied by Luttenberger [20], is a combination of the Björklund-Vorobyov strategy improvement algorithm for mean-payoff games [2], with the discrete strategy improvement valuation of Vöge and Jurdziński [30]. Strategy improvement algorithms select one of the two players to be the strategy improver. In this description, and throughout the rest of the paper, we will select player Even to take this role.

A Modified Game. At the start of the algorithm, we modify the game by introducing a new *sink* vertex s into the graph. For each vertex v of the Even player, we add a new edge from v to the sink. The idea is that, at any point player Even can choose to take the edge to s and terminate the game. The owner and priority of s are irrelevant, since the game stops once s is reached.

Admissible Strategies. A strategy $\sigma \in \Sigma_{\text{Even}}$ is said to be *admissible* if player Odd cannot force and odd cycle when playing against σ. More formally, σ is admissible if, for every strategy $\tau \in \Sigma_{\text{Odd}}$ we have that $\text{Play}(v, \sigma, \tau)$ either arrives at the sink s, or that $\text{MaxIo}(\text{Play}(v, \sigma, \tau))$ is even. The strategy improvement algorithm will only consider admissible strategies for player Even.

Valuations. The core of a strategy improvement algorithm is a *valuation*, which measures how good a given pair of strategies is from a given starting vertex. For our algorithm, the valuation will count how many times each priority occurs on a given path, so formally a valuation will be a function of the form $D_{\mathcal{G}} \to \mathbb{Z}$, and we define $\text{Vals}_{\mathcal{G}}$ to be the set of all functions of this form.

Given an admissible strategy $\sigma \in \Sigma_{\text{Even}}$ for Even, a strategy $\tau \in \Sigma_{\text{Odd}}$ for Odd, and a vertex $v \in V$, we define the *valuation function* $\text{Val}^{\sigma,\tau}(v) : V \to \text{Vals}_{\mathcal{G}} \cup \{\top\}$ as follows.

- If $\pi = \text{Play}(v, \sigma, \tau)$ is infinite, then we define $\text{Val}^{\sigma,\tau}(v) = \top$
- If $\pi = \text{Play}(v, \sigma, \tau)$ is finite, then it must end at the sink s. The valuation of v will count the number of times that each priority appears along π. Formally, if $\pi = v_0, v_1, \ldots, v_k, s$, then for each $p \in D_V$ we define a valuation $L \in \text{Vals}_{\mathcal{G}}$ as follows:
$$L(p) = \left| \{i \in \mathbb{N} : \text{pri}(v_i) = p\} \right|.$$

We set $\text{Val}^{\sigma,\tau}(v) = L$.

Observe that, since σ is an admissible strategy, $\text{Val}^{\sigma,\tau}(v) = \top$ implies that $\text{Play}(v, \sigma, \tau)$ is winning for Even.

Next, we introduce the operator $\sqsubseteq$ which will be used to compare valuations. We define $L \sqsubseteq \top$ for every $L \in \text{Vals}_{\mathcal{G}}$. When we compare two valuations, however, the procedure is more involved. Let $L_1, L_2 \in \text{Vals}_g$ be two valuations. If $L_1 = L_2$ then $L_1 \sqsubseteq L_2$ and $L_2 \sqsubseteq L_1$. Otherwise, we define $\text{Maxdiff}(L_1, L_2)$ to be the largest priority p such that $L_1(p) \neq L_2(p)$. Then, we have that $L_1 \sqsubseteq L_2$ if and only if one of the following is true: either $p = \text{Maxdiff}(L_1, L_2)$ is even and $L_1(p) < L_2(p)$, or $p = \text{Maxdiff}(L_1, L_2)$ is odd and $L_1(p) > L_2(p)$.

Best Responses. Given an admissible strategy $\sigma \in \Sigma_{\text{Even}}$, a *best response* is a strategy $\tau \in \Sigma_{\text{Odd}}$ that minimizes the valuation of each vertex. More formally, we define, $\text{br}(\sigma) \in \Sigma_{\text{Odd}}$ to be a strategy with the property that $\text{Val}^{\sigma, \text{br}(\sigma)}(v) \sqsubseteq \text{Val}^{\sigma, \tau}(v)$ for every strategy $\tau \in \Sigma_{\text{Odd}}$ and every vertex v. If there is more than one such strategy, then we pick one arbitrarily. Although it is not immediately clear, it can be shown that there is a single strategy $\tau \in \Sigma_{\text{Odd}}$ that simultaneously minimises the valuation of all vertices. Strategy improvement only ever considers an admissible strategy σ played against its best response, so we define the shorthand $\text{Val}^{\sigma} = \text{Val}^{\sigma, \text{br}(\sigma)}$.

The Algorithm. We are now ready to describe the strategy improvement algorithm. It begins by selecting the following *initial strategy* for Even. We define $\sigma_{\text{init}} \in \Sigma_{\text{Even}}$ so that $\sigma_{\text{init}}(v) = s$ for all $v \in V_{\text{Even}}$. Note that there is no guarantee that σ_{init} is admissible, because there may be a cycle with odd parity that contains only vertices belonging to player Odd. So, a preprocessing step must be performed to eliminate this possibility. One simple preprocessing procedure is to determine the set of vertices from which Odd can avoid visiting an Even vertex, and to insert enough dummy Even vertices into this subgame to prevent Odd from forming a cycle. As it happens, none of the games considered in our experimental study require preprocessing, so this is not a major issue in practice.

In each iteration, strategy improvement has a strategy for the improver. The first step is to compute the set of *switchable* edges for this strategy. An edge (v, u) is switchable in strategy σ if $u \neq \sigma(v)$ and $\text{Val}^{\sigma}(\sigma(v)) \sqsubset \text{Val}^{\sigma}(u)$. We define $\mathcal{S}^{\sigma}$ to be the set of edges that are switchable in σ.

The algorithm selects a non-empty subset of the switchable edges and *switches* them. We say that a set of edges $S \subseteq E$ is a *switchable set* if, for every pair of edges $(v, u), (v', u') \in S$, we have has $v \neq v'$, that is, S does not contain two outgoing edges for a single vertex. If S is a switchable set and σ is a strategy, then we can *switch* S in σ to create the new strategy $\sigma[S]$ where, for every vertex v:

$$\sigma[S](v) = \begin{cases} u & (v, u) \in S, \\ \sigma(v) & \text{otherwise.} \end{cases}$$

The key property of strategy improvement is that, if $S \subseteq \mathcal{S}^{\sigma}$ is a switchable set that contains only switchable edges, then we have that $\sigma[S]$ is better than σ in the $\sqsubseteq$ ordering. Formally, this means that $\text{Val}^{\sigma}(v) \sqsubseteq \text{Val}^{\sigma[S]}(v)$ for all vertices v, and there exists at least one vertex for which we have $\text{Val}^{\sigma}(v) \sqsubset \text{Val}^{\sigma[S]}(v)$.

The strict improvement property mentioned above implies that the algorithm cannot visit the same strategy twice, so it must eventually terminate. The algorithm can only terminate once it has reached a strategy with no switchable edges. We can use this strategy to determine winning sets for both players. That is, if σ^* is a strategy with no switchable edges, then we can prove that: $W_{\text{Even}} = \{v \in V : \text{Val}^{\sigma^*}(v) = \top\}$, and $W_{\text{Odd}} = \{v \in V : \text{Val}^{\sigma^*}(v) \neq \top\}$.

Luttenberger has given a direct proof that the algorithm is correct [20]. Actually, a simple proof of correctness can be obtained directly from the correctness of Björklund-Vorobyov (BV) algorithm. It is not difficult to show that if we turn the parity game into a mean-payoff game using the standard reduction, and then apply the BV algorithm to the resulting mean-payoff game, then the BV algorithm and this algorithm will pass through exactly the same sequence of strategies.

Theorem 2. *The following statements are true.*

- *For every strategy $\sigma \in \Sigma_{Even}$ there is at least one best response $\tau \in \Sigma_{Odd}$.*
- *Let σ be a strategy, and let $S \subseteq \mathcal{S}^\sigma$ be a switchable set that contains only switchable edges. We have $\mathrm{Val}^\sigma(v) \sqsubseteq \mathrm{Val}^{\sigma[S]}(v)$ for all vertices v, and there exists at least one vertex for which we have $\mathrm{Val}^\sigma(v) \sqsubset \mathrm{Val}^{\sigma[S]}(v)$.*
- *Let σ be a strategy that has no switchable edges. We have $W_{Even} = \{v \in V : \mathrm{Val}^\sigma(v) = \top\}$, and $W_{Odd} = \{v \in V : \mathrm{Val}^\sigma(v) \neq \top\}$.*

Switching Rules. Strategy improvement always switches a subset of switchable edges, but we have not discussed *which* set should be chosen. This decision is delegated to a *switching rule*, which for each strategy picks a subset of the switchable edges. In this paper we will focus on the *greedy all-switches* rule, which always switches every vertex that has a switchable edge. If a vertex has more than one switchable edge, then it picks an edge (v, u) that maximizes $\mathrm{Val}^\sigma(u)$ under the $\sqsubseteq$ ordering (arbitrarily if there is more than one such edge).

4   Computing Best Responses

To implement strategy improvement, we need a method for computing best responses. Since we only consider admissible strategies for Even, we know that Odd cannot create a cycle with odd parity, and so computing a best response simply requires us to find a shortest-path from each vertex to the sink, where path lengths are compared using the $\sqsubseteq$ ordering. Any vertex that has no path to the sink is winning for Even. The obvious way to do this is to apply a shortest-paths algorithm. Note that odd priorities correspond to negative edges weights, so a general algorithm, such as the Bellman-Ford algorithm, must be applied.

One-Player Strategy Improvement. In this paper, we propose an alternative: we will use one-player strategy improvement equipped with the greedy-all switches rule. We say that an edge (v, u) is *Odd-switchable* if $v \in V_{Odd}$ and $\mathrm{Val}^{\sigma,\tau}(\sigma(v)) \sqsupset \mathrm{Val}^{\sigma,\tau}(u)$. To find a best response against a fixed admissible strategy $\sigma \in \Sigma_{Even}$, the algorithm starts with an arbitrary Odd strategy $\tau \in \Sigma_{Odd}$, and repeatedly switches Odd-switchable edges until it arrives at an Odd strategy in which there are no Odd-switchable edges.

It is not difficult to see that if τ has no Odd-switchable edges when played against σ, then it is a best response against σ, because a strategy with no Odd-switchable edges satisfies the Bellman optimality equations for shortest paths.

One-player strategy improvement algorithms for solving shortest paths problems were studied by Cochet-Terrasson and Gaubert [3]. In particular, they proved that the all-switches variant of the algorithm always terminates after at most $O(|V||E|)$ steps. Hence, we have the following lemma.

Lemma 3. *Let σ be an admissible strategy. One-player strategy improvement will find a best-response against σ after at most $O(|V||E|)$ iterations.*

The Algorithm. We can now formally state the algorithm that we will study. Given a strategy $\sigma \in \Sigma_{\text{Even}}$, let $\text{All}_{\text{Even}}(\sigma)$ be the function that implements the greedy all-switches switching rule as described earlier. Moreover, given a pair of strategies $\sigma \in \Sigma_{\text{Even}}$ and $\tau \in \Sigma_{\text{Odd}}$, let $\text{All}_{\text{Odd}}(\sigma, \tau)$ be a set S of Odd-switchable edges (v, u) such that there is no edge $(v, w) \in E$ with $\text{Val}^{\sigma, \tau}(u) \sqsupset \text{Val}^{\sigma, \tau}(w)$, and such that each vertex has at most one outgoing edge in S.

Algorithm 1. The strategy improvement algorithm

Initialize $\sigma := \sigma_{\text{init}}$ and set τ to be an arbitrary strategy.
repeat
    repeat
        Compute $\text{Val}^{\sigma, \tau}(v)$ for every vertex v.
        Set $\tau := \tau[S_{\text{Odd}}]$ where $S_{\text{Odd}} = \text{All}_{\text{Odd}}(\sigma, \tau)$.
    until $S_{\text{Odd}} = \emptyset$
    Set $\sigma := \sigma[S_{\text{Even}}]$ where $S_{\text{Even}} = \text{All}_{\text{Even}}(\sigma)$.
until $S_{\text{Even}} = \emptyset$

The inner loop computes best responses using one-player strategy improvement, while the outer loop performs the two-player strategy improvement algorithm. Note, in particular, that after switching edges in σ, the first Odd strategy considered by the inner loop is the best response to the previous strategy.

5   Parallel Computation of Valuations

Most operations used by strategy improvement can naturally be carried out in parallel. In particular, if we have already computed a valuation, then deciding whether an edge is switchable at a particular vertex v, and finding the switchable edge that has the highest valuation at v, are both local properties that only depend on the outgoing edges of v. So these operations can trivially be carried out in parallel. This leaves the task of computing a valuation as the only task that does not have an obvious parallel algorithm.

In this section, we give an efficient parallel algorithm for computing a valuation. Given two strategies $\sigma \in \Sigma_{\text{Even}}$ and $\tau \in \Sigma_{\text{Odd}}$ in a game $\mathcal{G}$, we show how computing $\text{Val}^{\sigma, \tau}(v)$ can be parallelized in a work efficient manner. There is an obvious sequential algorithm for this task that runs in time $O(|V| \cdot |D_{\mathcal{G}}|)$ which works backwards on the tree defined by σ and τ and counts how many times each priority appears on each path to s. Every vertex not found by this procedure must have valuation $\top$.

List Ranking. The idea of our algorithm is to convert the problem of computing a valuation, into the well-known problem of computing prefix-sums on a linked list, which is known as *list ranking*. We will then adapt the efficient parallel algorithms that have been developed for this problem.

Given a sequence of integers $x_0, x_1, x_2, \ldots, x_k$, and a binary associative operator $\oplus$, the *prefix-sum* problem requires us to compute a sequence of integers $y_0, y_1, y_2, \ldots, y_k$ such that $y_i = x_1 \oplus x_2 \oplus \cdots \oplus x_{i-1}$. If the input sequence is given as an array, then efficient parallel algorithms have long been known [19].

If the input sequence is presented as a linked-list, then the problem is called the list ranking problem, and is more challenging. The first work optimal parallel algorithm for list ranking was given by Cole and Vishkin [4]. However, their algorithm is complex and difficult to implement in practice. Helman and Jájá give a simpler randomized algorithm that is work efficient with high probability [12].

Theorem 4 [12]. *There is a randomized algorithm for list ranking that, with high probability, runs in time $O(n/p)$ whenever $n > p^2 \ln n$, where n denotes the length of the list, and p denotes the number of processors.*

We now give a brief overview of the algorithm, as we will later modify it slightly. A full and detailed description can be found in [12]. The algorithm works randomly choosing $s = \frac{n}{p \log n}$ elements of the list to be *splitters*. Intuitively, each splitter defines a sublist that begins at the splitter, and ends at the next splitter that is encountered in the list (or the end of the list). These sublists are divided among the processors, and are ranked using the standard sequential algorithm. Once this has been completed, we can create a *reduced* list, in which each element is a splitter, and the value of each element is the prefix-sum of the corresponding sublist. The reduced list is ranked by a single processor, again using the standard sequential algorithm. Finally, we can complete the list ranking task as follows: if an element e of the list has rank x_r in its sublist, and the splitter at the start of sublist has rank x_s in the reduced list, then the rank of e is $x_s \oplus x_r$.

Pseudoforests and Euler Tours. We now show how the problem of computing a valuation can be reduced to list ranking. Let $\mathcal{G}^{\sigma,\tau} = (V, V_{\text{Even}}, V_{\text{Odd}}, E^{\sigma,\tau},$ pri) be the game $\mathcal{G}$ in which every edge not used by σ and τ is deleted. Since each vertex has exactly one outgoing edge in this game, the partition of V into V_{Even} and V_{Odd} are irrelevant, and we shall treat $\mathcal{G}^{\sigma,\tau}$ has a graph labelled by priorities.

First, we observe that $\mathcal{G}^{\sigma,\tau}$ is a *directed pseudoforest*. The set of vertices whose valuation is not $\top$ form a directed tree rooted at s. For these vertices, our task is to count the number of times each priority occurs on each path to the sink, and hence compute a valuation. Each other vertex is part of a *directed pseudotree*, which is a directed tree in which the root also has exactly one outgoing edge that leads back into the tree. Since we deal only with admissible strategies, every vertex in a pseudotree has valuation $\top$.

A standard technique for reducing problems on trees to list ranking is the *Euler tour* technique. We will describe this technique for the tree rooted at s,

Fig. 1. Converting a tree into a linked list using the Euler tour technique. Left: the original tree. Right: the corresponding linked list.

and show that it can be used to compute a valuation. We will also use the same technique for the other pseudo-trees in the graph, but since this portion of the algorithm is not standard, we defer the description until later.

In order to compute a valuation for every vertex v in the tree rooted at s, we need to count the number of times that a given priority p occurs on the path from v to the root. We create a linked list as follows. First we replace each directed edge (v, u) with two edges (v, u) and (u, v). Then we select an Euler tour of this modified graph that starts and ends at the root. We use this tour to create a linked list, in which each element of the list an edge of the original tree, and the successors of each element are determined by the Euler tour. The value associated with each element e is defined as follows:

- If $e = (u, v)$, then the value of e is 1 if $\mathrm{pri}(v) = p$, and 0 otherwise.
- If $e = (v, u)$, then the value of e is -1 if $\mathrm{pri}(v) = p$, and 0 otherwise.

If we then compute a list ranking on this list using $+$ as the operator $\oplus$, then the ranking of (v, u) gives the number of times p appears on the path from v to the sink. Obviously, to compute a valuation we must do the above procedure in parallel for each priority in the game.

Formal Reduction to List Ranking. We now give a formal definition of the technique that we just described. Recall that $E^{\sigma,\tau}$ gives the edges chosen by σ and τ. We define

$$\overleftarrow{E}^{\sigma,\tau} = \{(u, v) : (v, u) \in E^{\sigma,\tau}\},$$

to be the set of reversed edges. We call each edge in $E^{\sigma,\tau}$ an *up* edge, since it moves towards the root, and correspondingly we call each edge in $\overleftarrow{E}^{\sigma,\tau}$ a *down* edge. The set of elements in our linked list will be $L = E^{\sigma,\tau} \cup \overleftarrow{E}^{\sigma,\tau}$.

Next we define the successor function $\mathrm{succ} : L \to L \cup \{\epsilon\}$, which gives the structure of the list, and where ϵ is used to denote the end of the list. To do this, we take an arbitrary Euler tour of the tree, and define $\succ$ to be the function that follows this tour. Figure 1 gives an example of this construction.

In our overview, we described how to use list ranking to compute the number of times a given priority p appears on the path to the sink. In our formal definition, we will in fact compute a full valuation with a single call to a list ranking algorithm. To achieve this, we define the weight function $w : L \rightarrow \text{Vals}_{\mathcal{G}}$ as follows. For each priority $p \in D_{\mathcal{G}}$, we first define two valuations $A_p, A_{-p} \in \text{Vals}_{\mathcal{G}}$ so that, for every $q \in D_{\mathcal{G}}$:

$$A_p(q) = \begin{cases} 1 & \text{if } q = p, \\ 0 & \text{otherwise.} \end{cases} \qquad A_{-p}(q) = \begin{cases} -1 & \text{if } q = p, \\ 0 & \text{otherwise.} \end{cases}$$

Then, for every list element $e = (u, v) \in L$: if e is an up edge then we set $w(e) = A_{-\,\text{pri}(u)}$, and if e is a down edge then we set $w(e) = A_{\text{pri}(v)}$. Moreover, we define the binary operator $\oplus$ as follows. Given two valuations A_1, A_2, we define $A_1 \oplus A_2 = A_3$ where for every priority $p \in D_{\mathcal{G}}$ we have $A_3(p) = A_1(p) + A_2(p)$.

Modifications to the Helman-Jájá Algorithm. We must also handle the vertices that lie in pseudotrees. Our reduction turns every pseudotree into a pair of cycles. The Helman-Jájá algorithm can be adapted to deal with these, by ensuring that if a cycle is found in the reduced list, then all vertices on it are given a valuation of $\top$. Moreover, some vertices may not be part of a reduced list, because they may be part of a small pseudotree, and none of random splitters were in that pseudotree. Since the Helman-Jájá always picks the head of the list to be a splitter (in our case this would be an edge leaving the sink at the start of the Euler tour), every vertex in the tree rooted at s is in the reduced list. So any vertex not part of a reduced list can be assigned valuation $\top$.

Constructing the List Ranking Instance in Parallel. Since at least one of σ and τ will change between every iteration, we must construct a new list ranking instance in every iteration of our algorithm. Thus, in order to have a true parallel algorithm, we must be able to carry out the reduction in parallel as well.

We start by describing a sequential algorithm for the task. Each vertex in the tree maintains two pointers start_v and end_v. Initially, start_v points to the down edge of v, and end_v points to the up edge of v. Then, in an arbitrary order, we process each vertex v, and do the following:

1. Determine the parent of v in the tree, and call it u.
2. Connect the list element pointed to by start_u to the element pointed to by start_v.
3. Set $\text{start}_u = \text{end}_v$.

Once this has been completed, we then join the list element pointed to by start_v to the list element pointed to by end_v, for all vertices v.

Intuitively, this algorithm builds the tour of each subtree incrementally. The second step adds the tour of the subtree starting at v to the linked list associated with u. The third step ensures that any further children of u will place their tours after the tour of the subtree of v.

For example, let us consider the tree and corresponding Euler tour given in Fig. 1, and let us focus on the vertex b. Initially, start_v points to (a, b), while

end_v points to (b, a), which are the down and up edges of b, respectively. Let us suppose that d is processed before e. When d is processed, (a, b) is connected to (b, d) and $start_v$ is updated to point to (d, b). Subsequently, when e is processed (d, b) is connected to (b, e), and $start_v$ is updated to point to (e, b). Then, in the final step of the algorithm (b, d) is connected to (d, b) and (e, b) is connected to (b, a). So, the linked list corresponding to the subtree of b (shown on the right in Fig. 1) is created. Note that if e was processed before d, then a different linked list would be created, which would correspond to a different Euler tour of the tree. From the point of view of the algorithm, it is not relevant which Euler tour is used to construct the linked list.

In theory, this algorithm can be carried out in parallel in $O(n/p)$ time and $O(np)$ space by having each processor maintain its own copy of the pointers $start_v$ and end_v, and then after the algorithm has been completed, merging the p different sublists that were created.

In practice, the space blow up can be avoided by using atomic exchange operations, which are available on both CPU and GPU platforms. More precisely, we can use an atomic exchange instruction to set $start_u = end_v$, while copying the previous value of $start_u$ to a temporary variable, and then connect the list element that was pointed to by $start_u$ to $start_v$.

6   Experimental Results

Experimental Setup. Our experimental study uses four implementations.

- GPU-LR: a GPU implementation that uses the list-ranking algorithm to compute valuations. The GPU is responsible for ranking the sublists, while ranking the reduced list is carried sequentially on the CPU.
- CPU-Seq: a single-threaded implementation that uses the natural sequential algorithm for computing valuations.
- CPU-LR: a multi-threaded CPU implementation that uses the list-ranking algorithm to compute valuations. The sublists are ranked in parallel, while the reduced lists is ranked by a single thread.
- Bellman-Ford: a single-threaded CPU implementation that uses the Bellman-Ford algorithm to compute best responses.

All implementations are in C++, and the GPU portions are implemented using NVIDIA CUDA. The code is publicly available[2]. We also compare our results to PGSolver's recursive algorithm, with all of PGSolver's heuristics disabled in order to deliver a fair comparison. We chose the recursive algorithm because it was found to be the most competitive in the previous experimental study of Friedmann and Lange [10].

For our benchmark games we utilise the suite that was recently developed by Keiren [18]. This provides a wide array of parity games that have been used throughout the literature for model-checking and equivalence checking. Since there are over 1000 games, we have selected a subset of those games to use here,

---

[2] https://github.com/jfearnley/parallel-si.

Table 1. The games that we consider in our experimental study. The table displays the number of vertices, player Even vertices, player Odd vertices, edges, and distinct priorities.

Game	Property	Vertices	Σ_{Even}	Σ_{Odd}	Edges	Pris
CABP/Par 2	branching-bisim	167 k	79 k	88 k	434 k	2
CABP/Par 1	weak-bisim	147 k	122 k	25 k	501 k	2
ABP(BW)/CABP	weak-bisim	157 k	129 k	27 k	523 k	2
Elevator	fairness	862 k	503 k	359 k	1.4 m	3
Election	eventually-stable	2.3 m	343 k	2.0 m	7.9 m	4
Lift (Incorrect)	liveness	2.0 m	999 k	999 k	9.8 m	4
SWP/SWP 1	strong-bisim	3.8 m	1.5 m	2.2 m	11.5 m	2
SWP	io-read-write	6.8 m	4.2 m	2.6 m	15.8 m	3
CABP	io-receive	7.0 m	5.2 m	1.8 m	24.9 m	2
ABP/Onebit	weak-bisim	8.3 m	7.2 m	1.1 m	31.3 m	2
Hesselink/Hesselink	weak-bisim	29.9 m	22.9 m	7.0 m	78.8 m	2
SWP/SWP 2	branching-bisim	37.6 m	20.1 m	17.6 m	120.8 m	2
ABP(BW)/Onebit	weak-bisim	35.4 m	30.6 m	4.8 m	134.9 m	2
SWP/SWP 3	weak-bisim	32.9 m	29.0 m	3.9 m	167.5 m	2

and these are shown in Table 1. In particular, we have chosen a set of games that span a variety of sizes, and that cover a variety of tasks from verification. We found that strategy improvement solves many of the games in the suite in a very small number of iterations, so the results that we present here focus on the games upon which strategy improvement takes the largest number of iterations. The vast majority of the games in the suite have between 2 and 4 priorities, and the ones that do not are artificially constructed (eg. random games), so we believe that our sample is representative of real world verification tasks.

The test machine has an Intel Core i7-4770K CPU, clocked at 3.50 GHz (3.90 GHz boost), with 4 physical cores, and 16 GB of RAM. The GPU is an NVIDIA GeForce GTX 780, which has 2304 CUDA cores clocked at 1.05 GHz and 3 GB of RAM. At the time of purchase in 2013, the CPU cost £248.20 and the GPU cost £444.94. Since the CPU has 8 logical cores with hyper-threading enabled, we use 8 threads in our CPU multi-threaded implementations. When benchmarking for time, we ran each instance three times, and the reported results are the average of the three. We implemented a time limit of 10 min. We only report the amount of time needed to solve the game, discarding the time taken to parse the game.

Best Response Algorithms. Our first experiment is to determine which method for computing best responses is faster in practice. In this experiment we compare the single-core sequential implementation of one-player strategy improvement (SI) against a single-core sequential implementation of the Bellman-Ford algorithm.

Table 2. Experimental results comparing the algorithm used to compute a best response. The algorithms are (1) SI: one-player strategy improvement (2) SI (Reset): one-player strategy improvement starting from an arbitrary strategy (3) Bellman-Ford. For each algorithm we report the total time and the total number of iterations used by the best response algorithm.

Game	Maj.		SI		SI-Reset		Bellman-Ford	
	Edges	Iter	Time (s)	Iter	Time (s)	Iter	Time (s)	Iter
CABP/Par 2	434 k	8	0.33	53	0.49	100	1.65	161
CABP/Par 1	501 k	12	0.22	47	0.36	93	2.41	235
ABP(BW)/CABP	523 k	9	0.15	28	0.29	65	1.38	128
Elevator	1.4 m	33	13.18	231	17.88	364	216.36	2238
Election	7.9 m	77	41.43	364	57.66	585	157.5	842
Lift (Incorrect)	9.8 m	16	9.09	69	22.82	215	42.47	242
SWP/SWP 1	11.5 m	8	14.69	58	22.25	93	71.21	152
SWP	15.8 m	11	25.44	82	31.69	104	109.31	148
CABP	24.9 m	11	5.45	11	5.54	11	59.37	108
ABP/Onebit	31.3 m	20	34.15	57	93.78	234	494.97	604

As we have mentioned, our one-player strategy improvement starts with the optimal strategy against the previous strategy of the improver. To quantify the benefit of this, we have also include results for a version of the one-player strategy improvement algorithm that, at the start of each best response computation, resets to the initial arbitrarily chosen strategy. We refer to this as SI-Reset.

The results are displayed in Table 2. We only report results for games that Bellman-Ford solved within the 10 min time limit. We report the total number of *major iterations*, which are the iterations in which the improver's strategy is switched. The number of major iterations does not depend on the algorithm used to compute best responses. For each algorithm we report the overall time and the total number of iterations used computing best responses.

Before discussing the results in detail we should first note that these results paint a very positive picture for strategy improvement. All games were solved in at most 77 major iterations, with most being solved with significantly fewer major iterations. The number of iterations used on the Election instance was the most that we saw over any instance in our study, including those that we do not report here. This clearly shows that strategy improvement can scale to very large instances.

Moving on to the choice of best response algorithm, the most striking feature is that Bellman-Ford is on average 8.43 times slower than one-player strategy improvement (min 3.80, max 16.42). Some of this difference can be explained by the fact that Bellman-Ford is on average 1.72 times slower per iteration than one-player strategy improvement (min 1.11, max 2.38), which may be due to implementation inefficiencies. But most of the difference is due to the fact that Bellman-Ford uses on average 5.30 times more iterations than one-player strategy improvement (min 1.80, max 10.60).

The results with SI-Reset show that only some of this difference can be attributed to reusing the previous best response as SI-Reset uses on average 2.05 times more iterations than SI (min 1.00, max 4.11). Overall we found that SI used an average of 5.49 iterations to compute each best response (min 1.0 max 9.9), which again indicates that this method can scale to very large games.

Table 3. Experimental results comparing the running time of (1) GPU-LR: list ranking on the GPU (2) CPU-Seq: a sequential CPU implementation (3) CPU-LR: list ranking on a 4-core CPU (4) PGSolver: the recursive algorithm from PGSolver. † indicates a failure due to lack of memory.

Game	Edges	Iterations		Time (s)			
		Maj.	Tot.	GPU-LR	CPU-Seq	CPU-LR	PGSolver
CABP/Par 2	434.0 k	8	53	0.05	0.33	0.48	0.48
CABP/Par 1	501.0 k	12	47	0.04	0.22	0.4	0.46
ABP(BW)/CABP	523.0 k	9	28	0.03	0.15	0.25	0.49
Elevator	1.4 m	33	231	0.87	13.18	11.56	13.23
Election	7.9 m	77	364	4.37	41.43	58.43	30.45
Lift (Incorrect)	9.8 m	16	69	0.79	9.09	9.35	40.76
SWP/SWP 1	11.5 m	8	58	1.06	14.69	14.57	28.83
SWP	15.8 m	11	82	2.71	25.44	35.01	201.83
CABP	24.9 m	11	11	0.39	5.45	5.33	134.33
ABP/Onebit	31.3 m	20	57	2.28	34.15	32.46	—†
Hesselink/Hesselink	78.8 m	28	142	—†	318.98	299.43	—†
SWP/SWP 2	120.8 m	10	99	—†	282.17	265.62	—†
ABP(BW)/Onebit	134.9 m	20	57	—†	147.03	142.35	—†
SWP/SWP 3	167.5 m	10	71	—†	142.96	168.45	—†

Parallel Implementations. Our second set of experimental results concerns our parallel implementation of strategy improvement when best responses are computed by one-player strategy improvement. The results are displayed in Table 3.

The first thing to note is that the parallel algorithm does not deliver good performance when implemented on a CPU. On average the multi-threaded CPU list ranking algorithm was 1.25 times *slower* than the single-threaded sequential algorithm (min 0.88, max 1.77). This can be partially explained by the fact that the total amount of work done by the parallel algorithm is at least twice the amount of work performed by the sequential algorithm, since turning the strategy into a linked list doubles the number of vertices.

On the other hand, the GPU implementation delivers a significant speedup. To give a fair comparison between the GPU implementation and the CPU implementations, we compute the ratio between the time taken by GPU-LR, and the minimum of the times taken by CPU-Seq and CPU-LR. Using this metric we find that the average speedup is 10.37 (min 5.54, max 14.21). The average speedup increases to 12.17 if we discard instances with fewer than 1 million edges, where setup overhead makes the GPU algorithm less competitive.

The downside to the GPU implementation is that games with more than about 32 million edges are too large to fit within the 3 GB of memory on our test GPU. Obviously, there is a cost trade off between the extra speed delivered by a GPU and the cost of purchasing a GPU with enough memory. At the time of writing, relatively cheap consumer graphics cards can be bought with up to 8 GB of memory, while expensive dedicated compute cards are available with up to 24 GB of memory.

Finally, we compare our results to PGSolver's recursive algorithm. Here, to have a fair comparison, we should compare with the sequential CPU algorithm, as both algorithms are single-threaded. Unfortunately PGSolver ran out of memory for the very large games in our test set, but for the smaller games it can be seen that CPU-Seq is always competitive, and in many cases significantly faster than PGSolver.

References

1. Hoffman, A.J., Karp, R.M.: On nonterminating stochastic games. Manag. Sci. **12**(5), 359–370 (1966)
2. Björklund, H., Vorobyov, S.G.: A combinatorial strongly subexponential strategy improvement algorithm for mean payoff games. Discret. Appl. Math. **155**(2), 210–229 (2007)
3. Cochet-Terrasson, J., Gaubert, S.: Policy iteration algorithm for shortest path problems. Technical report (2000)
4. Cole, R., Vishkin, U.: Faster optimal parallel prefix sums and list ranking. Inf. Comput. **81**(3), 334–352 (1989)
5. Condon, A.: On algorithms for simple stochastic games. In: Proceedings of a DIMACS Workshop, Advances in Computational Complexity Theory, pp. 51–72 (1990)
6. Emerson, E.A., Jutla, C.S.: Tree automata, mu-calculus and determinacy. In: Proceedings of FOCS, pp. 368–377 (1991)
7. Emerson, E.A., Jutla, C.S., Sistla, A.P.: On model-checking for fragments of μ-calculus. In: Courcoubetis, C. (ed.) CAV 1993. LNCS, vol. 697, pp. 385–396. Springer, Heidelberg (1993). doi:10.1007/3-540-56922-7_32
8. Fearnley, J., Savani, R.: The complexity of all-switches strategy improvement. In: Proceedings of SODA, pp. 130–139 (2016)
9. Friedmann, O.: An exponential lower bound for the latest deterministic strategy iteration algorithms. Log. Methods Comput. Sci. **7**(3) (2011). Paper 23. http://www.lmcs-online.org/ojs/viewarticle.php?id=779&layout=abstract
10. Friedmann, O., Lange, M.: Solving parity games in practice. In: Liu, Z., Ravn, A.P. (eds.) ATVA 2009. LNCS, vol. 5799, pp. 182–196. Springer, Heidelberg (2009). doi:10.1007/978-3-642-04761-9_15
11. Grädel, E., Thomas, W., Wilke, T. (eds.): Automata Logics, and Infinite Games: A Guide to Current Research. LNCS, vol. 2500. Springer, Heidelberg (2002)
12. Helman, D.R., JáJá, J.: Designing practical efficient algorithms for symmetric multiprocessors. In: Goodrich, M.T., McGeoch, C.C. (eds.) ALENEX 1999. LNCS, vol. 1619, pp. 37–56. Springer, Heidelberg (1999). doi:10.1007/3-540-48518-X_3

13. Hoffmann, P., Luttenberger, M.: Solving parity games on the GPU. In: Hung, D., Ogawa, M. (eds.) ATVA 2013. LNCS, vol. 8172, pp. 455–459. Springer, Cham (2013). doi:10.1007/978-3-319-02444-8_34

14. Huth, M., Kuo, J.H.-P., Piterman, N.: Concurrent small progress measures. In: Eder, K., Lourenço, J., Shehory, O. (eds.) HVC 2011. LNCS, vol. 7261, pp. 130–144. Springer, Heidelberg (2012). doi:10.1007/978-3-642-34188-5_13

15. Jurdziński, M.: Deciding the winner in parity games is in UP ∩ co-UP. Inf. Process. Lett. **68**(3), 119–124 (1998)

16. Jurdziński, M.: Small progress measures for solving parity games. In: Reichel, H., Tison, S. (eds.) STACS 2000. LNCS, vol. 1770, pp. 290–301. Springer, Heidelberg (2000). doi:10.1007/3-540-46541-3_24

17. Kandziora, J.: Playing parity games on the playstation 3. In: Twente Student Conference (2009)

18. Keiren, J.J.A.: Benchmarks for parity games. In: Dastani, M., Sirjani, M. (eds.) FSEN 2015. LNCS, vol. 9392, pp. 127–142. Springer, Cham (2015). doi:10.1007/978-3-319-24644-4_9

19. Ladner, R.E., Fischer, M.J.: Parallel prefix computation. J. ACM **27**(4), 831–838 (1980)

20. Luttenberger, M.: Strategy iteration using non-deterministic strategies for solving parity games. CoRR, abs/0806.2923 (2008)

21. Matoušek, J., Sharir, M., Welzl, E.: A subexponential bound for linear programming. Algorithmica **16**(4–5), 498–516 (1996)

22. Meyer, P.J., Luttenberger, M.: Solving mean-payoff games on the GPU. In: Artho, C., Legay, A., Peled, D. (eds.) ATVA 2016. LNCS, vol. 9938, pp. 262–267. Springer, Cham (2016). doi:10.1007/978-3-319-46520-3_17

23. Mostowski, A.W.: Games with forbidden positions. Technical report 78, University of Gdańsk (1991)

24. Puri, A.: Theory of hybrid systems and discrete event systems. Ph.D. thesis, University of California, Berkeley (1995)

25. Puterman, M.L.: Markov Decision Processes: Discrete Stochastic Dynamic Programming. Wiley, New York (2005)

26. Schewe, S.: An optimal strategy improvement algorithm for solving parity and payoff games. In: Kaminski, M., Martini, S. (eds.) CSL 2008. LNCS, vol. 5213, pp. 369–384. Springer, Heidelberg (2008). doi:10.1007/978-3-540-87531-4_27

27. Stirling, C.: Local model checking games (extended abstract). In: Lee, I., Smolka, S.A. (eds.) CONCUR 1995. LNCS, vol. 962, pp. 1–11. Springer, Heidelberg (1995). doi:10.1007/3-540-60218-6_1

28. van de Pol, J., Weber, M.: A multi-core solver for parity games. Electr. Notes Theoret. Comput. Sci. **220**(2), 19–34 (2008)

29. van der Berg, F.: Solving parity games on the playstation 3. In: Twente Student Conference (2010)

30. Vöge, J., Jurdziński, M.: A discrete strategy improvement algorithm for solving parity games. In: Emerson, E.A., Sistla, A.P. (eds.) CAV 2000. LNCS, vol. 1855, pp. 202–215. Springer, Heidelberg (2000). doi:10.1007/10722167_18

31. Wei, Z., JáJá, J.: Optimization of linked list prefix computations on multithreaded GPUs using CUDA. Parallel Process. Lett. **22**(4), 1250012 (2012)

32. Zielonka, W.: Infinite games on finitely coloured graphs with applications to automata on infinite trees. Theoret. Comput. Sci. **200**, 135–183 (1998)

33. Zwick, U., Paterson, M.S.: The complexity of mean payoff games on graphs. Theoret. Comput. Sci. **158**(1–2), 343–359 (1996)

Model-Checking Linear-Time Properties of Parametrized Asynchronous Shared-Memory Pushdown Systems

Marie Fortin[1], Anca Muscholl[2], and Igor Walukiewicz[3(✉)]

[1] LSV, CNRS, ENS Paris-Saclay, Université Paris-Saclay, Cachan, France
[2] LaBRI, University of Bordeaux, Bordeaux, France
[3] CNRS, LaBRI, University of Bordeaux, Bordeaux, France
igor.walukiewicz@gmail.com

Abstract. A parametrized verification problem asks if a parallel composition of a leader process with some number of copies of a contributor process can exhibit a behavior satisfying a given property. We focus on the case of pushdown processes communicating via shared memory. In a series of recent papers it has been shown that reachability in this model is PSPACE-complete [Hague'11], [Esparza, Ganty, Majumdar'13], and that liveness is decidable in NEXPTIME [Durand-Gasselin, Esparza, Ganty, Majumdar'15]. We show that verification of general regular properties of traces of executions, satisfying some stuttering condition, is NEXPTIME-complete for this model. We also study two interesting subcases of this problem: we show that liveness is actually PSPACE-complete, and that safety is already NEXPTIME-complete.

1 Introduction

A parametrized verification problem asks if a given property holds for the parallel composition of a leader system with some arbitrary number of copies of a contributor system (see Fig. 1). This formulation appears already in a seminal paper of German and Sistla [19], see also the survey [3] for a recent overview of the literature. In this work, following [12,15,20,21,27], we consider parametric *pushdown* systems, where both the leader and contributors are pushdown automata, and communication is via shared variables without any locking primitives. Our primary motivation is the analysis of concurrent programs with procedure calls. While previous work on parametric pushdown systems focused mainly on reachability, or repeated reachability for the leader process, we show here that a large class of omega-regular properties is decidable for these systems.

In his pioneering work [21] Kahlon proposed parametrization as an abstraction step that avoids the undecidability barrier. A system composed of two copies of a pushdown automaton communicating via one register can simulate Turing machines [35], so no effective analysis of such systems is possible. Yet, if instead of two copies we ask if a system composed of an *arbitrary* number of copies of the pushdown automaton can write a specified value to a register, then the problem

© Springer International Publishing AG 2017
R. Majumdar and V. Kunčak (Eds.): CAV 2017, Part II, LNCS 10427, pp. 155–175, 2017.
DOI: 10.1007/978-3-319-63390-9_9

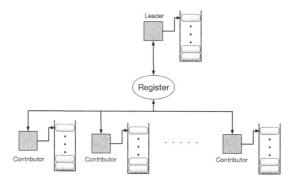

Fig. 1. A system consisting of one leader pushdown automaton and a number of copies of a contributor pushdown automaton.

becomes decidable. Later Hague [20] showed that reachability is also decidable for a more general architecture proposed by German and Sistla. Namely he considered systems with a leader pushdown automaton and an arbitrary number of copies of a contributor pushdown automaton; cf. Fig. 1. Consecutively, Esparza et al. [15] have proved that the problem is PSPACE-complete, thus surprisingly easy for such type of problem. La Torre et al. [27] showed that the reachability problem remains decidable if instead of pushdown automata one considers higher-order pushdown automata, or any other automata model with some weak decidability properties. Reachability was also shown to be decidable for parametric pushdown systems with *dynamic* thread creation [32].

Our motivating question is "what kind of linear-time properties are decidable for parametric pushdown systems?" Suppose that we want to check a universal reachability property: whether for every number of components, every run finally writes a specified value to the register? This problem translates into a safety query: does there exist some number of contributors, and some maximal run that does not write the specified value to the register? Maximality means here either an infinite run, or a finite run that cannot be prolonged. The maximality condition is clearly essential, as otherwise we could always take the empty run as a witness.

We show as our main result that verification of parametric pushdown systems is decidable for all regular properties subject to some stuttering condition linked to the fact that the number of contributors is not determined. We give precise complexities of the parametric verification problem for both the case when the property is given as a Büchi automaton, as well as when it is given by an LTL formula (NEXPTIME-complete). On the way we revisit the liveness problem studied in [12] and give a PSPACE algorithm for it. This answers the question left open by [12], that provided a PSPACE lower bound and a NEXPTIME upper bound for the liveness problem. It is somewhat surprising that for this kind of parametrized systems, checking liveness is not more difficult computationally than checking reachability, unlike for many other families of parametrized or, more generally, infinite-state systems (see e.g. Chap. 5 in [3] for a discussion and more references).

Another intermediate result of independent interest concerns universal reachability, which turns out to be coNEXPTIME-complete. The lower bound shows that it is actually possible to force a fair amount of synchronization in the parametric model; we can ensure that the first 2^n values written into the shared register are read in the correct order and none of them is skipped. So the coNEXPTIME-hardness result can be interpreted positively, as showing what can be implemented in this model.

Related Work. Parametrized verification of shared-memory, multi-threaded programs has been studied for finite-state threads e.g. in [2,23] and for pushdown threads in [1,5,25,26]. The decidability results in [1,5,25,26] fall in the category of reachability analysis up to a bounded number of execution contexts, and in [1,5], dynamic thread creation is allowed. The main difference with our setting is that synchronization primitives are allowed in those models, so decidability depends on restricting the set of executions. Our model does not restrict the executions, but has a weaker form of synchronization. In consequence our model rather over-approximates the set of executions while the approaches cited above under-approximate it.

In our model we have shared registers but no locks. Another option is to have locks and no registers. Analysis of pushdown systems with unrestricted locks is undecidable [22]. Interestingly, it becomes decidable for some locking disciplines like nested [22] or contextual locking [8]. This model remains decidable even when extended to dynamic pushdown networks [6]. Even reachability of regular sets of configurations is decidable in this model, provided it has a finitely many global locks together with nested locking [28,30] or contextual locking [29]. Regular sets of configurations can compensate to some extent the lack of communication in the model, for example they can describe globally inconsistent configurations.

Besides the cited papers, there are numerous results on the German and Sistla model beyond the reachability property, but restricted to finite state processes. German and Sistla have already considered LTL properties of the leader or of the contributors. They have also studied the setting without a leader and observed that it is much easier to handle. Emerson and Kahlon have considered stuttering-invariant properties [13] of the whole system of finite state processes. Recently, Bouyer et al. [7] considered a probabilistic version without leader and only finite-state contributors. They consider the problem of *almost-sure* reachability, which asks if a given state is reached by some process with probability 1 under a stochastic scheduler. They exhibit the existence of positive or negative cut-offs, and show that the problem can be decided in EXPSPACE, and is at least PSPACE-hard.

Finally, we should mention that there is a rich literature concerning the verification of *asynchronously-communicating* parametrized programs, that is mostly related to the verification of distributed protocols and varies for approaches and models (see e.g. [9,14,19,24] for some early work, and [3,11,31,33] and references therein). Most of these papers are concerned with finite-state programs only, which are not the main focus of our results.

Outline of the Paper. Section 2 starts by introducing the problems considered in this paper, and states our main results. In Sect. 3, we present the formal definitions of parametrized pushdown systems. In Sect. 4 we study the liveness problem, and in Sect. 5 the safety problem. Finally, we show in Sect. 6 how these results may be used to verify more general ω-regular properties. Throughout the paper we try to outline our arguments and give some intuitions for the proofs. The detailed proofs can be found in the in the full version of the paper [17].

2   Problem Statement and Overview of Results

The *parametrized pushdown systems* studied by [15,20,21] are described by two transition systems $\mathcal{D}$ and $\mathcal{C}$, traditionally called *leader* and *contributor*, which are both pushdown systems (cf. Fig. 1). Parametrization amounts to say that arbitrarily many contributor instances interact with one leader, and that contributors are anonymous. All participants communicate over lock-free, shared variables with finite domains. We distinguish read/write actions of the leader from those of contributors, for this we have two alphabets Σ_D and Σ_C. Since contributors do not have identities we do not distinguish between actions of different contributors.

The question we ask in this paper is which kind of linear-time properties of $(\Sigma_D \cup \Sigma_C)$-labeled traces of parametrized pushdown systems can be model-checked. Unsurprisingly, it turns out that we cannot hope for model-checking arbitrary regular properties. In general, model-checking is undecidable because the ability to refer to actions of both leader and contributors allows to single out exactly one contributor instance. Since two communicating pushdown systems [35] can simulate a Turing machine, undecidability follows then immediately.

The solution to the above problem is to consider properties that are adapted to the parametrized setting. Technically we consider linear-time properties $\mathcal{P}$ where actions of contributors can be replicated: if $u_0 a_0 u_1 a_1 u_2 \cdots \in \mathcal{P}$ with $a_i \in \Sigma_C$, $u_i \in \Sigma_D^*$, and $f : \mathbb{N} \to \mathbb{N}^+$, then $u_0 a_0^{f(0)} u_1 a_1^{f(1)} u_2 \cdots \in \mathcal{P}$, too. We call such properties *c-expanding*.

A related, classical notion is *stuttering*. A property $\mathcal{P}$ is stutter-invariant if for every finite or infinite sequence $a_0 a_1 \cdots$ and every function $f : \mathbb{N} \to \mathbb{N}^+$, we have $a_0 a_1 \cdots \in \mathcal{P}$ iff $a_0^{f(0)} a_1^{f(1)} \cdots \in \mathcal{P}$. Observe that every stutter-invariant property is c-expanding. Stutter-invariance is a natural requirement in the verification of general concurrent systems, and moreover well studied, e.g. for LTL they correspond to the fragment LTL$\backslash X$ [16,34]. Stutter-invariance is also common in parametrized verification [3], and for some synchronization primitives it allows to recover decidability in the finite-state case [13].

We will consider regular properties on both finite and infinite traces of parametrized systems, described either by LTL formulas or by Büchi automata with action labels from $\Sigma_C \cup \Sigma_D$.

Our main result is that model-checking c-expanding, ω-regular properties[1] of parametrized pushdown systems is decidable, and NEXPTIME-complete.

Theorem 1. *The following question is* NEXPTIME-*complete: given a parametrized pushdown system S and a c-expanding ω-regular property $\mathcal{P}$ over S (described by a Büchi automaton or by an LTL formula), determine if S has some maximal trace in $\mathcal{P}$.*

We list some particular instances of regular c-expanding ω-properties, that are both interesting on their own, and essential for our decision procedure:

1. The *reachability problem* asks if the parametrized pushdown system has some trace containing a given leader action T.
2. The *liveness (repeated reachability) problem* asks if the parametrized pushdown system has some trace with infinitely many occurrences of a given leader action T.
3. The *universal reachability problem* asks if every maximal trace of the parametrized pushdown system contains a given leader action T.
4. The complement of the previous question is the *max-safety problem*. It asks if the parametrized pushdown system has some maximal trace that does not contain a given leader action T.

Example 1. Let us imagine the system from Fig. 1 that works as follows: first some contributors propose values, then the leader chooses some proposed value and announces this choice to contributors so that afterwards all the contributors should use only this value. For such a system one may be interested to verify if for every number of contributors every run satisfies:

1. The leader eventually decides on the value.
2. If the leader decides on the value then the contributors use only this value.
3. On runs where only one value is used infinitely often, some correctness property holds.

Following other works on the subject we will rather prefer existentially quantified questions, where we ask whether there is some number of contributors and some run satisfying a property. Solutions to the reachability problem from the literature can be used to verify the second property, as its negation is "there is some run where the leader decides on a value and then a contributor uses a different value". The negation of the first property corresponds to max-safety: "there is some maximal run without the leader deciding on a value". The third property is a more complicated liveness property that is neither reachability nor safety. $\qquad\square$

Since max-safety and liveness problems are important steps towards our main result we also establish their exact complexities.

---

[1] By abuse of language we call them ω-regular although they may contain finite and infinite sequences.

Theorem 2. *The max-safety problem for parametrized pushdown systems is* NEXPTIME-*complete. It is* NP-*complete when contributors are finite-state systems.*

Theorem 3. *The liveness problem for parametrized pushdown systems is* PSPACE-*complete.*

The proof of Theorem 1 uses Theorems 2 and 3, and one more result, that is interesting on its own. Note that both the max-safety and liveness problems talk about one distinguished action of the leader, while c-expanding properties refer to actions of both leader and contributors. Perhaps a bit surprisingly, we show below that it suffices to consider only properties that refer to leader actions.

Theorem 4. *For every parametrized pushdown system S, there exists a parametrized pushdown system $\tilde{S}$ such that for every c-expanding property $\mathcal{P}$ over traces of S there exists a property $\tilde{\mathcal{P}}$ over sequences of leader actions of $\tilde{S}$ such that:*

1. *S has a finite (resp. infinite) maximal trace in $\mathcal{P}$ iff $\tilde{S}$ has a finite (resp. infinite) maximal trace whose projection on leader actions is in $\tilde{\mathcal{P}}$;*
2. *every infinite run of $\tilde{S}$ has infinitely many writes of the leader;*
3. *$\tilde{S}$ has an infinite run iff S has one.*

System $\tilde{S}$ has size linear in the size of S, and can be constructed in polynomial time. If $\mathcal{P}$ is a regular, respectively LTL property, then so is $\tilde{\mathcal{P}}$. An automaton or LTL formula of linear size for $\tilde{\mathcal{P}}$ is effectively computable from the one for $\mathcal{P}$.

3   Parametrized Pushdown Systems

In this section we recall the model of *parametrized pushdown systems* of [20] and its semantics. We start with some basic notations.

A *multiset* over a set E is a function $M : E \to \mathbb{N}$. We let $|M| = \sum_{x \in E} M(x)$. The *support* of M is the set $\{x \in E : M(x) > 0\}$. For $n \in \mathbb{N}$, we write nM, $M + M'$ and $M - M'$ for the multisets defined by $(nM)(x) = n \cdot M(x)$, $(M + M')(x) = M(x) + M'(x)$ and $(M - M')(x) = \max(0, M(x) - M'(x))$. We denote by $[x]$ the multiset containing a single copy of x, and $[x_1, \ldots, x_n]$ the multiset $[x_1] + \ldots + [x_n]$. We write $M \leq M'$ when $M(x) \leq M'(x)$ for all x.

A *transition system* with actions over a finite alphabet Σ is a tuple $\langle S, \delta, s_{init} \rangle$ where S is a (finite or infinite) set of states, $\delta \subseteq S \times \Sigma \times S$ is a set of transitions, and $s_{init} \in S$ the initial state. We write $s \xrightarrow{u} s'$ (for $u \in \Sigma^*$) when there exists a path from s to s' labeled by u. A *trace* is a sequence of actions labeling a path starting in s_{init}; so u is a trace if $s_{init} \xrightarrow{u} s'$ for some s'.

A *pushdown system* is a tuple $\langle Q, \Sigma, \Gamma, \Delta, q_{init}, A_{init} \rangle$ consisting of a finite set of states Q, a finite input alphabet Σ, a finite stack alphabet Γ, a set of transitions $\Delta \subseteq (Q \times \Gamma) \times (\Sigma \cup \{\varepsilon\}) \times (Q \times \Gamma^*)$, an initial state $q_{init} \in Q$, and an initial stack symbol $A_{init} \in \Gamma$. The associated transition system has $Q \times \Gamma^*$ as states, $q_{init} A_{init}$ as the initial state, and transitions $qA\alpha \xrightarrow{a} q'\alpha'\alpha$ for $(q, A, a, q', \alpha') \in \Delta$.

We proceed to the formal definition of parametrized pushdown systems. Given a leader process $\mathcal{D}$ and a contributor process $\mathcal{C}$, a system consists of one copy of $\mathcal{D}$ and arbitrarily many copies of $\mathcal{C}$ communicating via shared registers. For simplicity we assume that there is a single, finite-valued shared register (in the full version of the paper [17] we show how to reduce the case of several registers to that with one register). We write G for the finite set of register values, and use g, h to range over elements of G. The initial value of the register is g_{init}. Since only processes of type $\mathcal{C}$ are parametrized we distinguish the read/write actions of $\mathcal{C}$ and $\mathcal{D}$, by using disjoint action sets: $\Sigma_C = \{\bar{r}(g), \overline{w}(g) : g \in G\}$ and $\Sigma_D = \{r(g), w(g) : g \in G\}$. Both processes $\mathcal{C}$ and $\mathcal{D}$ are (possibly infinite) transition systems with read/write actions:

$$\mathcal{C} = \langle S, \delta \subseteq S \times \Sigma_C \times S, s_{init} \rangle \qquad \mathcal{D} = \langle T, \Delta \subseteq T \times \Sigma_D \times T, t_{init} \rangle \qquad (1)$$

In this paper we will consider the special case where $\mathcal{C}$ and $\mathcal{D}$ are pushdown transition systems:

$$\mathcal{A}_C = \langle P, \Sigma_C, \Gamma_C, \delta, p_{init}, A^C_{init} \rangle \qquad \mathcal{A}_D = \langle Q, \Sigma_D, \Gamma_D, \Delta, q_{init}, A^D_{init} \rangle \qquad (2)$$

In this case the transition system $\mathcal{C}$ from (1) is the transition system associated with $\mathcal{A}_C$: its set of states is $S = P \times (\Gamma_C)^*$ and the transition relation δ is defined by the push and pop operations. Similarly, the transition system $\mathcal{D}$ is determined by $\mathcal{A}_D$. When stating general results on parametrized pushdown systems we will use the notations from Eq. (1); when we need to refer to precise states, or use some particular property of pushdown transition systems, we will employ the notations from Eq. (2).

So a parametrized pushdown system $\mathcal{S}$ consists of an arbitrary number of copies of $\mathcal{C}$, one copy of $\mathcal{D}$, and a shared register. A *configuration* $(M \in \mathbb{N}^S, t \in T, g \in G)$ of $\mathcal{S}$ consists of a multiset M counting the number of instances of $\mathcal{C}$ in a given state, the state t of $\mathcal{D}$ and the current register value g.

To define the transitions of the parametrized pushdown system we need to extend the transition relation δ of $\mathcal{C}$ to multisets: let $M \xrightarrow{a} M'$ if $s \xrightarrow{a} s'$ in δ, $M(s) > 0$, and $M' = M - [s] + [s']$, for some $s, s' \in S$. Observe also that multiset transitions do not modify the size of the multiset. The transitions of the parametrized pushdown system are either transitions of $\mathcal{D}$ (the first two cases below) or transitions of $\mathcal{C}$ (the last two cases):

$$(M, t, g) \xrightarrow{w(h)} (M, t', h) \qquad \text{if } t \xrightarrow{w(h)} t' \text{ in } \Delta,$$

$$(M, t, g) \xrightarrow{r(h)} (M, t', h) \qquad \text{if } t \xrightarrow{r(h)} t' \text{ in } \Delta \text{ and } h = g,$$

$$(M, t, g) \xrightarrow{\overline{w}(h)} (M', t, h) \qquad \text{if } M \xrightarrow{\overline{w}(h)} M' \text{ in } \delta,$$

$$(M, t, g) \xrightarrow{\bar{r}(h)} (M', t, h) \qquad \text{if } M \xrightarrow{\bar{r}(h)} M' \text{ in } \delta \text{ and } h = g.$$

A *run* of $\mathcal{S}$ from a configuration (M, t, g) is a finite or an infinite sequence of transitions starting in (M, t, g). A run can start with any number n of contributors, but then the number of contributors is constant during the run. A run is *initial* if it starts in a configuration of the form $(n[s_{init}], t_{init}, g_{init})$, for some $n \in \mathbb{N}$. It is *maximal* if it is initial and cannot be extended to a longer run. In particular, every infinite initial run is maximal. A *(maximal) trace* of the parametrized pushdown system is a finite or an infinite sequence over $\Sigma_C \cup \Sigma_D$ labeling a (maximal) initial run.

4   Liveness

We show in this section that liveness for parametrized pushdown systems has the same complexity as reachability, namely PSPACE-complete (Theorem 3). The lower bound comes from reachability [15], and our contribution is to improve the upper bound from NEXPTIME [12] to PSPACE. We call a run of the parametrized pushdown system a *Büchi run* if it has infinitely many occurrences of the leader action ⊤. So the problem is to decide if a given parametrized pushdown system has a Büchi run.

Our proof has three steps. The first one relies on a result from [12], showing that it suffices to bound the stacks of contributors polynomially. This allows to search for ultimately periodic (lasso-shaped) runs of the parametrized pushdown system (Corollary 1), as in the case of a single pushdown system. The next step extends the technique introduced in [27] for the reachability problem, to Büchi runs: we reduce the search for Büchi runs to the existence of some run of the leader pushdown system, that is feasible in the global parametrized system (Lemma 2). The last step is the observation that we can replace the leader process by a finite-state system using downward closure (Lemma 3). Overall our procedure yields a PSPACE algorithm for the liveness problem (Theorem 3).

Finite-State Contributors. As observed in [12], parametrization allows to replace pushdown contributors by finite-state contributors, preserving all behaviors of the leader. The reason is that any behavior of some contributor instance can be replicated arbitrarily (but finitely many times). To state the result of [12] we need the notion of *effective stack-height* for a pushdown system. Consider a possibly infinite run $\rho = q_1\alpha_1 \xrightarrow{a_1} q_2\alpha_2 \xrightarrow{a_2} \dots$ of a pushdown system. We write $\alpha_i = \alpha_i'\alpha_i''$, where α_i'' is the longest suffix of α_i that is also a proper suffix of α_j for all $j > i$. The *effective stack-height* of a configuration $q_i\alpha_i$ in ρ is the length of α_i'. (Notice that even though it is never popped, the first element of the longest common suffix of the $(\alpha_i)_{j \geq i}$ may be read, hence the use of *proper* suffixes).

Remark 1. It is folklore that every infinite run of a *single* pushdown system contains infinitely many configurations with effective stack-height one.

By $\mathcal{C}_N$ we denote the restriction of the contributor pushdown $\mathcal{A}_C$ to runs in which all configurations have effective stack-height at most N. More precisely,

$\mathcal{C}_N$ is the finite-state system with set of states $\{p\alpha \in P\Gamma_C^* : |\alpha| \leq N\}$, and transitions $p\alpha \xrightarrow{a} q\alpha'$ if $p\alpha \xrightarrow{a} q\alpha'\alpha''$ in Δ for some α''. Note that $\mathcal{C}_N$ is effectively computable in PSPACE from $\mathcal{A}_C$ and N given in unary. One key idea in [12] is that when looking for Büchi runs of pushdown parametrized pushdown systems, $\mathcal{C}$ can be replaced by $\mathcal{C}_N$ for N polynomially bounded:

Theorem 5 (Theorem 4 in [12]). *Let $N > 2|P|^2|\Gamma_C|$. The parametrized pushdown system $\mathcal{S}$ has some Büchi run iff the parametrized pushdown system $\mathcal{S}_N$ obtained from $\mathcal{S}$ by replacing $\mathcal{C}$ by $\mathcal{C}_N$, has some Büchi run.*

The proof of the above theorem yields a similar result for finite runs. We state this in the next lemma, as we need to refer later to the form of configurations that are reachable in $\mathcal{S}_N$. The proof of the lemma relies on "distributing" the run of one contributor on the runs of two contributors, thereby decreasing the height of the stack. Recall that configurations of $\mathcal{S}$ are of the form $([s_1, \ldots, s_n], t, g)$, where the n contributor instances have states $s_1, \ldots, s_n$, the leader has state t, and the shared register has value g.

Lemma 1. *Let $N > 2|P|^2|\Gamma_C| + 1$. A configuration $([p_1\alpha_1, \ldots, p_n\alpha_n], t, g)$ of $\mathcal{S}_N$ is reachable iff there exists a reachable configuration of $\mathcal{S}$ of the form $([p_1\alpha_1\beta_1, \ldots, p_n\alpha_n\beta_n], t, g)$, for some $\beta_i \in \Gamma_C^*$.*

Notation. For the sake of clarity we write throughout the paper $\mathcal{C}_{fin}$ instead of $\mathcal{C}_N$ with $N = 2|P|^2|\Gamma_C| + 2$, and $\mathcal{S}_{fin}$ for the parametrized pushdown system with contributor process $\mathcal{C}_{fin}$ and leader process $\mathcal{D}$. We will use the notation $\langle P_{fin}, \Sigma_C, \delta, p_{init}^{fin} \rangle$ for the finite-state system $\mathcal{C}_{fin}$, and continue to write $\mathcal{A}_D = \langle Q, \Sigma_D, \Gamma_D, \Delta, q_{init}, A_{init}^D \rangle$ for the pushdown system $\mathcal{D}$.

Theorem 5 and Remark 1 show that the existence of Büchi runs boils down to the existence of "ultimately periodic runs":

Corollary 1. *The parametrized pushdown system $\mathcal{S}$ has a Büchi run iff there is a run of $\mathcal{S}_{fin}$ of the form*

$$(n[p_{init}^{fin}], t_{init}, g_{init}) \xrightarrow{u} (M, t_1, g) \xrightarrow{v} (M, t_2, g) \xrightarrow{v} \ldots$$

for some $n \in \mathbb{N}$, $g \in G$, $M \in (P_{fin})^n$, $u, v \in (\Sigma_C \cup \Sigma_D)^*$, where:

- *v ends by an action from Σ_D and contains $\top$, and*
- *all configurations $t_i \in Q\Gamma_D^*$ of $\mathcal{D}$ have effective stack-height one, the same control state, and the same top stack symbol.*

Capacities and Supported Loops. Our next goal is a PSPACE algorithm for the existence of ultimately periodic runs of $\mathcal{S}_{fin}$. Since the reachability problem is decidable in PSPACE, we will focus on loops in $\mathcal{S}_{fin}$ (i.e., runs of the form $(M, t, g) \xrightarrow{+} (M, t', g)$ as in Corollary 1) and adapt the proof for the reachability problem proposed in [27].

In a nutshell, the idea of [27] is to split a parametrized pushdown system into a part that concerns the leader, and a part that concerns the contributors. What actually matters are the values that the contributors can write into the register because once these values are written they can be repeatedly written on demand, since we are in a parametrized setting. This information will be summarized by the notion of *capacity*. The leader, resp. any individual contributor, can work with an additional capacity that abstracts the details of runs of other contributors, by recording only the effect on the shared register. Of course, the capacity needs to be validated at some point, leading to the notion of "supported run". The additional challenge is that this run should give a loop in the original system.

Following [27], $\mathcal{S}_{fin}$ splits into a finite-state system $\mathcal{C}^\kappa_{fin}$ representing the "capacity-aware" contributor, and a pushdown system $\mathcal{D}^\kappa$, representing the "capacity-aware" leader.

Formally, there is a new set of actions $\Sigma_\nu = \{\nu(g) : g \in G\}$ denoting first contributor writes. In addition, each of $\mathcal{C}^\kappa_{fin}$ and $\mathcal{D}^\kappa$ have a component K – the *capacity* – that stores the values that contributors have already written. The set of control states of $\mathcal{D}^\kappa$ is $\mathcal{P}(G) \times Q \times G$, and the initial state is $(\emptyset, q_{init}, g_{init})$. The input and the stack alphabets, Σ_D and Γ_D, are inherited from $\mathcal{D}$. So a configuration of $\mathcal{D}^\kappa$ has the form $(K \subseteq G, t \in Q\Gamma_D^*, g \in G)$. The transitions of $\mathcal{D}^\kappa$ are:

$$(K, t, g) \xrightarrow{w(h)} (K, t', h) \qquad \text{if } t \xrightarrow{w(h)} t' \text{ in } \Delta,$$

$$(K, t, g) \xrightarrow{r(h)} (K, t', h) \qquad \text{if } t \xrightarrow{r(h)} t' \text{ in } \Delta \text{ and } h \in K \cup \{g\},$$

$$(K, t, g) \xrightarrow{\nu(h)} (K \cup \{h\}, t, h) \qquad \text{if } h \notin K.$$

The finite transition system $\mathcal{C}^\kappa_{fin}$ is defined similarly, it just follows in addition the transitions of $\mathcal{D}^\kappa$ (first line below). The set of states of $\mathcal{C}^\kappa_{fin}$ is $\mathcal{P}(G) \times P_{fin} \times G$, input alphabet Σ_C, and initial state $(\emptyset, p^{fin}_{init}, g_{init})$. The transitions of $\mathcal{C}^\kappa_{fin}$ are:

$$(K, p, g) \xrightarrow{w(h)} (K, p, h), \quad (K, p, g) \xrightarrow{r(h)} (K, p, h), \quad (K, p, g) \xrightarrow{\nu(h)} (K \cup \{h\}, p, h)$$

$$(K, p, g) \xrightarrow{\overline{w}(h)} (K, p', h) \quad \text{if } p \xrightarrow{\overline{w}(h)} p' \text{ in } \delta \text{ and } h \in K$$

$$(K, p, g) \xrightarrow{\overline{r}(h)} (K, p', h) \quad \text{if } p \xrightarrow{\overline{r}(h)} p' \text{ in } \delta \text{ and } h \in K \cup \{g\}.$$

Note that in both $\mathcal{D}^\kappa$ and $\mathcal{C}^\kappa$ some additional reads $r(h), \overline{r}(h)$ are possible when $h \in K$ – these are called *capacity-reads*.

Notation. We write $\Sigma_{D,\nu}$ for $\Sigma_D \cup \Sigma_\nu$. Similarly for $\Sigma_{C,\nu}$ and $\Sigma_{C,D,\nu}$. By $v|_\Sigma$ we will denote the subword of v obtained by erasing the symbols not in Σ. Note that the value of the register after executing a trace v, in both $\mathcal{C}^\kappa_{fin}$ and $\mathcal{D}^\kappa$, is determined by the last action of v. We denote by $last(v)$ the register value of the last action of v (for v non-empty).

We now come back to examining when there exists an ultimately periodic run of $\mathcal{S}_{fin}$. Clearly, a run (or loop) of $\mathcal{S}_{fin}$ induces a run (or loop) of $\mathcal{D}^\kappa$, but the converse is not true. For the other direction we extend the notion of supported trace [27] to ω-*support*. Informally, a trace v of $\mathcal{D}^\kappa$ is called ω-*supported* when (1) for each first write $\nu(h)$ in v there is a trace of $\mathcal{C}^\kappa_{fin}$ witnessing the fact that a contributor run can produce the required action $\overline{w}(h)$, and (2) all witness traces can be completed to loops in $\mathcal{C}^\kappa_{fin}$.

Definition 1. *Consider a word* $v = v_1\nu(h_1)\cdots v_m\nu(h_m)v_{m+1} \in \Sigma^*_{D,\nu}$, *where* $v_1,\ldots,v_{m+1} \in \Sigma^*_D$, *and* $h_1,\ldots,h_m \in G$ *are pairwise different register values. Let* $p_1,\ldots,p_m \in P_{fin}$ *be states of* $\mathcal{C}_{fin}$.

We say that v *is* ω-*supported from* $(p_1,\ldots,p_m)$ *if for every* $1 \le i \le m$ *there is some trace* $u^i \in (\Sigma_{C,D,\nu})^*$ *of* $\mathcal{C}^\kappa_{fin}$ *of the form*

$$u^i = u^i_1\nu(h_1)\cdots u^i_i\nu(h_i)\,\overline{\boldsymbol{w}}(\boldsymbol{h_i})\,u^i_{i+1}\cdots u^i_m\nu(h_m)u^i_{m+1}$$

such that: (i) $u^i|_{\Sigma_{D,\nu}} = v$, *and (ii)* $(\emptyset, p_i, g) \xrightarrow{u^i} (K, p_i, g)$ *in* $\mathcal{C}^\kappa_{fin}$, *where* $g = last(v)$.

Note that $K = \{h_1,\ldots,h_m\}$ in the above definition, and that $u^i_j|_{\Sigma_{D,\nu}} = v_j$ holds for all j. The next lemma states that the notions of capacity and of ω-support suffice for checking the existence of Büchi runs. The intuition behind the proof of the lemma is that a *finite* number of contributor instances, starting in one of the states p_i, can simultaneously ensure that all capacity-reads are possible, and get back to state p_i.

Lemma 2. *The parametrized pushdown system* $\mathcal{S}$ *has some Büchi run iff there is some reachable configuration* $(M, qA\alpha, g)$ *of* $\mathcal{S}_{fin}$ *and a word* $v \in \Sigma^*_{D,\nu}$ *such that:*

1. $\mathcal{D}^\kappa$ *has a run of the form* $(\emptyset, qA, g) \xrightarrow{v} (K, qA\alpha', g)$, *and* $\top$ *appears in* v.
2. v *is* ω-*supported from some* $(p_1,\ldots,p_m)$ *such that* $[p_1,\ldots,p_m] \le M$.

Observe that by Definition 1, we have $m \le |G|$ in Lemma 2.

Algorithm. Recall that a word u is a subword of v, written $u \sqsubseteq v$, if u is obtained from v by erasing some symbols. The *downward closure* of a language $L \subseteq \Sigma^*$ is $L{\downarrow} = \{u \in \Sigma^* : \exists v \in L.\, u \sqsubseteq v\}$. By a classical result in combinatorics (Higman's lemma) we know that the downward closure of any language is regular, however not effective in general. For pushdown systems it is effective [10] and a finite-state automaton of exponential size can be computed on-the-fly in PSPACE.

For our PSPACE algorithm we first observe that the capacity-aware leader $\mathcal{D}^\kappa$ can be replaced by its downward closure, since adding some transitions of the leader does not affect the support of contributors:

Lemma 3. *Let* $v = v_1\nu(h_1)\cdots v_m\nu(h_m)v_{m+1}$ *be* ω-*supported from* $p_1,\ldots,p_m$, *and let* $v_j \sqsubseteq \overline{v}_j$ *for every* j. *Assume that* $\overline{v} = \overline{v}_1\nu(h_1)\cdots\overline{v}_m\nu(h_m)\overline{v}_{m+1}$ *satisfies* $last(v) = last(\overline{v})$. *Then* $\overline{v}$ *is also* ω-*supported from* $(p_1,\ldots,p_m)$.

The proof of Theorem 3 is based on Lemmas 2 and 3. The algorithm checks emptiness of the product of at most $|G| + 1$ finite-state automata of exponential size – the automaton for the downward closure, and the automata for ω-support. Together with a reachability check for the initial trace segment, we get a PSPACE algorithm for liveness.

5   Max-Safety

Recall that universal reachability amounts to ask that some special action $\top$ of the leader occurs in *every* trace, no matter how many contributor instances are around. This is a typical question to ask when we are interested in something that is computed by a parametrized system. The max-safety problem is just the complement of universal reachability. A (maximal) safe run is a (maximal) run that does not contain $\top$.

We show in this section that the max-safety problem is NP-complete when contributors are finite-state systems, and NEXPTIME-complete when contributors are pushdown systems (the leader is in both cases a pushdown system). As for liveness, we can reduce the second case to the first one, thus obtaining the NEXPTIME upper bound. The lower bound is more challenging.

Set Semantics. As a first step we will introduce a set semantics of parametrized pushdown systems that is equivalent to the multiset semantics of Sect. 3 when only finite traces are considered. The idea is that since the number of contributors is arbitrary, one can always add some contributor instances that copy all the actions of a given contributor. So once a state of $\mathcal{C}$ is reached, we can assume that we have arbitrarily (but finitely) many copies of $\mathcal{C}$ in that state. In consequence, multisets can be replaced by sets. Very similar ideas have been already used in [15,27]. Here we need to be a bit finer because we are interested in *maximal* runs.

Consider a parametrized pushdown system with the notations on page 7 (Eq. (1)):

$$\mathcal{C} = \langle S, \delta, s_{init} \rangle \qquad \mathcal{D} = \langle T, \Delta, t_{init} \rangle.$$

Instead of multisets $M \in \mathbb{N}^S$, we use sets $B \subseteq S$. As we have done for multisets, we lift the transitions from elements to sets of elements:

$$B \xrightarrow{a} B' \text{ in } \delta \quad \text{if } s \xrightarrow{a} s' \text{ in } \delta, \text{ and } B' \text{ is either } B \cup \{s'\} \text{ or } (B \cup \{s'\}) \setminus \{s\}$$
$$\text{for some } s \in B.$$

The intuition is that $B \xrightarrow{a} B \cup \{s'\}$ represents the case where *some* contributors in state s take the transition, and $B \xrightarrow{a} (B \cup \{s'\}) \setminus \{s\}$ corresponds to the case where *all* contributors in state s take the transition. The transitions in the *set semantics* are essentially the same as for the multiset case:

$$(B, t, g) \xrightarrow{w(h)} (B, t', h) \qquad \text{if } t \xrightarrow{w(h)} t' \text{ in } \Delta$$

$$(B, t, g) \xrightarrow{r(h)} (B, t', h) \qquad \text{if } t \xrightarrow{r(h)} t' \text{ in } \Delta \text{ and } h = g$$

$$(B, t, g) \xrightarrow{\overline{w}(h)} (B', t, h) \qquad \text{if } B \xrightarrow{\overline{w}(h)} B' \text{ in } \delta$$

$$(B, t, g) \xrightarrow{\overline{r}(h)} (B', t, h) \qquad \text{if } B \xrightarrow{\overline{r}(h)} B' \text{ in } \delta \text{ and } h = g$$

Remark 2. The set semantics is a variant of the *accumulator semantics* used in [27], in which only transitions of the form $B \xrightarrow{a} B \cup \{s'\}$ (but not $B \xrightarrow{a} (B \cup \{s'\}) \setminus \{s\}$) were used. The accumulator semantics is nice because it is monotonic, and it suffices for reachability. But it is not precise enough when dealing with *maximal* runs. □

Recall that a *support of a multiset* is the set of elements that appear in it with non-zero multiplicity. We have modified the accumulator semantics so that runs preserve the support as stated in the next lemma.

Lemma 4

1. If $(M_0, t_0, g_0) \xrightarrow{a_1} \ldots \xrightarrow{a_n} (M_n, t_n, g_n)$ in the multiset semantics, and B_j is the support of M_j, for every $j = 0, \ldots, n$, then $(B_0, t_0, g_0) \xrightarrow{a_1} \ldots \xrightarrow{a_n} (B_n, t_n, g_n)$ in the set semantics.

2. If $(B_0, t_0, g_0) \xrightarrow{a_1} \ldots \xrightarrow{a_n} (B_n, t_n, g_n)$ in the set semantics, then there exist multisets $M_0, \ldots, M_n$ such that M_j has support B_j, and for some $i_j > 0$,

$$(M_0, t_0, g_0) \xrightarrow{(a_1)^{i_1}} (M_1, t_1, g_1) \xrightarrow{(a_2)^{i_2}} \ldots \xrightarrow{(a_n)^{i_n}} (M_n, t_n, g_n)$$

in the multiset semantics.

Corollary 2. *Fix a parametrized pushdown system. In the multiset semantics the system has a finite maximal safe run ending in a configuration (M, t, g) iff in the set semantics the system has a finite maximal safe run ending in the configuration (B, t, g) with B being the support of M.*

Finite-State Contributors. We start with the case where contributors are finite-state. An easy reduction from 3-SAT shows:

Lemma 5. *The max-safety problem is NP-hard when contributor and leader are both finite-state systems.*

For the upper bound of the max-safety problem with finite-state contributors we need to distinguish between *finite* and *infinite* maximal safe runs.

The case of infinite safe runs reduces to the liveness problem, using Theorem 4 (items 2 and 3): we can construct from a given parametrized pushdown system S a parametrized pushdown system S' such that S has an infinite safe run iff S' has a run with infinitely many leader writes, but not $\top$. To decide if S' admits such a run, we remove $\top$ and test for each possible value g of the register if there is a run with infinitely many writes $w(g)$. Since liveness is in NP for finite-state contributors [12] we obtain:

Lemma 6. *For finite-state contributors and pushdown leader, it can be decided in NP whether a parametrized pushdown system has an infinite safe run.*

It remains to describe an algorithm for the existence of a *finite* maximal safe run. By Corollary 2 we can use our set semantics for this. From now on we will also exploit the fact that $\mathcal{D}$ is a pushdown system. Recall that the states of $\mathcal{D}$ are of the form $q\alpha$ where q is the state of the pushdown automaton defining $\mathcal{D}$ and α represents the stack. The question is to decide if there is a deadlock configuration $(B, q\alpha, g)$ in the parametrized pushdown system, such that $(B, q\alpha, g)$ is reachable without using the $\top$ action. Note that we can determine whether $(B, q\alpha, g)$ is a deadlock by looking only at B, q, g and the top symbol of α. Our algorithm will consist in guessing B, q, g and some $A \in \Gamma_D$, and then checking reachability.

To check reachability in NP we first show that it is sufficient to look for traces where the number of changes of the first component of configurations (the set-component) is polynomially bounded:

Lemma 7. *For every finite run ρ of the parametrized pushdown system in the set semantics, there exists some run ρ' with the same action labels, same end configuration and of the form $\rho' = \rho'_0 \cdots \rho'_k$ with $k \leq 2|S|$, where in each ρ'_j, all states have the same set-component.*

Proof. Take a run $\rho = (B_0, t_0, g_0) \xrightarrow{a_1} (B_1, t_1, g_1) \xrightarrow{a_2} \dots \xrightarrow{a_n} (B_n, t_n, g_n)$ of the parametrized pushdown system. We claim that there exists a run $\rho' = (B'_0, t_0, g_0) \xrightarrow{a_1} (B'_1, t_1, g_1) \xrightarrow{a_2} \dots \xrightarrow{a_n} (B'_n, t_n, g_n)$ such that $B_0 = B'_0$, $B_n = B'_n$, and for all $s \in S$ and $0 \leq i < n$, if $s \in B'_i$ and $s \notin B'_{i+1}$, then for all $j > i$, $s \notin B'_j$.

Indeed let us define B'_i by induction on i: $B'_0 = B_0$, and for $i > 1$,

- if $B_{i+1} = B_i$, then $B'_{i+1} = B'_i$.
- if $B_{i+1} = B_i \cup \{s\}$, then $B'_{i+1} = B'_i \cup \{s\}$.
- if $B_{i+1} = (B_i \backslash \{s\}) \cup \{s'\}$ and $s \notin B_j$ for all $j > i$, then $B'_{i+1} = (B'_i \backslash \{s\}) \cup \{s'\}$. If $s \in B_j$ for some $j > i$, then $B'_{i+1} = B'_i \cup \{s'\}$.

Clearly, ρ' is a run of the parametrized pushdown system. Moreover, for all i, $B_i \subseteq B'_i \subseteq \bigcup_{j=i}^{n} B_j$. So in particular, $B_n = B'_n$.

Now we take the run ρ'. Let $i_0 = 0$, and $i_1 < \cdots < i_k$ be the indices such that $B'_i \neq B'_{i-1}$. Then ρ' can be decomposed into $\rho' = \rho'_0 \cdots \rho'_k$, where for all j, the set-component of all states in ρ'_j is B'_{i_j}. Consider the sequence $B'_{i_0}, B'_{i_1}, \dots, B'_{i_k}$. There are states $s_1, \dots, s_k \in S$ such that for all $0 \leq j < k$, $B'_{i_{j+1}} = B'_{i_j} \cup \{s_j\}$ or $B'_{i_{j+1}} = (B'_{i_j} \cup \{s\}) \backslash \{s_j\}$ for some s. Moreover, each $s \in S$ is added at most once, and removed at most once from some B'_i, which means that there are at most two distinct indices j such that $s = s_j$. Hence $k \leq 2|S|$.   □

The next lemma follows now from Lemma 7: we first guess a sequence of sets of states $B_0, B_1, \dots, B_k = B$ of length $k \leq 2|S|$, then construct a pushdown automaton of polynomial size according to the guess, and finally check reachability in polynomial time [4]:

Lemma 8. *The following problem is in* NP*: given a parametrized pushdown system with finite-state contributors and a configuration* (B, qA, g) *in the set semantics, decide if there exists* α *such that* $(B, qA\alpha, g)$ *is reachable from the initial configuration.*

Proof. The set semantics of the parametrized pushdown system corresponds to a pushdown automaton $\mathcal{A}$ with set of control states $2^S \times Q \times G$, input alphabet $\Sigma_C \cup \Sigma_D$, and stack alphabet Γ_D. We first guess a sequence $\{s_{init}\} = B_0, B_1, \ldots, B_k = B$ of sets of contributor states, where $k \leq 2|S|$. Then we construct the restriction of $\mathcal{A}$ to runs where the first component of the state is equal to B_0, then B_1, up to B_k. The pushdown automaton thus obtained has polynomial size, and we can check in polynomial time whether it has some reachable configuration $(B, qA\alpha, g)$ [4]. $\qquad\square$

Combining Lemmas 5, 6 and 8 we obtain the complexity result for finite-state contributors:

Theorem 6. *The max-safety problem is* NP-*complete when contributors are finite-state systems.*

Pushdown Contributors. We now return to the case where contributors are pushdown systems, and show first a lower bound, by a reduction from a tiling problem [18]:

Lemma 9. *The max-safety problem is* NEXPTIME-*hard for parametrized pushdown systems.*

Proof. We reduce the following tiling problem [18] to the max-safety problem:

Input: A finite set of tiles Σ, horizontal and vertical compatibility relations $H, V \subseteq \Sigma^2$, and an initial row $x \in \Sigma^n$.

Question: Is there a tiling of the $2^n \times 2^n$ square respecting the compatibility relations and containing the initial row in the left corner?

A tiling is a function $t : \{1, \ldots, 2^n\}^2 \to \Sigma$ such that $(t(i, j), t(i, j + 1)) \in H$ and $(t(i, j), t(i + 1, j)) \in V$ for all i, j, and $t(1, 1)t(1, 2) \cdots t(1, n) = x$.

The idea of the reduction is that the system will have a maximal run without $\top$ if and only if the leader can guess a tiling respecting the horizontal compatibility, and the contributors check that the vertical compatibility is respected as well.

The leader will write down the tiling from left to right and from top to bottom, starting with the initial row. The sequence of values taken by the register on a (good) run will have the form

$$A_{1,1}, \overline{A_{1,1}}, A_{1,2}, \overline{A_{1,2}}, \ldots, A_{1,2^n}, \overline{A_{1,2^n}}, \ldots, A_{2^n,2^n} \overline{A_{2^n,2^n}} \ (\$\overline{\$})^{2^n} \ \diamond.$$

The $A_{i,j}$ are guessed and written by the leader, and the $\overline{A_{i,j}}$ are written by contributors. Letters $\overline{A_{i,j}}$ have two purposes: they ensure that at least one contributor has read the preceding letter, and prevent a contributor from reading the same letter twice. For technical reasons, this sequence is followed by a sequence $(\$\bar{\$})^{2^n} \diamond$ of writes from the leader (with $\$, \diamond \notin \Sigma$), and we will consider that $(A, \$) \in V$ for all $A \in \Sigma$.

The leader uses her stack to count the number i of rows (using the lower part of the stack), and the number j of tiles on each row (using the upper part of the stack). So, she repeats the following, up to reaching the values $i = 2^n, j = 2^n$: (i) guess a tile A compatible with the one on its left (if $j \neq 1$), and write A on the register, (ii) wait for an acknowledgment $\bar{A}$ from one of the contributors, (iii) increment j, (iv) if $j > 2^n$, increment i and set $j = 1$.

Finally, she repeats 2^n times the actions $w(\$)$, $w(\bar{\$})$, then finishes by writing $w(\diamond)$ and going to some distinguished state q_f.

Each contributor is supposed to read the entire sequence of values written in the register. He alternates between reading values of the form A and $\bar{A}$, which ensures that no value is read more than one time. At the same time, he uses his stack to count the number of writes $w(A)$ ($A \in \Sigma \cup \{\$\}$) of the leader, up to $(2^{2n} + 2^n)$, so that he can check that no value was missed. This operation will in fact be divided between counting up to 2^{2n}, and counting up to 2^n, as described below.

Every contributor decides non-deterministically to check vertical compatibility at some point. He chooses the current tile $A \neq \$$, and needs to check that the tile located below it (that is, occurring 2^n tiles later in the sequence of values written by the leader) is compatible with it. This is done as follows: after reading $A \neq \$$, the contributor writes $\bar{A}$ on the register (rather than waiting for another contributor to do so), and remembers the value. He interrupts his current counting, and starts counting anew on the top of the stack, up to 2^n. Upon reaching 2^n, he stores the value A' of the register, for later check. Then he resumes the first counting while reading the remaining of the sequence, up to 2^{2n}. At any moment, the contributor can read $\diamond$. If he reads $\diamond$ and either $(A, A') \notin V$ or the counting up to 2^n failed (i.e., his stack is not empty), then he writes $\#$ (with $\# \notin \Sigma \cup \bar{\Sigma} \cup \{\$, \diamond\}$) and stops; otherwise he simply stops. In state q_f, the leader may read any value $g \neq \diamond$, and she then does $\top$: $q_f \xrightarrow{r(g)} \xrightarrow{\top}$. From every other state $q \neq q_f$, the leader can do $\top$, too.

It can be verified [17] that there is a tiling of the $2^n \times 2^n$ square, if and only if there is a maximal run without any occurrence of $\top$. For the left-to-right implication the leader should write a sequence of register values corresponding to the tiling, and every contributor can end up with the empty stack upon reading $\diamond$, so no $\top$ will be generated. For the right-to-left direction, observe that in the maximal run the leader should reach q_f. In this case the acknowledgment mechanism is set up in such a way that all the values written by the leader should be successfully checked by contributors.   □

For the upper bound, similarly to the case of finite-state contributors we need to consider maximal finite and infinite runs separately. The case of infinite runs can be again reduced to liveness using Theorem 4, and turns out to be easier:

Lemma 10. *It can be decided in* PSPACE *whether a parametrized pushdown system has some infinite safe run.*

For *finite* maximal runs, we show that we match the NEXPTIME lower bound. For this we reduce the problem to the case of finite-state contributors, using Lemma 1 that gives a polynomial bound for contributor stacks. Then we can apply Lemma 8 that states that the complexity is NP for finite-state contributors:

Lemma 11. *It can be decided in* NEXPTIME *whether a parametrized pushdown system has some finite, maximal safe run.*

The three lemmas together prove Theorem 2.

6 Regular C-expanding Properties

In this section, we outline the proof of our general result stated in Theorem 1. The proof is based on Theorem 4, that says that we can focus on properties that refer only to leader actions. The proof idea for Theorem 4 is that in the new parametrized pushdown system, the register becomes part of the leader's state. This releases the register, that can be used now by contributors to communicate with the leader regarding the actions that they *intend* to perform, but the leader is in charge to execute them. Contributors in the new parametrized pushdown system write into the register the read/write action they want to execute; the leader executes the action and confirms this to the contributors by writing back into the register. The confirmation is read by contributors who at this point know that their action request has been read and executed. The simulation makes use of the fact that the property we want to check is c-expanding. The details of the construction, and the correctness proof, are a bit tedious since it is always possible that a value is overwritten before it gets read.

The proof of Theorem 1 is, once again, divided into two cases: one for finite and the other for infinite traces. For finite maximal traces we use the results about the max-safety problem, and for infinite traces we reduce the problem to liveness.

Lemma 12. *The following question is* NEXPTIME-*complete: given a parametrized pushdown system* S *and a c-expanding ω-regular property* P *over* S *(described by a Büchi automaton or by an LTL formula), determine if* S *has some maximal, finite trace in* P.

Proof Sketch. By Theorem 4 we can assume that we need to check a property P that refers only to actions of the leader. If P is given by an LTL formula, we start by constructing an equivalent finite automaton of exponential size. By taking the product of the leader D with this automaton representing P, we can assume that D has a distinguished set of final (control) states such that a finite run of the parametrized pushdown system satisfies P iff D reaches a final state.

The result then follows using Lemma 1, together with Lemma 8. Recall that in order to decide if a finite run is maximal it is enough to look at the top of its last configuration. Lemma 1 then tells us that there exists a maximal finite run in the parametrized pushdown system $\mathcal{S}$ with $\mathcal{D}$ ending in a final state iff there exists such a run in the parametrized pushdown system $\mathcal{S}_{fin}$, where contributors are finite-state; and by Lemma 8 the latter can be decided in NP in the size of $\mathcal{S}_{fin}$, so overall in NEXPTIME. The matching NEXPTIME-hardness lower bound follows from the proof of Lemma 9, as the parametrized pushdown system constructed there has no infinite safe trace, and the max-safety problem restricted to finite traces is a special instance of our problem.   □

As for the max-safety problem, the case of infinite runs turns out to be easier. It is also interesting to observe that the complexity now depends on whether the property is described by an automaton or by a formula.

Lemma 13. *The following question is* PSPACE-*complete: given a parametrized pushdown system* $\mathcal{S}$ *and a c-expanding ω-regular property* $\mathcal{P}$ *over* $\mathcal{S}$ *described by a Büchi automaton, determine if* $\mathcal{S}$ *has some* infinite *trace in* $\mathcal{P}$.

Proof Sketch. Applying again Theorem 4 and slightly modifying the parametrized pushdown system we can reduce the satisfaction of $\mathcal{P}$ to an instance of the liveness problem; observe also that liveness is a special case of our problem. With this reduction, PSPACE-completeness follows from Theorem 3.   □

Lemma 14. *The following question is* EXPTIME-*complete: given a parametrized pushdown system* $\mathcal{S}$ *and a c-expanding ω-regular property* $\mathcal{P}$ *over* $\mathcal{S}$ *described by an LTL formula, determine if* $\mathcal{S}$ *has some* infinite *trace in* $\mathcal{P}$.

Proof Sketch. The lower bound comes from the situation where there are no contributors at all [4]. For the upper bound: from an LTL formula we first construct a Büchi automaton of exponential size. As in Lemma 13, the first step is to reduce the problem of deciding if the parametrized pushdown system has a trace in $\mathcal{P}$ to the liveness of some parametrized pushdown system $\mathcal{S}'$. In the obtained system $\mathcal{S}'$ the leader $\mathcal{D}'$ is of exponential size, and $\mathcal{C}'$ is of polynomial size. As a second step we adapt the procedure given in the proof of Theorem 3: we do not build the downward closure of the leader, and we enumerate all possible sequences $\nu(h_1), \ldots, \nu(h_m)$ and intermediate states, instead of guessing them. Then we follow the lines of the proof of Theorem 3, checking emptiness of pushdown systems of exponential size in EXPTIME.   □

7   Conclusion

We have established the decidability and exact complexity for verifying linear-time properties of parametrized pushdown systems, a model introduced in [20] that can be seen as adapting a formulation from [19] to communicating pushdown processes as in [21]. For decidability we needed to require that properties are c-expanding, a lighter version of stuttering invariance. On the way to this result we have determined the exact complexity of deciding liveness properties, which turned out to be an easier problem than deciding the existence of maximal runs. Technically, our upper bound results for liveness as well as for maximal runs require to build on both the techniques from [12] and [27]. As pointed out in [12] the techniques for deciding reachability are not immediately applicable to the liveness problem. For reachability we can assume that for every write there is a separate contributor responsible to produce it. This is a very useful simplification that does not apply to repeated reachability, since we require that the number of contributors is bounded over the complete infinite run. For the case of maximal runs we introduced a simplification of the original semantics that is sensitive to divergence. The lower bound result for this case shows that being able to detect termination increases the complexity of the problem.

The model considered in this paper can be extended with dynamic thread creation. Reachability is still decidable for this extension [32]. The decidability proof is based on upper closures and well-quasi orders, so it does not provide any interesting complexity upper bounds. It is actually open whether the verification of regular properties of parametric systems with dynamic thread creation is decidable.

References

1. Atig, M.F., Bouajjani, A., Qadeer, S.: Context-bounded analysis for concurrent programs with dynamic creation of threads. Log. Methods Comput. Sci. **7**(4), 1–48 (2011)
2. Ball, T., Chaki, S., Rajamani, S.K.: Parameterized verification of multithreaded software libraries. In: Margaria, T., Yi, W. (eds.) TACAS 2001. LNCS, vol. 2031, pp. 158–173. Springer, Heidelberg (2001). doi:10.1007/3-540-45319-9_12
3. Bloem, R., Jacobs, S., Khalimov, A., Konnov, I., Rubin, S., Veith, H., Widder, J.: Decidability of Parameterized Verification. Morgan & Claypool Publishers, San Rafael (2015)
4. Bouajjani, A., Esparza, J., Maler, O.: Reachability analysis of pushdown automata: application to model-checking. In: Mazurkiewicz, A., Winkowski, J. (eds.) CONCUR 1997. LNCS, vol. 1243, pp. 135–150. Springer, Heidelberg (1997). doi:10.1007/3-540-63141-0_10
5. Bouajjani, A., Esparza, J., Schwoon, S., Strejček, J.: Reachability analysis of multithreaded software with asynchronous communication. In: Sarukkai, S., Sen, S. (eds.) FSTTCS 2005. LNCS, vol. 3821, pp. 348–359. Springer, Heidelberg (2005). doi:10.1007/11590156_28
6. Bouajjani, A., Müller-Olm, M., Touili, T.: Regular symbolic analysis of dynamic networks of pushdown systems. In: Abadi, M., Alfaro, L. (eds.) CONCUR 2005. LNCS, vol. 3653, pp. 473–487. Springer, Heidelberg (2005). doi:10.1007/11539452_36
7. Bouyer, P., Markey, N., Randour, M., Sangnier, A., Stan, D.: Reachability in networks of register protocols under stochastic schedulers. In: ICALP 2016, LIPIcs, pp. 106:1–106:14. Leibniz-Zentrum für Informatik (2016)
8. Chadha, R., Madhusudan, P., Viswanathan, M.: Reachability under contextual locking. In: Flanagan, C., König, B. (eds.) TACAS 2012. LNCS, vol. 7214, pp. 437–450. Springer, Heidelberg (2012). doi:10.1007/978-3-642-28756-5_30

9. Clarke, E.M., Grumberg, O., Jha, S.: Verifying parameterized networks. ACM Trans. Program. Lang. Syst. **19**(5), 726–750 (1997)
10. Courcelle, B.: On constructing obstruction sets of words. Bull. EATCS **44**, 178–186 (1991)
11. Delzanno, G.: Parameterized verification and model checking for distributed broadcast protocols. In: Giese, H., König, B. (eds.) ICGT 2014. LNCS, vol. 8571, pp. 1–16. Springer, Cham (2014). doi:10.1007/978-3-319-09108-2_1
12. Durand-Gasselin, A., Esparza, J., Ganty, P., Majumdar, R.: Model checking parameterized asynchronous shared-memory systems. Form. Methods Syst. Des. **50** (2–3), 140–167 (2017). Journal version of CAV 2015
13. Emerson, E.A., Kahlon, V.: Model checking guarded protocols. In: LICS 2003, pp. 361–370 (2003)
14. Esparza, J., Finkel, A., Mayr, R.: On the verification of broadcast protocols. In: LICS 1999, pp. 352–359. IEEE (1999)
15. Esparza, J., Ganty, P., Majumdar, R.: Parameterized verification of asynchronous shared-memory systems. J. ACM **63**(1), 10:1–10:48 (2016). Journal version of CAV 2013
16. Etessami, K.: A note on a question of Peled and Wilke regarding stutter-invariant LTL. Inf. Process. Lett. **75**(6), 261–263 (2000)
17. Fortin, M., Muscholl, A., Walukiewicz, I.: On parametrized verification of asynchronous, shared-memory pushdown systems. CoRR, abs/1606.08707 (2016)
18. Fürer, M.: The computational complexity of the unconstrained limited domino problem (with implications for logical decision problems). In: Börger, E., Hasenjaeger, G., Rödding, D. (eds.) LaM 1983. LNCS, vol. 171, pp. 312–319. Springer, Heidelberg (1984). doi:10.1007/3-540-13331-3_48
19. German, S.A., Sistla, P.A.: Reasoning about systems with many processes. J. ACM **39**(3), 675–735 (1992)
20. Hague, M.: Parameterised pushdown systems with non-atomic writes. In: FSTTCS 2011. LIPIcs, pp. 457–468. Schloss Dagstuhl - Leibniz-Zentrum für Informatik (2011)
21. Kahlon, V.: Parameterization as abstraction: a tractable approach to the dataflow analysis of concurrent programs. In: LICS 2008, pp. 181–192. IEEE (2008)
22. Kahlon, V., Ivančić, F., Gupta, A.: Reasoning about threads communicating via locks. In: Etessami, K., Rajamani, S.K. (eds.) CAV 2005. LNCS, vol. 3576, pp. 505–518. Springer, Heidelberg (2005). doi:10.1007/11513988_49
23. Kaiser, A., Kroening, D., Wahl, T.: Dynamic cutoff detection in parameterized concurrent programs. In: Touili, T., Cook, B., Jackson, P. (eds.) CAV 2010. LNCS, vol. 6174, pp. 645–659. Springer, Heidelberg (2010). doi:10.1007/978-3-642-14295-6_55
24. Kesten, Y., Pnueli, A., Shahar, E., Zuck, L.: Network invariants in action*. In: Brim, L., Křetínský, M., Kučera, A., Jančar, P. (eds.) CONCUR 2002. LNCS, vol. 2421, pp. 101–115. Springer, Heidelberg (2002). doi:10.1007/3-540-45694-5_8
25. La Torre, S., Madhusudan, P., Parlato, G.: Model-checking parameterized concurrent programs using linear interfaces. In: Touili, T., Cook, B., Jackson, P. (eds.) CAV 2010. LNCS, vol. 6174, pp. 629–644. Springer, Heidelberg (2010). doi:10.1007/978-3-642-14295-6_54
26. La Torre, S., Madhusudan, P., Parlato, G.: Sequentializing parameterized programs. In: FIT 2012. EPTCS, vol. 87, pp. 34–47 (2012)
27. La Torre, S., Muscholl, A., Walukiewicz, I.: Safety of parametrized asynchronous shared-memory systems is almost always decidable. In: CONCUR 2015. LIPIcs, vol. 42, pp. 72–84. Schloss Dagstuhl - Leibniz-Zentrum für Informatik (2015)

28. Lammich, P., Müller-Olm, M.: Conflict analysis of programs with procedures, dynamic thread creation, and monitors. In: Alpuente, M., Vidal, G. (eds.) SAS 2008. LNCS, vol. 5079, pp. 205–220. Springer, Heidelberg (2008). doi:10.1007/978-3-540-69166-2_14

29. Lammich, P., Müller-Olm, M., Seidl, H., Wenner, A.: Contextual locking for dynamic pushdown networks. In: Logozzo, F., Fähndrich, M. (eds.) SAS 2013. LNCS, vol. 7935, pp. 477–498. Springer, Heidelberg (2013). doi:10.1007/978-3-642-38856-9_25

30. Lammich, P., Müller-Olm, M., Wenner, A.: Predecessor sets of dynamic pushdown networks with tree-regular constraints. In: Bouajjani, A., Maler, O. (eds.) CAV 2009. LNCS, vol. 5643, pp. 525–539. Springer, Heidelberg (2009). doi:10.1007/978-3-642-02658-4_39

31. Lin, A.W., Rümmer, P.: Liveness of randomised parameterised systems under arbitrary schedulers. In: Chaudhuri, S., Farzan, A. (eds.) CAV 2016. LNCS, vol. 9780, pp. 112–133. Springer, Cham (2016). doi:10.1007/978-3-319-41540-6_7

32. Muscholl, A., Seidl, H., Walukiewicz, I.: Reachability for dynamic parametric processes. In: Bouajjani, A., Monniaux, D. (eds.) VMCAI 2017. LNCS, vol. 10145, pp. 424–441. Springer, Cham (2017). doi:10.1007/978-3-319-52234-0_23

33. Namjoshi, K.S., Trefler, R.J.: Analysis of dynamic process networks. In: Baier, C., Tinelli, C. (eds.) TACAS 2015. LNCS, vol. 9035, pp. 164–178. Springer, Heidelberg (2015). doi:10.1007/978-3-662-46681-0_11

34. Peled, D.A., Wilke, T.: Stutter-invariant temporal properties are expressible without the next-time operator. Inf. Process. Lett. **63**(5), 243–246 (1997)

35. Ramalingam, G.: Context-sensitive synchronization-sensitive analysis is undecidable. ACM Trans. Program. Lang. Syst. (TOPLAS) **22**(2), 416–430 (2000)

Minimization of Symbolic Transducers

Olli Saarikivi[1(✉)] and Margus Veanes[2]

[1] Aalto University and Helsinki Institute for Information Technology HIIT,
Helsinki, Finland
olli.saarikivi@aalto.fi
[2] Microsoft Research, Redmond, USA
margus@microsoft.com

Abstract. Symbolic transducers extend classical finite state transducers to infinite or large alphabets like Unicode, and are a popular tool in areas requiring reasoning over string transformations where traditional techniques do not scale. Here we develop the theory for and an algorithm for computing quotients of such transducers under indistinguishability preserving equivalence relations over states such as bisimulation. We show that the algorithm is a minimization algorithm in the deterministic finite state case. We evaluate the benefits of the proposed algorithm over real-world stream processing computations where symbolic transducers are formed as a result of repeated compositions.

1 Introduction

Finite state automata and transducers are used in a wide variety of applications, ranging from program compilation and verification [5,21] to computational linguistics [32]. A major limitation of classic automata is that their alphabets need to be finite (and small) for the algorithms to scale. To overcome this limitation several approaches have been proposed to accommodate *infinite* alphabets [28,37]. One approach is to use *predicates* instead of concrete characters on state transitions [37,41]. The theory and algorithms of such *symbolic finite automata* (SFAs) and *symbolic finite transducers* (SFTs) modulo *theories*, has recently received considerable attention [17,39] with applications in areas such as parameterized unit testing [38], web security [25], similarity analysis of binaries [16], and code parallelization [40]. Our interest in *symbolic transducers* (STs or SFTs with registers) is motivated by recent applications in string processing and streaming computations [35] where STs are used to express input to output transformations over data streams and UTF8-encoded text files, and STs are *fused* (composed serially) in order to eliminate intermediate streams.

In many applications the need to minimize the number of states without affecting the semantics is crucial for scalability. Much like product composition of classical finite state automata, for STs as well as SFTs, fusion implies a worst case quadratic blowup in the number of (control) states. Thus, similar to automata frameworks such as MONA [27], it is highly beneficial to be able to reduce the number of states after fusion. Concretely, our initial motivation for minimizing

© Springer International Publishing AG 2017
R. Majumdar and V. Kunčak (Eds.): CAV 2017, Part II, LNCS 10427, pp. 176–196, 2017.
DOI: 10.1007/978-3-319-63390-9_10

STs came from studying Huffman decoders [26], which we represented as SFTs. When an ST that implements Huffman decoding is fused with some other ST that ignores a part of the decoders output (e.g. everything that is not a digit), then a subgraph of the fused ST's states will resemble an SFA, i.e., have no outputs and no register updates. More generally, fusion might result in a lot of states being *indistinguishable*, i.e., have equivalent behavior for all inputs. This was the key insight that led us to a general algorithm for reducing the number of states of STs, presented here.

In the case of deterministic SFAs it is possible to reduce minimization to classical DFAs at an upfront exponential cost in the size of the SFA [17]. In the case of SFTs, a similar transformation to finite state transducers is not possible because SFTs allow *copying* of input into the output that breaks many of their classic properties [22]. Despite many differences, several algorithms are decidable for SFTs [39]. Whether SFTs can be *minimized* has been an open problem.

Here we develop a general state reduction algorithm that applies to all STs and guarantees minimality in the case of deterministic SFTs. In order to capture minimality we need to extend the definition of an ST [39] to allow *initial* outputs in addition to *final* outputs. The algorithm builds on and generalizes techniques from [33]. First, an ST A is *quasi-determinized* to an equivalent ST $\text{QD}(A)$ where all common outputs occur as early as possible. Second, $\text{QD}(A)$ is transformed into an SFA $\text{SFA}(\text{QD}(A))$ over a complex alphabet theory where in addition to the input, each complex character includes a list of output and a pair of current and next register values; A and $\text{SFA}(\text{QD}(A))$ have the same set of (control) states. Third, $\text{SFA}(\text{QD}(A))$ is used to compute a bisimulation relation $\sim$ over states through algorithms in [17,18]. Finally, the quotient $\text{QD}(A)/_\sim$ is formed to collapse bisimilar states. A series of theorems are stated to establish correctness of this algorithm. In particular, Mohri's minimization theorem [33, Theorem 2] is first generalized and used to show that, for deterministic SFTs, the algorithm produces a minimal SFT, where minimality is defined with respect to number of states. We show that, for STs in general, $\text{SFA}(A)$, accepts an *over-approximation* of all the valid transductions of the ST A, but the quotient $A/_\sim$ preserves the precise semantics of A for any equivalence relation $\sim$ over states that respects state indistinguishability in $\text{SFA}(A)$. We further generalize the algorithm to use register invariants. We evaluate the resulting algorithm on a set of STs produced by composing pipelines consisting of real-world stream processing computations. The results show that the state reduction algorithm is effective at reducing the size of symbolic transducers when applied after composition.

To summarize, our contributions are as follows:

- We extend the minimization theorem [33, Theorem 2] to a larger class of sequential functions (Theorem 1). We generalize the quasi-determinization algorithm from [33] to the symbolic setting (Sect. 3).
- We develop a theory of state reductions of STs through an over-approximating encoding to SFAs (Sects. 4 and 5).
- We describe how to strengthen STs using known invariants to enable register dependent state reductions (Sect. 6).

- We provide a construction of STs that implement decoders and encoders for prefix codes, e.g., Huffman codes (Sect. 7.1).
- We show the effectiveness of our state reduction approach on a varied set of STs obtained as compositions of stream processing pipelines (Sect. 8).

2 Symbolic Automata and Transducers

Here we recall the definitions of a symbolic finite automaton (SFA) and a symbolic transducer (ST) [39]. Before giving the formal definitions below, the underlying intuition behind symbolic automata and transducers is the following. An SFA is like a classical automaton whose concrete characters have been replaced by character predicates. The character predicates are symbolic representations of sets of characters. Such predicates may even denote infinite sets, e.g., when the character domain is the set of integers. The minimal requirements about such predicates are that they are closed under Boolean operations and that checking their satisfiability is decidable.

Example 1. Consider characters that are integers and character predicates as quantifier free formulas over integer linear arithmetic (with modulo-constant operator) containing one free variable x. Define P_{even} as the predicate $x \bmod 2 = 0$, and similarly, define P_{odd} as the predicate $x \bmod 2 = 1$. In this setting the predicate $P_{even} \wedge P_{odd}$ is unsatisfiable and the predicate $P_{even} \vee P_{odd}$ denotes the whole universe. The SFA in Fig. 1(a) accepts all sequences of numbers such that every element in an odd position is even and every element in an even position is odd. The first position of a sequence is 1 (thus odd) by definition.   ⊠

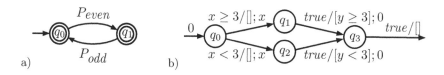

Fig. 1. (a) symbolic finite automaton; (b) symbolic transducer.

An ST has, in addition to an input predicate, also an output component, and it may potentially also use a *register*. An ST has finitely many *control states* similar to an SFA, but the register type may be infinite. Therefore an ST may have an infinite state space, where a state is defined as a pair of a control state and a register value. The outputs of an ST are represented symbolically using terms that denote functions from an input and a register to an output.

Example 2. Consider the symbolic transducer in Fig. 1(b). A label $\varphi/o; u$ reads as follows: φ is a predicate over (x, y) where x is the input and y the register; o is a sequence of terms denoting functions from (x, y) to output values; u is a function from (x, y) denoting a register update. For example, $true/[y \geq 3]; 0$ means that the output sequence is the singleton sequence containing the truth value of the current register y being greater than or equal to 3, and the register is reset to 0. A label ρ/o is the label of a *finalizer* leading to an implicit final state, with o being the output upon reaching the end of the input if ρ is true for the register.   ⊠

In the following we present formal definitions of SFAs and STs. The notations for SFAs are consistent with [17].

A sequence or list of n elements is denoted by $[e_1, \ldots, e_n]$ or $[e_i]_{i=1}^n$. The empty sequence is $[]$ or ϵ. Concatenation of two sequences u and v is denoted by juxtaposition uv and if e is an element and w a sequence then ew (resp. we) denotes the sequence $[e]w$ (resp. $w[e]$) provided that the types of e and w are clear from the context. Let u and v be sequences and $w = uv$. Then $u^{-1}w \stackrel{\text{def}}{=} v$ denotes the left division of w by u. The relation $u \preccurlyeq v$ means that u is a prefix of v. The operation $u \wedge v$ denotes the maximal common prefix of u and v.

We do not distinguish between a type and the universe that the type denotes, thus treating a type also as a semantic object or set. Given types σ and τ, we write $\mathcal{F}(\sigma{\rightarrow}\tau)$ for a given recursively enumerable (r.e.) set of terms f denoting functions $[\![f]\!]$ of type $\sigma \rightarrow \tau$. Let the Boolean type be $\mathbb{B}$. Terms in $\mathcal{P}(\sigma) \stackrel{\text{def}}{=} \mathcal{F}(\sigma{\rightarrow}\mathbb{B})$ are called $(\sigma\text{-})predicates$. The type $\sigma{\times}\tau$ is the Cartesian product type of σ and τ.

Example 3. Suppose we use a fixed variable x for the function argument (x is possibly a compound argument or a tuple of variables), then an expression such as $x_1 + x_2 \in \mathcal{F}(\mathbb{Z}{\times}\mathbb{Z}{\rightarrow}\mathbb{Z})$ represents addition, where x has type $\mathbb{Z}{\times}\mathbb{Z}$ and x_i represents the i'th element of x for $i \in \{1, 2\}$. E.g. $x_1 > 0 \wedge x_2 > 0 \in \mathcal{P}(\mathbb{Z}{\times}\mathbb{Z})$ restricts both elements of x to be positive.   ⊠

If S is a set then S^* denotes the Kleene closure of S, i.e., the set of all finite sequences of elements of S. The definitions of symbolic automata and transducers make use of effective Boolean algebras in place of concrete alphabets. An *effective Boolean algebra* $\mathcal{A}$ is a tuple $(U, \Psi, [\![\_]\!], \bot, \top, \vee, \wedge, \neg)$ where U is a non-empty recursively enumerable set of elements called the *universe* of $\mathcal{A}$. Ψ is an r.e. set of *predicates* that is closed under the Boolean connectives, $\vee, \wedge : \Psi \times \Psi \rightarrow \Psi, \neg : \Psi \rightarrow \Psi$, and $\bot, \top \in \Psi$. The *denotation function* $[\![\_]\!] : \Psi \rightarrow 2^U$ is r.e. and is such that, $[\![\bot]\!] = \emptyset$, $[\![\top]\!] = U$, for all $\varphi, \psi \in \Psi$, $[\![\varphi \vee \psi]\!] = [\![\varphi]\!] \cup [\![\psi]\!]$, $[\![\varphi \wedge \psi]\!] = [\![\varphi]\!] \cap [\![\psi]\!]$, and $[\![\neg\varphi]\!] = U \setminus [\![\varphi]\!]$. For $\varphi \in \Psi$, we write $\mathbf{Sat}(\varphi)$ when $[\![\varphi]\!] \neq \emptyset$ and say that φ is *satisfiable*. The algebra $\mathcal{A}$ is *decidable* if $\mathbf{Sat}$ is decidable. We say that $\mathcal{A}$ is *infinite* if U is infinite. In practice, an effective Boolean algebra is implemented with an API having methods that correspond to the Boolean operations.

2.1   Symbolic Finite Automata

Here we recall the definition of a symbolic finite automaton (SFA). The notations are consistent with [17]. We first define a Σ-*automaton* over a (possibly infinite) *alphabet* Σ, a (possibly infinite) *set of states* Q as a tuple $M = (\Sigma, Q, Q^0, F, \Delta)$ where $Q^0 \subseteq Q$ is the set of *initial states*, $F \subseteq Q$ is the set of *final states*, and $\Delta : Q \times \Sigma \times Q$ is the state *transition* relation. A single transition (p, a, q) in Δ is denoted by $p \xrightarrow{a} q$. The transition relation is lifted to $Q \times \Sigma^* \times Q$ as usual: for all $p, q, r \in Q$, $a \in \Sigma$ and $u \in \Sigma^*$: $q \xrightarrow{\epsilon} q$; if $p \xrightarrow{a} q$ and $q \xrightarrow{u} r$ then $p \xrightarrow{au} r$. The *language of* M *at* p is $\mathscr{L}(M, p) = \{w \in \Sigma^* \mid \exists q \in F : p \xrightarrow{w} q\}$. The *language of* M is $\mathscr{L}(M) = \bigcup_{q \in Q^0} \mathscr{L}(M, q)$. M is *deterministic* if $|Q^0| = 1$ and whenever $p \xrightarrow{a} q$ and $p \xrightarrow{a} r$ then $q = r$. M is *finite state* or *FA* if Q is finite. Σ-*DFA* stands for *deterministic finite (state) automaton* with alphabet Σ.

Definition 1. $p, q \in Q$ *are* indistinguishable, $p \equiv_M q$, *if* $\mathscr{L}(M, p) = \mathscr{L}(M, q)$.

If $\equiv$ is an equivalence relation over Q then for $q \in Q$, $q_{/\equiv}$ denotes the $\equiv$-equivalence class containing q and for $X \subseteq Q$, $X_{/\equiv}$ denotes the set of all $q_{/\equiv}$ for $q \in X$. Clearly, $\equiv_M$ is an equivalence relation. The $\equiv$-*quotient* of M is $M_{/\equiv} \stackrel{\text{def}}{=} (\Sigma, Q_{/\equiv}, q^0_{/\equiv}, F_{/\equiv}, \{q_{/\equiv} \xrightarrow{a} p_{/\equiv} \mid q \xrightarrow{a}_M p\})$. $M_{/\equiv_M}$ is *canonical* and *minimal* among all Σ-DFAs that accept the same language as M [17].

Definition 2. A *symbolic finite automaton* (*SFA*) M is a tuple $(\mathcal{A}, Q, Q^0, F, \Delta)$, where $\mathcal{A}$ is an effective Boolean algebra called the *alphabet*, Q is a finite set of states, $Q^0 \subseteq Q$ is the set of *initial states*, $F \subseteq Q$ is the set of *final states*, and Δ is a finite subset of $Q \times \Psi_{\mathcal{A}} \times Q$ called the *transition* relation.

Definition 3. Let $M = (\mathcal{A}, Q, Q^0, F, \Delta)$ be an SFA and $\Sigma = U_{\mathcal{A}}$. The *underlying* Σ-*FA* of M is $\llbracket M \rrbracket \stackrel{\text{def}}{=} (\Sigma, Q, Q^0, F, \{(p, a, q) \mid (p, \varphi, q) \in \Delta, a \in \llbracket \varphi \rrbracket\})$.

2.2 Transducers and Sequential Functions

Sequential functions are defined in [33] as functions that can be represented by deterministic finite state transducers that, in order to be algorithmically effective, operate over finite state spaces and finite input and output alphabets. Here we lift the definitions from [33] to the infinite and nondeterministic case. Fortunately, the key results that we need from [33] do not depend on finiteness of alphabets.[1]

Definition 4. A *transducer* is a tuple $\mathbf{f} = (Q, Q^0, F, I, O, \iota, \Delta, \$)$ where Q is a nonempty set of *states*, $Q^0 \subseteq Q$ is the set of *initial states*, $F \subseteq Q$ is the set of *final states*; I and O are nonempty sets called *input alphabet* and *output alphabet*, $\iota \subseteq Q^0 \times O^*$ is the *initial output relation* or the *initializer*, $\Delta \subseteq Q \times I \times O^* \times Q$ is the *transition relation*, and $\$ \subseteq F \times O^*$ is the *final output relation* or the *finalizer*. $\mathbf{f}$ is *deterministic* if $|Q^0| = 1$, $\iota : Q^0 \to O^*$ and $\$: F \to O^*$ are functions, and $\Delta : Q \times I \to O^* \times Q$ is a partial function.

---

[1] A technical difference is that Mohri [33] defines the state and the output components of a transition relation separately.

In the following let $\mathbf{f} = (Q, Q^0, F, I, O, \iota, \Delta, \$)$ be a fixed transducer. The following notations are used: $p \xrightarrow{a/u} q$ stands for $(p, a, u, q) \in \Delta$, and $p \xrightarrow{/u}$ stands for $(p, u) \in \$$, and $\xrightarrow{/u} p$ stands for $(p, u) \in \iota$. The transition relation is lifted to $Q \times I^* \times O^* \times Q$ as follows. For all $p, q, r \in Q, a \in I, v \in I^*, u, w \in O^* \colon p \xrightarrow{\epsilon/\epsilon} p$, if $p \xrightarrow{a/u} q$ and $q \xrightarrow{v/w} r$ then $p \xrightarrow{av/uw} r$. Further, for complete transductions the transition relation is lifted to $Q \times I^* \times O^*$. For all $p, q, \in Q, v \in I^*, u, w \in O^*$, if $p \xrightarrow{v/u} q$ and $q \xrightarrow{/w}$ then $p \xrightarrow{v/uw}$. The *transduction of* $\mathbf{f}$ *from state* p is the relation $\mathscr{T}(\mathbf{f}, p) \subseteq I^* \times O^*$ such that

$$\mathscr{T}(\mathbf{f}, p) \overset{\text{def}}{=} \{(v, w) \mid p \xrightarrow{v/w}\}$$

The *transduction of* $\mathbf{f}$ is the relation $\mathscr{T}(\mathbf{f}) \subseteq I^* \times O^*$ such that

$$\mathscr{T}(\mathbf{f}) \overset{\text{def}}{=} \{(v, w_0 w) \mid \exists p \in Q^0 \text{ such that } \xrightarrow{/w_0} p \xrightarrow{v/w}\}$$

Two transducers are *equivalent* if their transductions are equal. The *domain of* $\mathbf{f}$ *at state* p is the set $\mathscr{D}(\mathbf{f}, p) \overset{\text{def}}{=} \{v \in I^* \mid \exists w \in O^* : (v, w) \in \mathscr{T}(\mathbf{f}, p)\}$. The *domain of* $\mathbf{f}$ is $\mathscr{D}(\mathbf{f}) \overset{\text{def}}{=} \{v \in I^* \mid \exists w \in O^* : (v, w) \in \mathscr{T}(\mathbf{f})\}$. For any state $q \in Q$ define $P_{\mathbf{f},q}$, or P_q when $\mathbf{f}$ is clear, as the *longest common prefix* of all outputs from q in $\mathbf{f}$:

$$P_{\mathbf{f},q} \overset{\text{def}}{=} \bigwedge \{w \mid \exists v : (v, w) \in \mathscr{T}(\mathbf{f}, q)\} \quad \text{where } \bigwedge \emptyset \overset{\text{def}}{=} \epsilon.$$

Transform the initializer, the finalizer and the transition relation by promoting the common output prefixes to occur as early as possible as follows:

$$\hat{\iota} \overset{\text{def}}{=} \{(q, w P_q) \mid (q, w) \in \iota\}$$
$$\hat{\Delta} \overset{\text{def}}{=} \{(p, a, P_p^{-1} w P_q, q) \mid (p, a, w, q) \in \Delta\}$$
$$\hat{\$} \overset{\text{def}}{=} \{(q, P_q^{-1} w) \mid (q, w) \in \$\}$$

The corresponding transformation of $\mathbf{f}$ is defined as follows.

Definition 5. *Quasi-determinization* of $\mathbf{f}$ is $\mathbf{qd}(\mathbf{f}) \overset{\text{def}}{=} (Q, Q^0, F, I, O, \hat{\iota}, \hat{\Delta}, \hat{\$})$.

Quasi-determinization of $\mathbf{f}$ can be seen as a way to reduce nondeterminism in the output part and the following proposition follows from the definitions.

Proposition 1. $\mathscr{T}(\mathbf{f}) = \mathscr{T}(\mathbf{qd}(\mathbf{f}))$ *and* $\mathbf{qd}(\mathbf{qd}(\mathbf{f})) = \mathbf{qd}(\mathbf{f})$.

When $\mathbf{f}$ is deterministic we write $\mathscr{T}_{\mathbf{f},p} : \mathscr{D}(\mathbf{f}, p) \to O^*$ for $\mathscr{T}(\mathbf{f}, p)$ and $\mathscr{T}_{\mathbf{f}} : \mathscr{D}(\mathbf{f}) \to O^*$ for $\mathscr{T}(\mathbf{f})$ as functions. In particular, $\mathscr{T}_{\mathbf{f}}(v) = w$ means $(v, w) \in \mathscr{T}(\mathbf{f})$ and similarly for $\mathscr{T}(\mathbf{f}, p)$. Moreover, let $\mathbf{f}(v) \overset{\text{def}}{=} \mathscr{T}_{\mathbf{f}}(v)$ for $v \in \mathscr{D}(\mathbf{f})$.

Definition 6. A *sequential transducer* is a deterministic transducer with finitely many states. A *sequential function* is the transduction of some sequential transducer. A sequential transducer is *minimal* if there exists no equivalent sequential transducer with fewer states.

The initial output is needed for minimality, while the finalizer increases expressiveness.

Example 4. Consider an HTML decoder that replaces every pattern `&lt;` with `<`; e.g. the string `"&lt;&lt"` is mapped to `"<&lt"`. This is a sequential function whose sequential transducer requires the use of a finalizer, unless I is extended with a new end-of-input symbol that is used to terminate all input sequences. ⊠

Let $\mathbf{f} = (Q, Q^0, F, I, O, \iota, \Delta, \$)$ be a transducer. The underlying automaton of $\mathbf{f}$ combines inputs and outputs into single labels. Let $q^0, q^\bullet \notin Q$ be distinct new states and let Σ be the alphabet:

$$\Sigma = \{c_w \mid \exists q : (q, w) \in \iota \cup \$\} \cup \{c_w^a \mid \exists p, q : (p, a, w, q) \in \Delta\}$$

The Σ-*automaton of* $\mathbf{f}$ is $\mathbf{aut}(\mathbf{f}) \overset{\text{def}}{=} (\Sigma, Q \cup \{q^0, q^\bullet\}, \{q^0\}, \{q^\bullet\}, \Delta_0 \cup \Delta_1 \cup \Delta_2)$, where $\Delta_0 = \{(q^0, c_w, p) \mid (p, w) \in \iota\}$, $\Delta_1 = \{(p, c_w^a, q) \mid (p, a, w, q) \in \Delta\}$, and $\Delta_2 = \{(p, c_w, q^\bullet) \mid (p, w) \in \$\}$.

Minimization of a sequential transducer $\mathbf{f} = (Q, Q^0, F, I, O, \iota, \Delta, \$)$ proceeds now in two steps. First, $\mathbf{f}$ is quasi-determinized to $\mathbf{qd}(\mathbf{f})$. Second, $\mathbf{qd}(\mathbf{f})$ is minimized by collapsing states that are indistinguishable with respect to $\mathbf{aut}(\mathbf{qd}(\mathbf{f}))$. Let $\equiv$ be $\equiv_{\mathbf{aut}(\mathbf{qd}(\mathbf{f}))}$ in:

$$\mathbf{qd}(\mathbf{f})_{/\equiv} = (Q_{/\equiv}, Q^0_{/\equiv}, F_{/\equiv}, I, O, \hat{\iota}_{/\equiv}, \hat{\Delta}_{/\equiv}, \hat{\$}_{/\equiv})$$
$$\hat{\iota}_{/\equiv} = \{(q_{/\equiv}, w) \mid (q, w) \in \hat{\iota}\}$$
$$\hat{\$}_{/\equiv} = \{(q_{/\equiv}, w) \mid (q, w) \in \hat{\$}\}$$
$$\hat{\Delta}_{/\equiv} = \{(p_{/\equiv}, a, w, q_{/\equiv}) \mid (p, a, w, q) \in \hat{\Delta}\}$$

The following is a generalized form of Mohri's theorem that allows finalizers and infinite alphabets. For our purposes it therefore captures minimality at the semantic level rather than providing a decision procedure for minimization.

Theorem 1 (Mohri). *If* $\mathbf{f}$ *is a sequential transducer then* $\mathbf{qd}(\mathbf{f})_{/\equiv_{\mathbf{aut}(\mathbf{qd}(\mathbf{f}))}}$ *is a minimal sequential transducer that is equivalent to* $\mathbf{f}$.

2.3   Symbolic Transducers

A *symbolic transducer* (ST) represents a streaming computation over finite input sequences, where the input elements belong to some not-necessarily bounded domain. Let $X \subseteq_{\text{fin}} Y$ stand for X is a *finite subset* of Y.

Definition 7. A *symbolic transducer* is a tuple $A = (I, O, Q, q^0, o^0, T, F, R, r^0)$ where I is an *input element type*, O is an *output element type*, R is a *register type*, and Q is a *finite set of control states*, and where $q^0 \in Q$ is the *initial control state*, $r^0 \in R$ is the *initial register*, $o^0 \in O^*$ is the *initial output*,

$$T \subseteq_{\text{fin}} Q \times (\mathcal{P}(I \times R) \times \mathcal{F}(I \times R \rightarrow O)^* \times \mathcal{F}(I \times R \rightarrow R)) \times Q$$
$$F \subseteq_{\text{fin}} Q \times (\mathcal{P}(R) \times \mathcal{F}(R \rightarrow O)^*)$$

T is the *transition relation*, and F is the *finalizer*.

Let $\mathscr{D}(F)$ denote the set of all $(q, r) \in F \times R$ such that there exists a final rule $(q, \varphi, \bar{v}) \in F$ and $r \in [\![\varphi]\!]$. Given $\bar{v} = [v_i]_{i=1}^n \in \mathcal{F}(\tau_1 \to \tau_2)^*$ we let $[\![\bar{v}]\!]$ denote the function from τ_1 to τ_2^* such that for $a \in \tau_1$, $[\![\bar{v}]\!](a) = [[\![v_i]\!](a)]_{i=1}^n$.

Definition 8. The *underlying transducer of A*, denoted by $[\![A]\!]$, is defined as the transducer $(Q \times R, \{(q^0, r^0)\}, \mathscr{D}(F), I, O, \{(q^0, r^0) \mapsto o^0\}, \Delta, \$)$ where

$$\Delta = \{(p, r) \xrightarrow{a/[\![\bar{v}]\!](a, r)} (q, [\![u]\!](a, r)) \mid (p, (\varphi, \bar{v}, u), q) \in T, (a, r) \in [\![\varphi]\!]\}$$

$$\$ = \{(p, r) \xrightarrow{/[\![\bar{v}]\!](r)} \mid (p, (\varphi, \bar{v})) \in F, r \in [\![\varphi]\!]\}$$

A is *deterministic* if $[\![A]\!]$ is deterministic. Let $A = (I, O, Q, q^0, o^0, T, F, R, r^0)$ be a fixed deterministic ST.

Definition 9. A is a symbolic *finite* transducer or *SFT* if $|R| = 1$. We omit the trivial register type and omit the corresponding components when A is an SFT and let $A = (I, O, Q, q^0, o^0, T, F)$ where $T \subseteq_{\mathrm{fin}} Q \times (\mathcal{P}(I) \times \mathcal{F}(I \to O)^*) \times Q$ and $F \subseteq_{\mathrm{fin}} Q \times O^*$. A deterministic SFT A is *minimal* if $[\![A]\!]$ is minimal.

A deterministic SFT is the symbolic counterpart of a sequential transducer. Observe that in any symbolic transducer with a finite register type we can eliminate the register component by fusing it with the control state component and thus turn the ST into an SFT by using a state exploration algorithm [40].

Example 5. See Fig. 2. *Smileyfy* is a deterministic SFT whose input type and output type is Unicode.[2] The purpose of *Smileyfy* is to decode each pattern `:-)` into a smiley symbol[3] and to leave the input unchanged otherwise. For example *Smileyfy*`("☺:-):-")` = `"☺☺:-"`. *Unsmileyfy* is an SFT that replaces each smiley with the pattern `:-)` and leaves the input unchanged otherwise.   ⊠

3   Quasi-Determinization of Symbolic Transducers

Let $A = (I, O, Q, q^0, o^0, T, F, R, r^0)$ be a fixed ST. Assume that the ST is *clean*, meaning that all predicates that occur in the rules of A are satisfiable. Given a rule r in T or F we can effectively decide if some element of the output has a fixed value that is independent of the input and the register. Such constant value analysis is performed as follows. Consider $(p, (\lambda x.\varphi(x), [\lambda x.v_i(x)]_{i=1}^n, u), q) \in T$. Recall that $x : I \times R$ and $v_i(x) : O$. In order to decide if $\forall x x' : \varphi(x) \wedge \varphi(x') \Rightarrow v_i(x) = v_i(x')$ check unsatisfiability of $\varphi(x) \wedge \varphi(x') \wedge v_i(x) \neq v_i(x')$. If the formula is unsatisfiable we know that this implies that $v_i(x)$ is a fixed value for any x such that $\varphi(x)$ holds because $\varphi(x)$ is satisfiable since the ST is clean. We can then select an arbitrary model $\mathfrak{A} \models \varphi(x)$ and evaluate $v_i(x)$ in that model, say $a_i = v_i(x)^{\mathfrak{A}}$ and replace v_i by a_i in the output of the rule (as a preprocessing

---

[2] The Unicode alphabet is finite but very large, over a million characters. For most practical purposes it is considered as the set on natural numbers $\mathbb{N}$.

[3] For example Unicode codepoint 263A₁₆ or a smiley in the emoticon alphabet [2].

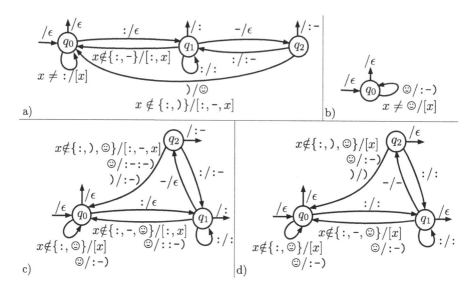

Fig. 2. SFTs: (a) *Smileyfy*; (b) *Unsmileyfy*; (c) SU = *Smileyfy* ∘ *Unsmileyfy*; (d) QD(SU).

step of A). If, on the other hand, $\varphi(x) \wedge \varphi(x') \wedge v_i(x) \neq v_i(x')$ is satisfiable it means that there exist at least two different outputs (for some different inputs for x and x', respectively). Let **1** and **2** be two fixed distinct symbols. Create multi-symbol NFA transitions $p \xrightarrow{c_1 \dots c_n} q$ where $c_i = a_i$ in the first case and $c_i \in \{1, 2\}$ in the second case. This yields an NFA over the finite alphabet $O \cup \{1, 2\}$ that can be quasi-determinized [33] to compute the maximal common prefixes $P_{A,p}$, or P_p when A is clear, for all $p \in Q$. Observe that $P_p \in O^*$ because the symbols **1** and **2** cannot occur in any common prefix since they conflict with each other. Next, the rules of A can be transformed to quasi-determinize A as follows. In each transition from p to q with output $\bar{v}$, replace $\bar{v}$ by $P_p^{-1} \bar{v} P_q$. In every final rule from p with output $\bar{v}$, replace $\bar{v}$ by $P_p^{-1} \bar{v}$. The initial output becomes $\hat{o}^0 = o^0 P_{q^0}$. Let the resulting ST be QD(A) $\overset{\text{def}}{=} (I, O, Q, q^0, \hat{o}^0, \hat{T}, \hat{F}, R, r^0)$.

Lemma 1. $\mathscr{T}([\![QD(A)]\!]) = \mathscr{T}(\mathbf{qd}([\![A]\!]))$.

Lemma 2. *If A is an SFT then* $[\![QD(A)]\!] = \mathbf{qd}([\![A]\!])$.

The following example illustrates the effect of quasi-determinization on SFTs. The example gives a simplified but realistic scenario involving composition of string manipulating functions. Chains of string transformations where data has been encoded and is being decoded before further analysis are frequent and may lead to extensive computation overheads [35].

Example 6. Recall Fig. 2. Composition of *Smileyfy* with *Unsmileyfy* is an SFT SU that first applies *Smileyfy* and then *Unsmileyfy*. SU is shown in Fig. 2(c).

If we calculate the maximal output prefixes for all the states in SU we get that $P_{q_0} = \epsilon$, $P_{q_1} = "\!:\!"$, and $P_{q_2} = "\!:\!-\!"$. After quasi-determinizing SU we get the SFT in Fig. 2(d). For example, consider the transition from q_2 to q_1 in SU. Then $P_{q_2}^{-1}"\!:\!-\!"P_{q_1} = "\!:\!-\!"^{-1}"\!:\!-\!:\!" = "\!:\!"$. So in QD($SU$) we have $q_2 \xrightarrow{:/:} q_1$.   ⊠

To enable more quasi-determinization in the presence of registers the QD-algorithm above can be modified to also move outputs that are only independent of the input, but not the register. Instead of checking for a constant value, yields are checked for input-independence: $\forall a, a', r : \varphi((a,r)) \wedge \varphi((a',r)) \Rightarrow v_i((a,r)) = v_i((a',r))$. The modified QD must also find common prefixes under the equivalence of yield formulas. To move register-dependent yields the register update of the transition the yield is moved over must be substituted into the formula. Furthermore, the yield formulas may be equivalent only under the context of their transitions' guards, and therefore a representative for an equivalence class of yields may need to be constructed from the constituent formulas.

4   SFA Encoding of Symbolic Transducers

Here we provide a translation that lifts STs to SFAs. This translation is used to reduce state reduction of STs to minimization of SFAs and plays therefore a central role in the paper. Given an ST $A = (I, O, Q, q^0, o^0, T, F, R, r^0)$ we construct an SFA SFA(A) for A by representing the labels of all the rules of A as predicates in a set $\mathcal{P}(L)$ where L is a type that encodes the labels. Let the effective Boolean algebra be $\mathcal{A}$, whose universe is L and whose set of predicates is $\mathcal{P}(L)$. We write $[\sigma]$ for the type of finite sequences or *lists* of elements of type σ. We access the i'th element of an element x having Cartesian product type (or tuple type) by x_1, x_2, x_3, etc. We define L as the disjoint union type $\mathtt{T}((I \times R) \times [O] \times R) \cup \mathtt{F}(R \times [O])$. The intent behind the type L is the following. A concrete label $\mathtt{T}((a,r), b, r')$ is an instance of the label of a transition such that for input a and register r the transition produces the output sequence b and the updated register r'. A concrete label $\mathtt{F}(r, b)$ is an instance of the label of a finalizer such that for register r the final output sequence is b.

Definition 10. The *predicate encoding of a label* l is the following L-predicate ϕ_l. For $l = (\varphi, [f_i]_{i=1}^n, g) \in \mathcal{P}(I \times R) \times \mathcal{F}(I \times R {\rightarrow} O)^* \times \mathcal{F}(I \times R {\rightarrow} R)$:

$$\phi_l(x) \stackrel{\text{def}}{=} \mathtt{IsT}(x) \wedge \varphi(x_1) \wedge x_2 = [f_i(x_1)]_{i=1}^n \wedge x_3 = g(x_1).$$

For $l = (\varphi, [f_i]_{i=1}^n) \in \mathcal{P}(R) \times \mathcal{F}(R {\rightarrow} O)^*$:

$$\phi_l(x) \stackrel{\text{def}}{=} \mathtt{IsF}(x) \wedge \varphi(x_1) \wedge x_2 = [f_i(x_1)]_{i=1}^n.$$

An important aspect of ϕ_l is that it is quantifier free and that its satisfiability is *decidable* provided that $\mathcal{A}$ is decidable. Moreover, $\neg\phi_l$ is a quantifier free predicate in $\mathcal{P}(L)$ by virtue of $\mathcal{P}(L)$ being closed under complement.

Definition 11. The *SFA of A*, denoted SFA(A), is the following SFA:

$$\text{SFA}(A) \stackrel{\text{def}}{=} (\mathcal{P}(L), Q \cup \{q^\bullet\}, q^0, \{q^\bullet\}, \Delta_{\text{SFA}(A)})$$
$$\Delta_{\text{SFA}(A)} = \{(p, \phi_l, q) \mid (p, l, q) \in T\} \cup \{(p, \phi_l, q^\bullet) \mid (p, l) \in F\}$$

The following theorem relates the transduction semantics of an ST with the language of the corresponding SFA.

Theorem 2 (Control State Abstraction). *The following are equivalent for all $u = (a_1 \cdots a_n) \in I^*$ and $v \in O^*$:*

1. $(u, o^0 v) \in \mathcal{T}(\llbracket A \rrbracket)$.
2. *There exist $r_0 = r_A^0$, $e \in O^*$, and, for $1 \le i \le n, v_i \in O^*, r_i \in R$, such that $[T((a_i, r_{i-1}), v_i, r_i)]_{i=1}^n [F(r_n, e)] \in \mathcal{L}(\text{SFA}(A))$ and $v = v_1 v_2 \cdots v_n e$.*

Proof. Any L-predicate over T-elements can be written equivalently as

$$\lambda \, T((x, y), z, w). \gamma(x, y) \wedge z = f(x, y) \wedge w = g(x, y)$$

which maps one-to-one with the ST transition label $\gamma/f; g$. Similarly for F-elements. We now state the following key property between A and SFA(A) that directly relates the trace semantics of A with the language of SFA(A). The proof of (*) follows from the definitions.

(*) For all $p, q \in Q, r, s \in R, a \in I$ and $v \in O^*$:

$$(p, r) \xrightarrow[\llbracket A \rrbracket]{a/v} (q, s) \Leftrightarrow p \xrightarrow[\llbracket \text{SFA}(A) \rrbracket]{T((a, r), v, s)} q \quad \text{and} \quad (p, r) \xrightarrow[\llbracket A \rrbracket]{\varepsilon} v \Leftrightarrow p \xrightarrow[\llbracket \text{SFA}(A) \rrbracket]{F(r, v)} q^\bullet.$$

Theorem 2 is proved by induction over the length of u and by using (*).   ⊠

We refer to Theorem 2 as the *ST control state abstraction theorem* because $\mathcal{L}(\text{SFA}(A))$ abstracts the use of the particular control states in any run of A. Note that while Theorem 2 ensures that $\mathcal{L}(\text{SFA}(A))$ includes all valid transductions, $\mathcal{L}(\text{SFA}(A))$ may also include sequences that do not correspond to valid transductions due to the register not evolving consistently, i.e., sequences containing a subsequence $[T((a_i, r_i), v_i, r_i), T((a_{i+1}, r_i'), v_{i+1}, r_{i+1})]$ where $r_i \neq r_i'$. We will see in the next section that it is still safe to use SFA(A) for control state reduction in A.

5   Minimization

We use the following algorithm for reducing the number of control states of an ST A. We first quasi-determinize A and then transform QD(A) into an SFA SFA(QD(A)) and use existing algorithms to reduce the number of states of SFA(QD(A)). The reduction of SFA(QD(A)) provides us with an equivalence relation $\sim$ over Q that can be used to merge $\sim$-equivalent states in A while preserving the transduction semantics of A. If $\sim$ is an equivalence relation over Q then the $\sim$-quotient of A is the ST

$$A_{/\sim} \stackrel{\text{def}}{=} (I, O, Q_{/\sim}, q^0_{/\sim}, o^0, \{(p_{/\sim}, l, q_{/\sim}) \mid (p, l, q) \in T\}, \{(p_{/\sim}, l) \mid (p, l) \in F\}, R, r^0).$$

The following theorem states that we can merge control states in A that are indistinguishable in $\text{SFA}(A)$ into one state, without affecting the transduction semantics of A.

Theorem 3. *For all $q \in Q_A, r \in R, u \in I^*, v \in O^*$, and equivalence relations $\sim \subseteq \equiv_{\text{SFA}(A)}$ this holds: $(u, v) \in \mathscr{T}(\llbracket A \rrbracket, (q, r)) \Leftrightarrow (u, v) \in \mathscr{T}(\llbracket A_{/\sim} \rrbracket, (q_{/\sim}, r))$.*

Proof. Let $u = [a_i]_{i=1}^n$. Suppose $p \sim q$. We have the following equivalences:

$$(p, r) \xrightarrow[\llbracket A \rrbracket]{u/v} \Leftrightarrow \exists p_1 \ldots p_n, r_1 \ldots r_n, v_1 \ldots v_n, e : v = v_1 + v_2 + \cdots + v_n + e,$$

$$(p, r) \xrightarrow[\llbracket A \rrbracket]{a_1/v_1} (p_1, r_1) \xrightarrow[\llbracket A \rrbracket]{a_2/v_2} (p_2, r_2) \cdots (p_n, r_n) \xrightarrow[\llbracket A \rrbracket]{e/e}$$

$$\Leftrightarrow \exists p_1 \ldots p_n, r_1 \ldots r_n, v_1 \ldots v_n, e : v = v_1 + v_2 + \cdots + v_n + e,$$

$$p \xrightarrow[\llbracket \text{SFA}(A) \rrbracket]{\text{T}((a_1, r), v_1, r_1)} p_1 \xrightarrow[\llbracket \text{SFA}(A) \rrbracket]{\text{T}((a_2, r_1), v_2, r_2)} p_2 \cdots p_n \xrightarrow[\llbracket \text{SFA}(A) \rrbracket]{\text{F}(r_n, e)} q^\bullet$$

$$\Leftrightarrow \exists p'_1 \ldots p'_n, r_1 \ldots r_n, v_1 \ldots v_n, e : v = v_1 + v_2 + \cdots + v_n + e,$$

$$q \xrightarrow[\llbracket \text{SFA}(A) \rrbracket]{\text{T}((a_1, r), v_1, r_1)} p'_1 \xrightarrow[\llbracket \text{SFA}(A) \rrbracket]{\text{T}((a_2, r_1), v_2, r_2)} p'_2 \cdots p'_n \xrightarrow[\llbracket \text{SFA}(A) \rrbracket]{\text{F}(r_n, e)} q^\bullet$$

$$\Leftrightarrow \exists p'_1 \ldots p'_n, r_1 \ldots r_n, v_1 \ldots v_n, e : v = v_1 + v_2 + \cdots + v_n + e,$$

$$(q, r) \xrightarrow[\llbracket A \rrbracket]{a_1/v_1} (p'_1, r_1) \xrightarrow[\llbracket A \rrbracket]{a_2/v_2} (p'_2, r_2) \cdots (p'_n, r_n) \xrightarrow[\llbracket A \rrbracket]{e/e}$$

$$\Leftrightarrow (q, r) \xrightarrow[\llbracket A \rrbracket]{u/v}$$

where the first equivalence holds by definition, the second equivalence uses Theorem 2(*), the third equivalence uses $p \equiv_{\text{SFA}(A)} q$, the fourth equivalence uses Theorem 2(*) again, and the last equivalence holds by definition. Therefore we can replace q by $q_{/\sim}$ without affecting the transduction semantics.   ⊠

The key implication for A is that we can replace all indistinguishable control states with a single fixed representative of the indistinguishability equivalence class. The most typical use for minimization arises as a post-processing step after composition. The following example illustrates a simplified scenario. The fusion composition of A and B, denoted $A \circ B$, has the classic semantics of relation composition: $(w, v) \in \mathscr{T}_{A \circ B} \Leftrightarrow \exists z : (w, z) \in \mathscr{T}_A \wedge (z, v) \in \mathscr{T}_B$.

Example 7. If we apply the SFA minimization algorithm from [17] to the SFA $\text{SFA}(\text{QD}(SU))$, with $\text{QD}(SU)$ as in in Fig. 2(c), we get an equivalence relation where all the states are indistinguishable. It turns out that the composed SFT in Fig. 2(d) is equivalent to the minimal SFT in Fig. 2(b).   ⊠

We get the following general state reduction theorem for STs by combining the above theorems. In the special case of deterministic SFTs it is a minimization theorem that provides a partial answer to the open problem of whether SFTs can be effectively minimized. For the case of functional (aka. single-valued) but possibly nondeterministic SFTs is still an open problem if an effective minimization procedure exists.

Theorem 4. *Let $A = (I, O, Q, q^0, o^0, T, F, R, r^0)$ be an ST. The following holds.*
(a) If $\sim\ \subseteq\ \equiv_{\text{SFA}(\text{QD}(A))}$ and $\sim$ is an equivalence relation then $\mathscr{T}(\text{QD}(A)_{/\sim}) = \mathscr{T}(A)$.
(b) If A is a deterministic SFT then $\text{QD}(A)_{/\equiv_{\text{SFA}(\text{QD}(A))}}$ is minimal.

Proof. We prove (a) first. Let $\sim\ \subseteq\ \equiv_{\text{SFA}(\text{QD}(A))}$ be an equivalence relation, $u \in I^*$, and $w \in O^*$. Recall that, for any ST B, $\mathscr{T}(B) \stackrel{\text{def}}{=} \mathscr{T}(\llbracket B \rrbracket)$. Let $o = o^0 P_{A,q^0}$. We get that

$$
\begin{aligned}
(u, w) \in \mathscr{T}(\llbracket \text{QD}(A)_{/\sim} \rrbracket) &\iff o \preccurlyeq w \text{ and } (u, o^{-1}w) \in \mathscr{T}(\llbracket \text{QD}(A)_{/\sim} \rrbracket, (q^0_{/\sim}, r^0)) \\
&\stackrel{\text{Thm 3}}{\iff} o \preccurlyeq w \text{ and } (u, o^{-1}w) \in \mathscr{T}(\llbracket \text{QD}(A) \rrbracket, (q^0, r^0)) \\
&\iff (u, w) \in \mathscr{T}(\llbracket \text{QD}(A) \rrbracket) \\
&\stackrel{\text{Lma 1}}{\iff} (u, w) \in \mathscr{T}(\mathbf{qd}(\llbracket A \rrbracket)) \\
&\stackrel{\text{Prop 1}}{\iff} (u, w) \in \mathscr{T}(\llbracket A \rrbracket)
\end{aligned}
$$

We prove (b) next. Let $\sim$ be $\equiv_{\text{SFA}(\text{QD}(A))}$. By [17, Theorem 2] and Lemma 2 we have that $\llbracket \text{QD}(A) \rrbracket = \mathbf{qd}(\llbracket A \rrbracket)$ and so $\sim\ =\ \equiv_{\mathbf{aut}(\mathbf{qd}(\llbracket A \rrbracket))}$. Theorem 1 implies now that $\mathbf{qd}(\llbracket A \rrbracket)_{/\sim}$ is minimal and $\mathscr{T}(\mathbf{qd}(\llbracket A \rrbracket)_{/\sim}) = \mathscr{T}(A)$ which implies that $\text{QD}(A)_{/\sim}$ is minimal since $\llbracket \text{QD}(A) \rrbracket_{/\sim} = \llbracket \text{QD}(A)_{/\sim} \rrbracket = \mathbf{qd}(\llbracket A \rrbracket)_{/\sim}$ where we may assume, without loss of generality, that the state space of an SFT A is Q.   ⊠

We can apply Theorem 4(a) to deterministic STs by using the minimization algorithms from [17] to compute $\equiv_{\text{SFA}(\text{QD}(A))}$, since determinism is preserved by the SFA transformation. It is also clear that $\text{QD}(\cdot)$ preserves determinism.

Theorem 4(a) also holds for nondeterministic STs. Practical significance of Theorem 4(b) is that most SFTs that are being used in the context of string encoding, string decoding and string sanitization routines [25] are indeed deterministic and composition of SFTs are used frequently for example for composing different encoding routines and minimization is one technique to optimize such generated code.

While Theorem 4 provides a way to minimize the number of states in an SFT, the transitions may still have a non-minimal representation. The techniques and complexity for minimizing guards and output formulas will depend on what the effective Boolean algebra in question is. For example for BDDs choosing the variable order that minimizes the size is NP-complete [11], while general Boolean formula minimization is NP^P-complete [13].

6   Register-Carried Indistinguishability

The SFA encoding presented in Sect. 4 does not handle indistinguishability arising from register carried dependencies.

Example 8. In the SFA encoding of the ST in Fig. 1(b) the states q_1 and q_2 are distinguishable, since the encoding of the transition $q_1 \xrightarrow{true/[x \geq 3];\, 0} q_3$ matches the set of concrete labels $\{\, \mathrm{T}((a, r), [b], 0) \mid a \in I, r \in R, b = (r \geq 3)\,\}$, which is distinct from the concrete labels $\{\, \mathrm{T}((a, r), [b], 0) \mid a \in I, r \in R, b = (r < 3)\,\}$ matched by the encoding of the transition $q_2 \xrightarrow{true/[x < 3];\, 0} q_3$. However, in the ST the transition $q_0 \xrightarrow{x \geq 3/[];\, x} q_1$ is the only incoming transition for q_1 and thus the register value at q_1 will always be ≥ 3, which implies that the transition from q_1 to q_3 can only output $[true]$. By a similar argument the same holds for the transition from q_2 to q_3. Therefore the two states are indistinguishable when the state invariants implied by the incoming transitions are taken into account.   ⊠

Assuming such invariants are available they can be used to strengthen an ST to make more state reduction available.

Definition 12. Let there be an ST $A = (I, O, Q, q^0, o^0, T, F, R, r^0)$ and a function $\zeta : Q \rightarrow \mathcal{P}(R)$ such that for all $p \in Q, r \in R, v \in I^*$ and $w \in O^*$ it holds that

$$(q^0, r^0) \xrightarrow[\llbracket A \rrbracket]{v/w} (p, r) \;\Rightarrow\; \zeta(p)(r)$$

Intuitively ζ gives per-control state invariants for all reachable register values. Now a corresponding strengthened ST $\mathrm{INV}^\zeta(A)$ can be constructed as:

$$\mathrm{INV}^\zeta(A) \stackrel{\mathrm{def}}{=} (I, O, Q, q^0, o^0, T', F', R, r^0)$$
$$T' = \{\, p \xrightarrow{\zeta(p) \,\wedge\, \varphi/v;\, u} q \mid (p, \varphi, v, u, q) \in T \,\}$$
$$F' = \{\, p \xrightarrow{\zeta(p) \wedge \varphi} v \mid (p, \varphi, v) \in F \,\}$$

Theorem 5. $\mathscr{T}(\mathrm{INV}^\zeta(A)) = \mathscr{T}(A)$.

Proof. Recall the assumption that for all $p \in Q, r \in R, v \in I^*$ and $w \in O^*$ it holds that $(q^0, r^0) \xrightarrow[\llbracket A \rrbracket]{v/w} (p, r) \;\Rightarrow\; \zeta(p)(r)$. Now for any (p, r) appearing in a trace of $\llbracket A \rrbracket$ we have $\zeta(p)(r)$ and, therefore, by Definition 8 $\llbracket A \rrbracket$ and $\llbracket \mathrm{INV}^\zeta(A) \rrbracket$ have the same outgoing transitions from (p, r). Thus for all $p \in Q, r \in R, v \in I$ and $w_0, w, w_1 \in O^*$ we have

$$\xrightarrow[\llbracket A \rrbracket]{/w_0} (p^0, r^0) \xrightarrow[\llbracket A \rrbracket]{v/w} (p, r) \xrightarrow[\llbracket A \rrbracket]{/w_1}$$
$$\Leftrightarrow \xrightarrow[\llbracket \mathrm{INV}^\zeta(A) \rrbracket]{/w_0} (p^0, r^0) \xrightarrow[\llbracket \mathrm{INV}^\zeta(A) \rrbracket]{v/w} (p, r) \xrightarrow[\llbracket \mathrm{INV}^\zeta(A) \rrbracket]{/w_1}$$

Therefore $\mathscr{T}(\mathrm{INV}^\zeta(A)) = \mathscr{T}(A)$.   ⊠

Using this strengthening the ST in Example 8 could be further reduced with the invariants $\zeta(q_1) \stackrel{\mathrm{def}}{=} y \geq 3, \zeta(q_2) \stackrel{\mathrm{def}}{=} y < 3$ and $\zeta(q_0) \stackrel{\mathrm{def}}{=} \zeta(q_3) \stackrel{\mathrm{def}}{=} y = 0$. In Example 8 these invariants immediately follow from the conjunction of constraints from incoming transitions for each control state. In general reachability analysis techniques, such as PDR [12], or other invariant condition generation algorithms could be used. This strengthening technique also implies that transitions for STs should be written in a non-defensive way to enable the most reduction.

7 Implementation

We have implemented an ST state reduction tool that builds upon a framework and algorithms developed in [35] that are available in the open source Microsoft Automata library [1]. The tool is an integrated part of a tool chain which composes pipelines of STs and generates efficient code for them.

   The tool allows STs to be specified as (i) imperative code in a subset of C#, (ii) XPath expressions or Regular expressions with capture groups hierarchically composed to other STs, (iii) compositions of other STs. For compositions the tool produces a single ST using a fusion algorithm that uses Z3 to prune unsatisfiable transitions.

7.1 Huffman Coding

We have extended the tool with support for generating SFTs that perform Huffman encoding and decoding [26]. Huffman coding is an optimal prefix code that assigns variable length bit patterns to symbols. Symbols are assigned bit patterns according to their frequency in such a way that more common symbols are represented with shorter bit patterns. Huffman coding is only one class of prefix codes. We will now give constructions of SFT decoders and encoders for any prefix code.

Definition 13. A *prefix code tree* is a tuple $(Q, E, q_0, \Sigma, S, l_\Sigma, l_S)$, where Q is a set of at least two vertices, $q_0 \in Q$ is the root, $E \subset Q \times Q$ s.t. (Q, E, q_0) is a tree rooted at q_0 with all edges in E directed away from the root, Σ is the *coding alphabet* and S is the *symbol alphabet*.

   $l_\Sigma : E \to \Sigma$ is a function s.t. $\forall (p, q), (p, q') \in E : l_\Sigma(p, q) \neq l_\Sigma(p, q')$. Let Q_{leaves} be the leaves of the tree (nodes with no outgoing edges). $l_S : Q_{leaves} \to S$ associates leaves to symbols.

Given a prefix code tree P the *decoder for P* is an SFT $(\Sigma, S, Q \setminus Q_{leaves}, q_0, \epsilon, T, \{(q_0, true, \epsilon)\})$ where:

$$
T = \{ p \xrightarrow{x = l_\Sigma(p, q)/\epsilon} q \mid (p, q) \in E \setminus (Q \times Q_{leaves}) \}
$$
$$
\cup \{ p \xrightarrow{x = l_\Sigma(p, q)/[l_S(q)]} q_0 \mid (p, q) \in E \cap (Q \times Q_{leaves}) \}
$$

The *encoder for P* is an SFT $(S, \Sigma, \{p_0\}, p_0, \epsilon, T, \{(p_0, true, \epsilon)\})$ where:

$$
T = \{ p_0 \xrightarrow{x = l_S(q)/code(q)} p_0 \mid q \in Q_{leaves} \}
$$
$$
code(q) = \text{let } q_1, \ldots, q_n \text{ be the unique path in } E \text{ from } q_0 \text{ to } q \text{ in}
$$
$$
[l_\Sigma(q_0, q_1), l_\Sigma(q_1, q_2), \ldots, l_\Sigma(q_n, q)]
$$

We will show in our evaluation that Huffman decoders in particular are very amenable to state reductions when composed with other transducers.

8   Evaluation

We evaluate the tool on STs drawn from [35]. These STs are fused pipelines consisting of real-world stream processing computations. The first four pipelines represent various stream processing scenarios: **Base64-avg** calculates a running average (window of 10) for Base64[4] encoded `ints` and re-encodes the results in Base64. **CSV-max** decodes an UTF-8 encoded CSV file to UTF-16, extracts the third column with a regular expression and finds the maximum length of these strings. The output is a single UTF-8 encoded decimal formatted integer. **Base64-delta** reads Base64 encoded `ints` and outputs deltas of successive inputs as UTF-8 encoded decimal integers on separate lines. **UTF8-lines** decodes an UTF-8 encoded file to UTF-16 and counts the number of newline characters. The output is a single UTF-8 encoded decimal formatted integer.

The following pipelines focus on CSV parsing scenarios using the regex based parsing offered by the tool: **CC-id** is written for a dataset of consumer complaints received by the U.S. Consumer Financial Protection Bureau. The pipeline produces the maximum value for the ID column. **CHSI-cancer** is written for a dataset on health indicators from the U.S. Department of Health & Human Services. The pipeline produces the average lung cancer deaths for counties in the dataset. **SBO-employees** is written for a dataset on business owners from the U.S. Census Bureau. The pipeline finds the maximum number of employees for businesses in the dataset.

Each of these pipelines consist of four phases: (i) decode UTF-8 to UTF-16, (ii) parse a column as an `int` using a regular expression based parser, (iii) run a query (maximum, minimum or average), and (iv) output the result as a sequence of bytes. The pipelines differ only in the regular expression and query used.

The following pipelines are written for XML processing scenarios and use an XPath based transducer for extracting the relevant data: **TPC-DI-SQL** The dataset was generated by a tool from the TPC-DI benchmark [34]. The pipeline extracts ids of accounts from customer records and for each outputs an SQL insert statement. **PIR-proteins** The dataset is a protein dataset from the U.S. based National Biomedical Research Foundation. The pipeline extracts the lengths of all proteins in the dataset and outputs the average length. **DBLP-oldest** The dataset is bibliographic information from the Digital Bibliography Library Project. The pipeline extracts the publication year of each article and outputs the earliest year. **MONDIAL-pop** Mondial is a dataset extracted from various geographical Web data sources. The pipeline extracts the population of each city in the dataset and outputs the highest population.

Additionally we evaluate one pipeline using the new Huffman decoding described in Sect. 7.1: **Huffman** decodes a Huffman encoded ASCII file and counts the newline characters. The data for creating the Huffman tree is Herman Melville's "Moby Dick".

For each pipeline in our evaluation we produce a single ST as the composition of the whole pipeline and apply the state reduction algorithm to it. In Fig. 3

---

[4] See https://en.wikipedia.org/wiki/Base64.

Pipeline	Removed	$|Q|$	Time	Pipeline	Removed	$|Q|$	Time
Base64-delta	10	18	39.9 s	SBO-employees	4	36	0.2 s
CSV-max	4	26	18.0 s	TPC-DI-SQL	68	457	44.1 s
Base64-avg	114	166	99.6 s	PIR-proteins	80	355	196.1 s
UTF8-lines	0	5	0.03 s	DBLP-oldest	36	219	9.8 s
CC-id	2024	983	4.4 s	MONDIAL-pop	56	319	12.4 s
CHSI-cancer	12	558	2.2 s	Huffman	915	360	2.6 s

Fig. 3. Control states removed and remaining, and total time taken.

we report the number of control states removed, the number of control states remaining and the time taken by the state reduction.

For the pipelines in Fig. 3 an average of 25% of the control states are removed. The amount of state reduction available is highly variable: for Huffman 72% of its control states are removed, as counting lines makes all control states that for all inputs output something else than an end-of-line character indistinguishable. On the other hand for UTF8-lines there is nothing left to remove as neither of the single control state line counting or integer formatting STs composed onto the UTF8 decoder make any control states (that correspond to encodings of different lengths) indistinguishable.

In general we see our state reduction algorithm being effective when some control states become indistinguishable due to composition. For example we can see great reduction in the regex and XML processing pipelines due to multi-byte encodings from the UTF8-to-UTF16 decoder being handled equivalently in parts of the regex or XPath matchers.

9   Related Work

Minimization of Finite State Transducers. Minimality of sequential transducers was first studied by Choffrut [14]. Mohri's original work on minimizing sequential finite state transducers appears in [31] and introduces the notion of quasi-determinization of NFAs, that is similar to classical shortest paths problems in weighted directed graphs. An incremental algorithm of minimizing acyclic finite state transducers is described in [30]. A notion of minimization of finite state transducers in natural language processing is studied in [20] by using flag diacritics. We stated Mohri's minimization algorithm so it applies to sequential transducers with final outputs. The notion of sequential functions with final outputs are often called *subsequential* functions and were originally introduced in [36]. Some algorithms for finitely subsequential transducers are investigated in [6].

Minimization of Symbolic Automata. The concept of automata with predicates instead of concrete symbols was first mentioned in [41] and was first discussed in [37] in the context of natural language processing. An algorithm for minimizing SFAs, based on Hopcroft's partition refinement, is developed in [17].

The MONA implementation [23] provides decision procedures for monadic second-order logic, and uses also highly-optimized and minimized BDD-based representation of automata [27]. The SFA minimization problem is also related to minimizing control flow graphs of programs, which is studied in [15] by reduction to a variant of classical automata minimization.

Nondeterministic Case. Our main theorem, Theorem 4, allows the ST or SFT to be nondeterministic and the resulting SFA may, likewise, be nondeterministic. Recently a state reduction algorithm has been developed for nondeterministic SFAs that is based on computing forward bisimulations [18]. A forward bisimulation $\sim$ preserves state indistinguishability and therefore Theorem 4(a) applies. There are numerous other algorithms, developed for nondeterministic automata [3,4,7,24,29] that may likewise be extensible for SFAs.

Transducers with Registers. Streaming string transducers [9] are another type of transducer that include a register as part of their state. A significant departure from symbolic transducers is that the contents of a string held in a register can be included in the output as a flattened part of the output sequence, thus making output in a single transition be potentially variable in length. It is unclear how our techniques would apply to streaming string transducers. In particular, streaming string transducers with data values are in general not closed under composition [9, Proposition 4]. Register minimization is a form of resource minimization that aims at reducing the number of registers and has been studied for streaming string transducers [10]. Register minimization has also been studied for cost register automata [8,19].

10   Conclusions

Similarly to products of DFAs and subset constructions of NFAs, compositions of symbolic transducers (STs) present an important target for minimization. Composition can often introduce indistinguishable control states, which makes it possible to leverage minimization algorithms for symbolic finite automata (SFAs) through an encoding approach. Combined with a quasi-determinization step our approach guarantees minimality for symbolic finite transducers (SFTs) when they are deterministic.

Minimizing an SFA encoding of an ST provides a very general control state reduction approach, which is agnostic to how the SFA is minimized as long as indistinguishable equivalence classes of control states are identified. The approach is even agnostic to nondeterminism and as such enables nondeterministic STs to be targeted as minimization algorithms for nondeterministic SFAs become available. To allow state reduction in STs where indistinguishability is due to register carried constraints, an ST can be strengthened using known invariants on the register.

On a set of STs composed from real-world streaming computations our state reduction algorithm removes an average of 25% showing that the approach is effective even with the over-approximation involved in the SFA encoding.

References

1. Automata library. https://github.com/AutomataDotNet/Automata
2. Emoticons, Unicode standard v9.0. http://unicode.org/charts/PDF/U1F600.pdf
3. Abdulla, P.A., Deneux, J., Kaati, L., Nilsson, M.: Minimization of non-deterministic automata with large alphabets. In: Farré, J., Litovsky, I., Schmitz, S. (eds.) CIAA 2005. LNCS, vol. 3845, pp. 31–42. Springer, Heidelberg (2006). doi:10.1007/11605157_3
4. Abdulla, P.A., Bouajjani, A., Holík, L., Kaati, L., Vojnar, T.: Composed bisimulation for tree automata. In: Ibarra, O.H., Ravikumar, B. (eds.) CIAA 2008. LNCS, vol. 5148, pp. 212–222. Springer, Heidelberg (2008). doi:10.1007/978-3-540-70844-5_22
5. Aho, A.V., Lam, M.S., Sethi, R., Ullman, J.D.: Compilers: Principles, Techniques, and Tools, 2nd edn. Addison-Wesley, Boston (2006)
6. Allauzen, C., Mohri, M.: Finitely subsequential transducers. Int. J. Found. Comput. Sci. **14**(6), 983–994 (2003)
7. Almeida, R., Holík, L., Mayr, R.: Reduction of nondeterministic tree automata. In: Chechik, M., Raskin, J.-F. (eds.) TACAS 2016. LNCS, vol. 9636, pp. 717–735. Springer, Heidelberg (2016). doi:10.1007/978-3-662-49674-9_46
8. Alur, R., Raghothaman, M.: Decision problems for additive regular functions. In: Fomin, F.V., Freivalds, R., Kwiatkowska, M., Peleg, D. (eds.) ICALP 2013. LNCS, vol. 7966, pp. 37–48. Springer, Heidelberg (2013). doi:10.1007/978-3-642-39212-2_7
9. Alur, R., Černý, P.: Streaming transducers for algorithmic verification of single-pass list-processing programs. SIGPLAN Not. - POPL 2011 **46**(1), 599–610 (2011)
10. Baschenis, F., Gauwin, O., Muscholl, A., Puppis, G.: Minimizing resources of sweeping and streaming string transducers. In: 43rd International Colloquium on Automata, Languages, and Programming (ICALP 2016). LIPIcs, vol. 55, pp. 114:1–114:14. Schloss Dagstuhl - Leibniz-Zentrum fuer Informatik (2016)
11. Bollig, B., Wegener, I.: Improving the variable ordering of OBDDs is NP-complete. IEEE Trans. Comput. **45**(9), 993–1002 (1996)
12. Bradley, A.R.: SAT-based model checking without unrolling. In: Jhala, R., Schmidt, D. (eds.) VMCAI 2011. LNCS, vol. 6538, pp. 70–87. Springer, Heidelberg (2011). doi:10.1007/978-3-642-18275-4_7
13. Buchfuhrer, D., Umans, C.: The complexity of Boolean formula minimization. J. Comput. Syst. Sci. **77**(1), 142–153 (2011)
14. Choffrut, C.: Contribution à l'étude de quelques familles remarquables de fonctions rationnelles. Ph.D. thesis, Universit Paris 7, Paris, France (1978)
15. Colcombet, T., Fradet, P.: Enforcing trace properties by program transformation. In: Proceedings of the 27th ACM SIGPLAN-SIGACT Symposium on Principles of Programming Languages (POPL 2000), pp. 54–66. ACM (2000)
16. Dalla Preda, M., Giacobazzi, R., Lakhotia, A., Mastroeni, I.: Abstract symbolic automata: mixed syntactic/semantic similarity analysis of executables. SIGPLAN Not. - POPL 2015 **50**(1), 329–341 (2015)
17. D'Antoni, L., Veanes, M.: Minimization of symbolic automata. SIGPLAN Not. - POPL 2014 **49**(1), 541–553 (2014)
18. D'Antoni, L., Veanes, M.: Forward bisimulations for nondeterministic symbolic finite automata. In: Legay, A., Margaria, T. (eds.) TACAS 201. LNCS, vol. 10205, pp. 518–534. Springer, Heidelberg (2017). doi:10.1007/978-3-662-54577-5_30

19. Daviaud, L., Reynier, P.-A., Talbot, J.-M.: A generalised twinning property for minimisation of cost register automata. In: Proceedings of the 31st Annual ACM/IEEE Symposium on Logic in Computer Science (LICS 2016), pp. 857–866. ACM (2016)

20. Drobac, S., Lindén, K., Pirinen, T., Silfverberg, M.: Heuristic hyper-minimization of finite state lexicons. In: Proceedings of the Ninth International Conference on Language Resources and Evaluation (LREC 2014). ELRA (2014)

21. D'Souza, D., Shankar, P. (eds.): Modern Applications of Automata Theory. IISc Research Monographs Series, vol. 2. World Scientific, Singapore (2012)

22. Fülöp, Z., Vogler, H.: Forward and backward application of symbolic tree transducers. Acta Informatica $51(5)$, 297–325 (2014)

23. Henriksen, J.G., Jensen, J., Jørgensen, M., Klarlund, N., Paige, R., Rauhe, T., Sandholm, A.: Mona: monadic second-order logic in practice. In: Brinksma, E., Cleaveland, W.R., Larsen, K.G., Margaria, T., Steffen, B. (eds.) TACAS 1995. LNCS, vol. 1019, pp. 89–110. Springer, Heidelberg (1995). doi:10.1007/3-540-60630-0_5

24. Högberg, J., Maletti, A., May, J.: Backward and forward bisimulation minimisation of tree automata. In: Holub, J., Žd'árek, J. (eds.) CIAA 2007. LNCS, vol. 4783, pp. 109–121. Springer, Heidelberg (2007). doi:10.1007/978-3-540-76336-9_12

25. Hooimeijer, P., Livshits, B., Molnar, D., Saxena, P., Veanes, M.: Fast and precise sanitizer analysis with Bek. In: Proceedings of the 20th USENIX Conference on Security (SEC 2011). USENIX Association (2011)

26. Huffman, D.A.: A method for the construction of minimum-redundancy codes. Proc. IRE $40(9)$, 1098–1101 (1952)

27. Klarlund, N., Møller, A., Schwartzbach, M.I.: MONA implementation secrets. Int. J. Found. Comput. Sci. $13(4)$, 571–586 (2002)

28. Manuel, A., Ramanujam, R.: Automata over infinite alphabets. In: D'Souza, D., Shankar, P. (eds.) Modern Applications of Automata Theory, pp. 529–554. World Scientific (2012)

29. Mayr, R., Clemente, L.: Advanced automata minimization. SIGPLAN Not. - POPL 2013 $48(1)$, 63–74 (2013)

30. Mesfar, S., Silberztein, M.: Transducer minimization and information compression for NooJ dictionaries. In: Proceedings of the 2009 Conference on Finite-State Methods and Natural Language Processing (FSMNLP 2008), pp. 110–121. IOS Press (2009)

31. Mohri, M.: Minimization of sequential transducers. In: Crochemore, M., Gusfield, D. (eds.) CPM 1994. LNCS, vol. 807, pp. 151–163. Springer, Heidelberg (1994). doi:10.1007/3-540-58094-8_14

32. Mohri, M.: Finite-state transducers in language and speech processing. Comput. Linguist. $23(2)$, 269–311 (1997)

33. Mohri, M.: Minimization algorithms for sequential transducers. Theoret. Comput. Sci. $234(1-2)$, 177–201 (2000)

34. Poess, M., Rabl, T., Jacobsen, H.-A., Caufield, B.: TPC-DI: the first industry benchmark for data integration. Proc. VLDB Endowment $7(13)$, 1367–1378 (2014)

35. Saarikivi, O., Veanes, M., Mytkowicz, T., Musuvathi, M.: Fusing effectful comprehensions. In: Proceedings of the 38th ACM SIGPLAN Conference on Programming Language Design and Implementation (PLDI 2017). ACM (2017)

36. Schützenberger, M.P.: Sur une variante des fonctions séquentielles. Theoret. Comput. Sci. 4, 47–57 (1977)

37. van Noord, G., Gerdemann, D.: Finite state transducers with predicates and identities. Grammars $4(3)$, 263–286 (2001)

38. Veanes, M., de Halleux, P., Tillmann, N.: Rex: symbolic regular expression explorer. In: Proceedings of the 2010 Third International Conference on Software Testing, Verification and Validation (ICST 2010), pp. 498–507. IEEE (2010)
39. Veanes, M., Hooimeijer, P., Livshits, B., Molnar, D., Bjorner, N.: Symbolic finite state transducers: algorithms and applications. SIGPLAN Not. - POPL 2012 **47**(1), 137–150 (2012)
40. Veanes, M., Mytkowicz, T., Molnar, D., Livshits, B.: Data-parallel string-manipulating programs. SIGPLAN Not. - POPL2015 **50**(1), 139–152 (2015)
41. Watson, B.W.: Implementing and using finite automata toolkits. In: Extended Finite State Models of Language, pp. 19–36. Cambridge University Press (1999)

Abstract Interpretation with Unfoldings

Marcelo Sousa[1]([✉]), César Rodríguez[2,3], Vijay D'Silva[4],
and Daniel Kroening[1,3]

[1] University of Oxford, Oxford, UK
marcelo.sousa@cs.ox.ac.uk
[2] Université Paris 13, Sorbonne Paris Cité,
LIPN, CNRS, Paris, France
[3] Diffblue Ltd., Oxford, UK
[4] Google Inc., San Francisco, USA

Abstract. We present and evaluate a technique for computing path-sensitive interference conditions during abstract interpretation of concurrent programs. In lieu of fixed point computation, we use prime event structures to compactly represent causal dependence and interference between sequences of transformers. Our main contribution is an unfolding algorithm that uses a new notion of independence to avoid redundant transformer application, thread-local fixed points to reduce the size of the unfolding, and a novel cutoff criterion based on subsumption to guarantee termination of the analysis. Our experiments show that the abstract unfolding produces an order of magnitude fewer false alarms than a mature abstract interpreter, while being several orders of magnitude faster than solver-based tools that have the same precision.

1 Introduction

This paper is concerned with the problem of extending an abstract interpreter for sequential programs to analyze concurrent programs. A naïve solution to this problem is a global fixed point analysis involving all threads in the program. An alternative that seeks to exploit the scalability of local analyses is to analyze each thread in isolation and exchange invariants on global variables between threads [3,18,19]. Much research on abstract interpretation of concurrent programs, including this paper, aims to discover analyses that combine the scalability of the local fixed point computation with the precision of a global fixed point.

The *abstract unfolding* data structure and algorithm presented in this paper combines an abstract domain with the type algorithm used to analyze Petri nets. An unfolding is a tree-like structure that uses partial orders to compactly represent concurrent executions and uses conflict relations to represent interference between executions. There are several obstacles to combining unfoldings with abstract domains. First, unfolding construction requires interference information that is absent from abstract domains. Second, an unfolding compactly

---

Supported by ERC project 280053 (CPROVER) and a Google Fellowship.

R. Majumdar and V. Kunčak (Eds.): CAV 2017, Part II, LNCS 10427, pp. 197–216, 2017.
DOI: 10.1007/978-3-319-63390-9_11

represents the traces of a system, while abstract domains approximate states and transitions. Finally, unfolding algorithms perform explicit-state analysis of deterministic systems while abstract domains are inherently symbolic and non-deterministic owing to abstraction.

The main idea of this paper is to construct an unfolding *of an analyzer*, rather than a program. An event is the application of a transformer in an analysis context, and concurrent executions are replaced by a partial order on transformer applications. We introduce independence for transformers and use this notion to construct an unfolding of a domain given a program and independence relation. The unfolding of a domain is typically large and we use thread-local fixed point computation to reduce its size without losing interference information.

Most pairs of transformers are not related by standard notions of independence. A counterintuitive observation in this paper is that by increasing the path-sensitivity of the analysis, we decrease interference, which reduces the number of interleavings to explore and improves scalability. From a static analysis perspective, our analyser uses the unfolding to represent a history abstraction (or trace partition) which is constructed using independence. From a dynamic analysis perspective, our approach is a form of partial-order reduction (POR) [23] that uses an abstract domain to collapse branches of the computation tree originating from thread-local control decisions.

Contribution. We make the following contributions towards reusing an abstract interpreter for sequential code for the analysis of a concurrent program.

1. A new notion of transformer independence for unfolding with domains (Sect. 4).
2. The unfolding of a domain, which provides a sound way to combine transformer application and partial-order reduction (Sect. 5.1).
3. A method to construct the unfolding using thread-local analysis and pruning techniques (Sects. 6 and 6.1).
4. An implementation and empirical evaluation demonstrating the trade-offs compared to an abstract interpreter and solver-based tools (Sect. 7).

The proofs of the formal results presented in this paper can be found in the extended version [24].

2   Motivating Example and Overview

Consider the program given in Fig. 1(a), which we wish to prove safe using an interval analysis. Thread 1 (resp. 2) increments i (resp. j) in a loop that can non-deterministically stop at any iteration. All variables are initialized to 0 and the program is safe, as the `assert` in thread 2 cannot be violated.

When we use a POR approach to prove safety of this program, the exploration algorithm exploits the fact that only the interference between statements that modify the variable g can lead to distinct final states. This interference is typically known as *independence* [10,22]. The practical relevance of independence is that one can use it to define a safe fragment, given in Fig. 1(b), of

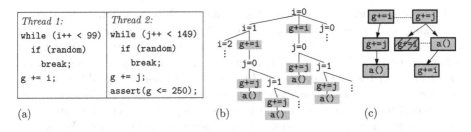

Fig. 1. (a) Example program (b) Its POR exploration tree (c) Our unfolding

the computation tree of the program which can be efficiently explored [1,23]. At every iteration of each loop, the conditionals open one more branch in the tree. Thus, each branch contains a different write to the global variable, which is dependent with the writes of the other thread as the order of their application reaches different states. As a result, the exploration tree becomes intractable very fast. It is of course possible to bound the depth of the exploration at the expense of completeness of the analysis.

The thread-modular static analysis that is implemented in ASTREEA [19] or FRAMA-C [26] incorrectly triggers an alarm for this program. These tools statically analyze each thread in isolation assuming that g equals 0. Both discover that thread 1 (resp. 2) can write $[0,100]$ (resp. $[0,150]$) to g when it reads 0 from it. Since each thread can modify the variable read by the other, they repeat the analysis starting from the join of the new interval with the initial interval. In this iteration, they discover that thread 2 can write $[0,250]$ to g when it reads $[0,150]$ from it. The analysis now incorrectly determines that it needs to re-analyze thread 2, because thread 1 also wrote $[0,250]$ in the previous iteration and that is a larger interval than that read by thread 2. This is the reasoning behind the false alarm. The core problem here is that these methods are path-insensitive across thread context switches and that is insufficient to prove this assertion. The analysis is accounting for a thread context switch that can never happen (the one that flows $[0,250]$ to thread 2 before thread 2 increments g). More recent approaches [15,20] can achieve a higher degree of flow-sensitivity but they either require manual annotations to guide the trace partitioning or are restricted to program locations outside of a loop body.

Our key contribution is an unfolding that is flow- and path-sensitive across interfering statements of the threads, and path-insensitive inside the non-interfering blocks of statements. Figure 1(c) shows the unfolding structure that our method explores for this program. The boxes in this structure are called *events* and they represent the action of firing a transformer after a history of firings. The arrows depict *causality* constraints between events, i.e., the *happens-before* relation. Dotted lines depict the immediate *conflict relation*, stating that two events cannot be simultaneously present in the same concurrent execution, known as *configuration*. This structure contains three maximal configurations (executions), which correspond to the three meaningful ways in which the statements reading or writing to variable g can interleave.

Conceptually, we can construct this unfolding using the following idea: start by picking an arbitrary interleaving. Initially we pick the empty one which reaches the initial state of the program. Now we run a sequential abstract interpreter on one thread, say thread 1, from that state and stop on every location that reads or writes a global variable. In this case, the analyzer would stop at the statement `g += i` with the invariant that $\langle g \mapsto [0,0], i \mapsto [0,100] \rangle$. This invariant corresponds to the first event of the unfolding (top-left corner). The unfolding contains now a new execution, so we iterate again the same procedure by picking the execution consisting of the event we just discovered. We run the analyser on thread 2 from the invariant reached by that execution and stop on any global action. That gives rise to the event `g+=j`, and in the next step using the execution composed of the two events we have seen, we discover its causal successor `a()` (representing the assert statement). Note however that before visiting that event, we could have added event `g+=j` corresponding to the invariant of running an analyser starting from the initial state on thread 2. Furthermore, since both invariants are related to the same shared variable, these two events must not be present in the same execution. We enforce that with the conflict relation.

Our method mitigates the aforementioned branching explosion of the POR tree because it never unfolds the conflicting branches of one thread (loop iterations in our example). In comparison to thread-modular analysis, it remains precise about the context switches because it uses a history-preserving data structure.

Another novelty of our approach is the observation that certain events are *equivalent* in the sense that the state associated with one is *subsumed* by the second. In our example, one of these events, known as a *cutoff event*, is labelled by `g+=i` and denoted with a striped pattern. Specifically, the configuration {`g+=i, g+=j`} reaches the same state as {`g+=j, g+=i`}. Thus, no causal successor of a cutoff event needs to be explored as any action that we can discover from the cutoff event can be found somewhere else in the structure.

Outline. The following diagram displays the various concepts and transformations presented in the paper:

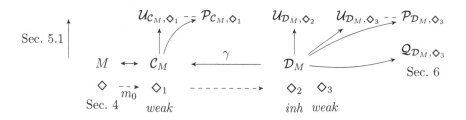

Fig. 2. Overview diagram

Let M be the program under analysis, whose concrete semantics $\mathcal{C}_M$ is abstracted by a domain $\mathcal{D}_M$. The relations $\Diamond$ and $\Diamond_i$ are independence relations with different levels of granularity over the transformers of M, $\mathcal{C}_M$, or $\mathcal{D}_M$.

We denote by $\mathcal{U}_{\mathcal{D}',\diamondsuit'}$ the *unfolding* of $\mathcal{D}'$ (either $\mathcal{C}_M$ or $\mathcal{D}_M$) under independence relation $\diamondsuit'$ (either $\diamondsuit_1$ or $\diamondsuit_2$). This transformation is defined in Sect. 5.1. Whenever we unfold a domain using a weak independence relation ($\diamondsuit_2$ on $\mathcal{C}_M$ and $\diamondsuit_3$ on $\mathcal{D}_M$), we can use cutoffs to prune the unfolding, represented by the dashed line between unfoldings. The resulting unfolding, defined in Sect. 6.1, is denoted by the letter $\mathcal{P}$. The main contribution of our work is the *compact unfolding*, $\mathcal{Q}_{\mathcal{D}_M,\diamondsuit_3}$, an example of which was given in Fig. 1(c).

3   Preliminaries

There is no new material in this section, but we recommend the reader to review the definition of an analysis instance, which is not standard.

Concurrent Programs. We model the semantics of a concurrent, non-deterministic program by a labelled transition system $M := \langle \Sigma, \to, A, s_0 \rangle$, where Σ is the set of *states*, A is the set of *program statements*, $\to \subseteq \Sigma \times A \times \Sigma$ is the transition relation, and s_0 is the *initial state*. The identifier of the thread containing a statement a is given by a function $p\colon A \to \mathbb{N}$. If $s \xrightarrow{a} s'$ is a transition, the statement a is *enabled* at s, and a can *fire* at s to produce s'. We let $enabl(s)$ denote the set of statements enabled at s. As statements may be non-deterministic, firing a may produce more than one such s'. A sequence $\sigma := a_1 \ldots a_n \in A^*$ is a *run* when there are states $s_1, \ldots, s_n$ satisfying $s_0 \xrightarrow{a_1} s_1 \ldots \xrightarrow{a_n} s_n$. For such σ we define $state(\sigma) := s_n$. We let $runs(M)$ denote the set of all runs of M, and $reach(M) := \{state(\sigma) \in \Sigma \colon \sigma \in runs(M)\}$ the set of all *reachable states* of M.

Analysis Instances. A lattice $\langle D, \sqsubseteq_D, \sqcup_D, \sqcap_D \rangle$ is a poset with a binary, least upper bound operator $\sqcup_D$ called *join* and a binary, greatest lower bound operator $\sqcap_D$ called *meet*. A *transformer* $f\colon D \to D$ is a monotone function on D. A *domain* $\langle D, \sqsubseteq, F \rangle$ consists of a lattice and a set of transformers. We adopt standard assumptions in the literature that D has a least element $\bot$, called *bottom*, and that transformers are *bottom-strict*, i.e. $f(\bot) = \bot$. To simplify presentation, we equip domains with sufficient structure to lift notions from transition systems to domains, and assume that domains represent control and data states.

Definition 1. *An analysis instance* $\mathcal{D} := \langle D, \sqsubseteq, F, d_0 \rangle$, *consists of a domain* $\langle D, \sqsubseteq, F \rangle$ *and an initial element* $d_0 \in D$.

A transformer f is *enabled* at an element d when $f(d) \neq \bot$, and the result of *firing* f at d is $f(d)$. The element *generated by* or *reached by* a sequence of transformers $\sigma := f_1, \ldots, f_m$ is the application $state(\sigma) := (f_m \circ \ldots \circ f_1)(d_0)$ of transformers in σ to d_0. Let $reach(\mathcal{D})$ be the set of reachable elements of $\mathcal{D}$. The sequence σ is a *run* if $state(\sigma) \neq \bot$ and $runs(\mathcal{D})$ is the set of all runs of $\mathcal{D}$.

The *collecting semantics* of a transition system M is the analysis instance $\mathcal{C}_M := \langle \mathscr{P}(\Sigma), \subseteq, F, \{s_0\} \rangle$, where F contains a transformer $f_a(S) :=$

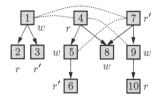

Fig. 3. A PES with 10 events, labelled by elements in $\{w, r, r'\}$.

$\left\{ s' \in \Sigma : s \in S \wedge s \xrightarrow{a} s' \right\}$ for every statement a of the program. The *pointwise-lifting* of a relation $R \subseteq A \times A$ on statements to transformers in $\mathcal{D}$ is $R_{\mathcal{D}} = \{\langle f_a, f_{a'} \rangle \mid \langle a, a' \rangle \in R\}$. Let $m_0 \colon A \to F$ be map from statements to transformers: $m_0(a) := f_a$. An analysis instance $\bar{\mathcal{D}} = \langle \bar{D}, \bar{\sqsubseteq}, \bar{F}, \bar{d}_0 \rangle$ is an *abstraction* of $\langle D, \sqsubseteq, F, d_0 \rangle$ if there exists a *concretization function* $\gamma \colon \bar{D} \to D$, which is monotone and satisfies that $d_0 \sqsubseteq \gamma(\bar{d}_0)$, and that $f \circ \gamma \sqsubseteq \gamma \circ \bar{f}$, where the order between functions is pointwise.

Labelled Prime Event Structures. Event structures are tree-like representations of system behaviour that use partial orders to represent concurrent interaction. Figure 3 depicts an event structure. The nodes are events and solid arrows, represent causal dependencies: events 4 and 7 must fire before 8 can fire. The dotted line represents conflicts: 4 and 7 are not in conflict and may occur in any order, but 4 and 9 are in conflict and cannot occur in the same execution.

A *labelled prime event structure* [21] (PES) is a tuple $\mathcal{E} := \langle E, <, \#, h \rangle$ with a set of events E, a causality relation $< \subseteq E \times E$, which is a strict partial order, a conflict relation $\# \subseteq E \times E$ that is symmetric and irreflexive, and a labelling function $h \colon E \to X$. The components of $\mathcal{E}$ satisfy (1) the *axiom of finite causes*, that for all $e \in E$, $\{e' \in E \colon e' < e\}$ is finite, and (2) the *axiom of hereditary conflict*, that for all $e, e', e'' \in E$, if $e \# e'$ and $e' < e''$, then $e \# e''$.

The *history* of an event $\lceil e \rceil := \{e' \in E \colon e' < e\}$ is the least set of events that must fire before e can fire. A *configuration* of $\mathcal{E}$ is a finite set $C \subseteq E$ that is (i) (causally closed) $\lceil e \rceil \subseteq C$ for all $e \in C$, and (ii) (conflict free) $\neg(e \# e')$ for all $e, e' \in C$. We let $conf(\mathcal{E})$ denote the set of all configurations of $\mathcal{E}$. For any $e \in E$, the *local configuration* of e is defined as $[e] := \lceil e \rceil \cup \{e\}$. In Fig. 3, the set $\{1, 2\}$ is a configuration, and in fact it is a local configuration, i.e., $[2] = \{1, 2\}$. The set $\{1, 2, 3\}$ is a $\subseteq$-maximal configuration. The local configuration of event 8 is $\{4, 7, 8\}$.

Given a configuration C, we define the *interleavings* of C as the set

$$inter(C) := \{h(e_1), \ldots, h(e_n) \colon \forall e_i, e_j \in C, e_i < e_j \implies i < j\}.$$

An interleaving corresponds to the sequence labelling any topological sorting (sequentialization) of the events in the configuration. We say that $\mathcal{E}$ is finite iff E is finite. In Fig. 3, the interleavings of configuration $\{1, 2, 3\}$ are wrr' and $wr'r$.

Event structures are naturally (partially) ordered by a *prefix* relation $\unlhd$. Given two PESs $\mathcal{E} := \langle E, <, \#, h \rangle$ and $\mathcal{E}' := \langle E', <', \#', h' \rangle$, we say that $\mathcal{E}$ is a *prefix* of $\mathcal{E}'$, written $\mathcal{E} \unlhd \mathcal{E}'$, when $E \subseteq E'$, $<$ and $\#$ are the projections of $<'$ and $\#'$ to E, and $E \supseteq \{e' \in E' : e' < e \wedge e \in E\}$. Moreover, the set of prefixes of a given PES $\mathcal{E}$ equipped with $\unlhd$ is a complete lattice.

4   Independence for Transformers

Partial-order reduction tools use a notion called independence to avoid exploring concurrent interleavings that lead to the same state. Our analyzer uses independence between transformers to compactly represent transformer applications that lead to the same result. The contribution of this section is a notion of independence for transformers (represented by the lowest horizontal arrows in Fig. 2) and a demonstration that abstraction may both create and violate independence relationships.

We recall a standard notion of independence for statements [10,22]. Two statements a, a' of a program M *commute at* a state s iff

- if $a \in enabl(s)$ and $s \xrightarrow{a} s'$, then $a' \in enabl(s)$ iff $a' \in enabl(s')$; and
- if $a, a' \in enabl(s)$, then there is a state s' such that $s \xrightarrow{a.a'} s'$ and $s \xrightarrow{a'.a} s'$.

Independence between statements is an underapproximation of commutativity. A relation $\diamondsuit \subseteq A \times A$ is an *independence* for M if it is symmetric, irreflexive, and satisfies that every $(a, a') \in \diamondsuit$ commute at every reachable state of M. In general, M has multiple independence relations; $\emptyset$ is always one of them.

Suppose that independence for transformers is defined by replacing statements and transitions with transformers and transformer application, respectively. Example 1 illustrates that an independence relation on statements cannot be lifted to obtain transformers that are independent under such a notion.

Example 1. Consider the collecting semantics $\mathcal{C}_M$ of a program M with two variables, x and y, two statements $a := \mathtt{assume(x==0)}$ and $a' := \mathtt{assume(y==0)}$, and initial element $d_0 := \{\langle x \mapsto 0, y \mapsto 1 \rangle, \langle x \mapsto 1, y \mapsto 0 \rangle\}$. Since a and a' read different variables, $R := \{\langle a, a' \rangle, \langle a', a \rangle\}$ is an independence relation on M. Now observe that $\{\langle f_a, f_{a'} \rangle, \langle f_{a'}, f_a \rangle\}$ is not an independence relation on $\mathcal{C}_M$, as f_a and $f_{a'}$ disable each other. Note, however, that $f_a(f_{a'}(d_0))$ and $f_{a'}(f_a(d_0))$ are both $\perp$.

Weak independence, defined below, allows transformers to be considered independent even if they disable each other.

Definition 2. *Let $\mathcal{D} := \langle D, \sqsubseteq, F, d_0 \rangle$ be an analysis instance. A relation $\diamondsuit \subseteq F \times F$ is a weak independence on transformers if it is symmetric, irreflexive, and satisfies that $f \diamondsuit f'$ implies $f(f'(d)) = f'(f(d))$ for every $d \in reach(\mathcal{D})$. Moreover, $\diamondsuit$ is an independence if it is a weak independence and satisfies that if $f(d) \neq \perp$, then $(f \circ f')(d) \neq \perp$ iff $f'(d) \neq \perp$, for all $d \in reach(\mathcal{D})$.*

Recall that $R_\mathcal{D}$ is the lifting of a relation on statements to transformers. Observe that the relation R in Example 1, when lifted to transformers is a weak independence on $\mathcal{C}_M$. The proposition below shows that independence relations on statements generate weak independence on transformers over $\mathcal{C}_M$.

Proposition 1 (Lifted independence). *If $\Diamond$ is an independence relation on M, the lifted relation $\Diamond_{\mathcal{C}_M}$ is a weak independence on the collecting semantics $\mathcal{C}_M$.*

Figure 2 graphically depicts the process of lifting an independence relation. Relation $\Diamond$ (on the left of the figure) is an independence relation on M. Relation $\Diamond_1 := \Diamond_{\mathcal{C}_M}$ is the lifting of $\Diamond$ to $\mathcal{C}_M$, and by Proposition 1 it is a weak independence relation on $\mathcal{C}_M$.

We now show that independence and abstraction are distinct notions in that transformers that are independent in a concrete domain may not be independent in the abstract, and those that are not independent in the concrete may become independent in the abstract.

Consider an analysis instance $\bar{\mathcal{D}} := \langle \bar{D}, \bar{\sqsubseteq}, \bar{F}, \bar{d}_0 \rangle$ that is an abstraction of $\mathcal{D} := \langle D, \sqsubseteq, F, d_0 \rangle$ and a weak independence $\Diamond \subseteq F \times F$. The *inherited relation* $\bar{\Diamond} \subseteq \bar{F} \times \bar{F}$ contains $\langle \bar{f}, \bar{f}' \rangle$ iff $\langle f, f' \rangle$ is in $\Diamond$.

Example 2 (Abstraction breaks independence). Consider a system M with the initial state $\langle x \mapsto 0, y \mapsto 0 \rangle$, and two threads $t_1 : \mathtt{x = 2}$, $t_2 : \mathtt{y = 7}$. Let $\mathcal{I}$ be the domain for interval analysis with elements $\langle i_x, i_y \rangle$ being intervals for values of x and y. The initial state is $\bar{d}_0 = \langle x \mapsto [0,0], y \mapsto [0,0] \rangle$. Abstract transformers for t_1 and t_2 are shown below. These transformers are deliberately imprecise to highlight that sound transformers are not the most precise ones.

$$f_1(\langle i_x, i_y \rangle) = \langle [2,4], i_y \rangle \qquad f_2(i_x, i_y) = \langle i_x, (\text{if } 3 \in i_x \text{ then } [7,9] \text{ else } [6,8]) \rangle$$

The relation $\Diamond := \{(t_1, t_2), (t_2, t_1)\}$ is an independence on M, and when lifted, $\Diamond_{\mathcal{C}_M}$ is a weak independence on $\mathcal{C}_M$ (in fact, $\Diamond_{\mathcal{C}_M}$ is an independence). However, the relation $\Diamond_{\mathcal{I}}$ is not a weak independence because f_1 and f_2 do not commute at d_0, due to the imprecision introduced by abstraction. Consider the statements $\mathtt{assume(x != 9)}$ and $\mathtt{assume(x < 10)}$ applied to $\langle x \mapsto [0, 10] \rangle$ to see that even best transformers may not commute.

On the other hand, even when certain transitions are not independent, their transformers may become independent in an abstract domain.

Example 3 (Abstraction creates independence). Consider two threads $t_1 : \mathtt{x = 2}$ and $t_2 : \mathtt{x = 3}$, with abstract transformers $f_1(i_x) = [2,3]$ and $f_2(i_x) = [2,3]$. The transitions t_1 and t_2 do not commute, but owing to imprecision, $R = \{(f_1, f_2), (f_2, f_1)\}$ is a weak independence on $\mathcal{I}$.

5   Unfolding of an Abstract Domain with Independence

This section shows that unfoldings, which have primarily been used to analyze Petri nets, can be applied to abstract interpretation. This section defines the vertical arrows of Fig. 2.

An abstract unfolding is an event structure in which an event is recursively defined as the application of a transformer after a minimal set of interfering events; and a configuration represent equivalent sequences of transformer applications (events). Analogous to an invariant map in abstract interpreters and an abstract reachability tree in software model checkers, our abstract unfolding allows for constructing an over-approximation of the set of fireable transitions in a program.

5.1   The Unfolding of a Domain

Our construction generates a PES $\mathcal{E} := \langle E, <, \#, h \rangle$. Recall that a configuration is a set of events that is closed with respect to $<$ and that is conflict-free. Events in $\mathcal{E}$ have the form $e = \langle f, C \rangle$, representing that the transformer f is applied after the transformers in configuration C are applied. The order in which transformers must be applied is given by $<$, while $\#$ encodes transformer applications that cannot belong to the same configuration.

The unfolding $\mathcal{U}_{\mathcal{D},\bowtie}$ of an analysis instance $\mathcal{D} := \langle D, \sqsubseteq, F, d_0 \rangle$ with respect to a relation $\bowtie \subseteq F \times F$ is defined inductively below. Recall that a configuration C generates a set of interleavings $inter(C)$, which define the *state* of the configuration,

$$state(C) := \bigsqcap_{\sigma \in inter(C)} state(\sigma)$$

If $\bowtie$ is a weak independence relation, all interleavings lead to the same state.

Definition 3 (Unfolding). *The unfolding $\mathcal{U}_{\mathcal{D},\bowtie}$ of $\mathcal{D}$ under the relation $\bowtie$ is the structure returned by the following procedure:*

1. *Start with a PES $\mathcal{E} := \langle E, <, \#, h \rangle$ equal to $\langle \emptyset, \emptyset, \emptyset, \emptyset \rangle$.*
2. *Add a new event $e := \langle f, C \rangle$ to E, where the configuration $C \in conf(\mathcal{E})$ and transformer f satisfy that f is enabled at $state(C)$, and $\neg(f \bowtie h(e))$ holds for every $<$-maximal event e in C.*
3. *Update $<$, $\#$, and h as follows:*
   - *for every $e' \in C$, set $e' < e$;*
   - *for every $e' \in E \setminus C$, if $e \neq e'$ and $\neg(f \bowtie h(e'))$, then set $e' \# e$;*
   - *set $h(e) := f$.*
4. *Repeat steps 2 and 3 until no new event can be added to E; return $\mathcal{E}$.*

Definition 3 defines the events, the causality, and conflict relations of $\mathcal{U}_{\mathcal{D},\bowtie}$ by means of a saturation procedure. Step 1 creates an empty PES. Step 2 defines a new event from a transformer f that can be applied after configuration C. Step 3 defines e to be a causal successor of every dependent event in C, and defines e

to be in conflict with dependent events not in C. Since conflicts are inherited in a PES, causal successors of e will also be in conflict with all e' satisfying $e \,\#\, e'$. Events from $E \backslash C$, which are unrelated to f in $\bowtie$, will remain concurrent to e.

Proposition 2. *The structure $\mathcal{U}_{\mathcal{D}, \diamondsuit}$ generated by Definition 3 is a uniquely defined PES.*

If $\bowtie$ is a weak independence, every configuration of $\mathcal{U}_{\mathcal{D}, \bowtie}$ represents sequences of transformer applications *that produce the same element.* If C is a configuration that is local, meaning it has a unique maximal event, or if C is generated by an independence, then $state(C)$ will not be $\bot$. Treating transformers as independent if they generate $\bot$ enables greater reduction during analysis.

Theorem 1 (Well-formedness of $\mathcal{U}_{\mathcal{D}, \diamondsuit}$). *Let $\diamondsuit$ be a weak independence on $\mathcal{D}$, let C be a configuration of $\mathcal{U}_{\mathcal{D}, \diamondsuit}$ and σ, σ' be interleavings of C. Then:*

1. *$state(\sigma) = state(\sigma')$;*
2. *$state(\sigma) \neq \bot$ when $\diamondsuit$ is additionally an independence relation;*
3. *If C is a local configuration, then also $state(\sigma) \neq \bot$.*

Theorem 2 shows that the unfolding is adequate for analysis in the sense that every sequence of transformer applications leading to non-$\bot$ elements that could be generated during standard analysis with a domain will be contained in the unfolding. We emphasize that these sequences are only symbolically represented.

Theorem 2 (Adequacy of $\mathcal{U}_{\mathcal{D}, \diamondsuit}$). *For every weak independence relation $\diamondsuit$ on $\mathcal{D}$, and sequence of transformers $\sigma \in runs(\mathcal{D})$, there is a unique configuration C of $\mathcal{U}_{\mathcal{D}, \diamondsuit}$ such that $\sigma \in inter(C)$.*

We discuss the above theorems in the context of Fig. 2. We know that $runs(M)$ is in bijective correspondence with $runs(\mathcal{C}_M)$. We said that $\diamondsuit_1$ is a weak independence in $\mathcal{C}_M$ (see Sect. 4). By Theorem 2, every run of M is represented by a unique configuration in $\mathcal{U}_{\mathcal{C}_M, \diamondsuit_1}$, and by Theorem 1 every configuration C of $\mathcal{U}_{\mathcal{C}_M, \diamondsuit_1}$ such that $state(C) \neq \bot$ is such that $inter(C) \subseteq runs(M)$.

5.2 Abstract Unfoldings

The soundness theorems of abstract interpretation show when a fixed point computed in an abstract domain soundly approximates fixed points in a concrete domain. Our analysis constructs unfoldings instead of fixed points. The soundness of our analysis *does not* follow from fixed point soundness because the abstract unfolding we construct depends on the independence relation used. Though independence may not be preserved under lifting, as shown in Example 2, lifted relations can still be used to obtain sound results.

Example 4. In Example 2, the transformer composition $f_1 \circ f_2$ produces $\langle x \mapsto [2,4], y \mapsto [6,8] \rangle$, while $f_2 \circ f_2$ produces $\langle x \mapsto [2,4], y \mapsto [7,9] \rangle$. If f_1 and f_2 are considered independent, the state of the configuration $\{f_1, f_2\}$ is $state(f_1, f_2) \sqcap state(f_2, f_1)$, which is the abstract element $\langle x \mapsto [2,4], y \mapsto [7,7] \rangle$ and contains the final state $\langle x \mapsto 2, y \mapsto 7 \rangle$ reached in the concrete.

Thus, with sound abstractions, abstract transformers can be treated as (weakly) independent if their concrete counterparts were (weakly) independent, without compromising soundness of the analysis. The soundness theorem below asserts a correspondence between sequences of concrete transformer applications and the abstract unfolding. The concrete and abstract objects in Theorem 3 have different type: we are not relating a concrete unfolding with an abstract unfolding, but concrete transformer sequences with abstract configurations. Since $state(C)$ is defined as a meet of transformer sequences, the proof of Theorem 3 relies on the independence relation and has a different structure from standard proofs of fixed point soundness from transformer soundness.

Theorem 3 (Soundness of the abstraction). *Let $\bar{\mathcal{D}}$ be a sound abstraction of the analysis instance $\mathcal{D}$, let $\Diamond$ be a weak independence on $\mathcal{D}$, and $\bar{\Diamond}$ be the lifted relation on $\bar{\mathcal{D}}$. For every sequence $\sigma \in runs(\mathcal{D})$ satisfying $state(\sigma) \neq \bot$, there is a unique configuration C of $\mathcal{U}_{\bar{\mathcal{D}},\bar{\Diamond}}$ such that $m(\sigma) \in inter(C)$.*

Theorems 2 and 3 are fundamentally different. Theorem 2 shows that, given a domain and a weak independence relation, the associated unfolding represents all sequences of transformer applications that may be generated during the analysis of that domain. Theorem 3 relates a concrete domain with the unfolding of an abstract one. Given a concrete domain, a concrete weak independence, and an abstract domain, Theorem 3 shows that every sequence of concrete transformers has a corresponding configuration in the unfolding of the abstract domain.

Surprisingly enough, the abstract unfolding in Theorem 3 may not represent all sequences of applications of the abstract domain in isolation (because the lifted relation $\bar{\Diamond}$ is not necessarily a weak independence in $\bar{\mathcal{D}}$), but will represent (this is what the theorem asserts) all transformer applications of the concrete domain.

In Fig. 2, let $\Diamond_2$ be the lifted independence of $\Diamond_1$. Theorem 3 asserts that for any $\sigma \in runs(\mathcal{C}_M)$ there is a configuration C of $\mathcal{U}_{\mathcal{D}_M,\Diamond_2}$ such that $m(\sigma) \in inter(C)$.

6 Plugging Thread-Local Analysis

Unfoldings compactly represent concurrent executions using partial orders. However, they are a branching structure and one extension of the unfolding can multiply the number of branches, leading to a blow-up in the number of branches. Static analyses of sequential programs often avoid this explosion (at the expense of precision) by over-approximating (using join or widening) the abstract state at the CFG locations where two or more program paths converge. Adequately lifting this simple idea of merging at CFG locations from sequential to concurrent programs is a highly non-trivial problem [8].

In this section, we present a method that addresses this challenge and can mitigate the blow-up in the size of the unfolding caused by conflicts between events of the same thread. The key idea of our method is to merge abstract states generated by statements that work on local data of one thread, i.e., those whose

---

Algorithm 1. Unfolding using thread-local fixpoint analysis

1 **Procedure** unfold($\mathcal{D}, \Diamond, n$)	9 **Procedure** mkevent($f, C, \Diamond$)
2 Set $\mathcal{E} := \langle E, <, \#, h \rangle$ to $\langle \emptyset, \emptyset, \emptyset, \emptyset \rangle$	10 **do**
3 **forall** i, C **in** $\mathbb{N}_n \times conf(\mathcal{E})$	11 Remove from C any $<$-maximal
4 **for** f *enabled on* tla($i, state(C)$)	event e such that $f \Diamond h(e)$
5 $e := $ mkevent($f, C, \Diamond$)	12 **while** C *changed*
6 **if** iscutoff($e, \mathcal{E}$) **continue**	13 **return** $\langle$mklabel(f)$, C \rangle$
7 Add e to E	14 **Procedure** mklabel(f)
8 Extend $<$, $\#$, and h with e.	15 **return** $d \mapsto f($tla($p(f), d$)$)$

---

impact over the memory/environment is invisible to other threads. Intuitively, the key insight is that we can merge certain configurations of the unfolding and still preserve its structural properties with respect to interference. The state of the resulting configuration will be a sound over-approximation of the states of the merged configurations at no loss of precision with respect to conflicts between events of different threads.

Our approach is to analyse M by constructing the unfolding of an abstract domain $\mathcal{D} := \langle D, \subseteq, F, d_0 \rangle$ and a weak independence relation $\Diamond$ using a thread-local procedure that over-approximates the effect of transformers altering local variables.

Assume that M has n threads. Let $F_1, \ldots, F_n$ be the partitioning of the set of transformers F by the thread to which they belong. For a transformer $f \in F_i$, we let $p(f) := i$ denote the thread to which f belongs. We define, per thread, the (local) transformers which can be used to run the merging analysis. A transformer $f \in F_i$ is *local* when, for all other threads $j \neq i$ and all transformers $f' \in F_j$ we have $f \Diamond f'$. A transformer is *global* if it is not local. We denote by F_i^{loc} and F_i^{glo}, respectively, the set of local and global transformers in F_i. In Fig. 1(a), the global transformers would be those representing the actions to the variable g. The remaining statements correspond to local transformers.

We formalize the thread-local analysis using the function tla: $\mathbb{N} \times D \to D$, which plays the role of an off-the-shelf static analyzer for sequential thread code. A call to tla(i, d) will run a static analyzer on thread i, restricted to F_i^{loc}, starting from d, and return its result which we assume to be a sound fixed point. Formally, we assume that if tla(i, d) returns $d' \in D$, then for every sequence $f_1 \ldots f_n \in (F_i^{\mathrm{loc}})^*$ we have $(f_n \circ \ldots \circ f_1)(d) \sqsubseteq d'$. This condition requires any implementation of tla(i, d) to return a sound approximation of the state that thread i could possibly reach after running only local transformers starting from d.

Algorithm 1 presents the overall approach proposed in this paper. Procedure unfold builds an *abstract unfolding* for $\mathcal{D}$ under independence relation $\Diamond$. It non-deterministically selects a thread i and a configuration C and runs a sequential static analyzer on thread i starting on the state reached by C. If a global transformer $f \in F_i^{\mathrm{glo}}$ is eventually enabled, the algorithm will try to insert it into the unfolding. For that it first calls the function mkevent, which constructs a history for f from C according to Definition 3, i.e., by removing from C events independent with f until all maximal events are dependent. Function mkevent then calls mklabel to construct a suitable label for the new event. Labels are functions in $D \to D$, we discuss them below. If the resulting event $e := \langle \bar{f}, H \rangle$ is a *cutoff*, i.e., an *equivalent* event is already in the unfolding prefix, then it will be ignored. Otherwise, we add it to E. Finally, we update relations $<$, $\#$, and h using exactly the same procedure as in Step 3 of Definition 3. In particular, we set $h(e) := \bar{f}$.

Unlike the unfolding $\mathcal{U}_{\mathcal{D},\Diamond}$ of Definition 3, the events of the PES constructed by Algorithm 1 are not labelled by transformers in F, but by ad-hoc functions constructed by mklabel. An event in this PES represents the aggregated application of multiple local transformers, summarized by tla into a fixed point, followed by the application of a global transformer. Function mklabel constructs a *collapsing transformer* that represents such transformation of the program state. Given a global transformer f it returns a function $\bar{f} \in D \to D$ that maps a state d to another state obtained by first running tla on f's thread starting from d and then running f. While an efficient implementation of Algorithm 1 does not need to actually construct this transformer, we formalize it here because it is necessary to define how to compute the state of a configuration, $state(C)$.

We denote by $\mathcal{Q}_{\mathcal{D},\Diamond}$ the PES constructed by a call to unfold$(\mathcal{D}, \Diamond, n)$. When the tla performs a path-insensitive analysis, the structure $\mathcal{Q}_{\mathcal{D},\Diamond}$ is (i) path-insensitive for runs that execute only local code, (ii) partially path-sensitive for runs that execute one or more global transformer, and (iii) flow-sensitive with respect to interference between threads. We refer to this analysis as a *causally-sensitive* analysis as it is precise with respect to the *dynamic* interference between threads.

Algorithm 1 embeds multiple constructions explained in this paper. For instance, when tla is implemented by the function $g(d, i) := d$ and the check of cutoffs is disabled (iscutoff systematically returns *false*), the algorithm is equivalent to Definition 3. We now show that $\mathcal{Q}_{\mathcal{D},\Diamond}$ is a safe abstraction of $\mathcal{D}$ when tla performs a non-trivial operation.

Theorem 4 (Soundness of the abstraction). *Let $\Diamond$ be a weak independence on $\mathcal{D}$ and $\mathcal{P}_{\mathcal{D},\Diamond}$ the PES computed by a call to* unfold $(\mathcal{D}, \Diamond, n)$ *with cutoff checking disabled. Then, for any execution $\sigma \in runs(\mathcal{D})$ there is a unique configuration C in $\mathcal{P}_{\mathcal{D},\Diamond}$ such that $\hat{\sigma} \in inter(C)$.*

6.1 Cutoff Events: Pruning the Unfolding

If we remove the conditional statement in line 6 of Algorithm 1, the algorithm would only terminate if every run of $\mathcal{D}$ contains finitely many global transformers. This conditional check has two purposes: (1) preventing infinite executions from inserting infinitely many events into $\mathcal{E}$; (2) pruning branches of the unfolding that start with *equivalent* events. The procedure iscutoff decides when an event is marked as a *cutoff* [17]. In such cases, no causal successor of the event will be explored. The implementation of `iscutoff` cannot prune "too often", as we want the computed PES to be a *complete* representation of behaviours of $\mathcal{D}$ (e.g., if a transformer is fireable, then some event in the PES will be labelled by it).

Formally, given $\mathcal{D}$, a PES $\mathcal{E}$ is $\mathcal{D}$-*complete* iff for every reachable element $d \in reach(\mathcal{D})$ there is a configuration C of $\mathcal{E}$ such that $state(C) \sqsupseteq d$. The key idea behind cutoff events is that, if event e is marked as a cutoff, then for any configuration C that includes e it must be possible to find a configuration C' without cutoff events such that $state(C) \sqsubseteq state(C')$. This can be achieved by defining $\texttt{iscutoff}(e, \mathcal{E})$ to be the predicate: $\exists e' \in \mathcal{E}$ such that $state([e]) \sqsubseteq state([e'])$ and $|[e']| < |[e]|$. When such e' exists, including the event e in $\mathcal{E}$ is unnecessary because any configuration C such that $e \in C$ can be replayed in $\mathcal{E}$ by first executing $[e']$ and then (copies of) the events in $C \backslash [e]$.

We now would like to prove that Algorithm 1 produces a $\mathcal{D}$-complete prefix when instantiated with the above definition of `iscutoff`. However, a subtle an unexpected interaction between the operators `tla` and `iscutoff` makes it possible to prove Theorem 5 only when `tla` *respects independence*. Formally, we require `tla` to satisfy the following property: for any $d \in reach(\mathcal{D})$ and any two global transformers $f \in F_i^{\text{glo}}$ and $f' \in F_j^{\text{glo}}$, if $f \Diamond f'$ then

$$(f' \circ \texttt{tla}(j) \circ f \circ \texttt{tla}(i))(d) = (f \circ \texttt{tla}(i) \circ f' \circ \texttt{tla}(j))(d)$$

When `tla` does not respect independence, it may over-approximate the global state (e.g. via joins and widening) in a way that breaks the independence of otherwise independent global transformers. This triggers the cutoff predicate to incorrectly prune necessary events.

Theorem 5. *Let $\Diamond$ be a weak independence in $\mathcal{D}$. Assume that `tla` respects independence and that `iscutoff` uses the procedure defined above. Then the PES $\mathcal{Q}_{\mathcal{D}, \Diamond}$ computed by Algorithm 1 is $\mathcal{D}$-complete.*

Note that Algorithm 1 terminates if the lattice order $\sqsubseteq$ is a well partial order (every infinite sequence contains an increasing pair). This includes, for instance, all finite domains. Furthermore, it is also possible to accelerate the termination of Algorithm 1 using widenings in `tla` to *force cutoffs*. Finally, notice that while we defined `iscutoff` using McMillan's size order [17], Theorem 5 also holds if `iscutoff` is defined using adequate orders [5], known to yield smaller prefixes. See [24] for additional details.

7   Experimental Evaluation

In this section we evaluate our approach based on abstract unfoldings. The goal of our experimental evaluation is to explore the following questions:

– Are abstract unfoldings practical? (i.e., is our approach able to yield efficient algorithms that can be used to prove properties of concurrent programs that require precise interference reasoning?)

– How does abstract unfoldings compare with competing approaches such as thread-modular analysis and symbolic partial order reduction?

Implementation. To address these questions, we have implemented a new program analyser based on abstract unfoldings baptized APOET, which implements an efficient variant of the exploration algorithm described in Algorithm 1. The exploration strategy is based on POET [23], an explicit-state model checker that implements a super-optimal partial order reduction method using unfoldings.

As described in Algorithm 1, APOET is an analyser parameterized by a domain and a set of procedures: `tla`, `iscutoff` and `mkevent`. As a proof of concept, we have implemented an interval analysis and a basic parametric segmentation functor for arrays [4], which we instantiate with intervals and concrete integers values (to represent offsets). In this way, we are able to precisely handle arrays of threads and mutexes. APOET supports dynamic thread creation and uses CIL to inline functions calls. The analyser receives as input a concurrent C program that uses the POSIX thread library and parameters to control the widening level and the use of cutoffs. We implemented cutoffs according to the definition in Sect. 6.1 using an hash table that maps control locations to abstract values and the size of the local configuration of events.

APOET is parameterized by a domain functor of actions that is used to define independence and control the `tla` procedure. We have implemented an instance of the domain of actions for memory accesses and thread synchronisations. Transformers *record* the segments of the memory, intervals of addresses or sets of addresses, that have been read or written and synchronisation actions related to thread creation, join and mutex lock and unlock operations. This approach is used to compute a conditional independence relation as transformers can perform different actions depending on the state. The conditional independence relation is dynamically computed and is used in the procedure `mkevent`.

Finally, the `tla` procedure was implemented with a worklist fixpoint algorithm which uses the widening level given as input. In the interval analysis, we guarantee that `tla` respects independence using a predicate over the actions that identifies whether a transformer is local or global. We currently support two modes in APOET: one that assumes programs are data-race free and considers any thread synchronisation (i.e., thread creation/join and mutex lock/unlock) a global transformer, and a second that considers any heap access or thread synchronisation a global transformer and can be used to detect data races.

Benchmark Selection. We used six benchmarks adapted from the SV-COMP'17 (corresponding to nine rows in Table 1) and four parametric programs (the remaining fifteen rows in Table 1) written by the authors: map-reduce DNA sequence analysis, producer-consumer, parallel sorting, and a thread pool. The majority of the SV-COMP benchmarks are not applicable for this evaluation since they are data deterministic (whereas our approach is primarily for data non-deterministic programs) or create unboundedly many threads, or use non-integer data types (e.g., structs, which are not currently supported by our prototype).

Thus, we devised parametric benchmarks that expose data non-determinism and complex synchronization patterns, where the correctness of assertions depend on the synchronization history. We believe that all new benchmarks are as complex as the most complex ones of the SV-COMP (excluding device drivers).

Each program was annotated with assertions enforcing, among others, properties related to thread synchronisation (e.g., after spawning the worker threads, the master analyses results only after all workers finished), or invariants about data (e.g., each thread accesses a non-overlapping segment of the input array).

Tool Selection. We compare our approach against the two approaches most closely related to ours: abstract interpretation based on thread-modular methods (represented by the tool AsTREEA) and partial-order reductions (PORs) handling data-nondeterminism (represented by two tools, IMPARA and CBMC 5.6). AsTREEA implements thread-modular abstract interpretation for concurrent programs [19], IMPARA combines POR with interpolation-based reasoning to cope with data non-determinism [25], and CBMC uses a symbolic encoding based on partial orders [2]. We sought to compare against symbolic execution approaches for multithreaded programs, but we were either unable to obtain the tools from the authors or the tools were unable to parse the benchmarks.

Experimental Results. Table 1 presents the experimental results. When the program contained non-terminating executions (e.g., spinlocks), we used 5 loop unwindings for CBMC as well as cutoffs in APOET and a widening level of 15. For the family of FMAX benchmarks, we were not able to run AsTREEA on all instances, so we report approximated execution times and warnings based on the results provided by Antoine Miné on some of the instances. With respect to the size of the abstract unfolding, our experiments show that APOET is able to explore unfoldings up to 33 K events and it was able to terminate on all benchmarks with an average execution time of 81 seconds. In comparison with AsTREEA, APOET is far more precise: we obtain only 12 warnings (of which 5 are false positives) with APOET compared to 43 (32 false positives) with AsTREEA. We observe a similar trend when comparing APOET with the MTHREAD plugin for FRAMA-C [26] and confirm that the main reason for the source of imprecision in AsTREEA is imprecise reasoning of thread interference. In the case of APOET, we obtain warnings in benchmarks that are buggy (LAZY*, SIGMA* and TPOLL* family), as expected. Furthermore, APOET reports warnings in the ATGC benchmarks caused by imprecise reasoning of arrays combined with widening and also in the COND benchmark as it contains non-relational assertions.

APOET is able to outperform IMPARA and CBMC on all benchmarks. We believe that these experiments demonstrate that effective symbolic reasoning with partial orders is challenging as CBMC only terminates on 46% of the benchmarks and IMPARA only on 17%.

Table 1. Experimental results. All experiments with APOET, IMPARA and CBMC were performed on an Intel Xeon CPU with 2.4 GHz and 4 GB memory with a timeout of 30 min; ASTREEA was ran on HP ZBook with 2.7 GHz i7 processor and 32 GB memory. Columns are: P: nr. of threads; A: nr. of assertions; $t(s)$: running time (TO - timeout); E: nr. of events in the unfolding; E_{cut}: nr. of cutoff events; W: nr. of warnings; V: verification result (S - safe; U - unsafe); N: nr. of node states; A $*$ marks programs containing bugs. < 2 reads as *"less than 2"*.

Benchmark			APOET				ASTREEA		IMPARA			CBMC 5.6	
Name	P	A	$t(s)$	E	E_{cut}	W	$t(s)$	W	V	$t(s)$	N	V	$t(s)$
ATGC(2)	3	7	0.37	47	0	1	1.07	2	–	TO	–	S	2.37
ATGC(3)	4	7	5.78	432	0	1	1.69	2	–	TO	–	S	6.6
ATGC(4)	5	7	132.08	7195	0	1	2.68	2	–	TO	–	S	20.22
COND	5	2	0.55	982	0	2	0.71	2	–	TO	–	S	34.39
FMAX(2,3)	2	8	0.70	100	15	0	0.31	0	–	TO	–	–	TO
FMAX(3,3)	2	8	0.58	85	11	0	<2	2	–	TO	–	–	TO
FMAX(5,3)	2	8	0.56	85	11	0	1.50	2	–	TO	–	–	TO
FMAX(2,4)	2	8	3.38	277	43	0	<2	2	–	TO	–	–	TO
FMAX(2,6)	2	8	45.82	1663	321	0	<2	2	–	TO	–	–	TO
FMAX(4,6)	2	8	61.32	2230	207	0	<2	2	–	TO	–	–	TO
FMAX(2,7)	2	8	146.19	3709	769	0	1.87	2	–	TO	–	–	TO
FMAX(4,7)	2	8	285.23	6966	671	0	<2	2	–	TO	–	–	TO
LAZY	4	2	0.01	72	0	0	0.50	2	–	TO	–	S	3.59
LAZY*	4	2	0.01	72	0	1	0.49	2	–	TO	–	U	3.50
MONAB1	5	1	0.27	982	0	0	0.61	0	–	TO	–	S	38.51
MONAB2	5	1	0.25	982	0	0	0.58	1	–	TO	–	S	37.34
RAND	5	1	0.40	657	0	0	3.32	0	–	TO	–	–	TO
SIGMA	5	5	2.62	7126	0	0	0.43	0	–	TO	–	S	189.09
SIGMA*	5	5	2.64	7126	0	1	0.43	1	–	TO	–	U	141.35
STF	3	2	0.01	69	0	0	0.66	2	S	5.93	250	S	2.12
TPOLL(2)*	3	11	1.23	141	7	1	1.97	2	U	0.64	80	–	TO
TPOLL(3)*	4	11	109.22	1712	90	2	3.77	3	U	0.72	113	–	TO
TPOLL(4)*	5	11	1111.46	33018	1762	2	8.06	3	U	0.78	152	–	TO
THPOOL	2	24	33.47	353	103	0	1.44	5	S	TO	–	–	TO

8 Related Work

In this section, we compare our approach with closely related program analysis techniques for (i) concurrent programs with (ii) a bounded number of threads and that (iii) handle data non-determinism.

The thread-modular approach in the style of rely-guarantee reasoning has been extensively studied in the past [3,9,12,15,16,18–20]. In [19], Miné proposes a flow-insensitive thread-modular analysis based on the interleaving semantics which forces the abstraction to cope with interleaving explosion. We address the interleaving explosion using the unfolding as an algorithmic approach to compute a flow and path-sensitive thread interference analysis. A recent approach [20] uses relational domains and trace partitioning to recover precision in thread modular analysis but requires manual annotations to guide the partitioning and does not scale with the number of global variables. The analysis in [7] is not as precise as our approach (confirmed by experiments with DUET on a simpler version of our benchmarks) as it employs an abstraction for unbounded parallelism. The work in [15] presents a thread modular analysis that uses a lightweight interference analysis to achieve an higher level of flow sensitivity similar to [7]. The interference analysis of [15] uses a constraint system to discard unfeasible pairs of read-write actions which is static and less precise than our approach based on independence. The approach is also flow-insensitive in the presence of loops with global read operations. Finally, the method in [12] focuses on manual thread-modular proofs, while our method is automatic.

The interprocedural analysis for recursive concurrent programs of [13] does not address the interleaving explosion. A related approach that uses unfoldings is the causality-based bitvector dataflow analysis proposed in [8]. There, unfoldings are used as a method to obtain dataflow information while in our approach they are the fundamental datastructure to drive the analysis. Thus we can apply thread-local fixpoint analysis while their unfolding suffers from path explosion due to local branching. Furthermore, we can build unfoldings for general domains even with invalid independence relations while their approach is restricted to the independence encoded in the syntax of a Petri net and bitvector domains.

Compared to dynamic analysis of concurrent programs [1,6,11,14], our approach builds on top of a (super-)optimal partial-order reduction [23] and is able to overcome a high degree of path explosion unrelated to thread interference.

9   Conclusion

We introduced a new algorithm for static analysis of concurrent programs based on the combination of abstract interpretation and unfoldings. Our algorithm explores an abstract unfolding using a new notion of independence to avoid redundant transformer application in an optimal POR strategy, thread-local fixed points to reduce the size of the unfolding, and a novel cutoff criterion based on subsumption to guarantee termination of the analysis.

Our experiments show that APOET generates about 10x fewer false positives than a mature thread modular abstract interpreter and is able to terminate on a large set of benchmarks as opposed to solver-based tools that have the same precision. We observed that the major reasons for the success of APOET are: (1) the use of cutoffs to cope with and prune cyclic explorations caused by spinlocks and (2) `tla` mitigates path explosion in the threads. Our analyser is able to scale with the number of threads as long as the interference between threads does not increase. As future work, we plan to experimentally evaluate the application of local widenings to force cutoffs to increase the scalability of our approach.

Acknowledgments. The authors would like to thank Antoine Miné for the invaluable help with ASTREEA and the anonymous reviewers for their helpful feedback.

References

1. Abdulla, P., Aronis, S., Jonsson, B., Sagonas, K.: Optimal dynamic partial order reduction. In: Principles of Programming Languages (POPL), pp. 373–384. ACM (2014)
2. Alglave, J., Kroening, D., Tautschnig, M.: Partial orders for efficient bounded model checking of concurrent software. In: Sharygina, N., Veith, H. (eds.) CAV 2013. LNCS, vol. 8044, pp. 141–157. Springer, Heidelberg (2013). doi:10.1007/978-3-642-39799-8_9
3. Carre, J.-L., Hymans, C.: From single-thread to multithreaded: an efficient static analysis algorithm. arXiv:0910.5833[cs], October 2009
4. Cousot, P., Cousot, R., Logozzo, F.: A parametric segmentation functor for fully automatic and scalable array content analysis. In: Principles of Programming Languages (POPL), pp. 105–118. ACM (2011)
5. Esparza, J., Römer, S., Vogler, W.: An improvement of McMillan's unfolding algorithm. Formal Methods Syst. Des. **20**, 285–310 (2002)
6. Farzan, A., Holzer, A., Razavi, N., Veith, H.: Con2Colic testing. In: Foundations of Software Engineering (FSE), pp. 37–47. ACM (2013)
7. Farzan, A., Kincaid, Z.: Verification of parameterized concurrent programs by modular reasoning about data and control. In: Principles of Programming Languages (POPL), pp. 297–308. ACM (2012)
8. Farzan, A., Madhusudan, P.: Causal dataflow analysis for concurrent programs. In: Grumberg, O., Huth, M. (eds.) TACAS 2007. LNCS, vol. 4424, pp. 102–116. Springer, Heidelberg (2007). doi:10.1007/978-3-540-71209-1_10
9. Flanagan, C., Qadeer, S.: Thread-modular model checking. In: Ball, T., Rajamani, S.K. (eds.) SPIN 2003. LNCS, vol. 2648, pp. 213–224. Springer, Heidelberg (2003). doi:10.1007/3-540-44829-2_14
10. Godefroid, P. (ed.): Partial-Order Methods for the Verification of Concurrent Systems. LNCS, vol. 1032. Springer, Heidelberg (1996). doi:10.1007/3-540-60761-7
11. Günther, H., Laarman, A., Sokolova, A., Weissenbacher, G.: Dynamic reductions for model checking concurrent software. In: Bouajjani, A., Monniaux, D. (eds.) VMCAI 2017. LNCS, vol. 10145, pp. 246–265. Springer, Cham (2017). doi:10.1007/978-3-319-52234-0_14
12. Hoenicke, J., Majumdar, R., Podelski, A.: Thread modularity at many levels: a pearl in compositional verification. In: Proceedings of the 44th ACM SIGPLAN Symposium on Principles of Programming Languages, POPL 2017, pp. 473–485. ACM, New York (2017)
13. Jeannet, B.: Relational interprocedural verification of concurrent programs. Softw. Syst. Model. **12**(2), 285–306 (2012)
14. Kähkänen, K., Saarikivi, O., Heljanko, K.: Unfolding based automated testing of multithreaded programs. Autom. Softw. Eng. **22**, 1–41 (2014)
15. Kusano, M., Wang, C.: Flow-sensitive composition of thread-modular abstract interpretation. In: Foundations of Software Engineering (FSE), pp. 799–809. ACM (2016)
16. Malkis, A., Podelski, A., Rybalchenko, A.: Precise thread-modular verification. In: Nielson, H.R., Filé, G. (eds.) SAS 2007. LNCS, vol. 4634, pp. 218–232. Springer, Heidelberg (2007). doi:10.1007/978-3-540-74061-2_14
17. McMillan, K.L.: Using unfoldings to avoid the state explosion problem in the verification of asynchronous circuits. In: Bochmann, G., Probst, D.K. (eds.) CAV 1992. LNCS, vol. 663, pp. 164–177. Springer, Heidelberg (1993). doi:10.1007/3-540-56496-9_14

18. Miné, A.: Static analysis of run-time errors in embedded real-time parallel C programs. Log. Methods Comput. Sci. **8**(1) (2012)
19. Miné, A.: Relational thread-modular static value analysis by abstract interpretation. In: McMillan, K.L., Rival, X. (eds.) VMCAI 2014. LNCS, vol. 8318, pp. 39–58. Springer, Heidelberg (2014). doi:10.1007/978-3-642-54013-4_3
20. Monat, R., Miné, A.: Precise thread-modular abstract interpretation of concurrent programs using relational interference abstractions. In: Bouajjani, A., Monniaux, D. (eds.) VMCAI 2017. LNCS, vol. 10145, pp. 386–404. Springer, Cham (2017). doi:10.1007/978-3-319-52234-0_21
21. Nielsen, M., Plotkin, G., Winskel, G.: Petri nets, event structures and domains, part I. Theoret. Comput. Sci. **13**(1), 85–108 (1981)
22. Peled, D.: All from one, one for all: on model checking using representatives. In: Courcoubetis, C. (ed.) CAV 1993. LNCS, vol. 697, pp. 409–423. Springer, Heidelberg (1993). doi:10.1007/3-540-56922-7_34
23. Rodríguez, C., Sousa, M., Sharma, S., Kroening, D.: Unfolding-based partial order reduction. In: Concurrency Theory (CONCUR). LIPIcs, vol. 42, pp. 456–469. Schloss Dagstuhl - Leibniz-Zentrum fuer Informatik (2015)
24. Sousa, M., Rodréguez, C., D'Silva, V., Kroening, D.: Abstract interpretation with unfoldings. CoRR abs/1705.00595 (2017)
25. Wachter, B., Kroening, D., Ouaknine, J.: Verifying multi-threaded software with impact. In: Formal Methods in Computer-Aided Design (FMCAD), pp. 210–217 (2013)
26. Yakobowski, B., Bonichon, R.: Frama-C's Mthread plug-in. Report, Software Reliability Laboratory (2012)

Cutoff Bounds for Consensus Algorithms

Ognjen Marić[✉], Christoph Sprenger[✉], and David Basin[✉]

Department of Computer Science, Institute of Information Security,
ETH Zurich, Zurich, Switzerland
`ogi.csb@mynosefroze.com`, {`sprenger,basin`}`@inf.ethz.ch`

Abstract. Consensus algorithms are fundamental building blocks for fault-tolerant distributed systems and their correctness is critical. However, there are currently no fully-automated methods for their verification. The main difficulty is that the algorithms are parameterized: they should work for any given number of processes. We provide an expressive language for consensus algorithms targeting the benign asynchronous setting. For this language, we give algorithm-dependent *cutoff bounds*. A cutoff bound B reduces the parameterized verification of consensus to a setting with B processes. For the algorithms in our case studies, we obtain bounds of 5 or 7, enabling us to model check them efficiently. This is the first cutoff result for fault-tolerant distributed systems.

1 Introduction

Fault-tolerant distributed systems are hard to get right: processes can stall, crash, or recover, and the network might lose, delay, or duplicate messages [6]. As the number and the cost of failures of these systems increase, industry is increasingly applying push-button verification methods to them, such as model checking [41] and testing [31]. These methods analyze individual system configurations with a small, fixed number of participating processes. However, many real distributed systems are intended to work for any given number of processes, i.e., they are *parameterized* in this number. The deployed instances are often larger than the analyzed ones, and the analyses then offer no a priori guarantees for the deployed system. Still, an informal observation known as the *small-scope hypothesis* [25] states that analyzing small system instances suffices in practice. Empirical studies [4,42,49] support this hypothesis in different settings. For example, in the distributed setting, a recent study [49] of 198 bug reports for several popular distributed systems found that 98% of those bugs could be triggered by three or fewer processes.

A crucial question is then: can we state and formally *prove* this hypothesis? That is, given a parameterized system and a property ψ, can we determine a *cutoff bound*: a number B such that whenever all systems with parameter values of B or less satisfy ψ, then systems with arbitrary parameter values also satisfy ψ? The answer is no in general as the parametric verification problem is undecidable even when we can decide the system's correctness for each parameter

© Springer International Publishing AG 2017
R. Majumdar and V. Kunčak (Eds.): CAV 2017, Part II, LNCS 10427, pp. 217–237, 2017.
DOI: 10.1007/978-3-319-63390-9_12

instance [5,45]. The best we can hope for is to find cutoff bounds for interesting classes of systems and properties. While such results exist [15–17,20,29,30], none apply to fault-tolerant distributed systems in general, and to algorithms for solving the *distributed consensus* problem in particular. Consensus algorithms are fundamental building blocks for distributed systems [22]: they are required whenever multiple processes want to maintain, in a fault-tolerant way, a consistent shared state or a consistent order of operations (for instance, in a database).

In addition to the lack of cutoff results, no fully automated method exists for the parametric verification of consensus algorithms. The invariant verification approach of [13] comes the closest, but it is not fully automated as the user must find inductive invariants that are automatically checked. Also, while the authors report good practical results, their main algorithm is only a semi-decision procedure. Other reported results have either performed bounded verification (e.g., [12,47,48]) or used interactive verification methods (e.g., [11,21,27,35,44]).

Contributions. Our main contribution is to prove the small scope hypothesis for an expressive class of consensus algorithms. In more detail:

1. We define a language *ConsL* (Sect. 3), capable of expressing numerous consensus algorithms that target the asynchronous and partially synchronous setting with benign (i.e., non-Byzantine) failures. The central feature of *ConsL* are guards based on fractional thresholds and selection predicates. These guards capture algorithm constructs such as "if messages have been received from more than $\frac{2}{3}$ of the processes, then select the smallest received value". We have specified the following algorithms in *ConsL*: Paxos [36], Chandra-Toueg [8], Ben-Or [7], $\frac{1}{3}$-rule and three algorithms from the Uniform Voting family [10], and the algorithm from [38].
2. For *ConsL* algorithms, we prove a *zero-one principle* for consensus (Sect. 4): the algorithm's correctness for binary inputs (from the set $\{0,1\}$) entails the algorithm's correctness for inputs from any ordered set, finite or infinite. This is an analogue of the same principle for sorting networks [32].
3. We give cutoff bounds for algorithms run on binary inputs (Sect. 5): given a *ConsL* algorithm $\mathcal{A}$, we show that $\mathcal{A}$ solves consensus on binary inputs if it solves it for *exactly* $B = 2d + 1$ processes, where d is the least common denominator of the fractional thresholds in $\mathcal{A}$'s guards. Together with Step 2, this proves the small scope hypothesis for *ConsL* algorithms.
4. The bounds we obtain for real-world algorithms are indeed small: 5 or 7 processes for all algorithms considered in this paper. We can thus leverage model checking to provide the first fully automated decision procedure applicable to a range of consensus algorithms, and we provide a tool (Sect. 6) that generates Promela/Spin [23] models from *ConsL* algorithms. The resulting verification times are competitive with the semi-automated method of [13].

2   Preliminaries

We start with set-theoretic preliminaries and briefly review the consensus problem and the Heard-Of (HO) model [10] for fault-tolerant distributed algorithms.

A multiset M over a set S is a function $S \to \mathbb{N}$, where $M(x)$ is the multiplicity of x in M. We define $|M| = \sum_{s \in S} M(s)$ and the multiset $M \setminus X$ for a *set* X by $(M \setminus X)(x) = 0$ if $x \in X$ and $(M \setminus X)(x) = M(x)$ otherwise. Note that this operation removes all occurrences of X's elements from M. The multiset image of a partial function $f \colon A \rightharpoonup B$, is the multiset $\#[f] \colon B \to \mathbb{N}$ defined by $\#[f](y) = |f^{-1}(y)|$. We introduce notation for specifying multisets. For example, $M = \{m_x \times x, m_y \times y\}$ denotes the multiset M where $M(x) = m_x$, $M(y) = m_y$, and $M(z) = 0$ for $z \notin \{x, y\}$. We also define $[a, b)_{\mathbb{Q}} = \{c \in \mathbb{Q} \mid a \leq c < b\}$.

2.1 Consensus

The consensus problem assumes a fixed set $\Pi = \{1, \ldots, n\}$ of communicating processes. Usually, we want an algorithm that solves this problem for any $n > 0$, i.e., an algorithm *parameterized* by n. Each process in Π receives an input from the value domain $\mathcal{V}$, and the goal is to have all processes decide on a common output. More precisely, a system *solves* the consensus problem [10] if it provides:

Uniform Agreement: No two processes ever decide on two different values.
Termination: Every process eventually decides on a value.
Non-triviality: Any value decided upon was input to some process.
Stability: Once a process decides, it never reverts to an undecided state.

Note that the termination requirement says nothing about execution stopping. In fact, to simplify modeling, we assume that all processes run forever. Furthermore, the requirements make no exemption for failed processes. We follow [10] where failed processes continue receiving and processing messages, and can thus still decide. However, the messages they send are no longer received by the other processes. We next explain this model in more detail.

2.2 The Heard-Of Model

We will define the semantics of our language via a translation into the HO model. This model characterizes round-based algorithms, where every process performs the following actions in each round: (1) send messages to other processes; (2) wait and collect messages from other processes; and (3) update the local state. The rounds must be *communication-closed*, such that the only messages collected in a round are the messages that are sent in that round.

A salient point of the HO model is that message collection (Step 2) is assumed to be performed by a lower-level *messaging layer* outside of the model. This layer ensures communication closedness (for example, by buffering early and dropping late messages) and handles issues such as message duplication. It decides when to stop the collection and advance the round (for instance, using a timeout), and hands over the received messages to the algorithm. Environment effects such as crashed or late senders or message loss or delay might prevent the delivery of some messages. The possible causes are indistinguishable to the receivers. The

Initially: inp_p is p's proposed value and dec_p is $\bot$
$\mathbf{send}_p^r$:
    send inp_p to all
$\mathbf{next}_p^r$:
    if $|HO_p^r| > \frac{2}{3}n$ and all received messages equal some v **then**
        $dec_p := v$
    if $|HO_p^r| > \frac{2}{3}n$ **then**
        $inp_p :=$ smallest most often received value

Fig. 1. The HO model of $\frac{1}{3}$-rule

HO model chooses to uniformly model all such effects, including process crashes, as message loss. The environment effects are thus encapsulated in the *heard-of sets* $HO_p^r \subseteq \Pi$, where HO_p^r models the set of processes whose messages are collected by the messaging layer for process p in round r.

Let $\mathcal{M}$ denote the message space. An *algorithm* in the HO model is specified by the following three elements, indexed by processes p and rounds r:

1. $I_p \subseteq S_p$ is the set of initial states of p (contained in p's state space S_p).
2. The *send function* $\mathbf{send}_p^r : S_p \times \Pi \to \mathcal{M}$, where $\mathbf{send}_p^r(s_p, q)$ determines the message p sends to q in round r, based on p's current state s_p. This function is total; not sending a message is modeled by a special dummy message $\star$.
3. The *update function* $\mathbf{next}_p^r : S_p \times (\Pi \rightharpoonup \mathcal{M}) \to 2^{S_p}$. Let $\mu_p^r : \Pi \rightharpoonup \mathcal{M}$ model the messages p receives in round r, i.e., given HO_p^r and s_q, let $\mu_p^r(q) = \mathbf{send}_q^r(s_q, p)$ if $q \in HO_p^r$ and let it be undefined otherwise. Then $\mathbf{next}_p^r(s_p, \mu_p^r)$ determines the set of possible successor states of p's current state s_p.

Example 1. Figure 1 shows the pseudo-code for the HO model of the $\frac{1}{3}$-rule consensus algorithm [10], where the state of each process consists of the fields inp and dec and $\mathbf{send}_p^r$ and $\mathbf{next}_p^r$ are the same for all processes p and rounds r. The updates of the inp and dec fields in $\mathbf{next}^r$ are done simultaneously. We do not explain here why this algorithm works; we just use it to showcase the HO model and motivate the design of our specification language, described shortly.

The semantics of an algorithm in the HO model is defined as the transition system $(S, \to, I)$, where each state $s \in S$ (respectively $s \in I$) consists of the local states $s_p \in S_p$ (respectively $s_p \in I_p$) of each process $p \in \Pi$ and a value $s.rnd \in \mathbb{N}$ recording the current round (initially 0). Given an *HO collection* $\{HO_p^r\}_{p \in \Pi}^{r \in \mathbb{N}}$, there is a *transition* $s \to s'$ in round $r = s.rnd$ if and only if $s'.rnd = r + 1$ and, for all processes $p \in \Pi$ and μ_p^r defined as above, $s_p' \in \mathbf{next}_p^r(s_p, \mu_p^r)$, i.e., all processes simultaneously execute an update. Each HO collection induces a set of infinite state sequences, called *traces*. The *width* of states and traces is $|\Pi|$. This *lockstep* semantics models HO algorithm executions in synchronous settings in an obvious way. But crucially, for consensus properties and communication-closed algorithms, it also soundly abstracts the *fine-grained* semantics [9,14], which models executions in asynchronous environments where processes progress independently of each other. Hence, we can verify consensus properties in the lockstep semantics of the HO model and conclude that they carry over to an asynchronous environment.

Solving consensus requires assumptions on the environment [18]; for instance, message loss can prevent consensus even with full synchrony [43]. As the HO model encapsulates environment effects in the HO collections, each algorithm states its environment assumptions using a *communication predicate*, a set of allowed HO collections. These then induce the algorithm's set of traces. To be useful, a predicate must reflect realistic assumptions on distributed systems, i.e., be implementable by a messaging layer using these assumptions. Two of the most important such assumptions can be reflected in two types of *round formulas* ϕ_{th} and ϕ_{uf} of the forms:

$$\phi_{th}(c,r) \triangleq \forall p. \ |HO_p^r| > c \cdot |\Pi| \qquad \text{and} \qquad \phi_{uf}(r) \triangleq \forall p, q. \ HO_p^r = HO_q^r.$$

The *threshold formula* $\phi_{th}(c,r)$ requires that, in round r, all processes receive messages from at least the fraction $c \in [0,1)_{\mathbb{Q}}$ of processes, reflecting the assumptions about the number of failures and timeouts in round r. The *uniformity formula* $\phi_{uf}(r)$ requires that all processes receive messages from the same set of processes in round r. This reflects the *partial synchrony* assumption of a *stable period* that spans an entire round. In stable periods, no crashes or recoveries occur, and all messages from non-crashed processes are delivered in a timely way. For example, the communication predicate for the $\frac{1}{3}$-rule algorithm is given by $\exists r_1, r_2. \ r_2 > r_1 \wedge \phi_{th}(\frac{2}{3}, r_1) \wedge \phi_{uf}(r_1) \wedge \phi_{th}(\frac{2}{3}, r_2)$.

While the modular construction of messaging layers implementing such predicates is an open question, provably correct ad-hoc implementations for partially synchronous environments exist [14,24], with modest proof complexity.

3   Specification Language

The HO model leverages the round structure present in many distributed algorithms to create a simple model for them. However, similarities between consensus algorithms for the asynchronous setting with benign failures run deeper than just their round structure. In this section, we exploit these similarities to define *ConsL*, a language that captures many algorithms for this setting.

3.1   Structural Commonalities Between Algorithms

To motivate the syntactic choices for *ConsL*, we use the $\frac{1}{3}$-rule algorithm to highlight the typical structural characteristics of consensus algorithms:

1. All processes are fully symmetric, i.e., execute the same code.
2. The state of each process p contains two distinguished fields *inp* (the input p receives) and *dec* (p's decision). Initially, *dec* is set to the distinguished value $\perp$, indicating that no decision has been made.
3. The **send** function always sends the value of a single state field.

⟨rspec⟩ ::= ⟨send-field⟩ ⟨cp⟩ ⟨instr⟩*

⟨send-field⟩ ::= *identifier*

⟨cp⟩ ::= ⤬ | ⤣ | ◁

⟨instr⟩ ::= ⟨guard⟩ ▷ ⟨upd-field⟩

⟨guard⟩ ::= (⟨th⟩,⟨pred⟩)

⟨th⟩ ::= *fraction*

⟨pred⟩ ::= **any** | **smor** | **min** | **all=** | maxts

⟨upd-field⟩ ::= *identifier*

(a) Syntax of *ConsL* round specifications.

inp ⤬
$(\frac{2}{3}, \texttt{all=}) \triangleright dec$
$(\frac{2}{3}, \texttt{smor}) \triangleright inp$

(b) The $\frac{1}{3}$-rule algorithm

$(0, inp)$

$(1, inp)$ $(1, dec)$

(c) The phase graph of $\frac{1}{3}$-rule

Fig. 2. *ConsL* syntax and example algorithm

4. In the **next** function, each state field is either left unchanged or is updated to some received value. No new values are produced; instead, values are simply propagated between fields. Moreover, their origins are irrelevant. The map $\mu_p^r : \Pi \rightharpoonup \mathcal{M}$ of received messages can hence be replaced by the *multiset* $R_p^r = \#[\mu_p^r]$. A field f is then updated to a value v from R_p^r if:

(a) $|R_p^r|$ is strictly larger than some threshold, expressed as a fraction of the total number of processes; in the example, this fraction is $\frac{2}{3}$ for the updates to both *inp* and *dec*, and

(b) v fulfills a particular predicate with respect to the set of received messages. In the example, the predicate for the *dec* update is that all messages in R_p^r equal v, and for the *inp* update that v is a value with the highest multiplicity in R_p^r and is the smallest such value.

3.2 Syntax

The above observations motivate the syntax for the basic building block of *ConsL*, the specification of a single round (Fig. 2a). Here, we focus on the core language, typeset in normal font; the greyed out parts are extensions (Sect. 3.4). A round specification starts with the state field that is sent in the round, followed by the communication pattern. In the ⤬ pattern, all process pairs exchange messages. The specification ends with a list of update *instructions*.

An instruction *instr* consists of a *guard* and the updated field. We assume that each *upd-field* appears at most once in the instruction list. The guard consists of a *threshold* $th \in [0,1)_{\mathbb{Q}}$, and a *predicate pred*. Intuitively, if messages are received from more than the given threshold of processes, the target field is updated with some value satisfying the predicate. The predicates are:

- **any:** any received value,
- **smor:** the smallest most often received value,
- **min:** the smallest received value, and
- **all=:** satisfied by v if all the received values equal v.

We will use the grammar symbols as projections where convenient; for example, given a guard G, we write $th(G)$ for its threshold. Figure 2b shows the (single) round specification of the $\frac{1}{3}$-rule algorithm.

While the $\frac{1}{3}$-rule algorithm repeats the same round indefinitely, many algorithms use finite sequences of rounds, called *phases*, as units of repetition.[1] A *ConsL algorithm* $\mathcal{A}$ consists of a finite set of phases, a *phase sequence*, specified by an infinite word w over this set, and a communication predicate, specified as below. The phase sequence determines the infinite sequence of round specifications to execute, reflecting our assumption that processes run forever. While our theorems also hold for arbitrary phase sequences, to obtain finite-state systems and enable model-checking, we require $w = uv^\omega$, for finite words u and v.

Communication Predicates. As we use an HO model semantics, *ConsL* algorithms must express their environment assumptions using communication predicates. Arbitrary predicates could make cutoff bounds unobtainable, so we provide a restricted but sufficient way to specify them. The building blocks are the round formulas $\phi_{th}(c,r)$ and $\phi_{uf}(r)$ from Sect. 2.2. Abusing notation, we associate the *round labels* $\phi_{th}(c)$ and ϕ_{uf} with the corresponding round formulas. Let $L = \{\phi_{uf}\} \cup \{\phi_{th}(c) \mid c \in [0,1)_\mathbb{Q}\}$ be the set of all round labels. A *ConsL* communication predicate is then specified by a language of infinite words over the alphabet $\Sigma = \mathcal{P}(L)$. Again, to ensure a finite representation, we require the language to be ω-regular. For example, the communication predicate of the $\frac{1}{3}$-rule algorithm is now specified as $\Sigma^* \Lambda_1 \Sigma^* \Lambda_2 \Sigma^\omega$, with $\Lambda_1 = \{\phi_{th}(\frac{2}{3}), \phi_{uf}\}$ and $\Lambda_2 = \{\phi_{th}(\frac{2}{3})\}$.

Restrictions. To ensure that cutoff bounds exist, *ConsL* has several syntactic restrictions. They are technical in nature and we provide some intuition for the two main ones here.

First, we constrain the data flow within a phase. Intuitively, a phase of a consensus algorithm is a single attempt to reach a decision on one of the input values. We exploit this by assuming that all data within a phase originates from the *inp* field, and that *inp* and *dec* are updated at most once. We formalize this using the notion of a *phase graph*. First, given a phase $\Phi = [rs_1, rs_2, \ldots, rs_n]$, and a field f, let f's *latest update before i*, denoted $lu(f,i)$, be the largest j, with $j < i$, such that f is updated in rs_j, and 0 if no such j exists. The phase graph is then a directed graph whose nodes are pairs (i,f) such that either the field f is updated in rs_i, or $i = 0$ and f is sent in some rs_j with $lu(f,j) = 0$. An edge $(i,f) \to (j,g)$ exists in the graph iff f is sent in rs_j, g is updated in rs_j, and $i = lu(f,j)$. Figure 2c shows $\frac{1}{3}$-rule's phase graph. Our first restriction is then:

(R1) The phase graph of each phase is a tree rooted at $(0, inp)$. For $f \in \{inp, dec\}$, at most one node (i,f) with $i > 0$ exists, and it must be a leaf. Moreover, these are the only leaves of the graph.

Hence, each phase has at most one round where two fields are simultaneously updated. In the phase graph, these rounds correspond to *fork points*, where the

---

[1] Some authors exchange the meanings of phases and rounds; we follow [10].

dec-path $(0, inp) \rightsquigarrow (j, dec)$ forks off from the *inp-path* $(0, inp) \rightsquigarrow (i, inp)$ (see Figs. 2c and 4). Handling these is the most challenging part of our proofs, as discussed later.

The second main restriction is based on the observation that, to ensure agreement, consensus algorithms require that decided values get stored as inputs for future phases. Hence, at the fork point, an update on the *dec-path* must imply an update on the *inp*-path. Therefore, the guard of the update on the *dec*-path must be stronger than the guard of the update on the *inp*-path. We exploit this and require a total ordering of the update guards in an algorithm. We start by defining a partial order $\sqsubseteq_{\mathcal{P}}$ on the predicates by $\texttt{any} \sqsubseteq_{\mathcal{P}} P$, $P \sqsubseteq_{\mathcal{P}} P$, and $P \sqsubseteq_{\mathcal{P}} \texttt{all=}$, for all predicates P. Hence, $P_1 \sqsubseteq_{\mathcal{P}} P_2$ iff whenever a value v satisfies P_2, then it also satisfies P_1. We extend this order to guards such that $G_1 \sqsubseteq G_2$ iff $th(G_1) \leq th(G_2)$ and $pred(G_1) \sqsubseteq_{\mathcal{P}} pred(G_2)$. The associated restriction is (R2), which we list along with the remaining restrictions (R3) and (R4):

(R2) The set of all guards used in the algorithm is totally ordered.
(R3) $\texttt{min}$ and $\texttt{smor}$ predicates only appear in instructions where *send-field* is *inp*.
(R4) If $th(G) = 0$, then $pred(G) = \texttt{any}$.

3.3 Semantics

Guards. We assume in the rest of the paper that the system is parameterized by a set Π of processes and a totally ordered set $\mathcal{V}$ of values. Given a multiset M of elements from the message space $\mathcal{M} \triangleq \mathcal{V} \cup \{\bot, \star\}$, define $vs(M) \triangleq M \setminus \{\bot, \star\}$. Then, given a guard $G = (t, p)$, a multiset M (of received messages), and a value $v \in \mathcal{V}$, we write $M \models G(v)$ if $|vs(M)| > t \cdot |\Pi|$, and one of the following four conditions holds:

1. $p = \texttt{any}$ and $vs(M)(v) > 0$,
2. $p = \texttt{all=}$ and $vs(M)(v) = |vs(M)|$,
3. $p = \texttt{min}$ and v is the smallest value in $vs(M)$, or
4. $p = \texttt{smor}$ and v is the smallest most frequent value in $M' = vs(M)$, i.e., $\forall v'.\ M'(v) \geq M'(v') \wedge (M'(v) = M'(v') \implies v \leq v')$.

Send and Next Functions. As mentioned earlier, the phase sequence of a *ConsL* algorithm uniquely determines a round specification $rs(r)$ for each round $r \in \mathbb{N}$ to be executed. We give an HO model semantics to such an algorithm by (1) specifying the same set of initial states for each process: *inp* takes an arbitrary value from $\mathcal{V}$ and all other fields are $\bot$; and (2) translating each round specification $rs(r)$ into a pair $(\texttt{send}_p^r, \texttt{next}_p^r)$ as follows:

- $\texttt{send}_p^r$ returns process p's current (in round r) value of the *send-field* of $rs(r)$.
- $\texttt{next}_p^r$ updates process p's state by selecting new values for all fields in the instruction list of $rs(r)$. Given an instruction $G \triangleright f$ and the partial function $\mu_p^r : \Pi \rightharpoonup \mathcal{M}$ of messages received by the process p, let $R_p^r = \#[\mu_p^r]$. The set of possible new values of the field f of process p is determined as follows:

- For all $v \in \mathcal{V}$ such that $R_p^r \models G(v)$, v is a possible new value for f.
- If no such value $v \in \mathcal{V}$ exists, the only possible value is the *fallback value*: the old value of f of process p if $f \in \{inp, dec\}$, and $\perp$ otherwise.

We call fields other than *inp* and *dec ephemeral* since their fallback value $\perp$ and the restriction (R1) jointly imply that they do not keep state between successive phases. Example 2 below presents an algorithm using ephemeral fields. Moreover, the semantics ensures that the *dec* field never reverts from a value in $\mathcal{V}$ to $\perp$. Hence, the stability requirement of consensus holds by construction for all *ConsL* algorithms, including those using the language extensions described later. We therefore do not further discuss this requirement.

Labeled Transition System Semantics. In Sect. 2.2 we introduced the unlabeled transition system semantics of the HO model. To restrict reasoning to those traces satisfying the communication predicates, we label the traces with round labels from Σ (Sect. 3.2). The r-th unlabeled transition $s \rightarrow s'$ of a trace generated by an HO collection $\{HO_p^r\}_{p \in \Pi}^{r \in \mathbb{N}}$ gives rise to a set of labeled transitions $s \xrightarrow{\Lambda} s'$, where $\Lambda \in \Sigma$, such that:

1. $\phi_{uf} \in \Lambda$ implies that the formula $\phi_{uf}(r)$ holds for $\{HO_p^r\}_{p \in \Pi}^{r \in \mathbb{N}}$.
2. $\phi_{th}(c) \in \Lambda$ implies that $\phi_{th}(c, r)$ holds, and that c appears as the threshold of some guard in the algorithm. For technical reasons, we also require that for all guards G in the transition, $th(G) = 0 \vee th(G) = c$.

A labeled trace includes both states and labels. The semantics of a *ConsL* algorithm $\mathcal{A}$ is the set of infinite traces whose labels form a word in the communication predicate of $\mathcal{A}$. Property satisfaction is relative to this semantics.

3.4 Extensions

To cover additional algorithms, we increase the expressiveness of *ConsL* by including three additional features: leaders (l), timestamps (t), and randomness (r). We write *ConsL^E* for a given set $E \subseteq \{l, t, r\}$ to denote the language with the corresponding extensions. An algorithm must specify the extensions it uses. As we do not know of any algorithms combining randomness and timestamps, for simplicity we assume $\{r, t\} \not\subseteq E$. The leaders and timestamp extensions are also subject to some syntactic restrictions required for our proofs. The restrictions and extensions' formal semantics are detailed in [39]; for space reasons, we only provide an informal overview here.

Leaders. Leaders are distinguished processes that act as coordinators: they collect the possible inputs and select one of them. Leaders add two new communication patterns:

- $\vartriangleleft$, where only the leader broadcasts a message in a round, and
- $\vartriangleright$, where all processes send a message exclusively to the leader.

1. $inp \gtrdot (\frac{1}{2}, \mathbf{maxts}) \triangleright lvote$
2. $lvote \lessdot (0, \mathbf{any}) \triangleright inp$
   $(0, \mathbf{any}) \triangleright vote$
3. $vote \gtrdot (\frac{1}{2}, \mathbf{any}) \triangleright ldec$
4. $ldec \lessdot (0, \mathbf{any}) \triangleright dec$

Communication predicate:
$(\Sigma^4)^* \{\phi_{lr}(\frac{1}{2})\}\{\phi_{ls}\}\{\phi_{lr}(\frac{1}{2})\}\{\phi_{ls}\}\Sigma^\omega$

Fig. 3. Paxos written in *ConsL*

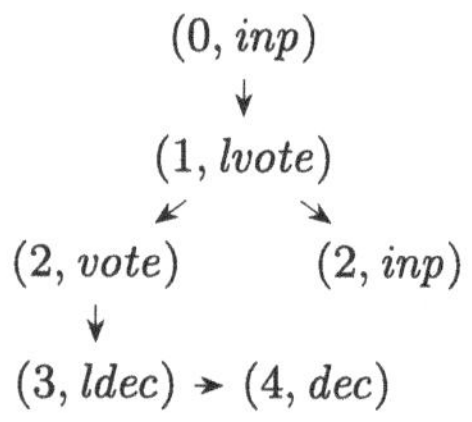

$(0, inp)$
$\downarrow$
$(1, lvote)$
$\swarrow \qquad \searrow$
$(2, vote) \qquad (2, inp)$
$\downarrow$
$(3, ldec) \rightarrow (4, dec)$

Fig. 4. Paxos phase graph

To prevent a failed leader from blocking progress, we assume that leaders can switch arbitrarily between phases. We also assume that the leader of each round is known in advance, as given by a function $ldr : \mathbb{N} \to \Pi$. This assumption is common (e.g., [8, 36]). Still, many algorithms work without it [10] as long as all processes eventually agree on the phase leader. We believe that our results also hold without the assumption, but we have not yet proved this. Next, to ensure progress, we add two new round formulas:

- a *leader send* formula $\phi_{ls}(r) \triangleq \forall p.\ ldr(r) \in HO_p^r$, requiring that all processes hear from the round leader, and
- a *leader receive* formula $\phi_{lr}(c, r) \triangleq |HO_{ldr(r)}^r| > c \cdot n$, requiring that the leader receives a sufficient number of messages in round r.

These formulas ensure that the algorithm is not stuck with a leader that has failed or is partitioned from the other processes. We also extend the set L of transition labels with the set $\{\phi_{ls}\} \cup \{\phi_{lr}(c) \mid c \in [0, 1)_\mathbb{Q}\}$.

Timestamps. A *timestamped field* stores a value together with the time of its last update, thereby recording information about the execution history. Time is logical, expressed by round numbers. When sending out a timestamped field, both the value and the timestamp are transmitted. A new predicate, $\mathbf{maxts}$, then selects a value with the highest timestamp; to break ties, the smallest such value is selected. In *ConsL*, timestamps only make sense with the *inp* field, since the other fields are either never sent out or do not persist between phases.

Example 2. To showcase the use of leaders and timestamps, Fig. 3 shows our *ConsL* model of the Paxos algorithm [36], or more precisely, its Synod part. The single four-round phase is repeated forever. Compared to [36], (1) our phases (called "ballots" there) appear to start automatically (by conceptually moving the *NextBallot* message of [36] to the messaging layer), (2) we assume that all processes receive an input instead of just the leader, and (3) we replace phase numbers by round numbers in *inp*'s timestamps (these are isomorphic by (R1)).

Randomness. Randomization is an alternative to partial synchrony for making consensus solvable [7]. Randomized algorithms normally have a probabilistic termination guarantee: all processes eventually decide with probability 1. The termination proof usually relies on an almost-sure "lucky toss", where all processes draw the same favorable randomness. We turn this into a standard termination guarantee by (1) modeling randomness as non-determinism: processes non-deterministically choose a bit for the fallback values; (2) providing a way to specify lucky tosses, inspired by the Ben-Or algorithm; and (3) extending the set L of transition labels with a special label λ, indicating that a lucky toss occurred. For randomized algorithms, we make the usual assumption that $\mathcal{V} = \{0, 1\}$.

4   The Zero-One Principle

The zero-one principle for sorting networks [32] is a well-known result stating that a sorting network correctly sorts all sequences of inputs if and only if it correctly sorts all sequences of elements from $\mathbb{B} \triangleq \{0, 1\}$. We prove an analogous result for our language and the consensus problem. We call the consensus problem for the binary domain $\mathcal{V} = \mathbb{B}$ the *binary consensus problem*. Since the randomization extension already assumes this domain, we restrict our attention here to non-randomized algorithms. We also need a further restriction on *ConsL*, listed separately as we need it only for the termination part of the 0-1 principle. The other results hold without this restriction.

RT min and all= guards do not appear in the same round specification.

Theorem 1. *An algorithm expressed in* $ConsL^E$ *(with* $r \notin E$*) that additionally obeys (RT) solves the consensus problem for an arbitrary value domain* $\mathcal{V}$ *if and only if it solves the binary consensus problem.*

There are intuitive reasons why the principle should hold. Since we assumed $r \notin E$, *ConsL*'s semantics immediately implies that all algorithms guarantee non-triviality (in addition to stability). We thus only have to consider agreement and termination, for which we prove that their violations are preserved when $\mathcal{V} = \mathbb{B}$. By definition, agreement requires only two values to disprove. We combine this with the earlier observation that *ConsL* algorithms simply propagate values between the processes' fields. Then it suffices to ensure that whenever two different values can be propagated in a multi-valued agreement counterexample, both 0 and 1 can be propagated when $\mathcal{V} = \mathbb{B}$. This is in general possible as the values themselves are irrelevant and only their relative ordering matters. Disproving termination requires showing that, whenever guards (in particular, those for updating *dec*) can fail in a multi-valued setting, they can fail in the binary setting. From the language semantics (Sect. 3.3), there are two ways for a guard to fail. The first way is to have the process receive insufficiently many non-$\perp$ messages. As this is independent of the size of $\mathcal{V}$, we can mimic this cause of failure in the binary setting. The second way is to have the process receive different values when the update is guarded by an all= predicate. In this case, two values also suffice.

Unfortunately, the proof (given in [39]) is more complex than this intuition might suggest. One example of its intricacies is the restriction (RT). The following problematic example shows why this restriction is necessary.

Phase Φ_1

$inp \; \diagdown\!\!\!\!\times \; (\frac{1}{2}, \mathtt{min}) \triangleright inp$

$\quad\quad (\frac{1}{2}, \mathtt{all=}) \triangleright vote$

$vote \; \diagdown\!\!\!\!\times \; (0, \mathtt{any}) \triangleright dec$

Phase Φ_2

$inp \; \diagdown\!\!\!\!\times$

$\quad\quad (\frac{1}{2}, \mathtt{min}) \triangleright inp$

Phase Φ_3

$inp \; \diagdown\!\!\!\!\times$

$\quad\quad (\frac{1}{2}, \mathtt{all=}) \triangleright dec$

Phase sequence: $\Phi_1\Phi_2\Phi_3^\omega$; communication predicate: $\{\phi_{th}(\frac{1}{2})\}^\omega$.

Fig. 5. Example showing the necessity of (RT)

Example 3. Consider the algorithm in Fig. 5. Note that the phase sequence is $\Phi_1\Phi_2\Phi_3^\omega$ and the communication predicate demands that all processes receive messages from a majority of processes in each round. Consequently, every round's threshold guard is satisfied. This algorithm violates termination in a three-valued setting, but not in the binary setting. To see this, first consider the binary setting. Assume that some process p is still undecided after Φ_3. This requires that p receives both 0's and 1's in Φ_3. Hence, some majority $P \subseteq \Pi$ of processes had inp set to 1 at the start of phase Φ_2. It follows that all processes in P have updated both inp and $vote$ to 1 in the first round of Φ_1. Due to the communication predicate, in the second round of Φ_1, p must have seen a message from at least one process from P and thus decided, which is a contradiction. Therefore, this algorithm terminates after at most four rounds in the binary setting.

In the multi-valued setting, the algorithm may not terminate. Consider a run of the algorithm where all processes have pairwise distinct values in their inp fields. In the first round, it is then possible that each process receives at least two different values and that there is no majority for a particular value in the inp fields at the end of the round. As a result, no process decides in the second round of phase Φ_1. Moreover, it is possible that different values still exist after phase Φ_2. Hence, phase Φ_3 does not guarantee termination.

The crux of the problem is round 1 of phase Φ_1, which (RT) prohibits. There, in a multi-valued setting, two processes p and q can update inp to two different values v and v', while the updates to $vote$ fail at both p and q. However, in the binary setting, any process p that updates inp to 1 must update $vote$ as well.

5   Cutoff Bounds for Binary Consensus

The zero-one principle shows that it suffices to verify consensus algorithms for the binary domain $\mathcal{V} = \mathbb{B}$. We now complete our proof of the small scope hypothesis by proving it for the binary case. For an algorithm $\mathcal{A}$ with the set of guards $\mathcal{G}$, let $T_{\mathcal{A}} = \{th(G) \mid G \in \mathcal{G} \wedge pred(G) \neq \mathtt{smor}\} \cup \{\frac{th(G)}{2} \mid G \in \mathcal{G} \wedge pred(G) = \mathtt{smor}\}$.

Theorem 2. *Let $\mathcal{A}$ be an algorithm written in $ConsL^E$ for some E. Let d be the least common denominator of the (reduced-form) fractions in $T_{\mathcal{A}}$. Then, $\mathcal{A}$ solves binary consensus for any number of processes if and only if $\mathcal{A}$ solves binary consensus for exactly $2d + 1$ processes.*

As an example, Theorem 2 yields a cutoff bound of 7 for the $\frac{1}{3}$-rule algorithm (Fig. 2) and a cutoff bound of 5 for Paxos (Fig. 3). Like with the 0-1 principle, we only sketch the main proof ideas; the details are in [39].

We start by giving an overview of our proof technique and providing intuition for the choice of our cutoff bound $B = 2d + 1$. The details differ slightly depending on the consensus property considered. We first explain the general approach, which is same for all the properties, and focus on the differences afterwards. We show that, given a (labeled) counterexample trace τ_l of a large width $k > B$ that violates a consensus property, we can create a counterexample τ_s of the small width B, with the same labels as τ_l. A *trace inflation* lemma allows us to ignore systems of widths below B by inflating small counterexamples.

Our proof is based on *simulations* in the style of [37]. These rely on a *simulation relation* R relating states s_l of the large system to states s_s of the small system. The main proof obligation for simulation requires that s_s can mimic all possible transitions from s_l; formally, given any s_s, s_l, s_l', and Λ, we must prove:

$$(s_s, s_l) \in R \wedge s_l \xrightarrow{\Lambda} s_l' \implies \exists s_s'. \, s_s \xrightarrow{\Lambda} s_s' \wedge (s_s', s_l') \in R. \qquad \text{(s-trans)}$$

To define the relation R, we observe that guards, and thus also transitions, are agnostic to the absolute numbers of processes; they only use fractional thresholds and compare the relative frequencies of values. Hence, we relate states of different sizes based on the frequencies of values from $\mathcal{V}_\perp$, expressed as fractions of the number of processes. We discretize these fractions into size-independent *slots* $\{0, \frac{1}{d}, \frac{2}{d}, \ldots \frac{d-1}{d}\}$, since only d-denominated fractions appear in the algorithm's guards. The state s_s must then be wide enough to accommodate the s_l-slot of each value from $\mathcal{V}_\perp$. In [39], we show that $2d + 1$ is the smallest such width. We now give more details of the simulation relation and our proof under the assumption that $\mathcal{V} = \mathbb{B}$.

5.1   Core Elements of the Simulation Relation

Given two natural numbers n (the system's width) and d (with $d \geq 2$), we define two sets $T \triangleq \{0, \frac{1}{d}, \ldots, \frac{d-1}{d}\}$ and $T_0 \triangleq T \cup \{-\frac{1}{3d}\}$, and a function $\gamma_n : \{0, \ldots, n\} \to T_0$, with $\gamma_n(c) = \frac{\lceil \frac{d}{n} c \rceil - 1}{d}$ when $c > 0$, and $\gamma_n(0) = -\frac{1}{3d}$. The function γ_n maps process counts to slots, where $\gamma_n(c)$ yields the smallest threshold in T_0 exceeded by the count c. These counts typically arise as $c = \#[s(f)](v)$, i.e., the number of processes holding value v in field f, where we write $s(f)$ for the function defined by $s(f)(p) = s_p.f$ for all $p \in \Pi$. If state s has width n, then $\gamma_n(\#[s(f)](v))$ denotes the corresponding slot in T_0. Given two multisets M_s and M_l of sizes B and k respectively, we define the following relations:

$$(M_s, M_l) \in cntMS_= \triangleq \forall v \in \mathcal{V}_\perp. \, \gamma_B(M_s(v)) = \gamma_k(M_l(v))$$

$$(M_s, M_l) \in cntMS_\geq(W) \triangleq \forall v \in W. \, \gamma_B(M_s(v)) \geq \gamma_k(M_l(v))$$

$$(M_s, M_l) \in cntMS_{\sum \geq}(W) \triangleq \gamma_B\left(\sum_{v \in W} M_s(v)\right) \geq \gamma_k\left(\sum_{v \in W} M_l(v)\right).$$

Table 1. Slots $\gamma_{|M|}(c)$ for different counts c and $T = \{0, \frac{1}{3}, \frac{2}{3}\}$.

Multiset M	$|M|$	$M(0)$	$M(1)$	$M(\perp)$	$M(0) + M(1)$
$M_s^1 = \{4 \times 0, 3 \times 1\}$	7	1/3	1/3	$-1/3d$	2/3
$M_l^1 = \{5 \times 0, 8 \times 1\}$	13	1/3	1/3	$-1/3d$	2/3
$M_l^2 = \{5 \times 0, 7 \times 1, 1 \times \perp\}$	13	1/3	1/3	0	2/3
$M_l^3 = \{4 \times 0, 9 \times 1\}$	13	0	2/3	$-1/3d$	2/3

The first relation requires the slot of each value from $\mathcal{V}_\perp$ to be exactly the same in both multisets. Sometimes this will be too strong a requirement, and we will switch to the other two relations, which are weaker (the first two relations can be expressed in terms of the last one, but we retain them for convenience).

Example 4. For the $\frac{1}{3}$-rule algorithm, we have $B = 7$ and $T = \{0, \frac{1}{3}, \frac{2}{3}\}$. Take $k = 13$ and consider the multisets M in the first column of Table 1. The second column of the table indicates their size and the remaining columns display for each of them the slots $\gamma_{|M|}(c)$ of the indicated counts c. Then, we have

- $(M_s^1, M_l^1) \in cntMS_=$,
- $(M_s^1, M_l^2) \in cntMS_\geq(\mathcal{V}) \cap cntMS_{\sum \geq}(\mathcal{V})$, but $(M_s^1, M_l^2) \notin cntMS_=$, and
- $(M_s^1, M_l^3) \in cntMS_{\sum \geq}(\mathcal{V})$, but $(M_s^1, M_l^3) \notin cntMS_\geq(\mathcal{V})$.

These relations form the basis of our simulation relation R. For space reasons, we focus on just the salient points of R. For example, we require:

$$(\#[s_s(inp)], \#[s_l(inp)]) \in cntMS_\geq(\mathcal{V}).$$ (inp-rel)

for all $(s_s, s_l) \in R$. Similar conditions relate the other fields. The exact relation used depends on both the property we are proving, and on the field's position in the phase graph. The next subsection provides additional details, focusing on the core language *ConsL* (without extensions) for simplicity.

5.2 Simulating Transitions

Given a transition $s \xrightarrow{\Lambda} s'$ in a trace, define U to be the set of all *upd-fields* appearing in the transition's instructions, and the *global update* associated with the transition to be a function $\mathcal{U} : U \to \Pi \to \mathcal{V}_\perp$, where $\mathcal{U}(f)(p)$ is $v \in \mathcal{V}$ if p updates the field f with v, and $\perp$ if p updates f with a fallback value. We let $u_p(f) = \mathcal{U}(f)(p)$ and call u_p the *local update* of the process p. Our simulation proofs proceed in three stages:

1. Simulate local updates: for any local update u_p possible from s_l, prove that there exists a set $P \subseteq \Pi$ such that any process whose HO set is P can also perform the local update u_p from s_s.

2. Simulate global updates: given any global update $\mathcal{U}_l$ associated with a transition $s_l \xrightarrow{\Lambda} s_l'$, combine the local updates from the previous stage to construct a global update $\mathcal{U}_s$ associated with a transition $s_s \xrightarrow{\Lambda} s_s'$, such that $\mathcal{U}_s$ is similar to $\mathcal{U}_l$. For example, for all fields f updated in a transition before the fork point, we require that $(\#[\mathcal{U}_s(f)], \#[\mathcal{U}_l(f)]) \in cntMS_=$.

3. Simulate state updates: given $s_l \xrightarrow{\Lambda} s_l'$, $\mathcal{U}_l$, and $\mathcal{U}_s$ as above, show that applying $\mathcal{U}_s$ to s_s yields an s_s' with $s_s \xrightarrow{\Lambda} s_s'$ and $(s_s', s_l') \in R$. When $\mathcal{U}_l$ updates inp, i.e., $inp \in U$, this is not always the case. The reason is that $\mathcal{U}_s$ alone does not completely determine $\#[s_s'(inp)]$, as the old values are used as a fallback. For instance, if $\#[s_s(inp)] = M_s^1 = \{4 \times 0, 3 \times 1\}$, we can construct two global updates $\mathcal{U}_1$ and $\mathcal{U}_2$ with $\#[\mathcal{U}_1(inp)] = \#[\mathcal{U}_2(inp)] = \{3 \times 0, 4 \times \bot\}$, such that applying $\mathcal{U}_1$ to s_s yields a state s_s' with $\#[s_s'(inp)] = \{7 \times 0\}$ ($\mathcal{U}_1$'s 3×0 overwrite all 1's in $s_s(inp)$), and $\mathcal{U}_2$ leaves s_s intact ($\mathcal{U}_2$'s 3×0 overwrite three 0's in $s_s(inp)$). Hence, to obtain the desired s_s' with $(s_s', s_l') \in R$, we might first have to transform $\mathcal{U}_s$ into some appropriate $\mathcal{U}_s'$ with $\#[\mathcal{U}_s(inp)] = \#[\mathcal{U}_s'(inp)]$ by permuting the processes' local updates. This is achieved by permuting their round HO sets. Note that this preserves the step label Λ.

Stage 1 is relatively straightforward, whereas the next two stages are significantly more involved. Stage 2 is complicated by the fork points (Sect. 3.2), which make constructing similar global updates a non-trivial combinatorial problem. The restriction (R2) is crucial in solving this problem. In Stage 3, a problem arises when the inp field is updated as the following example illustrates.

Example 5. Consider states s_s and s_l such that $\#[s_s(inp)] = M_s^1 = \{4 \times 0, 3 \times 1\}$ and $\#[s_l(inp)] = M_l^1 = \{5 \times 0, 8 \times 1\}$. There is an update $\mathcal{U}_l$ with $\#[\mathcal{U}_l(inp)] = \{1 \times 0, 1 \times 1, 11 \times \bot\}$ that yields a state s_l' with $\#[s_l'(inp)] = M_l^3 = \{4 \times 0, 9 \times 1\}$. The updates $\mathcal{U}_s$ with $\#[\mathcal{U}_s(inp)] = \{1 \times 0, 1 \times 1, 5 \times \bot\}$ are the only ones satisfying $(\#[\mathcal{U}_s(inp)], \#[\mathcal{U}_l(inp)]) \in cntMS_=$. However, none of these can be applied to s_s to yield a state s_s' such that (inp-rel) holds for s_l' and s_s', since attaining a fraction $\gamma_{13}(\#[s_l'(inp)](1)) = \gamma_{13}(9) = \frac{2}{3}$ of 1's in s_s' would require $\#[s_s'(inp)](1) \geq 5$. Hence, we might be forced to use a $\mathcal{U}_s$ such that $(\#[\mathcal{U}_s(inp)], \#[\mathcal{U}_l(inp)]) \notin cntMS_=$, which in turn might cause $(\#[\mathcal{U}_s(f)], \#[\mathcal{U}_l(f)]) \notin cntMS_=$ for the other fields updated by $\mathcal{U}_s$.

After the fork point, we therefore weaken the Stage 2 relation to

$$(\#[\mathcal{U}_s(f)], \#[\mathcal{U}_l(f)]) \in cntMS_\geq(W) \cap cntMS_{\sum\geq}(W),$$

for an appropriate $W \subset \mathcal{V}_\bot$. For ephemeral fields, this also implies that the simulation relation must use $cntMS_\geq(W)$ and $cntMS_{\sum\geq}(W)$ instead of $cntMS_=$. The choice of W depends on the property whose violation we want to preserve.

Agreement and Non-triviality. Preserving agreement and non-triviality violations requires the small system to make decisions whenever the large system makes them. Thus, we choose $W = \mathcal{V}$. This suffices to show that whenever a value $v \in \mathcal{V}$ satisfies a guard (in particular, for updating dec) in the large system, v also satisfies that guard in the small system. Our choice of W might force updates to happen in the small system where none happened in the large system, but this is acceptable for the violations we wish to preserve.

Termination. Preserving termination violations requires exactly the opposite: whenever an update guard (in particular, for updating dec) fails in the large system, its failure must also be possible in the small system. Recalling the semantics of $ConsL$, guards fail for two reasons: an insufficient number of non-$\perp$ messages have been received, or different values have been received and the guard uses an `all=` predicate. Choosing $W = \{\perp\}$ preserves the first cause of failure, but not the second. Choosing $W = \mathcal{V}$ preserves the second cause, but not the first. Thus, the correct choice depends on the transition $s_l \rightarrow s'_l$, and cannot be determined in advance. This is a well-known problem with *forward simulation*, the type of simulation that we described in (s-trans). To overcome this problem, we resort to *backward-forward simulations* [37], which enable us to switch between the two choices of W on-the-fly. As our transition systems are all finitely-branching, backward-forward simulation ensures the inclusion of infinite traces.

6   Experimental Results

We combine Theorems 1 and 2, the finite representations of the phase sequence and the communication predicates, and the techniques from [46] for handling unbounded timestamps to turn model checking into a decision procedure for $ConsL$ algorithms and consensus. Given a $ConsL$ algorithm $\mathcal{A}$ with a cutoff bound B, one encodes the HO model of $\mathcal{A}$ for $|\Pi| = B$ and $\mathcal{V} = \mathbb{B}$ in the model checker's input language and verifies it. We have built a tool that automatically translates a $ConsL$ algorithm into the appropriate Promela model and LTL properties for the Spin model checker [23]. As case studies, we generated models of different algorithms from the literature (Table 2). Our verification times confirm that the above decision procedure is applicable in practice, with modest resources.

The tool and the generated models are available for download [40]. For simplicity, our tool handles only a subset of phase sequence and communication predicate specifications described in Sect. 3.2. To improve performance, the tool implements two optimizations. First, it reduces the model's branching factor. In a naive modeling approach, in every round in which the uniformity formula ϕ_{uf} does not hold, each of the B processes first chooses its HO set independently and then performs a local update based on this HO set, yielding a branching factor of 2^{B^2}. Instead, the tool-generated models first calculate the possible local updates and let each process pick one of them, lowering the branching factor to typically 2 or 3. Second, the tool reduces the state space by exploiting symmetry in the system and applying a counter abstraction. The abstraction is sound and complete. For leaderless algorithms this is immediate since guard satisfaction (Sect. 3.3) is defined exactly on multisets; for leader-based algorithms, we need an additional variable to track the leader process' state in the abstraction.

Table 2. Experimental results. Time is given in seconds.

Algorithm	Bound	Agreement		Termination	
		Time	States	Time	States
Paxos	5	0.89	1,135,730	0.93	1,151,691
Paxos (3 rounds)	5	0.70	853,003	0.73	866,917
Chandra-Toueg	5	0.85	1,032,371	0.89	1,048,332
Algorithm from [38]	5	1.17	1,367,956	1.19	1,370,414
$\frac{1}{3}$-rule	7	0.04	67,578	0.04	70,070
Coordinated uniform voting	5	0.02	39,650	0.02	39,948
Simplified coord. uniform voting	5	0.01	27,304	0.01	27,616
Uniform voting (variant)	5	0.01	17,238	0.01	17,385
Ben-Or	5	0.03	42,478	0.03	45,348

7 Related Work

The general parametric verification problem was shown to be undecidable by Apt and Kozen [5]. Suzuki [45] showed that this holds also when the parameter is the number of replicated processes, each having a fixed state space. The small scope hypothesis is folklore, implicitly formulated by Jackson and Damon [26], and empirically studied for Java data structures by Andoni et al. [4], for answer-set programs by Oetsch et al. [42], and for distributed systems by Yuan et al. [49].

Cutoff Bounds. Cutoff bounds have been devised for several classes of algorithms and properties: for token-ring systems by Emerson and Namjoshi [17]; for systems with existential guards and systems with universal guards by Emerson and Kahlon [15]; for cache coherence protocols by Emerson and Kahlon [16]; for rectangular hybrid automata by Johnson and Mitra [29]; and for software transactional memories by Guerraoui et al. [20]. Kaiser et al. [30] devise a method for determining cutoff bounds for the thread-state reachability problem *dynamically*, by performing a partial search of the state space. Abdulla et al. [2] use similar ideas, but their results apply to a larger class of systems. None of these results applies to consensus algorithms or other types of fault-tolerant distributed systems. The only cutoff result that we are aware of in this area is by Delzanno et al. [12]. They derive cutoff bounds for the proposer and learner roles of Paxos, but not the acceptor role, for which they perform only bounded verification. We adopt the more common model where all processes play all the roles.

Other (Semi-)Automated Methods. Backward reachability analysis of well-quasi-ordered systems [1] and regular model checking [3] are two general approaches to the verification of parametric systems. Regular model checking has been used to verify some simple fault-tolerant algorithms [19]. However, no suitable well-quasi-ordering or regular transition relations are known to exist for fault-tolerant distributed systems that rely on threshold guards. Two recent works have explored alternative approaches for the parametric verification of such systems.

Konnov et al. [28] introduce an abstraction for systems based on a type of threshold guards, roughly similar to *ConsL* guards. Their technique yields a sound, but incomplete (due to abstraction) verification procedure for next-free LTL properties, and they successfully apply it to several simpler fault-tolerant algorithms. In [33,34] they propose additional verification methods for the abstraction and also apply them to a simplified version of the consensus problem.

Drăgoi et al. [13] introduce the consensus logic $\mathbb{CL}$, aimed at verifying the properties of round-based consensus algorithms, and a domain specific language for it [14]. $\mathbb{CL}$ is strictly more expressive than *ConsL*, and can encode algorithms for the synchronous and Byzantine settings. They provide a semi-decision procedure for invariant checking, which performs well in their experiments, and a full decision procedure for invariant checking for a fragment $\mathbb{CL}_{dec}$ whose expressive power is incomparable to *ConsL*. Their method is only semi-automated, since the user must find the appropriate invariants, and is not guaranteed to give an answer for $\mathbb{CL}$ (outside of $\mathbb{CL}_{dec}$), since it is based on a semi-decision procedure.

8   Conclusions

Our main contribution is the specification language *ConsL* for consensus algorithms, for which we derive a zero-one principle and cutoff bounds for verifying consensus properties. This language covers a relevant and non-trivial class of consensus algorithms. Our bounds are algorithm-dependent, but fairly small, either 5 or 7 for our case studies. This formally proves the small scope hypothesis for this class, and lends additional credibility to the hypothesis for other fault-tolerant distributed algorithms. Moreover, the bounds are small enough to be within the reach of standard model-checking methods, yielding the first fully automated verification procedure for consensus algorithms.

We see two directions for future work. The first is to extend our results to other algorithms. One possible extension is to Byzantine-tolerant algorithms. However, as these algorithms typically use thresholds with denominators in the range of 3 to 7, model checking them could become infeasible with $B = 2d + 1$. While lowering the factor 2 in B might be possible, we suspect that B's dependency on d is fundamental since in systems with fewer than $d + 1$ processes the notions "more than $\frac{d-1}{d}$ processes" and "all processes" coincide. Another possible extension is to target higher-level primitives that build on consensus algorithms in a white-box fashion, such as atomic (also called total-order) broadcast.

The second direction is to focus on the 0-1 principle. Putting aside the cutoff bounds might help to remove some of the more ad-hoc *ConsL* features (such as the restrictions in Sect. 3.2) and yield a simpler class of algorithms with hopefully simpler proofs. If such a class is obtained, one might consider generalizing the principle; for example, a 0-k principle could help decide k-set agreement.

Furthermore, we believe that the unbounded growth of the input (and thus also message) space with the increasing system width is a key obstacle for applying the method of [28] to general consensus algorithms, and that the 0-1 principle could provide the missing link.

Acknowledgments. We would like to thank the anonymous reviewers and Ralf Sasse for their useful feedback on the paper.

References

1. Abdulla, P., Cerans, K., Jonsson, B., Tsay, Y.-K.: General decidability theorems for infinite-state systems. In: LICS, pp. 313–321 (1996)
2. Abdulla, P., Haziza, F., Holík, L.: Parameterized verification through view abstraction. Int. J. Softw. Tools Technol. Transf., pp. 1–22 (2015)
3. Abdulla, P.A.: Regular model checking. Int. J. Softw. Tools Technol. Transf. **14**(2), 109–118 (2012)
4. Andoni, A., Daniliuc, D., Khurshid, S., Marinov, D.: Evaluating the "small scope hypothesis". In: POPL, vol. 2 (2003)
5. Apt, K.R., Kozen, D.C.: Limits for automatic verification of finite-state concurrent systems. Inf. Process. Lett. **22**(6), 307–309 (1986)
6. Bailis, P., Kingsbury, K.: The network is reliable. ACM Queue **12**(7), 20:20–20:32 (2014)
7. Ben-Or, M.: Another advantage of free choice: completely asynchronous agreement protocols. In: PODC, pp. 27–30 (1983)
8. Chandra, T.D., Toueg, S.: Unreliable failure detectors for reliable distributed systems. J. ACM (JACM) **43**(2), 225–267 (1996)
9. Chaouch-Saad, M., Charron-Bost, B., Merz, S.: A reduction theorem for the verification of round-based distributed algorithms. In: Bournez, O., Potapov, I. (eds.) RP 2009. LNCS, vol. 5797, pp. 93–106. Springer, Heidelberg (2009). doi:10.1007/978-3-642-04420-5_10
10. Charron-Bost, B., Schiper, A.: The Heard-Of model: computing in distributed systems with benign faults. Distrib. Comput. **22**(1), 49–71 (2009)
11. Debrat, H., Merz, S.: Verifying fault-tolerant distributed algorithms in the heard-of model. Archive of Formal Proofs (AFP) (2012). https://www.isa-afp.org/entries/Heard_Of.shtml
12. Delzanno, G., Tatarek, M., Traverso, R.: Model Checking Paxos in Spin. Electron. Proc. Theoret. Comput. Sci. **161**, 131–146 (2014)
13. Drăgoi, C., Henzinger, T.A., Veith, H., Widder, J., Zufferey, D.: A logic-based framework for verifying consensus algorithms. In: McMillan, K.L., Rival, X. (eds.) VMCAI 2014. LNCS, vol. 8318, pp. 161–181. Springer, Heidelberg (2014). doi:10.1007/978-3-642-54013-4_10
14. Drăgoi, C., Henzinger, T. A., Zufferey, D.: PSync: a partially synchronous language for fault-tolerant distributed algorithms. In: POPL, pp. 400–415 (2016)
15. Emerson, E.A., Kahlon, V.: Reducing model checking of the many to the few. In: McAllester, D. (ed.) CADE 2000. LNCS (LNAI), vol. 1831, pp. 236–254. Springer, Heidelberg (2000). doi:10.1007/10721959_19
16. Emerson, E.A., Kahlon, V.: Exact and efficient verification of parameterized cache coherence protocols. In: Geist, D., Tronci, E. (eds.) CHARME 2003. LNCS, vol. 2860, pp. 247–262. Springer, Heidelberg (2003). doi:10.1007/978-3-540-39724-3_22

17. Emerson, E.A., Namjoshi, K.S.: On reasoning about rings. Int. J. Found. Comput. Sci. **14**(04), 527–549 (2003)
18. Fischer, M.J., Lynch, N.A., Paterson, M.S.: Impossibility of distributed consensus with one faulty process. J. ACM **32**(2), 374–382 (1985)
19. Fisman, D., Kupferman, O., Lustig, Y.: On verifying fault tolerance of distributed protocols. In: Ramakrishnan, C.R., Rehof, J. (eds.) TACAS 2008. LNCS, vol. 4963, pp. 315–331. Springer, Heidelberg (2008). doi:10.1007/978-3-540-78800-3_22
20. Guerraoui, R., Henzinger, T.A., Jobstmann, B., Singh, V.: Model checking transactional memories. In: PLDI, pp. 372–382 (2008)
21. Hawblitzel, C., Howell, J., Kapritsos, M., Lorch, J.R., Parno, B., Roberts, M.L., Setty, S., Zill, B.: IronFleet: proving practical distributed systems correct. In SOSP, pp. 1–17 (2015)
22. Herlihy, M.: Wait-free synchronization. ACM Trans. Program. Lang. Syst. **13**(1), 124–149 (1991)
23. Holzmann, G.J.: The SPIN Model Checker - Primer and Reference Manual. Addison-Wesley, Boston (2004)
24. Hutle, M., Schiper, A.: Communication predicates: a high-level abstraction for coping with transient and dynamic faults. In: 37th Annual IEEE/IFIP International Conference on Dependable Systems and Networks, 2007, DSN 2007, pp. 92–101. IEEE (2007)
25. Jackson, D.: Software Abstractions: Logic, Language, and Analysis. MIT Press, Cambridge (2012)
26. Jackson, D., Damon, C.A.: Elements of style: analyzing a software design feature with a counterexample detector. IEEE Trans. Softw. Eng. **22**(7), 484–495 (1996)
27. Jaskelioff, M., Merz, S.: Proving the correctness of Disk Paxos. Archive of Formal Proofs (AFP) (2005). https://www.isa-afp.org/entries/DiskPaxos.shtml
28. John, A., Konnov, I., Schmid, U., Veith, H., Widder, J.: Parameterized model checking of fault-tolerant distributed algorithms by abstraction. In: FMCAD, pp. 201–209 (2013)
29. Johnson, T.T., Mitra, S.: A small model theorem for rectangular hybrid automata networks. In: Giese, H., Rosu, G. (eds.) FMOODS/FORTE -2012. LNCS, vol. 7273, pp. 18–34. Springer, Heidelberg (2012). doi:10.1007/978-3-642-30793-5_2
30. Kaiser, A., Kroening, D., Wahl, T.: Dynamic cutoff detection in parameterized concurrent programs. In: Touili, T., Cook, B., Jackson, P. (eds.) CAV 2010. LNCS, vol. 6174, pp. 645–659. Springer, Heidelberg (2010). doi:10.1007/978-3-642-14295-6_55
31. Kingsbury, K.: Jepsen: Testing the Partition Tolerance of PostgreSQL, Redis, MongoDB and Riak (2013). http://www.infoq.com/articles/jepsen
32. Knuth, D.E.: The Art of Computer Programming, Vol III: Sorting and Searching. Addison-Wesley, Boston (1973)
33. Konnov, I., Veith, H., Widder, J.: On the completeness of bounded model checking for threshold-based distributed algorithms: reachability. In: Baldan, P., Gorla, D. (eds.) CONCUR 2014. LNCS, vol. 8704, pp. 125–140. Springer, Heidelberg (2014). doi:10.1007/978-3-662-44584-6_10
34. Konnov, I., Veith, H., Widder, J.: SMT and POR beat counter abstraction: parameterized model checking of threshold-based distributed algorithms. In: Computer Aided Verification, pp. 85–102, July 2015
35. Küfner, P., Nestmann, U., Rickmann, C.: Formal verification of distributed algorithms. In: Baeten, J.C.M., Ball, T., Boer, F.S. (eds.) TCS 2012. LNCS, vol. 7604, pp. 209–224. Springer, Heidelberg (2012). doi:10.1007/978-3-642-33475-7_15
36. Lamport, L.: The part-time parliament. ACM Trans. Comput. Syst. **16**(2), 133–169 (1998)

37. Lynch, N., Vaandrager, F.: Forward and backward simulations part I: untimed systems. Inf. Comput. **121**, 214–233 (1995)
38. Marić, O., Sprenger, C., Basin, D.: Consensus Refined. In: DSN, pp. 391–402 (2015)
39. Marić, O.: Formal Verification of Fault-Tolerant Systems. Ph.D. thesis, Department of Computer Science, ETH Zurich (2017). http://dx.doi.org/10.3929/ethz-a-010892776
40. Marić, O.: The Consensus Verifier, May 2017. http://www.infsec.ethz.ch/research/software/consl-verifier
41. Newcombe, C.: Why Amazon Chose TLA$^+$. In: Ait, A.Y., Schewe, K.D. (eds.) Abstract State Machines, Alloy, B, TLA, VDM, and Z. ABZ 2014. LNCS, vol. 8477, pp. 25–39. Springer, Berlin (2014)
42. Oetsch, J., Prischink, M., Pührer, J., Schwengerer, M., Tompits, H.: On the small-scope hypothesis for testing answer-set programs. In: KR (2012)
43. Santoro, N., Widmayer, P.: Time is not a healer. In: Monien, B., Cori, R. (eds.) STACS 1989. LNCS, vol. 349, pp. 304–313. Springer, Heidelberg (1989). doi:10.1007/BFb0028994
44. Schiper, N., Rahli, V., van Renesse, R., Bickford, M., Constable, R.: Developing correctly replicated databases using formal tools. In: DSN, pp. 395–406 (2014)
45. Suzuki, I.: Proving properties of a ring of finite-state machines. Inf. Process. Lett. **28**(4), 213–214 (1988)
46. Tsuchiya, T., Schiper, A.: Model checking of consensus algorithms. In: SRDS, pp. 137–148, October 2007
47. Tsuchiya, T., Schiper, A.: Using bounded model checking to verify consensus algorithms. In: Taubenfeld, G. (ed.) DISC 2008. LNCS, vol. 5218, pp. 466–480. Springer, Heidelberg (2008). doi:10.1007/978-3-540-87779-0_32
48. Tsuchiya, T., Schiper, A.: Verification of consensus algorithms using satisfiability solving. Distrib. Comput. **23**(5–6), 341–358 (2010)
49. Yuan, D., Luo, Y., Zhuang, X., Rodrigues, G.R., Zhao, X., Zhang, Y., Jain, P.U., Stumm, M.: Simple testing can prevent most critical failures: an analysis of production failures in distributed dataintensive systems. In: OSDI (2014)

Towards Verifying Nonlinear Integer Arithmetic

Paul Beame[(✉)] and Vincent Liew[(✉)]

Computer Science and Engineering, University of Washington,
Seattle, WA 98195, USA
{beame,vliew}@cs.washington.edu

Abstract. We eliminate a key roadblock to efficient verification of non-linear integer arithmetic using CDCL SAT solvers, by showing how to construct short resolution proofs for many properties of the most widely used multiplier circuits. Such short proofs were conjectured not to exist. More precisely, we give $n^{O(1)}$ size regular resolution proofs for arbitrary degree 2 identities on array, diagonal, and Booth multipliers and $n^{O(\log n)}$ size proofs for these identities on Wallace tree multipliers.

1 Introduction

Recent decades have seen remarkable advances in our ability to verify hardware. Methods for hardware verification based on Ordered Binary Decision Diagrams (OBDDs) developed in the 1980s for hardware equivalence testing [16] were extended in the 1990s to produce general methods for symbolic model checking [18] to verify complex correctness properties of designs. More recently, several orders of magnitude of improvements in the efficiency of SAT solvers have brought new vistas of verification of hardware and software within reach.

Nonetheless, there is an important area of formal verification where road-blocks that were identified in the 1980s still remain: verification of data paths within designs for Arithmetic Logic Units (ALUs), or indeed any verification problem in hardware or software that involves the detailed properties of non-linear arithmetic. Natural examples of such verification problems in software include computations involving hashing or cryptographic constructions. At the highest level of abstraction, nonlinear arithmetic over the integers is undecidable, but the focus of these verification problems is on the decidable case of integers of bounded size, which is naturally described in the language of bit-vector arithmetic (see, e.g. [30,32]).

In particular, a notorious open problem is that of verifying properties of integer multipliers in a way that both is general purpose and avoids exponential scaling in the bit-width. Bryant [17] showed that this is impossible using OBDDs since they require exponential size in the bit-width just to represent the middle bit of the output of a multiplier. This lower bound has been improved [11] and extended to include very tight exponential lower bounds for much more

P. Beame and V. Liew—Research supported in part by NSF grant CCF-1524246.

R. Majumdar and V. Kunčak (Eds.): CAV 2017, Part II, LNCS 10427, pp. 238–258, 2017.
DOI: 10.1007/978-3-319-63390-9_13

general diagrams than OBDDs, and FBDDs [10,36] and general bounded-length branching programs [38]. With the flexibility of CNF formulas, efficient representation of multipliers is no longer a problem but, even with the advent of greatly improved SAT solvers, there has been no advance in verifying multipliers beyond exponential scaling.

One important technique for verifying software and hardware that includes multiplication has been to use methods of uninterpreted functions to handle multipliers (see [14,32]) – essentially converting them to black boxes and hoping that there is no need to look inside to check the details. Another important technique has been to observe that it is often the case that one input to a multiplier is a known constant and hence the resulting computation involves linear, rather than nonlinear arithmetic. These approaches have been combined with theories of arithmetic (e.g. [12,13,15,35]), including preprocessors that do some form of rewriting to eliminate nonlinear arithmetic, but these methods are not able, for example, to check the details of a multiplier implementation or handle nonlinearity.

Though the above approaches work in some contexts, they are very limited. The approach of verifying code with multiplication using uninterpreted functions is particularly problematic for hashing and cryptographic applications. For example, using uninterpreted functions in the actual hash function computation inherently can never consider the case that there is a hash collision, since it only can infer equality between terms with identical arguments. Concern about such applications is real: longstanding errors in multiplication in OpenSSL have recently come to light [34].

Recent presentations at verification conferences and workshops have highlighted the problem of verifying nonlinear arithmetic, and multipliers in particular, as one of the key gaps in our current verification methods [6,7,9,29].

Since bit-vector arithmetic is not itself a representation in Boolean variables, in order to apply SAT solvers to verify the designs, one must convert implementations and specifications to CNF formulas based on specified bit-widths. The process by which one does this is called *flattening* [32], or more commonly *bit-blasting*. The resulting CNF formulas are then sent to the SAT solvers. While the resulting bit-blasted CNF formulas for a multiplier may grow quadratically with the bit-width, this growth is not a significant problem. On the other hand, a major stumbling block for handling even modest bit-widths is the fact that existing SAT solvers run on these formulas experience exponential blow-up as the bit-width increases. This is true even for the best of recent methods, e.g., Boolector [13], MathSAT [15], STP [27], Z3 [25], and Yices [24].

In verifying a multiplier circuit one could try to compare it to a reference circuit that is known to be correct. This introduces a chicken-and-egg problem: how do we know that the reference circuit is correct? Another approach to verifying a multiplier circuit is to check that it satisfies the right properties. A correct multiplier circuit must obey the multiplication identities for a commutative ring. If we check that each of these *ring identities* holds then the multiplier cannot have an error. This approach has the advantage that the specification of a multiplier circuit can be written *a priori* in terms of its natural properties, rather than in terms of an external reference circuit.

Empirically, however, modern SAT-solvers perform badly using either approach to problems of multiplier verification. Biere, in the text accompanying benchmarks on the ring identities submitted to the 2016 SAT Competition [8] writes that when given as CNF formulas, no known technique is capable of handling bit-width larger than 16 for commutativity or associativity of multiplication or bit-width 12 for distributivity of multiplication over addition. These observations lead to the question: is the difficulty inherent in these verification problems, or are modern SAT-solvers just using the wrong tools for the job?

Modern SAT-solvers are based on a paradigm called conflict-directed clause-learning (CDCL) [33] which can be seen as a way of breaking out of the back-tracking search of traditional DPLL solvers [23]. When these solvers confirm the validity of an identity (by not finding a counterexample), their traces yield *resolution* proofs [4] of that identity. The size of such a proof is comparable to the running time of the solver; hence finding short resolution proofs of these identities is a necessary prerequisite for efficient verification via CDCL solvers. Although it is not known whether CDCL solvers are capable of efficiently simulating every resolution proof, all cases where short resolution proofs are known have also been shown to have short CDCL-style traces (e.g., [19–21]).

The extreme lack of success of general purpose solvers (in particular CDCL solvers) for verifying any non-trivial properties of bit-vector multiplication, recently led Biere to conjecture [9] that there is a fundamental proof-theoretic obstacle to succeeding on such problems; namely, verifying ring identities for multiplication circuits, such as commutativity, requires resolution proofs that are exponential in the bit-width n.

We show that such a roadblock to efficient verification of nonlinear arithmetic does not exist by giving a general method for finding short resolution proofs for verifying *any* degree 2 identity for Boolean circuits consisting of bit-vector adders and multipliers. This method is based on reducing the multiplier verification to finding a resolution refutation of one of a number of narrow *critical strips*. We apply this method to a number of the most widely used multiplier circuits, yielding $n^{O(1)}$ size proofs for array, diagonal, and Booth multipliers, and $n^{O(\log n)}$ size proofs for Wallace tree multipliers.

These resolution proofs are of a special simple form: they are *regular* resolution proofs[1]. Regular resolution proofs have been identified in theoretical models of CDCL solvers as one of the simplest kinds of proof that CDCL solvers naturally express [20]. Indeed, experience to date has been that the addition of some heuristics to CDCL suffices to find short regular resolution proofs that we know

---

[1] Some of these proofs are even more restricted *ordered* resolution proofs, also known as *DP* proofs, which are associated with the original Davis-Putnam procedure [22]. In contrast to the Davis-Putnam procedure, which eliminates variables one-by-one keeping all possible resolvents, ordered resolution (or DP) proofs only keep some minimal subset of these resolvents needed to derive a contradiction.

exist. The new regular resolution proofs that we produce are a key step towards developing such heuristics for verifying general nonlinear arithmetic.

Related Work: SAT solver-based techniques used in conjunction with case splitting previously were shown to achieve some success for certain multiplier verification problems in the work of Andrade et al. [3] improving on earlier work [2,37] which combined SAT solver and OBDD-based ideas for multiplier verification among other applications; however, there was no general understanding of when such methods will succeed.

Recently, two alternative approaches to multiplier verification have been considered: Kojevnikov [28] designed a mixed Boolean-algebraic solver, BASolver, that takes input CNF formulas in standard format. It uses algebraic rules on top of a DPLL solver. Though it can verify the equivalence of multipliers up to 32 bits in a reasonable time, in each instance it requires human input in order to find a suitable set of algebraic rules to help the solver. An alternative approach using Groebner basis algorithms has been considered [39]. This is a purely algebraic approach based on polynomials. Since the language of polynomials allows one to explicitly write down the algebraic specification for an n-bit multiplier, the verification problem is conveniently that of checking that the multiplier circuit computes a polynomial equivalent to the multiplier specification. [39] shows that Groebner basis algorithms can be used to verify 64-bit multipliers in less than ten minutes and 128-bit multipliers in less than two hours. However, this requires that the multipliers be identified and treated entirely separately from the rest of the circuit or software. Unfortunately, for the non-algebraic parts of circuits, Groebner basis methods can only handle problems several orders of magnitude smaller than can be handled by CDCL SAT-solvers and it remains to be seen whether it is possible to combine these to obtain effective verification for a general purpose software with nonlinear arithmetic or circuits that contain a multiplier as just one component of their design. In contrast, CDCL SAT solvers are already very effective for the non-algebraic aspects of circuits and are well-suited to handling the combination of different components; our work shows that there is no inherent limitation preventing them from being effective for verification of general purpose nonlinear arithmetic.

Roadmap: In Sect. 3 we introduce and give constructions of some standard multipliers, in particular the array multiplier and the Wallace tree multiplier. We give polynomial size regular resolution proofs for degree 2 identities for circuits constructed using array, diagonal, and Booth multipliers in Sect. 4 and give quasipolynomial size regular resolution proofs for circuits constructed using Wallace tree multipliers in Sect. 5.

2   Notation and Preliminaries

We represent Boolean variables in lowercase and denote clauses by uppercase letters and think of them as sets of literals, for example $C = \{x, \bar{y}, z\}$. We will work with length n *bit-vectors* of variables, denoted by $\mathbf{z} = z_{n-1} \ldots z_1 z_0$.

We consider identities from the commutative ring of integers $\mathbb{Z}$. We use a set $\sigma = \sigma(x_0, x_1 \ldots x_n) = \{x_0 = b_0, x_1 = b_1 \ldots x_n = b_n\}$, where each $b_i \in \{0,1\}$, to denote an assignment to the variables $x_0, x_1, \ldots x_n$.

Definition 1. *A* commutative ring $(\mathcal{R}, \oplus, \otimes, 0, 1)$ *consists of a nonempty set $\mathcal{R}$ with addition $(\oplus)$ and multiplication $(\otimes)$ operators that satisfy the following properties:*

1. *$(\mathcal{R}, \oplus)$ is associative and commutative and its identity element is 0.*
2. *For each $\mathbf{x} \in \mathcal{R}$ there exists an* additive inverse.
3. *$(\mathcal{R}, \otimes)$ is associative and commutative and its identity element is $1 \neq 0$.*
4. *(distributivity) For all $\mathbf{x}, \mathbf{y}, \mathbf{z} \in \mathcal{R}$, $\mathbf{x} \otimes (\mathbf{y} \oplus \mathbf{z}) = (\mathbf{x} \otimes \mathbf{y}) \oplus (\mathbf{x} \otimes \mathbf{z})$.*

A ring identity $L = R$ denotes a pair of expressions L, R that can be transformed into each other using commutativity, distributivity and associativity.

Note that both verifying integer $\oplus$ circuits and verifying that $\mathbf{x} \otimes \mathbf{1} = \mathbf{x}$ are easy in practice, so verifying an integer multiplier circuit $\otimes$ can be easily reduced to verifying its distributivity.

Definition 2. *A resolution proof consists of a sequence of clauses, each of which is either a clause of the input formula ϕ, or follows from two prior clauses via the* resolution rule *which produces clause $C \vee D$ from clauses $C \vee x$ and $D \vee \overline{x}$. We say that this inference* resolves *the clauses on x. The proof is a* refutation *of ϕ if it ends with the empty clause $\perp$. (With resolution we will use the terms "proof" and "refutation" interchangeably, since resolution provides proofs of unsatisfiability.)*

We can naturally represent a resolution proof P as a directed acyclic graph (DAG) of fan-in 2, with $\perp$ labelling the lone sink node. *Tree resolution* is the special subclass of resolution proofs where the DAG is a directed tree. Another restricted form of resolution is *regular resolution*: A resolution refutation is *regular* iff on any path in its DAG the inferences resolve on each variable at most once. The shortest tree resolution proofs are always regular. An *ordered* resolution refutation is a regular resolution refutation that has the further property that the order in which variables are resolved on along each path is consistent with a single total order of all variables. This is a very significant restriction and indeed the shortest tree resolution proofs do not necessarily have this property.

We will find it convenient to express our regular resolution proofs in the form of a *branching program* that solves the *conflict clause search problem*.

Definition 3. *Suppose that ϕ is an unsatisfiable formula. Then every assignment σ to its variables conflicts with some clause in ϕ. The* conflict clause search problem *is to map any assignment to some corresponding conflicting clause.*

Definition 4. *A* branching program *B on the Boolean variables $X = \{x_0, x_1, \ldots\}$ and output set ϕ (typically a set of clauses in this paper) is a finite directed acyclic graph with a unique source node and sink nodes at its leaves, each leaf labeled by an element from ϕ. Each non-sink node is labeled by a variable from X and* *has two outgoing edges, one labeled* 0 *and the other labeled* 1. *An assignment* σ *activates an edge labeled* $b \in \{0,1\}$ *outgoing from a node labeled by the variable* x_i *if* σ *contains the assignment* $x_i = b$. *If* σ *activates a path from the source to a sink labeled* $C \in \phi$, *we say that the branching program* B *outputs* C *(Fig. 1).*

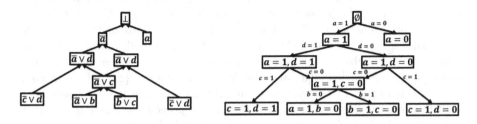

Fig. 1. A regular resolution refutation and the corresponding branching program.

A read-once branching program *(also known as a Free Binary Decision Diagram, or FBDD) is a branching program where each variable is read at most once on any path from source to leaf. An* Ordered Binary Decision Diagram (OBDD) *is a special case of an FBDD in which the variables read along any path are consistent with a single total order.*

The general case of the following theorem connecting regular resolution proofs and conflict clause search is due to Krajicek [31]; the special case connecting ordered resolution and OBDDs for the conflict clause search problem, which is a simple observation extending the original proof, does not seem to have been explicitly noted previously.

Theorem 1. *Let* ϕ *be an unsatisfiable formula. A regular resolution refutation* R *for* ϕ *of size* s *corresponds to a size* s *read-once branching program that solves the conflict clause search problem for* ϕ.

Suppose that B *is a read-once branching program of size* s *solving the conflict clause search problem for* ϕ. *Then there is a regular resolution refutation for* ϕ *of size* s.

Furthermore, if R *is an ordered resolution refutation then the resulting branching program is an OBDD and if* B *is an OBDD then the resulting resolution refutation is an ordered resolution refutation.*

Proof (Sketch). In this equivalence, the nodes of the read-once branching program are in one-to-one correspondence with the clauses in the proof and the edges of the read-once branching program correspond to the inference connections in the proof. That is, clauses $A \vee x$ and $B \vee \overline{x}$ resolve to yield clause C if and only if the node corresponding to C is labeled by x, its 0-outedge goes to the node corresponding to $A \vee x$ and its 1-outedge goes to the node corresponding to $B \vee \overline{x}$.

Moving from the proof to the branching program is immediate. For the reverse direction we label each node with the maximal clause that is falsified by every assignment reaching that node. It is not hard to check that all the needed properties are satisfied.

In our proofs we write each clause as the assignment it forbids. For example we write the clause $\{x, \bar{y}\}$ as the assignment $\{x = 0, y = 1\}$. We will build up branching programs for conflict clause search in ϕ in terms of three types of action, shown in Figs. 2, 3, 4. At a node labeled by an assignment $\sigma \not\ni z$, we *branch* on the variable z by adding a child node with assignment $\sigma \cup \{z = 0\}$, connected by a 0-labeled edge, and another child node $\sigma \cup \{z = 1\}$, connected by a 1-labeled edge. In the case that one of these children has an assignment conflicting with a clause $C \in \phi$, we say that we *propagated* the assignment σ to the other child's assignment. Lastly, for a set of leaf nodes with assignments $\sigma_0, \sigma_1, \ldots$ we can *merge* their branches based on a common assignment $\sigma \subset \cap_i \sigma_i$ by replacing these nodes with a single node labeled by σ.

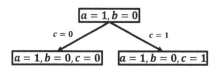

Fig. 2. Branching on c.

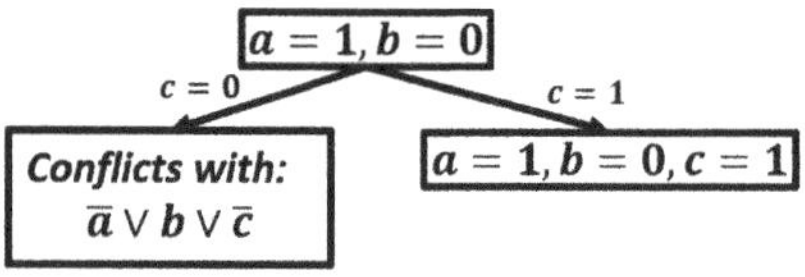

Fig. 3. Propagating to $c = 1$.

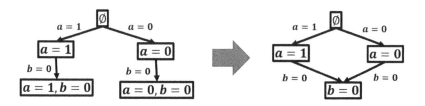

Fig. 4. Merging on the common assignment $\{b = 0\}$.

3   Multiplier Constructions

We describe our SAT instances as a set of constraints, where each constraint is a set of clauses. We build circuits out of *adders* that output, in binary, the sum of three input bits. An adder is encoded as follows:

Definition 5. *Suppose a_0, a_1, a_2 are inputs to an adder A. The outputs c, d of the adder A are encoded by the constraints:*

$$d = a_0 \oplus a_1 \oplus a_2 \qquad c = MAJ(a_0, a_1, a_2)$$

We call c and d the sum-bit *and c* carry-bit *respectively. If an adder has two constant inputs 0 it acts as a* wire. *If it has precisely one constant input 0, we call it a* half adder. *If no inputs are constant, we call it a* full adder.

Each circuit variable in our constructions has a *weight* of the form 2^i. Each adder will take in three bits of the same weight 2^i and output a *sum-bit* of weight 2^i and a *carry-bit* of weight 2^{i+1}. The adder's definition ensures that the weighted sum of its input bits is the same as the weighted sum of its output bits. In the constructions that follow, we divide the adders up into columns so that the i-th column contains all the adders with inputs of weight 2^i.

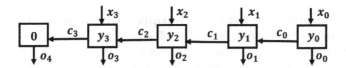

Fig. 5. 4-bit ripple-carry adder adding $\mathbf{x}, \mathbf{y}$. Each box represents a full adder with incoming arrows and outgoing arrows representing inputs and outputs.

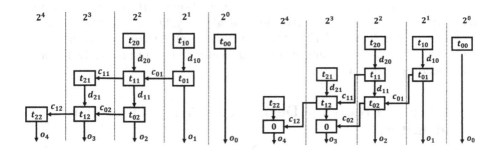

Fig. 6. Array multiplier tableau.   **Fig. 7.** Diagonal multiplier tableau.

Ripple-Carry Adder: A ripple-carry adder, shown in Fig. 5, takes in two bitvectors $\mathbf{x}, \mathbf{y}$ and outputs their sum in binary. In the i-th column, for $i \leq n$, we place an adder A_i that takes the three variables c_{i-1}, x_i, y_i and outputs the adder's carry variable and sum variable to c_i and o_i respectively. In the $n + 1$-st column we place a wire A_{n+1} taking c_n as input and outputting to o_{n+1}.

All the multipliers we describe perform two phases of computation to compute $\mathbf{xy}$ for length n bitvectors $\mathbf{x}, \mathbf{y}$. The first phase is the same in each multiplier: the circuit computes a *tableau* of values $x_i \wedge y_j$ for each pair of input bits x_i and y_j. In the second phase where the constructions differ, the circuit computes the weighted sum of the bits in the tableau.

Array Multiplier: An n-bit array multiplier works by arranging n ripple-carry adders in sequence in order to sum the n rows of the tableau. This multiplier has a simple gridlike architecture that is compact and easy to lay out physically. It has depth linear in its bitwidth. In the first phase, an array multiplier computes each tableau variable $t_{ij} = x_i \wedge y_j$, with associated weight 2^{i+j}.

Arrange a grid of full adders $A_{i,j}$, where $i,j \in [0,n]$, as shown in Fig. 6. Adder $A_{i,j}$ occupies the j-th row and the $i+j$-th column, takes inputs $t_{i,j}, d_{i+j,j-1}, c_{i-1,j}$ (replacing nonexisting variables with the constant 0), and outputs the carry and sum bits $c_{i,j}$ and $d_{i,j}$. Finally, we add constraints equating the sum-bits $d_{0,0}, d_{0,1}, \ldots, d_{0,n-1}, d_{1,n-1}, \ldots, d_{n-1,n-1}$ with the corresponding output bits $o_0, o_1, \ldots, o_{2n-1}$.

Diagonal Multiplier and Booth Multiplier: A diagonal multiplier uses a similar idea to the array multiplier. The difference is that the diagonal multiplier routes its carry bits to the next row instead of the same row as depicted in Fig. 7.

A Booth multiplier uses a similar idea to the array multiplier, but uses a telescoping sum identity to skip consecutive digits in one multiplicand.

Wallace Tree Multiplier: A Wallace tree multiplier takes a different approach to summing the tableau. Using carry-save adders (parallel 1-bit adders), it iteratively finds a new tableau with the same weighted sum as the previous tableau, but with 1/3 fewer rows. Upon reducing the original tableau to just two rows, it uses a carry-lookahead adder to obtain the final result. In contrast to the array multiplier, a Wallace tree multiplier is complicated to lay out physically, but has only logarithmic depth.

4 Efficient Proofs for Degree Two Array Multiplier Identities

We give polynomial-size resolution proofs that commutativity, distributivity, and $x(x+1) = x^2 + x$ hold for a correctly implemented array multiplier. We go on to give polynomial-size resolution proofs for general degree two identities.

Proof Overview: The main idea, common to our proofs for each circuit family including Wallace tree multipliers, is to start by branching according to the lowest order disagreeing output bit between the two circuits. In each of these branches, the subcircuit known as a *critical strip* consists of the constraints on a small number of columns behind the disagreeing bit. For a large enough choice of width this critical strip is unsatisfiable since the removed section of the tableau on the right does not have enough total weight to cause the disagreeing output bit. It then remains to refute each critical strip.

Our proofs inside each critical strip cycle through three steps: branching on the values of input bits, propagating those values as far in the circuit as possible, then saving the resulting assignment to the variables on the boundary of the propagation. We call each of these boundaries a *cut* in the circuit. We can think of the branching program as scanning the input bits, saving its progress with assignments to small cuts.

These *cuts* are sets of variables that, under any assignment, split the strip into a satisfiable and an unsatisfiable region. If our branching program holds a cut assignment that was propagated from an earlier portion of the circuit, then this cut assignment is consistent with this earlier subcircuit. But since the critical strip as a whole is unsatisfiable, this cut assignment must be inconsistent with the rest of the circuit. Using these cuts, we isolate a small unsatisfiable region in the critical strip that is easily refuted.

One can view our proof as showing that the constraints within each strip form a graph of *pathwidth* $O(\log n)$ which, by [26], implies that there is a polynomial-size ordered resolution refutation of the strip. In the case of commutativity, our argument implies that the constraint graphs for the strips can be combined to yield a single constraint graph of pathwidth $O(\log n)$. For the other identities, the orderings on the strips are different and the resulting constraint graphs only have small *branchwidth* which, by [1], still implies that there are small regular resolution proofs of the other identities. Rather than simply invoke these general arguments, we give the details of the resolution proofs, along with more precise size bounds.

4.1 Efficient Resolution Proofs for Commutativity

Definition 6. *We define a SAT instance $\phi_{\text{Comm}}^{\text{Array}}(n)$. The inputs are length n bitvectors $\mathbf{x}, \mathbf{y}$. Using the construction from Sect. 3, we define array multipliers L and R computing, respectively, the products $\mathbf{xy}$ and $\mathbf{yx}$. In this construction, the tableau variables in multipliers L and R are defined by the constraints*

$$t_{i,j}^{L} = x_i \wedge y_j, \qquad t_{i,j}^{R} = y_i \wedge x_j,$$

and in particular we can infer, through resolution, that $t_{i,j}^{L} = t_{j,i}^{R}$.

After specifying the subcircuits L and R, we add a final subcircuit E, a set of inequality-constraints *encoding that the two circuits disagree on some output bit:*

$$e_i = (\neg o_i^{L} \wedge o_i^{R}) \vee (o_i^{L} \wedge \neg o_i^{R}) \quad \forall i \in [0, 2n-1],$$

$$e_0 \vee e_1 \vee \ldots e_{2n-1}.$$

We give a small resolution proof for $\phi_{\text{Comm}}^{\text{Array}}(n)$ in the form of a labeled OBDD B, as described in Theorem 1. The variable order for B begins with the comparison bits in the order $e_0, e_1, \ldots$, followed by the output bits $o_0^{R}, o_1^{R}, \ldots$. Then B reads the variables associated with adders $A_{i,j}^{L}, A_{j,i}^{R}$ in order of increasing j, reading each row right to left. Finally, B reads the output bits $o_0^{L}, o_1^{L}, \ldots$, then the input bits $\mathbf{x}, \mathbf{y}$ in an arbitrary order.

At the root of B, we search for the first output bit that L and R disagree on by branching on the sequences of bits $e_k = 1, e_{k-1} = 0, \ldots e_0 = 0$ for each

$k \in [0, 2n]$. We will show that on each branch we can prove that $\phi_{\text{Comm}}^{\text{Array}}(n)$ is unsatisfiable using only the constraints from L and R on the variables inside columns $[k - \log n, k]$.

Definition 7. *Let* $\delta = \log n$. *Let* $\phi_{\text{Strip}}(k) \subset \phi_{\text{Comm}}^{\text{Array}}(n)$ *hold the constraints containing a tableau variable* $t_{i,j}^L$ *or* $t_{i,j}^R$ *for* $i + j \in [k - \delta, k]$. *Further, add unit clauses to* $\phi_{\text{Strip}}(k)$ *that encode the assignment:* $e_0 = 0, e_1 = 0, \ldots, e_{k-1} = 0, e_k = 1$ *to the first* k *bits of* **e**. *We call* $\phi_{\text{Strip}}(k)$ *a critical strip of* $\phi_{\text{Comm}}^{\text{Array}}(n)$. *We call the subset* $\phi_{\text{Strip}}(k) \cap L$ *the critical strip of circuit* L *and likewise for circuit* R.

Lemma 1. $\phi_{\text{Strip}}(k)$ *is unsatisfiable for all* k.

Proof. We interpret each critical strip as a circuit that outputs the weighted sum of the input variables in either circuit L, R. The assignment to **e** demands that the difference between the critical strip outputs is precisely 2^k. But by $t_{i,j}^L = t_{j,i}^R$, the weighted sum of the tableau variables is the same in both critical strips. The difference in the critical strip outputs is then bounded by the sum of the input carry bits to column $k - \delta$ in either strip. There are fewer than n input carry bits for either critical strip, each of weight $2^{k-\delta} = 2^k/n$, therefore the difference in critical strip outputs is less than 2^k, violating the assignment to **e**.

Observe that this proof only relied on the relation $t_{ij}^L = t_{ji}^R$ in the tableau variables. The additional requirement that the tableau variables came from an assignment to **x**, **y** is unnecessary to refute $\phi_{\text{Strip}}(k)$.

Lemma 2. *There is an* $O(n^7 \log n)$*-sized ordered resolution proof that* $\phi_{\text{Strip}}(k)$ *is unsatisfiable.*

Proof. For simplicity we assume $k \leq n$; the case where $k > n$ is similar. We will also preprocess $\phi_{\text{Strip}}(k)$ by resolving on **x**, **y** to obtain the tableau variable relations $t_{ji}^R = t_{ij}^L$, then replacing all the variables t_{ji}^R by t_{ij}^L in the clauses $\phi_{\text{Strip}}(k)$. Viewing the proof as a branching program, this amounts to querying **x**, **y** at the end. We will not resolve on **x**, **y** in the remainder of this proof.

We give this resolution proof in the form of a labeled read-once branching program B. We call the set of tableau variables of L, as well as the carry variables from column $k - \delta - 1$ of both L and R, the *input variables* to this critical strip. An assignment to the input variables, denoted by σ_{input}, determines the outputs of L and R.

The idea behind the branching program B is to verify circuit L by branching on input variables row-by-row, going from top-to-bottom, maintaining an assignment to a row of sum-variables. Since $t_{ij}^L = t_{ji}^R$, the tableau variables of circuit R simultaneously get revealed from bottom to top. In circuit R we maintain both a guess for its output values, and a row of sum-variables. From the proof of Lemma 1, if we have found that the outputs of L and R were computed correctly then they must violate one of the constraints $e_k = 0, \ldots, e_{k-\delta+1} = 0, e_{k-\delta} = 1$.

Definition 8. *Define* $\mathrm{Cut}(0)$ *as the set of variables containing*

$$d^R_{0,i}, o^R_{i-1} \quad for \quad i-1 \in [k-\delta, k].$$

For $j \in [1, k-\delta-1]$, *we define* $\mathrm{Cut}(j)$ *to be the set containing the variables:*

$$d^L_{i,j-1}, d^R_{j,i-1} \quad for \quad i+j-1 \in [k-\delta, k],$$
$$c^R_{j-1,i} \quad for \quad i+j-1 \in [k-\delta, k-1],$$
$$o^R_i \quad for \quad i \in [k-\delta, k].$$

Lastly, for $j \in [k-\delta, k]$, *we define* $\mathrm{Cut}(j)$ *to be the set containing the variables, when the indices are in-range:*

$$o^L_i \quad for \quad i \in [k-\delta, j-1],$$
$$d^L_{i+1,j-1}, d^R_{j,i}, c^R_{j-1,i} \quad for \quad i+j \in [k-\delta, k],$$
$$c^R_{j-1,i} \quad for \quad i+j-1 \in [k-\delta, k-1],$$
$$o^R_i \quad for \quad i \in [k-\delta, k].$$

We will label each node of B by the pair $(\mathrm{Cut}(j), \sigma)$ where $\mathrm{Cut}(j)$ keeps track of the previously seen cut (Fig. 8).

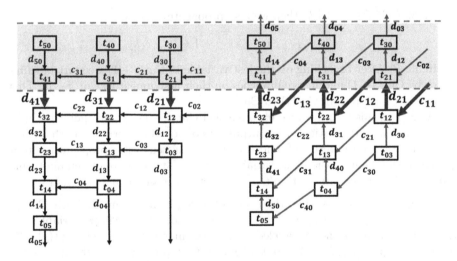

Fig. 8. The blue variables belong to $\mathrm{Cut}(2)$ of $\phi_{\mathrm{Strip}}(5)$. This cut divides the critical strip into a shaded satisfiable region and an unshaded unsatisfiable region. (Color figure online)

Initialization: Throughout, we work in terms of the tableau variables in circuit L, implicitly substituting t^L_{ij} for t^R_{ji}. We begin at the root node of the read-once branching program B, labeled $(\emptyset, \emptyset)$. For $i \in [k-\delta, k]$ we branch on the variable o^R_i, then propagate to $d^R_{0,i}$ using the constraint $o^R_i = d^R_{0,i}$. The surviving branches are those labeled by an assignment satisfying the constraints $o_i^R = d_{0,i}^R$. At this point we have reached nodes labeled Cut(0).

For each of the surviving branches, we branch on the tableau variables in the first row of L:

$$t_{i,0}^L \quad \text{for} \quad i \in [k - \delta, k].$$

Then we propagate to the variables, in sequence,

$$d_{1,i}^R, c_{0,i}^R \quad \text{for} \quad i + 1 \in [k - \delta, k]$$

from Cut(1) (notice that this does not include the input carry-bit $c_{0,k-\delta-1}^R$). We then merge on Cut(1).

Inductive Step: We now describe the transition from Cut(j) to Cut($j + 1$) for $j \in [1, k]$. Suppose that the branching program B has reached an assignment to Cut(j). From these nodes we branch on the next, j-th row of tableau variables

$$t_{i,j}^L \quad \text{for} \quad i + j \in [k - \delta, k]$$

and, when they exist, the pair of incoming input carry variables $c_{i,j}^L, c_{j-1,i}^R$ from column $k-\delta-1$, adjacent to the critical strip. We then propagate to the Cut($j+1$) and c^L variables in the sequence:

$$c_{i,j}^L, d_{i+1,j}^L \quad \text{for} \quad i + j + 1 \in [k - \delta, k]$$

in circuit L. If $j \in [k - \delta, k]$ then we also propagate to o_{j-1}.

$$c_{j,i}^R, d_{j+1,i}^R \quad \text{for} \quad i + j + 1 \in [k - \delta, k]$$

in circuit R. After branching on the last variable in Cut($j+1$) we start labeling nodes by Cut($j+1$) and merge branches on their assignment to Cut($j+1$). This completes the step from Cut(j) to Cut($j + 1$).

We repeat this step until we have reached Cut($k + 1$). At this point we have an assignment to the critical strip output bits $\mathbf{o}^L, \mathbf{o}^R$. Furthermore, both output assignments were the result of, and therefore consistent with, propagating from a single assignment on the input variables σ_{inputs}. By the proof of Lemma 1, this implies that our assignment to $\mathbf{o}^L, \mathbf{o}^R$ conflicts with an inequality constraint.

Size Bound: We show that there are $O(n^7 \log n)$ nodes in B. Each Cut(j) section of B begins with an assignment to at most $4\delta = 4 \log n$ variables, so there are at most n^4 nodes labeled by an assignment to precisely Cut(j). We branch on up to $\log(n) + 2$ input variables that propagate to the next cut's variables. So each cut has a full binary tree of $2 * (2^4 k^2)$ nodes branching on different configurations of input variables. For each leaf of this tree, B has a path of $O(\log n)$ nodes for propagating before the nodes get merged. Therefore each cut labels at most $O(n^6 \log n)$ nodes. There are $k + 1$ different cuts, thus B has at most $O((n + 1)n^6 \log n) = O(n^7 \log n)$ nodes.

Since the tableau variables were actually partial products of $\mathbf{x}$ and $\mathbf{y}$, we can make this proof smaller by branching on the bits of $\mathbf{x}, \mathbf{y}$ to determine the tableau variables in a row, maintaining a sliding window of δ bits of $\mathbf{x}$, yielding:

Corollary 1. $\phi_{\text{Strip}}(k)$ *has an* $O(n^6 \log n)$-*size regular resolution refutation.*

Theorem 2. *Let* $N = |\phi_{\text{Comm}}^{\text{Array}}| = O(n^2)$. *There is an* $O(N^{7/2} \log N)$ *size regular resolution proof that* $\phi_{\text{Comm}}^{\text{Array}}$ *is unsatisfiable. There is an* $O(N^4 \log N)$ *size ordered resolution proof that* $\phi_{\text{Comm}}^{\text{Array}}$ *is unsatisfiable.*

Proof. We can now describe the overall branching program B for $\phi_{\text{Comm}}^{\text{Array}}(n)$. The branching program branches on the inequality-constraint assignments $\sigma_e(k) = \{e_k = 1, e_{k-1} = 0, \ldots e_0 = 0\}$ for $k \in [0, 2n - 1]$. The k-th branch contains the clauses $\phi_{\text{Strip}}(k)$ so we can use the read-once branching program from either Corollary 1 or Lemma 2 (with each node augmented with the assignment $\sigma_e(k)$) to show that the branch is unsatisfiable. Corollary 1 yields the regular resolution proof and Lemma 2 yields the ordered resolution proof.

4.2   Efficient Resolution Proofs for Distributivity

Definition 9. *We define a SAT instance* $\phi_{\text{Dist}}^{\text{Array}}(n)$ *to verify the distributivity property*

$$x(y + z) = xy + xz$$

for an array multiplier in the natural way, using the constructions from Sect. 3. For the left hand expression we construct a ripple-carry adder L_{y+z}, *outputting* $(\mathbf{y} + \mathbf{z})$, *and array multiplier* $L_{x(y+z)}$ *outputting* $\mathbf{x}(\mathbf{y} + \mathbf{z})$. *For the right hand expression, we similarly define circuits* R_{xz}, R_{xy} *and* R_{xy+xz}.

We define $L = L_{y+z} \cup L_{x(y+z)}$ *and* $R = R_{xz} \cup R_{xy} \cup R_{xy+xz}$. *We let* E *contain the usual inequality constraints. The full distributivity instance is then* $\phi_{\text{Dist}}^{\text{Array}}(n) = L \cup R \cup E$.

We follow a similar strategy to the one used to refute $\phi_{\text{Comm}}^{\text{Array}}$. We again divide the instance into critical strips.

Definition 10. *Define the constant* $\delta = \log(2n)$. *Define the subset* $\phi_{\text{Strip}}(k) \subset \phi_{\text{Dist}}^{\text{Array}}(n)$ *to include, firstly, the full ripple-carry adder circuit* L_{y+z}. *Secondly, include the constraints containing one of the tableau variables* $t_{i,j}^{L_{x(y+z)}}, t_{i,j}^{R_{xy}}, t_{i,j}^{R_{xz}}$ *for* $i + j \in [k - \delta, k]$. *Thirdly, include the constraints on the carry-bits and sum-bits* $c_i^{R_{xy+xz}}, d_i^{R_{xy+xz}}$ *for* $i \in [k - \delta, k]$. *Lastly, add constraints to* $\phi_{\text{Strip}}(k)$ *that encode the assignment the bits:* $e_k = 1, e_{k-1} = 0, \ldots, e_0 = 0$.

Lemma 3. $\phi_{\text{Strip}}(k)$ *is unsatisfiable for all* k.

Proof (Sketch). Similarly to the proof of Lemma 1, the critical strip for $L_{x(y+z)}$ holds tableau bits with the same weighted sum (modulo 2^{k+1}) as those in R_{xz} and R_{xy} combined. The critical strip for $L_{x(y+z)}$ has at most n input carry-bits of weight $2^{k-\delta}$. The critical strips of the n-bit multipliers R_{xz} and R_{xy} each have at most $n - 1$ input carry variables of weight $2^{k-\delta}$. The critical strip of the adder R_{xy+xz} has one input carry variable, so the critical strip for R has $2n - 1$ input carry-bits. Since we set the width of the strip at $\delta = \log(2n)$, it is unsatisfiable.

Lemma 4. *For each k there is an $O(n^4 \log n)$ size regular resolution proof that $\phi_{\text{Strip}}(k)$ is unsatisfiable.*

Proof (Sketch). We construct a labeled branching program B that solves the conflict clause search problem for $\phi_{\text{Strip}}(k)$. The idea is similar to the one for the commutativity instance. We branch row-by-row in the critical strips, maintaining an assignment to cuts of variables in each multiplier. For each strip we will select a (different) variable ordering for $\mathbf{x}, \mathbf{y}, \mathbf{z}$ that reveals the tableau variables row-by-row. Assume that $k < n$ for simplicity; the case where $k \geq n$ is similar.

For an array multiplier $C \in \{L_{x(y+z)}, R_{xz}, R_{xy}\}$ and $j \in [1, k - \delta]$ we define $\text{Cut}^C(j)$ to be the set of variables

$$d_{i,j-1}^C \quad \text{for} \quad i + j - 1 \in [k - \delta, k],$$

and for $j \in [k - \delta + 1, k]$ we define $\text{Cut}^C(j)$ as the set of variables

$$d_{i,j-1}^C \quad \text{for} \quad i + j - 1 \in [k - \delta, k],$$
$$o_i^C \quad \text{for} \quad i \in [k - \delta, j - 2]$$

We define $\text{Cut}^{L_{y+z}}(j)$ to be the singleton set $\{c_{j-1}^{L_{y+z}}\}$. We also refer to a global cut, across the whole circuit: $\text{Cut}(j) = \cup_C \text{Cut}^C(j)$ (Fig. 9).

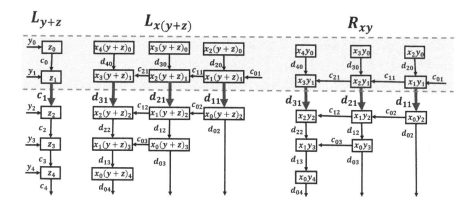

Fig. 9. Cut(2) for $\phi_{\text{Strip}}(4)$ consists of the blue variables.

As in the proof for commutativity, we sweep these cuts down each circuit. At row j, the branching program B will branch on x_{k-j}, y_j, z_j to reveal row j's tableau variables and then merge on the resulting propagated assignments to $\text{Cut}(j + 1)$.

Size Bound: There are $k+1$ different global cuts $\text{Cut}(j)$. Each $\text{Cut}(j)$ section of B begins with an assignment to at most $3\delta + 1$ variables. So each section $\text{Cut}(j)$ is initialized with at most $2^{3\delta + 1} = 8n^3$ branches. Each of these branches is a path with at most 10δ queried variables and therefore at most 20δ nodes. So there are at most $200\delta n^3$ nodes per cut and therefore at most $(k+1)200\delta n^3 = O(n^4 \log n)$ nodes in B.

Theorem 3. *Let* $N = |\phi_{\text{Dist}}^{\text{Array}}(n)| = O(n^2)$. *There is an* $O(N^{5/2} \log N)$ *size resolution proof that* $\phi_{\text{Dist}}^{\text{Array}}(k)$ *is unsatisfiable.*

Proof. At the root of this proof there are $2n$ branches each holding an assignment to $e_k, \ldots, e_1, e_0$. We refute each branch using the $O(n^4 \log n)$ size proof from Lemma 4.

4.3   Efficient Resolution Proofs for $x(x+1) = x^2 + x$

Define the SAT instance $\phi_{x(x+1)}^{\text{Array}}(n)$ for the identity $x(x+1) = x^2 + x$ in the usual way, with multipliers $L_{x(x+1)}$, R_{x^2} and ripple-carry adder L_{x+1}. While this identity looks like a special case of distributivity, its resolution proof is more complicated. This is because for distributivity: $x(y + z) = xy + xz$, the inputs to each multiplier were separate variables. This allowed us to scan the critical strip from one end to the other in a read-once fashion. If we try a similar strategy to scan the critical strip for the multiplier R_{x^2} from top to bottom, we will read each x_i twice. To avoid reading the same variable twice, we instead scan the critical strip from both ends, meeting in the middle. This strategy yields the following theorem, whose details can be found in the full version of this paper [5].

Theorem 4. *Let* $N = |\phi_{x(x+1)}^{\text{Array}}(n)| = O(n^2)$. *There is a size* $O(N^4 \log N)$ *regular resolution proof that* $\phi_{x(x+1)}^{\text{Array}}(n)$ *is unsatisfiable.*

4.4   Efficient Resolution Proofs for Degree Two Identities

Let $\phi_{L=R}^{\text{Array}}(n)$ denote a SAT instance corresponding to verifying the ring identity $L = R$. Similarly define $\phi_{L=R}^{\text{Diag}}(n)$ and $\phi_{L=R}^{\text{Booth}}(n)$ denote the diagonal and Booth multiplier versions. With the insight from the earlier proofs in this section, we can prove the general theorem:

Theorem 5. *For any degree two ring identity* $L = R$, *there are polynomial size regular refutations for* $\phi_{L=R}^{\text{Array}}(n)$.

Proof (Sketch). We divide $\phi_{L=R}^{\text{Array}}(n)$ into unsatisfiable critical strips of width $\delta = \log mn$, where m is the number of terms in the identity $L = R$. The ripple-carry adders that input to a multiplier remain intact, and for the rest we remove the columns outside the critical strip.

We begin by branching on guesses for the δ output bits from each multiplier and each truncated ripple-carry adder. In each multiplier we use a "meet-in-the-middle" strategy, similar to the proof for $x(x + 1) = x^2 + x$. We read all the input bitvectors in parallel, each in the same order. This branch order for each input bitvector $\mathbf{x}$ is $x_0, x_n, x_1, x_{n-1}, \ldots$. We can propagate these assignments to diagonal cuts in each multiplier that scan from the top and bottom edges towards the middle, and likewise for the intact ripple-carry adders. In each input bitvector we remember the assignment to just the most recently queried 2δ variables. Because of the symmetry of this variable order, it is compatible with swapping the order of inputs to any multiplier, as well as multipliers squaring an input.

Corollary 2. *For any degree two ring identity $L = R$, there are polynomial size regular resolution proofs for $\phi_{L=R}^{\mathrm{Diag}}(n)$ and $\phi_{L=R}^{\mathrm{Booth}}(n)$*

Proof. The proofs for diagonal and Booth multipliers follow the same ideas as the proof for an array multiplier.

5   Wallace Tree Multipliers

Like the proofs for array multipliers, our proofs for Wallace tree multipliers divide the instance into critical strips. In fact, our proofs branch on the input tableau in the same row-by-row order in both array and Wallace tree multipliers. However the size of the resulting cuts is $O(\log^2 n)$ for Wallace tree multipliers rather than the $O(\log n)$ size cuts for array multipliers. These cuts result in quasipolynomial size regular resolution proofs. The details of these resolution proofs and our Wallace tree multiplier construction are described in the full version of the paper [5].

Definition 11. *Let the SAT instance $\phi_{\mathrm{Comm}}^{\mathrm{Wall}}(n)$ encode two n-bit Wallace tree multipliers computing $\mathbf{xy}$ and $\mathbf{yx}$, as well as the usual inequality constraints. Similarly let $\phi_{\mathrm{Dist}}^{\mathrm{Wall}}(n)$ correspond to verifying distributivity. Finally, let the SAT instance $\phi_{L=R}^{\mathrm{Wall}}(n)$ correspond to verifying the ring identity $L = R$.*

Theorem 6. *The instance $\phi_{\mathrm{Comm}}^{\mathrm{Wall}}(n)$ has a size $O(n^{3\log n+3})$ regular resolution refutation. The instance $\phi_{\mathrm{Dist}}^{\mathrm{Wall}}(n)$ has a size $O(n^{4.5\log n+2})$ regular refutation.*

Using the same ordering on the input variables and ideas from the proof of Theorem 5, we can prove the analogous result for Wallace tree multipliers.

Theorem 7. *For any degree two ring identity $L = R$, there are quasipolynomial size regular refutations for $\phi_{L=R}^{\mathrm{Wall}}(n)$.*

6   Proving Equivalence Between Multipliers

Given any two n-bit multiplier circuits $\otimes_1$ and $\otimes_2$ we can define a Boolean formula $\phi_{\otimes_1 = \otimes_2}$ encoding the (negation of the) identity $\mathbf{x} \otimes_1 \mathbf{y} = \mathbf{x} \otimes_2 \mathbf{y}$ between length n bitvectors $\mathbf{x}$ and $\mathbf{y}$.

If they are both correct and compute using the typical tableau for multipliers then, as before, we can split $\phi_{\otimes_1 = \otimes_2}$ into unsatisfiable critical strips. We can scan down both strips row-by-row, as in the proofs for commutativity and distributivity. If we have reached the outputs of both multipliers without finding an error, these outputs will disagree with the inequality-constraints for the critical strip. For our examples this method yields polynomial-size proofs if neither is a Wallace tree multiplier, and quasi-polynomial size proofs otherwise.

On the other hand, if one multiplier is incorrect and the other is not, then the proof search will yield a satisfying assignment in the appropriate critical strip.

In the more general case where a multiplier does not use the typical tableau, one can label each internal gate by the index of the smallest output bit to which it is connected and focus on comparing subcircuits labeled by $O(\log n)$ consecutive output bits, as we do with critical strips. The complexity of this equivalence checking will depend somewhat on the similarity of the circuits involved.

7 Discussion

Despite significant advances in SAT solvers, one of their key persisting weaknesses has been in equivalence checking of arithmetic circuits. This pointed towards the conjecture that that the corresponding resolution proofs are exponentially large; if true, this would have been a fundamental obstacle putting nonlinear arithmetic out of reach for any CDCL SAT solver. We have shown that no such obstacle exists by giving the first small resolution proofs for verifying any degree two ring identity for the most common multiplier designs. Given the historical success of CDCL SAT solvers for finding specific proofs, our results suggest a new path towards verifying nonlinear arithmetic.

We introduced a method of dividing each instance into narrow, but still unsatisfiable, critical strips that is sufficiently general to yield short proofs for a wide variety of popular multiplier designs. The proof size upper bounds we derived were conservative; we did not try to optimize the parameters. A more important direction than doing so is to find the right guiding information to add, either to the formulas derived from the circuits or to CDCL SAT solver heuristics, to help them find such short proofs.

It also remains open to find a small resolution proof verifying the last ring property, associativity $(xy)z = x(yz)$. Our critical strip idea alone does not seem to work: while we can divide the outer multipliers into narrow critical strips, the yz or xy multipliers remain intact. These critical strips do not seem to have small cuts. Finding efficient proofs of associativity, combined with our results for degree two identities, could yield small proofs of any general ring identity.

References

1. Alekhnovich, M., Razborov, A.A.: Satisfiability, branch-width and Tseitin tautologies. In: Proceedings of 43rd Symposium on Foundations of Computer Science (FOCS 2002), Vancouver, BC, Canada, pp. 593–603. IEEE Computer Society, November 2002
2. Andersson, G., Bjesse, P., Cook, B., Hanna, Z.: A proof engine approach to solving combinational design automation problems. In: Proceedings of the 39th Design Automation Conference, DAC 2002, New Orleans, LA, USA, pp. 725–730. ACM, June 2002

3. Andrade, F.V., Oliveira, M.C.M., Fernandes, A.O., Coelho Jr., C.J.N.: SAT-based equivalence checking based on circuit partitioning and special approaches for conflict clause reuse. In: Girard, P., Krasniewski, A., Gramatová, E., Pawlak, A., Garbolino, T. (eds.) Proceedings of the 10th IEEE Workshop on Design & Diagnostics of Electronic Circuits & Systems (DDECS 2007), Kraków, Poland, pp. 397–402. IEEE Computer Society, April 2007

4. Beame, P., Kautz, H.A., Sabharwal, A.: Towards understanding and harnessing the potential of clause learning. J. Artif. Intell. Res. (JAIR) **22**, 319–351 (2004)

5. Beame, P., Liew, V.: Towards verifying nonlinear integer arithmetic. CoRR, abs/1705.04302 (2017)

6. Biere, A.: Challenges in bit-precise reasoning. In: Formal Methods in Computer-Aided Design, FMCAD 2014, Lausanne, Switzerland, p. 3, October 2014

7. Biere, A.: Where does SAT not work? In: BIRS Workshop on Theory and Applications of Applied SAT Solving, January 2014. http://www.birs.ca/events/2014/5-day-workshops/14w5101/videos/watch/201401201634-Biere.html

8. Biere, A.: Collection of combinational arithmetic miters submitted to the SAT competition 2016. In: Balyo, T., Heule, M., Järvisalo, M. (eds.) Proceedings of SAT Competition 2016 - Solver and Benchmark Descriptions, volume B-2016-1 of Department of Computer Science Series of Publications B, pp. 65–66. University of Helsinki (2016)

9. Biere, A.: Weaknesses of CDCL solvers. In: Fields Institute Workshop on Theoretical Foundations of SAT Solving, August 2016. http://www.fields.utoronto.ca/talks/weaknesses-cdcl-solvers

10. Bollig, B., Wooelfel, P.: A read-once branching program lower bound of $\Omega(2^{n/4})$ for integer multiplication using universal hashing. In: Proceedings of the Thirty-Third Annual ACM Symposium on the Theory of Computing, Hersonissos, Crete, Greece, pp. 419–424, July 2001

11. Bollig, B.: Larger lower bounds on the OBDD complexity of integer multiplication. Inf. Comput. **209**(3), 333–343 (2011)

12. Brinkmann, R., Drechsler, R.: RTL-datapath verification using integer linear programming. In: Proceedings of the ASPDAC 2002/VLSI Design 2002, Bangalore, India, pp. 741–746, January 2002

13. Brummayer, R., Biere, A.: Boolector: an efficient SMT solver for bit-vectors and arrays. In: Kowalewski, S., Philippou, A. (eds.) TACAS 2009. LNCS, vol. 5505, pp. 174–177. Springer, Heidelberg (2009). doi:10.1007/978-3-642-00768-2_16

14. Bruttomesso, R., Cimatti, A., Franzén, A., Griggio, A., Hanna, Z., Nadel, A., Palti, A., Sebastiani, R.: A lazy and layered SMT($\mathcal{BV}$) solver for hard industrial verification problems. In: Proceedings, Computer Aided Verification, 19th International Conference, CAV 2007, Berlin, Germany, pp. 547–560, July 2007

15. Bruttomesso, R., Cimatti, A., Franzén, A., Griggio, A., Sebastiani. R.: The Math-SAT 4 SMT solver. In: Proceedings, Computer Aided Verification, 20th International Conference, CAV 2008, pp. 299–303 (2008)

16. Bryant, R.E.: Graph-based algorithms for Boolean function manipulation. IEEE Trans. Comput. **35**(8), 677–691 (1986)

17. Bryant, R.E.: On the complexity of VLSI implementations and graph representations of Boolean functions with application to integer multiplication. IEEE Trans. Comput. **40**(2), 205–213 (1991)

18. Burch, J.R., Clarke, E.M., Long, D.E., McMillan, K.L., Dill, D.L.: Symbolic model checking for sequential circuit verification. IEEE Trans. Comput.-Aided Des. Integr. Circ. **13**(4), 401–424 (1994)

19. Bonet, M.L., Buss, S.: An improved separation of regular resolution from pool resolution and clause learning. In: Cimatti, A., Sebastiani, R. (eds.) SAT 2012. LNCS, vol. 7317, pp. 44–57. Springer, Heidelberg (2012). doi:10.1007/978-3-642-31612-8_5

20. Buss, S.R., Hoffmann, J., Johannsen, J.: Resolution trees with lemmas: resolution refinements that characterize DLL algorithms with clause learning. Log. Methods Comput. Sci. 4(4:13), 1–28 (2008)

21. Buss, S.R., Kolodziejczyk, L.: Small stone in pool. Log. Methods Comput. Sci. 10(2:16), 1–22 (2014)

22. Davis, M., Putnam, H.: A computing procedure for quantification theory. Commun. ACM 7, 201–215 (1960)

23. Davis, M., Logemann, G., Loveland, D.: A machine program for theorem-proving. Commun. ACM 5(7), 394–397 (1962)

24. de Moura, L.M.: System description: Yices 0.1. Technical report, Computer Science Laboratory, SRI International (2005)

25. Moura, L., Bjørner, N.: Z3: an efficient SMT solver. In: Ramakrishnan, C.R., Rehof, J. (eds.) TACAS 2008. LNCS, vol. 4963, pp. 337–340. Springer, Heidelberg (2008). doi:10.1007/978-3-540-78800-3_24

26. Dechter, R.: Bucket elimination: a unifying framework for probabilistic inference. In: Horvitz, E., Jensen, F.V. (eds.) UAI 1996: Proceedings of the Twelfth Annual Conference on Uncertainty in Artificial Intelligence, Portland, OR, USA, pp. 211–219. Morgan Kaufmann, August 1996

27. Ganesh, V., Dill, D.L.: A decision procedure for bit-vectors and arrays. In: Damm, W., Hermanns, H. (eds.) CAV 2007. LNCS, vol. 4590, pp. 519–531. Springer, Heidelberg (2007). doi:10.1007/978-3-540-73368-3_52

28. Hirsch, E., Itsykson, D., Kojevnikov, A., Kulikov, A., Nikolenko, S.: Report on the mixed Boolean-algebraic solver. Technical report, Laboratory of Mathematical Logic of St. Petersburg Department of Steklov Institute of Mathematics (2005)

29. Kalla, P.: Formal verification of arithmetic datapaths using algebraic geometry and symbolic computation. In: Proceedings, Formal Methods in Computer-Aided Design, FMCAD, p. 2. Austin, TX, September 2015

30. Kovásznai, G., Fröhlich, A., Biere, A.: Complexity of fixed-size bit-vector logics. Theory Comput. Syst. 59(2), 323–376 (2016)

31. Krajíček, J.: Bounded Arithmetic, Propositional Logic and Complexity Theory. Cambridge University Press, Cambridge (1996)

32. Kroening, D., Strichman, O.: Decision Procedures: An Algorithmic Point of View. Springer, Heidelberg (2008)

33. Marques-Silva, J.P., Lynce, I., Malik, S.: CDCL solvers. In: Biere, A., Heule, M., van Maaren, H., Walsh, T. (eds.) Handbook of Satisfiability, pp. 131–154. IOS Press (2009). Chap. 4

34. Openssl.org. Openssl bug cve-2016-7055 (2016)

35. Parthasarathy, G., Iyer, M.L., Cheng, K.-T., Wang, L.-C.: An efficient finite-domain constraint solver for circuits. In: Proceedings of the 41st Design Automation Conference, DAC, pp. 212–217 (2004)

36. Ponzio, S.: A lower bound for integer multiplication with read-once branching programs. In: Proceedings of the Twenty-Seventh Annual ACM Symposium on the Theory of Computing, pp. 130–139, Las Vegas, NV, May 1995

37. Reda, S., Salem, A.: Combinational equivalence checking using Boolean satisfiability and binary decision diagrams. In: Nebel, W., Jerraya, A. (eds.) Proceedings of the Conference on Design, Automation and Test in Europe, DATE 2001, Munich, Germany, pp. 122–126. IEEE Computer Society, March 2001

38. Sauerhoff, M., Woelfel, P.: Time-space tradeoff lower bounds for integer multiplication and graphs of arithmetic functions. In: Proceedings of the Thirty-Fifth Annual ACM Symposium on the Theory of Computing, pp. 186–195, San Diego, CA, June 2003
39. Sayed-Ahmed, A.A.R., Große, D., Kühne, U., Soeken, M., Drechsler, R.: Formal verification of integer multipliers by combining Gröbner basis with logic reduction. In: Fanucci, L., Teich, J. (eds.) 2016 Design, Automation & Test in Europe Conference & Exhibition, DATE 2016, pp. 1048–1053, Dresden, Germany. IEEE, March 2016

Distributed and Networked Systems

Network-Wide Configuration Synthesis

Ahmed El-Hassany$^{(\boxtimes)}$, Petar Tsankov, Laurent Vanbever,
and Martin Vechev

ETH Zürich, Zürich, Switzerland
eahmed@ethz.ch

Abstract. Computer networks are hard to manage. Given a set of high-level requirements (e.g., reachability, security), operators have to manually figure out the individual configuration of potentially hundreds of devices running complex distributed protocols so that they, collectively, compute a compatible forwarding state. Not surprisingly, operators often make mistakes which lead to downtimes.

To address this problem, we present a novel synthesis approach that automatically computes correct network configurations that comply with the operator's requirements. We capture the behavior of existing routers along with the distributed protocols they run in stratified Datalog. Our key insight is to reduce the problem of finding correct input configurations to the task of synthesizing inputs for a stratified Datalog program.

To solve this synthesis task, we introduce a new algorithm that synthesizes inputs for stratified Datalog programs. This algorithm is applicable beyond the domain of networks.

We leverage our synthesis algorithm to construct the first network-wide configuration synthesis system, called SyNET, that support multiple interacting routing protocols (OSPF and BGP) and static routes. We show that our system is practical and can infer correct input configurations, in a reasonable amount time, for networks of realistic size (>50 routers) that forward packets for multiple traffic classes.

1 Introduction

Despite being mission-critical for most organizations, managing a network is surprisingly hard and brittle.

A key reason is that network operators have to manually come up with a configuration, which ensures that the underlying distributed protocols compute a forwarding state that satisfies the operator's requirements.

Doing so requires operators to precisely understand: *(i)* the behavior of each distributed protocol; *(ii)* how the protocols interact with each other; and *(iii)* how each parameter in the configuration affects the distributed computation.

Because of this complexity, operators often make mistakes that can lead to severe network downtimes. As an illustration, Facebook (and Instagram) recently suffered from widespread issues for about an hour due to a misconfiguration [1]. In fact, studies show that most network downtimes are caused by humans, not equipment failures [2]. Such misconfigurations can have Internet-wide effects [3].

R. Majumdar and V. Kunčak (Eds.): CAV 2017, Part II, LNCS 10427, pp. 261–281, 2017.
DOI: 10.1007/978-3-319-63390-9_14

To prevent misconfigurations, researchers have developed tools that check if a given configuration is correct [4–7]. While useful, these works still require network operators to produce the configurations in the first place. Template-based approaches [8–11] along with vendor-agnostic abstractions [12–14] have been proposed to reduce the configuration burden. However, they still require operators to understand precisely the details of each protocol. Recently, Software-Defined Networks (SDNs) have emerged as another paradigm to manage networks by *programming* them from a central controller. Deploying SDN is, however, a major hurdle as it requires new network devices *and* management tools. Further, designing correct, robust and yet, scalable, SDN controllers is challenging [15–18]. Because of this, only a handful of networks are using SDN in production. As a result, configuring individual devices is by far the most widespread (and default) way to manage networks.

Problem Statement: Network-Wide Configuration Synthesis. Ideally, from a network operator perspective, one would like to solve what we refer to as the *Network-Wide Configuration Synthesis* problem: *Given a network specification $\mathcal{N}$, which defines the behavior of all routing protocols run by the routers, and a set $\mathcal{R}$ of requirements on the network-wide forwarding state, discover a configuration $\mathcal{C}$ such that the routers converge to a forwarding state compatible with $\mathcal{R}$.* That is, the operator simply provides the high-level requirements $\mathcal{R}$, and the configuration $\mathcal{C}$ is obtained automatically.

Distributed vs. Static Routing. Relying as much as possible on distributed protocols to compute the forwarding state is critical to ensure network reliability and scalability. A simpler problem would be to statically configure the forwarding entries of each router via static routes (e.g. see [19,20]). Relying solely on static routes is, however, undesirable for two reasons. First, they prevent routers from reacting locally upon failure. Second, they can be costly to update as routers often have a large number of static entries.

Key Challenges. Coming up with a solution to the network-wide synthesis problem is challenging for at least three reasons: *(i) Diversity*: protocols have different expressiveness in terms of the forwarding entries they compute. For instance, the Open Shortest Path First protocol (OSPF) can only direct traffic along shortest-paths, while the Border Gateway Protocol (BGP) can direct traffic along non-shortest paths. Conversely, BGP cannot forward traffic along multiple paths by default[1], while OSPF supports multi-path routing and is thus better suited for load-balancing traffic, a feature heavily used in practice. *(ii) Dependence:* distinct protocols often depend on one another, making it challenging to ensure that they collectively compute a compatible forwarding state. For instance, BGP depends on the network-wide intra-domain configuration; and *(iii) Feasibility*: the search space of configurations is massive and it is thus difficult to find one that leads to a forwarding state satisfying the requirements.

---

[1] While vendor-specific workarounds to make BGP multipath exist, these break the congruency between the control and data plane and could lead to correctness issues.

This Work. In this paper, we provide the first solution to the network-wide synthesis problem. Our approach is based on two steps. First, we use stratified Datalog to capture the behavior of the network, i.e. the distributed protocols ran by the routers together with any protocol dependencies. Datalog is indeed particularly well-suited for describing these protocols in a clear and declarative way. Here, the fixed point of a Datalog program represents the stable forwarding state of the network. Second, and a key insight of our work: we pose the network-wide synthesis problem as an instance of finding an input for a stratified Datalog program where the program's fixed point satisfies a given property. That is, the network operator simply provides the high-level requirements $\mathcal{R}$ on the forwarding state (i.e., which is the same as requiring the Datalog program' fixed point to satisfy $\mathcal{R}$), and our synthesizer automatically finds an input $\mathcal{C}$ to the Datalog program (i.e., which identifies the wanted network-wide configuration). We remark that our Datalog input synthesis algorithm is a general, independent contribution, and is applicable beyond networks.

Main Contributions. To summarize, our main contributions are:

- A formulation of the network-wide synthesis problem in terms of input synthesis for stratified Datalog (Sect. 2).
- The first input synthesis algorithm for stratified Datalog. This algorithm is of broader interest and is applicable beyond networks (Sect. 5).
- An instantiation and an end-to-end implementation of our input synthesis algorithm to the network-wide synthesis problem, along with network-specific optimizations, in a system called SyNET.
- An evaluation of SyNET on networks with multiple interacting widely-used protocols. In addition, we test the correctness of the generated configurations on an emulated network environment. Our results show that SyNET can automatically synthesize input configurations for networks of realistic size (>50 routers) carrying multiple traffic classes (Sect. 6).

2   Network-Wide Configuration Synthesis

We now illustrate our configuration synthesis approach on a simple example. We highlight how, given a network and a set of requirements, we can pose the synthesis problem as an instance of input synthesis for stratified Datalog.

2.1   Motivating Example

We consider the simple network topology, depicted in Fig. 1(b), composed of 4 routers denoted A, B, C and D. Routers B and C can reach the external network Ext, and router D is directly connected to two internal networks N1 and N2. In the following, we use the term traffic class to refer to a set of packets (e.g. packets destined to N1) that are handled analogously according to the requirements. In practice, each traffic class may contain thousands of IP prefixes [21].

```
Fwd(TC, Router, NextHop) :-
  Route(TC, Router, NextHop, Proto),
  SetAD(Proto, Router, Cost)
  minAD(TC, Router, Cost)
minAD(TC, Router, min<Cost>) :-
  Route(TC, Router, NextHop, Proto),
  SetAD(Proto, Router, Cost)
Route(TC, Router, Next, "static") :-
  SetStatic(TC, Router, NextHop)
Route(TC, Router, NextHop, "ospf") :-
  BestOSPFRoute(TC, Router, NextHop)
```

(a) Network Specification N

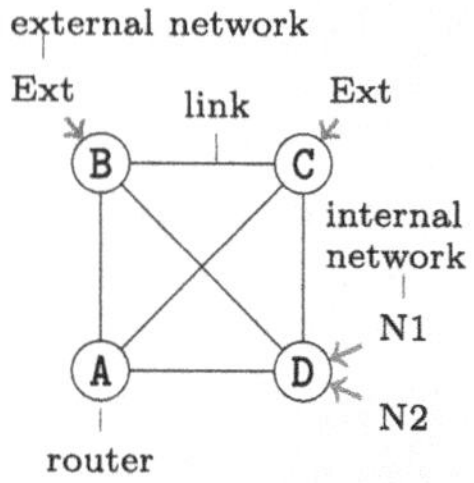

external network

Ext   link   Ext

internal network

Path requirements:

N1   Path(N1, A, [A,B,C,D])
       Path(N2, A, [A,D])
N2   Path(Ext, A, [A,C])
       Path(Ext, D, [D,B])

router

(b) Topology

(c) Requirements φ_R

Input Synthesis

```
SetAD("static", A, 10)
SetAD("ospf", A, 20)
...
SetStatic(N1, A, B)
...
SetOSPFEdgeCost(A, B, 10)
SetOSPFEdgeCost(A, C, 5)
SetOSPFEdgeCost(A, D, 5)
...
```

Derive

```
! 10G interface to B
interface TenGigabitEthernet1/1/1
...
ip ospf cost 10
! 10G interface to C
interface TenGigabitEthernet1/1/2
...
ip ospf cost 5
...
! static route to B
ip route 10.0.0.0 255.255.255.0 130.0.1.2
```

(d) Datalog Input I

(e) Configuration for Router A

Fig. 1. Network-wide Configuration Synthesis. The input is: (a) declarative network specification N in stratified Datalog (b) network topology, and (c) routing requirements φ_R. The output is: (d) a Datalog input I that results in a forwarding state satisfying the requirements. Configurations (e) are derived from I.

Computation of Forwarding State. We first informally describe how each router's forwarding entries are computed, assuming the configuration is provided.

Each router runs both, OSPF and BGP protocols, and in addition can also be configured with static routes. The computation of OSPF is based on finding least-cost paths to the internal destinations as well as to all routers in the network, where cost is the sum of the link weights defined in router configurations. The least-cost paths are then used to generate forwarding entries at each router to all internal destinations. In our example, these internal destinations are N1 and N2. In contrast, BGP computes forwarding entries to reach external destinations, Ext in our example. The computed forwarding entries define the next hop router for each destination. For example, BGP computes an entry at router A for Ext which forwards packets to a border router (i.e., either B or C). To decide which router the entry should forward to, each BGP router selects the egress point (i.e., border router) to reach an externally-learned prefix based on a preference value. This preference is (typically) defined in the configuration of each border router and propagated network-wide. If multiple routers announce the same preference for a prefix, internal BGP routers directs traffic to the closest egress point, according to the OSPF costs.

Once BGP and OSPF have finished computing their forwarding entries, each router takes these entries (along with those defined via static routes) and selects the OSPF-, BGP-, static route- produced forwarding entry with the highest preference (in networking terms, higher preference means lower administrative cost) defined in its local configuration. The union of all forwarding entries obtained at the routers is referred to as the forwarding state of the network.

Configuration Synthesis. Next, we illustrate the opposite direction (and one this work focuses on): given requirements φ_R, find a configuration which the protocols use to compute a forwarding state (as described above) that satisfies φ_R.

Let us consider the four path requirements given in Fig. 1(c). The first two state that A must forward packets for the traffic classes N1 and N2 along the paths $A \longrightarrow B \longrightarrow C \longrightarrow D$ and $A \longrightarrow D$, respectively. Note that these two requirements might reflect a security policy in the network or generated by a traffic engineering optimization tool [22,23]. These two requirements cannot be enforced using OSPF alone. The reason is that, as discussed, OSPF works by selecting the least-cost path (by summing the weights on the links) and there is no assignment of weights to links which would lead to least-cost paths that exactly match the two path requirements.

Yet, the two requirements can be enforced by: *(i)* generating a static route-based forwarding entry at A to forward packets for N1 to B; *(ii)* configuring link weights so paths $A \longrightarrow D$ and $B \longrightarrow C \longrightarrow D$ have the lowest OSPF costs from A to D and, respectively, from B to D; and *(iii)* on router A, configure a higher preference for forwarding entries based on static routes than OSPF forwarding entries. Because a static route forwarding entry is only generated for destination N1 (from *(i)*) and not N2, this means the entry for N1 will forward the traffic to router B while the entry for N2 will be the OSPF generated one (from *(ii)*).

The last two path requirements state that A and D must forward packets destined to the traffic class Ext to C and B, respectively. The two path requirements can by satisfied by: *(i)* setting identical BGP router preferences at the local configurations of B and C; and *(ii)* configuring link weights so that paths $A \longrightarrow C$ and $D \longrightarrow B$ have the lowest costs from A to C and from D to B, respectively. In this way, BGP will use the results from the OSPF least-cost paths to compute its forwarding entries to Ext. This is an example where BGP interacts with OSPF and uses information from its computation.

The following is the final configuration produced by our synthesizer (the synthesizer is discussed in later sections):

- weight 10 is assigned to link $A \longrightarrow B$,
- weight 5 is assigned to links $B \longrightarrow C$, $C \longrightarrow D$, and $A \longrightarrow C$,
- weight 4 is assigned to link $D \longrightarrow B$,
- weight 100 is assigned to the remaining links,
- a static route- based forwarding entry is defined at router A to forward traffic for $N1$ to B, and
- the router preference for all routers is set to 100.

In Fig. 1(e), we illustrate an excerpt of router A's local configuration.

Phrasing the Problem as Inputs Synthesis for Stratified Datalog. A key insight of our work is to pose the question of finding a network configuration as an instance of input synthesis for stratified Datalog.

First, we declaratively specify the behavior of the network, i.e. the distributed protocols that the routers run, the protocol interactions, and the network topology, as a stratified Datalog program N. As requirements usually pertain to the stable forwarding state, the stratified Datalog encoding captures the stable state of these routing protocols as opposed to intermediate computation steps. Few relevant Datalog rules are given in Fig. 1(a); we detail this specification step in Sect. 4. The resulting Datalog program derives a predicate Fwd that defines the forwarding entries computed by all routers, where Fwd(TC, Router, NextHop) is derived if Router forwards packets for traffic class TC to router NextHop.

Second, we can directly express routing requirements as constraints over the predicate Fwd. We denote these constraints with φ_R in Fig. 1.

Finally, an input I to the Datalog program N identifies a network-wide configuration. We formalize the network-wide configuration synthesis problem as:

Definition 1. *The network-wide configuration synthesis problem is:*
Input *A declarative network specification N and routing requirements φ_R.*
Output *A Datalog input I such that $[\![N]\!]_I \models \varphi_R$, if such an input exists; otherwise, return unsat.*

In our definition, $[\![N]\!]_I$ denotes the fixed point of the Datalog program N for the input I, and $[\![N]\!]_I \models \varphi_R$ holds if this fixed point satisfies the constraints φ_R.

Synthesizing inputs for stratified Datalog is, however, a difficult (and, in general, undecidable) problem [24]. The problem is, however, decidable if we fix a finite set of values to bound the set of inputs. This is reasonable in the context of networks, where values represent finitely many routers, interfaces, and configuration parameters.

To address the problem, we introduce a new iterative synthesis algorithm that partitions the Datalog program P into strata $P_1, \ldots, P_n$, finds an input I_i for each stratum P_i and then construct an input I for the Datalog program P. Each stratum P_i is a semi-positive Datalog program that enjoys the property that if a predicate is derived by the rules after some number of steps, then it must be contained in the fixed point. We describe this algorithm in Sect. 5.

3   Background: Stratified Datalog

We briefly overview the syntax and semantics of stratified Datalog.

Syntax. Datalog's syntax is given in Fig. 2. We use $\bar{r}$, $\bar{l}$, and $\bar{t}$ to denote zero or more rules, literals, and terms separated by commas, respectively. A Datalog program is *well-formed* if for any rule $a \leftarrow \bar{l}$, we have $vars(a) \subseteq vars(\bar{l})$, where $vars(\bar{l})$ returns the set of variables in $\bar{l}$.

(Program) $P ::= \bar{r}$	(Literal) $l ::= a \mid \neg a$	(Variables) $X, Y \in Vars$
(Rule) $r ::= a \leftarrow \bar{l}$	(Predicates) $p, q \in Preds$	(Values) $v \in Vals$
(Atom) $a ::= p(\bar{t})$	(Term) $t ::= X \mid v$	

Fig. 2. Syntax of stratified Datalog

A predicate is called *extensional* if it appears only in the bodies of rules (right side of the rule), otherwise (if it appears at least once in a rule head) it is called *intensional*. We denote the sets of extensional and intensional predicates of a program P by $edb(P)$ and $idb(P)$, respectively.

A Datalog program P is *stratified* if its rules can be partitioned into strata $P_1, \ldots, P_n$ such that if a predicate p occurs in a positive (negative) literal in the body of a rule in P_i, then all rules with p in their heads are in a stratum P_j with $j \leq i$ ($j < i$). Stratification ensures that predicates that appear in negative literals are fully defined in lower strata.

We syntactically extend stratified Datalog with aggregate functions such as `min` and `max`. This extension is possible as stratified Datalog is equally expressive to Datalog with stratified aggregate functions; for details see [25].

Semantics. Let $\mathcal{A} = \{p(\bar{t}) \mid \bar{t} \subseteq Vals\}$ denote the set of all ground (i.e. variable-free) atoms. The complete lattice $(\mathcal{P}(\mathcal{A}), \subseteq, \cap, \cup, \emptyset, \mathcal{A})$ partially orders the set of interpretations $\mathcal{P}(\mathcal{A})$.

Given a substitution $\sigma \in Vars \rightarrow Vals$ mapping variables to values. Given an atom a, we will write $\sigma(a)$ for the ground atom obtained by replacing the variables in a according to σ; e.g., $\sigma(p(X))$ returns the ground atom $p(\sigma(X))$. The consequence operator $T_P \in \mathcal{P}(\mathcal{A}) \rightarrow \mathcal{P}(\mathcal{A})$ for a program P is defined as

$$T_P(A) = A \cup \{\sigma(a) \mid a \leftarrow l_1 \ldots l_n \in P, \forall l_i \in \bar{l}.\ A \vdash \sigma(l_i)\}$$

where $A \vdash \sigma(a)$ if $\sigma(a) \in A$ and $A \vdash \sigma(\neg a)$ if $\sigma(a) \notin A$.

An input for P is a set of ground atoms constructed using P's extensional predicates. Let P be a program with strata $P_1, \ldots, P_n$ and I be an input for P. The model of P for I, denoted by $[\![P]\!]_I$, is M_n, where $M_0 = I$ and $M_i = \bigcap \{A \in \text{fp } T_{P_i} \mid A \subseteq M_{i-1}\}$ is the smallest fixed point of T_{P_i} that is greater than the lower stratum's model M_{i-1}.

4   Declarative Network Specification

In this section, we first describe how we declarative specify the behavior of the network as a Datalog program. Afterwards, we discuss how routing requirements are specified as constraints over the Datalog program's fixed point.

4.1   Specifying Networks

To faithfully capture a network's behavior, we model *(i)* the behavior of routing protocols and their interactions and *(ii)* the topology of the network.

Expressing Protocols in Stratified Datalog. We formalize individual routing protocols and how routers combine the forwarding entries computed by these protocols as a stratified Datalog program N. The Datalog program N derives the predicate `Fwd(TC, Router, NextHop)`, which represents the network's global forwarding state. In Fig. 1(a), for example, we show the relevant rules that define how the forwarding entries computed by OSPF are combined with those defined via static routes. The predicate `Route(TC, Router, NextHop, Proto)` captures the forwarding entries of OSPF and static routes. The top Datalog rule states that routers select, for each traffic class `TC`, the forwarding entry with the minimal administrative cost (`minAD`) calculated over all protocols via the second Datalog rule in Fig. 1(a). The bottom two rules define the predicate `Route`, which collects the forwarding entries defined via static routes and computed by OSPF. We remark that OSPF routes (represented by the predicate `BestOSPFRoute`) are defined through additional Datalog rules that capture the behavior of the OSPF protocol[2].

Network Topology. The network topology is also captured via Datalog rules in the program N. We model each router as a constant and use predicates to represent the topology. For example, the predicate `SetLink(R1, R2)` represents that two routers $R1$ and $R2$ are connected via a link, and we add the Datalog rule `SetLink(R1, R2) ← true` to define such a link.

4.2 Specifying Requirements

We specify the requirements as function-free first-order constraints over the predicate `Fwd(TC, Router, NextHop)`, which defines the network's forwarding state. We write $A \models \varphi$ to denote that a Datalog interpretation A satisfies φ. For illustration, we describe how common routing requirements can be specified:

`Path(TC, R1, [R1, R2,..., Rn])` (Path requirement): packets for traffic class `TC` must follow the path `R1,..., Rn`. These requirements are specified as a conjunction over the predicate `Fwd`.

$\forall R1, R2.$ `Fwd(TC1, R1, R2)` $\Rightarrow \neg$`Fwd(TC2, R1, R2)` (Traffic isolation): the paths for two distinct traffic classes `TC1` and `TC2` do not share links in the same direction.

`Reach(TC, R1, R2)` (Reachability): packets for traffic class `TC` can reach router `R2` from router `R1`. The predicate `Reach` is the transitive closure over the predicate `Fwd` (defined via Datalog rules).

$\forall TC, R.$ ($\neg$`Reach(TC, R, R)`) (Loop-freeness): generic requirement stipulating that the forwarding plane has no loops.

More complex requirements, such as way pointing, can be specified based on the core function-free first-order constraints provided by SyNET. Further, SyNET can be used as a backend for a high-level requirements language that is easier to use by a network operator.

---

[2] A detailed OSPF model can be found in the technical report [26].

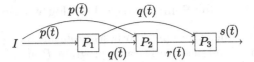

Fig. 3. A Datalog program with strata P_1, P_2, and P_3, and flow of predicates between the strata.

4.3 Network-Wide Configurations

The input protocol configurations deployed at the network's routers are represented as input *edb* predicates to the Datalog programs that formalize the protocols. For example, the local OSPF configuration for a router specifies the weights associated with the links connected to that router; this is represented by the *edb* predicate `SetOSPFEdgeCost(Router, NextHop, Weight)`.

A subset of the synthesized Datalog input for our motivating example is given in Fig. 1(d). Here, `SetAD` defines the administrative cost of static routes to be lower than that of OSPF (so static routes are prefered over forwarding entries computed by OSPF). The predicate `SetStatic(N1, A, B)`, which represents static routes, defines a static route for `N1` from A to B. The predicate `SetOSPFEdgeCost` defines the links' weights.

5 Input Synthesis for Stratified Datalog

We now present a new iterative algorithm for synthesizing inputs for stratified Datalog. We first describe the high-level flow of the algorithm before presenting the details.

High-Level Flow. Consider the stratified Datalog program with strata P_1, P_2, and P_3, depicted in Fig. 3. Incoming and outgoing edges of a stratum P_i indicate the *edb* predicates and, respectively, the *idb* predicates of that stratum. For example, the stratum P_3 takes as input predicates $q(\bar{t})$ and $r(\bar{t})$ and derives the predicate $s(\bar{t})$. Our iterative algorithm first synthesizes an input I_3 for P_3 which determines the predicates $q(\bar{t})$ and $r(\bar{t})$ that $P_1 \cup P_2$ must output. To synthesize such an input for a single stratum, we present an algorithm, called $\mathcal{S}_{SemiPos}$, that addresses the input synthesis problem for semi-positive Datalog programs [27, Chap. 15.2], i.e. Datalog programs where negation is restricted to *edb* predicates. After synthesizing an input I_3 for P_3, our iterative algorithm synthesizes an input I_2 for P_2 such that the fixed-point $[\![P_2]\!]_{I_2}$ produces the predicates $r(\bar{t})$ that are contained in the already synthesized input I_3 for P_3. We note that this iterative process may require backtracking, in case no input for P_2 can produce the desired predicates $r(\bar{t})$ contained in I_3. The algorithm terminates when it synthesizes inputs for all three strata.

In the following, we first present the algorithm $\mathcal{S}_{SemiPos}$ that is used to synthesize an input for a single stratum (which is a semi-positive program). Then, we present the general algorithm, called $\mathcal{S}_{Strat}$, that iteratively applies $\mathcal{S}_{SemiPos}$ for each stratum to synthesize inputs for stratified Datalog programs.

5.1 Input Synthesis for Semi-positive Datalog with SMT

The key idea is to reduce the input synthesis problem to satisfiability of SMT constraints: Given a semi-positive Datalog program P and a constraint φ, we encode the question $\exists I. \ [\![P]\!]_I \models \varphi$ into an SMT constraint ψ. If ψ is satisfiable, then from a model of ψ we can derive an input I such that $[\![P]\!]_I \models \varphi$.

SMT Encoding Challenges. Given a Datalog program P and a constraint φ, encoding the question $\exists I. \ [\![P]\!]_I \models \varphi$ with SMT constraints is non-trivial due to the mismatch between Datalog's program fixed point semantics and the classical semantics of first-order logic. This means that simply taking the conjunction of all Datalog rules into an SMT solver does not solve our problem. For example, consider the following Datalog program P_{tc}:

$$tc(X,Y) \leftarrow e(X,Y)$$
$$tc(X,Y) \leftarrow tc(X,Z), tc(Z,Y)$$

which computes the transitive closure of the predicate $e(X,Y)$. A naive way of encoding these Datalog rules with SMT constraints:

$$\forall X, Y. \ (e(X,Y) \Rightarrow tc(X,Y))$$
$$\forall X, Y. \ ((\exists Z. \ tc(X,Z) \wedge tc(Z,Y)) \Rightarrow tc(X,Y))$$

and we denote the conjunction of these two SMT constraints as $[P_{tc}]$. Now, suppose we have the fixed point constraint $\varphi_{tc} = (\neg e(v_0, v_2)) \wedge tc(v_0, v_2)$ and we want to generate an input I so that $[\![P_{tc}]\!]_I \models \varphi_{tc}$. A model that satisfies $[P_{tc}] \wedge \varphi_{tc}$ is

$$\mathcal{M} = \{e(v_0, v_1), tc(v_0, v_1), tc(v_0, v_2)\}$$

The input derived from this model, obtained by projecting $\mathcal{M}$ over the *edb* predicate e, is $I_{\mathcal{M}} = \{e(v_0, v_1)\}$. We get

$$[\![P_{tc}]\!]_{I_{\mathcal{M}}} = \{e(v_0, v_1), tc(v_0, v_1)\}$$

and so $[\![P_{tc}]\!]_{I_{\mathcal{M}}} \not\models \varphi_{tc}$, which is clearly not what is intended.

SMT Encoding. Our key insight is to split the constraint φ into a conjunction of positive and negative clauses, where a clause φ is positive (resp., negative) if $A \models \varphi$ implies that $A' \models \varphi$ for any interpretation $A' \supseteq A$ (resp., $A' \subseteq A$). We can then unroll recursive predicates to obtain a sound encoding for positive constraints, and we do not unroll them to get a sound encoding for negative constraints.

The encoding of a Datalog program P into an SMT constraint is defined in Fig. 4. The resulting SMT constraint is denoted by $[P]_k$, where the parameter k defines the number of unroll steps. In the encoding we assume that *(i)* all terms in rules' heads are variables and *(ii)* rules' heads with the same predicate have identical variable names. Note that any Datalog program can be converted into this form using rectification [28] and variable renaming.

$$[P]_k \quad = \bigwedge_{p \in idb(P)} \text{ENCODE}(P,p) \wedge \text{UNROLL}(P,p,k)$$

$$\text{ENCODE}(P,p) \quad = \bigwedge_{p(\overline{X}) \leftarrow \overline{l} \in P} \forall \overline{X}. \; ((\exists \overline{Y}. \bigwedge \overline{l}) \Rightarrow p(\overline{X})), \text{where } \overline{Y} = vars(\overline{l}) \setminus \overline{X}$$

$$\text{UNROLL}(P,p,k) = \bigwedge_{0 < i \leq k} \text{STEP}(P,p,i)$$

$$\text{STEP}(P,p,i) \quad = \forall \overline{X}. \; \Big(p_i(\overline{X}) \Leftrightarrow \big(\bigvee_{p(\overline{X}) \leftarrow \overline{l} \in P} \exists \overline{Y}. \; \tau(\overline{l}, i-1)\big)\Big), \text{where } \overline{Y} = vars(\overline{l}) \setminus \overline{X}$$

$$\tau(\overline{l}, k) \quad = \begin{cases} \tau(l_1, k) \wedge \cdots \tau(l_n, k) & \text{if } \overline{l} = l_1 \wedge \cdots \wedge l_n \\ \neg \tau(p(\overline{t}), k) & \text{if } \overline{l} = \neg p(\overline{t}) \\ \text{false} & \text{if } \overline{l} = p(\overline{t}), p \in idb(P), k = 0 \\ p_k(\overline{t}) & \text{if } \overline{l} = p(\overline{t}), p \in idb(P), k > 0 \\ l & \text{otherwise} \end{cases}$$

Fig. 4. Encoding a Datalog program P with constraints $[P]_k$

Function Encode. The constraint returned by $\text{ENCODE}(p, P)$ states that an atom $p(X)$ is derived if P has a rule that derives $p(\overline{X})$ and whose body evaluates to true. To capture Datalog's semantics, the variables in $p(\overline{X})$ are universally quantified, while those in the rules' bodies are existentially quantified. This constraint $\text{ENCODE}(p, P)$ is sound for negative requirements, but not for positive ones as it does not state that $p(\overline{X})$ is derived *only if* a rule body with $p(\overline{X})$ in the head evaluates to true.

Functions Unroll and Step. The constraint returned by $\text{STEP}(P, p, i)$ encodes whether an atom $p(X)$ is derived after i applications of P's rules; e.g., $p(X)$'s truth value after 3 steps is represented with the atom $p_3(X)$. Intuitively, $p(X)$ is true iff there is a rule that derives $p(X)$ and whose body evaluates to true using the atoms derived in previous iterations. Which atoms are derived in previous iterations is captured by the literal renaming function τ. Note that $\tau(l, 0)$ returns false for any *idb* literal l since all intensional predicates are initially false. Further, $\tau(l, k)$ returns l for any extensional literal l (the last case in Fig. 4) since their truth values do not change. Finally, the constraint returned by $\text{UNROLL}(P, p, k)$ conjoins $\text{STEP}(P, p, 0), \ldots, \text{STEP}(P, p, k)$ to capture the derivation of $p(X)$ after k steps. This is sound for positive requirements, but not for negative ones since more $p(X)$ atoms may be derived after k steps.

Example. To illustrate the encoding, we translate the Datalog program:

$$tc(X, Y) \leftarrow e(X, Y)$$
$$tc(X, Y) \leftarrow tc(X, Z), tc(Z, Y)$$

which computes the transitive closure of the predicate $e(X, Y)$. This program has one *idb* predicate, *tc*. The function $\text{ENCODE}(P, tc)$ returns

$$(\forall X, Y. \; e(X, Y) \Rightarrow tc(X, Y))$$
$$\wedge (\forall X, Y. \; (\exists Z. \; tc(X, Z) \wedge tc(Z, Y)) \Rightarrow tc(X, Y))$$

Algorithm 1. Algorithm $\mathcal{S}_{SemiPos}$ for semi-positive Datalog

---

Input: Semi-positive Datalog program P and a constraint φ
Output: An input I such that $[\![P]\!]_I \models \varphi$ or $\bot$

1 **begin**
2     $\varphi' \leftarrow \text{SIMPLIFY}(\varphi)$
3   **for** $k \in [1..bound_k]$ **do**
4         $\varphi_k \leftarrow \text{REWRITE}(\varphi', k)$
5         $\psi \leftarrow [\![P]\!]_k \wedge \varphi_k$
6   **if** $\exists J. \ J \models \psi$ **then**
7             $I \leftarrow \{p(\bar{t}) \in J \mid p \in edb(P)\}$, where $J \models \psi$
8   **return** I

9   **return** $\bot$

We apply function $\text{UNROLL}(P, tc, 2)$ for $k = 2$, which after simplifications returns

$$\forall X, Y. \ (tc_1(X, Y) \Leftrightarrow e(X, Y))$$
$$\forall X, Y. \ (tc_2(X, Y) \Leftrightarrow e(X, Y) \vee (\exists Z. \ tc_1(X, Z) \wedge tc_1(Z, Y)))$$

In the constraints, the predicates tc_1 and tc_2 encode the derived predicates tc after 1 and, respectively, 2, derivation steps.

Algorithm. Algorithm $\mathcal{S}_{SemiPos}(P, \varphi)$, given in Algorithm 1, first calls function $\text{SIMPLIFY}(\varphi)$ that *(i)* instantiates any quantifiers in φ and *(ii)* transforms the result into a conjunction of clauses, where each clause is a disjunction of literals.

Then, the algorithm iteratively unrolls the Datalog rules, up to a pre-defined bound, called $bound_k$. In each step of the for-loop, the algorithm generates an SMT constraint that captures *(i)* which atoms are derived after k applications of P's rules and *(ii)* which atoms are never derived by P. The resulting SMT constraint is denoted by $[\![P]\!]_k$. The algorithm also rewrites the simplified constraint φ' using the function $\text{REWRITE}(\varphi', k)$ which recursively traverses conjunctions and disjunctions in the simplified constraint φ' and maps positive literals to the k-unrolled predicate $p_k(\bar{t})$ and negative literals to $\neg p(\bar{t})$:

$$\text{REWRITE}(\varphi, k) = \begin{cases} p_k(\bar{t}) & \text{if } \varphi = p(\bar{t}) \\ \neg p(\bar{t}) & \text{if } \varphi = \neg p(\bar{t}) \\ \text{REWRITE}(\varphi_1, k) \vee \cdots \vee \text{REWRITE}(\varphi_n, k) & \text{if } \varphi = \varphi_1 \vee \ldots \vee \varphi_n \\ \text{REWRITE}(\varphi_1, k) \wedge \cdots \wedge \text{REWRITE}(\varphi_n, k) & \text{if } \varphi = \varphi_1 \wedge \ldots \wedge \varphi_n \end{cases}$$

Note that since $\vee$ and $\wedge$ are monotone, negative literals constitute negative constraints and positive literals constitute positive constraints.

If the resulting constraint $[\![P]\!]_k \wedge \psi_k$ is satisfiable, then an input is derived by projecting the interpretation I that satisfies the constraint over all edb predicates. Note that if there is an input I such that $[\![P]\!]_I \models \varphi$ and for which the fixed point $[\![P]\!]_I$ is reached in less than $bound_k$ steps, then $\mathcal{S}_{SemiPos}(P, \varphi)$ is guaranteed to return an input.

Algorithm 2. Input synthesis algorithm $\mathcal{S}_{Strat}$ for stratified Datalog

---

Input: Stratified Datalog program $P = P_1 \cup \cdots \cup P_n$, constraint φ over P_n
Output: An input I such that $[\![P]\!]_I \models \varphi$ or $\bot$

```
 1 begin
 2      F₁ ← ∅,...,Fₙ ← ∅; I₁ ← ⊥,...,Iₙ ← ⊥; i ← n
 3      while i > 0 do
 4          if |Fᵢ| > boundℱ then
 5              Fᵢ ← ∅; Fᵢ₊₁ ← Fᵢ₊₁ ∪ {Iᵢ₊₁}
 6              i ← i + 1;    // backtrack to higher stratum
 7              continue
```

8. $\quad\quad \psi_{\mathcal{F}} \leftarrow \bigwedge\limits_{I' \in \mathcal{F}_i} \left(\neg \bigwedge\limits_{p \in edb(P_i)} \text{ENCODEPRED}(I', p) \right)$

```
 9          if i = n then
10              ψᵢ ← φ
11          else
```

12. $\quad\quad\quad \psi_i \leftarrow \bigwedge\limits_{p \in \Delta_i} \text{ENCODEPRED}(I_{i+1} \cup \cdots \cup I_n, p)$

13. $\quad\quad\quad$ where $\Delta_i = (edb(P_i) \cup idb(P_i)) \cap (edb(P_{i+1}) \cup \cdots \cup edb(P_n))$

14. $\quad\quad I_i = \mathcal{S}_{SemiPos}(P_i, \psi_i \wedge \psi_{\mathcal{F}})$

```
15          if Iᵢ ≠ ⊥ then
16              i ← i - 1
17          else
18              if i < n then
19                  Fᵢ ← ∅; Fᵢ₊₁ ← Fᵢ₊₁ ∪ {Iᵢ₊₁}
20                  i ← i + 1    // backtrack to higher stratum
21              else
22                  return ⊥
```

23. $\quad$ **return** $I = \{ p(\bar{t}) \in I_1 \cup \cdots \cup I_n \mid p \in edb(P) \}$

Theorem 1. *Let P be a semi-positive Datalog program, φ a constraint. If $\mathcal{S}_{SemiPos}(P, \varphi) = I$ then $[\![P]\!]_I \models \varphi$.*[3]

5.2 Iterative Input Synthesis for Stratified Datalog

Our iterative input synthesis algorithm for stratified Datalog, called $\mathcal{S}_{Strat}$, is given in Algorithm 2. We assume that the fixed point constraint φ is defined over predicates that appear in the highest stratum P_n; this is without any loss of generality, as any constraint can be expressed using Datalog rules in the highest stratum, using a standard reduction to query satisfiability; cf. [24]. Starting with the highest stratum P_n, $\mathcal{S}_{Strat}$ generates an input I_n for P_n such that $[\![P_n]\!]_{I_n} \models \varphi$. Then, it iteratively synthesizes an input for the lower strata $P_{n-1}, \ldots, P_1$ using

---

[3] The theorem's proof can be found in the technical report [26].

the algorithm $\mathcal{S}_{SemiPos}$. Finally, to construct an input for P, the algorithm combines the inputs synthesized for all strata and returns this.

Recall that the fixed point of a stratum P_i is given as input to the higher strata $P_{i+1}, \ldots, P_n$. A key step when synthesizing an input I_i for P_i is thus to ensure that the idb predicates derived by P_i are identical to the edb predicates synthesized for the inputs $I_{i+1}, \ldots, I_n$ of the higher strata. Formally, let

$$\Delta_i = (edb(P_i) \cup idb(P_i)) \cap (edb(P_{i+1}) \cup \cdots \cup edb(P_n))$$

We must ensure that $\{p(\bar{t}) \in [\![P_i]\!]_{I_i} \mid p \in \Delta_i\} = \{p(\bar{t}) \in I_{i+1} \cup \cdots \cup I_n \mid p \in \Delta_i\}$.

Key Steps. The algorithm first partitions P into strata $P_1, \ldots P_n$. The strata can be computed using the predicates' dependency graph; see [27, Chap. 15.2]. For each stratum P_i, it maintains a set of inputs $\mathcal{F}_i$, which contains inputs for P_i for which the algorithm failed to synthesize inputs for the lower strata $P_1, \ldots, P_{i-1}$. We call the sets $\mathcal{F}_i$ *failed* inputs. All $\mathcal{F}_i$ are initially empty.

In each iteration of the while loop, the algorithm attempts to generate an input I_i for stratum P_i. At line 4, the algorithm checks whether $\mathcal{F}_i$ has exceeded a pre-defined bound $bound_{\mathcal{F}}$. If the bound is exceeded, it adds I_{i+1} to the failed inputs $\mathcal{F}_{i+1}$, re-initializes $\mathcal{F}_i$ to the empty set, and backtracks to a higher stratum by incrementing i. This avoids exhaustively searching through all inputs to find an input compatible with those synthesized for the higher strata.

At line 8, the algorithm uses the helper function $\text{ENCODEPRED}(I', p)$. This function returns the constraint $\forall \overline{X}. \left(\bigvee_{p(\bar{t}) \in I'} \overline{X} = \bar{t} \right) \Leftrightarrow p(\overline{X})$, which is satisfied by an interpretation I iff I contains identical $p(\bar{t})$ predicates as those in I'. That is, if $I \models \text{ENCODEPRED}(I', p)$ then for any $p(\bar{t})$ we have $p(\bar{t}) \in I$ iff $p(\bar{t}) \in I'$. Therefore, the constraint $\psi_{\mathcal{F}}$ constructed at line 8 is satisfied by an input I_i iff $I_i \notin \mathcal{F}_i$, which avoids synthesizing inputs from the set of failed inputs.

The constraint ψ_i in the algorithm constrains the fixed point of P_i. For the highest stratum P_n, ψ_i is set to the constraint φ given as input to the algorithm. For the remaining strata P_i, ψ_i is satisfied iff the fixed point of P_i is compatible with the synthesized inputs for the higher strata $P_{i+1}, \ldots, P_n$. In addition to constraining P_i's idb predicates, we also constrain the input edb predicates. This is necessary to eagerly constrain the inputs.

At line 14, the algorithm invokes $\mathcal{S}_{SemiPos}$ to generate an input I_i such that $[\![P_i]\!]_{I_i} \models \varphi_i \wedge \psi_{\mathcal{F}}$. The algorithm proceeds to the lower stratum if such an input is found ($I \neq \bot$); otherwise, if $i < n$ the algorithm backtracks to the higher stratum by increasing i and updating the sets $\mathcal{F}_{i+1}$, and if $i = n$ if returns $\bot$.

Finally, the while-loop terminates when the inputs of all strata have been generated. The algorithm constructs and returns the input I for P.

Theorem 2. *Let P be a stratified Datalog program with strata $P_1, \ldots, P_n$, and φ a constraint over predicates in P_n. If $\mathcal{S}_{Strat}(P, \varphi) = I$ then $[\![P]\!]_I \models \varphi$.*[4]

---

[4] The theorem's proof can be found in the technical report [26].

6   Implementation and Evaluation

In this section we first describe SyNET, and end-to-end implementation of our input synthesis algorithm applied to the network-wide synthesis problem. We then turn to our evaluation of SyNET on practical topologies and requirements.

6.1   Implementation

SyNET is implemented in Python and automatically encodes stratified Datalog programs specified in the LogicBlox language [29] into SMT constraints specified in the SMT-LIB v2 format [30]. It uses the Python API of Z3 [31] to check whether the generated SMT constraints are satisfiable and to obtain a model.

SyNET supports routers that run both, OSPF and BGP protocols, and that can be configured with static routes. SyNET uses natural splitting for protocols: external routes are handled by BGP, while internal routes are handled by IGP protocols (OSPF and static, where static routes are preferred over OSPF). We have partitioned the Datalog rules that capture these protocols and their dependencies into 8 strata. SyNET relies on additional SMT constraints to ensure the well-formedness of the OSPF, BGP, and static route configurations output by our synthesizer. For most topologies and requirements, the Datalog program reaches a fixed point within 20 iterations, and so we fixed the unroll and backtracking bounds ($bound_k$ and $bound_{\mathcal{F}}$) to 20.

SyNET is vendor agnostic with respect to the synthesized configurations. A simple script can be used to convert the output of SyNET into any vendor specific configuration format and then deploy them in production routers. Indeed, to test the correctness of SyNET, we implemented a small script to convert the input synthesized by SyNET to Cisco router configurations.

SyNET supports two key optimizations that improve its performance. The first optimization is *partial evaluation*: SyNET partially-evaluates Datalog rules with predicates whose truth values are known apriori. For example, all SetLink predicates are known and can be eliminated. This reduces the number of variables in the rules and, in turn, in the generated SMT constraints. The second optimization is *network-specific constraints*: we have configured SyNET with generic constraints, which are true for all forwarding states, and with protocol-specific constraints, i.e. constraints that hold for any input to a particular protocol. An example constraint is: *"No packet is forwarded out of the router if the destination network is directly connected to the router"*. These constraints are not specific to particular requirements or topology. They are thus defined one time and can be used to synthesize configurations for any requirements and networks.

6.2   Experiments

To investigate SyNET's performance and scalability, we experimented with different: *(i)* topologies, *(ii)* requirements; and *(iii)* protocol combinations. Further to test correctness, we ran all synthesized configurations on an emulated environment of Cisco routers [32] and we verified that the forwarding paths computed match the requirements for each experiment.

Network Topologies. We used network topologies that have between 4 and 64 routers. The 4-router network is our overview example where we considered the same requirements as those described in Sect. 2. The 9-router network is Internet2 (see Fig. 5), a US-based network that connects several major universities and research institutes. The remaining networks are $n \times n$ grids.

Routing Requirements. For each router and each traffic class, we generate a routing requirement that defines where the packets for that traffic class must be forwarded to. We consider 1, 5, and 10 traffic classes. For a topology with n routers and m traffic classes, we thus generate $n \times m$ requirements.

For topologies with multiple traffic classes, we add one external network announced by two randomly selected routers. We add requirements to enforce that all packets destined to the external networks are forwarded to one of the two routers. This models a scenario where the operator is planning maintenance downtime for one of the two routers. Further, to show that SyNET synthesizes configurations with partially defined input and protocol dependencies, we assume the local BGP preferences are fixed by the network operator and thus SyNET has to synthesize correct OSPF costs to meet the BGP requirements.

Protocols. We consider three different combinations of protocols: *(i)* static routes; *(ii)* OSPF and static routes; and *(iii)* OSPF, BGP, and static routes. The protocol combinations *(i)* and *(ii)* ignore requirements for external networks since only BGP computes routes for them.

Experimental Setup. We run SyNET on a machine with 128 GB of RAM and a modern 12-core dual-processors running at 2.3 GHz.

Fig. 5. Internet2 topology

Results. The synthesis times for the different networks and protocol combinations are shown in Table 1 (averaged over 10 runs). SyNET synthesizes the overview example's configuration described in Sect. 2 in 10 s. For the largest network (64 routers) and number of traffic classes (10 classes), SyNET synthesizes a configuration for static routes (protocol combination *(i)*) in less than 1 h, and for the combination of static routes and OSPF, SyNET takes less than 22 h. When using both OSPF and BGP protocols along with static routes, for all network topologies SyNET synthesizes configurations for 1 and 5 traffic classes within 8 h; for 10 traffic classes, SyNET times out after 24 h for the largest topologies with 49 and 64 routers.

Interpretation. Our results show that SyNET scales to real-world networks. Indeed, a longitudinal analysis of more than 260 production networks [33] revealed that 56% of them have less than 32 routers. SyNET would synthesize

Table 1. SyNET's synthesis times (averaged over 10 runs) for different number of routers, protocol combinations, and traffic classes in the requirements.

Protocol	# Routers	1 Traffic class		5 Traffic classes		10 Traffic classes	
		Avg	Std	Avg	Std	Avg	Std
Static	9	1.3 s	(0.5)	2.0 s	(0.1)	2.8 s	(0.4)
	9 (Internet2)	1.3 s	(0.5)	2.0 s	(0.0)	4.0 s	(0.8)
	16	5.9 s	(0.3)	7.8 s	(0.4)	11.2 s	(0.4)
	25	32.0 s	(0.6)	37.0 s	(0.6)	46.1 s	(0.9)
	36	2 m 49.7 s	(3.0)	3 m 1.5 s	(4.5)	3 m 27.0 s	(4.4)
	49	12 m 29.2 s	(7.0)	13 m 02.3 s	(10.6)	14 m 10.7 s	(15.0)
	64	46 m 36.2 s	(49.0)	47 m 23.8 s	(27.2)	49 m 22.2 s	(39.3)
OSPF+Static	9	9.4 s	(0.5)	19.8 s	(0.4)	39.9 s	(0.5)
	9 (Internet2)	9.0 s	(1.4)	21.3 s	(1.2)	49.3 s	(0.5)
	16	43.5 s	(0.7)	1 m 19.8 s	(0.6)	4 m 5.8 s	(1.6)
	25	2 m 55.2 s	(6.1)	7 m 3.8 s	(9.9)	15 m 56.4 s	(38.1)
	36	10 m 00.5 s	(9.5)	23 m 58.9 s	(22.5)	1 h 11 m 38.2 s	(127.5)
	49	24 m 11.6 s	(43.5)	1 h 30 m 00.3 s	(89.6)	5 h 22 m 55.8 s	(421.2)
	64	2 h 22 m 13.2 s	(209.9)	5 h 42 m 58.9 s	(619.4)	21 h 13 m 16.0 s	(1986.7)
BGP+OSPF+Static	9	15.3 s	(0.5)	27.7 s	(0.5)	1 m 0.5 s	(2.6)
	9 (Internet2)	13.3 s	(0.9)	22.7 s	(0.9)	1 m 19.7 s	(0.5)
	16	56.0 s	(1.6)	2 m 24.7 s	(0.9)	8 m 29.0 s	(10.7)
	25	3 m 56.3 s	(3.1)	8 m 46.3 s	(5.3)	40 m 09.3 s	(99.2)
	36	14 m 14.0 s	(15.0)	43 m 38.0 s	(5.7)	2 h 35 m 11.7 s	(197.7)
	49	1 h 23 m 20.7 s	(211.1)	2 h 15 m 18.0 s	(12.8)	timeout (>24h)	
	64	1 h 46 m 35.0 s	(165.8)	7 h 24 m 51.3 s	(519.2)	timeout (>24h)	

configurations for such networks within one hour. SyNET also already supports a reasonable amount of traffic classes. According to a study on real-world enterprise and WAN networks [21], even large networks with 100,000s of IP prefixes in their forwarding tables usually see less than 15 traffic classes in total.

While SyNET can take more than 24 h to synthesize a configuration for the largest networks (with all protocols activated and 10 traffic classes), we believe that this time can be reduced through divide-and-conquer. Real networks tend to be hierarchically organized around few regions (to ensure the scalability of the protocols [34]) whose configurations can be synthesized independently. We plan to explore the synthesis of such hierarchical configurations in future work.

7 Related Work

Analysis of Datalog Programs. Datalog has been successfully used to declaratively specify variety of static analyzers [35,36]. It has been also used to verify network-wide configurations for protocols such as OSPF and BGP [4]. Recent work [37] has extended Datalog to operate with richer classes of lattice structures. Further, the μZ tool [38] extends the Z3 SMT solver with support for fixed points. The focus of all these works is on computing the fixed point of a program P for a given input I and then checking a property φ on the fixed point. That is, they check whether $[\![P]\!]_I \models \varphi$. All of these works assume that the input is provided a priori. In contrast, our procedure discovers an input that produces a fixed point satisfying a given (user-provided) property on the fixed point.

The algorithm presented in [36] can be used to check whether certain tuples are not derived for a given set of inputs. Given a Datalog program P (without negation in the literals), a set Q of tuples, and a set $\mathcal{I}$ of inputs, the algorithm computes the set $Q \setminus \bigcap \{ \llbracket P \rrbracket_I \mid I \in \mathcal{I} \}$. This algorithm cannot address our problem because it does not support stratified Datalog programs, which are not monotone. While their encoding can be used to synthesize inputs for each stratum of a stratified Datalog program, it supports only negative properties, which require that certain tuples are not derived. Our approach is thus more general than [36] and can be used in their application domain.

The FORMULA system [39, 40] can synthesize inputs for non-recursive Dataog programs, as it supports non-recursive Horn clauses with stratified negation (even though [41] which uses FORMULA shows examples of recursive Horn clauses w/o negation). Handling recursion with stratified negation is nontrivial as bounded unrolling is unsound if applied to all strata together. Note that virtually all network specifications require recursive rules, which our system supports.

Symbolic Analysis and Synthesis. Our algorithm is similar in spirit to symbolic (or concolic) execution, which is used to automatically generate inputs for programs that violate a given assertion (e.g. division by zero); see [42–44] for an overview. These approaches unroll loops up to a bound and find inputs by calling an SMT solver on the symbolic path. While we also find inputs for a symbolic formula, the entire setting, techniques and algorithms, are all different from the standard symbolic execution setting.

Counter-example guided synthesis approaches are also related [45]. Typically, the goal of synthesis is to discover a program, while in our case the program is given and we synthesize an input for it. There is a connection, however, as a program can be represented as a vector of bits. Most such approaches have a single counter-example generator (i.e., the oracle), while we use a sequence of oracles. It would be interesting to investigate domains where such layered oracle counter-example generation can benefit and improve the efficiency of synthesis.

Network Configuration Synthesis. Propane [46] and Genesis [19] also produce network-wide configurations out of routing requirements. Unlike our approach, however, Propane only supports BGP and Genesis only supports static routes. In contrast to our system, Propane and Genesis support failure-resilience requirements. While we could directly capture such requirements by quantifying over links, this would make synthesis more expensive. A more efficient way to handle such requirements would be to synthesize a failure-resilient forwarding plane using a system like Genesis [19], and to then feed this as input to our synthesizer to get a network-wide configuration. In contrast to these approaches, our system is more general: one can directly extended it with additional routing protocols, by specifying them in stratified Datalog, and synthesize configurations for *any combination* of routing protocols.

ConfigAssure [47] is a general system that takes as input requirements in first-order constraints and outputs a configuration conforming to the requirements. The fixed point computation performed by routing protocols cannot be captured using the formalism used in ConfigAssure. Therefore, ConfigAssure cannot be used to specify networks and, in turn, to synthesize protocol configurations for networks.

8 Conclusion

We formulated the network-wide configuration synthesis problem as a problem of finding inputs of a Datalog program, and presented a new input synthesis algorithm to solve this challenge. Our algorithm is based on decomposing the Datalog rules into strata and iteratively synthesizing inputs for the individual strata using off-the-shelf SMT solvers. We implemented our approach in a system called SyNET and showed that it scales to realistic network size using any combination of OSPF, BGP and static routes.

References

1. Ryall, J.: Facebook, Tinder, Instagram suffer widespread issues. http://mashable.com/2015/01/27/facebook-tinder-instagram-issues/
2. Juniper Networks. What's Behind Network Downtime? Proactive Steps to Reduce Human Error and Improve Availability of Networks. Technical report, May 2008
3. BGPmon. Internet prefixes monitoring. http://www.bgpmon.net/blog/
4. Fogel, A., Fung, S., Pedrosa, L., Walraed-Sullivan, M., Govindan, R., Mahajan, R., Millstein, T.: A general approach to network configuration analysis. In: NSDI (2015)
5. Feamster, N., Balakrishnan, H.: Detecting BGP configuration faults with static analysis. In: NSDI (2005)
6. Nelson, T., Barratt, C., Dougherty, D.J., Fisler, K., Krishnamurthi, S.: The margrave tool for firewall analysis. In: LISA (2010)
7. Yuan, L., Chen, H., Mai, J., Chuah, C.-N., Su, Z., Mohapatra, P.: FIREMAN: a toolkit for firewall modeling and analysis. In: S&P (2006)
8. Vanbever, L., Quoitin, B., Bonaventure, O.: A hierarchical model for BGP routing policies. In: ACM SIGCOMM PRESTO (2009)
9. Chen, X., Mao, M., Van der Merwe, J.: PACMAN: a platform for automated and controlled network operations and configuration management. In: CoNEXT (2009)
10. Enck, W., Moyer, T., McDaniel, P., Sen, S., Sebos, P., Spoerel, S., Greenberg, A., Sung, Y.-W.E., Rao, S., Aiello, W.: Configuration management at massive scale: system design and experience. IEEE J. Sel. Areas Commun. (2009)
11. Gottlieb, J., Greenberg, A., Rexford, J., Wang, J.: Automated provisioning of BGP customers. IEEE Netw. **17**, 44–55 (2003)
12. Alaettinoglu, C., Villamizar, C., Gerich, E., Kessens, D., Meyer, D., Bates, T., Karrenberg, D., Terpstra, M.: Routing Policy Specification Language. RFC 2622
13. Bjorklund, M.: YANG - A Data Modeling Language for the Network Configuration Protocol (NETCONF). RFC 6020
14. Enns, R., et al.: Network Configuration Protocol (NETCONF). RFC 4741
15. El-Hassany, A., Miserez, J., Bielik, P., Vanbever, L., Vechev, M.: SDNRacer: concurrency analysis for SDNs. In: PLDI (2016)
16. Canini, M., Venzano, D., Peresini, P., Kostic, D., Rexford, J., et al.: A NICE way to test OpenFlow applications. In: NSDI (2012)
17. Scott, C., Wundsam, A., Raghavan, B., Panda, A., Or, A., Lai, J., Huang, E., Liu, Z., El-Hassany, A., Whitlock, S., Acharya, H.B., Zarifis, K., Shenker, S.: Troubleshooting Blackbox SDN control software with minimal causal sequences. In: ACM SIGCOMM (2014)

18. Ball, T., Bjørner, N., Gember, A., Itzhaky, S., Karbyshev, A., Sagiv, M., Schapira, M., Valadarsky, A.: VeriCon: towards verifying controller programs in software-defined networks. In: PLDI (2014)
19. Subramanian, K., D'Antoni, L., Akella, A.: Genesis: synthesizing forwarding tables in multi-tenant networks. In: POPL (2017)
20. Kang, N., Liu, Z., Rexford, J., Walker, D.: Optimizing the "One Big Switch" abstraction in software-defined networks. In: CoNEXT (2013)
21. Benson, T., Akella, A., Maltz, D.A.: Mining policies from enterprise network configuration. In: IMC (2009)
22. Awduche, D., et al.: Overview and Principles of Internet Traffic Engineering. RFC3272
23. Fortz, B., Rexford, J., Thorup, M.: Traffic engineering with traditional IP routing protocols. IEEE Commun. Mag. **40**, 118–124 (2002)
24. Halevy, A.Y., Mumick, I.S., Sagiv, Y., Shmueli, O.: Static analysis in datalog extensions. J. ACM **48**, 971–1012 (2001)
25. Mumick, I.S., Shmueli, O.: How expressive is stratified aggregation? Ann. Math. Artif. Intell. **15**, 407–435 (1995)
26. El-Hassany, A., Tsankov, P., Vanbever, L., Vechev, M.T.: Network-wide configuration synthesis. CoRR, abs/1611.02537 (2016). http://arxiv.org/abs/1611.02537
27. Abiteboul, S., Hull, R., Vianu, V. (eds.): Foundations of Databases: The Logical Level (1995)
28. Ullman, J.D.: Principles of Database and Knowledge-Base Systems. Computer Science Press, New York (1989)
29. https://logicblox.com/content/docs4/corereference/html/index.html
30. Barrett, C., et al.: The SMT-LIB Standard: Version 2.0 (2010)
31. De Moura, L., Bjørner, N.: Z3: an efficient SMT solver. In: TACAS (2008)
32. Graphical Network Simulator-3 (GNS3). https://www.gns3.com/
33. Knight, S., Nguyen, H.X., Falkner, N., Bowden, R.A., Roughan, M.: The internet topology zoo. IEEE J. Sel. Areas Commun. **29**, 1765–1775 (2011)
34. Doyle, J., Carroll, J.: Routing TCP/IP, vol. 1. Cisco Press, Indianapolis (2005)
35. Smaragdakis, Y., Bravenboer, M.: Using datalog for fast and easy program analysis. In: de Moor, O., Gottlob, G., Furche, T., Sellers, A. (eds.) Datalog Reloaded. LNCS, vol. 6702, pp. 245–251. Springer, Heidelberg (2011). doi:10.1007/978-3-642-24206-9_14
36. Zhang, X., Mangal, R., Grigore, R., Naik, M., Yang, H.: On abstraction refinement for program analyses in datalog. In: PLDI (2014)
37. Madsen, M., Yee, M.-H., Lhoták, O.: From datalog to flix: a declarative language for fixed points on lattices. In: PLDI (2016)
38. Hoder, K., Bjørner, N., De Moura, L.: μZ: an efficient engine for fixed points with constraints. In: CAV (2011)
39. Jackson, E.K., Sztipanovits, J.: Towards a formal foundation for domain specific modeling languages. In: EMSOFT (2006)
40. Jackson, E.K., Schulte, W.: Model generation for horn logic with stratified negation. In: Suzuki, K., Higashino, T., Yasumoto, K., El-Fakih, K. (eds.) FORTE 2008. LNCS, vol. 5048, pp. 1–20. Springer, Heidelberg (2008). doi:10.1007/978-3-540-68855-6_1
41. Jackson, E.K. Kang, E., Dahlweid, M., Seifert, D., Santen, T.: Components, platforms and possibilities: towards generic automation for MDA. In: EMSOFT (2010)
42. Cadar, C., Sen, K.: Symbolic execution for software testing: three decades later. Commun. ACM **26**, 82–90 (2013)

43. Kroening, D., Tautschnig, M.: CBMC – C bounded model checker. In: Ábrahám, E., Havelund, K. (eds.) TACAS 2014. TACAS 2014, vol. 8413, pp. 389–391. Springer, Heidelberg (2014). doi:10.1007/978-3-642-54862-8_26
44. Clarke, E., Kroening, D., Lerda, F.: A tool for checking ANSI-C programs. In: Jensen, K., Podelski, A. (eds.) TACAS 2004. LNCS, vol. 2988, pp. 168–176. Springer, Heidelberg (2004). doi:10.1007/978-3-540-24730-2_15
45. Solar-Lezama, A., Tancau, L., Bodik, R., Seshia, S., Saraswat, V.: Combinatorial Sketching for Finite Programs. In: ASPLOS (2006)
46. Beckett, R., Mahajan, R., Millstein, T., Padhye, J., Walker, D.: Don't mind the gap: bridging network-wide objectives and device-level configurations. In: SIGCOMM (2016)
47. Narain, S., Levin, G., Malik, S., Kaul, V.: Declarative infrastructure configuration synthesis and debugging. J. Netw. Syst. Manag. **16**, 235–258 (2008)

Verifying Equivalence of Spark Programs

Shelly Grossman[1(✉)], Sara Cohen[2], Shachar Itzhaky[3],
Noam Rinetzky[1], and Mooly Sagiv[1]

[1] Tel Aviv University, Tel Aviv, Israel
{shellygr,maon,msagiv}@tau.ac.il
[2] The Hebrew University of Jerusalem,
Jerusalem, Israel
sara@cs.huji.ac.il
[3] Massachusetts Institute of Technology, Cambridge, USA
shachari@mit.edu

Abstract. *Apache Spark* is a popular framework for writing large scale data processing applications. Our long term goal is to develop automatic tools for reasoning about Spark programs. This is challenging because Spark programs combine database-like relational algebraic operations and aggregate operations, corresponding to (nested) loops, with *User Defined Functions (UDFs)*. In this paper, we present a novel SMT-based technique for verifying the equivalence of Spark programs.

We model Spark as a programming language whose semantics imitates Relational Algebra queries (with aggregations) over bags (multisets) and allows for UDFs expressible in Presburger Arithmetics. We prove that the problem of checking equivalence is undecidable even for programs which use a single aggregation operator. Thus, we present sound techniques for verifying the equivalence of interesting classes of Spark programs, and show that it is complete under certain restrictions. We implemented our technique, and applied it to a few small, but intricate, test cases.

1 Introduction

Spark [17,29,30] is a popular framework for writing large scale data processing applications. It is an evolution of the Map-Reduce paradigm, which provides an abstraction of the distributed data as *bags* (multisets) of items. A bag r can be accessed using higher-order operations such as *map*, which applies a *user defined function (UDF)* to all items in r; *filter*, which filters items in r using a given boolean UDF; and *fold* which aggregates items together, again using a UDF. Intuitively, map, filter and fold can be seen as extensions to the standard database operations *project*, *select* and *aggregation*, respectively, with arbitrary

We would like to thank the reviewers for their helpful comments. The research leading to these results has received funding from the European Research Council under the European Union's Seventh Framework Programme (FP7/2007–2013)/ERC grant agreement n° [321174], by Len Blavatnik and the Blavatnik Family foundation, and by the Broadcom Foundation and Tel Aviv University Authentication Initiative.

R. Majumdar and V. Kunčak (Eds.): CAV 2017, Part II, LNCS 10427, pp. 282–300, 2017.
DOI: 10.1007/978-3-319-63390-9_15

UDFs applied. Bags also support by-key, *join* and *cartesian product* operators. A language such as *Scala* or *Python* is used as Spark's interface, allowing to embed calls to the underlying framework, as well as defining UDFs that Spark executes.

This paper shows how to harness SMT solvers to automatically reason about small subsets of Spark programs. Specifically, we are interested in developing tools that can check whether two Spark programs are equivalent and produce a witness input for the different behavior of inequivalent ones. Reasoning about the equivalence of Spark programs is challenging—not only is the problem undecidable even for programs containing a single aggregate operation, some specific intricacies arise from the fact that the input datasets are bags (rather than simple sets or individual items), and that the output might expose only a *partial* view of the results of UDF-based aggregations.

Our main tool for showing equivalence of Spark programs is reducing the equivalence question to the validity of a formula in Presburger arithmetic, which is a decidable theory [12,22]. More specifically, we present a simplified model of Spark by defining SparkLite, a functional programming language in which UDFs are expressed over a decidable theory. We show that SMT solvers can effectively verify equivalence of and detect potential differences between Spark programs. We present different verification techniques which leverage certain semantic restrictions which, in certain cases, make the problem decidable. These restrictions can also be validated through SMT. Arguably, the most interesting aspect of our technique is that it can reason about higher order operations such as *fold* and *foldByKey*, corresponding to limited usage of loops and nested loops, respectively. The key reason for the success of our techniques is that our restrictions make it possible to automatically infer inductive hypotheses simple enough to be mechanically checked by SMT solvers, e.g., [10].

Main Results. Our main technical contributions can be summarized as follows:

- We prove that verifying the equivalence of SparkLite programs is undecidable even in our limited setting.
- We identify several interesting restrictions of SparkLite programs, and develop sound, and in certain cases complete, methods for proving program equivalence. (See Table 1, which we gradually explain in Sect. 2).
- We implemented our approach on top of Z3 [10], and applied it to several interesting programs inspired by real-life Spark applications. When the implementation employs a complete method and determines that a pair of programs is not equivalent, it produces a (real) counterexample of bag elements which are witnesses for the difference between the programs. This counterexample is guaranteed to be valid for programs which have a complete verification method, and can help understand the differences between these programs.

2 Overview

For space considerations, we concentrate on presenting an informal overview through a series of simple examples, and formalize the results in [13].

Table 1. Sound methods for verifying equivalence of Spark programs, their syntactic and semantic prerequisites, and completeness. By abuse of notation, we refer to SparkLite programs adhering to the syntactic restriction of one of the first four verification methods as belonging to the *class of* SparkLite *programs* of the same name.

Method	Syntactic restriction	Semantic restriction	Complete?
$NoAgg$	No folds	-	✓
$AggOne^p$	Single fold, primitive output	-	-
$AggOne^b$	Single fold, bag output	-	-
$AggMult^p$	Non-nested folds, primitive output	-	-
$AggOne^p_{sync}$	Single fold, primitive output	Synchronous collapsible aggregations	✓
$AggOneK^b$	Single fold by key, bag output	Isomorphic keys	-

P1(R: Bag_{Int}):
$R'_1 = \texttt{map}(\lambda x.2 * x)(R)$
$R''_1 = \texttt{filter}(\lambda x.x \geq 100)(R'_1)$
return R''_1

P2(R: Bag_{Int}):
$R'_2 = \texttt{filter}(\lambda x.x \geq 50)(R)$
$R''_2 = \texttt{map}(\lambda x.2 * x)(R'_2)$
return R''_2

$$\forall x.ite(2 * x \geq 100, 2 * x, \bot) = 2 * ite(x \geq 50, x, \bot).$$

Fig. 1. Equivalent Spark programs and a formula attesting for their equivalence.

Figure 1 shows two equivalent Spark programs and the formula that we use for checking their equivalence. The programs accept a bag of integer elements. They return another bag where each element is twice the value of the original element, for elements which are at least 50. The programs operate differently: $P1$ first multiplies, then filters, while $P2$ goes the other way around. $\texttt{map}$ and $\texttt{filter}$ are operations that apply a function on each element in the bag, and yield a new bag. For example, let bag R be the bag $R = \{2, 2, 103, 64\}$ (note that repetitions are allowed). R is an input of both $P1$ and $P2$. The $\texttt{map}$ operator in the first line of $P1$ produces a new bag, R'_1, by doubling every element of R, i.e., $R'_1 = \{4, 4, 206, 128\}$. The $\texttt{filter}$ operator in the second line generates bag R''_1, containing the elements of R'_1 which are at least 100, i.e., $R''_1 = \{206, 128\}$. The second program first applies the filter operator, producing a bag R'_2 of all the elements in R which are not smaller than 50, resulting in the bag $R'_2 = \{103, 64\}$. $P2$ applies the map operator to produce bag R''_2 which contains the same elements as R''_1. Hence, both programs return the same value.

To verify that the programs are indeed *equivalent*, i.e., given the same inputs produce the same outputs, we encode them symbolically using formulae in first-order logic, such that the question of equivalence boils down to proving the validity of a formula. In this example, we encode $P1$ as a *program term*: $\phi(P1) = ite(2 * x \geq 100, 2 * x, \bot)$, and $P2$ as: $\phi(P2) = 2 * ite(x \geq 50, x, \bot)$, where ite denotes the if-then-else operator and $\bot$ is used to denote that the element has been removed. The variable symbol x can be thought of as an arbitrary element in the bag R, and the terms $\phi(P1)$ and $\phi(P2)$ record the effect of $P1$ and $P2$, respectively, on x. The constant symbol $\bot$ records the deletion of an element due to not satisfying the condition checked by the `filter` operation. The formula whose validity attests for the equivalence of $P1$ and $P2$ is $\forall x.\phi(P1) = \phi(P2)$. It is expressible in a decidable extension of Presburger Arithmetics, which supports the special $\bot$ symbol (see [13, Sect. 8]). Thus, its validity can be decided.

This example points out an important property of the *map* and *filter* operations, namely, their *locality*: they handle every element separately, with no regard to its multiplicity (the number of duplicates it has in the bag) or the presence of other elements. Thus, we can symbolically represent the effect of the program on any bag, by encoding its effect on a single arbitrary element from that bag. Interestingly, the locality property transcends to the *cartesian product* operator which conjoins items across bags.

Decidability. The validity of the aforementioned formula suffices to prove the equivalence of $P1$ and $P2$ due to a tacit fact: both programs operate on the same bag. Consider, however, programs $P1'$ and $P2'$ which receive bags R_1 and R_2 as inputs. $P1'$ maps all the elements of R_1 to 1 and $P2'$ does the same for R_2. Their symbolic encoding is $\phi(P1') = (\lambda x.1)x_1$ and $\phi(P1') = (\lambda x.1)x_2$, where x_1 and x_2 represent, respectively, arbitrary elements from R_1 and R_2. The formula $\forall x_1, x_2.\phi(P1') = \phi(P2')$ is valid. Alas, the programs produce different results if R_1 and R_2 have different sizes. Interestingly, we show that unless both programs always return the empty bag, they are equivalent *iff* their program terms are equivalent *and* use the same variable symbols.[1] Furthermore, it is possible to decide whether a program always returns the empty bag by determining if its program term is equivalent to $\bot$. Theorem 1 (Sect. 4.1) shows that the equivalence of *NoAgg* programs, i.e., ones not using aggregations, can be decided.

Usage of Inductive Reasoning. We use inductive reasoning to determine the equivalence of programs that use aggregations. Theorem 2 (presented later on) shows that equivalence in $AggOne^p$, that is, of programs that use a single `fold` operation and return a primitive value, is undecidable. Thus, we consider different classes of programs that use aggregations in limited ways.

Figure 2 contains an example of two simple equivalent $AggOne^p$ programs. The programs operate over a bag of pairs (product IDs, price). The programs check if the minimal price in the bag is at least 100. The second program does this by subtracting 20 from each price in the bag and comparing the minimum to 80. $P3$ computes the minimal price in R using `fold`, and then returns *true* if it is at least 100 and *false* otherwise. $P4$ first applies *discount* to every element, resulting in a temporary bag R', and then computes the minimum of R'. It returns *true* if the minimum is at least 80, and *false* otherwise.

The `fold` operation combines the elements of a bag by repeatedly applying a UDF. `fold` cannot be expressed in first order terms. Thus, we use induction

---

[1] Recall that intuitively, these variables pertain to arbitrary elements in the input bags. In our example, $\phi(P1')$ uses variable x_1 and $\phi(P2')$ uses x_2.

$$discount = \lambda(prod, p).(prod, p - 20)$$
$$min2 = \lambda A, (x, y).if\ A < y\ then\ A\ else\ y$$

P3(R: $Bag_{\mathtt{Prod \times Int}}$):   **P4**($R$: $Bag_{\mathtt{Prod \times Int}}$):

$minP = \mathtt{fold}(+\infty, min2)(R)$ $R' = \mathtt{map}(\lambda(prod, p).discount((prod, p)))(R)$

return $minP \geq 100$ $minDiscountP = \mathtt{fold}(+\infty, min2)(R')$

                                                return $minDiscountP \geq 80$

$$\left(\begin{array}{lr} prod' = prod \wedge p' = p - 20 & assumptions \\ \wedge M_2 = ite(M_1 < p, M_1, p) \wedge M_2' = ite(M_1' < p', M_1', p') & assumptions \end{array} \right)$$
$$\Longrightarrow (+\infty \geq 100 \iff +\infty \geq 80) \qquad\qquad base\ case$$
$$\wedge ((M_1 \geq 100 \iff M_1' \geq 80) \Longrightarrow (M_2 \geq 100 \iff M_2' \geq 80))\ induction\ step$$

Fig. 2. Equivalent Spark programs with aggregations and an inductive equivalence formula. Variables $prod, p, prod', p', M_1, M_1', M_2, M_2'$ are universally quantified.

to verify that two $\mathtt{fold}$ results are equal. Roughly speaking, the induction leverages the somewhat *local* nature of the $\mathtt{fold}$ operation, specifically, that it does not track *how* the temporarily accumulated value is obtained: Note that the elements of R' can be expressed by applying the *discount* function on the elements of R. Thus, intuitively, we can assume that in both programs, $\mathtt{fold}$ iterates on the *input* bag R in the same order. (It is permitted to assume a particular order because the applied UDFs must be commutative for the $\mathtt{fold}$ to be well-defined [17].[2]) The base of the induction hypothesis checks that the programs are equivalent when the input bags are empty, and the induction step verifies the equivalence is retained when we apply the $\mathtt{fold}$'s UDF on some arbitrary accumulated value and an element coming from each input bag.[3] In our example, when the bags are empty, both programs return *true*. (The $\mathtt{fold}$ operation returns $+\infty$.) Otherwise, we assume that after n prices checked, the minimum M_1 in $P3$ is at least 100 iff the minimum M_1' in $P4$ is at least 80. The programs are equivalent if this invariant is kept after checking the next product and price $((prod, p), (prod', p'))$ giving updated intermediate values M_2 and M_2'.

Completeness of the Inductive Reasoning. In the example in Fig. 2, we use a simple form of induction by proving that two higher-order operations are equivalent iff they are equivalent on every input element and arbitrary temporarily accumulated values (M_1 and M_1' in Fig. 2). Such an approach is incomplete. We now show an example for incompleteness, and a modified verification formula that is complete for a subset of $AggOne^p$, called $AggOne_{sync}^p$. In Fig. 3, $P3$ and

---

[2] We note that our results do not require UDFs to be associative, however, Spark does.

[3] Note that $AggOne^p$ programs can fold bags produced by a sequence of filter, map, and cartesian product operations. Our approach is applicable to such programs because if the program terms of two folded bags use the same variable symbols, then any selection of elements from the input bags produces an element in the bag being folded in one program iff it produces an element in the bag that the other program folds. (See Lemma 1).

$$min2 = \lambda A, (x, y).\ ite(A < y, A, y)$$

P5(R: $Bag_{Prod \times Int}$):

$minP = \texttt{fold}(+\infty, min2)(R)$

return $minP = 100$

P6(R: $Bag_{Prod \times Int}$):

$R' = \texttt{map}(\lambda(prod, p).discount((prod, p)))(R)$

$minDiscountP = \texttt{fold}(+\infty, min2)(R')$

return $minDiscountP = 80$

Naïve formula:

$$\left(\begin{array}{lr} prod' = prod \wedge p' = p - 20 & assumptions \\ \wedge\ M_2 = ite(M_1 < p, M_1, p) \wedge M_2' = ite(M_1' < p', M_1', p') & assumptions \end{array} \right)$$
$$\implies (+\infty = 100 \iff +\infty = 80) \qquad\qquad base\ case$$
$$\wedge((M_1 = 100 \iff M_1' = 80) \implies (M_2 = 100 \iff M_2' = 80))\ induction\ step$$

Revised formula:

$$\left(\begin{array}{lr} prod' = prod \wedge p' = p - 20 & assumptions \\ \wedge\ a = (a_0, a_1) \wedge M_1 = ite(+\infty < a_1, +\infty, a_1) & closure \\ \wedge\ M_1' = ite(+\infty < a_1 - 20, +\infty, a_1 - 20) & property \\ \wedge\ M_2 = ite(M_1 < p, M_1, p) \wedge M_2' = ite(M_1' < p', M_1', p') & assumptions \end{array} \right)$$
$$\implies (+\infty = 100 \iff +\infty = 80) \qquad\qquad base\ case$$
$$\wedge((M_1 = 100 \iff M_1' = 80) \implies (M_2 = 100 \iff M_2' = 80))\ induction\ step$$

Fig. 3. Equivalent Spark programs for which a more elaborate induction is required. All variables are universally quantified.

$P4$ were rewritten into $P5$ and $P6$, respectively, by using $=$ instead of $\geq$. The rewritten programs are equivalent. We show both the "naïve" formula, similar to the formula from Fig. 2, and a revised version of it. (We explain shortly how the revised formula is obtained.) The naïve formula is not valid, since it requires that the returned values be equivalent ignoring the history of applied $\texttt{fold}$ operations generating the intermediate values M_1 and M_1'. For example, for $M_1 = 60$, $M_1' = 120$, and $p = 100$, we get a spurious counterexample to equality, leading to the wrong conclusion that the programs may not be equivalent. In fact, if $P5$ and $P6$ iterate over the input bag in the same order, it is not possible that their (temporarily) accumulated values are 60 and 120 at the same time.

Luckily, we observe that, often, the $\texttt{fold}$ UDFs are somewhat restricted. One such natural property, is the ability to "collapse" any sequence of applications of the aggregation function f using a single application. We can leverage this property for more complete treatment of equivalence verification, if the programs collapse in *synchrony*; given their respective fold functions f_1, f_2, initial values i_1, i_2, and the symbolic representation of the program term pertaining to the folded bags φ_1, φ_2, the programs collapse in synchrony if the following holds:

$$\forall x, y. \exists a.\ f_1(f_1(i_1, \varphi_1(x)), \varphi_1(y)) = f_1(i_1, \varphi_1(a)) \tag{1}$$
$$\wedge\ f_2(f_2(i_2, \varphi_2(x)), \varphi_2(y)) = f_2(i_2, \varphi_2(a))$$

Note that the same input a is used to collapse both programs. In our example, $\min(\min(+\infty, x), y) = \min(+\infty, a)$, and $\min(\min(+\infty, x - 20), y - 20) =$

$$getDecile = \lambda(sId, g). \ (g/10, sId) \ ; \quad count = \lambda A, v. \ A + 1$$
$$isPassingDecile = \lambda(d, sId).d \geq 6 \ ; \quad isPassingGrade = \lambda(sId, g).g \geq 60$$

P7(R: $Bag_{\text{StudentID} \times \text{Int}}$):   **P8**($R$: $Bag_{\text{StudentID} \times \text{Int}}$):
$R' = \texttt{map}(getDecile)(R)$ $R' = \texttt{filter}(isPassingGrade)(R)$
$H = \texttt{foldByKey}(0, count)(R')$ $R'' = \texttt{map}(getDecile)(R')$
return $\texttt{filter}(isPassingDecile)(H)$ return $\texttt{foldByKey}(0, count)(R'')$

$$\left(d = g/10 \quad assumptions \right)$$
$$\implies \left(ite(d \geq 6, (d, 0), \bot) = (ite(g \geq 60, d, \bot), 0) \right. \qquad \qquad base \ case$$
$$\wedge \left(ite(d \geq 6, (d, C), \bot) = (ite(g \geq 60, d, \bot), C') \implies \qquad induction \ step \right.$$
$$\left. \left. ite(d \geq 6, (d, C+1), \bot) = (ite(g \geq 60, d, \bot), C'+1) \right) \right)$$

$$\forall g, g'.(g/10 = g'/10 \wedge g \neq \bot) \implies ite(g \geq 60, g/10, \bot) = ite(g' \geq 60, g'/10, \bot) \qquad (2)$$
$$\forall g, g'.ite(g \geq 60, g/10, \bot) = ite(g' \geq 60, g'/10, \bot) \wedge ite(g \geq 60, g/10, \bot) \neq \bot \implies g/10 = g'/10 \quad (3)$$

Fig. 4. Equivalent Spark programs with aggregation by-key. All variables are universally quantified. If any component of the tuple is $\bot$, then the entire tuple is considered as $\bot$.

$\min(+\infty, a - 20)$, for $a = \min(x, y)$. The reader may be concerned how this closure property can be checked. Interestingly, for formulas in Presburger arithmetic, an SMT solver can decide this property.

We utilized the above closure property by observing that any pair of intermediate results can be expressed as single applications of the UDF. Surely any M_1 must have been obtained by repeating applications of the form $f_1(f_1(\cdots))$, and similarly for M_1' with $f_2(f_2(\cdots))$. Therefore, in the revised formula, instead of quantifying on any M_1 and M_1', we quantify over the argument a to that single application, and introduce the assumption incurred by Eq. (1). We can then write an induction hypothesis that holds iff the two fold operations return an equal result.

Handling ByKey Operations. Spark is often used to aggregate values of groups of records identified by a shared key. For example, in Fig. 4 we present two equivalent programs that given a bag of pairs of student IDs and grades, return a histogram graph of all passing grades (≥ 60), in deciles. $P7$ first maps each student's grade to its decile, while making the decile the key. (The key is the first component in the pair.) Then, it computes the count of all students in a certain decile using the `foldByKey` operation, and filters out all non-passing deciles (<6) from the resulting histogram. $P8$ first filters out all failing grades, and then continues similarly with the histogram computation.

Verifying the equivalence of $P7$ and $P8$ is challenging because, intuitively, the by-key operation corresponds to a nested loop: It partitions the bag into *"buckets"* according to the key element of the bag and folds every bucket separately. Furthermore, note that the two programs fold bags which contain different keys.

Our approach to verify programs using by-key operations is based on a reduction to the problem of verifying programs using *fold*: We rewrite the programs, so instead of applying the fold operation on one bucket at a time (as `foldByKey` does), we apply it on the entire bag to get the global aggregated result. We then map each key to the global aggregated result, instead of the aggregated result for the bucket. It is then possible to write an inductive hypothesis based on the rewritten program. The reduction is sound if the two compared programs partition the bag's elements to buckets consistently: If program $Q1$ sends two elements to the same bucket, then $Q2$ must also send those two elements to the same bucket (although it does not have to be the same bucket as $Q1$), and vice versa. As with the property of collapsibility seen earlier, this property can also be expressed in Presburger arithmetic, and be verified using an SMT solver: for functions k_1 and k_2 that describe expressions for keys, we require:

$$\forall x, x'.\left((k_1(x) = k_1(x') \wedge k_1(x) \neq \bot) \implies (k_2(x) = k_2(x'))\right) \tag{2}$$

$$\forall x, x'.\left((k_2(x) = k_2(x') \wedge k_2(x) \neq \bot) \implies (k_1(x) = k_1(x'))\right) \tag{3}$$

Figure 4 shows the inductive hypothesis whose validity ensures the equivalence of $P7$ and $P8$, as well as the resulting instantiation of Eqs. (2) and (3). $AggOneK^b$ is a sound method for verifying equivalence of pairs of programs that use single `foldByKey` and satisfy Eqs. (2) and (3). (See [13, Lemma 7].)[4]

Decidability. Table 1 characterizes the programs for which our method is applicable, together with the strength of the method.[5] The example programs in Fig. 1 are representative of programs that belong to the *NoAgg* class of programs, for which we have a decision procedure for verifying equivalence. We consider five classes of programs containing `fold` operations. Equivalence in $AggOne^p$ is undecidable, and the result is extended naturally to the special cases of $AggOneK^b$, $AggOne^b$ and $AggMult^p$. On the other hand, $AggOne^p_{sync}$ is a complete verification method. The equivalence of the programs in Figs. 2 and 3 can be verified using $AggOne^p_{sync}$. Note that applying $AggOne^p_{sync}$ and $AggOneK^b$ require also checking the validity of Eq. (1), respectively Eqs. (2) and (3). Fortunately, these requirements are expressed in Presburger arithmetic and thus can be decided.

Limitations. We restrict ourselves to programs using *map, filter, cartesian product, fold,* and *foldByKey* where UDFs are defined in Presburger Arithmetic. We forbid self products—it is possible, but technically cumbersome, to extend our work to support self-products. However, supporting operators such as *union*

---

[4] Our approach is not sound if Eqs. (2) and (3) do not hold. To illustrate such a case, consider a hypothetical a case in which $P7'$ computes the histogram by deciles, $P8'$ by percentiles, and then both programs map all the elements to a constant, ignoring the aggregated value. $P7'$ produces at most 10 elements (one per decile), while $P8'$ produces at most 100, so they are clearly inequivalent.

[5] Due to space considerations, we do not discuss equivalence of programs from mixed syntactic classes with comparable output types. In essence, there is a reduction from these instances such that one of the methods presented here will be applicable.

and *subtract* can be tricky because of the bag semantics. Presburger arithmetic can be implemented with solvers such as Cooper's algorithm [9]. For simplicity we use Z3 which does not support full Presburger arithmetic, but supports the fragment of Presburger arithmetic used in this paper. Z3 also supports uninterpreted functions, which are useful to prove equivalence of other classes of Spark programs, but this is beyond the scope of this paper.

3   The SparkLite Language

In this section, we describe SparkLite, a simple functional programming language based on the operations provided by Spark [29].

Preliminaries. We denote a (possibly empty) sequence of elements coming from a set X by $\overline{X}$. An *if-then-else* expression $ite(p, e, e')$ denotes an expression that evaluates to e if p holds and to e' otherwise. A *bag* m over a domain X is a multiset, i.e., a set which allows for repetitions, with elements taken from X. We denote the *multiplicity* of an element x in bag m by $m(x)$, where for any x, either $0 < m(x)$ or $m(x)$ is undefined. We write $x \in m$ as a shorthand for $0 < m(x)$. We write $\{\!\!\{x; n(x) \mid x \in X \wedge \phi(x)\}\!\!\}$ to denote a bag with elements from X satisfying some property ϕ with multiplicity $n(x)$, and omit the conjunct $x \in X$ if X is clear from context. We denote the *size* (number of elements) of a bag m by $|m|$ and the empty bag by $\{\!\!\{\}\!\!\}$. We denote the i-th component of a tuple x by $p_i(x)$, and extend $p_i(\cdot)$ to bags containing tuples in the natural way.

SparkLite. The syntax of SparkLite is defined in Fig. 5. SparkLite supports two primitive types: *integers* (`Int`) and *booleans* (`Boolean`). On top of this, the user can define *record types* τ, which are tuples of primitive types, and *Bags*:[6] Bag_τ is (the type of) bags containing elements of type τ. We refer to primitive types and records as *basic types*, and, by abuse of notation, range over them using τ. We use e to denote a *basic expression* containing only basic types, written in Presburger arithmetics extended to include tuples in a straightforward way. (See [13, Sect. 8].) We range over variables using v and r for variables of basic types and *Bag*, respectively.

First-Order Functions	$Fdef$	$::=$ def $f = \lambda \overline{y:\tau}.e:\tau$
Second-Order Functions	$PFdef$	$::=$ def $F = \lambda \overline{x:\tau}.\lambda \overline{y:\tau}.e:\tau$
Function Expressions	f	$::= f \mid F(\overline{e})$
Bag Expressions	μ	$::=$ cartesian$(\mu, \mu') \mid$ map$(f)(\mu) \mid$ filter$(f)(\mu) \mid r$
General Expressions	η	$::= e \mid \mu \mid$ fold$(e, f)(\mu) \mid$ foldByKey$(e, f)(\mu)$
Let expressions	E	$::=$ let $x = \eta$ in $E \mid \epsilon$
Programs	$Prog$	$::= P(\overline{r:Bag_\tau}, \overline{v:\tau}) = \overline{Fdef} \; \overline{PFdef} \; E \; \eta$

Fig. 5. Syntax for SparkLite

---

[6] *Bags* is an abstraction of the main data-structure used in Spark, called *RDD* [17, 29,30].

A program $P(\overline{r : Bag_\tau}, \overline{v : \tau}) = \overline{Fdef} \; \overline{PFdef} \; E \; \eta$ is comprised of a *header* and a *body*, which are separated by the $=$ sign. The header contains the name of the program (P) and a sequence of the names and types of its input formal parameters, which may be *Bags* ($\overline{r}$) or records or primitive types ($\overline{v}$). The body of the program is comprised of two sequences of function declarations ($\overline{Fdef}$ and $\overline{PFdef}$), variable declarations (E), and the program's *main expression* (η). $\overline{Fdef}$ binds function names f with first-order lambda expressions, i.e., to a function which takes as input a sequence of arguments of basic types and returns a value of a basic type. $\overline{PFdef}$ associates function names F with a restricted form of second-order lambda expressions, which we refer to as *parametric functions*. As in the *Kappa Calculus* [15], a parametric function F receives a sequence of basic expressions and returns a first order function. Parametric functions can be instantiated to form an unbounded number of functions from a single pattern. For example, def addC $= \lambda x:$ Int. $\lambda y:$ Int. $x + y:$ Int can create any first order function which adds a constant to its argument, e.g., addC(1) $=$ $\lambda x:$ Int. $1 + x:$ Int and addC(2) $= \lambda x:$ Int. $2 + x:$ Int.

The program declares variables with a sequence of *let* expressions which bind general expressions to variables. A general expression is either a *basic expression* (e), a *bag expression* (μ), or an *aggregate expression* (fold$(e, f)(\mu)$ or foldByKey$(e, f)(\mu)$). The expression cartesian(μ, μ') returns the cartesian product of μ and μ'. map$(f)(\mu)$ produces a *Bag* by applying the unary UDF f to every element x of μ. filter$(f)(\mu)$ evaluates to a copy of μ, except that all elements in μ which do not satisfy f are removed. The aggregate expression fold$(e, f)(\mu)$ accumulates the results obtained by iteratively applying the binary UDF f to every element x in a *Bag* μ in some arbitrary order together with the accumulated result obtained so far, which is initialized to the *initial element* e. If μ is empty, then fold$(e, f)(\mu) = e$. The foldByKey(e, f) operation applied on a *Bag* μ of record type $K \times V$ produces a *Bag* of pairs, where every key $k \in K$ which appears in μ is associated with the result obtained by applying fold(e, f) to the *Bag* containing all the values associated with k in μ.

We denote the meaning of a SparkLite program P by $[\![P]\!]$, which receives *input environments* ρ_0, assigning values to P's formal variables, to either bags or basic types. (See [13, Sect. 7].)

Remarks. We assume that the signature of UDFs given to either *map, filter, fold* or *foldByKey* match the type of the *Bag* on which they are applied. Also, to ensure that the meaning of fold$(e, f)(r)$ and foldByKey$(e, f)(r)$ is well defined, i.e., we require, as Spark does [17], that f be commutative on its second argument: $\forall x, y_1, y_2. f(f(x, y_1), y_2) = f(f(x, y_2), y_1)$.

4 Verifying Equivalence of SparkLite Programs

Programs P_1 and P_2 are *comparable* if they receive the same sequence of formal input parameters, and produce the same output type. They are *equivalent* if, in addition, for any input environment ρ_0, it holds that $[\![P_1]\!](\rho_0) = [\![P_2]\!](\rho_0)$. We assume that we only check the equivalence of comparable programs. Also, without loss of generality, we define programs without *let* expressions; as variables are never reassigned, these can always be eliminated by substituting every variable by its definition. We can now state our result regarding decidability of *NoAgg* programs, defined as programs without aggregate terms. (cf. [13, Sect. 9].)

Theorem 1. *The equivalence of programs in the NoAgg class is decidable.*

Unsurprisingly, however, equivalence in the general case is undecidable. The reduction in [13, Theorem 2] from the halting problem for 2-counter machines shows that verifying equivalence of $AggOne^p$ programs, is an undecidable problem.

Theorem 2. *The problem of deciding whether two arbitrary $AggOne^p$ SparkLite programs are equivalent is undecidable.*

4.1   Program Terms

The first step of our technique is the construction of *program terms*: Given a program P with main expression η, we generate a *program term* $\phi(P)$ which, roughly speaking, reflects the effect of the program on arbitrary elements taken from its input bags. It is obtained by applying the translation function ϕ, shown in Fig. 6, on P's main expression. ϕ recursively traverses the expression and generates a logical term over the vocabulary of built-in operations and UDFs defined in P. The base case of the recursion is input bag variables r, which ϕ replaces with fresh variables $\mathbf{x}_r$. We refer to these variables as *representative variables*. Translation of a SparkLite operation on *Bags* produces a term corresponding to the application of its UDF on a single *Bag* element, which is a new bag expression: A $\texttt{map}(f)(\mu)$ operation is translated into the expression received by applying the lambda expression that corresponds to f, on the program term of μ. A $\texttt{filter}(f)(\mu)$ operation is translated to an *ite* expression which returns the program term of μ on the *then* branch and $\bot$ on the *else* branch. The $\texttt{cartesian}(\mu, \mu')$ operation is translated to a pair of program terms pertaining to its arguments. Note that in the absence of aggregate operations, $\phi(\cdot)$ is a first-order term and thus can be used directly in formulas.

Aggregate operations require iterating over all the elements of μ. Therefore, it is clear that the translation of $\texttt{fold}$ cannot be masqueraded as a first-order

$$
\begin{aligned}
\phi(r) &= \mathbf{x}_r & \phi(\texttt{filter}(f)(\mu)) &= ite(f(\phi(\mu)) = tt, \phi(\mu), \bot) \\
\phi(v) &= v & \phi(\texttt{cartesian}(\mu_1, \mu_2)) &= (\phi(\mu_1), \phi(\mu_2)) \\
\phi(c) &= c,\ c \text{ is const} & \phi(\texttt{fold}(e, f)(\mu)) &= [\phi(\mu)]_{e,f} \\
\phi(\texttt{map}(f)(\mu)) &= f(\phi(\mu))
\end{aligned}
$$

$\phi(e)$ is defined recursively based on the structure of e, e.g. $\phi(e_1 + e_2) = \phi(e_1) + \phi(e_2)$.

Fig. 6. A translation of a general expression to program terms.

term. For $\mathtt{fold}(e, f)(\mu)$ we are using a special operator $[\phi(\mu)]_{i,f}$, where $\phi(\mu)$ is the term pertaining to the bag being folded, i is the initial value, and f is the fold function. We refer to $[\phi(\mu)]_{i,f}$ as an aggregate term.

RepVarSet. For an expression μ consisting only of input bags and input parameters of basic types, $RepVarSet(\mu)$ denotes the set of all representative variables corresponding to the input bags appearing in μ. We can thus similarly define $RepVarSet(P)$ for the main expression of P. $\mathsf{FV}(P)$ denotes the entire set of free variables (both representative and non-bag inputs) in the program term of P.

Example 1. Consider the main expression $\eta = \mathtt{filter}(geq(100))(\mathtt{map}(double)(R))$ of the program $P1''$ obtained by inlining the *let* expressions in program $P1$ (see Sect. 2), defining the doubling function as $double = \lambda x.2 * x$, and instantiating the parametric function $geq = \lambda y.\lambda x.x \geq y$ to act as the condition of the filter. The program term of $P1''$ is $\phi(P1'') = ite(2 * \mathbf{x}_R \geq 100, 2 * \mathbf{x}_R, \bot)$. Intuitively, we can learn how $P1''$ affects every element of, e.g., input $Bag\{\!\{2, 2, 103, 64\}\!\}$, by treating $\phi(P1'')$ as a "function" of $\mathbf{x}_R$ and "applying" it to 2, 2, 103, and 64. It is easy to see that $\mathsf{FV}(P1'') = RepVarSet(P1'') = \{\mathbf{x}_R\}$. Consider now instead $P5'$ also obtained by inlining of the *let* expressions in $P5$. In this case, $\phi(P5'') = [\mathbf{x}_R]_{+\infty, \lambda A, (x,y).ite(A<y, A, y)} = 100$.

4.2 Verifying Equivalence of SparkLite Programs with Aggregation

In this section, we discuss the generation of inductive hypotheses for programs with aggregations. We focus on the $AggOne^p$ and $AggOne^p_{sync}$ methods (recall Table 1), applicable on programs with a single fold operation. For space reasons, we relegate to [13, Sects. 13 and 14] the discussion of the other methods: $AggOne^b$, $AggMult^p$ and $AggOneK^b$, which are all sound techniques generalizing $AggOne^p$.

We note that in the presence of $\mathtt{fold}$ operations, The resulting terms are no longer legal terms in first order logic, and thus, we cannot use them directly in formulae. Instead, we extract out of them a set of formulae whose validity, intuitively, amounts to the establishment of an inductive invariant regarding the effect of $\mathtt{fold}$ operations.

Verifying Equivalence of $AggOne^p$ Programs. Arguably, the simplest class of programs with aggregations is the class of programs that return a primitive expression that depends on the result of the aggregation operation. Technically, a pair of SparkLite programs is in class $AggOne^p$ if each program P in the pair belongs to $AggOne^p$, i.e., there is a an expression g in Presburger Arithmetic with a single free variable x such that the program term of P is of the form $g[[\phi(\mu)]_{i,f}/x]$, where μ is a bag expression that does not include $\mathtt{fold}$ or $\mathtt{foldByKey}$ operations; that is, if $\phi(P)$ can be obtained by substituting x in g with the aggregate term pertaining to the application of a $\mathtt{fold}$ operation on μ. In the following, we refer to g as P's *top expression*. By abuse of notation, we use the functional notation $g(t)$ as a shorthand for $g[t/x]$, the expression obtained by substituting the term t with g's free variable. Similarly, given an expression e with two free variables x and y, we write $e(t_1, t_2)$ as a shorthand for $e[t_1/x, t_2/y]$.

Lemma 1 formalizes the sound method that we used in Sect. 2 to show that $P3$ and $P4$ (see Fig. 2) are equivalent.

Lemma 1 (Sound Method for Verifying Equivalence of Agg^1 Programs). *Let P_1 and P_2 be $AggOne^p$ programs such that $\mathsf{FV}(P_1) = \mathsf{FV}(P_2)$. Assume that $\phi(P_1) = g_1([\phi(\mu_1)]_{i_1, f_1})$ and $\phi(P_2) = g_2([\phi(\mu_2)]_{i_2, f_2})$, where $f_1 = \lambda x, y. e_1$ and $f_2 = \lambda x, y. e_2$. P_1 and P_2 are equivalent if the following conditions hold:*

$$RepVarSet(\mu_1) = RepVarSet(\mu_2) \tag{4}$$

$$\mathbf{valid}\big(\forall \mathsf{FV}(P_1). g_1(i_1) = g_2(i_2)\big) \tag{5}$$

$$\mathbf{valid}\big(\forall \mathsf{FV}(P_1), M_1, M_2. g_1(M_1) = g_2(M_2) \implies \tag{6}$$
$$g_1(e_1(M_1, \phi(\mu_1))) = g_2(e_2(M_2, \phi(\mu_2))))\big)$$

Intuitively, Eqs. (5) and (6) formalize the concept of inductive reasoning described in Sect. 2 for the base of the induction and the induction step, respectively. Equation (4) requires that the free variables of the folded bag expressions use the same representative variables. It ensures that the two `fold` operations iterate over bags of the same size. Note that we do not require that the bag folded by the two programs be equivalent. However, in Eq. (6) we still use the fact that corresponding elements in the two folded bags can be produced by instantiating the program terms $e_{1,2}$ with corresponding elements from the input bags.

Complete Verification Techniques for Subclasses of $AggOne^p$. Lemma 1 provides a sound, but incomplete, verification technique. This means that there are cases in which a pair of equivalent programs does not satisfy one or more of the requirements of Lemma 1. Luckily, some of these cases can be identified and subsequently have their equivalence verified using other methods. As a simple example, in [13] we show that the equivalence of SparkLite programs whose `fold` operations return a constant value can be reduce to the (decidable) problem of verifying equivalence of $NoAgg$ programs. We now describe the $AggOne^p_{sync}$ verification method.

In Sect. 2 we showed that although programs $P5$ and $P6$ do not satisfy the requirements of Lemma 1, we can verify their equivalence using a more specialized verification technique, $AggOne^p_{sync}$. We now present a more detailed discussion of $AggOne^p_{sync}$. We recall that the three main properties of pairs of programs that $AggOne^p_{sync}$ applies to are (1) both belong to $AggOne^p$; (2) the folds in both programs can be collapsed; and (3) the process of collapsing the folds can be done in synchrony.

The collapsing property states that any value produced by consecutive applications of the `fold` UDF can be obtained by a single application. For example, if the UDF is $sum = \lambda x, y. x + y$ and the initial value is 0, then the result obtained by applying sum consecutively on any two elements a and b can also be obtained by applying sum once on $a + b$. Also, recall that the bag being folded contains elements which are obtained via a sequence of `map`, `filter` and `cartesian` operations applied to elements taken out of the input bags. Synchronized collapsing occurs when given the same input elements to two consecutive applications of the `fold` UDF, it is possible to collapse them both using the same input element.

Thus, *synchronized collapsing* is a semantic property of `fold` UDFs, aggregated terms, and initial values of a pair of programs that belong to $AggOne^p_{sync}$. In the following, we denote by $FV_r(P)$ and $FV_b(P)$ the subsets of $FV(P)$ comprised of bag, respectively, non-bag, input formal parameters.

Definition 1 (The $AggOne^p_{sync}$ Class). *Let P_1 and P_2 be $AggOne^p$ programs such that $FV(P_1) = FV(P_2)$. Assume that $\phi(P_1) = g_1([\phi(\mu_1)]_{i_1,f_1})$ and $\phi(P_2) = g_2([\phi(\mu_2)]_{i_2,f_2})$, where $f_1 = \lambda x, y. e_1$ and $f_2 = \lambda x, y. e_2$. We say that P_1 and P_2 belong together to $AggOne^p_{sync}$, denoted by $\langle P_1, P_2 \rangle \in AggOne^p_{sync}$, if the following conditions hold:*

$$RepVarSet(\mu_1) = RepVarSet(\mu_2) \tag{7}$$

$$\forall \bar{b}, \bar{u}, \bar{v}. \exists \bar{w}. \, e_1(i_1, \phi(\mu_1))[\bar{b}/FV_b, \bar{w}/FV_r] = \tag{8}$$
$$e_1((e_1(i_1, \phi(\mu_1))[\bar{b}/FV_b, \bar{u}/FV_r], \phi(\mu_1)[\bar{b}/FV_b, \bar{v}/FV_r])$$
$$\wedge \, e_2(i_2, \phi(\mu_2))[\bar{b}/FV_b, \bar{w}/FV_r] =$$
$$e_2((e_2(i_2, \phi(\mu_2))[\bar{b}/FV_b, \bar{u}/FV_r], \phi(\mu_2)[\bar{b}/FV_b, \bar{v}/FV_r])$$

Note that in Eq. (8), all applications of the `fold` UDF functions agree on the values of the non-bag input formal parameters used to "generate" the accumulated elements. Also note that checking if $\langle P_1, P_2 \rangle \in AggOne^p_{sync}$ involves determining the validity of an additional decidable formula, namely Eq. (8). Theorem 3 shows that verifying the equivalence of a pair of programs in $AggOne^p_{sync}$ effectively reduces to checking a single application of the `fold` UDFs.

Theorem 3 (Equivalence in $AggOne^p_{sync}$ is Decidable). *Let P_1 and P_2 be $AggOne^p$ programs as in Lemma 1, such that $\langle P_1, P_2 \rangle \in AggOne^p_{sync}$. P_1 and P_2 are equivalent if and only if the following holds:*

$$\mathbf{valid}(\forall FV(P_1). \, g_1(i_1) = g_2(i_2)) \tag{9}$$

$$\mathbf{valid}\left(\begin{array}{l} \forall \bar{v}, \bar{w}, M_1, M_2. \, (\, M_1 = e_1(i_1, \phi(\mu_1))[\bar{v}/FV(P_1)]) \wedge \\ M_2 = e_2(i_2, \phi(\mu_2))[\bar{v}/FV(P_1)])) \implies Ind \end{array} \right) \tag{10}$$

$$\text{where } Ind = \big(g_1(M_1) = g_2(M_2) \implies$$
$$g_1(e_1(M_1, \phi(\mu_1))) = g_2(e_2(M_2, \phi(\mu_2))))[\bar{w}/FV(P_1))]$$

5   Prototype Implementation

We developed a prototype implementation verifying the equivalence of Spark programs. The tool is written in Python 2.7 and uses the Z3 Python interface to prove formulas. We ran our experiments on a 64-bit Windows host with a quad core 3.40 GHz Intel Core i7-6700U processor, with 32 GB memory. The tool

Test	Description	Eq.	Ver.	Method
P1,P2	From Section 2. Showing map and filter commutativity.	Y	Y	$NoAgg$
P1,P2′	P2 changed to filter elements smaller than 100.	N	Y	$NoAgg$
P3, P4	From Section 2. Also proved using $AggOne^p_{sync}$.	Y	Y	$AggOne^p$
P5, P6	From Section 2.	Y	Y	$AggOne^p_{sync}$
P7, P8	From Section 2. Describe distribution of passing students' grades.	Y	Y	$AggOneK^b$
P9, P10	Distributivity of map UDFs with respect to join.	Y	Y	$NoAgg$
P9′, P10	Map UDFs which are not distributive with respect to join.	N	Y	$NoAgg$
P11, P12	Distributivity of filter UDFs with respect to join.	Y	Y	$NoAgg$
P13, P14	Count on a filtered bag / sum on a bag mapped to a constant (0/1).	Y	Y	$AggOne^p$
P15, P16	Modular arithmetic: Divisibility by 5 of the sum of the elements, vs. divisibility by 5 of the sum of the elements, each multiplied by 3.	Y	Y	$AggOne^p_{sync}$
P15′, P16′	Modular arithmetic: Divisibility by 6 instead of 5 is not retained.	N	Y	$AggOne^p_{sync}$
P15″, P16″	Modular arithmetic: Divisibility by 5 of the elements' count, vs. divisibility by 5 of the count after multiplying the elements by 3.	Y	N	$AggOne^p$
P17, P18	Maximum is expressed as inverted minimum of inverted elememts.	Y	Y	$AggOne^p_{sync}$
P17′, P18	As above, but there is a bug in the initial value of the maximum.	N	Y	$AggOne^p_{sync}$
P19, P20	Summation (by key) of positive vs. non-negative integers.	Y	Y	$AggOneK^b$
P21, P22	Summation of both keys and values in different ways.	Y	Y	$AggOneK^b$

Fig. 7. Highlighted test cases. Note that the join operator was implemented as a combination of `cartesian`, `filter` and `map` operations, with designated UDFs.

accepts pairs of Spark program written using the Python interface, determines the class of SparkLite program they belong to, and verifies their equivalence using the appropriate method.

A total of 23 test-cases of both equivalent and non-equivalent instances were tested, including all the examples from this paper. In Fig. 7, we highlight test cases inspired by real Spark uses taken from [17,28] and online resources (e.g., open-source Spark clients), and belong to one of the defined SparkLite classes. The full list of tested programs appears in [13, Sect. 15]. They include join optimizations, different aggregations, and various UDFs. For each instance, the tool either verifies that the given programs are equivalent, or produces a counterexample, that is, an input for which the programs produce different outputs. Each example was analyzed in less than 0.5 s. It is also interesting to note that most examples with a primitive aggregation output are verified using $AggOne^p_{sync}$ and not $AggOne^p$, indicating that the $AggOne^p_{sync}$ class is not esoteric, but wide enough to cover useful programs. Our tool was able to prove the equivalence of all equivalent programs, and find counterexamples for inequivalent ones, with the exception of $P15''$ and $P16''$ which belong to $AggOne^p$. While it is immediate that these programs are equivalent (we note the intermediate fold results in both programs are the same, and apply the same transformation on the fold result), our tool was not able to show the equivalence. This is because the $AggOne^p_{sync}$ technique is not applicable to this particular example, as $count$ is not a collapsible fold function, and the $AggOne^p$ technique is effective only when the equivalence claim is inductive, which is not the case here.

6 Related Work and Conclusion

The problem considered (i.e., determining equivalence of expressions accessing a dataset) is a classic topic in database theory. Query containment and equivalence were first studied in seminal work by Chandra and Merlin [2]. This work was extended in numerous papers, e.g., [18] for queries with inequalities and [4] for acyclic queries. Of most relevance to this paper are the extensions to queries evaluated under bag and bag-set semantics [3], and to aggregate queries, e.g., [7,8,14]. The latter papers consider specific aggregate functions, such as min, count, sum and average, or aggregate functions defined by operations over abelian monoids. In comparison, we do not restrict UDFs to monoids, and provide a different characterization for decidability.

In the field of verification and programming languages, several works address properties of relational algebra operators. Most notably, *Cosette* [6], is a fully automated prover for SQL equivalences, which provides a proof or a counterexample to equivalence by utilizing both a theorem prover and a solver. The approach supports standard SQL features as well as predetermined aggregation functions such as count, sum, and average. On the other hand, by addressing Spark programs, our approach focuses on custom UDFs for selects, projections, and aggregation. Similarly, *Spec#* [20] has a fixed set of comprehensions such as sum, count, min and max, fitted into templates with both filters and expression terms akin to map, which are encoded into the SMT solver using specialized axioms, e.g. the distribution of plus over min/max. Our techniques, on the other hand, extract automatically properties of comprehensions to define suitable verification conditions for equivalence. El Ghazi and Taghdiri [11] took the SMT solver approach to verify relational constraints in Alloy [16], in order to be able to provide proofs, and not just counterexamples. There is, however, no guarantee on completeness, or the ability of the solver to provide a proof. It differs from this work, which carefully defines criteria for decidability and soundness, even in the expense of expressivity. Loncaric et al. [21] utilize a small-model property of sets to verify synthesized data structures which is similar to the one we leverage in the *NoAgg* method. We extend this property to bags and aggregate operations. Smith and Albarghouthi [25] presented an algorithm for synthesizing Spark programs by analyzing user examples fitted into higher-order sketches. They use SMTs to verify commutativity of the *fold* UDFs. Chen et al. [5], studied the decidability of the latter problem. We use SMT to verify program equality assuming that the *fold* UDFs are commutative. In this sense, our approaches are complementary.

There are also generic frameworks for verifying functional programs, such as F^* [27] and *Liquid Types* [23,24]. These prove program safety via type checking, which also utilizes SMT to check validity of implications. Both approaches require additional manual effort to verify programs like the ones we explore: in *Liquid Types*, there is no notion of equivalence, so a suitable summary must be given that holds for both programs. In F^*, equivalence can be expressed via assertions, but verifying assertions in F^* is incomplete with respect to inductive data types, such as lists. Appropriate invariants must be provided manually, essentially the same ones that are constructed automatically in this paper. Another approach to verifying functional programs is applied by *Leon* [1,26], whose engine is based on decision procedures for the quantifier-free theory of algebraic data types with different fold functions, which allow handling recursive functions with first-order constraints. However, the approach relies on finite unrolling of the recursive calls, thus it cannot verify the equivalence of two programs when the equivalence property is not inductive by itself. In contrast, our approach is successful because of the novel specialized treatment of synchronous collapsible UDFs.

Dafny [19] supports functional programming, inductive data types, higher-order functions, and also provides some automatic induction. Dafny can automatically verify our *NoAgg* test cases. However, applying it to certain *AggOne^p* programs required supplying auxiliary lemmas. For example, verifying the equivalence of $P15$ and $P16$ required the use of a lemma asserting that multiplying the sum of elements in a bag by three produce the same result as summing the bag obtained by multiplying every element by three. Essentially, the lemma establishes equivalence relations between subprograms, and gives rise to a possible heuristic extension of our tool by searching for relations between subprograms.

Conclusion. The main conceptual contribution of this paper is that the problem of checking program equivalence of SparkLite programs, which reflect an interesting subset of Spark programs, can be addressed via a reduction to the validity of formulas in a decidable fragment of first-order logic. We believe the foundations laid in this paper will lead to the development of tools that handle formal verification and optimization of more classes of programs written in Spark and similar frameworks, e.g., ones with nested aggregations and unions.

References

1. Blanc, R., Kuncak, V., Kneuss, E., Suter, P.: An overview of the Leon verification system: verification by translation to recursive functions. In: Proceedings of the 4th Workshop on Scala, SCALA 2013, pp. 1:1–1:10. ACM, New York (2013)
2. Chandra, A.K., Merlin, P.M.: Optimal implementation of conjunctive queries in relational data bases. In: Proceedings of the Ninth Annual ACM Symposium on Theory of Computing, STOC 1977, pp. 77–90. ACM, New York (1977)
3. Chaudhuri, S., Vardi, M.Y.: Optimization of real conjunctive queries. In: Proceedings of the Twelfth ACM SIGACT-SIGMOD-SIGART Symposium on Principles of Database Systems, PODS 1993, pp. 59–70. ACM, New York (1993)
4. Chekuri, C., Rajaraman, A.: Conjunctive query containment revisited. Theoret. Comput. Sci. **239**(2), 211–229 (2000)
5. Chen, Y.-F., Hong, C.-D., Sinha, N., Wang, B.-Y.: Commutativity of reducers. In: Baier, C., Tinelli, C. (eds.) TACAS 2015. LNCS, vol. 9035, pp. 131–146. Springer, Heidelberg (2015). doi:10.1007/978-3-662-46681-0_9
6. Chu, S., Wang, C., Weitz, K., Cheung, A.: Cosette: an automated prover for SQL. In: Online Proceedings of the 8th Biennial Conference on Innovative Data Systems Research, CIDR 2017, 8–11 January 2017, Chaminade, CA, USA (2017)
7. Cohen, S., Nutt, W., Sagiv, Y.: Deciding equivalences among conjunctive aggregate queries. J. ACM **54**(2), 5 (2007)
8. Cohen, S., Sagiv, Y., Nutt, W.: Equivalences among aggregate queries with negation. ACM Trans. Comput. Logic **6**(2), 328–360 (2005)

9. Cooper, D.C.: Theorem proving in arithmetic without multiplication. Mach. Intell. **7**, 300 (1972)
10. De Moura, L., Bjørner, N.: Z3: an efficient SMT solver. In: Ramakrishnan, C.R., Rehof, J. (eds.) TACAS 2008. LNCS, vol. 4963, pp. 337–340. Springer, Heidelberg (2008). doi:10.1007/978-3-540-78800-3_24
11. El Ghazi, A.A., Taghdiri, M.: Relational reasoning via SMT solving. In: Butler, M., Schulte, W. (eds.) FM 2011. LNCS, vol. 6664, pp. 133–148. Springer, Heidelberg (2011). doi:10.1007/978-3-642-21437-0_12
12. Fischer, M.J., Rabin, M.O.: Super-exponential complexity of Presburger arithmetic. Technical report, Massachusetts Institue of Technology, Cambridge, MA, USA (1974)
13. Grossman, S., Cohen, S., Itzhaky, S., Rinetzky, N., Sagiv, M.: Verifying equivalence of spark programs. Technical report, Tel Aviv University, April 2017. http://www. cs.tau.ac.il/%7Eshellygr/pubs/sparkeq-tr.pdf
14. Grumbach, S., Rafanelli, M., Tininini, L.: On the equivalence and rewriting of aggregate queries. Acta Inf. **40**(8), 529–584 (2004)
15. Hasegawa, M.: Decomposing typed lambda calculus into a couple of categorical programming languages. In: Pitt, D., Rydeheard, D.E., Johnstone, P. (eds.) CTCS 1995. LNCS, vol. 953, pp. 200–219. Springer, Heidelberg (1995). doi:10. 1007/3-540-60164-3_28
16. Jackson, D.: Software Abstractions: Logic, Language, and Analysis. The MIT Press, Cambridge (2006)
17. Karau, H., Konwinski, A., Wendell, P., Zaharia, M.: Learning Spark: Lightning-Fast Big Data Analytics, 1st edn. O'Reilly Media Inc., Sebastopol (2015)
18. Klug, A.: On conjunctive queries containing inequalities. J. ACM **35**(1), 146–160 (1988)
19. Leino, K.R.M.: Dafny: an automatic program verifier for functional correctness. In: Clarke, E.M., Voronkov, A. (eds.) LPAR 2010. LNCS (LNAI), vol. 6355, pp. 348–370. Springer, Heidelberg (2010). doi:10.1007/978-3-642-17511-4_20
20. Leino, K.R.M., Monahan, R.: Reasoning about comprehensions with first-order SMT solvers. In: Proceedings of the 2009 ACM Symposium on Applied Computing, SAC 2009, pp. 615–622. ACM, New York (2009)
21. Loncaric, C., Torlak, E., Ernst, M.D.: Fast synthesis of fast collections. In: Proceedings of the 37th ACM SIGPLAN Conference on Programming Language Design and Implementation, PLDI 2016, pp. 355–368. ACM, New York (2016)
22. Presburger, M.: Über die vollständigkeit eines gewissen systems der arithmetik ganzer zahlen, in welchem die addition als einzige operation hervor. Comptes Rendus du I congrès de Mathématiciens des Pays Slaves, pp. 92–101 (1929)
23. Rondon, P.M., Kawaguchi, M., Jhala, R.: Liquid types. In: 35th ACM SIGPLAN-SIGACT Symposium on Principles of Programming Languages (POPL), pp. 159–169. ACM, January 2008
24. Rondon, P.M., Kawaguchi, M., Jhala, R.: Low-level liquid types. In: 37th ACM SIGPLAN-SIGACT Symposium on Principles of Programming Languages (POPL), pp. 131–144. ACM, January 2010
25. Smith, C., Albarghouthi, A.: Mapreduce program synthesis. In: Proceedings of the 37th ACM SIGPLAN Conference on Programming Language Design and Implementation, PLDI 2016, pp. 326–340. ACM, New York (2016)
26. Suter, P., Dotta, M., Kuncak, V.: Decision procedures for algebraic data types with abstractions. In: Proceedings of the 37th Annual ACM SIGPLAN-SIGACT Symposium on Principles of Programming Languages, POPL 2010, pp. 199–210. ACM, New York (2010)

27. Swamy, N., Hriţcu, C., Keller, C., Rastogi, A., Delignat-Lavaud, A., Forest, S., Bhargavan, K., Fournet, C., Strub, P.-Y., Kohlweiss, M., Zinzindohoue, J.-K., Zanella-Béguelin, S.: Dependent types and multi-monadic effects in F*. In: 43rd ACM SIGPLAN-SIGACT Symposium on Principles of Programming Languages (POPL), pp. 256–270. ACM, January 2016
28. Wills, J., Owen, S., Laserson, U., Ryza, S.: Advanced Analytics with Spark: Patterns for Learning from Data at Scale, 1st edn. O'Reilly Media Inc., Sebastopol (2015)
29. Zaharia, M., Chowdhury, M., Das, T., Dave, A., Ma, J., McCauly, M., Franklin, M.J., Shenker, S., Stoica, I.: Resilient distributed datasets: a fault-tolerant abstraction for in-memory cluster computing. In: Presented as Part of the 9th USENIX Symposium on Networked Systems Design and Implementation (NSDI 12), pp. 15–28. USENIX, San Jose (2012)
30. Zaharia, M., Chowdhury, M., Franklin, M.J., Shenker, S., Stoica, I.: Spark: cluster computing with working sets. In: Proceedings of the 2nd USENIX Conference on Hot Topics in Cloud Computing, HotCloud 2010, p. 10. USENIX Association, Berkeley (2010)

Synchronization Synthesis for Network Programs

Jedidiah McClurg[1]([✉]), Hossein Hojjat[2], and Pavol Černý[1]

[1] University of Colorado Boulder, Boulder, USA
jedidiah.mcclurg@colorado.edu
[2] Rochester Institute of Technology, Rochester, USA

Abstract. In software-defined networking (SDN), a controller program updates the forwarding rules installed on network packet-processing devices in response to events. Such programs are often physically distributed, running on several nodes of the network, and this distributed setting makes programming and debugging especially difficult. Furthermore, bugs in these programs can lead to serious problems such as packet loss and security violations. In this paper, we propose a program synthesis approach that makes it easier to write distributed controller programs. The programmer can specify each sequential process, and add a declarative specification of paths that packets are allowed to take. The synthesizer then inserts enough synchronization among the distributed controller processes such that the declarative specification will be satisfied by all packets traversing the network. Our key technical contribution is a counterexample-guided synthesis algorithm that furnishes network controller processes with the synchronization constructs required to prevent any races causing specification violations. Our programming model is based on Petri nets, and generalizes several models from the networking literature. Importantly, our programs can be implemented in a way that prevents races between updates to individual switches and in-flight packets. To our knowledge, this is the first counterexample-guided technique that automatically adds synchronization constructs to Petri-net-based programs. We demonstrate that our prototype implementation can fix realistic concurrency bugs described previously in the literature, and that our tool can readily scale to network topologies with 1000+ nodes.

1 Introduction

Software-defined networking (SDN) enables programmers or *network operators* to more easily implement important applications such as traffic engineering, distributed firewalls, network virtualization, etc. These applications are typically *event-driven*, in the sense that the packet-processing behavior can change in response to network events such as topology changes, shifts in traffic load, or arrival of packets at various network nodes. SDN enables this type of event-driven behavior via a *controller machine* that manages the network *configuration*, i.e., the set of *forwarding rules* installed on the network *switches*. The programmer can write code which runs on the controller, as well as instruct the switches to install custom forwarding rules, which inspect incoming packets and move them to other switches or send them to the controller for custom processing.

© Springer International Publishing AG 2017
R. Majumdar and V. Kunčak (Eds.): CAV 2017, Part II, LNCS 10427, pp. 301–321, 2017.
DOI: 10.1007/978-3-319-63390-9_16

Concurrency in Network Programs. Although SDN provides the abstraction of a *centralized* controller machine, in reality, network control is often physically distributed, with controller processes running on multiple network nodes [13]. The fact that these distributed programs control a network which is *itself* a distributed packet-forwarding system means that event-driven network applications can be especially difficult to write and debug. In particular, there are two types of races that can occur, resulting in incorrect behavior. First, there are races between updates of forwarding rules at individual switches, or between packets that are in-flight during updates. Second, there are races among the different processes of the distributed controller. We call the former *packet races*, and the latter *controller races*. Bugs resulting from either of these types of races can lead to serious problems such as packet loss and security violations.

Illustrative Example. Let us examine the difficulties of writing distributed controller programs, in regards to the two types of races. Consider the network topology in Fig. 1a. In the initial configuration, packets entering at $H1$ are forwarded through $S1, S5, S2$ to $H2$. There are two controllers (not shown), $C1$ and $C2$—controller $C1$ manages the upper part of the network ($H1, S1, S5, S3, H3$), and $C2$ manages the lower part ($H2, S2, S5, S4, H4$). Now imagine that the network operator wants to take down the forwarding rules that send packets from $H1$ to $H2$, and instead install rules to forward packets from $H3$ to $H4$. Furthermore, the operator wants to ensure that the following property ϕ holds at all times: *all packets entering the network from $H1$ must exit at $H2$*. When developing the program to do this, the network operator must consider the following:

- Packet race: If $C1$ removes the rule that forwards from $S1$ to $S5$ before removing the rule that forwards from $H1$ to $S5$, then a packet entering at $H1$ will be dropped at $S1$, violating specification ϕ.
- Controller race: Suppose $C1$ makes no changes, and $C2$ adds rules that forward from $S5$ to $S4$, and from $S4$ to $H4$. In the resulting configuration, a packet entering at $H1$ can be forwarded to $H4$, again violating ϕ.

Our Approach. We present a program synthesis approach that makes it easier to write distributed controller programs. The programmer can specify each sequential process (e.g., $C1$ and $C2$ in the previous example), and add a declarative specification of paths that packets are allowed to take (e.g., ϕ in the previous example). The synthesizer then inserts *synchronization constructs* that constrain the interactions among the controller processes to ensure that the specification is always satisfied by any packets traversing the network. Effectively, this allows the programmer to reduce the amount of effort spent on keeping track of possible interleavings of controller processes and inserting low-level synchronization constructs, and instead focus on writing a declarative specification which describes allowed packet paths. In the examples we have considered, we find these specifications to be a clear and easy way to write desired correctness properties.

Network Programming Model. In our approach, similar to network programming languages like OpenState [6], and Kinetic [20], we allow a network program to be described as a set of concurrently-operating finite state machines (FSMs) consisting of event-driven transitions between global network states. We generalize this by allowing the input network program to be a set of *event nets*, which are 1-safe Petri nets where each transition corresponds to a network event, and each place corresponds to a set of forwarding rules. This model extends network event structures [25] to enable straightforward modeling of programs with loops. An advantage of extending this particular programming model is that its programs can be efficiently implemented without packet races (see Sect. 3 for details).

Problem Statement. Our synthesizer has two inputs: (1) a set of event nets representing sequential processes of the distributed controller, and (2) a linear temporal logic (LTL) specification of paths that packets are allowed to take. For example, the programmer can specify properties such as "packets from $H1$ must pass through Middlebox $S5$ before exiting the network." The output is an event net consisting of the input event nets and added synchronization constructs, such that all packets traversing the network satisfy the specification. In other words, the added synchronization eliminates problems caused by controller races. Since we use event nets, which can be implemented without packet races, both types of races are eliminated in the final implementation of the distributed controller.

Algorithm. Our main contribution is a counterexample-guided inductive synthesis (CEGIS) algorithm for event nets. This consists of (1) a *repair engine* that synthesizes a candidate event net from the input event nets and a finite set of known counterexample traces, and (2) a *verifier* that checks whether the candidate satisfies the LTL property, producing a counterexample trace if not. The repair engine uses SMT to produce a candidate event net by adding synchronization constructs which ensure that it does not contain the counterexample traces discovered so far. Repairs are chosen from a variety of constructs (barriers, locks, condition variables). Given a candidate event net, the verifier checks whether it is deadlock-free (i.e., there is an execution where all processes can proceed without deadlock), whether it is 1-safe, and whether it satisfies the LTL property. We encode this as an LTL model-checking problem—the check fails (and returns a counterexample) if the event net exhibits an incorrect interleaving.

Contributions. This paper contains the following contributions:

- We describe *event nets*, a new model for representing concurrent network programs, which extends several previous approaches, enables using and reasoning about many synchronization constructs, and admits an efficient distributed implementation (Sects. 2 and 3).
- We present *synchronization synthesis for event nets*. To our knowledge, this is the first counterexample-guided technique that automatically adds synchronization constructs to Petri-net based programs. Our solution includes a *model checker for event nets*, and an SMT-based *repair engine for event nets* which can insert a variety of synchronization constructs (Sect. 4).
- We show the usefulness and efficiency of our prototype implementation, using several examples featuring network topologies of 1000+ switches (Sect. 5).

2   Network Programming Using Event Nets

Network programs change the network's global forwarding behavior in response to events. Recently proposed approaches such as OpenState [6] and Kinetic [20] allow a network program to be specified as a set of finite state machines, where each state is a static configuration (i.e., a set of forwarding rules at switches), and the transitions are driven by network events (packet arrivals, etc.). In this case, support for concurrency is enabled by allowing FSMs to execute in parallel, and any conflicts of the global forwarding state due to concurrency are avoided by either requiring the FSMs to be restricted to *disjoint* types of traffic, or by ignoring conflicts entirely. Neither of these options solves the problem—as we will see here (and in the Evaluation), serious bugs can arise due to unexpected interleavings. Overall, network programming languages typically do not have strong support for handling (and reasoning about) *concurrency*, and this is increasingly important, as SDNs are moving to distributed or multithreaded controllers.

Event Nets for Network Programming. We introduce a new approach which extends the finite-state view of network programming with support for concurrency and synchronization. Our model is called *event nets*, an extension of *1-safe Petri nets*, a well-studied framework for concurrency. An event net is a set of *places* (denoted as circles) which are connected via *directed edges* to *events* (denoted as squares). The current state of the program is indicated by a *marking* which assigns at most one *token* to each place, and an event can change the current marking by consuming a token from each of its input places and emitting a token to each of its output places. Since event nets model network programs, each place is labeled with a static network configuration, and at any time, the global configuration is taken as the union of the configurations at the marked places.

Figure 1b shows an example event net. We will use integer IDs (and alternatively, colors) to distinguish static configurations. Figure 1a shows the network topology corresponding to this example. In a given topology, the configurations associated with the event net are drawn in the color of the *places* which contain them, and also labeled with the corresponding place IDs. For example, place 3 in

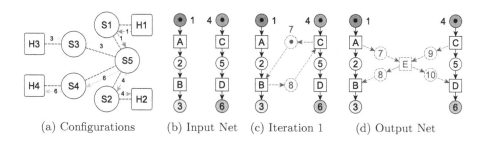

(a) Configurations   (b) Input Net   (c) Iteration 1   (d) Output Net

Fig. 1. Example #1 (Color figure online)

Fig. 1b is orange, and this corresponds to enabling forwarding along the orange path $H3, S3, S5$ (labeled with "3") in the topology shown in Fig. 1a. In the initial state of this event net, places $1, 4$ contain a token, meaning forwarding is initially enabled along the red (1) and green (4) paths.

Event Nets and Synchronization. Event nets allow us to specify synchronization easily. In Fig. 1c, we have added places $7, 8$—this makes event C unable to fire initially (since it does not have a token on input place 8), forcing it to wait until event B fires (B consumes a token from places $2, 7$ and emits a token at 8). Ultimately, we will show how these types of *synchronization skeletons* can be produced automatically. In Fig. 1(b, c, and d), the original event net is shown in black (solid lines), and synchronization constructs produced by our tool are shown in blue (dashed lines). We will now demonstrate by example how our tools works.

Example—Tenant Isolation in a Datacenter. Koponen et al. [21] describe an approach for providing *virtual networks* to *tenants* (users) of a datacenter, allowing them to connect virtual machines (VMs) using virtualized networking functionality (middleboxes, etc.). An important aspect is *isolation* between tenants—one tenant intercepting another tenant's traffic would be a severe security violation.

Let us extend the example described in the Introduction. In Fig. 1a, $S5$ is a physical device initially being used as a virtual middlebox processing Tenant X's traffic, which is being sent along the red (1) and green (4) paths. We wish to perform an update in the datacenter which allows Tenant Y to use $S5$, and moves the processing of Tenant X's traffic to a different physical device. For efficiency, let us use two controllers to execute this update—path 1 is taken down and path 3 is brought up by $C1$, and path 4 is taken down and path 6 is brought up by $C2$. The event net for this program is shown in Fig. 1b. The combinations of configurations $1, 6$ and $4, 3$ both allow traffic to flow between tenants, violating isolation. We can formalize the isolation specification as follows:

1. ϕ_1: *no packet originating at $H1$ should arrive at $H4$*, and
2. ϕ_2: *no packet originating at $H3$ should arrive at $H2$*.

Properties like these which describe *single-packet traces* can be encoded straightforwardly in linear temporal logic (LTL) (note that instead of LTL, we could use the more user-friendly PDL). Given an LTL specification, we ask a *verifier* whether the event net has any reachable marking whose configuration violates the specification. If so, a *counterexample trace* is provided, i.e., a sequence of events (starting from the initial state) which allows the violation. For example, using the specification $\phi_1 \wedge \phi_2$ and the Fig. 1b event net, our verifier informs us that the sequence of events C, D leads to a property violation—in particular, when the tokens are at places $6, 1$, traffic is allowed along the path $H1, S1, S5, S4, H4$, violating ϕ_1. Next, we ask a *repair engine* to suggest a fix for the event net which disallows the trace C, D, and in this case, our tool produces Fig. 1c. Again, we call the verifier, which now gives us the counterexample trace A, B (when the tokens are at $4, 3$, traffic is allowed along the path

$H3, S3, S5, S2, H2$, violating property ϕ_2). When we ask the repair engine to produce a fix which avoids *both* traces C, D and A, B, we obtain the event net shown in Fig. 1d. A final call to the verifier confirms that this event net satisfies both properties.

The synchronization skeleton produced in Fig. 1d functions as a *barrier*—it prevents tokens from arriving at 6 or 3 until *both* tokens have moved from $4, 1$. This ensures that $1, 4$ must *both* be taken down before bringing up paths $3, 6$. The following sections detail this synchronization synthesis approach.

3 Synchronization Synthesis for Event Nets

Before describing our synthesis algorithm in detail, we first need to formally define the concepts/terminology mentioned so far.

SDN Preliminaries. A *packet pkt* is a record of fields $\{f_1; f_2; \cdots; f_n\}$, where fields f represent properties such as source and destination address, protocol type, etc. The (numeric) values of fields are accessed via the notation $pkt.f$, and field updates are denoted $pkt[f \leftarrow n]$, where n is a numeric value. A *switch sw* is a node in the network with one or more *ports pt*. A *host* is a switch that can be a source or a sink of packets. A *location l* is a switch-port pair $n{:}m$. Locations may be connected by (bidirectional) physical *links* (l_1, l_2). The graph formed using the locations as nodes and links as edges is referred to as the *topology*. We fix the topology for the remainder of this section.

A *located packet lp* $= (pkt, sw, pt)$ is a packet and a location $sw{:}pt$. A *packet-trace (history) h* is a non-empty sequence of located packets. Packet forwarding is dictated by a *network configuration C*. We model C as a relation on located packets: if $C(lp, lp')$, then the network maps lp to lp', possibly changing its location and rewriting some of its fields. Since C is a relation, it allows multiple output packets to be generated from a single input. In a real network, the configuration only forwards packets between ports within each individual switch, but for convenience, we assume that C also captures link behavior (forwarding between switches), i.e. $C((pkt, n_1, m_1), (pkt, n_2, m_2))$ and $C((pkt, n_2, m_2), (pkt, n_1, m_1))$ hold for each link $(n_1{:}m_1, n_2{:}m_2)$. Consider a packet-trace $h = lp_0 lp_1 lp_2 \cdots lp_n$. We say that h is *allowed by* configuration C if and only if $\forall 1 \leq k \leq n.\ C(lp_{k-1}, lp_k)$, and we denote this as $h \in C$.

Petri Net Preliminaries. Our treatment of Petri nets closely follows that of Winskel [35] (Chap. 3). A *Petri net N* is a tuple (P, T, F, M_0), where P is a set of *places* (shown as circles), T is a set of *transitions* (shown as squares), $F \subseteq (P \times T) \cup (T \times P)$ is a set of *directed edges*, and M_0 is multiset of places denoting the *initial marking* (shown as dots on places). For notational convenience, we can view a multiset as a mapping from places to integers, i.e., $M(p)$ denotes the number of times place p appears in multiset M. We require that $P \neq \emptyset$, and $\forall p \in P.\ (M_0(p) > 0 \vee (\exists t \in T.\ ((p, t) \in F \vee (t, p) \in F)))$, and $\forall t \in T.\ \exists p_1, p_2 \in P.\ ((p_1, t) \in F \wedge (t, p_2) \in F)$. Given a transition t, we define its post- and pre-places as $t^\bullet = \{p \in P : (t, p) \in F\}$ and $^\bullet t = \{p \in P : (p, t) \in F\}$ respectively. This can be extended in the obvious way to $T'^\bullet$ and $^\bullet T'$, for subsets T' of T.

A marking indicates the number of *tokens* at each place. We say that a transition $t \in T$ is *enabled* by a marking M if and only if $\forall p \in P. ((p, t) \in F \implies M(p) > 0)$, and we use the notation $T' \subseteq M$ to mean that all $t \in T'$ are enabled by M. A marking M_i can transition into another marking M_{i+1} as dictated by the *firing rule*: $M_i \xrightarrow{T'} M_{i+1} \iff T' \subseteq M_i \wedge M_{i+1} = M_i - {}^\bullet T' + T'^\bullet$, where the $-/+$ operators denote multiset difference/union respectively. The *state graph* of a Petri net is a graph where each node is a marking (the initial node is M_0), and an edge $(M_i \xrightarrow{t} M_j)$ is in the graph if and only if we have $M_i \xrightarrow{\{t\}} M_j$ in the Petri net. A *trace* τ of a Petri net is a sequence $t_0 t_1 \cdots t_n$ such that there exist $M_i \xrightarrow{t_i} M_{i+1}$ in the Petri net's state graph, for all $0 \le i \le n$. We define $markings(t_0 t_1 \cdots t_n)$ to be the sequence $M_0 M_1 \cdots M_{n+1}$, where $M_0 \xrightarrow{t_0} M_1 \xrightarrow{t_1} \cdots \xrightarrow{t_n} M_{n+1}$ is in the state graph. We can *project* a trace onto a Petri net (denoted $\tau \triangleright N$) by removing any transitions in τ which are not in N. A *1-safe* Petri net is a Petri net in which for any marking M_j reachable from the initial marking M_0, we have $\forall x \in N. (0 \le M_j(x) \le 1)$, i.e., there is no more than 1 token at each place.

Event Nets. An *event* is a tuple (ψ, l), where l is a location, and ψ can be any predicate over network state, packet locations, etc. For instance, in [25], an event encodes an arrival of a packet with a header matching a given predicate to a given location. A *labeled net* L is a pair (N, λ), where N is a Petri net, and λ labels each place with a network configuration, and each transition with an event. An *event net* is a labeled net (N, λ) where N is 1-safe.

Semantics of Event Nets. Given event net marking M, we denote the *global configuration* of the network $C(M)$, given as $C(M) = \bigcup_{p \in M} \lambda(p)$. Given event net $E = (N, \lambda)$, let $Tr(E)$ be its set of traces (the set of traces of the underlying N). Given trace τ of an event net, we use $Configs(\tau)$ to denote $\{C(M) : M \in markings(\tau)\}$, i.e., the set of global configurations reachable along that trace.

Given event net E and trace τ in $Tr(E)$, we define $Traces(E, \tau)$, the packet traces allowed by τ and E, i.e., $Traces(E, \tau) = \{h : \exists C \in Configs(\tau). (h \in C)\}$. Note that labeling λ is not used here—we could define a more precise semantics by specifying consistency guarantees on how information about event occurrences propagates (as in [25]), but we instead choose an overapproximate semantics, to be independent of the precise definition of events and consistency guarantees.

Distributed Implementations of Event Nets. In general, an implementation of a network program specifies the initial network configuration, and dictates how the configuration changes (e.g., in response to events). We abstract away the details, defining the semantics of an *implemented network program Pr* as the set $W(Pr)$ of *program traces*, each of which is a set of packet traces. A program trace models a full execution, captured as the packet traces exhibited by the network as the program runs. We do not model packet trace interleavings, as this is not needed for the correctness notion we define. We say that Pr *implements* event net E if $\forall tr \in W(Pr). \exists \tau \in Tr(E). (tr \subseteq Traces(E, \tau))$. Intuitively, this means that each program trace can be explained by a trace of the event net E.

We now sketch a *distributed* implementation of event nets, i.e., one in which decisions and state changes are made locally at switches (and not, e.g., at a centralized controller). In order to produce a (distributed) implementation of event net E, we need to solve two issues (both related to the definition of $Traces(E, \tau)$).

First, we must ensure that each packet is processed by a single configuration (and not a mixture of several). This is solved by *edge* switches—those where packets enter the network from a host. An edge switch fixes the configuration in which a packet *pkt* will be processed, and attaches a corresponding tag to *pkt*.

Second, we must ensure that for each program trace, there exists a trace of E that explains it. The difficulty here stems from the possibility of *distributed conflicts* when the global state changes due to events. For example, in an application where two different switches listen for the same event, and *only the first* switch to detect the event should update the state, we can encounter a conflict where both switches think they are first, and both attempt to update the state. One way to resolve this is by using expensive coordination to reach agreement on which was "first." Another way is to use the following constraint. We define *local event net* to be an event net in which for any two events $e_1 = (\psi_1, l_1)$ and $e_2 = (\psi_2, l_2)$, we have $(^\bullet e_1 \cap {}^\bullet e_2 \neq \emptyset) \Rightarrow (l_1 = l_2)$, i.e., events sharing a common input place must be handled at the same location (*local labeled net* can be defined similarly). A local event net can be implemented without expensive coordination [25].

Theorem 1 (Implementability). *Given a local event net E, there exists a (distributed) implemented network program that implements E.*

The theorem implies that there are no packet races in the implementation, since it guarantees that each packet is never processed in a mix of configurations.

Packet-Trace Specifications. Beyond simply freedom from packet races, we wish to rule out *controller races*, i.e., unwanted interleavings of concurrent events in an event net. In particular, we use LTL to specify formulas that should be satisfied by each packet-trace possible in each global configuration. We use LTL because it is a very natural language for constructing formulas that describe *traces*. For example, if we want to describe traces for which some condition φ *eventually* holds, we can construct the LTL formula $\mathbf{F}\,\varphi$, and if we want to describe traces where φ holds *at each step (globally)*, we can construct the LTL formula $\mathbf{G}\,\varphi$.

Our LTL formulas are over a single packet *pkt*, which has a special field *pkt.loc* denoting its current location. For example, the property $(pkt.loc=H_1 \wedge pkt.dst=H_2 \implies \mathbf{F}\ pkt.loc=H_2)$ means that any packet located at Host 1 destined for Host 2 should eventually reach Host 2. Given a trace τ of an event net, we use $\tau \models \varphi$ to mean that φ holds in each configuration $C \in Configs(\tau)$.

For efficiency, we forbid the next operator. We have found this restricted form of LTL (usually referred to as *stutter-invariant* LTL) to be sufficient for expressing many properties about network configurations.

Processes and Synchronization Skeletons. The input to our algorithm is a set of disjoint local event nets, which we call *processes*—we can use simple pointwise-union of the tuples (denoted as $\bigsqcup$) to represent this as a single local event net

$E = \bigsqcup\{E_1, E_2, \cdots, E_n\}$. Given an event net $E = ((P, T, F, M_0), \lambda)$, a *synchronization skeleton* S for E is a tuple (P', T', F', M_0'), where $P \cap P' = \emptyset$, $T \cap T' = \emptyset$, $F \cap F' = \emptyset$, and $M_0 \cap M_0' = \emptyset$, and where $((P \cup P', T \cup T', F \cup F', M_0 \cup M_0'), \lambda)$ is a labeled net, which we denote $\bigsqcup\{E, S\}$.

Deadlock Freedom and 1-Safety. We want to avoid adding synchronization which fully deadlocks any process E_i. Let $L = \bigsqcup\{E, S\}$ be a labeled net where $E = \bigsqcup\{E_1, E_2, \cdots, E_n\}$, and let P_i, T_i be the places and transitions of each E_i. We say that L is *deadlock-free* if and only if there exists a trace $\tau \in L$ such that $\forall 0 \leq i \leq n, M_j \in markings(\tau), t \in T_i. (((\,^\bullet t \cap P_i) \subseteq M_j) \Rightarrow (\exists M_k \in markings(\tau). (k \geq j \wedge (t^\bullet \cap P_i) \subseteq M_k)))$, i.e. a trace of L where transitions t of each E_i fire as if they experienced no interference from the rest of L. We encode this as an LTL formula, obtaining a *progress* constraint φ_{progr} for E. Similarly, we want to avoid adding synchronization which produces a labeled net that is not 1-safe. We can also encode this as an LTL constraint φ_{1safe}.

Synchronization Synthesis Problem. Given φ and local event net $E = \bigsqcup\{E_1, E_2, \cdots, E_n\}$, find a local labeled net $L = \bigsqcup\{E, S\}$ which *correctly synchronizes* E:

1. $\forall \tau \in Tr(L). ((\tau \triangleright E) \in Tr(E))$, i.e., each τ of L (modulo added events) is a trace of E, and
2. $\forall \tau \in Tr(L). (\tau \models \varphi)$, i.e., all reachable configurations satisfy φ, and
3. $\forall \tau \in Tr(L). (\tau \models \varphi_{1safe})$, i.e., L is 1-safe (L is an event net), and
4. $\exists \tau \in Tr(L). (\tau \models \varphi_{progr})$, i.e., L deadlock-free.

4   Fixing and Checking Synchronization in Event Nets

Our approach is an instance of the CEGIS algorithm in [17], set up to solve problems of the form $\exists L. ((\forall \tau \in L. (\phi(\tau, E, \varphi, \varphi_{1safe}))) \wedge \neg(\forall \tau \in L. (\tau \not\models \varphi_{progr})))$, where E, L are input/output event nets, and ϕ captures 1–3 of the above specification. Our *event net repair engine* (Sect. 4.1) performs synthesis (producing candidates for $\exists$), and our *event net verifier* (Sect. 4.2) performs verification (checking $\forall$). Algorithm 1 shows the pseudocode of our synthesizer. The function *makeProperties* produces the $\varphi_{1safe}, \varphi_{progr}$ formulas discussed in Sect. 3. The following sections describe the other components of the algorithm.

4.1   Repairing Event Nets Using Counterexample Traces

We use SMT to find synchronization constructs to fix a finite set of bugs (given as unwanted event-net traces). Figure 2 shows *synchronization skeletons* which our repair engine adds between processes of the input event net. The *barrier* prevents events b, d from firing until *both* a, c have fired, *condition variable* requires a to fire before c can fire, and *mutex* ensures that events between a and b (inclusive) cannot interleave with the events between c and d (inclusive). Our algorithm explores different combinations of these skeletons, up to a given set of bounds.

Algorithm 1. Synchronization Synthesis Algorithm

Input: local event net $E = \bigsqcup\{E_1, E_2, \cdots, E_n\}$, LTL property φ, upper bound Y on the number of added places, upper bound X on the number of added transitions, upper bound I on the number of synchronization skeletons

Result: local labeled net L which correctly synchronizes E

1 $initRepairEngine(E_1, E_2, \cdots, E_n, X, Y, I)$ // initialize repair engine (Sect. 4.1)
2 $L \leftarrow E$; $(\varphi_{1safe}, \varphi_{progr}) \leftarrow makeProperties(E_1, E_2, \cdots, E_n)$
3 **while** *true* **do**
4      $ok \leftarrow true$; $props \leftarrow \{\varphi, \varphi_{1safe}, \varphi_{progr}\}$
5   **for** $\varphi' \in props$ **do**
6          $\tau_{ctex} \leftarrow verify(L, \varphi')$ // check the property (Sect. 4.2)
7   **if** $(\tau_{ctex} = \emptyset \wedge \varphi' = \varphi_{progr}) \vee (\tau_{ctex} \neq \emptyset \wedge \varphi' = \varphi_{1safe})$ **then**
8             $differentRepair()$; $ok \leftarrow false$ // try different repair (Sect. 4.1)
9   **else if** $\tau_{ctex} \neq \emptyset \wedge \varphi' \neq \varphi_{progr}$ **then**
10            $assertCtex(\tau_{ctex})$; $ok \leftarrow false$ // record counterexample (Sect. 4.1)
11   **if** ok **then**
12   **return** L // return correctly-synchronized event net
13     $L \leftarrow repair(L)$ // generate new candidate
14   **if** $L = \bot$ **then**
15   **return** *fail*   // cannot repair

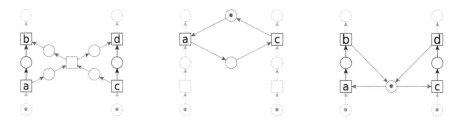

Fig. 2. Synchronization skeletons: (1) Barrier, (2) Condition Variable, (3) Mutex

Repair Engine Initialization. Algorithm 1 calls *initRepairEngine*, which initializes the function symbols shown in Fig. 3 and asserts well-formedness constraints. Labels in bold/blue are function symbol names, and cells are the corresponding values. For example, *Petri* is a 2-ary function symbol, and *Loc* is a 1-ary function symbol. Note that there is a separate *Ctex, Acc, Trans* for each k (where k is a counterexample index, as will be described shortly). The return type (i.e., the type of each cell) is indicated in parentheses after the name of each function symbol. For example, letting $\mathbb{B}$ denote the Boolean type $\{true, false\}$, the types of the function symbols are: $Petri : \mathbb{N} \times \mathbb{N} \rightarrow \mathbb{B} \times \mathbb{B}$, $Mark : \mathbb{N} \rightarrow \mathbb{N}$, $Loc : \mathbb{N} \rightarrow \mathbb{N} \times \mathbb{N}$, $Type : \mathbb{N} \rightarrow \mathbb{N}$, $Pair : \mathbb{N} \times \mathbb{N} \rightarrow \mathbb{N} \times \mathbb{N} \times \mathbb{N}$, $Range : \mathbb{N} \rightarrow \mathbb{N} \times \mathbb{N} \times \mathbb{N} \times \mathbb{N}$, $Ctex_k : \mathbb{N} \times \mathbb{N} \rightarrow \mathbb{N}$, $Acc_k : \mathbb{N} \rightarrow \mathbb{B}$, $Trans_k : \mathbb{N} \rightarrow \mathbb{N}$, $Len : \mathbb{N} \rightarrow \mathbb{N}$ (note that Len is not shown in the figure).

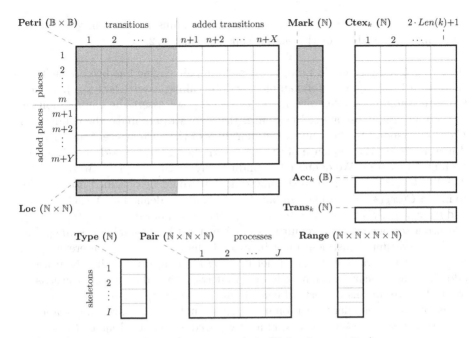

Fig. 3. SMT function symbols (Color figure online)

The regions highlighted in Fig. 3 are "set" (asserted equal) to values matching the input event net. In particular, $Petri(y, x)$ is of the form (b_1, b_2), where we set b_1 if and only if there is an edge from place y to transition x in E, and similarly set b_2 if and only if there is an edge from transition x to place y. $Mark(y)$ is set to 1 if and only if place y is marked in E. $Loc(x)$ is set to the location (switch/port pair) of the event at transition x. The bound Y limits how many places can be added, and X limits how many transitions can be added.

Bound I limits how many skeletons can be used simultaneously. Each "row" i of the $Type, Pair, Range$ symbols represents a single added skeleton. More specifically, $Type(i)$ identifies one of the three types of skeletons. Up to J processes can participate in each skeleton (Fig. 2 shows the skeletons for 2 processes, but they generalize to $j \geq 2$), and by default, J is set to the number of processes. Thus, $Pair(i, j)$ is a tuple (id, fst, snd), where id identifies a process, and fst, snd is a pair of events in that process. $Range(i)$ is a tuple $(pMin, pMax, tMin, tMax)$, where $pMin, pMax$ reserve a range of rows in the *added places* section of Fig. 3, and similarly, $tMin, tMax$ reserve a range of columns in the *added transitions*.

We assert a conjunction ϕ_{global} of well-formedness constraints to ensure that proper values are used to fill in the empty (un-highlighted) cells of Fig. 3. The primary constraint forces the *Petri* cells to be populated as dictated by any synchronization skeletons appearing in the $Type, Pair, Range$ rows. For example, given a row i where $Type(i) = 1$ (*barrier* synchronization skeleton), we would require that $Range(i) = (y_1, y_2, x_1, x_2)$, where $(y_2 - y_1) + 1 = 4$ and $(x_2 - x_1) + 1 = 1$, meaning 4 new places and 1 new transition would be reserved. Additionally, the values of *Petri* for rows y_1 through y_2 and columns x_1 through x_2 would be set to match the edges for the *barrier* construct in Fig. 2.

Asserting Counterexample Traces. Once the repair engine has been initialized, Algorithm 1 can add counterexample traces by calling $assertCtex(\tau_{ctex})$. To add the k-th counterexample trace $\tau_k = t_0 t_1 \cdots t_{n-1}$, we assert the conjunction ϕ_k of the following constraints. In essence, these constraints make the columns of $Ctex_k$ correspond to the sequence of markings of the current event net in *Petri* if it were to fire the sequence of transitions τ_k. Let $Ctex_k(*, x)$ denote the x-th "column" of $Ctex_k$. We define $Ctex_k$ inductively as $Ctex_k(*, 1) = Mark$ and for $x > 1$, $Ctex_k(*, x)$ is equal to the marking that would be obtained if t_{x-2} were to fire in $Ctex_k(*, x-1)$. The symbol Acc_k is similarly defined as $Acc_k(1) = true$ and for $x > 1$, $Acc_k(x) \iff (Acc_k(x-1) \wedge (t_{x-2}$ is enabled in $Ctex_k(*, x-1)))$. We also assert a constraint requiring that Acc_k must become false at some point.

An important adjustment must be made to handle *general* counterexamples. Specifically, if a trace of the event net in *Petri* is equal to τ_k modulo transitions added by the synchronization skeletons, that trace should be rejected just as τ_k would be. We do this by instead considering the trace $\tau'_k = \epsilon\, t_0\, \epsilon\, t_1\, \cdots\, \epsilon\, t_{n-1}$ (where ϵ is a placeholder transition used only for notational convenience), and for the ϵ transitions, we set $Ctex_k(*, x)$ as if we fired any enabled *added transitions* in $Ctex_k(*, x-1)$, and for the t transitions, we update $Ctex_k(*, x)$ as described previously. More specifically, the adjusted constraints ϕ_k are as follows:

1. $Ctex_k(*, 1) = Mark$.
2. $Len(k)=n \wedge Acc_k(1) \wedge \neg Acc_k(2 \cdot Len(k) + 1)$.
3. For $x \geq 2$, $Acc_k(x) \iff (Acc_k(x-1) \wedge (Trans_k(x)=\epsilon \vee (Trans_k(x)$ is enabled in $Ctex_k(*, x-1))))$.
4. For *odd* indices $x \geq 3$, $Trans_k(x) = t_{(x-3)/2}$, and $Ctex_k(*, x)$ is set as if $Trans_k(x)$ fired in $Ctex_k(*, x-1)$.
5. For *even* indices $x \geq 2$, $Trans_k(x) = \epsilon$, and $Ctex_k(*, x)$ is set as if all enabled *added transitions* fired in $Ctex_k(*, x-1)$.

The last constraint works because for our synchronization skeletons, any added transitions that occur immediately after each other in a trace can also occur in parallel. The negated acceptance constraint $\neg Acc_k(2 \cdot Len(k) + 1)$ makes sure that any synchronization generated by the SMT solver will not allow the counterexample trace τ_k to be accepted.

Trying a Different Repair. The *differentRepair*() function in Algorithm 1 makes sure the repair engine does not propose the current candidate again. When this is called, we prevent the current set of synchronization skeletons from appearing again by taking the conjunction of the *Type* and *Pair* values, as well as the values of *Mark* corresponding to the places reserved in *Range*, and asserting the negation. We denote the current set of all such assertions ϕ_{skip}.

Algorithm 2. Event Net Verifier (PROMELA Model)

---

1 $marked \leftarrow initMarking()$ `// initial marking from input event net`
2 **run** $singlePacket, transitions$ `// start both processes`
3 **Process** $singlePacket$:
4       $lock();\ status \leftarrow 1;\ pkt \leftarrow pickPacket();\ n \leftarrow pickHost()$
5   **do**
6           $pkt \leftarrow movePacket(pkt, marked)$ `// move according to current config.`
7   **while** $pkt.loc \neq drop \wedge \neg isHost(pkt.loc)$
8       $status \leftarrow 2;\ unlock()$

9 **Process** $transitions$:
10   **while** $true$ **do**
11          $lock()$
12          $t \leftarrow pickTransition(marked);\ marked \leftarrow updateMarking(t, marked)$
13          $unlock()$

Obtaining an Event Net. When the synthesizer calls $repair(L)$, we query the SMT solver for satisfiability of the current constraints. If satisfiable, values of $Petri, Mark$ in the model can be used to add synchronization skeletons to L. We can use *optimizing* functionality of the SMT solver (or a simple loop which asserts progressively smaller bounds for an objective function) to produce a minimal number of synchronization skeletons.

Note that formulas $\phi_{global}, \phi_{skip}, \phi_1, \cdots$ have polynomial size in terms of the input event net size and bounds Y, X, I, J, and are expressed in the decidable fragment QF_UFLIA (quantifier-free uninterpreted function symbols and linear integer arithmetic). We found this to scale well with modern SMT solvers (Sect. 5).

Lemma 1 (Correctness of the Repair Engine). *If the SMT solver finds that* $\phi = \phi_{global} \wedge \phi_{skip} \wedge \phi_1 \wedge \cdots \wedge \phi_k$ *is satisfiable, then the event net represented by the model does not contain any of the seen counterexample traces* $\tau_1, \cdots, \tau_k$. *If the SMT solver finds that* ϕ *is unsatisfiable, then all synchronization skeletons within the bounds fail to prevent some counterexample trace.*

4.2 Checking Event Nets

We now describe $verify(L, \varphi')$ in Algorithm 1. From L, we produce a PROMELA model for LTL model checking. Algorithm 2 shows the model pseudocode, which is an efficient implementation of the semantics described in Sect. 3. Variable $marked$ is a list of boolean flags, indicating which places currently contain a token. The $initMarking$ macro sets the initial values based on the initial marking of L. The $singlePacket$ process randomly selects a packet pkt and puts it at a random host, and then moves pkt until it either reaches another host, or is dropped ($pkt.loc = drop$). The $movePacket$ macro modifies/moves pkt according to the current marking's configuration. The $pickTransition$ macro randomly selects a transition $t \in L$, and $updateMarking$ updates the marking to reflect t firing.

We ask the model checker for a *counterexample trace* demonstrating a violation of φ'. This gives the sequence of transitions t chosen by *pickTransition*. We *generalize* this sequence by removing any transitions which are not in the original input event nets. This sequence is returned as τ_{ctex} to Algorithm 1.

Lemma 2 (Correctness of the Verifier). *If the verifier returns counterexample τ, then L violates φ in one of the global configurations in Configs(τ). If the verifier does not return a counterexample, then all traces of L satisfy φ.*

4.3   Overall Correctness Results

The proofs of the following theorems use Lemmas 1, 2, and Theorem 1.

Theorem 2 (Soundness of Algorithm 1). *Given E, φ, if an L is returned, then it is a local labeled net which correctly synchronizes E with respect to φ.*

Theorem 3 (Completeness of Algorithm 1). *If there exists a local labeled net $L = \bigsqcup\{E, S\}$, where $|S| \leq I$, and synchronization skeletons in S are each of the form shown in Fig. 2, and S has fewer than X total transitions and fewer than Y total places, and L correctly synchronizes E, then our algorithm will return such an L. Otherwise, the algorithm returns "fail."*

5   Implementation and Evaluation

We have implemented a prototype of our synthesizer. The repair engine (Sect. 4.1) utilizes the Z3 SMT solver, and the verifier (Sect. 4.2) utilizes the SPIN LTL model checker. In this section, we evaluate our system by addressing the following:

1. Can we use our approach to model a variety of real-world network programs?
2. Is our tool able to fix realistic concurrency-related bugs?
3. Is the performance of our tool reasonable when applied to real networks?

We address #1 and #2 via case studies based on real concurrency bugs described in the networking literature, and #3 by trying increasingly-large topologies for one of the studies. Figure 4 shows quantitative results for the case studies. The first group of columns denote number of switches (*switch*), CEGIS

benchmark	#number					time (sec.)				
	switch	iter	ctex	skip	SMT	build	verify	synth	misc	total
ex01-isolation	5	2	2	0	318	0.48	0.43	0.04	0.52	1.47
ex02-conflict	3	10	3	6	349	0.28	0.94	0.61	1.14	2.98
ex03-loop	4	2	1	0	257	0.48	0.43	0.01	0.45	1.37
ex04-composition	4	2	1	0	305	0.48	0.74	0.03	0.50	1.75
ex05-exclusive	3	5	3	3	583	5.17	4.48	0.10	1.00	10.74

Fig. 4. Performance of Examples 1–5

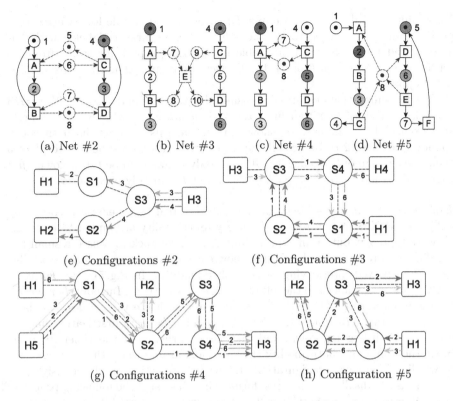

(a) Net #2   (b) Net #3   (c) Net #4   (d) Net #5

(e) Configurations #2   (f) Configurations #3

(g) Configurations #4   (h) Configuration #5

Fig. 5. Experiments—Event Nets and Configurations (Color figure online)

iterations (*iter*), SPIN counterexamples (*ctex*), event nets "skipped" due to a deadlock-freedom or 1-safety violation (*skip*), and formulas asserted to the SMT solver (*smt*). The remaining columns report runtime of the SPIN verifier generation/compilation (*build*), SPIN verification (*verify*), repair engine (*synth*), various auxiliary/initialization functionality (*misc*), and overall execution (*total*). Our experimental platform had 20 GB RAM and a 3.2 GHz 4-core Intel i5-4570 CPU.

Example #1—Tenant Isolation in a Datacenter. We used our tool on the example described in Sect. 2. We formalize the isolation property using the following LTL properties: $\phi_1 \triangleq G(loc{=}H1 \implies G(loc{\neq}H4))$ and $\phi_2 \triangleq G(loc{=}H3 \implies G(loc{\neq}H2))$. Our tool finds the *barrier* in Fig. 1d, which properly synchronizes the event net to avoid isolation violations, as described in Sect. 2.

Example #2—Conflicting Controller Modules. In a real bug (El-Hassany et al. [16]) encountered using the POX SDN controller, two concurrent controller modules *Discovery* and *Forwarding* made conflicting assumptions about which forwarding rules should be deleted, resulting in packet loss. Figure 5a shows a simplified version of such a scenario, where the left side $(1, A, 2, B)$ corresponds to the Discovery module, and the right side $(4, C, 3, D)$ corresponds to the

Forwarding module. In this example, Discovery is responsible for ensuring that packets can be forwarded to H1 (i.e., that the configuration labeled with 2 is active), and Forwarding is responsible for choosing a path for traffic from H3 (either the path labeled 3 or 4). In all cases, we require that traffic from H3 is not dropped.

We formalize this requirement using the LTL property $\phi_3 \triangleq \mathtt{G}(loc{=}H3 \implies \mathtt{G}(loc{\neq}drop))$. Our tool finds the *two condition variables* which properly synchronize the event net. As shown in Fig. 5a, this requires the path corresponding to place 2 to be brought up *before* the path corresponding to place 3 (i.e., event C can only occur after A), and only allows it to be taken down *after* the path 3 is moved back to path 4 (i.e., event B can only occur after D).

Example #3—Discovery Forwarding Loop. In a real bug scenario (Scott et al. [32]), the NOX SDN controller's discovery functionality attempted to learn the network topology, but an unexpected interleaving of packets caused a small forwarding loop to be created. We show how such a forwarding loop can arise due to an unexpected interleaving of controller modules. In Fig. 5b, the *Forwarding/Discovery* modules are the left/right sides respectively. Initially, *Forwarding* knows about the red (1) path in Fig. 5f, but will delete these rules, and later set up the orange (3) path. On the other hand, *Discovery* first learns that the green (4) path is going down, and then later learns about the violet (6) path. Since these modules both modify the same forwarding rules, they can create a forwarding loop when configurations 1, 6 or 4, 3 are active simultaneously.

We wish to disallow such loops, formalizing this using the following property: $\phi_4 \triangleq \mathtt{G}(status{=}1 \implies \mathtt{F}(status{=}2))$. As discussed in Sect. 4.2, *status* is set to 1 when the packet is injected into the network, and set to 2 when/if the packet subsequently exits or is dropped. Our tool enforces this by inserting a *barrier* (Fig. 5b), preventing the unwanted combinations of configurations.

Example #4—Policy Composition. In an update scenario (Canini et al. [9]) involving *overlapping* policies, one policy enforces HTTP traffic monitoring and the other requires traffic from a particular hosts(s) to *waypoint* through a device (e.g., an intrusion detection system or firewall). Problems arise for traffic processed by the *intersection* of these policies (e.g., HTTP packets from a particular host), causing a policy violation.

Figure 5g shows such a scenario. The left process of Fig. 5c is traffic monitoring, and the right is waypoint enforcement. HTTP traffic is initially enabled along the red (1) path. Traffic monitoring intercepts this traffic and diverts it to $H2$ by setting up the orange (2) path and subsequently bringing it down to form the blue path (3). Waypoint enforcement initially sets up the green path (5) through the waypoint $S3$, and finally allows traffic to enter by setting up the violet (6) path from $H1$. For *HTTP traffic from $H1$ destined for $H3$*, if traffic monitoring is not set up *before* waypoint enforcement enables the path from $H1$, this traffic can circumvent the waypoint (on the $S2 \rightarrow S4$ path), violating the policy.

We can encode this specification using the following LTL properties: $\phi_6 \triangleq \mathtt{G}((pkt.type{=}HTTP \wedge pkt.loc{=}H5) \Rightarrow \mathtt{F}(pkt.loc{=}H2 \vee pkt.loc{=}H3))$ and

$\phi_7 \triangleq (\neg(pkt.src{=}H1 \wedge pkt.dst{=}H3 \wedge pkt.loc{=}H3)$ W $(pkt.src{=}H1 \wedge pkt.dst{=}H3$
$\wedge\, pkt.loc{=}S3))$, where W is *weak until*. Our tool finds Fig. 5c, which forces traffic
monitoring to divert traffic *before* waypoint enforcement proceeds.

Example #5—Topology Changes During Update. Peresíni et al. [29] describe a
scenario in which a controller attempts to set up forwarding rules, and concurrently the topology changes, resulting in a forwarding loop being installed.

Figure 5h, examines a similar situation where the processes in Fig. 5d interleave improperly, resulting in a forwarding loop. The left process updates from
the red (2) to the orange (3) path, and the right process extends the green (5)
to the violet (6) path (potential forwarding loops: $S1, S3$ and $S1, S2, S3$).

We use the loop-freedom property ϕ_4 from Example #3. Our tool finds a
mutex synchronization skeleton (Fig. 5d). Note that both places 2, 3 are protected
by the mutex, since either would interact with place 6 to form a loop.

Scalability Experiments. Recall Example #1 (Fig. 1a). Instead of the short paths
between the pairs of hosts $H1, H2$ and $H3, H4$, we gathered a large set of
real network topologies, and randomly selected long host-to-host paths with
a single-switch intersection, corresponding to Example #1. We used datacenter FatTree topologies (e.g., Fig. 7a), scaling up the *depth* (number of layers)
and *fanout* (number of links per switch) to achieve a maximum size of 1088
switches, which would support a datacenter with 4096 hosts. We also used highly-
connected ("small-world") graphs, such as the one shown in Fig. 7b, and we
scaled up the number of switches (*ring size* in the Watts-Strogatz model) to 1000.
Additionally, we used 240 wide-area network topologies from the Topology Zoo
dataset—as an example, Fig. 7c shows the *NSFNET* topology, featuring physical
nodes across the United States. The results of these experiments are shown in
Figs. 6, 8a and b.

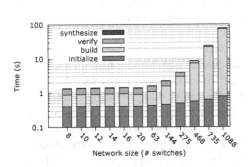

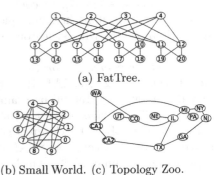

(a) FatTree.

(b) Small World. (c) Topology Zoo.

Fig. 6. Performance results: scalability of
Example #1 using Fat Tree topology

Fig. 7. Example network topologies

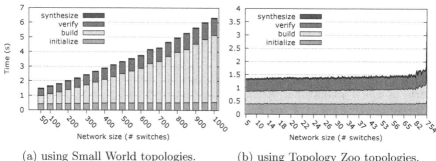

(a) using Small World topologies.   (b) using Topology Zoo topologies.

Fig. 8. Performance results: scalability of Example #1 (continued)

6   Related Work

Synthesis for Network Programs. Yuan et al. [36] present NetEgg, pioneering the approach of using examples to write network programs. In contrast, we focus on distributed programs and use specifications instead of examples. Additionally, different from our SMT-based strategy, NetEgg uses a backtracking search which may limit scalability. Padon et al. [28] "decentralize" a network program to work properly on distributed switches. Our work on the other hand takes a buggy decentralized program and inserts the necessary synchronization to make it correct. Saha et al. [31] and Hojjat et al. [18] present approaches for repairing a buggy network configuration using SMT and a Horn-clause-based synthesis algorithm respectively. Instead of repairing a static configuration, our event net repair engine repairs a network program. A *network update* is a simple network program—a situation where the global forwarding state of the network must change once. Many approaches solve the problem with respect to different consistency properties [23,37]. In contrast, we provide a new model (event nets) for succinctly describing how multiple updates can be composed, as well as an approach for synthesizing synchronization for this composition.

Concurrent Programming for Networks. Some well-known network programming languages (e.g., NetKAT [1]) only allow defining static configurations, and they do not support stateful programs and concurrency constructs. Many languages [20,27], provide support for stateful network programming (often with finite-state control), but lack direct support for synchronization. There are two recently-proposed exceptions: SNAP [2], which provides atomic blocks, and the approach by Canini et al. [9], which provides transactions. Both of these mechanisms are difficult to implement without damage to performance. In contrast, our solution is based on locality and synchronization synthesis, and is more fine-grained and efficiently implementable than previous approaches. It builds on and extends network event structures (NES) [25], which addresses the problem of rigorously defining correct event-driven behavior. From the *systems* side, basic support for stateful concurrent programming is provided by switch-level mechanisms [6,8], but global coordination still must be handled carefully at the language/compiler level.

Petri Net Synthesis. Ehrenfeucht et al. [15] introduce the "net synthesis" problem, i.e., producing a net whose state graph is *isomorphic to a given DFA*, and present the "regions" construction on which Petri net synthesis algorithms are based. Many researchers continued this theoretical line of work [3,11,12,19] and developed foundational (complexity-theoretic) results. Synthesis from examples for Petri nets was also considered [5], and examined in the slightly different setting of *process mining* [14,30]. Neither of these approaches is directly applicable to our problem of program repair by inserting synchronization to eliminate bugs. More closely related is *process enhancement* for Petri nets [4,24] but these works either modify the semantics of systems in arbitrary ways, whereas we only restrict behaviors by adding synchronization, or they rely on other abstractions (such as *timed* Petri nets) which are unsuitable for network programming.

Synthesis/Repair for Synchronization. There are many approaches for fixing concurrency bugs which use constraint (SAT/SMT) solving. Application areas include weak memory models [22,26], and repair of concurrency bugs [7,10,33,34]. The key difference is that while these works focus on shared-memory programs, we focus on message-passing Petri-net based programs. Our model is a general framework for synthesis of synchronization where many different types of synchronization constructs can be readily described and synthesized.

7 Conclusion

We have presented an approach for synthesis of synchronization to produce network programs which satisfy correctness properties. We allow the programmer to specify a network program as a set of concurrent behaviors, in addition to high-level temporal correctness properties, and our tool inserts synchronization constructs needed to remove unwanted interleavings. The advantages over previous work are that we provide (a) a language which leverages Petri nets' natural support for concurrency, and (b) an efficient counterexample-guided algorithm for synthesizing synchronization for programs in this language.

Acknowledgments. We would like to thank Nate Foster and P. Madhusudan for fruitful discussions. This research was supported in part by the NSF under award CCF 1421752, and by DARPA under agreement FA8750-14-2-0263.

References

1. Anderson, C.J., Foster, N., Guha, A., Jeannin, J.-B., Kozen, D., Schlesinger, C., Walker, D.: NetKAT: semantic foundations for networks. In: POPL (2014)
2. Arashloo, M.T., Koral, Y., Greenberg, M., Rexford, J., Walker, D.: SNAP: stateful network-wide abstractions for packet processing. In: SIGCOMM (2016)

3. Badouel, E., Bernardinello, L., Darondeau, P.: The synthesis problem for elementary net systems is NP-complete. Theor. Comput. Sci. **186**(1–2), 107–134 (1997)
4. Basile, F., Chiacchio, P., Coppola, J.: Model repair of time petri nets with temporal anomalies. In: IFAC (2015)
5. Bergenthum, R., Desel, J., Lorenz, R., Mauser, S.: Synthesis of petri nets from finite partial languages. Fundam. Inform. **88**(4), 437–468 (2008)
6. Bianchi, G., Bonola, M., Capone, A., Cascone, C.: Open-State: programming platform-independent stateful openflow applications inside the switch. In: ACM SIGCOMM CCR (2014)
7. Bloem, R., Hofferek, G., Könighofer, B., Könighofer, R., Ausserlechner, S., Spork, R.: Synthesis of synchronization using uninterpreted functions. In: FMCAD. IEEE (2014)
8. Bosshart, P., Daly, D., Gibb, G., Izzard, M., McKeown, N., Rexford, J., Schlesinger, C., Talayco, D., Vahdat, A., Varghese, G., et al.: P4: programming protocol-independent packet processors. In: ACM SIG- COMM CCR (2014)
9. Canini, M., Kuznetsov, P., Levin, D., Schmid, S.: Software transactional networking: concurrent and consistent policy composition. In: HotSDN (2013)
10. Černý, P., Henzinger, T.A., Radhakrishna, A., Ryzhyk, L., Tarrach, T.: Efficient synthesis for concurrency by semantics-preserving transformations. In: Sharygina, N., Veith, H. (eds.) CAV 2013. LNCS, vol. 8044, pp. 951–967. Springer, Heidelberg (2013). doi:10.1007/978-3-642-39799-8_68
11. Cortadella, J., Kishinevsky, M., Lavagno, L., Yakovlev, A.: Synthesizing petri nets from state-based models. In: ICCAD (1995)
12. Desel, J., Reisig, W.: The synthesis problem of petri nets. Acta Inf. **33**(4), 297–315 (1996)
13. Dixit, A.A., Hao, F., Mukherjee, S., Lakshman, T.V., Kompella, R.: ElastiCon: an elastic distributed SDN controller. In: ANCS (2014)
14. Dumas, M., García-Bañuelos, L.: Process mining reloaded: event structures as a unified representation of process models and event logs. In: Devillers, R., Valmari, A. (eds.) PETRI NETS 2015. LNCS, vol. 9115, pp. 33–48. Springer, Cham (2015). doi:10.1007/978-3-319-19488-2_2
15. Ehrenfeucht, A., Rozenberg, G.: Partial (Set) 2-structures. Part II: state spaces of concurrent systems. Acta Inf. **27**(4), 343–368 (1990)
16. El-Hassany, A., Miserez, J., Bielik, P., Vanbever, L., Vechev, M.T.: SDNRacer: concurrency analysis for software-defined networks. In: PLDI (2016)
17. Gulwani, S., Jha, S., Tiwari, A., Venkatesan, R.: Synthesis of loop-free programs. In: PLDI (2011)
18. Hojjat, H., Ruemmer, P., McClurg, J., Cerny, P., Foster, N.: Optimizing horn solvers for network repair. In: FMCAD (2016)
19. Hopkins, R.P.: Distributable nets. In: Rozenberg, G. (ed.) ICATPN 1990. LNCS, vol. 524, pp. 161–187. Springer, Heidelberg (1991). doi:10.1007/BFb0019974
20. Kim, H., Reich, J., Gupta, A., Shahbaz, M., Feamster, N., Clark, R.: Kinetic: verifiable dynamic network control. In: NSDI (2015)
21. Koponen, T., Amidon, K., Balland, P., Casado, M., Chanda, A., Fulton, B., Ganichev, I., Gross, J., Gude, N., Ingram, P., et al.: Network virtualization in multi-tenant datacenters. In: NSDI (2014)
22. Kuperstein, M., Vechev, M.T., Yahav, E.: Automatic inference of memory fences. In: FMCAD (2010)
23. Ludwig, A., Rost, M., Foucard, D., Schmid, S.: Good network updates for bad packets: waypoint enforcement beyond destination-based routing policies. In: HotNets (2014)

24. Martínez-Araiza, U., López-Mellado, E.: CTL model repair for bounded and deadlock free petri nets. In: IFAC (2015)
25. McClurg, J., Hojjat, H., Foster, N., Cerny, P.: Event-driven network programming. In: PLDI (2016)
26. Meshman, Y., Rinetzky, N., Yahav, E.: Pattern-based synthesis of synchronization for the C++ memory model. In: FMCAD (2015)
27. Nelson, T., Ferguson, A.D., Scheer, M.J., Krishnamurthi, S.: Tierless programming and reasoning for software-defined networks. In: NSDI (2014)
28. Padon, O., Immerman, N., Karbyshev, A., Lahav, O., Sagiv, M., Shoham, S.: Decentralizing SDN policies. In: POPL (2015)
29. Peresíni, P., Kuzniar, M., Vasic, N., Canini, M., Kostic, D.: OF.CPP: consistent packet processing for openflow. In: HotSDN (2013)
30. Ponce-de-León, H., Rodríguez, C., Carmona, J., Heljanko, K., Haar, S.: Unfolding-based process discovery. In: Finkbeiner, B., Pu, G., Zhang, L. (eds.) ATVA 2015. LNCS, vol. 9364, pp. 31–47. Springer, Cham (2015). doi:10.1007/978-3-319-24953-7_4
31. Saha, S., Prabhu, S., Madhusudan, P.: NetGen: synthesizing data-plane configurations for network policies. In: SOSR (2015)
32. Scott, C., Wundsam, A., Raghavan, B., Panda, A., Or, A., Lai, J., Huang, E., Liu, Z., El-Hassany, A., Whitlock, S., Acharya, H.B., Zarifis, K., Shenker, S.: Troubleshooting blackbox SDN control software with minimal causal sequences. In: SIGCOMM (2014)
33. Solar-Lezama, A., Jones, C.G., Bodík, R.: Sketching concurrent data structures. In: PLDI (2008)
34. Vechev, M., Yahav, E., Yorsh, G.: Abstraction-guided synthesis of synchronization. In: POPL (2010)
35. Winskel, G.: Event structures. In: Brauer, W., Reisig, W., Rozenberg, G. (eds.) ACPN 1986. LNCS, vol. 255, pp. 325–392. Springer, Heidelberg (1987). doi:10.1007/3-540-17906-2_31
36. Yuan, Y., Lin, D., Alur, R., Loo, B.T.: Scenario-based programming for SDN Policies. In: CoNEXT (2015)
37. Zhou, W., Jin, D., Croft, J., Caesar, M., Godfrey, P.B.: Enforcing generalized consistency properties in software-defined networks. In: NSDI (2015)

Synthesis

BoSy: An Experimentation Framework for Bounded Synthesis

Peter Faymonville, Bernd Finkbeiner, and Leander Tentrup[✉]

Saarland University, Saarbrücken, Germany
{faymonville,finkbeiner,
tentrup}@react.uni-saarland.de

Abstract. We present BoSy, a reactive synthesis tool based on the bounded synthesis approach. Bounded synthesis ensures the minimality of the synthesized implementation by incrementally increasing a bound on the size of the solutions it considers. For each bound, the existence of a solution is encoded as a logical constraint solving problem that is solved by an appropriate solver. BoSy constructs bounded synthesis encodings into SAT, QBF, DQBF, EPR, and SMT, and interfaces to solvers of the corresponding type. When supported by the solver, BoSy extracts solutions as circuits, which can, if desired, be verified with standard hardware model checkers. BoSy won the LTL synthesis track at SYNTCOMP 2016. In addition to its use as a synthesis tool, BoSy can also be used as an experimentation and performance evaluation framework for various types of satisfiability solvers.

1 Introduction

The reactive synthesis problem is to check whether a given ω-regular specification, usually presented as an LTL formula, has an implementation, and, if the answer is yes, to construct such an implementation. As a theoretical problem, reactive synthesis dates back all the way to Alonzo Church's solvability question [6] in the 1950s; as a practical engineering challenge, the problem is fairly new. Tools for reactive synthesis started to come out around 2007 [5,9,11,17]. The first SYNTCOMP tool competition took place at CAV 2014 and was originally restricted to safety specifications, and only later, starting with CAV 2016, extended with an LTL synthesis track [14].

In this paper, we present BoSy, the winner of the 2016 LTL synthesis track. BoSy is based on the bounded synthesis approach [12]. Bounded synthesis ensures the minimality of the synthesized implementation by incrementally increasing a bound on the size of the solutions it considers. For each bound, the existence of a solution is encoded as a logical constraint solving problem that is solved by an appropriate solver. If the solver returns "unsat", the bound is increased and a new constraint system is constructed; if the solver returns a satisfying assignment, an implementation is constructed.

Supported by the European Research Council (ERC) Grant OSARES (No. 683300).

R. Majumdar and V. Kunčak (Eds.): CAV 2017, Part II, LNCS 10427, pp. 325–332, 2017.
DOI: 10.1007/978-3-319-63390-9_17

From an engineering perspective, an interesting feature of the bounded synthesis approach is that it is highly modular. The construction of the constraint system involves a translation of the specification into an ω-automaton. Because the same type of translation is used in model checking, a lot of research has gone into optimizing this construction; well-known tools include ltl3ba [1] and spot [8]. On the solver side, the synthesis problem can be encoded in a range of logics, including boolean formulas (SAT), quantified boolean formulas (QBF), dependency quantified boolean formulas (DQBF), the effective propositional fragment of first-order logic (EPR), and logical formulas with background theories (SMT) (cf. [10]). For each of these encodings, there are again multiple competing solvers.

BoSy leverages the best tools for the LTL-to-automaton translation and the best tools for solving the resulting constraint systems. In addition to its main purpose, which is the highly effective synthesis of reactive implementations from LTL specifications, BoSy is therefore also an experimentation framework, which can be used to compare individual tools for each problem, and even to compare tools across different logical encodings. For example, the QBF encoding is more compact than the SAT encoding, because it treats the inputs of the synthesized system symbolically. BoSy can be used to validate, experimentally, whether QBF solvers translate this compactness into better performance (spoiler alert: in our experiments, they do). Likewise, the DQBF/EPR encoding is more compact than the QBF encoding, because this encoding treats the states of the synthesized system symbolically. In our experiments, the QBF solvers nevertheless outperform the currently available DQBF solvers.

In the remainder of this paper, we present the tool architecture, including the interfaces to other tools, and report on experimental results[1].

2   Tool Architecture

An overview of the architecture of BoSy is given in Fig. 1. For a given bounded synthesis instance, BoSy accepts a JSON-based input format that contains a specification φ given in LTL, the signature of the implementation given as a partition of the set of atomic propositions into inputs and outputs, and the target semantics as a Mealy or a Moore implementation. In the preprocessing component, the tool starts to search for a system *strategy* with φ and an environment *counter-strategy* with $\neg\varphi$ in parallel.[2]

After parsing, the LTL formula is translated into an equivalent universal co-Büchi automaton using an external automata translation tool. Currently, we support ltl3ba [1] and spot [8] for this conversion, but further translation tools can be integrated easily. Tools that output SPIN never-claims or the HOA format are supported.

---

[1] BoSy is available online at https://react.uni-saarland.de/tools/bosy/.

[2] The LTL reactive synthesis problem is not dual with respect to dualizing the LTL formula only, but the target semantics has to be adapted as well. If one searches for a transition-labeled (Mealy) implementation, a counterexample is state-labeled (Moore) and vice versa.

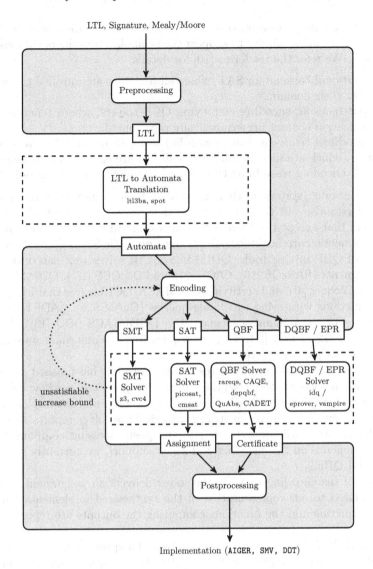

Fig. 1. Tool architecture of BoSy

To the resulting automaton, we apply some basic optimization steps like replacing rejecting terminal states with safety conditions and an analysis of strongly connected components to reduce the size of the constraint system [12].

The encoding component is responsible for creating the constraint system based on the selected encoding, the specification automaton, and the current bound on the number of states of the system. The component constructs a constraint system using a logic representation which supports propositional logic, different kinds of quantification, and comparison operators (between natural numbers). Our implementation contains the following encoding options. These encodings differ in their ability to support the symbolic encoding of the existence of functions. We refer the reader to [10] for details.

- A *propositional* backend for SAT, where all functions are unrolled to conjunctions over their domain.
- An *input-symbolic* encoding employing QBF solvers, where functions with one application context are symbolically represented.
- Two encodings (*state-symbolic*, *symbolic*) using DQBF/EPR solvers, where functions, which are used in multiple contexts, are encoded symbolically.
- An *SMT* encoding resembling the original bounded synthesis encoding [12].

This constraint system is then translated to a format that the selected solver understands, and the solver is called as an external tool. We support SAT solvers that accept the DIMACS input format and that can output satisfying assignments, currently PicoSAT [3] and CryptoMiniSat [24]. We have three categories of QBF solving tools: QDIMACS/QCIR solver that can output top-level assignments (RAReQS [16], CAQE [21], and DepQBF [18]), QDIMACS preprocessors (Bloqqer [4]), and certifying QDIMACS/QCIR solver that can provide boolean functions witnessing satisfiable queries (QuAbS [25], CADET [20], and CAQE [21]). For the remaining formats, i.e., DQDIMACS (iDQ [13]), TPTP3, and SMT (Z3 [19], CVC4 [2]), we only require format conformance as witness extraction is not supported, yet.

After the selected solver with corresponding encoding has finished processing the query and reports *unsatisfiable*, the *search strategy* determines how the bound for the next constraint encoding is increased. Currently, we have implemented a linear and an exponential search strategy. In case the solver reports *satisfiable*, the implementation will be extracted in the postprocessing component. The extraction depends on the encoding and solver support, we currently support it for SAT and QBF.

In case of the encoding to SAT, the solver delivers an assignment, which is then translated to our representation of the synthesized implementation. The transition function and the functions computing the outputs are represented as circuits.

In case of the QBF-encoding, we take a two-step approach for synthesis. The QBF query has the quantifier prefix $\exists\forall\exists$ [10]. In synthesis mode, the query is solved by a combination of QBF preprocessor and QBF solver. From a satisfiable query, the assignment of the top-level existential quantification is extracted [23] and then used to reduce the original query by eliminating the top level existential quantifier. The resulting query, now with a $\forall\exists$ prefix, is then solved using a certifying QBF solver that returns a certificate, that is a circuit representing the witnessing boolean functions. This certificate is then translated into the same functional representation of the synthesized implementation as in the SAT case.

This common representation of the implementations allows the translation into different output formats. From our representation, it is possible to translate the implementation into an AIGER circuit as required by the SYNTCOMP rules, to a SMV model for model checking, or to a graphical representation using the DOT format.

Further encodings can be integrated as extra components in the tool. Such an encoder component has access to the automaton, the semantics, and the input and output signals. The encoder must provide a method `solve` that takes as its parameter a bound and returns whether there is an implementation with the given bound that realizes the specification. The method is implemented by building the constraint system and solving it using a theory solver. One can either use our logic representation or build the textual solver representation directly. If the component supports synthesis, it implements a second method `extractSolution` that is called if `solve` returns true. It returns a representation of the realizing implementation as described above. In order to integrate new solver formats, one has to provide a translator from our logic representation to this format.

3 Experimentation

The reactive synthesis competition has a library of LTL benchmarks that can be transformed into the BoSy file format using the organizers' conversion tool [15]. The tool runsolver [22] is used in our experiments to get predictable timing results and to set appropriate time and memory limits. Figure 2 compares the performance of the different encodings for determining realizability on the SYNT-COMP benchmark set. Notably, the encoding employing QBF solving performed better than the SAT-based one and both solve more instances than the original SMT encoding. The two encodings using DQBF are not yet competitive due to limited availability of DQBF solvers.

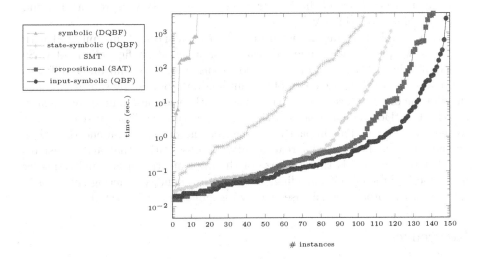

Fig. 2. Number of solved instances within 1 h among the 195 instances from SYNT-COMP 2016. The time axis has logarithmic scale. The experiment was run on a machine with a 3.6 GHz quad-core Intel Xeon processor.

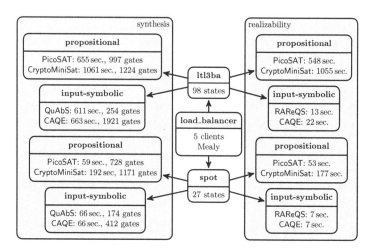

Fig. 3. The diagram shows the result on solving time and implementation quality for different configurations of BoSy on a sample specification.

Different configurations of BoSy may not only result in varying running times, but may also effect the *quality* of the synthesized implementation. A measurement of the quality of the implementation that has also been used in the reactive synthesis competition is the size of the implementation, measured in the number of gates in the circuit representation. The correctness of an implementation, i.e., whether the synthesized solution actually satisfies the original specification can be verified by model checking. One can either encode the solution as a circuit and use an AIGER model checker, or one can use the SMV representation and model check it with NuSMV [7].

For a sample benchmark, a parametric load-balancer [9] instantiated with 5 clients, we provide experimental results for different configurations of BoSy in Fig. 3. The two automaton conversion tools produce significantly different automata, where the state space of the automaton produced by spot is only one third of the one produced by ltl3ba. Consequently, the constraint system generated for the ltl3ba version is larger and thereby the running time worse compared to the spot version. This impact is stronger on the propositional encoding than on the input-symbolic one for realizability. An observation that also translates to other benchmarks is that the size of the implementation is usually smaller using the input-symbolic encoding. On the other hand, extracting solutions is cheaper in the propositional case as only assignments are extracted.

References

1. Babiak, T., Křetínský, M., Řehák, V., Strejček, J.: LTL to Büchi automata translation: fast and more deterministic. In: Flanagan, C., König, B. (eds.) TACAS 2012. LNCS, vol. 7214, pp. 95–109. Springer, Heidelberg (2012). doi:10.1007/978-3-642-28756-5_8

2. Barrett, C., Conway, C.L., Deters, M., Hadarean, L., Jovanović, D., King, T., Reynolds, A., Tinelli, C.: CVC4. In: Gopalakrishnan, G., Qadeer, S. (eds.) CAV 2011. LNCS, vol. 6806, pp. 171–177. Springer, Heidelberg (2011). doi:10.1007/978-3-642-22110-1_14

3. Biere, A.: Picosat essentials. JSAT **4**(2–4), 75–97 (2008)

4. Biere, A., Lonsing, F., Seidl, M.: Blocked clause elimination for QBF. In: Bjørner, N., Sofronie-Stokkermans, V. (eds.) CADE 2011. LNCS (LNAI), vol. 6803, pp. 101–115. Springer, Heidelberg (2011). doi:10.1007/978-3-642-22438-6_10

5. Bohy, A., Bruyère, V., Filiot, E., Jin, N., Raskin, J.-F.: Acacia+, a tool for LTL synthesis. In: Madhusudan, P., Seshia, S.A. (eds.) CAV 2012. LNCS, vol. 7358, pp. 652–657. Springer, Heidelberg (2012). doi:10.1007/978-3-642-31424-7_45

6. Church, A.: Application of recursive arithmetic to the problem of circuit synthesis. J. Symbolic Logic **28**(4), 289–290 (1963)

7. Cimatti, A., Clarke, E., Giunchiglia, E., Giunchiglia, F., Pistore, M., Roveri, M., Sebastiani, R., Tacchella, A.: NuSMV 2: an opensource tool for symbolic model checking. In: Brinksma, E., Larsen, K.G. (eds.) CAV 2002. LNCS, vol. 2404, pp. 359–364. Springer, Heidelberg (2002). doi:10.1007/3-540-45657-0_29

8. Duret-Lutz, A., Lewkowicz, A., Fauchille, A., Michaud, T., Renault, É., Xu, L.: Spot 2.0 — a framework for LTL and ω-automata manipulation. In: Artho, C., Legay, A., Peled, D. (eds.) ATVA 2016. LNCS, vol. 9938, pp. 122–129. Springer, Cham (2016). doi:10.1007/978-3-319-46520-3_8

9. Ehlers, R.: Unbeast: symbolic bounded synthesis. In: Abdulla, P.A., Leino, K.R.M. (eds.) TACAS 2011. LNCS, vol. 6605, pp. 272–275. Springer, Heidelberg (2011). doi:10.1007/978-3-642-19835-9_25

10. Faymonville, P., Finkbeiner, B., Rabe, M.N., Tentrup, L.: Encodings of bounded synthesis. In: Legay, A., Margaria, T. (eds.) TACAS 2017. LNCS, vol. 10205, pp. 354–370. Springer, Heidelberg (2017). doi:10.1007/978-3-662-54577-5_20

11. Filiot, E., Jin, N., Raskin, J.-F.: An antichain algorithm for LTL realizability. In: Bouajjani, A., Maler, O. (eds.) CAV 2009. LNCS, vol. 5643, pp. 263–277. Springer, Heidelberg (2009). doi:10.1007/978-3-642-02658-4_22

12. Finkbeiner, B., Schewe, S.: Bounded synthesis. STTT **15**(5–6), 519–539 (2013)

13. Fröhlich, A., Kovásznai, G., Biere, A., Veith, H.: iDQ: instantiation-based DQBF solving. In: Proceedings of POS@SAT. EPiC Series in Computing, vol. 27, pp. 103–116. EasyChair (2014)

14. Jacobs, S., Bloem, R., Brenguier, R., Khalimov, A., Klein, F., Könighofer, R., Kreber, J., Legg, A., Narodytska, N., Pérez, G.A., Raskin, J., Ryzhyk, L., Sankur, O., Seidl, M., Tentrup, L., Walker, A.: The 3rd reactive synthesis competition (SYNT-COMP 2016): Benchmarks, participants & results. In: Proceedings of SYNT@CAV. EPTCS, vol. 229, pp. 149–177 (2016)

15. Jacobs, S., Klein, F., Schirmer, S.: A high-level LTL synthesis format: TLSF v1.1. In: Proceedings of SYNT@CAV. EPTCS, vol. 229, pp. 112–132 (2016)

16. Janota, M., Klieber, W., Marques-Silva, J., Clarke, E.M.: Solving QBF with counterexample guided refinement. Artif. Intell. **234**, 1–25 (2016)

17. Jobstmann, B., Bloem, R.: Optimizations for LTL synthesis. In: FMCAD, pp. 117–124. IEEE Computer Society (2006)

18. Lonsing, F., Biere, A.: DepQBF: a dependency-aware QBF solver. JSAT **7**(2–3), 71–76 (2010)

19. Moura, L., Bjørner, N.: Z3: an efficient SMT solver. In: Ramakrishnan, C.R., Rehof, J. (eds.) TACAS 2008. LNCS, vol. 4963, pp. 337–340. Springer, Heidelberg (2008). doi:10.1007/978-3-540-78800-3_24

20. Rabe, M.N., Seshia, S.A.: Incremental determinization. In: Creignou, N., Le Berre, D. (eds.) SAT 2016. LNCS, vol. 9710, pp. 375–392. Springer, Cham (2016). doi:10. 1007/978-3-319-40970-2_23

21. Rabe, M.N., Tentrup, L.: CAQE: A certifying QBF solver. In: Proceedings of FMCAD, pp. 136–143. IEEE (2015)

22. Roussel, O.: Controlling a solver execution with the runsolver tool. JSAT **7**(4), 139–144 (2011)

23. Seidl, M., Könighofer, R.: Partial witnesses from preprocessed quantified boolean formulas. In: Proceedings of DATE, pp. 1–6. European Design and Automation Association (2014)

24. Soos, M., Nohl, K., Castelluccia, C.: Extending SAT solvers to cryptographic problems. In: Kullmann, O. (ed.) SAT 2009. LNCS, vol. 5584, pp. 244–257. Springer, Heidelberg (2009). doi:10.1007/978-3-642-02777-2_24

25. Tentrup, L.: Solving QBF by abstraction. CoRR abs/1604.06752 (2016)

Bounded Synthesis for Streett, Rabin, and CTL*

Ayrat Khalimov[✉] and Roderick Bloem

Graz University of Technology, Graz, Austria
ayrat.khalimov@iaik.tugraz.at

Abstract. SMT-based bounded synthesis uses an SMT solver to synthesize systems from LTL properties by going through co-Büchi automata. In this paper, we show how to extend the ranking functions used in Bounded Synthesis, and thus the bounded synthesis approach, to Büchi, Parity, Rabin, and Streett conditions. We show that we can handle both existential and universal properties this way, and therefore, that we can extend Bounded Synthesis to CTL*. Thus, we obtain the first Safraless synthesis approach and the first synthesis tool for (conjunctions of) the acceptance conditions mentioned above, and for CTL*.

1 Introduction

Reactive synthesis is the problem of constructing a correct system from a specification given as a temporal logic formula or an automaton. For Linear Temporal Logic [22], the standard approach to synthesis involves Safra's relatively complex construction [20,26] to determinize Büchi automata [23]. Over the last decade, alternatives to this approach have led to a boom in reactive synthesis. Besides methods that limit the expressibility of the logic [5] and complete methods including [12,28], Kupferman and Vardi's *Safraless* approach [17] and Finkbeiner and Schewe's *Bounded Synthesis* [27] provide relatively simple and efficient methods to synthesize LTL formulas.

The idea behind Bounded Synthesis is the following. LTL properties can be translated to Büchi automata [29] and verification of LTL properties can be reduced to deciding emptiness of the product of this automaton and the Kripke structure representing an implementation [19,30]. This product is a nondeterministic Büchi automaton in its own right. Finkbeiner and Schewe made two important observations: (1) Using a ranking function, the emptiness problem of nondeterministic Büchi automata can be encoded as a Satisfiability modulo Theories (SMT) query, and (2) by fixing its size, the Kripke structure can be left uninterpreted, resulting in an SMT query for a system that fulfills the property. Because the size of the system is bounded by Safra's construction, this yields an approach to LTL synthesis that is complete in principle. (Although proofs of unrealizability are usually computed differently.)

R. Bloem—Order was defined by a fair coin.

© Springer International Publishing AG 2017
R. Majumdar and V. Kunčak (Eds.): CAV 2017, Part II, LNCS 10427, pp. 333–352, 2017.
DOI: 10.1007/978-3-319-63390-9_18

The reduction to SMT used by Bounded Synthesis provides two benefits: the performance progress of SMT solvers and the flexibility. With the latter, it is easy to adapt the SMT constraints produced by Bounded Synthesis to build semi-complete synthesizers for distributed [27], self-stabilising [6], parameterized [13], assume-guarantee [7], probabilistic [3], and partially implemented systems.

In this paper, we extend Bounded Synthesis in two directions. First, we show how we can directly encode into SMT that some path of a system is accepted by an X automaton, for $X \in \{\text{Büchi, co-Büchi, Parity, Streett, Rabin}\}$. We do this by introducing new ranking functions, circumventing the need to explicitly translate these automata into Büchi automata.

Second, we extend Bounded Synthesis to branching logics. The branching logics allow the user to specify structural properties of the system. For example, if g is system output and r is system input, then the CTL^* formula $\text{AG EF}g$ says that a state satisfying g is always reachable; and the CTL^* formula $\text{EFG}(g \wedge r)$ roughly says that a state satisfying g is reachable and it has a self-loop satisfying r. In both cases, the existential path quantifier E allows us to refrain from specifying the exact path that leads to such states.

We show two approaches to the bounded synthesis for CTL^*. First, we show that we can use the ranking functions for X automata to either decide that some path of a system fulfills such a condition, or that *all* paths of the system do. Once we have established this fact, we can extend Bounded Synthesis to logics like CTL^* by replacing all state subformulas by fresh atomic propositions and encoding them each by a Büchi automaton. This approach follows the classical construction [9] of model checking CTL^*, extending it to synthesis setting. Alternative, we show that we can use a translation of CTL^* to Hesitant Alternating Automata [18] to obtain a relatively simple encoding to SMT.

Thus, we obtain a relatively simple, Safraless synthesis procedure to (conjunctions of) various acceptance conditions and CTL^*. This gives us a full decision procedure that is efficient when the specification is satisfied by a small system, but is admittedly impractical at showing unrealizability. Just like Bounded Synthesis does for LTL synthesis, it also gives us a semi-decision procedure for undecidable problems such as distributed [24] or parameterized synthesis [13,15]. We have implemented the CTL^* synthesis approach in a tool which to our knowledge is the only tool that supports CTL^* synthesis.

2   Definitions

Notation: $\mathbb{B} = \{\text{true}, \text{false}\}$ is the set of Boolean values, $\mathbb{N}$ is the set of natural numbers (excluding 0), $[k]$ is the set $\{i \in \mathbb{N} \mid i \leq k\}$ and $[0, k]$ is the set $[k] \cup \{0\}$ for $k \in \mathbb{N}$.

In this paper we consider *finite* systems and automata.

A *(Moore) system* M is a tuple $(I, O, T, t_0, \tau, out)$ where I and O are disjoint sets of input and output variables, T is the set of states, $t_0 \in T$ is the initial state, $\tau : T \times 2^I \to T$ is a transition function, $out : T \to 2^O$ is the output function that labels each state with a set of output variables. Note that systems have no dead ends and have a transition for every input.

For the rest of the section, fix a system $M = (I, O, T, t_0, \tau, out)$.

A *system path* is a sequence $t_1 t_2 \ldots \in T^\omega$ such that for every $i \in \mathbb{N}$ there is $e \in 2^I$ with $\tau(t_i, e) = t_{i+1}$. An *input-labeled system path* is a sequence $(t_1, e_1)(t_2, e_2) \ldots \in (T \times 2^I)^\omega$ where $\tau(t_i, e_i) = t_{i+1}$ for every $i \in \mathbb{N}$. A *system trace starting from* $t_1 \in T$ is a sequence $(o_1 \cup e_1)(o_2 \cup e_2) \ldots \in (2^{I \cup O})^\omega$ for which there exists an input-labeled system path $(t_1, e_1)(t_2, e_2) \ldots$ and $o_i = out(t_i)$ for every $i \in \mathbb{N}$. Note that since systems are Moore, the output o_i cannot "react" to input e_i, the outputs are "delayed" with respect to inputs.

A *word automaton* A is a tuple $(\Sigma, Q, q_0, \delta, acc)$ where Σ is an alphabet, Q is a set of states, $q_0 \in Q$ is initial, $\delta : Q \times \Sigma \to 2^Q$ is a transition relation, $acc : Q^\omega \to \mathbb{B}$ is a path acceptance condition. Note that automata have no dead ends and have a transition for every letter of the alphabet.

For the rest of the section, fix automaton $A = (\Sigma, Q, q_0, \delta, acc)$ with $\Sigma = 2^{I \cup O}$.

A *path in automaton* A is a sequence $q_0 q_1 \ldots \in Q^\omega$ starting in the initial state such that there exists $a_i \in \Sigma$ for every $i \geq 0$ such that $(q_i, a_i, q_{i+1}) \in \delta(q_i)$. A *sequence* $a_0 a_1 \cdots \in \Sigma^\omega$ *generates a path* $\pi = q_0 q_1 \ldots$ iff for every $i \geq 0$: $(q_i, a_i, q_{i+1}) \in \delta$. A *path* π *is accepted* iff $acc(\pi)$ holds.

We distinguish two types of automata: universal and non-deterministic. The type defines when the automaton accepts a given infinite sequence.

A *non-deterministic automaton* A accepts an infinite sequence from Σ^ω iff there exists an accepted path generated by the sequence. Universal automata require *all* paths generated by the sequence to be accepted. For an automaton A, write $L(A)$ for the set of all infinite sequences accepted by A.

The *product* $M \times A$ is the automaton $(Q \times T, (q_0, t_0), \Delta, acc')$ such that for all $(q, t) \in Q \times T$: $\Delta(q, t) = \{(\delta(q, a \cup out(t)), \tau(q, a)) \mid a \in 2^I\}$. Define acc' to return true for a given $\pi \in (Q \times T)^\omega$ iff acc returns true for the corresponding projection of π into Q. Note that $M \times A$ has the 1-letter alphabet (not shown in the tuple).

We distinguish between two *path quantifiers*, E and A: $M \models \mathsf{E}(A)$ iff there is a system trace $(o_0 \cup e_0)(o_1 \cup e_1) \ldots$ accepted by the automaton; $M \models \mathsf{A}(A)$ iff every system trace is accepted by the automaton.

Finally, we define different acceptance conditions. For a given infinite sequence $\pi \in Q^\omega$, let $Inf(\pi)$ be the elements of Q appearing in π infinitely often and let $Fin(\pi) = Q \setminus Inf(\pi)$. Then:

- *Büchi acceptance* is defined by a set $F \subseteq Q$: $acc(\pi)$ holds iff $Inf(\pi) \cap F \neq \emptyset$.
- *Co-Büchi acceptance* is defined by a set $F \subseteq Q$: $acc(\pi)$ holds iff $F \subseteq Fin(\pi)$.
- *Streett acceptance* is defined by pairs $\{(A_i \subseteq Q, G_i \subseteq Q)\}_{i \in [k]}$: $acc(\pi)$ holds iff $\forall i \in [k] : Inf(\pi) \cap A_i \neq \emptyset \to Inf(\pi) \cap G_i \neq \emptyset$.
- *Rabin acceptance* is defined by pairs $\{(F_i, I_i)\}_{i \in [k]}$: $acc(\pi)$ holds iff $\exists i \in [k] : F_i \subseteq Fin(\pi) \wedge Inf(\pi) \cap I_i \neq \emptyset$.
- *Parity acceptance* is defined by a priority function $p : Q \to [0, k]$: $acc(\pi)$ holds iff the minimal priority appearing infinitely often in $p(\pi)$ is even.

In addition to the above acceptance conditions, we define generalized versions. Generalized Büchi acceptance condition is defined by a set $\{F_i\}_{i \in [k]}$: $acc(\pi)$

holds iff the Büchi condition holds wrt. every F_i where $i \in [k]$. Similarly define Generalized co-Büchi, Streett, Rabin, and Parity conditions.

Abbreviations. We use the standard three letter abbreviation for automata $\{U, N, D\} \times \{B, C, S, P, R\} \times \{W\}$. For example, NBW means Nondeterministic Büchi Word automaton, UCW—Universal co-Büchi Word automaton.

3   Synthesis from Büchi, Streett, Rabin, Parity Automata

In this section we describe how to verify and synthesize properties described by Büchi, co-Büchi, Parity, Streett, and Rabin conditions. For each acceptance condition $X \in \{$Büchi, co-Büchi, Parity, Streett, Rabin$\}$, we can handle the question whether (the word defined by) some path of a system is in the language of a nondeterministic X automata, as well as the question of whether all paths of the system are in the language defined by a universal X automaton. There does not appear to be an easy way to mix these queries ("do all paths of the system fulfill the property defined by a given nondeterministic automaton?").

3.1   Ranking Functions

In the following, given a system $M = (I, O, T, t_0, \tau, out)$ and a nondeterministic (universal) automaton $A = (2^{I \cup O}, Q, q_0, \delta, acc)$, we will describe how to build an SMT query $\Phi_{M,A}$ that is satisfiable iff some path (all paths, resp.) of M are in $L(A)$. That is, we focus on the verification problem. When the verification problem is solved, we obtain the solution to the synthesis problem easily, following the Bounded Synthesis approach: Given an automaton A, we ask the SMT solver whether there is a system M such that $\Phi_{M,A}$ is satisfiable. More precisely, for increasing k, we fix a set of k states and ask the SMT solver for a transition relation τ and a labeling out for which $\Phi_{M,A}$ is satisfiable.

For the following, fix a system $M = (I, O, T, t_0, \tau, out)$ and an automaton $A = (2^{I \cup O}, Q, q_0, \delta, acc)$.

Our constructions use ranking functions. A *ranking function* is a function $\rho : Q \times T \to D$ for some well-founded domain D. A *rank comparison relation* is a relation $\rhd \subseteq Q \times D \times D$. In the following, we write $\rho(q, t) \rhd_q \rho(q', t')$ to mean $(q, \rho(q, t), \rho(q', t')) \in \rhd$.

We will first establish how to use these to check existential and universal properties and then define the ranking functions for the different acceptance conditions. Given a rank comparison function $\rhd$, we define the following formula to check an existential property:

$$\Phi_E^{\rhd}(M, A) = rch(q_0, t_0) \wedge$$
$$\bigwedge_{q,t \in Q \times T} rch(q, t) \rightarrow \bigvee_{(q, i \cup o, q') \in \delta} out(t) = o \wedge rch(q', \tau(t, i)) \wedge \rho(q, t) \rhd_q \rho(q', \tau(t, i)).$$

Similarly, to check universal properties, we define

$$\Phi_A^\triangleright(M, A) = rch(q_0, t_0) \wedge$$
$$\bigwedge_{q,t \in Q \times T} rch(q, t) \rightarrow \bigwedge_{(q, i \cup o, q') \in \delta} out(t) = o \rightarrow rch(q', \tau(t, i)) \wedge \rho(q, t) \triangleright_q \rho(q', \tau(t, i)).$$

In these formulas,

- the free variable $rch : Q \times T \rightarrow \mathbb{B}$ is an uninterpreted function that marks reachable states in the product of M and A, and
- the free variable $\rho : Q \times T \rightarrow \mathbb{N}$ is an uninterpreted ranking function.

Intuitively, $\Phi_E^\triangleright$ encodes that there is an accepting loop in the product automaton, while $\Phi_A^\triangleright$ ensures that all loops are accepting.

Given a path $\pi = (q_1, t_1)(q_2, t_2) \cdots \in (Q \times T)^\omega$ and a rank comparison relation $\triangleright$, we say that π *satisfies* $\triangleright$, denoted by $\pi \models \triangleright$, iff there exists a ranking function ρ such that $\rho(q_i, t_i) \triangleright_q \rho(q_{i+1}, t_{i+1})$ holds for every $i > 0$.

Let us look at the properties of these equations.

Lemma 1. *For any rank comparison relation* $\triangleright$: $\Phi_E^\triangleright(M, A)$ *is satisfiable iff* $M \times A$ *has an infinite path* $\pi = (q_1, t_1)(q_2, t_2) \ldots$ *that satisfies* $\triangleright$.

Proof Idea. Direction $\Leftarrow$. Assume that the product contains a path $\pi = (q_1, t_1) \ldots$ such that $\pi \models \triangleright$. By definition of $\pi \models \triangleright$, there is ρ such that $\rho(q_i, t_i) \triangleright \rho(q_{i+1}, t_{i+1})$ holds for every $i > 0$. If we use the same ρ for $\Phi_E^\triangleright(M, A)$ and set $rch(q, t)$ to true for $(q, t) \in \pi$ and to false for the other states, then the query is satisfied.

Direction $\Rightarrow$. Assume that $\Phi_E^\triangleright$ is satisfied. We use the ranking function ρ from the model of $\Phi_E^\triangleright$ to construct a lasso-shaped infinite path that satisfies $\triangleright$. $\square$

Let acc be an acceptance condition on $(Q \times T)^\omega$. We say that $\triangleright$ *expresses an acceptance condition* acc iff

$$\forall \pi \in (Q \times T)^\omega : \quad \pi \models \triangleright \quad \leftrightarrow \quad acc(\pi).$$

In words: (1) if an infinite path $\pi = (q_1, t_1) \ldots$ is accepted by acc, then there is $\rho : Q \times T \rightarrow \mathbb{N}$ such that $\rho(q_i, t_i) \triangleright_q \rho(q_{i+1}, t_{i+1})$ holds for all i; (2) if for an infinite path there is ρ such that $\rho(q_i, t_i) \triangleright_q \rho(q_{i+1}, t_{i+1})$ holds for all i, then the path is accepted by acc.

The following theorem connects the previous lemma with automata.

Theorem 1 (Soundness and Completeness for $\mathsf{E}(NXW)$). *Given a nondeterministic X automaton A and a system M. Let $\triangleright$ express* acc. *Then:* $\Phi_E^\triangleright(M, A)$ *is satisfiable iff* $M \models \mathsf{E}(A)$.

The formula $\Phi_A^\triangleright$ has similar properties, but in general only direction $\Rightarrow$ holds. The other direction we prove separately for each $\triangleright$ presented in the paper.

Lemma 2. *Given a system M, an automaton A, and any $\triangleright$: if $\Phi_A^{\triangleright}(M, A)$ is satisfiable, then all paths of $M \times A$ satisfy $\triangleright$.*

Proof Idea. Assume that $\Phi_A^{\triangleright}(M, A)$ is satisfied by ranking function ρ. Consider an arbitrary path π in $M \times A$. By the deinfition of $\Phi_A^{\triangleright}$, rch holds for every state of π and $\triangleright$ holds for every two consecutive states. Thus, π satisfies $\triangleright$. □

Theorem 2 (Soundness for A(UXW)). *Given a universal X automaton $A = (2^{I \cup O}, Q, q_0, \delta, acc)$ and a system $M = (I, O, T, t_0, \tau, out)$, let $\triangleright$ express acc. Then: if $\Phi_A^{\triangleright}(M, A)$ is satisfiable, then $M \models \mathsf{A}(A)$.*

3.2   Encoding for Büchi Automata

In the next sections, we describe rank comparison relations $\triangleright$ for the acceptance conditions Büchi, co-Büchi, Streett, Rabin, and Parity. We prove correctness only for Streett acceptance—the cases of Büchi, co-Büchi, and Parity follows as special cases. The correctness of $\triangleright$ constraints for Rabin acceptance follows from the work of Piterman et al. [21]. For didactical purposes, let us start with the relatively simple Büchi and co-Büchi conditions.

Büchi conditions were also presented in [8] and implicitly in [3]. Given a Büchi automaton $A = (2^{I \cup O}, Q, q_0, \delta, F)$, we define the rank comparison relation $\triangleright_B^A$ as

$$\rho(q, t) \triangleright_B^A \rho(q', t') = \begin{cases} true & \text{if } q \in F \\ \rho(q, t) > \rho(q', t') & \text{if } q \notin F \end{cases} \tag{1}$$

We have that $\triangleright_B$ expresses the Büchi condition. Intuitively, given an infinite path, we can use the natural numbers as the ranking domain and associate each state with the distance to the next acceptance condition on the path. If the path does not contain infinitely many accepting states, this ranking is not possible for a well-founded domain.

3.3   Encoding for Co-Büchi Automata

This case was presented in the original paper [27] on Bounded Synthesis. Given a co-Büchi automaton $A = (2^{I \cup O}, Q, q_0, \delta, F)$, the ranking constraint relation $\triangleright_C^A$ for co-Büchi is defined as

$$\rho(q, t) \triangleright_C^A \rho(q', t') = \begin{cases} \rho(q, t) > \rho(q', t) & \text{if } q \in F \\ \rho(q, t) \geq \rho(q', t') & \text{if } q \notin F. \end{cases} \tag{2}$$

We have that $\triangleright_C$ expresses the co-Büchi condition. Intuitively, a ranking of a path with infinitely many rejecting states is not possible, because the domain does not have an infinitely descending chain. If the number is finite, we can label each state with the number of rejecting states that are yet to come.

3.4 Encoding for Streett Automata

Given a Streett automaton $A = (2^{I \cup O}, Q, q_0, \delta, \{(A_i, G_i)\}_{i \in [k]})$, we take the domain $D = \mathbb{N}$ and define the rank comparison relation $\rhd_S = \bigwedge_i \rho(q, t) \rhd_S^{A,i} \rho(q', t')$, where

$$\rho(q,t) \rhd_S^{A,i} \rho(q',t') = \begin{cases} true & \text{if } q \in G_i \\ \rho_i(q,t) > \rho_i(q',t') & \text{if } q \in A_i \wedge q \notin G_i \\ \rho_i(q,t) \geq \rho_i(q',t') & \text{if } q \notin A_i \cup G_i \end{cases} \tag{3}$$

Theorem 3. *The rank comparison relation $\rhd_S$ expresses the Streett condition.*

In Sect. 3.1, we have shown that we can check for the existence of a path satisfying an acceptance condition if we are given a rank comparison relation that expresses the condition. We have also shown the soundness of the construction for checking whether all paths satisfy the condition. It remains to show that this construction is complete.

Theorem 4. *Given a Streett automaton $A = (2^{I \cup O}, Q, q_0, \delta, \{(A_i, G_i)\}_{i \in [k]})$ and a system $M = (I, O, T, t_0, \tau, out)$: if $M \models A(A)$, then $\Phi_A^{\rhd_S^A}(M, A)$ is satisfiable.*

Proof. Let $M \models A(A)$. We construct a model (ρ and rch) that satisfies the query. Let $rch(q, t) = \text{true}$ iff $(q, t) \in Q \times T$ is reachable in the product $\Gamma = M \times A$, and let $\rho_i(q, t) = 0$ for every unreachable $(q, t) \in Q \times T$. Now let us remove all unreachable states from Γ. Then for each $i \in [k]$, ρ_i is defined as follows.

- For every $(q, t) \in \cup_{i \in [k]} G_i \times T$, let $\rho_i(q, t) = 0$.
- Define an *SCC S of a graph* to be any maximal subset of the graph states such that for any $s \in S$, $s' \in S$, the graph has a path $\pi = s, \ldots, s'$ of length ≥ 2, where the length is the number of states appearing on the path. Thus, a single-state SCC can appear only if the state has a self-loop.
- Remove all outgoing edges from every state (q, t) of Γ with $q \in G_i$. The resulting graph Γ' has no SCCs that have a state (q, t) with $q \in \cup_{i \in [k]} A_i$.
- Let us define the graph Γ''. Let S be the set of all SCCs of Γ'. Then Γ'' has the states $V_{\Gamma''} = S \cup \{\{s\} \mid s \notin \cup_{S \in S} S\}$, i.e., each state is either an SCC or a singleton-set containing a state outside of any SCC (but in both cases, a state of Γ' is a set of states of Γ). The edges $E_{\Gamma''}$ of Γ'' are: $(S_1, S_2) \in E_{\Gamma''}$ iff $\exists s_1 \in S_1, s_2 \in S_2 : S_1 \neq S_2 \wedge (s_1, s_2) \in E_{\Gamma'}$. Intuitively, Γ'' is a graph derived from Γ by turning all accepting states into leafs, and by making SCCs the new states. Note that the graph Γ'' is a DAG.
- Given a path $\pi = S_1, \ldots, S_m$ in Γ'', let $nb(\pi)$ be the number of "bad" states visited on the path, i.e., $nb = |\pi \cap \{\{(q, t)\} : q \in \cup_{i \in [k]} A_i\}|$. Such a number exists since all paths of Γ'' are finite.
- For all $(q, t) \in S \in V_{\Gamma''}$ with $q \notin G_i$, let $\rho_i(q, t)$ be the max number of "bad" states visited on any path from S: $\rho_i(q, t) = max(\{nb(\pi) \mid \pi \text{ is a path from } S\})$. Such a number exists since the number of paths in Γ'' is finite. $\qquad \square$

Remark 1 (Comparison with ranking from [21]). Piterman et al. [21] introduced ranking functions to solve Streett *games*. Our ranking functions can be adapted to solve games, too. (Recall that our SMT encoding describes *model checking* with an uninterpreted system.) It may seem that in the case of games, our construction uses fewer counters than [21], but that is not the case. Given a DSW with k Streett pairs and n states, a winning strategy in the corresponding Streett game may require a memory of size $k!$. In this case, the size of system $\times$ automaton is $k!n$. Our construction introduces $2k$ counters with the domain $[k!n] \rightarrow [k!n]$ to associate a rank with each state. In contrast, [21] introduces $k!k$ counters with the domain $[n] \rightarrow [0, n]$. Encoding these counters into SAT would require $2k \cdot k!n \cdot log_2(k!n)$ bits for our construction, and $k!k \cdot n \cdot log_2(n)$ bits for the construction of [21]. Thus, our construction introduces $2(1 + log_2(k!)/log_2(n))$ times more bits. On the positive side, our construction is much simpler.

3.5   Encoding for Parity Automata

Given a Parity automaton $A = (2^{I \cup O}, Q, q_0, \delta, p)$ with indices $0, \ldots, k-1$, it is well known that we can translate it into the Streett automaton with pairs $(A_1, G_1), \ldots, (A_{m/2}, G_{m/2})$, where $A_i = \{q \mid p(q) = 2i - 1\}$, $G_i = \{q \mid p(q) \in \{0, 2, \ldots, 2i - 2\}\}$. We can then apply the encoding for Streett automata. The resulting ranking is essentially Jurdziński's progress measure [14].

3.6   Encoding for Rabin Automata

Given a Rabin automaton $A = (2^{I \cup O}, Q, q_0, \delta, \{F_i, I_i\}_{i \in [k]})$ and a system $M = (I, O, T, t_0, \tau, out)$, we use ranking contraints described by Piterman et al. [21] to construct a rank comparison relation. We define the ranking domain D to consist of tuples of numbers $(b, j_1, d_1, \ldots, j_k, d_k)$, where $\rho(q, t)$ has the following meaning. For each $l \in [k]$,

- $j_l \in [k]$ is the index of a Rabin pair,
- $b \in [0, |Q \times T|]$ is an upper bound on the number of times the set F_{j_1} can be visited from (q, t),
- $d_l \in [0, |Q \times T|]$ is the maximal distance from (q, t) to the set I_{j_l},

We define $\rhd_R^A$ as $\rho(q, t) \rhd_q \rho(q', t')$ iff there exists $l \in [k]$ such that one of the following holds:

$$b > b',$$
$$(b, \ldots, j_{l-1}, d_{l-1}) = (b', \ldots, j'_{l-1}, d'_{l-1}) \land j_l > j'_l \land q \notin \bigcup_{m \in [l-1]} F_{j_m},$$
$$(b, \ldots, j_l) = (b', \ldots, j'_l) \qquad \land d_l > d'_l \land q \notin \bigcup_{m \in [l]} F_{j_m} \qquad (4)$$
$$(b, \ldots, j_l) = (b', \ldots, j'_l) \qquad \land q \in I_{j_l} \land q \notin \bigcup_{m \in [l]} F_{j_m}$$

Here is the intuition. The first line bounds the number of visits to F_{j_1} (b decreases each time F_{j_1} is visited). The second line limits the changes of order $j_1, \ldots, j_k$

in rank b, $j_1, d_1, \ldots, j_k, d_k$ to a finite number. Together, these two lines ensure that on any path some F_m is not visited infinitely often. The third and fourth lines require I_{j_l} to be visited within d_l steps; once it is visited, the distance d_l can be reset to any number $\leq |Q \times T|$.

We can encode rank comparison constraints $\rhd$ in Eq. 4 into SMT as follows. For each of $j_1 \ldots j_k$ introduce an uninterpreted function: $Q \times T \to [k]$. For each of $b, d_1, \ldots, d_k$ introduce an uninterpreted function: $Q \times T \to [0, |Q \times T|]$. Finally, replace in Eq. 4 counters b, j, d, b', j', d' with expressions $b(q,t)$, $j(q,t)$, $d(q,t)$, $b(q',t')$, $j(q',t')$, $d(q',t')$ resp.

3.7 Generalized Automata

The extension to generalized automata is simple: replace $\rho(q,t) \rhd \rho(q',t')$ with $\bigwedge_i \rho_i(q,t) \rhd \rho_i(q',t')$ where ρ_i describes the ranking of ith automaton component. Note that all components use the same rch variables.

4 Synthesis for CTL*

We describe two ways to encode model checking for CTL* into SMT. The first one, direct encoding (Sect. 4.2), resembles bottom-up CTL* model checking [9]. The second encoding (Sect. 4.3) follows the automata-theoretic approach [18] and goes via hesitant tree automata. As usual, replacing a concrete system function with an uninterpreted one of a fixed size gives a bounded synthesis procedure.

Let us compare the approaches. In the direct encoding, the main difficulty is the procedure that generates the constraints: we need to walk through the formula and generate constraints for nondeterministic Büchi or universal co-Büchi subformulas. In the approach via hesitant tree automata, we first translate a given CTL* into a hesitant tree automaton A, and then encode the non-emptiness problem of the product of A and the system into an SMT query. In contrast to the direct encoding, the difficult part is to construct the automaton, while the definition of the rank comparison relation is very easy.

In the next section we define CTL* with inputs and then describe two approaches. The approaches are conceptually the same, thus automata fans are invited to read Sect. 4.3 about the approach using hesitant automata, while the reader who prefers bottom-up CTL* model checking is welcomed to Sect. 4.2.

4.1 CTL* with Inputs

For this section, fix a system $M = (I, O, T, t_0, \tau, out)$.

Below we define CTL* with inputs. The definition is slightly unusual (it differentiates inputs and outputs, see Remark 2) and is specific to Moore machines.

Syntax of CTL* with Inputs. *State formulas* have the grammar:

$$\Phi = \mathsf{true} \mid \mathsf{false} \mid o \mid \neg o \mid \Phi \wedge \Phi \mid \Phi \vee \Phi \mid \mathsf{A}\varphi \mid \mathsf{E}\varphi$$

where $o \in O$ and φ is a path formula. *Path formulas* are defined by the grammar:

$$\varphi = \Phi \mid i \mid \neg i \mid \varphi \wedge \varphi \mid \varphi \vee \varphi \mid \mathsf{X}\varphi \mid \varphi \mathsf{U} \varphi \mid \varphi \mathsf{R} \varphi,$$

where $i \in I$. The temporal operators G and F are defined as usual.

The above grammar describes the CTL^* formulas in the positive normal form. The general CTL^* formula (in which negations can appear anywhere) can be converted into the formula of this form with no size blowup, using equivalence $\neg(a \mathsf{U} b) \equiv \neg a \mathsf{R} \neg b$.

Semantics of CTL^* with Inputs. We define the semantics of CTL^* with respect to a system M. The definition is very similar to the standard one [2], except for a few cases involving inputs (marked with "+").

Let $t \in T$, and $o \in O$. Then:

- $t \not\models \Phi$ iff $t \models \Phi$ does not hold
- $t \models$ true and $t \not\models$ false
- $t \models o$ iff $o \in out(t)$, $t \models \neg o$ iff $o \notin out(t)$
- $t \models \Phi_1 \wedge \Phi_2$ iff $t \models \Phi_1$ and $t \models \Phi_2$. Similarly for $\Phi_1 \vee \Phi_2$.
+ $t \models \mathsf{A}\varphi$ iff for all *input-labeled* system paths π starting from t: $\pi \models \varphi$. For $\mathsf{E}\varphi$, replace "for all" with "there exists".

Let $\pi = (t_1, e_1)(t_2, e_2) \ldots \in (T \times 2^I)^\omega$ be an input-labeled system path and $i \in I$. For $k \in \mathbb{N}$, define $\pi_{[k:]} = (t_k, e_k) \ldots$, i.e., the suffix of π starting from (t_k, e_k). Then:

- $\pi \models \Phi$ iff $t_1 \models \Phi$
+ $\pi \models i$ iff $i \in e_1$, $\pi \models \neg i$ iff $i \notin e_1$
- $\pi \models \varphi_1 \wedge \varphi_2$ iff $\pi \models \varphi_1$ and $\pi \models \varphi_2$. Similarly for $\varphi_1 \vee \varphi_2$.
- $\pi \models \mathsf{X}\varphi$ iff $\pi_{[2:]} \models \varphi$
- $\pi \models \varphi_1 \mathsf{U} \varphi_2$ iff $\exists l \in \mathbb{N} : (\pi_{[l:]} \models \varphi_2 \wedge \forall m \in [1, l-1] : \pi_{[m:]} \models \varphi_1)$
- $\pi \models \varphi_1 \mathsf{R} \varphi_2$ iff $(\forall l \in \mathbb{N} : \pi_{[l:]} \models \varphi_2) \vee (\exists l \in \mathbb{N} : \pi_{[l:]} \models \varphi_1 \wedge \forall m \in [1, l] : \pi_{[m:]} \models \varphi_2)$

A system M satisfies a CTL^* *state formula* Φ, written $M \models \Phi$, iff the initial state satisfies it.

Note that $M \models i \wedge o$ is not defined, since $i \wedge o$ is not a state formula.

Remark 2 (Inputs vs. outputs). Let $r \in I$ and $g \in O$. According to the semantics, $\mathsf{E}r \wedge \mathsf{E}\neg r$ is valid, while $\mathsf{E}g \wedge \mathsf{E}\neg g$ ($\equiv g \wedge \neg g$) is unsatisfiable. Vice versa, $\mathsf{A}r \vee \mathsf{A}\neg r$ is unsatisfiable, while $\mathsf{A}g \vee \mathsf{A}\neg g$ ($\equiv g \vee \neg g$) is valid. This distinction is a consequence of the way we group inputs and outputs into traces.

4.2 Direct Encoding

We can encode CTL^* model checking in SMT following the classical model checking approach [9] with the exception that system is described by uninterpreted functions.

Let Φ be a CTL* state formula. We define the SMT query as follows.

(1) Replace each subformula f_i of Φ that starts with A or E with a new proposition p_i, and let $P = \{p_1, \ldots, p_k\}$. Thus, each p_i corresponds to some E/Aφ_i where φ_i is a path formula over $I \cup O \cup P$.

(2) For each $f \in \{f_1, \ldots, f_k\}$, we do the following. If f is of the form Aφ, we translate φ into a UCW[1], otherwise into an NBW; let the resulting automaton be $A_\varphi = (2^{I \cup O \cup P}, Q, q_0, \delta, F)$. Then for all $(q, t) \in Q \times T$ the query contains the constraints:

(2a) If A_φ is an NBW, then:

$$rch(q, t) \;\to\; \bigvee_{(i, q') \in \delta(q, out(t), P(t))} rch(q', t') \wedge \rho(q, t) \triangleright_B \rho(q', t')$$

(2b) If A_φ is a UCW, then:

$$rch(q, t) \;\to\; \bigwedge_{(i, q') \in \delta(q, out(t), P(t))} rch(q', t') \wedge \rho(q, t) \triangleright_C \rho(q', t')$$

In both cases, we have: $P(t) = \{p_i \in P \mid rch(q_0^{p_i}, t) = \text{true}\}$, $q_0^{p_i}$ is the initial state of A_{φ_i}, $\triangleright_B$ and $\triangleright_C$ are the Büchi and co-Büchi rank comparison functions wrt. A_φ (see Eqs. 1 and 2), and $t' = \tau(t, i)$. Intuitively, $P(t)$ under-approximates the subformulas that hold in t: if $p_i \in P(t)$, then $t \models f_i$.

(3) Let $\widetilde{\Phi}$ be the top-level Boolean formula of Φ. Then the query contains the constraint $\widetilde{\Phi}[p_i \leftarrow rch(q_0^{p_i}, t_0)]$, where $q_0^{p_i}$ is the initial state of A_{φ_i}. For example, for $\Phi = \neg g \wedge \text{AG EF} \neg g$ the constraint is $\neg g(t_0) \wedge rch(q_0^{p_2}, t_0)$ where: $g \in O$, p_2 corresponds to AGp_1, p_1 corresponds to EF$\neg g$.

Theorem 5 (Correctness of Direct Encoding). *Given a CTL* formula Φ over inputs I and outputs O and a system $M = (I, O, T, t_0, \tau, out)$: $M \models \Phi$ iff the query is satisfiable.*

Here is the intuition behind the proof. The standard bottom-up model checker marks every system state with state subformulas it satisfies. The model checker returns "Yes" iff the initial state satisfies the top-level Boolean formula. The direct encoding conceptually follows that approach. If for some system state t, $rch(q_0^{p_i}, t)$ holds, then t satisfies the corresponding to p_i state formula f_i. Thus, if the top-level Boolean constraint (3) holds, then $t_0 \models \Phi$. And vice versa: if model checker returns "Yes", then the marking it produced can be used to satisfy the SMT constraints. Finally, the positive normal form of Φ allows us to get away with encoding of positive obligations only ($rch(q_0^{p_i}, t) \Rightarrow t \models f_i$), eliminating the need to encode $\neg rch(q_0^{p_i}, t) \Rightarrow t \models \neg f_i$.

Example 1. Let $I = \{r\}$, $O = \{g\}$, $\Phi = g \wedge \text{AG EF} \neg g$. We associate p_1 with EF$\neg g$ and p_2 with AGp_1. Automata for p_1 and p_2 are in Fig. 1, the SMT constraints are in Fig. 2.

---

[1] To translate φ into a UCW, translate $\neg \varphi$ into an NBW and treat it as a UCW.

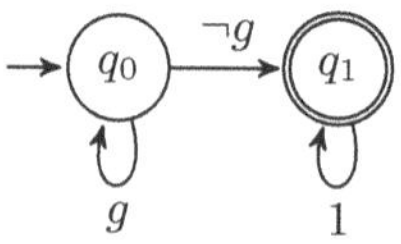

(a) NBW for $F \neg g$ 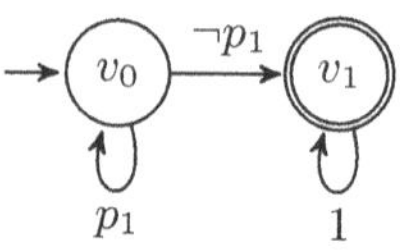   (b) UCW for Gp_1

Fig. 1. Automata for Example 1

$g(t) \wedge rch(q_0, t_0)$

$\displaystyle\bigwedge_{t \in T, r \in \mathbb{B}} rch(v_0, t) \wedge rch(q_0, t) \rightarrow rch(v_0, \tau(t, r)) \wedge \rho(v_0, t) \geq \rho(v_0, \tau(t, r))$

$\displaystyle\bigwedge_{t \in T, r \in \mathbb{B}} rch(v_0, t) \wedge \neg rch(q_0, t) \rightarrow rch(v_1, \tau(t, r)) \wedge \rho(v_0, t) \geq \rho(v_1, \tau(t, r))$

$\displaystyle\bigwedge_{t \in T, r \in \mathbb{B}} rch(v_1, t) \rightarrow rch(v_1, \tau(t, r)) \wedge \rho(v_1, t) > \rho(v_1, \tau(t, r))$

$\displaystyle\bigwedge_{t \in T, r \in \mathbb{B}} rch(q_0, t) \wedge g(t) \rightarrow rch(q_0, \tau(t, r)) \wedge \rho(q_0, t) > \rho(q_0, \tau(t, r))$

$\displaystyle\bigwedge_{t \in T, r \in \mathbb{B}} rch(q_0, t) \wedge \neg g(t) \rightarrow rch(q_1, \tau(t, r)) \wedge \rho(q_0, t) > \rho(q_1, \tau(t, r))$

$\displaystyle\bigwedge_{t \in T, r \in \mathbb{B}} rch(q_1, t) \rightarrow rch(q_1, \tau(t, r))$

Fig. 2. SMT constraints for Example 1

4.3   Encoding via Alternating Hesitant Tree Automata

A CTL* property can be converted into a hesitant tree automaton [18]. Then model checking a system with respect to a CTL* property is equivalent to checking non-emptiness of the product of the system and the hesitant automaton. The non-emptiness question can be reduced to solving a 1-Rabin game, and that is what the SMT query will express. The query will be satisfiable iff the product is non-empty. Below we define hesitant tree automata and describe the encoding.

Definitions. Intuitively, for a given CTL* formula, the alternating hesitant automaton expresses proof obligations encoded in (1)–(4) in Sect. 4.2, but in the form of an automaton. Thus, it is a mix of Büchi and co-Büchi automata.

Let $B^+(Q)$ be the set of all positive Boolean formulas over variables Q. Fix two disjoint finite sets, I and O. An *alternating hesitant tree automaton (AHT)* is a tuple $(\Sigma, D, Q, q_0, \delta, Acc)$, where $\Sigma = 2^O$, $D = 2^I$, $q_0 \in Q$ is the initial state, $\delta : Q \times \Sigma \rightarrow B^+(D \times Q)$ is the transition relation, $Acc \subseteq Q$ is the acceptance condition, and the following restrictions hold.

- Q can be partitioned into $Q_1^N, \ldots, Q_{k_N}^N$, $Q_1^U, \ldots, Q_{k_U}^U$, $Q_1^T, \ldots, Q_{k_T}^T$, where superscript N means nondeterministic, U means universal, and T means transient. Also, let $Q^N = \bigcup Q_i^N$, $Q^U = \bigcup Q_i^U$, and $Q^T = \bigcup Q_i^T$.

- There is a partial order on $\{Q_1^N, \ldots, Q_{k_N}^N, Q_1^U, \ldots, Q_{k_U}^U, Q_1^T, \ldots, Q_{k_T}^T\}$.
- The transition function δ satisfies: for any $q \in Q$, $a \in \Sigma$
  - if $q \in Q_i^T$, then: $\delta(q, a)$ contains no elements of Q_i^T; every element of $\delta(q, a)$ belongs to a lower set (with respect to the partial order);
  - if $q \in Q_i^N$, then: $\delta(q, a)$ contains only disjunctively related[2] elements of Q_i^N; every element of $\delta(q, a)$ outside of Q_i^N belongs to a lower set;
  - if $q \in Q_i^U$, then: $\delta(q, a)$ contains only conjunctively related (see footnote 2) elements of Q_i^U; every element of $\delta(q, a)$ outside of Q_i^U belongs to a lower set.

We later define the acceptance of a system by such an automaton.

A *1-letter alternating hesitant word automaton (1-AHW)* is an AHW $(Q, q_0, \delta : Q \to \mathcal{B}^+(Q), Acc \subseteq Q)$. Its alphabet has only one letter (not shown in the tuple) and the automaton satisfies restrictions on δ and Q similar to those for AHTs.

A *run of a 1-AHW* $(Q, q_0, \delta : Q \to \mathcal{B}^+(Q), Acc \subseteq Q)$ is a labeled tree defined in a standard way. Its nodes are from Q^*, the root is q_0, the labeling l maps a node (in Q^*) to the last element (in Q), and for any reachable node, $l(succ(n)) \models \delta(l(n))$ where $l(succ(n))$ is the set of labels of the successors of node n. A *run is accepting* if all paths of the tree satisfy the acceptance condition. A run tree *path satisfies the acceptance condition Acc* iff one of the following holds:

- the corresponding path in the 1-AHW gets trapped in some Q^U and visits $Acc \cap Q^U$ only finitely often, or
- the corresponding path in the 1-AHW gets trapped in some Q^N and visits some state of $Acc \cap Q^N$ infinitely often.

Intuitively, the 1-AHW acceptance condition is a mix of Büchi and co-Büchi acceptance conditions. It can also be seen as a Rabin acceptance with one pair (F, I) where $F = Acc \cap Q^U$ and $I = (Acc \cap Q^N) \cup (Q^U \setminus Acc)$.

Note that any path of a run tree of a 1-AHW is trapped in some Q_i^N or Q_i^U.

The *non-emptiness question of 1-AHW* is "does the automaton has an accepting run?".

A *product of an AHT* $(2^O, 2^I, Q, q_0, \delta, Acc)$ and a system $(I, O, T, t_0, \tau, out)$ is a 1-AHW $(Q \times T, (q_0, t_0), \Delta, Acc')$ s.t. $Acc' = \{(q, t) \mid q \in Acc\}$ and for all (q, t):

$$\Delta(q, t) = \delta(q, out(t))[(d, q') \mapsto (\tau(t, d), q')].$$

A *system is accepting by an AHT* iff their product (1-AHW) is non-empty.

Encoding. Given a system M and a CTL* formula φ, we convert ϕ into an AHT A [18]. Then, we encode the non-emptiness of the 1-AHW $M \times A$ into an SMT query:

---

[2] In a Boolean formula, atoms E are disjunctively (conjunctively) related iff the formula can be written into DNF (CNF) in such a way that each cube (clause) has at most one element from E.

$$rch(q_0, t_0) \wedge$$

$$\bigwedge_{q,t} rch(q,t) \rightarrow \delta(q, out(t)) \; [(d, q') \;\mapsto\; rch(q', \tau(t,d)) \wedge \rho(q,t) \rhd_{q,q'} \rho(q', \tau(t,d))] \tag{5}$$

where $\rhd_{q,q'}$ is:

- if q and q' are in the same Q_i^N, then the Büchi rank comparison $\rhd_B^{Q_i^N}$;
- if q and q' are in the same Q_i^U, then the co-Büchi rank comparison $\rhd_C^{Q_i^N}$;
- otherwise, true.

Note: For ease of explanation, $\rhd_{q,q'}$ depends on q and q', but it can also be defined to depend on q only. Intuitively, states from different Q_i correspond to different state subformulas of Φ.

Theorem 6. *Given a system $(I, O, T, t_0, \tau, out)$ and CTL* formula Φ over inputs I and outputs O: system $\models \Phi$ iff the SMT query in Eq. 5 is satisfiable.*

Proof Idea. Direction $\Rightarrow$. Let (Q, q_0, δ, Acc) be the 1-AHW representing the product system $\times$ AHT (AHT of Φ). We will use the following observation.

> Observation: *The 1-AHW non-emptiness can be reduced to solving the following 1-Rabin game.* The game states are Q, the game graph corresponds to δ, there is one Rabin pair (F, I) with $F = Acc \cap Q^U$, $I = (Acc \cap Q^N) \cup (Q^U \setminus Acc)$. Let us view δ to be in the DNF. Then, in state q of the game, the "existential" player (Automaton) chooses a disjunct in $\delta(q)$, while the "universal" player (Pathfinder) chooses a state in that disjunct. Automaton's strategy is winning iff for any Pathfinder's strategy the resulting play satisfies the Rabin acceptance (F, I). Note that Automaton has a winning strategy iff the 1-AHW is non-empty; also, memoryless strategies suffice for Automaton.

Since the 1-AHW is non-empty, Automaton has a memoryless winning strategy. We will construct rch and ρ from this strategy. For rch: set it to true if there is a strategy for Pathfinder such that the state will reached. Let us prove that ρ exists.

Since states from different Q_i can never form a cycle (due to the partial order), ρ of states from different Q_i are independent. Hence we consider two cases separately: ρ for some Q_i^N and for some Q_i^U.

- The case of Q_i^N is simple: by the definition of the 1-AHW, we can have only simple loops within Q_i^N. Any such reachable loop visits some state from $Acc \cap Q_i^N$. Consider such a loop: assign ρ for state q of the loop to be the minimal distance from any state $Acc \cap Q_i^N$.
- The case of Q_i^U: in contrast, we can have simple and non-simple loops within Q_i^U. But none of such loops visits $Acc \cap Q_i^U$. Then, for each $q \in Q_i^U$ assign ρ to be the maximum bad-distance from any state of Q_i^U. The bad-distance between q and q' is the maximum number of $Acc \cap Q^U$ states visited on any path from q to q'.

Direction ⇐. The query is satisfiable means there is a model for *rch*. Note that the query is Horn-like (... → ...), hence there is a minimal marking *rch* of states that still satisfies the query[3,4]. Wlog., assume *rch* is minimal. Consider the subset of the states of the 1-AHW that are marked with *rch*, and call it U. Note that U is a 1-AHW and it has only universal transitions (i.e., we never mark more than one disjunct of δ on the right side of ... → δ(...)). Intuitively, U represents a finite-state folding of the run tree of the original 1-AHW.

Claim: *the run tree (the unfolding of U) is accepting.* Suppose it is not: there is a run tree path that violates the acceptance. Consider the case when the path is trapped in some Q_i^U. Then the path visits a state in $Q_i^U \cap Acc$ infinitely often. But this is impossible since we use co-Büchi ranking for Q_i^U. Contradiction. The case when the path is trapped in some Q_i^N is similar—the Büchi ranking prevents from not visiting $Acc \cap Q_i^N$ infinitely often.

Thus, the 1-AHW is non-empty since it has an accepting run (U unfolded). □

5 Prototype Synthesizer for CTL*

We implemented both approaches to CTL* synthesis described in Sects. 4.2 and 4.3 inside the tool PARTY [15]: https://github.com/5nizza/party-elli (branch "cav17"). In this section we illustrate the approach via AHTs.

The synthesizer works as follows:

(1) Parse the specification that describes inputs, outputs, and CTL* formula Φ.
(2) Convert Φ into a hesitant tree automaton using the procedure described in [18], using LTL3BA [1] to convert path formulas into NBWs.
(3) For each system size k in increasing order:
  – encode "$\exists M_k : M_k \times AHT \neq \emptyset$?" into SMT using Eq. 5 where $|M_k| = k$
  – call Z3 solver [11]: if the solver returns "unsatisfiable", goto next iteration; otherwise print the model in the dot graph format.

This procedure is complete, because there is a $2^{2^{|\Phi|}}$ bound on the size of the system, although reaching it is impractical.

Running Example: Resettable 1-arbiter. Let $I = \{r\}$, $O = \{g\}$. Consider a simple CTL* property of an arbiter

$$\mathsf{EG}(\neg g) \wedge \mathsf{AG}(r \to \mathsf{F}g) \wedge \mathsf{AG}\,\mathsf{EF}\neg g.$$

---

[3] Minimal in the sense that it is not possible to reduce the number of *rch* truth values by falsifying some of *rch*.

[4] Non-minimality appears when δ of the alternating automaton has OR and the SMT solver marks with *rch* more than one OR argument. Another case is when the solver marks some state with *rch* but there is no antecedent requiring that.

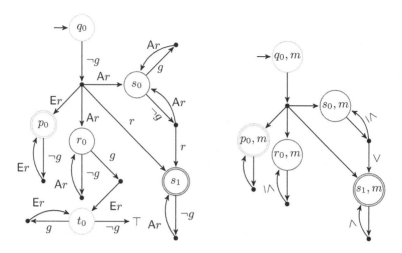

Fig. 3. On the left: AHT for the CTL* formula $\mathsf{EG}\neg g \wedge \mathsf{AG}\ \mathsf{EF}\neg g \wedge \mathsf{AG}(r \rightarrow \mathsf{F}g)$. Green states are from the nondeterministic partion, red states are from the universal partition, double states are final (a red final state is rejecting, a green final state is accepting). Falling out of red (universal) states is allowed, falling out of green (nondeterministic) states is not allowed. State $\top$ denotes an accepting state. In this automaton all transitions out of black dots are conjuncted. For example, $\delta(q_0, \neg g) = ((r, p_0) \vee (\neg r, p_0)) \wedge ((r, r_0) \wedge (\neg r, r_0)) \wedge (r, s_1) \wedge ((r, s_0) \wedge (\neg r, s_0))$. States s_0 and s_1 describe the property $\mathsf{AG}(r \rightarrow \mathsf{F}g)$, state p_0—$\mathsf{EG}\neg g$, states r_0 and t_0—$\mathsf{AG}\ \mathsf{EF}\neg g$, state t_0—$\mathsf{EF}\neg g$.

On the right side is the product (1-AHW) of the AHT with the one state system that never grants (thus it has $m \overset{true}{\rightarrow} m$ and $out(m) = \neg g$). The edges are labeled with the relation $\rhd_{q,q'}$ defined in Eq. 5. The product has no plausible annotatation due to the cycle $(s_1, m) \overset{\geq}{\rightarrow} (s_1, m)$, thus the system does not satisfy the property. (Color figure online)

The property says: there is a path from the initial state where the system never grants (including the initial state); every request should be granted; and finally, a state without the grant should always be reachable. We now invite the reader to Fig. 3. It contains the AHT produced by our tool, and on its right side we show the product of the AHT with the one-state system that does not satisfy the property. The correct system needs at least two states and is on the right.

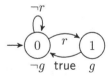

Resettable 2-arbiter. Let $I = \{r_1, r_2\}$, $O = \{g_1, g_2\}$. Consider the formula

$$\mathsf{EG}(\neg g_1 \wedge \neg g_2) \wedge \mathsf{AG}\ \mathsf{EF}(\neg g_1 \wedge \neg g_2) \wedge$$
$$\mathsf{AG}(r_1 \rightarrow \mathsf{F}g_1) \wedge \mathsf{AG}(r_2 \rightarrow \mathsf{F}g_2) \wedge \mathsf{AG}(\neg(g_1 \wedge g_2)).$$

Note that without the properties with E, the synthesizer can produce the system in Fig. 4a which starts in the state without grants and then always grants one or another client. Our synthesizer output the system in Fig. 4b (in one second).

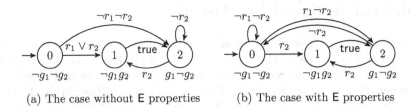

(a) The case without E properties   (b) The case with E properties

Fig. 4. Synthesized systems for the resettable arbiter example

Sender-Receiver System. Consider a sender-receiver system of the following structure. It has two modules, the sender (S) with inputs $\{i_1, i_2\}$ and output *wire* and the receiver (R) with input *wire* and outputs $\{o_1, o_2\}$. The sender can send one bit over the wire to the receiver. We would like to synthesize the sender and receiver modules that satisfy the following CTL* formula over $I = \{i_1, i_2\}$ and $O = \{o_1, o_2\}$:

$$AG((i_1 \wedge i_2) \rightarrow F(o_1 \wedge o_2)) \wedge$$
$$AG((i_1 \wedge i_2 \wedge o_1 \wedge o_2) \rightarrow X(o_1 \wedge o_2)) \wedge$$
$$AG(EF(o_1 \wedge \neg o_2) \wedge EF(\neg o_1 \wedge o_2) \wedge EF(\neg o_1 \wedge \neg o_2) \wedge EF(o_1 \wedge o_2)).$$

Our tool does not support the distributed synthesis, so we manually adapted the SMT query it produced, by introducing the following uninterpreted functions.

- For the sender: the transition function $\tau_s : T_s \times 2^{\{i_1, i_2\}} \rightarrow T_s$ and the output function $out_s : T_s \times 2^{\{i_1, i_2\}} \rightarrow \mathbb{B}$. We set T_s to have a single state.
- For the receiver: the transition function $\tau_r : T_r \times 2^{\{wire\}} \rightarrow T_r$ and the output functions $o_1 : T_r \rightarrow \mathbb{B}$ and $o_2 : T_r \rightarrow \mathbb{B}$. We set T_r to have four states.

It took Z3 solver about 1 min to find the solution shown in Fig. 5.

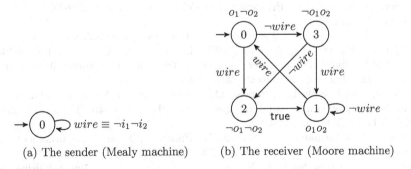

(a) The sender (Mealy machine)   (b) The receiver (Moore machine)

Fig. 5. The synthesized system for the sender-receiver example

6   Related Work and Conclusion

The closest is the work by Beyene et al. [4] on solving *infinite*-state games using SMT solvers. Conceptually, they use co-Büchi and Büchi ranking functions to encode game winning into SMT, which was also partially done by Schewe and Finkbeiner [27] a few years earlier (for finite-state systems). The authors focused on co-Büchi and Büchi automata, while we also considered Rabin and Streett automata (for finite-state systems). Although they claimed their approach can be extended to μ-calculus (and thus to CTL*), they did not elaborate beyond noting that CTL* verification can be reduced to games.

In this paper, we showed how the research on ranking functions [14,21] can be used to easily derive synthesis procedures. We also described two approaches to the CTL* synthesis and the only (to our knowledge) synthesizer supporting CTL*. (For CTL synthesis see [3,10,16,25] for PCTL.) The two approaches are conceptually similar. The approach via direct encoding is easier to code. The approach via alternating hesitant automata, for example, hints at how to reduce CTL* synthesis to solving safety games: via bounding the number of visits to co-Büchi final states and bounding the distance to Büchi final states, and then determinizing the resulting automaton. A possible future direction is to extend the approach to the logic ATL* and distributed systems.

Acknowledgements. We thank Swen Jacobs and Bernd Finkbeiner for early discussions on bounded synthesis for GR(1), Nir Piterman for explaining Streett/Rabin ranking constructions and alternating automata. This work was supported by the Austrian Science Fund (FWF) under the RiSE National Research Network (S11406).

References

1. Babiak, T., Křetínský, M., Řehák, V., Strejček, J.: LTL to büchi automata translation: fast and more deterministic. In: Flanagan, C., König, B. (eds.) TACAS 2012. LNCS, vol. 7214, pp. 95–109. Springer, Heidelberg (2012). doi:10.1007/978-3-642-28756-5_8
2. Baier, C., Katoen, J.P.: Principles of Model Checking, vol. 26202649. MIT Press, Cambridge (2008)
3. Bertrand, N., Fearnley, J., Schewe, S.: Bounded satisfiability for PCTL. In: Cégielski, P., Durand, A. (eds.) CSL. LIPICS, vol. 16, pp. 92–106. Schloss Dagstuhl-Leibniz-Zentrum fuer Informatik, Dagstuhl, Germany (2012). http://drops.dagstuhl.de/opus/volltexte/2012/3666
4. Beyene, T., Chaudhuri, S., Popeea, C., Rybalchenko, A.: A constraint-based approach to solving games on infinite graphs. SIGPLAN Not. **49**(1), 221–233 (2014). doi:10.1145/2578855.2535860
5. Bloem, R., Jobstmann, B., Piterman, N., Pnueli, A., Sa'ar, Y.: Synthesis of reactive(1) designs. J. Comput. Syst. Sci. **78**, 911–938 (2012)
6. Bloem, R., Braud-Santoni, N., Jacobs, S.: Synthesis of self-stabilising and byzantine-resilient distributed systems. In: Chaudhuri, S., Farzan, A. (eds.) CAV 2016. LNCS, vol. 9779, pp. 157–176. Springer, Cham (2016). doi:10.1007/978-3-319-41528-4_9

7. Bloem, R., Chatterjee, K., Jacobs, S., Könighofer, R.: Assume-guarantee synthesis for concurrent reactive programs with partial information. In: Baier, C., Tinelli, C. (eds.) TACAS 2015. LNCS, vol. 9035, pp. 517–532. Springer, Heidelberg (2015). doi:10.1007/978-3-662-46681-0_50

8. Bloem, R., Chockler, H., Ebrahimi, M., Strichman, O.: Synthesizing non-vacuous systems. In: Bouajjani, A., Monniaux, D. (eds.) VMCAI 2017. LNCS, vol. 10145, pp. 55–72. Springer, Cham (2017). doi:10.1007/978-3-319-52234-0_4

9. Clarke, E.M., Emerson, E.A., Sistla, A.P.: Automatic verification of finite-state concurrent systems using temporal logic specifications. ACM Trans. Program. Lang. Syst. 8(2), 244–263 (1986). doi:10.1145/5397.5399

10. De Angelis, E., Pettorossi, A., Proietti, M.: Synthesizing concurrent programs using answer set programming. Fundam. Inform. 120(3–4), 205–229 (2012)

11. de Moura, L., Bjørner, N.: Z3: an efficient SMT solver. In: Ramakrishnan, C.R., Rehof, J. (eds.) TACAS 2008. LNCS, vol. 4963, pp. 337–340. Springer, Heidelberg (2008). doi:10.1007/978-3-540-78800-3_24

12. Filiot, E., Jin, N., Raskin, J.: Antichains and compositional algorithms for LTL synthesis. Form. Methods Syst. Des. 39(3), 261–296 (2011). doi:10.1007/s10703-011-0115-3

13. Jacobs, S., Bloem, R.: Parameterized synthesis. In: Flanagan, C., König, B. (eds.) TACAS 2012. LNCS, vol. 7214, pp. 362–376. Springer, Heidelberg (2012). doi:10.1007/978-3-642-28756-5_25

14. Jurdziński, M.: Small progress measures for solving parity games. In: Reichel, H., Tison, S. (eds.) STACS 2000. LNCS, vol. 1770, pp. 290–301. Springer, Heidelberg (2000). doi:10.1007/3-540-46541-3_24

15. Khalimov, A., Jacobs, S., Bloem, R.: PARTY parameterized synthesis of token rings. In: Sharygina, N., Veith, H. (eds.) CAV 2013. LNCS, vol. 8044, pp. 928–933. Springer, Heidelberg (2013). doi:10.1007/978-3-642-39799-8_66

16. Klenze, T., Bayless, S., Hu, A.J.: Fast, flexible, and minimal CTL synthesis via SMT. In: Chaudhuri, S., Farzan, A. (eds.) CAV 2016. LNCS, vol. 9779, pp. 136–156. Springer, Cham (2016). doi:10.1007/978-3-319-41528-4_8

17. Kupferman, O., Vardi, M.Y.: Safraless decision procedures. In: FOCS. pp. 531–542 (2005)

18. Kupferman, O., Vardi, M.Y., Wolper, P.: An automata-theoretic approach to branching-time model checking. J. ACM 47(2), 312–360 (2000). doi:10.1145/333979.333987

19. Manna, Z., Wolper, P.: Synthesis of communicating processes from temporal logic specifications. In: Kozen, D. (ed.) Logic of Programs 1981. LNCS, vol. 131, pp. 253–281. Springer, Heidelberg (1982). doi:10.1007/BFb0025786

20. Piterman, N.: From nondeterministic Büchi and Streett automata to deterministic parity automata. In: LICS. pp. 255–264. IEEE Computer Society (2006). http://dx.doi.org/10.1109/LICS.2006.28

21. Piterman, N., Pnueli, A.: Faster solutions of Rabin and Streett games. In: Proceedings of the 21th IEEE Symposium on Logic in Computer Science (LICS 2006), 12–15 August 2006, Seattle, WA, USA, pp. 275–284 (2006). http://dx.doi.org/10.1109/LICS.2006.23

22. Pnueli, A.: The temporal logic of programs. In: 18th Annual Symposium on Foundations of Computer Science, 1977, pp. 46–57. IEEE (1977)

23. Pnueli, A., Rosner, R.: On the synthesis of a reactive module. In: Conference Record of the Sixteenth Annual ACM Symposium on Principles of Programming Languages, Austin, Texas, USA, 11–13 January 1989, pp. 179–190. ACM Press (1989). http://doi.acm.org/10.1145/75277.75293

24. Pnueli, A., Rosner, R.: Distributed reactive systems are hard to synthesize. In: 31st Annual Symposium on Foundations of Computer Science, St. Louis, Missouri, USA, 22–24 October 1990, Vol. 2, pp. 746–757. IEEE Computer Society (1990). http://dx.doi.org/10.1109/FSCS.1990.89597

25. Prezza, N.: CTL (Computation Tree Logic) sat solver. https://github.com/nicolaprezza/CTLSAT

26. Safra, S.: On the complexity of omega-automata. In: 29th Annual Symposium on Foundations of Computer Science, White Plains, New York, USA, 24–26 October 1988, pp. 319–327. IEEE Computer Society (1988). http://dx.doi.org/10.1109/SFCS.1988.21948

27. Schewe, S., Finkbeiner, B.: Bounded synthesis. In: Namjoshi, K.S., Yoneda, T., Higashino, T., Okamura, Y. (eds.) ATVA 2007. LNCS, vol. 4762, pp. 474–488. Springer, Heidelberg (2007). doi:10.1007/978-3-540-75596-8_33

28. Sohail, S., Somenzi, F.: Safety first: a two-stage algorithm for the synthesis of reactive systems. STTT 15(5–6), 433–454 (2013). doi:10.1007/s10009-012-0224-3

29. Vardi, M.Y., Wolper, P.: Reasoning about infinite computations. Inf. Comput. 115(1), 1–37 (1994). doi:10.1006/inco.1994.1092

30. Wolper, P., Vardi, M.Y., Sistla, A.P.: Reasoning about infinite computation paths (extended abstract). In: 24th Annual Symposium on Foundations of Computer Science, Tucson, Arizona, USA, 7–9 November 1983, pp. 185–194. IEEE Computer Society (1983). http://dx.doi.org/10.1109/SFCS.1983.51

Quantitative Assume Guarantee Synthesis

Shaull Almagor[1], Orna Kupferman[2], Jan Oliver Ringert[3],
and Yaron Velner[2(✉)]

[1] Department of Computer Science, Oxford University, Oxford, UK
[2] School of Computer Science and Engineering, The Hebrew University,
Jerusalem, Israel
yaron.welner@mail.huji.ac.il
[3] School of Computer Science, Tel Aviv University, Tel Aviv, Israel

Abstract. In *assume-guarantee synthesis*, we are given a specification
$\langle A, G \rangle$, describing an assumption on the environment and a guarantee
for the system, and we construct a system that interacts with an environment and is guaranteed to satisfy G whenever the environment satisfies A. While assume-guarantee synthesis is 2EXPTIME-complete for
specifications in LTL, researchers have identified the GR(1) fragment of
LTL, which supports assume-guarantee reasoning and for which synthesis has an efficient symbolic solution. In recent years we see a transition
to *quantitative synthesis*, in which the specification formalism is multi-
valued and the goal is to generate high-quality systems, namely ones that
maximize the satisfaction value of the specification.

We study quantitative assume-guarantee synthesis. We start with
specifications in LTL[$\mathcal{F}$], an extension of LTL by quality operators. The
satisfaction value of an LTL[$\mathcal{F}$] formula is a real value in $[0, 1]$, where
the higher the value is, the higher is the quality in which the computation satisfies the specification. We define the quantitative extension
GR(1)[$\mathcal{F}$] of GR(1). We show that the implication relation, which is at
the heart of assume-guarantee reasoning, has two natural semantics in
the quantitative setting. Indeed, in addition to $\max\{1 - A, G\}$, which is
the multi-valued counterpart of Boolean implication, there are settings
in which maximizing the ratio G/A is more appropriate. We show that
GR(1)[$\mathcal{F}$] formulas in both semantics are hard to synthesize. Still, in the
implication semantics, we can reduce GR(1)[$\mathcal{F}$] synthesis to GR(1) synthesis and apply its efficient symbolic algorithm. For the ratio semantics, we present a sound approximation, which can also be solved efficiently. Our experimental results show that our approach can successfully synthesize GR(1)[$\mathcal{F}$] specifications with over a million of concrete
states.

The research leading to these results has received funding from the Euro-
pean Research Council under the European Union's 7th Framework Programme
(FP7/2007-2013, ERC grant no 278410). Shaull Almagor is supported by ERC grant
AVS-ISS (648701).

R. Majumdar and V. Kunčak (Eds.): CAV 2017, Part II, LNCS 10427, pp. 353–374, 2017.
DOI: 10.1007/978-3-319-63390-9_19

1   Introduction

Synthesis is the automated construction of a system from its specification: given a linear temporal logic (LTL) formula ψ over sets I and O of input and output signals, we synthesize a finite-state system that *realizes* ψ [10,26]. At each moment in time, the system reads a truth assignment, generated by the environment, to the signals in I, and it generates a truth assignment to the signals in O. Thus, with every sequence of inputs, the system associates a sequence of outputs. The system realizes ψ if all the computations that are generated by the interaction satisfy ψ.

In recent years, researchers have considered extensions and variants of the classical setting of synthesis. One class of extensions originates from the *assume-guarantee* [1] approach that is taken in many settings of synthesis. There, the input to the synthesis problem consists of two parts: a behavior A that the environment is assumed to have, and a behavior G that the system is guaranteed to have [6].[2] Both A and G are over $I \cup O$. When A and G are in LTL, synthesis of the assume-guarantee pair $\langle A, G \rangle$ coincides with synthesis of the LTL formula $A \to G$. Still, the assume-guarantee approach brings with it new interesting problems. For example, one may study the weakest A that is required in order to make a given G realizable [6,21], and dually, the strongest G we can guarantee with a given A [11]. Indeed, the duality between the system and the environment in synthesis is intensified in light of the duality between A and G in assume-guarantee specifications [17]. In the more practical side, there is a challenge of finding expressive specification formalisms for which assume-guarantee synthesis is feasible in practice. Indeed, for LTL, the problem is 2EXPTIME-complete [26]. In [25], the authors introduce the *General Reactivity of Rank 1* fragment of LTL (GR(1), for short). Essentially, a GR(1) formula states that if some initial, safety, and fairness environment assumptions hold, then some initial, safety, and fairness system guarantees hold. The synthesis problem for GR(1) is in EXPTIME. It is shown, however, in [25], that GR(1) has an efficient symbolic synthesis algorithm, which is polynomial in the number of the concrete states of the specification. GR(1) synthesis has been used in various application domains and contexts, including robotics [18], scenario-based specifications [24], aspect languages [23], and event-based behavior models [12], to name a few. In addition, it is shown in [22] that almost all common LTL specification patterns can be specified in GR(1).

Another class of extensions to the classical synthesis problem addresses the quality of synthesized systems. Since LTL is Boolean, synthesized systems are correct, but there is no reference to their quality. This is a crucial drawback, as

---

[1] By "assume-guarantee" we refer to the notion of synthesis given environment assumptions and system guarantees, rather than the setting of multi-agent synthesis coined in [7].

[2] We note that an orthogonal line of work adds indirect assumptions about the environment, like *bounded synthesis*, where we assume that there is a bound on the size of the environment [19,28], or *rational synthesis*, in which the environment has its own objectives [14] and is assumed to behave rationally.

designers would be willing to give up manual design only if automated-synthesis algorithms return systems of comparable quality. Addressing this challenge, researchers have developed quantitative specification formalisms. For example, in [3], the input to the synthesis problem includes also Mealy machines that grade different realizing systems. In [1], the specification formalism is the multi-valued logic LTL[$\mathcal{F}$]. The satisfaction value of an LTL[$\mathcal{F}$] formula is a real value in $[0,1]$, where the higher the value is, the higher is the quality in which the computation satisfies the specification. LTL[$\mathcal{F}$] is really a family of logics, each parameterized by a set $\mathcal{F} \subseteq \{f : [0,1]^k \to [0,1] \mid k \in \mathbb{N}\}$ of functions (of arbitrary arity) over $[0,1]$. Using the functions in $\mathcal{F}$, a specifier can formally and easily prioritize different ways of satisfaction. For example, as in earlier work on multi-valued extensions of LTL (c.f., [13]), the set $\mathcal{F}$ may contain the min $\{x,y\}$, max $\{x,y\}$, and $1 - x$ functions, which are the standard quantitative analogues of the $\wedge$, $\vee$, and $\neg$ operators. The novelty of LTL[$\mathcal{F}$] is the ability to manipulate values by arbitrary functions. For example, $\mathcal{F}$ may contain the binary function $\oplus_\lambda$, for $\lambda \in [0,1]$. The satisfaction value of the formula $\varphi \oplus_\lambda \psi$ is the weighted (according to λ) average between the satisfaction values of φ and ψ. This enables the quality of the system to be an interpolation of different aspects of it. As an example, consider the LTL[$\mathcal{F}$] formula $\varphi = \mathsf{G}(req \to (grant \oplus_{\frac{2}{3}} \mathsf{X}grant))$. The formula specifies the fact that we want requests to be granted immediately and the grant to hold for two steps. When this always holds, the satisfaction value is $\frac{2}{3} + \frac{1}{3} = 1$. We are quite okay with grants that are given immediately and last for only one step, in which case the satisfaction value is $\frac{2}{3}$, and less content when grants arrive with a delay, in which case the satisfaction value is $\frac{1}{3}$.

Using a multi-valued specification formalism, synthesis is upgraded to generate not only correct, but also high-quality systems. In particular, the synthesis algorithm for LTL[$\mathcal{F}$] seeks systems of the highest possible satisfaction value. An extension of the Boolean setting to a quantitative one is of special interest in the case of assume-guarantee synthesis. Indeed, when A and G are multi-valued, there are several ways to define the satisfaction value of an assume-guarantee pair $\langle A, G \rangle$. If we adopt the semantics of LTL[$\mathcal{F}$] for $\to$, we get that the satisfaction value of $\langle A, G \rangle$ is the maximum between the "violation value" of A (that is, 1 minus its satisfaction value) and the satisfaction value of G. With this semantics we can, for example, synthesize a system that satisfies as many guarantees as possible when all the environment assumptions hold (see Example 2 in Sect. 5.2).

Sometimes, however, other semantics are more appropriate. Consider, for example, a specification where the environment assumption is the amount of gas in a fuel tank (normalized to $[0,1]$) and the guarantee is the distance a car can go. An optimal strategy in the max$\{1 - A, G\}$ semantics can assure a satisfaction value of $1/2$. However, the behavior of the strategy when the tank is more than half full need not be optimal and it could afford to drive only half of the maximal distance. On the other hand, in a *ratio semantics*, where the objective is to maximize G/A, the optimal strategy would strive to maximize the fuel consumption, which is more desirable.

Another interesting issue that arises in the setting of assume-guarantee synthesis and calls for a quantitative view is *cooperative reactive synthesis*, namely the ability of the system to influence the satisfaction value of A. Indeed, recall that both A and G are over $I \cup O$. While a system that causes A to fail does satisfy an $\langle A, G \rangle$ specification, it is very likely that a designer favors behaviors in which G holds over those in which A is violated. In [4], the authors study this issue and present a *hierarchy of cooperation levels* between the system and the environment. They also describe an algorithm that synthesizes systems with the highest possible cooperation level, namely ones that satisfy both A and G. With a quantitative approach to assume-guarantee synthesis, we can incorporate the hierarchy within the specification.

In this work we introduce and study *quantitative assume-guarantee synthesis*. The doubly-exponential solution for LTL[$\mathcal{F}$] synthesis applies to specifications of the form $A \rightarrow G$. We define and study GR(1)[$\mathcal{F}$], namely the fragment of LTL[$\mathcal{F}$] that is the multi-valued counterpart of GR(1). Recall that GR(1) formulas have two Boolean operators: conjunction (between the different components of A and G) and implication (between A and G). We discuss different possible multi-valued semantics to both operators. Our main contributions are as follows.

– We present a theoretical framework for quantitative assume-guarantee synthesis. We identify two natural special cases of interest, namely when implication stands for $\max\{1 - A, G\}$ or G/A (Sect. 2). For conjunction, we allow all monotonically increasing quantitative functions. We relate quantitative assume-guarantee synthesis with the solution of *quantitative two-player assume-guarantee games*. The winning values in these games correspond to the values with which a GR(1)[$\mathcal{F}$] specification can be realized, and winning strategies correspond to transducers that realize the specification in these values.

  • For the $\max\{1 - A, G\}$ semantics, we show an efficient synthesis algorithm for the case the number of fairness assumptions and guarantees is fixed. Further, we show that without this assumption, as well as in the case we allow a quantitative conjunction function that is not monotonically increasing, the corresponding quantitative assume-guarantee games cannot be solved efficiently, provided P$\neq$NP (Sect. 3).

  • For the G/A semantics, we show that even for a single assumption and guarantee, the corresponding quantitative assume-guarantee games are as hard as (Boolean) parity games. We present a sound approximation that has an efficient solution. Essentially, our approximation replaces the eventuality requirements in the fairness assumptions and guarantees by finitary-fairness ones [8,20] (Sect. 4).

  Our algorithms efficiently reduces the GR(1)[$\mathcal{F}$] synthesis problem to synthesis of a Boolean GR(1) specification. Hence, they work also in the symbolic setting.

– Finally, we present a series of experimental results that demonstrates the differences between the different semantics and the scalability of our solution in the symbolic setting (Sect. 5). Our experimental results also demonstrate the usefulness of the quantitative approach. Indeed, we handle specifications that are not realizable in the Boolean approach but have a high satisfaction value in the quantitative one.

Due to lack of space, in some cases the full proofs were omitted, and can be found in the full version in the authors' webpages.

2 Preliminaries

2.1 The Temporal Logic LTL[$\mathcal{F}$]

The linear temporal logic LTL[$\mathcal{F}$], introduced in [1], generalizes LTL by replacing the Boolean operators of LTL with arbitrary functions over $[0, 1]$. The logic is actually a family of logics, each parameterized by a set $\mathcal{F}$ of functions.

Syntax. Let AP be a set of Boolean atomic propositions, and let $\mathcal{F} \subseteq \{f : [0, 1]^k \to [0, 1] \mid k \in \mathbb{N}\}$ be a set of functions over $[0, 1]$. Note that the functions in $\mathcal{F}$ may have different arities. An LTL[$\mathcal{F}$] formula is one of the following:

- True, False, or p, for $p \in AP$.
- $f(\varphi_1, \ldots, \varphi_k)$, $X\varphi_1$, or $\varphi_1 U\varphi_2$, for LTL[$\mathcal{F}$] formulas $\varphi_1, \ldots, \varphi_k$ and a function $f \in \mathcal{F}$.

We define the description size $|\varphi|$ of an LTL[$\mathcal{F}$] formula φ to be the number of nodes in the generating tree of φ. Note that the function symbols in $\mathcal{F}$ are treated as constant-length symbols.

Semantics. We define the semantics of LTL[$\mathcal{F}$] formulas with respect to infinite computations over AP. A *computation* is a word $\pi = \pi_0, \pi_1, \ldots \in (2^{AP})^\omega$. We use π^i to denote the suffix $\pi_i, \pi_{i+1}, \ldots$. The semantics maps a computation π and an LTL[$\mathcal{F}$] formula φ to the *satisfaction value* of φ in π, denoted $[\![\pi, \varphi]\!]$. The satisfaction value is defined inductively as follows.[3]

- $[\![\pi, \text{True}]\!] = 1$ and $[\![\pi, \text{False}]\!] = 0$.
- For $p \in AP$, we have that $[\![\pi, p]\!] = 1$ if $p \in \pi_0$ and $[\![\pi, p]\!] = 0$ if $p \notin \pi_0$.
- For a function $f \in \mathcal{F}$, we have $[\![\pi, f(\varphi_1, \ldots, \varphi_k)]\!] = f([\![\pi, \varphi_1]\!], \ldots, [\![\pi, \varphi_k]\!])$.
- $[\![\pi, X\varphi_1]\!] = [\![\pi^1, \varphi_1]\!]$.
- $[\![\pi, \varphi_1 U\varphi_2]\!] = \max_{i \geq 0}\{\min\{[\![\pi^i, \varphi_2]\!], \min_{0 \leq j < i}[\![\pi^j, \varphi_1]\!]\}\}$.

It is not hard to prove, by induction on the structure of the formula, that for every computation π and formula φ, it holds that $[\![\pi, \varphi]\!] \in [0, 1]$. Also, the number of possible satisfaction values of φ is finite and is bounded by $2^{|\varphi|}$.

The logic LTL coincides with the logic LTL[$\mathcal{F}$] for $\mathcal{F}$ that corresponds to the usual Boolean operators. For simplicity, we use these operators as an abbreviation for the corresponding functions, as described below. In addition, we introduce notations for some useful functions. Let $x, y \in [0, 1]$ be satisfaction values and $\lambda \in [0, 1]$ be a parameter. Then,

---

[3] The observant reader may be concerned by our use of max and min where sup and inf are in order. It is proven in [1] that there are only finitely many satisfaction values for a formula φ, thus the semantics is well defined.

- $\neg x = 1 - x$
- $x \vee y = \max\{x, y\}$
- $x \wedge y = \min\{x, y\}$
- $x \rightarrow y = \max\{1 - x, y\}$
- $\nabla_\lambda x = \lambda \cdot x$
- $x \oplus_\lambda y = \lambda \cdot x + (1 - \lambda) \cdot y$

Other useful abbreviations are the "eventually" and "always" temporal operators, defined as follows.

- $\mathsf{F}\varphi_1 = \mathtt{True}\,\mathsf{U}\varphi_1$. Thus, $[\![\pi, \mathsf{F}\varphi_1]\!] = \max_{i \geq 0}\{[\![\pi^i, \varphi_1]\!]\}$.
- $\mathsf{G}\varphi_1 = \neg\mathsf{F}\neg\varphi_1$. Thus, $[\![\pi, \mathsf{G}\varphi_1]\!] = \min_{i \geq 0}\{[\![\pi^i, \varphi_1]\!]\}$.

2.2   GR(1) and GR(1)[$\mathcal{F}$]

A *propositional assertion* θ is a Boolean formula over AP, describing a single state in a computation. An *invariant* is an LTL formula φ over AP that uses only the X ("next") operator, and with no nesting of X's. Thus, φ relates a state in a computation and its successor.

The *General Reactivity of Rank 1* fragment of LTL (GR(1), for short), consists of formulas of the form[4]

$$(\theta^e \rightarrow \theta^s) \wedge (\theta^e \rightarrow \mathsf{G}((\mathsf{H}\varphi^e) \rightarrow \varphi^s)) \wedge ((\theta^e \wedge \mathsf{G}\varphi^e) \rightarrow (\bigwedge_{1 \leq i \leq k^e} \mathsf{GF}\psi_i^e \rightarrow \bigwedge_{1 \leq i \leq k^s} \mathsf{GF}\psi_i^s)),$$

for propositional assertions θ^e, θ^s, ψ_i^e, and ψ_i^s, and invariants φ^e and φ^s. We refer to θ^e and θ^s as the *initial assumption* and *initial guarantee*, respectively, refer to $\mathsf{G}\varphi^e$ and $\mathsf{G}\varphi^s$, as the *safety assumption* and *safety guarantee*, respectively, and refer to $\bigwedge_{1 \leq i \leq k^e} \mathsf{GF}\psi_i^e$ and $\bigwedge_{1 \leq i \leq k^s} \mathsf{GF}\psi_i^s$ as the *fairness assumption* and *fairness guarantee*, respectively.

The temporal operator H ("Henceforth") is the past variant of G. Thus, a position i in a computation π satisfies $\mathsf{H}\varphi$ if all suffixes π^j, for $j \leq i$, satisfy φ.

We proceed to the quantitative counterpart. A *quantitative propositional assertion* θ is an LTL[$\mathcal{F}$] propositional formula over AP, assigning a value to a single state in a computation. A *quantitative conjunction* is a monotonically increasing function $\otimes : [0, 1]^* \rightarrow [0, 1]$, which maps a vector of satisfaction values to a new satisfaction value. Formally, for every two vectors $v, u \in [0, 1]^n$, if $v \geq u$ (point wise), then $\otimes(v) \geq \otimes(u)$. A typical quantitative conjunction function is $\wedge$, where $x \wedge y = \min\{x, y\}$. A *quantitative implication* is a function $\mapsto : [0, 1] \times [0, 1] \rightarrow [0, \infty]$ that is monotonically decreasing in its first parameter and monotonically increasing in its second parameter. A typical quantitative implication function is $\rightarrow$, where $x \rightarrow y = \max\{1 - x, y\}$.

The GR(1)[$\mathcal{F}$] fragment of LTL[$\mathcal{F}$] consists of formulas of the form
$$(\theta^e \rightarrow \theta^s) \wedge (\theta^e \rightarrow \mathsf{G}((\mathsf{H}\varphi^e) \rightarrow \varphi^s)) \wedge ((\theta^e \wedge \mathsf{G}\varphi^e) \rightarrow (\otimes_{1 \leq i \leq k^e}\mathsf{GF}\psi_i^e \mapsto \otimes_{1 \leq i \leq k^s}\mathsf{GF}\psi_i^s),$$
for propositional assertions θ^e and θ^s, invariants φ^e and φ^s, and quantitative propositional assertions ψ_i^e and ψ_i^s.

---

[4] In some papers in the literature, GR(1) formulas have the following weaker form. $(\theta^e \wedge \mathsf{G}\varphi^e \wedge \bigwedge_{1 \leq i \leq k^e} \mathsf{GF}\psi_i^e) \rightarrow (\theta^s \wedge \mathsf{G}\varphi^s \wedge \bigwedge_{1 \leq i \leq k^s} \mathsf{GF}\psi_i^s)$. That is, if some safety and fairness environment assumptions hold, then some safety and fairness system guarantees hold. The original semantics of [25] as well as the symbolic implementation follow the stronger semantics.

Note that the subformulas that refer to the initial and safety assumptions and guarantees are Boolean. Indeed, the assumptions and guarantees are propositional assertions and invariants, their satisfaction values are in $\{0, 1\}$, and they are related by $\wedge$ and $\rightarrow$. The functions in $\mathcal{F}$ are these used in the quantitative propositional assertions ψ_i^e and ψ_i^s, as well as the functions $\mapsto$ and $\otimes$. It is easy to extend our results to a setting in which the initial and safety assumptions and guarantees are quantitative. We are going to focus on two quantitative implications: $x \rightarrow y$, mentioned above, which we are going to term *disjunctive implication*, and y/x, which we are going to term *ratio implication*. Note that the range of the ratio implication is $[0, \infty]$. We may consider variants of ratio implication with which the result is always in $[0, 1]$. One possibility is to be fully satisfied whenever $y \geq x$, which corresponds to defining y/x as $\min\{1, y/x\}$. Another possibility, especially given the finite ranges of x and y, is to map the possible values of y/x to $[0, 1]$ in a some monotonic way, for example by $1 - 1/(1 + y/x)$.

We may allow a $\text{GR}(1)[\mathcal{F}]$ formula to apply different quantitative conjunctions $\otimes^e$ and $\otimes^s$ to relate the components of the assumption and the guarantee.

We define the *width* of a quantitative propositional formula ψ, denoted *width* (ψ), as the number of different satisfaction values that ψ may have. We further denote the width of a $\text{GR}(1)[\mathcal{F}]$ specification by $\max\{\max_{1 \leq i \leq k^e} width(\psi_i^e),$ $\max_{1 \leq i \leq k^s} width(\psi_i^s)\}$, i.e., the least upper bound of the width of the quantitative propositional assertions appearing in the specification.

2.3   The Synthesis Problem

In the setting of open systems, the set AP of atomic propositions is partitioned into sets I and O of input and output signals. An (I, O)-transducer models the computations generated (deterministically) by a system when it interacts with an environment. The environment assigns values to the signals in I and the systems responds with an assignment to the signals in O. This process repeats forever. Formally, an (I, O)-*transducer* is a tuple $\mathcal{T} = \langle I, O, S, s_0, \rho, L \rangle$, where S is a finite set of states, $s_0 \in S$ is an initial state, $\rho : S \times 2^I \rightarrow S$ maps a state and an assignment for the input signals to a successor state, and $L : S \rightarrow 2^O$ is a labeling function that maps each state to an assignment for the output signals. Every sequence $i = i_0, i_1, \ldots \in (2^I)^\omega$ of assignments for the input signals induces a single trace $s = s_0, s_1, \ldots$ of $\mathcal{T}$, satisfying $s_{j+1} = \rho(s_j, i_j)$ for all $j \geq 0$, and induces the computation $\pi = \pi_0, \pi_1, \ldots$ over $2^{I \cup O}$ in which $\pi_j = i_j \cup L(s_j)$ for all $j \geq 0$.

In the Boolean setting, the *realizability* problem gets as input an LTL formula over $I \cup O$, and asks for the existence of an (I, O)-transducer all of whose computations satisfy the formula. In the quantitative analogue we seek the generation of high-quality systems. For a transducer $\mathcal{T}$ and an LTL$[\mathcal{F}]$ formula φ, we define the satisfaction value of φ in $\mathcal{T}$, denoted $[\![\mathcal{T}, \varphi]\!]$, as $\min\{[\![\pi, \varphi]\!] : \pi$ is a computation of $\mathcal{T}\}$. Accordingly, given an LTL$[\mathcal{F}]$ formula φ over $I \cup O$, the realizability problem is to find $\max\{[\![\mathcal{T}, \varphi]\!] : \mathcal{T}$ is an (I, O)-transducer$\}$. The synthesis problem is then to find a transducer that attains this value.[5] Moving from an optimization to a decision problem, we say, given a specification φ and a threshold $T \in [0, \infty]$, that φ is *realizable with value T* if there is a transducer $\mathcal{T}$ such that $[\![\mathcal{T}, \varphi]\!] \geq T$.

As shown in [1], the synthesis problem for LTL[$\mathcal{F}$] is 2EXPTIME-complete. Essentially, as in the Boolean setting, it is possible to construct, given an LTL[$\mathcal{F}$] formula φ and a predicate $P \subseteq [0, 1]$, a nondeterministic generalized Büchi automaton $\mathcal{A}_{\varphi,P}$ that accepts exactly all computations π such that $[\![\pi, \varphi]\!] \in P$. This automaton can be used for solving the decision problems that correspond to the optimization problems for LTL[$\mathcal{F}$]. In particular, in the case of synthesis, we can check the realizability of φ with value above some threshold $T \in [0, 1]$, by generating a game where the objective of the system is to generate only computations that are accepted by $\mathcal{A}_{\varphi,[T,1]}$.

Remark 1. Note that our definition for $[\![T, \varphi]\!]$ considered the worst-case setting, where the goal is to maximize the quality of the computation with the minimal quality. Alternatively, one can take a stochastic approach, where the goal is to generate a transducer that maximizes the expected quality of a computation, subject to a given distribution of the input signals [2]. As even simple stochastic reachability games are not known to have a polynomial solution [15] we leave it to future work.

Remark 2. In Sect. 1, we discussed the challenge of *cooperative reactive synthesis* [4], where a hierarchy of cooperation levels is used in order to favor behaviors in which the guarantee holds over these in which the assumption is violated. Using LTL[$\mathcal{F}$], the designer can easily specify her priorities in this issue. For example, if the assumption is φ^e and the guarantee is φ^s, then the LTL[$\mathcal{F}$] specification $\nabla_{0.9}(\neg\varphi^e) \vee \varphi^s$ has satisfaction value 0.9 in computations that only violate the assumption, and thus its synthesis would prefer transducers in which the guarantee is satisfied. Tuning down our satisfaction with violation of the assumption can also be achieved by taking some power of $(\neg\varphi^e)$, as in $(\neg\varphi^e)^2 \vee \varphi^s$. Dually, $(\neg\varphi^e) \vee \sqrt{\varphi^s}$ tunes up satisfaction of the guarantee. The extend to which we want to tune the assumption down or the guarantee up typically depends on the ability of the system to influence the satisfaction of the assumption. Note that by tuning down the assumptions, we incentivize the system to satisfy the guarantees, rather than to falsify the assumptions. This overcomes a common pitfall of assume-guarantee synthesis.

2.4   Games

A *two-player game* is $\mathcal{G} = \langle V = V_1 \cup V_2, E, v_0, W \rangle$, where V is a set of vertices partitioned to $V_1 \cup V_2$, $E \subseteq V \times V$ is a set of directed edges, and $v_0 \in V$ is an initial vertex, and W is a winning condition, to be defined below. We assume that E is total in its first element. The game is played between Player 1 and

---

[5] The specification of the problem does not require the transducer to be finite. As we shall show, however, as in the case of LTL, if some transducer that attains the value exists, there is also a finite-state one that does so.

Player 2. It starts in v_0. Whenever the current vertex v is in V_i, for $i \in \{1, 2\}$, Player i chooses an edge (v, u) and the game proceeds to u. Note that since E is total, there is always a legal move for the players. Formally, a *strategy* for Player i is a function $\tau_i : V^* \cdot V_i \to V$ such that for all $\pi \cdot v \in V^* \cdot V_i$, we have that $E(v, \tau_i(\pi \cdot v))$. The outcome of strategies τ_1 and τ_2 for the two players is the infinite path $v_0, v_1, v_2, \ldots$ where for all $j \geq 0$, we have that $v_{j+i} = \tau_i(v_0, \ldots, v_j)$, for the player i for which $v_j \in V_i$.

The winning condition W defines a subset of V^ω. The goal of Player 2 is to ensure that the outcome of the game is in W, while the goal of Player 1 is to make sure the outcome is not in W. Several types of winning conditions have been studied. In a *strong-fairness* game, the condition W is given by a formula $\bigwedge_{1 \leq i \leq k^e} \mathsf{GF}\psi_i^e \to \bigwedge_{1 \leq i \leq k^s} \mathsf{GF}\psi_i^s$, for predicates ψ_i^e and ψ_i^s over V. A path π in the game satisfies W if there is $1 \leq i \leq k^e$ such that π visits vertices that satisfy ψ_i^e only finitely often, or for all $1 \leq i \leq k^s$, it visits vertices that satisfy ψ_i^s infinitely often.

A *weighted game* augments $\mathcal{G}$ with a (multidimensional) *weight function* $w : V \to [0, 1]^k$, for some $k \in \mathbb{N}$. The *width* of a dimension $1 \leq i \leq k$ is $|\{w(v)[i] : v \in V\}|$, namely the number of different values that w may assign in the i-th dimension. Then, the width of w is the least upper bound on the widths of all dimensions. A weighted *strong-fairness* game is parameterized by quantitative conjunction and implication functions $\otimes$ and $\mapsto$. The winning condition is of the form $W = \otimes_{1 \leq i \leq k^e} \mathsf{GF}w[i] \mapsto \otimes_{1 \leq i \leq k^s} \mathsf{GF}w[k^e + i]$, for k^e and k^s such that $k = k^e + k^s$. The value of a path π is the evaluation of W in the path, where the value $w[i]$, for $1 \leq i \leq k$, in a vertex v, is $w(v)[i]$. Thus, the first k^e dimensions in $w(v)$ are associated with environment assumptions, and then k^s dimensions are associated with systems guarantees. Accordingly, we use $e[i]$, for $1 \leq i \leq k^e$, to denote $w[i]$, and use $s[i]$, for $1 \leq i \leq k^s$, to denote $w[k^e + i]$. For a threshold T and a weighted game $\mathcal{G}$ with winning condition W, we say that Player 2 wins $\mathcal{G}$ with value T iff Player 2 has a strategy to force the game into paths with value at least T.

For sets I and O of input and output signals, we say that a game $\mathcal{G}$ is an (I, O)-game if, intuitively, the moves of Player 1 (the environment) correspond to assignments to the signals in I and these of Player 2 (the system) correspond to assignments to the signals in O. Formally, there is a finite set S such that $V = 2^{I \cup O} \times S$, moves of Player 1 change only the 2^I component of a vertex, and then moves of Player 2 change only the 2^O and S components. It is not hard to see that a strategy of Player 2 in an (I, O)-game induces an (I, O)-transducer with state space S.

In the Boolean setting, LTL and GR(1) synthesis is reduced to the solution of a two-player game. For LTL, the construction of the game involves a translation of the specification to an automaton. The special structure of GR(1) formulas circumvents the need to construct an automaton. Instead, the initial and safety conditions determine the initial vertex of the game as well as the allowed transitions, and the fairness conditions induce the winning condition. In the full version we describe a similar construction from GR(1)$[\mathcal{F}]$ formulas to weighted strong-fairness games. Formally, we prove the following.

Theorem 1. *Consider a GR(1)[$\mathcal{F}$] formula $\varphi = \varphi_{init} \wedge \varphi_{safe} \wedge ((\theta^e \wedge G\varphi^e) \rightarrow (\otimes_{1 \leq i \leq k^e} GF\psi_i^e \mapsto \otimes_{1 \leq i \leq k^s} GF\psi_i^s)$ over $I \cup O$. We can construct a weighted strong-fairness (I, O)-game $\mathcal{G}$ with weight function $w : V \rightarrow [0,1]^{k^e+k^s}$ and winning condition of the form $\otimes_{1 \leq i \leq k^e} GFe[i] \mapsto \otimes_{1 \leq i \leq k^s} GFs[i]$, such that the state space of $\mathcal{G}$ is contained in $2^{I \cup O} \times \{1, 2\}$, the width of w is equal to the width of φ, and for every $T \in [0, \infty]$, we have that φ is realizable with value T iff Player 2 wins $\mathcal{G}$ with value T.*

3   Weighted Games with Disjunctive Implication

In this section we study weighted games with disjunctive implication, namely these induced by GR(1)[$\mathcal{F}$] formulas in which the satisfaction value of $x \mapsto y$ is $\max\{1 - x, y\}$.

3.1   Upper Bound

We start with good news and show that we can translate weighted strong-fairness games to Boolean ones. In Sect. 5, we describe a symbolic implementation of this translation. Then, combining it with a symbolic algorithm for Boolean GR(1) synthesis, we obtain a symbolic synthesis algorithm for GR(1)[$\mathcal{F}$].

Theorem 2. *Consider a weighted strong-fairness game $\mathcal{G}$ with n vertices, weight function $w : V \rightarrow [0,1]^{k^e+k^s}$ of width m, and winning condition $\otimes_{1 \leq i \leq k^e} GFe[i] \mapsto \otimes_{1 \leq i \leq k^s} GFs[i]$. Given a threshold T, we can construct a Boolean strong-fairness game $\mathcal{G}'$ with $O(n \cdot m^{k^e+k^s})$ vertices, such that Player 2 wins $\mathcal{G}$ with value at least T iff he wins $\mathcal{G}'$.*

Proof. Intuitively, at each step of $\mathcal{G}'$ we record the maximal values that were attained for $e[i]$ during a certain segment. Once $\otimes_{1 \leq i \leq k^e} GFe[i] \geq 1 - T$, we record that the assumptions have been fulfilled, and the environment visits a winning vertex and resets its record. Similarly, once $\otimes_{1 \leq i \leq k^s} GFs[i] \geq T$, we record that the guarantees have been fulfilled, so the system visits a winning vertex and resets its record. Then, the goal of the system is to generate only paths such that if the environment visits a winning vertex infinitely often, then so does the system.

We now turn to formalize this. Let $k = k^e + k^s$ and $\mathcal{G} = \langle V = V_1 \cup V_2, E, v_0, w, W \rangle$, with $w : V \rightarrow [0,1]^k$. We define $\mathcal{G}' = \langle S = S_1 \cup S_2, E', s_0, W' \rangle$ as follows. The vertices are (a finite subset of) $S = V \times [0,1]^k \times \{0, 1, 2\}$, with S_1 and S_2 determined by V_1 and V_2, respectively, in the first component, and the initial vertex is $s_0 = (v_0, r, 0)$ with $r \equiv 0$. Consider such a vertex $(v, r, b) \in S$. Intuitively, the game is played "mostly" on the $b = 0$ component, with visits to vertices with $b = 1$ whenever the environment assumptions hold, and to vertices with $b = 2$ whenever the system guarantees hold. We refer to r as a tuple $r = (r_1, \ldots, r_k)$.

We turn to define the edges. Consider vertices $s = (v, r, b)$ and $s' = (v', r', b')$. Then, $(s, s') \in E'$ if the following hold. First, if $b \in \{1, 2\}$, then we only reset the respective components of r. Thus, $v' = v, b' = 0$, and r' is obtained from r as follows: if $b = 1$ then $r'_i = 0$ for $1 \leq i \leq k^e$ and $r'_i = r_i$ for $k^e + 1 \leq i \leq k$, and similarly, if $b = 2$ then $r'_i = r_i$ for $1 \leq i \leq k^e$ and $r'_i = 0$ for $k^e + 1 \leq i \leq k$.

Next, for $b = 0$, the edges are induced by E. That is, v' is such that $(v, v') \in E$. In addition, we update the record by setting $r'_i = \max\{r_i, w(v')[i]\}$. Thus, r'_i records the maximal value seen by w in the i-th component since the last reset. Finally, for every $v \in V$, if $\otimes_{k^e + 1 \leq i \leq k} r_i \geq T$, we remove all outgoing edges from s, and set the only edge to $(v, r, 2)$. Otherwise, if $\otimes_{1 \leq i \leq k^e} r_i \geq 1 - T$, we remove all outgoing edges from s, and set the only edge to $(v, r, 1)$. Note that we give a priority to the guarantee, thus we go to a vertex with $b = 2$ whenever both $\otimes_{k^e + 1 \leq i \leq k} r_i \geq T$ and $\otimes_{1 \leq i \leq k^e} r_i \geq 1 - T$.

Observe that since the edges in the $b = 0$ component are determined by E, it is easy to draw a correspondence between paths in $\mathcal{G}$ and paths in $\mathcal{G}'$. Indeed, the only non-triviality in the correspondence is the reset operation. Since, however, resets do not change the first component of the vertex, the correspondence is maintained.

The winning condition in $\mathcal{G}'$ asserts that if vertices with $b = 1$ are visited infinitely often, then vertices with $b = 2$ should be visited infinitely often. That is, denoting $V \times [0, 1]^k \times \{j\}$ by V^j, we have $W' = \mathsf{GF}(V^1) \rightarrow \mathsf{GF}(V^2)$.

The correctness of the construction follows from the next argument: For every path ρ in $\mathcal{G}$ and a corresponding path ρ' in $\mathcal{G}'$.

– $[\![\rho, \otimes_{1 \leq i \leq k^e} \mathsf{GF}e[i]]\!] \geq 1 - T$ iff ρ' satisfies $\mathsf{GF}(V^1)$.
– $[\![\rho, \otimes_{1 \leq i \leq k^s} \mathsf{GF}s[i]]\!] \geq T$ iff ρ' satisfies $\mathsf{GF}(V^2)$.

Finally, we analyze the size of $\mathcal{G}'$. Consider a reachable vertex $(v, r, b) \in S$. Then, for every $1 \leq i \leq k$, we have that r_i is a value of $w[j]$ for some j. Accordingly, $|S| = O(|V| \cdot m^k \cdot |V|)$. In particular, if k is fixed, this is a polynomial blow-up with respect to $\mathcal{G}$. $\qquad\square$

By composing Theorems 1 and 2, we can conclude with the following.

Theorem 3. *Consider a GR(1)[$\mathcal{F}$] formula φ over $I \cup O$ with k^e assumptions, k^s guarantees, and width m. Given a threshold $T \in [0, \infty]$, we can construct a Boolean strong-fairness game $\mathcal{G}_\varphi$ whose winning condition has a single assumption and a single guarantee, such that Player 2 wins in $\mathcal{G}_\varphi$ iff φ is realizable with value T. Moreover, $\mathcal{G}_\varphi$ has $O(2^{|I \cup O|} m^{k^e + k^s})$ vertices.*

3.2   Lower Bounds

Theorem 3 reduces GR(1)[$\mathcal{F}$] realizability to the solution of strong-fairness games. The reduction relies on the monotonicity of the quantitative conjunctive operator $\otimes$. In addition, The obtained game is polynomial in $2^{|I \cup O|}$ whenever the number of assumptions and guarantees in the GR(1)[$\mathcal{F}$] formula is fixed. In this section, we show that if we drop either of the assumptions, then the corresponding weighted game becomes hard to solve. We start by dropping the monotonicity assumption.

Theorem 4. *Solving weighted strong-fairness games is NP-hard for non-monotonic $\otimes$ functions, even when there are no environment assumptions, and only two guarantees; i.e., when $k^e = 0$ and $k^s = 2$.*

Proof. We show a polynomial reduction from the problem of solving *two-dimensional parity games*. A two-dimensional parity game is $\mathcal{P} = \langle V = V_1 \cup V_2, E, v_0, p \rangle$, where V, E and v_0 describe a game graph, and $p : V \to \{1, \ldots, k\}^2$ is a priority function, assigning to every $v \in V$ two priorities $p(v) = (p_1(v), p_2(v))$. An infinite path is winning for Player 2 if the minimal priority that is visited infinitely often in each dimension is even. In Lemma 1 of [9], it is shown that solving such games is NP-hard.

Given a two-dimensional parity game $\mathcal{P}$, we construct a weighted strong-fairness game $\mathcal{G} = \langle V = V_1 \cup V_2, E, v_0, w, W \rangle$, where $w : V \to [0, 1]^2$ is of width k, and the winning condition W is of the form $\otimes(\mathsf{GF}w[1], \mathsf{GF}w[2])$, such that Player 2 wins $\mathcal{P}$ iff he wins $\mathcal{G}$ with value 1. Note that W has no environment assumption, and its system guarantee includes two conjuncts. For all $v \in V$, we define $w(v)[i] = \frac{1}{p_i(v)}$. The quantitative (non-monotonic) conjunction $\otimes$ is defined by $\otimes(x, y) = 1$ if $\frac{1}{x}$ and $\frac{1}{y}$ are even integers, and $\otimes(x, y) = 0$ otherwise.

We observe that for $i \in \{1, 2\}$, the satisfaction value of $\mathsf{GF}e[i]$ in a computation is $\frac{1}{x}$, where x is the minimal rank that occurs infinitely often in the computation in component i. Thus, a path has value 1 according to W iff it satisfies the parity condition. $\square$

Next, we show that dropping the assumption about the number of assumptions and guarantees being fixed yields co-NP-hardness, even for a monotonic $\otimes$ function. Specifically, the function we consider is the average function.

Theorem 5. *Solving weighted strong-fairness games is co-NP-hard.*

Proof. We show that the complement problem is NP-hard, by showing a polynomial reduction from the SET-COVER problem, which was shown to be NP-hard in [16]. In the SET-COVER problem, we are given a set $U = \{1, \ldots, m\}$, a collection of subsets $S \subseteq 2^U$ and a number $k \in \mathbb{N}$. The problem is to decide whether there exists a collection $T \subseteq S$ with $|T| = k$ such that $\bigcup_{s \in T} s = U$. The collection T is called a *cover* of U. We note that the problem is NP-hard also for the special case where $k = \frac{|S|}{2}$. Given a SET-COVER instance as above, we construct a weighted strong-fairness game $\mathcal{G} = \langle V = V_1 \cup V_2, E, v_0, w, W \rangle$, where $w : V \to [0, 1]^{|U| + |S|}$ is of width 3, $V_1 = S$, $V_2 = \emptyset$, and $E = V_1 \times V_1$. That is, Player 1 controls all the vertices of the graph, which is a clique of size $|S|$. Intuitively, Player 1 chooses a cover, i.e., subsets from S, and he wins iff the collection is of size at most $\frac{|S|}{2}$ and covers all the elements of U. We now formally define the weight function and the winning condition. The assumptions are the number of elements from U that are covered. Hence, for every $u \in U$, we add a dimension to the function e, and for every vertex $v \in V$ (recall that $V = S$), we define $e(v)[u] = 0.5$ if $u \in v$ and otherwise $e(v)[u] = 0$. The guarantees are the number of elements from S that are used in the cover. Hence, for every $r \in S$, we add a dimension to the function s, and for every vertex $v \in V$, we define $s(v)[r] = 1$ if $v = r$ and $s(v)[r] = 0$ otherwise. Finally, we set $\otimes$ to be the average function. A set cover of size at most $\frac{|S|}{2}$ exists iff Player 1 can violate the winning condition $\max(1 - \otimes(\mathsf{GF}e[1], \ldots, \mathsf{GF}e[|U|]), \otimes(\mathsf{GF}s[1], \ldots, \mathsf{GF}s[|S|])) > \frac{1}{2}$, and we are done. □

4   Weighted Games with Ratio Implication

In this section we study weighted games with ratio implication, namely these induced by $\mathrm{GR}(1)[\mathcal{F}]$ formulas in which the satisfaction value of $x \mapsto y$ is y/x. For this purpose we define $x/0 = \infty$ and allow quantitative values in $[0, \infty]$.

4.1   Lower Bound

We first show that deciding weighted games with ratio implication is hard even for the simple winning condition $\mathsf{GF}e[1] \mapsto \mathsf{GF}s[1]$, namely when the fairness assumption and guarantee consists of a single quantitative propositional assertion. For simplicity, we refer to $e[1]$ and $s[1]$ by e and s, respectively. Thus, each vertex in the graph is labeled by two weights, e and s with values in $[0, 1]$, and the value of a path π is the ratio $\frac{[\pi, \mathsf{GF}s]}{[\pi, \mathsf{GF}e]}$. We call weighted strong-fairness games with such a winning condition 1-*ratio games*. We show that deciding 1-ratio games is as hard as deciding parity games.

Theorem 6. *1-ratio games are polynomial-time inter-reducible with parity games.*

Proof. We first show a reduction from parity games to 1-ratio games. Let $\mathcal{G} = (V, E, p : V \to \{1, \ldots, n\})$ be a parity game. Consider weight functions $e, s : V \to \{0, 1, \ldots, n\}$, where $e(v) = p(v)$ if $p(v)$ is odd, and $e(v) = 0$ otherwise, and $s(v) = p(v)$ if $p(v)$ is even, and $s(v) = 0$ otherwise. For every infinite path, the maximal priority that is visited infinitely often is even if and only if $\frac{\mathsf{GF}s}{\mathsf{GF}e} \geq 1$.

We now show a reduction in the converse direction. W.l.o.g we consider a 1-ratio game with threshold 1 and with integer weights. A general threshold T can be simulated simply by multiplying environment weights by T. Rational weights can be transformed to integer weights by multiplying environment and system weights by the least common multiplier of the weights. Given a 1-ratio game $\mathcal{G} = \langle V, E, v_0, e, s \rangle$, consider the following priority function: If $s(v) \geq e(v)$, then $p(v) = 2s(v) + 2$, and otherwise $p(v) = 2e(v) + 1$. For every infinite path, the maximal priority that is visited infinitely often is even if and only if $\frac{\mathsf{GF}s}{\mathsf{GF}e} \geq 1$.

4.2   Upper Bound in a Finitary Semantics

Theorem 6 motivates an approximated solution for the case of $\mathrm{GR}(1)[\mathcal{F}]$ formulas with ratio implication. Inspired by finitary parity games [8, 20], we strengthen the winning condition in order to have a polynomial algorithm. Intuitively, the specification $\frac{\mathsf{GF}s}{\mathsf{GF}e} \geq T$ requires that whenever a computation visits a vertex v, where the value of the assumption is $e(v)$, then eventually it would visit also a vertex u in which the value of the guarantee is T times bigger than $e(v)$, i.e., $s(u) \geq T \cdot e(v)$. The finitary condition requires the existence of a bound b, such that whenever a vertex v is visited, then a vertex u with $s(u) \geq T \cdot e(v)$ is visited within at most b moves.

Chatterjee et al. showed that finitary parity games have a polynomial solution. Hence, by Theorem 6, synthesis over the finitary version of $\frac{\mathsf{GF}s}{\mathsf{GF}e} \geq T$ is also polynomial. Here, we present an alternative solution that has two advantages: (i) it involves a reduction to Boolean strong-fairness games (while the solution in [8] involves repeated iterations of winning region computation for a so called *weak parity* objective), and thus allow us to use existing tools for GR(1) symbolic synthesis; (ii) it naturally scales to winning conditions that involve a conjunction of objectives.

In Sect. 5, we describe a symbolic implementation of the GR(1)[$\mathcal{F}$] synthesis algorithm that follows from our solution.

From Finitary 1-ratio Games to Boolean Games. We first formally define the finitary winning condition. A path $\pi = \pi_0, \pi_1, \ldots$ satisfies a *finitary 1-ratio winning condition* $\frac{\mathsf{GF}s}{\mathsf{GF}e} \geq T$ if there is a bound $b \in \mathbb{N}$ such that for all $i \geq 0$, there is $0 \leq j_i \leq b$ such that $s(\pi_{i+j_i}) \geq e(\pi_i) \cdot T$. That is, whenever a vertex v is visited, a vertex u with $s(u) \geq e(v) \cdot T$ is visited within the next b rounds.

In order to obtain a reduction to Boolean strong-fairness games, we first consider a modified winning condition. Intuitively, the modified winning condition allows Player 2 to respond with a required guaranteed value within an unbounded number of rounds, yet he has to declare when he gives up and no longer tries to present a high guaranteed value, which is ok to do finitely often.

Formally, given a game $\mathcal{G}$ with a finitary 1-ratio winning condition with labels s and e, we define the game $\mathcal{G}'$ as follows:

- The vertices and edges are as in $\mathcal{G}$, except that Player 2 can always make a "give up" declaration when he takes a move.
- A Player 1 request is opened whenever a vertex is visited. A request can be either satisfied or closed.
  - A request of vertex v is satisfied when a vertex u with $s(u) \geq e(v) \cdot T$ is visited.
  - A request is closed when Player 2 gives up (and then, all requests are closed).
- A path satisfies the winning condition if Player 2 gives up only finitely many times and every request along the path is eventually satisfied or closed.

Clearly, if Player 2 wins $\mathcal{G}$, then the same strategy used there would be winning in $\mathcal{G}'$. In addition, taking b to be the size of the memory in a finite-memory winning strategy for Player 2 in $\mathcal{G}'$, we can prove that this strategy is winning also in $\mathcal{G}$. Formally, we have the following.

Lemma 1. *Player 2 wins $\mathcal{G}$ iff he wins $\mathcal{G}'$.*

We show that solving $\mathcal{G}'$, and in fact generating a winning strategy for Player 2, can be done in polynomial time. We do so by reducing $\mathcal{G}'$ to a Boolean strong-fairness game $\mathcal{G}''$. The latter games can be decided using Boolean GR(1) synthesis.

Given $\mathcal{G}'$, we label its vertices by 3 priorities. Indeed, the reduction is really to a parity game with 3 priorities (1, 2, and 3), which we can further translate to a strong-fairness winning condition. In order to label the vertices of $\mathcal{G}'$, the game $\mathcal{G}''$ keeps track of the maximal open request. This involves an $O(m)$ blow-up, for the width m of $\mathsf{GF}e \mapsto \mathsf{GF}s$. When the maximal request is satisfied, the vertex is labeled by priority 2. When the maximal request is closed, the vertex is labeled by priority 3. All other vertices are labeled by 1. Hence, if Player 2 gives up infinitely often or fails to eventually satisfy a request, then the outcome of the play is either 3 or 1, and the Player 2 loses. Otherwise, the outcome is 2 and Player 2 wins.

Lemma 2. *Player 2 wins $\mathcal{G}'$ iff he wins $\mathcal{G}''$.*

Lemmas 1 and 2 together imply that finitely 1-ratio games are polynomial time reducible to parity games with priority set $\{1, 2, 3\}$. It is not hard to see that winning in such games amounts to violating a strong-fairness condition, and thus can be specified as the negation of the GR(1) formula $\mathsf{GF}V^2 \to \mathsf{GF}V^3$, where V^j stands for vertices with priority j. Since synthesis tools for GR(1) specification generate also counter-strategies, namely, strategies for the environment in case the specification is not realizable, we have reduced finitely 1-ratio games to Boolean GR(1) synthesis.

From Finitely (k^e, k^s)-ratio Games to Boolean Games. In this section we extend the results above to conjunctions of objectives. Consider $\otimes$ functions that are monotonically increasing and the objective $\frac{\otimes_{1 \leq i \leq k^s} \mathsf{GF}s[i]}{\otimes_{1 \leq i \leq k^e} \mathsf{GF}e[i]} \geq T$. We first define a corresponding finitary condition. Let π be an infinite path in a graph. We say that a quantitative conjunction $\otimes_{1 \leq i \leq k} \mathsf{GF}w[i]$ gets value x in position r if along the segment between the previous time that $\otimes_{1 \leq i \leq k} \mathsf{GF}w[i]$ got a value x (or since the beginning of the path if it never got value x) and r, the path visited vertices $\{v_1, \ldots, v_k\}$ such that $\otimes(w(v_1)[1], \ldots, w(v_k)[k]) = x$. We note that in this segment the path may visit also other vertices other then $\{v_1, \ldots, v_k\}$, and the order of visits does not matter.

Winning a game $\mathcal{G}$ with finitely winning condition $W = \frac{\otimes_{1 \leq i \leq k^s} \mathsf{GF}s[i]}{\otimes_{1 \leq i \leq k^e} \mathsf{GF}e[i]} \geq T$, requires the existence of a bound $b \in \mathbb{N}$ such that a computation satisfies W if whenever $\otimes_{1 \leq i \leq k^e} \mathsf{GF}e[i]$ gets value x, then $\otimes_{1 \leq i \leq k^s} \mathsf{GF}s[i]$ gets value at least $x \cdot T$ at least once within the next b positions. We refer to W as a finitary (k^e, k^s)-ratio game.

It is not hard to see that the finitary ratio condition is a sound approximation of the ratio condition. Indeed, a winning strategy for the finitary version of W is also winning for its non-finitary version. In Sect. 5.2, we show an example where the approximation is not complete.

We now adjust the construction of $\mathcal{G}'$ in the 1-ratio case to finitary (k^e, k^s)-ratio games. The idea is similar, except that opening and closing of requests is now required for all values obtained along the computation.

- The vertices and edges are as in $\mathcal{G}$, except that Player 2 can always make a "give up" declaration when he takes a move.
- A Player 1 request for value x is opened whenever $\otimes_{1 \leq i \leq k^e} \mathsf{GF}e[i]$ gets value x. A request can be either satisfied or closed.
  - A request for value x is satisfied when $\otimes_{1 \leq i \leq k^s} \mathsf{GF}s[i]$ gets value greater or equal to $x \cdot T$.
  - A request is closed when Player 2 gives up (and then, all requests are closed).
- A path satisfies the winning condition if Player 2 gives up only finitely many times and every request along the path is eventually satisfied or closed.

By similar arguments as in Lemmas 1 and 2, Player 2 wins $\mathcal{G}'$ if and only if he wins $\mathcal{G}$. Moreover, a construction of $\mathcal{G}'$ and the reduction to GR(1) synthesis follows by the same arguments as in the proof of Lemma 2. As in the reduction in Theorem 2, the game $\mathcal{G}'$ needs to maintain of the values that $\otimes_{1 \leq i \leq k^s} \mathsf{GF}s[i]$ and $\otimes_{1 \leq i \leq k^e} \mathsf{GF}e[i]$ get. For this purpose we need to keep track of whether a request for value x was opened for every possible value of $\otimes_{1 \leq i \leq k^e} \mathsf{GF}e[i]$, i.e., we have to maintain a separate maximal record for every value of $\otimes_{1 \leq i \leq k^e}$. The reduction is explicitly described in Sect. 5.1. Let $m(\otimes^e)$ denote the number of different values that $\otimes_{1 \leq i \leq k^e} \mathsf{GF}e[i]$ can have. Note that $m(\otimes^e) \leq m^{k^e}$. By the above, the state blow-up required for maintaning the values is $(m^{k^s + k^e})^{m(\otimes^e)}$. Thus, when k^e, k^s, and $m(\otimes^e)$ are fixed, we get only a polynomial blowup.

5   Symbolic Solution

In this section we describe a symbolic implementation (Sect. 5.1) and experimental results (Sect. 5.2) for the GR(1)[$\mathcal{F}$] synthesis algorithm. In Sect. 3.1, we described a reduction from GR(1)[$\mathcal{F}$] synthesis to GR(1) synthesis. Our algorithm is based on combining a symbolic implementation of the reduction with the known symbolic algorithm for GR(1) synthesis. For synthesis we used the implementation of GR(1) from [5] based on JTLV [27] with CUDD 3.0 64Bit as a BDD engine. We ran the algorithms with Java 1.8 64Bit on a Windows 7 64Bit desktop computer with 16 GB and an Intel 3.2 GHz CPU. All the specifications are available in the supplementary material from http://tinyurl.com/m5s4hsn.

5.1   Symbolic Encoding

Our goal is to synthesize a reactive system that interacts with an environment that generates truth assignments to ℓ Boolean input signals (variables), thus $I = \{x_1, \ldots, x_\ell\}$, and generates assignments to ℓ Boolean output signals, thus $O = \{y_1, \ldots, y_\ell\}$. We use $\overline{x}$ to denote $x_1, \ldots, x_\ell$, and similarly for $\overline{y}$. Each state in the system is an assignment $(\overline{x}, \overline{y}) \in \{0, 1\}^{I \cup O}$ to the signals. A computation of the system is an infinite sequence of assignments to the signals. When a time t is known from the context we denote by x the value of a variable x in time t and by x' the value of x in time $t+1$.

Adjusting the basic notions to the symbolic setting, we get that an *invariant* is a propositional formula $\varphi(\overline{x}, \overline{y}, \overline{x}', \overline{y}')$, relating the current and the next values of the variables. Also, a *propositional quality function* is $\psi : \{0,1\}^{I \cup O} \to [0,1]$, mapping each assignment to the variables (that is, each state) to a value in $[0,1]$. Let $\varphi = (\theta^e \to \theta^s) \wedge (\theta^e \to \mathsf{G}((\mathsf{H}\varphi^e) \to \varphi^s)) \wedge ((\theta^e \wedge \mathsf{G}\varphi^e) \to (\otimes_{1 \leq i \leq k^e} \mathsf{GF}\psi_i^e \mapsto \otimes_{1 \leq i \leq k^s} \mathsf{GF}\psi_i^s)$. Let $m(\psi)$ be the width of a quantitative propositional assertion ψ. Recall that $m(\psi) \leq 2^{\min\{|\psi|, |I \cup O|\}}$. We encode each quantitative propositional assertion $\psi \in \{\psi_1^e, \ldots, \psi_{k^e}^e, \psi_1^s, \ldots, \psi_{k^s}^s\}$ by $m(\psi)$ Boolean functions $\psi^1, \ldots, \psi^{m(\psi)}$, where $\psi^j(\overline{x}, \overline{y})$ holds iff $\psi(\overline{x}, \overline{y}) = j$.

In the presence of a threshold T, the user can encode the $\otimes$ operator with two formulas $\chi_{\otimes \geq T}$ and $\chi_{\otimes \geq 1-T}$ that define when the value of a conjunction is greater or equal to T and when it is greater or equal to $1 - T$.

The symbolic solution is the reduction from Sects. 3 and 4. The maximal values record is constructed by automatically adding deterministic monitors to the GR(1) specification, similar to the temporal testers described in [5, Sect. 5.2]. These monitors add auxiliary variables and safety guarantees. In the reduction to Boolean GR(1), the fairness assumptions are determined according to the $\otimes$ function over the maximal values record.

Encoding Disjunctive Implication. The reduction of disjunctive implication from Sect. 3.1 generates GR(1) specifications with a single assumption and a single guarantee. Given φ as above, the reduction generates the GR(1) formula $(\hat{\theta}^e \to \hat{\theta}^s) \wedge (\hat{\theta}^e \to \mathsf{G}((\mathsf{H}\hat{\varphi}^e) \to \hat{\varphi}^s)) \wedge ((\hat{\theta}^e \wedge \mathsf{G}\hat{\varphi}^e) \to (\mathsf{GF}\hat{\psi}^e \to \mathsf{GF}\hat{\psi}^s))$, over the signals $\hat{I}$ and $\hat{O}$, where

- Let Aux be a set of auxiliary variables used for encoding maximal records. Thus, $\overline{a}^e = (a_1^e, \ldots, a_{k^e}^e)$ encodes the maximal record for $1 \leq i \leq k^e$, and $\overline{a}^s = (a_1^s, \ldots, a_{k^s}^s)$ encodes the maximal record for $1 \leq i \leq k^s$. Then, $\hat{I} = I$ and $\hat{O} = O \cup Aux$.
- $\hat{\theta}^e = \theta^e$ and $\hat{\theta}^s = \theta^s \wedge \bigwedge_{1 \leq i \leq k^e} a_i^e = 0 \wedge \bigwedge_{1 \leq i \leq k^s} a_i^s = 0$.
- $\hat{\varphi}^e = \varphi^e$ and $\hat{\varphi}^s = \varphi^s \wedge$
  $\bigwedge_{1 \leq i \leq k^e}(\text{if } \varphi_{\otimes \geq 1-T}(\overline{a}^e) \text{ then } a_i^{e\prime} = 0 \text{ else } a_i^{e\prime} = \max(a_i^e, \psi_i^e(\overline{x}', \overline{y}'))) \wedge$
  $\bigwedge_{1 \leq i \leq k^s}(\text{if } \varphi_{\otimes \geq T}(\overline{a}^s) \text{ then } a_i^{s\prime} = 0 \text{ else } a_i^{s\prime} = \max(a_i^s, \psi_i^s(\overline{x}', \overline{y}')))$.
- $\hat{\psi}^e = \varphi_{\otimes \geq 1-T}(\overline{a}^e)$ and $\hat{\psi}^s = \varphi_{\otimes \geq T}(\overline{a}^s)$.

The number of added Boolean auxiliary variables is $|Aux| = (k^e + k^s) \cdot log_2(m)$.

Encoding Ratio Objective. Recall that the reduction for the ratio implication from Sect. 4 leads to the negation of a GR(1) formula. Thus, in our experiments we used a variant of a GR(1) counter-strategy synthesis algorithm (see e.g., [17]). We denote the range of $\otimes_{1 \leq i \leq k^e}(\psi_i^e)$ by $range(\otimes^e)$. Given φ as above, the reduction generates a negated GR(1) specification $(\hat{\theta}^e \to \hat{\theta}^s) \wedge (\hat{\theta}^e \to \mathsf{G}((\mathsf{H}\hat{\varphi}^e) \to \hat{\varphi}^s)) \wedge ((\hat{\theta}^e \wedge \mathsf{G}\hat{\varphi}^e) \to (\bigwedge_{r \in range(\otimes^e)} \mathsf{GF}\hat{\psi}_r^s \wedge \mathsf{FG}\neg giveup))$, over the signals $\hat{I}$ and $\hat{O}$, where

- Let *giveup* be a variable for the system to declare giving up and *Aux* be a set of auxiliary variables used for encoding maximal records for every $r \in range(\otimes^e)$. Thus, $\overline{a}_r^e = (a_{1,r}^e, \ldots, a_{k^e,r}^e)$ encodes the maximal record for $1 \leq i \leq k^e$, and $\overline{a}_r^s = (a_{1,r}^s, \ldots, a_{k^s,r}^s)$ encodes the maximal record for $1 \leq i \leq k^s$. Then, $\hat{I} = I$ and $\hat{O} = O \cup \{giveup\} \cup Aux$.
- $\hat{\theta}^e = \theta^e$ and $\hat{\theta}^s = \theta^s \wedge \bigwedge_{r \in range(\otimes^e)} (\bigwedge_{1 \leq i \leq k^e} a_{i,r}^e = 0 \wedge \bigwedge_{1 \leq i \leq k^s} a_{i,r}^s = 0)$.
- $\hat{\varphi}^e = \varphi^e$ and $\hat{\varphi}^s = \varphi^s \wedge$
  $\bigwedge_{r \in range(\otimes^e)}$ if $\varphi_{\otimes \geq rT}(\overline{a}_r^s) \vee giveup$ then
  $\bigwedge_{1 \leq i \leq k^e} (a_{i,r}^{e\prime} = 0)$ else $a_{i,r}^{e\prime} = \max(a_{i,r}^e, \psi_i^e(\overline{x}', \overline{y}'))$
  $\bigwedge_{r \in range(\otimes^e)}$ if $\varphi_{\otimes \geq rT}(\overline{a}_r^s) \vee giveup$ then
  $\bigwedge_{1 \leq i \leq k^s} (a_{i,r}^{s\prime} = 0)$ else $a_{i,r}^{s\prime} = \max(a_{i,r}^s, \psi_i^s(\overline{x}', \overline{y}'))$.
- $\hat{\psi}_r^s = \varphi_{\otimes < r}(\overline{a}_r^e) \vee \varphi_{\otimes \geq rT}(\overline{a}_r^s))$.

The number of added Boolean auxiliary variables is $|Aux| = |range(\otimes^e)| \cdot (k^e + k^s) \cdot log_2(m)$.

5.2   Experimental Results

Beyond the feasibility of our algorithms, the examples below demonstrate the usefulness of the quantitative approach in assume-guarantee synthesis. Indeed, it involves specifications that are not realizable in the Boolean approach, but have high satisfaction values in the quantitative approach.

Example 1: Paint Robot. Consider a paint robot with two arms that paints parts of manufactured pieces (see Fig. 1). Each arm can paint using different colors. Colors can be changed, one at a time, when the environment (a human operator) supports the change. The goal of the robot is to always eventually paint pieces in a set of different color configurations expressed in its specification. A GR(1) specification of the robot controller is shown in List. 1.1. Essentially, the specification states that when the environment enables color change in the two arms, then the robot should produce all four combinations of colors. The colors used by each robot arm (`color[0]` and `color[1]`) are system controlled (output) and the respective supported color changes (`chg[0]` and `chg[1]`) are modeled as environment variables (input). The safety guarantees to not change colors unless supported are expressed in l.13–14. The safety assumption that a change of both colors does not occur at the same time is expressed in l.11. Finally, the fairness assumptions are to always eventually support color changes for each arm (l.16) and the fairness guarantees are that the system always eventually colors pieces in color combinations c1 to c4 (l.18).

The GR(1) specification of the robot is realizable. Notice that the GR(1) specification is unrealizable if one of the fairness assumptions was omitted; i.e., if one of the arms could have a constant color.

We obtain GR(1)[$\mathcal{F}$] specifications $\otimes^e(\psi_1^e, \psi_2^e) \to \otimes^s(\psi_1^s, \psi_2^s, \psi_3^s, \psi_4^s)$ with different semantics from the GR(1) specification, where for every fairness assumption and guarantee $\hat{\psi}_i$ we define a quantitative proposition ψ_i with value 1 if $\hat{\psi}_i$

```
1  module PaintJobRobot
2  // Robot with arms that color pieces.
3  out Int(0..255)[2] color; // colors of robot
4  in boolean[2] chg; // color change allowed
5  define // different colorings
6      c1 := color[0] < 128 & color[1] < 128;
7      c2 := color[0] < 128 & color[1] >= 128;
8      c3 := color[0] >= 128 & color[1] < 128;
9      c4 := color[0] >= 128 & color[1] >= 128;
10 // change support does not appear at same
        time
11 asm G !(chg[0] & chg[1]);
12 // no change support implies same color
13 gar G !chg[0] -> next(color[0])=color[0];
14 gar G !chg[1] -> next(color[1])=color[1];
15 // always eventually support change
16 asm GF chg[0]; asm GF chg[1];
17 // always eventually produce coloring
18 gar GF c1; gar GF c2; gar GF c3; gar GF c4;
```

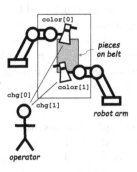

Fig. 1. Sketch of paint robot with two arms, different colors, and a human operator to support color changes. (Color figure online)

Listing 1.1. GR(1) specification with winning condition $(\mathsf{GFchg}[0] \wedge \mathsf{GFchg}[1]) \rightarrow (\mathsf{GFc1} \wedge \mathsf{GFc2} \wedge \mathsf{GFc3} \wedge \mathsf{GFc4})$

is satisfied and 0 otherwise. The specification has 2 environment variables and 16 system variables (Boolean variables). The reductions use 6 auxiliary variables for the disjunctive implication semantics and 12 ($\otimes^e = average$) or 6 ($\otimes^e = min$) auxiliary variables for the ratio implication. Table 1 shows maximal satisfaction values T for realizing the specifications, and the running times of realizability checks.

Table 1. Maximal value T and running time of $GR(1)[\mathcal{F}]$ realizability check for $\otimes^s = average$, different $\otimes^e$, and different implication semantics (all specifications in supplementary material).

	$\otimes^e = average$	$\otimes^e = min$
Disjunctive implication	1/2 (40 ms)	1 (50 ms)
Ratio implication	3/2 (121 ms)	3/1 (60 ms)

For $\otimes^e = average$, the maximal value of the disjunctive implication is $1/2$, as in the worst case if one assumption is violated the robot can only paint two colors, albeit the robot cannot commit on two specific colors. Note that even when both assumptions are satisfied, an optimal strategy need not paint more than two colors. For the ratio objective, the maximal value is $3/2$, therefore an optimal strategy paints 2 colors when one assumption holds and paints 3 colors when both assumptions hold. Thus, the optimal strategy for the ratio implication is more desirable in this case.[6]

---

[6] In the full version we explain why ratio 2 is impossible to obtain.

Intuitively, for $\otimes^e = \min$, the environment has to satisfy all assumptions and thus the system should be able to paint all four colors. Indeed, in the disjunctive implication semantics we get value 1. However, in the ratio semantics, the formed optimal strategy only paints 3 colors because of the finitary overapproximation metric. The finitary condition dictates a bound over the response time of the system and in this case the immediate consequence of two changes is only three different colors.

Example 2: Maximal Realizability. One interesting application of GR(1)[$\mathcal{F}$] synthesis is to compute *maximal realizability* of GR(1) specifications, i.e., the maximal number of guarantees that can be satisfied when all assumptions hold. This is naturally captured in a quantitative setting where the quantitative value of a Boolean assumption or guarantee is 1 if it is satisfied and 0 otherwise. Maximal realizability is expressed by the GR(1)[$\mathcal{F}$] specification $\max(1 - \min(\psi_i^e), average(\psi_i^s))$ (note that average is the normalized sum).

For example, for a specification with environment variable $x \in I$ and guarantees $\mathsf{GF}x \wedge \mathsf{GF}\neg x$, the maximal realizability is $1/2$. Note that a computation of realizable subsets would perform worse and yield result 0.

We have checked maximal realizability for unrealizable specifications of the AMBA case study from [11]. For AMBA variants of different sizes Table 2 shows the number of fairness assumptions $|\psi^e|$ and guarantees $|\psi^s|$, the number of system and environment variables $|I| + |O|$, and the running times of the GR(1) algorithm for checking realizability on the original problem in milli-seconds. We selected three different sizes (prefix 1 to 3) for each variant (wgf: added fairness guarantee, wgt: added safety guarantee, and woaf: removed fairness assumption) of AMBA provided by [11]. Table 2 also reports on the auxiliary Boolean variables $|Aux|$ our reduction adds (here $|Aux| = |\psi^s| + \log_2(|\psi^s|)$, see the full version), the optimal T the system can guarantee, the time $\hat{t}$ of checking realizability of the reduced GR(1) game, and the ratio between t and $\hat{t}$.

Table 2. Unrealizable specifications from [11], the maximal average of satisfiable fairness guarantees, and running times of computing the winning states.

Spec	$|\psi^e|$	$|\psi^s|$	$|I| + |O|$	t in ms	$|Aux|$	max T	$\hat{t}$ in ms	$\hat{t}/t$
amba_ahb_wgf_1	2	4	5 + 11	11	7	3/4	305	28
amba_ahb_wgf_2	2	6	7 + 15	72	9	5/6	6,337	88
amba_ahb_wgf_3	2	8	9 + 19	410	12	7/8	499,630	1,219
amba_ahb_wgt_1	2	3	5 + 11	10	5	0/3	9	1
amba_ahb_wgt_2	2	5	7 + 15	51	8	0/5	1,032	20
amba_ahb_wgt_3	2	7	9 + 19	92	10	0/7	4,653	51
amba_ahb_woaf_1	1	3	5 + 11	35	5	2/3	257	7
amba_ahb_woaf_2	1	5	7 + 15	175	8	4/5	2,058	12
amba_ahb_woaf_3	1	7	9 + 19	1,132	10	5/7	75,945	67

Table 2 shows that for many unrealizable AMBA specifications, the maximal realizable satisfaction value T is high. The times for computing all winning states of the GR(1)[$\mathcal{F}$] specification show an expected increase with growing specification size.

References

1. Almagor, S., Boker, U., Kupferman, O.: Formalizing and reasoning about quality. J. ACM **63**(3), 24:1–24:56 (2016)
2. Almagor, S., Kupferman, O.: High-quality synthesis against stochastic environments. In: CSL. LIPIcs, vol. 62, pp. 28:1–28:17 (2016)
3. Bloem, R., Chatterjee, K., Henzinger, T., Jobstmann, B.: Better quality in synthesis through quantitative objectives. In: CAV, pp. 140–156 (2009)
4. Bloem, R., Ehlers, R., Könighofer, R.: Cooperative reactive synthesis. In: Finkbeiner, B., Pu, G., Zhang, L. (eds.) ATVA 2015. LNCS, vol. 9364, pp. 394–410. Springer, Cham (2015). doi:10.1007/978-3-319-24953-7_29
5. Bloem, R., Jobstmann, B., Piterman, N., Pnueli, A., Sa'ar, Y.: Synthesis of reactive(1) designs. J. Comput. Syst. Sci. **78**(3), 911–938 (2012)
6. Chatterjee, K., Henzinger, T.A., Jobstmann, B.: Environment assumptions for synthesis. In: Breugel, F., Chechik, M. (eds.) CONCUR 2008. LNCS, vol. 5201, pp. 147–161. Springer, Heidelberg (2008). doi:10.1007/978-3-540-85361-9_14
7. Chatterjee, K., Henzinger, T.A.: Assume-guarantee synthesis. In: Grumberg, O., Huth, M. (eds.) TACAS 2007. LNCS, vol. 4424, pp. 261–275. Springer, Heidelberg (2007). doi:10.1007/978-3-540-71209-1_21
8. Chatterjee, K., Henzinger, T.A., Horn, F.: Finitary winning in omega-regular games. ACM Trans. Comput. Log. **11**(1), 1 (2009)
9. Chatterjee, K., Henzinger, T.A., Piterman, N.: Generalized parity games. In: Seidl, H. (ed.) FoSSaCS 2007. LNCS, vol. 4423, pp. 153–167. Springer, Heidelberg (2007). doi:10.1007/978-3-540-71389-0_12
10. Church, A.: Logic, arithmetics, and automata. In: Proceedings of the International Congress of Mathematicians, vol. 1962, pp. 23–35. Institut Mittag-Leffler (1963)
11. Cimatti, A., Roveri, M., Schuppan, V., Tchaltsev, A.: Diagnostic information for realizability. In: Logozzo, F., Peled, D.A., Zuck, L.D. (eds.) VMCAI 2008. LNCS, vol. 4905, pp. 52–67. Springer, Heidelberg (2008). doi:10.1007/978-3-540-78163-9_9
12. D'Ippolito, N., Braberman, V.A., Piterman, N., Uchitel, S.: Synthesizing nonanomalous event-based controllers for liveness goals. ACM Trans. Softw. Eng. Methodol. **22**(1), 9 (2013)
13. Faella, M., Legay, A., Stoelinga, M.: Model checking quantitative linear time logic. Electr. Notes Theor. Comput. Sci. **220**(3), 61–77 (2008)
14. Fisman, D., Kupferman, O., Lustig, Y.: Rational synthesis. In: Esparza, J., Majumdar, R. (eds.) TACAS 2010. LNCS, vol. 6015, pp. 190–204. Springer, Heidelberg (2010). doi:10.1007/978-3-642-12002-2_16
15. Gimbert, H., Horn, F.: Solving simple stochastic games with few random vertices. **5**(2) (2009). https://arxiv.org/abs/0712.1765
16. Karp, R.M.: Reducibility among combinatorial problems. In: Miller, R.E., Thatcher, J.W., Bohlinger, J.D. (eds.) Complexity of Computer Computations. The IBM Research Symposia Series, pp. 85–103. Springer, US, Newyork (1972). doi:10.1007/978-1-4684-2001-2_9

17. Könighofer, R., Hofferek, G., Bloem, R.: Debugging formal specifications: a practical approach using model-based diagnosis and counterstrategies. STTT **15**(5–6), 563–583 (2013)
18. Kress-Gazit, H., Fainekos, G.E., Pappas, G.J.: Temporal-logic-based reactive mission and motion planning. IEEE Trans. Robotics **25**(6), 1370–1381 (2009)
19. Kupferman, O., Lustig, Y., Vardi, M.Y., Yannakakis, M.: Temporal synthesis for bounded systems and environments. In: STACS, pp. 615–626 (2011)
20. Kupferman, O., Piterman, N., Vardi, M.Y.: From liveness to promptness. In: Damm, W., Hermanns, H. (eds.) CAV 2007. LNCS, vol. 4590, pp. 406–419. Springer, Heidelberg (2007). doi:10.1007/978-3-540-73368-3_44
21. Li, W., Dworkin, L., Seshia, S.A.: Mining assumptions for synthesis. In: MEMOCODE, pp. 43–50 (2011)
22. Maoz, S., Ringert, J.O.: GR(1) synthesis for LTL specification patterns. In: ESEC/FSE, pp. 96–106 (2015)
23. Maoz, S., Sa'ar, Y.: AspectLTL: an aspect language for LTL specifications. In: AOSD, pp. 19–30 (2011)
24. Maoz, S., Sa'ar, Y.: Assume-guarantee scenarios: semantics and synthesis. In: France, R.B., Kazmeier, J., Breu, R., Atkinson, C. (eds.) MODELS 2012. LNCS, vol. 7590, pp. 335–351. Springer, Heidelberg (2012). doi:10.1007/978-3-642-33666-9_22
25. Piterman, N., Pnueli, A., Sa'ar, Y.: Synthesis of reactive(1) designs. In: Emerson, E.A., Namjoshi, K.S. (eds.) VMCAI 2006. LNCS, vol. 3855, pp. 364–380. Springer, Heidelberg (2005). doi:10.1007/11609773_24
26. Pnueli, A., Rosner, R.: On the synthesis of a reactive module. In: POPL, pp. 179–190 (1989)
27. Pnueli, A., Sa'ar, Y., Zuck, L.D.: JTLV: a framework for developing verification algorithms. In: Touili, T., Cook, B., Jackson, P. (eds.) CAV 2010. LNCS, vol. 6174, pp. 171–174. Springer, Heidelberg (2010). doi:10.1007/978-3-642-14295-6_18
28. Schewe, S., Finkbeiner, B.: Bounded synthesis. In: Namjoshi, K.S., Yoneda, T., Higashino, T., Okamura, Y. (eds.) ATVA 2007. LNCS, vol. 4762, pp. 474–488. Springer, Heidelberg (2007). doi:10.1007/978-3-540-75596-8_33

Syntax-Guided Optimal Synthesis for Chemical Reaction Networks

Luca Cardelli[1,2], Milan Češka[3], Martin Fränzle[4], Marta Kwiatkowska[2],
Luca Laurenti[2], Nicola Paoletti[5], and Max Whitby[2(✉)]

[1] Microsoft Research Cambridge, Cambridge, UK
[2] Department of Computer Science, University of Oxford, Oxford, UK
max.whitby@keble.ox.ac.uk
[3] Faculty of Information Technology, Brno University of Technology,
Brno, Czech Republic
[4] Department of Computer Science, Carl von Ossietzky Universität Oldenburg,
Oldenburg, Germany
[5] Department of Computer Science, Stony Brook University, Stony Brook, USA

Abstract. We study the problem of optimal syntax-guided synthesis of
stochastic Chemical Reaction Networks (CRNs) that plays a fundamental role in design automation of molecular devices and in the construction of predictive biochemical models. We propose a sketching language
for CRNs that concisely captures syntactic constraints on the network
topology and allows its under-specification. Given a sketch, a correctness
specification, and a cost function defined over the CRN syntax, our goal
is to find a CRN that simultaneously meets the constraints, satisfies the
specification and minimizes the cost function. To ensure computational
feasibility of the synthesis process, we employ the Linear Noise Approximation allowing us to encode the synthesis problem as a satisfiability
modulo theories problem over a set of parametric Ordinary Differential Equations (ODEs). We design and implement a novel algorithm for
the optimal synthesis of CRNs that employs almost complete refutation
procedure for SMT over reals and ODEs, and exploits a meta-sketching
abstraction controlling the search strategy. Through relevant case studies
we demonstrate that our approach significantly improves the capability
of existing methods for synthesis of biochemical systems and paves the
way towards their automated and provably-correct design.

1 Introduction

Chemical Reaction Networks (CRNs) are a versatile language widely used for
modelling and analysis of biochemical systems. The power of CRNs derives from
the fact that they provide a compact formalism equivalent to Petri nets [42],
Vector Addition Systems (VAS) [36] and distributed population protocols [4].

This work has been partially supported by the Czech Grant Agency grant No. GA16-
17538S (M. Češka), Royal Society professorship, and EPSRC Programme on Mobile
Autonomy (EP/M019918/1).

© Springer International Publishing AG 2017
R. Majumdar and V. Kunčak (Eds.): CAV 2017, Part II, LNCS 10427, pp. 375–395, 2017.
DOI: 10.1007/978-3-319-63390-9_20

CRNs also serve as a high-level *programming language* for molecular devices [14, 49] in systems and synthetic biology. Motivated by numerous potential applications ranging from smart therapeutics to biosensors, the construction of CRNs that exhibit prescribed dynamics is a major goal of synthetic biology [17, 21, 52]. Formal verification methods are now commonly embodied in the design process of biological systems [32, 34, 40] in order to reason about their correctness and performance. However, there is still a costly gap between the design and verification process, exacerbated in cases where stochasticity must be considered, which is typically the case for molecular computation. Indeed, automated synthesis of *stochastic CRNs* is generally limited to the estimation or synthesis of rate parameters [20, 53], which neglect the network structure, and suffers from scalability issues [23].

Current research efforts in design automation aim to eliminate this gap and address the problem of *program synthesis* – automatic construction of programs from high-level specifications. The field of syntax-guided program synthesis [1] has made tremendous progress in recent years, based on the idea of supplementing the specification with a syntactic template that describes a high-level structure of the program and constrains the space of allowed programs. Applications range from bit-streaming programming [47] and concurrent data structures [46], to computational biology [37]. Often not only the correctness of synthesized programs is important, but also their optimality with respect to a given cost [8].

In this paper we consider the problem of optimal syntax-guided synthesis of CRNs. We work in the setting of *program sketching* [47], where the template is a partial program with holes (incomplete information) that are automatically resolved using a constraint solver. We define a sketching language for CRNs that allows designers to not only capture the high-level topology of the network and known dependencies among particular species and reactions, but also to compactly describe parts of the CRN where only limited knowledge is available or left unspecified (partially specified) in order to examine alternative topologies. A *CRN sketch* is therefore a parametric CRN, where the parameters can be unknown species, (real-valued) rates or (integer) stoichiometric constants. Our sketching language is well-suited for biological systems, where partial knowledge and uncertainties due to noisy or imprecise measurements are very common. We associate to a sketch a *cost* function that captures the structural complexity of the CRNs and reflects the cost of physically implementing it using DNA [14].

Traditionally, the dynamical behaviour of a CRN is represented as a *deterministic* time evolution of average species concentrations, described by a set of Ordinary Differential Equations (ODEs), or as a discrete-state *stochastic* process solved through the Chemical Master Equation (CME) [51]. Given the importance of faithfully modelling stochastic noise in biochemical systems [5, 27], we focus on the (continuous) Linear Noise Approximation (LNA) of the CME [28, 51]. It describes the time evolution of expectation and variance of the species in terms of ODEs, thus capturing the stochasticity intrinsic in CRNs, but, in contrast to solving the CME, scales well with respect to the molecular counts.

We can therefore represent the stochastic behaviour of a sketch as a set of parametric ODEs, which can be adequately solved as a satisfiability modulo theories (SMT) problem over the reals with ODEs. For this purpose, we employ the SMT solver iSAT(ODE) [26] that circumvents the well-known undecidability of this theory by a procedure generating either a certificate of unsatisfiability, or a solution that is precise up to an arbitrary user-defined precision.

To specify the desired *temporal behaviour* of the network, we support constraints about the expected number and variance of molecules, and, crucially, their derivatives over time. This allows us, for instance, to formalise that a given species shows a specific number of oscillations or has higher variability than another species, thus providing greater expressiveness compared to simple reachability specifications or temporal logic.

We therefore formulate and provide a solution to the following problem. For a given CRN sketch, a formal specification of the required temporal behaviour and a cost function, we seek a sketch instantiation (a concrete CRN) that satisfies the specification and minimizes the cost. The optimal solution for a given sketch is computed using the *meta-sketch* abstraction for CRNs inspired by [8]. It combines a representation of the syntactic search space with the cost function and defines an ordered set of sketches. This cost-based ordering allows us to effectively prune the search space during the synthesis process and guide the search towards the minimal cost.

In summary, this paper makes the following contributions:

- We propose the first sketching language for CRNs that supports partial specifications of the topology of the network and structural dependencies among species and reactions.
- We formulate a novel optimal synthesis problem that, thanks to the LNA interpretation of stochastic dynamics, can be solved as an almost complete decision/refutation problem over the reals involving parametric ODEs. In this way, our approach offers superior scalability with respect to the size of the system and the number of parameters and, crucially, supports the synthesis of the CRN structure and not just of rate parameters.
- We design a new synthesis algorithm that builds on the meta-sketch abstraction, ensuring the optimality of the solution, and the SMT solver iSAT.
- We develop a prototype implementation of the algorithm and evaluate the usefulness and performance of our approach on three case studies, demonstrating the feasibility of synthesising networks with complex dynamics in a matter of minutes.

We stress that CRNs provide not just a programming language for bio-systems, but a more general computational framework. In fact, CRNs are formally equivalent to population protocols and Petri nets. As a consequence, our methods enable effective program synthesis also in other non-biological domains [3].

Related Work. In the context of syntax-guided program synthesis (SyGuS) and program sketching, SMT-based approaches such as counter-example guided inductive synthesis [48] were shown to support the synthesis of deterministic programs for a variety of challenging problems [8,46]. Sketching for probabilistic programs is presented in [43], together with a synthesis algorithm that builds on stochastic search and approximate likelihood computation. A similar approach appears in [11,31], where genetic algorithms and probabilistic model checking are used to synthesise probabilistic models from model templates (an extension of the PRISM language [38]) and multi-objective specifications. SyGuS has also been used for data-constrained synthesis, as in [24,37,45], where (deterministic) biological models are derived from gene expression data.

A variety of methods exist for estimating and synthesising rate parameters of CRNs, based on either the deterministic or stochastic semantics [2,6,10,20, 35,41,53]. In contrast, our approach supports the synthesis of network structure and (uniquely) employs LNA.

Synthesis of CRNs from input-output functional specifications is considered in [23], via a method comprising two separate stages: (1) SMT-based generation of qualitative CRN models (candidates), and (2) for each candidate, parameter estimation of a parametric continuous time Markov chain (pCTMC). In contrast to our work, [23] do not consider solution optimality and require solving an optimisation problem for each concrete candidate on a pCTMC whose dimension is exponential in the number of molecules, making synthesis feasible only for very small numbers of molecules. On the other hand, our approach has complexity independent of the initial molecular population.

In [18], authors consider the problem of comparing CRNs of different size. They develop notions of bisimulations for CRNs in order to map a complex CRN into a simpler one, but with similar dynamical behaviour. Our optimal synthesis algorithm automatically guarantees that the synthesized CRN has the minimal size among all the CRNs consistent with the specification and the sketch.

2   Sketching Language for Chemical Reaction Networks

In this section, we introduce CRNs and the sketching language for their design.

2.1   Chemical Reaction Networks

CRN Syntax. A *chemical reaction network (CRN)* $\mathcal{C} = (\Lambda, \mathcal{R})$ is a pair of finite sets, where Λ is a set of *species*, $|\Lambda|$ denotes its size, and $\mathcal{R}$ is a set of reactions. Species in Λ interact according to the reactions in $\mathcal{R}$. A *reaction* $\tau \in \mathcal{R}$ is a triple $\tau = (r_\tau, p_\tau, k_\tau)$, where $r_\tau \in \mathbb{N}^{|\Lambda|}$ is the *reactant complex*, $p_\tau \in \mathbb{N}^{|\Lambda|}$ is the *product complex* and $k_\tau \in \mathbb{R}_{>0}$ is the coefficient associated with the rate of the reaction. r_τ and p_τ represent the stoichiometry of reactants and products. Given a reaction $\tau_1 = ([1,1,0],[0,0,2],k_1)$, we often refer to it as $\tau_1 : \lambda_1 + \lambda_2 \xrightarrow{k_1} 2\lambda_3$. The *state change* associated to τ is defined by $\upsilon_\tau = p_\tau - r_\tau$. For example, for τ_1 as above, we have $\upsilon_{\tau_1} = [-1,-1,2]$. The initial condition of a CRN is given by a vector of initial populations $x_0 \in \mathbb{N}^{|\Lambda|}$. A *chemical reaction system* (CRS) $C = (\Lambda, \mathcal{R}, x_0)$ is a tuple where (Λ, R) is a CRN and $x_0 \in \mathbb{N}^{|\Lambda|}$ represents its initial condition.

CRN Semantics. Under the usual assumption of mass action kinetics, the *stochastic* semantics of a CRN is generally given in terms of a discrete-state, continuous-time Markov process (CTMC) $(X(t), t \geq 0)$ [28], where the states, $x \in \mathbb{N}^{|A|}$, are vectors of molecular counts. Such a representation is accurate, but not scalable in practice because of the state space explosion problem [34,39]. An alternative *deterministic* model describes the evolution of the concentrations of the species as the solution $\Phi : \mathbb{R}_{\geq 0} \to \mathbb{R}^{|A|}$ of the following ODEs (the so called rate equations) [13]:

$$\frac{d\Phi(t)}{dt} = F(\Phi(t)) = \sum_{\tau \in \mathcal{R}} \upsilon_\tau \cdot (k_\tau \prod_{S \in A} \Phi_S^{r_{S,\tau}}(t)) \tag{1}$$

where Φ_S and $r_{S,\tau}$ are the components of vectors Φ and r_τ relative to species S. However, such a model does not take into account the stochasticity intrinsic in molecular interactions. In this paper, we work with the Linear Noise Approximation (LNA) [16,28,51], which describes the stochastic behaviour of a CRN in terms of a Gaussian process Y converging in distribution to X [9,28]. For a CRS $\mathcal{C} = (A, \mathcal{R}, x_0)$ contained in a system of volume N, we define $Y = N \cdot \Phi + \sqrt{N} \cdot Z$, where Φ is the solution of the rate equations (Eq. 1) with initial condition $\Phi(0) = \frac{x_0}{N}$. Z is a zero-mean Gaussian process with variance $C[Z(t)]$ described by

$$\frac{dC[Z(t)]}{dt} = J_F(\Phi(t))C[Z(t)] + C[Z(t)]J_F^T(\Phi(t)) + W(\Phi(t)) \tag{2}$$

where $J_F(\Phi(t))$ is the Jacobian of $F(\Phi(t))$, $J_F^T(\Phi(t))$ its transpose version, and $W(\Phi(t)) = \sum_{\tau \in \mathcal{R}} \upsilon_\tau \upsilon_\tau^T k_\tau \prod_{S \in A} (\Phi_S)^{r_{S,\tau}}(t)$. Y is a Gaussian process with expectation $E[Y(t)] = N\Phi(t)$ and covariance matrix $C[Y(t)] = NC[Z(t)]$. As a consequence, for any $t \in \mathbb{R}_{\geq 0}$, the distribution of $Y(t)$ is fully determined by its expectation and covariance. These are computed by solving the ODEs in Eq. 1–2, and thus avoiding the state space exploration. We denote by $[\![\mathcal{C}]\!]_N = (E[Y], C[Y])$ the solution of these equations for CRS $\mathcal{C}$ in a system of size N, henceforth called the *LNA model*. By using the LNA we can consider stochastic properties of CRNs whilst maintaining scalability comparable to that of the deterministic model [16]. In fact, the number of ODEs required for LNA is quadratic in the number of species and independent of the molecular counts.

2.2   CRN Sketching Language

CRN sketches are defined in a similar fashion to concrete CRNs, with the main difference being that species, stoichiometric constants and reaction rates are specified as unknown *variables*. The use of variables considerably increases the expressiveness of the language, allowing the modeller to specify *additional constraints* over them. Constraints facilitate the representation of key background knowledge of the underlying network, e.g. that a reaction is faster than another, or that it consumes more molecules than it produces.

Another important feature is that reactants and products of a reaction are lifted to *choices* of species (and corresponding stoichiometry). In this way, the modeller can explicitly incorporate in the reaction a set of admissible alternatives, letting the synthesiser resolve the choice.

Further, a sketch distinguishes between *optional* and *mandatory* reactions and species. These are used to express that some elements of the network *might* be present and that, on the other hand, other elements *must* be present. Our sketching language is well suited for synthesis of biological networks: it allows expressing key domain knowledge about the network, and, at the same time, it allows for network under-specification (holes, choices and variables). This is crucial for biological systems, where, due to inherent stochasticity or noisy measurements, the knowledge of the molecular interactions is often partial.

Definition 1 (Sketching language for CRNs). *A CRN sketch is a tuple* $\mathcal{S} = (\Lambda, \mathcal{R}, \mathsf{Var}, \mathsf{Dec}, \mathsf{Ini}, \mathsf{Con})$, *where:*

- $\Lambda = \Lambda_m \cup \Lambda_o$ *is a finite set of species, where* Λ_m *and* Λ_o *are sets of mandatory and optional species, respectively.*
- $\mathsf{Var} = \mathsf{Var}_\Lambda \cup \mathsf{Var}_c \cup \mathsf{Var}_r$ *is a finite set of variable names, where* Var_Λ, Var_c *and* Var_r *are sets of species, coefficient and rate variables, respectively.*
- Dec *is a finite set of variable declarations. Declarations bind variable names to their respective domains of evaluation and are of the form* $x : D$, *where* $x \in \mathsf{Var}$ *and* D *is the domain of* x. *Three types of declaration are supported:*
  - *Species, where* $x \in \mathsf{Var}_\Lambda$ *and* $D \subseteq \Lambda$ *is a finite non-empty set of species.*
  - *Stoichiometric coefficients, where* $x \in \mathsf{Var}_c$ *and* $D \subseteq \mathbb{N}$ *is a finite non-empty set of non-negative integers.*
  - *Rate parameters, where* $x \in \mathsf{Var}_r$ *and* $D \subseteq \mathbb{R}_{\geq 0}$ *is a bounded set of non-negative reals.*
- Ini *is the set of initial states, that is, a predicate on variables* $\{\lambda_0\}_{\lambda \in \Lambda}$ *describing the initial number of molecules for each species.*
- Con *is a finite set of additional constraints, specified as quantifier-free formulas over* Var.
- $\mathcal{R} = \mathcal{R}_m \cup \mathcal{R}_o$ *is a finite set of reactions, where* $\mathcal{R}_m$ *and* $\mathcal{R}_o$ *are sets of mandatory and optional reactions, respectively. As for a concrete CRNs, each* $\tau \in \mathcal{R}$ *is a triple* $\tau = (r_\tau, p_\tau, k_\tau)$, *where in this case* $k_\tau \in \mathsf{Var}_r$ *is a rate variable; the reaction complex* r_τ *and the product complex* p_τ *are sets of reactants and products, respectively. A reactant* $R \in r_\tau$ *(product* $P \in p_\tau$*) is a finite choice of species and coefficients, specified as a (non-empty) set* $R = \{c_i \lambda_i\}_{i=1,...,|R|}$, *where* $c_i \in \mathsf{Var}_c$ *and* $\lambda_i \in \mathsf{Var}_\Lambda$. *We denote with* f_{r_τ} *the uninterpreted choice function for the reactants of* τ, *that is, a function* $f_{r_\tau} : r_\tau \to \mathsf{Var}_c \times \mathsf{Var}_\Lambda$ *such that* $f_{r_\tau}(R) \in R$ *for each* $R \in r_\tau$. *The choice function for products,* f_{p_τ}, *is defined equivalently.*

As an example, reaction $\tau = (\{\{c_1\lambda_1, c_2\lambda_2\}, \{c_3\lambda_3\}\}, \{\{c_4\lambda_4, c_5\lambda_5\}\}, k)$ is preferably written as $\{c_1\lambda_1, c_2\lambda_2\} + c_3\lambda_3 \xrightarrow{k} \{c_4\lambda_4, c_5\lambda_5\}$, using the shortcut $c_3\lambda_3$ to indicate the single-option choice $\{c_3\lambda_3\}$. A possible concrete choice function for the reactants of τ is the function $\overline{f_{r_\tau}} = \{\{c_1\lambda_1, c_2\lambda_2\} \mapsto c_1\lambda_1, \{c_3\lambda_3\} \mapsto c_3\lambda_3\}$ that chooses option $c_1\lambda_1$ as first reactant.

Holes and Syntactic Sugar. Unknown information about the network can be also expressed using *holes*, i.e. portions of the model left "unfilled" and resolved by the synthesiser. Holes, denoted with ?, are implicitly encoded through sketch variables. To correctly interpret holes, we assume default domains, $D_r \subseteq \mathbb{R}$ bounded and $D_c \subseteq \mathbb{N}$ finite, for rate and coefficient variables, respectively. We also support the implicit declaration of variables, as shown in Example 1.

The following example illustrates the proposed sketching language and the optimal solution obtained using our synthesis algorithm introduced in Sect. 4.

Example 1 (Bell shape generator). *For a given species K, our goal is to synthesize a CRN such that the evolution of K, namely the expected number of molecules of K, has a bell-shaped profile during a given time interval, i.e. during an initial interval the population K increases, then reaches the maximum, and finally decreases, eventually dropping to 0. Table 1 (left) defines a sketch for the bell-shape generator inspired by the solution presented in [12].*

Table 1. Left: the sketch for bell-shape generator, with volume $N = 100$. Right: CRN producing the bell-shape profile (species K) synthesized by our algorithm

$\Lambda_m = \{K\}, \Lambda_o = \{A, B\}, \mathcal{R}_m = \{\tau_1, \tau_2\},$

$\mathcal{R}_o = \{\tau_3\}, \mathsf{Dec} = \{c_1, \dots, c_4 : [0, 2],$

$k_1, k_2, k_3 : [0, 0.1], \lambda_1, \lambda_2 : \{A, B\}\},$

$\mathsf{Con} = \{\lambda_1 \neq \lambda_2, c_1 < c_2, c_3 > c_4\},$

$\mathsf{Ini} = \{K_0 = 1 \wedge A_0 \in [0, 100] \wedge B_0 \in [0, 100]\}$

$\tau_1 = \lambda_1 + c_1 K \xrightarrow{k_1} c_2 K$

$\tau_2 = \{0, 1\}\lambda_2 + c_3 K \xrightarrow{k_2} ?\lambda_2 + c_4 K$

$\tau_3 = \emptyset \xrightarrow{k_3} \{\lambda_2, [1, 2]K\}$

$A + K \xrightarrow{56} 2K; \quad K + B \xrightarrow{43} 2B$

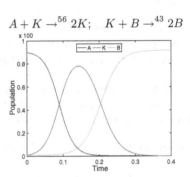

This sketch reflects our prior knowledge about the control mechanism of the production/degradation of K. It captures that the solution has to have a reaction generating K (τ_1) and a reaction where K is consumed (τ_2). We also know that τ_1 requires a species, represented by variable λ_1, that is consumed by τ_1, and thus τ_1 will be blocked after the initial population of the species is consumed. An additional species, λ_2, different from λ_1, may be required. However, the sketch does not specify its role exactly: reaction τ_2 consumes either none or one molecule of λ_2 and produces an unknown number of λ_2 molecules, as indicated by the hole ?. There is also an optional reaction, τ_3, that does not have any reactants and produces either 1 molecule of λ_2 or between 1 and 2 molecules of K. The sketch further defines the mandatory and optional sets of species, the domains of the variables, and the initial populations of species. We assume the default domain $D_c = [0, 2]$, meaning that the hole ? can take values from 0 to 2. Note that many sketch variables are implicitly declared, e.g. term $[1, 2]K$ corresponds to $c'\lambda'$ with fresh variables $c' : [1, 2]$ and $\lambda' : \{K\}$.

Table 1 (right) shows the optimal CRN computed by our algorithm for the cost function given in Definition 3 and the bell-shape profile produced by the CRN.

We now characterise when a concrete network is a valid instantiation of a sketch.

Definition 2 (Sketch instantiation). *A CRS $C = (\Lambda_C, \mathcal{R}_C, x_0)$ is a valid instantiation of a sketch $S = (\Lambda, \mathcal{R}, \mathsf{Var}, \mathsf{Dec}, \mathsf{Ini}, \mathsf{Con})$ if: $\mathsf{Ini}(x_0)$ holds; there exists an interpretation I of the variables in Var and choice functions such that:*

1. *all additional constraints are satisfied: $I \models \bigwedge_{\phi \in \mathsf{Con}} \phi$,*
2. *for each $\tau \in \mathcal{R}_m$ there is $\tau' \in \mathcal{R}_C$ that realises τ, i.e., τ' is obtained from τ by replacing variables and choice functions with their interpretation[1], and*
3. *for each $\tau' \in \mathcal{R}_C$ there is $\tau \in \mathcal{R}$ such that τ' realises τ;*

and the following conditions hold:

4. *for each $\tau' = (r_{\tau'}, p_{\tau'}, k_{\tau'}) \in \mathcal{R}_C$: $k_{\tau'} > 0$ and $r_{\tau'} + p_{\tau'} > 0$*
5. *$\Lambda_m \subseteq \Lambda_C$ and $\Lambda_C \subseteq \Lambda_m \cup \Lambda_o$ and*
6. *for each species $A \in \Lambda_C$ there is $r \in \mathcal{R}_C$ such that A appears in r as reactant or product.*

Such an interpretation is called consistent *for S. For sketch S and consistent interpretation I, we denote with $I(S)$ the instantiation of S through I. We denote with $L(S)$ the set of valid instantiations of S.*

Condition 4. states that there are no void reactions, i.e. having null rate ($k_{\tau'} = 0$), or having no reactants and products ($r_{\tau'} + p_{\tau'} = 0$). Further, condition 6. ensures that the concrete network contains only species occurring in some reactions.

Example 2. *A CRS $C_1 = \{\{A, B, K\}, \{\tau'_1, \tau'_2, \tau'_3\}, x_0\}$ where*

$$\tau'_1 = A + K \xrightarrow{0.01} 2K \quad \tau'_2 = B + K \xrightarrow{0.1} 2B \quad \tau'_3 = \emptyset \xrightarrow{0.001} K,$$

with $x_0 = (A_0 = 100, B_0 = K_0 = 1)$ is a valid instantiation of the bell shape sketch S from Example 1. Reactions τ'_1, τ'_2 and τ'_3 realise respectively reaction sketches τ_1, τ_2 and τ_3. The corresponding consistent interpretation is $I = \{\lambda_1 \mapsto A, c_1 \mapsto 1, k_1 \mapsto 0.01, c_2 \mapsto 2, c'_1 \mapsto 1, \lambda_2 \mapsto B, c_3 \mapsto 1, k_2 \mapsto 0.1, H \mapsto 2, c_4 \mapsto 0, k_3 \mapsto 0.001, f_{p_{\tau_3}} \mapsto \{\{\lambda_2, [1, 2]K\} \mapsto [1, 2]K\}, c'_2 \mapsto 1\}$, where c'_i is the i-th implicit stoichiometric variable and H is the only hole. The interpretation of $f_{p_{\tau_3}}$ indicates that the choice $\{\lambda_2, [1, 2]K\}$ is resolved as $[1, 2]K$.

Since a sketch instantiation corresponds to a CRS, we remark that its behaviour is given by the LNA model. Similarly, as we will show in Sect. 4, the SMT encoding of a sketch builds on a symbolic encoding of the LNA equations.

---

[1] When τ' realises sketch reaction τ, its reactants $r_{\tau'}$ is a set of the form $\{c_R \lambda_R\}_{R \in r_\tau}$, i.e. containing a concrete reactant for each choice R. Then, this is readily encoded in the reactant vector form $r_{\tau'} \in \mathbb{N}^{|\Lambda|}$ as per CRN definition (see Sect. 2.1). Similar reasoning applies for products $p_{\tau'}$.

3   Specification Language

We are interested in checking whether a CRN exhibits a given temporal profile. For this purpose, our specification language supports constraints about the expected number and variance of molecules, and, importantly, about their derivatives over time. This allows us, for instance, to synthesise a network where a given species shows a bell-shape profile (as in Example 1), or has variance greater than its expectation (considered in Sect. 5). Before explaining the specification language, we introduce the logical framework over which properties, together with CRN sketches, will be interpreted and evaluated.

3.1   Satisfiability Modulo ODEs

In syntax-guided synthesis, the synthesis problem typically reduces to an SMT problem [1]. Since we employ LNA, which generally involves non-linear ODEs, we resort to the framework of *satisfiability modulo ODEs* [25, 26, 30], which provides solving procedures for this theory that are sound and complete up to a user-specified precision. We stress that this framework allows for continuous encoding of the LNA equations, thus avoiding discrete approximations of its dynamics. Crucially, we can express arbitrary-order derivatives of the LNA variables, as these are smooth functions, and hence admit derivatives of all orders.

We employ the SMT solver iSAT(ODE) [25] that supports arithmetic constraint systems involving non-linear arithmetic and ODEs. The constraints solved are quantifier-free Boolean combinations of Boolean variables, arithmetic constraints over real- and integer-valued variables with bounded domains, and ODE constraints over real variables plus flow invariants. *Arithmetic constraints* are of the form $e_1 \sim e_2$, where $\sim \in \{<, \leq, =, \geq, >\}$ and $e_{1,2}$ are expressions built from real- and integer-valued variables and constants using functions from $\{+, -, \cdot, \sin, \cos, \mathrm{pow}_\mathbb{N}, \exp, \min, \max\}$. *ODE constraints* are time-invariant and given by $\frac{\mathrm{d}x}{\mathrm{d}t} = e$, where e is an expression as above[2] containing variables themselves defined by ODE constraints. *Flow invariant constraints* are of the form $x \leq c$ or $x \geq c$, with x being an ODE-defined variable and c being a constant. ODE constraints have to occur under positive polarity and are interpreted as first-order constraints on pre-values x and post-values x' of their variables, i.e., they relate those pairs (x, x') being connected by a trajectory satisfying $\frac{\mathrm{d}x}{\mathrm{d}t} = e$ and, if present, the flow invariant throughout.

Due to undecidability of the fragment of arithmetic addressed, iSAT(ODE) implements a sound, yet quantifiably incomplete, unsatisfiability check based on a combination of interval constraint propagation (ICP) for arithmetic constraints, safe numeric integration of ODEs, and conflict-driven clause learning (CDCL) for manipulating the Boolean structure of the formula. This procedure investigates "boxes", i.e. Cartesian products of intervals, in the solution space until it either finds a proof of unsatisfiability based on a set of boxes covering the original domain or finds some hull-consistent box [7], called a *candidate*

---

[2] Where we can additionally use non-total functions $/$, $\sqrt{}$ and $\ln$.

solution box, with edges smaller than a user-specified width $\delta > 0$. While the interval-based unsatisfiability proof implies unsatisfiability over the reals, thus rendering the procedure sound, the report of a candidate solution box only guarantees that a slight relaxation of the original problem is satisfiable. Within this relaxation, all original constraints are first rewritten to equi-satisfiable inequational form $t \sim 0$, with $\sim \in \{>, \geq\}$, and then relaxed to the strictly weaker constraint $t \sim -\delta$. In that sense, iSAT and related algorithms [30,50] provide reliable verdicts on either unsatisfiability of the original problem or satisfiability of its aforementioned δ-relaxation, and do in principle[3] always terminate with one of these two verdicts. Hence the name "δ-decidability" used by Gao et al. in [29].

3.2   Specification for CRNs

The class of properties we support are formulas describing a dynamical profile composed as a finite sequence of phases. Each phase i is characterised by an arithmetic predicate $\mathsf{pre} - \mathsf{post}_i$, describing the system state at its start and end points (including arithmetic relations between these two), as well as by flow invariants (formula inv_i) pertaining to the trajectory observed during the phase. Formally, a specification φ comprising $M \geq 1$ phases is defined by

$$\varphi = \bigwedge_{i=1}^{M} \mathsf{inv}_i \wedge \mathsf{pre} - \mathsf{post}_i \qquad (3)$$

Note that entry as well as target conditions of phases can be expressed within $\mathsf{pre} - \mathsf{post}_i$. Initial conditions are not part of the specification but, as explained in Sect. 4, the sketch definition.

CRS Correctness. For a CRS $\mathcal{C}$, Volume N, and property φ, we are interested in checking whether $\mathcal{C}$ is *correct* with respect to φ, written $[\![\mathcal{C}]\!]_N \models \varphi$, i.e., whether $\mathcal{C}$ at Volume N exhibits the dynamic behavior required by φ. Since $[\![\mathcal{C}]\!]_N$ is a set of ODEs, this corresponds to checking whether $\hat{\varphi} \wedge \varphi_{[\![\mathcal{C}]\!]_N}$ is satisfiable, where $\varphi_{[\![\mathcal{C}]\!]_N}$ is an SMT formula encoding the set of ODEs given by $[\![\mathcal{C}]\!]_N$ and their higher-order derivatives[4] by means of the corresponding ODE constraints, and $\hat{\varphi}$ is the usual bounded model checking (BMC) unwinding of the step relation $\bigwedge_{i=1}^{M}(\mathit{phase} = i \Rightarrow \mathsf{inv}_i \wedge \mathsf{pre} - \mathsf{post}_i) \wedge \mathit{phase}' = \mathit{phase} + 1$ encoding the phase sequencing and the pertinent phase constraints, together with the BMC target $\mathit{phase} = M$ enforcing all phases to be traversed. As this satisfiability problem is undecidable in general, we relax it to checking whether $\hat{\varphi} \wedge \varphi_{[\![\mathcal{C}]\!]_N}$ is δ-satisfiable in the sense of admitting a candidate solution box of width δ. In that case, we write $[\![\mathcal{C}]\!]_N \models^\delta \varphi$.

---

[3] i.e., when considering the abstract algorithms using unbounded precision rather than the safe rounding employed in their floating-point based actual implementations.

[4] Only the derivatives appearing in φ are included. These are encoded using the Faà di Bruno's formula [33].

Example 3 (Specification for the bell-shape generator). *The required bell-shaped profile for Example 1 can be formalized using a 2-phase specification as follows:*

$$\mathsf{inv}_1 \equiv E^{(1)}[K] \geq 0, \quad \mathsf{pre\text{-}post}_1 \equiv E^{(1)}[K]' = 0 \wedge E[K]' > 30,$$
$$\mathsf{inv}_2 \equiv E^{(1)}[K] \leq 0, \quad \mathsf{pre\text{-}post}_2 \equiv E[K]' \leq 1 \wedge T' = 1$$

where $E[K]$ is the expected value of species K and $E^{(1)}[K]$ its first derivative. T is the global time. Primed notation $(E[K]', E^{(1)}[K]', T')$ indicates the variable value at the end of the respective phase. Constraints inv_1 and inv_2 require, respectively, that $E[K]$ is not decreasing in the first phase, and not increasing in the second (and last) phase. $\mathsf{pre\text{-}post}_1$ states that, at the end of phase 1, $E[K]$ is a local optimum $(E^{(1)}[K]' = 0)$, and has an expected number of molecules greater than 30. $\mathsf{pre\text{-}post}_2$ states that, at the final phase, the expected number of molecules of K is at most 1 and that the final time is 1.

This example demonstrates that we can reason over complex temporal specifications including, for instance, a relevant fragment of bounded metric temporal logic [44].

4   Optimal Synthesis of Chemical Reaction Networks

In this section we formulate the optimal synthesis problem where we seek to find a concrete instantiation of the sketch (i.e. a CRN) that satisfies a given property and has a minimal cost. We further show the encoding of the problem using satisfiability modulo ODEs and present an algorithm scheme for its solution.

4.1   Problem Formulation

Before explaining our optimal synthesis problem, we first need to introduce the class of cost functions considered. A cost function G for a sketch $\mathcal{S}$ has signature $G : L(\mathcal{S}) \to \mathbb{N}$ and maps valid instantiations of $\mathcal{S}$ to a natural cost. A variety of interesting cost functions fit this description, and, depending on the particular application, the modeller can choose the most appropriate one. A special case is, for instance, the overall number of species and reactions, a measure of CRN complexity used in e.g. CRN comparison and reduction [18,19]. Importantly, cost functions are defined over the structure of the concrete instantiation, rather than its dynamics. As we shall see, this considerably simplifies the optimisation task, since it leads to a finite set of admissible costs. In the rest of the paper, we consider the following cost function, which captures the structural complexity of the CRN and the cost of physically implementing it using DNA [14,49].

Definition 3 (Cost function). *For a sketch $\mathcal{S} = (\Lambda, \mathcal{R}, \mathsf{Var}, \mathsf{Dec}, \mathsf{Ini}, \mathsf{Con})$, we consider the cost function $G_{\mathcal{S}} : L(\mathcal{S}) \to \mathbb{N}$ that, for any CRS instantiation $\mathcal{C} = (\Lambda, \mathcal{R}) \in L(\mathcal{S})$, is defined as:*

$$G_{\mathcal{S}}(\mathcal{C}) = 3 \cdot (|\Lambda \cap \Lambda_o|) + \sum_{\tau \in \mathcal{R}_{\mathcal{C}}} \sum_{S \in \Lambda} 6 \cdot r_{S,\tau} + 5 \cdot p_{S,\tau}$$

where $r_{S,\tau}$ $(p_{S,\tau})$ is the stoichiometry of species S as reactant (product) of τ.

This cost function penalizes the presence of optional species (Λ_o) and the number of reactants and products in each reaction. It does not explicitly include a penalty for optional reactions, but this is accounted for through an increased total number of reactants and products. We stress that different cost functions can be used, possibly conditioned also on the values of reaction rates.

Problem 1 *(Optimal synthesis of CRNs). Given a sketch S, cost function G_S, property φ, Volume N and precision δ, the optimal synthesis problem is to find CRS $C^* \in L(S)$, if it exists, such that $[\![C^*]\!]_N \models^\delta \varphi$ and, for each CRS $C \in L(S)$ such that $G_S(C) < G_S(C^*)$, it holds that $[\![C]\!]_N \not\models^\delta \varphi$.*

An important characteristic of the sketching language and the cost function is that for each sketch S the set $\{G_S(C) \mid C \in L(S)\}$ is finite. This follows from the fact that S restricts the maximal number of species and reactions as well as the maximal number of reactants and products for each reaction. Therefore, we can define for each sketch S the minimal cost μ_S and the maximal cost ν_S.

Example 4. *It is easy to verify that the cost of the CRS C of Example 2, a valid instantiation of the bell-shape generator sketch S, is $G_S(C) = 3 \cdot 2 + 6 \cdot 4 + 5 \cdot 5 = 55$, and that minimal and maximal costs of sketch S are, respectively, $\mu_S = 3 \cdot 1 + 6 \cdot 2 + 5 \cdot 2 = 25$ and $\nu_S = 3 \cdot 2 + 6 \cdot 5 + 5 \cdot 7 = 71$.*

We now define a meta-sketch abstraction for our sketching language that allows us to formulate an efficient optimal synthesis algorithm.

Definition 4 (Meta-sketch for CRNs). *Given a sketch S and a cost function G_S, we define the meta-sketch $\mathcal{M}_S = \{S(i) \mid \mu_S \leq i \leq \nu_S\}$, where $S(i)$ is a sketch whose instantiations have cost smaller than i, i.e. $L(S(i)) = \{C \in L(S) \mid G_S(C) < i\}$.*

A meta-sketch $\mathcal{M}_S$ establishes a hierarchy over the sketch S in the form of an ordered set of sketches $S(i)$. The ordering reflects the size of the search space for each $S(i)$ as well as the cost of implementing the CRNs described by $S(i)$. In contrast to the abstraction defined in [8], the ordering is given by the cost function and thus it can be directly used to guide the search towards the optimum.

4.2   Symbolic Encoding

Given a sketch of CRN $S = (\Lambda, \mathcal{R}, \mathsf{Var}, \mathsf{Dec}, \mathsf{Ini}, \mathsf{Con})$, we show that the dynamics of $L(S)$, set of possible instantiations of S, can be described symbolically by a set of parametric ODEs, plus additional constraints. These equations depend on the sketch variables and on the choice functions of each reaction, and describe the time evolution of mean and variance of the species.

For $S \in \Lambda, \lambda \in \mathsf{Var}$, we define the indicator function $\mathcal{I}_S(\lambda) = 1$ if $\lambda = S$, and 0 otherwise. For $S \in \Lambda$ and $\tau \in \mathcal{R}$, we define the following constants:

$$r_{S,\tau} = \sum_{\substack{R \in r_\tau \\ (c,\lambda)=f_{r_\tau}(R)}} c \cdot \mathcal{I}_S(\lambda), \qquad p_{S,\tau} = \sum_{\substack{P \in p_\tau \\ (c,\lambda)=f_{p_\tau}(P)}} c \cdot \mathcal{I}_S(\lambda), \qquad \upsilon_{S,\tau} = p_{S,\tau} - r_{S,\tau}$$

Note that these are equivalent to the corresponding coefficients for concrete CRNs, but now are parametric as they depend on the sketch variables. As for the LNA model of Sect. 2.1, symbolic expectation and variance together characterise the symbolic behaviour of sketch S, given as the set of parametric ODEs $[\![S]\!]_N = (N \cdot \Phi, N \cdot C[Z])$, for some Volume N.

The functions $\Phi(t)$ and $C[Z(t)]$ describe symbolically the time evolution of expected values and covariance of all instantiations of S, not just of valid instantiations. We restrict to valid instantiations by imposing the following formula:

$$\text{consist} \equiv \text{Ini}(x_0) \wedge \bigwedge_{\phi \in \text{Con}} \phi \wedge \bigwedge_{\tau \in \mathcal{R}_m} \neg\text{void}(\tau) \wedge \bigwedge_{S \in \Lambda_m} \text{used}(S)$$

which, based on Definition 2, states that initial state and additional constraints have to be met, all mandatory reactions must not be void, and all mandatory species must be "used", i.e. must appear in some (non-void) reactions. Note that we allow optional reactions to be void, in which case they are not included in the concrete network. Formally, $\text{void}(\tau) \equiv (k_\tau = 0) \vee \sum_{S \in \Lambda}(r_{S,\tau} + p_{S,\tau}) = 0$ and $\text{used}(S) \equiv \bigvee_{\tau \in \mathcal{R}} \neg\text{void}(\tau) \wedge (r_{S,\tau} + p_{S,\tau}) > 0$.

Sketch Correctness. Given an interpretation I consistent for S, call Φ_I and $C[Z]_I$, the concrete functions obtained from Φ and $C[Z]$ by substituting variables and functions with their assignments in I. The symbolic encoding ensures that the LNA model $[\![I(S)]\!]_N$ of CRS $I(S)$ (i.e. the instantiation of S through I, see Definition 2) is equivalent to $(\Phi_I, C[Z]_I)$.

With reference to our synthesis problem, this implies that the synthesis of a CRS C^* that satisfies a correctness specification φ from a sketch S corresponds to finding a consistent interpretation for S that satisfies φ. Similarly to the case for concrete CRSs, this corresponds to checking if $\hat{\varphi} \wedge \text{consist} \wedge \varphi_{[\![S]\!]_N}$ is δ-satisfiable for some precision δ, where $\hat{\varphi}$ is the BMC encoding of ϕ (see Sect. 3.2) and $\varphi_{[\![S]\!]_N}$ is the SMT encoding of the symbolic ODEs given by $[\![S]\!]_N$ and the corresponding derivatives.

Cost Constraints. For a sketch S and cost $i \in \mathbb{N}$, the following predicate encodes the cost function of Definition 3 in order to restrict S into $S(i)$, i.e. the sketch whose instantiations have cost smaller than i:

$$\text{Con}_G(i) \equiv \left(3 \cdot \sum_{S \in \Lambda_o} \mathcal{I}(\text{used}(S)) + \sum_{\tau \in \mathcal{R}} \mathcal{I}(\neg\text{void}(\tau)) \cdot \sum_{S \in \Lambda}(6 \cdot r_{S,\tau} + 5 \cdot p_{S,\tau})\right) < i$$

where $\mathcal{I}$ is the indicator function, and used and void are predicates defined above.

4.3   Algorithm Scheme for Optimal Synthesis

In Algorithm 1, we present an algorithm scheme for solving the optimal synthesis problem for CRNs. It builds on the meta-sketch abstraction described in Definition 4, which enables effective pruning of the search space through cost

---

Algorithm 1. Generalised synthesis scheme

Require: Meta-sketch $\mathcal{M}_S$, property φ, precision δ and initial precision δ_{init}
Ensure: C^* is a solution of Problem 1 if $\exists\, C \in L(\mathcal{M}_S^\omega) : C \vDash^\delta \varphi$, otherwise $C^* =$ null
1: $i^\top \leftarrow \nu_S; \ i^\perp \leftarrow \mu_S; \ i \leftarrow g(i^\perp, i^\top); \ C^* \leftarrow$ null
2: **repeat**
3:    $SAT_1 \leftarrow \delta\text{-Solver}(\mathcal{S}(i), \varphi, \delta_{init}); \ SAT_2 \leftarrow$ false
4:    **if** SAT_1 **then**
5:       $(M, SAT_2) \leftarrow \delta\text{-Solver}(\mathcal{S}(i), \varphi, \delta)$
6:       **if** SAT_2 **then** $C^* =$ getSoln$(\mathcal{S}(i), M)$
7:       **else** $\delta_{init} = (\delta_{init} - \delta)/2$
8:    $(i^\perp, i^\top) \leftarrow f(i, i^\perp, i^\top, SAT_2, \mathsf{G}_S(C^*)); \ i \leftarrow g(i^\perp, i^\top)$
9: **until** $i^\perp \leq i^\top$
10: **return** C^*

---

constraints, and the SMT-based encoding of Sect. 4.2, which allows for the automated derivation of meta-sketch instantiations (i.e. CRNs) that satisfy the specification and the cost constraints.

This scheme repeatedly invokes the SMT solver (δ-Solver) on the sketch encoding, and at each call the cost constraints are updated towards the optimal cost. We consider three approaches: (1) *top-down*: starting from the maximal cost ν_S, it solves meta-sketches with decreasing cost until no solution exists (UNSAT); (2) *bottom-up:* from the minimal cost μ_S, it increases the cost until a solution is found (SAT); (3) *binary search:* it bounds the upper estimate on the optimal solution using a SAT witness and the lower estimate with an UNSAT witness.

We further improve the algorithm by exploiting the fact that UNSAT witnesses can also be obtained at a lower precision δ_{init} ($\delta_{init} \gg \delta$), which consistently improves performance. Indeed, UNSAT outcomes are precise and thus valid for any precision. Note that the top-down strategy does not benefit from this speed-up since it only generates SAT witnesses.

At every iteration, variable i maintains the current cost. The solver is firstly called using the rough precision δ_{init} (line 3). If the solver returns SAT (potential false positive), we refine our query using the required precision δ (line 5). If this query is in turn satisfiable, then the solver also returns a candidate solution box M, where all discrete variables are instantiated to a single value and an interval smaller than δ is assigned to each real-valued variable. Function getSoln computes the actual sketch instantiation C^* as the centre point of M that δ-satisfies φ. The cost of C^* provides the upper bound on the optimal solution. If either query returns UNSAT, the current cost i provides the lower bound on the optimal solution. The second query being UNSAT implies that the rough precision δ_{init} produced a false positive, and thus it is refined for the next iteration (line 7).

The actual search strategy used in Algorithm 1 is given by the functions f controlling how the upper $(i^\top)$ and lower $(i^\perp)$ bounds on the cost are updated and by g determining the next cost to explore. Note that such bounds ensure the termination of the algorithm (line 9). In the bottom-up approach, f "terminates" the search (i.e. causes $i^\perp > i^\top$) if SAT_2 is true (i.e. when the first SAT witness is obtained), otherwise f sets $(i^{\perp}, i^{\top}) \leftarrow (i+1, i^{\top})$ and g sets $i \leftarrow i^{\perp}$. In the top-down case, f terminates the search if SAT_2 is false (i.e. at the first UNSAT witness), otherwise it sets $(i^{\perp}, i^{\top}) \leftarrow (i^{\perp}, G_S(C^*)-1)$ and $i \leftarrow i^{\top}$, where $G_S(C^*)$ is the cost of CRN C^*. Binary search is obtained with f that updates $(i^{\perp}, i^{\top})$ to $(i^{\perp}, G_S(C^*) - 1)$ if $SAT_2 = $ true, to $(i+1, i^{\top})$ otherwise, and with g that updates i to $i^{\perp} + \lfloor (i^{\top} - i^{\perp})/2 \rfloor$.

5 Experimental Evaluation

We evaluate the usefulness and performance of our optimal synthesis method on three case studies, representative of important problems studied in biology: (1) the **bell-shape generator**, a component occurring in signaling cascades; (2) **Super Poisson**, where we synthesize CRN implementations of stochastic processes with prescribed levels of process noise; and (3) **Phosphorelay network**, where we synthesize CRNs exhibiting switch-like sigmoidal profiles, which is the biochemical mechanism underlying cellular decision-making, driving in turn development and differentiation.

We employ the solver iSAT(ODE) [25,26][5], even if our algorithm supports any δ-solver. We ran preliminary experiments using the tool dReal [30], finding that iSAT performs significantly better on our instances. All experiments were run on a server with a Intel Xeon CPU E5645 @2.40 GHz processor (using a single core) and 24GB @1333 MHz RAM.

Bell-Shape Generator. We use the example described in Examples 1 and 3, resulting in 8 parametric ODEs, as the main benchmark. The synthesised CRN is shown in Fig. 1. In the first experiment, we evaluate the scalability of the solver with respect to precision δ and the size of the discrete search space, altered by changing the domains of species and coefficient variables of the sketch. We exclude cost constraints as they reduce the size of the search space. Runtimes, reported in Table 2 (left), correspond to a single call to iSAT with different δ values, leading to SAT outcomes in all cases. Note that the size of the continuous state space, given by the domains of rate variables, does not impose such a performance degradation, as shown in Table 3 (right) for a different model.

In the second experiment, we analyse how cost constraints and different variants of Algorithm 1 affect the performance of optimal synthesis. Table 2 (right) shows the number of iSAT calls with UNSAT/SAT outcomes (2nd column) and total runtimes without/with the improvement that attempts to obtain UNSAT witnesses at lower precision ($\delta_{init} = 10^{-1}$). Importantly, the average runtime for a single call to iSAT is significantly improved when we use cost constraints, since these reduce the discrete search space (between 216 s and 802 s with cost constraints, 1267 s without). Moreover, results clearly indicate that UNSAT cases are considerably faster to solve, because inconsistent cost constraints typically

---

[5] Version r2806. Parameters: `--maxdepth=k` (k is the BMC unrolling depth) and `--ode-opts=--continue-after-not-reaching-horizon`.

Table 2. Performance of bell-shape generator model. Left: runtimes for different precisions δ and discrete search space size. Right: optimal synthesis with different variants of Algorithm 1, fixed discrete search space size (1536) and $\delta = 10^{-3}$.

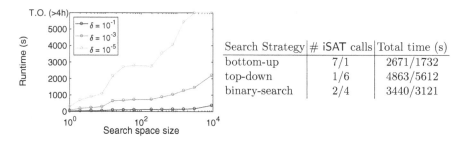

Search Strategy	# iSAT calls	Total time (s)
bottom-up	7/1	2671/1732
top-down	1/6	4863/5612
binary-search	2/4	3440/3121

lead to trivial UNSAT instances. This favours the bottom-up approach over the top-down. In this example, the bottom-up approach also outperforms binary-search, but we expect the opposite situation for synthesis problems with wider spectra of costs. As expected, we observe a speed-up when using a lower precision for UNSAT witnesses, except for the top-down approach.

Super Poisson. We demonstrate that our approach is able to synthesise a CRN that behaves as a stochastic process, namely, a super Poisson process having variance greater than its expectation. We formalise the behaviour on the interval $[0, 1]$ using a 1-phase specification as shown in Table 3 (left). For $N = 100$ we consider the sketch listed in Table 3 (center) where both reactions are mandatory, reflecting the knowledge that A is both produced and degraded.

Table 3. Left: the 1-phase specification of the super poisson process. Centre: the sketch. Right: runtimes for different precisions.

		Rate interval	Time (s)
$\mathsf{inv}_1 \equiv C[A] > E[A]$	$\Lambda = \{A, B\}, \Lambda_o = \{B\}, \lambda_1, \lambda_2 : \Lambda,$	$[0, 1]$	4
	$\mathcal{R}_m = \{\tau_1, \tau_2\}, A_0 = B_0 = 0,$	$[0, 10]$	18
$\mathsf{pre}\text{-}\mathsf{post}_1 \equiv T' = 1$	$k_1, k_2 : [0, 100], c_1, c_2, c_3 : [0, 2]$	$[0, 100]$	31
	$\tau_1 :\to^{k_1} c_1 A + c_2 \lambda_1; \quad \tau_2 : A \to^{k_2} c_3 \lambda_2;$		

Using precision $\delta = 10^{-3}$, we obtained the optimal solution $\{\xrightarrow{23} 2A, A \xrightarrow{94}\}$ (cost 16) in 4 s. Notably, the synthesis without the cost constraints took 19 s. Moreover, the ability to reason over the variance allows the solver to discard solution $\{\to A, A \to\}$ (implementation of a Poisson process [15]), which would have led to a variance equal to expectation. Table 3 (right) demonstrates the scalability of our approach with respect to the size of the continuous parameter space. Despite its non-trivial size (10 ODEs and discrete search space of size 288), we obtain remarkable performance, with runtimes in the order of seconds.

Phosphorelay Network. In the last case study we present a rate synthesis problem (i.e. all discrete parameters are instantiated) for a three-layer phosphorelay network [22]. In this network, each layer Li ($i = 1, 2, 3$) can be found in phosphorylated form, Lip, and there is the ligand B, acting as an input for the network. The authors of [22] were interested in finding rates such that the time dynamics of $L3p$ shows ultra-sensitivity – a sigmoid shape of the time evolution of $L3p$ – which they obtained by manually varying the parameters until the right profile was discovered. We show that our approach can automatically find these parameters, thus overcoming such a tedious and time-consuming task.

We formalise the required behaviour using the 2-phase specification as shown in Table 4 (left). In particular, we consider a time interval $[0, 1]$ during which $L3p$ never decreases ($E^{(1)}[L3p] \geq 0$), and we require that an inflection point in the second derivative occurs in the transition between the two phases. At the final time we require that the population of $L3p$ is above 100, to rule out trivial solutions. For $N = 1000$ we consider the sketch listed in Table 4 (center), inspired by [22]. Figure 1 lists the rates synthesised for $\delta = 10^{-3}$ and illustrates the obtained sigmoid profile.

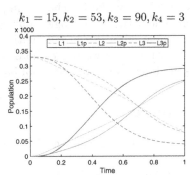

Fig. 1. The synthesised rates and the corresponding profile (without variance constraints).

We further consider a more complex variant of the problem, where we extend the specification to require that the variance of $L3p$ on its inflection point (the point where the variance is known to reach its maximum [22]) is limited by a threshold. This extension led to an encoding with 37 symbolic ODEs, compared to the 9 ODEs (7 species plus two ODEs for the derivatives of $L3p$) needed for the previous specification. Table 4 (right) shows the runtimes of the synthesis process for both variants of the model and different precisions δ. The results demonstrate that neither increasing the number of ODEs nor improving the precision leads to exponential slowdown of the synthesis process, indicating good scalability of our approach.

Table 4. Left: the 2-phase specification of the sigmoid profile (no variance constraints). Centre: the sketch. Right: runtimes for different precisions and the two variants (without and with covariances).

		ODEs	δ	Time (s)
$\mathsf{inv}_1 \equiv E^{(1)}[L3p] \geq 0 \wedge E^{(2)}[L3p] \geq 0$	$L1 + B \xrightarrow{k_1} B + L1p$	9	10^{-1}	53
	$L2 + L1p \xrightarrow{k_2} L1 + L2p$	9	10^{-3}	370
$\mathsf{pre\text{-}post}_1 \equiv E^{(2)}[L3p]' = 0$	$L2p + L3 \xrightarrow{k_3} L2 + L3p$	9	10^{-5}	719
	$L3p \xrightarrow{k_4} L3; \quad \emptyset \xrightarrow{1} B$	37	10^{-1}	1052
$\mathsf{inv}_2 \equiv E^{(1)}[L3p] \geq 0 \wedge E^{(2)}[L3p] \leq 0$	$k_1, \ldots, k_4 : (0, 100]$,	37	10^{-3}	11276
$\mathsf{pre\text{-}post}_2 \equiv E[L3p]' > 100 \wedge T' = 1$	$Li_0 = 330, Lip_0 = B_0 = 0$	37	10^{-5}	39047

Image caption (in figure): $k_1 = 15, k_2 = 53, k_3 = 90, k_4 = 3$

6   Conclusion

Automated synthesis of biochemical systems that exhibit prescribed behaviour is a landmark of synthetic and system biology. We presented a solution to this problem, introducing a novel method for SMT-based optimal synthesis of stochastic CRNs from rich temporal specifications and sketches (syntactic templates). By means of the LNA, we define the semantics of a sketch in terms of a set of parametric ODEs quadratic in the number of species, which allows us to reason about stochastic aspects not possible with the deterministic ODE-based semantics. Able to synthesize challenging systems with up to 37 ODEs and $\sim$10 K admissible network topologies, our method shows unprecedented scalability and paves the way for design automation for provably-correct molecular devices.

In future work we will explore alternative notions of optimality and encodings, and develop a software tool based on parallel search strategies.

References

1. Alur, R., et al.: Syntax-guided synthesis. Dependable Softw. Syst. Eng. **40**, 1–25 (2015)
2. Andreychenko, A., Mikeev, L., Spieler, D., Wolf, V.: Parameter identification for Markov models of biochemical reactions. In: Gopalakrishnan, G., Qadeer, S. (eds.) CAV 2011. LNCS, vol. 6806, pp. 83–98. Springer, Heidelberg (2011). doi:10.1007/978-3-642-22110-1_8
3. Angluin, D., Aspnes, J., Eisenstat, D.: Fast computation by population protocols with a leader. Distrib. Comput. **21**(3), 183–199 (2008)
4. Angluin, D., Aspnes, J., Eisenstat, D., Ruppert, E.: The computational power of population protocols. Distrib. Comput. **20**(4), 279–304 (2007)
5. Arkin, A., Ross, J., McAdams, H.H.: Stochastic kinetic analysis of developmental pathway bifurcation in phage λ-infected Escherichia coli cells. Genetics **149**(4), 1633–1648 (1998)
6. Barnat, J., et al.: On parameter synthesis by parallel model checking. IEEE/ACM Trans. Comput. Biol. Bioinf. **9**(3), 693–705 (2012)
7. Benhamou, F., Goualard, F., Granvilliers, L., Puget, J.F.: Revising hull and box consistency. In: ICLP 1999. MIT Press, pp. 230–244 (1999)
8. Bornholt, J., Torlak, E., Grossman, D., Ceze, L.: Optimizing synthesis with metasketches. In: POPL 2016. ACM, pp. 775–788 (2016)
9. Bortolussi, L., Cardelli, L., Kwiatkowska, M., Laurenti, L.: Approximation of probabilistic reachability for chemical reaction networks using the linear noise approximation. In: Agha, G., Houdt, B. (eds.) QEST 2016. LNCS, vol. 9826, pp. 72–88. Springer, Cham (2016). doi:10.1007/978-3-319-43425-4_5
10. Bortolussi, L., Milios, D., Sanguinetti, G.: Smoothed model checking for uncertain Continuous-Time Markov Chains. Inf. Comput. **247**, 235–253 (2016)
11. Calinescu, R.C., Češka, M., Gerasimou, S., Kwiatkowska, M., Paoletti, N.: Designing robust software systems through parametric markov chain synthesis. In: IEEE International Conference on Software Architecture (ICSA 2017). IEEE (2017)
12. Cardelli, L.: Artificial biochemistry. In: Condon, A., Harel, D., Kok, J.N., Salomaa, A., Winfree, E. (eds.) Algorithmic Bioprocesses, pp. 429–462. Springer, Heidelberg (2009)

13. Cardelli, L.: Morphisms of reaction networks that couple structure to function. BMC Syst. Biol. **8**(1), 84 (2014)
14. Cardelli, L.: Two-domain DNA strand displacement. Math. Struct. Comput. Sci. **23**(02), 247–271 (2013)
15. Cardelli, L., Kwiatkowska, M., Laurenti, L.: Programming discrete distributions with chemical reaction networks. In: Rondelez, Y., Woods, D. (eds.) DNA 2016. LNCS, vol. 9818, pp. 35–51. Springer, Cham (2016). doi:10.1007/978-3-319-43994-5_3
16. Cardelli, L., Kwiatkowska, M., Laurenti, L.: Stochastic analysis of chemical reaction networks using linear noise approximation. Biosystems **149**, 26–33 (2016)
17. Cardelli, L., Kwiatkowska, M., Whitby, M.: Chemical reaction network designs for asynchronous logic circuits. In: Rondelez, Y., Woods, D. (eds.) DNA 2016. LNCS, vol. 9818, pp. 67–81. Springer, Cham (2016). doi:10.1007/978-3-319-43994-5_5
18. Cardelli, L., Tribastone, M., Tschaikowski, M., Vandin, A.: Comparing chemical reaction networks: a categorical and algorithmic perspective. In: LICS 2016, pp. 485–494. ACM (2016)
19. Cardelli, L., Tribastone, M., Tschaikowski, M., Vandin, A.: Symbolic computation of differential equivalences. ACM SIGPLAN Notices **51**(1), 137–150 (2016). (ACM)
20. Češka, M., Dannenberg, F., Paoletti, N., Kwiatkowska, M., Brim, L.: Precise parameter synthesis for stochastic biochemical systems. Acta Inf. 1–35 (2016)
21. Chen, H.-L., Doty, D., Soloveichik, D.: Rate-independent computation in continuous chemical reaction networks. In: ITCS 2014, pp. 313–326. ACM (2014)
22. Csikász-Nagy, A., Cardelli, L., Soyer, O.S.: Response dynamics of phosphorelays suggest their potential utility in cell signalling. J. R. Soc. Interface **8**(57), 480–488 (2011)
23. Dalchau, N., Murphy, N., Petersen, R., Yordanov, B.: Synthesizing and tuning chemical reaction networks with specified behaviours. In: Phillips, A., Yin, P. (eds.) DNA 2015. LNCS, vol. 9211, pp. 16–33. Springer, Cham (2015). doi:10.1007/978-3-319-21999-8_2
24. Dunn, S.-J., Martello, G., Yordanov, B., Emmott, S., Smith, A.: Defining an essential transcription factor program for naive pluripotency. Science **344**(6188), 1156–1160 (2014)
25. Eggers, A., Fränzle, M., Herde, C.: SAT modulo ODE: a direct SAT approach to hybrid systems. In: Cha, S.S., Choi, J.-Y., Kim, M., Lee, I., Viswanathan, M. (eds.) ATVA 2008. LNCS, vol. 5311, pp. 171–185. Springer, Heidelberg (2008). doi:10.1007/978-3-540-88387-6_14
26. Eggers, A., Ramdani, N., Nedialkov, N.S., Fränzle, M.: Improving the SAT modulo ODE approach to hybrid systems analysis by combining different enclosure methods. Softw. Syst. Model. **14**(1), 121–148 (2015)
27. Eldar, A., Elowitz, M.B.: Functional roles for noise in genetic circuits. Nature **467**(7312), 167–173 (2010)
28. Ethier, S.N., Kurtz, T.G.: Markov Processes: Characterization and Convergence, vol. 282. Wiley, Hoboken (2009)
29. Gao, S., Avigad, J., Clarke, E.M.: δ-complete decision procedures for satisfiability over the reals. In: Gramlich, B., Miller, D., Sattler, U. (eds.) IJCAR 2012. LNCS, vol. 7364, pp. 286–300. Springer, Heidelberg (2012). doi:10.1007/978-3-642-31365-3_23
30. Gao, S., Kong, S., Clarke, E.M.: dReal: an SMT solver for nonlinear theories over the reals. In: Bonacina, M.P. (ed.) CADE 2013. LNCS (LNAI), vol. 7898, pp. 208–214. Springer, Heidelberg (2013). doi:10.1007/978-3-642-38574-2_14

31. Gerasimou, S., Tamburrelli, G., Calinescu, R.: Search-based synthesis of probabilistic models for quality-of-service software engineering. In: ASE 2015, pp. 319–330 (2015)
32. Giacobbe, M., Guet, C.C., Gupta, A., Henzinger, T.A., Paixão, T., Petrov, T.: Model checking gene regulatory networks. In: Baier, C., Tinelli, C. (eds.) TACAS 2015. LNCS, vol. 9035, pp. 469–483. Springer, Heidelberg (2015). doi:10.1007/978-3-662-46681-0_47
33. Hardy, M.: Combinatorics of partial derivatives. Electron. J. Combin. **13**(1), 13 (2006)
34. Heath, J., Kwiatkowska, M., Norman, G., Parker, D., Tymchyshyn, O.: Probabilistic model checking of complex biological pathways. Theoret. Comput. Sci. **391**(3), 239–257 (2008)
35. Hoops, S., et al.: COPASI - a complex pathway simulator. Bioinformatics **22**(24), 3067–3074 (2006)
36. Karp, R.M., Miller, R.E.: Parallel program schemata. J. Comput. Syst. Sci. **3**(2), 147–195 (1969)
37. Koksal, A.S., Pu, Y., Srivastava, S., Bodik, R., Fisher, J., Piterman, N.: Synthesis of Biological Models from Mutation Experiments. In: POPL 2013, pp. 469–482. ACM (2013)
38. Kwiatkowska, M., Norman, G., Parker, D.: PRISM 4.0: verification of probabilistic real-time systems. In: Gopalakrishnan, G., Qadeer, S. (eds.) CAV 2011. LNCS, vol. 6806, pp. 585–591. Springer, Heidelberg (2011). doi:10.1007/978-3-642-22110-1_47
39. Kwiatkowska, M., Thachuk, C.: Probabilistic model checking for biology. In: Software Systems Safety, vol, 36, p. 165 (2014)
40. Lakin, M.R., Parker, D., Cardelli, L., Kwiatkowska, M., Phillips, A.: Design and analysis of DNA strand displacement devices using probabilistic model checking. J. R. Soc. Interface **9**(72), 1470–1485 (2012)
41. Madsen, C., Shmarov, F., Zuliani, P.: BioPSy: an SMT-based tool for guaranteed parameter set synthesis of biological models. In: Roux, O., Bourdon, J. (eds.) CMSB 2015. LNCS, vol. 9308, pp. 182–194. Springer, Cham (2015). doi:10.1007/978-3-319-23401-4_16
42. Murata, T.: Petri nets: properties, analysis and applications. Proc. IEEE **77**(4), 541–580 (1989)
43. Nori, A.V., Ozair, S., Rajamani, S.K., Vijaykeerthy, D.: Effcient Synthesis of Probabilistic Programs. In: PLDI 2014, pp. 208–217. ACM (2015)
44. Ouaknine, J., Worrell, J.: Some recent results in metric temporal logic. In: Cassez, F., Jard, C. (eds.) FORMATS 2008. LNCS, vol. 5215, pp. 1–13. Springer, Heidelberg (2008). doi:10.1007/978-3-540-85778-5_1
45. Paoletti, N., Yordanov, B., Hamadi, Y., Wintersteiger, C.M., Kugler, H.: Analyzing and Synthesizing genomic logic functions. In: Biere, A., Bloem, R. (eds.) CAV 2014. LNCS, vol. 8559, pp. 343–357. Springer, Cham (2014). doi:10.1007/978-3-319-08867-9_23
46. Solar-Lezama, A., Jones, C.G., Bodik, R.: Sketching concurrent data structures. In: PLDI 2008, pp. 136–148. ACM (2008)
47. Solar-Lezama, A., Rabbah, R., Bodík, R., Ebcioğlu, K.: Programming by Sketching for bit-streaming programs. In: PLDI 2005, pp. 281–294. ACM (2005)
48. Solar-Lezama, A., Tancau, L., Bodik, R., Seshia, S., Saraswat, V.: Combinatorial sketching for finite programs. In: ASPLOS 2006, pp. 404–415. ACM (2006)
49. Soloveichik, D., Seelig, G., Winfree, E.: DNA as a universal substrate for chemical kinetics. Proc. Natl. Acad. Sci. U. S. A. **107**(12), 5393–5398 (2010)

50. Tung, V.X., Van Khanh, T., Ogawa, M.: raSAT: an SMT solver for polynomial constraints. In: Olivetti, N., Tiwari, A. (eds.) IJCAR 2016. LNCS (LNAI), vol. 9706, pp. 228–237. Springer, Cham (2016). doi:10.1007/978-3-319-40229-1_16

51. Van Kampen, N.G.: Stochastic Processes in Physics and Chemistry, Elsevier, vol. 1 (1992)

52. Yordanov, B., Kim, J., Petersen, R.L., Shudy, A., Kulkarni, V.V., Phillips, A.: Computational design of nucleic acid feedback control circuits. ACS Synth. Biol. **3**(8), 600–616 (2014)

53. Zimmer, C., Sahle, S.: Parameter estimation for stochastic models of biochemical reactions. J. Comput. Sci. Syst. Biol. **6**, 011–021 (2012)

Decision Procedures and Their Applications

Model Counting for Recursively-Defined Strings

Minh-Thai Trinh[1(✉)], Duc-Hiep Chu[2], and Joxan Jaffar[1]

[1] National University of Singapore, Singapore, Singapore
trinhmt@comp.nus.edu.sg
[2] Institute of Science and Technology, Klosterneuburg, Austria

Abstract. We present a new algorithm for model counting of a class of string constraints. In addition to the classic operation of concatenation, our class includes some *recursively defined* operations such as Kleene closure, and replacement of substrings. Additionally, our class also includes *length constraints* on the string expressions, which means, by requiring reasoning about numbers, that we face a *multi-sorted* logic. In the end, our string constraints are motivated by their use in programming for web applications.

Our algorithm comprises two novel features: the ability to use a technique of (1) *partial derivatives* for constraints that are already in a solved form, i.e. a form where its (string) satisfiability is clearly displayed, and (2) *non-progression*, where cyclic reasoning in the reduction process may be terminated (thus allowing for the algorithm to look elsewhere). Finally, we experimentally compare our model counter with two recent works on model counting of similar constraints, SMC [18] and ABC [5], to demonstrate its superior performance.

1 Introduction

In modern software, strings are not only ubiquitous, they also play a critical part: their improper use may cause serious security problems. For example, according to the Open Web Application Security Project [20], the most serious web application vulnerabilities include: (#1) Injection flaws (such as SQL injection) and (#3) Cross Site Scripting (XSS) flaws. Both vulnerabilities involve string-manipulating operations and occur due to inadequate sanitisation and inappropriate use of input *strings* provided by users.

The *model counting* problem, to count the number of *satisfiable assignments* for a constraint formula, continues to draw a lot of attention from security researchers. Specifically, model counters can be used directly by quantitative analyses of information flow (in order to determine how much secret information is leaked), combinatorial circuit designs, and probabilistic reasoning. For example, the constraints can be used to represent the relation between the inputs and outputs implied by the program in quantitative theories of information flow. This, in turn, has numerous applications such as quantitative information flow analysis [6,11,21,24], differential privacy [3], secure information flow [22], anonymity protocols [10], and side-channel analysis [16]. Recently, model

© Springer International Publishing AG 2017
R. Majumdar and V. Kunčak (Eds.): CAV 2017, Part II, LNCS 10427, pp. 399–418, 2017.
DOI: 10.1007/978-3-319-63390-9_21

counting has also been used by probabilistic symbolic execution where the goal is to compute the probability of the success and failure program paths [9,13].

Given the rise of web applications and their complicated manipulations of string inputs, model counting for string constraints naturally becomes a very important research problem [5,18]. There have been works on model counting for different kinds of domains such as boolean [8], and integer domains [19]. But they are not directly applicable to string constraints. The main difficulties are: (1) string constraints need to be *multi-sorted* because we need to reason about string lengths; and (2) each string length is either *unbounded*, or bounded by a very large number. For example, we can represent a bounded string as a bit vector and then employ the existing model counting for bit vector constraints to calculate the number of solutions. However, as highlighted in [18], the bit-vector representation of the regular expression S.match("(a | b)*") could grow exponentially w.r.t. the length of S, and the tools which employ this approach did not scale to strings of length beyond 20.

This work is inspired by two recent string model counters, SMC [18] and ABC [5][1], which have achieved very promising results. However, in contrast to these approaches, this paper *directly* addresses the two challenges of the string domain, (1) which is a multi-sorted theory, and (2) whose variables are generally unbounded. As a result, our model counter not only produces more precise counts, but also is generally more efficient.

We start by employing the infrastructure of the satisfiability solver S3P [26], which in turn builds on top of Z3 [12] to efficiently reason about multiple theories. S3P works by building its reduction tree, reducing the original formula into simpler formulas with the hope that it eventually encounter a *solved form* formula from which a satisfying assignment can be enumerated or proving that all the reduction paths lead to contradictions (i.e. the original formula is unsatisfiable). One key advancement of S3P is the ability to detect *non-progressive* scenarios with respect to a criterion of minimizing the "lexicographical length" of the returned solution, if a solution in fact exists. This helps avoiding infinite chains of reductions when dealing with unbounded strings. In other words, in the search process based on reduction rules, we can soundly prune a subproblem when the answer we seek can be found more efficiently elsewhere. If a subproblem is deemed non-progressive, it means that if the original input formula is satisfiable, then another satisfiable solution of shorter "length" will be found somewhere else. However, because a model counter needs to consider *all* solutions, what offered by S3P is not directly usable for model counting.

Our model counting algorithm proceeds by using the reduction rules of S3P, but to *exhaustively* build the reduction tree T. Each node will be associated with a "generating function" [18] representing its count. We compute the counts for all the leaf nodes, and propagate bottom-up to derive the count of the original input formula. There are four types of leaf nodes, i.e. a path is terminated when one of four scenarios is encountered:

---

[1] We will discuss them in more detail in the Related Work.

(1) A *contradiction* is derived. The leaf node is assigned a precise count of 0. (This holds for any variable of interest with any length.)
(2) The leaf node is in *solved form*[2]. We delegate to a helper function to precisely count a formula in solved form.
(3) The leaf node is a *non-progressive* formula, detected by S3P's rules. We can relate the count of that leaf to one of its ancestors via a recurrence relation.
(4) The path gets stuck or exceeds a predefined budget (often used to enforce termination), we resort to a baseline algorithm. In the implementation we choose SMC as the baseline algorithm.

Note however that counting the solutions of a formula in solved form, i.e., scenario (2), is not a trivial task. This is because the family of satisfiable strings might go beyond a regular language. Constraints on string lengths even further complicate the problem: a formula in solved form does not mean it is satisfiable. For this task, we adapt the notion of *partial derivative* function by Antimirov [4] to construct a tree, called an enumeration tree (for each leaf formula of T that is in solved form). The key distinction of an enumeration tree over the top-level reduction tree is that, because formulas are in solved form, we can perform specialized over/under-approximation techniques for the length constraints, in order to *direct* the enumeration process to repeated formulas, so that recurrence relations between the counts of them can be extracted. In the end, we use Mathematica to evaluate the count for the original formula, given a specific length to the string variable of interest.

Contributions: In summary, this paper proposes a new model counter, called S3#. We make the following theoretical contributions:

- We leverage the infrastructure of an existing string solver, namely S3P, to directly address the two main challenges of model counting for string constraints.
- We convert each non-progression scenario into a recurrence relation between the solution counts of formulas in our reduction tree.
- We propose a novel technique to precisely count the solutions of solved form formulas.

In our empirical evaluation of our implementation, we demonstrate the precision and efficiency of our model counting technique via real-world benchmarks against SMC and ABC, the two state-of-the-art model counting techniques for string constraints. Our first criterion is accuracy, and here we show clearly that our answers are more accurate in all cases. A second criterion is efficiency. We shall argue that we are in fact more efficient. However, there will be some counter-examples. But here we shall demonstrate that the counter-examples are themselves countered by a subsequent lack of accuracy. In the end, we demonstrate that S3# is for now better than the state-of-the-art.

---

[2] We will define "solved form" in Sect. 5.3.

2   Problem and Related Work

We will define the model counting problem for strings, discuss the implications in terms of soundness and precision. We also cover main related work in this Section.

2.1   Problem Definition

Suppose we have a formula F over free variables V. We shall defer defining the grammar for F for now. Let $\texttt{cvar} \in V$ be the string variable of interest and n denote the (symbolic) length of $\texttt{cvar}$. Let $S_{\texttt{cvar}}$ denote the set of solutions for $\texttt{cvar}$ that satisfies F. We define the model counting problem as finding an estimate of $|S_{\texttt{cvar}}|$ as a function of n, denoted by the quantity $S_{\texttt{cvar}}(n)$. In this paper, we focus on finding a precise *upper bound* $u(n)$ to $S_{\texttt{cvar}}(n)$. For certain applications, a *lower bound* estimate $l(n)$ is of more interest, but it can be defined analogously.

Even though our technique can also produce a precise lower bound, restricting the problem to an upper bound estimate helps in two ways: (1) it is easier to make comparison with ABC [5], which returns only an upper bound estimate; (2) the notions of soundness and precision are more intuitive as follows.

We say that an upper bound $u(n)$ is:

- *sound* iff $\forall i \geq 0, S_{\texttt{cvar}}(i) \leq u(i)$.
- *κ-precise* wrt. some $i \geq 0$ iff κ is the relative distance between $u(i)$ and $S_{\texttt{cvar}}(i)$, i.e. $\kappa = \frac{u(i) - S_{\texttt{cvar}}(i)}{S_{\texttt{cvar}}(i)}$; where $0/0 = 0$ and a positive number divided by zero equals to infinity.

Given a concrete length i of interest for $\texttt{cvar}$, we say an upper bound is the *exact* estimate/count if it is *0-precise* w.r.t. to i. Our definition also implies that it is extremely imprecise to provide a positive count for an unsatisfiable formula (in software testing, this leads to false positives). Furthermore, in the counting process, it is unsound to miss a satisfiable assignment, whereas counting an unsatisfiable assignment or counting one satisfiable assignment for multiple times (also called duplicate counting) are the main reasons that lead to imprecise estimates.

2.2   Related Work

There has been significant progress in building string solvers to support the reasoning of web applications. Recent notable works include [1,2,15,17,23,25, 26,29,30]. Some of these solvers bound the string length [15,23], whereas our approach handles strings of arbitrary length (as does ABC). Our solver also supports complicated string operations such as **replace**, which is commonly used in real-world programs (both in JavaScript [23] and Java [14]).

However, to the best of our knowledge, there are only two solvers that support model counting for strings, namely SMC [18] and ABC [5]. ABC has been used to quantify side-channel leakage in a more recent work [7].

The pioneering work [18] proposes to use "generating function" in model counting. Their treatment of string constraints is, however, rather simple. Briefly, a formula is *structurally* broken down into sub-formulas, until each sub-formula is in primitive form so that a generating function can be assigned. The rest of the effort is to appropriately (but routinely) combine the derived generating functions. The rules to combine are slightly different between computing upper bound and computing lower bound estimates. Importantly, these rules are *fixed*. For example, given a formula $F = F_1 \vee F_2$, SMC will count the upper bound for the number of solutions of F_1 and F_2 and then sum them up without taking into account the overlapping solutions between F_1 and F_2. Similarly, the lower bound for $F_1 \wedge F_2$ is simply 0. As highlighted in [5], SMC cannot determine a precise count for a simple regular expression constraint such as $x \in (\text{"}a\text{"} | \text{"}b\text{"})^* | \text{"}ab\text{"}$. It neither can *coordinate* the reasoning across logical connectives to infer precise counts for simple constraints such as $(x \in \text{"}a\text{"} | \text{"}b\text{"}) \vee (x \in \text{"}a\text{"} | \text{"}b\text{"} | \text{"}c\text{"} | \text{"}d\text{"})$ nor $(x \in \text{"}a\text{"} | \text{"}b\text{"}) \wedge (x \in \text{"}a\text{"} | \text{"}b\text{"} | \text{"}c\text{"} | \text{"}d\text{"})$. In short, the sources of the imprecision of SMC may be ambiguous grammars, conjunctions, disjunctions, length constraints, high-level string operations, etc.

ABC [5] enhances the precision by a rigorous method: representing the set of solution strings as an extended form of a deterministic finite automaton (DFA) and then precisely enumerating the count when a bound on string length is given. However, there are two issues with this approach. First, it might suffer from an up-front exponential blow-up, in the DFA construction phase. For example, a DFA that represents the concatenation of two DFA could be exponential in size of the input DFAs [28]. (Note that ABC's premise that "the number of paths to accepting states corresponds to the solution count" only holds for a DFA.) Second, to reason about web applications, the constraint language is required to be expressive. This frequently leads to cases that the set of solutions cannot be captured precisely with a regular language, e.g. what is called "relational constraints" in [5]. In such cases, ABC suffers from serious imprecision.

3 Motivating Examples

As stated in Sect. 1, model counting techniques for bounded domains are not directly applicable to the string domain. We now present some motivating examples where state-of-the-art string model counters are not precise.

First, we discuss the limitation of SMC. As pointed out in [5], it has a severe issue of *duplicate* counting. SMC focuses on the syntax structure of the input formula to recursively break it down into sub-formulas until these are in a primitive form. Then a generating function can be assigned independently to each of them. In other words, SMC does not have a semantics-based analysis on the actual solution set. Below are two simple examples showing imprecise bounds produced by SMC:

$$X \in ((\text{"}a\text{"} | \text{"}b\text{"})^* | \text{"}ab\text{"}) \qquad\qquad \Rightarrow 1 \leq S_X(2) \leq 5$$
$$X \in (\text{"}a\text{"} | \text{"}b\text{"}) \vee X \in (\text{"}a\text{"} | \text{"}b\text{"} | \text{"}c\text{"} | \text{"}d\text{"}) \Rightarrow 2 \leq S_X(1) \leq 6$$

The exact counts are 4 and 2 respectively. Both our tool S3# and ABC can produce these exact counts (as upper bounds). Next consider the following examples.

Example 1 (Regular language without length constraints). Count the number of solutions of X in:

$$X = Y \cdot Y \wedge Y \in (\text{``}a\text{''})^\star$$

Though the set of solutions for X can be captured by a regular language, the word equation $X = Y \cdot Y$ involves a concatenation operation, making the example non-trivial for existing tools. While ABC crashes, SMC returns an *unsound* estimate $[0; 0]$ – indicating that both the lower bound and the upper bound are 0. (We actually observe this behaviour in our evaluation with small benchmarks in Sect. 6, Table 1).

Example 2 (Non-regular language with length constraints). Count the number of solutions of X in:

$$X = Y \cdot Z \wedge Y \in (\text{``}a\text{''})^\star \wedge Z \in (\text{``}b\text{''})^\star \wedge \textbf{length}(Y) = \textbf{length}(Z)$$

It can be seen that the set of solutions of X is beyond a regular language. In fact, it is a context-free language: $\{a^m \cdot b^m \mid m \geq 0\}$.

For this example, SMC is not applicable because it cannot handle the constraint $\textbf{length}(Y) = \textbf{length}(Z)$ — its parser simply fails. Counting the solutions of length 2 for X, ABC gives 3 as an upper bound, while the exact count is 1. For length 500, ABC's answer is 501 though the exact count is still 1. Our tool S3# can produce the exact counts for all these scenarios.

In general, ABC does not handle well the cases where the solution set is not a regular language. The reason is that ABC needs to approximate all the solutions as an automaton before counting the accepting paths up to a given length bound. This limitation is quite serious because in practice, e.g. in web application, length constraints are often used. Therefore, the solution set is usually beyond a regular language. (This is realized frequently in our evaluation with Kaluza benchmarks in Sect. 6, Tables 2 and 3.)

4   The Core Language

We present the core constraint language in Fig. 1.

Variables: We deal with two types of variables: V_{str} consists of string variables (X, Y, Z, T, and possibly with subscripts); and V_{int} consists of integer variables (M, N, P, and possibly with subscripts).

Constants: Correspondingly, we have two types of constants: string and integer constants. Let C_{str} be a subset of $\xi^\star$ for some finite alphabet ξ. To make it easier to compare with other model counters, we choose the same alphabet size, that is 256. Elements of C_{str} are referred to as string constants or constant strings. They are denoted by a, b, and possibly with subscripts. The empty string is denoted ϵ. Elements of C_{int} are integers and denoted by m, n, possibly with subscripts.

$$
\begin{array}{lll}
Fml & ::= & Literal \mid \neg\, Literal \mid Fml \wedge Fml \\
Literal & ::= & A_s \mid A_l \\
A_s & ::= & T_{str} = T_{str} \\
A_l & ::= & T_{len} \leq m & (m \in C_{int}) \\
T_{str} & ::= & a & (a \in C_{str}) \\
& \mid & X & (X \in V_{str}) \\
& \mid & \mathbf{concat}(T_{str}, T_{str}) \\
& \mid & \mathbf{replace}(T_{str}, T_{regexpr}, T_{str}) \\
& \mid & \mathbf{star}(T_{regexpr}, M) & (M \in V_{int}, M \geq 0) \\
T_{regexpr} & ::= & a & (a \in C_{str}) \\
& \mid & (T_{regexpr})^{\star} \mid T_{regexpr} \cdot T_{regexpr} \\
& \mid & T_{regexpr} + T_{regexpr} \\
T_{len} & ::= & m & (m \in C_{int}) \\
& \mid & M & (M \in V_{int}) \\
& \mid & \mathbf{length}(T_{str}) \mid \Sigma_{i=1}^{n}(m_i * T_{len})
\end{array}
$$

Fig. 1. The syntax of our core constraint language

Terms: Terms may be string terms or length terms. A string T_{str} term (denoted D, E, and possibly with subscripts) is either an element of V_{str}, an element of C_{str}, or a function on terms. More specifically, we classify those functions into two groups: recursive and non-recursive functions. An example of recursive function is **replace** (which is used to replace *all* matches of a pattern in a string by a replacement), while an example of non-recursive function is **concat**. The concatenation of string terms is denoted by **concat** or interchangeably by · operator. For simplicity, we do not discuss string operations such as **match**, **split**, **exec** which return an array of strings. We note, however, these operations are fully supported in our implementation.

A length term (T_{len}) is an element of V_{int}, or an element of C_{int}, or a **length** function applied to a string term, or a constant integer multiple of a length term, or their sum. Furthermore, $T_{regexpr}$ represents regular expression terms. They are constructed from string constants by using operators such as concatenation ($\cdot$), union ($+$), and Kleene star ($\star$). Regular expression terms are only used as parameters of functions such as **replace** and **star**.

Following [25], we use the **star** function in order to reduce a membership predicate involving Kleene star to a word equation. The **star** function takes two input parameters. The first is a regular expression term, while the second is a non-negative integer variable. For example, $X \in (r)^{\star}$ is modeled as $X = \mathbf{star}(r, N)$, where N is a *fresh* variable denoting the number of times that r is repeated.

Literals: They are either string equations (A_s) or length constraints (A_l).

Formulas: Formulas (denoted F, G, H, K, I, and possibly with subscripts) are defined inductively over literals by using operators such as conjunction ($\wedge$), and negation ($\neg$). Note that, each theory solver of Z3 considers only a conjunction of literals at a time. The disjunction will be handled by the Z3 core. We use $\mathrm{Var}(F)$ to denote the set of all variables of F, including bound variables. Finally we can define the quantifier-free first-order two-sorted logic for our formulas as simply string equations involving some recursive and non-recursive functions, conjoined with some length constraints.

As shown in [25], to sufficiently reason about web applications, string solvers need to support formulas of quantifier-free first-order logic over string equations, membership predicates, string operations and length constraints. Given a formula of that logic, similarly to other approaches such as [25], our top level algorithm will reduce membership predicates into string equations where Kleene star operations are represented as recursive **star** functions. Other high level string operations can also be reduced to the above core constraint language. After such reductions, the new formula can be represented in our core constraint language in Fig. 1. Note that, our input language subsumes those of other tools. For example, compared with ABC, our **replace** operation can take as input string variables instead of just string constants.

5   Algorithm

We first present the top-level algorithm, and then more details on the helper functions.

5.1   Top-Level Algorithm

The top-level algorithm is the recursive function SOLVE presented in Algorithm 1. It takes two input arguments, a current formula F and γ, which is a list of pairs, each containing a formula and a sequence. γ is used to detect non-progressive formulas; we will discuss how γ is constructed and maintained in Sect. 5.2.

Given an input formula I and a variable of interest cvar, treated as global variables, an upper bound estimate $u(n)$ of the count is computed by invoking SOLVE$(I, \emptyset)$. When given a specific length len for cvar, we can get an integer estimate by evaluating $u(\text{len})$ using Mathematica. We discuss how to compute lower bound in our technical report [27].

Our algorithm constructs a reduction tree similar to the satisfiability checking algorithm in [26]. Specifically, the construction of the tree is driven by a set of *rules*.

Definition 1 (Reduction Rule). *Each rule is of the general form*

$$(RULE\text{-}NAME) \; \frac{F}{\bigvee_{i=1}^{m} G_i}$$

where F, G_i are conjunctions of literals[3], $F \equiv \bigvee_{i=1}^{m} G_i$, and $\text{Var}(F) \subseteq \text{Var}(G_i)$. □

An application of this rule transforms a formula at the top, F, into the formula at the bottom, which comprises a number (m) of *reducts* G_i.

---

[3] As per Fig. 1.

---

function SOLVE(F: *Fml*, γ: a list of pairs of a formula and a sequence)
⟨1⟩   **if** ($F \equiv \mathtt{false}$) **return** 0   /*..................... Case 1 ....*/
⟨2⟩ $\mathtt{cnstr_{cvar}} \leftarrow$ EXTRACT(F, cvar)
⟨3⟩   **if** (ISSOLVEDFORM($\mathtt{cnstr_{cvar}}$))
⟨4⟩   **return** COUNT($\mathtt{cnstr_{cvar}}$) /*...................... Case 2 ....*/
⟨5⟩   **if** (F contains a recursive term or a non-grounded concatenation)
⟨6⟩   **if** ($\exists \langle K, \sigma \rangle \in \gamma, \exists$ progressive substitution θ w.r.t. σ s.t. $F\theta \Rightarrow K$)
⟨7⟩   Mark K as an ancestor of a non-progressive formula
⟨8⟩   **return** RECURRENCE(K, F, θ) /*................. Case 3 ....*/
⟨9⟩   **if** (*depth* = *max_depth* OR there is no rule to apply)
⟨10⟩   **return** BASESOLVER(F, cvar)   /*................... Case 4 ....*/
⟨11⟩   **if** (F contains a recursive term or a non-grounded concatenation)
⟨12⟩   Let σ_F be a sequence on Var(F) s.t. τ is a prefix of σ_F
⟨13⟩ $\gamma \leftarrow \gamma \cup \langle F, \sigma_F \rangle$
⟨14⟩ $\bigvee G_i \leftarrow$ APPLYRULE(F)   /*.......... Apply a reduction rule ....*/
⟨15⟩   *sum* $\leftarrow 0$
⟨16⟩   **foreach** reduct G_i **do**
⟨17⟩   *sum* $\leftarrow$ *sum* + SOLVE(G_i, γ) /*................. Recursive Case ....*/
⟨18⟩   **return** EVALUATE(*sum*, F)
end function

Algorithm 1. Top-level algorithm

Our algorithm has four base cases that are mutually exclusive as follows:

- The current formula is unsatisfiable (line 1). We return 0 as the exact count.
- The current formula is in solved form (lines 2–4). We first extract the constraints that are relevant to cvar. If the extracted constraints are in solved form (which is defined in Sect. 5.3), then we use the helper function COUNT to precisely compute the count of $\mathtt{cnstr_{cvar}}$.
- The current formula is non-progressive (line 5–8), or the condition in line 6 holds. Intuitively, it means that there is an ancestor formula K that "subsumes" the current formula F (modulo a renaming θ). We then call the helper function RECURRENCE to express the count of F in terms of the count of K.
- The path is terminated because the maximum depth has been reached or no rule is applicable (lines 9–10). We then simply resort to an existing solver such as SMC.

It is important to note that except for case-1, where a contradiction is detected, a count in some other base case will generally be a "generating function" (e.g., as used in [18]).

Finally, lines 15–17 handle the recursive case, where we first apply a reduction rule to the current formula F, obtaining the reducts G_i. The estimate count for F is the sum of the estimate counts for those G_i. In line 18, if F is not marked as an ancestor of a non-progressive formula, then EVALUATE simply returns the expression *sum*, which is the summation of a number of generating functions.

Otherwise, there exists some descendant of F that is deemed non-progressive due to F. For such case, *sum* will be an expression that also involves the count of F, but with some smaller length. In other words, we have a recurrence equation to constrain the count of F. We rely on a function, EVALUATE, to add a recurrence equation into a global variable ϕ that tracks all collected recurrence equations, and prepare its base cases (see Sect. 5.2) so that concretization can be done when later we provide a concrete value of `len`.

5.2   Non-progressive Formulas

We now discuss the process of detecting non-progression. We first choose any sequence τ from all the variables of the input formula I. Then whenever we encounter a recursive term or a non-grounded concatenation, we add a pair, which consists of the current formula F and a sequence σ_F from all of F's variables, to γ (lines 11–13). The condition for choosing σ_F is that τ must be a prefix of σ_F. This is to help compare solution lengths "lexicographically" [26]. In line 6 of Algorithm 1, if we can find a pair $\langle K, \sigma \rangle \in \gamma$, and a progressive substitution θ w.r.t. σ (informally, θ will increase the solution length), such that $F\theta \Rightarrow K$ then we call F a non-progressive formula. We illustrate with the following example.

Example 3 (Non-progression). Count the number of solutions of X in:

$$\text{``}a\text{''} \cdot X = X \cdot \text{``}a\text{''}$$

See Fig. 2 where K is the formula of interest. By applying (SPLIT) rule to K, we obtain two reducts K_1 and K_2. In K_1, X is an empty string, whereas in K_2 we deduce that "a" must be a prefix of X. Next, by substituting X with "a"$\cdot X_1$ in K_2, we obtain F. If we keep on applying (SPLIT) and (SUB) rules, we will go into an infinite loop. As such, non-progression detection [26] is crucial to avoid non-termination. The technique will find $\theta = [X_1/X]$ s.t. $F\theta \Rightarrow K$ and conclude that F is non-progressive. For satisfiability checking, it is sound to prune F and continue the search for a solution in K_1.

$$\text{(SPLIT)} \frac{K \equiv \text{``}a\text{''} \cdot X = X \cdot \text{``}a\text{''}}{K_1 \equiv X = \epsilon \wedge \text{``}a\text{''} = \text{``}a\text{''} \quad \text{(SUB)} \frac{K_2 \equiv X = \text{``}a\text{''}\cdot X_1 \wedge \text{``}a\text{''} \cdot X = X \cdot \text{``}a\text{''}}{F \equiv X = \text{``}a\text{''}\cdot X_1 \wedge \text{``}a\text{''} \cdot X_1 = X_1 \cdot \text{``}a\text{''}}}$$

Fig. 2. Solving steps for Example 3

However, for model counting, we have to consider all solutions, including those contributed by F, if any. Thus we propose, instead of pruning F, we extract a relationship between the counts of F and of K, with RECURRENCE as a helper.

RECURRENCE is presented in Algorithm 2. It is important to note that based on θ, we can compute the length difference between `cvar` in K and the corresponding variable (for the substitution) in F. For the example above, it is the

---

function RECURRENCE(K: *Fml*, F: *Fml*, θ)
  $\langle 1 \rangle$ $d \leftarrow$ DIFF($K, F, \theta, \text{cvar}$)
  $\langle 2 \rangle$ Let f_K be a function over l_K, representing the estimate count of K
  $\langle 3 \rangle$ **return** $f_K(l_K - d)$
end function

Algorithm 2. RECURRENCE function

length difference between X and X_1, which is 1. We then can extract a relationship between the count of F and the count of K, thus further constraining the count of K with a recurrence equation.

Let f_K be the counting function for K; it takes as input the symbolic length l_K of cvar and returns the number of solutions of cvar for that length. In short, because $F\theta \implies K$, the count for F is (upper) bounded by $f_K(l_K - 1)$.

Now assume we compute the count of K (the variable of interest is still X) with len $= 3$. Following Algorithm 1, when we backtrack to node K, its *sum* is the expression $f_{K_1}(l_K) + f_K(l_K - 1)$; where $f_{K_1}(l_K)$ is a function that returns 1 when l_K is 0, and returns 0 otherwise. By calling EVALUATE($f_{K_1}(l_K) + f_K(l_K-1)$, K) in line 8, we will add a recurrence equation $f_K(l_K) = f_{K_1}(l_K) + f_K(l_K - 1)$ into ϕ. We also compute its base case $f_K(0)$, which is $f_{K_1}(0) + f_K(-1) = 1 + 0 = 1$. (Based on the distance d, a number of base cases might be required.) Finally, since K is the input formula of interest, when given query length len $= 3$, we can compute the value of $f_K(3) = 1$.

5.3 Solved Form Formulas

We now discuss how to compute an estimate count for a formula in solved form, i.e., the COUNT function.

As presented in Fig. 3, a formula is in solved form if it is a conjunction of atomic constraints and their negation. An atomic constraint is either an equality string constraint which is in solved form or a length constraint. To be in solved form, an equality string constraint can only be between a variable and a concatenation of *other* variables, between a variable and a constant, or between a variable and a **star** function. *Each variable can only appear once in the LHS of all equality constraints.*

In fact, one purpose of applying reduction rules is to obtain solved form formulas. For most cases, when no rule is applicable, the current formula is already in solved form. In this basic form, we can easily enumerate all the solutions for the string constraints. However, these solutions are also required to satisfy additional length constraints. As a result, a solved form formula system still might not have any solution.

Given a list of solved form formulas, we define its count as the count for the conjunction of all the formulas (note that the conjunction might not be in solved form). Now, given a solved form formula H, function COUNT will generate an enumeration tree rooted at $\{H\}$ (i.e. a singleton list with a formula H). Each node in the tree will be a list of solved form formulas, though as before, it is associated with a counting function, or *count* for short. Let β be a map between

$$
\begin{array}{llll}
SFml & ::= Atom & | \ \neg\, Atom & | \ SFml \wedge SFml \\
Atom & ::= A_{eq} & | \ A_l & \\
A_{eq} & ::= T_{var} = T_{concat} & | \ T_{var} = T_{ground} & \\
T_{var} & ::= X & & (X \in V_{str}) \\
T_{concat} & ::= X & & (X \in V_{str}) \\
& | \ \mathbf{concat}(T_{concat}, T_{concat}) & & \\
T_{ground} & ::= a & & (a \in C_{str}) \\
& | \ \mathbf{star}(T_{regexpr}, M) & & (M \in V_{int}, M \geq 0)
\end{array}
$$

Fig. 3. Solved form

a formula list (i.e. a node in the tree) and its count. E.g., the count of $\{H\}$ is $f_H = \beta(\{H\})$. We then use function RECUR_EQ to collect a set of recurrence equations (added into ϕ) between the counts for different nodes in the tree. These equations are parameterized by an integer variable l_H. In the end, COUNT(H) will return the count for H, denoted by $f_H(l_H)$.

In RECUR_EQ function, given a list of formulas α, we compute the count $f_\alpha(l_\alpha)$. Lines 6–8 handle the case when there exists an unsatisfiable formula in the list α. Lines 9–11 handle the case when we can reuse the result of an ancestor node. Lines 12–18 are to derive the child nodes by applying partial derivative functions, which are defined below. The count for a parent node is the sum of those for child nodes, which do not have the same starting character c_i. Those which share the same starting character c_i are put into λ_i, which is a list of $SFml$ list. For each λ_i, we use MOIVRE function to obtain the precise definition for the sum of the counts of all $\lambda_{ij}(1 \leq j \leq n)$ (to avoid overlapping solutions). MOIVRE function will then call RECUR_EQ with the first parameter is a list of formulas, which is the flattened combination of elements from λ_i.

In Algorithm 3, the TAIL function (line 16) is implemented via the variants of the partial derivative function of regular expressions by Antimirov [4]. The Antimirov's function can be denoted as δ_c which compute the partial derivative of the input regular expression w.r.t. character c. Concretely, $\delta_c(r)$ is a regular expression whose language is the set of all words w (including the empty one) such that $c \cdot w \in L(r)$. We now extend it by defining the partial derivative function for negation-free *formulas* in solved form. (We explain the handling of negation in our technical report.)

Definition 2 (Partial Derivative). *Given a string variable X, and a character $c \in \xi$, a partial derivative function $\delta_{X,c}$ of a solved form formula is defined as follows:*

$$
\delta_{X,c}(Y = T_1) \stackrel{def}{=} \{Y = T_1\} \qquad \delta_{X,c}(A_l) \stackrel{def}{=} \{A_l\} \qquad \delta_{X,c}(X = \epsilon) \stackrel{def}{=} \{\mathtt{false}\}
$$

$$
\delta_{X,c}(X = c \cdot s) \stackrel{def}{=} \{X = s\} \qquad \delta_{X,c}(X = d \cdot s) \stackrel{def}{=} \{\mathtt{false}\} \ \ \text{if} \ d \in \xi \ \text{and} \ d \neq c
$$

$$
\delta_{X,c}(X = \mathbf{star}(r, N)) \stackrel{def}{=} \{X = w \cdot \mathbf{star}(r, N-1)\}, \ \text{where} \ w \in \delta_c(r)
$$

$$
\delta_{X,c}(X = Y \wedge H_2) \stackrel{def}{=} \{X = Y\} \stackrel{*}{\wedge} \delta_{Y,c}(H_2)
$$

$$
\delta_{X,c}(X = Y \cdot Z \wedge H_2) \stackrel{def}{=} \{X = Y \cdot Z\} \stackrel{*}{\wedge} \delta_{Y,c}(H_2) \ \text{if} \ \neg e(Y)
$$

$$
\delta_{X,c}(X = Y \cdot Z \wedge H_2) \stackrel{def}{=} \{X = Y \cdot Z\} \stackrel{*}{\wedge} \delta_{Y,c}(H_2)
$$

$$
\cup \ \{X = Z \wedge Y = \epsilon\} \stackrel{*}{\wedge} \delta_{Z,c}(H_2) \ \text{if} \ e(Y)
$$

$$
\delta_{X,c}(H_1 \wedge H_2) \stackrel{def}{=} \delta_{X,c}(H_1) \stackrel{*}{\wedge} \delta_{X,c}(H_2)
$$

$\square$

---

function COUNT(H: *SFml*)
 ⟨1⟩ Let l_H be an integer variable and ϕ be a recurrence equation list
 ⟨2⟩ Let β be a mapping from *SFml* list to a counting function name
 ⟨3⟩ RECUR_EQ($\{H\}$, l_H, ϕ, β)
 ⟨4⟩ **return** $\beta(\{H\})(l_H)$
end function

function RECUR_EQ(α: *SFml* list, l_α: *int*, ϕ: recurrence equation list, β: a mapping)
 ⟨5⟩ Let f_α be a function from integer to integer
 ⟨6⟩ **if** ($\exists H \in \alpha : H \equiv \texttt{false}$)
 ⟨7⟩ $\phi \leftarrow \phi \cup \{f_\alpha(l_\alpha) = 0\}$
 ⟨8⟩ **return**
 ⟨9⟩ **if** ($\exists$ variable renaming $\theta : \beta[\theta(\alpha)] = f_{parent}$)
 ⟨10⟩ $\phi \leftarrow \phi \cup \{f_\alpha(l_\alpha) = f_{parent}(l_\alpha)\}$
 ⟨11⟩ **return**
 ⟨12⟩ $\beta[\alpha] \leftarrow f_\alpha$
 ⟨13⟩ Let ζ be the set of all the possible starting characters of **cvar**
 ⟨14⟩ $Sum \leftarrow 0$
 ⟨15⟩ **foreach** character $c_i \in \zeta$ **do**
 ⟨16⟩ $\lambda_i \leftarrow$ TAIL(α, **cvar**, c_i)   /* Each λ_i is a *SFml* list list */
 ⟨17⟩ $Sum \leftarrow Sum +$ MOIVRE($\lambda_i, l_\alpha - 1, \phi, \beta$)
 ⟨18⟩ $\phi \leftarrow \phi \cup \{f_\alpha(l_\alpha) = Sum\}$
end function

function MOIVRE(λ_i: *SFml* list list, N: *int*, ϕ: recurrence equation list, β: a mapping)
 ⟨19⟩ Let n be the size of λ_i
 ⟨20⟩ **for** $k = 1$ **to** n **do**
 ⟨21⟩ Let $Comb$ be all the combination $\binom{n}{k}$ of λ_i and m be its size
 ⟨22⟩ **foreach** combination $C \in Comb$ **do**
 ⟨23⟩ $\alpha_i \leftarrow$ FLATTEN(C)
 ⟨24⟩   RECUR_EQ(α_i, N, ϕ, β)
 ⟨25⟩ $a_k \leftarrow \Sigma_{i=1}^{m} f_{\alpha_i}$
 ⟨26⟩ **return** $\Sigma_{k=1}^{n}(-1)^{k-1} * a_k$
end function

Algorithm 3. COUNT function and its auxiliary functions

The function $e(Y)$ checks if a variable Y can be an empty string or not. For example, if we have $Y = \textbf{star}(\text{``}a\text{''}, N) \wedge N {\geq} 0$ then $e(Y) = \texttt{true}$, but if $Y = \text{``}a\text{''}$ then $e(Y) = \texttt{false}$. Meanwhile the operator $\overset{*}{\wedge}$ for two sets is the Cartesian product version of $\wedge$. We now explain Definition 2 via a simple example.

Example 4 (String-only constraints). Count the number of solutions of X in:

$$X = Y \cdot Z \wedge Y = \textbf{star}(\text{``}a\text{''}, N) \wedge Z = \textbf{star}(\text{``}b\text{''}, M)$$

Below is the counting tree for the input solved form formula. Suppose the count for the root node is $f_1(l_1)$. By applying $\delta_{X,\text{``}a\text{''}}$ for the formula in the root node, we obtain the left node where $Y = \textbf{star}(\text{``}a\text{''}, N-1)$. If we substitute $N-1$ with N, the formula in the left node becomes the formula in the root node. Therefore, the count for the left node is $f_1(l_1 - 1)$, since we have just removed a character "a" from X.

$$\boxed{\begin{array}{c} \{\ X{=}Y\cdot Z \wedge Y{=}\textbf{star}(\text{``}a\text{''}, N) \wedge \\ Z{=}\textbf{star}(\text{``}b\text{''}, M)\ \} \end{array}}\ f_1$$

$\delta_{X,\text{``}a\text{''}}$          $\delta_{X,\text{``}b\text{''}}$

$$\boxed{\begin{array}{c} \{\ X{=}Y\cdot Z \wedge Y{=}\textbf{star}(\text{``}a\text{''}, N{-}1)\wedge \\ Z{=}\textbf{star}(\text{``}b\text{''}, M)\ \} \end{array}}\ f_1 \qquad \boxed{\begin{array}{c} \{\ X{=}Z \wedge Z{=}\textbf{star}(\text{``}b\text{''}, M{-}1)\ \wedge \\ \underline{Y{=}\epsilon \wedge N{=}0}\ \} \end{array}}\ f_2$$

In short, we have a set of recurrence equations as below:

$$f_1(l_1) = f_1(l_1 - 1) + f_2(l_1 - 1)$$

Note that, we will remove redundant constraints which do not affect the final count (e.g. $Y = \epsilon \wedge N = 0$ in the right node). Similarly, we can have a counting tree for $X = Z \wedge Z = \textbf{star}(\text{``}b\text{''}, M - 1)$ and a recurrence equation for f_2. In addition, we also need to compute the base case for the definition of f_1, that is $f_1(0) = 1$.

The main technical issue that we have to overcome is non-termination of the counting tree construction (which leads to non-termination of REC_EQ function). Fortunately, because of the recursive structure of strings, in the case of string-only constraints, we can guarantee to terminate and to generate recurrence equations for every counting function (see Theorem 1). The difficulty here is of course when the constraints also include string lengths. To handle length constraints, we propose *over/under-approximation* techniques in order to give precise upper/lower bounds for counting functions. But first we need to propose another variant of the derivative function.

Definition 3 (Multi-head Partial Derivative). *Let* $s = \text{``}?\ldots?\text{''}\cdot c$ *be a concatenation between* i *copies of* "?" *and the character* c. *A multi-head partial derivative function* $\Delta_{X,s}$ *for the string variable* X *and the string* s *is defined as follows:*

$$\Delta_{X,c}(H) \stackrel{def}{=} \delta_{X,c}(H) \qquad \Delta_{X,s}(Y = T_1) \stackrel{def}{=} \{Y = T_1\} \qquad \Delta_{X,s}(A_l) \stackrel{def}{=} \{A_l\}$$

$$\Delta_{X,s}(X = Y \wedge H_2) \stackrel{def}{=} \{X = Y\} \stackrel{*}{\wedge} \Delta_{Y,s}(H_2)$$

$$\Delta_{X,s}(X = Y_0\ldots Y_n \wedge H_2) \stackrel{def}{=} \{X = Y_0\ldots Y_n\} \stackrel{*}{\wedge} \delta_{Y_i,c}(H_2) \qquad if\ \neg\text{CONCAT}(Y_j)$$
$$\qquad\qquad\qquad\qquad\qquad\qquad\qquad\qquad\qquad\qquad\qquad\qquad 0 \le j \le n$$

$$\Delta_{X,s}(H_1 \wedge H_2) \stackrel{def}{=} \Delta_{X,s}(H_1) \stackrel{*}{\wedge} \Delta_{X,s}(H_2)$$

$\square$

The function CONCAT(Y) checks if a variable Y is bound with any concatenation. For example, if we have $Y = Z_1 \cdot Z_2$ then CONCAT$(Y) = \texttt{true}$. Note that, given a negation-free formula in solved form, we can always transform it to the form $X = Y_0\ldots Y_n \wedge Y_0 = T_0 \wedge \ldots \wedge Y_n = T_n \wedge A_l$, where $\neg$CONCAT(Y_j) $(0 \le j \le n)$.

With the use of multi-head partial derivative function as the new implementation for the TAIL function (line 16), we now have to update Algorithm 3 correspondingly. Specifically, in line 13, instead of finding the starting characters

c_i of **cvar**, we now need to construct the set of string s_i, which is composed by i copies of "?" and the character c_i. This construction is guided by the length constraints.

Suppose we have a set of constraints on string lengths. By using inference rules, we can always transform the above set into a disjunction of conjunctive formulas on the second parameters of **star** functions. For example,

$$X = Y \cdot Z \wedge Y = \mathbf{star}(``a", N) \wedge Z = \mathbf{star}(``b", M) \wedge 2 * \mathbf{length}(Y) + \mathbf{length}(Z) = 4 * P$$

can be transformed into

$$X = Y \cdot Z \wedge Y = \mathbf{star}(``a", N) \wedge Z = \mathbf{star}(``b", M) \wedge 2N + M = 4P.$$

Thus, w.l.o.g., let us assume that the length constraints exist in the form of a conjunctive formula on the second parameters of **star** functions. Suppose we have a formula H composed by a conjunction of equality constraints A_k (in which the variable of interest X is constructed by concatenating constant strings and Y_i) and $Y_i = \mathbf{star}(s_i, N_i)$ ($0 \leq i \leq p$), along with linear arithmetic constraints on N_i ($0 \leq i \leq n$), where $N_0, ..., N_p$ are the second parameters of **star** functions, and $N_{p+1}, ..., N_n$ are integer variables.

$$H \equiv \bigwedge A_k \wedge \bigwedge Y_i = \mathbf{star}(s_i, N_i) \wedge \bigwedge \Sigma_{i=0}^{i \leq n} a_{ij} * N_i \leq b_j \quad \text{where} \quad 0 \leq j \leq m$$

Then we will try to solve the following set of constraints

$$\bigwedge \Sigma_{i=0}^{i \leq n} a_{ij} * N_i \geq 0 \quad \text{where} \quad 0 \leq j \leq m \tag{1}$$

If (1) has a solution $(l_0, \ldots l_n)$, then we know that we have to go the node where we have the constraint $\bigwedge_{i=0}^{i \leq p} Y_i = \mathbf{star}(s_i, N_i - l_i)$. Let G be the formula labelling that node. With the substitution $\theta = [N_0 - l_0/N_0, ..., N_n - l_n/N_n]$, we will have $G\theta \Rightarrow H$. Therefore $f_G(l_G) = f_H(l_H - |s_0| * l_0 - |s_1| * l_1... - |s_p| * l_p)$. This ensures the termination of the construction of the counting tree for H since other nodes are of less complexity than G.

Otherwise, we will try to remove as least as possible the integer constraints from (1) in order to make it become satisfiable. This is where the over-approximation applies. Suppose we have to remove the constraints where $j \in \mu$ to obtain a satisfiable formula

$$\bigwedge \Sigma_{i=0}^{i \leq n} a_{ij} * N_i \geq 0 \quad \text{where} \quad 0 \leq j \leq m \wedge j \notin \mu$$

then the upper bound for the number of solutions of H is the number of solutions of

$$H' \equiv \bigwedge A_k \wedge \bigwedge Y_i = \mathbf{star}(s_i, N_i) \wedge \bigwedge \Sigma_{i=0}^{i \leq n} a_{ij} * N_i \leq b_j \quad \text{where} \quad 0 \leq j \leq m \wedge j \notin \mu$$

It is obviously seen that the largest upper bound is the number of solutions of the string-only formula $H'' \equiv \bigwedge A_k \wedge \bigwedge Y_i = \mathbf{star}(s_i, N_i)$. (The lower bound for the number of solutions of H is the number of solutions of explored nodes in the counting tree for H. So the deeper we explore, the more precise lower bound we have. The smallest lower bound of course is 0.) To illustrate more, let us look at the following example.

Example 5 (String and length constraints). Count the number of solutions of X in:

$$X = Y \cdot Z \wedge Y = \mathbf{star}(\text{``}a\text{''}, N) \wedge Z = \mathbf{star}(\text{``}b\text{''}, M) \wedge 2N + M = 4P$$

First, we need to solve the equation $2N + M - 4P = 0$ in order to find the solution $N = 1$, $M = 2$, $P = 1$. Then we know that we need to drive the counting tree to the node that contains the constraint $Y = \mathbf{star}(\text{``}a\text{''}, N-1) \wedge Z = \mathbf{star}(\text{``}b\text{''}, M-2)$ as follows.

In short, we have a set of recurrence equations as below:

$$f_1(l_1) = f_1(l_1 - 3) + f_2(l_1 - 1) + f_3(l_1 - 1)$$
$$f_1(0) = 1; f_1(1) = 0; f_1(2) = 1; \forall n : f_4(n) = 0$$

Similarly, we can construct recurrence equations for f_2 and f_3.

Lastly, we make two formal statements about our algorithm. The proof sketch is in our technical report.

Theorem 1 (Soundness). *Given an input formula I, Algorithm 1 returns the sound upper bound (and lower bound) for the number of solutions of I.*   □

Theorem 2 (Precision). *Given a solved form formula H which does not contain any constraints of type A_l (i.e. length constraints), Algorithm 3 returns the exact number of solutions of H.*   □

6   Evaluation

We test our model counter S3# with two set of benchmarks, which have also been used for evaluating other string model counters. All experiments are run on a 3.2 GHz machine with 8 GB memory.

In the first case study, we use a small but popular set of benchmarks that are involved in different security contexts. For example, the experiments with 2 string manipulation utilities (wc and grep) from the BUSYBOX v.1.21.1 package, and one utility (csplit) from the COREUTILS v.8.21 package, demonstrate the quantification of how much information would be leaked if these utilities operate on homomorphically encrypted inputs as in AutoCrypt [18].

Table 1 summarizes the results of running S3# against SMC and ABC[4]. The first and second columns contain the input programs and the query lengths for the query variables. Given those inputs, we then report the bounds produced by each model counter along with its running time. Note that SMC and S3# can give both lower and upper bounds while ABC can only give upper bounds.

For each small benchmark, S3# can give the *exact* count (i.e. lower and upper bounds are equal). All input formulas here can in fact be transformed into solved form. This ultimately demonstrates the precision of our counting technique for solved form formulas. In Table 1, we highlight unsound bounds, generated by SMC and ABC, in bold with grey background.

In addition, the running time of S3# is small. It is much faster than SMC, and comparable to ABC. Among the three model counters, when ABC can produce an answer, it is often the fastest. In such cases, it is because an automaton can be quickly constructed to represent the solution set. However, ABC also crashes a few times with the "BDD is too large" error. For the ghttpd and

Table 1. Experiments with small benchmarks. The last column is to notify the bound is measured with a scale. The scale for marked rows are $10^{1465}, 10^{1465}, 10^{1129}, 10^{1289}, 10^{23}, 10^{14}$, resp.

Program	Len	SMC		ABC		S3#		
		Lower/Upper Bound	Time	Upper-Bound	Time	Exact Count	Time	
ghttpd	620	[10626.2;1031904473.2]	45.1	–	TO	1031904472.8	0.4	*
	11	[256;767]	28.3	**256**	0.3	767	0.3	
ghttpd_wo_len	620	[10626.2;1031904473.2]	45.1	**1023846357.2**	0.4	1031904472.8	0.4	*
	11	[256;767]	28.3	**765**	0.3	767	0.3	
nullhttpd	500	**[2.9**;1369.8]	24.8	0	0.5	0	0.3	*
csplit	629	**[5.9*10^{1460}**;3.1*10^{1481}]	160.5	Crash	–	0	0.4	
grep	629	**[0.7*10^{1408}**;0.1*10^{1435}]	255.0	Crash	–	0	0.4	
wc	629	[0.97;8.0]	245.9	Crash	–	0.97	5.6	*
obscure1	10	[11.2;11.6]	1.3	11.2	0.1	11.2	0.2	*
obscure2	6	[2.8;2.8]	8.9	2.8	0.5	2.8	0.3	*
strstr1	5	[196608;**196608**]	0.3	1099511431168	0.1	1099511431168	0.3	
strstr2	5	[16776960;16776960]	0.3	Crash	–	16776960	0.3	
regex	4	[0;**0**]	2.4	16	0.1	16	0.2	
contains	5	[67108096;67108096]	0.3	67108096	0.1	67108096	0.3	

---

[4] We used the latest versions from their websites, as of 20 Dec 2016.

length 620, ABC times out after 20 min. In these instances, the solution sets are beyond regular; ABC cannot effectively represent/over-approximate them using an automaton. In contrast, if we remove the length constraints from the `ghttpd` benchmark to obtain `ghttp_wo_len`, ABC can finish it within 0.4 seconds. This indicates that when the solution set is beyond regular, ABC not only loses it precision, but also loses its *robustness*.

We next consider Kaluza benchmarks, that was also used by SMC and ABC for their evaluations. These benchmarks were generated by Kudzu [23], when testing 18 web applications that include popular AJAX applications. The generated constraints are of boolean, integer and string types. Integer constraints also involve lengths of string variables, while string constraints include string equations, membership predicates.

Importantly, SMC cannot handle many constraints from the original benchmarks; instead SMC used an over-simplified version of Kaluza benchmarks where many important constraints are removed. (ABC [5] had also reported about the discrepancy when comparing with SMC.) As a result, we only compare S3# with ABC in this second case study, using the SMT-format version of Kaluza benchmarks as provided in [17].

Table 2. Kaluza UNSAT benchmarks

# Programs	ABC		S3#	
	Upper bound	Time	Count	Time
2700	0	1477	0	1130
9314	Crash			

Table 3. Kaluza SAT benchmarks

# Programs	ABC		S3#	
	Upper bound	Time	L&U	Time
24825	>0	6984	>0	46575
10445	Crash			

Tables 2 and 3 summarize the results of running S3# and ABC with two sets of Kaluza benchmarks: satisfiable and unsatisfiable ones. Note that ABC crashes often, nearly half the time[5]. Importantly, for the unsatisfiable benchmark examples, S3# produces the exact count 0. ABC, as in [5], managed to run more benchmarks, but failed to produce the upper bound 0 for 2,459 benchmark examples; thus they classified them as satisfiable. For the satisfiable examples, S3# is also more informative, always determining that the lower bound is positive.

7   Concluding Remarks and Future Work

We have presented a new algorithm for model counting of a class of string constraints, which are motivated by their use in programming for web applications. Our algorithm comprises two novel features: the ability to use a technique of (1) *partial derivatives* for constraints that are already in a solved form, i.e. a form where its (string) satisfiability is clearly displayed, and (2) *non-progression*, where cyclic reasoning in the reduction process may be terminated (thus allowing

---

[5] This differs from the report in [5]. Understandably, ABC has been under active development and there is significant difference in the version of ABC we used and the version had been evaluated in [5].

for the algorithm to look elsewhere). We have demonstrated the superior performance of our model counter in comparison with two recent works on model counting of similar constraints, SMC and ABC.

Though the algorithm is for model counting of string constraints, we believe it is applicable to other unbounded data structures such as lists, sequences. This is because both the solving and counting methods deal with recursive structures in a somewhat general manner. Specifically, the methods are applied to a general logic fragment of equality and recursive functions.

Acknowledgement. This research was supported by the Singapore MOE under Tier-2 grant R-252-000-591-112. It was also supported in part by the Austrian Science Fund (FWF) under grants S11402-N23 (RiSE/SHiNE) and Z211-N23 (Wittgenstein Award).

References

1. Abdulla, P.A., Atig, M.F., Chen, Y.-F., Holk, L., Rezine, A., Rümmer, P., Stenman, J.: String constraints for verification. In: Biere, A., Bloem, R. (eds.) CAV 2014. LNCS, vol. 8559, pp. 150–166. Springer, Cham (2014). doi:10.1007/978-3-319-08867-9_10

2. Abdulla, P.A., Atig, M.F., Chen, Y.-F., Holk, L., Rezine, A., Rümmer, P., Stenman, J.: Norn: an SMT solver for string constraints. In: Kroening, D., Păsăreanu, C.S. (eds.) CAV 2015. LNCS, vol. 9206, pp. 462–469. Springer, Cham (2015). doi:10.1007/978-3-319-21690-4_29

3. Alvim, M.S., Andrés, M.E., Chatzikokolakis, K., Palamidessi, C.: Quantitative information flow and applications to differential privacy. In: Aldini, A., Gorrieri, R. (eds.) FOSAD 2011. LNCS, vol. 6858, pp. 211–230. Springer, Heidelberg (2011). doi:10.1007/978-3-642-23082-0_8

4. Antimirov, V.: Partial derivatives of regular expressions and finite automaton constructions. Theoret. Comput. Sci. **155**(2), 291–319 (1996)

5. Aydin, A., Bang, L., Bultan, T.: Automata-based model counting for string constraints. In: Kroening, D., Păsăreanu, C.S. (eds.) CAV 2015. LNCS, vol. 9206, pp. 255–272. Springer, Cham (2015). doi:10.1007/978-3-319-21690-4_15

6. Backes, M., Köpf, B., Rybalchenko, A.: Automatic discovery and quantification of information leaks. In: 2009 30th IEEE Symposium on Security and Privacy, pp. 141–153, May 2009

7. Bang, L., Aydin, A., Phan, Q.-S., Pasareanu, C.S., Bultan, T.: String analysis for side channels with segmented oracles. In: FSE, pp. 193–204 (2016)

8. Biondi, F., Legay, A., Traonouez, L.-M., Wąsowski, A.: QUAIL: a quantitative security analyzer for imperative code. In: Sharygina, N., Veith, H. (eds.) CAV 2013. LNCS, vol. 8044, pp. 702–707. Springer, Heidelberg (2013). doi:10.1007/978-3-642-39799-8_49

9. Borges, M., Filieri, A., d'Amorim, M., Păsăreanu, C.S., Visser, W.: Compositional solution space quantification for probabilistic software analysis. In: Proceedings of the 35th ACM SIGPLAN Conference on Programming Language Design and Implementation, PLDI 2014, pp. 123–132. ACM, New York (2014)

10. Chatzikokolakis, K., Palamidessi, C., Panangaden, P.: Anonymity protocols as noisy channels. Inf. Comput. **206**(2–4), 378–401 (2008)

11. Clark, D., Hunt, S., Malacaria, P.: A static analysis for quantifying information flow in a simple imperative language. J. Comput. Secur. **15**(3), 321–371 (2007)

12. De Moura, L., Bjørner, N.: Z3: an efficient SMT solver. In: Ramakrishnan, C.R., Rehof, J. (eds.) TACAS 2008. LNCS, vol. 4963, pp. 337–340. Springer, Heidelberg (2008). doi:10.1007/978-3-540-78800-3_24

13. Filieri, A., Păsăreanu, C.S., Visser, W.: Reliability analysis in symbolic pathfinder. In: Proceedings of the 2013 International Conference on Software Engineering, ICSE 2013, Piscataway, NJ, USA, pp. 622–631. IEEE Press (2013)

14. Kausler, S., Sherman, E.: Evaluation of string constraint solvers in the context of symbolic execution. In: ASE, pp. 259–270 (2014)

15. Kiezun, A., Ganesh, V., Guo, P.J., Hooimeijer, P., Ernst, M.D.: Hampi: a solver for string constraints. In: ISSTA, pp. 105–116. ACM (2009)

16. Köpf, B., Basin, D.: An information-theoretic model for adaptive side-channel attacks. In: Proceedings of the 14th ACM Conference on Computer and Communications Security, CCS 2007, pp. 286–296. ACM, New York (2007)

17. Liang, T., Reynolds, A., Tinelli, C., Barrett, C., Deters, M.: A DPLL(T) theory solver for a theory of strings and regular expressions. In: Biere, A., Bloem, R. (eds.) CAV 2014. LNCS, vol. 8559, pp. 646–662. Springer, Cham (2014). doi:10.1007/978-3-319-08867-9_43

18. Luu, L., Shinde, S., Saxena, P., Demsky, B.: A model counter for constraints over unbounded strings. In: Proceedings of the 35th ACM SIGPLAN Conference on Programming Language Design and Implementation, PLDI 2014, pp. 565–576. ACM, New York (2014)

19. Morgado, A., Matos, P., Manquinho, V., Marques-Silva, J.: Counting models in integer domains. In: Biere, A., Gomes, C.P. (eds.) SAT 2006. LNCS, vol. 4121, pp. 410–423. Springer, Heidelberg (2006). doi:10.1007/11814948_37

20. OWASP: Top ten project, May 2013. http://www.owasp.org/

21. Phan, Q.-S., Malacaria, P., Tkachuk, O., Păsăreanu, C.S.: Symbolic quantitative information flow. SIGSOFT Softw. Eng. Notes 37(6), 1–5 (2012)

22. Sabelfeld, A., Myers, A.C.: Language-based information-flow security. IEEE J. Sel. A. Commun. 21(1), 5–19 (2006)

23. Saxena, P., Akhawe, D., Hanna, S., Mao, F., McCamant, S., Song, D.: A symbolic execution framework for JavaScript. In: SP, pp. 513–528 (2010)

24. Smith, G.: On the foundations of quantitative information flow. In: Alfaro, L. (ed.) FoSSaCS 2009. LNCS, vol. 5504, pp. 288–302. Springer, Heidelberg (2009). doi:10.1007/978-3-642-00596-1_21

25. Trinh, M.-T., Chu, D.-H., Jaffar, J.: S3: a symbolic string solver for vulnerability detection in web applications. In: ACM-CCS, pp. 1232–1243. ACM (2014)

26. Trinh, M.-T., Chu, D.-H., Jaffar, J.: Progressive reasoning over recursively-defined strings. In: Chaudhuri, S., Farzan, A. (eds.) CAV 2016. LNCS, vol. 9779, pp. 218–240. Springer, Cham (2016). doi:10.1007/978-3-319-41528-4_12

27. Trinh, M.-T., Chu, D.-H., Jaffar, J.: Technical report (2017). http://www.comp.nus.edu.sg/~trinhmt/

28. Yu, S., Zhuang, Q., Salomaa, K.: The state complexities of some basic operations on regular languages. Theor. Comput. Sci. 125, 315–328 (1994)

29. Zheng, Y., Ganesh, V., Subramanian, S., Tripp, O., Dolby, J., Zhang, X.: Effective search-space pruning for solvers of string equations, regular expressions and length constraints. In: Kroening, D., Păsăreanu, C.S. (eds.) CAV 2015. LNCS, vol. 9206, pp. 235–254. Springer, Cham (2015). doi:10.1007/978-3-319-21690-4_14

30. Zheng, Y., Zhang, X., Ganesh, V.: Z3-str: a z3-based string solver for web application analysis. In: ESEC/FSE, pp. 114–124 (2013)

A Three-Tier Strategy for Reasoning About Floating-Point Numbers in SMT

Sylvain Conchon[2,3]([✉]), Mohamed Iguernlala[1,2], Kailiang Ji[2],
Guillaume Melquiond[3], and Clément Fumex[2,3]

[1] OCamlPro SAS, 91190 Gif-sur-Yvette, France
[2] LRI (CNRS & Univ Paris-Sud), Université Paris-Saclay, 91405 Orsay, France
sylvain.conchon@lri.fr
[3] Inria, Université Paris-Saclay, 91120 Palaiseau, France

Abstract. The SMT-LIB standard defines a formal semantics for a theory of floating-point (FP) arithmetic (FPA). This formalization reduces FP operations to reals by means of a *rounding operator*, as done in the IEEE-754 standard. Closely following this description, we propose a three-tier strategy to reason about FPA in SMT solvers. The first layer is a purely axiomatic implementation of the automatable semantics of the SMT-LIB standard. It reasons with exceptional cases (*e.g.* overflows, division by zero, undefined operations) and reduces finite representable FP expressions to reals using the rounding operator. At the core of our strategy, a second layer handles a set of lemmas about the properties of rounding. For these lemmas to be used effectively, we extend the instantiation mechanism of SMT solvers to tightly cooperate with the third layer, the NRA engine of SMT solvers, which provides interval information. We implemented our strategy in the Alt-Ergo SMT solver and validated it on a set of benchmarks coming from the SMT-LIB competition, but also from the deductive verification of C and SPARK programs. The results show that our approach is promising and compete with existing techniques implemented in state-of-the-art SMT solvers.

Keywords: SMT · Floating-point arithmetic · Program verification

1 Introduction

Floating-point (FP) numbers is a common way of approximating reals in a computer. However, due to their finite and discrete representation, rounding errors are inherent to FP operations and the result of an FP computation may overflow or diverge from the exact value expected on reals. Because such deviations may cause serious software and hardware failures, it is important to develop tools that help analyze programs with FP numbers.

FP reasoning has been intensively investigated in the past in the context of theorem proving [6,7,10], abstract interpretation [9] or constraint solving [12].

This work is supported by the ANR projects SOPRANO (ANR-14-CE28-0020) and ProofInUse (ANR-14-LAB3-0007).

R. Majumdar and V. Kunčak (Eds.): CAV 2017, Part II, LNCS 10427, pp. 419–435, 2017.
DOI: 10.1007/978-3-319-63390-9_22

Recently, several decision procedures have been proposed in the context of *Satisfiability Modulo Theories* (SMT). In fact, the SMT-LIB standard [2] includes a formal semantics for a theory of floating-point arithmetic (FPA) [5] and some SMT solvers already support it (*e.g.* MathSAT5, REALIZER, SONOLAR, Z3).

There are three kinds of techniques for integrating FP reasoning in SMT. The first one interprets FP numbers as bit-vectors and FP operations as Boolean circuits. The second technique consists in lifting the CDCL procedure at the heart of SMT to an abstract algorithm (ACDCL) manipulating FP numbers as abstract values. In [4], real intervals are used to overapproximate FP values. The Boolean Constraint Propagations (BCP) of CDCL is extended with Interval Constraint Propagation (ICP) and decision steps make a case analysis by interval splitting. The third technique follows the IEEE-754 standard which reduces FP numbers to reals by means of a rounding operator. In [11], a two-layer decision procedure is presented. The first layer replaces FP terms by equal-valued exact-arithmetic terms in a fragment of real/integer arithmetic (RIA) extended by ceiling and floor functions. The second layer performs rounding which requires a case analysis to determine the binades of real values.

All these techniques suffer from drawbacks. Consider for instance the following FP formula[1] on binary64 FP numbers, where $\oplus$ is the FP addition with default *rounding to nearest with tie breaking to even* mode.

$$\text{-2.} \preceq u \preceq \text{2.} \ \wedge \ \text{-2.} \preceq v \preceq \text{2.} \ \wedge \ \text{-1.} \preceq w \preceq \text{1.} \ \wedge \ u \preceq v \wedge v \oplus w \prec u \oplus w \quad (1)$$

With bit-blasting, Z3 takes 5 min to prove unsatisfiability of this conjunction and MathSAT5 times out after 10 min. MathSAT5 also times out when using ACDCL, and so does REALIZER when using RIA. Possible explanations for these results are the following. On large bit-width FP numbers, bit-blasting techniques tend to generate very large propositional formulas hardly tractable even by very efficient SAT solvers. Concerning the second approach, ACDCL efficiency strongly depends on the choice of the abstract domain: the less precise (or expressive) the domain is, the more case splits are needed. On this example, the tool is forced to enumerate aggressively to offset the weakness of the interval-based domain. About the third technique, only few SMT solvers support RIA (with ceiling and floor functions) and providing an efficient and complete decision procedure for it is still an active domain of research. Here, to conclude rapidly, the RIA engine should be powerful enough to prove that the integral rounding functions used in the translation are monotonic.

In this paper, we propose another approach which takes the form of a three-tier strategy. Similarly to the third technique, we closely follow the SMT-LIB standard by reducing FP operations to reals using an explicit rounding operator. But instead of encoding rounded terms in RIA, we keep the operator and reason about it modulo a set of lemmas, mainly borrowed from a FP library of theorem prover such as Flocq [3].

Our first layer translates FP expressions into expressions mixing real numbers (for operations on finite FP inputs) and Booleans (for encoding exceptional

---

[1] Inspired by a discussion on https://github.com/Z3Prover/z3/issues/823.

values). For the example of Formula (1), some propositional simplifications reduce the translated expressions into the following real-only formula:

$$-2 \leq \overline{u} \leq 2 \ \wedge \ -2 \leq \overline{v} \leq 2 \ \wedge \ -1 \leq \overline{w} \leq 1 \ \wedge \ \overline{u} \leq \overline{v} \ \wedge \ \circ(\overline{v} + \overline{w}) < \circ(\overline{u} + \overline{w})$$

where $\overline{x}$ denotes the real value of a finite FP number x and where $\circ(x)$ is the FP number (seen as a real) chosen to represent a real x for a given format according to the default rounding mode. The second layer contains a lemma about the monotonicity of $\circ$, that is: $\forall x, y : \mathbb{R}. \ x \leq y \implies \circ(x) \leq \circ(y)$. Using contrapositive of monotonicity, we deduce from the last literal that $\overline{v} + \overline{w} < \overline{u} + \overline{w}$, which contradicts $\overline{u} \leq \overline{v}$, thanks to a simple reasoning over real numbers conducted by the third layer.

While our strategy only requires NRA support, the main challenge is to find the good instances of lemmas about rounding. Unfortunately, the syntactic (modulo uninterpreted equalities) matching algorithm of SMT is too weak to find relevant instances for some of them. Indeed, problematic lemmas require interval information to be instantiated efficiently. We expect the NRA decision procedure to abstract FP terms by real intervals, as in the ACDCL approach, and to export those intervals to the matching algorithm.

Since our approach is based on a generic instantiation mechanism, it is not meant to be complete. In practice, this is not a limitation, as we are mainly interested in discharging verification conditions coming from program verification, that is, in proving the unsatisfiability of formulas.

Contributions: We make the following contributions.

1. We propose a three-layer architecture for extending SMT solvers with FP reasoning. The heart of our approach is a new mechanism for reasoning about quantifiers modulo interval information.
2. We extend the matching modulo equality algorithm of SMT with a new matching algorithm based on intervals.
3. We present an implementation of our approach in the Alt-Ergo SMT solver. Results on benchmarks coming from deductive verification frameworks show that our strategy competes with tools based on other techniques.

Outline: We illustrate the general ideas of our approach by running a motivating example in Sect. 2. The design of the first layer is presented in Sect. 3. Section 4 gives an overview of the axioms about rounding, and intervals matching is detailed in Sect. 5. Benchmarks are given and discussed in Sect. 6 and we conclude in the last section.

2 Motivating Example

To illustrate the basic idea of our method, we consider a second simple example. We assume two binary32 FP variables u and v, a rounding operator $\circ(\cdot)$ and a mapping function $\overline{\cdot}$ from FP to reals. We will try to establish an upper bound for absolute error of the FP addition $u \oplus_m v$, assuming initial bounds for u and v. This (validity) problem can be expressed as follows:

$$(2. \preceq u \preceq 10. \ \wedge \ 2. \preceq v \preceq 10.) \implies (\overline{u \oplus v}) - (\overline{u} + \overline{v}) \leq 0.00000096$$

where 2. and 10. are syntactic sugar for the finite FP constants whose real values are 2 and 10 respectively. Note that we omit the rounding mode m when it is the default one or when it is irrelevant.

To establish the validity of the example with our approach, we rely on a three-layer extension of Alt-Ergo as shown in Fig. 1.

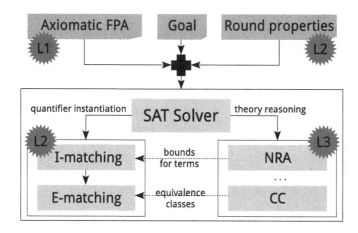

Fig. 1. A view of our framework inside the Alt-Ergo SMT solver. L1, L2, and L3, represent the different layers of our extension.

The first layer L1 consists of a set of "generic" axioms about FPA. It makes it possible to reason about the shape of FP expressions and to reduce FP constraints to real ones, using the rounding operator, when FP numbers are finite. More details about this layer are given in Sect. 3.

The second layer L2 plays an important role in our approach, as it enables effective cooperation between FP and real reasoning. It is made of two parts: an axiomatic part that provides properties about the rounding operator in an extended syntax of Alt-Ergo (see Sect. 4), and an interval-matching mechanism to instantiate these axioms (see Sect. 5).

The third layer L3 is a reasoning engine for non-linear real arithmetic that is able to provide bounds for terms. It is extended to partially handle some operators like rounding, exponentiation, integer logarithm, maximum, and absolute value. More precisely, this consists in enabling calculations when these operators are applied to constants, as we will see in the next sections.

To prove our example, six axioms from layer L1 and one axiom from layer L2 are required. These axioms are shown in Fig. 2. L1 axioms rely on a set of uninterpreted predicate symbols (is_finite, is_infinite, is_nan, is_positive, and

(L1-1) $\forall z.$ in_range$(z) \iff$ −0x1.FFFFFEp127 $\le z \le$ 0x1.FFFFFEp127

(L1-2) $\forall m.\forall x.\forall y.$ (is_finite$(x) \wedge$ is_finite$(y) \wedge$ in_range$(\circ_m(\overline{x} + \overline{y}))) \implies$
$$\overline{x \oplus_m y} = \circ_m(\overline{x} + \overline{y})$$

(L1-3) $\forall x.\forall y.$ $x \preceq y \implies$
$$\bigvee \begin{pmatrix} \text{is\_finite}(x) \wedge \text{is\_finite}(y) \\ \text{is\_infinite}(x) \wedge \text{is\_negative}(x) \wedge \neg\text{is\_nan}(y) \\ \text{is\_infinite}(y) \wedge \text{is\_positive}(y) \wedge \neg\text{is\_nan}(x) \end{pmatrix}$$

(L1-4) $\forall x.\forall y.$ (is_finite$(x) \wedge$ is_finite$(y) \wedge x \preceq y) \implies \overline{x} \le \overline{y}$

(L1-5) $\forall x.$ (is_infinite$(x) \vee$ is_nan$(x)) \implies \neg$ is_finite(x)

(L1-6) $\forall x.$ $\neg$ (is_negative$(x) \wedge$ is_positive(x))

(L2-1) $\forall z.\forall i.\forall j.$ $i \le z \le j \implies -2^\alpha \le \circ(z) - z \le 2^\alpha$
$$\text{where } \alpha = \text{ilog}_2(\max(|i|, |j|, 2^{e_{\min}+prec-1})) - prec$$

Fig. 2. Overview of axioms from L1 and L2 needed to prove the example.

is_negative) that are used to characterize the shape of FP expressions. L1-1 defines the range of real numbers that can be represented by finite binary32 FP numbers. When inputs are finite and the result does not overflow, the meaning of addition in terms of rounding operator is given by L1-2. Axioms L1-3 and L1-4 deal with the $\preceq$ relation: the first axiom enumerates the possible cases for a hypothesis $x \preceq y$, and the second one maps this predicate to its real counterpart when the arguments are finite. As for L1-5 and L1-6, they just impose some restrictions on the uninterpreted predicates. Finally, you may notice that axiom L2-1 from layer L2 is much more sophisticated. It bounds the distance between a real and its rounded value (when rounding to nearest) using some parameters $prec$ and $e_{\min}$ that depend on the format (see Sect. 3); function ilog_2 denotes the integer part of the base-2 logarithm.

The reasoning steps needed to prove the initial example within our framework are shown in Fig. 3. The initial hypotheses are named as follows: H1 $\equiv$ is_finite(2.), H2 $\equiv$ is_finite(10.), H3 $\equiv$ 2. $\preceq u$, H4 $\equiv$ 2. $\preceq v$, H5 $\equiv u \preceq$ 10., and H6 $\equiv v \preceq$ 10.. A property deduced at step i is named Di. Steps from 1 to 10 prove that u and v are finite using mainly E-matching (EM) and Boolean reasoning. Steps from 11 to 14 deduce bounds for $\overline{u}$ and $\overline{v}$ from those of u and v using the same reasoning engines. Step 15 instantiates the axiom that reduces FP addition to real addition, plus a rounding operation. However, to be able to use its conclusion, we should first show that the addition does not overflow: given bounds for $\overline{u} + \overline{v}$ (step 16), intervals-matching generates an instance from L2-1, which is simplified by the SAT (step 17). Thanks to an instance of L1-1, a combination of arithmetic and Boolean reasoning makes it possible to deduce that the addition does indeed not overflow (steps 18 and 19). Finally, using the deductions of steps 17 and 20, we derive that $\overline{u \oplus v} - (\overline{u} + \overline{v}) \le 2^{-20}$, which concludes the proof, since $2^{-20} = 0.000000953 \cdots < 0.00000096$.

IDs	used hypotheses	used axioms	used reasoners	produced deductions
1	H1	L1-5	EM, SAT	$\neg$is_infinite(2.)
2	H1	L1-5	EM, SAT	$\neg$is_nan(2.)
3	H2	L1-5	EM, SAT	$\neg$is_infinite(10.)
4	H2	L1-5	EM, SAT	$\neg$is_nan(10.)
5	H3, D{1,2}	L1-3	EM, SAT	is_finite(u)$\lor$ (is_infinite(u) $\land$ is_positive(u))
6	H4, D{1,2}	L1-3	EM, SAT	is_finite(v)$\lor$ (is_infinite(v) $\land$ is_positive(v))
7	H5, D{3,4}	L1-3	EM, SAT	is_finite(u)$\lor$ (is_infinite(u) $\land$ is_negative(u))
8	H6, D{3,4}	L1-3	EM, SAT	is_finite(v)$\lor$ (is_infinite(v) $\land$ is_negative(v))
9	D{5,7}	L1-6	EM, SAT	is_finite(u)
10	D{6,8}	L1-6	EM, SAT	is_finite(v)
11	H{1,3}, D9	L1-4	EM, SAT	$2 \leq \overline{u}$
12	H{1,4}, D10	L1-4	EM, SAT	$2 \leq \overline{v}$
13	H{2,5}, D9	L1-4	EM, SAT	$\overline{u} \leq 10$
14	H{2,6}, D10	L1-4	EM, SAT	$\overline{v} \leq 10$
15	D{9,10}	L1-2	EM, SAT	in_range($\circ(\overline{u}+\overline{v})$) $\Rightarrow \overline{u} \oplus \overline{v} = \circ(\overline{u}+\overline{v})$
16	D{11,12,13,14}		NRA	$\overline{u}+\overline{v} \in [4;20]$
17	D16	L2-1	EM, IM, SAT	$-2^{-20} \leq \circ(\overline{u}+\overline{v}) - (\overline{u}+\overline{v}) \leq 2^{-20}$
18	D{16,17}		NRA	$4-2^{-20} \leq \circ(\overline{u}+\overline{v}) \leq 20+2^{-20}$
19	D{18}	L1-1	EM, SAT, NRA	in_range($\circ(\overline{u}+\overline{v})$)
20	D{15,19}		SAT	$\overline{u} \oplus \overline{v} = \circ(\overline{u}+\overline{v})$
21	D{17,20}		NRA	$\overline{u} \oplus \overline{v} - (\overline{u}+\overline{v}) \leq 2^{-20}$

Fig. 3. Reasoning steps used to prove the example.

3   Layer 1: Generic Axiomatic FPA

The IEEE-754 standard defines several formats for representing FP numbers and gives the semantics of arithmetic operators over data of these formats [1]. The formats are specified at various abstraction levels. At Level 1, formats are just some subsets of real numbers to which $-\infty$ and $+\infty$ are added. At Level 2, zero is split into a positive zero and a negative zero, and a set of *Not-a-Number* (NaN) is added. The signed zeros behave as the multiplicative inverse of the infinities, while NaNs are the result of invalid operations such as $0 \times \infty$ or $\infty - \infty$. At Level 3, finite values get represented by their sign, significant, and exponent. The set of NaNs is also further refined. At Level 4, FP data get mapped to strings of bits. The IEEE-754 standard supports both binary and decimal formats, but we will focus on binary formats only.

The SMT-LIB theory follows a similar approach to describing FP formats [5], though it does not provide all the features of the IEEE-754 standard. Indeed, the latter is underspecified when it comes to NaNs: the standard tells when the result of an operation is NaN, but it does not tell which *payload* the NaN carries. So the SMT-LIB theory chose to have only one NaN to account for all the possible implementations. This also means that the theory provides a function for going from strings of bits to FP data, but not the other way around.

Taking advice of both the IEEE-754 standard and the SMT-LIB theory, we have formalized FP formats as a Why3 theory. The first step is to define an abstract type t which will be later instantiated for each format. We also give a few abstract predicates on this type:

```
predicate is_finite    t
predicate is_infinite  t
predicate is_nan       t
```

The Why3 syntax here means that these predicates take a single argument of type t. Then there are two axioms to make sure that a FP datum is either finite or infinite or NaN, of which axiom L1-5 of Fig. 2 is an implication.

```
axiom is_not_nan: forall x:t.
  (is_finite x \/ is_infinite x) <-> not (is_nan x)
axiom is_not_finite: forall x:t.
  not (is_finite x) <-> (is_infinite x \/ is_nan x)
```

Note that our formalization uses abstract predicates, but for SMT solvers that support enumerations, one could also imagine a less abstract formalization that does not require these two axioms.

Any finite FP datum has an associated real value. These values are of the form $m \cdot \beta^e$ with m an integer significand, e an exponent, and β the radix. The radix is 2 for the formats we are interested in. The ranges of allowed m and e are given by the format in the following way:

$$|m| < \beta^{prec} \wedge e_{\min} \leq e \wedge |m \cdot \beta^e| < \beta^{e_{\max}}.$$

The values of $prec$, $e_{\min}$, and $e_{\max}$ can be recovered from the Level 4 description of a format. For instance, if a binary format uses e_w bits for representing the exponent and m_w bits for representing the mantissa (that is, the significant without its most-significant bit for normal numbers), then

$$prec = m_w + 1 \wedge e_{\max} = 2^{e_w - 1} \wedge e_{\min} = 3 - e_{\max} - prec.$$

Our formalization does not give direct access to the significand or the exponent. It just provides an abstract function from t to the set of a real numbers, which is the function that was denoted $\overline{\cdot}$ in the previous section.

```
function to_real t : real
```

As for formats, the formalization uses an abstract real for the largest representable number (that is, $\beta^{e_{\max}} \cdot (1 - \beta^{-prec})$) and defines a predicate for characterizing real numbers in the range of finite numbers.

```
constant max_real : real
predicate in_range (x:real) = -max_real <= x <= max_real
```

Not all the real numbers that are in range are representable, so we arrive to the notion of rounding. It is present in both the IEEE-754 standard and the SMT-LIB theory. Let us first enumerate the five rounding modes supported by the standard:

```
type mode = RNE | RNA | RTP | RTN | RTZ
```

The first two modes round to nearest, with tie breaking to even (RNE) or away from zero (RNA). The last three modes are directed rounding: toward $+\infty$ (RTP), toward $-\infty$ (RTN), and toward zero (RTZ).

For a given target format, a rounding operator tells us which FP number should be used to represent a real number. If the real number is representable, then the choice is trivial; the only peculiarities come from the existence of signed zeros, which we will not detail here. Otherwise the FP number should be the closest one according to the rounding mode. For now, we follow the examples of the Gappa tool [7] and of the Flocq library [3], so we assume that the target format has an unbounded $e_{\max}$. That way, we do not have to bother with the issue of overflow yet. So the rounding operator can be given the following signature.

```
function round mode real : real
```

This is yet again declared as an abstract function, though it has a mathematical definition. If we denote $\circ_m$ the rounding operator with mode m, then we have

$$\circ_m (x) = \lceil x/\beta^e \rfloor_m \cdot \beta^e \tag{2}$$

with $e = \max(e_{\min}, \lfloor \log_\beta |x| \rfloor + 1 - prec)$. The integer part $\lceil \cdot \rfloor_m$ selects the integer the closest to a given real according to mode m. This definition of the rounding operator is sufficient to prove all the properties of Sect. 4, $e.g.$ monotonicity of the rounding operator, as done in Flocq.

Note that, if one wanted to use such a concrete definition in an SMT solver, one would also need $\log_\beta$ to be defined. This can be avoided by instead providing a function from $|x|$ to β^e, since this function can be finitely axiomatized using just inequalities for any format, as was done in [11]. In our case, we do not care about these details, as **round** is kept as an abstract function.

Our rounding operator ignores the issue of overflow, but this issue still has to be handled. We do so by defining the following predicate. It will be used to decide whether a rounded value is relevant or not as a result of an FP arithmetic operator.

```
predicate no_overflow (m:mode) (x:real) =
    in_range (round m x)
```

We now have enough definitions to state what the behavior of the FP addition is when its inputs are finite numbers. More precisely, the IEEE-754 standard states that an addition "shall be performed as if it first produced an intermediate result correct to infinite precision and with unbounded range, and then rounded that result". This trivially translates into the following specification (axiom L1-2 of Fig. 2) where + denotes the addition over real numbers.

```
function add mode t t : t
axiom add_finite: forall m:mode, x y:t.
  is_finite x -> is_finite y ->
  no_overflow m (to_real x + to_real y) ->
  is_finite (add m x y) /\
  to_real (add m x y) = round m (to_real x + to_real y)
```

As for the overflow case, here is a small excerpt of the add_special axiom which covers all the exceptional behaviors of the FP addition according to the standard:

```
axiom add_special: forall m:mode, x y:t.
  let r = add m x y in
  ... (* 6 other conjuncts *) ... /\
  (is_finite x /\ is_finite y /\
   not no_overflow m (to_real x + to_real y)
   -> same_sign_real r (to_real x + to_real y) /\
   overflow_value m r)
```

The same_sign_real relation tells which sign the final result has, assuming the infinitely-precise intermediate result is nonzero (which is the case if it overflowed). The overflow_value relation then selects the final result depending on the rounding mode and its sign.

An important property of our formalization, which we hope is apparent from the excerpts, is that it is a straightforward translation from the IEEE-754 standard. That does not mean that it is trivially error-free though, since we could well have forgotten some hypotheses or we could have mistyped an r for an x for instance. To prevent this issue, we have realized this formalization using the Coq proof assistant. What this means is that we have given concrete definition to all the abstract definitions (*e.g.* the Bplus function of Flocq for the FP addition) and then Why3 required us to formally prove in Coq that all the axioms hold. This gives a high level of confidence in the correctness of our formalization. A more detailed presentation of Layer 1 is given in this technical report [8].

4   Layers 2 and 3: Rounding Properties

Given a constraint mixing the rounding operator with non-linear real arithmetic terms, one can reduce it to an extension of non-linear real arithmetic with floor and ceiling functions using the encoding of the rounding operator given by Eq. (2). Then a solver that supports mixed real/integer non-linear arithmetic can be used to solve the resulting problem, as was done in [11].

In this paper, we adopt a different approach: instead of fully encoding the rounding operator, we reason modulo a set of its properties. Although theoretically incomplete compared to mixed non-linear integer/real encoding, our experimental evaluation shows that the method is effective in practice, in particular in the domain of program verification.

An overview of the rounding properties that are provided by Layer 2 are given in Fig. 4. Most of these axioms are borrowed from the Flocq formalization

(L2-1) $\forall x.\forall i.\forall j.\quad i \leq x \leq j \Rightarrow -2^\alpha \leq \mathrm{o}(x) - x \leq 2^\alpha$

where $\alpha = \mathtt{ilog_2}(\max(|i|, |j|, 2^{emin+prec-1})) - prec$

(L2-2) $\forall x.\forall i.\forall j.\forall m.\quad i \leq x \leq j \Rightarrow \mathrm{o}_m(i) \leq \mathrm{o}_m(x) \leq \mathrm{o}_m(j)$

(L2-3) $\forall x.\forall i.\forall j.\forall m.\quad i \leq x \leq j \Rightarrow \mathrm{o}_m^{\mathbb{Z}}(i) \leq \mathrm{o}_m^{\mathbb{Z}}(x) \leq \mathrm{o}_m^{\mathbb{Z}}(j)$

(L2-4) $\forall x.\forall m_1.\forall m_2.\quad \mathrm{o}_{m_1}(\mathrm{o}_{m_2}(x)) = \mathrm{o}_{m_2}(x)$

(L2-5) $\forall x.\forall y.\forall m.\quad x \leq y \Rightarrow \mathrm{o}_m(x) \leq \mathrm{o}_m(y)$

(L2-6) $\forall x.\forall y.\forall m.\quad \mathrm{o}_m(x) < \mathrm{o}_m(y) \Rightarrow x < \mathrm{o}_m(y)$

(L2-7) $\forall x.\forall y.\forall m.\quad \mathrm{o}_m(x) < \mathrm{o}_m(y) \Rightarrow \mathrm{o}_m(x) < y$

(L2-8) $\forall x.\forall i.\forall m.\quad \mathrm{o}_m(x) < i \Rightarrow x < \mathrm{o}_{\mathrm{RTP}}(i)$

(L2-9) $\forall x.\forall i.\forall m.\quad i \leq \mathrm{o}_m(x) \Rightarrow \mathrm{o}_{\mathrm{RTP}}(i) \leq \mathrm{o}_m(x)$

(L2-10) $\forall x.\forall y.\forall m.\quad |x| \geq 1 \Rightarrow |x| = 2^{\mathtt{ilog_2}(|x|)} \Rightarrow \mathrm{o}_m(x \cdot \mathrm{o}_m(y)) = x \cdot \mathrm{o}_m(y)$

(L2-11) $\forall x.\forall y.\forall m.\quad \mathrm{o}_m(x) < \mathrm{o}_m(y) \Rightarrow \mathrm{o}_m(\mathrm{o}_m(x) - \mathrm{o}_m(y)) < 0$

(L2-12) $\forall x.\forall y.\forall m.\quad \mathrm{o}_m(x) < -\mathrm{o}_m(y) \Rightarrow \mathrm{o}_m(\mathrm{o}_m(x) + \mathrm{o}_m(y)) < 0$

Fig. 4. Overview of the main axioms of Layer 2.

of FPA for the Coq proof assistant. Axiom L2-1 bounds the distance between a real and its rounded value (*i.e.* nearest float) with respect to the default rounding mode. Similar properties for other rounding modes are also provided. Axiom L2-2 states the monotonicity of rounding. This particular formulation is used to deduce numerical bounds for rounded values as we will see in the next section. Axiom L2-3 is similar to L2-2 except that operator $\mathrm{o}^{\mathbb{Z}}$ rounds to the nearest integer. Axiom L2-4 states the idempotency of rounding, independently of the rounding mode. Classical formulation of monotonicity is given by axiom L2-5, and the three next axioms are consequences of L2-5's contrapositive (modulo idempotency). Axiom L2-9 makes it possible to improve lower bounds of rounded expressions. A similar axiom is used to tighten upper bounds. The last three axioms provide some situations where arithmetic expressions can be simplified.

Several of those axioms are meant to be instantiated using some constant values (*e.g.* any occurrence of i and j) so that numerical computations can be performed. For instance, axiom L2-2 is akin to a *propagator* as found in CP techniques, while axiom L2-8 acts as a *contractor*. To do so, the SMT solver has to be able to compute an expression such as $\mathrm{o}_m(i)$ when i is a constant. We thus put a shallow preprocessor in front of the NRA engine to reduce these expressions to rational numbers that the NRA engine can make use of. This involves providing some code for evaluating o, $\mathrm{o}^{\mathbb{Z}}$, $2^{(\cdot)}$, $\mathtt{ilog_2}$, $\max$, $|\cdot|$.

5   Interval-Based Instantiation

Most of the axioms given in Fig. 4 cannot be efficiently instantiated using generic
E-matching techniques of SMT solvers, as it is not always possible to provide
good triggers for them. A trigger for an axiom $\forall \boldsymbol{x}.\varphi(\boldsymbol{x})$ is a term (or a set of
terms) that covers all variables $\boldsymbol{x}$. Based on this definition, a trigger-inference
algorithm would presumably compute $\{\circ_m(x), \circ_m(i), \circ_m(j)\}$ for the L2-2 axiom:

$$(\text{L2-2}) \quad \forall x.\forall i.\forall j.\forall m. \quad i \le x \le j \Rightarrow \circ_m(i) \le \circ_m(x) \le \circ_m(j).$$

This set of terms, however, is not suitable for this axiom, as it would prevent
its application when proving the following formula:

$$2 \le a \le 4 \implies 2 \le \circ(a) \le 4.$$

Indeed, the only way to instantiate the trigger is by choosing $x = i = j = a$ since
the only rounded value in the formula is $\circ(a)$. Yet the proper way to instantiate
the axiom is $x = a$, $i = 2$, $j = 4$. Then effectively computing $\circ(2)$ and $\circ(4)$ makes
it possible to conclude.

In order to efficiently reason modulo our rounding properties, we have decorated them with two kinds of triggers: *syntactic* and *interval* triggers. Syntactic
triggers are those that are already used by the generic E-matching mechanism.
For instance, the set of syntactic triggers of axiom L2-2 is the singleton $\{\circ_m(x)\}$.
Interval triggers are guards used to carefully instantiate the variables that are
not covered by syntactic triggers. The purpose of this kind of triggers is twofold:
(a) get rid of permissive or restrictive syntactic triggers, (b) take current arithmetic environment into account to guide the instantiation process. For instance,
a suitable interval trigger for axiom L2-2 is the set $\{i \le x, x \le j\}$.

The language of interval triggers is defined by the following grammar:

$$its ::= it \mid it, its \qquad it ::= b\,\mathcal{R}\,t \mid t\,\mathcal{R}\,b \qquad b ::= c \mid i \qquad \mathcal{R} ::= \le \mid <$$

where c is a numerical constant, i is a quantified variable, and t is a term. In the
rest of the paper, we assume that all the variables of the t terms (*resp.* none of
the variables in the b bounds) appear in syntactic triggers.

Let us illustrate the use of triggers with the Alt-Ergo statement of axiom
L2-8 from Fig. 4. (It has been simplified a bit for the sake of readability.)

```
axiom monotonicity_contrapositive_1 :
   forall x, i : real. forall m : mode
   [ round(m, x) ] { round(m, x) < i }.
   x < round(RTP, i)
```

The term between square brackets is a syntactic trigger: variables m and x
will be instantiated using any ground term $\circ(\cdot)$ found in the context. The term
between curly brackets is both an interval trigger and a hypothesis of the axiom:
variable i will be instantiated by any constant bound such that $\circ_m(x) < i$ holds.

Note that interval triggers are instantiated by querying the NRA engine, once
syntactic triggers have been instantiated. For instance, let us suppose that the

syntactic trigger gives $\circ_m(x)$ and that the NRA engine then tells that $\circ_m(x) < 5$ holds. Thus any number that is larger or equal to 5 satisfies the interval trigger $\circ_m(x) < i$. Since there are no other interval triggers about i, the most precise instance of i is 5. This leads to the following instance of the axiom being added:

$$\circ_m(x) < 5 \implies x < 5$$

since $\circ_{\text{RTP}}(5)$ evaluates to 5.

Now let us suppose that the current upper bound on $\circ_m(x)$ is just $\circ_m(x) \leq 5$. This time, any number that is strictly larger to 5 satisfies the interval trigger. There is no longer any most precise instance. So Alt-Ergo selects some arbitrary number $\varepsilon > 0$ and instantiates i with $5 + \varepsilon$. So some incompleteness creeps here. However, if ε is small enough, then $\circ_{\text{RTP}}(5 + \varepsilon)$ evaluates to the successor of 5 in the FP format, which leads to adding the following axiom instance:

$$\circ_m(x) < 5 + \varepsilon \implies x < 5 + 2^{3-\text{prec}}.$$

To conclude the section, some axioms of Layer 2 with their interval triggers are shown in Fig. 5. You may note that: (a) the verbose expression `let k = ...` in the second axiom actually reduces to a numerical constant by calculation when instantiating i and j with numerical values, (b) in the interval triggers of the third axiom, the bounds are constants. In this case, interval matching consists in simple numerical checks.

```
axiom integer_rounding_operator :
   forall x, i, j : real. forall m : mode.
   [ int_round(m, x) ] { i <= x, x <= j }.
   int_round(m, i) <= int_round(m, x) <= int_round(m, j)

axiom rounding_operator_absolute_error_RNE :
   forall x, i, j : real.
   [ round(RNE, x) ] { i <= x, x <= j }.
   let k =
    pow(2.,
      ilog2(max(abs(i),abs(j),pow(2., emin+prec-1))) - prec)
    in -k <= round(RNE, x) - x <= k

axiom round_of_int:
   forall x : int. forall m : mode.
   [ round(m, real_of_int(x))]
   { 0. <= real_of_int(x) + pow(2., prec),
     real_of_int(x) - pow(2., prec) <= 0. }.
   round(m, real_of_int(x)) = real_of_int(x)
```

Fig. 5. Some axioms of Layer 2 in Alt-Ergo's extended syntax.

6   Implementation and Evaluation

Implementation. To evaluate our approach, we have extended Alt-Ergo's instantiation engine with an interval-matching mechanism. The arithmetic engine has been strengthened to enable calculation with some function symbols (rounding operator, exponentiation, integer logarithm, etc.) when applied to numerical constants. Rounding properties are given as a list of axioms in a separate file, annotated with their triggers. Generic FPA axioms are provided by a Why3 FPA theory. Currently, the instances generated from the axioms of Layer 2 are given back to the SAT solver. The implementation will be available in the next release of Alt-Ergo.

Tools and Benchmarks Description. In addition to our implementation (denoted AE and AE+G in the result tables), we use three solvers for the evaluation: Z3 (v. 4.5.0), MathSAT5 (v. 5.3.14, denoted MS+A and MS+B), and Gappa (v. 1.3.1). While not an SMT solver, Gappa is included because it has significantly inspired our approach. We do not include REALIZER [11] as its input language is too limited to talk about infinities and NaNs.

Considered benchmarks consist of two sets of verification conditions (VC) extracted from numerical C[2] and SPARK programs, and of the QF-FP category of SMT-LIB benchmarks. Figure 6 explains how VCs are encoded to different solvers. In particular, notice that SMT-LIB benchmarks are directly fed to Z3 and MathSAT5, but they are translated to Why3 and combined with an axiomatic FPA before they are given to Alt-Ergo and Gappa.

VCs from C and SPARK programs are first extracted using Why3's weakest precondition calculus. They are then combined with generic FPA axioms and encoded to different solvers. For Z3 and MathSAT5, a faithful mapping from

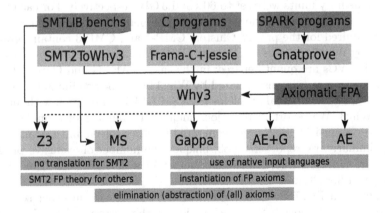

Fig. 6. Generation of verification conditions in the language of different solvers.

---

[2] See https://www.lri.fr/~sboldo/research.html and http://toccata.lri.fr/gallery/fp.
en.html for more details.

Why3 FPA axiomatization to the FP theory of SMT-LIB is used. In this case, first-order axiomatization of FP operations is removed. More generally, since MathSAT5 does not handle quantifiers, Why3 always eliminates the quantified parts of the VCs sent to it. The same elimination process is used for Gappa, except that Layer-1 axioms are first instantiated by Why3 since Gappa only knows about real numbers. This means that a set of ground instances is generated from FP operations' axioms using matching techniques and initial ground terms of the VCs.[3] To better evaluate the cost of Layer-1 axioms and to provide a fairer comparison with MathSAT5 and Gappa, we also generate Alt-Ergo benchmarks (denoted AE+G, where G stands for *ground*) where FP operations' axioms are instantiated and eliminated the same way they are for Gappa.

Since not all the VCs extracted for C and SPARK programs need FPA reasoning for them to be proved, we have filtered them as follows: if a VC is proved by Alt-Ergo without any reasoning modulo generic FPA axioms, rounding properties, or any other extension, it is removed from the benchmark. Filtering yields test-suites of 307 VCs (out of 1848 initially) from C programs and 1980 VCs (out of 23903) from SPARK programs. It should be noted that: (a) some VCs extracted from C and SPARK programs may require a combination of FPA reasoning with other theories and quantifiers instantiation to be proved, and (b) all the VCs are not provable.

For QF-FP benchmarks, we only keep formulas that are not known to be *satisfiable*, as we are interested in unsatisfiability (or dually in validity) in the context of program verification. Consequently *Wintersteiger* benchmarks with a SAT status, and *Griggio* benchmarks that are shown to be satisfiable by Z3 or MathSAT5 are filtered out. Schanda benchmarks are also discarded as they are already included in SPARK programs.

Experimental Results. The results of our evaluation are shown in Figs. 7 and 8. Time and memory limits were set to 60 s and 3 GB, respectively. For each prover (in the columns), we report the number and the percentage of proved VCs, and the time required for the proofs. Clusters CMP-1 and CMP-3 contain problems generated by Why3. Clusters CMP-2 and CMP-4 are also generated by Why3 but the resulting VCs are quantifier-free; in the case of AE+G and Gappa, Layer-1 axioms are automatically instantiated by Why3 before being eliminated. Cluster CMP-5 contains the original problems from SMT-LIB competition without going through Why3. We report in row "loc. unique" the number of formulas that a given solver exclusively discharges compared to other solvers in the same CMP-i cluster. Similarly, we report in "glob. unique" the number of exclusive proofs of each solver. Finally, we report the number of VCs that are proved by at least one prover in line "total".

We notice in Fig. 7 that Alt-Ergo and Gappa outperform other solvers on the C benchmark. Indeed, the specification of the corresponding C programs heavily uses reals for expressing pre- and post-conditions about FP numbers,

---

[3] Having Why3 instantiate some axioms in the VCs sent to Gappa is not specific to these benchmarks.

		CMP-1		CMP-2			
		AE	Z3	AE+G	Gappa	MS+B	MS+A
C	proved	194	2	194	199	4	2
	% proved	63.19%	0.65%	63.19%	64.82%	1.30%	0.65%
	time (secs)	566	< 1	348	78	4	< 1
	loc. unique	192	0	21	28	0	0
	glob. unique	8	0	2	25	0	0
	total	230/307 (74.92%) proved with at least one solver					
SPARK	proved	806	720	541	488	170	13
	% proved	40.71%	36.36%	27.32%	24.65%	8.59%	0.66%
	time (secs)	3090	4142	4769	305	301	1
	loc. unique	244	157	66	33	100	2
	glob. unique	151	105	31	33	7	0
	total	1136/1980 (57.37%) proved with at least one solver					

Fig. 7. Results on filtered VCs extracted from C and SPARK programs.

		CMP-3	CMP-4		CMP-5		
		AE	AE+G	Gappa	Z3	MS+B	MS+A
Wintersteiger unsat	proved	20012	19863	18102	20035	17201	17200
	% proved	99.89%	99.14%	90.35 %	100%	85.85%	85.85%
	time (secs)	876	487	44	65	66	63
	loc. unique	-	1784	23	2834	0	0
	glob. unique	0	0	0	0	0	0
	total	20035/20035 (100%) proved with at least one solver					
Griggio unknown + unsat	proved	2	33	0	50	49	5
	% proved	1.75%	28.95%	0%	43.86%	42.98%	4.39%
	time (secs)	18	621	0	1337	723	1
	loc. unique	-	33	0	6	3	1
	glob. unique	0	1	0	0	2	0
	total	57/114 (50.00%) proved with at least one solver					

Fig. 8. Results on QF-FP category of SMT-LIB benchmarks.

which impedes solvers that do not handle well the combination of FP and real reasoning. In particular, the fp.to_real function symbol is hardly supported. While Z3 parses it properly, it has troubles in solving problems involving it.[4]

On the opposite, SPARK programs are specified using FP numbers. Consequently, Z3's results are much closer to those of Alt-Ergo. Surprisingly, MathSAT5 with either bit-blasting (MS+B) or ACDCL (MS+A) does not perform well. This is probably due to the fact that MathSAT5 is not well tuned for the context of deductive program verification. One can notice two other interesting results on the SPARK benchmarks: first, AE+G's success rate is close to Gappa's but quite far from Alt-Ergo's. This is certainly due to the abstraction of quantified formulas, which prevents AE+G (and Gappa) from dynamically generating relevant instances to discharge some proofs. Second, the solvers are

---

[4] https://github.com/Z3Prover/z3/issues/14.

highly complementary. For instance, the SPARK results of Fig. 7 show that Alt-Ergo and Z3 together solve 963 VCs, but more than a third $(244 + 157)$ of these VCs are solved by only one prover.

Wintersteiger unsat benchmarks are very simple crafted formulas meant to stress compliance to the FP SMT-LIB standard and detect bugs in implementations. Z3 proves all the formulas of the benchmark. For Alt-Ergo, 23 formulas are not proved due to the inaccuracy of its NRA engine when bounding terms involving square root. For MathSAT5, unproved formulas are related to `fma` and `remainder` operators, which are apparently not supported yet. Gappa fails to prove approximately 2000 formulas due to the default reduced precision of its internal domains, since the infinitely-precise result of a binary64 `fma` might require up to 3122 bits so that its rounded value can be computed exactly.

Bit-blasting based techniques perform better on Griggio benchmarks. Since AE+G outperforms AE, the bad results likely come from a poor interaction between the E-matching and SAT engines of Alt-Ergo. As for Gappa, its inability to handle these benchmarks is due to the absence of any kind of SAT solver.

7   Conclusion and Future Work

We have presented a three-layer axiomatic strategy for reasoning about floating-point arithmetic in SMT. Experimental evaluations show that it is effective in practice for reasoning in a combination of FPA and real numbers, as required for instance to refer to the distance between FP and real computations.

We opted for the presented solution for different reasons: (a) it is lightweight, less intrusive and requires minimal changes in the solver, (b) potential bugs in most of the added code (mainly in interval matching) do not impact the soundness of our results, (c) axioms of Layer 1 have been verified with the Coq proof assistant for extra confidence, (d) rounding properties in Layer 2 are human-readable, can be reviewed and validated by experts, and are easily extensible, (e) our solution can be trivially extended to support decimal FP formats if need arises.

Future work. An interesting direction of research for improving performances could be to implement the generic FPA part as a built-in procedure, and inlining most of rounding properties as CP-like propagators. As the benchmarks show, the various approaches are complementary. We are thus planning to see how bit-blasting, ACDCL, and RIA techniques could be integrated in our framework, in particular to handle satisfiable formulas.

References

1. IEEE Standard for Floating-Point Arithmetic. Technical report. IEEE, August 2008
2. Barrett, C., Fontaine, P., Tinelli, C.: The SMT-LIB standard: version 2.5. Technical report, Department of Computer Science, The University of Iowa (2015)

3. Boldo, S., Melquiond, G.: Flocq: a unified library for proving floating-point algorithms in Coq. In: Antelo, E., Hough, D., Ienne, P. (eds.) Proceedings of the 20th IEEE Symposium on Computer Arithmetic, Tübingen, Germany, pp. 243–252 (2011)

4. Brain, M., D'Silva, V., Griggio, A., Haller, L., Kroening, D.: Deciding floating-point logic with abstract conflict driven clause learning. Form. Methods Syst. Des. 45(2), 213–245 (2014). doi:10.1007/s10703-013-0203-7

5. Brain, M., Tinelli, C., Rümmer, P., Wahl, T.: An automatable formal semantics for IEEE-754 floating-point arithmetic. In: Muller, J.-M., Tisserand, A., Villalba, J. (eds.) Proceedings of the 22nd IEEE Symposium on Computer Arithmetic, pp. 160–167. IEEE, Washington, D.C. (2015)

6. Daumas, M., Rideau, L., Théry, L.: A generic library for floating-point numbers and its application to exact computing. In: Boulton, R.J., Jackson, P.B. (eds.) TPHOLs 2001. LNCS, vol. 2152, pp. 169–184. Springer, Heidelberg (2001). doi:10.1007/3-540-44755-5_13

7. de Dinechin, F., Lauter, C., Melquiond, G.: Certifying the floating-point implementation of an elementary function using Gappa. Trans. Comput. 60(2), 242–253 (2011)

8. Fumex, C., Marché, C., Moy, Y.: Automated verification of floating-point computations in Ada programs. Research Report RR-9060, Inria Saclay-Île-de-France, April 2017

9. Goubault, E., Martel, M., Putot, S.: Asserting the precision of floating-point computations: a simple abstract interpreter. In: Métayer, D. (ed.) ESOP 2002. LNCS, vol. 2305, pp. 209–212. Springer, Heidelberg (2002). doi:10.1007/3-540-45927-8_15

10. Harrison, J.: A machine-checked theory of floating point arithmetic. In: Bertot, Y., Dowek, G., Théry, L., Hirschowitz, A., Paulin, C. (eds.) TPHOLs 1999. LNCS, vol. 1690, pp. 113–130. Springer, Heidelberg (1999). doi:10.1007/3-540-48256-3_9

11. Leeser, M., Mukherjee, S., Ramachandran, J., Wahl, T.: Make it real: effective floating-point reasoning via exact arithmetic. In: Design, Automation and Test in Europe Conference and Exhibition (DATE), Dresden, Germany, pp. 1–4, March 2014

12. Michel, C., Rueher, M., Lebbah, Y.: Solving constraints over floating-point numbers. In: Walsh, T. (ed.) CP 2001. LNCS, vol. 2239, pp. 524–538. Springer, Heidelberg (2001). doi:10.1007/3-540-45578-7_36

A Correct-by-Decision Solution for Simultaneous Place and Route

Alexander Nadel[(⊠)]

Intel Corporation, P.O. Box 1659, 31015 Haifa, Israel
alexander.nadel@intel.com

Abstract. To reduce a problem, provided in a human language, to constraint solving, one normally maps it to a set of constraints, written in the language of a suitable logic. This paper highlights a different paradigm, in which the original problem is converted into a set of constraints and a decision strategy, where the decision strategy is essential for guaranteeing the correctness of the modeling. We name such a paradigm Correct-by-Decision. Furthermore, we propose a Correct-by-Decision-based solution within a SAT solving framework for a critical industrial problem that shows up in the physical design stage of the CAD process: simultaneous place and route under arbitrary constraints (design rules). We demonstrate the usefulness of our approach experimentally on industrial and crafted instances.

1 Introduction

Nowadays, constraint solvers are widely applied to solve a rich variety of problems. Normally, reducing a problem, provided in a human language, to constraint solving involves the following steps:

1. Choosing the logic and the constraint solver most suitable for the problem at hand.
2. Reducing the problem to a set of constraints in the chosen logic, querying the solver, and mapping its results back to the original problem.

We call this generally accepted paradigm of reducing a problem to constraint solving *Correct-by-Constraint Paradigm (CBC)*.

Recently, a different paradigm has been identified and applied [8,12]. After choosing the logic and the solver, the problem is reduced to a set of constraints and a *decision strategy* for the solver. Both the constraints and the decision strategy are essential for guaranteeing correctness. We call such a paradigm the *Correct-by-Decision Paradigm (CBD)*. The difference between CBC and CBD paradigms is that in CBD the decision strategy is essential for guaranteeing the correctness of the modeling (in other words, reverting to the default decision strategy of the solver renders the modeling incorrect).

In [8,12], CBD-based solutions within a SAT solving framework were shown to outperform CBC-based solutions by four orders of magnitude for two industrial

© Springer International Publishing AG 2017
R. Majumdar and V. Kunčak (Eds.): CAV 2017, Part II, LNCS 10427, pp. 436–452, 2017.
DOI: 10.1007/978-3-319-63390-9_23

applications that show up in the physical design stage of Computer-Aided-Design (CAD): clock routing [8] and routing under constraints (RUC) [12]. Several factors were responsible for such an effect. First, the number of propositional clauses was drastically reduced. This is because many of the constraints were not required, their role being fulfilled by the decision strategy. In particular, the number of clauses was reduced by two orders of magnitude for clock routing [8]. Second, applying a problem-aware decision strategy helped make convergence substantially faster (a similar effect was observed in earlier works [3,18]). In addition, the decision strategy proved to be essential in meeting problem-specific optimization targets, e.g., reducing the routing cost in [12].

Interestingly, the widely applied scheme of incremental SAT solving under assumptions [2,7,13,14] can be thought of as an early unintentional application of CBD. Incremental SAT solving under assumptions is used when the initial problem can be solved with a series of SAT invocations over an incrementally constructed SAT instance, each time under different assumptions. It was found that instead of creating the SAT solver instance from scratch and using unit clauses to model assumptions, it is more effective to keep the solver instance alive and model the invocation-specific unit clauses as *assumptions*, that is, the first decisions taken by the solver. Such an approach falls into CBD category, since dropping the assumptions would render the approach unsound. Other examples of early unintentional CBD applications include [6,10], where a custom decision strategy was applied for efficient array reasoning and implicative simultaneous satisfiability, respectively.

The goal of this paper is twofold:

1. *To highlight the usefulness of* CBD *and provide more insight into it.* While previous works [8,12] identified that applying a decision strategy to simulate constraints is useful for their specific problems, we highlight CBD as a stand-alone paradigm. We wish to raise the awareness about CBD among the community, so that applying CBD for solving existing and new problems might become an explicit option to be considered by researchers.

2. *To propose a* CBD-*based solution to the critical industrial problem of Simultaneous Place and Route under Constraints (*PRUC*).* Both placement and routing are sub-stages in the physical design stage of CAD. Devices are placed in the placement stage and then connected (routed) in the routing stage (see [1,19] for a survey of the currently used approaches to both placement and routing). The eventual routing solution has to meet design rules which specify restrictions originating in manufacturing requirements. Currently placement and routing are carried out separately. The separation simplifies the physical design process significantly, but can very negatively impact execution time and solution quality. This is because the placer may come up with a solution that cannot be routed at all or cannot be routed cleanly w.r.t the design rules. In such a case additional place-and-route iterations are carried out, slowing down the process. Moreover, convergence is still not guaranteed. We propose a formal modeling and a CBD-based solution for the problem of *simultaneous* place and route under arbitrary bit-vector constraints that can be

applied to model simultaneous place and route under arbitrary design rules for integrated circuits [19] and printed circuit boards [1]. The advantages of simultaneous place and route were realized in previous work [15,16], where ad hoc place and route solutions were applied to two specific types of FPGA designs. [12] proposed a CBD-based solution for the routing stage only.

The rest of the paper is built as follows.

Section 2 sketches a CBD-based solution for the problem of Path-Finding under Constraints (PFUC) [4,12], that is, the problem of finding a path between two given vertices in a graph in the presence of constraints. Section 2 is important for two reasons. First, in it we illustrate the usefulness of CBD on a relatively simple application. Second, the PFUC solution that it sketches is a sub-component in both the RUC [12] and our proposed PRUC solutions.

Section 3 briefly reviews [12]'s approach to solving the RUC problem. This provides the background for our formulation and solution for the PRUC problem, which is introduced in Sect. 4. Section 5 provides the experimental results, and Sect. 6 concludes our paper.

We assume that the reader is familiar with the basics of bit-vector solving and SAT solving. See [9] for a recent overview.

2   Path-Finding Under Constraints

Consider the problem of *path-finding*, that is, finding a path from the source $s \in V$ to the target $t \in V$ in an undirected non-negatively weighted simple graph $G = (V, E)$.

Path-finding can be solved using the Dijkstra algorithm. Alternatively, one can reduce path-finding to propositional satisfiability as shown in Fig. 1. The formula in Fig. 1 can easily be translated to Conjunctive Normal Form (CNF), that is, a set of propositional clauses[1], and solved with a SAT solver. The active edges in the model returned by the solver (that is, the edges whose activity variables are assigned the value 1) comprise the sought-for path from s to t. Note that the neighbor constraints guarantee that s is connected to t.

Solving path-finding with a SAT solver is overkill since it can be solved with a polynomial algorithm, however SAT may be useful if the solution should satisfy additional user-given constraints. Consider the problem of Path-Finding under Constraints (PFUC) [12] defined as follows.

In PFUC, the input comprises a graph $G = (V, E)$, a source $s \in V$, a target $t \in V$, and an arbitrary bit-vector formula $F(E \cup V \cup A)$, where:

1. E are Boolean variables representing the edge activity.
2. V are Boolean variables representing the vertex activity.
3. A is a set of arbitrary auxiliary Boolean and bit-vector variables.

---

[1] Neighbor constraints are cardinality constraints, which can easily be translated to CNF (see [5] for a review).

---

1. Create a Boolean variable for every vertex and edge representing its *activity*, where a vertex/edge is active iff it appears on the solution path from s to t.
2. Create *edge consistency* constraints: for each edge $e = (v, u)$, create the following constraint: $e \implies v \wedge u$ (i.e., both vertices of an active edge are active).
3. Create *neighbor constraints*: ensure that each vertex v has exactly n active neighbor edges, where:
   (a) n=0 if the vertex is inactive
   (b) n=1 if v is the source or the target
   (c) n=2 if v is an active *internal* vertex (that is, neither the source nor the target)

Fig. 1. Modeling path-finding with constraints

Given a model for F, α, let $E^\alpha \subseteq E$ be the subset of edges assigned to 1 in α and $V(E^\alpha) \subseteq V$ be the subset of the vertices touched by E^α. We call the graph $G(V(E^\alpha), E^\alpha)$ the *solution graph* induced by α.

In PFUC, the output should be either a model α for F, such that there exists a path from s to t in the solution graph, or UNSAT, if no such model exists. If the problem is satisfiable, a desirable optimization requirement is to decrease the overall cost of the active edges.

PFUC can be solved by applying a SAT solver using the following two sets of clauses as input: those generated by path-finding encoding in Fig. 1 and the input bit-vector formula F translated to clauses. The problem is that such a CBC-based solution does not scale [12]. This is because neither the decision heuristic nor the conflict analysis components of the SAT solver are aware of the high-level problem at hand. Below we sketch a CBD-based solution that is based on the solution provided in [12]. It had previously been hinted at in [4].

First, activity variables and edge consistency constraints (entries 1 and 2 in Fig. 1) are created. The neighbor constraints (entry 3 in Fig. 1) are no longer required. Instead, the decision strategy will guarantee that there exists a (short) path from s to t in the solution graph.

Second, SAT solver's decision strategy is replaced by a strategy that builds an explicit walk from s to t using an incremental shortest-path algorithm, such as the Ramalingam-Reps algorithm [17] in [4] or the lazy A*-based flow in [12]. The new decision strategy strategy constructs such a walk in a stack $\pi = \left\{ s \xrightarrow{e_1} v_1 \ldots v_{k-1} \xrightarrow{e_k} l \right\}$. At the beginning, π contains the source s only. The algorithm will extend π following the suggestions of the shortest-path algorithm, where the shortest-path algorithm is allowed to use active and unassigned edges only. More specifically, assume that the solver has to take a decision; assume also that e is the next edge suggested by the shortest-path algorithm to be picked to connect the latest π's vertex l to t. If e is unassigned, the algorithm will push e to the back of π and activate e (by taking the decision which assigns e's activity variable the value 1). If e has already been assigned 1 by Boolean

Constraint Propagation (BCP), e is pushed to the back of π, and the shortest-path algorithm is queried for the next edge. After the SAT solver backtracks, the algorithm pops any unassigned edges from the back of π. After the walk from s to t is completed, the solver deactivates any unassigned edges to reduce the solution cost and then reverts to the default decision heuristic.

Third, the conflict analysis of the solver is extended as follows. Whenever there is no longer any path from the latest π's vertex l to t (because some vertices were deactivated as a result of propagation in F), the solver records a new clause that comprises the negation of the *conflict cut*–a subset of the inactive vertices that blocks any path from l (and s) to t.

Figure 2 illustrates the algorithm. Consider the initial position in Fig. 2a. The algorithm starts by extending π rightward from $s = (0,0)$ towards $t = (3,0)$ by activating the edge $(0,0)$–$(1,0)$. After that decision, two vertices become inactive as a result of Boolean Constraint Propagation as shown in Fig. 2b. The solver has to backtrack to $(0,0)$ and continue the walk towards t. As shown in Fig. 2c, when the solver reaches the vertex $(3,2)$ there is a conflict as no path from $(3,2)$ to t exists. The conflict cut comprises the following set $\{(2,0),(3,1)\}$. Note that when the conflict cut's vertices are inactive, any path from s to t is blocked. The solver records the conflict cut as a clause, which triggers the SAT solver's conflict analysis and backtracking engines. The situation after backtracking is shown in Fig. 2d. Extending the walk from that point on to t is straightforward. The eventual solution is shown in Fig. 2e.

After a solution is found, a simple post-processing algorithm can be applied to eliminate any cycles in the solution graph [12]. In our example this would have resulted in the active edge $(0,0)$–$(1,0)$ being deactivated.

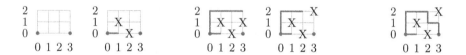

(a) Start   (b) Can't go right (c) A conflict (d) After backtracking   (e) Done

Fig. 2. Solving PFUC: trace example. Each intersection of the grid lines comprises a vertex. Assume that $s = (0,0)$ and $t = (3,0)$ and that the following CNF formula is provided: $\neg(1,0) \vee \neg(2,0)$, $\neg(1,0) \vee \neg(1,1)$, $\neg(3,2) \vee \neg(3,1)$. Bold red edges correspond to π. "X" marks inactive vertices. (Color figure online)

A CBD-based solution works well for the PFUC problem, since PFUC is comprised of two sub-problems, one better suited to a heuristic approach (finding a short path) and the other to constraint solving (solving the user-given constraints).

3   Routing Under Constraints

This section sketches [12]'s formulation and CBD-based solution to the problem of Routing under Constraints (RUC), which is required as background to our PRUC solution.

Consider first the following *routing* problem. Let $G = (V, E)$ be a non-negatively weighted simple graph. Let $N_{i \in \{0...m-1\}} \subseteq V$ be m pairwise disjoint non-empty subsets of G's vertices, called the *nets*, where the vertices of each net are called the *terminals*. A *routing* (comprising a solution for the routing problem) is a forest of *net routings* $E_{i \in \{0...m-1\}} \subseteq E$, such that all N_i's terminals are connected in N_i's net routing and all the net routings are pairwise vertex-disjoint. See an input example in Fig. 4a and an example of a solution in Fig. 4b. In practice, solutions minimizing the overall routing cost are preferred. To solve the routing problem, heuristic approaches are commonly applied – see [1] for a survey.

Consider now the RUC problem. In RUC, the input comprises an instance of the routing problem (that is, a graph $G = (V, E)$ and nets $N_{i \in \{0...m-1\}} \subseteq V$) and, in addition, a bit-vector formula $F(E \cup V \cup N \cup A)$, where the variables have the following semantics:

1. E are Boolean variables representing the edge activity.
2. V are Boolean variables representing the vertex activity.
3. N are bit-vector variables defined as follows: for every vertex v, a bit-vector variable $0 \le nid(v) \in N < m$ of width $\lceil log_2 m - 1 \rceil$ represents the unique net id of active vertices, where the *net id* of net N_i is the index i.
4. A is a set of arbitrary auxiliary Boolean and bit-vector variables.

Let R be an RUC instance and α be an assignment to $E \cup V \cup N \cup A$, then α satisfies R if and only if all the conditions in Fig. 3 hold.

---

1. *Routing correctness*: any two terminals of the same net N_i are connected in the solution graph $G(V(E^\alpha), E^\alpha)$ and any two terminals of two different nets are disconnected in $G(V(E^\alpha), E^\alpha)$
2. *Net boundary consistency*: for each vertex $v \in V : 0 \le nid(v) < m$
3. *Terminal consistency*: for each terminal $t \in N_i : nid(t) = i$
4. *Net edge consistency*: for each edge $e = (v, u)$, $e \implies v \wedge u \wedge (nid(v) = nid(u))$ (i.e., both vertices of an active edge are active and they share the net id)

Fig. 3. RUC consistency

We now sketch [12]'s CBD-based solution for RUC.

Recall that any CBD-based solution is comprised of constraints and a decision strategy. In our case, the constraints part is composed of net boundary consistency, terminal consistency, and net edge consistency shown in Fig. 3. The routing correctness is ensured by the decision strategy.

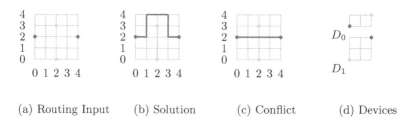

(a) Routing Input   (b) Solution   (c) Conflict   (d) Devices

Fig. 4. A routing example on a 5×5 solid grid graph, given two nets of two terminals each $N_0 = \{(0,2),(4,2)\}$ and $N_1 = \{(2,0),(2,3)\}$. It also serves as a place & route example, given two devices $D_0 = \{(2,1)_1,(0,0)_0\}$ and $D_1 = \{(2,2)_0,(0,0)_1\}$. Assume the edges' weights are 1. (Color figure online)

The basic idea behind the decision strategy is to route the nets one by one, where, within each net, the terminals are routed one by one. Specifically, assume that the terminal t_i of net $N_i = \{t_0, t_1, \ldots, t_{|N_i|-1}\}$ is to be routed. Let the current *net vertices* be the set $V(N_i)$ of vertices, connected to the already routed terminals $\{t_0, \ldots, t_{i-1}\}$ by active edges. The algorithm will connect t_i to the net vertices using the PFUC algorithm of Sect. 2 (with some extensions to conflict analysis, discussed below).

Consider, for example, the problem in Fig. 4a (no constraints are provided). Routing the blue net N_1, followed by the red net N_0 yields the solution in Fig. 4b. Assume the solver picked the other net ordering, i.e., that it started routing the red net N_0 first. That would result in the net conflict shown in Fig. 4c, where a *net conflict* is a situation in which a *conflicting net* N_c (N_1 in our example) is blocked by other nets and inactive vertices.

In case of a net conflict, let the *conflict cut* be a set of inactive vertices and vertices of net id $nid(v) \neq c$ which block the path from the current terminal of the conflicting net N_c to $V(N_c)$. In our example, the conflict cut is $\{(0,2),(1,2),(2,2),(3,2),(4,2)\}$. The solver will add a new clause, which disallows the conflict cut. The clause will contain the inactive vertices in the cut, and, in addition, any active vertex v of net id $nid(v) \neq c$ in the cut will contribute to the clause one bit on which the values of $nid(v)$ and c differ. In our example, the net id comprises a single bit, and the clause will look as follows: $\{nid(0,2), nid(1,2), nid(2,2), nid(3,2), nid(4,2)\}$. Adding the clause will trigger the solver's conflict analysis and backtracking engines. In our case, it will block the red path shown in Fig. 4c. The solver will keep constructing and blocking red paths until a red path going above the blue terminal $(2,3)$, and thus not blocking the blue net N_1, will be found.

Our example demonstrates that the order in which the nets are routed is critical. To speed up the algorithm, two net reordering algorithms were proposed in [12]: net swapping and net restarting. Both techniques are applied when a conflicting net N_c is blocked more times than a certain user-given threshold. Net swapping swaps the order between N_c and the latest net N_i blocking N_c. It then backtracks to the latest point where N_c is unassigned and starts routing

N_c. Net restarting moves N_c to the top of the net list and carries out a full restart. The algorithm will start routing N_c right after the restart. The combination of these techniques (where the net restarting threshold is higher than the net swapping threshold) has been shown to be extremely efficient [12]. Note that applying either one of the net reordering techniques would have solved the example instance in Fig. 4a after the conflict shown in Fig. 4c without any further conflicts.

4   Simultaneous Place and Route Under Constraints

As we have mentioned, the routing stage follows the placement stage in the CAD process. More specifically, placement lays out the user-given devices on a grid, and routing connects them. Below, for simplicity of presentation, we assume that the grid is 2-dimensional; our algorithms, however, are equally applicable to 3-dimensional grids.

The input to the Place and Route under Constraints (PRUC) problem contains the following components:

1. A rectangle $R = \{R_x, R_y\}$, serving as the grid.
2. A graph $G(V, E)$, whose each vertex $v_i \equiv (v_i^x \in [0, R_x - 1], v_i^y \in [0, R_y - 1]) \in V$ is a point in R. We do not apply any restrictions on the edges (normally, the edges are induced by the specific connectivity model of the input design).
3. A non-empty set of devices, where a *device* $D_i = \left\{ L_i^0, \ldots, L_i^{|D_i|-1} \right\}$ is a set of leaves, each *leaf* $L_i^j = (x_i^j, y_i^j)_{n_i^j}$ containing the leaf's *relative coordinates* (x_i^j, y_i^j) w.r.t to the device's root and the leaf's *net id* n_i^j. See the definition of D_0 and D_1 in Fig. 4's caption and their illustration in Fig. 4d for an example. An optional *placement rectangle* $R_i \subseteq R$, where the device's root is to be placed, is provided for each device. R_i defaults to R.
4. A bit-vector formula $F(E \cup V \cup N \cup A)$ (the semantics of the variables being similar to those presented in Sect. 3 in the context of RUC).

Informally, given a satisfiable PRUC instance, a PRUC solver should return a placement for all the devices (where a vertex cannot be occupied by more than one terminal) and a solution for the RUC instance, induced by the placement. We need some more notations to formalize PRUC's output.

Given a device D_i, the vertex $r_i \equiv (r_i[x], r_i[y]) \in V$ is a *potential root*, if, for each leaf $L_i^j = (x_i^j, y_i^j)_{n_i^j}$, the leaf's *terminal* $t(L_i^j, r_i) \equiv (r_i[x] + x_i^j, r_i[y] + y_i^j)$, given r_i, lies within R_i. The set of all potential roots of D_i is denoted by $roots(D_i)$.

The example device D_1 in Fig. 4 has the following potential roots, given a 5×5 solid grid graph: $roots(D_1) = \{(0,0), (1,0), (2,0), (0,1), (1,1), (2,1), (0,2), (1,2), (2,2)\}$.

Placing a device D_i at an *actual root* vertex $r_i \equiv (r_i[x], r_i[y]) \in V$, means creating a terminal $t(L_i^j, r_i) \equiv (r_i[x] + x_i^j, r_i[y] + y_i^j)$ for each leaf $L_i^j = (x_i^j, y_i^j)_{n_i^j}$.

It must hold that the terminal $t(L_i^j, r_i)$ is active (i.e., the activity variable of the terminal's vertex is turned on) and that its net id matches that of the leaf (that is, $nid(t(L_i^j, r_i)) = n_i^j$). In addition, each vertex can serve as a terminal for at most one leaf (in other words, at most one device can occupy a vertex).

For example, the routing instance in Fig. 4a could have been created by placing the two devices in Fig. 4d on a 5×5 solid grid graph as follows: D_0 is placed at $(0, 2)$ (creating the red terminal $(0,2)$ and the blue terminal $(2, 3)$), while D_1 is placed at $(2, 0)$ (creating the remaining two terminals).

Formally, a satisfying assignment to a PRUC instance comprises:

1. A placement for each device D_i (that is, each D_i is mapped to an actual root).
2. A solution for the RUC instance, comprising $G(V, E)$, the formula $F(E \cup V \cup N \cup A)$, and nets $N_{k \in \{0...m-1\}}$, where each net N_k is comprised of the terminals of all the leaves with net id k.

As in the case of PFUC and RUC, a desirable optimization requirement is to decrease the overall cost of the active edges. A PRUC should return UNSAT, given an unsatisfiable instance.

Note that RUC is a special case of PRUC, where all the devices are fixed (that is, their placement rectangle is fixed to one particular location). It was shown in [12] that RUC cannot be efficiently solved with either a CBC-based encoding or with the graph-aware solver Monosat [4]. Even more so, neither can PRUC be efficiently solved by these means. Below we introduce our CBD-based PRUC solution, which comprises a set of constraints (Sect. 4.1), a decision strategy (Sect. 4.2), and performance optimization heuristics (Sect. 4.3).

4.1   Constraints

For each device D_i and each potential root $r_i \in roots(D_i)$, we create a Boolean *potential root engagement* variable $e(r_i)$. Intuitively, $e(r_i)$ is 1 iff D_i is placed at r_i. Now we are ready to present the constraints:

1. Net boundary consistency and net edge consistency constraints are inherited from the RUC solution in Fig. 3.
2. *Placement consistency*: for each device D_i, exactly one of its potential root engagement variables holds.
3. *Leaf consistency*: for each device D_i and each potential root engagement variable $e(r_i)$: if $e(r_i)$ holds, then, for each leaf $L_i^j = (x_i^j, y_i^j)_{n_i^j} \in D_i$, the terminal vertex $t(L_i^j, r_i)$ is active, and it holds that $nid(t(L_i^j, r_i)) = n_i^j$.
4. *Placement uniqueness*: For every vertex v, if the vertex can serve as a terminal for more than one leaf, then at most one of the relevant potential root engagement variables (that is, the potential root engagement variables for roots, which, when used to place a device D_i, render v a terminal) holds. In our example in Fig. 4, the vertex $(4, 2)$ can serve as a terminal for the leaves $L_0^0 \equiv (2, 1)_1$ (if D_0 is placed at $(2, 1)$) and $L_1^0 \equiv (2, 2)_0$ (if D_1 is placed at $(2, 0)$). Hence, the following cardinality constraint is created for the vertex $(4, 2)$: at-most-1($e(r_0 \equiv (2, 1))$, $e(r_1 \equiv (2, 0))$).

Note that the high-level constraints are expressed in terms of standard bit-vector operators and cardinality constraints. Thus, the constraints can easily be translated to propositional clauses [5, 9].

4.2 Decision Strategy

Our basic decision strategy goes as follows. For each device D_i, in the user-given order, we place the device at some potential root r_i (by turning on r_i's potential root engagement variable) and then route the device. To route a device D_i we proceed as follows: for every leaf $L_i^j = (x_i^j, y_i^j)_{n_i^j} \in D_i$ in the user-given order, we connect the newly created terminal $t(L_i^j, r_i)$ to n_i^j's net vertices $V(n_i^j)$ (net vertices are all the vertices connected to the already routed terminals of net n_i^j by active edges) using the PFUC algorithm, explained in Sect. 2 (with some modifications to net conflict analysis, explained below).

Placement Heuristic. We introduce our placement heuristic (that is, the heuristic the decision strategy uses for picking the actual root for the device) after providing some additional notations.

Assume the decision strategy is about to place a device D_i. We call a potential root $r_i \in roots(D_i)$ *available*, if its engagement variable $e(r_i)$ is unassigned or assigned 1[2]. For a device D_i, let D_i's net id's $N(D_i)$ be the set of the nets associated with D_i's leaves. A net N_h is *fresh* if N_h does not belong to $N(D_j)$ for any of the already placed devices D_j. D_i is *fresh* if all of D_i's nets are fresh (in other words, a device D_i is fresh if and only if none of net ids of the already placed terminals belongs to $N(D_i)$).

Assume we need to place a fresh device D_i. In this case we place the device as close to the center of the grid R as possible. More specifically, we strive to minimize the overall cost of the shortest paths in G from the terminals, created by placing the device, to the center[3]. The reason we chose this heuristic is because the closer the device is to the border of the grid the more difficult it is to route (since the borders restrict the routing options). More specifically, our algorithm works as follows. We run Breadth-First-Search (BFS) starting at the center of the grid and working outwards towards its borders. We pick the first available root $r_i \in roots(D_i)$, such that all D_i's terminals, given r_i, were visited by BFS. Note that the placement consistency constraints ensure that one of the roots must be available. Placement uniqueness constraints ensure that there exists a location, not occupied by another device.

Now assume we are about to place a non-fresh device D_i. We place D_i so as to minimize the overall cost of the paths from the terminals, generated by placing

---

[2] Let r_i be a potential root of a device D_i that is about to be placed by the decision strategy. The engagement variable $e(r_i)$ can already be assigned 1 at this point if Boolean Constraint Propagation (BCP) has been able to conclude that r_i is the only potential root of D_i where the device can be placed.

[3] The center is the vertex $(R_x/2, R_y/2)$, if available, or, otherwise, the vertex whose Manhattan distance from $(R_x/2, R_y/2)$ is as small as possible.

D_i, to the net vertices of the non-fresh nets. Such a heuristic is useful both for increasing the odds that the placement will be routable and for decreasing the overall routing cost to meet the optimization requirement. More specifically, our algorithm works as follows. For every vertex v and non-fresh net N_h, we calculate the cost $c(v, N_h)$ of the shortest path from v to N_h's net vertices $V(N_h)$. This can be done by running BFS starting from $V(N_h)$ for each non-fresh net N_h. For every v, let $c(v)$ be the sum of the costs $c(v, N_h)$ across all the non-fresh nets. We place D_i at the root $r_i \in roots(D_i)$ which minimizes the sum of the $c(v)$'s for all D_i's terminals, given r_i. To further improve efficiency, one can run the BFS searches which start at the non-fresh nets in parallel and halt once the first available root is reached.

Net Conflict Analysis. Our PRUC algorithm applies the PFUC algorithm, presented in Sect. 2, to connect the current terminal t of net N_h (created by placing leaf $L_i^j = (x_i^j, y_i^j)_{h \equiv n_i^j}$ of the currently routed device D_i) to $V(N_h)$. Assume that PFUC encounters a net conflict, that is, that all the paths from t to $V(N_h)$ are blocked by the conflict cut, which comprises inactive vertices and vertices of net id $nid(v) \neq h$. Our proposed conflict analysis algorithm is based on the conflict analysis algorithm of the RUC solution, described in Sect. 3.

Recall that the RUC solution records a conflict clause C comprising the inactive vertices in the cut, and that any active vertex v of net id $nid(v) \neq h$ in the cut contributes to the clause one bit on which the values of $nid(v)$ and h differ. Note that, unlike in the case of RUC, where the terminals are static, the terminals are created by placing devices for PRUC. For the net conflict to occur, two dynamically created terminals of net N_h must be separated by the conflict cut. One such terminal is created by placing the currently routed device D_i, while the other terminal can belong to any previously placed device whose set of nets includes N_h. Hence, we must augment the conflict clause C with two additional literals:

1. The negation of the actual root's engagement variable $e(r_i)$ of the currently routed device D_i, and
2. The negation of the actual root's engagement variable $e(r_w)$ of one of the previously placed devices D_w, whose set of nets includes N_h.

Example. Consider Fig. 4. Assume the algorithm is given a 5×5 grid and the devices D_0 and D_1 (in that order). The algorithm will start by placing the device D_0 as close as possible to the center. The minimal distance to the center is 3 for several potential roots, $(0, 2)$ included. Assume $(0, 2)$ is picked as the actual root, so D_0 is placed as shown in Fig. 4a. The set of net vertices is empty for both nets before placing D_0, so no routing is required for the newly created terminals. The algorithm will continue by placing D_1. The minimal combined distance to the net vertices of both nets is 7 for several roots, including $(2, 0)$. Assume the algorithm picks the root $(2, 0)$ for placing D_1. Figure 4a reflects the situation after the placement. Next, the algorithm will route the red terminal

$(4, 2)$ (of the leaf $L_1^0 \equiv (2, 2)_0$) to connect it to $V(N_0) = \{(0, 2)\}$. The situation after completing this routing is shown in Fig. 4c.

The algorithm will then attempt to connect the blue terminal $(2, 0)$ (of the leaf $L_1^1 \equiv (0, 0)_1$) to $V(N_1) = \{(2, 3)\}$. It will immediately encounter a net conflict (since the path from $(2, 0)$ to $(2, 3)$ is blocked by the red net N_0), and record a conflict clause. The clause will include the net id variables' bits $\{nid(0,2),$ $nid(1,2), nid(2,2), nid(3,2), nid(4,2)\}$ and the negation of the actual root engagement variables for both devices, namely, $\neg e(r_0 \equiv (0, 2))$ and $\neg e(r_1 \equiv (2, 0))$.

The algorithm will then keep routing the terminals generated by the first placement it chose, and will, eventually, succeed. More specifically, the solver will keep constructing and blocking red paths until a red path going above the blue terminal $(2, 3)$ (and thus not blocking the blue net N_1) is found (exactly as in the RUC case).

The basic PRUC algorithm presented so far is functional but inefficient. As our example demonstrates, the algorithm will preserve the current device ordering, leaf ordering and the initial placement picked by the algorithm. Such an approach is not sufficiently dynamic.

4.3 Performance Optimization Heuristics

We propose three performance optimization heuristics to improve the efficiency of the algorithm. As we shall see, each of the proposed techniques solves the example we discussed at the end of Sect. 4.2 right after the first conflict and without any further conflicts.

For the currently routed device D_i, let its *root decision level* be the decision level of its actual root engagement variable.

Consider each technique separately for now. We will discuss how to combine the heuristics a bit later.

Leaf Reordering. *Leaf reordering* is about reordering the leaves of the currently routed device D_i when routing the terminal of a certain leaf L_i^j. Leaf reordering is applied after encountering a user-given number of conflicts, initialized with 0 each time the algorithm starts routing the device. The technique simply moves L_i^j to the beginning of the leaf list of D_i, backtracks to D_i's root decision level, and starts routing D_i in the new order.

Consider the conflict shown in Fig. 4c and discussed at the end of Sect. 4.2. Applying leaf reordering at that point would switch the order of D_1's leaves. The algorithm would then route the blue terminal $(2, 0)$ first, followed by the red terminal $(4, 2)$. That would yield the solution in Fig. 4b without further conflicts.

Device Replacement. *Device replacement* is about trying out different placements for the currently routed device, rather than sticking to one particular placement. Device replacement works as follows: when a certain conflict threshold is reached, after the algorithm starts routing the currently routed device D_i, the algorithm backtracks to D_i's root decision level and places D_i at the *next* available root w.r.t to the current ordering: that is, either the distance from the center, if D_i is fresh, or, otherwise, the overall distance to the net vertices of the non-fresh nets of the device. If no next available root is available, replacement cycles back to the *first* root in the current ordering.

In our example, the device replacement algorithm could have moved device D_1 to several possible locations equidistant from the existing nets, $(2, 2)$ being one of them. Assume that D_1 is placed at $(2, 2)$. The following solution would then be generated without any further conflicts:

Device Reordering. *Device reordering* is about reordering the devices right after a certain conflict threshold is encountered after the algorithm starts routing the currently routed device D_i. The technique moves D_i to the top of the list of devices, carries out a full restart (that is, backtracks to decision level 0) and starts placing and routing in the new order, i.e., D_i will be the first one to be placed and routed.

In our example, switching the order of the devices, placing D_1 first followed by D_0, will still result in the placement in Fig. 4a. However, the algorithm will route without any further conflicts, since the blue leaf comes first for device D_0; hence the blue net N_1 will be routed first, followed by the red net N_0, yielding the solution in Fig. 4b.

Combining Performance Optimization Heuristics. The three heuristics differ w.r.t to their locality.

Leaf reordering is the most local of the three, since it is applied given one particular device and one concrete placement. Device replacement is more global, since it can change the actual placement of the current device. Device reordering is the most global of the three techniques, since it changes the global device ordering, and also requires a full restart.

To combine the three heuristics, one can try them all out starting with the more local leaf reordering, followed by the more global device replacement, followed by the yet more global device reordering. To this end, the leaf reordering conflict threshold should be the smallest, followed by the device replacement threshold, and finally by the device reordering threshold.

For the combination to work, conflict counting towards the next device replacement and the next device reordering must *not* be restarted when leaf reordering occurs for the currently routed device. Likewise, conflict counting towards the next device reordering must not be restarted when device replacement occurs.

5 Experimental Results

Our experiments on industrial and crafted instances are described below. We used machines with 32 GB of memory running Intel® Xeon® processors with 3 GHz CPU frequency. The timeout was set to 20 min for all the experiments.

5.1 Industrial

We experimented with 48 clips of Intel's designs. Each such clip is currently solved by a proprietary industrial place and route flow that applies placement first followed by routing. On average it takes about 24 hours to solve one clip with 60 to 85 invocations of the place and route flow. Multiple invocations are needed since the placer sometimes fails to generate a routable routing instance.

In our experiments, we aim to demonstrate the potential usefulness of applying our algorithms in industrial settings. Another goal is to study the impact of applying and combining the three performance optimization heuristics presented in Sect. 4.3: leaf reordering, device replacement, and device reordering. We generated 48 different configurations by combining the following conflict thresholds for the three heuristics, where ∞ means that the technique is not applied at all:

1: **for all** $lro \in \{3, 10, 25, \infty\}$ **do**
2:     **for all** $drp \in \{3, 10, 25, 100, \infty\}$ **do**
3:         **for all** $dro \in \{3, 10, 25, 100, 1000, \infty\}$ **do**
4:             **if** $(lro = \infty$ or $(lro < drp$ and $lro < dro))$ and $(drp = \infty$ or $drp < dro)$ **then**
5:             Generate a configuration (lro, drp, dro) with leaf reordering threshold lro, device replacing threshold drp, and device reordering threshold dro.

Note that based on the conclusions of Sect. 4.3 we let the leaf reordering conflict threshold always be the smallest one, followed by the device replacement threshold, and then by the device reordering threshold.

Table 1 shows the results for the best 12 configurations in terms of solved instances within the time-out of 20 min (the 'Time in sec.' column shows the overall run-time, where the time-out value of 1200 s is added for unsolved instances).

The best performing configuration, solving 44/48 instances within 20 min, is $(\infty, 3, 25)$. Hence, combining frequent device replacement with frequent device reordering yields the best results. Leaf reordering, on the other hand, does not contribute, based on these results. The configuration (∞, ∞, ∞) (that is, none of the three performance optimization heuristics is applied) does not appear in the table, since it solved only 14 instances.

Additional analysis revealed that the 4 instances that remained unsolved by the best configuration $(\infty, 3, 25)$ are solved by at least one of the following 3 configurations: $(\infty, 10, 100)$, $(\infty, 10, 25)$, and $(10, 25, 100)$. Interestingly, one of the instances is solved solely by two configurations which apply leaf reordering– $(10, 25, 100)$ and $(10, \infty, 25)$. This result hints that although leaf reordering was not found to be useful overall, it can still contribute to solving some instances.

<table>
<tr><td colspan="5">**Table 1.** Best configs for industrial</td></tr>
</table>

lro	drp	dro	Solved	Time in sec.
∞	3	25	44	16823
∞	∞	10	40	18641
∞	10	25	40	16463
∞	∞	25	40	16880
3	∞	10	39	19593
10	∞	25	39	18068
∞	3	10	38	17763
3	∞	25	38	16675
∞	10	100	36	24422
∞	∞	3	36	22623
10	25	100	35	24346
∞	3	100	35	23824

Table 2. Best configs for crafted

lro	drp	dro	Solved	Time in sec.
∞	3	10	30	1914
∞	3	25	30	8932
∞	∞	3	30	16046
3	10	25	29	10683
∞	3	100	29	12503
∞	∞	10	29	15459
3	10	100	28	19598
∞	10	25	27	15008
3	∞	25	22	17558
3	∞	10	20	16734
∞	25	100	19	24116
10	∞	25	18	27598

The new CBD-based tool is as good as the existing industrial solution in terms of quality. The average wire length is almost identical; the difference is 0.6% (the new approach being slightly better). This is ultimately because both the existing heuristical solution and the new CBD-based tool are based on shortest-path algorithms. In addition, physical design experts have confirmed that the quality of the new tool is as good as that of the existing solution.

5.2 Crafted

This section analyzes the performance of our algorithms on PRUC instances we crafted. All the benchmarks and detailed results are publicly available at [11]. We pursued two goals:

1. To generate challenging yet solvable publicly available PRUC instances to encourage further PRUC research, and
2. To further analyze the performance of leaf reordering, device replacement, and device reordering.

The instances were generated as follows.

First, we used a 100×100 solid grid graph. It was shown in [12] that reducing RUC (being PRUC's special case) to either bit-vector reasoning or Monosat [4] solver input does not scale to grids of such a size, even on simple instances.

Second, we used 5×5 devices with 4 leaves, each leaf using random relative coordinates (within the rectangle $(0,0)$–$(4,4)$) and a random net.

Third, according to our preliminary experiments, it made sense to use 10 devices and 40 nets for each instance in order to create instances which are challenging enough yet not too difficult to solve.

Fourth, each instance was augmented with $(C/100) * |V|$ binary clauses, where $|V| = 10000$ and C is a parameter. The clauses are generated as follows: pick a random vertex $v = (x, y)$ and another random vertex u sharing either the x or y coordinate with v, and add the clause $\neg v \vee \neg u$.

All in all, we generated 30 random instances as follows:

1: **for all** $C \in \{0, 15, 30\}$ **do**
2:     **for all** $i \in \{1, 2, 3, 4, 5, 6, 7, 8, 9, 10\}$ **do**
3:         Generate a PRUC instance on a 100×100 grid with 10 5×5 devices with 4 leaves each, each leaf using random relative coordinates within the rectangle $(0, 0)$–$(4, 4)$ and a random net with net id in the interval $[0 - 39]$. In addition, generate $(C/100) * 10000$ random binary clauses as described above.

We used the same 48 configurations we had experimented with in Sect. 5.1. Consider the results in Table 2, showing the best 12 configurations in terms of the number of instances solved. The absolutely best configuration, which solved all the instances 4.5 times faster than the next best configuration, is $(\infty, 3, 10)$. Hence, combining frequent device replacement with frequent device reordering yields the best results for crafted instances, similarly to our experiments with industrial instances, with an even smaller device reordering conflict threshold. Leaf reordering does not seem to be helpful for the crafted instances. The configuration (∞, ∞, ∞), which applies none of the three performance optimization techniques, solved none of the instances.

6   Conclusion

This paper highlights a novel paradigm for reducing a problem to constraint solving, which we called Correct-by-Decision (CBD). In CBD, the problem is reduced to a set of constraints and a decision strategy, where the decision strategy is essential for guaranteeing correctness. We saw that CBD is useful when the problem is composed of two interleaved sub-problems, one of which has an easy heuristical solution, while the other requires solving a set of constraints.

Furthermore, we proposed a CBD-based solution to a critical industrial problem that shows up in the physical design stage of the CAD process: simultaneous place and route under arbitrary constraints (design rules), which we called PRUC. We demonstrated that our approach can successfully cope with industrial instances and analyzed the performance of different heuristics we proposed on these instances. We also crafted challenging publicly available PRUC instances and studied the performance of our algorithms on these instances.

References

1. Abboud, N., Grötschel, M., Koch, T.: Mathematical methods for physical layout of printed circuit boards: an overview. OR Spectr. **30**(3), 453–468 (2008)
2. Audemard, G., Lagniez, J.-M., Simon, L.: Improving glucose for incremental SAT solving with assumptions: application to MUS extraction. In: Järvisalo, M., Van Gelder, A. (eds.) SAT 2013. LNCS, vol. 7962, pp. 309–317. Springer, Heidelberg (2013). doi:10.1007/978-3-642-39071-5_23

3. Barrett, C., Donham, J.: Combining SAT methods with non-clausal decision heuristics. Electr. Notes Theor. Comput. Sci. **125**(3), 3–12 (2005)
4. Bayless, S., Bayless, N., Hoos, H.H., Hu, A.J.: SAT modulo monotonic theories. In: Bonet, B., Koenig, S. (eds.) Proceedings of the Twenty-Ninth AAAI Conference on Artificial Intelligence, 25–30 January 2015, Austin, Texas, USA, pp. 3702–3709. AAAI Press, New York (2015)
5. Biere, A., Le Berre, D., Lonca, E., Manthey, N.: Detecting cardinality constraints in CNF. In: Sinz, C., Egly, U. (eds.) [20], pp. 285–301
6. Brummayer, R., Biere, A.: Lemmas on demand for the extensional theory of arrays. JSAT **6**(1–3), 165–201 (2009)
7. Eén, N., Sörensson, N.: An extensible SAT-solver. In: Giunchiglia, E., Tacchella, A. (eds.) SAT 2003. LNCS, vol. 2919, pp. 502–518. Springer, Heidelberg (2004). doi:10.1007/978-3-540-24605-3_37
8. Erez, A., Nadel, A.: Finding bounded path in graph using SMT for automatic clock routing. In: Kroening, D., Păsăreanu, C.S. (eds.) CAV 2015. LNCS, vol. 9207, pp. 20–36. Springer, Cham (2015). doi:10.1007/978-3-319-21668-3_2
9. Hadarean, L.: An efficient and trustworthy theory solver for bit-vectors in satisfiability modulo theories. Dissertation, New York University (2015)
10. Khasidashvili, Z., Nadel, A.: Implicative simultaneous satisfiability and applications. In: Eder, K., Lourenço, J., Shehory, O. (eds.) HVC 2011. LNCS, vol. 7261, pp. 66–79. Springer, Heidelberg (2012). doi:10.1007/978-3-642-34188-5_9
11. Nadel, A.: A correct-by-decision solution for simultaneous place and route: benchmarks and detailed results. https://goo.gl/MNl1PE
12. Nadel, A.: Routing under constraints. In: Piskac, R., Talupur, M. (eds.) 2016 Formal Methods in Computer-Aided Design, FMCAD 2016, Mountain View, CA, USA, 3–6 October 2016, pp. 125–132. IEEE, Washington, D.C. (2016)
13. Nadel, A., Ryvchin, V.: Efficient SAT solving under assumptions. In: Cimatti, A., Sebastiani, R. (eds.) SAT 2012. LNCS, vol. 7317, pp. 242–255. Springer, Heidelberg (2012). doi:10.1007/978-3-642-31612-8_19
14. Nadel, A., Ryvchin, V., Strichman, O.: Ultimately incremental SAT. In: Sinz, C., Egly, U. (eds.) [20], pp. 206–218
15. Nag, S., Rutenbar, R.A.: Performance-driven simultaneous place and route for row-based FPGAs. In: DAC, pp. 301–307 (1994)
16. Nag, S.K., Rutenbar, R.A.: Performance-driven simultaneous place and route for island-style FPGAs. In: Rudell, R.L., (eds.) Proceedings of the 1995 IEEE/ACM International Conference on Computer-Aided Design, ICCAD 1995, San Jose, California, USA, 5–9 November 1995, pp. 332–338. IEEE Computer Society/ACM, Washington, D.C. (1995)
17. Ramalingam, G., Reps, T.W.: An incremental algorithm for a generalization of the shortest-path problem. J. Algorithms **21**(2), 267–305 (1996)
18. Sabharwal, A.: Symchaff: a structure-aware satisfiability solver. In: Veloso, M.M., Kambhampati, S. (eds.) Proceedings of the Twentieth National Conference on Artificial Intelligence and the Seventeenth Innovative Applications of Artificial Intelligence Conference, 9–13 July 2005, Pittsburgh, Pennsylvania, USA, pp. 467–474. AAAI Press/The MIT Press, Austin (2005)
19. Sherwani, N.A.: Algorithms for VLSI Physical Design Automation, 3rd edn. Kluwer, Dordrecht (1998)
20. Sinz, C., Egly, U. (eds.): SAT 2014. LNCS, vol. 8561. Springer, Cham (2014)

Scaling Up DPLL(T) String Solvers Using Context-Dependent Simplification

Andrew Reynolds[1], Maverick Woo[2],
Clark Barrett[3], David Brumley[2], Tianyi Liang[4],
and Cesare Tinelli[1(✉)]

[1] Department of Computer Science,
The University of Iowa, Iowa City, USA
`cesare-tinelli@uiowa.edu`
[2] CyLab, Carnegie Mellon University, Pittsburgh, USA
[3] Department of Computer Science, Stanford University, Stanford, USA
[4] Two Sigma, New York, USA

Abstract. Efficient reasoning about strings is essential to a growing number of security and verification applications. We describe satisfiability checking techniques in an extended theory of strings that includes operators commonly occurring in these applications, such as contains, index_of and replace. We introduce a novel context-dependent simplification technique that improves the scalability of string solvers on challenging constraints coming from real-world problems. Our evaluation shows that an implementation of these techniques in the SMT solver CVC4 significantly outperforms state-of-the-art string solvers on benchmarks generated using PyEx, a symbolic execution engine for Python programs. Using a test suite sampled from four popular Python packages, we show that PyEx uses only 41% of the runtime when coupled with CVC4 than when coupled with CVC4's closest competitor while achieving comparable program coverage.

1 Introduction

A growing number of applications of static analysis techniques have benefited from automated reasoning tools for string constraints. The effect of such tools on symbolic execution in particular has been transformative. At a high level, symbolic execution *runs* a program under analysis by representing its input values symbolically and tracking the program variables as expressions over these symbolic values, together with other concrete values in the program. The collected expressions are then analyzed by an automated reasoning tool to determine path feasibility at branches or other properties such as security vulnerabilities at points of interest. With the ever-increasing hardware and automated reasoning capabilities, symbolic execution has enjoyed much success in practice. A recent example in the cybersecurity realm was the DARPA Cyber Grand Challenge,[1] which featured a number of Cyber Reasoning Systems that heavily relied on symbolic execution techniques (see, e.g., [7,24]).

---

[1] See http://www.darpa.mil/program/cyber-grand-challenge.

© Springer International Publishing AG 2017
R. Majumdar and V. Kunčak (Eds.): CAV 2017, Part II, LNCS 10427, pp. 453–474, 2017.
DOI: 10.1007/978-3-319-63390-9_24

Prior to the availability of string-capable reasoning tools, developers of symbolic execution engines had to adopt various ad-hoc heuristics to cope with strings and other variable-length inputs. One popular heuristic is to impose an artificial upper-bound on the length of these inputs. Unfortunately, this not only compromises analysis accuracy, since the chosen upper bounds may be too low in face of adversarial inputs, but it also leads to inefficiencies in solvers when practitioners, in an attempt to mitigate this problem, may end up setting the upper bounds too high. To address this issue, a number of SMT solvers have been extended recently with native support for *unbounded* strings and length constraints [2,19,26,30]. These solvers have dramatically improved both in performance and robustness over the past few years, enabling a new generation of symbolic execution tools that support faithful string reasoning.

This paper revisits approaches for solving *extended string constraints*, which allow a rich language of string terms over operators such as contains, index_of and replace. Earlier techniques for extended string constraints [5,18,27,30] often rely on eager reductions to a core language of constraints, with the effect of requiring the solver to deal with fairly large or complex combination of basic constraints. For instance, encoding the constraint $\neg$contains(x, y) commonly involves bounded universal quantification over the integers, to state that string y does not occur at any position in x. In this work, we start with the observation that DPLL(T)-based SMT solvers [12] often reason in contexts where string variables are equated to (partially) concrete values. Based on this, we have developed a way to leverage efficient context-dependent simplification techniques and reduce extended constraints to a core language lazily instead.

Contribution and Significance. We extend a calculus by Liang et al. [19] to handle *extended string constraints* (i.e. constraints over substr, contains, index_of and replace) using a combination of two techniques:

- a reduction of extended string constraints to basic ones involving bounded quantification (Sect. 3.1), and
- an inference technique based on context-dependent simplification (Sect. 3.2) which supplements this reduction and in practice significantly improves the scalability of our approach on constraints coming from symbolic execution.

Additionally, we provide a new set of 25,421 publicly-available benchmarks over extended string constraints. These benchmarks were generated by running PyEx, a new symbolic executor for Python programs based on PyExZ3 [3], over a test suite of 19 target functions sampled from four popular Python packages. We discuss an experimental evaluation showing that our implementation in the SMT solver CVC4 significantly outperforms other state-of-the-art string solvers in finding models for these benchmarks.

Finally, we discuss how the superior performance of CVC4 in comparison to other solvers translates into real-life benefits for Python developers using PyEx.

Structure of the Paper. After some formal preliminaries, we briefly review a calculus for basic string constraints in Sect. 2 that is an abbreviated version of [19].

We present new techniques for extended string constraints in Sect. 3, and evaluate these techniques on real-world queries generated by PyEx σ in Sect. 5.

1.1 Related Work

The satisfiability of word equations was proven decidable by Makanin [21] and then given a PSPACE algorithm by Plandowski [22]. The decidability of the fairly restricted language of word equations with length constraints is an open problem [11]. In practice, a number of approaches for solving string and regular expression constraints rely on reductions to automata [10,15,28] or bit-vector constraints for fixed-length strings [16]. More recently, new approaches have been developed for the satisfiability problem for (unbounded) word equations and memberships with length [2,19,20,27,30] within SMT solvers. Among these, z3-STR [30] and S3 [27] are third-party extensions of the SMT solver z3 [9] adding support for string constraints via reductions to linear arithmetic and uninterpreted functions. This support includes extended string constraints over a signature similar to the one we consider in this paper. With respect to these solvers, our string solver is fully integrated into the architecture of CVC4, meaning it can be combined with other theories of CVC4, such as algebraic datatypes and arrays.

This paper is similar in scope to work by Bjørner et al. [5], which gives decidability results and an approach for string library functions, including contains and replace. As in that work, we reduce the satisfiability problem for extended string constraints to a core language with bounded quantification. We also incorporate simplification techniques that improve performance by completely or partially avoiding this reduction.

Our target application, symbolic execution, has a rich history, starting from the seminal work of King [17]. Common modern symbolic execution tools include SAGE [13], KLEE [6], S2E [8], and Mayhem [7], which are all designed to analyze low-level binary or source code. In contrast, this paper considers constraints generated from the symbolic executor PyEx, which is designed to analyze Python code and includes support for string variables.

1.2 Formal Preliminaries

We work in the context of many-sorted first-order logic with equality and assume the reader is familiar with the notions signature, term, literal, (quantified) formula, and free variable. We consider many-sorted signatures Σ that contain an (infix) logical symbol $\approx$ for equality—which has type $\sigma \times \sigma$ for all sorts σ in Σ and is always interpreted as the identity relation. We also assume signatures Σ contain the Boolean sort Bool and Boolean constant symbols $\top$ and $\bot$ for true and false. Without loss of generality, we assume $\approx$ is the only predicate symbol in Σ, as all other predicates may be modeled as functions with return sort Bool. If P is a function with return sort Bool, we will commonly write $P(t)$ as shorthand for $P(t) \approx \top$. If e is a term or a formula, we denote by $\mathcal{V}(e)$ and $\mathcal{T}(e)$ the set of free variables and subterms of e respectively, extending these notations to tuples and sets of terms or formulas as expected.

Σ_A $n :$ Int for all $n \in \mathbb{N}$ $+ :$ Int $\times$ Int $\to$ Int $- :$ Int $\to$ Int $\geqslant :$ Int $\times$ Int $\to$ Bool

Σ_S $l :$ Str for all $l \in \mathcal{A}^*$ con : Str $\times \cdots \times$ Str $\to$ Str   len : Str $\to$ Int

Σ_X substr :   Str $\times$ Int $\times$ Int $\to$ Str   contains : Str $\times$ Str $\to$ Bool
      index_of : Str $\times$ Str $\times$ Int $\to$ Int   replace :   Str $\times$ Str $\times$ Str $\to$ Str

Fig. 1. Functions in signature Σ_{ASX}. Str and Int denote strings and integers respectively.

A *theory* is a pair $T = (\Sigma, \mathbf{I})$ where Σ is a signature and $\mathbf{I}$ is a class of Σ-interpretations, the *models* of T. A Σ-formula φ is *satisfiable* (resp., *unsatisfiable*) in T if it is satisfied by some (resp., no) interpretation in $\mathbf{I}$. A set Γ of Σ-formulas *entails in* T a Σ-formula φ, written $\Gamma \models_T \varphi$, if every interpretation in $\mathbf{I}$ that satisfies all formulas in Γ satisfies φ as well. We write $\Gamma \models \varphi$ to denote entailment in the (empty) theory of equality. We say Γ *propositionally entails* φ, written $\Gamma \models_p \varphi$, if Γ entails φ when considering all atoms in γ and φ as propositional variables. Two Σ-terms or Σ-formulas are *equivalent in* T if they are satisfied by the same models of T. Two formulas φ_1 and φ_2 are *equisatisfiable in* T if $\exists \boldsymbol{x}_1. \varphi_1$ and $\exists \boldsymbol{x}_2. \varphi_2$ are equivalent in T where $\boldsymbol{x}_i$ collects the free variables of φ_i that do not occur free in φ_j with $i \neq j$.

We consider an extended theory T_{ASX} of strings and length equations, whose signature Σ_{ASX} is given in Fig. 1. We assume a fixed finite alphabet $\mathcal{A}$ of characters. The signature includes the sorts Str and Int denoting strings and integers respectively. Figure 1 divides the signature Σ_{ASX} into three parts, which we denote by Σ_A, Σ_S and Σ_X. We will write Σ_{AS} to denote $\Sigma_A \cup \Sigma_S$ and so on. The subsignature Σ_A is provided on the top line of Fig. 1 and includes the usual symbols of *linear* integer arithmetic, interpreted as expected. We will commonly write $t_1 \bowtie t_2$, with $\bowtie \in \{>, <, \leqslant\}$, as syntactic sugar for the equivalent inequality between t_1 and t_2 expressed using only $\geqslant$. The subsignature Σ_S is provided on the second line and includes: a constant symbol, or *string constant*, for each word of $\mathcal{A}^*$ (including ϵ for the empty word), interpreted as that word; a variadic function symbol con : Str $\times \ldots \times$ Str $\to$ Str, interpreted as word concatenation; and a function symbol len : Str $\to$ Int, interpreted as the word length function. The subsignature Σ_X is provided in the remainder of the figure.

We refer to the function symbols in Σ_X as *extended functions*, and terms whose top symbol is in Σ_X as *extended function terms*. A *position* in a string x is a non-negative integer smaller than the length of x that identifies a character in x — with 0 identifying the first character, 1 the second, and so on. For all x, y, z, n, m, the term substr(x, n, m) is interpreted as the maximal substring of x starting at position n with length at most m, or the empty string if n is an invalid position; contains(x, y) is interpreted as true if and only if string x contains string y; index_of(x, y, n) is interpreted as the position of the first occurrence of y in x starting at position n, or -1 if y is empty, n is an invalid position, or if no such occurrence exists; replace(x, y, z) is interpreted as the result of replacing the first occurrence in x of y by z, or just x if y is empty or x does not contain y.

An *atomic term* is either a constant or a variable. A *flat term* is a term of the form $f(x_1, \ldots, x_n)$, where $x_1, \ldots, x_n$ are variables. A *string term* is one

$$\mathsf{con}(s, \epsilon, u) \to \mathsf{con}(s, u) \qquad \mathsf{con}() \to \epsilon \quad \mathsf{con}(s) \to s$$
$$\mathsf{con}(s, \mathsf{con}(t), u) \to \mathsf{con}(s, t, u) \qquad \mathsf{con}(s, c_1 \cdots c_i, c_{i+1} \cdots c_n, u) \to \mathsf{con}(s, c_1 \cdots c_n, u)$$
$$\mathsf{len}(c_1 \cdots c_n) \to n \qquad \mathsf{len}(\mathsf{con}(s_1, \ldots, s_n)) \to \mathsf{len}\, s_1 + \cdots + \mathsf{len}\, s_n$$

Fig. 2. Simplification rules for Σ_{AS}-terms.

that contains function symbols from Σ_{SX} only. A string term is *basic* if contains function symbols from Σ_{S} only, and *extended* otherwise. A *(basic, extended) string constraint* is a (dis)equality between (basic, extended) string terms. An *arithmetic constraint* is an inequality or (dis)equality between linear combinations of atomic and/or string terms with integer sort. Notice that (dis)equalities between integer variables and constraints such as $\mathsf{len}\, x \approx \mathsf{len}\, y$ are both string and arithmetic constraints. A T_{ASX}-constraint is either a string or an arithmetic constraint. Without loss of generality, we consider the satisfiability problem for Σ_{ASX}-formulas composed of T_{ASX}-constraints only.

If E is a finite set of basic string constraints, the *congruence closure* of E is the set

$$\widehat{E} = \{s \approx t \mid s, t \in \mathcal{T}(E), E \models s \approx t\} \cup$$
$$\{s \not\approx t \mid s, t \in \mathcal{T}(E), s' \not\approx t' \in E \cup L, E \models s \approx s' \wedge t \approx t' \text{ for some } s', t'\}$$

where $L = \{l_1 \not\approx l_2 \mid \text{for all distinct } l_1, l_2 \in \mathcal{A}^*\} \cup \{\top \not\approx \bot\}$. The congruence closure of E induces an equivalence relation over $\mathcal{T}(E)$ where two terms s, t are equivalent iff $s \approx t \in \widehat{E}$. For all $t \in \mathcal{T}(E)$, we denote its equivalence class in $\widehat{E}$ by $[t]_E$ or just $[t]$ when E is clear.

Given a term t, we write $t{\downarrow}$ to denote its *simplified form*, where $t{\downarrow}$ is a term that is equivalent to t in T_{ASX} and is not simplifiable further (i.e., $(t{\downarrow}){\downarrow} = t{\downarrow}$). We do not insist that simplified forms be canonical, that is, equivalent terms need not have the same simplified form. Rules for computing the simplified form of Σ_{AS}-terms are given in Fig. 2. Rules for computing the simplified form of other Σ_{ASX}-terms are fairly sophisticated and will be described in detail in Sect. 3.2. Given a tuple of basic string terms t, we write $t{\downarrow}$ to denote a tuple of atomic string terms corresponding to the arguments of $\mathsf{con}(t){\downarrow}$. For example, if $c_1, c_2 \in \mathcal{A}$, $(c_1, \mathsf{con}(c_2, x), y){\downarrow} = (c_1 c_2, x, y)$ and $(x, \epsilon){\downarrow} = (x)$. Given an arbitrary Σ_{ASX}-formula φ, we write $\lfloor \varphi \rfloor$ to denote an equisatisfiable (purified) formula whose atoms are T_{ASX}-constraints, and where t is in simplified form (i.e., $t = t{\downarrow}$) for all its subterms t. For example, $\lfloor \mathsf{substr}(x, n_0, n_1+1) \approx y \rfloor$ is $\mathsf{substr}(x, n_0, n_2) \approx y \wedge n_2 \approx n_1 + 1$ for a fresh integer variable n_2.

2   A Calculus for Basic String Constraints

Liang et al. [19] developed a calculus for the satisfiability of finite conjunctions of constraints in a theory of strings with length and regular expressions. This section presents a modified version of that calculus. We focus on the portion of that calculus that handles string equalities and length constraints, and omit discussion of its other aspects. Furthermore, we extend that calculus with support for constraints involving extended functions. To simplify the description of this extension and make it self-contained, we also extend the calculus to model propositional reasoning as well, making it applicable to Σ_{ASX}-formulas instead of just conjunctions of T_{ASX}-constraints.

Definition 1 (Configurations). *A configuration is either the distinguished symbol* unsat *or a tuple of the form* $\langle \mathsf{G}, \mathsf{S}, \mathsf{A} \rangle$ *where* G *is a set of* Σ_{ASX}-formulas, A *is a set of arithmetic constraints, and* S *is a tuple of the form* $(\mathsf{E}, \mathsf{X}, \mathsf{F}, \mathsf{N})$, *where:*

- E *is a set of basic string equalities;*
- X *is a set of equalities of the form* $x \approx t$, *where* x *is a variable and* t *is a flat extended function term;*
- F *is a set of pairs* $s \mapsto \boldsymbol{a}$ *where* $s \in \mathcal{T}(\mathsf{E})$ *and* $\boldsymbol{a}$ *is a tuple of atomic string terms;*
- N *is a set of pairs* $e \mapsto \boldsymbol{a}$ *where* e *is an equivalence class of* $\widehat{\mathsf{E}}$ *and* $\boldsymbol{a}$ *is a tuple of atomic string terms.* □

A configuration $\langle \mathsf{G}, \mathsf{S}, \mathsf{A} \rangle$ models the internal state of various modules of a DPLL(T)-based solver. The component G collects the formulas being processed by the solver's propositional satisfiability (SAT) engine; S models the state of a theory solver for strings; and A collects the constraints given to a solver for linear integer arithmetic. Initial configurations have the form $\langle \{\varphi\}, \overline{\varnothing}, \varnothing \rangle$ where φ is a *quantifier-free* T_{ASX}-formula to be checked for satisfiability and $\overline{\varnothing}$ abbreviates the tuple $(\varnothing, \varnothing, \varnothing, \varnothing)$.

We describe a calculus for the satisfiability of string constraints by a set of derivation rules that modify configurations. The rules are given in *guarded assignment form*, where the top of the rule describes the conditions under which the rule can be applied, and the bottom of the rule either is unsat, or otherwise describes the resulting modifications to the components of our configuration. A rule may have multiple, alternative conclusions separated by ∥. An application of a rule is *redundant* if it has a conclusion where each component in the derived configuration is a subset of the corresponding component in the premise configuration. A configuration other than unsat is *saturated* if every possible application of a derivation rule to it is redundant. A *derivation tree* is a tree where each node is a configuration whose children, if any, are obtained by a non-redundant application of a rule of the calculus. A *closed* derivation tree (where all terminal nodes are unsat) with root node $\langle \{\varphi\}, \overline{\varnothing}, \varnothing \rangle$ is a proof that φ is unsatisfiable in T_{ASX}. A derivation tree with root node $\langle \{\varphi\}, \overline{\varnothing}, \varnothing \rangle$ and a saturated leaf is, under certain assumptions (see Theorem 1) a witness that φ is satisfiable in T_{ASX}.

To discuss the rules, we first introduce the notation for updating the internal state $S = (E, X, F, N)$ of our string solver. Let M be a set of T_{ASX}-constraints. By introducing enough fresh variables, we can construct an equisatisfiable set $M_E \cup M_X$ where M_E is a set of Σ_{AS}-literals and M_X is a set of equalities of the form $y \approx t$, with y a variable and t a flat extended function term. For simplicity,

$$\text{Prop-Assign} \; \frac{\mathsf{G} = \mathsf{G}', \varphi \quad \varphi \text{ is quantifier-free}}{\|_{M \models_p \varphi} \; \mathsf{G} := \mathsf{G}' \quad \mathsf{S} := \mathsf{S} \oplus M|_S \quad \mathsf{A} := \mathsf{A} \cup M|_A} \qquad \text{A-Conf} \; \frac{\mathsf{A} \models_{\mathsf{LIA}} \bot}{\mathsf{unsat}}$$

$$\text{A-Prop} \; \frac{\mathsf{S} \models s \approx t \quad s, t : \mathsf{Int}}{\mathsf{A} := \mathsf{A}, s \approx t} \qquad \text{S-Prop} \; \frac{\mathsf{A} \models_{\mathsf{LIA}} s \approx t \quad s, t : \mathsf{Int}}{\mathsf{S} := \mathsf{S} \oplus \{s \approx t\}} \qquad \text{S-Conf} \; \frac{s \not\approx s \in \hat{\mathsf{E}}}{\mathsf{unsat}}$$

$$\text{L-Eq} \; \frac{x \approx t \in \hat{\mathsf{E}} \quad x : \mathsf{Str}}{\mathsf{A} := \mathsf{A}, \mathsf{len}\, x \approx (\mathsf{len}\, t)\!\downarrow} \qquad \text{L-Geq} \; \frac{x \in \mathcal{V}(\mathsf{S} \cup \mathsf{A}) \quad x : \mathsf{Str}}{\mathsf{S} := \mathsf{S} \oplus \{x \approx \epsilon\} \quad \| \quad \mathsf{A} := \mathsf{A}, \mathsf{len}\, x > 0}$$

Fig. 3. Rules modeling the interaction between the propositional, string and arithmetic subsolvers.

we assume here that M_E does not contain string disequalities.[2] We define the *external update* of S with M, written $S \oplus M$, to be the tuple $(E \cup M_E, X \cup M_X, \varnothing, \varnothing)$. For Σ_{AS}-terms t_1, t_2, we define the *internal update* of S with $t_1 \approx t_2$, written $S \odot t_1 \approx t_2$, to be the tuple $(E \cup \{t_1 \approx t_2\}, X, F\sigma, \varnothing)$, where σ is the substitution $\{t_1 \mapsto t_2\}$ if t_1 is a string variable and is the empty substitution otherwise, and $F\sigma$ is the result of replacing the right hand side of all pairs $y \mapsto a$ in F with $(a\sigma)\!\downarrow$.

The rules in Fig. 3 model the basic interaction between the various subsolvers in our approach. The rule Prop-Assign considers each *propositional satisfying assignment* M for a quantifier-free formula $\varphi \in \mathsf{G}$, i.e., each set M of literals such as every atom of φ occurs either positively or negatively (but not both) in M, all the atoms in M occur in φ, and $M \models_p \varphi$. For each such M, Prop-Assign has a conclusion where the string constraints in M (denoted as $M|_S$) are given to the string subsolver and the arithmetic constraints (denoted as $M|_A$) are given to the arithmetic subsolver. The arithmetic and string solvers use rules A-Prop and S-Prop to share equalities between (shared) arithmetic terms, and use A-Conf and S-Conf to report that their respective set of constraints is unsatisfiable. In those rules and in the rest of the paper, $\models_{\mathsf{LIA}}$ denotes entailment in linear integer arithmetic. The rules L-Eq and L-Geq respectively infer and guess arithmetic constraints involving string length.

Example 1. Consider the formula φ of the form $\mathsf{len}\, x > \mathsf{len}\, y \wedge y \approx \mathsf{con}(x, \mathsf{a})$. Starting from configuration $\langle \{\varphi\}, \varnothing, \varnothing \rangle$, we may apply Prop-Assign to remove φ from G and update S and A based the propositional satisfying assignment for φ. We obtain a configuration where A is $\{\mathsf{len}\, x > \mathsf{len}\, y\}$ and the E component of S is $\{y \approx \mathsf{con}(x, \mathsf{a})\}$. Since $(\mathsf{len}(\mathsf{con}(x, \mathsf{a})))\!\downarrow = \mathsf{len}\, x + 1$, we may add $\mathsf{len}\, y \approx \mathsf{len}\, x + 1$ to A by the rule L-Eq. Since $\mathsf{len}\, x > \mathsf{len}\, y, \mathsf{len}\, y \approx \mathsf{len}\, x + 1 \models_{\mathsf{LIA}} \bot$, we may apply A-Conf to derive the unsat configuration, establishing that φ is unsatisfiable in T_{ASX}. $\qquad\qquad \square$

---

[2] String disequalities can be reduced to a finite disjunction of equalities, e.g. see [1]. More sophisticated and efficient methods for handling string disequalities are given in [19].

$$\text{F-Form1} \; \frac{\text{con}(t_1,\ldots,t_n) \in \mathcal{T}(\mathsf{E}) \quad \mathsf{N}\,[t_i] = s_i \text{ for } i = 1,\ldots,n}{\mathsf{F} := \mathsf{F}, \text{con}(t_1,\ldots,t_n) \mapsto (s_1,\ldots,s_n)\!\downarrow} \qquad \text{F-Form2} \; \frac{l \in \mathcal{T}(\mathsf{E})}{\mathsf{F} := \mathsf{F}, l \mapsto (l)\!\downarrow}$$

$$\text{N-Form1} \; \frac{e \not\subseteq \mathcal{V}(\mathsf{E}) \quad \mathsf{F}\,t = a \text{ for all } t \in e \backslash \mathcal{V}(\mathsf{E})}{\mathsf{N} := \mathsf{N}, e \mapsto a} \qquad \text{N-Form2} \; \frac{[x] \subseteq \mathcal{V}(\mathsf{E}) \quad x \preceq y \text{ for all } y \in [x]}{\mathsf{N} := \mathsf{N}, [x] \mapsto (x)}$$

$$\text{F-Unify} \; \frac{\mathsf{F}\,s = (\boldsymbol{w},u,\boldsymbol{u}_1) \quad \mathsf{F}\,t = (\boldsymbol{w},v,\boldsymbol{v}_1) \quad s \approx t \in \hat{\mathsf{E}} \quad u < v \quad \mathsf{E} \models \text{len}\,u \approx \text{len}\,v}{\mathsf{S} := \mathsf{S} \odot v \approx u}$$

$$\text{F-Split} \; \frac{\mathsf{F}\,s = (\boldsymbol{w},u,\boldsymbol{u}_1) \quad \mathsf{F}\,t = (\boldsymbol{w},v,\boldsymbol{v}_1) \quad s \approx t \in \hat{\mathsf{E}} \quad \mathsf{E} \models \text{len}\,u \not\approx \text{len}\,v}{\mathsf{S} := \mathsf{S} \odot u \approx \text{con}(v,z) \quad \| \quad \mathsf{S} := \mathsf{S} \odot v \approx \text{con}(u,z)} \quad \frac{u \notin \mathcal{V}(\boldsymbol{v}_1) \quad v \notin \mathcal{V}(\boldsymbol{u}_1)}{}$$

$$\text{L-Split} \; \frac{x,y \in \mathcal{V}(\mathsf{E}) \quad x,y : \text{Str}}{\mathsf{E} := \mathsf{E}, \text{len}\,x \approx \text{len}\,y \quad \| \quad \mathsf{E} := \mathsf{E}, \text{len}\,x \not\approx \text{len}\,y}$$

Fig. 4. String derivation rules. The rules construct flat forms F and normal forms N for string terms. The letter l denotes a string constant, and z denotes a fresh string variable.

The rules in Fig. 4 are used by the string solver for building the mappings F and N. We defer discussion of the X component of configurations until Sect. 3. In the rules, we assume a total ordering $\prec$ on string terms, whose only restriction is that $t_1 \prec t_2$ if t_1 is variable and t_2 is not. For a term t, we call $\mathsf{F}\,t$ the *flat form* of t, and for an equivalence class e, we call $\mathsf{N}\,e$ the *normal form* of e. We construct the mappings F and N using the rules F-Form1, F-Form2, N-Form1 and N-Form2 in a mutually recursive fashion. The remaining three rules apply to cases where the above rules do not result in complete mappings for F and N. In the case where we compute flat forms for two terms s and t in the same equivalence class that share a common prefix $\boldsymbol{w}$ followed by two distinct variables u and v, we apply F-Unify to infer $u \approx v$ in the case that the lengths of u and v are equal, otherwise we apply F-Split to infer that u is a prefix of v or vice versa in the case that the lengths of u and v are disequal. The rule L-Split splits the derivation based on equality between the lengths of string variables x and y, which we use to derive configurations where one of these two rules applies.

Example 2. Consider a configuration where E is $\{y \approx \text{con}(a,x), x \approx \text{con}(u,z),$ $y \approx \text{con}(a,v,z), w \approx a, \text{len}\,u \approx \text{len}\,v\}$. The equivalence classes of $\hat{\mathsf{E}}$ are

$$\{y, \text{con}(a,x), \text{con}(a,v,a)\} \quad \{x, \text{con}(u,a)\} \quad \{u\} \quad \{v\} \quad \{w,a\}$$

Using N-Form2, we obtain $\mathsf{N}\,[u] = (u)$ and $\mathsf{N}\,[v] = (v)$. Using F-Form1 and N-Form1, we obtain $\mathsf{F}\,\text{con}(u,a) = \mathsf{N}\,[x] = (u,z)$ and $\mathsf{F}\,a = \mathsf{N}\,[w] = (a)$. For $[y]$, we use F-Form1 to obtain $\mathsf{F}\operatorname{con}(\mathsf{a}, x) = (\mathsf{a}, u, \mathsf{a})$ and $\mathsf{F}\operatorname{con}(\mathsf{a}, v, \mathsf{a}) = (\mathsf{a}, v, \mathsf{a})$. Since the flat forms of these terms are not the same and $\operatorname{len} u \approx \operatorname{len} v \in \mathsf{E}$, we may apply F-Unify to conclude $v \approx u$. We update S to $\mathsf{S} \odot u \approx v$, after which the equivalence classes are:

$$\{y, \operatorname{con}(\mathsf{a}, x), \operatorname{con}(\mathsf{a}, v, \mathsf{a})\} \quad \{x, \operatorname{con}(u, \mathsf{a})\} \quad \{u, v\} \quad \{w, \mathsf{a}\}$$

and $\mathsf{F}\operatorname{con}(\mathsf{a}, v, \mathsf{a})$ is now $(\mathsf{a}, u, \mathsf{a})$. Then we can use N-Form1 and N-Form2 to reconstruct N. Since $\mathsf{F}\operatorname{con}(\mathsf{a}, x) = \mathsf{F}\operatorname{con}(\mathsf{a}, v, \mathsf{a}) = (\mathsf{a}, u, \mathsf{a})$, we can obtain $\mathsf{N}[y] = (\mathsf{a}, u, \mathsf{a})$. This results in a configuration where N is a complete mapping over the equivalence classes and no more rules apply, indicating that E is satisfiable in T_{ASX}. $\qquad\square$

We say a configuration is *cyclic* if $\widehat{\mathsf{E}}$ either contains a chain of equalities of the form $s \approx \operatorname{con}(t_1), s_1 \approx \operatorname{con}(t_2), \ldots, s_{n-1} \approx \operatorname{con}(t_n), s_n \approx s$ where s_i is a term from t_i for each i, or an equality of the form $s \approx t$ where $\mathsf{F}\, s = (w, u), \mathsf{F}\, t = (w, v)$, w is the maximal common prefix of $\mathsf{F}\, s$, and $\mathsf{F}\, t$ and $\mathcal{V}(u) \cap \mathcal{V}(v)$ is non-empty. Recent techniques have been proposed for cyclic string constraints [19, 29]. We instead focus primarily on acyclic string constraints in the following result.

Theorem 1. *For all quantifier-free Σ_{AS}-formulas φ, the following hold.*

1. *There is a closed derivation tree with root $\langle\{\varphi\}, \overline{\varnothing}, \varnothing\rangle$ only if φ is unsat in T_{ASX}.*
2. *There is a derivation tree with root $\langle\{\varphi\}, \overline{\varnothing}, \varnothing\rangle$ containing an acyclic saturated configuration only if φ is sat in T_{ASX}.*

3   Techniques for Extended String Constraints

This section gives a novel extension of the calculus in the previous section for determining the satisfiability of T_{ASX}-constraints. While the decidability of this problem is not known [5], we focus on techniques that are both refutation-sound and model-sound but guaranteed to terminate in general. We introduce two techniques for establishing the (un)satisfiability of T_{ASX}-constraints S, described by the additional derivation rules in Figs. 5 and 6 which supplement those from Sect. 2.

3.1   Expanding Extended Function Terms to Bounded Integer Quantification

The satisfiability problem for equalities over Σ_{ASX}-terms can be reduced to the satisfiability problem for possibly quantified Σ_{AS}-formulas. This reduction is provided by rule Ext-Expand in Fig. 5 which, given $x \approx t \in \mathsf{X}$, adds an equisatisfiable formula $[\![x \approx t]\!]$ to G, the *expanded form* of $x \approx t$. The rules also removes $x \approx t$ from X, effectively marking it as processed. Since $[\![x \approx t]\!]$ keeps the (free) variables of $x \approx t$, any interpretation later found to satisfy $[\![x \approx t]\!]$ will also satisfy $x \approx t$.

$$\text{Ext-Expand} \quad \frac{x \approx t \in \mathsf{X}}{\mathsf{G} := \mathsf{G}, \lfloor [\![x \approx t]\!] \rfloor \quad \mathsf{X} := \mathsf{X} \backslash \{ x \approx t \}} \qquad \text{where}$$

$$[\![x \approx \mathsf{substr}(y, n, m)]\!] = \mathsf{ite}(\, 0 \leqslant n < \mathsf{len}\, y \wedge 0 < m,\ y \approx \mathsf{con}(z_1, x, z_2) \wedge \mathsf{len}\, z_1 \approx n \wedge$$
$$\mathsf{len}\, z_2 \approx \mathsf{len}\, y \,\dot{-}\, m,\ x \approx \epsilon\,)$$

$$[\![x \approx \mathsf{contains}(y, z)]\!] = (x \not\approx \top) \Leftrightarrow \forall k.\, 0 \leqslant k \leqslant \mathsf{len}\, y - \mathsf{len}\, z \Rightarrow \mathsf{substr}(y, k, \mathsf{len}\, z) \not\approx z$$

$$[\![x \approx \mathsf{index\_of}(y, z, n)]\!] = \mathsf{ite}(\, 0 \leqslant n \wedge z \not\approx \epsilon \wedge \mathsf{contains}(y', z),\ \mathsf{substr}(y', x', \mathsf{len}\, z) \approx z \wedge$$
$$\neg\mathsf{contains}(\mathsf{substr}(y', 0, x' + \mathsf{len}\, z - 1), z),\ x \approx -1\,)$$
$$\text{with } y' = \mathsf{substr}(y, n, \mathsf{len}\, y - n) \text{ and } x' = x - n$$

$$[\![x \approx \mathsf{replace}(y, z, w)]\!] = \mathsf{ite}(\, \mathsf{contains}(y, z) \wedge z \not\approx \epsilon,\ x \approx \mathsf{con}(z_1, w, z_2) \wedge$$
$$y \approx \mathsf{con}(z_1, z, z_2) \wedge \mathsf{index\_of}(y, z, 0) \approx \mathsf{len}\, z_1,\ x \approx y\,)$$

$$\text{B-Val} \quad \frac{t : \mathsf{Int} \quad n \text{ is a numeral}}{\mathsf{A} := \mathsf{A}, t \leqslant n \quad \| \quad \mathsf{A} := \mathsf{A}, t > n} \qquad \text{B-Inst} \quad \frac{\begin{array}{c} \mathsf{G} = \mathsf{G}', \varphi[\forall k.\, 0 \leqslant k \leqslant t \Rightarrow \psi] \\ \mathsf{A} \models_{\mathsf{LIA}} t \leqslant n \text{ for some numeral } n \end{array}}{\mathsf{G} := \mathsf{G}', \lfloor \varphi[\wedge_{i=0}^{n} \psi\{k \mapsto i\}] \rfloor}$$

Fig. 5. Rules for reducing Σ_{ASX}-constraints to Σ_{AS}-constraints, where z_1, z_2 are fresh variables, $n_1 \,\dot{-}\, n_2$ denotes the maximum of $n_1 - n_2$ and 0, and ite is the if-then-else connective.

The definition of expanded form for the possible cases of t are given below rule Ext-Expand.[3] We remark that this rule can be applied only finitely many times. For an intuition of why, consider any ordering $\prec$ on function symbols such that $f \prec g$ if g is an extended function and f is not, and substr $\prec$ contains $\prec$ index_of $\prec$ replace. In all cases, all function symbols of $[\![x \approx f(t)]\!]$ are smaller than f in this ordering.

Note that the reduction introduces formulas with *bounded integer quantification*, that is, formulas of the form $\forall k.\, 0 \leqslant k \leqslant t \Rightarrow \varphi$, where t does not contain k and φ is quantifier-free. Special consideration is needed to handle formulas of this form. We employ a pragmatic approach, modeled by the other two rules in Fig. 5, which guesses upper bounds on certain arithmetic terms and eliminates those quantified formulas based on these bounds. Specifically, rule B-Val splits the search into two cases $t \leqslant n$ and $t > n$, where t is an integer term and n is a numeral. In the rule B-Inst, if G contains a formula φ having a subformula $\forall k.\, 0 \leqslant k \leqslant t \Rightarrow \psi$ and A entails a (concrete) upper bound on t, then that subformula is replaced by a finite conjunction. Since all quantifiers introduced in a configuration are bounded, these two rules used in combination suffice to eliminate them.

Example 3. Consider the formula $\varphi = \mathsf{contains}(y, z) \wedge 0 < \mathsf{len}\, y \leqslant 3 \wedge 0 < \mathsf{len}\, z$. Applying Prop-Assign to φ results in a configuration where E, X and A respectively are $\{x \approx \top\}$, $\{x \approx \mathsf{contains}(y, z)\}$, and $\{0 < \mathsf{len}\, y \leqslant 3, 0 < \mathsf{len}\, z\}$. Using Ext-Expand, we remove $x \approx \top$ from X and add to G, $[\![x \approx \mathsf{contains}(y, z)]\!]$ which is:

$$(x \not\approx \top) \Leftrightarrow \forall k.\, 0 \leqslant k \leqslant \mathsf{len}\, y - \mathsf{len}\, z \Rightarrow \mathsf{substr}(y, k, \mathsf{len}\, z) \not\approx z.$$

---

[3] We use a number of optimizations of this encoding in our implementation.

Since $A \models_{\mathsf{LIA}} \mathsf{len}\, y - \mathsf{len}\, z \leqslant 2$, by B-Inst we can replace this formula with:

$$((x \not\approx \top) \Leftrightarrow \wedge_{j=0}^{2} \mathsf{substr}(y, n_j, \mathsf{len}\, z) \not\approx z) \wedge \bigwedge_{j=0}^{2} n_j \approx j$$

where n_j is a fresh integer variable for $j = 0, 1, 2$. Applying Prop-Assign to this formula gives a branch where E and X are updated to $\{x \approx \top, m_0 \approx \mathsf{len}\, z, x_0 \approx z\}$ and $\{x_0 \approx \mathsf{substr}(y, n_0, m_0)\}$ for fresh variables x_0 and m_0. Using the rule Ext-Expand, we remove the equality from X and add $[\![x_0 \approx \mathsf{substr}(y, n_0, m_0)]\!]$ to G, which is:

$$\mathsf{ite}(\, 0 \leqslant n_0 < \mathsf{len}\, y \wedge 0 \leqslant m_0,$$
$$y \approx \mathsf{con}(z_1, x_0, z_2) \wedge \mathsf{len}\, z_1 \approx 0 \wedge \mathsf{len}\, z_2 \approx \mathsf{len}\, y \dot- m_0, \, x_0 \approx \epsilon)$$

with z_1, z_2 fresh string variables. Applying Prop-Assign again produces a branch with $\mathsf{E} = \{x \approx \top, x_0 \approx z, m_0 \approx \mathsf{len}\, z, y \approx \mathsf{con}(z_1, x_0, z_2)\}$ and X empty. The set E is satisfiable in T_{ASX}. Deriving a saturated configuration from this point indicates that φ is satisfiable in T_{ASX} as well. Indeed, all interpretations that satisfy both $y \approx \mathsf{con}(z_1, x_0, z_2)$ and $x_0 \approx z$ also satisfy $\mathsf{contains}(y, z)$.   □

Although these rules give the general idea of our approach, our implementation actually handles the bounded quantifiers in a more sophisticated way, using model-based quantifier instantiation [23]. In a nutshell, we avoid generating all the instances of a quantified formula either by backtracking when a subset of them are unsatisfiable, or by determining that (sets of) instances are already satisfied by a candidate model.

3.2   Context-Dependent Simplification of Extended Function Terms

The reductions described above may be impractical due to the size and complexity of the formulas they introduce. For this reason, we have developed techniques for recognizing when the interpretation of an extended function term can be deduced based on the constraints in the current context. As a simple example, if $\mathsf{contains}(\mathsf{abc}, x)$ is a term belonging to the string theory (with abc a string constant), and the string solver has inferred that x is equal to a concrete value (e.g., d) or even a partially concrete value (e.g., $\mathsf{con}(\mathsf{d}, y)$), then we can already infer that $\mathsf{contains}(\mathsf{abc}, x)$ is equivalent to $\bot$, thereby avoiding the construction of its expanded form. We present next a generic technique for inferring such facts that has a substantial performance impact in practice.

The rule Ext-Simplify from Fig. 6 applies to configurations in which an extended function term t can be simplified to an equivalent form, modulo the current set of constraints, that does not involve extended functions. In this rule, we derive a set of equalities $\boldsymbol{y} \approx \boldsymbol{s}$ that are consequences of our current set of string constraints E, where typically $\boldsymbol{y}$ are the (free) variables of t. We will refer to $\{\boldsymbol{y} \mapsto \boldsymbol{s}\}$ as a *derivable substitution* (in E). If the simplified form of t under this substitution is a Σ_{AS}-term, then we add the equality $x \approx (t\{\boldsymbol{y} \mapsto \boldsymbol{s}\})\!\downarrow$ to G, and remove $x \approx t$ from X. Similarly when t is of sort Bool, the rule Ext-Simplify-Pred adds an equivalence to G based on the result of simplifying the formula

$$\text{Ext-Simplify} \; \frac{x \approx t \in \mathsf{X} \qquad \mathsf{E} \models \boldsymbol{y} \approx \boldsymbol{s} \qquad (t\{\boldsymbol{y} \mapsto \boldsymbol{s}\})\!\downarrow \text{ is a } \varSigma_{\mathsf{AS}}\text{-term}}{\mathsf{G} := \mathsf{G}, \lfloor x \approx (t\{\boldsymbol{y} \mapsto \boldsymbol{s}\})\!\downarrow \rfloor \qquad \mathsf{X} := \mathsf{X}\backslash\{x \approx t\}}$$

$$\text{Ext-Simplify-Pred} \; \frac{x \approx t \in \mathsf{X} \qquad \mathsf{E} \models \boldsymbol{y} \approx \boldsymbol{s} \qquad t : \mathsf{Bool}}{\mathsf{G} := \mathsf{G}, \lfloor (x \approx \top) \Leftrightarrow ((t \approx \top)\{\boldsymbol{y} \mapsto \boldsymbol{s}\})\!\downarrow \rfloor \qquad \mathsf{X} := \mathsf{X}\backslash\{x \approx t\}}$$

$$\text{Ext-Eq} \; \frac{x_1 \approx t_1, x_2 \approx t_2 \in \mathsf{X} \qquad \mathsf{E} \models \boldsymbol{y} \approx \boldsymbol{s} \qquad (t_1\{\boldsymbol{y} \mapsto \boldsymbol{s}\})\!\downarrow = (t_2\{\boldsymbol{y} \mapsto \boldsymbol{s}\})\!\downarrow}{\mathsf{S} := \mathsf{S} \oplus \{x_1 \approx x_2\}}$$

Fig. 6. Rules for context-dependent simplification of extended functions terms.

$$
\begin{array}{rcll}
\text{contains}(l_1, l_2) & \to & \top & \text{if } l_1 \text{ contains } l_2 \\
\text{contains}(l_1, l_2) & \to & \bot & \text{if } l_1 \text{ does not contain } l_2 \\
\text{contains}(l_1, \text{con}(l_2, t)) & \to & \bot & \text{if } l_1 \text{ does not contain } l_2 \\
\text{contains}(l_1, \text{con}(l_2, t)) & \to & \bot & \text{if } \text{contains}(l_1\backslash l_2, \text{con}(t)) \to^* \bot \\
\text{contains}(l_1, \text{con}(x, t)) & \to & \bot & \text{if } \text{contains}(l_1, \text{con}(t)) \to^* \bot \\
\text{contains}(\text{con}(l_1, t), l_2) & \to & \top & \text{if } l_1 \text{ contains } l_2 \\
\text{contains}(\text{con}(x, t), s) & \to & \top & \text{if } \text{contains}(\text{con}(t), s) \to^* \top \\
\text{contains}(\text{con}(t, \boldsymbol{s}), \text{con}(t, \boldsymbol{u})) & \to & \top & \text{if } \text{contains}(\text{con}(\boldsymbol{s}), \text{con}(\boldsymbol{u})) \to^* \top \\
\text{contains}(\text{con}(l_1, t), l_2) & \to & \text{contains}(\text{con}(t), l_2) & \text{if } l_1 \sqcup_l l_2 = \epsilon \\
\text{contains}(\text{con}(t, l_1), l_2) & \to & \text{contains}(\text{con}(t), l_2) & \text{if } l_1 \sqcup_r l_2 = \epsilon
\end{array}
$$

$$
\begin{array}{rcl}
\text{contains}(\epsilon, t) \approx \top & \to & \epsilon \approx t \\
\text{contains}(\text{con}(t_1, l_1, t_2), l_2) \approx \top & \to & \vee_{i=1}^{2}\text{contains}(\text{con}(t_i), l_2) \approx \top \quad \text{if } l_1 \sqcup_r l_2 = l_1 \sqcup_l l_2 = \epsilon
\end{array}
$$

Fig. 7. Examples of simplification rules for contains.

$t \approx \top$ under a derivable substitution, and removes $x \approx t$ from X. The rule Ext-Eq is used to deduce equalities between extended terms that are syntactically identical after simplification under a derivable substitution.

These rules require methods for computing the simplified form $t\!\downarrow$ of $\varSigma_{\mathsf{ASX}}$-terms t, as well as for choosing substitutions $\{\boldsymbol{y} \mapsto \boldsymbol{s}\}$. We describe these methods in the following, and give several examples.

Simplification Rules for Extended String Functions. Recall that by construction, a term t and its simplified form $t\!\downarrow$ are equivalent in T_{ASX}. It is generally advantageous to use techniques that often simplify $\varSigma_{\mathsf{ASX}}$-terms t to $\varSigma_{\mathsf{AS}}$-terms $t\!\downarrow$, since this eliminates the need to apply Ext-Expand to compute the expanded form of t. For this reason, we use aggressive and non-trivial simplification techniques when considering $\varSigma_{\mathsf{ASX}}$-terms.

Examples of some of the simplification rules for contains are given in Fig. 7. There, for string constants l_1, l_2, we write $l_1 \setminus l_2$ to denote the empty string if l_1 does not contain l_2, and the remainder obtained from removing the largest prefix of l_1 containing l_2 otherwise. We use $l_1 \sqcup_l l_2$ (resp. $l_1 \sqcup_r l_2$) to denote l_2 if l_1 contains l_2, and the largest suffix (resp. prefix) of l_1 that is a prefix (resp. suffix) of l_2 otherwise. For example, $(\text{abcde} \setminus \text{cd}) = \text{e}$, $(\text{abcde} \setminus \text{ba}) = \epsilon$, $(\text{abcde} \sqcup_l \text{def}) = \text{de}$, $(\text{abcde} \sqcup_r \text{def}) = \epsilon$, and $(\text{abcdc} \sqcup_l \text{cd}) = \text{cd}$. Also, $s \to^* t$ indicates that t can be obtained from s by zero or more applications of the rules in the figure. One can prove that his rewrite system is terminating by noting that all conditions and right hand side of each non-trivial rule involve only concatenation terms with strictly fewer arguments than its left hand side.

In practice, the rules are implemented by a handful of recursive passes over the arguments of contains terms. Computing the simplified form of other operators is also fairly sophisticated and not shown here. (Our simplifier is around 2000 lines of C++ code.) Despite its complexity, simplification often results in significant performance improvements, by eliminating the need to generate the expanded form of Σ_{ASX}-terms. We illustrate this in the following examples.

Example 4. Given input $y \approx \mathsf{bc} \wedge \mathsf{contains}(\mathsf{con}(\mathsf{a}, y), \mathsf{con}(\mathsf{b}, z, \mathsf{a}))$, our calculus considers a configuration where E and X respectively are

$$\{y \approx \mathsf{bc}, x_1 \approx \top, z_1 \approx \mathsf{con}(\mathsf{a}, y), z_2 \approx \mathsf{con}(\mathsf{b}, z, \mathsf{a})\} \text{ and } \{x_1 \approx \mathsf{contains}(z_1, z_2)\}$$

where x_1, z_1, z_2 are fresh string variables. We have that $\mathsf{E} \models z_1 \approx \mathsf{abc} \wedge z_2 \approx \mathsf{con}(\mathsf{b}, z, \mathsf{a})$. Hence the substitution $\sigma = \{z_1 \mapsto \mathsf{abc}, z_2 \mapsto \mathsf{con}(\mathsf{b}, z, \mathsf{a})\}$ is derivable in this configuration. Since $(\mathsf{contains}(z_1, z_2)\sigma){\downarrow} = \mathsf{contains}(\mathsf{abc}, \mathsf{con}(\mathsf{b}, z, \mathsf{a})){\downarrow} = \bot$, we may apply Ext-Simplify to remove $x_1 \approx \mathsf{contains}(z_1, z_2)$ from X and add $x_1 \approx \bot$ to E, after which unsat may be derived, since $x_1 \approx \top \in \mathsf{E}$. In this example, we have avoided expanding the input formula by reasoning that $\mathsf{con}(\mathsf{a}, y)$ does not contain $\mathsf{con}(\mathsf{b}, z, \mathsf{a})$ in the context where y is bc. □

Example 5. Given input $y \approx \mathsf{con}(\mathsf{a}, z) \wedge \mathsf{contains}(\mathsf{con}(x, y), \mathsf{bc})$, our calculus considers the configuration where E and X respectively are

$$\{y \approx \mathsf{con}(\mathsf{a}, z), x_1 \approx \top, z_1 \approx \mathsf{con}(x, y), z_2 \approx \mathsf{bc}\} \text{ and } \{x_1 \approx \mathsf{contains}(z_1, z_2)\}$$

The substitution $\sigma = \{z_1 \approx \mathsf{con}(x, \mathsf{a}, z), z_2 \mapsto \mathsf{bc}\}$ is derivable in this configuration. Computing $(\mathsf{contains}(z_1, z_2)\sigma){\downarrow}$ results in $\mathsf{contains}(x, \mathsf{bc}) \vee \mathsf{contains}(z, \mathsf{bc})$. We may apply Ext-Simplify-Pred to remove $x_1 \approx \mathsf{contains}(z_1, z_2)$ from X and add this formula to G, after which we consider the two disjuncts independently. □

Example 6. Given input $y \approx \mathsf{ab} \wedge \mathsf{contains}(\mathsf{con}(\mathsf{b}, z), y) \wedge \neg\mathsf{contains}(z, y)$, our calculus considers the configuration where E and X respectively are

$$\{y \approx \mathsf{ab}, x_1 \approx \top, x_2 \approx \bot, z_1 \approx \mathsf{con}(\mathsf{b}, z)\} \text{ and } \{x_1 \approx \mathsf{contains}(z_1, y), x_2 \approx \mathsf{contains}(z, y)\}$$

The substitution $\sigma = \{y \approx \mathsf{ab}, z_1 \approx \mathsf{con}(\mathsf{b}, z)\}$ is derivable in this configuration, and $(\mathsf{contains}(z_1, y)\sigma){\downarrow} = \mathsf{contains}(z, \mathsf{ab}) = (\mathsf{contains}(z, y)\sigma){\downarrow}$. Hence we can apply Ext-Eq to add $x_1 \approx x_2$ to E, after which unsat can be derived. □

Choosing Substitutions. A simple and general heuristic for choosing substitutions $\{y \mapsto s\}$ for terms t in the rules from Fig. 6 is to map each variable y in t to some representative of its equivalence class $[y]$. We assume string constants are chosen as representatives whenever possible. We call this the *representative substitution* for t (in E). Representative substitutions are both easy to compute and often enough for reducing Σ_{ASX}-terms. A more powerful method for choosing substitutions is to consider substitutions that map each free variable y in t to $\mathsf{con}(a_1, \ldots, a_n)\downarrow$ where $\mathsf{N}\,[y] = (a_1, \ldots, a_n)$. We call this the *normal form substitution* for t. Intuitively, the normal form of t is a schema representing all known information about t. In this sense, a substitution mapping variables to their normal forms gives the highest likelihood of enabling our simplification techniques. In practice, our implementation takes advantage of both of these heuristics for choosing substitutions.

Example 7. Say we are in a configuration where the equivalence classes of $\widehat{\mathsf{E}}$ are:

$$\{y, \mathsf{con}(\mathsf{a}, x)\} \quad \{x, \mathsf{con}(z, \mathsf{c}), u\} \quad \{z, w, \mathsf{b}\}$$

and the normal forms are $\mathsf{N}[y] = \mathsf{abc}, \mathsf{N}[x] = \mathsf{bc}$ and $\mathsf{N}[z] = \mathsf{b}$. If y, x, and b are chosen as the representatives of these classes, the representative substitution σ_r for this configuration is $\{y \mapsto y, x \mapsto x, u \mapsto x, z \mapsto \mathsf{b}, w \mapsto \mathsf{b}\}$, whereas the normal form substitution σ_n is $\{y \mapsto \mathsf{abc}, x \mapsto \mathsf{bc}, u \mapsto \mathsf{bc}, z \mapsto \mathsf{b}, w \mapsto \mathsf{b}\}$. Only the latter substitution suffices to show that $\mathsf{contains}(y, \mathsf{con}(z, z))$ is false in the current context, noting $(\mathsf{contains}(y, \mathsf{con}(z, z))\sigma_r)\downarrow = \mathsf{contains}(y, \mathsf{bb})$ and $(\mathsf{contains}(y, \mathsf{con}(z, z))\sigma_n)\downarrow = \bot$. □

4   Implementation

We have implemented all of these techniques in the DPLL(T)-based SMT solver CVC4 [4]. At a high level, our implementation can be summarized as a particular strategy for applying the rules of the calculus, which we outline in the following.

Strategy 1. *Start with a derivation tree consisting of (root) node $\langle\{\varphi\}, \varnothing, \varnothing\rangle$.*
Let t_{len} be $\mathsf{len}\,x_1 + \ldots + \mathsf{len}\,x_m$ where $x_1, \ldots, x_m$ are the string variables of φ.
While the tree is not closed, consider as current configuration the left-most leaf in the tree that is not unsat *and apply to it a derivation rule to that configuration, based on the steps below.*

1. *Let* n *be the smallest numeral such that* $t_{\mathsf{len}} > \mathsf{n} \notin A$. *If* $t_{\mathsf{len}} \leqslant \mathsf{n} \notin A$, *apply B-Val for* t_{len} *and* n.
2. *If* G *contains a formula* φ *with subformula* $\forall k. 0 \leqslant k \leqslant t \Rightarrow \psi$, *then let* n *be the smallest numeral such that* $t > \mathsf{n} \notin A$. *If* $t \leqslant \mathsf{n} \in A$, *apply B-Inst for* φ *and* n. *Otherwise, apply B-Val for* t *and* n.
3. *If possible, apply a rule from Fig. 3, giving priority to A-Conf and S-Conf.*
4. *If possible, apply a rule from Fig. 6 based on representative substitutions.*
5. *If possible, apply a rule from Fig. 4.*
6. *If possible, apply a rule from Fig. 6 based on normal form substitutions.*
7. *If* X *is non-empty, apply the rule* Ext-Expand *for some equality* $x \approx t$ *in* X.

If no rule applies and the current configuration is acyclic, return sat. *If the tree is closed, return* unsat. □

The strategy above is sound both for refutations and models, although it is not terminating in general.

Theorem 2. *For all initial configurations* $\langle\{\varphi\}, \varnothing, \varnothing\rangle$ *where* φ *is a quantifier-free* Σ_{ASX}-*formula:*

1. *Strategy 1 returns* unsat *only if* φ *is unsatisfiable in* T_{ASX}.
2. *Strategy 1 returns* sat *only if* φ *is satisfiable in* T_{ASX}.

Implementation. While a comprehensive description of our implementation is beyond the scope of this work, we mention a few salient implementation details. The rule Prop-Assign is implemented by converting G to clausal normal form and giving the resulting clauses to a SAT solver with support for conflict-driven clause learning. The rule A-Conf is implemented by a standard theory solver for linear integer arithmetic. The rules of the calculus that modify the S component of our configuration are implemented in a dedicated DPLL(T) *theory solver* for strings which generates *conflict clauses* when branches of a derivation tree are closed, and *theory lemmas* for rules that add formulas to G or A and those that have multiple conclusions. Conflict clauses are generated by tracking *explanations* so that each literal internally added to S can be justified in terms of input literals. Finally, we do not explicitly introduce fresh variables when constructing the set X, and instead record the set of extended terms that occur in E, which are implicitly treated as variables. We now revisit a few of the examples, giving concrete details on the operation of the solver.

Example 8. In Example 1, our input was $\mathsf{len}\, x > \mathsf{len}\, y \wedge y \approx \mathsf{con}(x, \mathsf{a})$. For this input, the SAT solver finds a propositionally satisfying assignment that assigns both conjuncts to true, which causes the literal $\mathsf{len}\, x > \mathsf{len}\, y$ to be given to the theory solver for linear integer arithmetic, and $y \approx \mathsf{con}(x, \mathsf{a})$ to be given to the theory solver for strings. This corresponds to an application of the rule Prop-Assign. The string solver sends $(\neg y \approx \mathsf{con}(x, \mathsf{a}) \vee \mathsf{len}\, y \approx \mathsf{len}\, x + 1)$ as a theory lemma to the SAT solver, corresponding to an application of the rule L-Eq. After that, the SAT solver assigns $\mathsf{len}\, y \approx \mathsf{len}\, x + 1$ to true, causing that literal to be asserted to the arithmetic solver, which subsequently generates a conflict clause of the form $(\neg\mathsf{len}\, x > \mathsf{len}\, y \vee \neg\mathsf{len}\, y \approx \mathsf{len}\, x + 1)$ corresponding to an application of A-Conf. After receiving this clause, the SAT solver is unable to find another satisfying assignment and causes the system to terminate with "unsat." □

Example 9. In Example 4, the string solver is given as input the literals $y \approx \mathsf{bc}$ and $\mathsf{contains}(\mathsf{con}(\mathsf{a}, y), \mathsf{con}(\mathsf{b}, z, \mathsf{a})) \approx \top$. The intermediate variables z_1 and z_2 are not explicitly introduced. Instead, using the substitution $\sigma = \{y \mapsto \mathsf{bc}\}$, the solver directly infers that $\mathsf{contains}(\mathsf{con}(\mathsf{a}, y), \mathsf{con}(\mathsf{b}, z, \mathsf{a}))\sigma{\downarrow} = \bot$. Based on this simplification, it infers $\mathsf{contains}(\mathsf{con}(\mathsf{a}, y), \mathsf{con}(\mathsf{b}, z, \mathsf{a})) \approx \bot$ with the explanation $y \approx \mathsf{bc}$. Since the inferred literal conflicts with the second input literal, the string solver reports the conflict clause $\neg y \approx \mathsf{bc} \vee \mathsf{contains}(\mathsf{con}(\mathsf{a}, y), \mathsf{con}(\mathsf{b}, z, \mathsf{a})) \approx \top$. □

Example 10. In Example 6, the equality $y \approx \mathsf{ab}$ is the explanation for the substitution $\sigma = \{y \mapsto \mathsf{ab}\}$ under which $\mathsf{contains}(\mathsf{con}(\mathsf{b}, z), y)\sigma{\downarrow} = \mathsf{contains}(z, \mathsf{ab}) = \mathsf{contains}(\mathsf{con}(z, y))\sigma{\downarrow}$. Hence, the solver reports $(\neg y \approx \mathsf{ab} \vee \neg\mathsf{contains}(\mathsf{con}(\mathsf{b}, z), y) \vee \mathsf{contains}(z, y))$ as a conflict clause in this example. □

Example 11. Explanations are tracked for normal form substitutions as well. In Example 7, a possible explanation for the substitution σ_n is $y \approx \mathsf{con}(\mathsf{a}, x) \wedge x \approx \mathsf{con}(z, \mathsf{c}) \wedge u \approx x \wedge z \approx \mathsf{b} \wedge w \approx z$. Explanations for simplifications that occur under the substitution σ_n must include these equalities.   □

In practice, we minimize explanations by only including the variables in substitutions that are relevant for certain inferences. In particular, the domain of derivable substitutions is restricted to the free variables of the terms they apply to. We further reduce this set based on dependency analysis. For example, $\mathsf{contains}(\mathsf{abc}, \mathsf{con}(x, y)) \approx \bot$ can be explained by $x \approx \mathsf{d} \wedge y \approx \mathsf{a}$. However, $x \approx \mathsf{d}$ alone is enough.

5   Evaluation

This section reports on our experimental evaluation of our approach for extended string constraints as implemented in the SMT solver CVC4.[4] We used benchmark queries generated by running PyEx, a symbolic executor for Python programs, over a test suite that mimics the usage by a real-world Python developer. The technical details of our benchmark generation process are provided in Sect. 5.2.

We considered several configurations of CVC4 that differ in the subset of steps from Strategy 1 they apply. The default configuration, denoted **cvc4**, performs Steps 2, 3, 5 and 7 only. Configurations with suffix **f** (for "finite model finding") perform Step 1, and configurations with suffix **s** (for "simplification") perform Steps 4 and 6. For example, configuration **cvc4+fs** performs all seven steps. We consider other solvers for string constraints, including Z3-STR [30] (git revision e398f81) and Z3 [9] (version 4.5, git revision 24eae3f) which was recently extended with native support for strings.

5.1   Comparison with Other String Solvers

We first evaluated the raw performance of CVC4, Z3, and Z3-STR on the string benchmarks we collected with PyEx. We considered three sets of benchmarks produced by PyEx using **cvc4+fs**, Z3, and Z3-STR as the path constraint solver during program exploration. We denote these sets, which collectively consisted of 25,421 benchmark problems, as **PyEx-cfs**, **PyEx-z3** and **PyEx-z32**, respectively. We omit a small number (35) of these benchmarks for the following reasons: for 13 of them, at least one of the solvers produced a parse error; for the other 22, one solver returned a model (i.e., a satisfying assignment for the variables in the input problem) and agreed with its own model, but another solver answered "unsat" and disagreed with the model of the first solver.[5] We attribute the parse errors to how the solvers process certain escape sequences in string constants, and the model discrepancies to minor differences in the semantics of substr when input indices are out of bounds.

---

[4] For details, see http://cvc4.cs.stanford.edu/papers/CAV2017-strings/.

[5] We say solver A *(dis)agrees* with solver B's model for input formula φ if A finds that $\varphi \wedge \mathcal{M}_B$ is (un)sat, where $\mathcal{M}_B$ is a conjunction of equalities encoding B's.

Solver	PyEx-cfs (5557)			PyEx-z3 (8399)			PyEx-z32 (11430)			Total (25386)			
	sat	unsat	×	sat	unsat	×	sat	unsat	×	sat	time	unsat	time
cvc4+fs	**4229**	1256	72	**5694**	1325	1380	**10104**	1194	132	**20027**	5h1m	3775	7m
cvc4+s	4133	1270	154	5461	1325	1613	9884	1193	353	19478	8h40m	3788	6m
cvc4+f	4160	1217	180	5571	1308	1520	9210	1145	1075	18941	6h38m	3670	6m
cvc4	4160	1213	184	5570	1308	1521	9211	1145	1074	18941	6h32m	3666	6m
z3	3421	1274	862	4925	**1333**	2141	7219	**1196**	3015	15565	11h30m	**3803**	3m
z3str2	2013	**1278**	2266	2803	1333	4263	4726	1182	5522	9542	15h47m	3793	13m

Fig. 8. Results of running each solver over benchmarks generated by PyEx over our test suite. All benchmarks run with a 30 s timeout.

All results were produced on StarExec [25], a public execution service for running comparative evaluations of logical solvers. The results for the three solvers on the three benchmark sets are shown in Fig. 8 based on a 30 s timeout. The columns show the number of benchmarks that were determined to be satisfiable and unsatisfiable by each solver. The column with heading × indicates the number of times the solver either timed out or terminated with an inconclusive response such as "unknown." The best configuration of CVC4 (**cvc4+fs**) had a factor of 3.8 fewer timeouts than Z3, and a factor of 7.6 fewer timeouts or failures than Z3-STR in total over all benchmark sets. In particular, we note that **cvc4+fs** solved 1,451 unique benchmarks with respect to Z3 among those generated during a symbolic execution run using Z3 as the solver (**PyEx-z3**). Since PyEx supports concurrent solver invocation, this suggests a mixed-solver strategy that employs both **cvc+fs** and Z3 would likely have reduced the number of failed queries for that run. For unsatisfiable benchmarks, the solvers were relatively closer in performance, where Z3 solved 24 more unsatisfiable benchmarks than **cvc4+fs**, which is not tuned for the unsatisfiable case due to its use of finite model finding. This further suggests a mixed-solver strategy would likely be beneficial for symbolic execution since it is often used for both program exploration (where sat leads to progress) and vulnerability checking (where unsat implies safety).

In addition to solving more benchmarks, **cvc4+fs** was significantly faster over them. Figure 9 plots the cumulative run time of the three solvers on benchmarks that each solves. With respect to Z3, which took 11 h and 33 min on the 19,368 benchmarks its solves, **cvc4+fs** solved its first 19,368 benchmarks in 1 h and 23 min, and overall took only 5 h and 8 min on the 23,802 benchmarks it solves.

Using the context-dependent simplification techniques from Sect. 3.2, **cvc4+s** was able to solve 663 more benchmarks than **cvc4**, which does not apply simplification. By incorporating finite model finding, **cvc4+fs** was able to solve 536 more benchmarks in significantly less time, with a cumulative difference of more than 3 h on solved benchmarks compared to **cvc4+s**. Taking the virtual best configuration of CVC4, our techniques find 20,594 benchmarks to be satisfiable, 567 more than **cvc4+fs**, indicating that a portfolio approach for the various configurations would be advantageous.

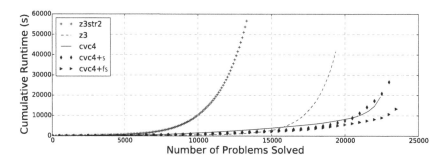

Fig. 9. Cactus plot of configurations of CVC4, Z3 and Z3-STR on solved benchmarks across all three benchmark sets.

We also measured how often CVC4 resorted to expanding extended function terms. We considered a modified configuration **cvc4+fs'** that is identical to **cvc4+fs** except that it does not use the rule Ext-Simplify. The 23,738 benchmarks solved by both **cvc4+fs** and **cvc4+fs'** had 619.2 extended function terms on average. On average over these benchmarks, the configuration **cvc4+fs'** found that 63.5 unique extended functions terms were relevant to satisfiability (e.g., were added to a configuration), and of these 24.3 were expanded (38%). Likewise, **cvc4+fs** found that 66.4 unique extended functions terms were relevant to satisfiability, and of these 12.6 were expanded (19%). With Ext-Simplify, it inferred 405.2 equalities per benchmark on average based on context-dependent simplification, showing that simplification is possible in a majority of contexts (97%). Limited to expansions that introduce universal quantification, which excludes expansions of substr and positively asserted contains, **cvc4+fs'** considered 11.4 expansions on average compared to 2.7 considered by **cvc4+fs**. This means that approximately 4 times fewer quantified formulas were introduced thanks to context-dependent simplification in **cvc4+fs**.

5.2   Symbolic Execution for Python

Our benchmarks were generated by PyEx, which is a symbolic executor designed to assist Python developers achieve high-coverage testing in their daily development routine, e.g., as part of the nightly tests run on the most recent version of a code base. To demonstrate the relative performance of CVC4, Z3, and Z3-STR in our nightly tests scenario, we ran PyEx on a test suite of 19 functions sampled from 4 popular Python packages: httplib2, pip, pymongo, and requests. The set of queries generated during this experiment was used for our evaluation of the raw solver performance in Sect. 5.1. In this section, we show that the superior raw performance of CVC4 over other current solvers also translates into *real-life benefits* for PyEx users.

Our experiment was conducted on a developer machine featuring an Intel E3-1275 v3 quad-core processor (3.5 GHz) and 32 GB of memory. PyEx was run on each of the 19 functions for a maximum CPU time of 2 h. By design, PyEx issues concurrent queries using Python multiprocessing when multiple queries are pending. To reflect the configuration of our test machine, we capped the number of concurrent processes to 8. Note that, due to the nature of our test infrastructure, each of the 19 functions was tested in sequence and thus concurrency happened only within the testing of each individual function. In addition, PyEx has a notion of a per-path timeout, which is a heuristic to steer code exploration away from code paths that are stuck with hard queries. For this experiment, that timeout was set to 10 min.

We argue that the most important metrics for a developer are (i) the wall-clock time to run PyEx over the test suite and (ii) the coverage achieved over this time. In our experiments, PyEx with z3 and with z3-STR finished in 717 min and 829 min, respectively. By comparison, PyEx with the recommended configuration of CVC4 (**cvc4+fs**) finished in 295 min, which represents a speedup of 59% and 64% respectively over the other solvers. To compare coverage, we used the Python coverage library to measure both *line coverage*, the percentage of executed source lines, and *branch coverage*, the number of witnessed branch outcomes, of the test suite during symbolic execution. The line coverage of PyEx with **cvc4+fs**, z3, and z3-STR was respectively 8.48%, 8.41%, and 8.34%,[6] whereas the branch coverage was 3612, 3895, and 3500. Taking both metrics into account, we conclude that **cvc4+fs** is highly effective for PyEx since it achieves similar coverage as the other tools while running significantly faster.

6   Concluding Remarks and Future Work

We have presented a calculus for extended string constraints that relies on both bounded quantifier elimination and context-dependent simplification techniques. The latter led to significant performance benefits for constraints coming from symbolic execution of Python programs. An implementation of these techniques in CVC4 has 3.8 times fewer timeouts and enables the PyEx symbolic executor to achieve comparable program coverage on our test suite while using only 41% of the runtime compared to other solvers.

Our analysis on program coverage indicates that an interesting research avenue for future work would be to determine correlations between certain features of models generated by string solvers and their utility in a symbolic executor, since different models may lead to different symbolic executions and hence different overall analyses.

We plan to develop context-dependent simplification techniques for other string functions, including conversion functions str_to_int and int_to_str, and to adapt these techniques to other SMT theories. Notably, we would like to use context-dependent simplification to optimize lazy approaches for fixed-width bit-vectors [14] where it is beneficial to avoid bit-blasting bit-vector operators, such as multiplication, that require elaborate encodings.

---

[6] Overall coverage appears to be low because we tested only some functions from each library.

Acknowledgments. This work was supported in part by the National Science Foundation under grants CNS-1228765, CNS-1228768, and CNS-1228827. We express our immense gratitude to Peter Chapman, who served as the first lead developer of PyEx.

References

1. Abdulla, P.A., Atig, M.F., Chen, Y.-F., Holík, L., Rezine, A., Rümmer, P., Stenman, J.: String constraints for verification. In: Biere, A., Bloem, R. (eds.) CAV 2014. LNCS, vol. 8559, pp. 150–166. Springer, Cham (2014). doi:10.1007/978-3-319-08867-9_10

2. Abdulla, P.A., Atig, M.F., Chen, Y.-F., Holík, L., Rezine, A., Rümmer, P., Stenman, J.: Norn: an SMT solver for string constraints. In: Kroening, D., Păsăreanu, C.S. (eds.) CAV 2015. LNCS, vol. 9206, pp. 462–469. Springer, Cham (2015). doi:10.1007/978-3-319-21690-4_29

3. Ball, T., Daniel, J.: Deconstructing dynamic symbolic execution. In: Proceedings of the 2014 Marktoberdorf Summer School on Dependable Software Systems Engineering. IOS Press (2014)

4. Barrett, C., Conway, C.L., Deters, M., Hadarean, L., Jovanović, D., King, T., Reynolds, A., Tinelli, C.: CVC4. In: Gopalakrishnan, G., Qadeer, S. (eds.) CAV 2011. LNCS, vol. 6806, pp. 171–177. Springer, Heidelberg (2011). doi:10.1007/978-3-642-22110-1_14

5. Bjørner, N., Tillmann, N., Voronkov, A.: Path feasibility analysis for string-manipulating programs. In: Kowalewski, S., Philippou, A. (eds.) TACAS 2009. LNCS, vol. 5505, pp. 307–321. Springer, Heidelberg (2009). doi:10.1007/978-3-642-00768-2_27

6. Cadar, C., Dunbar, D., Engler, D.: KLEE: unassisted and automatic generation of high-coverage tests for complex systems programs. In: Proceedings of the 8th USENIX Symposium on Operating System Design and Implementation, pp. 209–224. USENIX (2008)

7. Cha, S.K., Avgerinos, T., Rebert, A., Brumley, D.: Unleashing Mayhem on binary code. In: Proceedings of the 2012 IEEE Symposium on Security and Privacy, pp. 380–394. IEEE (2012)

8. Chipounov, V., Kuznetsov, V., Candea, G.: S2E: a platform for in-vivo multi-path analysis of software systems. In: Proceedings of the 16th International Conference on Architectural Support for Programming Languages and Operating Systems, pp. 265–278. ACM (2011)

9. De Moura, L., Bjørner, N.: Z3: an efficient SMT solver. In: Ramakrishnan, C.R., Rehof, J. (eds.) TACAS 2008. LNCS, vol. 4963, pp. 337–340. Springer, Heidelberg (2008). doi:10.1007/978-3-540-78800-3_24

10. Fu, X., Li, C.: A string constraint solver for detecting web application vulnerability. In: Proceedings of the 22nd International Conference on Software Engineering and Knowledge Engineering, SEKE 2010. Knowledge Systems Institute Graduate School (2010)

11. Ganesh, V., Minnes, M., Solar-Lezama, A., Rinard, M.: Word equations with length constraints: what's decidable? In: Biere, A., Nahir, A., Vos, T. (eds.) HVC 2012. LNCS, vol. 7857, pp. 209–226. Springer, Heidelberg (2013). doi:10.1007/978-3-642-39611-3_21

12. Ganzinger, H., Hagen, G., Nieuwenhuis, R., Oliveras, A., Tinelli, C.: DPLL(T): fast decision procedures. In: Alur, R., Peled, D.A. (eds.) CAV 2004. LNCS, vol. 3114, pp. 175–188. Springer, Heidelberg (2004). doi:10.1007/978-3-540-27813-9_14

13. Godefroid, P., Levin, M.Y., Molnar, D.: Automated whitebox fuzz testing. In: Proceedings of the 16th Annual Network and Distributed System Security Symposium. Internet Society (2008)

14. Hadarean, L., Bansal, K., Jovanović, D., Barrett, C., Tinelli, C.: A tale of two solvers: eager and lazy approaches to bit-vectors. In: Biere, A., Bloem, R. (eds.) CAV 2014. LNCS, vol. 8559, pp. 680–695. Springer, Cham (2014). doi:10.1007/978-3-319-08867-9_45

15. Hooimeijer, P., Veanes, M.: An evaluation of automata algorithms for string analysis. In: Jhala, R., Schmidt, D. (eds.) VMCAI 2011. LNCS, vol. 6538, pp. 248–262. Springer, Heidelberg (2011). doi:10.1007/978-3-642-18275-4_18

16. Kiezun, A., Ganesh, V., Guo, P.J., Hooimeijer, P., Ernst, M.D.: HAMPI: a solver for string constraints. In: Proceedings of the Eighteenth International Symposium on Software Testing and Analysis, pp. 105–116. ACM (2009)

17. King, J.C.: Symbolic execution and program testing. Commun. ACM 19(7), 385–394 (1976)

18. Li, G., Ghosh, I.: PASS: string solving with parameterized array and interval automaton. In: Bertacco, V., Legay, A. (eds.) HVC 2013. LNCS, vol. 8244, pp. 15–31. Springer, Cham (2013). doi:10.1007/978-3-319-03077-7_2

19. Liang, T., Reynolds, A., Tinelli, C., Barrett, C., Deters, M.: A DPLL(T) theory solver for a theory of strings and regular expressions. In: Biere, A., Bloem, R. (eds.) CAV 2014. LNCS, vol. 8559, pp. 646–662. Springer, Cham (2014). doi:10.1007/978-3-319-08867-9_43

20. Liang, T., Tsiskaridze, N., Reynolds, A., Tinelli, C., Barrett, C.: A decision procedure for regular membership and length constraints over unbounded strings. In: Lutz, C., Ranise, S. (eds.) FroCoS 2015. LNCS, vol. 9322, pp. 135–150. Springer, Cham (2015). doi:10.1007/978-3-319-24246-0_9

21. Makanin, G.S.: The problem of solvability of equations in a free semigroup. English transl. in Math USSR Sbornik 32, 147–236 (1977)

22. Plandowski, W.: Satisfiability of word equations with constants is in PSPACE. J. ACM 51(3), 483–496 (2004)

23. Reynolds, A., Tinelli, C., Goel, A., Krstić, S., Deters, M., Barrett, C.: Quantifier instantiation techniques for finite model finding in SMT. In: Bonacina, M.P. (ed.) CADE 2013. LNCS, vol. 7898, pp. 377–391. Springer, Heidelberg (2013). doi:10.1007/978-3-642-38574-2_26

24. Stephens, N., Grosen, J., Salls, C., Dutcher, A., Wang, R., Corbetta, J., Shoshitaishvili, Y., Kruegel, C., Vigna, G.: Driller: augmenting fuzzing through selective symbolic execution. In: Proceedings of the Network and Distributed System Security Symposium (2016)

25. Stump, A., Sutcliffe, G., Tinelli, C.: StarExec: a cross-community infrastructure for logic solving. In: Demri, S., Kapur, D., Weidenbach, C. (eds.) IJCAR 2014. LNCS, vol. 8562, pp. 367–373. Springer, Cham (2014). doi:10.1007/978-3-319-08587-6_28

26. Trinh, M.-T., Chu, D.-H., Jaffar, J.: Progressive reasoning over recursively-defined strings. In: Chaudhuri, S., Farzan, A. (eds.) CAV 2016. LNCS, vol. 9779, pp. 218–240. Springer, Cham (2016). doi:10.1007/978-3-319-41528-4_12

27. Trinh, M.-T., Chu, D.-H., Jaffar, J.: S3: a symbolic string solver for vulnerability detection in web applications. In: Yung, M., Li, N. (eds.) Proceedings of the 21st ACM Conference on Computer and Communications Security (2014)

28. Veanes, M., Bjørner, N., Moura, L.: Symbolic automata constraint solving. In: Fermüller, C.G., Voronkov, A. (eds.) LPAR 2010. LNCS, vol. 6397, pp. 640–654. Springer, Heidelberg (2010). doi:10.1007/978-3-642-16242-8_45

29. Zheng, Y., Ganesh, V., Subramanian, S., Tripp, O., Dolby, J., Zhang, X.: Effective search-space pruning for solvers of string equations, regular expressions and length constraints. In: Kroening, D., Păsăreanu, C.S. (eds.) CAV 2015. LNCS, vol. 9206, pp. 235–254. Springer, Cham (2015). doi:10.1007/978-3-319-21690-4_14
30. Zheng, Y., Zhang, X., Ganesh, V.: Z3-str: a z3-based string solver for web application analysis. In: Proceedings of the 2013 9th Joint Meeting on Foundations of Software Engineering, ESEC/FSE 2013, pp. 114–124. ACM (2013)

On Expansion and Resolution in CEGAR Based QBF Solving

Leander Tentrup[✉]

Saarland University, Saarbrücken, Germany
`tentrup@react.uni-saarland.de`

Abstract. A quantified Boolean formula (QBF) is a propositional formula extended with universal and existential quantification over propositions. There are two methodologies in CEGAR based QBF solving techniques, one that is based on a refinement loop that builds partial expansions and a more recent one that is based on the communication of satisfied clauses. Despite their algorithmic similarity, their performance characteristics in experimental evaluations are very different and in many cases orthogonal. We compare those CEGAR approaches using proof theory developed around QBF solving and present a unified calculus that combines the strength of both approaches. Lastly, we implement the new calculus and confirm experimentally that the theoretical improvements lead to improved performance.

1 Introduction

Efficient solving techniques for Boolean theories are an integral part of modern verification and synthesis methods. Especially in synthesis, the amount of choice in the solution space leads to propositional problems of enormous size. Quantified Boolean formulas (QBFs) have repeatedly been considered as a candidate theory for synthesis approaches [6, 7, 10–12, 24] and recent advances in QBF solvers give rise to hope that QBF may help to increase the scalability of those approaches.

Solving quantified Boolean formulas (QBF) using partial expansions in a counterexample guided abstraction and refinement (CEGAR) loop [16] has proven to be very successful. From its introduction, the corresponding solver RAReQS won several QBF competitions. In recent work, a different kind of CEGAR algorithms have been proposed [18, 25], implemented in the solvers Qesto and CAQE. All those CEGAR approaches share algorithmic similarities like working recursively over the structure of the quantifier prefix and using SAT solver to enumerate candidate solutions. However, instead of using partial expansions of the QBF as RAReQS does, newer approaches base their refinements on whether a set of clauses is satisfied or not. Despite those algorithmic similarities, the performance characteristics of the resulting solver in experimental

Supported by the European Research Council (ERC) Grant OSARES (No. 683300).

R. Majumdar and V. Kunčak (Eds.): CAV 2017, Part II, LNCS 10427, pp. 475–494, 2017.
DOI: 10.1007/978-3-319-63390-9_25

evaluations are very different and in many cases orthogonal: While RAReQS tends to perform best on instances with a low number of quantifier alternations, Qesto and CAQE have an advantage in instances with many alternations [25].

Proof theory has been repeatedly used to improve the understanding of different solving techniques. For example, the proof calculus ∀Exp+Res [17] has been developed to characterize aspects of expansion-based solving. In this paper, we introduce a new calculus ∀Red+Res that corresponds to the clausal-based CEGAR approaches [18,25]. The levelized nature of those algorithms are reflected by the rules of this calculus, universal reduction and propositional resolution, which are applied to blocks of quantifiers. We show that this calculus is inherently different to ∀Exp+Res explaining the empirical performance results. In detail, we show that ∀Red+Res polynomial simulates level-ordered Q-resolution. We also discuss an extension to ∀Red+Res that was already proposed as solving optimizations [25] and show that this extension makes the resulting calculus exponential more concise.

Further, we integrate the ∀Exp+Res calculus as a rule that can be used within the ∀Red+Res calculus, leading to a unified proof calculus for all current CEGAR approaches. We show that the unified calculus is exponential stronger than both ∀Exp+Res and ∀Red+Res, as well as just applying both simultaneously. This unified calculus serves as a base for implementing an expansion refinement in the QBF solver CAQE. On standard benchmark sets, the combined approach leads to a significant empirical improvement over the previous implementation.

2   Preliminaries

2.1   Quantified Boolean Formulas

We consider quantified Boolean formulas in prenex conjunctive normal form (PCNF), that is a formula consisting of a linear and consecutive quantifier prefix as well as a propositional matrix. A *matrix* is a set of clauses, and a clause is a disjunctive combination of *literals* l, that is either a variable or its negation.

Given a clause $C = (l_1 \vee l_2 \vee \ldots \vee l_n)$, we use set notation interchangeably, that is C is also represented by the set $\{l_1, l_2, \ldots, l_n\}$. Furthermore, we use standard set operations, such as union and intersection, to work with clauses.

For readability, we lift the quantification over variables to the quantification over sets of variables and denote a maximal consecutive block of quantifiers of the same type $\forall x_1. \forall x_2. \cdots \forall x_n. \varphi$ by $\forall X. \varphi$ and $\exists x_1. \exists x_2. \cdots \exists x_n. \varphi$ by $\exists X. \varphi$, accordingly, where $X = \{x_1, \ldots, x_n\}$.

Given a set of variables X, an *assignment* of X is a function $\alpha : X \to \mathbb{B}$ that maps each variable $x \in X$ to either true ($\top$) or false ($\bot$). When the domain of α is not clear from context, we write α_X. We use the instantiation of a QBF Φ by assignment α, written $\Phi[\alpha]$ which removes quantification over variables in $\mathrm{dom}(\alpha)$ and replaces occurrences of $x \in \mathrm{dom}(\alpha)$ by $\alpha(x)$. We write $\alpha \vDash \varphi$ if the assignment α satisfies a propositional formula φ, i.e., $\varphi[\alpha] \equiv \top$.

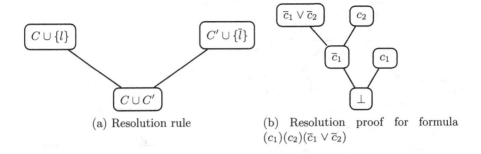

(a) Resolution rule

(b) Resolution proof for formula $(c_1)(c_2)(\bar{c}_1 \vee \bar{c}_2)$

Fig. 1. Visualization of the resolution rule as a graph.

2.2 Resolution

Propositional resolution is a well-known method for refuting propositional formulas in conjunctive normal form (CNF). The resolution rule allows to *merge* two clauses that contain the same variable, but in opposite signs.

$$\frac{C \cup \{l\} \quad C' \cup \{\bar{l}\}}{C \cup C'} \ \text{res}$$

A resolution proof π is a series of applications of the resolution rule. A propositional formula is unsatisfiable if there is a resolution proof that derives the empty clause. We visualize resolution proofs by a graph where the nodes with indegree 0 are called the leaves and the unique node with outdegree 0 is called the root. We depict the graph representation of a resolution proof in Fig. 1(b). The *size* of a resolution proof is the number of nodes in the graph.

2.3 Proof Systems

We consider proof systems that are able to refute quantified Boolean formulas. To enable comparison between proof systems, one uses the concept of *polynomial simulation*. A proof system P polynomially simulates (p-simulates) P' if there is a polynomial p such that for every number n and every formula Φ it holds that if there is a proof of Φ in P' of size n, then there is a proof of Φ in P whose size is less than $p(n)$. We call P and P' polynomial equivalent, if P' additionally p-simulates P.

A refutation based calculus (such as resolution) is regarded as a proof system because it can refute the negation of a formula.

Figure 2 gives an overview over the proof systems introduced in this paper and their relation. An edge $P \rightarrow P'$ means that P p-simulates P' (transitive edges are omitted). A dashed line indicates incomparability results.

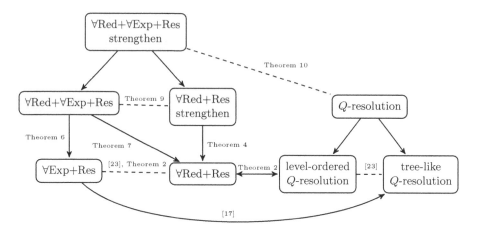

Fig. 2. Overview of the proof systems and their relations. Solid arrows indicate p-simulation relation. Dashed lines indicate incomparability results. The gray boxes are the ones introduced in this paper.

3   Proof Calculi

Given a PCNF formula $Q X_1 \ldots Q X_n . \bigwedge_{1 \leq i \leq m} C_i$. We define a function $lit(i, k)$ that returns the literals of clause C_i that are bound at quantifier level k ($1 \leq k \leq n$). Further, we generalize this definition to $lit(i, > k)$ and $lit(i, < k)$ that return the literals bound after (before) level k. We define $lit(i, 0) = lit(i, n + 1) = \emptyset$ for every $1 \leq i \leq m$. We use $\mathcal{C}$ to denote a set of clauses and $Q_k \in \{\exists, \forall\}$ to denote the quantification type of level k.

3.1   A Proof System for Clausal Abstractions

We start by defining the object on which our proof system $\forall$Red+Res is based on. A *proof object* $\mathcal{P}^k$ consists of a set of indices $\mathcal{P}$ where an index $i \in \mathcal{P}$ represents the i-th clause in the original matrix and k denotes the k-th level of the quantifier hierarchy. We define an operation $lit(\mathcal{P}^k) = \bigcup_{i \in \mathcal{P}} lit(i, k)$, that gives access to the literals of clauses contained in $\mathcal{P}^k$. The leaves in our proof system are singleton sets $\{i\}^z$ where z is the maximum quantification level of all literals in clause C_i. The root of a refutation proof is the proof object $\mathcal{P}^0$ that represents the empty set, i.e., $lit(\mathcal{P}^0) = \emptyset$.

The rules of the proof system is given in Fig. 3. It consists of three rules, an axiom rule (init) that generates leaves, a resolution rule (res), and a universal reduction rule ($\forall$red). The latter two rules enable to transform a premise that is related to quantifier level k into a conclusion that is related to quantifier level $k - 1$. The universal reduction rule and the resolution rule are used for universal and existential quantifier blocks, respectively.

$$\frac{\mathcal{P}_1^k \quad \cdots \quad \mathcal{P}_j^k \quad \pi}{\left(\bigcup_{i \in \{1,\ldots,j\}} \mathcal{P}_i\right)^{k-1}} \ \text{res} \qquad \begin{array}{l} Q_k = \exists \\ \pi \text{ is a resolution refutation proof for } \bigwedge_{1 \leq i \leq j} lit(\mathcal{P}_i^k) \end{array}$$

$$\frac{\mathcal{P}^k}{\mathcal{P}^{k-1}} \ \forall\text{red} \qquad \begin{array}{l} Q_k = \forall \\ \forall l \in lit(\mathcal{P}^k). \bar{l} \notin lit(\mathcal{P}^k) \end{array}$$

$$\frac{}{\{i\}^k} \ \text{init} \qquad \begin{array}{l} 1 \leq i \leq m \\ lit(i, > k) = \emptyset \end{array}$$

Fig. 3. The rules of the ∀Red+Res calculus.

Resolution Rule. There is a close connection between (res) and the propositional resolution as (res) merges a number of proof objects $\mathcal{P}_i^k$ of level k into a single proof object of level $k - 1$. It does so by using a resolution proof for a propositional formula that is constructed from the premises $\mathcal{P}_i^k$. This propositional formula $\bigwedge_{1 \leq i \leq j} lit(\mathcal{P}_i^k)$ contains *only* literals of level k. Intuitively, this rule can be interpreted as follows: a resolution proof over those clauses rules out any possible existential assignment at quantifier level k, thus, one of those clauses has to be satisfied at an earlier level.

Universal Reduction Rule. In contrast to (res), (∀red) works on single proof objects. It can be applied if level k is universal and the premise does not encode a universal tautology, i.e., for every literal $l \in lit(\mathcal{P}^k)$, the negated literal $\bar{l}$ is not contained in $lit(\mathcal{P}^k)$.

Graph Representation. A proof in the ∀Red+Res calculus can be represented as a directed acyclic graph (DAG). The nodes in the DAG are proof objects $\mathcal{P}^k$ and the edges represent applications of (res) and (∀red). The rule (res) is represented by a hyper-edge that is labeled with the propositional resolution proof π. Edges representing the universal reduction can thus remain unlabeled without introducing ambiguity. The *size* of a ∀Red+Res proof is the number of nodes in the graph together with the number of inner (non-leaf, non-root) nodes of the containing propositional resolution proofs.

A *refutation* in the ∀Red+Res calculus is a proof that derives a proof object $\mathcal{P}^0$ at level 0. A proof for some $\mathcal{P}^k$ is a ∀Red+Res proof with root $\mathcal{P}^k$. Thus, a proof for $\mathcal{P}^k$ can be also viewed as a refutation for the formula $Q\,X_{k+1} \ldots Q\,X_n$. $\bigwedge_{i \in \mathcal{P}} lit(i, > k)$ starting with quantifier level $k + 1$ and containing clauses represented by $\mathcal{P}$.

Example 1. Consider the following QBF

$$\underbrace{\exists e_1}_{1} . \underbrace{\forall u_1}_{2} . \underbrace{\exists c_1, c_2}_{3} . \underbrace{(\bar{e}_1 \vee c_1)}_{C_1} \underbrace{(\bar{u}_1 \vee c_1)}_{C_2} \underbrace{(e_1 \vee c_2)}_{C_3} \underbrace{(u_1 \vee c_2)}_{C_4} \underbrace{(\bar{c}_1 \vee \bar{c}_2)}_{C_5}. \tag{1}$$

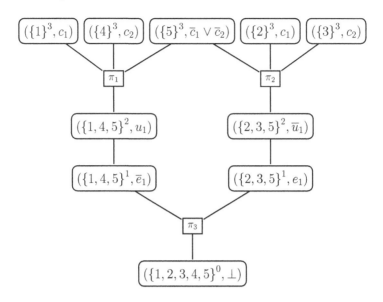

Fig. 4. A ∀Red+Res refutation for formula (1).

The refutation in the ∀Red+Res calculus is given in Fig. 4. In the nodes, we represent the proof objects $\mathcal{P}^k$ in the first component and the represented clause in the second component. The proof follows the structure of the quantifier prefix, i.e., it needs four levels to derive a refutation. The resolution proof π_1 for propositional formula

$$lit(\{1\}^3) \wedge lit(\{4\}^3) \wedge lit(\{5\}^3) \equiv (c_1)(c_2)(\overline{c}_1 \vee \overline{c}_2)$$

is depicted in Fig. 1(b).

In the following, we give a formal correctness argument and compare our calculus to established proof systems. A QBF proof system is *sound* if deriving a proof implies that the QBF is false and it is *refutational complete* if every false QBF has a proof.

Theorem 1. *∀Red+Res is sound and refutational complete for QBF.*

Proof. The completeness proof is carried out by induction over the quantifier prefix.

Induction Base. Let $\exists X. \varphi$ be a false QBF and φ be propositional. Then (res) derives some $\mathcal{P}^0$ because resolution is complete for propositional formulas. Let $\forall X. \varphi$ be a false QBF and φ be propositional. Picking an arbitrary (non-tautological) clause C_i and applying (∀red) leads to $\{i\}^0$.

Induction Step. Let $\exists X. \Phi$ be a false QBF, i.e., for all assignments α_X the QBF $\Phi[\alpha_X]$ is false. Hence, by induction hypothesis, there exists a ∀Red+Res proof for every $\Phi[\alpha_X]$. We transform those proofs in a way that they can be used to build a proof for Φ. Let P be a proof of $\Phi[\alpha_X]$. P has a distinct root node (representing the empty set), that was derived using ($\forall$red) as $\Phi[\alpha_X]$ starts with a universal quantifier. To embed P in Φ, we increment every level in P by one, as Φ has one additional (existential) quantifier level. Then, instead of deriving the empty set, the former root node derives a proof object of the form $\mathcal{P}^1$. Let N be the set of those former root nodes. By construction, there exists a resolution proof π such that the empty set can be derived by (res) using N (or a subset thereof). Assuming otherwise leads to the contradiction that some $\Phi[\alpha_X]$ is true.

Let $\forall X.\,\Phi$ be a false QBF, i.e., there is an assignment α_X such that the QBF $\Phi[\alpha_X]$ is false. Hence, by induction hypothesis, there exists a $\forall$Red+Res proof for $\Phi[\alpha_X]$. Applying ($\forall$red) using α_X is a $\forall$Red+Res proof for Φ.

For soundness it is enough to show that one cannot derive a clause using this calculus that changes the satisfiability. Let $\Phi = Q\,X_1\dots Q\,X_n.\bigwedge_{1\le i\le m} C_i$ be an arbitrary QBF. For every level k and every $\mathcal{P}^k$ generated by the application of the $\forall$Red+Res calculus, it holds that Φ and $Q\,X_1\dots Q\,X_n.\bigwedge_{1\le i\le m} C_i \wedge$ $(\bigvee_{i\in\mathcal{P}}\bigvee_{l\in lit(i,\le k)} l)$ are equisatisfiable. Assume otherwise, then either ($\forall$red) or (res) have derived a $\mathcal{P}^k$ that would make Φ false. Again, by induction, one can show that if ($\forall$red) derived a $\mathcal{P}^k$ that makes Φ false, the original premise $\mathcal{P}^{k+1}$ would have made Φ false; likewise, if (res) derived a $\mathcal{P}^k$ that makes Φ false, the conjunction of the premises have made Φ false. $\square$

Comparison to Q-resolution Calculus. Q-resolution [19] is an extension of the (propositional) resolution rule to handle universal quantification. The universal reduction rule allows the removal of universal literal u from a clause C if no existential literal $l \in C$ depends on u. There are also additional rules on when the resolution rule can be applied, i.e., it is not allowed to produce tautology clauses using the resolution rule. The definitions of Q-resolution proof and refutation are analogous to the propositional case.

There are two restricted classes of Q-resolution that are commonly considered, that is *level-ordered* and *tree-like* Q-resolution. A Q-resolution proof is level-ordered if resolution of an existential literal l at level k happens before every other existential literal with level $<k$. A Q-resolution proof is tree-like if the graph representing the proof has a tree shape.

As a first result, we show that $\forall$Red+Res is polynomially equivalent to level-ordered Q-resolution, i.e., a proof in our calculus can be polynomially simulated in level-ordered Q-resolution and vice versa. While this is straightforward from the definitions of both calculi, this is much less obvious if one looks at the underlying algorithms of the CEGAR approaches [18,25] and QCDCL [27].

Theorem 2. *$\forall$Red+Res and level-ordered Q-resolution are p-sim. equivalent.*

Proof. A $\forall$Red+Res proof can be transformed into a Q-resolution proof by replacing every node $\mathcal{P}^k$ by the clause $(\bigvee_{i\in\mathcal{P}}\bigvee_{l\in lit(i,\le k)} l)$ and by replacing the hyper-edge labeled with π by a graph representing the applications of the resolution rule. Similarly, a level-ordered Q-resolution proof can be transformed into a ∀Red+Res proof by a step-wise transformation from leaves to the root. This way, one can track the clauses needed for constructing the proof objects $\mathcal{P}^k$ at every level k.   □

Despite being equally powerful, the differences are important and enable the expansion based extension that we will introduce in the next section. One difference is that our calculus only reasons about literals of one quantifier level, which allows us to use plain resolution without any changes (as are needed in Q-resolution). Further, the proof rules capture the fact that only proof obligations are communicated between the quantifier levels of the QBF. An immediate consequence is that every refutation in the proof system is DAG-like and has exactly depth $k + 1$.

Since the level-ordering constraint imposes an order on the resolution, the size of the refutation proof may be exponentially larger for some formulas [14]. Hence, also ∀Red+Res is in general exponentially weaker than unrestricted Q-resolution. In practice, and already noted by Janota and Marques-Silva [17], solvers that are based on Q-resolution proofs produce level-ordered Q-resolution.

In the initial version of CAQE [25] an optimization that can generate new resolvents at level k without recursion into deeper levels was described. We model this optimization as a new rule extending the ∀Red+Res calculus and show that this rule leads to an exponential separation.

Strong UNSAT Rule. In the implementation of CAQE, we used an optimization which we called *strong UNSAT refinement* [25], that allowed the solver to strengthen a certain type of refinements. The basic idea behind this optimization is that if the solver determines that, at an existential level k, a certain set of clauses $\mathcal{C}$ cannot be satisfied at the same time, then every alternative set of clauses $\mathcal{C}'$, that is equivalent with respect to the literals in levels $> k$, cannot be satisfied as well. We introduce the following proof rule that formalizes this intuition. We extend proof objects $\mathcal{P}^k$ such that they can additionally contain fresh literals, i.e., literals that were not part of the original QBF. Those literals are treated as they were bound at level k, i.e., they are contained in $lit(\mathcal{P}^k)$ and can thus be used in the premise of the rule (res), but are not contained in the conclusion $\mathcal{P}^{k-1}$.

$$\frac{(\mathcal{P} \cup \{i\})^k}{(\{a\} \cup \mathcal{P})^k \quad \{\bar{a}, j_1\}^k \quad \cdots \quad \{\bar{a}, j_n\}^k} \text{ strengthen} \quad \begin{array}{l} Q_k = \exists, \\ lit(j, > k) \subseteq lit(i, > k) \\ \text{for all } j \in \{j_1, \ldots, j_n\}, \\ a \text{ a fresh var.} \end{array}$$

Theorem 3. *The strengthening rule is sound.*

Proof. In a resolution proof at level k, one can derive the proof objects $(\mathcal{P} \cup \{j\})^k$ for $j \in \{j_1, \ldots, j_n\}$ using the conclusion of the strengthening rule. Assume we have a proof for $(\mathcal{P} \cup \{i\})^k$ (premise), then the quantified formula $\forall X_{k+1} \ldots Q X_n . \bigwedge_{i^* \in \mathcal{P}} lit(i^*, > k) \wedge lit(i, > k)$ is false. Thus, the QBF with the same quantifier prefix and matrix, extended by some clause $lit(j, > k)$ for

$j \in \{j_1, \ldots, j_n\}$, is still false. Since every C_j subsumes C_i with respect to quantifier level greater than k ($lit(j, > k) \subseteq lit(i, > k)$), the clause $lit(i, > k)$ can be eliminated without changing satisfiability. Thus, the resulting quantified formula $\forall X_{k+1} \ldots Q X_n . \bigwedge_{i^* \in \mathcal{P}} lit(i^*, > k) \wedge lit(j, > k)$ is false and there exists a $\forall$Red+Res proof for $(\mathcal{P} \cup \{j\})^k$. $\qquad\square$

Theorem 4. *The proof system without strengthening rule does not p-simulate the proof system with strengthening rule.*

Proof. We use the family of formulas CR_n that was used to show that level-ordered Q-resolution cannot p-simulate $\forall$Exp+Res [17]. We show that CR_n has a polynomial refutation in the $\forall$Red+Res calculus with strengthening rule, but has only exponential refutations without it. The latter follows from Theorem 2 and the results by Janota and Marques-Silva [17].

The formula CR_n has the quantifier prefix $\exists x_{11} \ldots x_{nn} \forall z \exists a_1 \ldots a_n b_1 \ldots b_n$ and the matrix is given by

$$\left(\bigvee_{i \in 1..n} \overline{a}_i \right) \wedge \left(\bigvee_{i \in 1..n} \overline{b}_i \right) \wedge \bigwedge_{i,j \in 1..n} \underbrace{(x_{ij} \vee z \vee a_i)}_{C_{ij}} \wedge \underbrace{(\overline{x}_{ij} \vee \overline{z} \vee b_j)}_{C_{\overline{ij}}}. \qquad (2)$$

One can interpret the constraints as selecting rows and columns in a matrix where i selects the row and j selects the column, e.g., for $n = 3$ it can be visualized as follows:

$x_{11} \vee z \vee a_1$	$\overline{x}_{11} \vee \overline{z} \vee b_1$	$x_{12} \vee z \vee a_1$	$\overline{x}_{12} \vee \overline{z} \vee b_2$	$x_{13} \vee z \vee a_1$	$\overline{x}_{13} \vee \overline{z} \vee b_3$
$x_{21} \vee z \vee a_2$	$\overline{x}_{21} \vee \overline{z} \vee b_1$	$x_{22} \vee z \vee a_2$	$\overline{x}_{22} \vee \overline{z} \vee b_2$	$x_{23} \vee z \vee a_2$	$\overline{x}_{23} \vee \overline{z} \vee b_3$
$x_{31} \vee z \vee a_3$	$\overline{x}_{31} \vee \overline{z} \vee b_1$	$x_{32} \vee z \vee a_3$	$\overline{x}_{32} \vee \overline{z} \vee b_2$	$x_{33} \vee z \vee a_3$	$\overline{x}_{33} \vee \overline{z} \vee b_3$

Assume $z \to 0$, then we derive the proof object $\mathcal{P}^1 = \{i1 \mid i \in 1..n\}^1$ ($lit(\mathcal{P}^1) = \bigvee_{i \in 1..n} x_{i1}$) by applying the resolution and reduction rule. Likewise, for $z \to 1$, we derive the proof object $\mathcal{P}_0^1 = \{\overline{1j} \mid j \in 1..n\}^1$ ($lit(\mathcal{P}_0^1) = \bigvee_{j \in 1..n} \overline{x}_{1j}$). Applying the strengthening rule on $\mathcal{P}_0^1$ results in $\mathcal{P}_1^1 = (\{c_1\} \cup \{\overline{1j} \mid j \in 2..n\})^1$ and $\{\overline{c}_1, \overline{11}\}^1, \{\overline{c}_1, \overline{21}\}^1, \ldots, \{\overline{c}_1, \overline{n1}\}^1$ where c_1 is a fresh variable. Further $n-1$ applications of the strengthening rule starting on $\mathcal{P}_1^1$ lead to $\mathcal{P}_n^1 = \{c_j \mid j \in 1..n\}^1$ and the proof objects $\{\overline{c}_j, \overline{ij} \mid i,j \in 1..n\}^1$, where c_j are fresh variables, as all clauses in a column are equivalent with respect to the inner quantifiers (contain $\overline{z} \vee b_j$).

Using $\mathcal{P}^1$ and $\{\overline{c}_1, \overline{11}\}^1, \{\overline{c}_1, \overline{21}\}^1, \ldots, \{\overline{c}_1, \overline{n1}\}^1$ from the first strengthening application, we derive the singleton set $\{\overline{c}_1\}$ using n resolution steps ($lit(\mathcal{P}^1) = \bigvee_{i \in 1..n} x_{i1}$ and $lit(\{\overline{c}_1, \overline{i1}\}^1) = \{\overline{c}_1, \overline{x}_{i1}\}$). Analogously, one derives the singletons $\{\overline{c}_2\} \ldots \{\overline{c}_n\}$ and together with $\mathcal{P}_n^1 = \{c_j \mid j \in 1..n\}$ the empty set is derived. Thus, there exists a polynomial resolution proof leading to a proof object $\mathcal{P}^0$ and the size of the overall proof is polynomial, too. $\qquad\square$

We note that despite being stronger than plain $\forall$Red+Res, the extended calculus is still incomparable to $\forall$Exp+Res.

Corollary 1. ∀*Red+Res with strengthening rule does not p-simulate* ∀*Exp+Res.*

Proof. We use a modification of formula CR_n (2), which we call CR_n' in the following. The single universal variable z is replaced by a number of variables z_{ij} for every pair $i, j \in 1..N$. It follows that the strengthening rule is never applicable and hence, the proof system is as strong as level-ordered Q-resolution which has an exponential refutation of CR_n while ∀Exp+Res has a polynomial refutation since the expansion tree has still only two branches [17].   □

When compared to Q-resolution, the strengthening rule can be interpreted as a step towards breaking the level-ordered constraint inherent to ∀Red+Res. The calculus, however, is not as strong as Q-resolution.

Corollary 2. ∀*Red+Res with strengthening rule does not p-sim. Q-resolution.*

Proof. The formula CR_n' from the previous proof has a polynomial (tree-like) Q-resolution proof. The proof for CR_n given by Mahajan and Shukla [23] can be modified for CR_n'.   □

Both results follow from the fact that the strengthening rule as presented is not applicable to the formula CR_n'. Where in CR_n, the clauses $C_{\overline{ij}}$ are equal with respect to the inner quantifier when j is fixed ($\overline{z} \vee b_j$), in CR_n' they are all different ($\overline{z}_{ij} \vee b_j$). This difference is only due to the universal variables z_{ij}. Thus, we propose a stronger version of the strengthening rule that does the subset check only on the existential variables. For the universal literals, one additionally has to make sure that no resolvent produces a tautology (as it is the case in CR_n'). We leave the formalization to future work.

3.2   Expansion

The levelized nature of the proof system allows us to introduce additional rules that can reason about quantified subformulas. In the following, we introduce such a rule that allows us to use the ∀Exp+Res calculus [17] within a ∀Red+Res proof.

We start by giving necessary notations used to define ∀Exp+Res. We refer the reader to [17] for further information.

Definition 1 (adapted from [17])

- *A* ∀-*expansion tree for QBF* Φ *with* u *universal quantifier blocks is a rooted tree* $\mathcal{T}$ *such that every path* $p_0 \xrightarrow{\alpha_1} p_1 \cdots \xrightarrow{\alpha_u} p_u$ *in* $\mathcal{T}$ *from the root* p_0 *to some leaf* p_u *has exactly* u *edges and each edge* $p_{i-1} \xrightarrow{\alpha_i} p_i$ *is labeled with a total assignment* α_u *to the universal variables at universal level* u. *Each path in* $\mathcal{T}$ *is uniquely defined by its labeling.*
- *Let* $\mathcal{T}$ *be a* ∀-*expansion tree and* $P = p_0 \xrightarrow{\alpha_1} p_1 \cdots \xrightarrow{\alpha_u} p_u$ *be a path from the root* p_0 *to some leaf* p_u.
  1. *For an existential variable* x *we define* $expand\text{-}var(P, x) = x^\alpha$ *where* x^α *is a fresh variable and* α *is the universal assignment of the dependencies of* x.

2. *For a propositional formula φ define $expand(P, \varphi)$ as instantiating φ with $\alpha_1, \ldots, \alpha_u$ and replacing every existential variable x by $expand\text{-}var(P, x)$.*
3. *Define $expand(\mathcal{T}, \Phi)$ as the conjunction of all $expand(P, \varphi)$ for each root-to-leaf P in $\mathcal{T}$.*

In difference to previous work, we allow to use the expansion rule on quantified subformulas of Φ additionally to applying it to Φ directly. By $\mathcal{C}^{\geq k}$ we denote a set of clauses that only contain literals bound at level $\geq k$.

$$\frac{\mathcal{T} \quad \mathcal{C}^{\geq k} \quad \pi}{\mathcal{P}^{k-1}} \;\forall\text{exp-res} \qquad \begin{array}{l} Q_k = \exists, \pi \text{ is a resolution refutation of the expansion} \\ \text{formula } expand(\mathcal{T}, \exists X_k.\forall X_{k+1} \ldots \exists X_m.\mathcal{C}^{\geq k}) \\ \mathcal{P}^{k-1} = \{i \mid C_i \in \mathcal{C}\}^{k-1} \end{array}$$

The rule states that if there is a universal expansion of the quantified Boolean formula $\exists X_k.\forall X_{k+1} \ldots \exists X_m.\mathcal{C}^{\geq k}$ and a resolution refutation π for this expansion, then there is no existential assignment that satisfies clauses $\mathcal{C}$ from level k. The size of the expansion rule is the sum of the size of the expansion tree and resolution proof [17].

Example 2. We demonstrate the interplay between ($\forall$exp-res) and the $\forall$Red+Res calculus on the following formula

$$\overbrace{\exists e_1}^{1}.\overbrace{\forall u_1}^{2}.\overbrace{\exists c_1, c_2}^{3}.\overbrace{\forall a}^{4}.\overbrace{\exists b}^{5}.\overbrace{\exists x}^{6}.\overbrace{\forall z}^{7}.\;\exists t\;.$$

$$\underbrace{(\bar{e}_1 \vee c_1)}_{1}\underbrace{(\bar{u}_1 \vee c_1)}_{2}\underbrace{(e_1 \vee c_2)}_{3}\underbrace{(u_1 \vee c_2)}_{4}\underbrace{(\bar{c}_1 \vee \bar{c}_2 \vee \bar{b} \vee \bar{a})}_{5}\underbrace{(z \vee t \vee b)}_{6}\underbrace{(\bar{z} \vee \bar{t})}_{7}\underbrace{(x \vee \bar{t})}_{8}\underbrace{(\bar{x} \vee t)}_{9}$$

To apply ($\forall$exp-res), we use the clauses 5–9 from quantifier level 5, i.e., $\mathcal{C}^{\geq 5} = \{(\bar{b})(z \vee t \vee b)(\bar{z} \vee \bar{t})(x \vee \bar{t})(\bar{x} \vee t)\}$. The corresponding quantifier prefix is $\exists b \exists x \forall z \exists t$. Using the complete expansion of z ($\{z \to 0, z \to 1\}$) as the expansion tree $\mathcal{T}$, we get the following expansion formula

$$(\bar{b})(t^{\{z \to 0\}} \vee b)(x \vee \bar{t}^{\{z \to 0\}})(\bar{x} \vee t^{\{z \to 0\}})(\bar{t}^{\{z \to 1\}})(x \vee \bar{t}^{\{z \to 1\}})(\bar{x} \vee t^{\{z \to 1\}}),$$

which has a simple resolution proof π. The conclusion of ($\forall$exp-res) leads to the proof object $\{5, 6, 7, 8, 9\}^4$, but only clause 5 contains literals bound before quantification level 5. After a universal reduction, the proof continues as described in Example 1.

Theorem 5. *The $\forall$exp-res rule is sound.*

Proof. Assume otherwise, then one would be able to derive a proof object $\mathcal{P}^{k-1}$ that is part of a $\forall$Red+Res refutation proof for true QBF Φ. Thus, the clause corresponding to $\mathcal{P}^{k-1}$ (cf. proof of Theorem 1) $(\bigvee_{i \in \mathcal{P}} \bigvee_{l \in lit(i, <k)} l)$ made Φ false. However, the same clause can be derived directly by applying the expansion $\mathcal{T}$ to the original QBF, i.e., expanding universal variables beginning with quantification level $k+1$, and propositional resolution on the resulting expansion formula. Thus, this clause can be conjunctively added to the matrix without changing satisfiability, leading to a contradiction. $\qquad\square$

The resulting proof system can be viewed as a unification of the currently known CEGAR approaches for solving quantified Boolean formulas [16,18,25].

Theorem 6. *∀Exp+Res does not p-simulate ∀Red+∀Exp+Res.*

Proof. ∀Exp+Res does not p-simulate level-ordered Q-resolution [23].   □

The combination of both rules makes the proof system stronger than merely choosing between expansion and resolution proof upfront.

Theorem 7. *There is a QBF that has polynomial refutation in ∀Red+∀Exp+ Res, but has only exponential refutations in ∀Red+Res and ∀Exp+Res.*

Proof. For this proof, we take two formulas that are hard for Q-resolution and ∀Exp+Res, respectively. We build a new family of formulas that has a polynomial refutation in ∀Red+∀Exp+Res, but only exponential refutations in ∀Red+Res and ∀Exp+Res.

The first formula we consider is formula (2) form [17], that we call DAG_n in the following:

$$\exists e_1 \forall u_1 \exists c_1 c_2 \ldots \exists e_n \forall u_n \exists c_{2n-1} c_{2n}.$$

$$\left(\bigvee_{i\in 1\ldots 2n} \overline{c}_i \right) \wedge \bigwedge_{i\in 1\ldots n} (\overline{e}_i \vee c_{2i-1}) \wedge (\overline{u}_i \vee c_{2i-1}) \wedge (e_i \vee c_{2i}) \wedge (u_i \vee c_{2i})$$

It is known that DAG_n has a polynomial level-ordered Q-resolution proof and only exponential ∀Exp+Res proofs [17]. As a second formula, we use the $QParity_n$ formula [2]

$$\exists x_1 \ldots x_n \forall z \exists t_2 \ldots t_n. \operatorname{xor}(x_1, x_2, t_2) \wedge \bigwedge_{i\in 3\ldots n} \operatorname{xor}(t_{i-1}, x_i, t_i) \wedge (z \vee t_n) \wedge (\overline{z} \vee \overline{t}_n)$$

where $\operatorname{xor}(o_1, o_2, o) = (\overline{o}_1 \vee \overline{o}_2 \vee \overline{o}) \wedge (o_1 \vee o_2 \vee \overline{o}) \wedge (\overline{o}_1 \vee o_2 \vee o) \wedge (o_1 \vee \overline{o}_2 \vee o)$ defines o to be equal to $o_1 \oplus o_2$. $QParity_n$ has a polynomial ∀Exp+Res refutation but only exponential Q-resolution refutations [2]. We construct the following formula

$$\exists e_1 \forall u_1 \exists c_1 c_2 \ldots \exists e_n \forall u_n \exists c_{2n-1} c_{2n}. \forall a \exists b. \exists x_1 \ldots x_n \forall z \exists t_2 \ldots t_n.$$

$$\bigwedge_{i\in 1\ldots n} (\overline{e}_i \vee c_{2i-1}) \wedge (\overline{u}_i \vee c_{2i-1}) \wedge (e_i \vee c_{2i}) \wedge (u_i \vee c_{2i}) \wedge$$

$$(\overline{a} \vee \overline{b} \vee \bigvee_{i\in 1\ldots 2n} \overline{c}_i) \wedge \operatorname{xor}(x_1, x_2, t_2) \wedge \bigwedge_{i\in 3\ldots n} \operatorname{xor}(t_{i-1}, x_i, t_i) \wedge (z \vee t_n \vee b) \wedge (\overline{z} \vee \overline{t}_n)$$

We argue in the following that this formula has a polynomial refutation in ∀Red+∀Exp+Res. First, using (∀exp-res) we can derive the proof object containing the clause $(\overline{a} \vee \bigvee_{i\in\{1\ldots 2n\}} \overline{c}_i)$ using the expansion tree $\mathcal{T} = \{z \to 0, z \to 1\}$ and the clauses from the last row (analogue to Example 2). After applying universal reduction, the proof object representing clause $(\bigvee_{i\in\{1\ldots 2n\}} \overline{c}_i)$ can be derived. For the remaining formula, there is a polynomial and level-ordered resolution proof [17], thus, the formula has a polynomial ∀Red+∀Exp+Res proof.

There is no polynomial Q-resolution proof, because deriving $(\bigvee_{i \in \{1...2n\}} \bar{c}_i)$ is exponential in Q-resolution. Likewise, there is no polynomial $\forall$Exp+Res proof as the formula after deriving this clause has only exponential $\forall$Exp+Res refutations.   □

One question that remains open, is how the new proof system compares to unrestricted Q-resolution. We already know that the new proof system polynomially simulates both tree-like Q-resolution as well as level-ordered Q-resolution.

Theorem 8. *$\forall$Red+$\forall$Exp+Res does not p-simulate Q-resolution.*

Proof (Sketch). We construct a formula that is hard for expansion and level-ordered Q-resolution, but easy for (unrestricted) Q-resolution. We have already seen in the proof of Theorem 7 that DAG_n is hard for $\forall$Exp+Res but easy for Q-resolution. However, the Q-resolution proof of DAG_n is level-ordered. Hence, we need an additional formula that is hard to refute for level-ordered Q-resolution. We use the modified pigeon hole formula from [14] where unrestricted resolution has polynomial proofs and resolution proofs that are restricted to a certain variable ordering are exponential. Using universal quantification, one can impose an arbitrary order on a level-ordered Q-resolution proof, thus, there is a quantified Boolean formula which has only exponential level-ordered Q-resolution but has a polynomial Q-resolution proof. The disjunction of those two formulas gives the required witness. This formula is easy to refute for Q-resolution, but the first one is hard for $\forall$Exp+Res and the second is hard for level-ordered Q-resolution.   □

3.3 Comparison Between Extensions

We conclude this section by comparing the two extensions of the $\forall$Red+Res calculus introduced in this paper.

Theorem 9. *$\forall$Red+$\forall$Exp+Res and $\forall$Red+Res with strengthening rule are incomparable.*

Proof (Sketch). The family of formulas CR'_n from proof of Corollary 1 separates $\forall$Red+$\forall$Exp+Res and $\forall$Red+Res with strengthening rule. Since the strengthening rule is not applicable, all $\forall$Red+Res proofs are exponential while there is a polynomial proof in $\forall$Red+$\forall$Exp+Res.

The other direction is shown by using a similar construction as the one used in the proof of Theorem 7. We use a combination of CR_n and DAG_n to construct a formula that has only exponential refutations in $\forall$Red+$\forall$Exp+Res, but a polynomial refutation using the strengthening rule. The formula DAG_n is used to generate the premise for the application of the strengthening rule to solve CR_n. To generate this premise using the rule ($\forall$exp-res) one needs an exponential proof. There is a polynomial proof for DAG_n in $\forall$Red+Res, but there is none for CR_n, thus, $\forall$Red+$\forall$Exp+Res has only exponential refutations.   □

Algorithm 1. Modified CEGAR solving loop for existential quantifier

---
1: φ_k is the propositional abstraction for quantifier $\exists X_k$
2: **procedure** SOLVE$_\exists(\exists X_k.\Psi, \mathcal{P}^k)$
3:     **while** *true* **do**
4:         disable clauses C_i^k of φ_k where $i \notin \mathcal{P}^k$ ▷ those C_i are already satisfied $< k$
5:         generate candidate solution $\mathcal{P}_*^{k+1}$ using SAT solver and abstraction φ_k
6:         **if** no candidate exists **then**   ▷ there is a resolution proof π
7:             **return** UNSAT, $\mathcal{P}^{k-1}$
8:         **else if** Ψ is propositional **then**   ▷ base case for structural recursion
9:             **return** SAT, witness
10:         verify candidate recursively, call SOLVE$_\forall(\Psi, \mathcal{P}_*^{k+1})$
11:         **if** candidate correct **then**
12:             **return** SAT, witness
13:         **else**
14:             counterexample consists of $\mathcal{P}_{ce}^k$ and **expansion tree** $\mathcal{T}$
15:             refine φ_k such that one clause C_i^k in with $i \in \mathcal{P}_{ce}$ must be satisfied
16:             **refine φ_k with abstraction of expansion of Φ with respect to $\mathcal{T}$**

Theorem 10. *$\forall Red+\forall Exp+Res$ with strengthening rule and Q-resolution are incomparable.*

Proof. Follows from the proof of Theorem 8 as the witnessing formula can be constructed such that the strengthening rule is not applicable. The other direction follows from the separation of Q-resolution and $\forall$Exp+Res by Beyersdorff et al. [2].   ☐

4   Experimental Evaluation

4.1   Implementation

We extended the implementation of CAQE with the possibility to use the rule ($\forall$exp-res) as introduced in Sect. 3.2[1]. While the rule is applicable at every level in the QBF in principle, the effectiveness decreases when applying it to deeply nested formulas where CAQE tends to perform better [25] than RAReQS. We aim to strike a balance between expansion and clausal-abstraction, i.e., keeping the best performance characteristics of both solving methods. Thus, in our implementation, we apply the expansion refinement (additional to the clausal-abstraction refinement) to the innermost universal quantifier.

An overview of the CEGAR algorithm is given in Algorithm 1. There is a close connection between the rules of the $\forall$Red+Res calculus and the presented algorithm. Especially, we use a SAT solver to prove the refutation needed in the rule (res). We refer to [25] for algorithmic details. Changes to the original algorithm are written in bold text.

---
[1] CAQE is available online at https://react.uni-saarland.de/tools/caqe/.

Abstraction. The abstraction for quantifier $\exists X_k$, written φ_k is the projection of the clauses of the matrix to variables in X_k, i.e., $\bigwedge_{1 \leq i \leq m} lit(i, k)$. We assume that there is a operation to "disable" clauses in φ_k which corresponds to the situation where a clause C_i is satisfied by some variable bound before k. Likewise, for every clause we allow the assumption that this clause will be satisfied by a some variable bound after k. This is used to generate candidate proof objects $\mathcal{P}_*^{k+1}$ for inner levels. In the refinement step, this assumption can be invalidated, i.e., there is a way to force satisfaction of a clause at level k. Those operations can be implemented by an incremental SAT solver and two additional literals controlling the satisfaction of clauses [25].

Algorithm. The algorithm recurses on the structure of the quantifier prefix and communicates proof objects $\mathcal{P}$, which indicate the clauses of the matrix that are satisfied. At an existential quantifier, the abstraction generates a candidate solution (line 5) and checks recursively whether the candidate is correct (line 10). If not, the counterexample originally consists of a set of clauses (which could not be satisfied from the inner existential quantifiers). We extend this counterexample to also include an expansion tree $\mathcal{T}$ from the levels below. Additionally to the original refinement, we also build the expansion of the QBF with respect to the expansion tree $\mathcal{T}$, resulting in a QBF with the same quantifier prefix as the current level (with additional existential variables due to expansion). This QBF is then translated into a propositional formula in the same way as the original QBF. Lastly, the abstraction φ_k is then conjunctively combined with this propositional formula. Note that if the function returns UNSAT (line 7), the corresponding resolution proof from the SAT solver can be used to apply the rule (res) form the $\forall$Red+Res calculus.

As the underlying SAT solver in the implementation, we use PicoSAT [3], MiniSat [8], cryptominisat [26], or Lingeling [4].

4.2 Evaluation

In our evaluation, we show that the established theoretical separations shown in the last section translate to a significant empirical improvement. The evaluation is structured by the following three hypothesizes: First, the strengthen and expansion refinement give a significant improvement over the plain version of CAQE. Combining both refinements is overall better than only applying one of them. Second, we show that the improvement provided by the those refinements is independently of the underlying SAT solver. Third, when comparing on a per instance basis, the combined refinement effects the runtime mostly positively. We show that the improvement is up to three orders of magnitude.

We compare our implementation against RAReQS [16], Qesto [18], DepQBF in version 5.0 [21], and GhostQ [20]. For every solver except GhostQ, we use Bloqqer [5] in version 031 as preprocessor. For our experiments, we used a machine with a 3.6 GHz quad-core Intel Xeon processor and 32 GB of memory. The timeout and memout were set to 10 min and 8 GB, respectively.

Table 1. Number of solved instances of the QBFGallery 2014 and QBFEval 2016 benchmark sets.

Family	Total	CAQE-cryptominisat				RAReQS	Qesto	DepQBF	GhostQ
		Plain	Strengthen	Expansion	Both				
Eval2012r2	276	128	129	146	**149**	134	132	139	145
Bomb	132	94	**95**	94	94	82	78	80	82
Complexity	104	60	68	86	85	**90**	76	51	43
Dungeon	107	60	65	**70**	70	61	57	67	50
Hardness	114	108	102	**109**	101	69	106	80	51
Planning	147	45	93	65	95	**144**	55	38	13
Testing	131	91	86	93	91	95	90	99	**113**
Preprocessing	242	86	93	105	**110**	107	104	108	60
Gallery2014	1253	672	731	768	**795**	782	698	662	557
Eval2016	825	607	611	635	636	**644**	623	598	595
All	2078	1279	1342	1403	**1431**	1426	1321	1260	1152

Table 1 shows number of solved instances on the QBFGallery 2014 benchmark set, broken down by benchmark family, as well as the more recent QBFEval 2016 benchmark set. For CAQE, we only report on the best performing version, that is the one using cryptominisat as a backend solver.

The table shows that the strengthen and expansion refinement individually improve over the plain version of CAQE in the number of solved instances. Further, the combination of both refinements is the overall best solver, followed by RAReQS.

In the following, we refer to the combination of strengthen and expansion refinement as extended refinements. We want to detail the improvements due to the extended refinements and show their independence of the backend solver. The plot in Fig. 5 depicts the effect of the extended refinements with respect to the solved instances. The improvements in the number of solved instances are independent from the choice of the underlying SAT solver and range between 100 to 150 more instances solved compared to the plain version of CAQE.

The scatter plot depicted in Fig. 6 compares the running times of plain CAQE to the one using extended refinements (both using cryptominisat) on a per instance basis. Marks below the diagonal means that the variant using extended refinements is faster. It is remarkable that the extended refinements have mostly positive effect on the solving times. Only a few instances saw a significant increase in solving time and even less timed out with extended refinements while being solved before. On the other hand, we see improvements in solving time that exceed three orders of magnitude. This is an empirical confirmation of our goal stated before that our implementation of expansion-refinement adds performance characteristic of expansion-based solvers while keeping the characteristics of the clausal-abstraction algorithm.

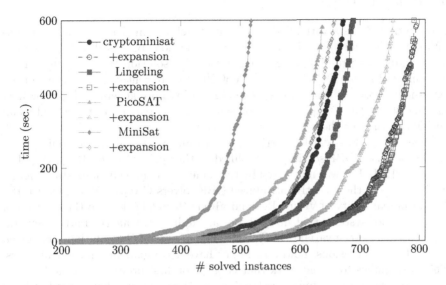

Fig. 5. Effect of the expansion refinement on the different configurations of CAQE on the GBFGallery 2014 benchmark sets.

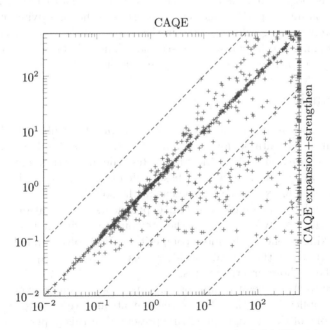

Fig. 6. Scatter plot comparing the solving time (in sec.) of CAQE with and without extended refinement.

5 Related Work

Q-resolution [19] is a variant of propositional refutation that is sound and refutation complete for QBF. There have been extensions proposed to Q-resolution, like long-distance resolution [27] and universal resolution [13], some which are implemented in the QCDCL solver DepQBF [21]. Recently, there has also been extensions proposed that extend Q-resolution by more generalized axioms [22]. In some sense, the ($\forall$exp-res) rule presented in this paper can be viewed as an new axiom rule for the $\forall$Red+Res calculus.

The $\forall$Exp+Res calculus [17] was introduced to allow reasoning over expansion-based QBF solving, exemplified by the QBF solver RAReQS [16]. The work on $\forall$Red+Res was motivated by the same desire, namely understanding the performance of the recently introduced QBF solvers CAQE [25] and Qesto [18]. The incomparability of $\forall$Exp+Res and $\forall$Red+Res [2,17] lead to the creation of stronger proof systems that unify those calculi, like IR-Calc [1]. Further separation results, between variants of IR-Calc and variants of Q-resolution, were given in [2]. Those extensions, however, do not have accompanying implementations. This also applies to recent work that is based on first-order resolution [9].

There are two well-known restrictions to Q-resolution, that is level-ordered and tree-like Q-resolution. Those restricted calculi were shown to be incomparable [23]. QCDCL based solver exhibit level-ordered proofs [15] and it was shown that $\forall$Exp+Res p-simulates tree-like Q-resolution [17]. We showed that $\forall$Red+Res is polynomial simulation equivalent to level-ordered Q-resolution, which explains similar performance characteristics of the underlying solvers. Further, the strengthening rule presented in this paper can be viewed as a first step towards breaking the level-ordered restriction. The $\forall$Red+$\forall$Exp+Res calculus p-simulates level-ordered and tree-like Q-resolution.

6 Conclusion

In this paper, we have introduced a new QBF proof calculus $\forall$Red+Res and showed that it is suitable for describing CEGAR based solving algorithms. We defined two extensions of the $\forall$Red+Res calculus and showed that there is a theoretical advantage over the basic calculus. Based on this foundation, we implemented an expansion refinement in the solver CAQE and evaluated it on standard QBF benchmark sets. Our experiments show that our new implementation significantly outperforms the previous one, with little to no negative impact, making it one of the most competitive QBF solver available. We have also shown that our theoretical considerations and the consequent algorithmic change explains those practical gains.

In future work, we want to improve the implementation by exploring heuristics for the application of the different refinements and we want to explore alternative versions of the strengthening rule presented in this paper.

Acknowledgments. I thank Christopher Hahn and the anonymous reviewers for their comments on earlier versions of this paper.

References

1. Beyersdorff, O., Chew, L., Janota, M.: On unification of QBF resolution-based calculi. In: Csuhaj-Varjú, E., Dietzfelbinger, M., Ésik, Z. (eds.) MFCS 2014. LNCS, vol. 8635, pp. 81–93. Springer, Heidelberg (2014). doi:10.1007/978-3-662-44465-8_8
2. Beyersdorff, O., Chew, L., Janota, M.: Proof complexity of resolution-based QBF calculi. In: Proceedings of STACS. LIPIcs, vol. 30, pp. 76–89. Schloss Dagstuhl - Leibniz-Zentrum fuer Informatik (2015)
3. Biere, A.: PicoSAT essentials. JSAT **4**(2–4), 75–97 (2008)
4. Biere, A.: Lingeling essentials, a tutorial on design and implementation aspects of the the SAT solver lingeling. In: Proceedings of POS@SAT. EPiC Series in Computing, vol. 27, p. 88. EasyChair (2014)
5. Biere, A., Lonsing, F., Seidl, M.: Blocked clause elimination for QBF. In: Bjørner, N., Sofronie-Stokkermans, V. (eds.) CADE 2011. LNCS, vol. 6803, pp. 101–115. Springer, Heidelberg (2011). doi:10.1007/978-3-642-22438-6_10
6. Bloem, R., Egly, U., Klampfl, P., Könighofer, R., Lonsing, F.: SAT-based methods for circuit synthesis. In: Proceedings of FMCAD, pp. 31–34. IEEE (2014)
7. Bloem, R., Könighofer, R., Seidl, M.: SAT-based synthesis methods for safety specs. In: McMillan, K.L., Rival, X. (eds.) VMCAI 2014. LNCS, vol. 8318, pp. 1–20. Springer, Heidelberg (2014). doi:10.1007/978-3-642-54013-4_1
8. Eén, N., Sörensson, N.: An extensible SAT-solver. In: Giunchiglia, E., Tacchella, A. (eds.) SAT 2003. LNCS, vol. 2919, pp. 502–518. Springer, Heidelberg (2004). doi:10.1007/978-3-540-24605-3_37
9. Egly, U.: On stronger calculi for QBFs. In: Creignou, N., Le Berre, D. (eds.) SAT 2016. LNCS, vol. 9710, pp. 419–434. Springer, Cham (2016). doi:10.1007/978-3-319-40970-2_26
10. Faymonville, P., Finkbeiner, B., Rabe, M.N., Tentrup, L.: Encodings of bounded synthesis. In: Legay, A., Margaria, T. (eds.) TACAS 2017. LNCS, vol. 10205, pp. 354–370. Springer, Heidelberg (2017). doi:10.1007/978-3-662-54577-5_20
11. Finkbeiner, B.: Bounded synthesis for petri games. In: Meyer, R., Platzer, A., Wehrheim, H. (eds.) Correct System Design. LNCS, vol. 9360, pp. 223–237. Springer, Cham (2015). doi:10.1007/978-3-319-23506-6_15
12. Finkbeiner, B., Tentrup, L.: Detecting unrealizability of distributed fault-tolerant systems. Logical Methods Comput. Sci. **11**(3) (2015)
13. Gelder, A.: Contributions to the theory of practical quantified boolean formula solving. In: Milano, M. (ed.) CP 2012. LNCS, pp. 647–663. Springer, Heidelberg (2012). doi:10.1007/978-3-642-33558-7_47
14. Goerdt, A.: Davis-Putnam resolution versus unrestricted resolution. Ann. Math. Artif. Intell. **6**(1–3), 169–184 (1992)
15. Janota, M.: On Q-resolution and CDCL QBF solving. In: Creignou, N., Le Berre, D. (eds.) SAT 2016. LNCS, vol. 9710, pp. 402–418. Springer, Cham (2016). doi:10.1007/978-3-319-40970-2_25
16. Janota, M., Klieber, W., Marques-Silva, J., Clarke, E.M.: Solving QBF with counterexample guided refinement. Artif. Intell. **234**, 1–25 (2016)
17. Janota, M., Marques-Silva, J.: Expansion-based QBF solving versus Q-resolution. Theor. Comput. Sci. **577**, 25–42 (2015)
18. Janota, M., Marques-Silva, J.: Solving QBF by clause selection. In: Proceedings of IJCAI, pp. 325–331. AAAI Press (2015)
19. Büning, H.K., Karpinski, M., Flögel, A.: Resolution for quantified Boolean formulas. Inf. Comput. **117**(1), 12–18 (1995)

20. Klieber, W., Sapra, S., Gao, S., Clarke, E.: A non-prenex, non-clausal QBF solver with game-state learning. In: Strichman, O., Szeider, S. (eds.) SAT 2010. LNCS, vol. 6175, pp. 128–142. Springer, Heidelberg (2010). doi:10.1007/978-3-642-14186-7_12

21. Lonsing, F., Biere, A.: DepQBF: a dependency-aware QBF solver. JSAT **7**(2–3), 71–76 (2010)

22. Lonsing, F., Egly, U., Seidl, M.: Q-resolution with generalized axioms. In: Creignou, N., Le Berre, D. (eds.) SAT 2016. LNCS, vol. 9710, pp. 435–452. Springer, Cham (2016). doi:10.1007/978-3-319-40970-2_27

23. Mahajan, M., Shukla, A.: Level-ordered Q-resolution and tree-like Q-resolution are incomparable. Inf. Process. Lett. **116**(3), 256–258 (2016)

24. Miller, C., Scholl, C., Becker, B.: Proving QBF-hardness in bounded model checking for incomplete designs. In: Proceedings of MTV, pp. 23–28. IEEE Computer Society (2013)

25. Rabe, M.N., Tentrup, L.: CAQE: a certifying QBF solver. In: Proceedings of FMCAD, pp. 136–143. IEEE (2015)

26. Soos, M., Nohl, K., Castelluccia, C.: Extending SAT solvers to cryptographic problems. In: Kullmann, O. (ed.) SAT 2009. LNCS, vol. 5584, pp. 244–257. Springer, Heidelberg (2009). doi:10.1007/978-3-642-02777-2_24

27. Zhang, L., Malik, S.: Conflict driven learning in a quantified Boolean satisfiability solver. In: Proceedings of ICCAD, pp. 442–449. ACM/IEEE Computer Society (2002)

A Decidable Fragment in Separation Logic with Inductive Predicates and Arithmetic

Quang Loc Le[1]([⊠]), Makoto Tatsuta[2], Jun Sun[3], and Wei-Ngan Chin[4]

[1] School of Computing, Teesside University, Middlesbrough, UK
Q.Le@tees.ac.uk
[2] National Institute of Informatics/Sokendai, Tokyo, Japan
[3] Singapore University of Technology and Design, Singapore, Singapore
[4] National University of Singapore, Singapore, Singapore

Abstract. We consider the satisfiability problem for a fragment of separation logic including inductive predicates with shape and arithmetic properties. We show that the fragment is decidable if the arithmetic properties can be represented as *semilinear* sets. Our decision procedure is based on a novel algorithm to infer a finite representation for each inductive predicate which precisely characterises its satisfiability. Our analysis shows that the proposed algorithm runs in exponential time in the worst case. We have implemented our decision procedure and integrated it into an existing verification system. Our experiment on benchmarks shows that our procedure helps to verify the benchmarks effectively.

Keywords: Satisfiability solving · Decidability · Separation logic · Inductive predicates

1 Introduction

Separation logic [14,27] is a well-established assertion language designed for reasoning about heap-manipulating programs. Combined with inductive predicates, separation logic has been shown to capture semantics of loops and recursive procedures naturally and succinctly. A decision procedure for satisfiability of separation logic with inductive predicates could be useful for multiple analysis problems associated with heap-manipulating programs, e.g., compositional verification [8,19,26], shape analysis [15], termination analysis [6] as well as to uncover reachability in bug finding tools [17]. It has been shown that the satisfiability of the fragment of separation logic which does not include inductive (user-defined) predicates is decidable [7,17,22,23]. The main challenge on satisfiability checking of separation logic with inductive predicates is that it often requires reasoning about infinite heaps as well as infinite integer domain. Indeed, the problem in the full fragment of inductive predicates with shape and arithmetic properties is shown to be undecidable [29]. One research goal is thus to identify decidable yet expressive fragment of the logic, based on which we can have precise and always-terminating reasoning over heap-manipulating programs.

© Springer International Publishing AG 2017
R. Majumdar and V. Kunčak (Eds.): CAV 2017, Part II, LNCS 10427, pp. 495–517, 2017.
DOI: 10.1007/978-3-319-63390-9_26

One way to show that a fragment of separation logic with inductive predicates is decidable is to infer, for each inductive predicate, a finite representation without any inductive predicates which precisely characterizes its satisfiability. For example, the authors in [1] showed that inductive predicates on linked lists can be precisely characterised by models of length zero or two and thus concludes that the fragment of separation logic with inductive predicates on linked lists only is decidable. Later, Brotherston *et al.* proposed SLSAT [5], a decision procedure to compute for every arbitrary heap-only inductive predicate a finite (disjunctive) set of base formulas which exactly characterises its satisfiability, and consequently showed that the fragment of separation logic with heap-only inductive predicates is decidable. Finally, the work in [29] extended SLSAT to show that a fragment of separation logic with inductive predicates and arithmetic properties under several restrictions is decidable. In particular, their fragment only allows inductive predicates satisfying the following conditions: for each inductive predicate, its heap part has two disjuncts and the arithmetic part is restricted in DPI predicates.

In this work, we present a decidable fragment of separation logic including inductive predicates with shape and arithmetic properties, which is more expressive than all fragments which have been shown to be decidable previously. The decidability is shown through a novel algorithm which computes for each inductive predicate a base formula (i.e. one without inductive predicates) which exactly characterizes its satisfiability. The idea is to compute for each heap-only inductive predicate a non-recursive base formula regardless of the infinite domains. In the case that the inductive predicate includes shape and arithmetic properties, if the arithmetical properties can be precisely computed in the form of arithmetic closures, we derive a combination of the base formula and the arithmetic closures which precisely characterises satisfiability for the inductive predicate.

In particular, we show how to derive a disjunctive base formula for each inductive predicate based on *flat formulas*, which are designed to capture the notion of a (infinite) set of formulas which can be represented by the same base formula (allocated memory, (dis)equalities and arithmetic closures). First, we describe a novel algorithm to derive for each inductive predicate a cyclic unfolding tree prior to flattening the tree into a disjunctive set of *regular* formulas. Every regular formula in this set has the same base pair of the allocated memory and (dis)equalities over a set of free variables (similar to [5]). Secondly, we define a decidable fragment where every regular formula derived for inductive predicates is flattable i.e., its arithmetic part is a conjunction of periodic constraints and the closure of the union of these conjunctions can be represented by some semilinear sets and thus is Presburger-definable (similar to [4,29]). As a result, our algorithm derives for each inductive predicate a disjunctive set of flat formulas, and then a disjunctive set of base formulas.

Contributions. We make the following technical contributions.

– Firstly, we present a novel algorithm to generate cyclic unfolding trees for inductive predicates with shape and arithmetic properties. Our complexity analysis shows that the proposed algorithm runs in exponential time in the worst case.

- Secondly, based on the algorithm, we present a decision procedure for satisfiability checking of the fragment of separation logic with inductive predicates where arithmetic properties can be represented as semilinear sets.
- Thirdly, we have implemented our algorithm and applied it to verify several benchmark programs. In our implementation, we generate under-/over-approximated bases for those inductive predicates beyond the decidable fragment systematically.

Organization. The rest of the paper is organized as follows. Section 2 presents relevant definition. Section 3 shows an overview of our approach through an example. We show how to compute bases of regular formulas in Sect. 4 and subsequently compute regular formulas of inductive predicates in Sect. 5. Section 6 describes a decision procedure. Our implementation and evaluation are presented in Sect. 7. Section 8 reviews related work and lastly Sect. 9 concludes. For space reason, all missing proofs are presented in [20].

2 Preliminaries

We use $\bar{x}$ to denote a sequence of variables and x_i to denote its ith element. We write $\bar{x}^N$ and $\bar{x}^S$ to denote the sequence of integer variables and pointer variables in $\bar{x}$, resp.

Syntax. A formula is defined by the syntax presented in Fig. 1. A symbolic heap Δ is an existentially quantified conjunction of some spatial formula κ, some pointer (dis)equality α and some formula in Presburger arithmetic ϕ. All free variables in Δ, denoted by function $FV(\Delta)$, are implicitly universally quantified at the outermost level. The spatial formula κ may be conjoined ($*$) by emp predicate, points-to predicates $x{\mapsto}c(f_i{:}v_i)$ and inductive predicate $P(\bar{v})_u^o$ where o and u are labels used for constructing unfolding trees in a breadth-first manner. While o captures the ordering number, u is the number of unfolding. We occasionally omit these numbers if there is no ambiguity. Whenever possible, we discard f_i of the points-to predicate and use its short form as $x{\mapsto}c(\bar{v})$. We often

Predicates	$Pred$	$::=$	$\mathrm{pred}\ \mathrm{P}_1(\bar{v}){\equiv}\Phi_1;\ \cdots;\mathrm{pred}\ \mathrm{P}_n(\bar{v}){\equiv}\Phi_n$
Formula	Φ	$::=$	$\Delta\mid\Phi_1\vee\Phi_2$ $\qquad\Delta::=\exists\bar{v}{\cdot}\ (\kappa{\wedge}\alpha{\wedge}\phi)$
Spatial formula	κ	$::=$	$\mathrm{emp}\mid x{\mapsto}c(f_i{:}v_i)\mid\mathrm{P}(\bar{v})_u^o\mid\kappa_1{*}\kappa_2$
Ptr (Dis)Equality	α	$::=$	$\mathtt{true}\mid\mathtt{false}\mid v_1{=}v_2\mid v{=}\mathtt{null}\mid v_1{\neq}v_2\mid v{\neq}\mathtt{null}\mid\alpha_1{\wedge}\alpha_2$
Presburger arith.	ϕ	$::=$	$\mathtt{true}\mid i\mid\exists v{\cdot}\ \phi\mid\neg\phi\mid\phi_1{\wedge}\phi_2\mid\phi_1{\vee}\phi_2$
Linear arithmetic	i	$::=$	$a_1{=}a_2\mid a_1{\leq}a_2$
	a	$::=$	$k^{\mathtt{int}}\mid v\mid k^{\mathtt{int}}{\times}a\mid a_1{+}a_2\mid-a\mid max(a_1,a_2)\mid min(a_1,a_2)$
$\mathcal{P}{=}\{\mathrm{P}_1,...,\mathrm{P}_n\}$		$c\in Node$	$f_i\in Fields\quad v,v_i,x,y\in Var\quad\bar{v}\equiv v_1,...,v_n$

Fig. 1. Syntax.

use π to denote a conjunction of α and ϕ formulas. Note that $v_1 \neq v_2$ and $v \neq \texttt{null}$ are short forms for $\neg(v_1 = v_2)$ and $\neg(v = \texttt{null})$ respectively. _ is used to denote a "don't care" term.

We write $\mathcal{P}$ to denote a set of n predicates in our system. Each inductive predicate is defined by a disjunction Φ using the key word $\texttt{pred}$. In each disjunct, we require that variables which are not formal parameters must be existentially quantified.

Example 1. We define an increasingly sorted list using the fragment above.

$$\texttt{pred sortll(root},n,mi) \equiv \texttt{root} \mapsto node2(mi, \texttt{null}) \land n=1$$
$$\lor \exists\ q,n_1,mi_1\cdot \texttt{root} \mapsto node2(mi, q) * \texttt{sortll}(q, n_1, mi_1) \land n=n_1+1 \land mi \leq mi_1;$$

where the data structure $node2$ is declared as: *data node2 { int val; node2 next;}*. In the sorted list $\texttt{sortll(root},n,mi)$, $\texttt{root}$ is the pointer pointing to the head of the list, n is the length of the list and mi is the minimal value stored in the list.

We use $\Delta[t_1/t_2]$ for a substitution of all occurrences of t_2 in Δ to t_1. Note that we always apply the following normalization after predicate unfolding: $(\exists \bar{w}_1\cdot\ \kappa_1 \land \pi_1) * (\exists \bar{w}_2\cdot\ \kappa_2 \land \pi_2) \equiv (\exists \bar{w}_1, \bar{v}_2\cdot\ \kappa_1 * (\kappa_2\rho) \land \pi_1 \land (\pi_2\rho))$ where $\bar{v}_2$ is a vector of fresh variables and has the same length n as $\bar{w}_2$; and ρ is a substitution: $\rho= \circ \{[v_i/w_i] \mid \forall i \in \{1...n\}\}$.

Our proposal relies on the following definitions. $\texttt{P}(\bar{v})$ is called (heap) observable if there is at least one free *pointer-typed* variable in $\bar{v}$. Otherwise, it is called *unobservable*. $v \mapsto c(\bar{t})$ is called (heap) observable if v is free. Otherwise, it is *unobservable*.

- **(base formula)** Φ is a *base* formula (or base for short) if it does not include any occurrences of inductive predicates. Otherwise, it is an inductive formula.
- **($\Delta^{\exists}$ formula)** Let $\Delta^{\exists}$ be a base formula and is of the form:

$$\Delta^{\exists} \equiv \exists \bar{w}\cdot x_1 \mapsto c_1(\bar{v}_1) * \ldots * x_n \mapsto c_n(\bar{v}_n) \land \alpha \land \phi$$

  $\Delta^{\exists}$ is a totally (existentially) quantified heap base formula if $x_i \in \bar{w}$ for all $i \in \{1, \ldots, n\}$ and $FV(\alpha) \subseteq \bar{w}$. We show that existentially quantified pointer-typed variables are not externally visible wrt. the satisfiability problem (Sect. 4). This is the fundamental for the transformation of an inductive predicate into an equi-satisfiable set of base formulas.
- **(regular formula)** Φ is a regular formula if it is of the form: $\Phi \equiv \Delta^b * \Upsilon^{\exists}$ where Δ^b is a base formula and $\Upsilon^{\exists}$ is a disjunctive (possibly infinite) set of $\Delta^{\exists}$ formulas. For example $\Delta^b * (\exists \bar{w}\cdot \texttt{P}_1(\bar{v}_1) * \ldots * \texttt{P}_n(\bar{v}_n))$, where $\bar{v}_i^S \subseteq \bar{w} \forall i \in \{1...n\}$, is a regular formula.
- **(flat formula)** Φ is a flat formula if it is a regular formula and is flattable, i.e. can be represented by a base formula.

We use Δ^b to denote a conjunctive base formula, Δ^{re} a regular formula and Δ^{flat} a flat formula. The following definition is critical for the computation of base formulas.

Definition 1. *The numeric projection* $(\Phi)^N$ *is defined inductively as follows.*

$$(\Delta_1 \vee \Delta_2)^N \equiv (\Delta_1)^N \vee (\Delta_2)^N \qquad (\kappa_1 * \kappa_2)^N \qquad\qquad \equiv (\kappa_1)^N \wedge (\kappa_2)^N$$
$$(\exists \bar{x} \cdot \Delta)^N \quad \equiv \exists \bar{x}^N \cdot (\Delta)^N \qquad (P(\bar{v}))^N \qquad\qquad \equiv P^N(\bar{v}^N)$$
$$(\kappa \wedge \alpha \wedge \phi)^N \equiv (\kappa)^N \wedge \phi \qquad (x \mapsto c(\bar{v}))^N \equiv (\texttt{emp})^N \equiv \texttt{true}$$

For each inductive predicate $P(\bar{t}) \equiv \Phi$, we assume the inductive predicate symbols P^N and predicate $P^N(\bar{t}^N)$ for its numeric projection satisfy $P^N(\bar{t}^N) \equiv \Phi^N$. The semantics of the numeric projection $P^N(\bar{t}^N)$ is as follows. Let Υ_P^b be a (infinite) set base formulas derived from $P(\bar{t})$. If all variables in $\bar{t}$ are pointer-typed, then $P^N(\bar{t}^N) \equiv \texttt{true}$. Otherwise, $P^N(\bar{t}^N) \equiv \bigvee\{(\Delta^b)^N \mid \Delta^b \in \Upsilon_P^b\}$.

Example 2. The numeric definition $\texttt{sortll}^N$ corresponding to the above increasingly sorted list $\texttt{sortll}$ is defined as follows.

$$\texttt{pred sortll}^N(n, mi) \equiv n{=}1$$
$$\vee \ \exists\ n_1, mi_1 \cdot \texttt{sortll}^N(n_1, mi_1) \wedge n{=}n_1{+}1 \wedge mi{\leq}mi_1;$$

Semantics. Concrete heap models assume a fixed finite collection *Node*, a fixed finite collection *Fields*, a disjoint set *Loc* of locations (heap addresses), a set of non-address values *Val*, such that $\texttt{null} \in Val$ and $Val \cap Loc = \emptyset$. Further, we define:

$$Heaps \overset{\text{def}}{=} Loc \rightharpoonup_{fin}(Node \rightarrow Fields \rightarrow Val \cup Loc)$$
$$Stacks \overset{\text{def}}{=} Var \rightarrow Val \cup Loc$$

The semantics is given by a forcing relation: $s, h \models \Phi$ that forces the stack s and heap h to satisfy the constraint Φ where $h \in Heaps$, $s \in Stacks$, and Φ is a formula.

The semantics is presented in Fig. 2. $dom(f)$ is the domain of function f; $h_1 \# h_2$ denotes that heaps h_1 and h_2 are disjoint, i.e., $dom(h_1) \cap dom(h_2) = \emptyset$; and $h_1 \cdot h_2$ denotes the union of two disjoint heaps. Semantics of pure formulas depend on stack valuations. It is straightforward and omitted for simplicity.

$s, h \models \texttt{emp}$	iff $h = \emptyset$
$s, h \models v \mapsto c(f_i : v_i)$	iff $l = s(v), dom(h) = \{l \to r\}$ and $r(c, f_i) = s(v_i)$
$s, h \models P(\bar{t})$	iff $s, h \models P(\bar{t})^m$ for some $m \geq 0$
$s, h \models P(\bar{t})^{k+1}$	iff $s, h \models \Delta[P(\bar{t})^k / P(\bar{t})]$ for some definition branch Δ of P
$s, h \models P(\bar{t})^0$	iff never
$s, h \models \kappa_1 * \kappa_2$	iff $\exists h_1, h_2 \cdot h_1 \# h_2$ and $h = h_1 \cdot h_2$ and
	$\qquad s, h_1 \models \kappa_1$ and $s, h_2 \models \kappa_2$
$s, h \models \texttt{true}$	iff always $\qquad\quad s, h \models \texttt{false}$ iff never
$s, h \models \exists v_1, ..., v_n \cdot (\kappa \wedge \pi)$	iff $\exists \alpha_1 ... \alpha_n \cdot s(v_1 {\mapsto} \alpha_1 * ... * v_n {\mapsto} \alpha_n), h \models \kappa$
	$\qquad$ and $s(v_1 {\mapsto} \alpha_1 * ... * v_n {\mapsto} \alpha_n) \models \pi$
$s, h \models \Phi_1 \vee \Phi_2$	iff $s, h \models \Phi_1$ or $s, h \models \Phi_2$

Fig. 2. Semantics.

3   Overview and Illustration

In this section, we illustrate how our decision procedure works through checking the satisfiability of the following inductive predicate over the data structure *node* which is declared as: *data node {node left; node right;}*.

$$\texttt{pred } \mathtt{Q}(x,y,n) \equiv \exists\ y_1 \cdot x \mapsto node(\mathtt{null},y_1) \wedge y{=}\mathtt{null} \wedge x{\neq}\mathtt{null} \wedge n{=}1$$
$$\vee\ \exists\ x_1,y_1,n_1 \cdot y \mapsto node(x_1,y_1) * \mathtt{Q}(x,y_1,n_1)^0_- \wedge y{\neq}\mathtt{null} \wedge n{=}n_1{+}2;$$

First, we infer a disjunctive set of base formulas for the predicate Q which precisely characterizes Q's satisfiability. After that, we check satisfiability of each disjunct in the set. If one of the disjuncts is satisfied, so is Q. We remark that as the base formulas do not contain any occurrences of inductive predicates, their satisfiability is decidable [17,23]. We generate the base formulas for each inductive predicate by: (i) constructing a cyclic unfolding tree and (ii) extracting base formulas from the leaf nodes in the tree.

Constructing Cyclic Unfolding Tree. We construct the cyclic unfolding tree for inductive predicate Q as shown in Fig. 3. In an unfolding tree, a node v is a conjunctive formula. An edge from v_1 to v_2 where v_2 is a child of v_1 is obtained by unfolding v_1, i.e., substituting an occurrence of an inductive predicate in v_1 with one disjunct in the predicate's definition (after proper actual/formal parameter

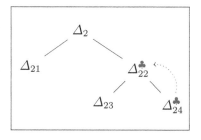

Fig. 3. Cyclic unfolding tree $\mathcal{T}_2^Q$.

substitutions). For instance, in Fig. 3, the root of the tree is $\Delta_2 \equiv \mathtt{Q}(x,y,n)^0_0$. We remark that the ordering number and unfolding number of the root are initially set to 0. The root has two children, Δ_{21} and Δ_{22}, which are obtained by unfolding the occurrence of Q with its two branches.

$$\Delta_{21} \equiv \exists\ y_1 \cdot x \mapsto node(\mathtt{null}, y_1) \wedge y{=}\mathtt{null} \wedge x{\neq}\mathtt{null} \wedge n{=}1$$
$$\Delta_{22} \equiv \exists\ x_1,y_1,n_1 \cdot y \mapsto node(x_1,y_1) * \mathtt{Q}(x,y_1,n_1)^0_1 \wedge y{\neq}\mathtt{null} \wedge n{=}n_1{+}2$$

In turn, Δ_{22} has two children, Δ_{23} and Δ_{24}, which are obtained by unfolding the occurrence of Q again.

$$\Delta_{23} \equiv \exists\ x_1,y_1,n_1,y_2 \cdot y \mapsto node(x_1,y_1) * x \mapsto node(\mathtt{null}, y_2)\ \wedge$$
$$y_1{=}\mathtt{null} \wedge x{\neq}\mathtt{null} \wedge n_1{=}1 \wedge y{\neq}\mathtt{null} \wedge n{=}n_1{+}2$$
$$\Delta_{24} \equiv \exists\ x_1,y_1,n_1,x_2,y_2,n_2 \cdot y \mapsto node(x_1,y_1)*y_1 \mapsto node(x_2,y_2)*\mathtt{Q}(x,y_2,n_2)^0_2\ \wedge$$
$$y_1{\neq}\mathtt{null} \wedge n_1{=}n_2{+}2 \wedge y{\neq}\mathtt{null} \wedge n{=}n_1{+}2$$

We remark that unfolding numbers annotated for occurrences of recursive predicates (e.g., $\mathtt{Q}(x,y_1,n_1)^0_1$ in Δ_{22} and $\mathtt{Q}(x,y_2,n_2)^0_2$ in Δ_{24}) are increased by one after each unfolding.

A leaf in the unfolding tree is either a base formula (e.g., Δ_{21} and Δ_{23}), or one whose all occurrences of inductive predicates are unobservable, or one which is linked back to an interior node (e.g., Δ_{24}). Intuitively, a leaf node v is linked back to an interior node v' only if v is subsumed (wrt. the satisfiability problem) by v' in terms of the constraint on the heap. These back-links generate (virtual) cycles in the tree. A leaf is marked either closed or open. It is marked closed if it is either unsatisfiable or is linked back to some interior node. Otherwise, it is marked open. For instance, Δ_{24} is linked back to Δ_{22} and thus marked closed. These two nodes are labeled with the fresh symbol ♣ in Fig. 3. They are linked as they have (i) the same *observable* points-to predicate $y \mapsto node(\_,\_)$, (ii) the same *observable* occurrence of inductive predicate $Q(x,\_,\_)$ and (iii) the same disequalities over free variables (i.e., $y \neq null$).

Each path ending with a leaf node which is not involved in any back-link represents (a way to derive) a formula which can be obtained by unfolding the inductive predicates according to the edges in the path. A cycle in the tree thus represents an infinite set of formulas, since we can construct infinitely many paths by iterating through the cycle an unbounded number of times. For instance, in Fig. 3, we can obtain a different formula following the cycle from Δ_{22} to Δ_{24} and back to Δ_{22} for a different number of times and then following the edge from Δ_{22} to Δ_{23}. We show that all formulas obtained by iterating through the same cycle a different number of times have the same *spatial* base. Furthermore, if the closure of the arithmetic part of these formulas is Presburger-definable, we can construct one formula to represent this infinite set of formulas.

Flattening Cyclic Unfolding Tree. After constructing the tree, we derive the **base** for the inductive predicates, e.g. Q in this example. To do that, we flatten the tree iteratively until there is no cycle left. To flatten the tree iteratively, we keep flattening the minimal cyclic sub-trees, i.e. the sub-trees without nested cycles, in a bottom-up manner. For instance, in Fig. 3 the sub-tree in which Δ_{22} is the root is a minimal cyclic sub-tree. In principle, we can derive an infinite number of base formulae, each of which corresponds to the formula constructed by iterating the cyclic a different number of times. For instance, the following is the disjunctive set of the formulas obtained by following the cycle zero or more times (and then visiting Δ_{23}).

$$
\begin{aligned}
\Delta_{23}^{flat} \equiv\ & \exists x_1,y_1,n_1,y_2 \cdot (y \mapsto node(x_1,y_1) * x \mapsto node(null, y_2) \wedge x \neq null \wedge \\
& y \neq null \wedge n = n_1 + 1) \wedge (y_1 = null \wedge n_1 = 1) \\
\vee\ & \exists x_1,y_1,n_1,x_2,y_2,n_2,y_3 \cdot (y \mapsto node(x_1,y_1) * x \mapsto node(null, y_3) \wedge x \neq null \wedge \\
& y \neq null \wedge n = n_1 + 1) * (y_1 \mapsto node(x_2,y_2) * \wedge y_2 = null \wedge n_1 = n_2 + 2 \\
& n_2 = 1) \\
\vee\ & \dots
\end{aligned}
$$

Notice that each iteration of this cycle results in a formula which conjuncts Δ_{23} with unobservable heaps (e.g., $y_1 \mapsto node(\_,y_2) \wedge y_2 = null$ where y_1, y_2 are existentially quantified variables) and a constraint which requires that the third parameter of Q

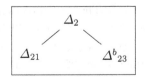

Fig. 4. Flattened tree.

is increased by two. We refer to Δ_{23}^{flat} as a flat formula. One of our main contribution in this work is to show that all formulae in the set have the same base. In particular, we state that a quantified heap base formula $\Delta_i^\exists$ is equi-satisfiable to its numeric projection, i.e. $(\Delta_i^\exists)^N$. As a result, a flat formula is equi-satisfiable to a conjunction of a base formula (i.e., Δ_{23}) and the set of the numeric projections. Furthermore, in the proposed decidable fragment, closure of this numeric set is Presburger-definable. In this example, this numeric set can be represented by the arithmetic predicate: $P_{cyc}(n_1) \equiv n_1 = 1 \vee \exists n_2 \cdot n_1 = n_2 + 2 \wedge P_{cyc}(n_2)$. Following [29], we can show that this predicate is equivalent to the following Presburger formula: $\exists k \cdot n_1 = 2k+1 \wedge k \geq 0$. As a result, Δ_{23}^{flat} is equi-satisfiable to the following base formula:

$$\Delta^b_{23} \equiv \exists\ x_1, y_1, x_2, y_2, n_1 \cdot (y \mapsto node(x_1, y_1) * x \mapsto node(\texttt{null}, y_2) \wedge x \neq \texttt{null} \wedge$$
$$y \neq \texttt{null} \wedge n = n_1 + 1) \wedge (\exists k \cdot n_1 = 2k+1 \wedge k \geq 0)$$

T_2^Q is flattened as the tree presented in Fig. 4 which has no cycle. Finally, the base of Q is computed based on the open leaf nodes of the tree shown in Fig. 4. It is the disjunction of Δ_{21} and Δ^b_{23} as:

$\{\exists\ y_1 \cdot x \mapsto node(\texttt{null}, y_1) \wedge y = \texttt{null} \wedge x \neq \texttt{null} \wedge n = 1;$
$\exists\ x_1, y_1, y_2, k \cdot y \mapsto node(x_1, y_1) * x \mapsto node(\texttt{null}, y_2) \wedge x \neq \texttt{null} \wedge y \neq \texttt{null} \wedge n = 2k+2 \wedge k \geq 0\}$

Since either disjunct of the set above is satisfiable, so is Q.

4   Foundation of Base Computation

In this section, we show that existentially quantified pointer-typed variables are not externally visible wrt. the satisfiability problem. This finding is fundamental for the transformation of an inductive predicate into regular formulas and then flat formulas. The following two functions: $\mathbf{eXPure}(\Delta^b)$ and $\Pi(\pi, \bar{w})$, are relevant in our argument.

Reduction. We first define a function called $\mathbf{eXPure}$, which transforms a base formula into an *equi-satisfiable* first-order formula. $\mathbf{eXPure}$ is defined as follows:

$$\mathbf{eXPure}(\exists \bar{w} \cdot\ x_1 \mapsto c_1(\bar{v}_1) * ... * x_n \mapsto c_n(\bar{v}_n) \wedge \pi) \equiv$$
$$\exists\ \bar{w} \cdot \bigwedge\{x_i \neq \texttt{null} \mid i \in \{1...n\}\} \wedge \bigwedge\{x_i \neq x_j \mid i, j \in \{1...n\}\ \text{and}\ i \neq j\} \wedge \pi$$

Proposition 1. *For all s such that* $s \models \mathbf{eXPure}(\Delta^b)$*, there exists s′,h such that* $s \subseteq s'$*,* $|dom(h)| = n + |\bar{w}|$*,* $(s(x_i) \to \_) \in dom(h)\ \forall i \in \{1...n\}$*, and* $s', h \models \Delta^b$ *where* $|dom(h)|$ *is the size of heap* $dom(h)$ *and* $|\bar{w}|$ *is the length of sequence* $\bar{w}$*.*

Proposition 2. *For all s,h such that* $s, h \models \Delta^b$*,* $s \models \mathbf{eXPure}(\Delta^b)$*.*

Lemma 1. Δ^b *is satisfiable if only if* $\mathbf{eXPure}(\Delta^b)$ *is satisfiable.*

Proof. The "if" direction follows immediately from Proposition 1. The "only if" direction follows immediately from Proposition 2.   □

We remark that the proposed function $\mathbf{eXPure}$ is similar to the well-formed function in [22]. Indeed, the well-formed function is more general than $\mathbf{eXPure}$ as it additionally supports singly-linked lists *lseg*.

Quantifier Elimination. Function $\Pi(\pi, \bar{w})$ eliminates the existential quantifiers on pointer-typed variables $\bar{w}^S$. It is defined as follows.

Definition 2. $\Pi(\text{true}, \bar{w}) = \text{true}$, $\Pi(\text{false}, \bar{w}) = \text{false}$, $\Pi(v_1 \neq v_1 \wedge \pi_1, \bar{w}) = \text{false}$, $\Pi(\exists \bar{w} \cdot \alpha \wedge \phi, \bar{w}) = \exists \bar{w} \cdot \Pi(\alpha, \bar{w}) \wedge \phi$. *Otherwise,*

$$\Pi(v_1 = v_2 \wedge \alpha_1, \bar{w}) = \begin{cases} \Pi(\alpha_1[v_1/v_2], \bar{w}) & if\ v_1 \in \bar{w}^S \\ \Pi(\alpha_1[v_2/v_1], \bar{w}) & if\ v_2 \in \bar{w}^S\ and\ v_1 \notin \bar{w}^S \\ v_1 = v_2 \wedge \Pi(\alpha_1, \bar{w}) & otherwise \end{cases}$$

$$\Pi(v_1 \neq v_2 \wedge \alpha_1, \bar{w}) = \begin{cases} v_1 \neq v_2 \wedge \Pi(\alpha_1, \bar{w}) & if\ v_i \notin \bar{w}^S, i = \{1, 2\} \\ \Pi(\alpha_1, \bar{w}) & otherwise \end{cases}$$

For soundness, we assume that α is sorted s.t. equality conjuncts are processed before disequality ones.

Lemma 2. *For all s, $s \models \exists \bar{w} \cdot \alpha$ iff there exists $s' \subseteq s$ and $s' \models \Pi(\alpha, \bar{w})$.*

We remark that quantifier elimination in equality logic has been studied well and can be done in SMT solvers (i.e., Z3 [10]). In this paper, we present a simplified implementation for efficiency.

Lemmas 1 and 2 imply that it is sound and complete to discard existentially quantified heaps while solving satisfiability in our fragment. The base of a regular formula is computed as follows.

Lemma 3. *For all s and h, $s, h \models \Delta^b * \Upsilon^\exists$ iff there exist $s' \subseteq s$, $h' \subseteq h$ and $s', h' \models \Delta^b \wedge \bigvee \{(\Delta^\exists)^N \mid \Delta^\exists \in \Upsilon^\exists\}$.*

The proof, based on structural induction on the number of base formulas $\Delta^\exists$ of $\Upsilon^\exists$, is presented in [20]. We remark that this result can be implicitly implied from the results presented in [6,17,18]. Now, the problem of base computation in separation logic is reduced to the problem of closure computation for arithmetic constraints. We formally define this reduction as follows.

Definition 3 (Base Computation). *Let $\Delta^{re} \equiv \Delta^b * \Upsilon^\exists$ be a regular formula. Δ^{re} is flattable, i.e. can be represented as a base formula, if $\bigvee \{(\Delta^\exists)^N \mid \Delta^\exists \in \Upsilon^\exists\}$ is equivalent to a Presburger formula.*

We note that the disjunction set $\Upsilon^\exists$ may be infinite. In the next section we transform each inductive predicate into a set of regular formulas; each of these regular formulas is of the form: $\Delta^{re} \equiv \Delta^b * (\exists \bar{w} \cdot P_1(\bar{v}_1) * ... * P_n(\bar{v}_n))$, where $\bar{v}_i^S \subseteq \bar{w}$ for all $i \in \{1...n\}$. Based on Definition 3, Δ^{re} is equivalent to $\Delta^{re} \equiv \Delta^b * (\exists \bar{w} \cdot P_1{}^N(\bar{v}_1^N) \wedge ... \wedge P_n{}^N(\bar{v}_n^N))$. Thus, the problem of base computation for inductive predicates is reduced to the problem of closure computation for numeric predicates.

5   Transformation of Inductive Predicates

In this section, we present an algorithm, named `pred2reg`, to transform each inductive predicate into a disjunctive set of regular formulas. Each of these regular formulas is of the form: $\Delta^{re} \equiv \Delta^b * (\exists \bar{w} \cdot P_1(\bar{v}_1) * ... * P_n(\bar{v}_n))$, where $\bar{v}_i^S \subseteq \bar{w}$ for all $i \in \{1...n\}$. For each inductive predicate in $\mathcal{P}$, `pred2reg` first uses procedure `utree` to construct a cyclic unfolding tree to characterise its satisfiability (Sect. 5.1). After that, `pred2reg` uses procedure `extract_regular` to flatten the tree into a set of regular formulas in a bottom-up manner (Sect. 5.2). The correctness of the transformation is presented in Sect. 5.3.

5.1   Constructing Cyclic Unfolding Tree

Procedure `utree` presented in Algorithm 1 aims to construct an unfolding tree given an inductive predicate. This algorithm is an instantiation of the S2SAT algorithm described in [17]. While S2SAT is designed for decision problems (`SAT` or `UNSAT`), `utree` works as a re-write procedure. It transforms an user-defined predicate into an unfolding tree with (virtual) cycles. Given an inductive predicate, say $P(\bar{v})$, it constructs a cyclic unfolding tree for the formula $\Delta \equiv P(\bar{v})_0^0$. Each iteration (lines 2–12) conducts one of the following four actions. Function `OA` over-approximates every leaf node and checks whether it is unsatisfiable. If it is the case, the function marks the leaf closed. Function `link_back` links a leaf back to an interior node if they have the same free (externally) pointer-based variables. In each such back-link, the leaf node is called a bud and the interior node is called a companion. Function `choose_bfs` chooses an open leaf for the unfolding with function `unfold`.

Algorithm 1. Procedure `utree`

---

    input : Δ
    output: $\mathcal{T}_n$
1 $i \leftarrow 0; \mathcal{T}_0 \leftarrow \{\Delta\}$;   `/* initialize */`
2 **while** true **do**
3      $\mathcal{T}_i \leftarrow \text{OA}(\mathcal{T}_i)$;   `/* mark unsat and closed */`
4      $\mathcal{T}_i \leftarrow \text{link\_back}(\mathcal{T}_i)$;   `/* detect similarly */`
5      $(\text{is\_exists}, \Delta_i) \leftarrow \text{choose\_bfs}(\mathcal{T}_i)$;   `/* open leaf for unfolding */`
6   **if** *not* is_exists **then**
7   **return** $\mathcal{T}_i$;
8   **else**
9           $i \leftarrow i+1$;
10         $\mathcal{T}_i \leftarrow \text{unfold}(\Delta_i)$;
11   **end**
12 **end**

Over-Approximation. Given an input tree $\mathcal{T}_i$, for each its leaf node Δ, function OA obtains the over-approximation Δ' by substituting all occurrences of inductive predicates appearing in Δ with true prior to transforming Δ' into an equi-satisfiable first-order formula π' using function eXPure (defined in Sect. 4). Finally, π' is discharged using an SMT solver. If π' is unsatisfiable, so is Δ.

Unfolding. In each iteration, our algorithm selects one open leaf node including some occurrences of inductive predicates to expand the tree. The node is selected in a breadth-first manner. Among all open leaf nodes, a node is selected if it contains at least one *observable* occurrence of an inductive predicate, e.g. $P(\bar{v})_u^o$, where u is the smallest unfolding number. If there are more than one such occurrences, the one with the smallest ordering number is chosen. We remark that a leaf node whose occurrences of inductive predicates are all unobservable is never unfolded as this leaf is already a regular formula. For each new node derived, unfold marks it open and creates a new edge accordingly. Let $Q(\bar{t})^{o_l}$ denote a predicate occurrence of the derived node, its unfolding number is set to $u+1$ if it is (not necessary directly) recursive. Otherwise, it is u. Its sequence number is set to o_l+o.

Linking Back. Function link_back connects an open leaf with at least one observable occurrence of inductive predicate (say, $\exists \bar{w}_1 \cdot \kappa_1 \wedge \alpha_1 \wedge \phi_1$) to an interior node (say, $\exists \bar{w}_2 \cdot \kappa_2 \wedge \alpha_2 \wedge \phi_2$) as follows.

1. First, it discards all unobservable points-to predicates and all unobservable inductive predicates, and then eliminates existentially quantified variables for pointer equalities and disequalities in the two formulas. Afterwards, the two formulas become $\kappa_1' \wedge \alpha_{1a} \wedge \phi_1$ and $\kappa_2' \wedge \alpha_{2a} \wedge \phi_2$ where $\alpha_{1a} \equiv \Pi(\alpha_1, \bar{w}_1^S)$, $\alpha_{2a} \equiv \Pi(\alpha_2, \bar{w}_2^S)$.
2. Secondly, it constructs α_{1b} (resp., α_{2b}) by augmenting the closure for equalities on pointers into α_{1a} (resp., α_{2a}): if $x=y \in \alpha$ and $y=z \in \alpha$ then $x=z \in \alpha$.
3. Thirdly, it builds a set of addresses, i.e. B_1, B_2, for each formula. Given a formula $\exists \bar{w} \cdot \kappa \wedge \alpha \wedge \phi$, its set of addresses B is collected as follows. If $x \mapsto c(\_) \in \kappa$ then $x \in B$; if $x \in B$ and $x=y \in \alpha$ then $y \in B$.
4. Next, it adds into α_{1b} (resp. α_{2b}) the Boolean abstraction of separating predicates, e.g. $\alpha_{1c} \equiv \alpha_{1b} \wedge \bigwedge \{x \neq \text{null} \mid x \in B_1\} \wedge \bigwedge \{x \neq y \mid x,y \in B_1\}$ and similarly for α_{2c}. Note that we assume redundant constraints in α_{1c} and α_{2c} are discarded.
5. Finally, $\kappa_1' \wedge \alpha_{1c} \wedge \phi_1$ is linked to $\kappa_2' \wedge \alpha_{2c} \wedge \phi_2$ if the following conditions hold:
   - (i) B_1 and B_2 are identical; and
   - (ii) α_{1c} and α_{2c} are identical; and
   - (iii) For all occurrence $P_i(\bar{t})_{u_2}^{o_2}$ in κ_2', there exists one occurrence $P_i(\bar{v})_{u_1}^{o_1}$ in κ_1' such that $u_1 > u_2$ and for all free variable $v_i \in \bar{v}$, t_i is a free variable and $\alpha_{1c} \implies t_i = v_i$.

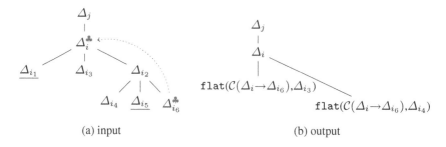

(a) input   (b) output

Fig. 5. Flattening minimal cyclic sub-tree.

5.2   Flattening Cyclic Unfolding Tree

To compute a set of regular formulas for a cyclic tree, procedure `extract_regular` flattens its cycles using procedure `flat_tree` iteratively in a bottom-up manner until there is no cycle left. Afterward, the set is derived from the disjunctive set of flattened open leaf nodes. In particular, it repeatedly applies `flat_tree` on minimal cyclic sub-trees. A cyclic sub-tree is minimal if it does not include any (nested) cyclic sub-trees and among other companion nodes, its companion node is the one which is closest to a leaf node. We use $\mathcal{C}(\Delta_c \rightarrow \{\Delta_b^1, .., \Delta_b^n\})$ to denote a minimal cyclic sub-tree where back-links are formed between companion Δ_c and buds Δ_b^i. If there is only one bud in the tree, we write $\mathcal{C}(\Delta_c \rightarrow \Delta_b)$ for simplicity. Function `flat_tree` takes a minimal cyclic sub-tree as an input and returns a set of regular formulas, each of them corresponds to an open leaf node in the tree.

We illustrate procedure `flat_tree` through the example in Fig. 5 where the tree in the left (Fig. 5(a)) is a minimal cyclic sub-tree $\mathcal{C}(\Delta_i \rightarrow \Delta_{i_6})$ and is the input of `flat_tree`. For a minimal cyclic sub-tree, `flat_tree` first eliminates all closed leaf nodes (e.g., Δ_{i_1} and Δ_{i_5}). We remark that if all leaf nodes of a cyclic sub-tree are unsatisfiable, the whole sub-tree is pruned i.e. replaced by a closed node with `false`. After that, the open leaf nodes (e.g., Δ_{i_3} and Δ_{i_4}) are flattened by the function `flat`. Finally, flattened nodes (e.g., `flat`$(\mathcal{C}(\Delta_i \rightarrow \Delta_{i_6}), \Delta_{i_3})$ and `flat`$(\mathcal{C}(\Delta_i \rightarrow \Delta_{i_6}), \Delta_{i_5})$) are connected directly to the root of the minimal cyclic sub-tree (e.g., Δ_i); all other nodes (e.g., Δ_{i_2} and Δ_{i_6}) are discarded. The result is presented in Fig. 5(b).

Function `flat` takes a minimal cyclic sub-tree, e.g. $\mathcal{C}(\Delta_c \rightarrow \Delta_b)$, and an open leaf node in the sub-tree, e.g. $\Delta_j^{re} \equiv \exists \bar{w} \cdot \Delta^b * P_1(\bar{t}_1) * ... * P_n(\bar{t}_n)$ where $\bar{t}_i^S \subseteq \bar{w}$ $\forall i \in \{1...n\}$, as inputs. It generates a regular formula representing the set of formulas which can be obtained by unfolding according to the path which iterates the cycle (from Δ_c to Δ_b and back to Δ_c) an arbitrary number of times and finally follows the path from Δ_c to Δ_j^{re}. As the formulas obtained by unfolding according to the paths of the cycle are existentially heap-quantified, following Lemma 3, they are equi-satisfiable with their numeric part. As so, `flat` constructs a new arithmetical inductive predicate, called P_{cyc}, to extrapolate the arithmetic constraints over the path from Δ_c to Δ_b. The generation of P_{cyc} only

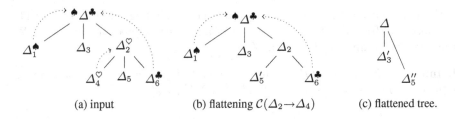

(a) input   (b) flattening $\mathcal{C}(\Delta_2 \rightarrow \Delta_4)$ (c) flattened tree.

Fig. 6. Flattening a complex cyclic tree.

succeeds if the arithmetical constraints of Δ_c, Δ_j^{re} and Δ_b are of the form ϕ_c, $\phi_c \wedge \phi_{base}$ and $\phi_c \wedge \phi_{rec}$, respectively. Let $t_1,..,t_i$ be a sequence of integer-typed parameters of the matched inductive predicates in Δ_c and $t'_1,..,t'_i$ be the corresponding sequence of integer-typed parameters of the matched inductive predicates in Δ_b. Then, flat generates the predicate $P_{cyc}(t_1,...,t_i)$ defined as follows.

$$\text{pred } P_{cyc}(t_1,...,t_i) \equiv \exists \bar{w}_b \cdot \phi_{base} \vee \exists \bar{w}_c \cdot \phi_{rec} \wedge P_{cyc}(t'_1,...,t'_i)$$

where $\bar{w}_b = FV(\phi_{base}) \setminus \{t_1,...,t_i\}$ and $\bar{w}_c = FV(\phi_{rec}) \setminus \{t_1,...,t_i\} \setminus \{t'_1,...,t'_i\}$. Afterward, flat produces the output as: $\exists \bar{w} \cdot \Delta^b \wedge P_1^N(\bar{t}_1^N) \wedge ... \wedge P_n^N(\bar{t}_n^N) \wedge P_{cyc}(t_1,..,t_i)$.

Finally, we highlight the flattening procedure with a fairly complex example in Fig. 6. The input tree, presented in Fig. 6(a), has three cycles. First, flat_tree flattens the lower tree $\mathcal{C}(\Delta_2 \rightarrow \Delta_4)$ and produces the tree in the middle, Fig. 6(b), where $\Delta'_5 \equiv \text{flat}(\mathcal{C}(\Delta_2 \rightarrow \Delta_4), \Delta_5)$. After that, it flattens the intermediate tree and produces a cyclic-free tree in Fig. 6(c). In the final tree, $\Delta'_3 \equiv \text{flat}(\mathcal{C}(\Delta \rightarrow \{\Delta_1, \Delta_6\}), \Delta_3)$ and $\Delta''_5 \equiv \text{flat}(\mathcal{C}(\Delta \rightarrow \{\Delta_1, \Delta_6\}), \Delta'_5)$. As the latter tree has two back-links, the corresponding arithmetic predicate generated for it has two recursive branches.

5.3 Correctness

Procedure utree. First, it is easy to verify that the cyclic unfolding tree derived by the procedure utree preserves satisfiability and unsatisfiability of the given predicate.

Lemma 4. *Let $\mathcal{T}_i$ be the cyclic unfolding tree derived by procedure* utree *for predicate $P_i(\bar{t}_i)$. $\mathcal{T}_i$ contains at least one satisfiable leaf node iff $P_i(\bar{t}_i)$ is satisfiable.*

Next, we provide a complexity analysis for procedure utree. Intuitively, the procedure terminates if there is no more leaf node for unfolding. This happens when all leaf nodes are either base formulas, or formulas with unobservable occurrences of inductive predicates or linked back. The last case occurs if two nodes involved in a back link have similar arrangement over free predicate arguments. As the number of these free arguments are finite, so is the number of arrangements. In particular, suppose we have N inductive predicates (e.g., $P_1,...,P_N$), and m

is the maximal length of predicate parameters (including one more for `null`). The maximal free *pointer-typed* variables of an inductive predicate is also m. We compute the complexity based on N and m.

Lemma 5. *Every path of the cyclic unfolding tree generated by procedure* `utree` *(Algorithm 1) has at most* $\mathcal{O}(2^m \times (2^m)^N \times 2^{2m^2})$ *nodes.*

Procedure `extract_regular`. For simplicity, we only discuss the minimal cyclic sub-trees including one cycle. Let $\mathcal{C}(\Delta_c \rightarrow \Delta_b)$ be a minimal cyclic sub-tree and $\Delta^b{}_j$ be a satisfiable leaf node in the tree. Let $\mathtt{lassos}(\Delta_c, \Delta_b, \Delta^b{}_j, k)$ be a formula which is obtained by unfolding the tree following the cycle (from Δ_c to Δ_b and back to Δ_c) k times and finally following the path from Δ_c to $\Delta^b{}_j$.

Lemma 6. $s, h \models \bigvee_{k \geq 0} \mathtt{lassos}(\Delta_c, \Delta_b, \Delta^b{}_j, k)$ *iff there exist* $s' \subseteq s$ *and* $h' \subseteq h$ *such that* $s', h' \models \mathtt{flat}(\mathcal{C}(\Delta_c \rightarrow \Delta_b), \Delta^b{}_j)$.

Proof. By structural induction on k and Lemma 3.   □

The correctness of function `flat_tree` immediately follows Lemma 6.

Lemma 7. *Let* $\mathcal{C}(\Delta_c \rightarrow \Delta_b)$ *be a minimal cyclic sub-tree.* $\mathcal{C}(\Delta_c \rightarrow \Delta_b)$ *is satisfiable iff there exist* $\Delta^{re} \in \mathtt{flat\_tree}(\mathcal{C}(\Delta_c \rightarrow \Delta_b))$ *and* s, h *such that* $s, h \models \Delta^{re}$.

6   Decision Procedure

Satisfiability of inductive predicates is solvable if all cycles of their unfolding trees can be flattened into regular formulas and all these regular formulas are flattable.

6.1   Decidable Fragment

Our decidable fragment is based on classes of regular formulas where each formula is flattable. We focus on the special class of regular formulas generated from the procedure `pred2reg` in the previous section (i.e., based on inductive predicates) and show how to compute bases for this class. In particular, each regular formula in this class is a set of base formulas unfolded from inductive predicates, e.g. $\Delta^{re} \equiv \Delta^b * (\exists \bar{w} \cdot \mathtt{P_1}(\bar{v}_1) * ... * \mathtt{P_n}(\bar{v}_n))$, where $\bar{v}_i^S \subseteq \bar{w}$ for all $i \in \{1...n\}$. Following Lemma 3, we have: Δ^{re} is equi-satisfiable with $\Delta^b \wedge (\exists \bar{w} \cdot \mathtt{P_1}^N(\bar{t}_1^N) * ... \wedge \mathtt{P_n}^N(\bar{t}_n^N))$. Hence, Δ^{re} is flattable, i.e. can be represented by a base formula, if every $\mathtt{P_i}^N(\bar{t}_i^N)$ is equivalent with a Presburger formula ϕ_i for all $i \in \{1...n\}$. As so, Δ^{re} is equi-satisfiable to the base formula: $\Delta^b \wedge (\exists \bar{w} \cdot \phi_1 \wedge ... \wedge \phi_n)$. In consequence, we define a class of flattable formulas, called flat DPI formula, based on DPI predicates where each predicate is equivalent to a Presburger formula [29].

An arithmetic inductive predicate is DPI if it is not inductive or is defined as follows.

$$\mathtt{pred}\ P^N(\bar{x}) \equiv \bigwedge_{1 \leq i \leq m} \phi_{0,i} \vee \exists \bar{z} \cdot \bigwedge_{1 \leq i \leq m} \phi_i \wedge \bigwedge_{1 \leq l \leq L} P^N(\bar{z}^l)$$

where m is the arity of P^N, $FV(\phi_{0,i}) \subseteq \{x_i\}$, $\bar{z} \supseteq \bar{z}^l$, and there exists j such that ϕ_i is either of $x_i = f(\bar{z}_i)$, $x_i \geq f(\bar{z}_i)$, or $x_i \leq f(\bar{z}_i)$ for all $i \neq j$, and ϕ_j is either of the following:

(1) $x_j = f(\bar{z}_j) + c \wedge \phi'$ (2) $x_j \geq f(\bar{z}_j) + c \wedge \phi'$ (3) $x_j \leq f(\bar{z}_j) + c \wedge \phi'$

(4) a conjunction of the following forms with some integer constant $n > 0$:
$$\phi', nx_j = f(\bar{z}_j), nx_j \geq f(\bar{z}_j), or \ nx_j \leq f(\bar{z}_j)$$

where c is some integer constant, $\bar{z}_j$ is $z_j^1, \ldots, z_j^L$, ϕ' is an arithmetical formula such that $FV(\phi') \subseteq \bar{z}_j$ and $\phi'[z/\bar{z}_j]$ is true for any z, $f(\bar{z}_j)$ is a combination of $z_j^1, \ldots, z_j^L$ with max, min, defined by $f(\bar{z}_j) := z_j^l \mid max(f(\bar{z}_j), f(\bar{z}_j)) \mid min(f(\bar{z}_j), f(\bar{z}_j))$, and f's may be different from each other in the conjunction of (4).

The authors in [29] showed that each inductive predicate DPI exactly represents some eventually periodic sets which are equivalent to some sets characterized by some Presburger arithmetical formulas.

Lemma 8 [29]. *For every DPI inductive predicate $P(\bar{x})$, there is a formula ϕ equivalent to $P(\bar{x})$ such that ϕ does not contain any inductive predicates.*

Finally, we define flat DPI formulas based on the DPI predicates as follows.

Definition 4 (Flat DPI Formula). *Let $\Delta \equiv \Delta^b * (\exists \bar{w} \cdot P_1(\bar{v}_1) * \ldots * P_n(\bar{v}_n))$ where $\bar{v}_i^S \subseteq \bar{w}$ for all $i \in \{1 \ldots n\}$. Δ is flattable if, for all $i \in \{1 \ldots n\}$, the arithmetic predicate $P_i{}^N(\bar{v}_i^N)$ is a DPI predicate.*

We remark that flat formulas can be extended to any class of inductive predicates whose numeric projections can be defined in Presburger arithmetic.

Now, we define a decidable fragment based on the flattable formulas.

Definition 5 (Decidable Fragment). *Let $\mathcal{P} = \{P_1, \ldots, P_n\}$ and $\mathcal{P}^{cyc} = \{P_1^{cyc}, \ldots, P_m^{cyc}\}$ be arithmetic predicates generated by function flat_tree while transforming the predicates in $\mathcal{P}$ using pred2reg. Solving satisfiability for every inductive predicate P_i in $\mathcal{P}$ is decidable iff every arithmetic predicate in $\mathcal{P}^N \cup \mathcal{P}^{cyc}$ is DPI where $\mathcal{P}^N = \{P_1{}^N, \ldots, P_n{}^N\}$.*

We remark that the decidable fragment is parameterized by the classes of flattable formulas. It is extensible to any decidable fragment of arithmetic inductive predicates.

6.2 Decision Algorithm

Computing Bases for Inductive Predicates. We present a procedure, called pred2base, to compute for each inductive predicate in $\mathcal{P}$ a set of base formulas. pred2base is described in Algorithm 2. It takes a set of predicates $\mathcal{P}$ as input and produces a mapping base$^{\mathcal{P}}$ which maps each inductive predicate to a set

---

Algorithm 2. Deriving Bases.

```
input  : P
output: base^P
1  base^P←∅; P^cyc←∅; Pres←∅;
2  foreach Pi(t̄i) ∈ P do
3  |    (reg(Pi(t̄i)), P^cyc_Pi)←pred2reg(Pi(t̄i));        /* to regular formulas */
4  |    P^cyc←P^cyc∪P^cyc_Pi;                     /* and numeric predicates for cycles */
5  end
6  foreach P^N_j(t̄j) ∈ P^N∪P^cyc do
7  |    Pres(P^N_j(t̄j))←pred2pres(pred P^N_j(t̄j));      /* compute fixed points */
8  end
9  foreach Pi(t̄i) ∈ P do
10 |    base^P(Pi(t̄i))←subst(Pres, reg(Pi(t̄i)));
11 end
12 return base^P;
```

---

of base formulas. `pred2base` first uses procedure `pred2reg` (lines 2–5) to transform the predicates into regular formulas (which are stored in `reg`) together with a set of arithmetic inductive predicates (which are stored in P^{cyc}) while flattening cycles. We recap that for each inductive predicate function `pred2reg` first uses procedure `utree` in Sect. 5.1 to construct a cyclic unfolding tree and then uses procedure `extract_regular` in Sect. 5.2 to flatten the tree into a set of regular formulas. After that, it uses function `pred2pres` (lines 6–8) to compute for each inductive predicate in $P^N∪P^{cyc}$ an equivalent Presburger formula. These relations is stored in the mapping `Pres`. Finally, at lines 9–11 it obtains a set of base formulas from substituting all arithmetic inductive predicates in the corresponding regular formulas by their equivalent Presburger formulas.

Satisfiability Solving. Let Δ be a formula over a set of user-defined predicates P where $P=\{P_1, ..., P_m\}$. The satisfiability of Δ is reduced to the satisfiability of the predicate: `pred` $P_0(\bar{t}_0) \equiv \Delta$; where P_0 is a fresh symbol and $\bar{t}_0$ is the set of free variables in Δ: $\bar{t}_0 \equiv FV(\Delta)$.

6.3   Correctness

We now show the correctness of our procedure in the decidable fragment.

Theorem 1. *Procedure `pred2base` terminates for the decidable fragment.*

Proposition 3. *Let $P_i(\bar{t}_i)$ be an inductive predicate in the decidable fragment. If $P_i(\bar{t}_i)$ is satisfiable, $reg(P_i(\bar{v}_i))$ produced by procedure `pred2reg` contains at least one satisfiable formula.*

Proposition 4. *Let $P_i(\bar{t}_i)$ be an inductive predicate in the decidable fragment. If procedure `pred2reg` can derive for it a non-empty set of satisfiable regular formulas, then there exists an unfolding tree of $P_i(\bar{t}_i)$ containing at least one satisfiable leaf node.*

The proof is trivial.

Theorem 2. *Suppose that $\mathcal{P}$ is a system of inductive predicates in the proposed decidable fragment. Assume that procedure* `pred2base` *can derive for every* $P_i(\bar{t}_i)$ *a base* $\mathsf{base}^{\mathcal{P}}P_i(\bar{t}_i)$. *For all* s, h *and* $P_i \in \mathcal{P}$, $s,h \models P_i(\bar{t}_i)$ *iff there exist* $s' \subseteq s$, $h' \subseteq h$, *and* $\Delta^b \in \mathsf{base}^{\mathcal{P}}P_i(\bar{t}_i)$ *such that* $s',h' \models \Delta^b$.

Proof. The "if" direction follows immediately from Lemmas 3, 8 and Proposition 3. The "only if" direction follows immediately from Lemmas 3, 8 and Proposition 4. □

The above theorem implies that base generation for a system of heap-only inductive predicates is decidable with the complexity $\mathcal{O}(2^m \times 2^{2m^2} \times (2^m)^N)$ time in the worst case. This finding is consistent with the one in [5].

7   Implementation and Evaluation

The proposed solver has been implemented based on the S2SAT framework [17]. We use Fixcalc [25] to compute closure for arithmetic relations. The SMT solver Z3 [10] is used for satisfiability problems over arithmetic. In the following, we first describe how to infer over-/under-approximated bases for those predicates beyond the decidable fragment. While over-approximated bases are important for unsatisfiability in verifying safety [8,15,26], under-approximated bases are critical for satisfiability in finding bugs [16]. After that, we show experimental results on the base computation and the satisfiability problem.

We sometimes over-approximate a base formula in order to show unsatisfiability, which helps to prune infeasible disjunctive program states and discharge entailment problems with empty heap in RHS [8]. In particular, the validity of the entailment checking $\Delta \vdash \mathsf{emp} \wedge \pi_c$ is equivalent to the unsatisfiability of the satisfiability problem $\Delta \wedge \neg \pi_c$. Similarly, we sometimes under-approximate a base formula in order to show satisfiability, which helps to generate counter-examples that highlight scenarios for real errors. For the latter, our approach is coupled with an error calculus [16] to affirm a real bug in HIP/S2 system [8,15]. When an error (which may be a false positive) is detected, we perform an additional satisfiability check on its pre-condition to check its feasibility. If it is satisfied, we invoke an error explanation procedure to identify a sequence of reachable code statements leading to the error [16]. With our new satisfiability procedure, we can confirm true bugs (which were not previously possible) so as to provide support towards fixing program errors.

It can be implied from Sect. 6 that generating approximated base for a formula relies on the approximation of the arithmetic part of inductive predicates, and then of regular formulas. To compute an under-approximation, we adopt the k-index bound approach from [4]. In particular, to compute a closure for a predicate P^N, we only consider all unfolded formulas which have at most k occurrences of inductive predicates. As the disjunction of the bounded formulas is an under-approximation, the closure computed is an under-approximated base.

To compute an over-approximation, we adopt the approach in [30]. In particular, first we transform the system of arithmetic inductive predicates into a system of constrained Horn clauses. After that, we use Fixcalc [25] to solve the constraints and compute an over-approximated base.

In the rest, we show the capability of our base inference and its application in program verification. We remark that, in [17] we show how a satisfiability solver in separation logic is applied into the verification system S2_{td}. The experiments were performed on a machine with the Intel i7-960 (3.2 GHz) processor and 16 GB of RAM.

Base Inference. Using our proposed procedure, we have inferred bases for a broad range of data structures. The results are shown in Table 1. The first column shows the names of inductive predicates including cyclic linked-list, list segment, linked-list with even size, binary trees. TLL is binary trees whose nodes point to their parent and all leave nodes are linked as a singly-linked list. In all these predicates, n is the length. The second column shows the inferred bases. Note that we use _ for existentially quantified variables for simplicity. The third column presents type of the base (exact base or over-approximated base). The last column captures time (in seconds) of the computation.

While our proposal can infer bases for most predicates, there are also predicates where we have inferred approximated bases (AVL tree, heap tree, complete tree and red-black tree). These typically occur when they are outside of the decidable fragments. In all these cases, we had to infer over-approximation and under-approximations by k-index (under-approximated bases are not shown for brevity).

Table 1. Bases inference for data structures

Data structure	Base inferred	Type	Sec.
Singly llist (size)	$\{\texttt{emp} \wedge \texttt{root} = \texttt{null} \wedge n = 0; \texttt{root} \mapsto c_1(\_,\_) \wedge n > 0\}$	exact	0.15
Even llist (size)	$\{\texttt{emp} \wedge \texttt{root} = \texttt{null} \wedge n = 0; \exists i \cdot \texttt{root} \mapsto c_1(\_,\_) \wedge i > 0 \wedge n = 2*i\}$	exact	0.28
Sorted llist (size, sorted)	$\{\texttt{emp} \wedge \texttt{root} = \texttt{null} \wedge n = 0 \wedge sm \leq lg;$ $\texttt{root} \mapsto c_1(\_,\_) \wedge n > 0 \wedge sm \leq lg\}$	exact	0.14
Doubly llist (size)	$\{\texttt{emp} \wedge \texttt{root} = \texttt{null} \wedge n = 0; \texttt{root} \mapsto c_1(\_,\_) \wedge n > 0\}$	exact	0.16
CompleteT (size, minheight)	$\{\texttt{emp} \wedge \texttt{root} = \texttt{null} \wedge n = 0 \wedge minh = 0;$ $\texttt{root} \mapsto c_2(\_,\_) \wedge n \leq 2*minh - 1 \wedge nmin \leq n; \}$	over	2.3
Heap trees (size, maxelem)	$\{\texttt{emp} \wedge \texttt{root} = \texttt{null} \wedge n = 0 \wedge mx = 0;$ $\texttt{root} \mapsto c_2(\_,\_) \wedge n > 0 \wedge mx \geq 0\}$	over	0.3
AVL (height, size)	$\{\texttt{emp} \wedge \texttt{root} = \texttt{null} \wedge n = 0 \wedge bal = 1;$ $\texttt{root} \mapsto c_2(\_,\_) \wedge h > 0 \wedge n \geq h \wedge n \geq 2*h - 2\}$	over	0.67
RBT(size, color, blackheight)	$\{\texttt{emp} \wedge \texttt{root} = \texttt{null} \wedge n = 0 \wedge bh = 1 \wedge cl = 0;$ $\texttt{root} \mapsto c_2(\_,\_) \wedge n > 0 \wedge cl = 1; \texttt{root} \mapsto c_2(\_,\_) \wedge n > 0 \wedge cl = 0\}$	over	0.61
TLL	$\{\texttt{root} \mapsto c_4(\_,\_,\_,\_) \wedge \texttt{root} = \texttt{ll}; \texttt{root} \mapsto c_4(\_,\_,\_,\_) * ll \mapsto c_4(\_,\_,\_,\_)\}$	exact	0.14

Table 2. Experimental results on satisfiability problems

Data structure (pure properties)	#query	#unsat	#sat	Time (seconds)
Singly llist (size)	666	75	591	0.85
Even llist (size)	139	125	14	1.04
Sorted llist (size, sorted)	217	21	196	0.46
Doubly llist (size)	452	50	402	1.08
CompleteT (size, minheight)	387	33	354	55.41
Heap trees (size, maxelem)	487	67	400	7.22
AVL (height, size)	881	64	817	52.15
RBT (size, blackheight, color)	1741	217	1524	40.85
TLL	128	13	115	0.39

Satisfiability Solving. We have implemented a new satisfiability solver based on the base inference. Our solver supports input as presented in Sect. 2 as well as in SMT2 format based on the description in [28]. We have integrated our proposed satisfiability procedure into HIP/S2 [8,15], a verification system based on separation logic. Table 2 shows the experimental results on a set of satisfiability problems generated from the verification of heap-manipulating programs. The first column lists the data structures and their pure properties. The second column lists the total number of satisfiability queries sent to the decision procedure. The next two columns show the amount of unsat and sat queries, respectively. We use $k=10$ for the inference of under-approximation. The last column captures the processed time (in seconds) for queries of each data structure. The experimental results show that our satisfiability solver could exactly decide all sat and unsat problems from our suite of verification tasks for complex data structures. This is despite the use of approximated bases for four examples, namely Heap trees, Complete trees, AVL and RBT, that are outside of the decidable fragment.

8   Related Work

Solving satisfiability in fragments of separation logic with inductive predicates has been studied extensively. Several decidable fragments were proposed with some restrictions over either shape of inductive predicates, or arithmetic, or satisfiability queries. Proposals in [2,5,9,11,13,17,21,29][1] presented decision procedures for fragments including inductive predicates with heap properties, pure equalities but without arithmetic. Initial attempts like [2,9,21] focus only on linked lists. Smallfoot [2] exploits the small model property of linked lists. SPEN [11] enhances the decidable fragment above with nested lists and skip lists.

---

[1] We remark that works in [2,9,11,13,21] also discussed decision procedures for the entailment problem which is beyond the scope of this paper.

[13] extends the decidable fragment with tree structures. The satisfiability problem is reduced to decidability of Monadic Second Order Logic on graphs with bounded tree width. Finally, SLSAT [5] proposes a decision procedure for arbitrary inductive definitions. The essence of SLSAT is an algorithm to derive for each predicate an equi-satisfiable base. Our work is an extension of SLSAT to support a combination of inductive predicates and arithmetic. To support arithmetical properties, instead of computing a least fixed point for heap property, our procedure first constructs a cyclic unfolding tree and then flattens the tree to derives the base. The decidable fragment in [29] has the following restrictions: for each inductive definition, (1) it has only a single induction case, (2) its inductive case has only a single occurrence of the inductive predicate unless the satisfiability of the spatial part becomes trivial, and (3) mutual inductive definitions are not allowed. Our decidable fragment removes these restrictions. Finally, [17] supports satisfiability checking of the universal fragment restricted in both shape and arithmetic. In comparison, our procedure supports arbitrary inductive definitions with relations based on semilinear sets over arithmetical parameters.

In terms of decision procedures supporting inductive predicates and arithmetic, GRASShoper [23] and Asterix [22] are among the first decision procedures where shape definitions are restricted to linked lists. The decidable fragments have been recently widened in extended GRASShoper [24], CompSPEN [12], S2SAT$_{SL}$ [17,18,29]. While CompSPEN extends the graph-based algorithm [9] to doubly-linked list, S2SAT$_{SL}$ is an instantiation of S2SAT [17]. For back-link construction, the instantiations [17,18] are based on both heap and arithmetic constraints. Our algorithm in this work is more compositional i.e., it first forms back-links based only on the heap domain and then reduces the satisfiability problems into the satisfiability problems over arithmetic. By doing so, we can exploit well-developed results for the arithmetic domain. In this work, we reuse the result based on semilinear sets [29] for the arithmetic. In [20], we show how to adapt results based on periodic relations [4]. We are currently investigating how to use regular model checking [3] to enhance our decision procedure. The procedure S2SAT$_{SL}$ presented in [17] constructs back-links based on a combination of heap and arithmetic domains. In this work, back-links are constructed based on heap domain only. The satisfiability of the arithmetic part is processed in a separate phase. By doing so, the decidable fragment proposed in this paper is much more expressive when compared with the decidable fragment in [17]. For instance, while the decidable fragment in [17] includes a restricted fragment of heap-only predicates, the decidable fragment presented in this work includes arbitrary heap-only predicates. Our proposal may be viewed as an extension of the work [29] with the construction of cyclic unfolding trees to support arbitrary spatial predicates. To the best of our knowledge, our proposal is the most powerful decision procedure for satisfiability in separation logic.

9 Conclusion

We have presented a novel decision procedure for an expressive fragment of separation logic including shape and arithmetic properties. Our procedure is based on computing an equi-satisfiable base formula for each inductive predicate. This base computation, in turn, relies on the computation of the base for a set of flat formulas. We provide a complexity analysis to show that the decision problem for heap-based fragment is, in the worst case, in exponential time. We have implemented our proposal in a prototype tool and integrated it into an existing verification system. Experimental results shows that our procedure works effectively over the set of satisfiability benchmarks.

Acknowledgements. Quang Loc and Jun Sun are partially supported by NRF grant RGNRF1501 and Wei-Ngan by MoE Tier-2 grant MOE2013-T2-2-146.

References

1. Berdine, J., Calcagno, C., O'Hearn, P.W.: A decidable fragment of separation logic. In: Lodaya, K., Mahajan, M. (eds.) FSTTCS 2004. LNCS, vol. 3328, pp. 97–109. Springer, Heidelberg (2004). doi:10.1007/978-3-540-30538-5_9
2. Berdine, J., Calcagno, C., O'Hearn, P.W.: Symbolic execution with separation logic. In: Yi, K. (ed.) APLAS 2005. LNCS, vol. 3780, pp. 52–68. Springer, Heidelberg (2005). doi:10.1007/11575467_5
3. Bouajjani, A., Jonsson, B., Nilsson, M., Touili, T.: Regular model checking. In: Emerson, E.A., Sistla, A.P. (eds.) CAV 2000. LNCS, vol. 1855, pp. 403–418. Springer, Heidelberg (2000). doi:10.1007/10722167_31
4. Bozga, M., Iosif, R., Konečný, F.: Fast acceleration of ultimately periodic relations. In: Touili, T., Cook, B., Jackson, P. (eds.) CAV 2010. LNCS, vol. 6174, pp. 227–242. Springer, Heidelberg (2010). doi:10.1007/978-3-642-14295-6_23
5. Brotherston, J., Fuhs, C., Pérez, J.A.N., Gorogiannis, N.: A decision procedure for satisfiability in separation logic with inductive predicates. In: CSL-LICS 2014, pp. 25:1–25:10, (2014). ACM, New York
6. Brotherston, J., Gorogiannis, N.: Cyclic abduction of inductively defined safety and termination preconditions. In: Müller-Olm, M., Seidl, H. (eds.) SAS 2014. LNCS, vol. 8723, pp. 68–84. Springer, Cham (2014). doi:10.1007/978-3-319-10936-7_5
7. Calcagno, C., Yang, H., O'Hearn, P.W.: Computability and complexity results for a spatial assertion language for data structures. In: Hariharan, R., Vinay, V., Mukund, M. (eds.) FSTTCS 2001. LNCS, vol. 2245, pp. 108–119. Springer, Heidelberg (2001). doi:10.1007/3-540-45294-X_10
8. Chin, W.N., David, C., Nguyen, H.H., Qin, S.: Automated verification of shape, size and bag properties via user-defined predicates in separation logic. SCP **77**(9), 1006–1036 (2012)
9. Cook, B., Haase, C., Ouaknine, J., Parkinson, M., Worrell, J.: Tractable reasoning in a fragment of separation logic. In: Katoen, J.-P., König, B. (eds.) CONCUR 2011. LNCS, vol. 6901, pp. 235–249. Springer, Heidelberg (2011). doi:10.1007/978-3-642-23217-6_16

10. de Moura, L., Bjørner, N.: Z3: an efficient smt solver. In: Ramakrishnan, C.R., Rehof, J. (eds.) TACAS 2008. LNCS, vol. 4963, pp. 337–340. Springer, Heidelberg (2008). doi:10.1007/978-3-540-78800-3_24

11. Enea, C., Lengál, O., Sighireanu, M., Vojnar, T.: Compositional entailment checking for a fragment of separation logic. In: Garrigue, J. (ed.) APLAS 2014. LNCS, vol. 8858, pp. 314–333. Springer, Cham (2014). doi:10.1007/978-3-319-12736-1_17

12. Gu, X., Chen, T., Wu, Z.: A complete decision procedure for linearly compositional separation logic with data constraints. In: Olivetti, N., Tiwari, A. (eds.) IJCAR 2016. LNCS (LNAI), vol. 9706, pp. 532–549. Springer, Cham (2016). doi:10.1007/978-3-319-40229-1_36

13. Iosif, R., Rogalewicz, A., Simacek, J.: The tree width of separation logic with recursive definitions. In: Bonacina, M.P. (ed.) CADE 2013. LNCS (LNAI), vol. 7898, pp. 21–38. Springer, Heidelberg (2013). doi:10.1007/978-3-642-38574-2_2

14. Ishtiaq, S., O'Hearn, P.W.: BI as an assertion language for mutable data structures. In: ACM POPL, pp. 14–26, London, January 2001

15. Le, Q.L., Gherghina, C., Qin, S., Chin, W.-N.: Shape analysis via second-order bi-abduction. In: Biere, A., Bloem, R. (eds.) CAV 2014. LNCS, vol. 8559, pp. 52–68. Springer, Cham (2014). doi:10.1007/978-3-319-08867-9_4

16. Le, Q.L., Sharma, A., Craciun, F., Chin, W.-N.: Towards complete specifications with an error calculus. In: Brat, G., Rungta, N., Venet, A. (eds.) NFM 2013. LNCS, vol. 7871, pp. 291–306. Springer, Heidelberg (2013). doi:10.1007/978-3-642-38088-4_20

17. Le, Q.L., Sun, J., Chin, W.-N.: Satisfiability modulo heap-based programs. In: Chaudhuri, S., Farzan, A. (eds.) CAV 2016. LNCS, vol. 9779, pp. 382–404. Springer, Cham (2016). doi:10.1007/978-3-319-41528-4_21

18. Le, Q.L., Sun, J., Qin, S.: Verifying heap-manipulating programs using constrained horn clauses (technical report) (2017)

19. Le, Q.L., Sun, J., Qin, S., Chin, W.-N.: Frame inference for inductive entailment proofs in separation logic (technical report), May 2016

20. Le, Q.L., Tatsuta, M., Jun, S., Chin, W.-N.: A decidable fragment in separation logic with inductive predicates and arithmetic (technical report) (2017)

21. Navarro Pérez, J.A., Rybalchenko, A.: Separation logic + superposition calculus = heap theorem prover. In: PLDI 2011, pp. 556–566. ACM (2011)

22. Navarro Pérez, J.A., Rybalchenko, A.: Separation logic modulo theories. In: Shan, C. (ed.) APLAS 2013. LNCS, vol. 8301, pp. 90–106. Springer, Cham (2013). doi:10.1007/978-3-319-03542-0_7

23. Piskac, R., Wies, T., Zufferey, D.: Automating separation logic using SMT. In: Sharygina, N., Veith, H. (eds.) CAV 2013. LNCS, vol. 8044, pp. 773–789. Springer, Heidelberg (2013). doi:10.1007/978-3-642-39799-8_54

24. Piskac, R., Wies, T., Zufferey, D.: GRASShopper: complete heap verification with mixed specifications. In: Ábrahám, E., Havelund, K. (eds.) TACAS 2014. LNCS, vol. 8413, pp. 124–139. Springer, Heidelberg (2014). doi:10.1007/978-3-642-54862-8_9

25. Popeea, C., Chin, W.-N.: Inferring disjunctive postconditions. In: Okada, M., Satoh, I. (eds.) ASIAN 2006. LNCS, vol. 4435, pp. 331–345. Springer, Heidelberg (2007). doi:10.1007/978-3-540-77505-8_26

26. Qiu, X., Garg, P., Ştefănescu, A., Madhusudan, P.: Natural proofs for structure, data, and separation. In: PLDI, pp. 231–242 (2013). ACM, New York

27. Reynolds, J.: Separation logic: a logic for shared mutable data structures. In: IEEE LICS, pp. 55–74 (2002)

28. Serban, C.: A formalization of separation logic in SMT-LIB v2.5 syntax, types and semantics. Technical report, Verimag (2015) Accessed Jan 2017
29. Tatsuta, M., Le, Q.L., Chin, W.-N.: Decision procedure for separation logic with inductive definitions and Presburger arithmetic. In: Igarashi, A. (ed.) APLAS 2016. LNCS, vol. 10017, pp. 423–443. Springer, Cham (2016). doi:10.1007/ 978-3-319-47958-3_22
30. Trinh, M.-T., Le, Q.L., David, C., Chin, W.-N.: Bi-abduction with pure properties for specification inference. In: Shan, C. (ed.) APLAS 2013. LNCS, vol. 8301, pp. 107–123. Springer, Cham (2013). doi:10.1007/978-3-319-03542-0_8

Software Analysis

Finding Fix Locations for CFL-Reachability Analyses via Minimum Cuts

Andrei Marian Dan[1]([✉]), Manu Sridharan[2], Satish Chandra[2],
Jean-Baptiste Jeannin[2], and Martin Vechev[1]

[1] Department of Computer Science, ETH Zurich, Zürich, Switzerland
{andrei.dan,martin.vechev}@inf.ethz.ch
[2] Samsung Research America, Mountain View, USA
manu@sridharan.net, schandra@schandra.org, jb.jeannin@gmail.com

Abstract. Static analysis tools are increasingly important for ensuring code quality. Ideally, all warnings from a static analysis would be addressed, but the volume of warnings and false positives usually makes this effort prohibitive. We present techniques for finding *fix locations*, a small set of program locations where fixes can be applied to address all static analysis warnings. We focus on analyses expressible as context-free-language reachability, where a set of fix locations is naturally expressed as a min-cut of the CFL graph. We show, surprisingly, that computing such a CFL min-cut is NP-hard. We then phrase the problem of finding CFL min-cuts as an optimization problem which allows us to trade-off the size of the cut vs. the preservation of computed information. We then show how to solve the optimization problem via a MaxSAT encoding.

Our evaluation shows that we compute fix location sets that are significantly smaller than both the number of warnings and, in the case of a true CFL min-cut, the fix location sets from a normal min-cut.

1 Introduction

Static analysis tools are playing an increasingly important role in ensuring code quality of real-world software. They are able to detect a wide variety of defects, from low-level memory errors to violations of typestate properties. In an ideal setting, code would be made "clean" with respect to these tools: all warnings would be addressed either with a fix of the underlying defect, or a combination of code restructuring and annotations to show the tool no defect exists.

Unfortunately, this ideal is rarely achieved in practice. One issue is that the volume of warnings emitted by these tools can be large, with each issue potentially requiring significant time to inspect and understand. Further, as is inevitable in static analysis, many of the warnings are false positives, and expending significant effort in annotating and restructuring code to avoid false positive reports may overburden the developer.

M. Sridharan—Currently affiliated with Uber.
S. Chandra—Currently affiliated with Facebook.

© Springer International Publishing AG 2017
R. Majumdar and V. Kunčak (Eds.): CAV 2017, Part II, LNCS 10427, pp. 521–541, 2017.
DOI: 10.1007/978-3-319-63390-9_27

This paper presents a technique for computing a small set of *fix locations*, such that code changes at or near those locations can address *all* warnings emitted by a static analysis. Previous work (e.g., Fink et al. [7]) has observed that many static analysis warnings (particularly false positives) can stem from a small amount of buggy or difficult-to-analyze code that leads to cascading warnings. Producing a small set of fix locations would help pinpoint this crucial code, which could significantly ease the process of addressing a large set of warnings. Similarly, recent work provides succinct explanations for type inference errors [14, 17, 22].

A trend in large companies is to only allow committing code that is warning free. It is deemed acceptable that false positives may need a small refactoring, or an annotation to silence the analyzer. Addressing all warnings results in a program that is error free with respect to the analyser that is used. Note that the user can potentially insert an assumption, instead of modifying the fix location code. This way, the analyzer gains precision and eliminates false positives.

We focus on analyses expressible as context-free-language reachability (CFL-reachability) problems [18]. The CFL-reachability framework can express a wide variety of program analyses, including points-to analysis and inter-procedural dataflow analysis [18]. In a CFL-reachability-based analysis, an error report typically corresponds to the existence of corresponding (CFL) paths in a graph representing the program and analysis problem. Hence, the problem of computing fix locations maps naturally to the problem of computing a cut of the graph that removes the paths corresponding to the errors. Intuitively, the fix locations are the program locations corresponding to the edges in this cut.

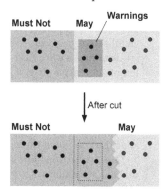

Fig. 1. A cut causes "may" facts that trigger warnings to become "must-not" facts.

Figure 1 gives an overview of our goal. A CFL-reachability analysis typically computes a set of "may" facts that hold for the input program, corresponding to CFL paths in the graph. The absence of a path then corresponds to a complementary "must-not" fact, and a cut of the graph changes some facts from "may" to "must-not" (while preserving "must-not" facts). Certain "may" facts trigger analysis warnings, and our goal is to compute a small cut that turns all such "may" facts into "must-not" facts, thereby eliminating all warnings.

A promising component of computing fix locations would be to compute a *CFL min-cut* of a graph (we will discuss shortly why the CFL min-cut may not be the optimal solution in all cases). A CFL min-cut is distinguished from a standard graph min-cut in that it need only cut CFL paths in the graph. For a CFL-reachability problem, the CFL min-cut may be smaller than a standard min-cut that ignores edge labels (see Sect. 2). As CFL-reachability is computable in polynomial time [18], a natural question is:

Can a CFL min-cut be computed in polynomial time?

A key result of this work is that (perhaps surprisingly) it is not possible to compute a CFL-min-cut in polynomial time for an arbitrary CFL language.[1] Towards that, we prove that computing the CFL min-cut problem for the restricted language of balanced parentheses is NP-hard. Moreover, we prove that for a language with multiple types of parentheses, computing the CFL min-cut on graphs resulting from applying an IFDS null analysis on programs is also NP-hard. We expect that similar techniques will work for other realistic analyses like pointer analysis.

CFL-reachability problems correspond to Datalog programs consisting entirely of chain rules [18]. For such programs, the CFL min-cut problem maps to finding the smallest set of input facts that, when removed, make a specified set of output facts underivable. Our hardness result implies that finding this smallest set for Datalog chain programs is also NP-hard.

Beyond computational hardness, a CFL min-cut may not always provide the most desirable set of fix locations, as it does not consider the degree of unnecessary change to the (abstract) program behavior. Notice that in Fig. 1, the cut caused some "may" facts that did not correspond to warnings to become "must-not" facts. If this set of needlessly-transformed "may" facts becomes too large, the fix locations corresponding to a CFL min-cut may not be desirable (see Sect. 2 for an example). On the other hand, an approach that strictly minimizes the number of transformed "may" facts (while still fixing all warnings) may yield an excessively large set of fix locations. Hence, we require a technique that allows for a tunable tradeoff between these two factors, analogous to tradeoffs between syntactic and semantic change in program repair [6].

To achieve this flexible tradeoff, we first define an *abstract distance* that measures how many of the "may" facts are transformed for a given cut. Second, we formulate the problem of computing the best cut of a CFL graph as an optimization problem. In the process, we show how this formulation can be constructed with a simple instrumentation of an optimized IFDS solver, requiring no changes to analysis clients using the solver. The optimization formulation combines the goal to minimize the cut size (formulated for IFDS problems based on the Reps-Horwitz-Sagiv tabulation algorithm [19]) with the minimization of the abstract distance. Finally, we solve the optimization problem via an encoding to a weighted MaxSAT formula. MaxSAT solvers have improved dramatically in recent years, and the framework of weighted MaxSAT allows us to concisely express the relevant tradeoffs in our problem.

We have implemented our technique and evaluated it on a realistic null dereference analysis for Java programs. We found that our proposed fix location sets were often smaller than the total number of warnings (up to 11 times smaller). Moreover, we discover that the size of a CFL min-cut is significantly smaller (up to 50%) than the size of a normal min-cut. We also evaluated the tradeoffs between cut vs. abstract distance sizes. To our best knowledge, our system is the first to be able to suggest a minimal number of fix locations for errors found by a static analysis.

---

[1] Assuming $P \neq NP$.

Contributions. This paper presents the following contributions:

- We prove that computing a CFL min-cut is NP-hard, even for a simple balanced-parentheses language and acyclic graphs (Sect. 3).
- We define the notion of abstract distance and define an optimization problem between the CFL min-cut vs. abstract distance sizes and show how to solve this problem via (MaxSAT Sect. 4).
- We evaluate our approach on an IFDS-based null-pointer analysis on several benchmark programs, showing the benefits of CFL min-cuts and exploring the tradeoffs involved (Sect. 5).

2   Overview

In this section we provide an overview of our approach on a motivating program analysis example, illustrating the usefulness of CFL min-cuts and the tradeoffs involved. We start with some core definitions.

2.1   CFL Reachability

Let us consider the context-free grammar of balanced parenthesis $H = \{\{S\}, \Sigma, R, S\}$, where $\Sigma = \{(,), \epsilon\}$ is a set of symbols; S is the non-terminal starting variable; and $R = \{S \rightarrow SS, S \rightarrow (S), S \rightarrow \epsilon\}$ is the set of production rules. Let $G = (V, E)$ be a graph with vertices V and edges E, each edge labelled with a symbol from Σ; Fig. 2 gives an example.

Given a graph G and a context-free grammar H, CFL reachability from a source vertex u to a destination vertex v is conceptually established as follows. Given a path p, we define word W_p as the concatenation of the edge labels of p. Then, v is CFL-reachable from u iff there exists a path p from u to v s.t. W_p is in the language defined by H. In the graph of Fig. 2, only vertices d and f are CFL-reachable from vertex a.

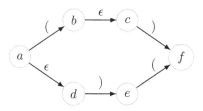

Fig. 2. Edges of the graph are labelled with symbols from the context-free grammar of balanced parenthesis H.

2.2   CFL Min-Cuts

Min-Cut. A standard min-cut between two nodes a and f of a graph is defined as a minimal set of edges M such that if all edges in M are removed, no path remains from a to f. For Fig. 2, any min-cut between nodes a and f must have size 2, as it must cut the path $a \rightarrow b \rightarrow c \rightarrow f$ and and the path $a \rightarrow d \rightarrow e \rightarrow f$. Computing a min-cut is polynomial in the size of the graph and several algorithms have been developed [8, 21].

CFL Min-Cut. Similarly, a CFL min-cut between two nodes a and f of a graph is defined as a minimal-size set of edges that, when removed, ensure no CFL path exists from a to f. Any min-cut is also a CFL cut. However, it is possible that a min-cut is not a CFL min-cut. For Fig. 2, the only CFL path from a to f is $a \rightarrow b \rightarrow c \rightarrow f$. ($a \rightarrow d \rightarrow e \rightarrow f$ is not a CFL path because the word "ϵ)(" has mismatched parentheses.) Therefore, for this example the CFL min-cuts are of size one ($\{ab\}$, $\{bc\}$ or $\{cf\}$). Though computing a standard min-cut has a polynomial time complexity, in Sect. 3 we prove that computing a CFL min-cut is NP-hard even for a simple balanced parentheses language.

2.3 Min-Cuts for Program Analysis

Here, we detail how our technique applies CFL min-cuts to finding fix locations for a static analysis, focusing on an analysis expressed atop the well-known IFDS framework [19].

Figure 3 shows an example program. We use ... to omit parts of the program, for simplification purposes. The program consists of a class with three static methods (f, g, main) and one static field (a).

Null Dereference IFDS Analysis. A null dereference analysis for Java checks that field accesses and method invocations do not dereference null, causing a NullPointerException. Such an analysis can be encoded in the IFDS (interprocedural, finite, distributive, subset) framework [19]. IFDS problems can be solved by computing CFL-reachability over an exploded super-graph repre-

```
1:  class Hello {
2:      static Object a;
3:      static void f() { ... }
4:      static void g() { ... }

5:  public static
        void main(String[] args) {
6:          a = null;
7:          if (...) { f(); }
8:          else { g(); }

9:          a = new Object();
10:         if (...) { a = null; }
11:         ...
12:         if (...) {f(); a.toString();}
13:         else {g(); a.getClass(); }}}
```

Fig. 3. On this example, a null dereference analysis reports 2 warnings at lines 12 and 13. Depending on *if* conditions, these could be bugs or false positives.

sentation of the program. We briefly describe the technique here; see Reps et al. for further details [19].

Super-Graph. Starting from the input program P, the analysis constructs a *supergraph*, a type of interprocedural control-flow graph. The supergraph nodes for the example in Fig. 3 are the boxes in Fig. 4. In addition to the usual nodes of the intra-procedural flow graphs, each procedure has a distinguished entry and exit node (e.g., s_f and e_f). Each function call is represented by a call and return node at the caller (e.g., n_3 and n_4), and by edges from the call node to the callee entry and from the callee exit to the return node. A detailed description of supergraphs is available in [19].

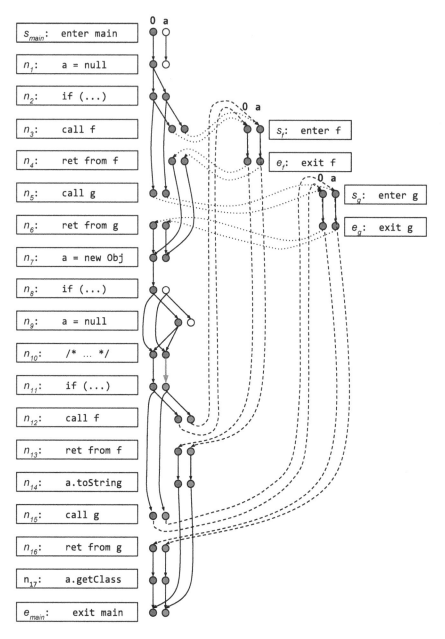

Fig. 4. Exploded super-graph for the program in Fig. 3. The emphasized blue edge represents a CFL min-cut in this graph such that the fact a is not reachable at statements a.toString and a.getClass. The white circles represent facts that are not reachable from the fact **0** of the main procedure's entry node. The grey and blue circles represent reachable facts from the fact **0** of the main procedure's entry node. The blue nodes become CFL unreachable if we remove the blue edge. A reachable node a means that the variable a may be null at that program point. (Color figure online)

Exploded Super-Graph. Given the supergraph, the IFDS analysis constructs an *exploded supergraph*, with nodes representing facts at program points and edges representing control flow and transfer functions. The exploded supergraph for null dereference analysis of Fig. 3 is shown in Fig. 4. Here, the analysis only needs to track nullness of global variable a. So, for each node in the supergraph, the exploded supergraph has two nodes: a **0** node and an **a** node. (The number of nodes depends on the number of facts in the abstract domain.) The **0** nodes are required for well-formedness, and the **a** node tracks whether the variable a *may be null*. The solid edges represent the transfer function for the corresponding program statement. E.g. edges $\langle n_1, 0\rangle \rightarrow \langle n_2, 0\rangle$ and $\langle n_1, 0\rangle \rightarrow \langle n_2, a\rangle$ show that statement a = null "gens" a fact that a may be null. The dotted and dashed edges correspond to function calls and returns. We use dotted edges for the first (in program order) calls and return for functions f and g (e.g., $\langle n_3, 0\rangle \cdots\rightarrow \langle s_f, 0\rangle$ and $\langle e_f, 0\rangle \cdots\rightarrow \langle n_4, 0\rangle$) and we use dashed edges for the second calls to these functions. Any *realizable path* through the graph must exit a function call via the same type of edge (dotted or dashed) as it entered. Checking for realizable paths is equivalent to computing CFL reachability with a parenthesis labeling for call and return edges. Each call site gets a unique pair of open and close parentheses, e.g., $(^1_f$ for n_3 to s_f edges and $)^1_f$ for e_f to n_4 edges, and the language ensures any CFL path has matched parentheses.

Warnings as CFL-Reachability. The IFDS analysis computes CFL-reachability of nodes in the exploded super-graph using the tabulation algorithm [19]. In our example, if an **a** node is CFL-reachable from node $\langle s_{main}, 0\rangle$, then variable a may be null at the corresponding program point. In Fig. 4, all of the grey and blue nodes are CFL-reachable from $\langle s_{main}, 0\rangle$, while the white nodes are not. In particular, the nodes $\langle n_{14}, a\rangle$ and $\langle n_{17}, a\rangle$ corresponding to the statements a.toString and a.getClass are CFL-reachable (blue color). The analysis thus triggers two warnings, indicating possible null dereferences at lines 12 and 13 of Fig. 3. These warnings could be real bugs or false positives, depending on the actual conditions in the if statements.

Fix Locations. To remove all warnings, the corresponding exploded supergraph nodes must be made unreachable from the **0** entry node. For our example, making an **a** node unreachable corresponds to proving a *must not* be null at the corresponding program point. A CFL min-cut gives a minimal set of edges to make the warning nodes unreachable, and the corresponding program locations are the suggested fix locations. In Fig. 4, the blue solid edge $\langle n_{10}, a\rangle \rightarrow \langle n_{11}, a\rangle$ is a CFL min-cut between node $\langle s_{main}, 0\rangle$ and the warning nodes ($\langle n_{14}, a\rangle$ and $\langle n_{17}, a\rangle$). If we remove this edge, then all blue nodes become CFL-unreachable from node $\langle s_{main}, 0\rangle$.

Min-Cut vs. CFL Min-Cut. Notice that if we consider regular reachability instead of CFL reachability, then the nodes corresponding to warnings are still reachable from $\langle s_{main}, 0\rangle$ in Fig. 4, even after removing the CFL min-cut (blue edge). For example, node $\langle n_{14}, a\rangle$ can be reached through the path: $\langle s_{main}, 0\rangle \rightarrow \langle n_1, 0\rangle \rightarrow$

$\langle n_2, \mathbf{a} \rangle \longrightarrow \langle n_3, \mathbf{a} \rangle \cdots\!\!\rightarrow \langle s_f, \mathbf{a} \rangle \longrightarrow \langle e_f, \mathbf{a} \rangle \dashrightarrow \langle n_{13}, \mathbf{a} \rangle \longrightarrow \langle n_{14}, \mathbf{a} \rangle$. However, this is not a realizable program path because the call edge $\langle n_3, \mathbf{a} \rangle \cdots\!\!\rightarrow \langle s_f, \mathbf{a} \rangle$ does not correspond to the return edge $\langle e_f, \mathbf{a} \rangle \dashrightarrow \langle n_{13}, \mathbf{a} \rangle$. For this example, a regular min-cut has size two.[2] Hence, if only regular min-cuts were considered, the number of fix locations could be unnecessarily higher than a CFL min-cut, leading to needless fixing effort from the programmer.

CFL Min-Cut Selection. In general, a graph can have several CFL min-cuts. We choose to select the cut that preserves the most reachability facts in the exploded super-graph. Choosing in this manner converts as few may facts to must-not facts as possible (see Fig. 1), retaining as much of the original safe behavior as possible. The blue edge CFL min-cut in Fig. 4 only makes the eight blue nodes in the graph CFL unreachable. The actual fix can be implemented by simply introducing a line `a = new Object()` (or a more realistic fix) between lines 11 and 12 of Fig. 3. Note that suggesting a concrete *repair* is future work and out of scope for this paper.

Consider another possible CFL min-cut, $\langle n_9, \mathbf{0} \rangle$ to $\langle n_{10}, \mathbf{a} \rangle$. Since node n_{10} can correspond to a large code fragment (that potentially does not write to variable $\mathbf{a}$), this alternate cut could correspond to a much more disruptive change. Further trade-offs between preserving semantics and min-cut sizes are presented in Sect. 4. Next, we study the complexity of finding a CFL min-cut.

3   CFL Min-Cut Complexity

The time complexity for CFL-reachability is $O(|\varSigma|^3 n^3)$ when using dynamic programming, where n is the number of graph vertices and $|\varSigma|$ the size of the CFL [16], compared to normal reachability which is $O(n)$ (graph traversal). Computing a normal min-cut has the complexity $O(mn \times log(n^2/m))$ (m is the number of graph edges) [8], and one might expect only a polynomial additional cost for computing a CFL min-cut. But, here we show that computing a CFL min-cut is *NP-hard* even for a restricted version of the problem (Table 1).

Table 1. Time complexity for the reachability and min-cut problems.

	Reachability	Min-cut
Normal	$O(n)$	$O(mn \times log(n^2/m))$ [8]
CFL	$O(|\varSigma|^3 n^3)$ [16]	*NP-hard* (this work)

When considering this problem, we focused on balanced parentheses languages (as defined in Sect. 2.1), as most popular and important CFL-reachability-based program analyses we know of use balanced parentheses. Theorem 1 shows

---

[2] Note that an edge between two $\mathbf{0}$ nodes (e.g. $\langle s_{main}, \mathbf{0} \rangle \longrightarrow \langle n_1, \mathbf{0} \rangle$) cannot be cut as such an edge is required for the well-formedness of the exploded supergraph [19].

NP-hardness of CFL min-cut for the restricted language of balanced parenthe-ses. Theorem 1 also shows that the hardness result holds *even for acyclic graphs* and it is our best result in terms of the most restricted CFL and graph struc-ture. In practice, when applying a CFL-reachability analysis to graphs from real programs, the resulting graphs may not allow for the structure used in the proof of Theorem 1. Still, most popular CFL-reachability analyses allow for mul-tiple parentheses types and we show an example in Theorem 2 that for graphs resulting from an IFDS null analysis the CFL min-cut problem is NP-hard. We believe that similar proof techniques can be extended to other realistic analyses like pointer analysis.

Preliminaries. Let L be a context-free language over the alphabet Σ and a directed graph $G = (V, E)$ such that the edges in E are labelled with members of Σ (*label* : $E \rightarrow \Sigma$). Henceforth CFL paths, CFL reachability and CFL min-cuts are understood with respect to the language L. Let $s \in V$ be the source node and $t \in V$ the target node. Each path from s to t in G defines a word over the alphabet Σ. A path is a CFL path if the word corresponding to the path is a member of L. We consider directed graphs. The s, t CFL min-cut problem is defined as finding the smallest subset $E' \subseteq E$ such that there exists no CFL path from s to t in the graph $G' = (V, E \setminus E')$.

Theorem 1. *If L is the language of balanced parentheses, finding the s, t CFL min-cut in acyclic directed graphs with edges labelled by symbols of L is NP-hard.*

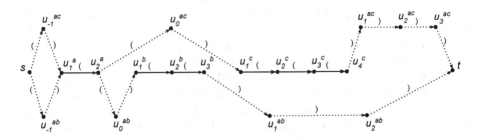

Fig. 5. Acyclic labelled graph for which finding the CFL min-cut between s and t leads to finding the vertex cover for the graph with three vertices and two edges ($\{a, b, c\}, \{ab, ac\}$).

Proof. We reduce the vertex cover problem to s, t CFL min-cut in acyclic graphs. Given an undirected graph $G = (V, E)$, the vertex cover problem [10] computes the smallest set $C \subseteq V$ such that $\forall uv \in E \Rightarrow u \in C \vee v \in C$. We map each element of V to a number in $\{1 \ldots n\}$, where $|V| = n$ ($id : V \rightarrow \{1 \ldots n\}$). Notice that if initially G contains $vv \in E$, where $v \in V$, then v has to be in the vertex cover. Therefore, we add v to the solution and remove all the edges containing v from E. From now we can assume that E does not contain vv edges, $v \in V$.

Starting from the graph (V, E), we construct the new graph (V', E') on which we compute the s, t CFL min-cut. First, we introduce two distinguished vertices $\{s, t\} \subseteq V'$. Then for each vertex $v \in V$ we create $id(v) + 1$ vertices in V': $\{u_1^v, \ldots, u_{id(v)+1}^v\}$. Additionally, we add $id(v)$ edges to E', labelled with the symbol "(": $\{u_1^v u_2^v, \ldots, u_{id(v)}^v u_{id(v)+1}^v\}$.

For each edge $vv' \in E$, ordered (without loss of generality) such that $id(v) < id(v')$, we first create 2 new vertices in V': $\{u_{-1}^{vv'}, u_0^{vv'}\}$, and 4 new edges in E': $su_{-1}^{vv'}, u_{id(v)+1}^v u_0^{vv'}$, labelled with "(" and $u_{-1}^{vv'} u_1^v, u_0^{vv'} u_1^{v'}$ labelled with ")".

Finally, for each edge $vv' \in E$, we introduce $id(v) + id(v') - 1$ vertices $\{u_1^{vv'}, \ldots u_{id(v)+id(v')-1}^{vv'}\}$ and $id(v) + id(v')$ edges labelled by ")":

$$\{u_{id(v')+1}^{v'} u_1^{vv'}, u_1^{vv'} u_2^{vv'}, \ldots, u_{id(v)+id(v')-2}^{vv'} u_{id(v)+id(v')-1}^{vv'}, u_{id(v)+id(v')-1}^{vv'} t\}$$

Overall, if $|E| = m$, the number of vertices in V' is $O(n^2 + mn)$ and the number of edges in E' is $O(n^2 + mn)$.

We illustrate the construction for a small graph $(\{a, b, c\}, \{ab, ac\})$ for which we want to find the vertex cover. First, we associate 1 to vertex a, 2 to b and 3 to c. Next, following the steps described above, we construct the graph shown in Fig. 5.

For each edge $vv' \in E$, there exists a corresponding CFL path from s to t in the graph (G', E'). This path contains all the $id(v) + id(v')$ edges corresponding to v and v'. Additionally, the CFL path will contain the sub-CFL-paths of length 2 between s and the first vertex corresponding to v (u_1^v) and from the last vertex corresponding to v ($u_{id(v)+1}^v$) to the first vertex corresponding to v' ($u_1^{v'}$).

There exist additional CFL paths from s to t. Given $vv' \in E$ and $v_1, v_2 \in V$ such that $v_1 v_2 \in E$ and $v_2 v' \in E$ and $id(v_1) + id(v_2) = id(v)$, there is an CFL path from s to t containing the edges added for the vertices v_1, v_2 and v'. An important observation is that any cut for the CFL paths corresponding to edges in E will also be a cut for the additional CFL paths described above. Therefore, the additional CFL paths do not increase the size of the s, t CFL min-cut.

Finding an s, t CFL min-cut in this newly constructed graph is equivalent to finding a vertex cover in the original graph. We show how to obtain the vertex cover given an s, t CFL min-cut $M = \{e_1, \ldots, e_k\}$.

The first step is to transform M such that it contains only edges of type $u_i^v u_{i+1}^v$, where $v \in V$ and $i < id(v) + 1$.

If $e \in M$ is of type $u_i^{vv'} u_{i+1}^{vv'}$, we replace it with $u_{id(v')}^{v'} u_{id(v')+1}^{v'}$. It is impossible that the new edge already exists in M, because all CFL paths that contain $u_i^{vv'} u_{i+1}^{vv'}$ also contain $u_{id(v')}^{v'} u_{id(v')+1}^{v'}$ and this would contradict the minimality of the cut size. Additionally, M remains an s, t CFL cut and has the same size.

If e is of type $su_{-1}^{vv'}$, $u_{-1}^{vv'} u_1^v$, $u_{id(v)+1}^v u_0^{vv'}$ or $u_0^{vv'} u_1^{v'}$ then we replace it with the edge $u_{id(v)}^v u_{id(v)+1}^v$. Similarly to the previous case, all the CFL paths that contain e also contain its replacement $(u_{id(v)}^v u_{id(v)+1}^v)$.

Next, to each edge $u_i^v u_{i+1}^v$ in the s, t CFL min-cut corresponds the vertex v in the cover set. For the example in Fig. 5, the CFL min-cut is edge $u_1^a u_2^a$, which corresponds to $\{a\}$ as the result for the vertex cover problem for the graph $(\{a, b, c\}, \{ab, ac\})$.

The s, t CFL min-cut contains at least one edge from each CFL path from s to t. This implies that the vertex cover will contain at least one vertex of each edge in E. The minimality of the cut implies the minimality of the vertex cover.   □

Theorem 2. *If L is the language of balanced multiple types of parentheses, finding the s, t CFL min-cut in exploded supergraphs resulted from applying a CFL analysis is NP-hard, considering that the edges between two **0** nodes cannot be part of the cut.*

Proof. We prove this theorem by reduction from the vertex cover problem. The proof has two steps. First, given an undirected graph $G = (V, E)$ for which we want to compute the vertex cover, we construct a program P. Second, given a null analysis like the one in Sect. 2, we show that finding a CFL min-cut of the exploded super-graph of program P implies finding a vertex cover for graph G.

Constructing the Program P. Let $n = |V|$ be the number of vertices in the graph G. The program P has a variable x of type Obj and $n + 1$ methods. We assume the class Obj declares a method $f()$. For each vertice $u \in V$ we declare in P a method $m_u()$ that does not modify x. Additionally, we introduce a method $prog$ that has a local integer i, initialized to a random value between 1 and m, where $m = |E|$ is the number of edges in G. The method $prog$ contains a switch statement that takes as argument i and has m cases, one for each edge in G. For the case corresponding to the edge $uv \in E$, the variable x is set to $null$, then the methods $m_u()$ and $m_v()$ are invoked and the variable x is dereferenced by invoking the function $x.f()$. Finally, each case ends with a *break* statement. For example, given the small graph $(\{a, b, c\}, \{ab, ac\})$, we construct the following program:

Exploded Supergraph Using the Null Analysis. Next, consider the null analysis used in Sect. 2. For each node in the supergraph of program P, the exploded super-graph contains two nodes: a **0** node and an **x** node (meaning x may be null at that program point). Initially, there exists one CFL path from the **0** node at the entry in method $prog$ to each dereference $x.f()$ in P (exactly one CFL path for each edge in G). Each path contains a prefix of edges between **0** nodes, and a suffix of edges between **x** nodes. The edge between a **0** and an **x** node corresponds to the statements x = null that precede the dereference. Since the cut may not contain edges between two **0** nodes, the CFL min-cut will contain edges that are part of the suffixes of each CFL path that leads to a dereference of x or edges between a **0** and an **x** node. For a CFL min-cut, we replace the edges that are not between **x** nodes inside one of the methods m_u, for $u \in V$, with edges between nodes inside one of the m_u functions. For instance, if the CFL cut contains an edge between a **0** and an **x** node, we will replace it with an edge between two **x** nodes inside the first method that is called after the corresponding x = null statement. This does not increase the size of the cut.

```
1:  class P {
2:    Obj x = new Obj();
3:    void m_a() { ... }
4:    void m_b() { ... }
5:    void m_c() { ... }

6:  void prog() {
7:      i = random(2);
8:      switch(i) {
9:      case 1: x = null; m_a(); m_b(); x.f(); break;
10:     case 2: x = null; m_a(); m_c(); x.f(); break; }}
```

Fig. 6. Program for which finding the CFL min-cut in its exploded supergraph for a null analysis leads to finding the vertex cover for the graph with three vertices and two edges ($\{a, b, c\}, \{ab, ac\}$).

Each CFL min-cut has at most one edge from each method m_u. Given a CFL min-cut, we can build the vertex cover by selecting the vertices corresponding to the methods that contain edges of the CFL min-cut. The CFL cut is minimal and there exists exactly one CFL path for each edge in G, therefore the obtained vertex cover is minimal.

Given a vertex cover, we can construct a CFL cut by selecting a cut edge in each method m_u corresponding to a vertex u in the cover.

For the program in Fig. 6, the CFL min-cut is an edge in function m_a, which corresponds to the vertex cover $\{a\}$. Intuitively, adding the line x = new Obj(); in method m_a will lead to eliminating all null dereference warnings that the null analysis would trigger.

As an observation, for acyclic directed graphs with normal cut-sizes of up to 2, the CFL min-cut size is equal to the normal min-cut size. This implies that any min-cut of size at most 2 is also a CFL min-cut.

Proposition 1. *If the s, t min-cut has the size at most 2 in an acyclic graph, then this is also an s, t CFL min-cut.*

Proof. Any s, t min-cut is also an s, t CFL cut because if all paths from s to t are removed, then all the CFL paths are also removed. If the graph G', where we remove all edges that are not part of a CFL path from s to t, has a min cut of size 1, then it is also an s, t CFL min-cut.

If G' has a min-cut of size 2, we show that there cannot exist a smaller s, t CFL min-cut. Assuming an s, t CFL -min-cut of size 1 exists, then all CFL paths from s to t contain the cut edge c. We show that all the non-CFL paths from s to t also contain c. Let p be a non-CFL path from s to t. The first edge of p is either c or comes before c on an CFL path from s to t. It cannot come after c, because we would obtain a cycle in the graph. Similarly, for all the edges of p not equal to c, they must appear before c in an CFL path from s to t. Assume no edge is equal to c, then the last edge of the path, reaching t is before c, which creates a cycle. Since all paths contain c, then the s, t min-cut is of size 1, contradicting the hypothesis.

4   Solving the CFL Min-Cut for IFDS

In this section we present our approach to solve the CFL min-cut problem for an IFDS analysis. First, we instrument the IFDS analysis, recording the relevant information while it computes CFL reachability in the exploded super-graph. Second, based on the recorded information and the warnings found by the analysis, we formulate and solve the CFL min-cut as an optimization problem.

4.1   IFDS Analysis Instrumentation

Types of Edges. The tabulation algorithm [19] solves CFL reachability from the **0** entry node to all nodes in the exploded supergraph. In the process, it derives two types of edges: path edges and summary edges. If the algorithm derives a path edge between nodes n_1 and n_2, it means n_2 is actually CFL reachable from the **0** entry node. Summary edges are derived between fact nodes corresponding to a function call and a matching return from call. For instance, in Fig. 4, a summary edge would be introduced between nodes $\langle n_3, \mathbf{0} \rangle$ and $\langle n_4, \mathbf{0} \rangle$.

Derivation Rules. The tabulation algorithm maintains a worklist of recently derived path edges and applies a set of rules to derive additional path edges. The newly derived path edges are implied by existing path edges, exploded supergraph edges and summary edges. The complete description of the derivation rules can be found in [19]. For the example in Fig. 4, the tabulation algorithm starts with path edge $pathEdge_1$ $\langle s_{main}, \mathbf{0} \rangle \longrightarrow \langle s_{main}, \mathbf{0} \rangle$ in the worklist. Next, based on $pathEdge_1$ and the exploded super-graph edge $\langle s_{main}, \mathbf{0} \rangle \longrightarrow \langle n_1, \mathbf{0} \rangle$ ($graphEdge_1$), the algorithm derives $pathEdge_2$ $\langle s_{main}, \mathbf{0} \rangle \longrightarrow \langle n_1, \mathbf{0} \rangle$, and adds it to the worklist.

Recording All Derivations. During the execution of the tabulation algorithm, we record all derivations (a derivation is an instance of a rule application) and keep track of all path edges (PE), summary edges (SE) and edges of the exploded super-graph (GE) that were used in these derivations. The set of all derivations is D and each derivation is stored as an implication. The following is an example of a derivation:

$$pathEdge_1 \wedge graphEdge_1 \Rightarrow pathEdge_2$$

An important property of our instrumentation is that we record all possible derivations for each path edge and summary edge (in case such an edge can be derived in more than one way). This ensures that we capture all derivations and the CFL min-cut we will compute in the next step is guaranteed to be correct (covers all CFL paths). Let $W \subseteq PE$ be the set of path edges (warnings always correspond to path edges) which corresponds to warnings of the analysis. Given the PE, SE, GE, D and W sets, we proceed to find the CFL min-cut.

4.2   Optimization Objective

Let $Edges = PE \cup SE \cup GE$ and let $\sigma: Edges \rightarrow \{true, false\}$ map an edge to $true$ or $false$. For a given σ, let $[\![\,]\!]_\sigma: D \rightarrow \{true, false\}$ compute the boolean value of each derivation with respect to σ. That is, the truth value of a derivation (such as the one listed above) is computed by simply applying basic logical rules on the truth values of the edges as defined in σ. We define Q as:

$$Q(D, W) = \{\sigma \mid \forall d \in D : [\![d]\!]_\sigma \wedge \forall w \in W : \neg\sigma(w)\}$$

Here, $Q(D, W)$ denotes the set of valuations that satisfy all derivations in D and for which all warning edges in W are mapped to $false$.

Let $f_\sigma : Edges \rightarrow \{0, 1\}$ such that:

$$\forall e \in Edges : (\sigma(e) \equiv f_\sigma(e) = 1) \wedge (\neg\sigma(e) \equiv f_\sigma(e) = 0)$$

Using this auxiliary function we can now express the CFL min-cut problem as the following optimization objective:

$$\operatorname*{argmax}_{\sigma \in Q(D,W)} \sum_{p \in GE} f_\sigma(p)$$

The solution of this problem will be a valuation in Q that maps the highest number of graph edges to $true$. The graph edges mapped to $false$ are the edges of the CFL min-cut. Note that the optimization problem above can have several possible solutions. We describe next a possible criteria to select a solution.

Minimize Abstract Distance. Given a program P and an IFDS analysis, we consider an abstract program as the exploded super-graph esg_P corresponding to P. Let $nr(esg)$ be the number of nodes of the exploded super-graph esg that are CFL reachable from the **0** entry node. We define the distance between two exploded supergraphs as: $d(esg_1, esg_2) = |nr(esg_1) - nr(esg_2)|$. Given esg_P, one intuitive criteria is to select a CFL min-cut C such that the distance $d(esg_P, esg_P \setminus C)$ is minimal, where $esg_P \setminus C$ is the same as esg_P except we remove the edges in C. As discussed in Sect. 2.3, this criteria leads to a CFL min-cut where we try to preserve as many CFL-reachable nodes in the exploded super-graph as possible. For example, in Fig. 4, the abstract distance between the exploded supergraph before and after removing the cut (blue edge) is 8 (there are 8 nodes, shown in blue, that become CFL unreachable). This criterion can be seen as a proxy for reducing the number of changes to the program (as more changes would likely lead to more changes in the computed abstract facts). We now extend our optimization problem with this criterion.

The goal is to select the valuation σ such that it corresponds to a CFL min-cut and it has a maximal number of path edges mapped to $true$. As mentioned before, each path edge corresponds to an abstract fact that holds at a certain program point. The challenge is that, if we simply add the sum of $f_\sigma(p)$ for all $p \in PE$ to the formula above, it will not be sound. The problem is that the result may have path edges mapped to *true* even if the left hand sides of all their corresponding derivations are *false*. This would lead to incorrect results.

To address this challenge, we create a new set of derivations, $\hat{D}$, that contains all derivations in D as well as new derivations, described next. Given a path or a summary edge $p \in PE \cup SE$, let $D_p \subseteq D$ be the derivations in D that have the right hand side of the implication equal to p: $D_p = \{d \in D \mid rhs(d) = p\}$. All derivations $d \in D_p$ are of the form $lhs(d) \Rightarrow p$, where lhs represents the left hand side of the implication. For all $p \in PE \cup SE$, we add to the set $\hat{D}$ the derivation: $p \Rightarrow \bigvee_{d \in D_p} lhs(d)$. This avoids valuations that map a path or a summary edge to *true* even if all left hand sides of their corresponding derivations are *false*.

We define $w \colon GE \cup PE \to \mathbb{R}$ as a function assigning a value to a path or a graph edge. The new optimization objective is:

$$\underset{\sigma \in Q(\hat{D}, W)}{\operatorname{argmax}} \sum_{p \in GE \cup PE} w(p) \times f_\sigma(p)$$

In particular, if $\forall p \in GE : w(p) = |PE| + 1$ and $\forall p \in PE : w(p) = 1$, then the priority of the optimization problem is to find a CFL min-cut, and then select the cut that maximizes the number of path edges. Additionally, we can implement a trade-off between the size of the CFL cut and the number of path edges, if the sum of weights of PE edges is greater than the weight of at least one GE edge. Maximizing the number of path edges corresponds to minimizing the "may" facts from Fig. 1 that are transformed to "must-not" facts.

4.3 Solution via MaxSAT

We solve the above optimization problems via a translation to MaxSAT.

Variables. For each edge in *Edges* we introduce a boolean variable in the MaxSAT formula. Additionally, for each derivation in D, we introduce a new boolean variable. Let B be the set of all the boolean variables of the formula and let $b_e \colon Edges \to B$ map edges to the correspondin boolean variables and $b_d \colon D \to B$ map derivations to boolean variables.

Clauses. For each edge $p \in GE \cup PE$, we add to the boolean formula one unit clause - $b_e(p)$, of weight $w(p)$. For each derivation $d \in D$, we add two clauses: (i) a clause contains, for each edge p appearing in $lhs(d)$, the literal $\neg b_e(p)$ and the literal $b_d(d)$, and (ii) a second clause that contains $\neg b_d(d)$ and $b_e(p)$. The weight of these clauses is set to ∞. Further, for each edge $p \in PE \cup SE$, we add a clause containing the literal $\neg b_e(p)$ and the literals $b_d(d)$, for all $d \in D_p$. This clause has the weight ∞. Finally, for each edge $p \in W$, we add the unit clause $\neg b_e(p)$ with weight ∞.

5 Evaluation

In this section, we present an evaluation of the CFL min-cut approach described in Sect. 4, leveraging a null-deference analysis similar to the one in Sect. 2.

Table 2. Benchmarks showing the differences between the number of warnings, CFL and normal min-cut sizes for the null pointer analysis.

Benchmark	Null pointer analysis		CFL min-cut			Normal min-cut		
	Time (s)	Warnings	Time (s)	Size	Distance	Time (s)	Size	Distance
Antlr	13	114	32	19	401	28	28	588
Eclipse	9	41	13	12	260	11	12	351
Hsqldb	1	22	1	2	120	0.6	2	122
Luindex	11	92	60	9	1519	8	10	1636
Pmd	1	22	2	2	124	0.3	2	126
Xalan	1	40	3	3	232	0.4	3	234
Javasrc-p	12	28	16	11	167	10	14	309
Kawa-c	27	14	34	9	226	23	10	726
Rhino-a	64	59	173	15	2154	87	18	3282
Schroeder-m	2	40	3	5	382	0.8	5	420
Toba-s	1	1	0.4	1	2	0.3	1	30

Null Dereference Analysis. We first implemented an IFDS-based analysis for detecting null-pointer dereferences (as described in Sect. 2), leveraging the WALA analysis framework [1]. The analysis runs in the forward direction, tracking access paths that either may be null (if some statement may have written null to the location) or may-not be null (some statement wrote a non-null value into the location; if the may-not be null fact is unreachable, then the variable must be null). A null-pointer error is reported when a variable that may (or must) be null is de-referenced. The analysis includes basic interpretation of branch conditions comparing variables to null. The analysis does not track all aliasing exactly, and hence is unsound—soundness is not required to evaluate our current techniques. In our evaluation, we used the WPM-3-2015.co MaxSAT solver [2].

Benchmarks. We ran the analysis on a suite of 11 open-source Java benchmarks. The set of benchmarks includes programs from the DaCapo suite [3], and also programs used in other recent work on static analysis [7,23].

Results. Table 2 summarizes the results from our experiments. The first column indicates the name of the benchmark program. The next two columns show the running time in seconds of the null dereference analysis and the number of warnings it generates for each program. As described in Sect. 4, the analysis is instrumented and all possible derivations are recorded during its execution. The next three columns present information about the CFL min-cut computation: the running time in seconds, the size of the cut, and the abstract distance between the exploded supergraphs before and after the cut (defined in Sect. 4.2). The final three columns present the same information as before, this time for computing a normal min-cut, instead of a CFL min-cut.

Table 3. Abstract distance vs. CFL cut size trade-off, for Antlr and Rhino-a.

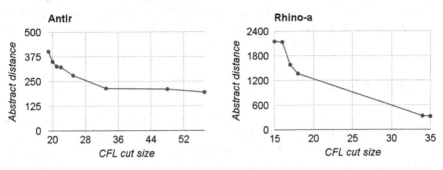

Number of Warnings vs. Number of Fix Locations. For several benchmarks (Hsqldb, Luindex, Pmd, Xalan, Schroeder-m), the size of the min-cut is approximately 10 times smaller than the number of warnings of the analysis. This confirms our hypothesis that a small number of fix locations has the potential to address all warnings—computing a min-cut is beneficial in such cases.

CFL Min-Cut Size. Computing a CFL min-cut can often reduce the size of the cut over a normal min-cut. For benchmarks such as Antlr, Luindex, Javasrc-p, Kawa-c, Rhino-a, the normal min-cut is between 10%–50% larger than the CFL min-cut. This is a non-trivial difference, as each report requires manual effort from the end user.

Program Fixes. We inspected manually the fix locations proposed by our system for several benchmarks and discovered that identifying the concrete fix was straightforward. Adding these fixes removed all the initial warnings. Constructing the fixes can become more complex in the case of other IFDS analyses. We consider that to be an interesting future work item.

Implementation Details. To simplify the boolean formulas that are generated, we exclude identity edges (propagating the same fact) from the possible cuts. This reduces greatly the burden of the MaxSAT solver, enabling a more scalable implementation. Intuitively this The MaxSAT solver can take advantage of the stratification optimization [2] to compute faster the min-cuts with maximized path edges.

Case Study: Cut Size - Abstract Distance Tradeoffs. We investigated the tradeoff between the CFL cut size and the abstract distance. We kept the weight for all edges $p \in PE$ as $w(p) = 1$ and we set the weight of $p \in GE : w(p) = k$, where k is a constant between 1 and $|PE| + 1$. We illustrate our results on two of the benchmarks, Antlr and Rhino-a. For each benchmark, we show in Table 3 the CFL cut size (on the X axis) and the abstract distance (on the Y axis) for several values of k. (Note that the CFL cuts for different values of k are not subsets of each other.) For both benchmarks we observe that allowing a larger cut size leads to a smaller abstract distance. This makes intuitive sense: as cuts are allowed to grow larger, fix locations can be more "specialized" to warnings, reducing effects on other may facts. In the limit, a cut could include a fix location specific to each warning, minimizing abstract distance.

6   Related Work

Our work bears some similarity to recent work on finding minimal explanations for type inference errors. Pavlinovic et al. leverage MaxSMT for computing small explanations [17], while Loncaric et al. leverage MaxSAT [14]. Zhang and Myers [22] takes a probabilistic approach based on constraint graphs from type inference. These techniques may also benefit from factoring in a notion of abstract distance, rather than purely minimizing the number of fix locations.

Given an error trace that violates an assertion, Jose and Majumdar [9] use MaxSAT to localize the error causes. Their work identifies potential error causes of the concrete test execution that violates an assertion, whereas our approach focuses on warnings of static analyses.

Merlin [12] automatically classifies methods into sources, sinks and sanitizers, for taint analysis. Their sanitizer inference could be viewed as finding ways to "cut" flows from sources to sinks, but our problem differs in that we allow many more graph edges to be cut. Livshits and Chong [11] aim to find a valid sanitization of a given data-flow graph. Their approach leverages static and dynamic analysis, whereas our work is purely static.

The complexity class for the view update problem is studied in Buneman et al. [4]. The paper investigates the complexity of identifying a minimal set tuples in the database whose deletion will eliminate a given tuple from a query view; this problem bears some similarity to the CFL min-cut problem as applied to chain Datalog programs (see Sect. 1). The paper proves the problem is NP-hard for several types of queries.

D'Antoni et al. [6] aim to find repairs of small programs such that both the syntactic and the semantic difference between the original and the fixed programs is minimal, leveraging the Sketch synthesis tool [20]. The semantic difference is the distance between concrete traces of the programs. In contrast, our work focuses on minimizing abstract distances. Moreover, our system suggests fix locations (corresponding to abstract transitions) and runs on large benchmarks, as opposed to computing concrete program fixes for small input programs.

The system in Mangal et al. [15] infers weights for rules of a static analysis in order to classify the warnings of the analysis, based on feedback collected from users on previous analysis runs. It is interesting to apply similar techniques to automatically infer weights for edges in the cut so to explore further the min-cut vs. abstract distance tradeoff. In our work, we directly determine possible fix locations that will address all the warnings. Our experiments show that the number of fix locations can be several times smaller than the number of warnings.

Recent work [5,13] presents a system that infers necessary preconditions (when such a precondition does not hold, the program is guaranteed to be wrong) on large-scale programs. Their work considers non-null, array out of bounds and contracts analyses. Our system can be viewed as inferring a minimal number of sufficient preconditions for IFDS analyses.

7 Conclusion

The CFL min-cut is a fundamental building block for suggesting fix locations for both false positive warnings caused by over-approximations of the analysis and true bugs of the program. In this work, we first proved that computing CFL min-cuts is NP-hard. Next, we phrased the CFL min-cut as an optimization problem and solved it via MaxSAT. Using a null dereference analysis, we experimentally showed that in practice the CFL min-cut frequently yields fewer fix locations and smaller abstract program distances than a normal min-cut. In future work, we plan to apply CFL min-cuts to more program analysis problems and investigate faster CFL min-cut algorithms for common graph structures.

Acknowledgements. We thank Dimitar Dimitrov from ETH Zurich for comments on earlier proofs of the theorems in this paper.

References

1. Watson, T.J.: Libraries for Analysis (WALA). http://wala.sf.net. Accessed 22 Jan 2017
2. Ansótegui, C., Bonet, M.L., Gabàs, J., Levy, J.: Improving SAT-based weighted maxSAT solvers. In: Milano, M. (ed.) CP 2012. LNCS, pp. 86–101. Springer, Heidelberg (2012). doi:10.1007/978-3-642-33558-7_9
3. Blackburn, S.M., Garner, R., Hoffmann, C., Khang, A.M., McKinley, K.S., Bentzur, R., Diwan, A., Feinberg, D., Frampton, D., Guyer, S.Z., Hirzel, M., Hosking, A., Jump, M., Lee, H., Moss, J.E.B., Phansalkar, A., Stefanović, D., VanDrunen, T., von Dincklage, D., Wiedermann, B.: The DaCapo benchmarks: Java benchmarking development and analysis. In: Proceedings of the 21st Annual ACM SIGPLAN Conference on Object-Oriented Programming Systems, Languages, and Applications, OOPSLA 2006, pp. 169–190. ACM, New York (2006)
4. Buneman, P., Khanna, S., Tan, W.-C.: On propagation of deletions and annotations through views. In: Proceedings of the Twenty-First ACM SIGMOD-SIGACT-SIGART Symposium on Principles of Database Systems, PODS 2002, pp. 150–158. ACM, New York (2002)
5. Cousot, P., Cousot, R., Fähndrich, M., Logozzo, F.: Automatic inference of necessary preconditions. In: Giacobazzi, R., Berdine, J., Mastroeni, I. (eds.) VMCAI 2013. LNCS, vol. 7737, pp. 128–148. Springer, Heidelberg (2013). doi:10.1007/978-3-642-35873-9_10
6. D'Antoni, L., Samanta, R., Singh, R.: QLOSE: program repair with quantitative objectives. In: Chaudhuri, S., Farzan, A. (eds.) CAV 2016. LNCS, vol. 9780, pp. 383–401. Springer, Cham (2016). doi:10.1007/978-3-319-41540-6_21
7. Fink, S.J., Yahav, E., Dor, N., Ramalingam, G., Geay, E.: Effective typestate verification in the presence of aliasing. In: Pollock, L.L., Pezzè, M. (eds.) Proceedings of the ACM/SIGSOFT International Symposium on Software Testing and Analysis, ISSTA 2006, Portland, Maine, USA, 17–20 July 2006, pp. 133–144. ACM (2006)

8. Hao, J., Orlin, J.B.: A faster algorithm for finding the minimum cut in a graph. In: Proceedings of the Third Annual ACM-SIAM Symposium on Discrete Algorithms, SODA 1992, pp. 165–174. Society for Industrial and Applied Mathematics, Philadelphia (1992)

9. Jose, M., Majumdar, R.: Cause clue clauses: error localization using maximum satisfiability. In: Proceedings of the 32nd ACM SIGPLAN Conference on Programming Language Design and Implementation, PLDI 2011, pp. 437–446. ACM, New York (2011)

10. Karp, R.M.: Reducibility among combinatorial problems. In: Miller, R.E., Thatcher, J.W. (eds.) Proceedings of a Symposium on the Complexity of Computer Computations, 20–22 March 1972, IBM Thomas J. Watson Research Center, Yorktown Heights, New York. The IBM Research Symposia Series, pp. 85–103. Plenum Press, New York (1972)

11. Livshits, B., Chong, S.: Towards fully automatic placement of security sanitizers and declassifiers. In: Proceedings of the 40th Annual ACM SIGPLAN-SIGACT Symposium on Principles of Programming Languages, POPL 2013, pp. 385–398. ACM, New York (2013)

12. Livshits, B., Nori, A.V., Rajamani, S.K., Banerjee, A.: Merlin: specification inference for explicit information flow problems. In: Proceedings of the 30th ACM SIGPLAN Conference on Programming Language Design and Implementation, PLDI 2009, pp. 75–86. ACM, New York (2009)

13. Logozzo, F., Ball, T.: Modular and verified automatic program repair. In: Leavens, G.T., Dwyer, M.B. (eds.) Proceedings of the 27th Annual ACM SIGPLAN Conference on Object-Oriented Programming, Systems, Languages, and Applications, OOPSLA 2012, part of SPLASH 2012, Tucson, AZ, USA, 21–25 October 2012, pp. 133–146. ACM (2012)

14. Loncaric, C., Chandra, S., Schlesinger, C., Sridharan, M.: A practical framework for type inference error explanation. In: Proceedings of the 2016 ACM SIGPLAN International Conference on Object-Oriented Programming, Systems, Languages, and Applications, OOPSLA 2016, pp. 781–799. ACM, New York (2016)

15. Mangal, R., Zhang, X., Nori, A.V., Naik, M.: A user-guided approach to program analysis. In: Proceedings of the 2015 10th Joint Meeting on Foundations of Software Engineering, ESEC/FSE 2015, pp. 462–473. ACM, New York (2015)

16. Melski, D., Reps, T.W.: Interconvertibility of a class of set constraints and context-free-language reachability. Theoret. Comput. Sci. **248**(1–2), 29–98 (2000)

17. Pavlinovic, Z., King, T., Wies, T.: Practical SMT-based type error localization. In: Proceedings of the 20th ACM SIGPLAN International Conference on Functional Programming, ICFP 2015, pp. 412–423. ACM, New York (2015)

18. Reps, T.: Program analysis via graph reachability. In: Proceedings of the 1997 International Symposium on Logic Programming, ILPS 1997, pp. 5–19. MIT Press, Cambridge (1997)

19. Reps, T.W., Horwitz, S., Sagiv, S.: Precise interprocedural dataflow analysis via graph reachability. In: Cytron, R.K., Lee, P. (eds.) Conference Record of POPL 1995: 22nd ACM SIGPLAN-SIGACT Symposium on Principles of Programming Languages, San Francisco, California, USA, 23–25 January 1995, pp. 49–61. ACM Press (1995)

20. Solar-Lezama, A., Tancau, L., Bodik, R., Seshia, S., Saraswat, V.: Combinatorial sketching for finite programs. In: Proceedings of the 12th International Conference on Architectural Support for Programming Languages and Operating Systems, ASPLOS XII, pp. 404–415. ACM, New York (2006)

21. Stoer, M., Wagner, F.: A simple min-cut algorithm. J. ACM **44**(4), 585–591 (1997)
22. Zhang, D., Myers, A.C.: Toward general diagnosis of static errors. In: Proceedings of the 41st ACM SIGPLAN-SIGACT Symposium on Principles of Programming Languages, POPL 2014, pp. 569–581. ACM, New York (2014)
23. Zhang, X., Mangal, R., Grigore, R., Naik, M., Yang, H.: On abstraction refinement for program analyses in datalog. In: ACM SIGPLAN Conference on Programming Language Design and Implementation, PLDI 2014, Edinburgh, United Kingdom - 09–11 June 2014, p. 27 (2014)

Proving Linearizability Using Forward Simulations

Ahmed Bouajjani[1], Michael Emmi[2], Constantin Enea[1(✉)],
and Suha Orhun Mutluergil[3]

[1] IRIF, Univ. Paris Diderot, Paris, France
{abou,cenea}@irif.fr
[2] Nokia Bell Labs, Murray Hill, USA
michael.emmi@nokia.com
[3] Koc University, Sarıyer, Turkey
smutluergil@ku.edu.tr

Abstract. Linearizability is the standard correctness criterion for concurrent data structures such as stacks and queues. It allows to establish observational refinement between a concurrent implementation and an atomic reference implementation. Proving linearizability requires identifying linearization points for each method invocation along all possible computations, leading to valid sequential executions, or alternatively, establishing forward *and* backward simulations. In both cases, carrying out proofs is hard and complex in general. In particular, backward reasoning is difficult in the context of programs with data structures, and strategies for identifying statically linearization points cannot be defined for all existing implementations. In this paper, we show that, contrary to common belief, many such complex implementations, including, e.g., the Herlihy and Wing Queue and the Time-Stamped Stack, can be proved correct using only forward simulation arguments. This leads to simple and natural correctness proofs for these implementations that are amenable to automation.

1 Introduction

Programming efficient concurrent implementations of atomic collections, e.g., stacks and queues, is error prone. To minimize synchronization overhead between concurrent method invocations, implementors avoid blocking operations like lock acquisition, allowing methods to execute concurrently. However, concurrency risks unintended inter-operation interference, and risks conformance to atomic reference implementations. Conformance is formally captured by *(observational) refinement*, which assures that all behaviors of programs using these efficient implementations would also be possible were the atomic reference implementations used instead.

An extended version of this paper including the missing proofs can be found at [8].

© Springer International Publishing AG 2017
R. Majumdar and V. Kunčak (Eds.): CAV 2017, Part II, LNCS 10427, pp. 542–563, 2017.
DOI: 10.1007/978-3-319-63390-9_28

Observational refinement can be formalized as a trace inclusion problem, and the latter can itself be reduced to an invariant checking problem, but this requires in general introducing history and prophecy variables [1]. Alternatively, verifying refinement requires in general establishing a forward simulation *and* a backward simulation [21]. While simulations are natural concepts, backward reasoning, corresponding to the use of prophecy variables, is in general hard and complex for programs manipulating data structures. Therefore, a crucial issue is to understand the limits of forward reasoning in establishing refinement. More precisely, an important question is to determine for which concurrent abstract data structures, and for which classes of implementations, it is possible to carry out a refinement proof using only forward simulations.

To get rid of backward simulations (or prophecy variables) while preserving completeness w.r.t. refinement, it is necessary to have reference implementations that are *deterministic*. Interestingly, determinism allows also to simplify the forward simulation checking problem. Indeed, in this case, this problem can be reduced to an invariant checking problem. Basically, the simulation relation can be seen as an invariant of the system composed of the two compared programs. Therefore, existing methods and tools for invariant checking can be leveraged in this context.

But, in order to determine precisely what is meant by determinism, an important point is to fix the alphabet of observable events along computations. Typically, to reason about refinement between two library implementations, the only observable events are the calls and returns corresponding to the method invocations along computations. This means that only the external interface of the library is considered to compare behaviors, and nothing else from the implementations is exposed. Unfortunately, it can be shown that in this case, it is impossible to have deterministic atomic reference implementations for common data structures such as stacks and queues (see, e.g., [24]). Then, an important question is what is the necessary amount of information that should be exposed by the implementations to overcome this problem?

One approach addressing this question is based on linearizability [18] and its correspondence with refinement [7,12]. Linearizability of a computation (of some implementation) means that each of the method invocations can be seen as happening at some point, called *linearization point*, occurring somewhere between the call and return events of that invocation. The obtained sequence of linearization points along the computation should define a sequence of operations that is possible in the atomic reference implementation. Proving the existence of such sequences of linearization points, for all the computations of a concurrent library, is a complex problem [3,5,14]. However, proving linearizability becomes less complex when linearization points are fixed for each method, i.e., associated with the execution of a designated statement in its source code [5]. In this case, we can consider that libraries expose in addition to calls and returns, events signaling linearization points. By extending this way the alphabet of observable events, it becomes straightforward to define *deterministic* atomic reference implementations. Therefore, proving linearizability can be carried out using forward simulations when linearization points are fixed, e.g., [2, 4, 27, 28]. Unfortunately, this approach is not applicable to efficient implementations such as the LCRQ queue [22] (based on the principle of the Herlihy and Wing queue [18]), and the Time-Stamped Stack [10]. The proofs of linearizability of these implementations are highly nontrivial, very involved, and hard to read, understand and automatize. Therefore, the crucial question we address is what is precisely the kind of information that is necessary to expose in order to obtain deterministic atomic reference implementations for such data structures, allowing to derive simple and natural linearizability proofs for such complex implementations, based on forward simulations, that are amenable to automation?

We observe that the main difficulty in reasoning about these implementations is that, linearization points of enqueue/push operations occurring along some given computation, depend in general on the linearization points of dequeue/pop operations that occur arbitrarily far in the future. Therefore, since linearization points for enqueue/push operations cannot be determined in advance, the information that could be fixed and exposed can concern only the dequeue/pop operations.

One first idea is to consider that linearization points are fixed for dequeue/pop methods and only for these methods. We show that under the assumption that implementations expose linearizations points for these methods, it is possible to define deterministic atomic reference implementations for both queues and stacks. We show that this is indeed useful by providing a simple proof of the Herlihy and Wing queue (based on establishing a forward simulation) that can be carried out as an invariant checking proof.

However, in the case of Time-Stamped Stack, fixing linearization points of pop operations is actually too restrictive. Nevertheless, we show that our approach can be generalized to handle this case. The key idea is to reason about what we call *commit points*, and that correspond roughly speaking to the last point a method accesses to the shared data structure during its execution. We prove that by exposing commit points (instead of linearization points) for pop methods, we can still provide deterministic reference implementations. We show that using this approach leads to a quite simple proof of the Time-Stamped Stack, based on forward simulations.

2   Preliminaries

We formalize several abstraction relations between libraries using a simple yet universal model of computation, namely labeled transition systems (LTS). This model captures shared-memory programs with an arbitrary number of threads, abstracting away the details of any particular programming language irrelevant to our development.

A *labeled transition system* (LTS) $A = (Q, \Sigma, s_0, \delta)$ over the possibly-infinite alphabet Σ is a possibly-infinite set Q of states with initial state $s_0 \in Q$, and a transition relation $\delta \subseteq Q \times \Sigma \times Q$. The ith symbol of a sequence $\tau \in \Sigma^*$ is denoted τ_i, and ε denotes the empty sequence. An *execution* of A

is an alternating sequence of states and transition labels (also called actions) $\rho = s_0, e_0, s_1 \dots e_{k-1}, s_k$ for some $k > 0$ such that $\delta(s_i, e_i, s_{i+1})$ for each i such that $0 \leq i < k$. We write $s_i \xrightarrow{e_i \dots e_{j-1}}_A s_j$ as shorthand for the subsequence $s_i, e_i, \dots, s_{j-1}, e_{j-1}, s_j$ of ρ, for any $0 \leq i \leq j < k$ (in particular $s_i \xrightarrow{\varepsilon} s_i$). The projection $\tau | \Gamma$ of a sequence τ is the maximum subsequence of τ over alphabet Γ. This notation is extended to sets of sequences as usual. A *trace* of A is the projection $\rho | \Sigma$ of an execution ρ of A. The set of executions, resp., traces, of an LTS A is denoted by $E(A)$, resp., $Tr(A)$. An LTS is *deterministic* if for any state s and any sequence $\tau \in \Sigma^*$, there is at most one state s' such that $s \xrightarrow{\tau} s'$. More generally, for an alphabet $\Gamma \subseteq \Sigma$, an LTS is Γ-*deterministic* if for any state s and any sequence $\tau \in \Gamma^*$, there is at most one state s' such that $s \xrightarrow{\tau'} s'$ and τ is a subsequence of τ'.

2.1   Libraries

Programs interact with libraries by calling named library *methods*, which receive *arguments* and yield *return values* upon completion. We fix arbitrary sets $\mathbb{M}$ and $\mathbb{V}$ of method names and argument/return values. We fix an arbitrary set $\mathbb{O}$ of operation identifiers, and for given sets $\mathbb{M}$ and $\mathbb{V}$ of methods and values, we fix the sets

$$C = \{inv(m, d, k) : m \in \mathbb{M}, d \in \mathbb{V}, k \in \mathbb{O}\} \text{ and } R = \{ret(m, d, k) : m \in \mathbb{M}, d \in \mathbb{V}, k \in \mathbb{O}\}$$

of *call actions* and *return actions*; each call action $inv(m, d, k)$ combines a method $m \in \mathbb{M}$ and value $d \in \mathbb{V}$ with an *operation identifier* $k \in \mathbb{O}$. Operation identifiers are used to pair call and return actions. We may omit the second field from a call/return action for methods that have no arguments or return values. For notational convenience, we take $\mathbb{O} = \mathbb{N}$ for the rest of the paper.

A *library* is an LTS over alphabet Σ such that $C \cup R \subseteq \Sigma$. We assume that the traces of a library satisfy standard well-formedness properties, e.g., return actions correspond to previous call actions. Given a standard library description as a set of methods, the LTS represents the executions of its most general client (that calls an arbitrary set of methods with an arbitrary set of threads in an unbounded loop). The states of this LTS consist of the shared state of the library together with the local state of each thread. The transitions correspond to statements in the methods' bodies, or call and return actions. An operation k is called *completed* in a trace τ when $ret(m, d, k)$ occurs in τ, for some m and d. Otherwise, it is called *pending*.

The projection of a library trace over $C \cup R$ is called a *history*. The set of histories of a library L is denoted by $H(L)$. Since libraries only dictate methods executions between their respective calls and returns, for any history they admit, they must also admit histories with weaker inter-operation ordering, in which calls may happen earlier, and/or returns later. A history h_1 is *weaker* than a history h_2, written $h_1 \sqsubseteq h_2$, iff there exists a history h_1' obtained from h_1 by appending return actions, and deleting call actions, s.t.: h_2 is a permutation of

h'_1 that preserves the order between return and call actions, i.e., if a given return action occurs before a given call action in h'_1, then the same holds in h_2.

A library L is called *atomic* when there exists a set S of sequential histories such that $H(L)$ contains every weakening of a history in S. Atomic libraries are often considered as specifications for concurrent objects. Libraries can be made atomic by guarding their methods bodies with global lock acquisitions.

A library L is called a *queue implementation* when $\mathbb{M} = \{enq, deq\}$ (enq is the method that enqueues a value and deq is the method removing a value) and $\mathbb{V} = \mathbb{N} \cup \{\texttt{EMPTY}\}$ where $\texttt{EMPTY}$ is the value returned by deq when the queue is empty. Similarly, a library L is called a *stack implementation* when $\mathbb{M} = \{push, pop\}$ and $\mathbb{V} = \mathbb{N} \cup \{\texttt{EMPTY}\}$. For queue and stack implementations, we assume that the same value is never added twice, i.e., for every trace τ of such a library and every two call actions $inv(m, d_1, k_1)$ and $inv(m, d_2, k_2)$ where $m \in \{enq, push\}$ we have that $d_1 \neq d_2$. As shown in several works [2,6], this assumption is without loss of generality for libraries that are data independent, i.e., their behaviors are not influenced by the values added to the collection. All the queue and stack implementations that we are aware of are data independent. On a technical note, this assumption is used to define (Γ-)deterministic abstract implementations of stacks and queues in Sects. 4 and 5.

2.2   Refinement and Linearizability

Conformance of a library L_1 to a specification given as an "abstract" library L_2 is formally captured by *(observational) refinement*. Informally, we say L_1 refines L_2 iff every computation of every program using L_1 would also be possible were L_2 used instead. We assume that a program can interact with the library only through call and return actions, and thus refinement can be defined as history set inclusion. Refinement is equivalent to the *linearizability* criterion [18] when L_2 is an atomic library [7,12].

Definition 1. *A library L_1 refines another library L_2 iff $H(L_1) \subseteq H(L_2)$.*

Linearizability [18] requires that every history of a concurrent library L_1 can be "linearized" to a sequential history admitted by a library L_2 used as a specification. Formally, a sequential history h_2 with only complete operations is called a *linearization* of a history h_1 when $h_1 \sqsubseteq h_2$. A history h_1 is *linearizable* w.r.t. a library L_2 iff there exists a linearization h_2 of h_1 such that $h_2 \in H(L_2)$. A library L_1 is *linearizable* w.r.t. L_2, written $L_1 \sqsubseteq L_2$, iff each history $h_1 \in H(L_1)$ is linearizable w.r.t. L_2.

Theorem 1 [7,12]. *Let L_1 and L_2 be two libraries, such that L_2 is atomic. Then, $L_1 \sqsubseteq L_2$ iff L_1 refines L_2.*

In the rest of the paper, we discuss methods for proving refinement (and thus, linearizability) focusing mainly on queue and stack implementations.

3   Refinement Proofs

Library refinement is an instance of a more general notion of refinement between LTSs, which for some alphabet Γ of *observable actions* is defined as the inclusion of sets of traces projected on Γ. Library refinement corresponds to the case $\Gamma = C \cup R$. Typically, Γ-refinement between two LTSs A_1 and A_2 is proved using *simulation relations* which roughly, require that A_2 can mimic every step of A_1 using a (possibly empty) sequence of steps. Mainly, there are two kinds of simulation relations, forward or backward, depending on whether the preservation of steps is proved starting from a similar state forward or backward. It has been shown that Γ-refinement is equivalent to the existence of *backward simulations*, modulo the addition of history variables that record events in the implementation, and to the existence of *forward simulations* provided that the right-hand side LTS, A_2, is Γ-deterministic [1,21]. We focus on proofs based on forward simulations because they are easier to automatize.

In general, forward simulations are *not* a complete proof method for library refinement because libraries are not $C \cup R$-deterministic (the same sequence of call/return actions can lead to different states depending on the interleaving of the internal actions). However, there are classes of atomic libraries, e.g., libraries with "fixed linearization points" (defined later in this section), for which it is possible to identify a larger alphabet Γ of observable actions (including call/return actions), and implementations that are Γ-deterministic. For queues and stacks, Sects. 4 and 5 define other such classes of implementations that cover all the implementations that we are aware of.

Let $A_1 = (Q_1, \Sigma, s_0^1, \delta_1)$ and $A_2 = (Q_2, \Sigma, s_0^2, \delta_2)$ be two LTSs over Σ_1 and Σ_2, respectively, and Γ an alphabet, such that $\Gamma \subseteq \Sigma_1 \cap \Sigma_2$.

Definition 2. *The LTS A_1 Γ-refines A_2 iff $Tr(A_1)|\Gamma \subseteq Tr(A_2)|\Gamma$.*

The notion of Γ-refinement instantiated to libraries (i.e., to LTSs defining libraries) implies the notion of refinement in Definition 1 for every Γ such that $C \cup R \subseteq \Gamma$.

We define a notion of *forward* simulation that can be used to prove Γ-refinement

Definition 3. *A relation $F \subseteq Q_1 \times Q_2$ is called a Γ-forward simulation from A_1 to A_2 iff $F(s_0^1, s_0^2)$ and:*

- *For all $s, s' \in Q_1$, $\gamma \in \Gamma$, and $u \in Q_2$, such that $(s, \gamma, s') \in \delta_1$ and $F(s, u)$, we have that there exists $u' \in Q_2$ such that $F(s', u')$ and $u \xrightarrow{\sigma} u'$ where $\sigma_i = \gamma$, for some i, and $\sigma_j \in \Sigma_2 \setminus \Gamma$, for all $j \neq i$.*
- *For all $s, s' \in Q_1$, $e \in \Sigma_1 \setminus \Gamma$, and $u \in Q_2$, such that $(s, e, s') \in \delta_1$ and $F(s, u)$, we have that there exists $u' \in Q_2$ such that $F(s', u')$ and $u \xrightarrow{\sigma} u'$ where $\sigma \in (\Sigma_2 \setminus \Gamma)^*$.*

A Γ-forward simulation states that every step of A_1 is simulated by a sequence of steps of A_2. To imply Γ-refinement, every step of A_1 labeled by an observable action $\gamma \in \Gamma$ should be simulated by a sequence of steps of A_2 where exactly one transition is labeled by γ and all the other transitions are labeled by non-observable actions. The dual notion of *backward* simulation where steps are simulated backwards can be defined similarly.

The following shows the soundness and the completeness of Γ-forward simulations (when A_2 is Γ-deterministic). It is an instantiation of previous results [1,21].

Theorem 2. *If there is a Γ-forward simulation from A_1 to A_2, then A_1 Γ-refines A_2. Also, if A_1 Γ-refines A_2 and A_2 is Γ-deterministic, then there is a Γ-forward simulation from A_1 to A_2.*

The linearization of a concurrent history can be also defined in terms of *linearization points*. Informally, a linearization point of an operation in an execution is a point in time where the operation is conceptually effectuated; given the linearization points of each operation, the linearization of a concurrent history is the sequential history which takes operations in the order of their linearization points. For some libraries, the linearization points of all the invocations of a method m correspond to the execution of a fixed statement in m's body. For instance, when method bodies are guarded with a global-lock acquisition, the linearization point of every method invocation corresponds to the execution of the body. When the linearization points are fixed, we assume that the library is an LTS over an alphabet that includes actions $lin(m, d, k)$ with $m \in \mathbb{M}$, $d \in \mathbb{V}$ and $k \in \mathbb{O}$, representing the linearization point of the operation k returning value d. Let Lin denote the set of such actions. The projection of a library trace over $C \cup R \cup Lin$ is called an *extended history*. A trace or extended history is called Lin-complete when every completed operation has a linearization point, i.e., each return action $ret(m, d, k)$ is preceded by an action $lin(m, d, k)$. A library L over alphabet Σ is called *with fixed linearization points* iff $C \cup R \cup Lin \subseteq \Sigma$ and every trace $\tau \in Tr(L)$ is Lin-complete.

Proving the correctness of an implementation L_1 of a concurrent object such as a queue or a stack with fixed linearization points reduces to proving that L_1 is a $(C \cup R \cup Lin)$-refinement of an abstract implementation L_2 of the same object where method bodies are guarded with a global-lock acquisition. As a direct consequence of Theorem 2, since the abstract implementation is $(C \cup R \cup Lin)$-deterministic, proving $(C \cup R \cup Lin)$-refinement is equivalent to finding a $(C \cup R \cup Lin)$-forward simulation from L_1 to L_2.

Sections 4 and 5 extend this result to queue and stack implementations where the linearization point of the methods *adding* values to the collection is *not* fixed.

4   Queues with Fixed Dequeue Linearization Points

The classical abstract queue implementation, denoted $AbsQ_0$, maintains a sequence of enqueued values; dequeues return the oldest non-dequeued value, at the time of their linearization points, or EMPTY. Some implementations, like the queue of Herlihy and Wing [18], denoted HWQ and listed in Fig. 1, are not forward-simulated by $AbsQ_0$, even though they refine $AbsQ_0$, since the order in

```
void enq(int x) {
  i = back++; items[i] = x;
}
int deq() {
  while (1) {
    range = back - 1;
    for (int i = 0; i <= range; i++) {
      x = swap(items[i],null);
      if (x != null) return x;
} } }
```

Fig. 1. The Herlihy and Wing Queue [18].

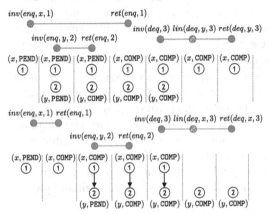

Fig. 2. Forward simulation with *AbsQ*. Lines depict operations, and circles depict call, return, and linearization point actions.

```
function loc: 𝕆 → {inv,lin,ret,⊥}
function arg, ret: 𝕆 → V
function present, pending: 𝕆 → 𝔹
function before: 𝕆 × 𝕆 → 𝔹

rule inv(enq,v,k):
  arg(k) := v
  present(k) := true
  pending(k) := true
  forall k1 with present(k1):
    if ¬pending(k1):
      before(k1,k) := true

rule ret(enq,k):
  pending(k) := false

rule inv(deq,k):
  pass

rule lin(deq,v,k):
  ret(k) := v
  if v = EMPTY:
    forall k' with present(k'):
      assert pending(k')
  else:
    let k1 = arg⁻¹(v)
    assert present(k1)
    forall k2 with present(k2):
      assert ¬before(k2,k1)
    present(k1) := false

rule ret(deq,v,k):
  assert ret(k) = v
```

Fig. 3. The *AbsQ* implementation; each rule α(_, k) implicitly begins with assert loc(k) = α and ends with the appropriate loc(k) := β.

which their enqueues are linearized to form $AbsQ_0$s sequence is not determined until later, when their values are dequeued.

In this section we develop an abstract queue implementation, denoted *AbsQ*, which maintains a partial order of enqueues, rather than a linear sequence. Since *AbsQ* does not force refining implementations to eagerly pick among linearizations of their enqueues, it forward-simulates many more queue implementations. In fact, *AbsQ* forward-simulates all queue implementations of which we are aware that are not forward-simulated by $AbsQ_0$, including HWQ, The Baskets Queue [19], The Linked Concurrent Ring Queue (LCRQ) [22], and The Time-Stamped Queue [10].

4.1 Enqueue Methods with Non-Fixed Linearization Points

We describe *HWQ* where the linearization points of the enqueue methods are not fixed. The shared state consists of an array items storing the values in the queue and a counter back storing the index of the first unused position in items. Initially, all the positions in the array are null and back is 0. An enqueue method starts by reserving a position in `items` (`i` stores the index of this position and `back` is incremented so the same position cannot be used by other enqueues) and then, stores the argument `x` at this position. The dequeue method traverses the array `items` starting from the beginning and atomically swaps `null` with the encountered value. If the value is not `null`, then the dequeue returns that value. If it reaches the end of the array, then it restarts.

The linearization points of the enqueues are not fixed, they depend on dequeues executing in the future. Consider the following trace with two concurrent enqueues ($i(k)$ represents the value of `i` in operation k): $inv(enq, x, 1)$, $inv(enq, y, 2)$, $i(1) = bck++$, $i(2) = bck++$, $items[i(2)] = y$. Assuming that the linearization point corresponds to the assignment of `i`, the history of this trace should be linearized to $inv(enq, x, 1)$, $ret(enq, 1)$, $inv(enq, y, 2)$, $ret(enq, 2)$. However, a dequeue executing until completion after this trace will return y (only position 1 is filled in the array `items`) which is not consistent with this linearization. On the other hand, assuming that enqueues should be linearized at the assignment of `items[i]` and extending the trace with $items[i(1)] = x$ and a completed dequeue that in this case returns x, leads to the incorrect linearization: $inv(enq, y, 2)$, $ret(enq, 2)$, $inv(enq, x, 1)$, $ret(enq, 1)$, $inv(deq, 3)$, $ret(deq, x, 3)$.

The dequeue method has a fixed linearization point which corresponds to an execution of `swap` returning a non-null value. This action alone contributes to the effect of that value being removed from the queue. Every concurrent history can be linearized to a sequential history where dequeues occur in the order of their linearization points in the concurrent history. This claim is formally proved in Sect. 4.3.

Since the linearization points of the enqueues are determined by future dequeue invocations, there exists no forward simulation from HWQ to $AbsQ_0$. In the following, we describe the abstract implementation $AbsQ$ for which such a forward simulation does exist.

4.2 Abstract Queue Implementation

Informally, $AbsQ$ records the set of enqueue operations, whose argument has not yet been removed by a matching dequeue operation. In addition, it records the happens-before order between those enqueue operations: this is a partial order ordering an enqueue k_1 before another enqueue k_2 iff k_1 returned before k_2 was invoked. The linearization point of a dequeue can either remove a minimal enqueue k (w.r.t. the happens-before stored in the state) and fix the return value to the value d added by k, or fix the return value to `EMPTY` provided that the current state stores only pending enqueues (intuitively, the dequeue overlaps with all the enqueue operations stored in the current state and it can be linearized before all of them).

Figure 2 pictures two executions of $AbsQ$ for two extended histories (that include dequeue linearization points). The state of $AbsQ$ after each action is pictured as a graph below the action. The nodes of this graph represent enqueue operations and the edges happens-before constraints. Each node is labeled by a value (the argument of the enqueue) and a flag `PEND` or `COMP` showing whether the operation is pending or completed. For instance, in the case of the first history, the dequeue linearization point $lin(deq, y, 3)$ is enabled because the current happens-before contains a *minimal* enqueue operation with argument y. Note that a linearization point $lin(deq, x, 3)$ is also enabled at this state.

We define $AbsQ$ with the abstract state machine given in Fig. 3 which defines an LTS over the alphabet $C \cup R \cup Lin(deq)$. The state of $AbsQ$ consists of several updatable functions: `loc` indicates the abstract control point of a given operation; `arg` and `ret` indicate the argument or return value of a given operation, respectively; `present` indicates whether a given enqueue operation has yet to be removed, and `pending` indicates whether it has yet to complete; `before` indicates the happens-before order between operations. Initially, `loc(k) = inv` for all k, and `present(k1) = pending(k1) = before(k1,k2) = false` for all k1, k2. Each rule determines the next state of $AbsQ$ for the corresponding action. For instance, the `lin(deq,v,k)` rule updates the state of $AbsQ$ for the linearization action of a dequeue operation with identifier k returning value v: when v = EMPTY then $AbsQ$ insists via an assertion that any still-present enqueue must still be pending; otherwise, when v $\neq$ k then $AbsQ$ insists that a corresponding enqueue is present, and that it is minimal in the happens-before order, before marking that enqueue as not present. Updates to the `loc` function, implicit in Fig. 3, ensure that the invocation, linearization-point, and return actions of each operation occur in the correct order.

The following result states that the library $AbsQ$ has exactly the same set of histories as the standard abstract library $AbsQ_0$.

Theorem 3. *$AbsQ$ is a refinement of $AbsQ_0$ and vice-versa.*

A trace of a queue implementation is called $Lin(deq)$-*complete* when every completed dequeue has a linearization point, i.e., each return action $ret(deq, d, k)$ is preceded by an action $lin(deq, d, k)$. A queue implementation L over alphabet Σ, such that $C \cup R \cup Lin(deq) \subseteq \Sigma$, is called *with fixed dequeue linearization points* when every trace $\tau \in Tr(L)$ is $Lin(deq)$-complete.

The following result shows that $C \cup R \cup Lin(deq)$-forward simulations are a sound and complete proof method for showing the correctness of a queue implementation with fixed dequeue linearization points (up to the correctness of the linearization points). It is obtained from Theorem 3 and Theorem 2 using the fact that the alphabet of $AbsQ$ is exactly $C \cup R \cup Lin(deq)$ and $AbsQ$ is deterministic. The determinism of $AbsQ$ relies on the assumption that every value is added at most once. Without this assumption, $AbsQ$ may reach a state with two enqueues adding the same value being both minimal in the happens-before. A transition corresponding to the linearization point of a dequeue from this state can remove any of these two enqueues leading to two different states. Therefore, $AbsQ$ becomes non-deterministic. Note that this is independent of the fact that $AbsQ$ manipulates operation identifiers.

Corollary 1. *A queue implementation L with fixed dequeue linearization points is a $C \cup R \cup Lin(deq)$-refinement of $AbsQ_0$ iff there exists a $C \cup R \cup Lin(deq)$-forward simulation from L to $AbsQ$.*

4.3   A Correctness Proof for Herlihy and Wing Queue

We describe a forward simulation F_1 from HWQ to $AbsQ$. The description of HWQ in Fig. 1 defines an LTS whose states contain the shared array items and the shared counter back together with a valuation for the local variables i, x, and range, and the control location of each operation. A transition is either a call or a return action, or a statement in one of the two methods enq or deq.

An HWQ state s is related by F_1 to $AbsQ$ states t where the predicate present is true for all the enqueues in s whose argument is stored in the array items, and all the pending enqueues that have not yet written to the array items (and only for these enqueues). We refer to such enqueues in s as present enqueues. Also, pending(k) is true in t whenever k is a pending enqueue in s, arg$(k) = d$ in t whenever the argument of the enqueue k in s is d, and for every dequeue operation k such that x$(k) = d \neq$ null, we have that y$(k) = d$ (recall that y is a local variable of the dequeue method in $AbsQ$). The order relation before in t satisfies the following constraints:

(a) pending enqueues are maximal, i.e., for every two present enqueues k and k' such that k' is pending, we have that $\neg$before(k', k),
(b) before is consistent with the order in which positions of items have been reserved, i.e., for every two present enqueues k and k' such that i$(k) <$ i(k'), we have that $\neg$before(k', k),
(c) if the position i reserved by an enqueue k has been "observed" by a non-linearized dequeue that in the current array traversal may "observe" a later position j reserved by another enqueue k', then k can't be ordered before k', i.e., for every two present enqueues k and k', and a dequeue k_d, such that

$$\texttt{canRemove}(k_d, k') \wedge (\texttt{i}(k) < \texttt{i}(k_d) \vee (\texttt{i}(k) = \texttt{i}(k_d) \wedge \texttt{afterSwapNull}(k_d))) \quad (1)$$

we have that $\neg$before(k, k'). The predicate canRemove(k_d, k') holds when k_d visited a null item in items and the position $i(k')$ reserved by k' is in the range of (k_d) i.e., (x$(k_d) =$ null $\wedge$ i$(k_d) <$ i$(k') \leq$ range(k_d)) $\vee$ (i(k_d) = i$(k') \wedge$ beforeSwap$(k_d) \wedge$ items$[i(k')]! =$ null). The predicate afterSwapNull(k_d) (resp., beforeSwap(k_d)) holds when the dequeue k_d is at the control point after a swap returning null (resp., before a swap).

The constraints on before ensure that a present enqueue whose argument is about to be removed by a dequeue operation is minimal. Thus, let k' be a present enqueue that inserted its argument to items, and k_d a pending dequeue such that canRemove(k_d, k') holds and k_d is just before its swap action at the reserved position of k' i.e., i$(k_d) =$ i(k'). Another pending enqueue k cannot be ordered before k' since pending enqueues are maximal by (a) Regarding the completed and present enqueues k, we consider two cases: $i(k) > i(k')$ and $i(k) < i(k')$. For the former case, the constraint (b) ensures $\neg$before(k, k') and for the latter case the constraint (c) ensures $\neg$before(k, k'). Consequently, k' is a minimal element w.r.t. before just before k_d removes its argument.

Next, we show that F_1 is indeed a $C \cup R \cup Lin(deq)$-forward simulation. Let s and t be states of HWQ and $AbsQ$, respectively, such that $(s, t) \in F_1$. We omit discussing the trivial case of transitions labeled by call and return actions which are simulated by similar transitions of $AbsQ$.

We show that each internal step of an enqueue or dequeue, except a swap returning a non-null value in dequeue (which represents its linearization point), is simulated by an *empty* sequence of $AbsQ$ transitions, i.e., for every state s' obtained through one of these steps, if $(s, t) \in F_1$, then $(s', t) \in F_1$ for each $AbsQ$ state t. Essentially, this consists in proving the following property, called *monotonicity*: the set of possible before relations associated by F_1 to s' doesn't exclude any order before associated to s.

Concerning enqueue rules, let s' be the state obtained from s when a pending enqueue k reserves an array position. This enqueue must be maximal in both t and any state t' related to s' (since it's pending). Moreover, there is no dequeue that can "observe" this position before restarting the array traversal. Therefore, item (c) in the definition of F_1 doesn't constrain the order between k and some other enqueue neither in s nor in s'. Since this transition doesn't affect the constraints on the order between enqueues different from k (their local variables remain unchanged), monotonicity holds. This property is trivially satisfied by the second step of enqueue which doesn't affect i.

To prove monotonicity in the case of dequeue internal steps different from its linearization point, it is important to track the non-trivial instantiations of item (c) in the definition of before over the two states s and s', i.e., the triples (k, k', k_d) for which (1) holds. Instantiations that are enabled only in s' may in principle lead to a violation of monotonicity (since they restrict the orders before associated to s'). For the two steps that begin an array traversal, i.e., reading the index of the last used position and setting i to 0, there exist no such new instantiations in s' because the value of i is either not set or 0. The same is true for the increment of i in a dequeue k_d since the predicate afterSwapNull(k_d) holds in state s. The execution of swap returning null in a dequeue k_d enables new instantiations (k, k', k_d) in s', thus adding potentially new constraints $\neg$before(k, k'). We show that these instantiations are however vacuous because k must be pending in s and thus maximal in every order before associated by F_1 to s. Let k and k' be two enqueues such that together with the dequeue k_d they satisfy the property (1) in s' but not in s. We write $i_s(k)$ for the value of the variable i of operation k in state s. We have that $i_{s'}(k) = i_{s'}(k_d) \leq i_{s'}(k')$ and items$[i_{s'}(k_d)] = $ null. The latter implies that the enqueue k didn't execute the second statement (since the position it reserved is still null) and it is pending in s'. The step that swaps the null item does not modify anything except the control point of k_d that makes afterSwapNull(k_d) true in s'. Hence, $i_s(k) = i_s(k_d) \leq i_s(k')$ and items$[i_s(k_d)] = $ null is also true. Therefore, k is pending in s and maximal. Hence, before(k, k') is not true in both s and s'.

Finally, we show that the linearization point of a dequeue k of HWQ, i.e., an execution of swap returning a non-null value d, from state s and leading to a state s' is simulated by a transition labeled by $lin(deq, d, k)$ of $AbsQ$ from state t. By the definition of HWQ, there is a unique enqueue k_e which filled the position updated by k, i.e., $i_s(k_e) = i_s(k)$ and $x_{s'}(k) = x_s(k_e)$.

We show that k_e is minimal in the order before of t which implies that k_e could be chosen by $lin(deq, d, k)$ step applied on t. As explained previously, instantiating item (c) in the definition of before with $k' = k_e$ and $k_d = k$, and instantiating item (b) with $k = k_e$, we ensure the minimality of k_e. Moreover, the state t' obtained from t through a $lin(deq, d, k)$ transition is related to s' because the value added by k_e is not anymore present in items and present(k_e) doesn't hold in t'.

5   Stacks with Fixed Pop Commit Points

The abstract implementation in Sect. 4 can be adapted to stacks, the main modification being that the linearization point $lin(pop, d, k)$ with $d \neq$ EMPTY is enabled when k is added by a push which is maximal in the happens-before order stored in the state. However, there are stack implementations, e.g., Time-Stamped Stack [10] (TSS, for short), which cannot be proved correct using forward simulations to this abstract implementation because the linearization points of the pop operations are not fixed. Exploiting particular properties of the stack semantics, we refine the ideas used in $AbsQ$ and define a new abstract implementation for stacks, denoted as $AbsS$, which is able to simulate such implementations. Forward simulations to $AbsS$ are complete for proving the correctness of stack implementations provided that the point in time where the return value of a pop operation is determined, called *commit point*, corresponds to a fixed statement in the pop method.

5.1   Pop Methods with Fixed Commit Points

We explain the meaning of the commit points on a simplified version of the Time-Stamped Stack [10] (TSS, for short) given in Fig. 4. This implementation

```
struct Node{                              int pop() {
  int data;                                 bool success = false;
  int ts;                                   int maxTS = -1;
  Node* next;                               Node* youngest = null;
  bool taken;                               while ( !success ) {
};                                            maxTS = -1; youngest = null;
                                              for(int i=0; i<maxThreads; i++) {
bool CAS(bool data, bool a, bool b);            Node* n = pools[i];
                                                while (n->taken && n->next != n)
Node* pools[maxThreads];                          n = n->next;
int TS = 0;                                       if(maxTS < n->ts) {
                                                    maxTS = n->ts; youngest = n;
void push(int x) {                                }
  Node* n =                                     }
    new Node(x,MAX_INT, null,false);          if (youngest != null)
  n->next = pools[myTID];                        success =
  pools[myTID] = n;                               CAS(youngest->taken, false, true);
  int i = TS++;                               }
  n->ts = i;                                  return youngest->data;
}                                           }
```

Fig. 4. The time-stamped stack [10].

maintains an array of singly-linked lists, one for each thread, where list nodes contain a data value (field **data**), a timestamp (field **ts**), the next pointer (field **next**), and a Boolean flag indicating whether the node represents a value removed from the stack (field **taken**). Initially, each list contains a sentinel dummy node pointing to itself with timestamp -1 and the flag **taken** set to **false**.

Pushing a value to the stack proceeds in several steps: adding a node with maximal timestamp in the list associated to the thread executing the push (given by the special variable **myTID**), asking for a new timestamp (given by the shared variable **TS**), and updating the timestamp of the added node. Popping a value from the stack consists in traversing all the lists, finding the first element which doesn't represent a removed value (i.e., **taken** is **false**) in each list, and selecting the element with the maximal timestamp. A compare-and-swap (CAS) is used to set the **taken** flag of this element to **true**. The procedure restarts if the CAS fails.

The push operations don't have a fixed linearization point because adding a node to a list and updating its timestamp are not executed in a single atomic step. The nodes can be added in an order which is not consistent with the order between the timestamps assigned later in the execution. Also, the value added by a push that just added an element to a list can be popped before the value added by a completed push (since it has a maximal timestamp). The same holds for pop operations: The only reasonable choice for a linearization point is a successful CAS (that results in updating the field **taken**). Figure 5 pictures an execution showing that this action doesn't correspond to a linearization point, i.e., an execution for which the pop operations in every correct linearization are

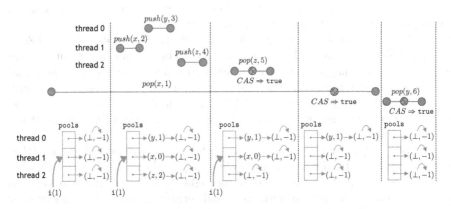

Fig. 5. An execution of *TSS*. An operation is pictured by a line delimited by two circles denoting the call and respectively, the return action. Pop operations with identifier k and removing value d are labeled $pop(d,k)$. Their representation includes another circle that stands for a successful CAS which is their commit point. The library state after an execution prefix delimited at the right by a dotted line is pictured in the bottom part (the picture immediately to the left of the dotted line). A pair (d,t) represents a list node with **data** $= d$ and **ts** $= t$, and $i(1)$ denotes the value of i in the pop with identifier 1. We omit the nodes where the field **taken** is **true**.

not ordered according to the order between successful CASs. In every correct linearization of that execution, the pop operation removing x is ordered before the one removing z although they perform a successful CAS in the opposite order.

An interesting property of the successful CASs in pop operations is that they fix the return value, i.e., the return value is `youngest->data` where `youngest` is the node updated by the CAS. We call such actions *commit points*. More generally, commit points are actions that access shared variables, from which every control-flow path leads to the return control point and contains no more accesses to the shared memory (i.e., after a commit point, the return value is computed using only local variables).

When the commit points of pop operations are fixed to particular implementation actions (e.g., a successful CAS) we assume that the library is an LTS over an alphabet that contains actions $com(pop, d, k)$ with $d \in \mathbb{V}$ and $k \in \mathbb{O}$ (denoting the commit point of the pop with identifier k and returning d). Let $Com(pop)$ be the set of such actions.

5.2   Abstract Stack Implementation

We define an abstract stack $AbsS$ over alphabet $C \cup R \cup Com(pop)$ that essentially, similarly to $AbsQ$, maintains the happens-before order of the pushes whose value has not yet been removed by a matching pop. Pop operations are treated differently since the commit points are not necessarily linearization points. Intuitively, a pop can be linearized before its commit point. Each pop operation starts by taking a snapshot of the completed push operations which are maximal in the happens-before, more precisely, which don't happen before another completed push operation. Also, the library maintains the set of push operations overlapping with each pop operation. The commit point $com(pop, d, k)$ with $d \neq$ EMPTY is enabled if either d was added by one of the push operations in the initial snapshot, or by a push happening earlier when arguments of pushes from the initial snapshot have been removed, or by one of the push operations that overlaps with pop k. The commit point $com(pop, \text{EMPTY}, k)$ is enabled if all the values added by push operations happening before k have been removed. The effect of the commit points is explained below through examples.

Figure 6 pictures two executions of $AbsS$ for two extended histories (that include pop commit points). For readability, we give the state of $AbsS$ only after several execution prefixes delimited at the right by a dotted line. We focus on pop operations – the effect of push calls and returns is similar to enqueue calls and returns in $AbsQ$. Let us first consider the history on the top part. The first state we give is reached after the call of pop with identifier 3. This shows the effect of a pop invocation: the greatest completed pushes according to the current happens-before (here, the push with identifier 1) are marked as maxAtInvoc(3), and the pending pushes are marked as overlap(3). As a side remark, any other push operation that starts after pop 3 would be also marked as overlap(3). The commit point $com(pop, x, 3)$ (pictured with a red circle) is enabled because x was added by a push marked as maxAtInvoc(3). The effect of the commit point

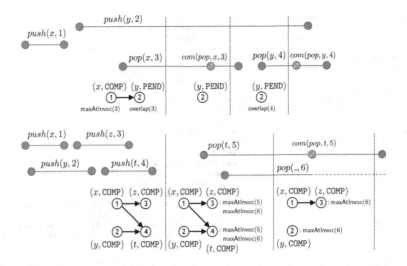

Fig. 6. Simulating stack histories with *AbsS*.

is that push 1 is removed from the state (the execution on the bottom shows a more complicated case). For the second pop, the commit point $com(pop, y, 4)$ is enabled because y was added by a push marked as overlap(4). The execution on the bottom shows an example where the marking maxAtInvoc(k) for some pop k is updated at commit points. The pushes 3 and 4 are marked as maxAtInvoc(5) and maxAtInvoc(6) when the pops 5 and 6 start. Then, $com(pop, t, 5)$ is enabled since t was added by $push(t, 4)$ which is marked as maxAtInvoc(5). Besides removing $push(t, 4)$, the commit point produces a state where a pop committing later, e.g., pop 6, can remove y which was added by a predecessor of $push(t, 4)$ in the happens-before (y could become the top of the stack when t is removed). This history is valid because $push(y, 2)$ can be linearized after $push(x, 1)$ and $push(z, 3)$. Thus, push 2, a predecessor of the push which is removed, is marked as maxAtInvoc(6). Push 1 which is also a predecessor of the removed push is not marked as maxAtInvoc(6) because it happens before another push, i.e., push 3, which is already marked as maxAtInvoc(6) (the value added by push 3 should be removed before the value added by push 1 could become the top of the stack).

The description of *AbsS* as an abstract state machine is given in Fig. 7. Compared to *AbsQ*, the state contains two more updatable functions maxAtInvoc and overlap. For each pop operation k, maxAtInvoc(k) records the set of completed push operations which were maximal in the happens-before (defined by before) when pop k was invoked, or happening earlier provided that the values of all the pushes happening later than one of these maximal ones and before pop k have been removed. Also, overlap(k) contains the push operations overlapping with a pop k. Initially, loc(k) = inv for all k, present(k1) = pending(k1) = before(k1,k2) = false, and maxAtInvoc(k1) = overlap(k1) = $\emptyset$, for all k1, k2. The rules for actions of push methods are similar to those for enqueues

```
function loc: ℚ → {inv,com,ret,⊥}    rule inv(pop,k):
function arg, ret: ℚ → V                forall k1 with present(k1):
function present, pending: ℚ → 𝔹        if pending(k1):
function before: ℚ × ℚ → 𝔹                 overlap(k) := overlap(k) ∪ {k1}
function maxAtInvoc: ℚ → ℘(ℚ)           else:
function overlap: ℚ → ℘(ℚ)                 if ∀k2.present(k2)∧before(k1,k2)⇒pending(k2):
                                              maxAtInvoc(k) = maxAtInvoc(k) ∪ {k1}
rule inv(push,x,k):
  present(k) := true                  rule com(pop,y,k):
  pending(k) := true                    ret(k) := y
  arg(k) := x                           if y = EMPTY:
  forall k1 with present(k1):            assert maxAtInvoc(k) = ∅
    if ¬pending(k1):                    else:
      before(k1,k) := true              let k1 := arg⁻¹(y)
  forall k1:                            assert present(k1)
    overlap(k1) := overlap(k1)∪{k}      assert k1 ∈ maxAtInvoc(k) ∪ overlap(k)
                                        present(k1) := false
rule ret(push,k):                       forall k2 with k1 ∈ maxAtInvoc(k2):
  pending(k) := false                     maxAtInvoc(k2) := maxAtInvoc(k2) \ {k1}
                                          forall k3 with before₁(k3,k1):
rule ret(pop,y,k):                          if ∀k4≠k1.before₁(k3,k4) ⇒ k4∈overlap(k2):
  assert ret(k) = y                           maxAtInvoc(k2) := maxAtInvoc(k2) ∪ {k3}
```

Fig. 7. The *AbsS* implementation; each rule $\alpha(\_, k)$ implicitly begins with assert $loc(k) = \alpha$ and ends with the appropriate $loc(k) := \beta$; and $before_1$ denotes the transitive reduction of before.

in *AbsQ*, except that every newly invoked push operation k is added to the set overlap(k1) for all pop operations k1 (since k overlaps with all the currently pending pops). The rule inv(pop,k), marking the invocation of a pop, sets maxAtInvoc(k) and overlap(k) as explained above. The rule com(pop,EMPTY,k) is enabled when the set maxAtInvoc(k) is empty (otherwise, there would be push operations happening before pop k which makes the return value EMPTY incorrect). Also, com(pop,y,k) with y ≠ EMPTY is enabled when y was added by a push k1 which belongs to maxAtInvoc(k) ∪ overlap(k). This rule may also update maxAtInvoc(k2) for other pending pops k2. More precisely, whenever maxAtInvoc(k2) contains the push k1, the latter is replaced by the immediate predecessors of k1 (according to before) that are followed exclusively by pushes overlapping with k2.

The abstract state machine in Fig. 7 defines an LTS over the alphabet $C \cup R \cup Com(pop)$. Let $AbsS_0$ be the standard abstract implementation of a stack where elements are stored in a sequence, push and pop operations adding and removing an element from the beginning of the sequence in one atomic step, respectively. For $\mathbb{M} = \{push, pop\}$, the alphabet of $AbsS_0$ is $C \cup R \cup Lin$. The following result states that the library *AbsS* has exactly the same set of histories as $AbsS_0$.

Theorem 4. *AbsS is a refinement of $AbsS_0$ and vice-versa.*

A trace of a stack implementation is called *Com(pop)-complete* when every completed pop has a commit point, i.e., each return $ret(pop, d, k)$ is preceded by an action $com(pop, d, k)$. A stack implementation L over Σ, such that $C \cup R \cup Com(pop) \subseteq \Sigma$, is called *with fixed pop commit points* when every trace $\tau \in Tr(L)$ is *Com(pop)-complete*.

As a consequence of Theorem 2, $C \cup R \cup Com(pop)$-forward simulations are a sound and complete proof method for showing the correctness of a stack implementation with fixed pop commit points (up to the correctness of the commit points).

Corollary 2. *A stack L with fixed pop commit points is a $C \cup R \cup Com(pop)$-refinement of AbsS iff there is a $C \cup R \cup Com(pop)$-forward simulation from L to AbsS.*

Linearization points can also be seen as commit points and thus the following holds.

Corollary 3. *A stack implementation L with fixed pop linearization points where transition labels lin(pop, d, k) are substituted with com(pop, d, k) is a $C \cup R \cup Com(pop)$-refinement of $AbsS_0$ iff there is a $C \cup R \cup Com(pop)$-forward simulation from L to AbsS.*

5.3   A Correctness Proof for Time-Stamped Stack

We describe a forward simulation F_2 from TSS to $AbsS$, which is similar to the one from HWQ to $AbsQ$ for the components of an $AbsS$ state which exist also in $AbsQ$ (i.e., different from maxAtInvoc and overlap).

Thus, a TSS state s is related by F_2 to $AbsS$ states t where present(k) is true for every push operation k in s such that k has not yet added a node to pools or its node is still present in pools (i.e., the node created by the push has taken set to false). Also, pending(k) is true in t iff k is pending in s.

To describe the constraints on the order relation before and the sets maxAtInvoc and overlap in t, we consider the following notations: $ts_s(k)$, resp., $TID_s(k)$, denotes the timestamp of the node created by the push k in state s (the ts field of this node), resp., the id of the thread executing k. By an abuse of terminology, we call $ts_s(k)$ the timestamp of k in state s. Also, $k \leadsto_s k'$ when intuitively, a traversal of pools would encounter the node created by k before the one created by k'. More precisely, $k \leadsto_s k'$ when $TID_s(k) < TID_s(k')$, or $TID_s(k) = TID_s(k')$ and the node created by k' is reachable from the one created by k in the list pointed to by $pools[TID_s(k)]$.

The order relation before satisfies the following: (1) pending pushes are maximal, (2) before is consistent with the order between node timestamps, i.e., $ts_s(k) \leq ts_s(k')$ implies $\neg before(k', k)$, and (3) before includes the order between pushes executed in the same thread, i.e., $TID_s(k) = TID_s(k')$ and $ts_s(k) < ts_s(k')$ implies $before(k, k')$.

The components maxAtInvoc and overlap satisfy the following constraints (their domain is the set of identifiers of pending pops):

Frontiers: By the definition of TSS, a pending pop p in s could, in the future, remove the value added by a push k which is maximal (w.r.t. before) or a push k which is completed but followed only by pending pushes (in the order relation before). Therefore, for all pop operations p which are pending in s, we have that $k \in$ overlap$(p) \cup$ maxAtInvoc(p), for every push k such that present$(k) \wedge$ (pending$(k) \vee (\forall k'.$present$(k') \wedge$ before$(k, k') \rightarrow$ pending$(k'))$).

TraverseBefore: A pop p with youngest$(p) \neq$ null that reached the node n overlaps with every present push that created a node with a timestamp greater than youngest$(p)- >$ ts and which occurs in pools before the node n. Formally, if youngest$_s(p) = n_s(k) \neq$ null, $n_s(p) = n_s(k_1)$, $k_2 \rightsquigarrow_s k_1$, present$(k_2)$, and ts$_s(k_2) \geq$ ts$_s(k)$, then $k_2 \in$ overlap(p), for each p, k_1, k_2.

TraverseBeforeNull: A pop p with youngest$(p) =$ null overlaps with every push that created a node which occurs in pools before the node reached by p, i.e., youngest$_s(p) =$ null, $n_s(p) = n_s(k_1)$, $k_2 \rightsquigarrow_s k_1$, and present$(k_2)$ implies $k_2 \in$ overlap(p), for each p, k_1, k_2.

TraverseAfter: If the variable youngest of a pop p points to a node which is not taken, then this node was created by a push in maxAtInvoc$(p) \cup$ overlap(p) or the node currently reached by p is followed in pools by another node which was created by a push in maxAtInvoc$(p) \cup$ overlap(p). Formally, for each p, k_1, k_2, if youngest$_s(p) = n_s(k_1)$, $n_s(k_1)$->taken $=$ false, and $n_s(p) = n_s(k_2)$, then one of the following holds:

- $k_1 \in$ maxAtInvoc$(p) \cup$ overlap(p), or
- there exists a push k_3 in s such that present(k_3), $k_3 \in$ maxAtInvoc$(p) \cup$ overlap(p), ts$_s(k_3) >$ ts$_s(k_1)$, and either $k_2 \rightsquigarrow_s k_3$ or $n_s(k_2) = n_s(k_3)$ and p is at a control point before the assignment statement that changes the variable youngest.

The functions maxAtInvoc and overlap satisfy more constraints which can be seen as invariants of *AbsS*, e.g., maxAtInvoc(p) and overlap(p) do not contain predecessors of pushes from maxAtInvoc(p) (for each p, k_1, k_2, before(k_1, k_2) and $k_2 \in$ maxAtInvoc(p) implies $k_1 \notin$ maxAtInvoc$(p) \cup$ overlap(p)). They can be found in [8].

Note that F_2 cannot satisfy the reverse of ***Frontiers***, i.e., every push in overlap$(p) \cup$ maxAtInvoc(p), for some p, is maximal or followed only by pending pushes (w.r.t., before). This is because the linearization points of pop operations are not fixed and they can occur anywhere in between their invocation and commit points. Hence, any push operation which was maximal or followed only by pending pushes in the happens-before in between the invocation and the commit can be removed by a pop. And such a push may no longer satisfy the same properties in the state s.

Based on the values stored in *youngest*$_s(p)$ and $n_s(p)$, for some pop p, the other three constraints identify other push operations that overlap with p, or they were followed only by pending pushes when p was invoked. ***TraverseBefore*** and ***TraverseBeforeNull*** state that pushes which add new nodes to the pools seen by p in the past, are overlapping with p. ***TraverseAfter*** states that either the push adding the current youngest node *youngest*$_s(p)$ is in overlap$_s(p) \cup$ maxAtInvoc$_s(p)$, or there is a node that p will visit in the future which is in overlap$_s(p) \cup$ maxAtInvoc$_s(p)$.

The proof that F_2 is indeed a forward simulation from *TSS* to *AbsS* follows the same lines as the one given for the Herlihy and Wing Queue. It can be found in [8].

6 Related Work

Many techniques for linearizability verification, e.g., [2,4,27,28], are based on forward simulation arguments, and typically only work for libraries where the linearization point of every invocation of a method m is fixed to a particular statement in the code of m. The works in [9,11,25,29] deal with *external* linearization points where the action of an operation k can be the linearization point of a concurrently executing operation k'. We say that the linearization point of k' is external. This situation arises in read-only methods like the contains method of an optimistic set [23], libraries based on the elimination back-off scheme, e.g., [15], or flat combining [13,16]. In these implementations, an operation can do an update on the shared state that becomes the linearization point of a concurrent read-only method (e.g., a contains returning true may be linearized when an add method adds a new value to the shared state) or an operation may update the data structure on behalf of other concurrently executing operations (whose updates are published in the shared state). In all these cases, every linearization point can still be associated syntactically to a statement in the code of a method and doesn't depend on operations executed in the future (unlike *HWQ* and *TSS*). However, identifying the set of operations for which such a statement is a linearization point can only be done by looking at the whole program state (the local states of all the active operations). This poses a problem in the context of compositional reasoning (where auxiliary variables are required), but still admits a forward simulation argument. For manual proofs, such implementations with external linearization points can still be defined as LTSs that produce *Lin*-complete traces and thus still fall in the class of implementations for which forward simulations are enough for proving refinement. These proof methods are not complete and they are not able to deal with implementations like *HWQ* or *TSS*.

There also exist linearizability proof techniques based on backward simulations or alternatively, prophecy variables, e.g., [20,24,26]. These works can deal with implementations where the linearization points are not fixed, but the proofs are conceptually more complex and less amenable to automation.

The works in [6,17] propose reductions of linearizability to assertion checking where the idea is to define finite-state automata that recognize violations of concurrent queues and stacks. These automata are simple enough in the case of queues and there is a proof of *HWQ* based on this reduction [17]. However, in the case of stacks, the automata become much more complicated and we are not aware of a proof for an implementation such as *TSS* which is based on this reduction.

Acknowledgements. This work is supported in part by the European Research Council (ERC) under the European Union's Horizon 2020 research and innovation program (grant agreement No. 678177).

References

1. Abadi, M., Lamport, L.: The existence of refinement mappings. Theoret. Comput. Sci. **82**(2), 253–284 (1991)
2. Abdulla, P.A., Haziza, F., Holík, L., Jonsson, B., Rezine, A.: An integrated specification and verification technique for highly concurrent data structures. In: Piterman, N., Smolka, S.A. (eds.) TACAS 2013. LNCS, vol. 7795, pp. 324–338. Springer, Heidelberg (2013). doi:10.1007/978-3-642-36742-7_23
3. Alur, R., McMillan, K.L., Peled, D.: Model-checking of correctness conditions for concurrent objects. Inf. Comput. **160**(1–2), 167–188 (2000)
4. Amit, D., Rinetzky, N., Reps, T.W., Sagiv, M., Yahav, E.: Comparison under abstraction for verifying linearizability. In: Damm, W., Hermanns, H. (eds.) CAV 2007. LNCS, vol. 4590, pp. 477–490. Springer, Heidelberg (2007). doi:10.1007/978-3-540-73368-3_49
5. Bouajjani, A., Emmi, M., Enea, C., Hamza, J.: Verifying concurrent programs against sequential specifications. In: Felleisen, M., Gardner, P. (eds.) ESOP 2013. LNCS, vol. 7792, pp. 290–309. Springer, Heidelberg (2013). doi:10.1007/978-3-642-37036-6_17
6. Bouajjani, A., Emmi, M., Enea, C., Hamza, J.: On reducing linearizability to state reachability. In: Halldórsson, M.M., Iwama, K., Kobayashi, N., Speckmann, B. (eds.) ICALP 2015. LNCS, vol. 9135, pp. 95–107. Springer, Heidelberg (2015). doi:10.1007/978-3-662-47666-6_8
7. Bouajjani, A., Emmi, M., Enea, C., Hamza, J.: Tractable refinement checking for concurrent objects. In: Proceedings of the 42nd Annual ACM SIGPLAN-SIGACT Symposium on Principles of Programming Languages, POPL 2015, Mumbai, India, 15–17 January 2015, pp. 651–662 (2015)
8. Bouajjani, A., Emmi, M., Enea, C., Mutluergil, S.O.: Proving linearizability using forward simulations. CoRR, abs/1702.02705 (2017). http://arxiv.org/abs/1702.02705
9. Derrick, J., Schellhorn, G., Wehrheim, H.: Verifying linearisability with potential linearisation points. In: Butler, M., Schulte, W. (eds.) FM 2011. LNCS, vol. 6664, pp. 323–337. Springer, Heidelberg (2011). doi:10.1007/978-3-642-21437-0_25. ISBN 978-3-642-21437-0
10. Dodds, M., Haas, A., Kirsch, C.M.: A scalable, correct time-stamped stack. In: Proceedings of the 42nd Annual ACM SIGPLAN-SIGACT Symposium on Principles of Programming Languages, POPL 2015, Mumbai, India, 15–17 January 2015, pp. 233–246 (2015)
11. Drăgoi, C., Gupta, A., Henzinger, T.A.: Automatic linearizability proofs of concurrent objects with cooperating updates. In: Sharygina, N., Veith, H. (eds.) CAV 2013. LNCS, vol. 8044, pp. 174–190. Springer, Heidelberg (2013). doi:10.1007/978-3-642-39799-8_11
12. Filipovic, I., O'Hearn, P.W., Rinetzky, N., Yang, H.: Abstraction for concurrent objects. Theoret. Comput. Sci. **411**(51–52), 4379–4398 (2010)
13. Gorelik, M., Hendler, D.: Brief announcement: an asymmetric flat-combining based queue algorithm. In: ACM Symposium on Principles of Distributed Computing, PODC 2013, Montreal, QC, Canada, 22–24 July 2013, pp. 319–321 (2013)
14. Hamza, J.: On the complexity of linearizability. In: Bouajjani, A., Fauconnier, H. (eds.) NETYS 2015. LNCS, vol. 9466, pp. 308–321. Springer, Cham (2015). doi:10.1007/978-3-319-26850-7_21

15. Hendler, D., Shavit, N., Yerushalmi, L.: A scalable lock-free stack algorithm. In: SPAA 2004, pp. 206–215. ACM (2004)
16. Hendler, D., Incze, I., Shavit, N., Tzafrir, M.: Flat combining and the synchronization-parallelism tradeoff. In: SPAA 2010: Proceedings of the 22nd Annual ACM Symposium on Parallelism in Algorithms and Architectures, Thira, Santorini, Greece, 13–15 June 2010, pp. 355–364 (2010)
17. Henzinger, T.A., Sezgin, A., Vafeiadis, V.: Aspect-oriented linearizability proofs. In: CONCUR, pp. 242–256 (2013)
18. Herlihy, M., Wing, J.M.: Linearizability: a correctness condition for concurrent objects. ACM Trans. Program. Lang. Syst. 12(3), 463–492 (1990)
19. Hoffman, M., Shalev, O., Shavit, N.: The baskets queue. In: Tovar, E., Tsigas, P., Fouchal, H. (eds.) OPODIS 2007. LNCS, vol. 4878, pp. 401–414. Springer, Heidelberg (2007). doi:10.1007/978-3-540-77096-1_29. ISBN 978-3-540-77095-4
20. Liang, H., Feng, X.: Modular verification of linearizability with non-fixed linearization points. In: ACM SIGPLAN Conference on Programming Language Design and Implementation, PLDI 2013, Seattle, WA, USA, 16–19 June 2013, pp. 459–470 (2013)
21. Lynch, N.A., Vaandrager, F.W.: Forward and backward simulations: I. untimed systems. Inf. Comput. 121(2), 214–233 (1995)
22. Morrison, A., Afek, Y.: Fast concurrent queues for x86 processors. In: ACM SIGPLAN Symposium on Principles and Practice of Parallel Programming, PPoPP 2013, Shenzhen, China, 23–27 February 2013, pp. 103–112 (2013)
23. O'Hearn, P.W., Rinetzky, N., Vechev, M.T., Yahav, E., Yorsh, G.: Verifying linearizability with hindsight. In: PODC 2010, pp. 85–94. ACM (2010)
24. Schellhorn, G., Wehrheim, H., Derrick, J.: How to prove algorithms linearisable. In: Madhusudan, P., Seshia, S.A. (eds.) CAV 2012. LNCS, vol. 7358, pp. 243–259. Springer, Heidelberg (2012). doi:10.1007/978-3-642-31424-7_21
25. Vafeiadis, V.: Automatically proving linearizability. In: Touili, T., Cook, B., Jackson, P. (eds.) CAV 2010. LNCS, vol. 6174, pp. 450–464. Springer, Heidelberg (2010). doi:10.1007/978-3-642-14295-6_40
26. Vafeiadis, V.: Modular fine-grained concurrency verification. Ph.D. thesis, University of Cambridge (2008)
27. Vafeiadis, V.: Shape-value abstraction for verifying linearizability. In: Jones, N.D., Müller-Olm, M. (eds.) VMCAI 2009. LNCS, vol. 5403, pp. 335–348. Springer, Heidelberg (2008). doi:10.1007/978-3-540-93900-9_27
28. Vafeiadis, V., Herlihy, M., Hoare, T., Shapiro, M.: Proving correctness of highly-concurrent linearisable objects. In: PPoPP 2006, pp. 129–136. ACM (2006)
29. Zhu, H., Petri, G., Jagannathan, S.: POLING: SMT aided linearizability proofs. In: Kroening, D., Păsăreanu, C.S. (eds.) CAV 2015. LNCS, vol. 9207, pp. 3–19. Springer, Cham (2015). doi:10.1007/978-3-319-21668-3_1

EAHyper: Satisfiability, Implication, and Equivalence Checking of Hyperproperties

Bernd Finkbeiner, Christopher Hahn[(✉)],
and Marvin Stenger

Saarland Informatics Campus, Saarland University,
Saarbrücken, Germany
{finkbeiner,hahn,stenger}@react.uni-saarland.de

Abstract. We introduce EAHyper, the first tool for the automatic checking of satisfiability, implication, and equivalence of hyperproperties. Hyperproperties are system properties that relate multiple computation traces. A typical example is an information flow policy that compares the observations made by an external observer on execution traces that result from different values of a secret variable. EAHyper analyzes hyperproperties that are specified in HyperLTL, a recently introduced extension of linear-time temporal logic (LTL). HyperLTL uses trace variables and trace quantifiers to refer to multiple execution traces simultaneously. Applications of EAHyper include the automatic detection of specifications that are inconsistent or vacuously true, as well as the comparison of multiple formalizations of the same policy, such as different notions of observational determinism.

1 Introduction

HyperLTL [3] is a recently introduced temporal logic for the specification of hyperproperties [4]. HyperLTL characterizes the secrecy and integrity of a system by comparing two or more execution traces. For example, we might express that the contents of a variable is secret by specifying that an external observer makes the same observations on all execution traces that result from different values of the variable. Such a specification cannot be expressed as a standard trace property, because it refers to multiple traces. The specification can, however, be expressed as a hyperproperty, which is a *set of sets* of traces.

HyperLTL has been used to specify and verify the information flow in communication protocols and web applications, the symmetric access to critical resources in mutex protocols, and Hamming distances between code words in error resistant codes [8,9,13]. The logic is already supported by both model checking [8] and runtime verification [1] tools. In this paper, we present the first tool for HyperLTL *satisfiability*. Our tool, which we call EAHyper, can be used

This work was partially supported by the German Research Foundation (DFG) in the Collaborative Research Center 1223 and by the Graduate School of Computer Science at Saarland University.

© Springer International Publishing AG 2017
R. Majumdar and V. Kunčak (Eds.): CAV 2017, Part II, LNCS 10427, pp. 564–570, 2017.
DOI: 10.1007/978-3-319-63390-9_29

to automatically detect specifications that are inconsistent or vacuously true, and to check implication and equivalence between multiple formalizations of the same requirement.

HyperLTL extends linear-time temporal logic (LTL) with trace variables and trace quantifiers. The requirement that the external observer makes the same observations on all traces is, for example, expressed as the HyperLTL formula $\forall \pi. \forall \pi'.\ \mathsf{G}(O_\pi = O_{\pi'})$, where O is the set of observable outputs. A more general property is *observational determinism* [12,14,17], which requires that a system appears deterministic to an observer who sees inputs I and outputs O. Observational determinism can be formalized as the HyperLTL formula $\forall \pi. \forall \pi'.\ \mathsf{G}(I_\pi = I_{\pi'}) \rightarrow \mathsf{G}(O_\pi = O_{\pi'})$, or, alternatively, as the HyperLTL formula $\forall \pi. \forall \pi'.\ (O_\pi = O_{\pi'})\ \mathsf{W}\ (I_\pi \neq I_{\pi'})$. The first formalization states that on any pair of traces, where the inputs are the same, the outputs must be the same as well; the second formalization states that differences in the observable output may only occur *after* differences in the observable input have occurred. As can be easily checked with EAHyper, the second formalization is the stronger requirement.

EAHyper implements the decision procedure for the $\exists^* \forall^*$ fragment of Hyper-LTL [7]. The $\exists^* \forall^*$ fragment consists of all HyperLTL formulas with at most one quantifier alternation, where no existential quantifier is in the scope of a universal quantifier. Many practical HyperLTL specifications are in fact alternation-free, i.e., they contain either only universal or only existential quantifiers. The $\exists^* \forall^*$ fragment is the largest decidable fragment. It contains in particular all alternation-free formulas and also all implications and equivalences between alternation-free formulas.

In the remainder of this paper, we give a quick summary of the syntax and semantics of HyperLTL, describe the implementation of EAHyper, and report on experimental results.

2 HyperLTL

HyperLTL Syntax. HyperLTL extends LTL with trace variables and trace quantifiers. Let $\mathcal{V}$ be an infinite supply of trace variables, AP the set of atomic propositions, and TR the set of infinite traces over AP. The syntax of HyperLTL is given by the following grammar:

$$\psi ::= \exists \pi.\ \psi\ |\ \forall \pi.\ \psi\ |\ \varphi$$
$$\varphi ::= a_\pi\ |\ \neg\varphi\ |\ \varphi \vee \varphi\ |\ \mathsf{X}\,\varphi\ |\ \varphi\,\mathsf{U}\,\varphi$$

where $a \in AP$ is an atomic proposition and $\pi \in \mathcal{V}$ is a trace variable. The derived temporal operators F, G, and W are defined as for LTL. Logical connectives, i.e., $\wedge$, $\rightarrow$, and $\leftrightarrow$ are derived in the usual way. We also use syntactic sugar like $O_\pi = O_{\pi'}$, which abbreviates $\bigwedge_{a \in O} a_\pi \leftrightarrow a_{\pi'}$ for a set O of atomic propositions.

The $\exists^*$ fragment of HyperLTL consists of all formulas that only contain existential quantifiers. The $\forall^*$ fragment of HyperLTL consists of all formulas that only contain universal quantifiers. The union of the two fragments is the *alternation-free fragment*. The $\exists^*\forall^*$ *fragment* consists of all formulas with at most one quantifier alternation, where no existential quantifier is in the scope of a universal quantifier.

HyperLTL Semantics. A HyperLTL formula defines a *hyperproperty*, which is a set of sets of traces. A set T of traces satisfies the hyperproperty if it is an element of this set of sets. Formally, the semantics of HyperLTL formulas is given with respect to *trace assignment* Π from $\mathcal{V}$ to TR, i.e., a partial function mapping trace variables to actual traces. $\Pi[\pi \mapsto t]$ denotes that π is mapped to t, with everything else mapped according to Π. $\Pi[i, \infty]$ denotes the trace assignment that is equal to $\Pi(\pi)[i, \infty]$ for all π.

$\Pi \models_T \exists\pi.\psi$	iff	there exists $t \in T : \Pi[\pi \mapsto t] \models_T \psi$
$\Pi \models_T \forall\pi.\psi$	iff	for all $t \in T : \Pi[\pi \mapsto t] \models_T \psi$
$\Pi \models_T a_\pi$	iff	$a \in \Pi(\pi)[0]$
$\Pi \models_T \neg\psi$	iff	$\Pi \not\models_T \psi$
$\Pi \models_T \psi_1 \vee \psi_2$	iff	$\Pi \models_T \psi_1$ or $\Pi \models_T \psi_2$
$\Pi \models_T \mathsf{X}\psi$	iff	$\Pi[1, \infty] \models_T \psi$
$\Pi \models_T \psi_1 \mathsf{U} \psi_2$	iff	there exists $i \geq 0 : \Pi[i, \infty] \models_T \psi_2$
		and for all $0 \leq j < i$ we have $\Pi[j, \infty] \models_T \psi_1$

A HyperLTL formula φ is *satisfiable* if and only if there exists a non-empty trace set T, such that $\Pi \models_T \psi$, where Π is the empty trace assignment. The formula φ is *valid* if and only if for all non-empty trace sets T it holds that $\Pi \models_T \psi$.

3   EAHyper

The input of EAHyper is either a HyperLTL formula in the $\exists^*\forall^*$ fragment, or an implication between two alternation-free formulas. For $\exists^*\forall^*$ formulas, EAHyper reports satisfiability; for implications between alternation-free formulas, validity. EAHyper proceeds in three steps:

1. *Translation into the $\exists^*\forall^*$ fragment:* If the input is an implication between two alternation-free formulas, we construct a formula in the $\exists^*\forall^*$ fragment that represents the *negation* of the implication. For example, for the implication of $\forall\pi_1\ldots\forall\pi_n.\ \psi$ and $\forall\pi'_1\ldots\forall\pi'_m.\ \varphi$, we construct the $\exists^*\forall^*$ formula $\exists\pi'_1\ldots\exists\pi'_m\forall\pi_1\ldots\forall\pi_n.\ \psi \wedge \neg\varphi$. The implication is valid if and only if the resulting $\exists^*\forall^*$ formula is unsatisfiable.

2. *Reduction to LTL satisfiability:* EAHyper implements the decision procedure for the $\exists^*\forall^*$ fragment of HyperLTL [7]. The satisfiability of the HyperLTL formula is reduced to the satisfiability of an LTL formula:
   - Formulas in the $\forall^*$ fragment are translated to LTL formulas by discarding the quantifier prefix and all trace variables. For example, $\forall\pi_1.\forall\pi_2.\ \mathsf{G}b_{\pi_1} \wedge \mathsf{G}\neg b_{\pi_2}$ is translated to the equisatisfiable LTL formula $\mathsf{G}b \wedge \mathsf{G}\neg b$.

- Formulas in the $\exists^*$ fragment are translated to LTL formulas by introducing a fresh atomic proposition a_i for every atomic proposition a and every trace variable π_i. For example, $\exists \pi_1.\exists \pi_2.\ a_{\pi_1} \wedge G\neg b_{\pi_1} \wedge Gb_{\pi_2}$ is translated to the equisatisfiable LTL formula $a_1 \wedge G\neg b_1 \wedge Gb_2$.
- Formulas in the $\exists^*\forall^*$ fragment are translated into the $\exists^*$ fragment (and then on into LTL) by unrolling the universal quantifiers. For example, $\exists \pi_1.\exists \pi_2.\forall \pi'_1.\forall \pi'_2.\ Ga_{\pi'_1} \wedge Gb_{\pi'_2} \wedge Gc_{\pi_1} \wedge Gd_{\pi_2}$ is translated to the equisatisfiable $\exists^*$ formula $\exists \pi_1.\exists \pi_2.\ (Ga_{\pi_1} \wedge Gb_{\pi_1} \wedge Gc_{\pi_1} \wedge Gd_{\pi_2}) \wedge (Ga_{\pi_2} \wedge Gb_{\pi_1} \wedge Gc_{\pi_1} \wedge Gd_{\pi_2}) \wedge (Ga_{\pi_1} \wedge Gb_{\pi_2} \wedge Gc_{\pi_1} \wedge Gd_{\pi_2}) \wedge (Ga_{\pi_2} \wedge Gb_{\pi_2} \wedge Gc_{\pi_1} \wedge Gd_{\pi_2})$.

3. *LTL satisfiability:* The satisfiability of the resulting LTL formula is checked through an external tool. Currently, EAHyper is linked to two LTL satisfiability checkers, pltl and Aalta.
   - Pltl [15] is a one-pass tableaux-based decision procedure for LTL, which not necessarily explores the full tableaux.
   - Aalta_2.0 [11] is a decision procedure for LTL based on a reduction to the Boolean satisfiability problem, which is in turn solved by minisat [6]. Aalta's on-the-fly approach is based on so-called obligation sets and outperforms model-checking-based LTL satisfiability solvers.

EAHyper is implemented in OCaml and supports UNIX-based operating systems. Batch-processing of HyperLTL formulas is provided. Options such as the choice of the LTL satisfiability checker are provided via a command-line interface.

4 Experimental Results

We report on the performance of EAHyper on a range of benchmarks, including observational determinism, symmetry, error resistant code, as well as randomly generated formulas. The experiments were carried out in a virtual machine running Ubuntu 14.04 LTS on an Intel Core i5-2500K CPU with 3.3 GHZ and 2 GB RAM. We chose to run EAHyper in a virtual machine to make our results easily reproducible; running EAHyper natively results in (even) better performance.[1]

- *Observational Determinism* [12,14,17]. Our first benchmark compares the following formalizations of observational determinism, with $|I| = |O| = 1$: $(OD1) : \forall \pi_1.\forall \pi'_1.\ G(I_{\pi_1} = I_{\pi'_1}) \rightarrow G(O_{\pi_1} = O_{\pi'_1})$, $(OD2) : \forall \pi_2.\forall \pi'_2.\ (I_{\pi_2} = I_{\pi'_2}) \rightarrow G(O_{\pi_2} = O_{\pi'_2})$, and $(OD3) : \forall \pi_3.\forall \pi'_3.\ (O_{\pi_3} = O_{\pi'_3})\ W\ (I_{\pi_3} \neq I_{\pi'_3})$. EAHyper needs less then a second to order the formalizations with respect to implication: $OD2 \rightarrow OD1$, $OD2 \rightarrow OD3$, and $OD3 \rightarrow OD1$.
- *Quantitative Noninterference* [2]. The bounding problem of quantitative noninterference asks whether the amount of information leaked by a system is bounded by a constant c. This is expressed in HyperLTL as the requirement that there are no $c + 1$ distinguishable traces for a *low-security* observer [16].

$$QN(c) := \forall \pi_0 \ldots \forall \pi_c.\ \neg((\bigwedge_i I_{\pi_i} = I_{\pi_0}) \wedge \bigwedge_{i \neq j} O_{\pi_i} \neq O_{\pi_j})$$

---

[1] EAHyper is available online at https://react.uni-saarland.de/tools/eahyper/.

Table 1. Quantitative noninterference benchmark: wall clock time in seconds for checking whether QN(row) implies QN(column). "–" denotes that the instance was not solved in 120 s.

(a) Aalta

QN	1	2	3	4	5
1	0.04	0.04	0.54	–	–
2	0.03	0.09	1.58	–	–
3	0.03	0.05	0.68	–	–
4	0.03	0.11	0.34	8.68	–
5	0.06	0.34	–	–	–

(b) pltl

QN	1	2	3	4	5
1	0.05	0.05	0.08	0.13	0.23
2	0.05	0.11	0.25	0.39	0.79
3	0.07	0.25	0.77	2.02	5.12
4	0.16	0.73	3.12	17.73	43.26
5	0.26	2.57	15.67	71.82	–

In the benchmark, we check implications between different bounds. The performance of EAHyper is shown in Table 1. Using Aalta as the LTL satisfiability checker generally produces faster results, but pltl scales to larger bounds.

- *Symmetry* [8]. A violation of symmetry in a mutual exclusion protocol indicates that some concurrent process has an unfair advantage in accessing a critical section. The benchmark is derived from a model checking case study, in which various symmetry claims were verified and falsified for the Bakery protocol. EAHyper checks the implications between the four main symmetry properties from the case study in 13.86 s. Exactly one of the implications turns out to be true.

- *Error resistant code* [8]. Error resistant codes enable the transmission of data over noisy channels. A typical model of errors bounds the number of flipped bits that may happen for a given code word length. Then, error correction coding schemes must guarantee that all code words have a minimal Hamming distance. The following HyperLTL formula specifies that all code words $o \in O$ produced by an encoder have a minimal Hamming distance [10] of d: $\forall \pi. \ \forall \pi'. \ F(\bigvee_{i \in I} \neg(i_\pi \leftrightarrow i_{\pi'})) \rightarrow \neg Ham_O(d - 1, \pi, \pi')$. Ham_O is recursively defined as $Ham_O(-1, \pi, \pi') = false$ and $Ham_O(d, \pi, \pi') = (\bigwedge_{o \in O} o_\pi \leftrightarrow o_{\pi'}) \ W \ (\bigvee_{o \in O} \neg(o_\pi \leftrightarrow o_{\pi'}) \wedge X \ Ham_O(d - 1, \pi, \pi'))$. The benchmark checks implications between the HyperLTL formulas for different minimal Hamming distances. The performance of EAHyper is shown in Table 2.

- *Random formulas.* In the last benchmark, we randomly generated sets of 250 HyperLTL formulas containing five atomic propositions, using randltl [5] and assigning trace variables randomly to atomic propositions. As shown in Table 3, EAHyper reaches its limits, by running out of memory, after approximately five existential and five universal quantifiers.

5   Discussion

EAHyper is the first implementation of the decision procedure for the $\exists^*\forall^*$ fragment of HyperLTL [7]. For formulas with up to approximately five universal quantifiers, EAHyper performs reliably well on our broad range of benchmarks, which represent different types of hyperproperties studied in the literature as well as randomly generated formulas.

Table 2. Error resistant codes benchmark: wall clock time in seconds for checking whether Ham(row) implies Ham(column).

Ham	0	1	2	3	4	5	6	7	8	9	10	11	12	13	14	15	16
0	0.03	0.02	0.03	0.02	0.02	0.02	0.03	0.03	0.04	0.08	0.10	0.18	0.25	0.46	0.74	1.35	2.62
1	0.03	0.02	0.03	0.03	0.04	0.03	0.05	0.04	0.06	0.08	0.13	0.21	0.40	0.49	0.82	1.50	2.99
2	0.01	0.03	0.03	0.03	0.04	0.02	0.03	0.04	0.04	0.07	0.12	0.21	0.36	0.55	0.88	1.59	3.09
3	0.03	0.04	0.04	0.05	0.04	0.04	0.03	0.04	0.05	0.07	0.12	0.23	0.36	0.52	0.87	1.56	3.12
4	0.04	0.04	0.04	0.06	0.10	0.02	0.03	0.05	0.08	0.08	0.16	0.21	0.36	0.52	0.86	1.66	3.05
5	0.03	0.03	0.05	0.07	0.07	0.19	0.14	0.17	0.05	0.08	0.14	0.22	0.30	0.52	0.92	1.55	2.99
6	0.03	0.04	0.05	0.06	0.09	0.22	0.35	0.21	0.25	0.11	0.25	0.26	0.36	0.53	0.87	1.57	3.00
7	0.04	0.05	0.05	0.05	0.14	0.24	0.32	0.37	0.38	0.42	0.14	0.20	0.37	0.52	0.89	1.65	3.05
8	0.05	0.05	0.07	0.10	0.17	0.23	0.26	0.36	0.50	0.56	0.47	0.40	0.53	0.53	1.13	1.61	3.18
9	0.07	0.08	0.08	0.10	0.16	0.19	0.21	0.43	0.70	0.64	0.48	0.52	0.90	0.65	1.03	1.71	3.08
10	0.09	0.13	0.15	0.15	0.21	0.20	0.34	0.43	0.54	0.76	1.38	1.55	0.61	0.89	1.03	1.78	3.22
11	0.16	0.23	0.22	0.24	0.24	0.26	0.41	0.53	0.62	0.81	1.30	1.29	1.81	1.05	1.86	2.33	3.17
12	0.27	0.30	0.36	0.30	0.32	0.41	0.45	0.46	0.85	0.91	1.69	1.28	2.81	2.82	1.14	3.91	4.49
13	0.38	0.46	0.51	0.47	0.57	0.52	0.57	0.86	1.03	1.27	1.47	2.16	3.19	8.22	5.48	8.64	7.08
14	0.69	0.87	0.91	0.84	0.84	0.98	0.94	1.02	1.46	1.30	2.01	3.82	3.96	6.35	7.50	9.06	11.11
15	1.22	1.52	1.58	1.70	1.69	1.65	1.67	1.74	1.87	2.73	3.02	3.08	5.87	7.25	13.04	34.17	12.26
16	2.26	3.04	2.97	3.00	3.10	3.11	3.35	3.29	3.57	4.17	3.76	5.78	7.45	17.31	17.75	31.51	48.09

Table 3. Random formulas benchmark: instances solved in 120 s and average wall clock time in seconds for 250 random formulas. Size denotes the tree-size argument for randltl.

size	40	60	40	60	40	60	40	60	40	60	40	60	40	60	40	60	40	60
	$\exists^0\forall^0$		$\exists^1\forall^0$		$\exists^2\forall^0$		$\exists^3\forall^0$		$\exists^4\forall^0$		$\exists^5\forall^0$		$\exists^6\forall^0$		$\exists^7\forall^0$		$\exists^8\forall^0$	
solved			250	250	250	250	250	250	250	250	250	250	250	250	250	250	250	250
avgt			0.01	0.01	0.01	0.01	0.01	0.01	0.01	0.01	0.01	0.01	0.01	0.01	0.01	0.01	0.01	0.01
	$\exists^0\forall^1$		$\exists^1\forall^1$		$\exists^2\forall^1$		$\exists^3\forall^1$		$\exists^4\forall^1$		$\exists^5\forall^1$		$\exists^6\forall^1$		$\exists^7\forall^1$		$\exists^8\forall^1$	
solved	250	250	250	250	250	250	250	249	250	250	249	247	250	248	249	247	247	248
avgt	0.01	0.01	0.01	0.01	0.02	0.02	0.02	0.05	0.02	0.06	0.02	0.01	0.02	0.01	0.13	0.02	0.04	0.08
	$\exists^0\forall^2$		$\exists^1\forall^2$		$\exists^2\forall^2$		$\exists^3\forall^2$		$\exists^4\forall^2$		$\exists^5\forall^2$		$\exists^6\forall^2$		$\exists^7\forall^2$		$\exists^8\forall^2$	
solved	250	250	250	250	248	249	249	247	247	247	248	246	246	246	244	246	244	247
avgt	0.01	0.01	0.01	0.01	0.03	0.12	0.03	0.01	0.26	0.02	0.32	0.02	0.09	0.02	0.02	0.02	0.05	0.03
	$\exists^0\forall^3$		$\exists^1\forall^3$		$\exists^2\forall^3$		$\exists^3\forall^3$		$\exists^4\forall^3$		$\exists^5\forall^3$		$\exists^6\forall^3$		$\exists^7\forall^3$		$\exists^8\forall^3$	
solved	250	250	250	250	249	247	248	246	247	245	245	246	245	246	244	247	243	246
avgt	0.01	0.01	0.01	0.01	0.03	0.02	0.07	0.02	0.06	0.03	0.14	0.05	0.17	0.08	0.23	0.16	0.45	0.25
	$\exists^0\forall^4$		$\exists^1\forall^4$		$\exists^2\forall^4$		$\exists^3\forall^4$		$\exists^4\forall^4$		$\exists^5\forall^4$		$\exists^6\forall^4$		$\exists^7\forall^4$		$\exists^8\forall^4$	
solved	250	250	250	250	250	246	247	246	245	246	244	247	245	247	244	245	0	0
avgt	0.01	0.1	0.01	0.01	0.02	0.01	0.21	0.03	0.35	0.09	0.23	0.28	0.46	1.01	0.98	2.41	–	–
	$\exists^0\forall^5$		$\exists^1\forall^5$		$\exists^2\forall^5$		$\exists^3\forall^5$		$\exists^4\forall^5$		$\exists^5\forall^5$		$\exists^6\forall^5$		$\exists^7\forall^5$		$\exists^8\forall^5$	
solved	250	250	250	250	249	247	248	247	243	245	245	246	0	0	0	0	0	0
avgt	0.01	0.01	0.01	0.01	0.26	0.02	0.18	0.07	0.27	0.37	0.51	2.81	–	–	–	–	–	–

References

1. Bonakdarpour, B., Finkbeiner, B.: Runtime verification for HyperLTL. In: Falcone, Y., Sánchez, C. (eds.) RV 2016. LNCS, vol. 10012, pp. 41–45. Springer, Cham (2016)

2. Clark, D., Hunt, S., Malacaria, P.: Quantified interference for a while language. Electron. Notes Theoret. Comput. Sci. **112**, 149–166 (2005)
3. Clarkson, M.R., Finkbeiner, B., Koleini, M., Micinski, K.K., Rabe, M.N., Sánchez, C.: Temporal logics for hyperproperties. In: Abadi, M., Kremer, S. (eds.) POST 2014. LNCS, vol. 8414, pp. 265–284. Springer, Heidelberg (2014). doi:10.1007/978-3-642-54792-8_15
4. Clarkson, M.R., Schneider, F.B.: Hyperproperties. J. Comput. Secur. **18**(6), 1157–1210 (2010)
5. Duret-Lutz, A.: Manipulating LTL formulas using spot 1.0. In: Hung, D., Ogawa, M. (eds.) ATVA 2013. LNCS, vol. 8172, pp. 442–445. Springer, Cham (2013). doi:10.1007/978-3-319-02444-8_31
6. Eén, N., Sörensson, N.: An extensible SAT-solver. In: Giunchiglia, E., Tacchella, A. (eds.) SAT 2003. LNCS, vol. 2919, pp. 502–518. Springer, Heidelberg (2004). doi:10.1007/978-3-540-24605-3_37
7. Finkbeiner, B., Hahn, C.: Deciding hyperproperties. In: Proceedings of the 27th International Conference on Concurrency Theory, CONCUR 2016, pp. 13:1–13:14 (2016)
8. Finkbeiner, B., Rabe, M.N., Sánchez, C.: Algorithms for model checking Hyper-LTL and HyperCTL*. In: Kroening, D., Păsăreanu, C. (eds.) Computer Aided Verification. LNCS, vol. 9206, pp. 30–48. Springer, Cham (2015)
9. Finkbeiner, B., Seidl, H., Müller, C.: Specifying and verifying secrecy in work-flows with arbitrarily many agents. In: Artho, C., Legay, A., Peled, D. (eds.) ATVA 2016. LNCS, vol. 9938, pp. 157–173. Springer, Cham (2016). doi:10.1007/978-3-319-46520-3_11
10. Hamming, R.W.: Error detecting and error correcting codes. Bell Labs Tech. J. **29**(2), 147–160 (1950)
11. Li, J., Zhang, L., Pu, G., Vardi, M.Y., He, J.: LTL satisfiability checking revisited. In: 2013 20th International Symposium on Temporal Representation and Reasoning, TIME 2013, pp. 91–98 (2013)
12. McLean, J.: Proving noninterference and functional correctness using traces. J. Comput. Secur. **1**(1), 37–58 (1992)
13. Rabe, M.N.: A Temporal Logic Approach to Information-flow Control. Ph.D. thesis, Saarland University (2016)
14. Roscoe, A.W.: CSP and determinism in security modelling. In: Proceedings of the 1995 IEEE Symposium on Security and Privacy, pp. 114–127 (1995)
15. Schwendimann, S.: A new one-pass tableau calculus for **PLTL**. In: Swart, H. (ed.) TABLEAUX 1998. LNCS (LNAI), vol. 1397, pp. 277–291. Springer, Heidelberg (1998). doi:10.1007/3-540-69778-0_28
16. Smith, G.: On the foundations of quantitative information flow. In: Proceedings of the 12th International Conference on Foundations of Software Science and Computational Structures, FOSSACS 2009, pp. 288–302 (2009)
17. Zdancewic, S., Myers, A.C.: Observational determinism for concurrent program security. In: 16th IEEE Computer Security Foundations Workshop CSFW-16 2003, p. 29 (2003)

Automating Induction for Solving Horn Clauses

Hiroshi Unno$^{(\boxtimes)}$, Sho Torii, and Hiroki Sakamoto

University of Tsukuba, Tsukuba, Japan
{uhiro,sho,sakamoto}@logic.cs.tsukuba.ac.jp

Abstract. Verification problems of programs in various paradigms can be reduced to problems of solving Horn clause constraints on predicate variables that represent unknown inductive invariants. This paper presents a novel Horn constraint solving method based on inductive theorem proving: the method reduces Horn constraint solving to validity checking of first-order formulas with inductively defined predicates, which are then checked by induction on the derivation of the predicates. To automate inductive proofs, we introduce a novel proof system tailored to Horn constraint solving, and use a PDR-based Horn constraint solver as well as an SMT solver to discharge proof obligations arising in the proof search. We prove that our proof system satisfies the soundness and relative completeness with respect to ordinary Horn constraint solving schemes. The two main advantages of the proposed method are that (1) it can deal with constraints over any background theories supported by the underlying SMT solver, including nonlinear arithmetic and algebraic data structures, and (2) the method can verify *relational specifications* across programs in various paradigms where multiple function calls need to be analyzed simultaneously. The class of specifications includes practically important ones such as functional equivalence, associativity, commutativity, distributivity, monotonicity, idempotency, and non-interference. Our novel combination of Horn clause constraints with inductive theorem proving enables us to naturally and automatically axiomatize recursive functions that are possibly non-terminating, non-deterministic, higher-order, exception-raising, and over non-inductively defined data types. We have implemented a relational verification tool for the OCaml functional language based on the proposed method and obtained promising results in preliminary experiments.

1 Introduction

Verification problems of programs written in various paradigms, including imperative [30], logic, concurrent [28], functional [47,54,55,59], and object-oriented [36] ones, can be reduced to problems of solving Horn clause constraints on predicate variables that represent unknown inductive invariants. A given program is guaranteed to satisfy its specification if the Horn constraints generated from the program have a solution (see [27] for an overview of the approach).

© Springer International Publishing AG 2017
R. Majumdar and V. Kunčak (Eds.): CAV 2017, Part II, LNCS 10427, pp. 571–591, 2017.
DOI: 10.1007/978-3-319-63390-9_30

This paper presents a novel Horn constraint solving method based on inductive theorem proving: the method reduces Horn constraint solving to validity checking of first-order formulas with inductively defined predicates, which are then checked by induction on the derivation of the predicates. The main technical challenge here is how to automate inductive proofs. To this end, we propose an inductive proof system tailored for Horn constraint solving and a technique based on SMT and PDR [10] to automate proof search in the system. Furthermore, we prove that the proof system satisfies the soundness and relative completeness with respect to ordinary Horn constraint solving schemes.

Compared to previous Horn constraint solving methods [27,29,32,33,41,48, 52,55,57] based on Craig interpolation [21,42], abstract interpretation [20], and PDR, the proposed method has two major advantages:

1. It can solve Horn clause constraints over any background theories supported by the underlying SMT solver. Our method solved constraints over the theories of nonlinear arithmetic and algebraic data structures, which are not supported by most existing Horn constraint solvers.
2. It can verify *relational specifications* where multiple function calls need to be analyzed simultaneously. The class of specifications includes practically important ones such as functional equivalence, associativity, commutativity, distributivity, monotonicity, idempotency, and non-interference.

To show the usefulness of our approach, we have implemented a relational verification tool for the OCaml functional language based on the proposed method and obtained promising results in preliminary experiments.

For an example of the reduction from (relational) verification to Horn constraint solving, consider the following OCaml program D_{mult}.[1]

```
let rec mult x y = if y=0 then 0 else x + mult x (y-1)
let rec mult_acc x y a = if y=0 then a else mult_acc x (y-1) (a+x)
let main x y a = assert (mult x y + a = mult_acc x y a)
```

Here, the function `mult` takes two integer arguments x, y and recursively computes $x \times y$ (note that `mult` never terminates if y < 0). `mult_acc` is a tail-recursive version of `mult` with an accumulator a. The function `main` contains an assertion with the condition mult x y + a = mult_acc x y a, which represents a relational specification, namely, the functional equivalence of `mult` and `mult_acc`. Our verification problem here is whether for any integers x, y, and a, the evaluation of main x y a, under the call-by-value evaluation strategy adopted by OCaml, never causes an assertion failure, that is $\forall x, y, a \in \mathbb{N}$. main $x\ y\ a \not\hookrightarrow^*$assert false. By using a constraint generation method for functional programs [55], the relational verification problem is reduced to the constraint solving problem of the following Horn clause constraint set $\mathcal{H}_{mult}$:

---

[1] Our work also applies to programs that require a path-sensitive analysis of intricate control flows caused by non-termination, non-determinism, higher-order functions, and exceptions but, for illustration purposes, we use this as a running example.

$$\left\{ \begin{array}{l} P(x,0,0), \quad P(x,y,x+r) \Leftarrow P(x,y-1,r) \wedge (y \neq 0), \\ Q(x,0,a,a), \quad Q(x,y,a,r) \Leftarrow Q(x,y-1,a+x,r) \wedge (y \neq 0), \\ \bot \Leftarrow P(x,y,r_1) \wedge Q(x,y,a,r_2) \wedge (r_1 + a \neq r_2) \end{array} \right\}$$

Here, the predicate variable P (resp. Q) represents an inductive invariant among the arguments and the return value of the function mult (resp. mult_acc). The first Horn clause $P(x,0,0)$ is generated from the then-branch of the definition of mult and expresses that mult returns 0 if 0 is given as the second argument. The second clause in $\mathcal{H}_{mult}$, $P(x,y,x+r) \Leftarrow P(x,y-1,r) \wedge (y \neq 0)$ is generated from the else-branch and represents that mult returns $x+r$ if the second argument y is non-zero and r is returned by the recursive call mult x (y-1). The other Horn clauses are similarly generated from the then- and else- branches of mult_acc and the assertion in main. Because $\mathcal{H}_{mult}$ has a satisfying substitution (i.e., solution) $\theta_{mult} = \{P \mapsto \lambda(x,y,r).x \times y = r, Q \mapsto \lambda(x,y,a,r).x \times y + a = r\}$ for the predicate variables P and Q, the correctness of the constraint generation [55] guarantees that the evaluation of main x y a never causes an assertion failure.

The previous Horn constraint solving methods, however, cannot solve this kind of constraints that require a relational analysis of multiple predicates. To see why, recall the constraint in $\mathcal{H}_{mult}$, $\bot \Leftarrow P(x,y,r_1) \wedge Q(x,y,a,r_2) \wedge (r_1 + a \neq r_2)$ which asserts the equivalence of mult and mult_acc, where a relational analysis of the two predicates P and Q is required. The previous methods, however, analyze each predicate P and Q separately, and therefore must infer nonlinear invariants $r_1 = x \times y$ and $r_2 = x \times y + a$ respectively for the predicate applications $P(x,y,r_1)$ and $Q(x,y,a,r_2)$ to conclude $r_1 + a = r_2$ by canceling $x \times y$, because x and y are the only shared arguments between $P(x,y,r_1)$ and $Q(x,y,a,r_2)$. The previous methods can only find solutions that are expressible by efficiently decidable theories such as the quantifier-free linear real (QF_LRA) and integer (QF_LIA) arithmetic[2], which are not powerful enough to express the above nonlinear invariants and the solution θ_{mult} of $\mathcal{H}_{mult}$.

By contrast, our induction-based Horn constraint solving method can directly and automatically show that the predicate applications $P(x,y,r_1)$ and $Q(x,y,a,r_2)$ imply $r_1 + a = r_2$ (i.e., $\mathcal{H}_{mult}$ is solvable), by simultaneously analyzing the two. More precisely, our method interprets P,Q as the predicates inductively defined by the definite clauses (i.e., the clauses whose head is a predicate application), and uses induction on the derivation of $P(x,y,r_1)$ to prove the conjecture $\forall x,y,r_1,a,r_2.(P(x,y,r_1) \wedge Q(x,y,a,r_2) \wedge (r_1 + a \neq r_2) \Rightarrow \bot)$ denoted by the goal clause (i.e., the clause whose head is *not* a predicate application).

The use of Horn clause constraints, which can be considered as an Intermediate Verification Language (IVL) common to Horn constraint solvers and target languages, enables our method to verify relational specifications across programs written in various paradigms. Horn constraints can naturally axiomatize various advanced language features including recursive functions that are partial (i.e., possibly non-terminating), non-deterministic, higher-order, exception-raising, and over non-inductively defined data types (recall that $\mathcal{H}_{mult}$ axiomatizes the

---

[2] See http://smt-lib.org/ for the definition of the theories.

partial functions `mult` and `mult_acc`, and see the full version [58] for more examples). Furthermore, we can automate the axiomatization process by using program logics such as Hoare logics for imperative and refinement type systems [47,54,55,60] for functional programs. In fact, researchers have developed and made available tools such as SeaHorn [30] and JayHorn [36], respectively for translating C and Java programs into Horn constraints. Despite their expressiveness, Horn constraints have a simpler logical semantics than other popular IVLs like Boogie [3] and Why3 [8]. The simplicity enabled us to directly apply inductive theorem proving and made the proofs and implementation easier.

In contrast to our method based on the logic of predicates defined by Horn clause constraints, most state-of-the-art automated inductive theorem provers such as ACL2s [15], Leon [50], Dafny [40], Zeno [49], HipSpec [18], and CVC4 [46] are based on logics of pure total functions over inductively-defined data structures. Some of them support powerful induction schemes such as recursion induction [43] and well-founded induction (if the termination arguments for the recursive functions are given). However, the axiomatization process often requires users' manual intervention and possibly has a negative effect on the automation of induction later, because one needs to take into consideration the evaluation strategies and complex control flows caused by higher-order functions and side-effects such as non-termination, exceptions, and non-determinism. Furthermore, the process needs to preserve branching and calling context information for path- and context-sensitive verification. Thus, our approach complements automated inductive theorem proving with the expressive power of Horn clause constraints and, from the opposite point of view, opens the way to leveraging the achievements of the automated induction community into Horn constraint solving.

The rest of the paper is organized as follows. In Sect. 2, we will give an overview of our induction-based Horn constraint solving method. Section 3 defines Horn constraint solving problems and proves the correctness of the reduction from constraint solving to inductive theorem proving. Section 4 formalizes our constraint solving method and proves its soundness and relative completeness. Section 5 reports on our prototype implementation based on the proposed method and the results of preliminary experiments. We compare our method with related work in Sect. 6 and conclude the paper with some remarks on future work in Sect. 7. The full version [58] contains omitted proofs, example constraints generated from verification problems, and implementation details.

2   Overview of Induction-Based Horn Constraint Solving

In this section, we use the constraint set $\mathcal{H}_{mult}$ in Sect. 1 as a running example to give an overview of our induction-based Horn constraint solving method (more formal treatment is provided in Sects. 3 and 4). Our method interprets the definite clauses of a given constraint set as derivation rules for *atoms* $P(\tilde{t})$, namely, applications of a predicate variable P to a sequence $\tilde{t}$ of terms $t_1, \ldots, t_m$.

For example, the definite clauses $\mathcal{D}_{mult} \subseteq \mathcal{H}_{mult}$ are interpreted as the rules:

$$\frac{\models y = 0 \wedge r = 0}{P(x,y,r)} \qquad \frac{P(x,y-1,r-x) \qquad \models y \neq 0}{P(x,y,r)}$$

$$\frac{\models y = 0 \wedge r = a}{Q(x,y,a,r)} \qquad \frac{Q(x,y-1,a+x,r) \qquad \models y \neq 0}{Q(x,y,a,r)}$$

Here, the heads of the clauses are changed into the uniform representations $P(x,y,r)$ and $Q(x,y,a,r)$ of atoms over variables. These rules inductively define the least interpretation ρ_{mult} for P and Q that satisfies the definite clauses $\mathcal{D}_{mult}$. We thus get $\rho_{mult} = \{P \mapsto \{(x,y,r) \in \mathbb{Z}^3 \mid x \times y = r \wedge y \geq 0\}, Q \mapsto \{(x,y,a,r) \in \mathbb{Z}^4 \mid x \times y + a = r \wedge y \geq 0\}\}$, and $\mathcal{H}_{mult}$ has a solution iff the goal clause

$$\forall x,y,r_1,a,r_2. \left(P(x,y,r_1) \wedge Q(x,y,a,r_2) \wedge (r_1 + a \neq r_2) \Rightarrow \bot \right)$$

is valid under ρ_{mult} (see Sect. 3 for a correctness proof of the reduction). We then check the validity of the goal by induction on the derivation of atoms.

Principle 1 (Induction on Derivations). *Let $\mathcal{P}$ be a property on derivations D of atoms. We then have $\forall D.\mathcal{P}(D)$ if and only if $\forall D. ((\forall D' \prec D.\mathcal{P}(D')) \Rightarrow \mathcal{P}(D))$, where $D' \prec D$ represents that D' is a strict sub-derivation of D.*

Formally, we propose an inductive proof system for deriving judgments of the form $\mathcal{D}; \Gamma; A; \phi \vdash \bot$, where $\bot$ represents the contradiction, ϕ represents a formula without atoms, A represents a set of atoms, Γ represents a set of induction hypotheses and user-specified lemmas, and $\mathcal{D}$ represents a set of definite clauses that define the least interpretation of the predicate variables in Γ or A. Here, Γ, A, and ϕ are allowed to have common free term variables. The free term variables of a clause in $\mathcal{D}$ have the scope within the clause, and are considered to be universally quantified. Intuitively, a judgment $\mathcal{D}; \Gamma; A; \phi \vdash \bot$ means that the formula $\bigwedge \Gamma \wedge \bigwedge A \wedge \phi \Rightarrow \bot$ is valid under the least interpretation induced by $\mathcal{D}$. For example, consider the following judgment J_{mult}:

$$J_{mult} \triangleq \mathcal{D}_{mult}; \emptyset; \{P(x,y,r_1), Q(x,y,a,r_2)\}; (r_1 + a \neq r_2) \vdash \bot$$

If J_{mult} is derivable, $P(x,y,r_1) \wedge Q(x,y,a,r_2) \wedge (r_1 + a \neq r_2) \Rightarrow \bot$ is valid under the least predicate interpretation by $\mathcal{D}_{mult}$, and hence $\mathcal{H}_{mult}$ has a solution.

The inference rules for the judgment $\mathcal{D}; \Gamma; A; \phi \vdash \bot$ are shown in Sect. 4, Fig. 2. The rules there, however, are too general and formal for the purpose of providing an overview of the idea. Therefore, we defer a detailed explanation of the rules to Sect. 4, and here explain a simplified version shown below, obtained from the complete version by eliding some conditions and subtleties while retaining the essence. The rules are designed to exploit Γ and $\mathcal{D}$ for iteratively updating the current *knowledge* represented by the formula $\bigwedge A \wedge \phi$ until a contradiction is implied. The first rule INDUCT

$$\frac{P(\tilde{t}) \in A \qquad \{\tilde{y}\} = fvs(A) \cup fvs(\phi) \qquad \tilde{x} : \text{fresh} \qquad \sigma = \{\tilde{y} \mapsto \tilde{x}\}}{\mathcal{D}; \Gamma; A; \phi \vdash \bot}$$

$$\psi = \forall \tilde{x}. \left((P(\sigma\tilde{t}) \prec P(\tilde{t})) \wedge \bigwedge \sigma A \Rightarrow \neg(\sigma\phi) \right) \qquad \mathcal{D}; \Gamma \cup \{\psi\}; A; \phi \vdash \bot$$

selects an atom $P(\widetilde{t}) \in A$ and performs induction on the derivation of the atom by adding a new induction hypothesis ψ to Γ, which is obtained from the current proof obligation $\bigwedge A \wedge \phi \Rightarrow \bot$ by generalizing its free term variables (denoted by $fvs(A) \cup fvs(\phi)$) into fresh ones $\widetilde{x}$ using a map σ, and adding a guard $P(\sigma \widetilde{t}) \prec P(\widetilde{t})$, requiring the derivation of $P(\sigma \widetilde{t})$ to be a strict sub-derivation of that of $P(\widetilde{t})$, to avoid an unsound application of ψ. The second rule UNFOLD

$$\frac{P(\widetilde{t}) \in A \qquad \mathcal{D}; \Gamma; A \cup [\widetilde{t}/\widetilde{x}]A'; \phi \wedge [\widetilde{t}/\widetilde{x}]\phi' \vdash \bot \qquad (\text{for each } (P(\widetilde{x}) \Leftarrow A' \wedge \phi') \in \mathcal{D})}{\mathcal{D}; \Gamma; A; \phi \vdash \bot}$$

selects an atom $P(\widetilde{t}) \in A$, performs a case analysis on the last rule used to derive the atom, which is represented by a definite clause in $\mathcal{D}$. The third rule APPLY$\bot$

$$\frac{\forall \widetilde{x}. \left(\left(P(\widetilde{t'}) \prec P(\widetilde{t}) \right) \wedge \bigwedge A' \Rightarrow \phi' \right) \in \Gamma \qquad dom(\sigma) = \{\widetilde{x}\} \qquad P(\sigma \widetilde{t'}) \prec P(\widetilde{t})}{\models \bigwedge A \wedge \phi \Rightarrow \bigwedge \sigma A' \qquad \mathcal{D}; \Gamma; A; \phi \wedge \sigma \phi' \vdash \bot}{\mathcal{D}; \Gamma; A; \phi \vdash \bot}$$

selects an induction hypothesis in Γ, and tries to find an instantiation σ of the quantified variables $\widetilde{x}$ such that

- the instantiated premise $\bigwedge \sigma A'$ of the hypothesis is implied by the current knowledge $\bigwedge A \wedge \phi$ and
- the derivation of the atom $P(\sigma \widetilde{t'}) \in \sigma A'$ to which the hypothesis is being applied is a strict sub-derivation of that of the atom $P(\widetilde{t})$ on which the induction (that has introduced the hypothesis) has been performed.

If such a σ is found, $\sigma \phi'$ is added to the current knowledge. The fourth rule VALID$\bot$ checks whether the current knowledge implies $\bot$, and if so, closes the proof branch under consideration.

Figure 1 shows the structure (with side-conditions omitted) of a derivation of the judgment J_{mult}, constructed by using the simplified version of the inference rules. We below explain how the derivation is constructed. First, by performing induction on the atom $P(x, y, r_1)$ in J_{mult} using the rule INDUCT, we obtain the subgoal J_0, where the induction hypothesis $\forall x', y', r'_1, a', r'_2. \phi_{ind}$ is added. We then apply UNFOLD to perform a case analysis on the last rule used to derive the atom $P(x, y, r_1)$, and obtain the two subgoals J_1 and J_2. We here got two subgoals because D_{mult} has two clauses with the head that matches with the atom $P(x, y, r_1)$. The two subgoals are then discharged as follows.

- **Subgoal 1:** By performing a case analysis on $Q(x, y, a, r_2)$ in J_1 using the rule UNFOLD, we further get two subgoals J_3 and J_4. Both J_3 and J_4 are derived by the rule VALID$\bot$ because $\models \phi_3 \Rightarrow \bot$ and $\models \phi_4 \Rightarrow \bot$ hold.
- **Subgoal 2:** By performing a case analysis on $Q(x, y, a, r_2)$ in J_2 using the rule UNFOLD, we obtain two subgoals J_5 and J_6. J_5 is derived by the rule VALID$\bot$ because $\models \phi_5 \Rightarrow \bot$ holds. To derive J_6, we use the rule APPLY$\bot$ to

$$\cfrac{\cfrac{\cfrac{\cfrac{}{J_3}\text{(Valid$\perp$)}\quad\cfrac{}{J_4}\text{(Valid$\perp$)}}{J_1}\text{(Unfold)}\quad\cfrac{\cfrac{}{J_5}\text{(Valid$\perp$)}\quad\cfrac{\cfrac{}{J_7}\text{(Valid$\perp$)}}{J_6}\text{(Apply$\perp$)}}{J_2}\text{(Unfold)}}{J_0}}{J_{mult}}\text{(Induct)}$$

Here, J_i's are of the form $J_i \triangleq \mathcal{D}_{mult}; \{\forall x', y', r'_1, a', r'_2.\ \phi_{ind}\}\,; A_i; \phi_i \vdash \perp$ where:

$$\phi_{ind} = (P(x', y', r'_1) \prec P(x, y, r_1)) \wedge P(x', y', r'_1) \wedge Q(x', y', a', r'_2) \Rightarrow r'_1 + a' = r'_2$$

$\phi_0 = r_1 + a \neq r_2$	$\phi_6 = \phi_2 \wedge y \neq 0$
$\phi_1 = \phi_0 \wedge y = 0 \wedge r_1 = 0$	$\phi_7 = \phi_6 \wedge \sigma(r'_1 + a' = r'_2)$
$\phi_2 = \phi_0 \wedge y \neq 0$	$A_0 = A_1 = A_3 = \{P(x, y, r_1), Q(x, y, a, r_2)\}$
$\phi_3 = \phi_1 \wedge y = 0 \wedge r_2 = a$	$A_2 = A_5 = A_0 \cup \{P(x, y-1, r_1 - x)\}$
$\phi_4 = \phi_1 \wedge y \neq 0$	$A_4 = A_1 \cup \{Q(x, y-1, a+x, r_2)\}$
$\phi_5 = \phi_2 \wedge y = 0 \wedge r_2 = a$	$A_6 = A_7 = A_2 \cup \{Q(x, y-1, a+x, r_2)\}$

Fig. 1. The structure of an example derivation of J_{mult}.

apply the induction hypothesis to the atom $P(x, y-1, r_1 - x) \in A_6$ in J_6. Note that this can be done by using the quantifier instantiation

$$\sigma = \{x' \mapsto x, y' \mapsto y-1, r'_1 \mapsto r_1 - x, a' \mapsto a + x, r'_2 \mapsto r_2\},$$

because $\sigma(P(x', y', r'_1)) = P(x, y-1, r_1 - x) \prec P(x, y, r_1)$ holds and the premise $\sigma(P(x', y', r'_1) \wedge Q(x', y', a', r'_2)) = P(x, y-1, r_1 - x) \wedge Q(x, y-1, a + x, r_2)$ of the instantiated hypothesis is implied by the current knowledge $\bigwedge A_6 \wedge r_1 + a \neq r_2 \wedge y \neq 0$. We thus obtain the subgoal J_7, whose ϕ-part is equivalent to $r_1 + a \neq r_2 \wedge y \neq 0 \wedge r_1 + a = r_2$. Because this implies a contradiction, J_7 is finally derived by using the rule Valid$\perp$.

To automate proof search in the system, we use either an off-the-shelf SMT solver or a PDR-based Horn constraint solver for checking whether the current knowledge implies a contradiction (in the rule Valid$\perp$). An SMT solver is also used to check whether each element of Γ can be used to update the current knowledge, by finding a quantifier instantiation σ (in the rule Apply$\perp$). The use of an SMT solver provides our method with efficient and powerful reasoning about data structures, including integers, real numbers, arrays, algebraic data types, and uninterpreted functions. However, there still remain two challenges to be addressed towards full automation:

1. **Challenge:** How to check (in the rule Apply$\perp$) the strict sub-derivation relation $P(\widetilde{t'}) \prec P(\widetilde{t})$ between the derivation of an atom $P(\widetilde{t'})$ to which an induction hypothesis in Γ is being applied, and the derivation of the atom

$P(\widetilde{t})$ on which the induction has been performed? Recall that in the above derivation of J_{mult}, we needed to check $P(x, y-1, r_1-x) \prec P(x, y, r_1)$ before applying the rule APPLY$\perp$ to J_6.

Our solution: The formalized rules presented in Sect. 4 keep sufficient information for checking the strict sub-derivation relation: we associate each induction hypothesis in Γ with an *induction identifier* α, and each atom in A with a set M of identifiers indicating which hypotheses can be applied to the atom. Further details are explained in Sect. 4.

2. **Challenge:** In which order should the rules be applied?

   Our solution: We here adopt the following simple strategy, and evaluate it by experiments in Sect. 5.

   – Repeatedly apply the rule APPLY$\perp$ if possible, until no new knowledge is obtained. (Even if the rule does not apply, applications of INDUCT and UNFOLD explained in the following items may make APPLY$\perp$ applicable.)
   – If the knowledge cannot be updated by APPLY$\perp$, select some atom from A in a breadth-first manner, and apply the rule INDUCT to the atom.
   – Apply the rule UNFOLD whenever INDUCT is applied.
   – Try to apply the rule VALID$\perp$ whenever the knowledge is updated.

3   Horn Constraint Solving Problems

This section formalizes Horn constraint solving problems and proves the correctness of our reduction from constraint solving to inductive theorem proving. We here restrict ourselves to constraint Horn clauses over the theory $\mathcal{T}_{\mathbb{Z}}$ of quantifier-free linear integer arithmetic for simplicity, although our induction-based Horn constraint solving method formalized in Sect. 4 supports constraints over any background theories supported by the underlying SMT solver. A $\mathcal{T}_{\mathbb{Z}}$-*formula* ϕ is a Boolean combination of atomic formulas $t_1 \leq t_2$, $t_1 < t_2$, $t_1 = t_2$, and $t_1 \neq t_2$. We write $\top$ and $\perp$ respectively for tautology and contradiction. A $\mathcal{T}_{\mathbb{Z}}$-*term* t is either a term variable x, an integer constant n, $t_1 + t_2$, or $t_1 - t_2$.

3.1   Notation for HCSs

A *Horn Constraint Set (HCS)* $\mathcal{H}$ is a finite set $\{hc_1, \ldots, hc_m\}$ of Horn clauses. A *Horn clause* hc is defined to be $h \Leftarrow b$, consisting of a head h and a body b. A *head* h is either of the form $P(\widetilde{t})$ or $\perp$, and a *body* b is of the form $P_1(\widetilde{t}_1) \wedge \cdots \wedge P_m(\widetilde{t}_m) \wedge \phi$. Here, P is a meta-variable ranging over predicate variables. We write $ar(P)$ for the arity of P. We often abbreviate a Horn clause $h \Leftarrow \top$ as h. We write $pvs(hc)$ for the set of the predicate variables that occur in hc and define $pvs(\mathcal{H}) = \bigcup_{hc \in \mathcal{H}} pvs(hc)$. Similarly, we write $fvs(hc)$ for the set of the term variables in hc and define $fvs(\mathcal{H}) = \bigcup_{hc \in \mathcal{H}} fvs(hc)$. We assume that for any $hc_1, hc_2 \in \mathcal{H}$, $hc_1 \neq hc_2$ implies $fvs(hc_1) \cap fvs(hc_2) = \emptyset$. We write $\mathcal{H}{\upharpoonright}_P$ for the set of Horn clauses in $\mathcal{H}$ of the form $P(\widetilde{t}) \Leftarrow b$. We define $\mathcal{H}(P) = \lambda \widetilde{x}. \exists \widetilde{y}. \bigvee_{i=1}^m (b_i \wedge \widetilde{x} = \widetilde{t}_i)$ if $\mathcal{H}{\upharpoonright}_P = \{P(\widetilde{t}_i) \Leftarrow b_i\}_{i \in \{1,\ldots,m\}}$ where $\{\widetilde{y}\} = fvs(\mathcal{H}{\upharpoonright}_P)$ and $\{\widetilde{x}\} \cap \{\widetilde{y}\} = \emptyset$. By using $\mathcal{H}(P)$, an HCS $\mathcal{H}$ is logically interpreted as the formula $\bigwedge_{P \in pvs(\mathcal{H})} \forall \tilde{x}_P. (\mathcal{H}(P)(\tilde{x}_P) \Rightarrow P(\tilde{x}_P))$, where $\tilde{x}_P = x_1, \ldots, x_{ar(P)}$. A Horn clause with the head of the form $P(\tilde{t})$ (resp. $\bot$) is called a *definite clause* (resp. a *goal* clause). We write $def(\mathcal{H})$ (resp. $goal(\mathcal{H})$) for the subset of $\mathcal{H}$ consisting of only the definite (resp. goal) clauses. Note that $\mathcal{H} = def(\mathcal{H}) \cup goal(\mathcal{H})$ and $def(\mathcal{H}) \cap goal(\mathcal{H}) = \emptyset$.

3.2   Predicate Interpretation

A *predicate interpretation* ρ for an HCS $\mathcal{H}$ is a map from each predicate variable $P \in pvs(\mathcal{H})$ to a subset of $\mathbb{Z}^{ar(P)}$. We write the domain of ρ as $\mathrm{dom}(\rho)$. We write $\rho_1 \subseteq \rho_2$ if $\rho_1(P) \subseteq \rho_2(P)$ for all $P \in pvs(\mathcal{H})$. We call an interpretation ρ a *solution of* $\mathcal{H}$ and write $\rho \models \mathcal{H}$ if $\rho \models hc$ holds for all $hc \in \mathcal{H}$. For example, $\rho'_{mult} = \{P \mapsto \{(x, y, r) \in \mathbb{Z}^3 \mid x \times y = r\}, Q \mapsto \{(x, y, a, r) \in \mathbb{Z}^4 \mid x \times y + a = r\}\}$ is a solution of the HCS $\mathcal{H}_{mult}$ in Sect. 1.

Definition 1 (Horn Constraint Solving Problems). *A* Horn constraint solving problem *is the problem of checking if a given HCS $\mathcal{H}$ has a solution.*

We now establish the reduction from Horn constraint solving to inductive theorem proving, which is the foundation of our induction-based Horn constraint solving method. The definite clauses $def(\mathcal{H})$ are considered to inductively define the *least predicate interpretation* for $\mathcal{H}$ as the least fixed-point $\mu F_{\mathcal{H}}$ of the following function on predicate interpretations.

$$F_{\mathcal{H}}(\rho) = \left\{ P \mapsto \left\{ (\tilde{x}) \in \mathbb{Z}^{ar(P)} \;\middle|\; \rho \models \mathcal{H}(P)(\tilde{x}) \right\} \;\middle|\; P \in \mathrm{dom}(\rho) \right\}$$

Because $F_{\mathcal{H}}$ is continuous [35], the least fixed-point $\mu F_{\mathcal{H}}$ of $F_{\mathcal{H}}$ exists. Furthermore, we can express it as $\mu F_{\mathcal{H}} = \bigcup_{i \in \mathbb{N}} F^i_{\mathcal{H}}(\{P \mapsto \emptyset \mid P \in pvs(\mathcal{H})\})$, where $F^i_{\mathcal{H}}$ means i-times application of $F_{\mathcal{H}}$. It immediately follows that the least predicate interpretation $\mu F_{\mathcal{H}}$ is a solution of $def(\mathcal{H})$ because any fixed-point of $F_{\mathcal{H}}$ is a solution of $def(\mathcal{H})$. Furthermore, $\mu F_{\mathcal{H}}$ is the least solution. Formally, we can prove the following proposition.

Proposition 1. $\mu F_{\mathcal{H}} \models def(\mathcal{H})$ *holds, and for all ρ such that $\rho \models def(\mathcal{H})$, $\mu F_{\mathcal{H}} \subseteq \rho$ holds.*

On the other hand, the goal clauses $goal(\mathcal{H})$ are considered as specifications of the least predicate interpretation $\mu F_{\mathcal{H}}$. As a corollary of Proposition 1, it follows that $\mathcal{H}$ has a solution if and only if $\mu F_{\mathcal{H}}$ satisfies the specifications $goal(\mathcal{H})$.

Corollary 1. $\rho \models \mathcal{H}$ *for some ρ if and only if $\mu F_{\mathcal{H}} \models goal(\mathcal{H})$*

In Sect. 4, we present an induction-based method for proving $\mu F_{\mathcal{H}} \models goal(\mathcal{H})$.

4   Induction-Based Horn Constraint Solving Method

As explained in Sect. 2, our method is based on the reduction from Horn constraint solving into inductive theorem proving. The remaining task is to develop

Perform induction on the derivation of the atom $P(\tilde{t})$:

$$\frac{P_o^M(\tilde{t}) \in A \qquad \Gamma' = \Gamma \cup \left\{(\alpha \rhd P(\tilde{t}), A, \phi, h)\right\} \qquad}{\mathcal{D}; \Gamma; A; \phi \vdash h} \frac{\mathcal{D}; \Gamma'; (A \setminus P_o^M(\tilde{t})) \cup \left\{P_\alpha^M(\tilde{t})\right\}; \phi \vdash h \qquad (\alpha : \text{fresh})}{} \quad (\textsc{Induct})$$

Case-analyze the last rule used (where m rules are possible):

$$\frac{P_\alpha^M(\tilde{t}) \in A \qquad \mathcal{D}(P)(\tilde{t}) = \bigvee_{i=1}^m \exists \tilde{x}_i. \, (\phi_i \wedge \bigwedge A_i)}{\mathcal{D}; \Gamma; A \cup A_{io}^{M \cup \{\alpha\}}; \phi \wedge \phi_i \vdash h \qquad (\text{for each } i \in \{1, \ldots, m\})}{\mathcal{D}; \Gamma; A; \phi \vdash h}} \quad (\textsc{Unfold})$$

Apply an induction hypothesis or a user-specified lemma in Γ:

$$\frac{(g, A', \phi', \bot) \in \Gamma \qquad \text{dom}(\sigma) = fvs(A') \qquad \models \phi \Rightarrow [\![\sigma g \in A]\!] \qquad \models \phi \Rightarrow [\![\sigma A' \subseteq A]\!] \qquad \{\tilde{x}\} = fvs(\phi') \setminus \text{dom}(\sigma) \qquad \mathcal{D}; \Gamma; A; \phi \wedge \forall \tilde{x}.\neg(\sigma \phi') \vdash h}{\mathcal{D}; \Gamma; A; \phi \vdash h} \quad (\textsc{Apply}\bot)$$

Apply an induction hypothesis or a user-specified lemma in Γ:

$$\frac{(g, A', \phi', P(\tilde{t})) \in \Gamma \qquad \text{dom}(\sigma) = fvs(A') \cup fvs(\tilde{t}) \qquad \models \phi \Rightarrow [\![\sigma g \in A]\!] \qquad \models \phi \Rightarrow \exists \tilde{x}.(\sigma \phi') \qquad \models \phi \Rightarrow [\![\sigma A' \subseteq A]\!] \qquad \{\tilde{x}\} = fvs(\phi') \setminus \text{dom}(\sigma) \qquad \mathcal{D}; \Gamma; A \cup \left\{P_o^\emptyset(\sigma \tilde{t})\right\}; \phi \vdash h}{\mathcal{D}; \Gamma; A; \phi \vdash h} \quad (\textsc{Apply}P)$$

Apply a definite clause in $\mathcal{D}$:

$$\frac{(P(\tilde{t}) \Leftarrow \phi' \wedge \bigwedge A') \in \mathcal{D} \qquad \text{dom}(\sigma) = fvs(A') \cup fvs(\tilde{t}) \qquad \models \phi \Rightarrow \exists \tilde{x}.(\sigma \phi') \qquad \models \phi \Rightarrow [\![\sigma A' \subseteq A]\!] \qquad \{\tilde{x}\} = fvs(\phi') \setminus \text{dom}(\sigma) \qquad \mathcal{D}; \Gamma; A \cup \left\{P_o^\emptyset(\sigma \tilde{t})\right\}; \phi \vdash h}{\mathcal{D}; \Gamma; A; \phi \vdash h} \quad (\textsc{Fold})$$

Check if the current knowledge entails the asserted proposition:

$$\frac{\mu F_{\mathcal{D}} \models \bigwedge A \wedge \phi \Rightarrow \bot}{\mathcal{D}; \Gamma; A; \phi \vdash \bot} \; (\textsc{Valid}\bot) \qquad \frac{\mu F_{\mathcal{D}} \models \bigwedge A \wedge \phi \Rightarrow [\![P(\tilde{t}) \in A]\!]}{\mathcal{D}; \Gamma; A; \phi \vdash P(\tilde{t})} \; (\textsc{Valid}P)$$

Auxiliary functions:

$$[\![P(\tilde{t}) \in A]\!] \triangleq \bigvee_{P(\tilde{t}') \in A} \tilde{t} = \tilde{t}' \qquad [\![A_1 \subseteq A_2]\!] \triangleq \bigwedge_{P(\tilde{t}) \in A_1} [\![P(\tilde{t}) \in A_2]\!]$$

$$[\![\bullet \in A]\!] \triangleq \top \qquad [\![\alpha \rhd P(\tilde{t}) \in A]\!] \triangleq [\![P(\tilde{t}) \in \left\{P^M(\tilde{t}') \in A \mid \alpha \in M\right\}]\!]$$

Fig. 2. The inference rules for the judgment $\mathcal{D}; \Gamma; A; \phi \vdash h$.

an automated method for proving the inductive conjectures obtained from Horn constraints. We thus formalize our inductive proof system tailored to Horn constraint solving and proves its soundness and relative completeness. To automate proof search in the system, we adopt the rule application strategy in Sect. 2.

We formalize a general and more elaborate version of the inductive proof system explained in Sect. 2. A judgment of the extended system is of the form

$\mathcal{D}; \Gamma; A; \phi \vdash h$, where $\mathcal{D}$ is a set of definite clauses and ϕ represents a formula without atoms. We here assume that $\mathcal{D}(P)$ is defined similarly as $\mathcal{H}(P)$. The asserted proposition h on the right is now allowed to be an atom $P(\tilde{t})$ instead of $\perp$. For deriving such judgments, we will introduce new rules FOLD and VALIDP later in this section. Γ represents a set $\{(g_1, A_1, \phi_1, h_1), \ldots, (g_m, A_m, \phi_m, h_m)\}$ consisting of user-specified lemmas and induction hypotheses, where g_i is either $\bullet$ or $\alpha \triangleright P(\tilde{t})$. $(\bullet, A, \phi, h) \in \Gamma$ represents the user-specified lemma $\forall \tilde{x}. (\bigwedge A \wedge \phi \Rightarrow h)$ where $\{\tilde{x}\} = fvs(A, \phi, h)$, while $(\alpha \triangleright P(\tilde{t}), A, \phi, h) \in \Gamma$ represents the induction hypothesis $\forall \tilde{x}. ((P(\tilde{t}) \prec P(\tilde{t}')) \wedge \bigwedge A \wedge \phi \Rightarrow h)$ with $\{\tilde{x}\} = fvs(P(\tilde{t}), A, \phi, h)$ that has been introduced by induction on the derivation of the atom $P(\tilde{t}')$. Here, α represents the *induction identifier* assigned to the application of induction that has introduced the hypothesis. Note that h on the right-hand side of $\Rightarrow$ is now allowed to be an atom of the form $Q(\tilde{t})$. We will introduce a new rule APPLYP later in this section for using such lemmas and hypotheses to obtain new knowledge. A is also extended to be a set $\{P_{1\alpha_1}^{M_1}(\tilde{t}_1), \ldots, P_{m\alpha_m}^{M_m}(\tilde{t}_m)\}$ of annotated atoms. Each element $P_\alpha^M(\tilde{t})$ has two annotations:

- an induction identifier α indicating that the induction with the identifier α is performed on the atom by the rule INDUCT. If the rule INDUCT has never been applied to the atom, α is set to be a special identifier denoted by $\circ$.
- a set of induction identifiers M indicating that if $\alpha' \in M$, the derivation D of the atom $P_\alpha^M(\tilde{t})$ satisfies $D \prec D'$ for the derivation D' of the atom $P(\tilde{t}')$ on which the induction with the identifier α' is performed. Thus, an induction hypothesis $(\alpha' \triangleright P(\tilde{t}'), A', \phi', h') \in \Gamma$ can be applied to the atom $P_\alpha^M(\tilde{t}) \in A$ only if $\alpha' \in M$ holds.

Note that we use these annotations only for guiding inductive proofs and $P_\alpha^M(\tilde{t})$ is logically equivalent to $P(\tilde{t})$. We often omit these annotations when they are clear from the context.

Given a Horn constraint solving problem $\mathcal{H}$, our method reduces the problem into an inductive theorem proving problem as follows. For each goal clause in $goal(\mathcal{H}) = \{\bigwedge A_i \wedge \phi_i \Rightarrow \perp\}_{i=1}^m$, we check the judgment $def(\mathcal{H}); \emptyset; A_{i\circ}^\emptyset; \phi_i \vdash \perp$ is derivable by the inductive proof system. Here, each atom in A_i is initially annotated with $\emptyset$ and $\circ$.

The inference rules for the judgment $\mathcal{D}; \Gamma; A; \phi \vdash h$ are defined in Fig. 2. The rule INDUCT selects an atom $P_\circ^M(\tilde{t}) \in A$ and performs induction on the derivation of the atom. This rule generates a fresh induction identifier $\alpha \neq \circ$, adds a new induction hypothesis $(\alpha \triangleright P(\tilde{t}), A, \phi, h)$ to Γ, and replaces the atom $P_\circ^M(\tilde{t})$ with the annotated one $P_\alpha^M(\tilde{t})$ for remembering that the induction with the identifier α is performed on it. The rule UNFOLD selects an atom $P_\alpha^M(\tilde{t}) \in A$ and performs a case analysis on the last rule $P(\tilde{t}) \Leftarrow \phi_i \wedge \bigwedge A_i$ used to derive the atom. As the result, the goal is broken into m-subgoals if there are m rules possibly used to derive the atom. The rule adds $A_{i\circ}^{M \cup \{\alpha\}}$ and ϕ_i respectively to A and ϕ in the i-th subgoal, where A_α^M represents $\{P_\alpha^M(\tilde{t}) \mid P(\tilde{t}) \in A\}$. Note here that each atom in A_i is annotated with $M \cup \{\alpha\}$ because the derivation of the atom A_i is a strict sub-derivation of that of the atom $P_\alpha^M(\tilde{t})$ on which the induction with the identifier α has been performed. If $\alpha = \circ$, it is the case that the rule INDUCT has never been applied to the atom $P_\alpha^M(\widetilde{t})$ yet. The rules APPLY$\bot$ and APPLYP select $(g, A', \phi', h) \in \Gamma$, which represents a user-specified lemma if $g = \bullet$ and an induction hypothesis otherwise, and try to add new knowledge respectively to the ϕ- and the A-part of the current knowledge: the rules try to find an instantiation σ for the free term variables in (g, A', ϕ', h), which are considered to be universally quantified, and then use $\sigma(g, A', \phi', h)$ to obtain new knowledge. Contrary to the rule UNFOLD, the rule FOLD tries to use a definite clause $P(\widetilde{t}) \Leftarrow \phi' \wedge \bigwedge A' \in \mathcal{D}$ from the body to the head direction: FOLD tries to find σ such that $\sigma(\phi' \wedge \bigwedge A')$ is implied by the current knowledge, and updates it with $P(\sigma\widetilde{t})$. This rule is useful when we check the correctness of user specified lemmas. The rule VALID$\bot$ checks if the current knowledge $\bigwedge A \wedge \phi$ implies a contradiction, while the rule VALIDP checks if the asserted proposition $P(\widetilde{t})$ on the right-hand side of the judgment is implied by the current knowledge. Here, we can use either an SMT solver or a (PDR-based) Horn constraint solver. The former is much faster because the validity checking problem $\mu F_\mathcal{D} \models \bigwedge A \wedge \phi \Rightarrow \psi$ is approximated to $\models \bigwedge \phi \Rightarrow \psi$. By contrast, the latter is much more precise because we reduce $\mu F_\mathcal{D} \models \bigwedge A \wedge \phi \Rightarrow \psi$ to Horn constraint solving of $\mathcal{D} \cup \{\bot \Leftarrow \bigwedge A \wedge \phi \wedge \neg\psi\}$. The soundness of the inductive proof system is shown as follows.

Lemma 1 (Soundness). *If $\mathcal{D}; \Gamma; A; \phi \vdash h$ is derivable, then there is k such that $\mu F_\mathcal{D} \models [\![\Gamma, A]\!]^k \wedge \bigwedge A \wedge \phi \Rightarrow h$ holds. Here, $[\![\Gamma, A]\!]^k$ represents the conjunction of user-specified lemmas and induction hypotheses in Γ instantiated for the atoms occurring in the k-times unfolding of A.*

The correctness of our Horn constraint solving method follows immediately from Lemma 1 and Corollary 1 as follows.

Theorem 1. *Suppose that $\mathcal{H}$ is an HCS with $goal(\mathcal{H}) = \{\bigwedge A_i \wedge \phi_i \Rightarrow \bot\}_{i=1}^m$ and $def(\mathcal{H}); \emptyset; A_i; \phi_i \vdash \bot$ for all $i = 1, \ldots, m$. It then follows $\rho \models \mathcal{H}$ for some ρ.*

Proof. By Lemma 1 and the fact that $\mu F_{def(\mathcal{H})} \models \bigwedge A_i \Rightarrow [\![\emptyset, A_i]\!]^k$, we get $\mu F_{def(\mathcal{H})} \models \bigwedge A_i \wedge \phi_i \Rightarrow \bot$. We therefore have $\mu F_{def(\mathcal{H})} \models goal(\mathcal{H})$. It then follows that $\rho \models \mathcal{H}$ for some ρ by Corollary 1. ∎

We can also prove the following relative completeness of our system with respect to ordinary Horn constraint solving schemes that find solutions explicitly.

Lemma 2 (Relative Completeness). *Suppose that ρ is a solution of a given HCS $\mathcal{H}$ with $goal(\mathcal{H}) = \{\bot \Leftarrow \bigwedge A \wedge \phi\}$. Let $\Gamma = \{\phi_P \mid P \in dom(\rho)\}$ where $\phi_P = (\forall \widetilde{x}. \ P(\widetilde{x}) \Rightarrow \rho(P)(\widetilde{x}))$. Then, $def(\mathcal{H}); \Gamma; A; \phi \vdash \bot$ and $def(\mathcal{H}); \Gamma \setminus \{\phi_P\}; P(\widetilde{x}); \neg\rho(P)(\widetilde{x}) \vdash \bot$ hold for all $P \in dom(\rho)$.*

Note that our method can exploit over-approximations of the predicates computed by an existing Horn constraint solver as lemmas for checking the validity of the goal clauses, even if the existing solver failed to find a complete solution.

5   Implementation and Preliminary Experiments

We have implemented a Horn constraint solver based on the proposed method and integrated it, as a backend solver, with a refinement type-based verification tool RCaml [54,55,57] for the OCaml functional language. Our solver generates a proof tree like the one shown in Fig. 1 as a certificate if the given constraint set is judged to have a solution, and a counterexample if the constraint set is judged unsolvable. We adopted Z3 [22] and its PDR engine [32] respectively as the underlying SMT and Horn constraint solvers of the inductive proof system. In addition, our solver is extended to generate conjectures on the determinacy of the predicates, which are then checked and used as lemmas. This extension is particularly useful for verification of deterministic functions. The details of the implementation are explained in the full version [58]. The web interface to the verification tool as well as all the benchmark programs used in the experiments reported below are available from http://www.cs.tsukuba.ac.jp/~uhiro/.

We have tested our tool on two benchmark sets. The first set is obtained from the test suite for automated induction provided by the authors of the IsaPlanner system [23]. The benchmark set consists of 85 (mostly) relational verification problems of pure mathematical functions on algebraic data types (ADTs) such as natural numbers, lists, and binary trees. Most of the problems cannot be verified by using the previous Horn constraint solvers [27,29,33,41, 48,52,55,57] because they support neither relational verification nor ADTs. The benchmark set has also been used to evaluate the automated inductive theorem provers [18,40,46,49]. The experiment results on this benchmark set are reported in Sect. 5.1.

To demonstrate advantages of our novel combination of Horn constraint solving with inductive theorem proving, we have prepared the second benchmark set consisting of 30 assertion safety verification problems of (mostly relational) specifications of OCaml programs that use various advanced language features such as partial (i.e., possibly non-terminating) functions, higher-order functions, exceptions, non-determinism, ADTs, and non-inductively defined data types (e.g., real numbers). The benchmark set also includes integer functions with complex recursion and a verification problem concerning the equivalence of programs written in different language paradigms. All the verification problems except 4 are relational ones where safe inductive invariants are not expressible in QF_LIA, and therefore not solvable by the previous Horn constraint solvers. These verification problems are naturally and automatically axiomatized by our method using predicates defined by Horn constraints as the least interpretation. By contrast, these problems cannot be straightforwardly axiomatized by the previous automated inductive theorem provers based on logics of pure total functions on ADTs. The experiment results on this benchmark set are reported in Sect. 5.2.

5.1   Experiments on IsaPlanner Benchmark Set

We manually translated the IsaPlanner benchmarks into assertion safety verification problems of OCaml programs, where we encoded natural numbers using integer primitives, and defined lists and binary trees as ADTs in OCaml. RCaml reduced the verification problems into Horn constraint solving problems using the constraint generation method proposed in [55]. Our solver then automatically solved 68 out of 85 verification problems without using lemmas, and 73 problems with the extension for conjecturing the determinacy of predicates enabled. We have manually analyzed the experiment results and found that 9 out of 12 failed problems require lemmas. The other 3 problems caused timeout of Z3. It was because the rule application strategy implemented in our solver caused useless detours in proofs and put heavier burden on Z3 than necessary.

The experiment results on the IsaPlanner benchmark set show that our Horn-clause-based axiomatization of total recursive functions does not have significant negative impact on the automation of induction; According to the comparison in [49] of state-of-the-art automated inductive theorem provers, which are based on logics of pure total functions over ADTs, IsaPlanner [23] proved 47 out of the 85 IsaPlanner benchmarks, Dafny [40] proved 45, ACL2s [15] proved 74, and Zeno [49] proved 82. The HipSpec [18] inductive prover and the SMT solver CVC4 extended with induction [46] are reported to have proved 80. In contrast to our Horn-clause-based method, these inductive theorem provers can be, and in fact are directly applied to prove the conjectures in the benchmark set, because the benchmark set contains only pure total functions over ADTs.

It is also worth noting that, all the inductive provers that achieved better results than ours support automatic lemma discovery (beyond the determinacy), in a stark contrast to our solver. For example, the above result (80 out of 85) of CVC4 is obtained when they enable an automatic lemma discovery technique proposed in [46] and use a different encoding (called **dti** in [46]) of natural numbers than ours. When they disable the technique and use a similar encoding to ours (called **dtt** in [46]), CVC4 is reported to have proved 64. Thus, we believe that extending our method with automatic lemma discovery, which has been comprehensively studied by the automated induction community [15,18, 34,37,46,49], further makes induction-based Horn constraint solving powerful.

5.2 Experiments on Benchmark Set that Uses Advanced Features

Table 1 summarizes the experiment results on the benchmark set. The column "specification" shows the verified specification and the column "kind" shows its kind, where "equiv", "assoc", "comm", "dist", "mono", "idem", "nonint", and "nonrel" respectively represent the equivalence, associativity, commutativity, distributivity, monotonicity, idempotency, non-interference, and non-relational. The column "features" shows the language features used in the verification problem, where each character has the following meaning: H: higher-order functions, E: exceptions, P: partial (i.e., possibly non-terminating) functions, D: demonic non-determinism, R: real functions, I: integer functions with complex recursion, N: nonlinear functions, C: procedures written in different programming paradigms. The column "result" represents whether our tool succeeded ✓ or failed ✗. The column "time" represents the elapsed time for verification in seconds.

Our tool successfully solved 28 out of 30 problems. Overall, the results show that our tool can solve relational verification problems that use various advanced language features, in a practical time with surprisingly few user-specified lemmas. We also want to emphasize that the problem ID5, which required a lemma, is a relational verification problem involving two function calls with significantly different control flows: one recurses on x and the other on y. Thus, the result demonstrates an advantage of our induction-based method that it can exploit lemmas to fill the gap between function calls with different control flows. Another interesting result we obtain is that the distributivity ID7 of mult is solved thanks to our combination of inductive theorem proving and PDR-based Horn constraint solving, and just using either of them failed.

Our tool, however, failed to verify the associativity ID8 of mult and the equivalence ID15 of sum_down and sum_up. ID8 requires two lemmas $P_{\text{mult}}(x, y, r) \Rightarrow P_{\text{mult}}(y, x, r)$, which represents the commutativity of mult, and $P_{\text{mult}}(x + y, z, r) \Rightarrow \exists s_1, s_2.(P_{\text{mult}}(x, z, s_1) \wedge P_{\text{mult}}(y, z, s_2) \wedge r = s_1 + s_2)$. The latter lemma, however, is not of the form currently supported by our proof system. In ID15, the functions sum_down and sum_up use different recursion parameters (resp. y and x), and requires $P_{\text{sum\_down}}(x, y, s) \wedge a < x \Rightarrow \exists s_1, s_2.(P_{\text{sum\_down}}(a, y, s_1) \wedge P_{\text{sum\_down}}(a, x-1, s_2) \wedge s = s_1 - s_2)$ and $P_{\text{sum\_up}}(x, y, s) \wedge a < x \Rightarrow \exists s_1, s_2.(P_{\text{sum\_down}}(a, y, s_1) \wedge P_{\text{sum\_down}}(a, x-1, s_2) \wedge s = s_1 - s_2)$. These lemmas are provable by induction on the derivation of $P_{\text{sum\_down}}(x, y, s)$ and $P_{\text{sum\_up}}(x, y, s)$, respectively. However, as in the case of ID8, our system does not support the form of the lemmas. Future work thus includes an extension to more general form of lemmas and judgments.

6   Related Work

Automated inductive theorem proving techniques and tools have long been studied, for example and to name a few: the Boyer-Moore theorem provers [37] ACL2s [15], rewriting induction provers [45] SPIKE [9], proof planners CLAM [14,34] and IsaPlanner [23], and SMT-based induction provers Leon [50], Dafny [40], Zeno [49], HipSpec [18], and CVC4 extended with induction [46]. These automated provers are mostly based on logics of pure total functions over inductive data types. Consequently, users of these provers are required to axiomatize advanced language features and specifications using pure total functions as necessary. The axiomatization process, however, is non-trivial, error-prone, and possibly causes a negative effect on the automation of induction. For example, if a partial function (e.g., $f(x) = f(x) + 1$) is input, Zeno goes into an infinite loop and CVC4 is unsound (unless control literals proposed in [50] are used in the axiomatization). We have also confirmed that CVC4 failed to verify complex integer functions like the McCarthy 91 and the Ackermann functions (resp. ID19 and ID20 in Table 1). By contrast, our method supports advanced language features and specifications via Horn-clause encoding of their semantics based on program logics. Compared to cyclic proofs [11] and widely-supported structural induction on derivation trees, our proof system uses induction explicitly by maintaining a set of induction hypotheses and annotating atoms with

Table 1. Experiment results on programs that use various language features

ID	specification	kind	features	result	time (sec.)
1	mult x y + a = mult_acc x y a	equiv	P	✓	0.378
2	mult x y = mult_acc x y 0	equiv	P	✓[†]	0.803
3	mult $(1 + x)$ y = y + mult x y	equiv	P	✓	0.403
4	$y \geq 0$ ⇒ mult x $(1 + y)$ = x + mult x y	equiv	P	✓	0.426
5	mult x y = mult y x	comm	P	✓[‡]	0.389
6	mult $(x + y)$ z = mult x z + mult y z	dist	P	✓	1.964
7	mult x $(y + z)$ = mult x y + mult x z	dist	P	✓	4.360
8	mult (mult x y) z = mult x (mult y z)	assoc	P	✗	n/a
9	$0 \leq x_1 \leq x_2 \wedge 0 \leq y_1 \leq y_2$ ⇒ mult x_1 y_1 ≤ mult x_2 y_2	mono	P	✓	0.416
10	sum x + a = sum_acc x a	equiv		✓	0.576
11	sum x = x + sum $(x - 1)$	equiv		✓	0.452
12	$x \leq y$ ⇒ sum x ≤ sum y	mono		✓	0.593
13	$x \geq 0$ ⇒ sum x = sum_down 0 x	equiv	P	✓	0.444
14	$x < 0$ ⇒ sum x = sum_up x 0	equiv	P	✓	0.530
15	sum_down x y = sum_up x y	equiv	P	✗	n/a
16	sum x = apply sum x	equiv	H	✓	0.430
17	mult x y = apply2 mult x y	equiv	H, P	✓	0.416
18	repeat x (add x) a y = a + mult x y	equiv	H, P	✓	0.455
19	$x \leq 101$ ⇒ mc91 x = 91	nonrel	I	✓	0.233
20	$x \geq 0 \wedge y \geq 0$ ⇒ ack x y > y	nonrel	I	✓	0.316
21	$x \geq 0$ ⇒ 2 × sum x = x × $(x + 1)$	nonrel	N	✓	0.275
22	dyn_sys 0. $\not\longrightarrow^*$ assert false	nonrel	R, N	✓	0.189
23	flip_mod y x = flip_mod y (flip_mod y x)	idem	P	✓	13.290
24	noninter h_1 l_1 l_2 l_3 = noninter h_2 l_1 l_2 l_3	nonint	P	✓	1.203
25	try find_opt p l = Some (find p l) with Not_Found → find_opt p l = None	equiv	H, E	✓	1.065
26	try mem (find ((=) x) l) l with Not_Found → ¬(mem x l)	equiv	H, E	✓	1.056
27	sum_list l = fold_left (+) 0 l	equiv	H	✓	6.148
28	sum_list l = fold_right (+) l 0	equiv	H	✓	0.508
29	sum_fun randpos n > 0	equiv	H, D	✓	0.319
30	mult x y = mult_Ccode(x, y)	equiv	P, C	✓	0.303

[†] A lemma $P_{\mathtt{mult\_acc}}(x, y, a, r) \Rightarrow P_{\mathtt{mult\_acc}}(x, y, a - x, r - x)$ is used
[‡] A lemma $P_{\mathtt{mult}}(x, y, r) \Rightarrow P_{\mathtt{mult}}(x - 1, y, r - y)$ is used
Used a machine with Intel(R) Xeon(R) CPU (2.50 GHz, 16 GB of memory).

induction identifiers so that we can apply the hypotheses soundly. This enables our system to introduce multiple induction hypotheses within a single proof path from dynamically generated formulas. Another advantage is the support of user-supplied lemmas, which are useful in relational verification involving function calls with different control flows (e.g., ID5). To address entailment checking problems in separation logic, researchers have recently proposed induction-based methods [12,13,16,39,51] to go beyond the popular unfold-and-match paradigm (see e.g. [44]). It seems fruitful to incorporate their techniques into our approach to Horn constraint solving to enable verification of heap-manipulating higher-order functional programs.

To aid verification of relational specifications of functional programs, Giesl [25] proposed context-moving transformations and Asada et al. [2] proposed a kind of tupling transformation. SymDiff [38] is a transformation-based tool built on top of Boogie [3] for equivalence verification of imperative programs. Self-composition [5] is a program transformation technique to reduce k-safety [19,53] verification into ordinary safety verification, and has been applied to non-interference [4,5,53,56] and regression verification [24] of imperative programs. These transformations are useful for some patterns of relational verification problems, which are, however, less flexible in some cases than our approach based on a more general principle of induction. For example, Asada et al.'s transformation enables verification of the functional equivalence of recursive functions with the same recursion pattern (e.g., ID1), but does not help verification of the commutativity of `mult` (ID5). Because most of the transformations are designed for a particular target language, they cannot be applied to aid relational verification across programs written in different paradigms (e.g., ID30). Concurrently to our work, De Angelis et al. [1] recently proposed a predicate pairing transformation in the setting of Horn constraints for relational verification of imperative programs. We tested our tool with some of their benchmark constraint solving problems. There were some problems our tool successfully solved but their tool VERIMAP failed, and vice versa: only our tool solved "barthe2" in MON category (if its goal clause is generalized) and "product" in INJ category. We also confirmed that VERIMAP failed to solve our benchmark ID5 involving function calls with different control flows. On the contrary, VERIMAP solved ID15.

There have also been proposed program logics that allow precise relational verification [6,7,17,26]. In particular, the relational refinement type system proposed in [6] can be applied to differential privacy and other relational security verification problems of higher-order functional programs. This approach, however, is not automated.

7   Conclusion and Future Work

We have proposed a novel Horn constraint solving method based on an inductive proof system and a PDR and SMT-based technique to automate proof search in the system. We have shown that our method can solve Horn clause constraints obtained from relational verification problems that were not possible with the previous methods based on Craig interpolation, abstract interpretation, and PDR. Furthermore, our novel combination of Horn clause constraints with inductive theorem proving enabled our method to automatically axiomatize and verify relational specifications of programs that use various advanced language features.

As a future work, we are planning to extend our inductive proof system to support more general form of lemmas and judgments. We are also planning to extend our proof search method to support automatic lemma discovery as in the state-of-the-art inductive theorem provers [15,18,46,49]. To aid users to better understand verification results of our method, it is important to generate a symbolic representation of a solution of the original Horn constraint set from the found inductive proof. It is however often the case that a solution of Horn constraint sets that require relational analysis (e.g., $\mathcal{H}_{mult}$) is not expressible by a formula of the underlying logic. It therefore seems fruitful to generate a symbolic representation of mutual summaries in the sense of [31] across multiple predicates (e.g., P, Q of $\mathcal{H}_{mult}$).

Acknowledgments. We would like to thank Tachio Terauchi for useful discussions, and anonymous referees for their constructive comments. This work was partially supported by Kakenhi 16H05856 and 15H05706.

References

1. Angelis, E., Fioravanti, F., Pettorossi, A., Proietti, M.: Relational verification through horn clause transformation. In: Rival, X. (ed.) SAS 2016. LNCS, vol. 9837, pp. 147–169. Springer, Heidelberg (2016). doi:10.1007/978-3-662-53413-7_8
2. Asada, K., Sato, R., Kobayashi, N.: Verifying relational properties of functional programs by first-order refinement. In: PEPM 2015, pp. 61–72. ACM (2015)
3. Barnett, M., Chang, B.-Y.E., DeLine, R., Jacobs, B., Leino, K.R.M.: Boogie: a modular reusable verifier for object-oriented programs. In: Boer, F.S., Bonsangue, M.M., Graf, S., Roever, W.-P. (eds.) FMCO 2005. LNCS, vol. 4111, pp. 364–387. Springer, Heidelberg (2006). doi:10.1007/11804192_17
4. Barthe, G., Crespo, J.M., Kunz, C.: Relational verification using product programs. In: Butler, M., Schulte, W. (eds.) FM 2011. LNCS, vol. 6664, pp. 200–214. Springer, Heidelberg (2011). doi:10.1007/978-3-642-21437-0_17
5. Barthe, G., D'Argenio, P.R., Rezk, T.: Secure information flow by self-composition. In: CSFW 2004, pp. 100–114. IEEE (2004)
6. Barthe, G., Gaboardi, M., Gallego Arias, E.J., Hsu, J., Roth, A., Strub, P.-Y.: Higher-order approximate relational refinement types for mechanism design and differential privacy. In: POPL 2015, pp. 55–68. ACM (2015)
7. Barthe, G., Köpf, B., Olmedo, F., Zanella Béguelin, S.: Probabilistic relational reasoning for differential privacy. In: POPL 2012, pp. 97–110. ACM (2012)
8. Bobot, F., Filliâtre, J.-C., Marché, C., Paskevich, A.: Why3: Shepherd your herd of provers. In: Boogie 2011, pp. 53–64 (2011)
9. Bouhoula, A., Kounalis, E., Rusinowitch, M.: SPIKE, an automatic theorem prover. In: Voronkov, A. (ed.) LPAR 1992. LNCS, vol. 624, pp. 460–462. Springer, Heidelberg (1992). doi:10.1007/BFb0013087
10. Bradley, A.R.: SAT-based model checking without unrolling. In: Jhala, R., Schmidt, D. (eds.) VMCAI 2011. LNCS, vol. 6538, pp. 70–87. Springer, Heidelberg (2011). doi:10.1007/978-3-642-18275-4_7
11. Brotherston, J.: Cyclic proofs for first-order logic with inductive definitions. In: Beckert, B. (ed.) TABLEAUX 2005. LNCS (LNAI), vol. 3702, pp. 78–92. Springer, Heidelberg (2005). doi:10.1007/11554554_8
12. Brotherston, J., Distefano, D., Petersen, R.L.: Automated cyclic entailment proofs in separation logic. In: Bjørner, N., Sofronie-Stokkermans, V. (eds.) CADE 2011. LNCS (LNAI), vol. 6803, pp. 131–146. Springer, Heidelberg (2011). doi:10.1007/978-3-642-22438-6_12

13. Brotherston, J., Fuhs, C., Navarro, J.A.P., Gorogiannis, N.: A decision procedure for satisfiability in separation logic with inductive predicates. In: CSL-LICS 2014, pp. 25:1–25:10. ACM (2014)

14. Bundy, A., van Harmelen, F., Horn, C., Smaill, A.: The O^YS^TER-CL^AM system. In: Stickel, M.E. (ed.) CADE 1990. LNCS, vol. 449, pp. 647–648. Springer, Heidelberg (1990). doi:10.1007/3-540-52885-7_123

15. Chamarthi, H.R., Dillinger, P., Manolios, P., Vroon, D.: The ACL2 sedan theorem proving system. In: Abdulla, P.A., Leino, K.R.M. (eds.) TACAS 2011. LNCS, vol. 6605, pp. 291–295. Springer, Heidelberg (2011). doi:10.1007/978-3-642-19835-9_27

16. Chu, D.-H., Jaffar, J., Trinh, M.-T.: Automatic induction proofs of data-structures in imperative programs. In: PLDI 2015, pp. 457–466. ACM (2015)

17. Ciobâcă, Ş., Lucanu, D., Rusu, V., Roşu, G.: A language-independent proof system for mutual program equivalence. In: Merz, S., Pang, J. (eds.) ICFEM 2014. LNCS, vol. 8829, pp. 75–90. Springer, Cham (2014). doi:10.1007/978-3-319-11737-9_6

18. Claessen, K., Johansson, M., Rosén, D., Smallbone, N.: Automating inductive proofs using theory exploration. In: Bonacina, M.P. (ed.) CADE 2013. LNCS (LNAI), vol. 7898, pp. 392–406. Springer, Heidelberg (2013). doi:10.1007/978-3-642-38574-2_27

19. Clarkson, M.R., Schneider, F.B.: Hyperproperties. In: CSF 2008, pp. 51–65. IEEE (2008)

20. Cousot, P., Cousot, R.: Abstract interpretation: a unified lattice model for static analysis of programs by construction or approximation of fixpoints. In: POPL 1977, pp. 238–252. ACM (1977)

21. Craig, W.: Three uses of the Herbrand-Gentzen theorem in relating model theory and proof theory. J. Symbolic Logic **22**, 269–285 (1957)

22. de Moura, L., Bjørner, N.: Z3: an efficient SMT solver. In: Ramakrishnan, C.R., Rehof, J. (eds.) TACAS 2008. LNCS, vol. 4963, pp. 337–340. Springer, Heidelberg (2008). doi:10.1007/978-3-540-78800-3_24

23. Dixon, L., Fleuriot, J.: IsaPlanner: a prototype proof planner in isabelle. In: Baader, F. (ed.) CADE 2003. LNCS (LNAI), vol. 2741, pp. 279–283. Springer, Heidelberg (2003). doi:10.1007/978-3-540-45085-6_22

24. Felsing, D., Grebing, S., Klebanov, V., Rümmer, P., Ulbrich, M.: Automating regression verification. In: ASE 2014, pp. 349–360. ACM (2014)

25. Giesl, J.: Context-moving transformations for function verification. In: Bossi, A. (ed.) LOPSTR 1999. LNCS, vol. 1817, pp. 293–312. Springer, Heidelberg (2000). doi:10.1007/10720327_17

26. Godlin, B., Strichman, O.: Regression verification: proving the equivalence of similar programs. Softw. Test. Verification Reliab. **23**(3), 241–258 (2013)

27. Grebenshchikov, S., Lopes, N.P., Popeea, C., Rybalchenko, A.: Synthesizing software verifiers from proof rules. In: PLDI 2012, pp. 405–416. ACM (2012)

28. Gupta, A., Popeea, C., Rybalchenko, A.: Predicate abstraction and refinement for verifying multi-threaded programs. In: POPL 2011, pp. 331–344. ACM (2011)

29. Gupta, A., Popeea, C., Rybalchenko, A.: Solving recursion-free horn clauses over LI+UIF. In: Yang, H. (ed.) APLAS 2011. LNCS, vol. 7078, pp. 188–203. Springer, Heidelberg (2011). doi:10.1007/978-3-642-25318-8_16

30. Gurfinkel, A., Kahsai, T., Komuravelli, A., Navas, J.A.: The seahorn verification framework. In: Kroening, D., Păsăreanu, C.S. (eds.) CAV 2015. LNCS, vol. 9206, pp. 343–361. Springer, Cham (2015). doi:10.1007/978-3-319-21690-4_20

31. Hawblitzel, C., Kawaguchi, M., Lahiri, S.K., Rebêlo, H.: Towards modularly comparing programs using automated theorem provers. In: Bonacina, M.P. (ed.) CADE 2013. LNCS (LNAI), vol. 7898, pp. 282–299. Springer, Heidelberg (2013). doi:10.1007/978-3-642-38574-2_20

32. Hoder, K., Bjørner, N.: Generalized property directed reachability. In: Cimatti, A., Sebastiani, R. (eds.) SAT 2012. LNCS, vol. 7317, pp. 157–171. Springer, Heidelberg (2012). doi:10.1007/978-3-642-31612-8_13

33. Hoder, K., Bjørner, N., de Moura, L.: μZ – an efficient engine for fixed points with constraints. In: Gopalakrishnan, G., Qadeer, S. (eds.) CAV 2011. LNCS, vol. 6806, pp. 457–462. Springer, Heidelberg (2011). doi:10.1007/978-3-642-22110-1_36

34. Ireland, A., Bundy, A.: Productive use of failure in inductive proof. J. Autom. Reas. 16(1–2), 79–111 (1996)

35. Jaffar, J., Maher, M.J.: Constraint logic programming: a survey. J. Logic Program. 19, 503–581 (1994)

36. Kahsai, T., Rümmer, P., Sanchez, H., Schäf, M.: JayHorn: a framework for verifying java programs. In: Chaudhuri, S., Farzan, A. (eds.) CAV 2016. LNCS, vol. 9779, pp. 352–358. Springer, Cham (2016). doi:10.1007/978-3-319-41528-4_19

37. Kaufmann, M., Moore, J.S., Manolios, P.: Computer Aided-Reasoning: An Approach. Kluwer Academic Publishers, Heidelberg (2000)

38. Lahiri, S.K., Hawblitzel, C., Kawaguchi, M., Rebêlo, H.: SYMDIFF: a language-agnostic semantic diff tool for imperative programs. In: Madhusudan, P., Seshia, S.A. (eds.) CAV 2012. LNCS, vol. 7358, pp. 712–717. Springer, Heidelberg (2012). doi:10.1007/978-3-642-31424-7_54

39. Le, Q.L., Sun, J., Chin, W.-N.: Satisfiability modulo heap-based programs. In: Chaudhuri, S., Farzan, A. (eds.) CAV 2016. LNCS, vol. 9779, pp. 382–404. Springer, Cham (2016). doi:10.1007/978-3-319-41528-4_21

40. Leino, K.R.M.: Automating induction with an SMT solver. In: Kuncak, V., Rybalchenko, A. (eds.) VMCAI 2012. LNCS, vol. 7148, pp. 315–331. Springer, Heidelberg (2012). doi:10.1007/978-3-642-27940-9_21

41. McMillan, K., Rybalchenko, A.: Computing relational fixed points using interpolation. Technical report MSR-TR-2013-6, Microsoft Research (2013)

42. McMillan, K.L.: An interpolating theorem prover. Theor. Comput. Sci. 345(1), 101–121 (2005)

43. Nipkow, T., Wenzel, M., Paulson, L.C. (eds.): Isabelle/HOL: A Proof Assistant for Higher-Order Logic. LNCS, vol. 2283. Springer, Heidelberg (2002). doi:10.1007/3-540-45949-9

44. Pek, E., Qiu, X., Madhusudan, P.: Natural proofs for data structure manipulation in C using separation logic. In: PLDI 2014, pp. 440–451. ACM (2014)

45. Reddy, U.S.: Term rewriting induction. In: Stickel, M.E. (ed.) CADE 1990. LNCS, vol. 449, pp. 162–177. Springer, Heidelberg (1990). doi:10.1007/3-540-52885-7_86

46. Reynolds, A., Kuncak, V.: Induction for SMT solvers. In: D'Souza, D., Lal, A., Larsen, K.G. (eds.) VMCAI 2015. LNCS, vol. 8931, pp. 80–98. Springer, Heidelberg (2015). doi:10.1007/978-3-662-46081-8_5

47. Rondon, P., Kawaguchi, M., Jhala, R.: Liquid types. In: PLDI 2008, pp. 159–169. ACM (2008)

48. Rümmer, P., Hojjat, H., Kuncak, V.: Disjunctive interpolants for horn-clause verification. In: Sharygina, N., Veith, H. (eds.) CAV 2013. LNCS, vol. 8044, pp. 347–363. Springer, Heidelberg (2013). doi:10.1007/978-3-642-39799-8_24

49. Sonnex, W., Drossopoulou, S., Eisenbach, S.: Zeno: an automated prover for properties of recursive data structures. In: Flanagan, C., König, B. (eds.) TACAS 2012. LNCS, vol. 7214, pp. 407–421. Springer, Heidelberg (2012). doi:10.1007/978-3-642-28756-5_28

50. Suter, P., Köksal, A.S., Kuncak, V.: Satisfiability modulo recursive programs. In: Yahav, E. (ed.) SAS 2011. LNCS, vol. 6887, pp. 298–315. Springer, Heidelberg (2011). doi:10.1007/978-3-642-23702-7_23

51. Ta, Q.-T., Le, T.C., Khoo, S.-C., Chin, W.-N.: Automated mutual explicit induction proof in separation logic. In: Fitzgerald, J., Heitmeyer, C., Gnesi, S., Philippou, A. (eds.) FM 2016. LNCS, vol. 9995, pp. 659–676. Springer, Cham (2016). doi:10.1007/978-3-319-48989-6_40

52. Terauchi, T.: Dependent types from counterexamples. In: POPL 2010, pp. 119–130. ACM (2010)

53. Terauchi, T., Aiken, A.: Secure information flow as a safety problem. In: Hankin, C., Siveroni, I. (eds.) SAS 2005. LNCS, vol. 3672, pp. 352–367. Springer, Heidelberg (2005). doi:10.1007/11547662_24

54. Unno, H., Kobayashi, N.: On-demand refinement of dependent types. In: Garrigue, J., Hermenegildo, M.V. (eds.) FLOPS 2008. LNCS, vol. 4989, pp. 81–96. Springer, Heidelberg (2008). doi:10.1007/978-3-540-78969-7_8

55. Unno, H., Kobayashi, N.: Dependent type inference with interpolants. In: PPDP 2009, pp. 277–288. ACM (2009)

56. Unno, H., Kobayashi, N., Yonezawa, A.: Combining type-based analysis and model checking for finding counterexamples against non-interference. In: PLAS 2006, pp. 17–26. ACM (2006)

57. Unno, H., Terauchi, T.: Inferring simple solutions to recursion-free horn clauses via sampling. In: Baier, C., Tinelli, C. (eds.) TACAS 2015. LNCS, vol. 9035, pp. 149–163. Springer, Heidelberg (2015). doi:10.1007/978-3-662-46681-0_10

58. Unno, H., Torii, S., Sakamoto, H.: Automating induction for solving horn clauses. (2017) http://www.cs.tsukuba.ac.jp/~uhiro/

59. Vazou, N., Seidel, E.L., Jhala, R., Vytiniotis, D., Peyton Jones, S.L.: Refinement types for Haskell. In: ICFP 2014, pp. 269–282. ACM (2014)

60. Xi, H., Pfenning, F.: Dependent types in practical programming. In: POPL 1999, pp. 214–227. ACM (1999)

A Storm is Coming:
A Modern Probabilistic Model Checker

Christian Dehnert[(✉)], Sebastian Junges,
Joost-Pieter Katoen, and Matthias Volk

RWTH Aachen University, Aachen, Germany
dehnert@cs.rwth-aachen.de

Abstract. We launch the new probabilistic model checker Storm. It features the analysis of discrete- and continuous-time variants of both Markov chains and MDPs. It supports the Prism and JANI modeling languages, probabilistic programs, dynamic fault trees and generalized stochastic Petri nets. It has a modular set-up in which solvers and symbolic engines can easily be exchanged. It offers a Python API for rapid prototyping by encapsulating Storm's fast and scalable algorithms. Experiments on a variety of benchmarks show its competitive performance.

1 Introduction

In the last five years, we have developed our in-house probabilistic model checker with the aim to have an easy-to-use platform for experimenting with new verification algorithms, richer probabilistic models, algorithmic improvements, different modeling formalisms, various new features, and so forth. Although open-source probabilistic model checkers do exist, most are not flexible and modular enough to easily support this. Our efforts have led to a toolkit with mature building bricks with simple interfaces for possible extensions, and a modular set-up. It comprises about 100,000 lines of C++ code. The time has come to make this toolkit available to a wider audience: this paper presents Storm.

Like its main competitors Prism [1], MRMC [2], and iscasMC [3], Storm relies on numerical and symbolic computations. It does not support discrete-event simulation, known as statistical model checking [4]. The main characteristic features of Storm are:

- it supports *various native input formats*: the Prism input format, generalized stochastic Petri nets, dynamic fault trees, and conditioned probabilistic programs. This is not just providing another parser; state-space reduction and generation techniques as well as analysis algorithms are partly tailored to these modeling formalisms;
- in addition to Markov chains and MDPs, it supports *Markov automata* [5], a model containing probabilistic branching, non-determinism, and exponentially distributed delays;

© Springer International Publishing AG 2017
R. Majumdar and V. Kunčak (Eds.): CAV 2017, Part II, LNCS 10427, pp. 592–600, 2017.
DOI: 10.1007/978-3-319-63390-9_31

- it can do *explicit state* and *fully symbolic* (BDD-based) model checking as well as a *mixture* of these modes;
- it has a *modular* set-up, enabling the easy exchange of different solvers and distinct decision diagram packages; its current release supports about 15 solvers, and the BDD packages `CUDD` [6] and multi-threaded `Sylvan` [7];
- it provides a *Python API* facilitating easy and rapid prototyping of other tools using the engines and algorithms in STORM;
- it provides the following functionalities under one roof: the synthesis of counterexamples and permissive schedulers (both MILP- and SMT-based), game-based abstraction of infinite-state MDPs, efficient algorithms for conditional probabilities and rewards [8], and long-run averages on MDPs [9];
- its performance in terms of verification speed and memory footprint on the PRISM benchmark suite is mostly better compared to PRISM.

Although many functionalities of PRISM are covered by STORM, there are significant differences. STORM does not support LTL model checking (as in ISCASMC and PRISM) and does not support the PRISM features: probabilistic timed automata, and an equivalent of PRISM's "hybrid" engine (a crossover between full MTBDD and STORM's "hybrid" engine), a fully symbolic engine for continuous-time models, statistical model checking, and the analysis of stochastic games as in PRISM-GAMES [10].

2   Features

Model Types. STORM supports Markov chains and Markov decision processes (MDPs), both in two forms: discrete time and continuous time. This yields four different models: classical discrete-time (DTMCs) and continuous-time Markov chains (CTMCs), as well as MDPs and Markov automata (MA) [5], a compositional variant of continuous-time MDPs. The MA is the richest model. CTMCs are MAs without non-determinism, while MDPs are MAs without delays; DTMCs are CTMCs without delays, cf. [11]. All these models are extensible with rewards (or dually: costs) to states, and – for non-deterministic models – to actions. Most probabilistic model checkers support Markov chains and/or MDPs; MAs so far have only been supported by few tools [12,13].

Modeling Languages. STORM supports various symbolic and an explicit input format to specify the aforementioned model types: (i) Most prominently, the PRISM input language [1] (ii) the recently defined JANI format [14], a universal probabilistic modeling language; (iii) as the first tool *every*[1] generalized stochastic Petri net (GSPN) [17] via both a dedicated model builder as well as an encoding in JANI; (iv) dynamic fault trees (DFTs) [18,19] – due to dedicated state-space generation and reduction techniques for DFTs, STORM significantly

---

[1] Existing CSL model checkers for GSPNs such as GreatSPN [15] and MARCIE [16] are restricted to confusion-free Petri nets; STORM does not have this restriction as it supports MA.

outperforms competing tools in this domain [20]; (v) pGCL probabilistic programs [21] extended with observe-statements [22], an essential feature to describe and analyze e.g., Bayesian networks; (vi) in the spirit of MRMC [2], models can be provided in a format that explicitly enumerates transitions.

Properties. STORM focusses on probabilistic branching-time logics, i.e. PCTL [23] and CSL [24] for discrete-time and continuous-time models, respectively. To enable the treatment of reward objectives such as expected and long-run rewards, STORM supports reward extensions of these logics in a similar way as PRISM. In addition, STORM supports conditional probabilities and conditional rewards [8]; these are, e.g., important for the analysis of cpGCL programs.

Engines. STORM features two distinct in-memory representations of probabilistic models: *sparse matrices* allow for fast operations on small and moderately sized models, multi-terminal binary decision diagrams (MTBDDs) are able to represent gigantic models, however with slightly more expensive operations. A variety of engines built around the in-memory representations is available, which allows for the more efficient treatment of input models. Both STORM's *sparse* and the *exploration* engine purely use a sparse matrix-based representation. While the former amounts to an efficient implementation of the standard approaches, the latter one implements the ideas of [25] which scrutinizes the state space with machine learning methods. Three other engines, *dd*, *hybrid* and *abstraction-refinement*, use MTBDDs as their primary representation. While *dd* exclusively uses decision diagrams, *hybrid* also uses sparse matrices for operations deemed more suitable on this format. The *abstraction-refinement* engine abstracts (possibly infinite) discrete-time Markov models to (finite) stochastic games and automatically refines the abstraction as necessary.

Parametric Models. STORM was used as backend in [26,27]. By using the dedicated library CARL [28] for the representation of rational functions and applying novel algorithms for the analysis of parametric discrete-time models, it has proven to significantly outperform the dedicated tool PARAM [29] and parametric model checking in PRISM.

Exact Arithmetic. Several works [30,31] observed that the numerical methods applied by probabilistic model checkers are prone to numerical problems. STORM therefore supports enabling exact arithmetic to obtain *precise results.*

Counterexample Generation. For probabilistic models, several counterexample representations have been proposed [32]. STORM implements the MILP-based counterexample technique [33], as well as the MAXSAT-based generation of high-level counterexamples on PRISM models [34]. These algorithms go beyond the capabilities of dedicated, stand-alone counterexample generation tools such as DiPro [35] and COMICS [36]. In particular, the synthesis of high-level counterexamples facilitates to obtain counterexamples as PRISM code, starting from a PRISM model and a refuted property.

APIs. Storm can be used via *three* interfaces: a command-line interface, a C++ API, and a Python API. The command-line interface consists of several binaries that provide end-users access to the available settings for different tasks. Advanced users can utilize the many settings to tune the performance. Developers may either use the C++ API that offers fine-grained and performance-oriented access to Storm's functionality, or the Python API which allows rapid prototyping and encapsulates the high-performance implementations within Storm.

Availability. Storm's source code is available as open source and can be obtained along with additional information at http://www.stormchecker.org.

3   Architecture

Figure 1 depicts the architecture of Storm. Solid arrows indicate the flow of control and data, dashed lines represent a "uses" relationship. After the initial parsing step, it depends on the selected engine whether a model building step is performed: for all but the *exploration* and *abstraction-refinement* engines, it is necessary to build a full in-memory representation of the model upfront. Note that the available engines depend on the input format and that both PRISM and GSPN input can be either treated natively or transformed to JANI.

Solvers. Storm's infrastructure is built around the notion of a *solver*. For instance, solvers are available for sets of linear or Bellman equations (both using sparse matrices as well as MTBDDs), (mixed-integer) linear programming (MILP) and satisfiability modulo theories (SMT). Note that Storm does not support stochastic games as input models, yet, but solvers for them are available because they are used in the *abstraction-refinement* engine. Offering these interfaces has several key advantages. First, it provides easy and coherent access to the tasks commonly involved in probabilistic model checking. Secondly, it

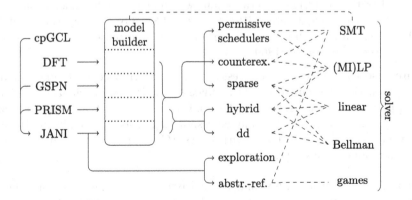

Fig. 1. Storm's architecture.

Table 1. Solvers offered by STORM.

Solver type	Available solvers
Linear equations (sparse)	Eigen [37], gmm++ [38], elim. [39], built-in
Linear equations (MTBDD)	CUDD [6], Sylvan [7]
Bellman equations (sparse)	Eigen, gmm++, built-in
Bellman equations (MTBDD)	CUDD, Sylvan
Stochastic games (sparse)	built-in
Stochastic games (MTBDD)	CUDD, Sylvan
(MI)LP	Gurobi [40], glpk [41]
SMT	Z3 [42], MathSAT [43], SMT-LIB

enables the use of dedicated state-of-the-art high-performance libraries for the task at hand. More specifically, as the performance characteristics of different backend solvers can vary drastically for the same input, this permits choosing the best solver for a given task. Licensing problems are avoided, because implementations can be easily enabled and disabled, depending on whether or not the particular license fits the requirements. Implementing new solver functionality is easy and can be done without knowledge about the global code base. Finally, it allows to embed new state-of-the-art solvers in the future. For each of those interfaces, several actual implementations exist. Table 1 gives an overview over the currently available implementations. Almost all engines and all other key modules make use of *solvers*. The most prominent example is the use of the equation solvers for answering standard verification queries. However, other modules use them too, e.g. model building (SMT), counterexample generation [33,34] (SMT, MILP) and permissive scheduler generation [44,45] (SMT, MILP).

4   Evaluation

Set-up. For the performance evaluation, we conducted experiments on a HP BL685C G7. Up to eight cores with 2.0 GHz and 8 GB of memory were available to the tools, but only PRISM's garbage collection used more than one core at a time. We set a time-out of 1800 s.

Comparison with PRISM. To assess STORM's performance on standard model-checking queries, we compare it with PRISM on the PRISM benchmark suite [46]. More specifically, we consider all DTMCs, CTMCs and MDPs (24 in total, and several instances per model) and all corresponding properties (82 in total). Note that we do not compare STORM with ISCASMC as the latter one has a strong focus on more complex LTL properties.

Methodology. As both PRISM and STORM offer several engines with different strengths and weaknesses, we choose the following comparison methodology. We compare engines that "match" in terms of the general approach. For example,

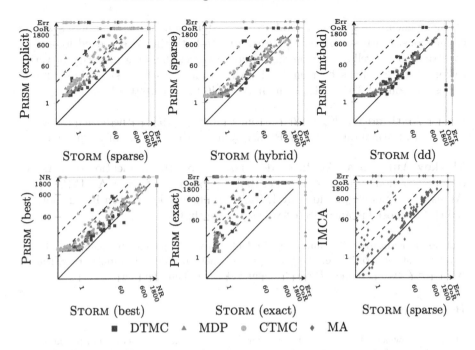

Fig. 2. Run-time comparison (seconds) of different engines/features.

Prism's *explicit* engine first builds the model in terms of a sparse matrix directly and then performs the model checking on this representation, which matches the approach of Storm's *sparse* engine. In the same manner, Prism's *sparse* engine is comparable to Storm's *hybrid* one and Prism's *mtbdd* engine corresponds to Storm's *dd* engine. Finally, we compare the run-times of Prism and Storm when selecting the best engine for each individual benchmark instance.

Results. Figure 2 (top-row) summarizes the results of the experiments in log-log scale. We plot the total time taken by the Storm engines versus the "matching" Prism engines. Data points above the main diagonal indicate that Storm solved the task faster. The two dashed lines indicate a speed-up of 10 and 100, respectively; "OoR" denotes memory- or time-outs, "Err" denotes that a tool was not able to complete the task for any other reason and "NR" stands for "no result".

Discussion. We observe that Storm is competitive on all compared engines. Even though the MTBDD-based engines are very similar and even use the same MTBDD library (CUDD), most of the time Storm is able to outperform Prism. Note that Storm currently does not support CTMCs in this engine. We observe a slightly clearer advantage of Storm' hybrid engine in comparison to Prism's sparse engine. Here, model building times tend to be similar, but most often the numerical solution is done more efficiently by Storm. However, for large

CTMC benchmarks, PRISM tends to be faster than STORM. STORM's *sparse* engine consistently outperforms PRISM due to both the time needed for model construction as well as solving times. For the overwhelming majority of verification tasks, STORM's best engine is faster than PRISM's best engine. STORM solves 361 (out of 380) tasks, compared to 346 tasks PRISM solves.

Exact Arithmetic. Figure 2 (bottom center) compares the *exact* modes of both tools. STORM outperforms PRISM by up to three orders of magnitude.

Markov Automata. As PRISM does not support the verification of MAs, we compare STORM with the only other tool capable of verifying MAs: IMCA [12]. We used the models provided by IMCA, results are depicted in Fig. 2 (bottom right). For most instances, STORM is significantly faster.

Acknowledgments. The authors would like to thank people that support(ed) the development of STORM over the years (in alphabetical order): Philipp Berger, Harold Bruintjes, Gereon Kremer, David Korzeniewski, and Tim Quatmann.

References

1. Kwiatkowska, M., Norman, G., Parker, D.: PRISM 4.0: Verification of probabilistic real-time systems. In: Gopalakrishnan, G., Qadeer, S. (eds.) CAV 2011. LNCS, vol. 6806, pp. 585–591. Springer, Heidelberg (2011). doi:10.1007/978-3-642-22110-1_47
2. Katoen, J.P., Zapreev, I.S., Hahn, E.M., Hermanns, H., Jansen, D.N.: The ins and outs of the probabilistic model checker MRMC. Perform. Eval. **68**(2), 90–104 (2011)
3. Hahn, E.M., Li, Y., Schewe, S., Turrini, A., Zhang, L.: ISCASMC: a web-based probabilistic model checker. In: Jones, C., Pihlajasaari, P., Sun, J. (eds.) FM 2014. LNCS, vol. 8442, pp. 312–317. Springer, Cham (2014). doi:10.1007/978-3-319-06410-9_22
4. Larsen, K.G., Legay, A.: Statistical model checking: past, present, and future. In: Margaria, T., Steffen, B. (eds.) ISoLA 2016. LNCS, vol. 9952, pp. 3–15. Springer, Cham (2016). doi:10.1007/978-3-319-47166-2_1
5. Eisentraut, C., Hermanns, H., Zhang, L.: On probabilistic automata in continuous time. In: Proceedings of LICS, pp. 342–351. IEEE CS (2010)
6. CUDD (2016). http://vlsi.colorado.edu/~fabio/CUDD/cudd.pdf
7. Dijk, T., Pol, J.: Sylvan: multi-core decision diagrams. In: Baier, C., Tinelli, C. (eds.) TACAS 2015. LNCS, vol. 9035, pp. 677–691. Springer, Heidelberg (2015). doi:10.1007/978-3-662-46681-0_60
8. Baier, C., Klein, J., Klüppelholz, S., Märcker, S.: Computing conditional probabilities in markovian models efficiently. In: Ábrahám, E., Havelund, K. (eds.) TACAS 2014. LNCS, vol. 8413, pp. 515–530. Springer, Heidelberg (2014). doi:10.1007/978-3-642-54862-8_43
9. de Alfaro, L.: How to specify and verify the long-run average behavior of probabilistic systems. In: Proceedings of LICS, pp. 454–465. IEEE CS (1998)
10. Chen, T., Forejt, V., Kwiatkowska, M., Parker, D., Simaitis, A.: PRISM-games: a model checker for stochastic multi-player games. In: Piterman, N., Smolka, S.A. (eds.) TACAS 2013. LNCS, vol. 7795, pp. 185–191. Springer, Heidelberg (2013). doi:10.1007/978-3-642-36742-7_13

11. Katoen, J.P.: The probabilistic model checking landscape. In: Proceedings of LICS, pp. 31–46. ACM (2016)
12. Guck, D., Timmer, M., Hatefi, H., Ruijters, E., Stoelinga, M.: Modelling and analysis of markov reward automata. In: Cassez, F., Raskin, J.-F. (eds.) ATVA 2014. LNCS, vol. 8837, pp. 168–184. Springer, Cham (2014). doi:10.1007/978-3-319-11936-6_13
13. Guck, D., Hatefi, H., Hermanns, H., Katoen, J., Timmer, M.: Analysis of timed and long-run objectives for Markov automata. LMCS **10**(3), 1–29 (2014)
14. Budde, C.E., Dehnert, C., Hahn, E.M., Hartmanns, A., Junges, S., Turrini, A.: JANI: quantitative model and tool interaction. In: Legay, A., Margaria, T. (eds.) TACAS 2017. LNCS, vol. 10206, pp. 151–168. Springer, Heidelberg (2017). doi:10.1007/978-3-662-54580-5_9
15. Amparore, E.G., Beccuti, M., Donatelli, S.: (Stochastic) model checking in great-SPN. In: Ciardo, G., Kindler, E. (eds.) PETRI NETS 2014. LNCS, vol. 8489, pp. 354–363. Springer, Cham (2014). doi:10.1007/978-3-319-07734-5_19
16. Schwarick, M., Heiner, M., Rohr, C.: MARCIE - model checking and reachability analysis done efficiently. In: Proceedings of QEST, pp. 91–100. IEEE CS (2011)
17. Eisentraut, C., Hermanns, H., Katoen, J.-P., Zhang, L.: A semantics for every GSPN. In: Colom, J.-M., Desel, J. (eds.) PETRI NETS 2013. LNCS, vol. 7927, pp. 90–109. Springer, Heidelberg (2013). doi:10.1007/978-3-642-38697-8_6
18. Dugan, J.B., Bavuso, S.J., Boyd, M.A.: Dynamic fault-tree models for fault-tolerant computer systems. IEEE Trans. Reliab. **41**(3), 363–377 (1992)
19. Boudali, H., Crouzen, P., Stoelinga, M.I.A.: A rigorous, compositional, and extensible framework for dynamic fault tree analysis. IEEE Trans. Secure Distr. Comput. **7**(2), 128–143 (2010)
20. Volk, M., Junges, S., Katoen, J.-P.: Advancing dynamic fault tree analysis - get succinct state spaces fast and synthesise failure rates. In: Skavhaug, A., Guiochet, J., Bitsch, F. (eds.) SAFECOMP 2016. LNCS, vol. 9922, pp. 253–265. Springer, Cham (2016). doi:10.1007/978-3-319-45477-1_20
21. McIver, A., Morgan, C.: Abstraction, Refinement and Proof for Probabilistic Systems. Monographs in Computer Science. Springer, Heidelberg (2005). doi:10.1007/b138392
22. Gordon, A.D., Henzinger, T.A., Nori, A.V., Rajamani.K.: Probabilistic programming. In: FOSE, pp. 167–181. ACM (2014)
23. Hansson, H., Jonsson, B.: A logic for reasoning about time and reliability. Formal Aspects Comput. **6**(5), 512–535 (1994)
24. Baier, C., Haverkort, B.R., Hermanns, H., Katoen, J.P.: Model-checking algorithms for continuous-time Markov chains. IEEE Trans. Softw. Eng. **29**(6), 524–541 (2003)
25. Brázdil, T., Chatterjee, K., Chmelík, M., Forejt, V., Křetínský, J., Kwiatkowska, M., Parker, D., Ujma, M.: Verification of markov decision processes using learning algorithms. In: Cassez, F., Raskin, J.-F. (eds.) ATVA 2014. LNCS, vol. 8837, pp. 98–114. Springer, Cham (2014). doi:10.1007/978-3-319-11936-6_8
26. Dehnert, C., Junges, S., Jansen, N., Corzilius, F., Volk, M., Bruintjes, H., Katoen, J.-P., Ábrahám, E.: PROPhESY: A PRObabilistic ParamEter SYnthesis Tool. In: Kroening, D., Păsăreanu, C.S. (eds.) CAV 2015. LNCS, vol. 9206, pp. 214–231. Springer, Cham (2015). doi:10.1007/978-3-319-21690-4_13
27. Quatmann, T., Dehnert, C., Jansen, N., Junges, S., Katoen, J.-P.: Parameter synthesis for markov models: faster than ever. In: Artho, C., Legay, A., Peled, D. (eds.) ATVA 2016. LNCS, vol. 9938, pp. 50–67. Springer, Cham (2016). doi:10.1007/978-3-319-46520-3_4

28. CARL Website: http://smtrat.github.io/carl/ (2015)
29. Hahn, E.M., Hermanns, H., Zhang, L.: Probabilistic reachability for parametric Markov models. STTT **13**(1), 3–19 (2010)
30. Haddad, S., Monmege, B.: Reachability in MDPs: refining convergence of value iteration. In: Ouaknine, J., Potapov, I., Worrell, J. (eds.) RP 2014. LNCS, vol. 8762, pp. 125–137. Springer, Cham (2014). doi:10.1007/978-3-319-11439-2_10
31. Wimmer, R., Becker, B.: Correctness issues of symbolic bisimulation computation-for Markov chains. In: Müller-Clostermann, B., Echtle, K., Rathgeb, E.P. (eds.) MMB & DFT 2010. LNCS, vol. 5987, pp. 287–301. Springer, Berlin (2010)
32. Ábrahám, E., Becker, B., Dehnert, C., Jansen, N., Katoen, J.-P., Wimmer, R.: Counterexample generation for discrete-time Markov models: an introductory survey. In: Bernardo, M., Damiani, F., Hähnle, R., Johnsen, E.B., Schaefer, I. (eds.) SFM 2014. LNCS, vol. 8483, pp. 65–121. Springer, Cham (2014). doi:10.1007/978-3-319-07317-0_3
33. Wimmer, R., Jansen, N., Vorpahl, A., Ábrahám, E., Katoen, J.P., Becker, B.: High-level counterexamples for probabilistic automata. LMCS **11**(1), 1–23 (2015)
34. Dehnert, C., Jansen, N., Wimmer, R., Ábrahám, E., Katoen, J.-P.: Fast debugging of PRISM models. In: Cassez, F., Raskin, J.-F. (eds.) ATVA 2014. LNCS, vol. 8837, pp. 146–162. Springer, Cham (2014). doi:10.1007/978-3-319-11936-6_11
35. Aljazzar, H., Leitner-Fischer, F., Leue, S., Simeonov, D.: DiPro - a tool for probabilistic counterexample generation. In: Groce, A., Musuvathi, M. (eds.) SPIN 2011. LNCS, vol. 6823, pp. 183–187. Springer, Heidelberg (2011). doi:10.1007/978-3-642-22306-8_13
36. Jansen, N., Ábrahám, E., Volk, M., Wimmer, R., Katoen, J.P., Becker, B.: The COMICS tool - Computing minimal counterexamples for DTMCs. In: Chakraborty, S., Mukund, M. (eds.) ATVA 2012, vol. 7561, pp. 349–353. Springer, Heidelberg (2012)
37. Guennebaud, G., Jacob, B., et al.: Eigen v3. (2017). http://eigen.tuxfamily.org
38. GMM++ Website: (2015). http://getfem.org/gmm/index.html
39. Daws, C.: Symbolic and parametric model checking of discrete-time Markov chains. In: Liu, Z., Araki, K. (eds.) ICTAC 2004. LNCS, vol. 3407, pp. 280–294. Springer, Heidelberg (2005). doi:10.1007/978-3-540-31862-0_21
40. Gurobi Optimization Inc.: Gurobi optimizer reference manual (2015). http://www.gurobi.com
41. GNU project: Linear programming kit, version 4.6 (2016). http://www.gnu.org/software/glpk/glpk.html
42. Moura, L., Bjørner, N.: Z3: an efficient SMT solver. In: Ramakrishnan, C.R., Rehof, J. (eds.) TACAS 2008. LNCS, vol. 4963, pp. 337–340. Springer, Heidelberg (2008). doi:10.1007/978-3-540-78800-3_24
43. Cimatti, A., Griggio, A., Schaafsma, B.J., Sebastiani, R.: The mathSAT5 SMT solver. In: Piterman, N., Smolka, S.A. (eds.) TACAS 2013. LNCS, vol. 7795, pp. 93–107. Springer, Heidelberg (2013). doi:10.1007/978-3-642-36742-7_7
44. Dräger, K., Forejt, V., Kwiatkowska, M., Parker, D., Ujma, M.: Permissive controller synthesis for probabilistic systems. LMCS **11**(2), 1–34 (2015)
45. Junges, S., Jansen, N., Dehnert, C., Topcu, U., Katoen, J.-P.: Safety-constrained reinforcement learning for MDPs. In: Chechik, M., Raskin, J.-F. (eds.) TACAS 2016. LNCS, vol. 9636, pp. 130–146. Springer, Heidelberg (2016). doi:10.1007/978-3-662-49674-9_8
46. Kwiatkowska, M., Norman, G., Parker, D.: The PRISM benchmark suite. In: Proceedings of QEST, pp. 203–204. IEEE CS (2012)

On Multiphase-Linear Ranking Functions

Amir M. Ben-Amram[1] and Samir Genaim[2(✉)]

[1] School of Computer Science, The Tel-Aviv Academic College, Tel Aviv, Israel
[2] DSIC, Complutense University of Madrid (UCM), Madrid, Spain
genaim@gmail.com

Abstract. Multiphase ranking functions ($M\Phi$RFs) were proposed as a means to prove the termination of a loop in which the computation progresses through a number of "phases", and the progress of each phase is described by a different linear ranking function. Our work provides new insights regarding such functions for loops described by a conjunction of linear constraints (single-path loops). We provide a complete polynomial-time solution to the problem of existence and of synthesis of $M\Phi$RF of bounded depth (number of phases), when variables range over rational or real numbers; a complete solution for the (harder) case that variables are integer, with a matching lower-bound proof, showing that the problem is coNP-complete; and a new theorem which bounds the number of iterations for loops with $M\Phi$RFs. Surprisingly, the bound is linear, even when the variables involved change in non-linear way. We also consider a type of *lexicographic* ranking functions more expressive than types of lexicographic functions for which complete solutions have been given so far. We prove that for the above type of loops, lexicographic functions can be reduced to $M\Phi$RFs, and thus the questions of complexity of detection, synthesis, and iteration bounds are also answered for this class.

1 Introduction

Proving that a program will not go into an infinite loop is one of the most fundamental tasks of program verification, and has been the subject of voluminous research. Perhaps the best known, and often used, technique for proving termination is the *ranking function*. This is a function f that maps program states into the elements of a well-founded ordered set, such that $f(s) > f(s')$ holds whenever state s' follows state s. This implies termination since infinite descent in a well-founded order is impossible.

Unlike termination of programs in general, which is the fundamental example of undecidability, the algorithmic problems of detection (deciding the existence) or generation (synthesis) of a ranking function can well be solvable, given certain choices of the program representation, and the class of ranking function.

This work was funded partially by the Spanish MINECO projects TIN2012-38137 and TIN2015-69175-C4-2-R, and by the CM project S2013/ICE-3006. We thank Mooly Sagiv for providing us with a working space at Tel-Aviv University, which was crucial for completing this work.

© Springer International Publishing AG 2017
R. Majumdar and V. Kunčak (Eds.): CAV 2017, Part II, LNCS 10427, pp. 601–620, 2017.
DOI: 10.1007/978-3-319-63390-9_32

Numerous researchers have proposed such classes, with an eye towards decidability; in some cases the algorithmic problems have been completely settled, and efficient algorithms provided, while other cases remain as open problems. Thus, in designing ranking functions, we look for expressivity (to capture more program behaviors) but also want (efficient) computability. Besides proving termination, some classes of ranking functions also serve to bound the length of the computation (an *iteration bound*), useful in applications such as *cost analysis* (execution-time analysis, resource analysis) and loop optimization [1,2,7,14].

We focus on *single-path linear-constraint loops* (*SLC* loops for short), where a state is described by the values of a finite set of numerical variables, and the effect of a transition (one iteration of the loop) is described by a conjunction of *linear constraints*. We consider the setting of integer-valued variables, as well as rational-valued (or real-valued) variables[1]. Here is an example of this loop representation (a formal definition is in Sect. 2); primed variables $x', y', \dots$ refer to the state following the transition.

$$\texttt{while } (x \geq -z) \texttt{ do } x' = x + y,\ y' = y + z,\ z' = z - 1 \qquad (1)$$

Note that by $x' = x + y$ we mean an equation, not an assignment statement; it is a standard procedure to compile sequential code into such equations (if the operations used are linear), or to approximate it using various techniques.

This constraint representation may be extended to represent branching in the loop body, a so-called *multiple-path loop*; in the current work we do not consider such loops. However, *SLC* loops are important, e.g., in approaches that reduce a question about a whole program to questions about simple loops [10,11,13,16,19]; see [21] for references that show the importance of such loops in other fields.

We assume the "constraint loop" to be given, and do not concern ourselves with the orthogonal topic of extracting such loops from general programs.

Types of Ranking Functions. Several types of ranking functions have been suggested; linear ranking functions (*LRFs*) are probably the most widely used and well-understood. In this case, we seek a function $f(x_1, \dots, x_n) = a_1 x_1 + \cdots + a_n x_n + a_0$, with the rationals as a co-domain, such that (i) $f(\bar{x}) \geq 0$ for any valuation $\bar{x}$ that satisfies the loop constraints (i.e., an enabled state); and (ii) $f(\bar{x}) - f(\bar{x}') \geq 1$ for any transition leading from $\bar{x}$ to $\bar{x}'$. Technically, the rationals are not a well-founded set under the usual order, but we can refer to the partial order $a \succeq b$ if and only if $a \geq 0$ and $a \geq b + 1$, which is well-founded. Given a linear-constraint loop, it is possible to find a linear ranking function (if one exists) using linear programming (*LP*). This method was found by multiple researchers in different contexts and in some alternative versions [9,14,22,24]. Since *LP* has a polynomial-time complexity, most of these methods yield polynomial-time algorithms. This method is sound (any ranking function produced is valid), and complete (if there is a ranking function, it will find one), when variables are

---

[1] For the results in this paper, the real-number case is equivalent to the rational-number case, and in the sequel we refer just to rationals.

assumed to range over the rationals. When variables range over the integers, treating the domain as $\mathbb{Q}$ is safe, but completeness is not guaranteed. Consider the following loop:

$$\texttt{while } (x_2 - x_1 \leq 0,\ x_1 + x_2 \geq 1) \texttt{ do } x_2' = x_2 - 2x_1 + 1,\ x_1' = x_1 \qquad (2)$$

and observe that it does not terminate over the rationals at all (try $x_1 = x_2 = \frac{1}{2}$); but it has a LRF that is valid for all integer valuations, e.g., $f(x_1, x_2) = x_1 + x_2$. Several authors noted this issue, and finally the complexity of a complete solution for the integers was settled by [4], who proved that the detection problem is coNP-*complete* and gave matching algorithms.

However, not all terminating loops have a LRF; and to handle more loops, one may resort to an argument that combines several $LRFs$ to capture a more complex behavior. Two types of such behavior that re-occur in the literature on termination are lexicographic ranking and multiphase ranking.

Lexicographic Ranking. One can prove the termination of a loop by considering a tuple, say a pair $\langle f_1, f_2 \rangle$ of linear functions, such that either f_1 decreases, or f_1 does not change and f_2 decreases. There are some variants of the definition [2, 4, 5, 17] regarding whether both functions have to be non-negative at all times, or "just when necessary." The most permissive definition [17] allows any component to be negative, and technically, it ranks states in the lexicographic extension of the order $\succeq$ mentioned above. We refer to this class as $LLRFs$. For example, the following loop

$$\texttt{while } (x \geq 0, y \leq 10, z \geq 0, z \leq 1) \texttt{ do } x' = x+y+z-10, y' = y+z, z' = 1-z \quad (3)$$

has the $LLRF$ $\langle 4y, 4x - 4z + 1 \rangle$, which is valid only according to [17].

Multiphase Ranking. Consider loop (1) above. Clearly, the loop goes through three phases—in the first, z descends, while the other variables may increase; in the second (which begins once z becomes negative), y decreases; in the last phase (beginning when y becomes negative), x decreases. Note that since there is no lower bound on y or on z, they cannot be used in a LRF; however, each phase is clearly finite, as it is associated with a value that is non-negative and decreasing during that phase. In other words, each phase is linearly ranked. We shall say that this loop has the *multiphase ranking function* ($M\Phi RF$) $\langle z+1, y+1, x \rangle$. The general definition (Sect. 2) allows for an arbitrary number d of linear components; we refer to d as *depth*, intuitively it is the number of phases.

Some loops have multiphase behavior which is not so evident as in the last example. Consider the following loop, that we will discuss further in Sect. 6, with $M\Phi RF$ $\langle x - 4y, x - 2y, x - y \rangle$

$$\texttt{while } (x \geq 1,\ y \geq 1,\ x \geq y,\ 4y \geq x) \texttt{ do } x' = 2x,\ y' = 3y \qquad (4)$$

Technically, under which ordering is a $M\Phi RF$ a ranking function? It is quite easy to see that the pairs used in the examples above descend in the lexicographic extension of $\succeq$. This means that $M\Phi RFs$ are a sub-class of $LLRFs$. Note that, intuitively, a lexicographic ranking function also has "phases", namely, steps where the first component decreases, steps where the second component decreases, etc.; but these phases may alternate an unbounded number of times.

Complete Solutions and Complexity. Complete solutions for $M\Phi$RFs (over the rationals) appear in [18,20]. Both use non-linear constraint solving, and therefore do not achieve a polynomial time complexity. [3] study "eventual linear ranking functions," which are $M\Phi$RFs of depth 2, and pose the questions of a polynomial-time solution and complete solution for the integers as open problems.

In this paper, we provide complete solutions to the existence and synthesis problems for both $M\Phi$RFs and *LLRFs*, for rational and integer *SLC* loops, where the algorithm is parameterized by a depth bound. Over the rationals, the decision problem is PTIME and the synthesis can be done in polynomial time; over the integers, the existence problem is coNP-complete, and our synthesis procedure is deterministic exponential-time.

While such algorithms would be a contribution in itself, we find it even more interesting that our results are mostly based on discovering unexpected *equivalences* between classes of ranking functions. We prove two such results: Theorem 3 in Sect. 4 shows that *LLRFs* are not stronger than $M\Phi$RFs for *SLC* loops. Thus, the complete solution for *LLRFs* is just to solve for $M\Phi$RFs (for the loop (3), we find the $M\Phi$RF $\langle 4y + x - z, 4x - 4z + 4\rangle$). Theorem 1 in Sect. 3 shows that one can further reduce the search for $M\Phi$RFs to a proper sub-class, called *nested* $M\Phi$RFs. This class was introduced in [18] because its definition is simpler and allows for a polynomial-time solution (over $\mathbb{Q}$)[2].

Our complete solution for the *integers* is also a reduction—transforming the problem so that solving over the rationals cannot give false alarms. The transformation consists of computing the *integer hull* of the transition polyhedron. This transformation is well-known in the case of *LRFs* [4,12,14], so it was a natural approach to try, however its proof in the case of $M\Phi$RFs is more involved.

We also make a contribution towards the use of $M\Phi$RFs in deriving *iteration bounds*. As the loop (1) demonstrates, it is possible for the variables that control subsequent phases to grow (at a polynomial rate) during the first phase. Nonetheless, we prove that *any $M\Phi$RF implies a linear bound on the number of iterations* for a *SLC* loop (in terms of the initial values of the variables). Thus, it is also the case that any *LLRF* implies a linear bound.

An open problem raised by our work is whether one can precompute a bound on the depth of a $M\Phi$RF for a given loop (if there is one); for example [4] prove a depth bound of n (the number of variables) on their notion of *LLRFs* (which is more restrictive); however their class is known to be weaker than $M\Phi$RFs and *LLRFs*. In Sect. 6 we discuss this problem.

The article is organized as follows. Section 2 gives precise definitions and necessary background. Sections 3 and 4 give our equivalence results for different types of ranking functions (over the rationals) and the algorithmic implications.

---

[2] This definition is also implicit in [6], where multi-path loops are considered, but each path should have a nested $M\Phi$RF.

Section 5 covers the integer setting, Sect. 6 discusses depth bounds, Sect. 7 discusses the iteration bound, and Sect. 8 concludes. For closely related work, see the above-mentioned references, while for further background on algorithmic and complexity aspects of linear/lexicographic ranking, we refer the reader to [4].

2 Preliminaries

In this section we define the class of loops we study, the type of ranking functions, and recall some definitions, and properties, regarding (integer) polyhedra.

Single-Path Linear-Constraint Loops. A *single-path* linear-constraint loop (*SLC* for short) over n variables $x_1, \ldots, x_n$ has the form

$$\texttt{while } (B\mathbf{x} \leq \mathbf{b}) \texttt{ do } A\begin{pmatrix} \mathbf{x} \\ \mathbf{x}' \end{pmatrix} \leq \mathbf{c}$$

where $\mathbf{x} = (x_1, \ldots, x_n)^{\mathsf{T}}$ and $\mathbf{x}' = (x_1', \ldots, x_n')^{\mathsf{T}}$ are column vectors, and for some $p, q > 0$, $B \in \mathbb{Q}^{p \times n}$, $A \in \mathbb{Q}^{q \times 2n}$, $\mathbf{b} \in \mathbb{Q}^p$, $\mathbf{c} \in \mathbb{Q}^q$. The constraint $B\mathbf{x} \leq \mathbf{b}$ is called *the loop condition* (a.k.a. the loop guard) and the other constraint is called *the update*. We say that the loop is a *rational loop* if $\mathbf{x}$ and $\mathbf{x}'$ range over $\mathbb{Q}^n$, and that it is an *integer loop* if they range over $\mathbb{Z}^n$. One could also allow variables to take any real-number value, but as long as the constraints are expressed by rational numbers, our results for $\mathbb{Q}$ also apply to $\mathbb{R}$.

We say that there is a transition from a state $\mathbf{x} \in \mathbb{Q}^n$ to a state $\mathbf{x}' \in \mathbb{Q}^n$, if $\mathbf{x}$ satisfies the condition and $\mathbf{x}$ and $\mathbf{x}'$ satisfy the update. A transition can be seen as a point $\begin{pmatrix} \mathbf{x} \\ \mathbf{x}' \end{pmatrix} \in \mathbb{Q}^{2n}$, where its first n components correspond to $\mathbf{x}$ and its last n components to $\mathbf{x}'$. For ease of notation, we denote $\begin{pmatrix} \mathbf{x} \\ \mathbf{x}' \end{pmatrix}$ by $\mathbf{x}''$. The set of all transitions $\mathbf{x}'' \in \mathbb{Q}^{2n}$, of a given *SLC* loop, will be denoted by $\mathcal{Q}$ and is specified by the constraints in the loop body and update. It is a polyhedron (see below), which we call *the transition polyhedron*. For the purpose of this article, the essence of the loop is this polyhedron, even if the loop is presented in a more readable form as above.

Multi-phase Ranking Functions. An affine function $f : \mathbb{Q}^n \to \mathbb{Q}$ is of the form $f(\mathbf{x}) = \vec{a} \cdot \mathbf{x} + a_0$ where $\vec{a} \in \mathbb{Q}^n$ is a row vector and $a_0 \in \mathbb{Q}$. For a given function f, we define the function $\Delta f : \mathbb{Q}^{2n} \mapsto \mathbb{Q}$ as $\Delta f(\mathbf{x}'') = f(\mathbf{x}) - f(\mathbf{x}')$.

Definition 1. *Given a set of transitions $T \subseteq \mathbb{Q}^{2n}$, we say that $\tau = \langle f_1, \ldots, f_d \rangle$ is a MΦRF (of depth d) for T if for every $\mathbf{x}'' \in T$ there is an index $i \in [1, d]$ such that:*

$$\forall j \leq i. \ \Delta f_j(\mathbf{x}'') \geq 1, \tag{5}$$
$$f_i(\mathbf{x}) \geq 0, \tag{6}$$
$$\forall j < i. \quad f_j(\mathbf{x}) \leq 0. \tag{7}$$

We say that $\mathbf{x}''$ is ranked by f_i (for the minimal such i).

It is not hard to see that this definition, for $d = 1$, means that f_1 is a linear ranking function, and for $d > 1$, it implies that as long as $f_1(\mathbf{x}) \geq 0$, transition $\mathbf{x}''$ must be ranked by f_1, and when $f_1(\mathbf{x}) < 0$, $\langle f_2, \ldots, f_d \rangle$ becomes a $M\Phi RF$. This agrees with the intuitive notion of "phases." We further note that, for loops specified by polyhedra, making the inequality (7) strict results in the same class of ranking functions (we chose the definition that is easier to work with), and, similarly, we can replace (5) by $\Delta f_j(\mathbf{x}'') > 0$, obtaining an equivalent definition (up to multiplication of the f_i by some constants). We say that τ is *irredundant* if removing any component invalidates the $M\Phi RF$.

The decision problem *Existence of a $M\Phi RF$* asks to determine whether a given SLC loop admits a $M\Phi RF$. The *bounded* decision problem, denoted by $BM\Phi RF(\mathbb{Q})$ and $BM\Phi RF(\mathbb{Z})$, restricts the search to $M\Phi RFs$ of depth at most d, where the parameter d is part of the input.

Polyhedra. A *rational convex polyhedron* $\mathcal{P} \subseteq \mathbb{Q}^n$ (*polyhedron* for short) is the set of solutions of a set of inequalities $A\mathbf{x} \leq \mathbf{b}$, namely $\mathcal{P} = \{\mathbf{x} \in \mathbb{Q}^n \mid A\mathbf{x} \leq \mathbf{b}\}$, where $A \in \mathbb{Q}^{m \times n}$ is a rational matrix of n columns and m rows, $\mathbf{x} \in \mathbb{Q}^n$ and $\mathbf{b} \in \mathbb{Q}^m$ are column vectors of n and m rational values respectively. We say that $\mathcal{P}$ is specified by $A\mathbf{x} \leq \mathbf{b}$. If $\mathbf{b} = \mathbf{0}$, then $\mathcal{P}$ is a *cone*. The set of *recession directions* of a polyhedron $\mathcal{P}$ specified by $A\mathbf{x} \leq \mathbf{b}$, also know as its *recession cone*, is the set $\{\mathbf{y} \in \mathbb{Q}^n \mid A\mathbf{y} \leq \mathbf{0}\}$. For a given polyhedron $\mathcal{P} \subseteq \mathbb{Q}^n$ we let $I(\mathcal{P})$ be $\mathcal{P} \cap \mathbb{Z}^n$, i.e., the set of integer points of $\mathcal{P}$. The *integer hull* of $\mathcal{P}$, commonly denoted by $\mathcal{P}_I$, is defined as the convex hull of $I(\mathcal{P})$, i.e., every rational point of $\mathcal{P}_I$ is a convex combination of integer points. It is known that $\mathcal{P}_I$ is also a polyhedron, and that $\texttt{rec.cone}(\mathcal{P}) = \texttt{rec.cone}(\mathcal{P}_I)$ [23, Theorem 16.1, p. 231]. An *integer polyhedron* is a polyhedron $\mathcal{P}$ such that $\mathcal{P} = \mathcal{P}_I$. We also say that $\mathcal{P}$ is *integral*.

Next we state a lemma that is fundamental for many proofs in this article. Given a polyhedron $\mathcal{P}$, the lemma shows that if a disjunction of constraints of the form $f_i > 0$, or $f_i \geq 0$, holds over $\mathcal{P}$, then a certain conic combination of these functions is non-negative over $\mathcal{P}$.

Lemma 1. *Fix $\rhd$ to be either $>$ or $\geq$. Given a polyhedron $\mathcal{P} \neq \emptyset$, and linear functions $f_1, \ldots, f_k$ such that*

(i) $\mathbf{x} \in \mathcal{P} \rightarrow f_1(\mathbf{x}) \rhd 0 \vee \cdots \vee f_{k-1}(\mathbf{x}) \rhd 0 \vee f_k(\mathbf{x}) \geq 0$
(ii) $\mathbf{x} \in \mathcal{P} \nrightarrow f_1(\mathbf{x}) \rhd 0 \vee \cdots \vee f_{k-1}(\mathbf{x}) \rhd 0$

There exist non-negative constants $\mu_1, \ldots, \mu_{k-1}$ such that $\mathbf{x} \in \mathcal{P} \rightarrow \mu_1 f_1(\mathbf{x}) + \cdots + \mu_{k-1} f_{k-1}(\mathbf{x}) + f_k(\mathbf{x}) \geq 0$.

Proof. We prove the lemma in one version; the other is very similar. Specifically, we assume:

(i) $\mathbf{x} \in \mathcal{P} \rightarrow f_1(\mathbf{x}) > 0 \vee \cdots \vee f_{k-1}(\mathbf{x}) > 0 \vee f_k(\mathbf{x}) \geq 0$
(ii) $\mathbf{x} \in \mathcal{P} \nrightarrow f_1(\mathbf{x}) > 0 \vee \cdots \vee f_{k-1}(\mathbf{x}) > 0$.

Let $\mathcal{P}$ be $B\mathbf{x} \leq \mathbf{c}$, $f_i = \vec{a}_i \cdot \mathbf{x} - b_i$, then (i) is equivalent to infeasibility of

$$B\mathbf{x} \leq \mathbf{c} \wedge A\mathbf{x} \leq \mathbf{b} \wedge \vec{a}_k \cdot \mathbf{x} < b_k \tag{8}$$

where A consists of the $k-1$ rows $\vec{a}_i$, and $\mathbf{b}$ of corresponding b_i. However, $B\mathbf{x} \leq \mathbf{c} \wedge A\mathbf{x} \leq \mathbf{b}$ is assumed to be feasible.

According to Motzkin's transposition theorem [23, Corollary 7.1k, p. 94], this implies that there are row vectors $\vec{\lambda}, \vec{\lambda}' \geq 0$ and a constant $\mu \geq 0$ such that the following is true:

$$\vec{\lambda}B + \vec{\lambda}'A + \mu a_k = 0 \wedge \vec{\lambda}\mathbf{c} + \vec{\lambda}'\mathbf{b} + \mu b_k \leq 0 \wedge (\mu \neq 0 \vee \vec{\lambda}\mathbf{c} + \vec{\lambda}'\mathbf{b} + \mu b_k < 0) \tag{9}$$

Now, if (9) is true, then for all $\mathbf{x} \in \mathcal{P}$,

$$\left(\sum_i \lambda_i' f_i(\mathbf{x})\right) + \mu f_k(\mathbf{x}) = \vec{\lambda}'A\mathbf{x} - \vec{\lambda}'\mathbf{b} + \mu a_k\mathbf{x} - \mu b_k$$

$$= -\vec{\lambda}B\mathbf{x} - \vec{\lambda}'\mathbf{b} - \mu b_k \geq -\vec{\lambda}\mathbf{c} - \vec{\lambda}'\mathbf{b} - \mu b_k \geq 0$$

where if $\mu = 0$, the last inequality must be strict. However, if $\mu = 0$, then $\vec{\lambda}B + \vec{\lambda}'A = 0$, so by feasibility of $B\mathbf{x} \leq \mathbf{c}$ and $A\mathbf{x} \leq \mathbf{b}$, this implies $\vec{\lambda}\mathbf{c} + \vec{\lambda}'\mathbf{b} \geq 0$, a contradiction. Thus, $(\sum_i \lambda_i' f_i) + \mu f_k \geq 0$ on $\mathcal{P}$ and $\mu > 0$. Dividing by μ we obtain the conclusion of the lemma. $\qquad \square$

3   Complexity of Synthesis of $M\Phi$RFs over the Rationals

In this section we study the complexity of deciding if a given rational SLC loop has a $M\Phi$RF of depth d, and show that this can be done in polynomial time. These results follow from an equivalence between $M\Phi$RFs and a sub-class called *nested ranking functions* [18]. In the rest of this article we assume a given SLC loop specified by a transition polyhedron $\mathcal{Q}$. The complexity results are in terms of the bit-size of the a constraint representation of $\mathcal{Q}$ (see Sect. 2 of [4]).

Definition 2. *A d-tuple $\tau = \langle f_1, \ldots, f_d \rangle$ is a* nested ranking function *for $\mathcal{Q}$ if the following are satisfied for all $\mathbf{x}'' \in \mathcal{Q}$ (where $f_0 \equiv 0$ for uniformity)*

$$f_d(\mathbf{x}) \geq 0 \tag{10}$$

$$(\Delta f_i(\mathbf{x}'') - 1) + f_{i-1}(\mathbf{x}) \geq 0 \qquad \text{for all } i = 1, \ldots, d. \tag{11}$$

It is easy to see that a nested ranking function is a $M\Phi$RF. Indeed, f_1 is decreasing, and when it becomes negative f_2 starts to decrease, etc. Moreover, the loop must stop by the time that f_d becomes negative, since f_d is non-negative over $\mathcal{Q}$ (more precisely, on the projection of $\mathcal{Q}$ to its first n coordinates—as f_i is a function of state).

Example 1. Consider loop (1) (at Page 2). It has the $M\Phi$RF $\langle z+1, y+1, x \rangle$ which is not nested because, among other things, last component x might be negative, e.g., for the state $x = -1, y = 0, z = 1$. However, it has the nested ranking function $\langle z+1, y+1, z+x \rangle$, which is $M\Phi$RF.

The above example shows that there are $M\Phi RFs$ which are not nested ranking functions, however, next we show that if a loop has a $M\Phi RF$ then it has a (possibly different) nested ranking function of the same depth. We first state an auxiliary lemma, and then prove the main result.

Lemma 2. *Let $\tau = \langle f_1, \dots, f_d \rangle$ be an irredundant $M\Phi RF$ for Q, such that $\langle f_2, \dots, f_d \rangle$ is a nested ranking function for $Q' = Q \cap \{ \mathbf{x}'' \in \mathbb{Q}^{2n} \mid f_1(\mathbf{x}) \leq 0 \}$. Then there is a nested ranking function of depth d for Q.*

Proof. First recall that, by definition of $M\Phi RF$, we have $\Delta f_1(\mathbf{x}'') \geq 1$ for any $\mathbf{x}'' \in Q$, and since $\langle f_2, \dots, f_d \rangle$ is a nested ranking function for Q' we have

$$\mathbf{x}'' \in Q' \rightarrow f_d(\mathbf{x}) \geq 0$$
$$\mathbf{x}'' \in Q' \rightarrow (\Delta f_2(\mathbf{x}'') - 1) \geq 0 \land$$
$$(\Delta f_3(\mathbf{x}'') - 1) + f_2(\mathbf{x}'') \geq 0 \land \qquad (12)$$
$$\cdots$$
$$(\Delta f_d(\mathbf{x}'') - 1) + f_{d-1}(\mathbf{x}'') \geq 0$$

Next we construct a nested ranking function $\langle f_1', \dots, f_d' \rangle$ for Q, i.e., such that (10) is satisfied for f_d', and (11) is satisfied for each f_i' and f_{i-1}' — we refer to the instance of (11) for a specific i as (11_i).

We start with the condition (10). If f_d is non-negative over Q we let $f_d' = f_d$, otherwise, clearly $\mathbf{x}'' \in Q \rightarrow f_d(\mathbf{x}) \geq 0 \lor f_1(\mathbf{x}) > 0$. Then, by Lemma 1 there is a constant $\mu_d > 0$ such that $\mathbf{x}'' \in Q \rightarrow f_d(\mathbf{x}) + \mu_d f_1(\mathbf{x}) \geq 0$ and we define $f_d'(\mathbf{x}) = f_d(\mathbf{x}) + \mu_d f_1(\mathbf{x})$. Clearly (10) holds for f_d'.

Next, we handle the conditions (11_i) for $i = d, \dots, 3$ in this order. When we handle (11_i), we shall define $f_{i-1}'(\mathbf{x}) = f_{i-1}(\mathbf{x}) + \mu_{i-1} f_1(\mathbf{x})$ for some $\mu_{i-1} \geq 0$. Note that f_d' has this form. Suppose we have computed $f_d', \dots, f_i'$. The construction of f_{i-1}' will ensure that (11_i) holds over Q. From (12) we know that

$$\mathbf{x}'' \in Q' \rightarrow (\Delta f_i(\mathbf{x}'') - 1) + f_{i-1}(\mathbf{x}'') \geq 0.$$

Now since $f_i'(\mathbf{x}) = f_i(\mathbf{x}) + \mu_i f_1(\mathbf{x})$, and $\Delta f_1(\mathbf{x}'') \geq 1$ over Q, we have

$$\mathbf{x}'' \in Q' \rightarrow (\Delta f_i'(\mathbf{x}'') - 1) + f_{i-1}(\mathbf{x}'') \geq 0.$$

Now if $(\Delta f_i'(\mathbf{x}'') - 1) + f_{i-1}(\mathbf{x}'') \geq 0$ holds over Q as well, we let $f_{i-1}' = f_{i-1}$. Otherwise, we have

$$\mathbf{x}'' \in Q \rightarrow (\Delta f_i'(\mathbf{x}'') - 1) + f_{i-1}(\mathbf{x}) \geq 0 \lor f_1(\mathbf{x}) > 0,$$

and by Lemma 1 there is $\mu_{i-1} > 0$ such that

$$\mathbf{x}'' \in Q \rightarrow (\Delta f_i'(\mathbf{x}'') - 1) + f_{i-1}(\mathbf{x}) + \mu_{i-1} f_1(\mathbf{x}) \geq 0.$$

In this case, we let $f_{i-1}'(\mathbf{x}) = f_{i-1}(\mathbf{x}) + \mu_{i-1} f_1(\mathbf{x})$. Clearly (11_i) holds.

We proceed to (11_2). From (12) we know that

$$\mathbf{x}'' \in Q' \rightarrow (\Delta f_2(\mathbf{x}'') - 1) \geq 0.$$

Since $f_2'(\mathbf{x}) = f_2(\mathbf{x}) + \mu_2 f_1(\mathbf{x})$ and $\Delta f_1(\mathbf{x}'') \geq 1$ we have

$$\mathbf{x}'' \in \mathcal{Q}' \rightarrow (\Delta f_2'(\mathbf{x}'') - 1) \geq 0.$$

Next, by definition of $\mathcal{Q}'$ and the Lemma's assumption we have

$$\mathbf{x}'' \in \mathcal{Q} \rightarrow (\Delta f_2'(\mathbf{x}'') - 1) \geq 0 \vee f_1(\mathbf{x}) > 0$$

and we also know that $(\Delta f_2'(\mathbf{x}'') - 1) \geq 0$ does not hold over $\mathcal{Q}$, because then f_1 would be redundant. Now by Lemma 1 there is $\mu_1 > 0$ such that

$$\mathbf{x}'' \in \mathcal{Q} \rightarrow (\Delta f_2'(\mathbf{x}'') - 1) + \mu_1 f_1(\mathbf{x}) \geq 0.$$

We let $f_1'(\mathbf{x}) = \mu_1 f_1(\mathbf{x})$. For ($11_1$) we need to show that $\Delta f_1'(\mathbf{x}'') - 1 \geq 0$ holds over $\mathcal{Q}$, which clearly holds if $\mu_1 \geq 1$ since $\Delta f_1(\mathbf{x}'') \geq 1$; otherwise we multiply all f_i' by $\frac{1}{\mu_1}$, which does not affect any (11_i) and makes (11_1) true.   □

Theorem 1. *If $\mathcal{Q}$ has a MΦRF of depth d, then it has a nested ranking function of depth at most d.*

Proof. The proof is by induction on d. We assume a MΦRF $\langle f_1, \ldots, f_d \rangle$ for $\mathcal{Q}$. For $d = 1$ there is no difference between a general MΦRF and a nested one. For $d > 1$, we consider $\langle f_2, \ldots, f_d \rangle$ as a MΦRF for $\mathcal{Q}' = \mathcal{Q} \cap \{\mathbf{x}'' \in \mathbb{Q}^{2n} \mid f_1(\mathbf{x}) \leq 0\}$, we apply the induction hypothesis to turn $\langle f_2, \ldots, f_d \rangle$ into a nested MΦRF. Either f_1 becomes redundant, or we can apply Lemma 2.   □

The above theorem gives us a complete algorithm for the synthesis of MΦRFs of a given depth d for $\mathcal{Q}$, namely, just synthesize a nested MΦRF.

Theorem 2. *BMΦRF($\mathbb{Q}$) ∈ PTIME.*

Proof. We describe, concisely, how to determine if a nested MΦRF exists, and then synthesize one, in polynomial time (this actually appears in [18]). Given $\mathcal{Q}$, our goal is to find $f_1, \ldots, f_d$ such that (10), (11) hold. If we take just one of the conjuncts, our task is to find coefficients for the functions involved (f_d, or f_i and f_{i-1}), such that the desired inequality is implied by $\mathcal{Q}$. Using Farkas' lemma [23], this problem can be formulated as a *LP* problem, where the coefficients we seek are unknowns. By conjoing all these *LP* problems, we obtain a single *LP* problem, of polynomial size, whose solution—if there is one—provides the coefficients of all the f_i; and if there is no solution, then no nested MΦRF exists. Since *LP* is polynomial-time, this procedure has polynomial time complexity.   □

Clearly, if d is considered as constant, then BMΦRF($\mathbb{Q}$) is polynomial in the bit-size of $\mathcal{Q}$. When considering d as variable, then the complexity is polynomial in the bit-size of $\mathcal{Q}$ plus d—equivalently, it is polynomial in the bit-size of the input if we assume that d is given in unary representation (which is a reasonable assumption since d describes the number of components of the MΦRF sought).

4 Multiphase vs Lexicographic-Linear Ranking Functions

$M\Phi$RFs are similar to $LLRFs$, and a natural question is: which one is more powerful for proving termination of SLC loops? In this section we show that they have the same power, by proving that an SLC has a $M\Phi$RF if and only if it has a $LLRF$. We first note that there are several definitions for $LLRFs$ [2,4,5,17]. The following is the most general [17].

Definition 3. *Given a set of transitions $T \subseteq \mathbb{Q}^{2n}$, we say that $\langle f_1, \ldots, f_d \rangle$ is a LLRF (of depth d) for T if for every $\mathbf{x}'' \in T$ there is an index i such that:*

$$\forall j < i. \; \Delta f_j(\mathbf{x}'') \geq 0, \tag{13}$$
$$\Delta f_i(\mathbf{x}'') \geq 1, \tag{14}$$
$$f_i(\mathbf{x}) \geq 0, \tag{15}$$

We say that $\mathbf{x}''$ is ranked by f_i (for the minimal such i).

Regarding other definitions: [4] requires $f_j(\mathbf{x}) \geq 0$ for all f_j with $j \leq i$, and [2] requires it for all components. Actually [2] shows that an SLC loop has a $LLRF$ according to their definition if and only if it has a LRF, which is not the case of [4]. The definition in [5] (which do not present here) is equivalent to a LRF when considering SLC loops, as their main interest is in multipath loops.

It is easy to see that a $M\Phi$RF is also a $LLRF$ as in Definition 3. Next we show that for SLC loops any $LLRF$ can be converted to a $M\Phi$RF, proving that these classes of ranking functions have the same power for SLC loops. We start with an auxiliary lemma.

Lemma 3. *Let f be a non-negative linear function over $\mathbb{Q}$. If $\mathbb{Q}' = \mathbb{Q} \cap \{\mathbf{x}'' \mid \Delta f(\mathbf{x}'') \leq 0\}$ has a $M\Phi$RF of depth d, then $\mathbb{Q}$ has one of depth at most $d + 1$.*

Proof. Note that appending f to a $M\Phi$RF τ of $\mathbb{Q}'$ does not always produce a $M\Phi$RF, since the components of τ are not guaranteed to decrease over $\mathbb{Q} \setminus \mathbb{Q}'$. Let $\tau = \langle g_1, \ldots, g_d \rangle$ be a $M\Phi$RF for $\mathbb{Q}'$, we construct a $M\Phi$RF $\langle g_1', \ldots, g_d', f \rangle$ for $\mathbb{Q}$. If g_1 is decreasing over $\mathbb{Q}$, we define $g_1'(\mathbf{x}) = g_1(\mathbf{x})$. Otherwise, we have

$$\mathbf{x}'' \in \mathbb{Q} \to \Delta f(\mathbf{x}'') > 0 \lor \Delta g_1(\mathbf{x}'') \geq 1.$$

Therefore, by Lemma 1, we can construct $g_1'(\mathbf{x}) = g_1(\mathbf{x}) + \mu f(\mathbf{x})$ such that $\mathbf{x}'' \in \mathbb{Q} \to \Delta g_1'(\mathbf{x}'') \geq 1$. Moreover, since f is non-negative, g_1' is non-negative on the transitions on which g_1 is non-negative. If $d > 1$, we proceed with $\mathbb{Q}^{(1)} = \mathbb{Q} \cap \{\mathbf{x}'' \mid g_1'(\mathbf{x}) \leq (-1)\}$. Note that these transitions must be ranked, in $\mathbb{Q}'$, by $\langle g_2, \ldots, g_d \rangle$. If g_2 is decreasing over $\mathbb{Q}^{(1)}$, let $g_2' = g_2$, otherwise

$$\mathbf{x}'' \in \mathbb{Q}^{(1)} \to \Delta f(\mathbf{x}'') > 0 \lor \Delta g_2(\mathbf{x}'') \geq 1,$$

and again by Lemma 1 we can construct the desired g_2'. In general for any $j \leq d$ we construct g_{j+1}' such that $\Delta g_{j+1}' \geq 1$ over

$$\mathbb{Q}^{(j)} = \mathbb{Q} \cap \{\mathbf{x}'' \in \mathbb{Q}^{2n} \mid g_1'(\mathbf{x}) \leq (-1) \land \cdots \land g_j'(\mathbf{x}) \leq (-1)\}$$

and $\mathbf{x}'' \in \mathcal{Q} \wedge g_j(\mathbf{x}) \geq 0 \rightarrow g'_j(\mathbf{x}) \geq 0$. Finally we define

$$\mathcal{Q}^{(d)} = \mathcal{Q} \cap \{\mathbf{x}'' \in \mathbb{Q}^{2n} \mid g'_1(\mathbf{x}) \leq (-1) \wedge g'_d(\mathbf{x}) \leq (-1)\},$$

each transition $\mathbf{x}'' \in \mathcal{Q}^{(d)}$ must satisfy $\Delta f(\mathbf{x}'') > 0$, and in such case $\Delta f(\mathbf{x}'')$ must have a minimum $c > 0$ since $\mathcal{Q}^{(d)}$ is a polyhedron. Without loss of generality we assume $c \geq 1$, otherwise take $\frac{1}{c}f$ instead of f. Now $\tau' = \langle g'_1+1, \ldots, g'_d+1, f \rangle$ is a $M\Phi RF$ for $\mathcal{Q}$. Note that if we arrive to $\mathcal{Q}^{(j)}$ that is empty, we can stop since we already have a $M\Phi RF$. □

In what follows, by a *weak LLRF* we mean the class of ranking functions obtained by changing condition (14) to $\Delta f_i(\mathbf{x}'') > 0$. Clearly it is more general than *LLRFs*, and as we will see next it suffices to guarantee termination, since we show how to convert them to $M\Phi RFs$. We prefer to use this class as it simplifies the proof for the integer case that we present in Sect. 5.

Lemma 4. *Let $\langle f_1, \ldots, f_d \rangle$ be a* weak *LLRF for $\mathcal{Q}$. There is a linear function g that is positive over $\mathcal{Q}$, and decreasing on (at least) the same transitions of f_i, for some $1 \leq i \leq d$.*

Proof. If any f_i is positive over $\mathcal{Q}$, we take $g = f_i$. Otherwise, we have $\mathbf{x}'' \in \mathcal{Q} \rightarrow f_1(\mathbf{x}) \geq 0 \vee \cdots \vee f_d(\mathbf{x}) \geq 0$ since every transition is ranked by some f_i. If this implication satisfies the conditions of Lemma 1 then we can construct $g(\mathbf{x}) = f_d(\mathbf{x}) + \sum_{i=1}^{d-1} \mu_i f_i(\mathbf{x})$ that is non-negative over $\mathcal{Q}$, and, moreover, decreases on the transitions ranked by f_d. If the conditions of Lemma 1 are not satisfied, then the second condition must be false, that is, $\mathbf{x}'' \in \mathcal{Q} \rightarrow f_1(\mathbf{x}) \geq 0 \vee \cdots \vee f_{d-1}(\mathbf{x}) \geq 0$. Now we repeat the same reasoning as above for this implication. Eventually we either construct g that corresponds for some f_i as above, or we arrive to $\mathbf{x}'' \in \mathcal{Q} \rightarrow f_1(\mathbf{x}) \geq 0$, and then take $g = f_1$. □

Theorem 3. *If $\mathcal{Q}$ has a weak LLRF of depth d, it has a $M\Phi RF$ of depth d.*

Proof. Let $\langle f_1, \ldots, f_d \rangle$ be a weak *LLRF* for $\mathcal{Q}$. We construct a corresponding $M\Phi RF$. The proof is by induction on the depth d of the *LLRF*. For $d = 1$ it is clear since it is an *LRF*.[3] Now let $d > 1$, by Lemma 4 we can find g that is positive over $\mathcal{Q}$ and decreasing at least on the same transitions as f_i. Now $\langle f_1, \ldots, f_{i-1}, f_{i+1}, \ldots, f_d \rangle$ is a weak *LLRF* of depth $d - 1$ for $\mathcal{Q}' = \mathcal{Q} \cap \{\mathbf{x}'' \mid \Delta g(\mathbf{x}'') \leq 0\}$. By the induction hypothesis we can construct a weak $M\Phi RF$ for $\mathcal{Q}'$ of depth $d - 1$, and by Lemma 3 we can lift it to one of depth d for $\mathcal{Q}$. □

Example 2. Let $\mathcal{Q}$ be the transition polyhedron of the loop (3) (on Page 3), which admits the *LLRF* $\langle 4y, 4x - 4z + 4 \rangle$, and note that it is not a $M\Phi RF$. Following the proof of above theorem, we can convert it to the $M\Phi RF$ $\langle 4y + x - z, 4x - 4z + 4 \rangle$.

---

[3] If $\Delta f_i(\mathbf{x}'') > 0$ holds over $\mathcal{Q}$, then there must be $c > 0$ such that $\Delta f_i(\mathbf{x}'') \geq c$ holds over $\mathcal{Q}$. This is because a bounded LP problem (with non-strict inequalities only) attains its extremal value [23, p. 92].

5 $M\Phi$RFs and *LLRFs* over the Integers

The procedure of Sect. 3 for synthesizing $M\Phi$RFs, i.e., use LP to synthesize a nested ranking function, is complete for rational loops but not for integer loops. That is because it might be the case that $I(\mathcal{Q})$ has a $M\Phi$RF but $\mathcal{Q}$ does not.

Example 3. Consider the loop

while $(x_2 - x_1 \leq 0, x_1 + x_2 \geq 1, x_3 \geq 0)$ do $x_2' = x_2 - 2x_1 + 1; x_3' = x_3 + 10x_2 + 9$

When interpreted over the integers, it has the $M\Phi$RF $\langle 10x_2, x_3 \rangle$. However, when interpreted over the rationals, the loop does not even terminate, e.g., for $(\frac{1}{2}, \frac{1}{2}, 0)$.

For *LRFs*, completeness for the integer case was achieved by reducing the problem to the rational case, using the integer hull $\mathcal{Q}_I$ [4,12]. In fact, it is quite easy to see why this reduction works for *LRFs*, as the requirements that a *LRF* has to satisfy are a conjunction of linear inequalities and if they are satisfied by $I(\mathcal{Q})$, they will be satisfied by convex combinations of such points, i.e., $\mathcal{Q}_I$.

Since we have reduced the problem of finding a $M\Phi$RF to finding a nested ranking function, and the requirements from a nested ranking function are conjunctions of linear inequalities that should be implied by $\mathcal{Q}$, it is tempting to assume that this argument applies also for $M\Phi$RFs. However, to justify the use of nested functions, specifically in proving Lemma 2, we relied on Lemma 1, which we applied to $\mathcal{Q}$ (it is quite easy to see that the lemma fails if instead of quantifying over a polyhedron, one quantifies only on its integer points). This means that we did not prove that the existence of a $M\Phi$RF for $I(\mathcal{Q})$ implies the existence of a nested ranking function over $I(\mathcal{Q})$. A similar observation also holds for the results of Sect. 4, where we proved that any (weak) *LLRF* can be converted to a $M\Phi$RF. Those results are valid only for rational loops, since in the corresponding proofs we used Lemma 1.

In this section we show that reduction of the integer case to the rational one, via the integer hull, does work also for $M\Phi$RFs, and for converting *LLRFs* to $M\Phi$RFs, thus extending our result to integer loops. We do so by showing that if $I(\mathcal{Q})$ has a weak *LLRF*, then $\mathcal{Q}_I$ has a weak *LLRF* (over the rationals).

Theorem 4. *Let* $\langle f_1, \ldots, f_d \rangle$ *be a weak LLRF for* $I(\mathcal{Q})$. *There are constants* $c_1, \ldots, c_d$ *such that* $\langle f_1 + c_1, \ldots, f_d + c_d \rangle$ *is a weak LLRF for* $\mathcal{Q}_I$.

Proof. The proof is by induction on d. The base case, $d = 1$, concerns a *LRF*, and as already mentioned, is trivial (and $c_1 = 0$). For $d > 1$, define:

$$\boxed{\mathcal{Q}' = \mathcal{Q}_I \cap \{\mathbf{x}'' \in \mathbb{Q}^{2n} \mid f_1(\mathbf{x}) \leq -1\}} \quad \boxed{\mathcal{Q}'' = \mathcal{Q}_I \cap \{\mathbf{x}'' \in \mathbb{Q}^{2n} \mid \Delta f_1(\mathbf{x}'') = 0\}}$$

Note that $\mathcal{Q}'$ includes only integer points of $\mathcal{Q}_I$ that are not ranked at the first component, due to violating $f_1(\mathbf{x}) \geq 0$. By changing the first component into $f_1 + 1$, we take care of points where $-1 < f_1(\mathbf{x}) < 0$. Thus we will have that for every integer point $\mathbf{x}'' \in \mathcal{Q}$, if it is not in $\mathcal{Q}'$, then the first component is non-negative, and otherwise $\mathbf{x}''$ is ranked by $\langle f_2, \ldots, f_d \rangle$. Similarly $\mathcal{Q}''$ includes all the integer points of $\mathcal{Q}_I$ that are not ranked by the first component due to violating $\Delta f_1(\mathbf{x}'') > 0$. Note also that $\mathcal{Q}''$ is integral, since it is a face of $\mathcal{Q}_I$. On the other hand, $\mathcal{Q}'$ is not necessarily integral, so we have to distinguish $\mathcal{Q}'_I$ from $\mathcal{Q}'$. By the induction hypothesis there are

- $c'_2, \ldots, c'_d$ such that $\langle f_2 + c'_2, \ldots, f_d + c'_d \rangle$ is a weak LLRF for $\mathcal{Q}'_I$; and
- $c''_2, \ldots, c''_d$ such that $\langle f_2 + c''_2, \ldots, f_d + c''_d \rangle$ is a weak LLRF for $\mathcal{Q}''_I$.

Next we prove that f_1 has a lower bound on $\mathcal{Q}_I \setminus \mathcal{Q}'_I$, i.e., there is $c_1 \geq 1$ such that $f_1 + c_1$ is non-negative on this set. Before proceeding to the proof, note that this implies that $\langle f_1 + c_1, f_2 + \max(c'_2, c''_2), \ldots, f_d + \max(c'_d, c''_d) \rangle$ is a weak LLRF for $\mathcal{Q}_I$. To see this, take any rational $\mathbf{x}'' \in \mathcal{Q}_I$, then either $\mathbf{x}''$ is ranked by the first component, or $\mathbf{x}'' \in \mathcal{Q}''$ or $\mathbf{x}'' \in \mathcal{Q}'_I$; in the last two cases, it is ranked by a component $f_i + \max(c'_i, c''_i)$ for $i > 1$.

It remains to prove that f_1 has a lower bound on $\mathcal{Q}_I \setminus \mathcal{Q}'_I$. We assume that $\mathcal{Q}'_I$ is non-empty, since otherwise, by the definition of $\mathcal{Q}'$, it is easy to see that $f_1 \geq -1$ over all of $\mathcal{Q}_I$. Thus, we consider $\mathcal{Q}'_I$ in an irredundant constraint representation: $\mathcal{Q}'_I = \{\mathbf{x}'' \in \mathbb{Q}^{2n} \mid \vec{a}_i \cdot \mathbf{x}'' \leq b_i, \ i = 1, \ldots, m\}$, and define

$$\boxed{\mathcal{P}_i = \mathcal{Q}_I \cap \{\mathbf{x}'' \in \mathbb{Q}^{2n} \mid \vec{a}_i \cdot \mathbf{x}'' > b_i\}} \quad \boxed{\mathcal{P}'_i = \mathcal{Q}_I \cap \{\mathbf{x}'' \in \mathbb{Q}^{2n} \mid \vec{a}_i \cdot \mathbf{x}'' \geq b_i\}}$$

for $i = 1, \ldots, m$. Then, clearly, $\mathcal{Q}_I \setminus \mathcal{Q}'_I \subseteq \bigcup_{i=1}^m \mathcal{P}_i$. It suffices to prove that f_1 has a lower bound over $\mathcal{P}_i$, for every i. Fix i, such that $\mathcal{P}_i$ is not empty. It is important to note that, by construction, all integer points of $\mathcal{P}_i$ are in $\mathcal{Q}_I \setminus \mathcal{Q}'_I$.

Let H be the half-space $\{\mathbf{x}'' \mid \vec{a}_i \cdot \mathbf{x} \leq b_i\}$. We first claim that $\mathcal{P}_i = \mathcal{P}'_i \setminus H$ contains an integer point. Equivalently, there is an integer point of $\mathcal{Q}_I$ not contained in H. There has to be such a point, for otherwise, $\mathcal{Q}_I$, being integral, would be contained in H, and $\mathcal{P}_i$ would be empty. Let $\mathbf{x}''_0$ be such a point.

Next, assume (by way of contradiction) that f_1 is *not* lower bounded on $\mathcal{P}_i$. Express f_1 as $f_1(\mathbf{x}) = \vec{\lambda} \cdot \mathbf{x} + \lambda_0$, then $\vec{\lambda} \cdot \mathbf{x}$ is not lower bounded on $\mathcal{P}_i$ and thus not on $\mathcal{P}'_i$. This means that $\mathcal{P}'_i$ is not a polytope, and thus can be expressed as $\mathcal{O} + \mathcal{C}$, where $\mathcal{O}$ is a polytope and $\mathcal{C}$ is a cone [23, Corollary 7.1b, p. 88]. There must be a rational $\mathbf{y}'' \in \mathcal{C}$ such that $\vec{\lambda} \cdot \mathbf{y} < 0$, since otherwise f_1 would be bounded on $\mathcal{P}'_i$.

For $k \in \mathbb{Z}_+$, consider the point $\mathbf{x}''_0 + k\mathbf{y}''$. Clearly it is in P'_i. Since $\mathbf{y}'' \in \mathcal{C}$, we have $\vec{a}_i \cdot \mathbf{y}'' \geq 0$; Since $\mathbf{x}''_0 \in \mathcal{P}_i$, we have $\vec{a}_i \cdot \mathbf{x}''_0 > b_i$; adding up, we get $\vec{a}_i \cdot (\mathbf{x}''_0 + k\mathbf{y}'') > b_i$ for all k. We conclude that the set $S = \{\mathbf{x}''_0 + k\mathbf{y}'' \mid k \in \mathbb{Z}_+\}$ is contained in $\mathcal{P}_i$. Clearly, it includes an infinite number of integer points. Moreover f_1 obtains arbitrarily negative values on S (the larger k, the smaller the value), in particular on its integer points. Recall that these points are included $\mathcal{Q}_I \setminus \mathcal{Q}'_I$, thus f_1 is not lower bounded on the *integer points of* $\mathcal{Q}_I \setminus \mathcal{Q}'_I$, a contradiction to the way $\mathcal{Q}'_I$ was defined. $\qquad\square$

Corollary 1. *If $I(\mathcal{Q})$ has a weak LLRF of depth d, then $\mathcal{Q}_I$ has a MΦRF, of depth at most d.*

Proof. By Theorem 4 we know that $\mathcal{Q}_I$ has a weak LLRF (of the same depth), which in turn can be converted to a MΦRF by Theorem 3. $\qquad\square$

Since $M\Phi$RFs are also weak $LLRF$, the above corollary provides a complete procedure for synthesizing $M\Phi$RFs over the integers, simply by seeking a nested ranking function for Q_I.

Example 4. For the loop of Example 3, computing the integer hull results in the addition of $x_1 \geq 1$. Now seeking a $M\Phi$RF as in Sect. 3 we find, for example, $\langle 10x_2 + 10, x_3 \rangle$. Note that $\langle 10x_2, x_3 \rangle$, which a $M\Phi$RF for $I(Q)$, is not a $M\Phi$RF for Q_I according to Definition 1, e.g., for any $0 < \varepsilon < 1$ the transition $(1 + \varepsilon, -\varepsilon, 0, 1, -3\varepsilon - 1, -10\varepsilon + 9) \in Q_I$ is not ranked, since $10x_2 < 0$ and $x_3 - x_3' = 10\varepsilon - 9 < 1$.

The procedure described above has exponential-time complexity, because computing the integer hull requires exponential time. However, it is polynomial for the cases in which the integer hull can be computed in polynomial time [4, Sect. 4]. The next theorem shows that the exponential time complexity is unavoidable for the general case (unless P = NP). The proof repeats the arguments in the coNP-completes proof for $LRFs$ [4, Sect. 3]. We omit the details.

Theorem 5. $BM\Phi RF(\mathbb{Z})$ *is* coNP-*complete.*

As in Sect. 3, we consider d as constant, or as input given in unary.

6 The Depth of a $M\Phi$RF

A wishful thought: If we could pre-compute an upper bound on the depth of optimal $M\Phi$RFs, and use it to bound the recursion, we would obtain a complete decision procedure for $M\Phi$RFs in general, since we can seek a $M\Phi$RF, as in Sect. 3, of this specific depth. This thought is motivated by results for *lexicographic ranking functions*, for example, [4] shows that the number of components in such functions is bounded by the number of variables in the loop. For $M\Phi$RFs, we were not able to find a similar upper bound, and we can show that the problem is more complicated than in the lexicographic case as a bound, if one exists, must depend not only on the number of variables or constraints, but also on the values of the coefficients in the loop constraints.

Theorem 6. *For integer $B > 0$, the following loop Q_B*

$$\text{while } (x \geq 1,\ y \geq 1,\ x \geq y,\ 2^B y \geq x) \text{ do } x' = 2x,\ y' = 3y$$

needs at least $B + 1$ components in any $M\Phi RF$.

Proof. Define $R_i = \{(2^i c, c, 2^{i+1}c, 3c) \mid c \geq 1\}$ and note that for $i = 0 \ldots B$, we have $R_i \subset Q_B$. Moreover, $R_i \neq R_j$ for different i and j. Next we prove that in any $M\Phi$RF $\langle f_1, \ldots, f_d \rangle$ for Q_B, and R_i with $i = 0 \ldots B$, there must be a component f_k such that $\mathbf{x}'' \in R_i \to f_k(\mathbf{x}) - f(0,0) \geq 0 \wedge \Delta f_k(\mathbf{x}'') > 0$. To prove this, fix i. We argue by the pigeonhole principle that, for some k, $f_k(2^i c, c) = c f_k(2^i, 1) + (1 - c)f_k(0,0) \geq 0$ and $f_k(2^i c, c) - f_k(2^{i+1}c, 3c) = c(f_k(2^i, 1) - f_k(2^{i+1}, 3)) > 0$

for infinite number of values of c, and thus $f_k(2^i, 1) - f_k(0, 0) \geq 0$, and $f_k(2^i, 1) - f_k(2^{i+1}, 3) > 0$, leading to the above statement. We say that R_i is "ranked" by f_k.

If $d < B+1$, then, by the pigeonhole principle, there are different R_i and R_j that are "ranked" by the same f_k. We show that this leads to a contradiction. Consider R_i and R_j, with $j > i$, and assume that they are "ranked" by $f_k(x, y) = a_1 x + a_2 y + a_0$. Applying the conclusion of the last paragraph to R_i and R_j, we have:

$$f_k(2^i, 1) - f_k(2^{i+1}, 3) = -a_1 2^i - a_2 2 > 0 \tag{16}$$

$$f_k(2^j, 1) - f_k(2^{j+1}, 3) = -a_1 2^j - a_2 2 > 0 \tag{17}$$

$$f_k(2^i, 1) - f_k(0, 0) = a_1 2^i + a_2 \quad \geq 0 \tag{18}$$

$$f_k(2^j, 1) - f_k(0, 0) = a_1 2^j + a_2 \quad \geq 0 \tag{19}$$

Adding $\frac{1}{2} \cdot$(17) to (19) we get $a_1 2^{j-1} > 0$. Thus, a_1 must be positive. From the sum of $\frac{1}{2} \cdot$(17) and (18), we get $a_1(2^i - 2^{j-1}) > 0$, which implies $j > i+1$, and $a_1 < 0$, a contradiction. Note that the bound $B+1$ is tight. This is confirmed by the $M\Phi$RF $\langle x - 2^B y, x - 2^{B-1} y, x - 2^{B-2} y, \ldots, x - y \rangle$. $\quad\square$

7   Iteration Bounds from $M\Phi$RFs

Automatic complexity analysis techniques are often based on bounding the number of iterations of loops, using ranking functions. Thus, it is natural to ask if a $M\Phi$RF implies a bound on the number of iterations of a given SLC loop. For $LRFs$, the implied bound is trivially linear, and in the case of SLC loops, it is known to be linear also for a class of lexicographic ranking functions [4]. In this section we show that $M\Phi$RFs, too, imply a linear iteration bound, despite the fact that the variables involved may grow non-linearly during the loop. Below we concentrate on its existence, but the bound can also be computed explicitly.

Example 5. Consider the following loop with the corresponding $M\Phi$RF $\langle y+1, x \rangle$

$$\texttt{while } (x \geq 0) \texttt{ do } x' = x + y,\ y' = y - 1$$

Let us consider an execution starting from positive values x_0 and y_0, and note that when $y+1$ reaches 0, i.e., when moving to the second phase, the value of x would be $x_0 - 1 + \sum_{i=-1}^{y_0} i = x_0 - 1 + \frac{y_0(y_0+1)}{2}$, which is polynomial in the input. It may seem that the next phase would be super-linear, since it is ranked by x, however, note that x decreases first by 1, then by 2, then by 3, etc. Therefore the quantity $\frac{y_0(y_0+1)}{2}$ is eliminated in y_0 iterations.

In what follows we generalize the observation of the above example. We consider an SLC loop $\mathcal{Q}$, and a corresponding irredundant $M\Phi$RF $\tau = \langle f_1, \ldots, f_d \rangle$. Let us start with an outline of the proof. We first define a function $F_k(t)$ that corresponds to the value of f_k after iteration t. We then bound each F_k by some expression $UB_k(t)$, and observe that for t greater than some number T_k, that depends linearly on the input, $UB_k(T_k)$ becomes negative. This means that T_k is an upper bound on the time in which the k-th phase ends; the whole loop must terminate before $\max_k T_k$ iterations.

Let $\mathbf{x}_t$ be the state after iteration t, and define $F_k(t) = f_k(\mathbf{x}_t)$, i.e., the value of the k-th component f_k after t iterations. For the initial state $\mathbf{x}_0$, we let $M = \max\{f_1(\mathbf{x}_0), \ldots, f_d(\mathbf{x}_0), 1\}$. Note that M is linear in $\|\mathbf{x}_0\|_\infty$ (i.e., in the maximum absolute value of the components of $\mathbf{x}_0$). We first state an auxiliary lemma, and then a lemma that bounds F_k.

Lemma 5. *For all $1 < k \le d$, there are $\mu_1, \ldots, \mu_{k-2} \ge 0$ and $\mu_{k-1} > 0$ such that $\mathbf{x}'' \in \mathcal{Q} \rightarrow \mu_1 f_1(\mathbf{x}) + \cdots + \mu_{k-1} f_{k-1}(\mathbf{x}) + (\Delta f_k(\mathbf{x}'') - 1) \ge 0$.*

Proof. From the definition of $M\Phi RF$ we have

$$\mathbf{x}'' \in \mathcal{Q} \rightarrow f_1(\mathbf{x}) \ge 0 \vee \cdots \vee f_{k-1}(\mathbf{x}) \ge 0 \vee \Delta f_k(\mathbf{x}'') \ge 1.$$

Moreover the conditions of Lemma 1 hold since f_k is not redundant, thus there are non-negative constants $\mu_1, \ldots, \mu_{k-1}$ such that

$$\mathbf{x}'' \in \mathcal{Q} \rightarrow \mu_1 f_1(\mathbf{x}) + \cdots + \mu_{k-1} f_{k-1}(\mathbf{x}) + (\Delta f_k(\mathbf{x}'') - 1) \ge 0.$$

Moreover, at least μ_{k-1} must be non-zero, otherwise it means that $\Delta f_k(\mathbf{x}'') \ge 1$ holds already when $f_1, \ldots, f_{k-2}$ are negative, so f_{k-1} would be redundant.   □

Lemma 6. *For all $1 \le k \le d$, there are constants $c_k, d_k > 0$ such that $F_k(t) \le c_k M t^{k-1} - d_k t^k$, for all $t \ge 1$.*

Proof. The proof is by induction. For $k = 1$ we let $c_1 = d_1 = 1$ and get $F_1(t) \le M - t$, which is trivially true. For $k \ge 2$ we assume that the lemma holds for smaller indexes and show that it holds for k. Note that the change in the value of $F_k(t)$ in the i-th iteration is $f_k(\mathbf{x}_{i+1}) - f_k(\mathbf{x}_i) = -\Delta f_k(\mathbf{x}_i'')$. By Lemma 5 and the definition of F_k, we have $\mu_1, \ldots, \mu_{k-2} \ge 0$ and $\mu_{k-1} > 0$ such that (over $\mathcal{Q}$)

$$f_k(\mathbf{x}_{i+1}) - f_k(\mathbf{x}_i) < \mu_1 F_1(i) + \cdots + \mu_{k-1} F_{k-1}(i). \tag{20}$$

Now we bound F_k (explanation follows):

$$F_k(t) = f_k(\mathbf{x}_0) + \Sigma_{i=0}^{t-1}(f_k(\mathbf{x}_{i+1}) - f_k(\mathbf{x}_i)) \tag{21}$$

$$< M + \Sigma_{i=0}^{t-1}\left(\mu_1 F_1(i) + \cdots + \mu_{k-1} F_{k-1}(i)\right) \tag{22}$$

$$\le M(1+\mu) + \Sigma_{i=1}^{t-1}\left(\mu_1 F_1(i) + \cdots + \mu_{k-1} F_{k-1}(i)\right) \tag{23}$$

$$\le M(1+\mu) + \Sigma_{i=1}^{t-1}\Sigma_{j=1}^{k-1}\left(\mu_j c_j M i^{j-1} - \mu_j d_j i^j\right) \tag{24}$$

$$\le M(1+\mu) + \Sigma_{i=1}^{t-1}\left((\Sigma_{j=1}^{k-1}\mu_j c_j M i^{j-1}) - \mu_{k-1} d_{k-1} i^{k-1}\right) \tag{25}$$

$$\le M(1+\mu) + \Sigma_{i=1}^{t-1}\left(M(\Sigma_{j=1}^{k-1}\mu_j c_j) i^{k-2} - \mu_{k-1} d_{k-1} i^{k-1}\right) \tag{26}$$

$$= M(1+\mu) + M(\Sigma_{j=1}^{k-1}\mu_j c_j)(\Sigma_{i=1}^{t-1} i^{k-2}) - \mu_{k-1} d_{k-1} \Sigma_{i=1}^{t-1} i^{k-1} \tag{27}$$

$$\le M(1+\mu) + M(\Sigma_{j=1}^{k-1}\mu_j c_j)(\frac{t^{k-1}}{k-1}) - \mu_{k-1} d_{k-1}(\frac{t^k}{k} - t^{k-1}) \tag{28}$$

$$= c_k M t^{k-1} - d_k t^k \tag{29}$$

Each step above is obtained from the previous one as follows: (22) by replacing $f_k(\mathbf{x}_0)$ by M, since $f_k(\mathbf{x}_0) \leq M$, and applying (20); (23) by separating the term for $i = 0$ from the sum; this term is bounded by μM, where $\mu = \sum_{j=1}^{k-1} \mu_j$, because $F_k(0) = f_k(\mathbf{x}_0) \leq M$ by definition; (24) by applying the induction hypothesis; (25) by removing all negative values $-\mu_j d_j i^j$, except the last one $-\mu_{k-1} d_{k-1} i^{k-1}$; (26) by replacing i^{j-1} by an upper bound i^{k-2}; (27) by opening parentheses; (28) replacing $\Sigma_{i=1}^{t-1} i^{k-2}$ by an upper bound $\frac{t^{k-1}}{k-1}$, and $\Sigma_{i=1}^{t-1} i^{k-1}$ by a lower bound $\frac{t^k}{k} - t^{k-1}$; finally for (28), take $c_k = (1 + \mu) + (\Sigma_{j=1}^{k-1} \mu_j c_j)/(k-1) + \mu_{k-1} d_{k-1}$, and $d_k = \mu_{k-1} d_{k-1}/k$ and note that both are positive. □

Theorem 7. *An SLC loop that has a MΦRF terminates in a number of iterations bounded by $O(\|\mathbf{x}_0\|_\infty)$.*

Proof. For $t > \max\{1, (c_k/d_k)M\}$, we have $F_k(t) < 0$, proving that the k-th phase terminates by this time (since it remains negative). Thus, by the time $\max\{1, (c_1/d_1)M, \ldots, (c_d/d_d)M\}$, which is linear in $\|\mathbf{x}_0\|_\infty$, all phases must have terminated. Note that c_k and d_k can be computed explicitly, if desired. □

We remark that the above result also holds for multi-path loops if they have a nested MΦRF, but does not hold for any MΦRF.

8   Conclusion

LRFs, *LLRFs* and *MΦRFs* have all been proposed in earlier work. The original purpose of this work has been to improve our understanding of *MΦRFs*, and answer open problems regarding the complexity of obtaining such functions from linear-constraint loops, the difference between the integer case and the rational case, and the possibility of inferring an iteration bound from such ranking functions. Similarly, we wanted to understand a natural class of lexicographic ranking functions, which removes a restriction of previous definitions regarding negative values. Surprisingly, it turned out that our main results are *equivalences* which show that, for *SLC* loops, both *MΦRFs* and *LLRFs* reduce to a simple kind of *MΦRFs*, that has been known to allow polynomial-time solution (over ℚ). Thus, our result collapsed, in essence, these above classes of ranking functions.

The implication of having a polynomial-time solution, which is hardly more complex than the standard algorithm to find *LRFs*, is that whenever one considers using *LRFs* in one's work, one should consider using *MΦRFs*. By controlling the depth of the *MΦRFs* one trades expressivity for processing cost. We believe that it would be sensible to start with depth 1 (i.e., seeking a *LRF*) and increase the depth upon failure. Similarly, since a complete solution for the integers is inherently more costly, it makes sense to begin with the solution that is complete over the rationals, since it is safe for the integer case. If this fail, one can also consider special cases in which the inherent hardness can be avoided [4, Sect. 4].

Theoretically, some tantalizing open problems remain. Is it possible to decide whether a given loop admits a *MΦRF*, without a depth bound? This is related to

Table 1. Experiments on loops taken from [15]—loops (1–5) originate from [11] and (6–41) originate from [8].

♯	loop	Nested $M\Phi$RF
1	`while (x≥0) x'=-2x+10;`	None
2	`while (x>0) x'=x+y; y'=y+z;`	None
3	`while (x≤N)` `  if (*) { x'=2*x+y; y'=y+1; } else x'=x+1;`	None
4	`while (1)` `  if (x<n) { x'=x+y; if (x'≥200) break; }`	None
5	`while (x<>y) if (x>y) x'=x-y; else y'=y-x;`	None
6	`while (x<0) x'=x+y; y'=y-1;`	None
7	`while (x>0) x'=x+y; y'=-2y;`	None
8	`while (x<y) x'=x+y; y'=-2y;`	None
9	`while (x<y) x'=x+y; 2y'=y;`	None
10	`while (4x-5y>0) x'=2x+4y; y'=4x;`	None
11	`while (x<5) x'=x-y; y'=x+y;`	None
12	`while (x>0, y>0) x'=-2x+10y;`	None
13	`while (x>0) x'=x+y;`	None
14	`while (x<10) x'=-y; y'=y+1;`	None
15	`while (x<0) x'=x+z; y'=y+1; z'=-2y`	None
16	`while (x>0, x<100) x'≥2x+10;`	$\langle -\frac{1}{11}x + \frac{111}{11} \rangle$
17	`while (x>1) -2x'=x;`	$\langle \frac{2}{4}x \rangle$
18	`while (x>1) 2x'≤x;`	$\langle x \rangle$
19	`while (x>0) 2x'≤x;`	$\langle 2x \rangle$
20	`while (x>0) x'=x+y; y'=y-1;`	$\langle y+1, x \rangle$
21	`while (4x+y>0) x'=-2x+4y; y'=4x;`	None
22	`while (x>0, x<y) x'=2x; y'=y+1;`	$\langle -3x+2y, -x+y \rangle$
23	`while (x>0) x'=x-2y; y'=y+1;`	$\langle -2y+1, x \rangle$
24	`while (x>0, x<n) x'=-x+y-5; y'=2y; n'=n;`	$\langle \frac{2}{14}x - \frac{1}{7}y + \frac{13}{14}n, -\frac{2}{14}x + \frac{8}{14}n \rangle$
25	`while (x>0, y<0) x'=x+y; y'=y-1;`	$\langle x \rangle$
26	`while (x-y>0) x'=-x+y; y'=y+1;`	$\langle -y, x-y \rangle$
27	`while (x>0) x'=y; y'=y-1;`	$\langle y, x \rangle$
28	`while (x>0) x'=x+y-5; y'=-2y;`	$\langle \frac{3}{8}x + \frac{1}{8}y, \frac{1}{8}x + \frac{7}{8} \rangle$
29	`while (x+y>0) x'=x-1; y'=-2y;`	$\langle x, \frac{1}{3}y + \frac{1}{3}y + \frac{2}{3} \rangle$
30	`while (x>y) x'=x-y; 1≤y'≤2`	$\langle x-y \rangle$
31	`while (x>0) x'=x+y; y'=-y-1;`	$\langle 2x+y, x \rangle$
32	`while (x>0) x'=y; y'≤-y;`	$\langle x + \frac{1}{2}y, \frac{1}{2}x + \frac{1}{2} \rangle$
33	`while (x<y) x'=x+1; y'=z; z'=z;`	$\langle -x+z, -x+y \rangle$
34	`while (x>0) x'=x+y; y'=y+z; z'=z-1;`	$\langle z+1, y+1, x \rangle$
35	`while (x+y≥0, x≤z) x'=2x+y; y'=y+1; z'=z`	$\langle -x-y+1, -x+z+1 \rangle$
36	`while (x>0, x≤z) x'=2x+y; y'=y+1; z'=z`	$\langle -y, -x+2z \rangle$
37	`while (x≥0) x'=x+y; y'=z; z'=-z-1;`	$\langle 2x+2y+z+1, 3x+y+1, x+1 \rangle$
38	`while (x-y>0) x'=-x+y; y'=z; z'=z+1;`	$\langle -z, x-y \rangle$
39	`while (x>0, x<y) x'>2x; y'=z; z'=z;`	$\langle -\frac{6}{12}x + \frac{7}{12}z, -\frac{2}{12}x + \frac{7}{12}y \rangle$
40	`while (x≥0, x+y≥0) x'=x+y+z; y'=-z-1; z'=z;`	$\langle x+y+1 \rangle$
41	`while (x+y≥0, x≤n) x'=2x+y; y'=z; z'=z+1; n'=n;`	$\langle -x-z+1, -x-y+1, -x+n+1 \rangle$

the question, discussed in Sect. 6, whether it is possible to precompute a depth bound. What is the complexity of the $M\Phi RF$ problems over multi-path loops? For such loops, the equivalence of $M\Phi RFs$, nested r.f.s and $LLRFs$ does not hold. Finally (generalizing the first question), we think that there is need for further exploration of single-path loops and of the plethora of "termination witnesses" based on linear functions (a notable reference is [18]).

We have implemented the *nested ranking function* procedure of Sect. 3, and applied it on a set of terminating and non-terminating SLC loops taken from [15]. Table 1 (at Page 18) summarizes these experiments. All loops marked with "None" have no $M\Phi RF$, and they are mostly non-terminating: Loop 1 is terminating over the integers, but does not have $M\Phi RF$, and Loop 21 is terminating over both integers and rationals but does not have $M\Phi RF$. Note that loops 3–5 are multi-path, in such case we seek a nested $M\Phi RF$ that is valid for all paths. In all cases, a strict inequality $x > y$ was translated to $x \geq y + 1$ before applying out procedure. Interestingly, all 25 terminating loops in this set have a $M\Phi RF$. These experiments can be tried at http://loopkiller.com/irankfinder.

References

1. Albert, E., Arenas, P., Genaim, S., Puebla, G.: Closed-form upper bounds in static cost analysis. J. Autom. Reason. **46**(2), 161–203 (2011)
2. Alias, C., Darte, A., Feautrier, P., Gonnord, L.: Multi-dimensional rankings, program termination, and complexity bounds of flowchart programs. In: Cousot, R., Martel, M. (eds.) SAS 2010. LNCS, vol. 6337, pp. 117–133. Springer, Heidelberg (2010). doi:10.1007/978-3-642-15769-1_8
3. Bagnara, R., Mesnard, F.: Eventual linear ranking functions. In: Proceedings of the 15th International Symposium on Principles and Practice of Declarative Programming, PPDP 2013, pp. 229–238. ACM Press (2013)
4. Ben-Amram, A.M., Genaim, S.: Ranking functions for linear-constraint loops. J. ACM **61**(4), 26:1–26:55 (2014)
5. Bradley, A.R., Manna, Z., Sipma, H.B.: Linear ranking with reachability. In: Etessami, K., Rajamani, S.K. (eds.) CAV 2005. LNCS, vol. 3576, pp. 491–504. Springer, Heidelberg (2005). doi:10.1007/11513988_48
6. Bradley, A.R., Manna, Z., Sipma, H.B.: The polyranking principle. In: Caires, L., Italiano, G.F., Monteiro, L., Palamidessi, C., Yung, M. (eds.) ICALP 2005. LNCS, vol. 3580, pp. 1349–1361. Springer, Heidelberg (2005). doi:10.1007/11523468_109
7. Brockschmidt, M., Emmes, F., Falke, S., Fuhs, C., Giesl, J.: Analyzing runtime and size complexity of integer programs. ACM Trans. Program. Lang. Syst. **38**(4), 13 (2016)
8. Chen, H.Y., Flur, S., Mukhopadhyay, S.: Termination proofs for linear simple loops. STTT **17**(1), 47–57 (2015)
9. Colóon, M.A., Sipma, H.B.: Synthesis of linear ranking functions. In: Margaria, T., Yi, W. (eds.) TACAS 2001. LNCS, vol. 2031, pp. 67–81. Springer, Heidelberg (2001). doi:10.1007/3-540-45319-9_6
10. Cook, B., Gotsman, A., Podelski, A., Rybalchenko, A., Vardi, M.Y.: Proving that programs eventually do something good. In: Proceedings of the 34th ACM SIGPLAN-SIGACT Symposium on Principles of Programming Languages, POPL 2007, Nice, France, 17–19 January 2007, pp. 265–276 (2007)

11. Cook, B., Gulwani, S., Lev-Ami, T., Rybalchenko, A., Sagiv, M.: Proving conditional termination. In: Gupta, A., Malik, S. (eds.) CAV 2008. LNCS, vol. 5123, pp. 328–340. Springer, Heidelberg (2008). doi:10.1007/978-3-540-70545-1_32

12. Cook, B., Kroening, D., Rümmer, P., Wintersteiger, C.M.: Ranking function synthesis for bit-vector relations. Formal Methods Syst. Des. **43**(1), 93–120 (2013)

13. Cook, B., Podelski, A., Rybalchenko, A.: Termination proofs for systems code. In: Schwartzbach, M.I., Ball, T., (eds.) Programming Language Design and Implementation, PLDI 2006, pp. 415–426. ACM (2006)

14. Feautrier, P.: Some efficient solutions to the affine scheduling problem I. One-dimensional time. Int. J. Parallel Prog. **21**(5), 313–347 (1992)

15. Ganty, P., Genaim, S.: Proving termination starting from the end. In: Sharygina, N., Veith, H. (eds.) CAV 2013. LNCS, vol. 8044, pp. 397–412. Springer, Heidelberg (2013). doi:10.1007/978-3-642-39799-8_27

16. Harrison, M.: Lectures on Sequential Machines. Academic Press, Cambridge (1969)

17. Larraz, D., Oliveras, A., Rodríguez-Carbonell, E., Rubio, A.: Proving termination of imperative programs using Max-SMT. In: Formal Methods in Computer-Aided Design, FMCAD 2013, pp. 218–225. IEEE (2013)

18. Leike, J., Heizmann, M.: Ranking templates for linear loops. Log. Methods Comput. Sci. **11**(1), 1–27 (2015)

19. Leroux, J., Sutre, G.: Flat counter automata almost everywhere!. In: Peled, D.A., Tsay, Y.-K. (eds.) ATVA 2005. LNCS, vol. 3707, pp. 489–503. Springer, Heidelberg (2005). doi:10.1007/11562948_36

20. Li, Y., Zhu, G., Feng, Y.: The L-depth eventual linear ranking functions for single-path linear constraint loops. In: 10th International Symposium on Theoretical Aspects of Software Engineering (TASE 2016), pp. 30–37. IEEE (2016)

21. Ouaknine, J., Worrell, J.: On linear recurrence sequences and loop termination. ACM SIGLOG News **2**(2), 4–13 (2015)

22. Podelski, A., Rybalchenko, A.: A complete method for the synthesis of linear ranking functions. In: Steffen, B., Levi, G. (eds.) VMCAI 2004. LNCS, vol. 2937, pp. 239–251. Springer, Heidelberg (2004). doi:10.1007/978-3-540-24622-0_20

23. Schrijver, A.: Theory of Linear and Integer Programming. Wiley, New York (1986)

24. Sohn, K., Van Gelder, A.: Termination detection in logic programs using argument sizes. In: Rosenkrantz, D.J. (ed.) Symposium on Principles of Database Systems, pp. 216–226. ACM Press (1991)

Author Index

Printed in the United States
By Bookmasters